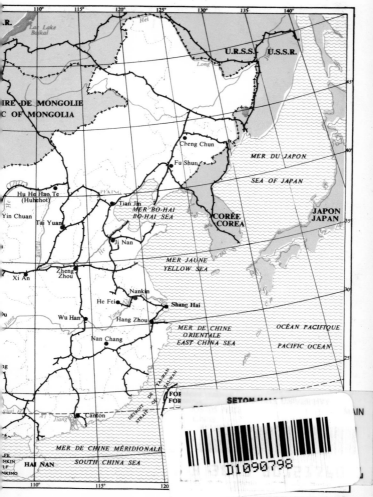

8f10b 6500

CARTOGRAPHIE NAGEL

CHINA

NAGEL'S
ENCYCLOPEDIA - GUIDE

AWARDS
ROME, 1958 PARIS, 1961 VIENNA, 1968, 1972

CHINA

1504 pages
92 plans in black and white
15 large coloured maps and plans
Atlas of 25 pages in colour
Fourth edition

NAGEL PUBLISHERS
GENEVA · PARIS · MUNICH

English version by **Anne L. Destenay**

ISBN 2–8263–0731–2

CONTENTS

INTRODUCTION

Page

CONTENTS

CONTENTS

CONTENTS

CONTENTS

MAPS AND PLANS

Maps in colour

Atlas (see end of book)

Maps in black and white

FOREWORD

The writing of a guide book on China is a real challenge in this age in which we live. Apart from the difficulties arising from the size of the country, its complex nature and its language, the political situation does not simplify the task. The limited travelling facilities and difficulty of access to many sources of information made it seem at first that it would be impossible to produce an objective and useful work.

In 1964, France renewed diplomatic relations with China, after an interruption of fifteen years. Monsieur L. Paye was appointed Ambassador to Peking. A former Minister of Education, he at once began to develop cultural relations and contacts between the universities of the two countries. Chinese students were sent to Paris, and at the same time, the Chinese invited twenty French students and about fifty teachers, as a prelude to exchanges on a larger scale in 1965. They were all young people who were passionately interested in the country's civilisation. Although they had been brought up on the ancient philosophical, artistic and literary traditions, they did not allow this to interfere with their interest in the new realities of modern China. When travelling, and in a general effort to understand, several of them pooled their knowledge and sources of information. Several other people made spontaneous contributions on their own special fields. The first idea, and the possibility of producing this work, grew out of this joint effort. I myself merely made up the team and directed their work, drew up the plan, combined the various contributions and composed the outline of the analysis of modern Chinese culture.

The reader will find the names of the chief contributors elsewhere. Special mention must be made, however, of the part played by two of them, Monsieur and Madame Denys and Claudine Lombard. They are students of history and sinology; their contribution to this book is a truly scientific and original piece of work, based on information from Chinese sources, and checked on the spot where possible. They are responsible for the whole chapter on Peking, as well as most of those on the provinces, and the accounts of Chinese history and the National Minority Races, all of which represents a total of well over 500 pages.

The most recent general guide books in English, German or Japanese are at least 40 years old. Yet China has changed more over the last thirty years than during several centuries of her history. As Etiemble said, to recognise China is not enough, we must get to know her as well. This book makes an honest and objective contribution. It is hoped that even at its own modest level, it will help towards spiritual communion between the different peoples, and towards mutual understanding and peace among men.

                                        Marcel GIRARD

LIST OF CONTRIBUTORS

Jean-François Billeter:
  Chinese Religion and Philosophy
  The Provinces of He bei, Shan dong, He nan, Shan xi and
  Shân xi

Jean-François Billeter and Jacques Dars:
  The Calendar, Chinese Names
  The Chinese Script

Claude Chayet:
  Chinese Cooking

Jacques Dars:
  The Abacus, Chinese Games
  The Autonomous Regions of Tibet, Xin jiang, Ning xia,
  Inner Mongolia; the Provinces of Qing hai and Gan su

François Dell:
  The Chinese Language

Jean-Pierre Dieny:
  Chinese literature

Marcel Girard:
  Modern Chinese Culture
  The Former Legation Quarter
  Canton
  Hong Kong

Jacques Guillermaz:
  China from 1911 to 1966
  Governmental and Administrative Institutions
  The Communist Party
  The Province of Si chuan

Claudine and Denys Lombard:
  History
  The Minorities
  The City of Peking
  The Towns of Tian jin, Luo yang, Xi an, Nanking, Su zhou,
  Shang hai, Hang zhou, Chang sha.
  The Southern Provinces

Eliane Richard:
  Practical Information

Michelle t'Serstevens:
  Chinese Art

Paul Wagret:
  Geography
  China Since 1966.

The following contributed to the maps:

Jean-François Billeter   Corine Löchen
Daniel Chauvin   Claudine and Denys Lombard
Jacques Dars   Jean-François Papet
Catherine Gipoulon   Marie-Annick Lancelot

IMPORTANT

The transcription used for the Chinese terms in this work is the official one adopted by the People's Republic of China, known as pin yin. It is the only one used in place names on railway stations. on street signs, etc. (see introduction, p. 94).

A triple index at the end of the book will help the reader to recognise Chinese terms, drawn up in:

  1) the official transcription (pin yin);

  2) the transcription adopted by the Ecole Française d'Extrême-Orient (E.F.E.O.), which is the one generally used in France:

  3) the Wade transcription, used in Anglo-Saxon countries.

INTRODUCTION

GEOGRAPHY

3,657,765 square miles (9,561,000 km²): China is as big as the whole continent of Europe. 3,000 miles (5,000 km) from east to west, 3,400 miles (5,500 km) from north to south: China stretches over four time-belts, and in terms of latitude, it stretches from Denmark to Hoggar. It is a world in itself, the Chinese subcontinent, inhabited by about 900 million people, representing a quarter of all humanity.

General Remarks. Like the Ancient Greeks, the Ancient Chinese considered that their country was the centre of the world; barbarian countries stretched round all sides of it. The traditional names: "Middle Kingdom", *Zhong guo*, or "Flowery Middle Country", *Zhong hua*, still in use today, sprang from this idea.

During the European Middle Ages, China was known, thanks to travellers like Marco Polo, by the name of *Cathay*, which became *Kitaï* in Russian. It no doubt comes from a deformation of the name of a mediaeval Chinese dynasty originating from the north, the Khitan. Our word *China* comes from the name of the Qin Dynasty, which ruled in the 3rd century B.C.; it was short-lived, but its influence was considerable.

Until fairly recently, China proper, or "the China of the eighteen provinces" was considered apart from its dependencies (Manchuria, Mongolia, Tibet, Xin jiang—or Sin kiang). These divisions have in fact been obsolete since the 1911 Revolution. They corresponded roughly to two areas which were unevenly inhabited and unequally developed. Formosa (Tai wan), Macao (belonging to Portugal) and Hong Kong (Britain) should be included in any consideration of China as a whole. Some frontiers are contested by the People's Republic of China, particularly in the direction of Indian Assam.

Although influenced by Chinese civilisation, Korea and Vietnam are distinct from China. Even so, China takes a special interest in them, as was borne out by events tied up with the Korean war (1950-1953) and in Vietnam. Within China itself live several ethnic minorities: Mongols, Manchu, Tibetans, Uighurs, etc.

Relief

Roughly speaking, China can be split into *east China*, which consists mainly of plains and hills, with a relatively humid climate, the home of the traditional peasantry, and *west* or *inland China*, made up of dry, thinly populated plateaux and mountains, the home of the ethnic minorities.

East China. Four large sectors fill this part; from north to south, they are:

a) Former Manchuria, now called *North East China*, a fertile sedimentary basin, where the soil is mainly black, of the chernozem type. Mountains surround it, cutting it off from the neighbouring regions: the Great Khingan Mountains to the west separate it from Inner Mongolia, the Little Khingan Mountains to the north slope down to the River Amur, and the Chang bai shan Mountains lie eastwards along the Korean frontier. The Manchurian sedimentary gulf is narrow to the south where it gives on to the Bo hai (formerly the Gulf of Chihli) and grows wider to the north; the northern part is unfortunately the part where the climate is coldest and most unfavourable to agriculture.

b) The Yellow River (Huang he) Alluvial Plain embraces the provinces of He bei, Shan dong, He nan and An hui. This vast plain, half as big as France, is made up of loess and fertile alluvium. The rocky mass of the Shan dong mountains (18,000 feet) rises out of the plain to the east.

c) The Graduated Plateaux of Shan xi and Shân xi and those of Gan su, which are an extension continuing eastwards, are made of hardened loess, sometimes several hundreds of feet thick; the loess has been re-modelled by water and has a tabular structure broken here and there by faults (the Tai yuan basin) or by the passage which the Huang he has cut through it.

d) South China begins south of the Qin ling Mountains and the River Huai: a profusion of hills and valleys lie beyond the Yang zi; some of the hills are over 3,000 feet high. The Red Basin, lying at an altitude of about 1,300 feet, forms an enclave among the mountains. To the south-west stretch the limestone plateaux of Guang xi and Yun nan, which are continued by the mountains of Burma, Laos and Tong King.

West China. This inland part of China, made up of mountain ranges and highlands which are among the highest in the world, is beset by dry, cold erosion: it is an area of naked landscapes of sand and stones.

a) Tibet, the "Roof of the World", covers an area of 228,000 square miles (600,000 km²); its altitude is 16,000 feet or more. It is a series of mountain chains and depressions lying from east to west, rather than a plateau. To the north, the Kun

lun and Altyn Tagh ranges stand between it and Xin jiang;
the Karakorum is an extension of them stretching westwards to
Kashmir. The impressive barrier of the Himalayas rises to the
south, dominated by Mount Chomolungma (Everest), about
26,000 feet high. Valleys are few and usually inhospitable,
as they often follow a zigzag pattern, lying at the bottom of
impassible gorges (upper reaches of the Indus and the Brahmaputra—Tsangpo in Tibetan).

b) "*The Si chuan Alps*" which rise to 20,000 feet, are the
extension of the folds forming the Himalayas, which change
direction slightly, and run south-eastwards: "row upon row
of sharp ridges, with narrow, precipitous valleys lying between
them, up to 10,000 feet deep" (J. Chesneaux). These gashes
through the mountains, accommodating the Salween, the Mekong,
and the upper Yang zi, represent an almost insurmountable
obstacle to communication between east and west.

c) *The Xin jiang Basin* (Sin kiang) is in fact double: two
depressions are separated by a mountain ridge in the middle:
the "celestial mountains" (Tian shan), 12,000 feet high. Faulted
structure predominates in this area; the Tian shan are an
enormous *horst*, like a block which has been tilted, with the
strange, steep Turfan depression hollowed out of the heart of it
(470 feet below sea level). The Dzungaria basin is north of the
mountains; it is only 800 feet above sea level, and throughout
the centuries, it has always been the route taken by invaders
and merchants. The huge Tarim basin lies to the south, with
the River Tarim flowing through it into the Lob nor; it was
in this region of endless desert that the "Croisière Jaune",
the Citroën expedition, got into difficulties in 1930 or so.

d) *The Gobi Desert*, north of the Huang he, constitutes Inner
Mongolia. It is a sandy plain with dunes formed by the wind,
broken here and there by stony plateaux, such as the Nan shan
along the southern edge. It is fairly high; the altitude varies
between 3,000 and 4,500 feet.

Conclusion. On the whole, the land slopes from west to
east, as is borne out by the fact that the continent is drained
by rivers emptying into the China Sea. Plateaux fall away
step by step towards the sea, without coming across any obstacles
in the way of mountain chains lying in a north—south direction.
Another difference exists, however, over and above the one
just described between east and west China: that between
north and South China.

because they are breached deliberately (1938, to check the Japanese invasion), the result is widespread devastation; not for nothing is the Yellow River called "China's Sorrow". The position of the mouth of the Yellow River has changed 26 times in 3000 years; sometimes it is to the north, sometimes to the south of Shan dong.

When the river is low, the flow is sometimes less than 150 cu. m. per s., which makes regular irrigation impossible. The same is true of navigation. The present regime has started work on a vast plan to regulate the river: it was begun in 1957, and will not be finished before the very end of the 20th century. It includes the building of 46 large dams, the creation of navigable reaches, work on soil conservation, and the production of 110 thousand million kWh. Some sections are already completed, such as the work on San men ("the three gates") at the point where the river flows out on to the plain; 600,000 people east of Xi an have been or will be moved from their homes as a result of drowning some parts of the valley.

The Yang zi. The Blue River, as it was incorrectly called by Westerners, is a little longer than the Yellow River: 3,494 miles. The Chinese never call it the Blue River, and its waters are often full of silt. Its catchment basin covers 714,000 square miles and includes numerous tributaries, unlike the Yellow River, which is more solitary. As a result of the tributaries and of the more generous rain the discharge of the Yang zi is ten times that of the Yellow River: it has a flow of 30,000 cubic metres per second, which earns it third place among the rivers of the world, after the Amazon and the Congo.

Even in the winter, the river is never very low, and at high water in the summer, it never has a flow of less than 80,000 cubic metres per second. Its size is less striking than in the case of the Huang he, partly because of the Lakes Po yang and Dong ting, which regulate it and absorb some of the excess when the river is high. Even so, disastrous floods have been known, such as the 1931 catastrophe when an area the size of Great Britain was flooded, and 3 million people died. The Yang zi delta moves forward about 60 feet a year.

The Yang zi is used for irrigation and is also highly navigable. Sea-going boats go as far upstream as Wu han; once the work going on in the Yi chang narrows is completed, they will be able to go as far as Sui fu, in the heart of the Red Basin.

The Xi jiang. The Xi jiang or *Western River* is much shorter than the other two, as it measures only 1650 miles. Its basin is almost as large as Spain and its flow is three times that of the

Yellow River! The reason for this is that monsoon rains are particularly plentiful in this area of southern China. It is not surprising, therefore, to find that sometimes the rise of the river can be compared with the Yang zi. It is called "Western River" because of its position compared with the Bei jiang and the Dong jiang, which like it are both tributaries of the Canton River.

It should be remembered that rivers are of immense importance in the agricultural life and in the history of China in general. "The need for an organised watch on the dykes and for a collective effort to maintain the irrigation canal system resulted in the appearance of politically centralised states very early on in the middle Yellow River basin or on the lower reaches of the Yang zi. For centuries, the best criterion of good administration and the prosperity of the empire was the state of the dykes, reservoirs and canals; conversely, the chroniclers included the deterioration of the dykes and canals among the signs heralding the fall of dynasties, alongside famines, uprisings and signs in the heavens." (J. Chesneaux).

The Regions of China

The Chinese world is extremely varied, owing to the vast territory which it covers and the contrasts in climate. Diversity cannot, however, efface the unity of its civilisation. Paul Claudel wrote: "... China is not divided into compartments like Europe. No frontier, no special organisms stood in the way of the spread of human waves".

North China and South China. The two Chinas, one on each side of the River Huai and the Qin ling Mountains, are very different in appearance. The North consists of plateaux and broad plains, the South of hills, mountains and basins. The North is colder and drier, with icy winds and snow in the winter; the South enjoys an almost tropical climate with mild winters. The North receives scanty rain, and experiences frequent famines; the South has regular and plentiful rain. The North is the country of loess, yellow earth, of open countryside and dust; the Southern deltas and valleys are covered with alluvial soils, red soils produced by sandstone and clay. The North is the country of wheat, millet, gaoliang and the soy-bean, the South that of rice, cotton and the tea plant. Finally, the Northerners live in villages of houses of puddled clay, whereas the Southerners live in villages built of brick; in the North towns are often surrounded by walls, with broad streets laid out like a chess board, and little low houses scattered among gardens; the South has towns with

POPULATION

P. Gourou, in his masterly study entitled *La Terre et l'homme en Extrême-Orient*, stresses the fundamental importance of the human element in this civilisation: "The Far-Eastern countryside is dominated by man and his work. Long strings of porters, bending under the weight of the carrying pole, trot along narrow paths; others stand patiently on the river bank, fishing; peasants busy themselves in the fields; a funeral procession conducts a body to its last resting-place to the sound of fifes and cymbals. Every tree was planted by man, every pond was dug out by the peasants, every inch of cultivable ground has been carefully worked by man for thousands of years."

The Demographic Problem

900 million Chinese? When the Empire fell in 1911, a reliable estimate put China's population at 374 million. No other census took place before 1953, when it was thought that the population was anything between 450 to 500 million, depending on different opinions. The results of the 1953 census knocked all the forecasts sideways, as they revealed the existence of 602 million Chinese (12 million of whom were living abroad). The world suddenly awoke to the vast numbers of Chinese: three times as many Chinese as Russians, four times as many Chinese as Americans in the United States. China is the most heavily populated country in the world, with half as many people again as India, and a more homogeneous population at that.

The birth-rate has fallen from about 35 per thousand in the 1950's to approximately 26 per thousand today. As the death rate is approximately 10 per thousand, the possible annual surplus is probably round about 10 million. In five years, China acquires more new inhabitants than the entire population of France! In 1979 the population may be reckoned at approximately 885 million, which amounts to between a quarter and a fifth of humanity.

Density and Distribution. The density of population in China is not a new phenomenon. It is estimated that the Chinese masses must already have represented a third of the world's population at certain periods. This presents a sharp contrast with the much more recent development in population in Europe (19th century) and in the United States (end of the 19th and 20th centuries). It is also well-known that the Chinese civilisation is one of the oldest on earth. The superabundance of humanity explains narrow, paved streets, overlooked by tall houses. North China is the country of the mule, the donkey and sometimes the camel, South China is that of the water-buffalo.

Chinese Central Asia. This is an area which is infinitely more hostile to man than the other two. Stones, sand, tall grass at best replace the fields. Stock-raising is the chief source of livelihood, providing as it does milk, yoghourt, meat, and material for clothes and tents. This China of deserts (Mongolia, Xin jiang) was however the centre of great empires earlier on: "Attila, Genghis Khan, Tamerlane emerged in the midst of civilised periods, and suddenly, within a few years, reduced the Roman, Iranian or Chinese world to a heap of ruins.

"The reverse is true as well: Chinese colonisation of the grasslands brought with it the advance of cultivation and the retreat of the prairie. The Mongol shepherd or the Tungus woodsman retreated further and further in the face of this invasion, like the Red Indians in their flight westwards before the American farmer..." (R. Grousset, *Bilan de l'histoire.*) For more reasons than one, these inland regions of Asia deserve the name of the "Chinese Far West".

the strenuous work of the countless masses building dams, like millions of ants. Calling men into action balances the scarcity of machines, uses surplus man-power, and constitutes part of the originality of "Chinese methods", as they have been called: a paradox in a century in which machines are all-powerful.

These masses of human beings are by no means evenly distributed over all the $3\frac{1}{2}$ million square miles: this means that average density of population—195 inhabitants per square mile—is scarcely more than a theoretical figure. The most densely populated areas (over 250 per square mile) are the great North China plain, the Yang zi valley, the South China coastline, and the Red Basin. Some regions reach fantastic figures: 1024 or more in Chong ming Island at the mouth of the Yang zi, and even more in some cantons of Guang dong province. These are no doubt record figures for rural areas, as they are even higher than the figures for Bengal.

Population density, at its highest in the south—where two crops of rice can be grown per year—decreases further north, where only one crop of wheat, which is less nourishing than rice, can be grown per year. The population decreases towards the west as well, and eventually falls below 25 per square mile in Tibet and Xin jiang. These contrasts correspond to the difference in agricultural possibilities: intensive cultivation to the east, and marginal or almost non-existant cultivation in the west. One look at the rain distribution and the demographic maps is enough to see that they correspond almost exactly. For the moment, the vast majority of the Chinese are concentrated in the rural areas and earn a living from agriculture: 80 per cent.

Problems. China has an extremely young population, as two Chinese out of five are under eighteen. An age pyramid which is very wide at the base reveals a country of great demographic vitality, but at the same time it presents numerous difficulties for a State which is still developing: will the standard of living increase more rapidly than the population?

The Chinese leaders were brought face to face with the gravity of the situation by the famine of 1959–1962. Whereas in 1950 it was officially stated that China had nothing to fear from over-population, for several years now this optimism has been less marked. The problem of birth control has come out into the open; young men and women are "advised" to marry fairly late, after 25, and it is not unusual to find husbands and wives living apart, as they work far away from each other. The disadvantages of over-frequent pregnancies are stressed too, for they prevent women from working for the construction of socialism.

Women are slightly fewer in proportion to men: 48% as against 52%. This is due to the consequences of the inferior position of women, which lasted for centuries, and can still be felt today; the mortality rate was distinctly higher among girls than boys: baby girls were abandoned more often than boys at birth, for only male heirs could continue the cult of the ancestors and take over the family farm. It should be emphasised that this inequality of the sexes has completely disappeared now, and has been replaced by rigorous equality.

The Racial Elements

Strictly speaking, no Chinese *race* exists as such. The group usually known as the Chinese people is made up of extremely varied racial elements, some of which still retain marked individuality: the "National Minorities" (see p. 58). The Minorities do not exceed 45 million people, however, which represents 5% of the total number of inhabitants of present-day China. The vast majority of the Chinese people are *Han:* they are the ones traditionally known as "the Chinese".

North China, that is, the great Yellow River plain, the loess plateaux of Shan xi and Shân xi, the Shan dong mountains, and broadly speaking, as far as the Yang zi, is inhabited by Chinese in the true sense of the word, or *Han*. The name comes from that of the dynasty which reigned from the 2nd century B.C. to the 2nd century A.D. They constitute a homogeneous block, and have gradually assimilated all foreign elements over the centuries; they speak the same dialect, "mandarin", or Peking dialect, now the official language.

South China, that is, roughly from the Yang zi southwards, is also inhabited by *Han*. The situation is different here however: the Han moved southwards over the first thousand years A.D., and had to absorb numerous non-Chinese elements. This mingling of races explains the existence of a southern physical type which differs considerably from the northern type. The southern Chinese have shown themselves to be more turbulent than their northern brothers, as most of the revolutionary movements of the 19 thand 20th centuries originated there: the Tai ping uprising in the 1850's, the reform movement started by Kang You wei in 1899, and the work of Sun Yat sen in the early years of the 20th century. Mao Ze dong himself was a native of Hu nan and his first Chinese Soviet Republic was in Jiang xi. The language spoken in the south is often very different from that of the north: the main southern dialect is Cantonese.

In the South-West, which includes Yun nan, Si chuan, Gui zhou and Guang xi, the Chinese influence spread much less rapidly: the nature of the country makes travelling and communication difficult, so that the original peoples have retained their individuality; the Han have no real foothold in the area except along the valleys and routes leading into the region, and in the towns. The biggest racial element is constituted by the Zhuang of Guang xi, who form an autonomous region, and amount to about 7 million altogether. The Miao, Li su, etc. form other groups. The Minorities, who retain their own languages and folklore, show an infinitely lower rate of population increase than the Han; what is more, they are often split into scattered tribes.

The West, which was included in the Chinese State relatively late, still contains the original peoples, who are relatively homogeneous: Mongols in Inner Mongolia (related to the Mongols of the Republic of Mongolia), Tibetans, Kazaks and Kirghiz of Dzungaria (related to those who live in Soviet Central Asia), Uighur Turks of Xin jiang. Most of them are Moslems.

Altogether, the Minorities occupy nearly two thirds of the total surface area of China, although they account for only 5% of the population. The Han are above all plain-dwellers, dependent on agriculture, whereas the Minorities have settled in the mountains, on the steppe and in the deserts.

The almost exclusive preponderance of the *Han* ensures great unity in the human geography of China. It is very different from India, divided up by its caste system, with its 800 languages and countless religions. It is very different too from the Soviet Union, where over 25% of the inhabitants are not Slav. This no doubt goes a long way to explain the strong influence of both China and her civilisation.

THE MINORITIES

It is often said that the People's Republic of China is a "state made up of countless National Minorities". As well as the Han, who represent the overwhelming majority of the population, about fifty non-Han "Minorities" exist, numbering about 45 million people altogether. Our term "Chinese" covers and often mixes up two ideas which are carefully distinguished from each other in modern China; "Chinese" means a citizen of the People's Republic *(Zhong guo ren)* and a man who is a member of the largest racial group, the Han *(Han zu ren)*. In some cases it would be helpful if the distinction observed in Chinese were indicated in our languages as well.

This multitude of nationalities is the result of a long historical process which began with the dawn of Chinese history and continued over the centuries which followed. Chinese civilisation originated in the middle Yellow River valley area and gradually spread; the history of China is also partly the history of this gradual extension of Chinese culture. Little by little, as the populations living on the boundaries were assimilated, they entered the Chinese community and once a few generations had passed, they were considered as Han. Texts dating from the Zhou period mention "barbarians" called *rong* and *yi* who lived on the edge of the Chinese territory and sometimes between different spheres of Chinese culture. Little is known of these "barbarians"; they seem to have been assimilated from the beginning of the empire.

The phenomenon continued as time went on; a list of these «barbarians» living on the edge of the Chinese world can be drawn up for each historical period (modern historical textbooks refer to them as "National Minorities"). Virtually nothing is known of their early history beyond what the Chinese textbooks record, which is not much. Although little is known about their civilisations, they must have played an important part in the development of Chinese civilisation, which was perpetually influenced by contact with them. It is known, for instance, that from the 3rd to the 6th century, the mixing process was particularly active in the north of China (see Historical introduction); although all trace of the non-Han population which played a vital part has disappeared by now (Qiang, Di, Xiong nu, Xian bei, etc.), their influence should not be neglected for that reason. As early as the 8th century, but above all from the 13th century onwards, the names of several "Minorities" appear in the texts; they now figure in the official catalogue of the People's Republic

(Tibetans, Zhuang, Mongols, Uighurs, etc.). From the Ming onwards, the documents are more numerous, and it would be possible to make a closer study of the fascinating history of the relationships and contacts between the Han and the populations of the marches.

This explains fairly adequately why most of the Minorities now live on the edges of Chinese territory, on the northern, western and southern borders or in other words, in regions which have only comparatively recently come fully under Chinese influence. To give an accurate idea of the question, a more detailed explanation is needed, for the term "National Minority" can be used under widely differing circumstances.

Some of the races developed their own, highly complex civilisations over the years, on the edge of the Chinese civilisation strictly speaking, and they could not be expected to accept wholesale assimilation. The Tibetans, the Mongols and the Uighurs, for instance, have a long historic tradition behind them, and now live in large groups in vast, unbroken stretches of territory. Language, the scripts and religion (Lamaism and Islam) represent indisputable conditions for autonomy.

The Minorities living in the south-west are very different, particularly those in Yun nan and Gui zhou; they are infinitely varied and present a challenge to the ethnographer (over half of all the Minorities recorded in China are in the province of Yun nan). Their geographical distribution and their linguistic differences have prevented the formation of solid units. Each race is represented by relatively few individuals, sometimes scattered and living miles away from each other (the Miao, for example). From the 19th century onwards, these areas have been on the edge of regions which have been systematically developed; their society and economy were very backward by the eve of 1949 ("primitive" or "feudal" age, according to the Chinese works on the subject). The Zhuang should be considered apart from this group, as they have been known since the 11th century, are the strongest Minority, numerically speaking, and live in a compact body in Guang xi.

Special mention must be made of the two original "Minorities", the Manchu and the Hui. The history of the Manchu is an excellent example of rapid assimilation; their evolution is easier to follow than most, as they appeared late in the history of China, and are well documented. The Manchu, related to the Tungus, entered China in about the middle of the 17th century and founded the last imperial dynasty, the Qing. To start with, the Manchu, who were divided into "banners", remained faithful to their language and traditions. But Chinese influence gained on them so rapidly that their descendants even forgot the Manchu tongue; the last Emperor, Pu yi, knew only one expression: "Get up!", which he pronounced during audiences, when the officials prostrated themselves in front of him. European sinologues recruited their teachers of Peking dialect from among the Manchu round about 1930. The two hundred thousand or so individuals who still claim Manchu nationality today are completely sinicized and show nothing to distinguish them from the Han.

The history of the Hui is more complex. Their name appeared under the Yuan dynasty; it is related etymologically to that of the Uighur. Moslems, most of them merchants from Central Asia, were known as Hui (or Hui hui). Gradually it became usual to refer to all Moslems by this name, whether they came from the west, or were Han converts (the Uighur Moslems are not considered as part of the Hui, however). Communities of them existed throughout the empire, in towns (Peking, Xi an, etc.) or in certain particular regions (Ning xia, Gan su, Yun nan). The Hui speak Chinese only (a few understand a little Arabic) and in most cases, nothing distinguishes them from the Han physically (though their faces sometimes reveal western blood). Since 1950, most of the young Hui have stopped frequenting the mosques, but they still observe the taboo on pork. The traveller in China will notice numerous restaurants in all towns reserved mainly for the Hui, and indicated by the two characters: *Qing zhen* ("pure").

An effort has been made since the revolution to bring out a new policy towards the Minorities, by stressing equality and condemning the "pan-Hanism" which was tending to develop after the fall of the Qing. History books and museums both afforded an important place to the "Minorities", who have contributed to the building of China alongside the Han. The Museum of the Minorities' Cultural Palace in Peking gives a somewhat stylised outline of the past history and the future of the different racial groups (see p. 523). Two illustrated magazines are devoted to the problems of the Minorities, and troupes of singers and dancers from one or other of the Minorities are often to be seen performing in the big towns. These efforts have no doubt helped to bring about a change in attitude and offer the rights of citizenship to people who only several decades ago were considered, if not as barbarians, at least as minors.

For administrative purposes, autonomous regions, zones and districts have been created. Five big autonomous regions exist:

the Autonomous Region of Tibet, the Uighur Autonomous Region of Xin jiang, the Inner Mongolian Autonomous Region, the Hui Autonomous Region of Ning xia, the Zhuang Autonomous Region of Guang xi. The autonomous zones and districts are within the autonomous regions and the provinces; Yun nan has large numbers of them (see p. 1233) and more were created there as late as 1964. The list is still open. Future cadres are recruited in the autonomous regions and sent to special institutes (National Minorities' Institutes, *Min zu xue yuan*), where they learn the Chinese language, along with the principles of communist administration.

The regions where the Minorities live have gained from economic measures, particularly from the agrarian reform and the improvement of communications (railway, roads, airlines). Light industry is now gradually replacing the age-old handicrafts which were often the only source of manufactured articles. By no means all the resources have been tapped as yet, and they are generally to be found in profusion in areas which have not been subjected to the needs of modern life (forests, mines, hydro-electricity).

The most rapid changes of all have taken place on the cultural plane. A great effort has been made to ensure that all the languages which up till now had never been written down should be furnished with an alphabet (particularly the languages of the south-western Minorites: Zhuang, Miao, Bu yi, Li su, Jing po, etc.); most of these new alphabets are based on adaptations of the Latin alphabet. Where traditional scripts existed, an effort is being made to spread the knowledge of them, as many were scarcely known outside a small elite (Tibetan, Mongol, Korean, Tai scripts). Uighur (which has affinities with Turkish) used to be written in Arabic script, and was romanised in 1965. Elementary manuals, and the works of Chairman Mao, have been published in these languages. This campaign against illiteracy, which enabled each Minority to establish links with its past once more, was backed up by an effort to spread the knowledge of Chinese, the only language giving access to secondary education. Several bilingual dictionaries have been published over the last few years, but there is not yet one for each language. The Scientific Research Centre for National Minorities conducted several linguistic and ethnographic enquiries, particularly before 1960, which threw light on the civilisations of the Minorities (oral traditions were collected); the archaeological services drew up an inventory of the historical monuments in Tibet, Xin jiang and Inner Mongolia. At the same time, an attempt was made to develop a new cultural life based on modern themes (creation of the great opera *Princess Wen cheng* on the theme of Sino-Tibetan friendship). In 1965, a small troupe of actors from Inner Mongolia, known as the "Wu lu mu qi" was acclaimed throughout the country; they travelled the steppes, giving evening performances of playlets designed to illustrate new principles.

List of Minorities

Figures for 1957 as published in the *Xin hua zi dian* dictionary.

Name	Population	Distribution
Zhuang	7,780,000	Guang xi Autonomous Region, Yun nan, Guang dong.
Hui	3,930,000	Ning xia and Xin jiang Autonomous Regions, Gan su.
Uighur	3,900,000	Xin jiang Autonomous Region.
Yi	3,260,000	Yun nan, Si chuan, Gui zhou.
Tibetan	2,770,000	Tibetan Autonomous Region, Qing hai, Si chuan, Gan su, Yun nan.
Miao	2,680,000	Gui zhou, Hu nan, Yun nan, Guang xi Autonomous Region, Si chuan, Guang dong.
Manchu	2,430,000	Liao ning, Hei long jiang, Ji lin, He bei, the City of Peking, the Inner Mongolian Autonomous Region.
Mongol	1,640,000	Inner Mongolian and Xin jiang Autonomous Regions, Liao ning, Ji lin, Hei long jiang, Gan su, Qing hai, He bei, He nan.
Bu yi	1,310,000	Gui zhou.
Korean	1,250,000	Ji lin, Hei long jiang, Liao ning.
Dong	820,000	Gui zhou, Hu nan, Guang xi Autonomous Region.

Name	Population	Distribution
Yao	740,000	Guang xi Autonomous Region Hu nan, Yun nan, Guang dong, Gui zhou.
Bai	680,000	Yun nan.
Tu jia	600,000	Hu nan, Hu bei.
Ha ni	540,000	Yun nan.
Kazakh	530,000	Xin jiang Autonomous Region, Gan su, Qing hai.
Dai (Tai)	500,000	Yun nan.
Li	390,000	Guang dong (Hai nan).
Li su	310,000	Yun nan.
Ka wa	280,000	Yun nan.
She	220,000	Fu jian, Zhe jiang, Jiang xi, Guang dong.
Gao shan	200,000	Tai wan.
La hu	180,000	Yun nan.
Shui	160,000	Gui zhou.
Dong xiang	150,000	Gan su.
Na xi	150,000	Yun nan.
Jing po	100,000	Yun nan.
Ke er ke zi	68,000	Xin jiang Autonomous Region.
Tu	63,000	Qing hai.
Da wor	50,000	Inner Mongolian and Xin jiang Autonomous Regions, Hei long jiang.
Mu lao	44,000	Guang xi Autonomous Region.
Qiang	42,000	Si chuan.
Bu lang	41,000	Yun nan.
Sa la	31,000	Qing hai, Gan su.
Mao nan	24,000	Guang xi Autonomous Region,
Ge lao	23,000	Gui zhou.
Xi bo	21,000	Xin jiang Autonomous Region. Liao ning.

Name	Population	Distribution
A chang	17,000	Yun nan.
Pu mi	15,000	Yun nan.
Tadjik (Tadzhik)	15,000	Xin jiang Autonomous Region.
Nu	13,000	Yun nan.
Uzbek	11,000	Xin jiang Autonomous Region.
Russians	9,700	Xin jiang Autonomous Region.
E wen ke	7,200	Inner Mongolian Autonomous Region.
Beng long	6,300	Yun nan.
Bao an	5,500	Gan su.
Yu gu	4,600	Gan su.
Jing	4,400	Guang dong.
Tartar	4,300	Xin jiang Autonomous Region.
Du long	2,700	Yun nan.
E lun chun	2,400	Hei long jiang, Inner Mongolian Autonomous Region.
He zhe	600	Hei long jiang.
Men ba	3,800	Tibet.

THE CHINESE LANGUAGE

The languages spoken in the People's Republic of China can be divided into two groups: Chinese proper (spoken by over 90% of the population) and the non-Chinese languages spoken by some of the minorities. Spoken Chinese varies widely from one region to another, so much so that without a common national language, people from different areas would be unable to understand each other. The common language is, broadly speaking, Peking dialect.

The languages spoken by the minorities will be dealt with briefly first, followed by:

I Spoken Chinese: a historical outline and the dialects as they are today.

II The Common Language: Phonetics and grammar.

III Chinese script.

The Minorities' languages

The political frontiers of the People's Republic of China are by no means linguistic frontiers. Countless non-Chinese languages are to be found in the border areas, varying enormously as far as the number of speakers (from several million to several thousand), their homogeneity, and the knowledge available about them today, are concerned. Only the most important of them can be discussed here. They belong to four language groups:

I. *The Altaic group* includes the Mongol dialects and the Turkic languages spoken in Xin jiang (Uighur, Kazakh).

II. *The Tibeto-Burmese group* includes Tibetan, Yi (or Lolo), Hani and Tujia.

III. *The Thai group* includes Zhuang, Dai, Bu yi and Dong.

IV. Yao and Miao form a separate group.

It should be remembered that some ethnic groups which are considered as minorities, such as the Hui (Moslems), speak Chinese only.

I. CHINESE

A. The Development of the Language

The Chinese script ceased to develop at the beginning of the Christian era and shows virtually no trace of the linguistic development which followed. The information to be gleaned from the script on the earlier stages of the language is extremely scanty; whereas alphabetic scripts analyse words into elementary sounds to which the letters correspond, Chinese script limits this analysis to the word itself, formerly monosyllabic (formed of one syllable alone). A character, giving no indication of the pronunciation, represents each word as a whole (syllable). At the same time, the written texts which have survived are mainly in an artificial language used solely for writing, bearing little resemblance to the spoken language. The linguist must therefore use them with the utmost wariness.

1. From the beginning up to the end of the Han

The area of Chinese gradually spread southwards from the middle Yellow River region. From the Warring States period onwards, considerable differences existed between the speech of the middle and lower Yellow River and that of the middle and lower Yang zi River.

Even before the Qin unified the empire and imposed their centralisation policy, a common written language, transcending all dialectal differences, was already coming into being. The minister Li Si unified the script and put an end to the confusions produced by local usages. The reform, and the appearance of the scholar class, both helped in the development of the common written language; the spoken language corresponding to it gradually grew further and further away from this developing written language. *The existence of a common written language alongside local forms of speech and at the same time independent of them*, is a phenomenon still to be found today; it is a constant and essential feature in the history of Chinese culture.

2. From the end of the Han to the end of the Song

Politically, these ten centuries consist of periods of division alternating with periods of renewed unity. The barbarians occupied the north, causing large-scale migrations towards the south on several different occasions; large sections of the population carried the Chinese language south of the Yang zi. As far as can be judged, the languages of the barbarian occupiers had no perceptible influence on the Chinese speech of the northern areas.

According to Bernhard Karlgren: "We have reason to believe that the vernacular of North China of the sixth century A.D., (. . .), in the lapse of the Tang dynasty spread over the larger part of the China of those days at the expense of other ancient dialects and became what linguists call a *koine*, a general language..."

(The Chinese Language, p. 44*).* Linguists have reconstructed this language with the help of contemporary rhyme books, and except for a few features of some of the Fu jian dialects, modern dialects can be explained by going back to this common Ancient Chinese, which later developed in different ways according to the different regions.

The introduction of Buddhism in China was also extremely important for the history of the language. The written language used by the officials grew daily further away from spoken usage, and was unsuitable as a vehicle for Buddhist propaganda. From the Tang dynasty onwards, Buddhist texts were written in a language which was as close as possible to the spoken language, and which developed alongside the scholars' written language.

At the same time, the Chinese discovered the Indian grammatical tradition, which was to have a lasting effect on the drawing up of rhyme tables, where the words are classed systematically according to their phonetic characteristics, and not according to the characters representing them. The countless Chinese translations of Indian texts also give transcriptions in Chinese characters of Indian words whose pronunciation is known to us through other sources; all this represents precious material for linguists wanting to reconstruct the pronunciation of that time.

3. Modern times

When the Yuan came to power (13th century), Peking became the capital of the empire and was to remain so for over six centuries. The centre of gravity of the linguistic map, which up till then had been fixed in the Yellow River Valley, except for a few interruptions due to barbarian invasions, moved northwards. As the state grew more centralised, *the northern dialect, known as "guanhua" (Mandarin) came to be the spoken language used by the administration and the scholars throughout the empire.* It exerted an increasing influence over the local speech forms.

The implantation of the northern dialect in the south west (Yun nan, Gui zhou, Guang xi) and the north east dates from this period.

Wenyan and baihua

The preponderance of the northern language may also be explained by the flowering of literary works written in the spoken language. The great novels were written in what was essentially the northern language, and were consequently accessible to a much larger section of the public than were writings in the tradi-

tional written language (or *wenyan*), virtually a dead language,
needing long years of study before it could be mastered.

Two written languages, *wenyan* and *baihua*, existed side by
side throughout this period. *Wenyan* was the written language
of the mandarin class, the instrument of its administrative power
and the expression of its ideology. It was maintained systematically by the state examinations, which required candidates to
learn it. *Baihua* is the term for the language used, save for
a few exceptions, for all new and living works of Chinese literature from the Yuan Dynasty until this century: these include
chiefly novels and plays. As a language, it is close to spoken
usage, which is its main source.

When compared with *baihua*, the most striking feature of
wenyan is its conciseness. Its vocabulary, based on ancient texts,
is essentially monosyllabic (one character for each word) and
completely different from that of the spoken language. The grammar makes the greatest possible use of word-order. *Wenyan* is a
written language only, much less liable to redundance than the
spoken word. At the same time, the character once written has a
far greater distinguishing power than the syllable in spoken
language, and this difference is growing more accentuated as the
northern dialects grow more impoverished phonetically. A text
in *wenyan* read aloud in Peking dialect is often completely in-
comprehensible now: modern Peking dialect possesses about
thirteen hundred different syllables altogether. The number of
characters likely to appear in a text in *wenyan* of any given period
exceeds this figure, however. Many characters therefore share
the same pronunciation, and the listener, on the other hand, is
faced with a choice between several characters for each syllable
of the text as it is read. As the language is extremely concise, the
context gives little help in distinguishing between these homonyms.

The movement of political and cultural renewal at the beginning of the 20th century began the gradual suppression of
wenyan, while *baihua* was more and more widely used. The pressure of modern, democratic ideals dealt the death-blow to
wenyan, the language of the initiated and instrument of cultural
domination. Once *wenyan* had disappeared, *baihua* came to be
the only language in use for books and newpapers.

The first measures designed to spread Mandarin systematically
throughout the whole country, under the name of *guoyu* (National Language), date from the same time. The measures taken
before 1949 met with only limited success. Not until the present
regime was established did the government's decisions finally
take effect: a common spoken language, now known as *putonghua*

(Common Language) was imposed throughout China, by means of education, wireless broadcasts, public entertainment. *Putonghua* is based on the northern dialect; its pronunciation is that of Peking, and its grammar that of the modern works in *baihua*. Within the space of a few generations, all Chinese will, theoretically, speak the same language; the dialects will then become regional patois, doomed to disappear little by little.

B. Modern Dialects

The complex state of the dialects at present is generally explained by referring back to a hypothetical common Chinese supposed to have existed in the 6th century, which developed differently in different regions.

The syllable is at its most impoverished in the northern dialects; the Peking dialect in particular, has lost all trace of the consonants -*p*, *t*, and -*k* which used to occur at the end of the syllable in Ancient Chinese. The sound system of a language such as that spoken in Canton has undergone less drastic changes, and is nearer the 6th century pronunciation.

Different forms of speech which share some of the main features of the phonetic development are collected under the heading of a few important "dialects". The classification given here is the most widely accepted. It is however a broad one, as people who understand each other with difficulty or even not at all are often to be found within the same area. Here is a list of the dialects and their distribution:

1. *Northern dialect* (also called: *Mandarin dialect*). It includes the speech of *over 70% of the Han population:* all the regions north of the Yang zi, the south western point of Hu bei, the north western part of Hu nan, Gui zhou, Yun nan and Si chuan. It can be divided further into (see map):

   northern Mandarin,
   lower Yang zi Mandarin,
   south western Mandarin.

In contrast with the relatively homogeneous mass of the Mandarin forms, south China is divided up even further:

2. WU dialect: part of Jiang su, south of the Yang zi River and most of Zhe jiang;

3. XIANG dialect: Hu nan, except for north west Hu nan.

4. GAN dialect: Jiang xi and the south eastern point of Hu bei.

5. NORTHERN MIN dialect: north Fu jian and a small part of Tai wan.

6. SOUTHERN MIN dialect: south Fu jian, most of Tai
wan, part of Hai nan and east Guang dong.

7. YUE dialect: most of Guang dong and south eastern
Guang xi.

8. KE JIA dialect (or HAKKA): this embraces a handful
of forms of speech found in the north and east of Guang dong
mainly. They are also to be found scattered through south
eastern Guang xi, eastern Fu jian, southern Guang dong,
Si chuan and Hu nan.

Most of the Chinese of south east Asia speak the Yue and
Min dialects. Those in America and elsewhere usually speak
the Yue dialect.

The grammatical systems of all these dialects differ only on
secondary points, such as a few differences in word-order or
particles, all differences which in themselves would not prevent
speakers of one dialect from understanding speakers of other
dialects. The same is not true of the sound systems and vocabulary, however.

"to cry" is *ku* at Peking and *huk* at Canton. Both forms go
back to the word **k'uk* ("to cry") in Ancient Chinese (6th century). "north" is *bei* at Peking and *pak* at Canton; both forms
come from the Ancient Chinese **pek*. In these cases the words
have developed parallel to one another. They form part of a
simple pattern of phonetic similarities between one dialect
and another, like those which exist between French and Italian,
both of which derive from Latin: *homme* and *huomo* (Latin
homo), *père* and *padre* (Latin *pater*). In cases such as these,
where both forms share the same origin in Ancient Chinese,
and the meanings are still roughly the same today, the Chinese
usually say that the difference is phonetic; the same written
character is used for both *ku* and *huk*, *bei* and *pak*. This gives
rise to an illusion that is widespread in China, namely that
the chief, fundamental linguistic reality is contained in writing,
and that differences between dialects are essentially differences
in reading, or vocal interpretation of the characters.

But linguistic development does not follow a straight line;
it remoulds the very structure of the vocabulary; little connection
exists between the French word *voleur* and the Italian equivalent
ladro, or between the French *ville* and the Italian *città*. "the
neck" is *bozi* at Peking and *geng* at Canton; these two words
obviously do not share the same origin in ancient Chinese.
Differences like these can apply to a large area of vocabulary,
quite apart from the cases where a word in language A is

LES DIALECTES CHINOIS
THE CHINESE DIALECTS
d'après Sun Chang xu «Han yu ci hui»
(Le vocabulaire chinois), Chang Chun, 1957
page 270, «The Chinese Vocabulary»

Dialecte Mandarin du nord
Northern Mandarin dialect

Dialecte Mandarin du bas Yang Zi
Lower Yang Zi Mandarin dialect

Dialecte Mandarin du sud-ouest
South-west Mandarin Dialect

Dialecte Wu
Wu dialect

Dialecte Xiang
Xiang dialect

Dialecte Gan
Gan dialect

Dialecte Min du nord
Northern Min dialect

Dialecte Min du Sud
Southern Min dialect

Dialecte Yue
Yue dialect

Dialecte Ke Jia (Hakka)
Ke Jia (Hakka) dialect

Langues non-chinoises
Non-chinese languages

represented by different equivalents in language B according
to the context. Generally speaking, this re-organisation of
the vocabulary has been carried further in the northern dialects
than in those of the south. Two different forms of Chinese
may differ as widely as far as their sound systems and vocabulary are concerned as do French and Spanish.

The Chinese realised at the beginning of this century that
they would never succeed in building a great, modern country
until their linguistic divisions could be eliminated. One of
the basic tasks which the present regime has set itself in the
cultural field is that of the spreading of a common spoken

language throughout the country. The Common Language *(putonghua)* is based on the northern dialect, purged of all regional characteristics in grammar and vocabulary. The pronunciation is that of Peking.

II. THE COMMON LANGUAGE

Chinese[1] has the reputation of being a particularly difficult and complicated language. In fact it is *different*. Our languages use certain grammatical processes to analyse and describe experience; Chinese uses others which analyse and describe them in a different way. Considered in themselves, these methods are as simple and as efficient as the ones which we are used to. Before embarking on the grammar and vocabulary of the common language, the sound system (that of Peking speech) will be briefly discussed.

A. Sound System

From the point of view of phonology, vocabulary and writing, the fundamental unit of Chinese is the syllable. It consists of three elements: the initial, the final and the tone. Each will be discussed separately.

The initial is a consonant. Initials include two sets of consonants, "aspirated" and "non-aspirated". An aspirated consonant is one whose release is followed by a voiceless puff of breath (like the *k-* of *kill*, or the *p-* of the German *Puppe*). The initial consonants are as follows:

p	t	c	ch	k	q
b	d	z	zh	g	j

f l s sh h x
m n

r

The aspirated and non-aspirated consonants are boxed in.

---

[1] "Chinese" or the "Chinese language" both refer to *putonghua* in this text when used with no further qualification. The transcription used is that of *pinyin fang'an*, the only one in use in China since 1958.

The *final* can be denoted by the formula *(A) + B + (C)*, in which *B* represents the middle vowel, sometimes preceded by the vowel *A*, which can be *i, ü* or *u*, and *C* which can be *i, u, n* or *ng*. For example:

	initial	final		
		A	B	C
chē (vehicle) consists of:	*ch*		*e*	
lèi (tired)	*l*		*e*	*i*
duō (many)...................	*d*	*u*	*o*	
huáng (yellow)	*h*	*u*	*a*	*ng*
màn (slow)	*m*		*a*	*n*
ài (to love)			*a*	*i*

If they are listed systematically, it will be found that Peking dialect possesses slightly more than thirty different finals. A final may also form a syllable on its own, without an initial. Each initial does not necessarily combine with every final; some are incompatible. For example, *q, j* and *x* precede only finals beginning with *i* or *ü; c, z* and *s, ch, zh, sh* and *r, k, g* and *h* appear everywhere else.

The vowel is the most important component in the syllable in Peking dialect. As the only final consonants are -*n* and -*ng*, the consonant clusters which occur frequently in our languages do not exist. *Marx*, a monosyllabic word, becomes three syllables in Chinese, because *k* and *s* cannot belong to the same syllable, and unless the speaker has learned a foreign language, he is incapable of pronouncing them together without an additional vowel. Nor can *s* be pronounced as a final: it too needs an additional vowel. The result is *măkèsī*. When the Chinese begin to learn English or French, for example, they have a tendency to pronounce every final mute *e* and to add a number of vowels to separate consonant clusters. This explains their characteristic, hesitant pronunciation.

The tones: Peking dialect has four different pitch variations whose function it is to distinguish one word from another in the same way as vowels and consonants do. Take the syllable *ma* for instance. When pronounced without varying the pitch of the voice (level tone), it is *mā* (Mother); with a rising inflexion (rising tone, *má*), it means hemp; with a falling inflexion (falling tone), *mà*, it means to abuse. If the pitch of the voice falls and then rises (falling and rising tone), *mǎ*, it means horse. *mā*, *má*, *mǎ* and *mà* are not homonyms any more than *hill*, *fill*, *mill* and *pill* are in English; they count as four different syllables.

The tone is applied to the syllable as a whole, and not to one component only. Every syllable has to be pronounced on one of the four tones, except when it occurs in an unstressed position, when differences in the tone disappear, along with certain qualities of the vowel itself; in these cases the *pinyin* transcription leaves out the tone sign: *ma* is an unstressed particle indicating a question.

Tones and *intonation* are two completely different things. In English, for example, the word *mother* may be pronounced in a level tone of voice (neutral), with a rising inflexion (questioning), or with a falling inflexion (emphatic). Whatever the inflexion, however, the identity of the word remains the same. It merely takes on a different colour.

The use of tones to differentiate between words is fairly widespread and occurs in several Asian, African and S. American languages; it even occurs in Swedish.

B. Vocabulary and Grammar

1. General principles

Some languages, such as German and Latin, use different case-endings to indicate the function of a word in a sentence; in the Latin sentence *Petrus Paulum videt* (Peter sees Paul), for example, the case-endings *-us* and *-um* are the only indications given to show that *Petrus* is the subject and *Paulum* the object. English and French, on the other hand, both of which have lost all but a few remains of their case systems, rely on *word order:* in the sentence *Peter sees Paul*, the position of each word is the only indication given to show that *Peter* is the subject and *Paul* the object. When the word-order is reversed, the meaning changes: *Paul sees Peter*. In Chinese this is still more systematic:

wō dǎ nǐ "I beat you"   *nǐ dǎ wō* "you beat me"

I to beat you   you to beat me

Chinese words are generally invariable. Chinese makes no distinction between singular and plural, gender, agreement of subject and verb, etc.., most of which in English would be indicated by differences within the word itself or in its ending.

The Chinese verb goes further than the English verb in ignoring differences in person:

je vais	*tu vas*	*il va*	*nous allons*	*vous allez*	*ils vont*
I go	you go	he goes	we go	you go	they go
wǒ qù	*nǐ qù*	*tā qù*	*wǒmen qù*	*nǐmen qù*	*tāmen qù*

The Chinese morphological system, if it can be called that, is reduced to a few suffixes, some grammatical, some derivative.

wǒ (I)   → *wǒmen* (we)
chī (eat)   → *chīle* (to have finished eating)
xiàndài (modern)   → *xiàndàihuà* (to modernise)

When French uses, for example:

a) *finis, finissons,* b) *crains, craignons,* c) *bois, buvons,*

the first person plural suffix *-ons* is added and is accompanied by changes in the root:

a) *fini-* → *finiss-*, b) *crain-* → *craign-*, c) *boi-* → *buv-*.

The same thing applies to the derivation of words:

comprendre → *compréhension, opprimer* → *oppression, sale* → *saleté, probe* → *probité.*

Chinese possesses no variants such as these, whose function it is to bind the different parts of the words together. Each word, each suffix exists in one unchangeable form, unaffected by differences in the contexts.

In fact, the relationship between the elements within the word itself or between words in a sentence in English or French, for example, makes each element or word like a piece in a jigsaw puzzle, fitting in with the next one; Chinese is more like a game of dominoes, where the pieces are merely placed next to one another.

2. Vocabulary

A short digression is necessary here to give a brief, though not over-simplified, explanation of the main principles governing Chinese language and writing.

In the English sentence: *Mary washes the tea-pot, tea-pot* is one word; it is an indivisible whole, subject to the same syntactic rules which govern simple words like *cup* or *knife*. The function of "object of the verb *to wash*" and the definite article *the* apply to the word as a whole and not to *tea* and *pot* separately. On the other hand, in the sentence: *She puts the tea in the pot,* the two elements *tea* and *pot* are independent units each with its own syntactic function in the sentence; they are complete words. A unit which constitutes a word in any given sentence A does not necessarily do so in sentence B.

Take a word like *geology*, for instance. Unlike *tea* and *pot*, the two component parts, *geo-* and *-logy* never appear alone as separate words, but always combined with something else, as in *geo-graphy, geo-physics*, or *psycho-logy, astro-logy*.

A more precise idea than that of the word is needed, standing for the basic components of the language in general, making no distinction between those which can be used alone (*tea, pot*) and those which can be used only in conjunction with others, within a larger unit (*geo-* and *-logy*).

The next unit after the word, as defined by general linguistics, is the *morpheme*, the smallest unit with a meaning of its own. The word *unkindness* consists of three morphemes, only one of which, *kind*, can be used as a word on its own. Simple words like *kind, man, down* consist of one morpheme only, as they cannot be broken down into smaller elements which still retain a meaning. To simplify matters here, it can be said that "morpheme" is a generic term embracing the ideas of root and affix (prefixes, derivative suffixes, verb and noun endings).

In English, the morphemes form fixed groups, sanctioned by usage, which are words. In Chinese, on the other hand, it could be said that the morphemes are completely free. They are joined on to each other with great flexibility, forming syntactical units whose cohesiveness varies considerably. No essential difference exists between the principles governing the combining of morphemes into words, and those governing the combining of the words themselves. The dividing line between what should still be termed "compound words" and what is already a "word group" is therefore often extremely vague. Traditional ideas of "simple words" and "compound words" bring only rigid, fixed groups to mind. If these alone are used, it is impossible to convey the fluidity of Chinese vocabulary. where every morpheme is available for use in new combinations,

The importance of the syllable in Chinese derives from the fact that *the morphemes generally consist of single syllables*. In this sentence:

1	2	3	4	5	6	7
tā	*chīle*	*yì*	*wǎn*	*mǐfàn*		
he	eat	a	bowl	rice		
	-suffix					

("he has eaten a bowl of rice"), seven morphemes are grouped in five words. The word *chīle* consists of the verb *chī* (to eat), which can stand alone, and the suffix *-le*, which indicates a finished action, and which can only be used added on to a verb. The word *mǐfàn* (cooked rice) is made up of *mǐ* (rice) and *fàn* (cooked rice), each of which may be used separately as a complete word.

Morphemes of more than one syllable are relatively rare. Examples of this are: *késou* (to cough), *dōngxi* (thing), *tàiyang* (sun). It is impossible to break down *tàiyang*, for instance, into two syllables, *tài* and *yang*, whose combined meaning gives idea of the sun. *Tàiyang*, both in meaning and form, is an indivisible whole; it is a morpheme.

The *words*, however, *are for the most part disyllabic*, at least as far as *the vocabulary* is concerned. This superiority in numbers on the part of disyllabic words scarcely makes itself felt in speech, as the most frequently used words are often monosyllables, grammatical elements or ones belonging to the basic vocabulary; hardly any new ones are being created. Some examples of this are: *dǎ* (to hit); *kàn* (to look); *hē* (to drink); *mén* (door); *shuǐ* (water); *kuài* (fast); *hǎo* (good); etc.

Two-syllable words, which are by far the most numerous, are usually composed of two morphemes of one syllable each, like the word *mǐfàn* already mentioned.

Prefixes and suffixes are relatively few; *most of the vocabulary consists of compound words* of a type similar to English words like *ant-eater*, *classroom*, *blackboard*, *geology*, etc. Examples of two of the most usual methods of formation will be given here:

1. Juxtaposition of two antonyms or two synonyms. *mǎi* means "to buy" and *mài* means "to sell". The compound word *mǎimai* means "trade".

Other similar words are:

duō (many) + *shǎo* (few)	→ *duōshao* (how many?)
cháng (long) + *duǎn* (short	→ *chángduǎn* (length)
gǎi (modify) + *biàn* (change)	→ *gǎibiàn* (to modify)
xūn (to look for) + *zhǎo* (to look for)	→ *xūnzhǎo* (to look for)

II. The first morpheme qualifies the second:

rè (warm) + *ài* (to love)	→ *rèài* (to love ardently)
kè (class) + *běn* (notebook)	→ *kèběn* (exercise book)
diàn (electric) + *huà* (word)	→ *diànhuà* (telephone)
tiě (iron) + *lù* (road)	→ *tiělù* (railway)

Many other methods of word-formation exist as well as
these. In modern Chinese, compounding is the very soul of
vocabulary. The links binding the element of a compound word
are often fairly weak. The proof of this lies in the way in which
the Chinese break up some word groups and retain only a few
morphemes to form a new word. Take the expression *gāojí
zhōngxué* (higher secondary school) for instance: it consists
of two words:

gāojí (higher), made up of two morphemes, *gāo* (high) and
jí (degree) *zhōngxué* (secondary school), made up of *zhōng*
(middle) and *xué* (study).

The Chinese have made up another word by using the first
and third morphemes only: *gāozhōng*, where *gāo* and *zhōng*
have both kept their individuality. Another example of this
is the expression *tǔdí gǎigé* (agrarian reform), which can be
broken down into:

tǔ (earth) + *dì* (earth)   → *tǔdì* (earth)
gǎi (modify) + *gé* (reform)→ (reform);   the   first   and   third
morphemes have combined to form the word *tǔgǎi* (agrarian
reform).

3. Syntax

3–1. *Word Classes.* We usually divide the words of a language
into different classes according to their morphology and the
part they play in the sentence (nouns, verbs, adjectives, etc.).
In English, for instance, words fulfil different functions: the
verb "describes a state or an action" and is conjugated; the
noun "represents a thing or an idea" and is preceded by an
article or a pronoun, etc. A Chinese word contains nothing
to indicate whether it is a noun, a verb or another part of
speech. The same word often fulfils different roles according
to the context. Take the following two sentences, for example:

yīnggāi nǔlì gōngzuò   one must work diligently
(must)   (diligently)   (to work)

nǐde   gōngzuò   zěnmeyàng?   how is your work going?
(your)   (work)   (how is)

Generally speaking, *gōngzuò* is translated by a verb (to
work) in the first sentence, and by a noun (work) in the second;
we cannot conceive of a word which can be alternately a noun
and a verb without a morphological change: *work*, for instance,
appears as *work* or *works* when used as a noun, and as *work,
works, working, worked* when used as a verb. The first sentence

can be translated either as: "one must work diligently" or "diligent work is necessary". In both cases, we are trying to force the Chinese sentence into the mould of English word classes, thinking that they are universal.

This does not mean, however, that Chinese contains no distinction between the word classes, and that every word can alternately act as a noun, a verb, an adjective, etc. It means simply that the classes are divided off in a different way, and that the relationship between them is not the same as that which we are accustomed to. Strictly speaking, other terms should be used, rather than "noun", "verb", "adjective", all of which have too many associations with Indo-European languages. To make things easier, and also because some analogies exist, however rough, between the classification of the word classes in Chinese and the Indo-European languages, the traditional terminology is generally used. It should not be forgotten, though, that the two realities involved can neither of them be reduced to the other.

3–2. *Word-order.* The order of the simple Chinese sentence is usually as follows:

subject — verb — object

for example:

(1) (2) (3) (4) (5) (6)
wǒ gěi dìdi yí kuài táng

(1) (2) (3) (4) (5) (6)
(I) (to give) (younger brother) (a) (piece) (sugar)
«I give my little brother a piece of sugar»

(1) (2) (3)
nǐ kàn shénme?

(1) (2) (3)
(you) (to look) (what?)
«What are you looking at?»

Within this basic pattern, the words are arranged to fit in with the basic principle that the *qualifier precedes the qualified;* in *jiù shū,* "old book", the adjective *jiù* "old" (qualifier) precedes *shū* "book", which it qualifies. In the same way, in *nǔlì gōngzuò* "to work diligently", the qualifier *nǔlì* "diligently" precedes *gōngzuò,* which it qualifies. In the group:

zhōnghuá rénmín gònghéguó   "People's Republic of China"
(China)   (people)   (republic)

the qualifier "China" precedes what it qualifies, the "People's Republic", which in turn can be broken down in the same way.

Qualifiers of nouns may be made up into fairly complicated groups. They are often accompanied by the unstressed particle -*de*, which is attached to the last word in the group:

[*wǒ*]-*de shū*   "my book"
(I)   (book)

[*nǐ gěi wǒ*]-*de shū*   "the book which you give me"
(you) (to give) (I) (book)

[*wǒ qùnián zhù*]-*de fángzi* "the room which I lived in last year"
(I) (last year) (to live)   (room)

The square brackets denote the part of the sentence which the particle -*de* pertains to.

Chinese has different kinds of verb modifiers: adverbs, and groups of words introduced by a proposition, which could be called "circumstantial complements":

nǐ kuài qù (you) (quickly) (to go)   "go quickly!"
nǐ gēn tā qù (you) (with) (he) (to go)   "go with him"
nǐ dào nǎli qù (you) (to) (where?) (to go) "where are you going?"

3–3. *Grammatical Categories (grammatical determinatives)*

The Chinese noun does not indicate number. The sentence:

zhuōzi shang yǒu shū
(table) (on) (there is) (book (s)

gives no hint whether books or a book are meant. The context, or the situation in which the remark is made, provide the clarification, if necessary. In English, a choice has to be made between singular and plural every time a noun is used; if need be, the singular can be used in the case of uncertainty, or when the thing in question cannot be counted. In the sentence: "The chicken is a domestic bird", the singular is not used in the sense of one and one only, as opposed to two or more, as the speaker is talking about the species of chickens in general, without specifying their number, as in the sentence: "We eat chicken on Sundays". The literal translation of the Chinese sentence ought then to be: "There is book on the table". The language has the means of indicating the exact number if it is found to be necessary. In the example given, the determinative *yīxiē* would be used, giving: *zhuōzi shang yǒu yīxiē shū*, which can only mean: "There are some books on the table". Chinese can make as clear a distinction as our own languages between "one" and "several", but only when it is judged necessary.

The verb is the next thing to be studied. Chinese has a large variety of ways in which an action may be situated in time, described in the course of its development, or in its relationship with other actions. The methods used to make any given distinction do not resemble ours, however. Basically, they do not stress the same aspects of experience; a few examples will help to illustrate this:

1) Chinese uses the plain form of the verb, or the verb with suffixes attached. The suffixes *-le* and *-guo* alone will be mentioned here.

tā chī (plain form)
(he) (to eat)

wǒ chīguo jī "I have already eaten chicken" (once or several times in the past)

wǒ chīle jī "I have eaten (finished) the chicken".

The suffix *-guo* stresses the fact that the action has already happened once or several times in the past. The suffix *-le* emphasises the completed aspect of the action and its repercussions. English possesses only one verb form (the perfect) to express this distinction, and has to use the adverb "already", or another verb, "to finish". The two sentences in English lay stress on the past aspect, as opposed to the present or the future. Chinese, on the other hand, makes a careful distinction between the completed aspect indicated by *-le* and the "experiential" aspect shown by *-guo*. The dividing line between completed and non-completed does not fall in with our division of past on the one hand and present and future on the other, as this sentence shows:

míngtiān tā chīle fàn jiù zǒu
(tomorrow) (he) (to eat) (meal) (then) (to go)

which means: "he will go tomorrow when he has finished his meal".

The plain form of the verb presents the action considered from a general aspect, without specifying the circumstances:

tā míngtiān lái "he will come tomorrow" (or "he hopes to come tomorrow")
(he) (tomorrow) (to come)

(*zuótiān   lái*)-*de rén*　　　　　"the man who came yesterday"
(yesterday) (to come) (man)

tā   xiǎng   lái　　　　　　　　"he wants to come"
(he) (to want) (to come)

When the form *lái* is translated by "he will come", "he came"
and "to come", the whole sentence has to be re-arranged to
fit in with our own linguistic habits, which oblige us to use
the form of the verb to convey some of the indications supplied
by the context in Chinese. The form *lái* is felt to be the same
in all the different contexts.

II) Chinese uses:

wǒ suǒle mén　　　　　　　　　"I have locked the door"
(I) (to lock) (door)

mén suǒle　　"the door is locked" (literally "has been locked")
(door) (to lock)

The verb *suǒle* contains no change in its form corresponding
to the distinction between active and passive as illustrated by
"to lock" and "to be locked". The context alone is enough.
Chinese stresses the distinction by using a special morpheme
only when a risk of ambiguity arises.

III) To indicate a new state of affairs or one not fully realised by
the speaker before, the particle -*le* is added to the last word in
the sentence (it should not be confused with the suffix -*le* mentioned earlier on); Chinese opposes:

wǒ pàng "I am fat" and *wǒ pàngle* "I have got fatter" (literally:
(I) (fat)　　　　　　　　　　　　　　　　"now I am fat)

wǒ méiyou qián　　　　　　"I haven't any money"
(I) (no) (have) (money)

and *wo méiyou qiánle*　　"I haven't **any** *more* money"
(I) (no) (have) (money)

English, in similar cases, uses "to be fat" as opposed to "to
have got fatter" and "any" and "any more", which proves
once more that neither of the two means of expression can be
reduced to the other, and that neither can furnish a word for
word equivalent for the other. To isolate the Chinese verbal
system from the rest of the language and show up its poverty
compared with the English system is a risky undertaking. Each
language ascribes its own set of values to the verb, which forms
a whole with its context. It is possible to feel and express the

most subtle distinctions between present and past, and real or imaginary happenings without possessing as complex a system of tenses and moods as our own.

III. THE SCRIPT

A. Chinese Characters

Scripts which use an alphabet analyse each spoken word into a succession of "elementary sounds" which can be rendered by twenty to thirty letters only. The principle of the Chinese script is different; this is due to the unusual structure of the language, and to the historical conditions in which it developed.

In old Chinese, as opposed to Modern Chinese, most of the words consisted of a single monosyllabic morpheme. A sentence was constructed of a succession of invariable words, each of one syllable. The script assigned a separate sign (character) to each word. Each character therefore represented a fraction of the meaning and a given syllable at the same time. Nothing in the structure of the language obliged the script to carry the analysis further than the syllable, since the syllable represented the smallest unit of meaning, and existed in an unchangeable form. This type of script would be inconvenient for Indo-European languages, where the form of a morpheme often varies from one context to another, and several morphemes often form closely-knit segments which defy analysis; the script would be inadequate to reflect the alternations in the morphology. In the case of English verbs, for instance, root changes often occur in different parts of the verb; if characters were used, the character for the morpheme "to sink" would have to be pronounced in a different way for "sank" and "sunk". The juxtaposition of Chinese characters corresponds to the juxtaposition of morphemes with fixed forms in words.

As time went on, the proportion of two-syllable words increased considerably; monosyllabic words which were originally independent were joined up to form words like *any-thing*, *mean-while*, *some-one* in English. The written language kept as near as possible to the old state of affairs and still used a vocabulary which was essentially made up of words of one syllable. The spread of written styles which are nearer to the spoken language has all but eliminated the old orderly system in which the word, the morpheme, the syllable and the character coincided. One feature of this has remained unchanged: each spoken syllable is represented by a character, and *a sentence, once written down, contains as many characters as it does syllables.*

As most morphemes in modern Chinese are monosyllabic, it can be said that in most cases a character stands for a morpheme, which has a meaning when it stands on its own. In the sentence already quoted: *wǒ chīle yí wǎn mǐfàn* (I have eaten a bowl of rice), seven characters (Fig. I) (I) correspond to the seven syllables, all of which are morphemes. Each time that the Chinese use the morpheme *wǒ* (I), they write the character No. 1; each time that they use the morpheme *chī* (to eat), they write the character No. 2, etc...[1]

我　　吃　　了　　一　　碗　　米　　飯

| 1 | 2 | 3 | 4 | 5 | 6 | 7 |
| wǒ | chī | le | yì | wǎn | mǐ | fàn |

Fig. 1

The morphemes and characters certainly do not always correspond as perfectly as this, however, as beginners of Chinese learn all too soon. First of all, a number of morphemes exist with more than one syllable. For example character No. 8 (Fig. 2) generally stands for the morpheme *dōng* (east); character No. 9 (Fig. 2) generally stands for the morpheme *xī* (west). But the two characters, when combined, generally give the two-syllabled morpheme *dōngxi*, whose vague meaning (thing) has nothing to do with the meanings of the morphemes *dōng* and *xī* in modern Chinese. Readers have to pass over the usual meanings of the two and retain their pronunciation only.

東　　　西　　　長　　　重　　　馬

| 8 | 9 | 10 | 11 | 12 |

Fig. 2

---

[1] The characters in Chinese script are always evenly spaced, with no reference to the way in which the morphemes join to form words. They are traditionally arranged in vertical columns reading from top to bottom and from right to left. Almost all books and newspapers in the People's Republic of China are now printed horizontally, and read from left to right, as in the West.

At the same time, one character may stand for different morphemes, according to its context, which are often homophones or sounds which closely resemble each other: character 10 (Fig. 3) can stand for the morphemes *cháng* (long), *zhǎng* (to grow) and *zhǎng* (chief); character No. 11 stands for the morphemes *chóng* (again) and *zhòng* (heavy), depending on the context. The most frequent characters of this type were recently collected in a dictionary, and cover seventy finely printed pages.

Irregularities like these have always existed. To understand the reason for them, the relationship between each character and the morpheme which it stands for must be grasped. A comparison might be helpful here: the symbol "2" stands at the same time for the English word "two", the French "deux", the Spanish "dos", etc..; the link in each case is not between the symbol and the formal features (the sound) of each word, for this varies from one language to another, but with their meaning. No link exists necessarily between the form of the symbol "2" and its meaning; the Roman figure "II" or any other symbol adopted by mathematicians would, in theory, fill the role just as well.

The same goes for Chinese characters and the morphemes which they represent. The links between character No. 12 and the morpheme *mǎ* (horse) are purely a matter of convention: the character cannot be broken down into smaller units whose combined meaning would represent the idea of "horse", nor can it be broken into smaller units whose combined pronunciation would produce the syllable *mǎ* (the principle of phonetic script). In short, *the form of each character contains nothing to suggest its meaning or pronunciation*.

In the case of phonetic script, which is associated with the formal features (the sound) of words, about thirty or so letters associated with the *sounds* of the language have to be memorised, along with the rules governing their combinations; to be able to read means to be able to make out new words (names and rare technical terms, for instance). The Chinese have to memorise the characters associated with the morphemes one by one. A character contains nothing to enable it to be read when seen for the first time, even if it stands for a morpheme in constant use in everyday speech.

As it is not associated with the formal features of the language, *the Chinese script is incapable of any direct reflection of sound changes*. Sound changes in alphabetic scripts always involve a change in spelling sooner or later; in the case of the Chinese script, each character has remained linked with the word it originally stood for, without any change in form, which partly explains why the situation is so complicated at the moment. If Latin had used the same type of script, and it had survived until now, the character for the Latin word *caput* (head) would also now stand for *chief, captain, capital,* and *decapitate,* all of which are derived from it. According to the context, it would have four different meanings, none of which had anything to do with each other in the language of today.

The fact that the Chinese script has never responded to the direct influence of phonetic development, combined with its complex nature, which reduced it to a privilege reserved to a small minority of people, are both factors which helped to maintain a universal written language, known all over China. The very nature of the script made it incapable of reflecting the diverging phonetic development of the dialects; as it was used only by the administration and the ruling classes, it was further away from the spoken usage of the mass of the population than any other style of language. Memorising the characters and learning the universal written language were two inseparable operations. As has already been said, the written language *(wenyan)* did not correspond to any spoken language, and this state of affairs lasted right up to the 20th century. Now that *wenyan* has been replaced by *baihua* (the literary form of the northern dialect), the universal written language is backed up by a spoken language which, with the help of the policy of the present regime, should gradually extend throughout China, relegating all the dialects to the status of patois. Not until then will the written language faithfully reflect the spoken language for all Chinese.

As the script has only slender connections with spoken usage, the form of the characters has not changed much since the beginning of the Christian era. This has always brought the Chinese into closer contact with their cultural heritage, enabling them to draw on it continually to enrich their language. A large proportion of the characters in the old texts no longer correspond to words in current use, but their pronunciation has been handed down, following the general lines of phonetic development. They can be called back into use when needed, and combined with others to forms new term (the phonetic structure of Chinese makes it particularly difficult to assimilate foreign words). Most of the technical, scientific, and political etc... vocabulary which has appeared since the end of the last century has been created by borrowing from ancient texts, just

strokes in order of writing

basic components

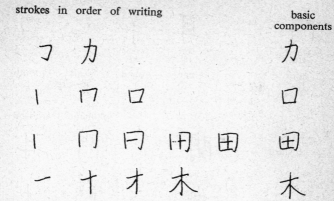

the components combine to form the following characters:

Fig. 3

as the European languages have made borrowings from Latin and Greek.

It is generally considered that to be able to read fluently, one must know between three and four thousand characters (which represents many more words, in fact, since each character is to be found combined with others to form polysyllabic words). For a script like this to be workable, each character has to have its own form, its own set of strokes which can survive all possible distorsion by rapid writing, and be easily recognisable and therefore easy to remember. The strokes (Fig. 3) can be arranged in several hundred basic graphic combinations, which are *devoid of all meaning* in themselves. These are then combined in different ways to form characters. This systematisation is a great help in reading and learning. The principle is as old as the characters themselves: when new characters were needed, the Chinese combined already existing characters, instead of adding new, original forms. The characters made up of a *radical*

門

耳　　手　　心　　口

13

18　　19　　20　　21
door

ear　hand　heart　mouth

		phonétic	radical
to hear	聞 14	ˊ 門	耳
to cover	捫 15	門	扌
melancholy	悶 16	門	心
to ask	問 17	門	口

Fig. 4

and a *phonetic*, especially, which now fill most of the dictionary,
were created in this way. It was noticed, for example, that
the word "door" which already had a character (No. 13, Fig. 4),
and the word "to hear", for which a character was needed,
were pronounced in much the same way. Character No. 13 was
combined with another (No. 18) standing for "ear" and a
new character for "to hear" was created (No. 14). Character
No. 14 was described as consisting of a phonetic and a radical;
the phonetic showed the reader that the word was pronounced
in much the same way as "door", and the radical showed that
the meaning was linked with "ear". Characters No. 15, 16 and
17 were formed according to the same principle, to represent
other words which resembled "door" in sound: "to cover,

27	28	29	30	31
shuān	shǎn	xián	bì	kāi

Fig. 5

22	23	24	25	26	phonetic	
xī	jié	cuò	cuò	cù		

Fig. 6

smooth out", "melancholy" and "to ask" respectively. All three characters contain the phonetic taken from character No. 13 standing for "door"; their radicals were derived from characters already in existence, No. 19, 20 and 21, standing for "hand", "heart" and "mouth" respectively. Over 90% of the characters in common use today were created in this way.

Unfortunately, phonetic development has often produced considerable changes in the pronunciation of characters which were originally similar in sound. The phonetics now give only vague indications of the pronunciation of characters. Today, characters No. 13, 14, 15, 16 and 17 are read as *mén, wén, mèn, mén* and *wèn* respectively. The pronunciation of the characters in Fig. 6 show much greater differences. The division of a character into radical and phonetic is by no means always as clear as in the examples given; a part which acts as the phonetic

24	=	radical "metal"	+	phonetic

Fig. 7

in one character is not necessarily the phonetic in another one.
Nothing enables the reader to guess that the element derived
from character No. 13 is the phonetic in characters 14, 15, 16
and 17, but not in characters 27, 28, 29, 30 and 31, which are
pronounced *shuān*, *shǎn*, *xián*, *bì* and *kāi* respectively (Fig. 5).

As for the radical, from the very beginning it gave only
rough indications of the meaning; when the phonetic gives
no indications of the sound, it gives little help towards identifying the morpheme represented. The semantic development
has made things more difficult here too: the connections existing today between the meaning of the radical and that of the
character as a whole are often obvious to philologists alone.
The method for forming new characters, which is in constant
use, has to be taken into account too, for is at the root of
many irregularities to be found today: a character already

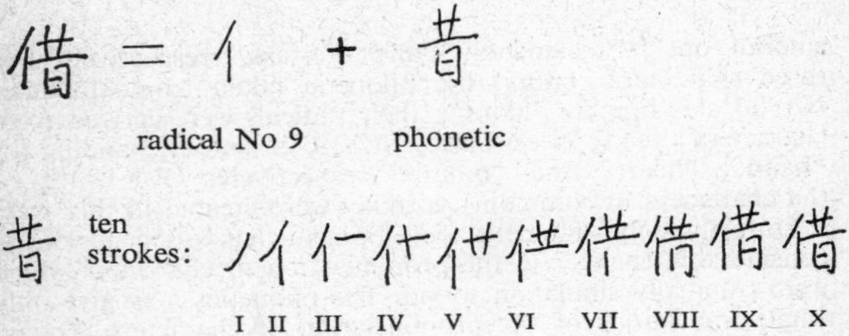

借 ＝ 亻 ＋ 昔

radical No 9   phonetic

借 ten
strokes: ノ 亻 亻 什 卅 供 供 借 借 借

I   II   III   IV   V   VI   VII   VIII   IX   X

Fig. 8

in existence was borrowed to represent a new word of identical
or similar pronunciation, to avoid creating a new one. Character
No. 24 (Fig. 7) originally stood for a word meaning "to inlay",
as the radical "metal" indicates. Then it was borrowed to
represent another word, whose pronunciation was similar,
meaning "mistake". The radical "metal" has obviously nothing
to do with this new meaning.

Characters are customarily classed according to their radicals
in dictionaries. Chinese lexicographers have drawn up a list —
which varied from one period to another — containing the most
usual and easily recognisable radicals. The list in the great
Kang Xi dictionary (18th century), for instance, which is still
in use today, contains two hundred and fourteen radicals,

arranged according to the number of strokes in each one, starting with the lowest number. All the characters with the same radical are collected under the same heading, again arranged according to the number of strokes. Three basic operations have to be carried out to look up a character (take character No. 23, Fig. 8, for example):

I. Find the radical and turn to the list with that heading. In the case of character 23, this is easy, as the radical is "man", one of the most frequent; it is ninth on the list. (The radical is not always as easy to find, however. All good dictionaries contain an appendix listing characters with obscure radicals!)

II. Having turned to heading number nine, the number of strokes in the character have to be counted. The example contains ten. The next step is to find the list of characters, in section nine, containing ten strokes.

III. Finally, the character has to be found in the list.

Many other classification systems are in use, but none can compare with the simplicity and strict accuracy of alphabetic classifications.

B. *The Simplifying of characters. Transcriptions*

The reform of the Chinese script plays an essential role in the tremendous effort towards widespread education to which the present regime has committed itself. Two main factors are involved.

1. The Simplifying of Characters

The traditional characters are difficult to remember and to write, and often hard to recognise and tell from one another. A superhuman effort would be needed before they could be

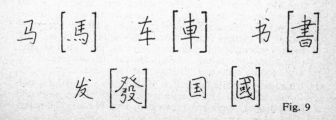

Fig. 9

assimilated by six hundred million people, and the task had to be rendered as easy as possible. The simplifying of characters is no innovation; examples of it have recurred constantly throughout the history of China. Highly simplified variants for numbers of characters appeared as early as the first millenary B.C., often in the margin of official texts. In cases such as these, the simplified form is recognised officially, and the original, complicated form is eliminated. When no simplified form has existed in the past for a character, it is created by referring to traditional methods. As soon as they are adopted, the simplified characters replace the old ones for educational purposes and in books. They are introduced gradually, so that people who can read already are not suddenly faced with a mass of new forms. The dictionaries give both forms. Figure 9 gives several examples of simplified characters; the traditional forms are in square brackets.

2. Introduction of an Alphabetic Script

The simplifying of the characters is merely a process of alteration which affects the formal shape of the characters individually; as it does not touch on the fundamental principle of the Chinese script, it can do nothing to remedy its basic difficulties:

I.   To read a Chinese text is to remember the morpheme attached by convention to each character. However simplified these characters may be, a far greater effort of memory is needed to learn them than to learn phonetic scripts, for there only a few general *rules* governing spelling have to be applied.

II. The number of characters and the fact that they do not lend themselves easily to simple, systematic classification constitute a source of difficulties which grow daily more numerous with the development of modern means of communication, and the spread of written information. Whereas words written in alphabetic script are combinations of a limited number of elements (letters), each Chinese character has to be chosen from among thousands of others; this creates severe complications in printing, in the postal services (the telegraph among others), and in the drawing up of any kind of catalogue, directory or table, etc.

III. Characters are also a source of difficulty in relations with foreign countries. In Chinese texts, foreign place names and other proper names are transcribed using as many characters

馬 克 思
mǎ　kè　sī

馬 賽 倫 敦
mǎ　sài　lún　dūn

Fig. 10

as they contain syllables to the Chinese ear; the characters play a purely phonetic role; the reader takes no notice of their usual meaning, and concentrates on their pronunciation only. (See the transcriptions usually found for *Marx, Marseilles* and *London*, Fig. 10). The method is in complete confusion at the moment, and the phonetic poverty of Peking dialect produces ambiguities which could never be entirely eliminated, however systematised it became. The same chaos reigns abroad when Chinese has to be transcribed by an alphabetic script. To put an end to it, the Chinese themselves must first adopt one coherent system, and one alone, in their publications intended for foreigners.

This last, albeit minor problem of transcriptions for the use of foreigners gave birth to the first attempts at writing Chinese alphabetically. The first transcription in Latin letters was invented at the beginning of the 17th century by the Italian Jesuit, Matteo Ricci. Since then literally dozens of different transcriptions have been put forward. Most of them date from the 19th and early 20th centuries. They can be divided into two groups:

a) The systems for use by foreigners.

They were invented by foreigners to make it easier for their compatriots to learn a dialect of Chinese (usually Mandarin) and to enable dictionaries giving the pronunciation of characters or be compiled. Each method was drawn up using the sound and spelling systems of one language alone, and as no single one has won universal approbation, readers have to be able to switch from one to another, depending on the origin of the publication which they are reading (English, French, German, etc.). Even the individual countries have failed to agree to use one system alone; newspapers, atlases and historical works do not generally use the same transcription. Sinologues have drawn up sound tables to enable themselves to switch easily from systems which they know well to the more unfamiliar ones. The modest table which follows this passage is limited to four transcriptions: *pinyin*, which will be discussed here; Wade, which is probably the most widely used at present, particularly in the Anglo-Saxon world, and which is used by the Chinese postal services in a modified form; that of the Ecole Française de l'Extrême-Orient, used in most French works on sinology; and Lessing, the German system.

b) The systems used by the Chinese

The first of these were invented in the 19th century by English and American missionaries, who wanted to spread their written propaganda as far as possible. Transcriptions were drawn up for the speech of the main towns, and the Bible was translated into the local dialects by means of them. Some missionaries intended that these alphabetic scripts, which were much easier to learn than the characters, as they were directly linked to local usage, should gradually replace the traditional script. Their failure is obviously linked with the widespread failure of the missions in China. In all events, had countless local scripts developed at the expense of characters, they would have deprived China of an instrument and symbol of her cultural unity.

A strong movement among intellectuals in favour of a phonetic script developed in the last decade of the 19th century, and at the beginning of the 20th century. They considered that the difficulty of the Chinese script was one of the main causes of the widespread illiteracy, and the weakness and backwardness of their country. Several systems were created, some for different dialects and some for mandarin. All this intense activity was crowned in 1918 by the offical adoption of *zhuyin zimu* (literally: "alphabet to indicate the sound"), which was invented to indicate the pronunciation of *guoyu* ("the national language"), already mentioned earlier on. It should be stressed that *zhuyin zimu* was not intended to replace the traditional script, but to act as an *auxiliary system of phonetic notation* to allow *guoyu* to be spread, and to note the pronunciation of the characters. The thirty-nine letters of the *zhuyin zimu* alphabet were taken from old, very simple Chinese characters.

The present regime, naturally, has taken up the policy of its predecessors in this respect and broadened it; even before they came to power, the Communists were always fervent and active supporters of a phonetic script. In 1958, after long and careful preparatory work, the *hanyu pinyin fang'an* ("Scheme for a Chinese Phonetic Alphabet"; it will be referred to here as *pinyin* from now on), was adopted. It should be pointed out straight away that it is a preliminary draft which will be changed later on if experience shows it to be unsatisfactory, and not a definitive system. It has one great advantage over *zhuyin zimu*: it uses the Latin alphabet, which avoids many problems in relations with foreign countries and with the national minorities, most of whose writing systems use the Latin alphabet too. But, as was the case with *zhuyin zimu*, for the moment it is no more than an auxiliary system; the characters still predominate in written communication. The *pinyin* script is without doubt gaining ground every day, as it appears in the titles of newspapers, on signs, posters and wrappings of commercial goods, etc., but it is always accompanied by characters, and its role is simply to give their pronunciation.

Pinyin was designed above all to record the Peking dialect pronunciation of the characters, and to act generally as an educational instrument to help in the spreading of *putonghua* (common language). Although, for the sake of convenience, they have been treated separately here, *the adoption of a common spoken language and of a single phonetic script are two aspects of the same problem*, las the use of a single universally accepted phonetic script by al Chinese implies that a standard common pronunciation has already been chosen, and will be recorded by the script in question. Before the characters can be completely replaced by one phonetic script (standing for Peking pronunciation), *putonghua* win probably have to have become the second language, common to all Chinese, so that the phonetic script will represent a spoken language for every one of them.

The authors of this guide book have chosen to use the *pinyin* transcription rather than one of the ones traditionally in use is, the West. The fact that the Chinese have themselves adopted this alphabetic script, which was invented above all for their use, should gradually put an end to the confusion and arbitrary decisions which govern the question of transcriptions outside China today. *Pinyin* is already in use in the teaching of Chinese in several European universities and schools, and there can be no doubt but that it will spread still further. The choice of *pinyin* also means that the same system can be used in both the French and English editions of this book.

The table which follows gives approximate phonetic equivalents in English, French and German for the sounds represented by the letters used in *pinyin*. These sounds sometimes differ widely from those represented by each letter in the three languages concerned; the reader is invited to make the necessary effort to learn them, just as he would presumably take the trouble to learn the Greek alphabet before going to Greece, or simply to learn a different reading for the Latin alphabet when travelling in other European countries. The names of places and people, and the various Chinese expressions to be found in this guide book will then come alive for him, and he will be able to relate what he has read here to what he hears spoken by the Chinese around him.

Sound Tables

I. Initials

pinyin	EFEO	Wade	Lessing
b	p	p	b
p	p'	p'	p
m	m	m	m
f	f	f	f
d	t	t	d
t	t'	t'	t
n	n	n	n
l	l	l	l
g	k	k	g
k	k'	k'	k
h	h	h	h
j	k, ts	ch	dj
q	k', ts'	ch'	tj
x	h, s	hs	s
zh	tch	ch	dsch
ch	tch'	ch'	tsch
sh	ch	sh	sch
r	j	j	j
z	ts	ts	ds
c	ts'	ts'	ts
s	s	s	s

II. Finals[1]

pinyin	EFEO	Wade	Lessing
a	a	a	a
o, uo, e[2]	o	o	o
e	ö, o[3] (ngo)	ê	ö
-i	e, eu[4]	ih, u[5]	ĭ
er	eul	êrh	örl
ai	ai (ngai)	ai	ai
ei	ei	ei	e
ao	ao (ngao)	ao	au
ou	eou (ngeou)	ou	ou
an	an (ngan)	an	an
en	en (ngen)	ên	ën
ang	ang (ngang)	ang	ang
eng	eng	êng	ëng
ong (weng)	ong (wong)	ung (wêng)	ung (wëng)
i (yi)	i (yi)	i	i
ia (ya)	ia, ea (ya)	ia (ya)	ia (ya)
iao (yao)	iao, eao (yao)	iao (yao)	iau (yau)
ie (ye)	ie, iai (ye)	ieh (yeh)	iä (yä)
iu (you)	ieou (yeou)	iu (yu)	iu (yu)
ian (yan)	ien (yen)	ien (yen)	iän (yän)
in (yin)	in (yin)	in (yin)	in (yin)
iang (yang)	iang, eang (yang)	iang (yang)	iang (yang)
ing (ying)	ing (ying)	ing (ying)	ing (ying)
iong (yong)	iong (yong)	iung (yung)	iung (yung)
u (wu)	ou (wou)	u (wu)	u (wu)
ua (wa)	oua (wa)	ua (wa)	ua (wa)
uo (wo)	ouo (wo)	uo (wo)	uo (wo)

[1] The forms in brackets represent the same final when it has no initial consonant preceding it. The use of a special graph in this case does not usually reflect any difference in pronunciation. The group *ng-* used in the EFEO system shows that the syllable contains no initial consonant; it should not be pronounced.

[2] When preceded by the equivalent of the *pinyin b. p. f. m.* the *o* in Wade, EFEO and Lessing corresponds to the *o* in *pinyin*. When preceded by the equivalents of the *pinyin g. k. h* gor in a syllable with no initial consonant, the *o* in Wade, EFEO and Lessing corresponds to the *pinyin e*. Everywhere else, the *o* in Wade, EFEO and Lessing corresponds to *uo* in *pinyin*.

pinyin	EFEO	Wade	Lessing
uai (wai)	ouai (wai)	uai (wai)	uai (wai)
uei (wei)	ouei (wei)	uei, ui (wei)	ue, ui (we)
uan (wan)	ouan (wan)	uan (wan)	uan (wan)
un (wen)	ouen (wen)	un (wên)	un (wën)
uang	ouang	uang	uang
(wang)	(wang)	(wang)	(wang)
u, ü[6] (yu)	iu (yu)	ü (yü)	ü (yü)
ue, üe[6] (yue)	iue, io (yue)	üeh, io (yüeh)	üä (yüä)
uan[7] (yuan)	iuan (yuan)	üan (yüan)	üan (yüan)
un[7] (yun)	iun (yun)	ün (yün)	ün (yün)

General Remarks on the sound tables:

Generally speaking, the transcription systems differ not only in the letters or groups of letters which they ascribe to the sound elements of the language, but also in the way the sounds are interpreted. Thus (note 4) in *pinyin* the same final, *-i*, is given for both *shi* and *zi*, whereas in EFEO they are *che* and *tseu* respectively, with two different finals, *-e* and *-eu*. It should not be forgotten, however, that transcription systems are subject to practical restraints which may go against the needs of theoretical coherence. In EFEO, for instance, *-eu* does not represent two consecutive sound elements, the first represented by *-e* and the second by *-u;* it forms a group, which when read as though it were French (as in *bleu* or *creux*) gives an acceptable approximation of the Chinese sound it represents. It is therefore impossible to draw up a sound table giving letter for letter equivalences; to retain some measure of accuracy, while avoiding over-complication, initials and finals must be treated separately.

---

[3] The *ŏ* in EFEO represents the *e* in *pinyin*, except when preceded by the equivalents of *g, k, h* and in syllables with no initial consonant, where EFEO *o = pinyin e*.

[4] The syllables written as *zhi, chi, shi, ri* in pinyin are written as *tche, tch'e, che* and *je* by the EFEO; the syllables written as *zi, ci, si* in pinyin are written as *tseu, ts'eu, sseu* by the EFEO.

[5] The syllables written as *zhi, chi, shi, ri,* in pinyin are written as *chih, ch'ih, shih, ji,* by Wade; the syllables written as *zi, ci, si,* in pinyin are written as *tzu, tz'u, ssu,* by Wade.

[6] In *pinyin* the umlaut symbol is not used above *u* when it follows *j, q, x* and *y*.

[7] When preceded by *pinyin j, q, x* and *y* only.

The tones are usually marked only in transcriptions of a specifically linguistic nature. For this reason they have been marked in examples used as illustrations of the language, and omitted in terms like *putonghua, wenyan, guoyu,* etc., denoting something specifically Chinese, for which no satisfactory English equivalent exists.

The Chinese use this method themselves: tones are omitted on signs giving names of shops, streets etc., and are reserved for use in dictionaries and school textbooks only.

The four tones—level, rising, falling and rising, falling—are shown in *pinyin* by the symbols: —, /, ∪, \ placed above the central vowel, and in EFEO by the symbols: —, ∧, \, /. Wade and Lessing both prefer to use the Arabic numerals 1, 2, 3, 4 to the right above each syllable.

Pronunciation Table

I. Initials

the sound represented in *pinyin* by the letter	is pronounced roughly like:		
	English	French	German
b	bill	bal	Bach
p	pike[1]	pelle[1]	Puppe
m	mad	mare	Mass
f	fall	fort	Feder
d	dull	doux	Dach
t	talk[1]	toux[1]	Teller
n	nose	noix	nass
l	last	loi	Leder
g	go	gare	Gast
k	cold[1]	car[1]	Keller
h	hand	roc	lachen
z	needs	tsar	entsetzt
c	czar[1]	tsar[1]	Zeit
s	sell	sale	Fass
zh	jug	budget	Dschungel

---

[1] Strongly aspirated.

ch	church[1]	tchèque[1]	*Tsch*eche
sh	show	chat	Schatten
r	plea*s*ure	*j*oue	Eta*g*e
j	jeep	dz -(i)[2]	
q	cheese[1]	ts -(i)[1]	Ziel
x	she	s -(i)	i*ch*

II. Finals

the sound represented in *pinyin* by the letters	is pronounced roughly like:		
	English	French	German
a	father	sac	Saal
ai	like	ail	Zeit
an	man	panne	mahnen
ang		langue	Drang
ao	out	chaos[3]	Haus
e	cup	heure	möchte
ei	lake	oseille	
en	giv*en*	jeune	lach*en*
eng	lung		eng
i (yi)	see	scie	Sieb
ia (ya)		fiacre	Jahr
ian (yan)	cayenne	Et*ienne*	Jänner
iang (yang)	young	étud*iant*	iang
iao (yao)	yowl	iao	jauchzen
ie (ye)	yes	feu*illet*	Projekt
iu (you)	yoke	mai*llot*	johlen
in (yin)	keen	fine	Sinn
ing (ying)	sing	camping	singen
iong (yong)	"*Jung*frau"	lion	jung
o	stop	sol	sollen
ong	song	longue	Stimmung
ou	coat	saule	Hof
u (wu)	moon	boue	Kuh
ü; u[4] (yu)		rue	Flüh

[1] Strongly aspirated.
[2] Groups of letters with no proper meaning should be read according to the rules usual governing spelling.
[3] Pronounced as one syllable.
[4] After *j*, *q*, *x*, and *y*.

ua (wa)		ouate	ua
uai (wai)	wife	ouailles	uai
uan (wan)	wan	Ant*oine*	uan
uan² (wan)		suinter[1]	üan
uang (wang)		Rouen[1]	uang
üe, ue² (yue)		fluet[1]	üä
ui (wei)	way	doué	ue
un (wen)	soon	guitoune	*Un*heil
un² (yun)		lune	Düne
uo (wo)	wall	Drouot[1]	uo

IV. VOCABULARY

I	wǒ
you (sing.)	nǐ
he, she	tā
we	wǒmen
you (plur.)	nǐmen
they	tāmen
you (polite form)	nín
my, mine	wǒde
your, yours	nǐde
his, hers	tāde
our, ours	wǒmende
your, yours	nǐmende
your, yours (polite form)	nínde
their, theirs	tāmende
Good morning (afternoon, evening)	ní hǎo
good-bye	zài jiàn
no	bù
yes	shì, duì
I beg your pardon (I'm sorry)	duìbuqǐ
Excuse me	láojià
alright	hǎo
its not alright	bù xíng

---

[1] Pronounced as one syllable.
After *j, q, x,* and *y.*

thank you	xièxie
its allowed, one can	kěyi
its not allowed, one cannot	bù kěyi
I want	wǒ yào
I don't want	(wǒ) bù yào
I don't understand	wǒ bù dǒng
don't forget	bié wàngji
comrade	tóngzhì
its very interesting	hěn yǒuyìsi
I have, you have, he has	yǒu
I haven't, you haven't, he hasn't	méiyǒu
careful!	zhùyì
What time is it?	jǐ diǎnle?
early	zǎo
late	wǎn
now	xiànzài
after	yǐhòu
immediately	mǎshàng
quickly	kuài
the day (daytime)	báitiān
the night	yèli
morning (early)	zǎoshang
morning	shàngwu
midday	zhōngwu
afternoon	xiàwu
evening	wǎnshang
day	tiān
the day before yesterday	qiántiān
yesterday	jzuótian
today	intian
tomorrow	míngtian
the day after tomorrow	hòutian
when?	shénme shíhou?
Sunday	lǐbaitiān
Monday	lǐbaiyī
Tuesday	lǐbaièr
Wednesday	lǐbaisān
Thursday	lǐbaisì
Friday	lǐbaiwǔ
Saturday	lǐbailiù
week	lǐbài
month	yuè
year	nián

one	yī
two	èr (liǎng)
three	sān
four	sì
five	wǔ
six	liù
seven	qī
eight	bā
nine	jiǔ
ten	shí
eleven	shí yī
twelve	shí 'èr
thirteen	shí sān, etc...
twenty	èrshí
thirty	sānshí
forty	sìshí
forty-three	sìshí sān
a hundred	yìbǎi
two hundred	èrbǎi
three hundred	sānbǎi, etc.
five hundred and sixty-five	wǔbǎi liùshíwǔ
a thousand	yìqiān
ten thousand	yíwàn
a hundred thousand	shíwàn
a million	yìbǎiwàn
how many?, how much?	duōshao
how much is this?	duōshao qián?
beef	niúròu
beer	píjiǔ
bowl	wǎnzi
bread	miànbāo
breakfast	zǎodiǎn
butter	huángyóu
cake	diǎnxin
Chinese food	zhōngcān
chopsticks	kuàizi
coffee	kāfēi
cold water	liáng kāishuǐ
cup (or glass)	bēizi
dinner	wǎnfàn
egg	jīdàn
fish	yú
fork	chāzi

fruit	shuǐguǒ
ice-cream	bīngqílín
jam	guǒzijiàng
knife	dāozi
lemonade	qishuǐ
lunch	wǔfàn
menu	càidān
milk	niúnǎi
mutton	yángròu
plate	pánzi
pork	zhūròu
potato	tǔdòur
rice	mǐfàn
salt	yán
soup	tāng
spoon	sháozi
sugar	táng
tea (green)	lüchá
tea (black)	hóngchá
vinegar	cù
western food	xīcān
wine	pútaojiǔ
yoghourt	suān niúnǎi
bath (to have a bath)	xǐzǎo
blanket	bèizi
chair	yǐzi
clean	gānjing
clothes-hanger	yījià
cold	lěng
dining-room	cāntīng
dirty	bù gānjing
fan (electric)	diànshàn
ground floor	yī lóu
first floor	èr lóu
second floor	sān lóu, etc.
hot	rè
too hot	tài rè
hotel	lüguǎn
key	yàoshi
mirror	jìngzi
mosquito-net	wénzhàng
pillow	zhěntou
post-card	míngxinpiàn

room	fángjiān
sheet	chuángdān
to sleep, to go to bed	shuìjiào
stamp (postage)	yóupiào
telephone	diànhuà
towel	máojīn
waiter	fúwùyuán
to wash clothes	xǐ yīfu
W.C.	cèsuǒ

HISTORY

A brief outline will be given here, which can be filled out by the description of the Peking Historical Museum (see p. 426), the historical introductions to the sections on the chief towns (particularly Peking, Nanking, Luo yang, Xi an, Hang zhou), and by the books whose titles are given in the bibliography.

Paleolithic Era

The Lower Paleolithic era is represented in north China by the famous Peking Man (middle Pleistocene), whose bones were discovered in 1921 at Zhou kou dian, south west of Peking (alongside stone tools and traces of fire), and by numerous remains found in Shan xi, and more recently still at Lan tian, in Shân xi; in south China it is represented by various remains discovered in Guang xi in 1956 and 1957. The Middle and Upper Paleolithic are not so well represented (remains found in the Ordos region).

Neolithic Era

(From the fourth millennium B.C.). Remains of a large microlithic industry have been found in the sandy regions (to the north). Three Neolithic cultures developed, one after the other, in the loess region (the Yellow River valley), which from then on appears to have been more advanced than the surrounding areas. They are called after the colour of the pottery found in each case: Red or Painted Pottery belonging to the Yang shao Culture (He nan site, see p. 429), known most of all because of the Ban po site (near Xi an, in Shân xi, see p. 430, 946), and found as far as Gan su (Ban shan); Black Pottery belonging to the Long shan Culture (site in Shan dong); and finally Grey Pottery (known mainly from sites found in He nan). Proof of cultivation of cereals, stock-rearing and fishing exists from the Yang shao period onwards; wood seems to have been used extensively from the Long shan period onwards. The first dynasty in Chinese history is traditionally supposed to have existed from about 2200–1800 B.C., at the end of the Neolithic Era; it is known as the Xia, and its founder was the mythical hero Yu the Great, said to have appeared after a flood. A link may yet be found some day between some site in Shân xi or Henan and this pre-bronze age "dynasty".

The Bronze Age: the Shang and the beginning of the Zhou (1800-800 B.C.).

A phenomenon of the greatest importance occurred in central China towards the beginning of the second millenium: the technique of bronze casting appeared. External influences (Central Asia) cannot be entirely excluded, but it has been proved that the technique used was gradually developed within China itself. The chief centres of this culture were in present He nan (Zheng zhou and An yang) and the Wei valley (Shân xi). Several other prominent features of ancient Chinese civilisation appeared at the same time as the use of bronze, such as the "fundamental dichotomy", as it has been called, between the nobles living in their "city-palaces" (J. Gernet) and the peasants who worked on their lands, round the walls of the town. Little is known about the peasants' life, apart from what may be gleaned from fragments of legends, and songs (interpreted by M. Granet): forests still covered most of the country; grain cultivation held second place, after stock-rearing and above all hunting; silk-worms were reared. The nobles' life is better known as the remains of complete towns have been uncovered by excavations (such as An yang, see p. 826). The nobles devoted their lives to hunting or going to war (the two pursuits were linked as prisoners were considered as game); they used chariots drawn by two or four horses; the characteristic weapon was the ge, a sort of hook mounted on a handle. They also fulfilled religious duties, which included ancestor worship and worship of the god of the earth, they performed sacrifices, presented offerings in bronze ritual vessels, mimed plays and practised divination (using tortoiseshell covered with pictograms, a rudimentary form of writing, which were subjected to fire, and the cracks produced were then interpreted). The dwellings faced south and already included features which are characteristic of later Chinese houses; large numbers of human victims have been found in the richest tombs, obviously sacrificed during the funeral ceremonies. The nobles acknowledged the authority of a sovereign who was their religious head (the "son of heaven", who was responsible for cosmic order) first and foremost, as well as their ruler. All this, however, represents only a small part of what later became the area occupied by China: centres of Chinese civilisation (the city-palaces and their immediate suburbs) were fairly frequent in the middle Yellow River valley, but became more scattered further away from it, and between them lived peoples of whom little is known, considered as barbarians by the Chinese, but gradually assimilated by them.

Chinese chronicles contain a list of Shang dynasty rulers (traditional dates: 1766-1112 B.C.) which has been found to correspond almost exactly to the list which has been drawn up from inscriptions found at An yang. Their capital was moved several times within the area which is now the north and north-east of modern He nan, until they finally settled at An yang, where their civilisation blossomed (14th-11th century). Then, weakened by constant campaigns against the other peoples of the Huai region who were not as yet under Chinese influence, the Shang were overthrown by the Zhou, who came from the Wei region (Shân xi). The Zhou established their capital near the site of modern Xi an first of all, but in about 750 B.C. they were pushed out by neighbouring barbarian peoples and fled to He nan, near Luo yang. Xi an and Luo yang, their two capitals, were to remain the centre of what was then China for many years (until the end of the Tang, in the 9th century).

A Period of Transition: the Hegemons

(The period known as the "Spring and Autumn" period). "There is good reason to believe that between the end of the second millenium and the 7th century, land in North China was gradually brought under cultivation and populated" (J. Gernet). Little by little the forests receded before the patches of burned land and the fauna, which abounded under the Shang (hunting was an extremely important activity) became more rare; stock-rearing also declined. The functions of the noble class also changed gradually: its members began to take an interest in agriculture, which consequently began to grow in importance. A different outlook developed at the same time: the "extra-vagance" of the Shang (large-scale slaughter of game, wastage), which corresponded to plentiful resources, was replaced by the "ritualism" which was to exert a moderating and restraining influence familiar throughout the history of Chinese civilisation.

Little by little "city-palaces" were scattered throughout Central China, as far south as the Yang zi; the Chinese world had become so large that the Zhou kings could not make their authority adequately felt. Several autonomous principalities formed in the border areas and began to try to enlarge their territories (cultivated land became extremely important) and claim hegemony. The local population played a big part in the forming of these principalities; each new state grew aware of its own individuality, endangering the unity of the Chinese world. Three large principalities assumed power in turn during the 7th and 6th centuries B.C.: Qi (in Shan dong), Jin (Shan xi), and above all Chu, whose territories reached south of the Yang zi. The wars between them resulted in the creation of the first internal state structures (tax reforms, publication of penal laws) and the organisation of relations between the states (subtle diplomacy, defence alliances, oaths to promote solidarity). Princes were forced into awareness of military and economic difficulties, while at the same time the peasants' conditions deteriorated. The period is known as the "Spring and Autumn Period" (Chinese: *Chun qiu*), after the title of a chronicle recording the events from 722 to 481.

The Iron Age: The Warring States

From the 5th to the 3rd century B.C., Chinese economy and society both underwent profound changes, whose importance cannot be too heavily stressed. The evolution which is noticeable as early on as the 6th century crystallised into the discovery of the technique of casting iron, which is testified for the first time in 513 (1600 years before it became known in Europe), and the traction plough. The forests receded even further thanks to the claiming of new land, carried out more efficiently than before with better agricultural tools; the nuclei of Chinese civilisation, which had previously been separated by empty spaces, grew larger until they touched each other. The principalities became large states depending mainly on agriculture; large-scale collective irrigation work was begun in the Wei valley, in Jiang su and in Si chuan. Various reformatory measures were carried out, aimed at destroying the remains of the old nobility and organising a centralised power (the prince was to nominate his officials). The peasants were formed into regiments (they were divided into groups of five or six families, and the principle of collective responsibility was introduced); taxes and loans were created; sections of the population were transferred to uninhabited areas. The wars of conquest continued, prolonging those already under way in the era of the hegemons (hence the name of the period, the "Warring States"), but the techniques of war developed further; the main body of the army no longer consisted of nobles' chariots, but of infantry recruited from the peasantry; a cavalry came into being (a borrowing from the nomads on the northern borders); the states built walls round their territories to protect themselves from "barbarian" invasions (they began to threaten in the 4th century) and from the attacks of their rivals. The workshops attached to the old "city-palaces" expanded into large centres of handicrafts (foundries, pottery, salt works, lacquer); the towns grew and trade developed (the first elements of a merchant class came into being; four types of money were used in the 4th and 3rd centuries). These economic and social transformations were accompanied by great progress in political and philosophical thought; the period was known as the "hundred schools" (Confucius, Mo Zi, Taoists, Legalists, etc...).

The last Zhou kings took refuge at Luo yang, having lost their authority completely, while the states fought among themselves to gain power. Finally, the prince of Qin (Shân xi) who had won power through early reforms, the conquest of Si chuan and skilful water-engineering works, emerged victorious; he imposed his principles of government on the other Chinese countries (taking the Legalists as his source of inspiration) and founded the empire in 221 B.C.

The Foundation of the Empire, Qin shi Huang di (221-210)

The prince of Qin was the promoter of an idea which was to survive him for two thousand years: that of a unified empire with an emperor (Chinese: *Huang di*, "August sovereign") whose authority extended over all the Chinese territories which otherwise tended to be disunited by distance, regionalism and rivalry. The prince who was later to be known as Qin shi Huang di ("Qin, the first emperor") carried out his plan in three stages; he took over the power in the state of Qin in 238 and prepared his victories through cunning and diplomacy; from 230 to 221 he crushed his rivals one by one, and pushed out the borders of the Chinese world in several masterly campaigns, driving eastwards as far as the pass of Shan hai guan (see p. 667), northwards as far as the steppeland where the Xiong nu (assimilated to the Huns) roamed, and southwards as far as the sea (four armies met near the site of modern Canton); from 221 until his death in 210, he organised his conquests: thirty-six commanderies were created, a network of roads was formed (in the shape of a star, radiating from Xian yang, the capital), weights and measures, coinage and the script were standardised; the fortifications separating the states were destroyed, but the Great Wall was built along the northern frontier to protect the new empire from the nomad invasions; privately owned weapons were confiscated, the classics, which "discredited the present in favour of the past" were destroyed and the followers of Confucius were persecuted; the system of groups of families was strengthened and a moral order imposed.

The measures taken by Qin shi Huang di were too severe, however; the population of the eastern regions, used to a more refined civilisation, found the restraint forced on them by these harsh laws hard to bear; the huge work projects (the Great Wall, the A fang gong Palace near Xi an, see p. 927, and the Emperor's tumulus) exhausted the manpower and drained the treasury. An uprising broke out (led by Chen Sheng and Wu Guang); regional particularities re-appeared, and the local ruling houses came together again; the son of Qin shi Huang di was de-throned in 206. The Qin Dynasty was a short one, but it left behind it memories which nothing could obliterate: it is almost certain that it was through silk from "Qin" that China first became known to the West.

The Han Empire (2nd century B.C. -2nd century A.D.)

The four centuries which correspond roughly to the Han empire saw considerable progress in agriculture; the process which was begun under the Warring States continued and developed. Iron tools became widely used, more irrigation work was carried out and grain production increased, which allowed for an increase in population (towards the beginning of the Christian era the empire had 57 million inhabitants). One of the first results of this economic prosperity was the rise of a landed class who gradually took over from the old nobility which had been suppressed under the Qin; large estates were formed, whose owners sometimes tended to make themselves independent of the central authority.

The merchants also benefited from the general prosperity as a large home market developed; they grew rich by transporting grain or by working the monopolies which the state entrusted to them (salt, iron). The first emperors set up the elements of a government which was to act as a model for later dynasties: three advisers, a chancellor, a secretariat and several ministries worked alongside the emperor; Confucian ideas were brought back into favour, and future officials, recruited from then on by an examination system, were required to study them; at the same time, work was begun on codification. The emperors were not content merely to collect all former Chinese territories under their authority, they wanted to push out the frontiers of their empire further still; they made light work of annexing the autonomous state of Nan Yue (the area round modern Canton) in the south; they tried to bring the Tarim basin in the north west (modern Xin jiang) under their suzerainty, but there they met with more or less permanent opposition from the Xiong nu; defeats and victories followed in close succession (short-lived success won by the Generals Huo Qu bing and Ban Chao; the envoy Zhang Qian was sent to explore central Asia, 138-125 B.C.). The Han Empire also saw great cultural development: the growth of learning and the study of history (Si ma Qian wrote his *Historical Records*), philosophic thought, the sciences (the first seismograph was built by Zhang Heng), poetry (the "court-poet", Si ma Xiang ru); the figurines and furnishings found in the tombs give a better idea of the standard of luxury of the times than do the architectural remains, for they have largely disappeared.

After several years of warfare against different "kings" (parti-cularly Xiang yu, King of Chu), Liu Bang, the son of an eastern land-owning family, founded the new Han Dynasty (206 B.C.). As their capital was in the west until the beginning of the Chris-tian era, at Chang an (modern Xi an, Shân xi), the early Han are known as the "Western Han". Emperor Wu di (140—87) tried to enrich the treasury in order to conquer the Xiong nu (selling of ranks, recoinage, creation of monopolies). The victories were expensive, however, and the great land-owners continued to remove ever-increasing numbers of free peasants from the control of the state. From 8 to 22 A.D. a high-ranking official, Wang Mang, managed to overthrow the Han and create the shortlived Xin ("new") dynasty; he attempted to make large numbers of reforms, whose meaning was not always clear, and which were all doomed to failure. An uprising broke out, known as the "Red Eyebrows" (the rebels dyed their eyebrows red, as a sign of gratitude). A prince belonging to the Han family took advantage of the situation and managed to restore the dynasty to power. From 23 to 186, the Han established their capital further east, at Luo yang, and were therefore known as the "Eastern Han". The large estates grew larger every day, for the emperors could find no means to check them; the court itself was hemmed in by plotting eunuchs. In 184 a new uprising broke out in the west: the Yellow Turbans uprising, whose leaders were imbued with Taoist doctrine. At the same time, the barbarians renewed their attacks on the northern

di was not able to put down the rebellions which flared up in many areas from 615 onwards. In 618, the Sui Dynasty fell, and the Tang took over, continuing the work of unification and centralisation which the other had begun.

The Tang Empire (618-917)

This was a period of culmination; China was one of the most powerful states in east Asia, and probably one of the most powerful in the world. The vital centres of the empire, as under the Zhou and the Han, were Chang an first of all (modern Xi an; the town then had a population of a million) and then Luo yang; the lower Yang zi region continued to develop. The Tang emperors wanted to extend their rule north east (campaigns in Korea), south west (suzerainty over the state of Nan chao, Yun nan), and above all north west, as far as the Tarim oasis (wars against the Turks; travels of the Buddhist pilgrim Xuan zang who went to India and came back through central Asia). The merchants benefited from the unification and spread of the empire; money became so widely used that taxes were collected in cash and no longer in kind from 780 onwards; a kind of money draft was also in use, known as *fei qian* ("flying cash"). The chief problem, as before, was the agrarian question; in 624 an agrarian statute was issued, based on the one issued by the Northern Wei, which redistributed some of the lands which were ownerless as a result of the disturbances of the previous reign (some were granted for life); the statute seems to have been put into effect (proof exists for the Dun huang oasis) and to have resulted in a renewal of agriculture; the central authority was however powerless to prevent a dual tendency which was to upset the balance of the country regions: "migrations" of peasants who fled exorbitant taxation and set out to look for new lands, and often swelled the ranks of bands of bandits or rebels; and the enlarging of the great estates whose owners tended to avoid the central authority (one case of this was furnished by the large estates belonging to the monasteries). Culture flourished under the Tang dynasty; the great poets: Li Bai, Du Fu, Bai Ju yi, and the magnificent ceramic tomb figurines (horses, camels, ethnic), many examples of which are to be found in Western museums, are quoted most often of all; the development of Confucian thought (with the great prose-writer, Han Yu) and of Buddhist thought (rise of the "Meditation" school, from the Sanskrit: *Dhyana*, Chinese:

Chan, Japanese: *Zen*) must also be mentioned, as well as scientific progress (cartography, astronomy), the birth of an original style of painting (little is left of it now) and the flowering of countless "court arts" (dancing, music, the theatre), which were mainly influenced by central Asia.

Three great figures dominate the beginning of the Tang empire 1) Li Shi min (Emperor Tai zong, 627–649), the true founder of the Tang Dynasty, who overcame the Sui by skilful campaigns, and although he put his father Li Yuan on the throne, he himself exercised the power; in 627, he made his father abdicate, eliminated his brothers, who claimed the succession, and reigned alone. He re-organised the administration and the coinage and overcame the Turks and the Koreans. 2) Empress Wu Ze tian (684–710): she was the secondary wife of Emperor Tai zong and then of Emperor Gao zong; in 680, she proclaimed her son to be the rightful heir and took the throne herself, as "emperor" of a new Zhou Dynasty. The empress was supported by eastern clans, who were in favour of the Buddhist church; she transferred the capital to Luo yang and ordered an enormous temple to be built at Long men. During her reign, the Turks broke away from Chinese domination and even tried to intervene in Chinese domestic affairs. Finally, the empress' supporters were put down by a prince from the Tang family, who re-gained power once more. 3) Emperor Xuan zong (713–756): he was a great patron and lover of literature and music; his reign encouraged a great blossoming of the arts. Misfortune seemed to pursue him, however. The Chinese armies were beaten by the Arabs at Talas, near the Ili, in 751, and by the Nan zhao in the south west; a general of Turkish origin called An Lu shan rose in rebellion and marched on Chang an (755); the emperor had to flee to Si chuan, but the soldiers of his escort forced his favourite concubine, the beautiful Yang gui fei, to commit suicide, as they considered her to be responsible for the disaster (the life and separation of the lovers, whose story has now become legend, has always been a favourite subject for poets). The revolt of An Lu shan was a critical turning-point in the history of the Tang; although many attempts were made to carry out reforms (tax reforms, measures counteracting the power and wealth of the Buddhist monasteries), the dynasty never restored its authority or managed to check the centrifugal forces which were threatening the unity of the empire. An uprising led by Huang Chao broke out in 875; his armies overran the whole empire, from north to south, and precipitated the splintering process.

The "Five Dynasties" (907-960)

The empire was split up once more, this time for about half a century. Five short-lived dynasties reigned in the north (hence the name of the period), while the south was ruled by ten "kingdoms". It was a period of gestation for China, during which several facts emerged which were to gain great importance later on. The lower Yang zi and Si chuan provinces continued to develop (tea trade, manufacture of porcelain); rich tombs found in the Nanking or Cheng du areas give an idea of the extent of the luxury pervading these towns. In the north, the capital was transferred from Luo yang to the site of modern Kai feng (where it was to remain under the first Song emperors, before being moved to Hang zhou). The "barbarian" Khitan founded an empire in the north east, with a town on the site of modern Peking as their capital; in 937 they founded the Liao Dynasty and began to cherish aspirations to gaining power over the rest of China as well. The northern peoples grew more and more threatening as the centuries went on. This period saw the beginning of paper money and the origins of printing, both of which were to come into their own under the Song.

The Song Empire (960-1276)

Three main phenomena dominated this period: 1) a permanent threat in the form of a great "barbarian" state in the north east (in the area round Peking, which first became an important own at this point); the Jürched (founders of the Jin dynasty) succeeded the Khitan (founders of the Liao Dynasty) in 1125; the Mongols (founders of the Yuan Dynasty) succeeded the Jürched from 1215–1217. 2) The centres in the lower Yang zi region grew more and more important, and the capital of the Song Dynasty was established in this area for a century and a half (for the first time, the centre of Chinese culture was not in the middle Yellow River region). 3) The merchant class came to constitute an important section of the urban population; it developed its own culture, which could be described as "bourgeois" (literature using the spoken language). In spite of wars between north and south, the periods of peace were long enough to enable a great civilisation to develop; groups of scholars and private schools grew up all over the empire, and printing facilitated learning. The "Neo-Confucian" synthesis of the philosopher Zhu Xi (about 1200), the scientific meditations of the scholar Chen Gua (who gives the first description of printing), the literature produced by the school of Shu (whose greatest representative was the poet Su Dong po), and the flowering of the schools of painting, all bear witness to the creativeness of the period.

The founder of the Song Dynasty preferred to turn towards the southern states and annex them, for they were easier and more tempting prey than the Khitan to the north. Difficulties arose immediately after the re-unification was accomplished, however: the court had to "buy peace" by regular payment of a large tribute to the north eastern barbarians, and at the same time keep up a standing army big enough to protect the empire. At the capital itself, the difficulty was to find a sound policy; in the 9th century, the conservative element (led by Si Ma guang) opposed the would-be innovators (represented by Wang An shi) and inflation was unavoidable. In 1126, the Jin took Kai feng, captured the emperor and carried off a rich haul (in particular, some astronomical instruments and the famous "stone drums" which were taken to Peking (see p. 477). A prince belonging to the imperial house settled at Hang zhou, where the dynasty continued, known as the "Southern Song". Warfare continued against the Jin, in which General Yue Fei distinguished himself by inflicting resounding defeats on the northerners, and was himself defeated only by the plots of his rival (see p. 1080). When the Jin gave way to Genghis Khan, the Southern Song were doomed. Hang zhou fell to the Mongols in 1276 and the southern provinces were gathered into the Yuan empire.

The Yuan Empire (1276-1368)

Now, for the first time, China as a whole came under foreign rule. Chinese historians can generally find little to say in favour of the Yuan, though it is by no means certain that China did nothing but suffer at the hands of the new occupiers. The capital was established at Khanbaliq (modern Peking), in the region which had already been developed under the Liao. The road through central Asia which had for a long time been closed to Chinese trade was re-opened; the frontiers were enlarged (suzerainty over Tibet and Yun nan); large military expeditions were organised against Burma, Champa, Java and Japan, most of which ended in failure. The towns prospered, but the country areas were in difficulties (lands were confiscated to be handed over to the Mongols, and agrarian movements occurred, like that of the Red Turbans which dealt the death blow to the dynasty in the middle of the 14th century). As far as culture was concerned, it was a cosmopolitan age: numerous Moslems and Europeans arrived (Marco Polo, Franciscan missionaries); Western ideas and technical skills permeated to China, and at the same time, Chinese discoveries (gun-powder, printing) were introduced in the West.

The Ming Empire (1368-1644)

A peasant from An hui, Zhu Yan zhang, took advantage of the disturbances resulting from the Red Turbans uprising to establish the new Ming Dynasty (the name, which means "bright", is said to have something to do with Manichean beliefs). Under his reign (the Hong wu era, 1368–1399) and that of his younger son (the Yong le era, 1403–1425), the empire went through a period of great expansion. The Mongols were driven back north of the Great Wall, which was restored. The economy was re-organised, particularly agriculture (a cadastral survey was introduced); the central power was reinforced (a council and a secret police force were created); the capital, which under Hong wu had been at Nanking, was transferred to Peking for good under Yong le. Large sea expeditions were sent to the south seas, and as far as east Africa, to revive foreign trade (seven expeditions were led by the eunuch Zheng He between 1405 and 1435). Difficulties arose from the end of the 15th century onwards: the Mongols were threatening from the north, and the east coasts were harried by Japanese pirates; large estates were formed, disturbing the balance in the country regions; strikes and workers' movements arose in handicraft centres; the emperors' authority began to wane, and the court came under the power of the eunuchs. After the long reign of Wan li (1573–1620), the opposing forces broke into the open and the armies led by Li Zi cheng entered Peking and forced the last Ming emperor to commit suicide. The Manchus took the opportunity created by the disturbances to invade northern China and proclaim the Qing Dynasty; the rest of the empire had to be conquered gradually ("Southern Ming" resistance in the southern provinces; resistance led by Zheng Cheng gong, known by the Europeans as "Koxinga", in Fu jian and the island of Formosa).

The Beginning of the Qing Dynasty (1644-c. 1850)

The increase in population is the most important factor during this period. Estimated at 150 million in about 1600, the population rose to 300 million in 1787, and then to 430 million just before 1850. The factor of quantity was to play a leading part from then on. The corollary of the increase was emigration; for several centuries, numbers of the less fortunate had been leaving Fu jian and Guang dong every year to swell the Chinese colonies in Indo-China or the Indian Archipelago; under the Qing, the numbers increased. The arrival of the Europeans constituted another deciding factor: the Russians to the north (the tsars conquered Siberia), and the Dutch and the English, particularly, to the south (the Netherlands East Indies and the Empire of India were formed); China had new neighbours to take into account. The empire experienced an era of prosperity under the long reigns of Kang xi (1662–1723) and Qian long (1736–1796). Agriculture progressed (new crops such as maize and tobacco were introduced, and a system of state granaries was put into effect); industry developed (state and private enterprises employed large numbers of salaried workers; Hang zhou was famous for its silk, Fo shan near Canton for its forges, and Jing de zhen, in Jiang xi, for its pottery kilns); the empire expanded its frontiers (wars in central Asia against the Eleuths and in the south west against Burma). From the end of the eighteenth century onwards, the life-giving forces seem to have begun to ebb, the population appears to have grown faster than production, the Manchu authority waned, and their opponents began to form into the famous secret societies. The Europeans, who were waiting for the Chinese market to "open", tried to make the most of the situation.

European Ascendancy

The English had been in Canton for a long time by 1839; they imported large quantities of opium from India to balance trade, which would otherwise have shown a deficit. In 1839, the mandarin Lin Ze xu decided to deal severely with this illegal import, and had a large consignment of it destroyed. The English, who for several years had been wanting to increase the volume of trade with China, took advantage of the incident to start a military campaign. They bombarded forts in the mouth of the Xi jiang, then took Shang hai (June 1842) and Nanking.

A treaty signed at Nanking opened five ports to British trade: Canton, Shang hai, Amoy, Fu zhou and Ning bo, and ceded Hong kong to England.

The threat which Europe represented was not the main source of worry for the Manchu court, for uprisings occurred which nearly undermined its authority: Moslem uprisings in Yun nan and Turkestan, and even more serious, the **Tai ping revolt**. It began in Guang xi and soon spread to several provinces in south China. Its leader, Hong Xiu quan wanted to overthrow the Qing and establish the Heavenly Kingdom of Great Peace *(Tai ping tian guo)*. In 1852, his supporters took Han kou; in 1853, Nanking became the capital of the new empire. Edicts issued by Hong Xiu quan have been preserved; they were designed to create an entirely new society: redistribution of land, reform of the tax system, the emancipation of women, the suppression of the pigtail. The Tai ping tried to gain control over north China, but failed in their attempt to take Peking. Finally the British and the French decided to take advantage of the difficulties experienced by the government in Peking and impose their own will on it. A military campaign began (the burning of the Summer Palace in Peking in October 1860, see p. 598) and ended in the signing of the treaty of Peking which "opened" eleven new ports and granted numerous privileges to foreign residents (the right to organise concessions, extraterritorial rights, freedom for missionaries). Once all this had been obtained, the Europeans supported the Manchus against the Tai ping. The Tai ping, weakened by rivalry within its ranks, gave way; in July 1864, Nanking was won back once more.

China, as the suzerain of Annam, was worried by the French progress in Tongking. War broke out in 1883; in 1885 |the treaty of Tian jin ended the war and opened two towns on the south west frontier to French trade. China also had suzerainty over Korea; her opponent there was Japan, which was galvanised by the "Meiji Reform" (1868), and tried to take Korea. War broke out there in 1894; the Japanese won the control of the seas, occupied Port Arthur and advanced into Manchuria. According to the terms of the treaty of Shimonoseki (1895), China ceded Formosa, the Pescadores Islands and the Liao dong Peninsula, undertook to pay an indemnity and granted trade benefits. But these military defeats were by no means the most serious events; the Western countries already controlled the empire's customs, and went on to obtain land on lease, concessions in the shape of railway lines, and finally they divided China into "spheres of influence" (the Russians in the north, the Germans in Shan dong, the British in the Yang zi valley, the French in the south west). The "break up of China" was complete.

Although the Chinese, unlike the Japanese, did not go in for "Westernisation" and modernisation from the very beginning, they certainly did not remain inactive. Their reactions took several forms. Some of the great mandarins, such as Li Hong zhang, for instance, wanted to take over certain European technical skills for use in China (arsenals, the formation of a modern army). A few enlightened scholars saw even further and supported the adoption of changes in China similar to those chosen by Japan; Kang You wei and his disciples (one of whom was Liang Qi chao) won the approval of Emperor Guang xu and from June to September 1898 ("the Hundred Days") they drew up edicts of reform (without touching on the political regime of the empire). The empress, Ci xi (Tz'u-hsi), managed to regain the authority which the reformers had removed from her; the emperor was imprisoned in a palace in the Forbidden City, where he stayed until his death in 1908; Kang You wei managed to escape, but several of his friends were executed; most of the edicts were revoked.

The secret societies had been active for some time, and now initiated armed movements, some of them xenophobic. The most spectacular of these was the one organised by the members of the society known as the Yi he tuan (which the Europeans called the "Boxers") in Peking in 1900. They laid seige to the foreigners, who withstood them for fifty days in the "Legation Quarter" (see p. 531), which they had barricaded as best they could; they were relieved eventually by an expeditionary force consisting of soldiers belonging to seven Western powers and Japan. Empress Ci xi fled to Xi an and the conquerors occupied the Imperial Palace (see the descriptions given by P. Loti in *Les derniers jours de Pékin*). A protocol was signed in 1901; China was required to pay an indemnity amounting to 540 000 taels, among other things ("the Boxer indemnity"). The victory of 1900 was followed by an era of prosperity for the European residents and the Japanese; business continued until the eve of the revolution. Most of the lines belonging to the first Chinese railways (which were mainly in the north and near the ports) were built between 1900 and 1911, by Western companies.

The 1911 Revolution

Japan's victory over the Russian empire (1906) had repercussions in China, as it did elsewhere. It inspired new courage in revolutionaries who were determined to oppose the "unequal treaties" and the European ascendancy. The progress in means of communication made it easier to spread new ideas. Even Empress Ci xi herself had to allow a few reforms through from 1905 onwards (the old examinations system was abandoned, European style curricula were introduced in secondary schools, and a constitution was promised). These concessions did not however satisfy the more advanced elements, who led by Dr. Sun Yat sen (known by the Chinese as Sun Zhong shan) aimed at overthrowing the Qing and inaugurating a modern type of government. Sun Yat sen, who was born near Canton in 1866, had the support of the southern bourgeoisie, of students who had returned to China after studying in Europe, and above all of the Overseas Chinese, who contributed funds; he founded an association, the Tong meng hui, and then a party, the Guo min dang; the revolutionaries used every opportunity to turn incidents of discontent to their advantage, and to provoke uprisings. Empress Ci xi died in 1908, after proclaiming the young Pu yi, then two years old, as her successor; within the court itself, the supporters of the Regent (the second Prince Chun, Pu yi's father) vied with the supporters of General Yuan Shi kai; intrigues flourished and the authority of the Manchu waned in consequence. In May 1911, the government decided to nationalise all provincial and private railways, a measure which could not fail to attack the independence and the interests of Chinese capitalists. It was a signal for revolt: demonstrations and a strike took place in Si chuan, and an armed uprising broke out at Wu chang (see p. 1123). The Manchu court found itself obliged to appeal for help to Yuan Shi kai, who preferred to side with the revolutionaries. Delegations from all the provinces met at Nanking in December to elect Sun Yat sen president. Early on in 1912, however, Sun Yat sen gave way to make room for the "strong man", Yuan Shi kai, who, it was thought, would have support from the West; he procured the abdication of the last Qing emperor in 1912 (February). Yuan was appointed temporary president of the Chinese Republic. China then became a republic; "this fact was important in itself, at this particular moment, when from one end of the ancient continent to the other, France, Switzerland and Portugal were the only other states no longer under the rule of a hereditary monarchy"

(J. Chesneaux). It was the first act of a slow transformation, at times a difficult one, which was to take place over the next years.

CHINA FROM 1911 TO 1949

The fall of the Empire in October 1911 heralded nearly half a century of political and military confusion within the country. Japan, with the help of the international state of affairs, was to exert economic control over China at several different times and in different ways, detach Manchuria for a time, and finally attack and invade the country from 1937 to 1945.

Internal Events

From 1912 to 1916, Yuan Shi kai did his best to accede to the throne of the Empire himself. With this aim in view, he dissolved the Guo min dang founded by Sun Yat sen, and then the Parliament which had been formed in April 1913. Finally, in December 1915, a senate of his supporters offered him the throne, to enable him to found a new dynasty. A series of rebellions in the southern provinces (uprising led by Zai Ao in Yun nan) prevented his plan from being put into action, and he decided against it before he died on June 6th 1916.

For over ten years, from 1916 until the "Northern Expedition" in 1926, China was torn by various military cliques, who gained support from provincial particularism.

A government with purely artificial authority was set up in Peking; the An fu clique led by Duan Qi rui, the Zhi li clique under Wu Pei fu, and the Feng tian clique with Zhang Zuo lin, to mention only the main ones, shared the power and fought among themselves, mixing warfare and compromise.

At the same time, nationalist and revolutionary feelings still progressed, at least in towns and among students, workers and in some sections of the Army.

Several times Sun Yat sen managed to form a "National Government" in Canton, and finally, with considerable difficulty, he won the whole province of Guang dong over to his cause.

Several important events occured during this period.

The May the Fourth Movement, 1919, which began in Peking as a reaction against decisions taken at the Versailles Peace Conference, was both a patriotic and a cultural movement. It spread to several large towns and became in fact a national movement.

The Chinese Communist Party, which was to survive countless vissicitudes in its rise to power, and set up the present regime on October 1st 1949, was founded in Shang hai on July 1st 1921.

On January 1st 1924, the Guo min dang of Sun Yat sen was re-organised on a Bolshevik pattern, following advice from Borodin. It acquired strictness and efficiency which had been unknown before. A revolutionary army was created with the help of Soviet advisers and material. The Guo min dang and the young Communist Party worked in close collaboration; those who were members of the second belonged to the first as well.

On April 12th 1925, Sun Yat sen died in Peking.

Several incidents in Shang hai (May 30th 1925) and Canton (June 23rd) involving concessions authorities and Chinese demonstrators, combined to excite and develop nationalist feeling which was directed both against the presence of foreigners in China and against the military cliques.

After the death of Sun Yat sen, the Canton National Government came under the control of Chiang Kai shek. The revolutionary movement became strong enough to promote the "Northern Expedition" (June 1926). The nationalist armies, with the support of several provincial cliques, rapidly took the provinces of central China (Hu nan; Hu bei, Jiang xi) and later eastern China (An hui, Zhe jiang, Jiang su).

In spring 1927, the right wing of the Guo min dang, led by Chiang Kai shek, broke with the Communist Party and executed or imprisoned its members, particularly in Shang hai (April 12th 1927). During the summer, the left wing of the Guo min dang, under Wang Jing wei, at Wu han, did the same thing. The Chinese Communist Party tried in vain to stir up support in the Army (the Nan chang Uprising, August 1st 1927) and to take Canton (December 12th 1927), but had to go underground or shelter in mountainous districts of central China.

After a period of disunion, the nationalist generals, supported by some feudal military elements who had come over to them, took Peking. Meanwhile a central nationalist government had been created at Nanking on April 18th 1927; the law which governed it was proclaimed on October 4th 1928.

Chiang Kai shek tried to unify the country in the face of opposition from provincial governors and dissidents of the Guo min dang, and from the communists. The latter, led by Mao Ze dong and Zhou En lai, founded a Chinese Soviet Republic in Jiang xi. When threatened with destruction, they set out on the Long March, which lasted from October 1934 until mid 1935; after covering 10,000 kilometres, they reached Yan an (Yenan) in North China. Japanese pressure increased— Manchuria became a Japanese protectorate in 1931 under the name of Manchukuo—and a slight *rapprochement* took place between Chiang and Mao. Chiang was captured and agreed to stop fighting the communists (the Xi an incident, December 1936). When the Sino-Japanese War broke out in July 1937, China was more or less united to resist the attack. Few Chinese were ready to collaborate with the Japanese, apart from the Nanking puppet government, led by Wang Jing wei, a former disciple of Sun Yat sen (see above).

The Sino-Japanese War (1937-1945)

At first, the war was limited to North China and the Shang hai area; the Chinese armies resisted with great courage and tenacity from August to November 1937. In October 1938, the Japanese army held the main towns and communication channels in North China, as well as Wu han, the Yang zi valley as far as the Yi chang Gorges, and Canton; it had reached the limits of its expansion, more or less. Elements of the communist Eighth Route Army, and later of the New Fourth Army, spread out behind the Japanese lines in the southern provinces and the lower Yang zi valley respectively, creating administrative and military bases. As the scope of the Sino-Japanese war and of the European war in the Pacific (December 1941) grew larger, the military situation changed. China triumphed, backed up by powerful allies. In August 1945, the Japanese armies in China capitulated. China regained control over Manchuria and Tai wan.

Peace was short-lived, however. The central government, the Communist Party, and a representative of American diplomacy (General Marshall) tried in vain to reach an agreement on a formula for a coalition government and the re-organisation of the army. The agreements which had been drawn up laboriously in 1946 were not respected and civil war flared up once more between the Nanking government's forces and those of the Communist Party. In the autumn of 1948, the government armies suffered a series of resounding defeats, in Manchuria, north China and east China. After a short armistice, the Communist armies crossed the Yang zi on April 21st 1949; nothing further stood in their way as they marched southwards and westwards, taking Canton in October, and Chong qing in November; the war was virtually over. The remains of the nationalist armies fled to Tai wan, where they set up a nationalist government once more.

The People's Republic of China

The first actions taken by the Government of the Republic of China after its proclamation on October 1st 1949 were directed towards the founding of new institutions and the restoring of the economy, which had suffered badly from twelve years' warfare. The agrarian reform of June 30th 1950 allowed for a better distribution of land, and helped to encourage a revolutionary spirit in the countryside. The marriage law (passed on April 30th 1950) freed individuals of both sexes from all restraints imposed by the family, and therefore had far-reaching social consequences. Various "mass campaigns" were carried out to help change the structure of society and its mentality. The Korean War (1950–1953) marked China's return to the fields of Asian and even world politics.

From 1953 to 1957, People's China launched the first five-year plan, designed to build up basic heavy industry with Soviet help. Agriculture was organised on a collective basis at the same time (semi-socialist and later socialist co-operatives), as well as industry and trade.

A new constitution was adopted (September 20th 1954); the Eighth Congress of the Chinese Communist Party was held in September 1956, and the movement known as the "Hundred Flowers" developed briefly in 1957.

From 1958 onwards, the second five-year plan was launched, at the same time as the phase known as the "Great Leap Forward". This was marked by frenzied speeding-up of production rhythms and by the creation of "People's Production Communes", which were organisations fulfilling several functions, divided into production brigades and teams.

The People's Communes as they were in 1958 underwent considerable re-adjustment, both in their working and their size (25,000 communes in 1958, 70,000 in 1962).

The international role played by China has assumed increasing (mportance. This was made clear during the Geneva Conference i1954 and 1961–2) and the Bandung Conference in 1955, as well as by positions taken up with regard to various important questions. China is particularly opposed to the "neo-revisionist" tendency displayed by certain socialist countries; she upholds the revolutionary movements in the developing countries, and has been involved in disputes with India over the exact demarcation of the frontier; she is attempting to drive the United States out of the Far East, and intends to preserve her right to make her own nuclear weapons[1].

A new era began in 1966, with the Cultural Revolution. The Great Leap Forward had been a disaster, accentuated by natural calamities (floods, drought and locusts). Mao went into semi-retirement, leaving the office of President of the Republic to Liu Shao qi.

The gulf between the Chinese and the Soviet Union grew larger. From 1960 onwards, the quarrel developed in three different fields: ideology (the Chinese were not afraid of war against the "paper tiger", as they called American imperialism, and they disapproved of Kruschev's revisionism); politics (organization of the communist bloc; should the U.S.S.R. monopolize the leadership of it ?); and the territorial question (Peking claimed that the regions of Siberia ceded to the Czar in 1881 should be given back to China). As the Russians saw it, China was heading for danger and the people's communes were Utopian; the Chinese considered the U.S.S.R. as a rich country which had abandoned all revolutionary urges. In 1960, the U.S.S.R. put an end to all financial and technical help; in 1965 the Chinese students in Moscow were expelled; in 1969 serious clashes occurred on the frontier, on the Ussuri and in Xin jiang. The quarrel seems to have been toned down since then, but the break between the Soviet Union and China is deep-seated and apparently irreparable.

The first visible sign of the Cultural Revolution dates from 25 May 1966, when a wall-poster *(dazibao)* asked for the mayor of Peking to be dismissed from office. An unprecedented wave of revolutionary activity broke over the country during the months that followed, and thousands of red guards, aged between nine and seventeen were let loose, with the battle cry of "Everything that does not reflect the thought of Mao must be burned". People were forced to make public self-criticisms, successions of purges took place, and fierce fighting broke out.

---

[1] The first three Chinese nuclear explosions occurred on October 16th 1964, May 14th 1965 and May 9th 1966. China exploded her first thermo-nuclear bomb on June 17th 1967.

Mao Ze dong came back into the forefront; his "little red book" was constantly brandished. Liu Shao qi was evinced in 1968, while Lin Biao, the leader of the army, became second in command of the state, before he too was eliminated (he died in 1971, in an attempt to escape to the Soviet Union). The Cultural Revolution eventually came to an end in 1972-73, leaving an aftermath of anarchy which lasted for some time longer.

Thanks to the efforts of the Prime Minister, Zhou En lai, China turned to the West once more after quarrelling with Moscow. President Nixon was entertained in great pomp in Peking in 1972, followed shortly afterwards by the Japanese Prime Minister, Tanaka, and the French President, Pompidou. In 1971 China was admitted to the United Nations, where it replaced Taiwan.

In 1976 Zhou En lai and Mao Ze dong, the two giants who built the People's Republic of China, died one after the other. The ultra-revolutionaries of the Gang of Four, led by Mao's widow Jiang Jing, were quickly dislodged. With Hua Guo feng as president and Deng Xiao ping as second in command, China seems anxious to work at the improvement of its economy. The spectacular reconciliation with Japan in 1978, and the overtures made to the West in the domain of economic cooperation, are perhaps the beginning of a new era in the long history of China.

CHRONOLOGICAL LIST
OF MING AND QING EMPERORS

Temple name	*Year Period*	*Date of accession*

Ming Dynasty (1368-1644)

Tai zu	Hong wu	1368
Hui di	Jian wen	1399
Cheng zu	Yong le	1403
Ren zong	Hong xi	1425
Xuan zong	Xuan de	1426
Ying zong	Zheng tong	1436
Dai zong	Jing tai	1450
Ying zong	Tian shun	1457
Xian zong	Cheng hua	1465
Xiao zong	Hong zhi	1488
Wu zong	Zheng de	1506
Shi zong	Jia jing	1522
Mu zong	Long qing	1567
Shen zong	Wan li	1573
Guang zong	Tai chang	1620
Xi zong	Tian qi	1621
Si zong	Chong zhen	1628

Qing Dynasty (1644-1911)

Temple name	Year Period	Date
Shi zu	Shun zhi	1644
Sheng zu	Kang xi	1622
Shi zong	Yong zheng	1723
Gao zong	Qian long	1736
Ren zong	Jia qing	1796
Xuan zong	Dao guang	1821
Wen zong	Xian feng	1851
Mu zong	Tong zhi	1862
De zong	Guang xu	1875
	Xuan tong	1909

CHINESE RELIGION AND PHILOSOPHY

I. INTRODUCTION

It is often said that China has had three great religions: Confucianism, Taoism and Buddhism. This conception is justified up to a certain point. No one could contest the fact that these three exerted great influence on Chinese history and thought, and that they became privileged expressions of it. It would be wrong, however, to consider them as three similar terms, an abstract, unchangeable triad to be found in all eras in Chinese history. Not until the 19th century, and wrongly at that, was Confucianism assimilated to a religion properly speaking. It was above all a moral system and a political ideology, that of the scholar-official class. As for Taoism and Buddhism, the relationship here was complicated and variable. After years of struggle between the two, and of mutual influence, they finally became merged in a popular religion which borrowed elements from each one freely, without depending directly on either. From the Song and the Yuan onwards, the two were indistinguishable, except in the forms practised in monasteries or upheld during theological discussions. In the religious life of the people they were inextricably mingled and constituted elements of a synthesis which went beyond both of them. A description of Buddhism and Taoism as separate entities would not cover the religious life of the Chinese. Confucianism, although essentially agnostic and rationalistic when serving as the ideology of the ruling classes, did in fact embrace numerous religious elements and made its contribution to the vast synthesis which will be referred to here as "popular religion", for want of an accepted term. It cannot, therefore, be thought of as constantly and systematically opposed to Buddhism and Taoism. This opposition had true meaning in the eyes of a few intolerant scholars only, and not in daily life.

The formula of three religions, although justified in the abstract, is not a true reflection of historical reality, and if each of the three terms is considered in isolation from the others, it is hard to realise what religious life in China really was. Several of its fundamental characteristics made it extremely different from religious life as known in Europe.

One feature of the history of religion in China is continuity. New ideas, whether introduced from abroad or produced by the evolution of society, always came in gradually enough to be fitted into the existing framework of society without disturbing

it too much. When Buddhism penetrated China, it did not result
in the upheaval which the birth of Christianity provoked in the
West; it was a rich addition to Chinese civilisation, but it did not
alter its foundations. China has known none of the great dramas
(schisms, conversions, reforms) and holy wars which were a permanent feature of religious evolution in the West. Those who
search Chinese history for the bitter struggle between temporal
and spiritual power which was such a strong characteristic of the
Christian Middle Ages look in vain. The opposition between
Emperor and Pope created a gulf between real political power and
the ideal of a universal community embracing the whole human
race. This universalist ideal was then gradually transposed to a
purely religious plane. Politics were set free from religious and
moral tutelage (if not from all religious and moral justification)
and became a positive technique of government in the service
of the state or states. In China the universalist idea of the state
survived until the beginning of the 20th century, and disappeared
only with the fall of the empire. One of the constant and fundamental concepts of Chinese thought, from the beginnings until
the modern age, was in fact that the human world was one; that
it constituted one great family, whose only sovereign was the
Emperor, the Son of Heaven. As the sovereign was himself the
symbol of the human species in general, his authority was to be
respected by all men. Those who did not acknowledge him were
considered rebels or at best misguided. The emperor was morally
responsible for the smooth conduct of human affairs, and for
social order. He was supposed to reign by setting an example
through his own virtue rather than by means of institutions or
laws. For the Chinese, the social order was above all a *moral*
order, spreading progressively from the summit to the smallest
social units, without a break. As collective morality was considered more important than anything else, it has withstood all
upsets, both past and present; this permanent quality may explain
the continuity in the history of Chinese religion. None of the
religions practised in China could break it down, whether they
originated in the country or came from outside. When they attacked it or threatened the moral order of the state, they were
ruthlessly suppressed. But when they were found to be compa-
tible with the order, they were tolerated, no matter where they
came from, or what their underlying concepts were. Consequently Chinese society acted as a framework within which
countless beliefs and religions confronted each other, to be
collected, superimposed and mingled with each other. They
existed side by side, and elements from different ones were com-

bined freely. Officials would often observe Confucian rites during their public life, and practise Taoism in private. Until recently, it was common practice to ask Buddhist monks to perform funeral ceremonies, but to turn to Taoist monks to combat spirits and diseases. Ancestor worship was practised by all Chinese, regardless of their other loyalties. Because they were able to remain indifferent to doctrinal incompatibilities in different religions and to use them all with no difficulty, some people have held that the Chinese are not a religious people. Their conception of faith has never involved the intransigence and intolerance which characterise Islam and Christianity. In China, religious faith had no metaphysical preoccupations, no idea of the individual face to face with the deity, conversing with him or in anguish when abandoned by him. Chinese religious writings appear to contain nothing comparable with the psalms or the great Christian mystic writings. Instead of the contrast between the deity and the human being, the creator and the created, there exists in Chinese religions a tendency to link the natural and the supernatural worlds and to look on them as two systems which influence each other, each one an extension of the other, belonging to one and the same world, bound by the same laws. The hierarchy of the gods, the administration of heaven and hell, were based on the pattern of the officials' hierarchy and the imperial administration system. The emperor of China awarded titles to the deities; he promoted them, or punished them by demoting them. Many of the deities in the Chinese pantheon were canonised historical figures or ones who had become gods by chance. Furthermore, countless gods of fields, mountains, rivers, the kitchen, doors and walls were venerated. The whole of nature was inhabited by spirits who made sure that everything ran smoothly. Generally speaking, it could be said that in China religious feeling is feeling for harmony in nature, and that all religious practices were directed towards preserving this harmony. Spiritual anguish springs not from the fear of individual damnation, but from the idea that a disturbance of nature, or cosmic disorder, is always possible. This could perhaps be regarded as the expression of an agricultural civilisation depending for its existence on the regular rhythm of the seasons, a civilisation whose work calls for a constant collective effort, and an understanding between men reflecting harmony in nature. One of the most striking features of Chinese thought is the concept that the moral order reigning in society and the natural order governing the world are of the same nature and interdependent. The Emperor blamed himself for the natural catastrophes which overtook his country; they were due to his lack of virtue. On the other hand, such disasters always preceded the fall of a dynasty: they were symptoms of its moral weakness and heralded its decline.

Everything was linked: the moral and natural orders, the natural and the supernatural. Metaphysical anguish and passion seem to be missing from this conciliating religious life. It would be wrong to conclude, however, that China has never known any religion but one of simplicity and the formalist ritual of state worship. Plenty of Messianic movements have existed and sects of all kinds have flourished at all times. Religion has sometimes been sombre, satanic or fanatic. Great ages of faith and religious fervour have existed too: innumerable Buddhist pilgrims left Tang China to travel to India across the deserts and glaciers of Central Asia, spurred on by the hope of seeing the country of the Buddha with their own eyes.

It should not be forgotten that Chinese religions did not develop in a vacuum. The oldest Chinese conceptions of the universe seem to bear traces of Middle Eastern influence, which came to China by way of Central Asia. Buddhism came from India along the same route through Central Asia at the beginning of the Christian era. Christianity (Nestorianism) existed in China as early as the Tang. Under the Ming and the early Qing it became fairly widespread among the ruling class, thanks to the skilful policy of the Jesuit mission. Then, as European power grew, presenting more and more of a threat to the country, Christianity fell out of favour: the Western powers were suspected of using it as a kind of Trojan horse. In spite of interdictions and persecutions, however, it survived until modern times. Islam has always played an important part and still does. The numbers of Moslems make China the greatest Moslem power in the world.

Some of the fundamental features which give an unusual aspect to the history of Chinese religions can be found in the history of *philosophy* as well. For two or three centuries before the foundation of the empire, China passed through a period of creative activity which resulted, on the intellectual plane, in the formation of numerous schools of philosophy. The "Hundred Schools" inspired all Chinese philosophic thought right up to the modern era and the penetration of ideas from the West. The history of philosophy, like the history of religion, shows remarkable continuity. This feature has been reinforced by the fact that for 2000 years, from the foundation of the empire until its fall, philosophical thought was almost entirely the prerogative of the scholar-official class. This means that for over 2000 years all Chinese philosophical thought was based on Confucianism. Even the most revolutionary ideas were attributed to him, for the sake of form, or were introduced as a commentary on his thought. From Confucius himself up to his last great exponent, Kang You wei, no philosopher openly put forward new ideas. Chinese philosophy of the imperial era could be described as the "hand-maid of Confucian principles" just as Mediaeval philosophy could be described as the "hand-maid of theology". This uniformity hid profound changes, divergences and numerous contradictions. The philosophy of the Tang and the Song was strongly influenced by Buddhist and Taoist ideas. Under the Ming and the Qing, a few philosophers who were influenced indirectly by the West questioned the Confucian moral system. Chinese philosophy, however, has never had a Descartes to make a clean sweep of all old ideas and begin again from nothing; the vocabulary alone has changed, and that only slightly. The weight of Confucian tradition prevented change so efficiently that it is often difficult to perceive the evolution of real concepts beneath the ideas used. This difficulty alone is enough to make it hard for a European to study. Another one exists too: the inaccuracy of the philosophical concepts used, and the unusual logic, evocative rather than analytic, which Chinese used in assembling them. Other more serious difficulties arise from the inspiration of Chinese philosophy combined with difficulties of form. The great problems at the heart of Western philosophy, such as the disputes on the relationship of free will and necessity, between perception and reality, are not to be found here. Save for a few rare examples, Chinese philosophy is apparently little concerned with an abstract search for truth. The organising of the world is more important that the knowledge of it. The same practical attitude and anxiety to promote social efficiency which permeated religion is present here as well.

The problem of social organisation is at the centre of Chinese philosophical thought. If this is described as a *practical* problem, some of its implications for a Chinese mind may be overlooked, for as has been said already, moral (i.e. social) order is bound up with natural order. No conflict exists between the natural law and that of human liberty. Freedom, if it exists for the Chinese, is not thought of as free will (which would involve *arbitrary* decisions), but as freedom to follow a natural tendency, to join spontaneously into a whole. This whole, whether it be the universe, nature or human society, does not appear as an artificial construction, but as a living organism whose parts adapt themselves spontaneously to each other, through a virtue which is inherent in them. Consequently, it is essential to recognise this virtue, and then to encourage its awakening, by education if necessary. Harmony in society will be the natural result. This concept makes no break between knowledge of human nature and moral and social preoccupations. The study of human nature should give rise to a morality which merely needs to be cultivated for order to reign. Western traditions place much importance on institutions, right, and the contract which limits individual liberty in the common interest. These ideas have never been prevalent in China: laws were considered as a last resort to be appealed to when morality failed to find an answer to all difficulties. Philosophy was concerned above all with the principles of social organisation, and was consequently the expression of all that is deepest and most original in Chinese thought. But as the problems reflected are those of a society very different from Western societies, it is usually extremely difficult for Europeans to grasp. This is true of Confucianist philosophy of the imperial era. The philosophers of the Warring States period are nearer to our ways of thought as their means of expression is much less rigid. Their thought is not disguised in commentaries of the classics; they indulge in lively digressions and dialogues on extremely varied subjects. Like Plato or Lucretius, they deserve to be considered as great authors as well as philosophers. The *Analects* of Confucius *(Lun yu)*, *Mencius (Meng zi)*, and the work known as *Zhuang zi (Chuang-tzu)*, one of the great master-pieces of Chinese prose, held to be a classic in the Taoist tradition, all deserve to be mentioned here. Among the philosophers who wrote after the foundation of the empire, the most accessible and attractive is probably Wang Chong (27–91 A.D.), a rationalist and materialist who wrote violent attacks on the obscuranticism of his time (his book is entitled *Lun Heng*).

The history of Chinese religions and philosophy seems to be closely linked to the history of Chinese society. A brief account of their origins, evolution and relationship will be given here, rather than a systematic description of their different doctrines. Explanations of the doctrines can be found in the works mentioned in the bibliography (see p. 389).

II. ANCIENT RELIGIOUS CONCEPTS

"Religion" is a misleading term when applied to the ancient China of the Shang and the Zhou dynasties; "religious world" would probably be a better expression, for it represents a complex collection of cosmological concepts, myths, beliefs, magic rites and divinatory practices. Archaeology and written sources give fairly extensive information about some aspects of the religious life of this period. The inscriptions on bone and tortoiseshell found in large quantities at An yang (see p. 824) since the beginning of the century, and which were used for divination, give valuable information on the Shang dynasty. Historical chronicles like the *Zuo zhuan*, which covers the years from 722–453 B.C. (the Chun qiu period) contain numerous passages dealing with Heaven, Destiny, miracles of good or bad omen, and sacrifices accepted or refused by the gods. The Confucian classics are rich in religious teachings. Large areas are still buried in shadow, however. Only fragments of ancient mythology remain, and nothing which can be compared with the Graeco-Roman pantheon. A few late works like the *Chu ci* (the *Elegies of Chu*, poems by Qu yuan, dating from the beginning of the 3rd century B.C.) contain a last glimpse of what ancient Chinese mythology must have been. Its disappearance is due to the Han dynasty Confucian scholars. Instead of preserving it as some Greek and Latin authors did, they transformed it to create, *a posteriori*, a vast system by which to justify their own power. They wanted above all to prove that Confucius was the heir of great sovereigns belonging to an age of gold, so that they themselves represented the continuation of a venerable tradition. To illustrate these claims, they re-cast the mythology, eliminating everything which did not serve their own purposes. Some of the great old myths have survived, however: the story of Hou yi, the archer who shot down nine suns, leaving one alone to continue on its way; and the story of Nü wa, a goddess with a serdent's tail who repaired one of the eight pillars supporting the vault of the heavens. The best known myths are those which were taken up for use in the Confucian tradition, for instance the account of the five mythical emperors who are traditionally supposed to have reigned between 2550 and 2140 B.C. They were: the Yellow Emperor (Huang di), Zhuan xu, Di ku, Yao and Shun. The last two were considered by the Confucians as model sovereigns, whose devotion to public affairs knew no bounds.

A few fundamental notions emerge from the religious world of Ancient China, which the French sinologue Marcel Granet calls the "basis of Chinese thought". They were already well formed by the Zhou period. The first Chinese philosophical schools took their inspiration from them; from the last three centuries before the birth of Christ onwards, the Taoist religion and the Confucian system both drew on them for their fundamental concepts. Marcel Granet has made a penetrating analysis of them in his book *La Pensée chinoise*. The ones to appear most frequently afterwards are perhaps the notion of *dao* and the double idea of *yin* and *yang*. Although they have varied in content in different periods and during different tendencies, they run through the entire history of Chinese thought like an unbroken thread. *Dao* originally meant "way, road" (it still does in spoken language). By extension it took on the meaning of "course of things"; it referred to the principle of movement at work in all natural processes. This movement was not conceived of as a mechanical movement, but as a natural, continuous flow forming the very tissue of reality. In this way it became the first element of the universe for the Taoists, in which they immersed themselves to escape the restraints of social life and the limitations of discursive reasoning. The name of their religion: "taoism" is the equivalent of the Chinese *dao jiao*, "the religion (or teaching) of *dao*". It should be remembered that *dao* is far from being an idea peculiar to Taoism; it plays its part in all aspects of Chinese thought. It is present in Confucian writings just as often as in Taoist ones. The English translation is generally "Road" or "Way", which renders the highly abstract level of the idea, but not the dynamic element. *Dao* is a movement: the alternating movement of two complementary forces, *yin* and *yang*, whose combined action moves every aspect of the universe: life and death, summer and winter, day and night. *Yin* and *yang* are not however thought of as two opposing and independent sources of energy, but rather as two abstract categories used to express, or expressing all alternation and duality. The swing of the seasons, of day and night, are the result of the action of *yin* and *yang;* antitheses, and everything double, also comes under the categories of *yin* and *yang:* light, heat and movement are due to *yang;* darkness, cold and motionlessness are due to *yin.* Man and the heavens are assimilated to *yang,* earth and woman to *yin.* All movement and life everywhere are born of the interaction of *yin* and *yang.*

Yin originally meant the part of a valley south of the river, which the sun never reached, but left in shadow. *Yang* was the sunny part north of the river (the word can be found used in this sense in many Chinese place names). In *Fêtes et chansons de la Chine ancienne*, Marcel Granet shows that the two abstract notions of *yin* and *yang* probably came from old peasant festivals which were held in certain spots on either side of a river. During these festivals, held in spring and autumn, marriages were arranged by games: the girls danced and sang on one side of the river, and the boys on the other. At the end, the two groups joined up and formed engaged couples, after exchanging signs during the dance. The marriages were celebrated at the next festival. The religious emotion and the social importance of these festivals resulted in a special meaning being attached to the terms used to denote the two sides of the river, and to oppose them as the dancers themselves were opposed.

Some of the oldest notions seem to be of peasant origin (dao, yin and yang). Others, however, were born of the religious life of the nobility; the chief of these is the worship of the ancestors. The nobles' power was hereditary under the Zhou. The perpetuating of the lines was the guarantee and the justification of power. It was indicated first of all by surnames (xing) which were handed down from one generation to another. Only the nobles bore family names; the people had none. Complicated rites controlled the relationships within the family between one generation and another, and particularly between the living generations and the dead. The presence of the dead ancestors was symbolised by tablets bearing their names. The number of tablets arranged on the family altar depended on the rank of the family: seven tablets in the royal family, five in high-ranking officials' families, and three in the case of the lower nobility. The souls of the ancestors had to be fed by the living. If the offerings and sacrifices were neglected, they suffered and might take revenge. They were supposed to share the same needs as the living. For this reason, the first Shang kings were buried with their wives, servants, their dogs, horses, chariots, weapons, jewels and provisions. Burial of this kind was still practised, on a smaller scale, and less often, under the Zhou dynasty. Passages in the Zuo zhuan (mentioned above) show that this practice of collective burial aroused disapproval during the Chun qiu period; it was already considered barbarous.

The court ceremonies should be mentioned among the religious practices peculiar to the ruling class. The Zhou dynasty kings offered large sacrifices every year to Heaven and Earth, for they were considered to be the centre of the universe, and were supposed to control its order by symbolic rites. One of these was the publication of the calendar. To help the king draw up the calendar and resolve spiritual questions in general, several colleges of specialists were formed round the court. They learned the arts of writing, mathematics, astronomy and astrology. Some of them were specialists in divination. The books which were handed down by Confucius, and which became Confucian "classics" (jing) under the Han, contain countless details about the official religion. One of them, the *Yi jing (Classic of Changes)*, dating from the beginning of the Zhou dynasty, is a treatise on the art of divination based on a system of symbolic representations. A hexagram is supposed to correspond to every situation. Each hexagram is composed of six horizontal lines, one above the other. Some lines are broken (two lines placed end to end), some are unbroken (a single line). The broken lines are assimilated to *yin*, the unbroken ones to *yang*. 64 different hexagrams can be made by combining them in different ways, forming a symbol of reality. Each hexagram is accompanied by a commentary. Although hard to understand, the *Yi jing* is important, for it contains numerous terms which were later taken up for use in Chinese philosophy, especially metaphysics. Writing a commentary on the *Yi jing* came to be a way of writing on metaphysical questions.

III. THE HUNDRED SCHOOLS

During the Chun qiu period (770–481 B.C.), the fiefs of th Zhou dynasty kingdom gradually became independent states. The border states expanded outwards, conquering new territory and adding to their power. They soon started fighting agains¹ each other, and wars were frequent. The battlefields were generally territories belonging to the small states in the centre who had been unable to expand and therefore were less highly developed than the great outer states; their societies were more traditional and more attached to the old religious and ritual concept of political power.

This concept was abandoned by the larger states. They owed their new power not to Heaven's favour or to the moral perfection of their princes, but to their skill in the art of war and the stability of their economy (relative autonomy conceded to the peasants, efficient tax system). Their conception of politics and technical skills was therefore much more practical. The old colleges of offerers of sacrifices, scribes and astrologers were bypassed by new men, considered more important: strategists, politicians, diplomatists, archivists, technicians. The colleges, which considered themselves to enshrine a sacred tradition, were relegated to second place, and even became inactive.

Confucius' thought emerged against this background (Chinese: Kong zi, 551–479 B.C.). He was born in Shan dong, in the little state of Lu (see Qu fu, p. 742), and he belonged through his origins to the now decadent and traditionalist class which once had been the right hand of religious power. His aim was to save it by finding it a new task to fulfil, which would be in harmony with the new time. Hence the disconcerting and contradictory aspect of his ideas, which are those of a traditionalist and a reformer at the same time.

His first task was to save the aristocratic morality which was steeped in religious values whose failure seemed imminent, if not already under way. The old hereditary nobility found that its power was threatened by social upsets of ever-widening scope. The instruments of political power were in the hands of men who put the state above all moral considerations. Confucius realised that the nobility would be able to keep its position only if it managed to found its power on moral authority instead of hereditary claims. It would rule through morality. At the same time it would stem the "baneful tendency" towards governing by laws, and founding the power of the state on political restraint and military strength. In order to rule through moral example, the nobility must renew its vigour by adequate education: every able man would be accepted by the schools, whatever his social origin. After wandering for years through all of China in the hope of finding a prince enlightened enough to adopt his ideas on government, Confucius himself put this broad vision into practice at the end of his life. As he found no such prince, he went back to his native country, the state of Lu, and devoted himself to teaching. Confucius himself left no written works. His disciples, however, collected the words of their master: the result was the *Analects (Lun yu)*, which consists of slightly over 500 fragments written in the spoken language of the time. Most of them take the form of short dialogues between Confucius and his disciples. Although they are easily approachable, their incoherence is at first disconcerting. The pattern which holds them together is not obvious at first sight.

This apparent incoherence of thought and the scanty information in existence about his life (a few indications to be gleaned from the *Analects* and a biography, mainly legendary, in the *Historical Records* by Si ma Qian) have enabled people to interpret the philosophy of Confucius in the most contradictory ways possible: he has been found alternately to be an execrable reactionary and the first democrat. These divergencies are obviously due to the political convictions of the exponents, first and foremost; but to a certain extent, their germs are to be found in the thought of Confucius himself. He was after all a daring educationalist and at the same time, a conservative who wanted to ensure domination by a traditional aristocracy (even though he wanted to give it new foundations). His thought is in fact characterised by a fundamental ambiguity. The over-riding importance conceded to the moral qualities of the rulers could work for progress and become a factor for democracy. It could also, as was seen to be the case later, become the ideological justification for moral conformity imposed by the state.

The importance acquired by Confucius' thought from the Han dynasty onwards and its status of official doctrine for over 2000 years should not obliterate the fact that when it was introduced, and until the foundation of the empire, it was but one school of thought among many others, and not even the most important. The aristocracy to whom Confucius entrusted a new mission were soon superseded. The Warring States period (481–221 B.C.) was an era of bitter political and military struggles in China. The large states used power politics against each other, each trying to re-create a unified kingdom of Zhou to its own advantage. These four centuries of permanent upset and rapid social transformation produced an unprecedented intellectual ferment in China. The powerful nobles, ministers and heads of state maintained courts at their own expense frequented by musicians, entertainers, painters, and also fencing masters and teachers of strategy, as well as politicians, philosophers, teachers of rhetoric, diplomatists. They sometimes amounted to several thousand followers. The holders of power vied with each other to attract the most able diplomatists, the most clear-sighted politicians, the most prudent advisers. All available resources in terms of policy and intelligence had to be brought into play in the struggle for hegemony.

The first schools of Chinese philosophy were born into this historical context. Confucius had already travelled from one end of China to the other, accompanied by a group of disciples, proposing his maxims of government to the princes of the period. For two or three centuries after his death, until the unification of the empire, large numbers of philosophers wandered from one court to another trying to get their political concepts accepted, and each hoping to be taken on as adviser to a minister or a king. Apart from the originality of their views, one of their main trump cards was their eloquence and dialectic ability. Some of them were not simply clients of influential people: they maintained their own clientele in the form of a court of devoted disciples, and were often heads of schools. They launched stinging campaigns of polemics against each other. The intellectual effervescence which this encouraged is comparable from all points of view with the flowering of Greek philosophic thought, which happened at roughly the same time.

The schools of philosophy of the Warring States period, often called the "Hundred Schools" *(bai jia)* were divided into ten groups by the Han dynasty historian, Si ma Qian (given in the chapter headed *Yi wen zhi* in the *Historical Records*). The study of these groups is extremely interesting from a historical point of view, as the ideas which they uphold in many cases express the interests of different classes of the population. Chinese society became more and more complex during the centuries preceding the unification. The officials of the ruling class, the great merchants, the peasants and the craftsmen belonged to distinct social categories. This is one of the factors which contributed to the birth of different or contradictory political doctrines, and which resulted in their confrontation.

The Confucianist school, or rather the philosophers openly supporting Confucius' thought (they were not conscious themselves of having formed a "school") included Mencius (Chinese Meng zi, 372–289 B.C.) and Xun zi (often transcribed as Hsün-tzu, 3rd century B.C.). Mencius' work consisted of dialogues which were often brilliant and full of attack. Mencius himself is portrayed discussing points with his disciples, his rivals or the king of the kingdom of Qi. The tone which the philosopher adopts when speaking to the king is so free and easy that it sometimes borders on impertinence; it would have been unthinkable during Confucius' lifetime. Mencius developed the doctrine considerably, in a way that Confucius himself would never have allowed: a sovereign's moral qualities mean nothing, he says, unless they result in a policy which brings good to the people; such a policy is in fact in the sovereign's interest, as power which acts contrary to the will of the people will not last; in the last resort, the people have a perfect right to overthrow incapable sovereigns. Mencius appears to have been tempted to add: all rulers cannot but take my advice or if not, withstand the consequences. This daring doctrine came to nothing, as it did not take account of the fact that the Chinese states were involved in bitter fighting at that time, and none of them had the time to devote itself to the building up of a just society. Mencius' philosophy, from this point of view, is tinged with idealism, whereas that of his successor, Xun zi, is free of all illusions. He has no hope of converting the sovereign to any particular policy, but wants to formulate a general theory of society to serve as a basis for all political thought. This change in viewpoint is reflected in the form of the work: Xun zi abandons the dialogue form and writes a systematic account of his doctrine. He forced himself to have no recourse whatsoever to religious and irrational factors when explaining natural and social phenomena. He showed that social order was a necessity imposed by the communal life and division of labour; that human nature, if not corrected by education, runs a continual risk of being led astray by baneful instincts and passions; that stable institutions are needed to preserve peace, as well as education. This philosophy contains little trace of Confucius' serene confidence in the moral virtue of the individual. The continuity of the inspiration is revealed in one point, however: like Confucius, Xun zi considered that it was useless to impose order by means of laws, that the only way of governing was to control morality by education; that self-control and sound habits inculcated by education were the only sure foundation of social order. Confucius' aim was to form an elite. Xun zi proposes a complete theory of society.

The school of Mo zi (480–420 B.C.) was one of the most influential of the philosophical schools which flourished during the Warring States period. Mo zi attacked the social injustices of his time, protesting vehemently against the privileges enjoyed by the great families, their clannishness, their exaggerated extravagance (a polemic against music at court, and against luxurious funerals), the seizing of wealth by the powerful, the murderous struggles in which the princes engaged among themselves, in which the people were the chief losers; he proclaimed an ideal, equalitarian society in which everything to do with expenditure and way of life would be regulated to follow a uniform pattern. He held that autocratic power should be given to the poor, a class close to the peasantry, and not to the nobility. His ideas aroused more of a reaction than did those of the Confucianist school. They were furthermore spread systematically by an organisation of active militants. Dressed like the peasants and craftsmen of the day, they intervened to avoid war, came to the defense of towns which were unjustly attacked, and approached prime ministers to persuade them to abandon plans which promised to turn out badly. The art of persuasion was therefore as important to them as the art of war. The philosophic works of Mo zi contain treatises on other matter as well.

Unlike the aristocratic ideal of the Confucianist and the equalitarian ideal of Mo zi, the theory of the Legalists *(fa jia)* had a direct and decisive influence on politics. They considered that it was an established fact that morality is powerless to govern society. The politics of the time had taught them that interest alone moves the world. They drew up clear-sighted theories about a state based on a system of rewards and punishment, maintaining its hold over people by playing on their vanity and desire for honour and their fear of punishment. The ruler should merely apply an impartial and invariable order by instituting a system of public laws, well-known by all his subjects. He himself would hold absolute power, never delegating any of it for fear that the unity of the state be threatened by internal strife. This concept of power enfeebled the hereditary noble families, suppressed their privilege and submitted state politics to one criterion, that of practical efficiency (social order, military strength, economic power). It is easy to assume that the Legalist had a blind faith in laws as such, and considered them all-powerful, but this is not so. Their political theory laid great store by flair, adroitness and initiative. They did not think of law as a system of repression, but as a carefully-judged pattern of warning and reward which in the long run would act as an education. They anticipated a gradual transformation of society. They had one point at least in common with the Confucians: their ideal was never to have to apply the law, but to create social harmony through education. Unlike the Confucians, however, they thought out efficient educational methods. The greatest philosopher of the Legalist school was Han fei (died 233 B.C.). His work, *Han fei zi*, is remarkable for the inflexible strictness of its reasoning.

Most of the schools of philosophy in ancient China were chiefly concerned with finding a solution to the political crisis which their country was experiencing. Some looked for the solution in the rejection of all forms of tyranny, others in the accession of a strong state. The gravity and urgency of the political difficulties and the constant war, of which society bore the main brunt, engendered an individualistic and anarchic trend of thought as well. Several schools held that political ambition and preoccupation with public affairs were but vanity, that the refinements of civilisation led the mind astray and should be rejected, that social institutions led to confusion in morals and should be abolished, that morality was sheer imposture and ought to be forgotten. The most important of these was the Taoist school *(dao jia)*. Zhuang zi (often transcribed as Chuang-tzu, c. 350–270 B.C.) was its most brilliant defender. In his philosophical work, called *Zhuang zi* after its author, he uses every possible form: exposition, dialogue, polemic, satire, fable, story, to throw his enemies into confusion and bring them into disrepute. *Zhuang zi* contains a complete social theory: the holders of power are all robbers; robbers, on the other hand are aristocrats in their way; as for politicians and reformers of all kinds, they do nothing but spread confusion, Confucius included; for this reason, whether they like it or not, they are accomplices of highwaymen who constantly threaten to seize power. The only hope of salvation is to return to the primitive state when man, ignorant of all artifice and convention, lived in perfect peace with himself and nature. The Taoists considered all distinctions artificial: life and death, happiness and unhappiness, small and large, everything came to the same thing; all reasoning was trickery. This rejection of reasoning, the refusal of all social restraints, the search for a state of mind older than all civilisation, verged on mysticism. Their aim was to strip off all the elaborate trappings of life so as to discover in themselves the universal movement of *dao*, to accept it and merge with it, losing individual consciousness. From that moment, so the Taoists said, the body became light, so that it could fly with the wind, live on dew and exist for thousands of years.

One of the merits of the Taoist school is that its members preserved and handed down an inheritance of magic and religious practices which were threatened by the development of moral thought and reasoning and likely to be entirely forgotten. It contained a motley collection of traditions from the old colleges of soothsayers, from theorists of *yin* and *yang*, from sorcerers who worked miracles, from rain-doctors and popular healers. The trend also carried with it an astonishing volume of empirical knowledge alongside numerous superstitions. The Taoist ascetics used various auxiliary techniques (diatetics, breath-control, concentration) in which modern science recognises many established facts. As they constantly aspired to a return to nature, the Taoists played an advanced role in the development of some of the natural sciences. Chinese medicine and its pharmacopoeia owes an enormous debt to Taoism (this aspect of Taoism has been studied by Joseph Needham in *Science and Civilisation in China*).

These remarks on Taoism show that the development of the great rationalist schools of thought during the Warring States period did not involve the disappearance of popular beliefs and religion (ancient Greece also had its mysteries, cults and superstitions). One of the most interesting sources of information on the religious life of this time is the works of the greatest poet of ancient China, Qu Yuan (340–278 B.C.). Several of his poems seem to have been inspired by a Shamanist liturgy:

the priest invites the goddess to descend to the dwelling which he has prepared for her, using a song rich in imagery: when she has left him once more, he feels all the melancholy of an abandoned lover. One of the poems is a long speech calling the soul of a dead person back to the world of the living (cf. *The Nine Songs. A Study in Shamanism in Ancient China*, by A. Waley, London 1955; *The Elegies of Ch'u*, translated by D. Hawkes, Oxford 1959).

IV. THE HAN DYNASTY: FORMATION OF THE CONFUCIAN SYSTEM AND THE TAOIST RELIGION

The last years of the 3rd century B.C. saw the rapid development of events which decided the course of the later history of China: the king of Qin conquered the whole of China by a few crushing campaigns and proclaimed himself emperor in 221 B.C. (Qin shi Huang di). He consolidated the unity of the empire by a series of ruthless reforms; but after his death (209 B.C.) the new state disintegrated into anarchy. Revolts flared up almost everywhere; their leaders quarrelled over the power for a time, and the unity of the empire seemed to be threatened. In 206 B.C. Liu Bang triumphed over all the opposition and founded the Han dynasty. During these events and the time which followed them several philosophical tendencies which had formed over the preceding years came into violent competition, reflecting the political and social opposition.

The rise of the kingdom of Qin had been made possible by a series of widespread internal reforms inspired by the Legalist theorists. It is no exaggeration to say that the victory of Qin shi Huang di, and therefore the unification of the empire was in fact the victory of their doctrine. The military, political and administrative measures taken by Qin shi Huang di to consolidate the new imperial power were a systematic application of their theories (absolute power of the sovereign, highly centralised state, administered by a class of officials, the unification of the coinage, measures, the script, etc.). Stern measures were taken against the social class which seemed likely, sooner or later, to endanger the new state: the hereditary nobility and the princely families. They had lost their power but still retained some of their influence, and represented centrifugal forces which were always to be feared, particularly as they enshrined the prestige of the old literary and intellectual traditions, and were extremely conscious of their political vocation. In 213 B.C., Qin shi Huang di ordered that Confucian books be burned and the scholars persecuted, in the hope of subduing this class once and for all. All traces of their aristocratic ideal, their theory of government, and the ideological justification of the privileges they enjoyed in the past were to be wiped out completely.

Through the application of intelligent reforms, the Legalist theories had made it possible to transform the backward state of Qin into a formidable military power. They also helped to create the political and administrative structures of one of the greatest and most long-lasting empires of all history, over the space of a few years. They were not destined to last for long however. No room was left for family and religious traditions, or for the arts. When the Qin dynasty fell, the theories were discredited, and no other dynasty ever dared to bring them back into play. On the accession of the Han dynasty, Confucian ideas were brought back into favour and rose to the position of supreme importance which they were to occupy as long as the empire lasted: until the beginning of the 20th century.

Of all the old philosophical schools, none suited the new needs as well as Confucianism. The value placed on social hierarchy insured the return to power of the great land-owning families. The old tradition which it quoted as its authority provided the titles for the new dynasty and gave it an ideological foundation. With the return of the idea that only the morality of the ruling class can insure good government, the land-owning class prevented the rising merchant class from forming any pretentions to sharing in the government of the state. It is not pure chance that the morality of the time relegated the merchants to the bottom of the social scale, regardless of their real economic power. The scholar-official appeared; he owed a certain debt to the state official as conceived by the Legalists, but his education was based on the study of the Confucian classics (Shi jing, the Classic of Songs; Shu jing, the Classic of Documents; Yi jing, the Classic of Changes; Li ji, the Record of Rituals). The classics were taught in an imperial academy and provided the material for the offical examinations by which the state recruited its servants. Each pupil studied one classic only at first, under the direction of one teacher. The interpretation varied with each teacher. In accordance with the outlook of the times, the main aim was to hand down the teaching of the sages of old, not to discover new theories based on it. This explains the existence of varying interpretations and the apparent lack of method. The fundamental ideas were the same everywhere, however: the sovereign must regulate his own conduct according to the cosmic order; his example will influence his ministers, the people surrounding him, and, by degrees, all his subjects; he will become the mediator between the natural and social orders through his own virtue. If the social order disintegrates, it will be concluded that the emperor is at fault; he has not set a good enough example. Dissatisfaction among the people is considered as a warning to the emperor from Heaven: if he is incapable of imposing harmony, he will lose the mandate of heaven and be overthrown.

The Confucianism of the Han must not be thought of as a rigid, unified doctrine. Numerous scholastic disputes arose, and the appearance of apocryphal texts attributed to Confucius inspired interminable debates. The theorists of the period borrowed elements from different doctrines and gradually formed a vast synthesis where Confucius' theories were mingled with teachings from the classics, Taoist ideas, theories of *yin* and *yang* and of the five elements. All this was a long way from the intellectual debates of the Hundred Schools period. Obscurantism prevailed. The works of the only philosopher to try to oppose it, Wan Chong, bear witness to this. His rejection of whimsical theories, of irrational explanations, and his scepticism and good sense, were not followed by others. His philosophical work, *Lun heng*, stands alone; paradoxically enough, it is the only one of that period which still holds interest for the modern reader (see the English translation by Forke).

While the power of the land-owners and the scholar-officials was gaining ground on the intellectual plane through the creation of a vast scholastic synthesis, a religion was coming into being: Taoism. Contrary to what is generally held to be the case, this Taoism had little to do with the philosophical and mystical theories formulated by the great masters of the Taoist school of the Warring States period: Lao zi, Zhuang zi. The aim was no longer to reach a state of union with *dao*, the primary cause of the universe, through practising asceticism. The religion which was born under the Han dynasty promised physical immortality to the faithful. Numerous recipes were suggested: dieting, alchemists' drugs or pills, breathing techniques, magic formulae, cults of all kinds. Troubled spirits who found no consolation in the austere Confucian doctrines turned to these practices, searching for liberation from death. At the end of the Han, Taoism was a popular religion preaching the remission of sins, and organising ceremonies of penitance in public.

Believers were organised into communities; they paid a remittance
of five bushels of rice a year, met regularly to celebrate festivals,
and wore yellow turbans. The movement became so powerful
in eastern China that it turned into a revolt against the power
of the emperor: in 184 A.D. the revolt of the Yellow Turbans
heralded the fall of the Han dynasty. During the four centuries
of disunity which China then suffered, Taoism became an
organised religion, with monastic orders, clergy, scriptural
writings and a large pantheon of deities. Under the Han it
was still a sect, but it later became a Church in the true sense
of the word. This transformation took place under the influence
of a foreign religion: Buddhism.

V. BUDDHISM

Buddhism originated in India in about the 6th or 5th century
B.C., triumphed briefly under the reign of king Asoka in the
3rd century, and continued for several centuries more in north
and north west India. From there it spread towards central
Asia and into the little oasis kingdoms of present-day Xin jiang.
During the 2nd and 1st centuries B.C., the Han dynasty extended
its sphere of influence westwards and opened the silk route:
the highway by which Buddhism was gradually to penetrate
China was created. Trade relations grew up between China
and the small kingdoms of central Asia, Kashmir and India;
as a result, Buddhist missionaries appeared in China and
founded several communities there. One is known to have existed
as early as the 1st century A.D. in the present province of
Jiang su. A century later, a community at Luo yang was so
flourishing that Emperor Huan (147–168 A.D.) had Buddhist
ceremonies performed in his palace under its influence. The
new religion penetrated by slow degrees, and almost
without the Chinese realising it. At first they thought that
it was a variety of Taoism, and explained its origins by attributing it to Lao zi: the old philosopher was supposed to have
left China, riding an ox, to go and expound his doctrines to
the western barbarians; Buddhism was the barbarian version
of Taoism. The confusion between the two at first may have
arisen from the fact that both proposed a doctrine of salvation,
and that their doctrinal differences, although fundamental,
could not be clearly understood by the Chinese. Their language
was inadequately equipped to express the abstract theories of
Buddhism. It had already been refined by a long literary tradition, but as it had nothing to compare with the Sanskrit inflexions

and grammatical classifications, it could with great difficulty convey the subtle reasoning underlying the Indian speculation. Not until masters emerged capable of writing both Sanskrit and Chinese did the full originality of Buddhism become apparent. The first great translator was a monk from central Asia, Kumârajîva, who lived in the 5th century. After him translations from Sanskrit became more and more frequent and accurate until about the 8th century. The greatest translators were Xuan zang (second half of the 7th century) and Yi jing (end of the 7th and beginning of the 8th century). The gigantic work accomplished by these men had no mean influence on the evolution of Chinese thought: the speculations in Confucianist philosophy under the Song would have been inconceivable, had it not been for the discovery of Indian metaphysics and the logical equipment which it used. The translations also had an effect on Taoism for by revealing the imposing collection of deities embraced by Buddhism, they encouraged the Taoists to create a similar pantheon to keep up with the other faith. Although the translations from the Sanskrit had a great influence on the development of Taoism and on Confucianist philosophy, they had much less influence on the religious life itself. Only the simplest ideas were retained here, such as the transmigration of souls, and the merit acquired by performing charitable acts (alms). Buddhism, in introducing the practice of giving alms to the Chinese community, played a special part in the Chinese economy: as monasteries were exempt from taxation, the peasants were tempted to give their land to them, and then be engaged by the monasteries as tenants. Thus they escaped taxation, forced labour, and military service, while the monasteries themselves grew rich. Their economic power under the Tang was such that the imperial power was threatened; in 845 the Emperor ordered the suppression of Buddhism, accompanied by the dissolution of the monasteries and the return of all monks to secular life. Chinese Buddhism never fully recovered from this blow. In the space of a few centuries, however, it had penetrated all aspects of Chinese civilisation to such an extent that its imprint was indelible. It had inspired an unprecedented development of the plastic arts (sculpture at Dun huang, Yun gang, Long men, etc.), played a considerable part in the birth of a Chinese literature written in the spoken language (the first Chinese novels are very close to the Buddhist sermons from which they originated), and encouraged the first use of printing to spread written texts (the *Diamond Sutra*, printed in 869 A.D. is the oldest known example of printing).

Its influence on the intellectual plane was considerable, but
indirect. Buddhism arrived in China in a late form, known as
the Greater Vehicle, a form in which metaphysical speculation
which the Buddha himself had not included in his teaching,
had made great progress. The Chinese transformed these
abstract and rigorous speculations to fit in with their own
habits of thought, more down to earth, but giving considerable
importance to intuition. The most characteristic products
of this marriage of Buddhism to the Chinese mentality include
the concepts upheld by the Chan sect, better known in Europe
under its Japanese name, Zen (founded in the 6th century by
the Indian monk Boddhidarma, see p. 809): all reasoning should
be rejected, all doctrines are simply as many useless burdens
imposed on the mind, salvation rests in a sudden realisation
of the vanity of everything. The spirit of Chan is very close
to the Taoist thought of Zhuang zi in some respects (rejection
of all intellectual speculation, all worship, social restraints, etc.).
Another characteristic form of Buddhism in China was the
Pure Land sect (Jing tu), whose teaching proclaimed that it
was enough to believe in Amitābha (Chinese: *O mi tuo fo*,
Japanese: *Amida*), a Bodhisattva who reigned in the Western
Paradise *(xi tian)*, to be certain of eternal life spent in the
same paradise. Originally Buddhism denied life after death;
nothing was permanent. The Pure Land sect introduced the
idea of eternal life, and drew nearer to Taoism in this respect
(the Western Paradise was itself a borrowing from Taoism).
Buddhism had to undergo these profound changes before it
could become a religion which had a real hold on the people
of China. Doctrines and sects such as Chan or the Pure Land
Sect are so far removed from Indian Buddhism that they are
barely the same religion.

Both Buddhism and Taoism went through their greatest
periods of development during the four centuries of division
in China from the fall of the Han dynasty (220 A.D.), to the
founding of the Tang dynasty (618 A.D.). With the re-unification
of the empire by the Sui, and the culmination of its power under
the Tang, Confucianism came into its own again. The Tang re-
organised the administration, and reinforced the imperial examination system. The teaching of the classics practised under the
Han no longer satisfied the new needs: one explanation of the
classics alone was published throughout the empire, and a
thorough knowledge of this was enough, in theory, to enable
a candidate to pass the examinations, which were no longer
held in the capital alone, but throughout the empire. Confucian-

ism became a system, but this found expression only in an "authorised commentary" *(zheng yi)* of the classics. Not until the Song dynasty did any true innovation in philosophical thought appear. Under the Tang, the reinforcement of Confucianism showed itself above all in a literary movement, led by the prose writers Han yu (768–824) and Liu Zong yuan (773–819). Their wish to reform prose writing and to give it back the vigour which it had in the writings of Confucius and Mencius came from a desire to spread the maxims of Confucianism more efficiently.

VI. CONFUCIANISM AT ITS ZENITH UNDER THE SONG

When the central power was strengthened under the Tang the imperial administration also strengthened its control over the Buddhist and Taoist monasteries. The object was to impose limits on the development of the two religions to prevent unbounded extension of their economic and social power. By this time, they had been in opposition to each other for so long, and had influenced each other so far, that in the minds of most people they were no longer two separate, opposed religions. The cosmopolitanism which reigned under the Tang provided a climate of thought in which different religions could easily co-exist (Nestorian Christians at Chang an). The evolution continued under the Song: the ascendancy of Confucian thought in official life was finally established for good, while cosmopolitanism and religious tolerance grew still more marked. At Quan zhou (Fu jian), a great maritime trading centre under the Song, Buddhist, Brahman, Arab and Christian tomb stones have been found. Jewish communities and Manicheist sects appeared in China. Taoism and Buddhism formed new sects. Religious life grew more varied, but it lost its impetus and creative energy at the same time. Chinese society had undergone a transformation. The Tang were military conquerors. During the Song dynasty's reign, China withdrew into herself again and created a society which was essentially urban and based on commerce. The scholar-official class grew larger numerically than it had ever been under the Tang. Several factors can account for this, among them the intention of the imperial throne to remove all power from the military leaders and hand it over in its entirety to highly efficient civil administrators. The Tang dynasty foundered in the midst of struggles between military factions; the Song dynasty intended this to serve as a lesson. The scholars, now that they were more numerous, and because the Chinese world was growing richer in general, formed a leisure class with time to develop study and scholarship. The result was a renewal of philosophic thought. The greatest of the Song thinkers was Zhi Xi (1130–1200): with Confucianism as a basis, he created a philosophy whose influence was as widespread in China as was that of St. Thomas Aquinas in Europe. Until then, Confucianism had assumed that close links existed between the natural and the moral orders; no systematic explanation of these links had ever been put forward (a few attempts had been made under the Han). Zhu Xi worked out a metaphysical theory which resolved the contradiction between the two: the whole universe, in its ultimate reality and all its manifestations, is the product of two distinct, infinite principles, which are at the same time inseparable, called *li* and *qi*. *Li* (literally: design, pattern, form) can be translated by "principle"; *qi* (literally: ether) by "matter". The English scholar Joseph Needham sees some of the intuitions of modern science in this philosophical system (see *Science and Civilisation in China*, vol. II). By basing his system on the two ideas of *li* and *qi*, Zhu Xi fixed the fundamental terms for all great philosophical debates which came after him (Ming and Qing eras). Although a slight risk of altering the meanings is involved, *li* can be assimilated to mind and *qi* to matter, and an idealistic or materialistic tendency can be attributed to the Song, Ming and Qing philosophers, depending on whether they lay greater importance on one or other of the terms. Other philosophers had used this formula before him, particularly Cheng Hao (1032–1085) and Cheng Yi (1033–1107), two brothers whose philosophy is closely linked with that of Zhu Xi in the Chinese tradition. Zhu Xi had enemies: the best known of them is Lu Jiu yuan (1139–1192), an upholder of absolute subjectivism. He held that all knowledge of reality could come only from introspection; his ideas were clearly influenced by Chan Buddhism. Zhu Xi's philosophical system was attacked by the Zhe jiang school of philosophy at the end of the Song, and chiefly by Chen Liang (1143–1194). The critical condition in which the Chinese state then found itself, and its imminent collapse, inspired them to devote themselves to practical tasks (politics, science). They condemned the philosophy of Zhu Xi as vain amusement.

VII. MING AND QING ORTHODOXY

No new developments occurred in Confucianist thought during the Yuan dynasty; the scholar class, shorn of its status by the Mongols, was not given to philosophizing. It preferred to indulge in literary amusement (opera), as this was more prudent. The accession of the Ming dynasty provoked a reaction of nationalist feeling, and the state then formed was even more strict and dictatorial than that of the Song. On the intellectual plane, this strictness resulted in the adoption of Song Confucianism as orthodox and in a growing intolerance of all forms of independent thought. The interpretation of the Confucian classics given by Zhu Xi was the only one accepted in the imperial examinations: it became a dogma. Its philosophy, known as *li xue* ("doctrine of the spiritual principle, *li*"), became the equivalent of a state religion, austere and puritanical, reminiscent of the ideas accompanying the Counter-Reformation. The great philosopher of the time was Wang Yang ming (Wang Shou ren, 1472–1528), a high-ranking official and general at the imperial court. He opposed the theories of Zhu Xi and refused to look for the principle of the universe in exterior reality, as he did. Referring back to the thought of Lu Jiu yuan, he claimed to find it within himself, in an inborn knowledge of reality. His ideas provoked widespread reaction and a school of philosophy grew up from them *(Wang xue)*. Wang Gen (1483–1541), a disciple of Wang Yang ming, drew new conclusions from the philosophy of the master: since all wisdom and knowledge spring from the consciousness of each individual person, man cannot be the victim of his own ignorance or of an unknown destiny; he is free to act and direct his life according to his own will. The ideology of a rising class of merchants and craftsmen can be seen appearing in the ideas of Wang Gen; for them free enterprise seemed still to be a far-off ideal (the first workmen's strikes occurred under the Ming). The ideas of Wang Gen were taken to their logical consequence by Li Zhi (1527–1602), the son of a great South China merchant family. His thought was like a challenge flung in the face of the upholders of Confucian orthodoxy, the ideological expression of a class of great land-owners and scholar-officials. If each man is capable of judgement, why should such over-riding importance be accorded to Confucius, Mencius and their teachings? What right have they to impose their maxims on other men? What proof is there that Confucius intended to form a school?

These ideas met with success and became a direct threat to the
order of the state as understood by its rulers. The works of
Li Zhi were forbidden and he himself was threatened, then
persecuted. Finally he was arrested and committed suicide
in prison at the age of 75. The violent reaction of the court proves
that they felt themselves endangered. It is tempting to wonder
whether these ideas would have undermined the imperial
regime, given time. The regime, now insecure, was saved by
the Manchu, forty years after the death of Li Zhi, and maintained
by them until the beginning of the 20th century. The arrival
of the Manchu struck a hard blow at the evolution of Chinese
philosophy. To break down the bitter resistance of the scholar-
officials, they adopted a double policy which consisted in
attracting the scholars over to them by large rewards and at
the same time instituting a ruthless inquisition system to muzzle
public opinion. Thus the movement of ideas which arose at
the end of the Ming among the scholars, promising a far-reaching
renewal of Chinese philosophy, as well as a development of the
political concepts of the ruling class, was cut short. Among
the philosophers alive at the end of the Ming dynasty, special
mention should be made of Wang Fu zhi (1619–1692), who
worked out a dynamic materialistic theory and claimed that
all nature and human society was in a state of permanent
evolution. He held that the earth should belong to those who
cultivated it, not to the emperor. Wang Fu zhi led an army of
resistance against the Qing. Then, when he saw that the Qing
were there to stay and that the Ming cause was lost, he retired to
Hu nan and devoted his life to study. Huang Zong xi (1610–
1695) belonged to the same generation and shared much the
same fate. His political writings constitute a violent criticism of
the dictatorial regime, and contain a germ of democratic thought.
He was the author of the first historical work in Chinese philosophy (a history of Confucian thought under the Song and
the Ming). Gu Yan wu (1613–1682) was the third great figure
belonging to the same generation; his influence was by far
the strongest. He was a scholar and a great reformer. He attributed the defeat of the Ming to Confucian orthodoxy, to its
idealist and quietist orientation; he blamed the Song philosophers
for this and showed that they had mis-represented the true
meaning of Confucius' thought, which, he held, was originally
practical, active and deeply committed. Gu Yan wu, like the
reformers and humanists of the European Renaissance, went
back to the sources in question. As in Europe, this move gave
rise to a philological method of study and gave great impetus

to the study of history. Gu Yan wu was a distinguished scholar in almost every branch of the sciences of his time (history, archaeology, philosophy, phonetics, mathematics, astronomy, geography, etc.). He was the originator of a vast movement of critical learning which was the summit of intellectual life under the Qing. The strict control exercised by the inquisition forbade the questioning of orthodox views and institutions. Archaeology and history provided loop-holes, and in some cases an indirect way of expressing philosophical ideas which it would have been dangerous to uphold openly. The Qing era had many great scholars, but few original thinkers. Among them, the most remarkable was probably Dai Zhen (1734–1777), a materialist whose theory of knowledge through meaning recalled the French age of enlightenment. He was opposed to morality imposed by orthodox thought and held that the satisfaction of the natural needs (alimentary, sexual, security) of each man was the only way to bring about social harmony, and that these needs, instead of being opposed to moral and spiritual life, are in fact at the base of it. Another eminent figure was above all a pedagogue: Yan Yuan (1635–1704). He was a son of the people, an enemy of theories and books, who compared the Confucianist scholasticism of the Song to a pig's bladder full of air. In 1694, he founded a gymnasium in the province of He bei, where the subjects taught were the military arts, archery, horsemanship, boxing, history, mathematics, astronomy, hydraulic engineering and botany. The gymnasium was probably the most modern of its kind in the world. Unfortunately it was destroyed by floods a few months after it was founded. The writings of Yan Yuan were handed down by his disciple, Li Gong.

The Jesuits, who arrived in China under the Ming and settled in Peking brought with them scientific knowledge of which the Chinese had no inkling and awoke their curiosity by showing them European techniques. As the political, commercial and military influences from Europe gradually permeated Asia, this curiosity was backed up by vague uncertainty. In the 17th and 18th centuries, it never occurred to the Chinese that they would one day have to confront the West. The ferment brought by the Jesuits had its effect on some minds even so.

The thought of Dai Zhen and Yan Yuan reveals an anxiety to re-consider the society of their time and to transfer it to a more solid rational foundation. Their work was ignored, however, and was almost forgotten until the fall of the empire.

VIII. POPULAR RELIGION
AND NON-CHINESE RELIGION

It has already been pointed out that from the Tang onwards, Taoism and Buddhism gradually stopped being considered as two different religions. The clergy of each were still opposed the other, and ceremonies were carried out according to different rites. But the main body of the faithful detached itself little by little from both religions, creating an independent religious life, a vast syncretic system, elements of which were borrowed from Taoism, Buddhism, local cults and the world of legends. This tendency had appeared under the Song, and then progressed under the Yuan and the Ming; the clergy were considered as two classes of superior sorcerers, whose practical roles differed. Buddhist priests, helped by supernatural powers, could deliver the souls of the dead from the tortures of hell, by redeeming their sins. Taoist monks could deliver the living from the demons, illnesses and mysterious influences which assailed them. These respective attributions are nowhere clearly defined; they grew up gradually out of custom. This popular religion is hard to describe. Henri Maspéro says of it: "...the tendency to change all religious forces into personal deities continued, constituting a vast, confused body of popular mythology with the form of a hierarchy similar to that of the imperial administrative organisations, with temporary gods who were promoted or demoted like the officials of this world, who were a curious mixture of Taoist Immortals and Buddhist Saints. Ancestor worship is the only element to have remained more or less unchanged, although ideas about the dead have changed, and the Buddhist belief in transmigration has been universally adopted, which makes the cult itself hard to explain" (Les Religions chinoises, Mélanges posthumes, vol. I, p. 114). "All the supernatural beings in popular religion, whether they are known by the title of Fo (Buddha), Pu sa (Bodhisattva), Lo han (Arhat), Tian zun (Heavenly Venerable One), Xian (Immortal), Di (Emperor), Hou (Empress), Wang (King), or even the lowliest of all, Shen (god or goddess) are of the same nature and only distinguishable from each other by the lesser or greater powers attributed to them; the titles given to them simply denote ranks in a rather loosely-knit hierarchy. Worshippers of the Sun and the Moon give them the title of Buddha; Emperor Guan, one of the most popular gods, is often called Bodhisattva" (ibid. p. 116).

The names of some of the most important popular deities are given further on (see p. 160, and also the section on the

Tai shan, p. 715, and the Yong le gong, p. 912). The reader wanting a complete description of all popular deities may consult *A Dictionary of Chinese Mythology*, by E.T.C. Warner, Kelly and Welsh Ltd., Shanghai 1932, 627 pages, repub. New York, 1961. The best way to obtain a living picture of all this is to read the satirical novel entitled *Xi you ji: Journey to the West*, written under the Ming by Wu Cheng en (1510?–1528?). The novel has a Buddhist theme, and describes a journey to India undertaken by Xuan zang, the Tang dynasty monk, who went there in search of holy writings (see p. 151). Countless Taoist and other themes are added to it, with stories of demons and sorcerers, of the Western Paradise and the under-world, of the assembly of the gods, of good and bad dragons. The Monkey King, who is the central figure in the book, has nothing to do with the Buddhist theme which underlies the work (English translation by A. Waley, *Monkey*).

Other classics of Chinese literature give invaluable information on the beliefs in spirits and demons, and particularly the collection of fantastic tales called *Strange Stories from a Chinese Studio (Liao zhai zhi yi)* by Pu Song ling (1640–1715) (English translation by H. Giles).

To give a complete picture of religious life under the Ming, the Qing and in the first half of the 20th century, a description of the numerous customs and superstitions, and the festivals which spread over the whole year (see p. 336) would be essential; a description of the countless deities would have to be included too. Certain religious movements expressed particular forces in society. At the end of the Song and under the Yuan, some Taoist groups led movements of popular resistance to foreign domination. Under the Ming and the Qing, these sects changed into secret societies. The peasant movement led by Zhu Yuan zhang at the end of Yuan was inspired by Manicheism, and it is extremely probable that when Zhu Yuan zhang, as emperor, chose the name *Ming* for the new dynasty which he founded, he was paying homage to this religion of Iranian origin.

Manicheism was not the only foreign religion to play its part in China. Islam seems to have arrived in China under the Tang through the Arab mercenaries taken on by the imperial court. It began to play an important part under the Yuan. Under the Qing, it inspired the inhabitants of Turkestan to carry on a violent struggle against Chinese domination. Judaism, which appeared in China under the Song, is often confused with Islam, or taken to be a tendency of Islam. Christianity existed in Tang China; it arrived from Persia, in the form of

Nestorianism. The Roman Catholic Church took root under the Yuan (the Franciscan Giovanni de Piano Carpini was sent to Peking by the Pope in 1425). With the Italian Matteo Ricci (1552–1610) who was at the head of the Jesuit mission in Peking, Christianity won influence among members of the court and the high-ranking officials. Matteo Ricci, who managed to be accepted by the Chinese by becoming a mandarin, thought that he could convert China to Christianity by converting the emperor; he was without any doubt the most outstanding of all European missionaries to visit China. His successors, who had not the same wide-ranging mind and approach, eventually lost all hope of winning the Chinese leaders over to the Christian faith. The rulers were in fact more interested in the scientific knowledge imparted by Ricci than in the faith he brought with him, and the privileges which they allowed him are largely explainable by the great admiration in which they held him. Ricci's career, and the presence of the Jesuits in China, resulted in the first great intellectual meeting between China and Europe (scientific ideas reached China, the French thought they had found an example of the ideal of the enlightened monarchy in China; influence of ideas taken from Chinese philosophy in the philosophy of Leibnitz, etc.).

A new religion, a variety of Buddhism, appeared in China under the Ming: Lamaism. Strictly speaking, this religion was founded under the Tang in Tibet, in 747 A.D. During the Yong le era (1403–1425), it split into two. The old church, whose clergy wore red, was called the "Red Sect" from then on *(hong jiao)*; the new one, whose clergy wore yellow, was known as the "Yellow Sect" *(huang jiao)*. Emperor Qian long, anxious to reinforce the political unity of the empire, went into collaboration with the reformed branch of Lamaism *(huang jiao)*, as it was particularly powerful in Tibet and Mongolia. This explains the presence of Lamaism in Peking (see Yong he gong, p. 501).

GLOSSARY: CHINESE DEITIES AND RELIGIOUS TERMS

A MI TUO FO

In Chinese: Amitābha (or Fa Bao, Treasure of the Law, Dharma). The name A mi tuo fo was introduced by the Nepalese sect of Mahāyāna in about 300 A.D., but became important in the 5th century only, when the Western Paradise *(Xi tian)* was invented as a substitute for Nirvana.

BA XIAN

The Eight Immortals, also known as *jiu zhong ba xian*, or the Eight Drunken Immortals, or the Eight Immortals in the wine glass. They were people who for some reason or other became immortal; three of them (Zhong Li quan, Zhang Guo and Lu Yan) were historical figures and the rest are purely legendary. They were constantly depicted and their portraits can be found on countless objects (vases, tea-pots, scrolls, embroidery, etc.). The expedition which they undertook all together is also very well known *(ba xian guo hai:* "the eight immortals cross the sea"): they decided to go and admire the marvels of the sea; the usual form of heavenly locomotion—sitting on a cloud—was turned down by Lu Yan, who proposed that each one should show the infinite variety of his powers by placing an object on the surface of the sea and walking on it. One used a walking-stick, another a sword, another a feather fan, etc. and they floated rapidly over the waves. Next they fought the Dragon King, defeated him, and continued their wanderings over the sea, encountering thousands of adventures. Their "biographies" are arranged in the order in which they became immortal.

1. Li Tie Kuai

He is also known as Kong Mu, and is always depicted with his cane and his gourd full of magic medicines. Xi Wang Mu (see further on) taught him the art of becoming immortal. His likeness was often used as an emblem by chemists' shops. He is also identified with Li Ning yang, whose soul left his body to go and visit the *Hua shan* Mountains. He left his body to the care of his disciple Lang Ling, asking him to burn it if he was not back in a week's time. On the sixth day the disciple was called to his mother's bedside, for she was dying, so he burned the body before he left: when the soul returned, it found nothing but a heap of ashes. At the same moment, a beggar died nearby; the wandering soul entered his body. It then noticed that the body it inhabited had a long, pointed head, a black face, and bushy, untidy beard and hair, and wished to leave this not very tempting shelter; but Lao zi advised him not to try, giving him a golden band to bind his hair, and an iron walking stick to make up for the paralysed leg.

Li Tie Kuai (Li of the iron cane) felt his eyes with his hand and found that his eye sockets were as big as belt buckles (hence his name of Kong Mu: Hollow Eyes). It is also said that Li Tie Kuai then went to see his disciple's mother: he poured the contents of his gourd into her mouth, and the dead woman came to life again. Then there was a gust of wind: the Immortal disappeared. During his wanderings over the earth, he used to hang a bottle up on the wall of his room; he jumped into it for the night, and left it again the next morning.

2. Zhong Li quan

He was born in Shân xi, and became a marshal under the empire; when he was an old man, he retired to the Yang jiao Mountains to live the life of a hermit. According to other sources, he was nothing more than an officer in the service of Duke Zhou Xiao: having suffered a defeat, he took refuge in the *Zhong nan shan*, where he met the Five Heroes who taught him the doctrine of immortality. Later on he took the pompous title of "The Only Independent One Under Heaven". It is said that for a long time he turned copper into silver with the help of a certain drug, and that he gave the silver to the poor. One day, as he was meditating, the stone wall of his house fell down, revealing a jade box containing secret instructions on how to become immortal: he followed them for a time, and one day his room filled with multicoloured clouds and music: a celestial crane arrived and carried him off to the country of immortality. He is shown sometimes carrying his feather fan, sometimes a peach of immortality.

3. Lan Cai he

Zhong Li quan was the soldier; Lan Cai he was the mountebank. He is sometimes described as a hermaphrodite, sometimes as a woman. She is usually depicted playing the flute or cymbals and is supposed to have been Yang su, of the Tang dynasty, originally. She wandered through the empire, singing in the streets, one shoe on and one shoe off, and could sleep in the snow: her breath formed a shining mist like the steam off a pot of boiling water. One day she was found drunk in an inn in An hui, and suddenly disappeared on a cloud, after throwing her shoe, her dress, her belt and her castanets to the ground.

4. Zhang Guo Lao

He was the Old Man. He is said to have lived in the middle or the end of the 8th century. He was first of all a hermit in the

Shan xi mountains; when invited to attend the court by the Emperors Tai zong and Gao zong, he stubbornly refused to go. Finally, pressed into it by Empress Wu (684–705), he left his retreat, but died suddenly at the gate of the Temple of the Jealous Woman. His body was already being eaten by worms when he reappeared, alive and well, in the Heng zhou mountains. He rode a white mule which could cover thousands of leagues in a single day: once he had reached his destination, he folded it up like a sheet of paper and put it into his bag. When he needed it again, he filled his mouth with water and showered the paper with it: the animal was ready once more. He is usually depicted riding his mule, sometimes facing its head, sometimes its tail; he carries a phoenix feather or a peach of immortality. When in the presence of Emperor Ming Huang (713–756), he would perform tricks to amuse him: he would make himself invisible, swallow a cup of deadly poison, kill birds by pretending simply to take aim at them, etc. He also distinguished himself in the art of necromancy. Some pictures also show him bringing an offspring to newly married couples.

5. He Xian gu

She was shown holding a magic lotus flower in her hand (the flower which opened the heart) and sometimes playing the *sheng* (mouth-organ) and drinking wine. She lived during the reign of the Tang Empress Wu (684–705): when she was born, she had only six hairs on the top of her head and it is said that she never had any more, in spite of the hair which she has in her pictures. She chose to live in the Mother of Pearl Mountains: there, a spirit told her in a dream to grind one of the stones of the mountains to powder to acquire agility and immortality: she did so, and spent her life from then on floating from one peak to another, bringing back the fruit she had collected in the mountains to her mother in the evenings. Little by little she realised that she did not need to eat to live... Her fame reached the ears of Empress Wu, who invited her to the court: she started on her way there, but suddenly disappeared during the journey and became an Immortal. She is said to have appeared again later, in 750, floating on coloured clouds near the temple of Ma Gu, the famous Taoist witch.

6. Lü Dong bin

He was born in Shan xi in 755, into a family of officials; he was five feet two inches high. When he twenty, he left on a journey to Lu shan in Jiang xi, and met the fire dragon, who gave him a sword thanks to which he could hide in the air as he wished. He visited Chang an, the capital, where he met the Immortal Han Zhong li who revealed to him the mysteries of alchemy and of the elixir of life. Next he was given supernatural powers and magic weapons: he travelled throughout the empire for four hundred years, killing dragons and freeing the earth from various catastrophes. In 1115, Emperor Hui zong gave him the title of Hero of Marvellous Wisdom. He is often depicted with his "devil-killing sabre", carrying a fly-whisk called *yun zhou* ("cloud broom"), which is also a Taoist symbol indicating that one can walk on the clouds and fly through the air at will. He had considerable literary gifts, and was venerated by scholars; under the name of Patriarch Luo, he was the patron god of ink-makers.

7. Han Xiang zi

He is said to have been the grand nephew of Han Yu, the great Tang statesman and writer, who prepared him for the examinations himself; the pupil surpassed his master, both by his intelligence and by his unusual gifts which enabled him, for example, to make wonderful plants grow in a handful of earth. Other sources have it that he was the disciple of Lü Dong bin, and that he was carried right up to the branches of the spirits' supernatural peach trees: he fell out of the branches and became Immortal during the fall.

8. Cao Guo jiu

He became Immortal because the seven other Immortals who lived in seven of the eight caves of the Upper Spheres wanted to find a tenant for the eighth: he was elected because he had qualities resembling a spirit; he was related to the imperial family and is often depicted holding his tablet giving him admission to the court. Another legend tells that Empress Cao, widow of Emperor Ren zong of the Song dynasty (1023–1064) had two younger brothers: the elder one would have nothing to do with the affairs of the State, and the second was unfortunately renowned for his bad behaviour: after many talkings to, he refused to mend his ways, and finally he was condemned to death, accused of murder. His brother, ashamed of the situation, went into hiding in the mountains where he covered his head and body with wild plants and resolved to live as a hermit. One day, the two Immortals Han Zhong li and Lü Dong bin met him in his retreat and asked him what he was doing there: "I am looking for the Way" was his reply. "Which Way... and where is it?" He pointed to his heart. The two visitors smiled with satisfaction: "The heart is heaven and heaven is the Way: you understand the origin of things." They gave him a recipe which enabled him to become Immortal in a few days himself.

BI XIA YUAN JUN

The First Princess of Purple and Blue Clouds who presides over births. There are in fact two principal deities with this name: one lived in Fu jian, the other on the Tai shan.

The first one, who was born, so the legend goes, in the Fu zhou district, was the daughter of an illustrious magician at the court of Wang Yan jun (10th century). She went to live in an unknown place, "in the middle of the seas", and no one knows what became of her after that.

The legend about the second one reports that the government of Jiang Tai gong was so perfect and peaceful that the wind never blew in his region. One night, Wen Wang (1231–1135 B.C.) saw in a dream a weeping woman who said she was the daughter of the God of the Tai shan and the wife of the Spirit of the Western Sea; when she travelled, she added, she was usually escorted by the winds and the rains; but she could no longer cross the territories of Jiang Tai gong, because her virtue was so powerful. The next day, Wen had Jiang sent for; a violent wind blew up and the region was drenched with rain, showing that the deity and her escort had been able to go through. The daughter of the God of the Tai shan in this legend is Bi Xia Yuan Jun.

CAI SHEN

The God of Riches. As in many cases, this deity covers several people. One of them is Zhao Gong ming, a hero of the Three Kingdoms. Another is Zhao Gong ming, of the Zhou dynasty: it is said that when Jiang Zi ya was fighting for Wu Wang (1121–1114 B.C.) against the last emperor of the Shang dynasty, Zhao Gong ming, who was then a hermit living in the E mei Mountains, took up the cause of the Shang emperor. He is known to have been able to ride a black tiger, and to throw pearls for a great distance, which then exploded like bombs. But Jiang Zi ya overcame him by the following means: he made a straw image of his enemy, wrote his name on the image, and worshipped it for twenty days; on the twenty-first day, he shot arrows of peach wood into the heart and eyes of the image.

At the same time, Zhao Gong ming, in the other camp, felt ill, gave one cry and died. Later on, Jiang Zi ya persuaded the Jade Emperor to give up the souls of the heroes who died in the battle: when Zhao Gong ming was brought before him, he praised his bravery, deplored the circumstances of his death, and canonised him under the title of Minister of Riches and Prosperity.

CHANG E

She stole from Hou Yi, her husband (see Shen Yi), the drug of immortality which Xi Wang mu (see further on) had given him, and fled to the moon, where she lived in a wonderful palace. Then she became goddess of the moon. Shen Yi went to visit her in the moon, and built her a palace; afterwards, they met regularly on the 15th day of every month. A legend adds that Chang E was eventually changed into a tortoise, whose shape can be seen on the moon's surface.

CHENG HUANG

God of Ramparts and Moats, God of the City, Celestial Mandarin. The ramparts and moats were the ones surrounding every Chinese town. Cheng Huang was also the spiritual "mandarin" of each town; each city, town and village had its own deity: all these Cheng Huang taken as a whole constituted the Celestial Ministry of Justice, over which a chief Cheng Huang presided.

The worship of Cheng Huang goes back to the time of Emperor Yao (2357–2255, according to the legendary chronology), who instituted a sacrifice called *ba zha* (God of Grass-hoppers) in honour of the eight spirits, the seventh of whom, Shui Yong, was the one who presided over the moats full of water surrounding the towns. Later on, the human defenders of various towns were represented under the form of this spirit: the cult of the city gods was thus handed on; they defended towns from their spiritual enemies, acted as governor, judge, magistrate, tax-collector, etc. The Cheng Huang controlled the demons of the area, and could order them to deliver the country from drought or other calamities. These duties were performed in collaboration with the human magistrate of the town, who shared the same rank: if the magistrate burned incense in honour of Cheng Huang, it was an act of pure courtesy.

FAN TIAN WANG

Chinese name for Brahma, the "father of all living beings".

FAN WANG

The father of all living beings, the essence permeating the universe. Later on he became "the soul of the universe", an impersonal being, who woke from an eternity of apathy to hatch the cosmic egg from which emerged this world.

FENG BO

Count of the wind; he is depicted as an old man with a white beard, a yellow coat and a red and white cap, holding a sack and sending the wind, which proceeds from his mouth, in whatever direction he wishes.

FO, FO TUO

Chinese for Buddha.

FU SHEN

The God of happiness. He was originally Judge of Criminal Affairs in Dao zhou (Hu nan). His career arose from the fact that Emperor Wu di of the Liang dynasty (502–550) was particularly fond of dwarves, whom he employed as servants and jesters at his court. The Judge pointed out to the emperor that his collections of dwarves were dangerous for family relationships, and that they were his subjects, not his slaves; the emperor agreed to stop collecting then. The population were so relieved that they published pictures of him, which they put into circulation, made sacrifices to him to show their gratitude, and he was worshipped everywhere as the god of happiness. He is often associated with another god of happiness, Guo Zi yi, one of the greatest figures in Chinese history. Guo Zi yi saved the dynasty from the ravages of the Turfan under the reign of Emperor Xuan zong (713–765).

GUAN DI

He is also known as Guan gong, Wu di, Guan Yu, etc... He was the God of war. He was originally Guan Yu, a hero belonging to the Three Kingdoms. He swore an oath of brotherhood with Zhang Fei and Liu Bei (see History) known as the Peach-tree Garden Oath. Finally he was captured and executed by Sun Quan, a general who revolted against Cao Cao. He was venerated for a long time as the most famous Chinese soldier hero, until the Ming emperor Shen zong granted him the title of Pillar of Heaven and Protector of the Kingdom; from then on, he became a god and the temples dedicated to him can be seen all over China. He became the patron of soldiers and of various corporations, (such as the corporation of soybean merchants, as he had belonged to the profession in his youth), of Literature (because he was said to be able to recite the whole of the *Zuo zhuan*), and of Riches. The temples dedicated to him were known as Wu sheng miao, temples to the God of War.

GUAN YIN

The Goddess of Mercy, also known as *Guan shi yin zi zai* or *Guan yin pu sa*. She may be an old Chinese deity, worshipped before the introduction of Buddhism. Later on, the Buddhists adopted her as the incarnation of Avalokiteshvara (or Padmapāni), and called her Guan Yin; the name means literally "who listens to the world's request". She is Captain of the Boat of Salvation which carries men's souls over the seas of life and death to the Pure Land. According to the legends, she was originally the third daughter of Miao Zhuang wang (8th century B.C.); she decided to give up her life to religion, and finally got her father's permission to enter the White Bird Convent at Lung shu xian. Her father had her employed for all the most degrading tasks possible, and eventually, unable to break his daughter's will, he ordered that she be put to the sword; the sword broke into a thousand pieces. Next he ordered her to be suffocated, without allowing her soul to leave her body, so that she would go to hell; hell was changed into paradise. To save her, Yama transported her miraculaously on a lotus flower and she was reborn on the Island of Pu tuo (Potala) near Ning bo, where she lived for nine years, healing the sick and saving sailors from perdition. Her father fell ill; she healed him be applying to him a piece of flesh cut from her own arm. Her father, in gratitude, ordered a statue to be erected in her honour, which was to be a statue complete with arms and eyes, *quan shou quan yan*. The sculptor understood *qian shou qian yan*, and the result was a statue of Guan Yin with a thousand arms and a thousand eyes, which was to perpetuate the memory of the goddess.

HENG and HA

They are called "Heng Ha er jiang", the two officers, Heng and Ha. In 1121, when the Yin dynasty was being overthrown and the Zhou dynasty founded, there were two officers, Zhen

Lun and Chen qi; they were known as He-who-blows-through-his-nose and He-who-blows-through-his-mouth respectively. The first of the two was the grand superintendant of of the armies of Zhou the tyrant, and the second was in charge of provisions. Heng had received miraculous power from his teacher Du E, the famous Taoist magician of the Kun lun Mountains: when he breathed out through his nose, his nostrils made a noise like a bell, and gave out two rays of white light which destroyed his enemies, body and soul; with Heng's help, Zhou the tyrant won several battles. One day Heng was taken prisoner, however, thrown into chains, and taken to the general of the enemy dynasty: his life was spared, and he was even appointed general superintendant and generalissimo of five armies. This brought him face to face with Ha: the latter had been taught by the magician how to fill his chest with a quantity of yellow gas which wiped out everything within his reach.

The two champions set to and a fierce fight of gas and rays of light began; then Ha was wounded in the shoulder by No Zha, and in the stomach by Yellow Flying Tiger, both Zhou dynasty soldiers. Heng too was wounded by Marshal Great Golden Pint (an ox spirit who had the mysterious power of being able to produce the famous bezoar in his entrails): he stood in front of Heng, and with a noise like thunder, he spat a piece of bezoar the size of a rice bowl into his face; Heng was hit on the nose, collapsed and was immediately cut in two by his opponent. Later on, when the Zhou dynasty was finally established, Jiang Zi ya canonised the two officesr Heng and Ha, and entrusted them with the task of guarding Buddhist temples, where colossal statues or pictures of them are often to be seen.

HUANG DI

The Yellow Emperor (2698–2598 B.C.), venerated as the god of architecture. He was one of the legendary sovereigns who suceeded Pan gu (see further on), and founded the Chinese empire after his victory over the Miao tribes and their chief, Chi Yu. Before that, his name was Xuan Yuan. He is supposed to have invented wheeled vehicles, armour, boats, pottery, etc... and to have improved the agricultural work of Shen nong (see further on) by deciding on the moment when trees should be planted and seeds sown. He also studied astronomy, mineralogy, built roads, etc... and became emperor because of his unsurpassed energy. At the end of his reign, the phoenix and the *qi lin* (a sort of unicorn) appeared to show their satisfaction at this wise and good reign.

JU LAI FO

The "Buddha who came thus" (Sanskrit: Tathagata): one of the titles of the Buddha, and at the same time, the highest name given to each Buddha.

LEI GONG

The Duke of Thunder. He is depicted as a hideous black demon, with bat's wings, a monkey's face and an eagle's beak; in one hand, he holds a steel chisel, in the other a spiritual hammer with which he beats the numerous drums round him (the Chinese believed that the sound of these drums, not the lightning, caused death).

LEI ZU

The Thunder Ancestor, also President of the Ministry of Thunder *(lei bu)*. He has three eyes, one of which is in the middle of his forehead, and gives out a ray of light over two feet long when it opens. He rides a black unicorn, and can cover millions of leagues in one moment. He is often confused with Lei Gong. He is the god of sowers, grain merchants and inn-keepers.

LONG

Usually translated as Dragon. Popular zoology placed the dragon just after man in the hieriarchy of living beings (the "unicorn" and the phoenix were higher than all animals living on earth and in the air). The dragon is equally at ease in the air, on the ground or in the sea; the Chinese were firm believers in dragons: when an enquiry was made at the beginning of this century, out of a hundred people asked: "Do you believe that dragons exist?", 82 replied that they did.

The origin of dragons seems to go back to the existence of antediluvian monsters like the ones illustrated in works on paleontology. The discovery of fossilized skeletons may also have been enough to make people attribute supernatural powers to them; at the same time, the appearance of a dragon was considered a good omen (for they were the symbol of life-giving rain), particularly for affairs of the State. (When Yuan Shi kai was thinking of restoring the empire, he thought the time had come to see a dragon and sent off teams of men to try to discover a skeleton, for this would have showed the people that his wish was in agreement with the law of Heaven). The exact appearance of dragons has been described as follows: a camel's head, fallow deer's horns, cow's ears, snake's neck, a fish's body, carp's scales, eagles' claws, a devil's eyes and tiger's paws; a dragon's body falls into three sections: from the nose to the shoulder, from the shoulder to the thighs, from the thighs to the tail; dragons may be red, yellow, blue, black and white. The number of their claws varies from three to five according to the period. Until recently, many people claimed to have seen dragons, and could describe them in detail; towards 1920, for instance, a Nanking teacher declared that when he was young, a dragon fell from the sky and stayed, exhausted, near his house for 24 hours; the people round covered it respectfully with matting; the teacher himself, more curious than the rest, had managed to see that the dragon had four feet, a cow's head and a scaly body; what was more, it was 50 feet long, and blue...

LONG WANG

Sometimes *Hai Long Wang:* the Dragon King, or the Dragon King of the Sea. The name for guardian spirits of the sea, rivers, lakes and water in general.

LU BAN

God of Carpenters and President of the Celestial Ministry of Public Works. Originally, he was Ban of the state of Lu (Shan dong province) born in 506 B.C. He was an expert in working metal, stone and wood, but retired at the age of 40 to live a hermit's life on Mount Li. He was granted supernatural powers, and became able to rise into the air and bestride the clouds. During the Yong le period of the Ming dynasty (1403–1425), he received the title of Great Master, Pillar of the Empire. Craftsmen who wanted their wishes executed immediately prayed to him.

According to other biographies, the person in question was Gong Shu zi, a skilful man of the state of Lu who carved wooden magpies which were able to stay in the air for three days; he also made a wooden charioteer who drove a sort of automobile, and engines of war which broke down city walls. A third source states that the god was Lu Ban, a native of Gan su: he built a wooden kite which could carry his father for long distances through the air; when he landed at Wu hui, the people mistook him for a demon and killed him; Lu Ban, who was furious, made a wooden Immortal whose arm pointed towards the

town, causing a three years' drought. When the people discovered the reason for these disasters, they sent presents to Lu Ban
to calm his anger and cut off the statue's hand; plentiful rain
fell at once.

LUO HAN

The name comes from the Sanskrit *arhan* or *arhat*, which
indicated the ideal state which each man should try to attain:
an arhat is one who has accomplished the eightfold way, has
attained illumination, and is saved for all eternity.

MI LO FO

In Chinese, Maitreya.

NÜ WA

The goddess of go-betweens, daughter of the Water Spirit,
born three months after her brother Fu Xi (2953–2838 B.C.).
Her body was like that of a snail (hence her name, Nü Wa,
snail-girl). She is also described as having a human head and a
snake's body. When her brother became emperor, she followed
him to Shan xi and then He nan, and noticed that young people
were living together, which was bad for the general morality;
she advised Fu Xi to forbid marriages between members of the
same family, to draw up laws on concluding engagements
through the action of a go-between, on buying presents, and
on marriage ceremonies, etc. This was done, and from then on,
Nü Wa was given the title of goddess of go-betweens. When her
brother died, she reigned herself, under the title of Nü huang.
At the end of her reign, Gong Gong, who administered punishments, rebelled and tried to make the influence of water predominate over that of wood (under whose influence Nü Wa reigned).
Nü Wa ordered Mo Pei (later on the fire god) to balance the
influence of water and Gong Gong fled to the west; he reached
an enormously high mountain and climbed it; at the top he
found the eight stone pillars which bear the vault of heaven.
The rebel seized one and shook it until it fell, taking a corner
of the vault of heaven with it, and destroying the southern
slope of the mountain as it fell. Nü Wa managed to build up
scaffolding to repair the damage; she took Gong Gong prisoner
and put him to death. The mountain which had sheltered him
was called the Bu zhou shan from then on, the imperfect mountain; it was steep and inaccessible: above their heads, people

saw an enormous black hole from which issued violent winds
and pelting rain. Nü Wa then melted down stones of five colours
to repair the vault of heaven, and cut off the feet of the celestial
tortoise to straighten the four edges of the world (then thought
to be square).

PAN GU

He who put chaos in order, or the creator of universe, himself
the offspring of the two great principles of *yin* and *yang*. He is
shown as a dwarf dressed in a bear's skin, or in leaves. He has
two horns on his head; he carries a hammer in his right hand,
and a sculptor's chisel in his left hand. Supernatural creatures
help him in his work: the unicorn, phoenix and dragon. The
creation took 18,000 years; after it was over, he disintegrated,
and the different parts of his body formed different parts of
the visible universe (constellations, mountains, etc.).

PU SA

Abbreviation of Pu ti sa tuo, the Chinese translation of
Bodhisattva.

QING LONG and BAI HU

The Blue Dragon and the White Tiger. The duties fulfilled
by Heng and Ha (see above) at the entrance to Buddhist temples
are fulfilled by these two at the entrance to Taoist temples.
The first one is the spirit of the blue dragon star, and was Deng
Jiu' gong, a general in chief of the last emperor of the Yin
dynasty; he was wounded by Heng and executed. The second
is the white star spirit, and was Yin Cheng xiu, son of a high-
ranking official under the last tyrant of the Yin dynasty, who
was sent to negotiate with Jiang Zi ya and was executed by
him; his son tried to avenge the death of his father, but was
killed; his head was born in triumph to Jiang Zi ya. He was
canonised later.

SAN QING

The Three Pure Ones. A triad of Taoist gods: Yu Qing
(Jade Azure) Shang Qing (High Azure) and Tai Qing (Supreme
Azure). These deities live in the three skies which correspond
to the three original divisions of the cosmic ether.

SHANG DI

The Supreme Sovereign, the Universal Ancestor. No details of his nature exist, but he has anthropomorphic characteristics. He governs, fixes fate and gives his mandate to the king or emperor. He is represented as just and provident; he punishes, rewards, and likes to receive sacrifices and offerings from mortals. He appears in men's dreams, gives audience to the privileged, listens to the complaints of the oppressed; he is constant and unequalled, different from the transcendental beings, whom he dominates. Nothing happens or is done without his will. He was an ancestral deity which remained unchanged until the era of Confucius and his disciples, when he became more distant and abstract: he was then the Supreme Being, the Pure August One: his ministers on earth were Guan Yu (see above), the Cheng Huang (see above), the Tu di (see further on), or local gods of each village, and the *Zao jun*, hearth gods of every family.

SHE JI

The God of Earth and Harvests. The worship of this god combined gratitude for the past and a prayer for the future; the spirits of the earth and millet have been venerated since the earliest times of all. As time went on, human beings were chosen as patrons of the earth and agriculture: they are divided into two categories, universal and local. The first category embraces, for instance, Gong Gong (see under Nü Wa), a powerful prince in the reign of Emperor Fu Xi (2953–1838 B.C.), and Emperors Tai zu (1368–1399) and Ren zong (1425–1426).

The Emperor alone could perform the rites to the Sovereign of the Earth: the other believers addressed local deities (see Tu di) who passed it on.

SHEN NONG

The God of Agriculture: the title attributed to the successor of Fu Xi (2953–2838 B.C.). He was the first person to analyse the harmful and beneficial properties of plants, and was also one of the gods of apothecaries.

SHEN YI

The Divine Archer. One day when Emperor Yao (see further on) was walking in the street of Huai yang in the second year of his reign (2436 B.C.) he met a man carrying a bow and arrows;

the bow was covered with a kind of red fabric. The man was Chi jiang Zi yu; he said he was a skilled archer, and could fly on the wings of the wind. To test his skill, Yao asked him to shoot at a pine-tree on one of the neighbouring hills; Chi shot an arrow through the tree, and then jumped on to a breath of wind to go and fetch his arrow. The Emperor gave him the name of "Divine Archer", took him into his train, and gave him the title of Engineer of all wood work. Chi lived by eating flowers only.

Then he accomplished various other exploits: he overcame the god of the wind, killed dangerous creatures, built a palace for Jin Mu, etc. He married Chang E, the sister of the water spirit; she fled to the moon (see Chang E) where he went to see her and built a palace for her; they met on the fifteenth day of every month. Then Shen Yi returned to his empire on the sun, and built himself a wonderful palace there: from then on, the sun and the moon each had their sovereign. Shen Yi and Chang E are often depicted holding the sun and the moon respectively.

SHENG REN

Usually translated as "Saint"; it refers in fact to the highest category of canonised mortals; they live in the highest of the San Qing regions (see above), in the Jade Azure.

SI DA TIAN WANG

The Four Great Celestial Kings (the four Maharajas); they are a sort of guardian spirit belonging to the group of *hu shi zhe*, guardians of the universe (Lokapolas). In China they were temple guardians, but they symbolised the seasons at the same time, and controlled the four elements (fire, air, earth and water). As guardians, they stand at the entrance to temples: enormous, fantastic creatures, armed from head to foot and carrying their respective symbols.

The Four Kings are obviously the Taoist version of the four Jin gang belonging to Buddhism: the Taoists call them by name: Li, Ma, Zhao and Wen: they are shown carrying a pagoda, a sword, two swords and a pointed stick respectively.

SUN HOU ZI

Sun the monkey, who became a god. He was the hero of the *Xi you ji* ("A Journey to the West"), known to everyone;

the novel tells the story of the adventures of the monk Xuan zang and his acolytes in their search for Buddhist sacred books.

Sun is also called Sun Wu kong (who penetrates the void), Qi tian da sheng (Great Saint, equal to Heaven). He was born from an egg which formed on top of the Mountain of Flowers and Fruit in the kingdom of Ao lai, over the sea; the egg, fertilised by the wind, gave birth to a stone monkey, who greeted the four points of the compass: beams of golden light flowed from his eyes and lit up the Palace of the Pole Star; the light lasted until Sun was able to feed himself. Yu huang (see further on) said to himself: "I will complete the wonderful diversity of creatures engendered by the earth and the heavens: this monkey will run and gambol on the mountain peaks, jump and frisk in the waters and feeding on fruit from the trees, he will be a companion for the gibbon and the crane...".

The exploits of the Monkey were such that he was proclaimed Monkey King. He then set about finding a way to become immortal. After various extraordinary adventures, he finally acquired transcendant powers, became converted to Buddhism, and accompanied Xuan zang on his journey. Eventually he was rewarded during a banquet of the Immortals presided over by Mi luo fo, and appointed God of Victorious Combat. He was the patron of official messengers.

TIAN NÜ

Sanskrit: dēvi, a female dēva.

TU DI

The guardian spirit of the countryside; his jurisdiction was limited to certain small areas (whereas the She Ji—see above—controlled prefectures and even provinces).

WEN CHANG

The God of Literature. He is made up of two people; one is vaguely historical, the other entirely mythical.

The historical figure was Zhang Ya, born under the Tang dynasty in what is now Zhe jiang. He went to live in Si chuan, at Zi tong, where he was afterwards worshipped as a god. He was a brilliant scholar and writer, with a post at the Board of Rites. In his old age, he disappeared suddenly (or was killed in battle). According to the legends, the god was Zhong Kui, a scholar. He was first in the examinations at the Capital, and went to see the Emperor to receive his prize, as the custom was. But his face was so repulsively ugly that the Emperor refused to give him his reward. Zhong Kui, in despair, threw himself into the sea. As he was on the point of drowning, a sea monster took him on its back and brought him back to the surface; from there, Zhong Kui went straight to the sky and went to live in the star called Kui (the "house" between Andromeda and the Fish). Soon scholars were making offerings and worshipping Kui, god of literature. The god which they worshipped was the constellation Kui (the name was a homophone of the scholar's own) and eventually the god of the constellation was depicted in the form of a demon carrying a bushel (another play on words, based on the character for *kui* which means a demon and is made up of two ideograms, one meaning demon and the other bushel). This still does not explain how Zhang Ya acquired the title of Wen Chang, god of literature. It was the result of a Taoist subterfuge: they are responsible for the fable of Zhong Kui being saved by the monster. They claim furthermore that the Supreme Sovereign, Sheng di (see above) had asked the son of Zhang Ya to fit up his palace on Wen Chang (Wen Chang was the oblong part of the Great Bear constellation). Little by little, the scholars got into the habit of saying that their success was due to the spirit of Zi tong (Zhang Ya), and they depicted him, wrongly, as the incarnation of the group of stars, Wen Chang.

As a result of this highly involved confusion based on the stars, Wen Chang was represented in the popular imagination as surrounded by four acolytes: a servant on one side (to help him on journeys) and two other figures (the Celestial Deaf Man and the Earthly Dumb Man, both incapable of revealing their master's secrets), and on the other a shapeless individual who is none other than Kui xing (Kui star): a fat dwarf with a demon's face, with one leg raised, a scholar's brush in one hand and a bushel in the other. Kui xing was held to be the one who distributed diplomas and success in examinations; temples were dedicated to him all over China.

XI WANG MU

The Western Queen Mother (or Jin Mu, Golden Mother). This deity was formed from the pure quintessence of the Western Air, in the legendary continent of Shen zhou. She is the female, passive principle *(yin)* which corresponds to the male principle *(yang)* represented by Dong Wang Gong. The two principles engendered the heavens and the earth, and all the beings in the universe. Xi Wang mu is the leader of the armies of spirits which live in the Kun lun Mountains (The Taoist equivalent of the Buddhist Sumeru). Sometimes she is depicted in human form, with a panther's tail, tiger's teeth and untidy hair. The legends tell how in 110 B.C. she came in person to the palace of Emperor Wu di, and presented him with the seven peaches of immortality. Her own palace is on the snow-covered peaks of the Kun lun Mountains; it is 1,000 *li* round, with solid gold ramparts and battlements of precious stones; it is also the place where the Immortals usually live, and their banquets are held there *(Pan tao hui)*, on the shores of the Jasper Lake. Delicacies are served, such as bears' paws, monkeys' lips, dragons' liver, etc. and peaches, which have the mystic virtue of imparting immortality to those who eat them, and whose ripening determines the date of the banquets. The adventurous career of Sun Wu kong began with the stealing of these peaches (see above).

XIAN, XIAN REN

An Immortal, or the Taoist Immortals, who live in the mountains. Whereas the Buddhists promised the Western Paradise *(Xi tian)* to their believers, the Taoists promised immortality. This immortality was acquired by means of *nei tan:* this mixture formed a little invisible being, who gradually grew larger, inside a man's body; once it had reached the size of a man, it could remain on earth or leave for better places: in this case, it shed its earthly body like a cicada, and was then a celestial immortal: if it stayed in this world, it became an immortal spirit. Sometimes Immortals die, but only in appearance: the bodies are metamorphosed, the bones are transformed. After "death", the Immortals retain the properties of living beings, the skin keeps its freshness, and their eyes the keenness: although they are apparently dead, they are more living than ever. Some Immortals are capable of flying freely through the air as soon as their hair begins to fall out. Metamorphosis of *xian ren* happens in broad daylight (in the case of *zhen ren*, perfect men, it happens at midnight).

YAN LUO WANG

The President of the fifth court of hell. He was originally president of the first court, but was demoted because he was not severe enough. Buddhism borrowed this god and his duties from Brahmanism, for Yan Luo Wang is the same as Yama, god of death and king of demons in the Vedic system.

YAO and SHUN

Yao is the legendary emperor of the age of gold. After a miraculous birth, he came to the throne in 2357 B.C., and after 70 or 90 years abdicated in favour of Shun (2317–2208), a model of filial piety and the inventor of the paintbrush.

YAO WANG

The King of Medicine. Originally he was Sun Si miao; he gave proof of amazing abilities from childhood: he could learn 1000 characters in one day! Later on, he was initiated into the secrets of *yin* and *yang*, and immortality, etc. He lived on wine and air alone. The Dragon King of the Water Palace presented him with 30 chapters of Long cang, "the Dragon's Secrets", in return for a service which he rendered, so that mankind should profit by it. He was the friend, adviser and doctor of all the great figures of the reign of Emperor Gao zong of the Tang (650–684). He died in 682; after a whole month, his body was still in perfect condition. When it was to be put into the coffin it was found to have disappeared; only the clothes were left. He is usually depicted accompanied by two young servants, one with a gourd full of miraculous pills, the other holding a leaf of a medecinal herb out to him.

YU

Yü the Great, minister of Emperors Yao and Shun (see above), was called "regulator of the Flood" by the latter; he carried out his task conscientiously, over nine hard-working years. In 2205 B.C., he succeeded Shun as first emperor of the Xia dynasty.

YU DI

The Pearl Emperor, principal deity of the Taoist pantheon. He also had a place in the Buddhist pantheon, where he was in a lower position than Brahma. He is also known as Yu Huang. He was popularly believed to command all the Buddhas, spirits, genies and the ten kings of hell.

YU HUANG

The Jade Emperor, the Pure August One (jade is a symbol of purity). He is the supreme sovereign of the universe, and the saviour of men. A member of the Taoist pantheon, he corresponds to Shang di, who belongs to the Confucians (see above). The history of this extremely popular deity is as follows: after Emperor Zhen zong (998–1123) had signed a humiliating peace treaty with the Tungus, his dynasty seemed about to lose the nation's support. The Emperor announced with great pomp that he was in direct contact with Heaven; he called a meeting of his ministers in the tenth month of 1102 and declared: "An Immortal came to me in a dream, bringing a letter from the Jade Emperor, who said: 'I have already sent you two celestial messages through your ancestor, Tai Zu; now I am going to send him to you.'" Shortly afterwards, the ancestor Tai Zu (founder of the dynasty) appeared as Yu Huang had promised, and Emperor Zhen zong quickly told his ministers. This is the origin of Yu Wang, who was born of an imperial nocturnal meditation. In 1013, Zhen zong had a statue of Yu Huang made, and had it put in the Pure Jade Palace (Yu qing gong) where it was worshipped by the whole court; in 1015, he conferred the titles of Supreme Author of Heaven, of the Universe, of human fate, of rites, etc. on Yu Huang, as well as that of Great Sovereign of Heaven. The deity later became extremely popular.

ZAO JUN

The God of the Hearth. This Taoist invention was adopted throughout China: every Chinese family worshipped him regularly. The gullible Emperor Xiao Wu di of the Han (140–86 B.C.) was the first to worship the Hearth God. A Taoist monk, Li Shao jun, promised him that he would acquire divine powers if he agreed to favour religion; the Emperor asked him to bring his divine patron to see him where upon the image of Zao jun appeared to him in a dream one night. The Emperor made a solemn sacrifice to him. Between the Han and Song dynasties, Zao jun, the god of furnaces, who was important for alchemy, was changed into the Hearth God, Zao Shen (the word *zao* means both hearth and furnace).

ZHANG DAO LING

He was born in 35 A.D. at Tian mu shan (Zhe jiang) under the reign of the Han Emperor Guang wu di (25-58 A.D.). He is said to have understood the *Dao de jing*, geomancy, the mysteries of water, and astronomy, when he was only seven. He was the founder of modern Taoism, for he decided its orientation and gave it ways to survive (first of all by his new, mysterious recipes using alchemy and magic for making immortality pills, and then by the invention of talismans to heal all kinds of disease).

He was a great scholar, and one day said: "What good is literature in prolonging life?!" From then on, he devoted himself to the study of alchemy and the preparation of immortality drugs; he went to live in the Bei mang Hills, north of He nan fu, the capital of He nan. He declined the invitations of Emperor Zhang di (76–89 A.D.) and Emperor He di (89–106 A.D.) to visit the court, and after going to see several famous mountains, he went to Yun jin dong, a cave of Immortals. He continued his research there for three years, and finally found the way to unite "the blue dragon and the white tiger", and from then on was able to make the immortality pill; he ate it, and although he was 60 by that time, his face took on its youthful look once more. He also was given a mysterious book by a god, containing recipes for changing shape and for chasing away demons and goblins. Then he left for Si chuan, where he settled on the Cloud Plateau (Yun tai), and from there went up to heaven, leaving a magic book, a collection of talismans, his seal and his magic sword to his children. All this happened in 157 A.D. (which means that Zhang Dao ling was 123).

ZHANG XIAN

The Provider of Children, and patron of pregnant women. He is depicted as an old man with a white face and a long beard, and a child at his side. He carries a bow and arrow, for shooting the Celestial Dog. (The Dog Star: if the destiny of a family fell under the influence of the star, the family would have no more children, or if children were born, they would die when still small).

ZHEN REN

The perfect being, or ideal being. They constituted the second class of deified mortals, and lived in the High Azure (see San Qing); they are men who have subjected themselves to the Taoist mystic discipline, and have acquired perfect control over themselves and nature.

ZHI NÜ

The Spinner, the Goddess of Spinners. Countless stories arose in China out of star-gazing: one of them tells of the Herdsman and the Spinner (Aquila and Vega). The Spinner was the daughter of the sun god, who was tired of seeing her sitting at her spinning-wheel day and night, and thought that if he married her to a neighbour who kept his flocks on the other side of the Silver Way (the Milky Way), she would perhaps change.

She was married forthwith; her habits did in fact change, but not as her father had hoped, for she became gay and happy, forgetting her wheel and her needle, and spending her days and nights in amusement and idleness. The sun god was angry, and thinking that the fault lay with the husband, decided to separate them. He ordered the husband to take his flocks to feed on the other side of the river of stars and told him that from then on, he would meet his wife once a year, on the seventh night of the seventh month. To make a bridge over the river, he called myriads of magpies to spread their wings and provide a bridge for the poor lover; the husband went back to his flocks, and his wife took up her spinning-wheel and needle again. The sun god was happy to see them both busy once more.

When the time came for them to see each other again, the wife began to worry: supposing it should rain! The Heavenly River was full up to the top of its banks, so that the slightest drop might produce a flood, and there would be no bridge of birds! But the sky was clear, the magpies came in their hundreds to make a way for the tiny Lady to go and join the Herdsman. As long as it did not rain, she met her husband every year. On earth people always hoped that the weather would be fine on that day, and the festival was celebrated by young and old alike. The two constellations were venerated particularly by women, who hoped to be granted greater ability in needle work and making artificial flowers.

ZU

The "Patriarchs" of Chinese Buddhism: those who have reached the heart of Buddhist doctrine, who have acquired magic powers, whose perception is sharpest of all, who have the greatest intellectual capacity, etc. They are also defenders of the faith against heretics and enemies of religion. The six greatest Chinese patriarchs are:
—Da mo da shi (or Pu ti duo luo): Bodhidharma
—Shen Guang alias Hui Ke
—Seng can
—Dao xin
—Hong ren
—Hui neng

CHINESE LITERATURE

General Remarks

If you have never been inside a Chinese library, and you find yourself one day in Peking, looking round the bazaar in Wang fu jing or the antique shops in Liu li chang, you should take the opportunity of going into a secondhand bookshop which specialises in selling old books. Our plebian paperbacks, with their narrow shoulders and torn covers, and the rich bourgeois volumes with their gay or sober bindings, have no equivalent here. Slim volumes in sets of four or eight with a cloth-bound cover round them lie in orderly piles on the shelves, revealing nothing but a greyish, dusty strip of paper which sometimes bears the title. The austerity of this display will discourage you from looking further and you will leave quickly, feeling a suggestion of the panic which seizes all students of Chinese when first confronted by this spectacle. These piles of paper, this mass with no gold lettering or leather bindings to make one's gaze linger constitute a true likeness of the enormous volumes of Chinese literature. If a French student of Chinese is interested in poetry, for instance, and if he goes straight to the Tang dynasty, which was contemporary with the Carolingians, and richer in poetry than any other era, he will be confronted by the *Collected Poetry of the Tang*, containing 50,000 pieces of poetry by 2,300 authors. It is not easy to find a way through this jungle of poetry. The historian, whatever his field may be, has to venture into the labyrinth of the "Collections" containing texts of all kinds, and "Encyclopedias" where knowledge and literature in their entirety have been poured time and time again, under different headings.

These texts which have been accumulating for 2,500 years represent all the literary *genres* which have flourished in Europe, with one exception: the epic. It was thought that the Chinese were not interested in epic poetry. However, judging by the success which always greets story-tellers, and by the length and zest of their stories, it seems more likely that the epic did exist in China after all, but never in a fixed written form. To understand this point, as with many others too, the circumstances of the creation of Chinese literature must be taken into account.

For a long time, Chinese literature shared the fate of one class, that of the scholars. Its greatness and its weaknesses result from this. The word *wen* meaning literature also stood for civil power, as opposed to military power, or *wu*. In peace-time, the scholar was responsible for organising the city. From very early on, philosophers of differing schools of thought, all rivals, wandered from one court to another, looking for a monarch with an enlightened turn of mind who would accept their advice. The scholars' power must have been considerable as early as the 3rd century B.C., for Qin shi Huang di, who unified the empire by force of arms and wanted to introduce government based on laws, ordered books everywhere to be burned. The scholars, if not the texts themselves, made a rapid recovery from this disaster, in spite of the gnashing of teeth which the memory of it excited for centuries afterwards. The Han dynasty, whose work inspired 2000 years of Chinese history, witnessed both the victory of the Confucians over supporters of other doctrines and their rise to the key positions in the running of state affairs. Liu Bang, the founder of the dynasty, was a man straight from the people, however, with a hearty dislike of scholars. When the learned Lu Jia spoke of the sacred texts of the Confucian school, he replied that he had won his empire on horseback and cared little for these books. "You won it on horseback", Lu Jia replied, "but will you be able to govern it on horseback?" Overcome by this, the Emperor agreed to listen to the advice given to him by Confucius' heirs. That day marked the beginning of their ascendancy. The famous examinations system later consolidated their hold on the government and the administration. As candidates for administrative posts were judged on their literary ability, particularly in the realm of poetry, the scholars were men of letters as well. The domination of these literary men in politics was eclipsed once or twice, but it did not finally come to an end until the 20th century, when the empire itself fell.

The scholar class owed its power first and foremost to its mastery of the technique of writing. The difficulty of the Chinese language and the strain which it imposes on the memory is well known. The fact that it did not only transcribe spoken language, but was a language in itself, at least until the 20th century, is less widely known. It did not abide by the same rules and conventions as the spoken language. It evolved much more slowly, and followed its own way. The writer was concerned not with words but with "characters"; he worked in an artificial world like that of colours or notes. The art of writing, cultivated to the limit of its possibilities by a class whose supremacy it ensured, produced admirable masterpieces, and, it must be admitted, large numbers of works of high technical perfection completely devoid of inspiration as well. Very early on, the scholar class used advanced techniques to serve this art, whose splendour was proof of their own success. Craftsmen pitted their wits against each other in the making of paper, brushes and ink, which the scholars then used to rival each other on a higher plane. Printing was invented in China several centuries before Gutenberg. To make sure that the classics and other texts were preserved, stone engravers equalled the art of the printers and covered the country with countless steles. The respect for tradition and the enthusiastic study of antiquity gave birth to and fostered philology, lexicography, and bibliography. With such care lavished on it, literature naturally flowered and the heritage of the old masters was handed down regularly, except for times of catastrophe, and was held up as a model from one generation to another.

A glance at a dictionary of writers' biographies is enough to show that most of them held posts as officials, either at the capital itself, or in local administration. When fortune smiled upon them, they became upholders of the political system and of social order. This is the reason why moral conformism and literary academicism had such widespread support. The most powerful minds made violent criticisms of abuses, not in a revolutionary spirit, but with the majesty befitting guardians of tradition moved by the wish to return to ancient art or wisdom. On the other hand, those who waited in vain for an opening, or who vegetated in minor posts, or whose career was destroyed and ended in exile, turned their backs on the official doctrine and looked for a new way of life in religion, alchemy, music, wine or nature. Beneath the calm waters of academicism flowed another current, sometimes individualistic and inclined to anarchy, sometimes mystic or epicurean. Both currents were often mingled in the same author: many scholars lived a double life, sometimes joining in public life, the only source of true glory, and sometimes disappearing into the solitude of the mountains or the gaiety of the amusement quarters.

Even so, whatever their tastes may have been, the scholars had some points in common: pride in their knowledge and love, or at least respect, for the art of writing. Since the 20th century literary revolution, they have been accused of failing to appreciate drama and the novel written in spoken language, and of excluding them from the main body of literature; these two literary *genres*, both of popular origin, were the only ones in which the last imperial dynasties, the Ming and the Qing, really excelled. It is said that they developed late in China thanks to the scholar class, who despised them and were hostile towards them. But when the same accusers praise the creative genius of the Chinese people and credit it with the invention of all the different kinds of poetry which formed the glory of the classical era, stressing the fact that their country's literature has been renewed periodically by borrowings from popular lyricism, they are making an implicit admission of the lucidity of the scholars who were the renovators. Each time that a poetic *genre* was moribund after constant repetition, the most competent scholars discovered new forms among the mass of oral literature, which had great potentialities, and which would have disappeared but for them. None could doubt that the Chinese people has particular talents for poetry, drama and dancing. Modern plays and films often show singers or choirs of boys or girls who joke, tease each other, or ask each other riddles, exactly like the peasants whose poetic joustings are reflected in the *Classic of Songs (Shi jing)*, which dates from the beginning of Chinese civilisation, and is the oldest anthology of poetry and one of the best loved "classics". The crowds love story-tellers and opera singers so much that the government of the People's Republic of China, in its efforts to create a new literature which should "serve the people", relies more on the traditional techniques of these performers than on innovations in the field of drama or the novel. In encouraging amateur troupes and reviving popular art forms on the decline, the present regime is in fact repeating a process which is customary in China, a return to original sources, which has often instilled new life into Chinese literature. It would be absurd, however, when considering classical literature, to stress merely the origins of each form— the people itself—and its decadence in the sterile scholars' milieu. Each literary form has gone through a period of full bloom between its rise and fall, when it has yielded its finest fruits, thanks to a few writers of genius, most of whom were scholars. Chinese literature owes its masterpieces to an unusual sort of collaboration between the people and the educated elite. However refined and steeped in culture, the great authors always remained in close touch with popular forms. Their genius lay in a balance between what was traditional and what was natural.

Chinese literature, particularly poetry, oscillates between periods of splendour and decline, depending on whether the creative imagination of the masses and the artistic experience of the educated class coincided or not; other factors have influenced its development too, however. Chinese literature did not develop in a vacuum any more than did the rest of Chinese civilisation as a whole. The spread of Buddhism in China brought with it consequences of considerable importance. The missionary impetus stimulated intellectual and artistic life and encouraged the invention of printing, and drama and the novel in spoken language seem to have arisen out of religious preaching. After the 1920 literary revolution, writers tried to renew the novel, poetry and the theatre by imitating foreign works. For thirty years, people were feeling their way, fascinated by the examples which they found in the shape of numerous translations, and yet having the greatest difficulty in adapting them to China. Although the start of the People's Republic marks the abandoning of the foreign masters respected by the previous generation, the principles which have guided literary creation since then, for example the doctrine of "socialist realism", are not Chinese in origin either.

The Literary Role of the Philosophers

A separate section of the introduction of this guide is rightly devoted to philosophy. However, no introduction to Chinese literature would be complete without a mention of the philosophers, any more than histories of other literatures would be with no mention of Plato or Descartes. During the last centuries before Christ, before the accession of the empire, the different schools which vied with each other in a ferment of rival doctrines made a vital contribution to the formation of both language and literature. Like Socrates, Confucius left no works written by his own hand, but only compilations in which he may not even have had any true part. His disciples, however, defended and illustrated the master's doctrine with considerable brilliance. Mencius in particular, in the work which is called after him *(Meng zi)*, combined sparkling discussions, lively dialogue and flexible expositions written in a prose which for centuries afterwards was a source of admiration for men of letters. Redoubtable writers of polemics appeared outside the Confucian school. Whereas Han Fei zi, the Legalist, produced a model of clarity, the work of Mo Di is verbose and heavy, and that of the sophists and dialecticians attracted attention to language problems. The most attractive writers are to be found among the Taoists, however. The *Way and Power Classic (Dao de jing)*, written by Lao zi, has fascinated students of oriental languages for centuries: it has probably been translated more often in the West than any other Chinese text, although the attraction of its hermetic style, paradoxes and brilliant imagery is not always entirely genuine. Zhuang Zhou, the author of the *Zhuang zi*, is accepted as the greatest writer of Chinese antiquity. He is a poet of vision, as well as a writer of biting and ironic polemics. Interpretations of the *Dao de jing* abound, but no translator has yet honestly completed one of the *Zhuang zi*.

All the great names appear at the dawn of Chinese literature. For over 2000 years afterwards, they were taken as guides; their genius inspired or smothered hundreds of imitators. The books which constituted the Confucian canon did not only form the basis of society; every scholar, and therefore every writer, had to learn them by heart as a child. They covered such a varied field that each author found later, when he reached maturity, that they confirmed his personal experiences, so that he was tempted to quote from them. Most poets, and even more prose-writers, used this common heritage, even if they merely alluded to it. The Canon was built up little by little, and in its final form of 13 books, it dates from the Song. It is an incongruous collection, as it includes an ancient manual of divination, the *Yi jing*, which Confucius recommended highly, but which is a source of despair to modern scholars; a set of three rituals, one of which, the *Zhou li*, is a detailed picture of the governmental structure of the ideal kingdom of Zhou; the first four historic works in Chinese, that is, the *Classic of Documents (Shu jing)* and the *Spring and Autumn Annals (Chun qiu)*, repeated three times with three different commentaries, one of which was the *Zuo zhuan;* an anthology of the *Analects (Lun yu)* of Confucius and his disciples, which is no doubt a fairly faithful record of the master's thought, which was studied avidly in Japan under the Tokugawa and has often been translated in the West; the work by Mencius which has already been mentioned; a brief work on filial piety, the *Xiao jing;* a lexicon, the *Er ya;* and finally the *Classic of Songs (Shi jing)*, the first anthology of poetry to appear in China, and a living source which has been used by writers of every era.

The art of writing was for a long time exercised in a closed world. The written language was its form and the classics its substance. It was easier to elaborate an ancient theme than to understand reality. A description of reality alone would have seemed flat or incongruous. It was possible only through the classifications which had provided the framework for the vision of the ancients. This explains why so many authors never speak of themselves, or even of original thoughts or situations except by means of allusions to deeds and gestures of the ancients or by quotations; it gives some idea of the overbearing influence which the weight of tradition exerted on Chinese classical literature. The cult of antiquity has disappeared today, but the teaching of Marxist "classics" has replaced the teaching of the Confucian "classics". The use of the argument of authority and the taste for quotation seems to be more rife in modern China than it ever was before.

The Writing of History

Historical works hold a key position in the body of Chinese prose, for close links bind them to philosophy on one hand and to imaginative literature on the other. The art of narrative prose flourished, as all writers showed a particular weakness for it. As the oldest known specimens of Chinese script are divinatory texts, engraved on bone or tortoiseshell, it seems reasonable to suppose that the scholar class first began to form round the soothsayers. It must also have included secretaries at an early date, working at the rulers' courts, drawing up official edicts or recording events, treaties, natural calamities and eclipses. Old chronicles such as the *Spring and Autumn Annals*, which cover the history of the kingdom of Lu from 722 to 481 B.C. consist merely of a collection of documents like these, all disappointingly dry. The chronicles of another classical work, the *Classic of Documents*, show more evidence of style; the authentic chapters contain an attempt to rationalise the myths and build up historical figures for the legendary first sovereigns of China. Among ancient works in prose are some masterpieces, written in a pseudo-historical vein, intended partly as fiction, partly as philosophical teaching, which had a lasting influence on later works. They are collections of stories with morals, or conversations on politics or society, whose themes and heroes, although often based on fact, may be imaginary. One of these works, the *Zuo zhuan*, is famous for its vigorous style, the dramatic conciseness of its narratives, and for the accuracy of the documentation; it is one of the set of Confucian classics. It is, to all appearances, merely a commentary on the *Spring and Autumn Annals*, but it goes so much further than the limits imposed by them that it has sometimes been thought to be the remains of a larger work, clumsily re-adapted to fit as a commentary to the annals of the kingdom of Lu. Whatever the case may be, the *Zuo zhuan* in its present form lacks unity of conception and method, and so does not deserve to be considered as the first history of China. This title is reserved for a work written under the Han, the *Historical Records (Shi ji)* by Si ma Qian (born 145 B.C.). The author, who is one of China's greatest writers, was historiographer at the court of Emperor Wu. The power and prosperity of China then, her policy of expansion, the splendour of her court and the development of the arts and humanities, made this particular reign one of exceptional brilliance. Si ma Qian, with the help of the imperial archives and libraries, completed a general history of China from the beginnings until his own day. He resorted to the chronicles already mentioned for information on the early stages of history, in which the fantastic is inextricably mingled with political theory, providing an impenetrable disguise for historical truth. As he comes nearer his own times, documentation increases in volume. He includes extracts from the archives in his own text; he quotes all kinds of works, some of them long, in prose and verse, which but for him would have disappeared, and which now appear intact to be expounded by modern scholars. As it is a compilation of original documents, recorded with scrupulous care, the history of Si ma Qian justifies varied and tendentious interpretations of the past. It is an invaluable source in itself. It has other merits too, of which the first and foremost is its orderliness. It it divided into five sections: 1) the "Basic Annals" recording the principal events of each reign; 2) Chronological and genealogical tables; 3) 8 treatises on specialised, basic subjects, such as the history of rites, music, astronomy, canals, trade, etc..; 4) 30 monographs devoted above all to the histories of the great feudal families; 5) 70 monographs chiefly on important figures and their families. These different series of compositions have one point in common: they are straight narratives, which keep strictly to the chronological order of events. Repetition inevitably occurs between the annals, the treatises and the monographs; the narratives overlap in such a way that the facts are presented from several different angles, and gradually acquire their true relief for the reader. Although the author narrates rather than interprets, it is clear all the same that the choice of episodes is not left to chance. He allows suitable importance to imperial decrees and governmental decisions, and then lingers long on court intrigues or the ups and downs of great political careers. He is virtually uninterested in the lives and standards of living of the peasants and town-dwellers in general. On the other hand, the lives of the great men themselves are presented as a series of examples, either good or bad. History is a lesson for posterity, a compilation of edifying anecdotes illustrating the principles of official standards of morality. This function of history justifies its literary aspirations. Si ma Qian is as great a writer as Tacitus or Theucydides. The power and density of his style renders him equal to the earlier writers, whom he took as his model, and the life and colour which he breathes into his narrative far outstrips them.

Few writers in the history of literature have influenced posterity for as long as Si ma Qian. For nearly twenty centuries, historians based their work on his, though they were never capable of equalling it. The *History of the Earlier Han (Han shu)* by Ban Gu (1st century A.D.) is modelled on the *Historical Records* and even borrows large passages from them, which are quoted. It was the first of a series of official works, known as the twenty-four "standard histories" which constitute a continuous picture of China from the Han to the end of the Ming. Each book in the collection, which shows astonishing continuity and uniformity, was prepared by the archovists of the dynasty which it covers and written by the historiographers of the following dynasty. The rulings as to the fom, laid down by Si ma Qian, have scarcely varied at all, even though the plan of the whole was adjusted once or twice: the fourth section, for instance, devoted to the feudal families, disappeared, and specialised treatises on new subjects swelled the volume of the third section. Most of the countless other historical works which flourished alongside the twenty-four "standard histories" were closely dependant on them too. They complement the official texts, or discuss or resume them, but never question their superiority. In short, the whole tree of Chinese historiography and its countless ramifications spring from one stock alone, the *Historical Records* by Si ma Qian.

Novels and Short Stories

No real frontier exists between history and fiction, any more than between history and philosophy. If the epic did not develop in China, it may be because unlike the Western courts where bards and troubadours transformed the deeds of the nobles' ancestors for their entertainment, men of letters in China have been left to change myths into lessons for history since the dawning of Chinese literature. Immense stores of ancient mythology existed originally, but only fragments of it have survived, in the form of pieces which the philosophers saved to illustrate their doctrines. As they were subject to both history and morality, centuries passed before imaginative works attained independence. Even after scholars like Si ma Qian had undertaken to separate history from mythology, apocryphal chronicles existed alongside the first dynastic histories, taking material from them to make an artistic mixture of the true and the false. The novel did no more than ornament history, while remaining dependant on it. Even the fantastic narratives which flourished a little later, under the Six Dynasties, were not thought at the time to be imaginary, according to Lu Xun—the greatest modern Chinese writer was also the first historian of the novel. During this period of upheavals, one of the most brilliant in the history of Chinese religions, the development of Buddhism and Taoism encouraged people to turn their minds to meditate on the supernatural world. Good authors collected anecdotes, and recorded the wonders performed by alchemists, the metamorphoses of spirits, the miracles wrought by Buddhist deities, the appearances of ghosts. They were the precursors of the tales of the fantastic, one of the most lively forms of novelistic narrative writing in China. At the same time another genre appeared, also with a great future: the study of manners, and social satires, born of the conversations and intellectual joustings of the educated circles. Several collections of anecdotes have preserved the sharp observations or un-self-conscious criticisms which constituted the greatest charm of these groups.

Novelistic prose really developed under the Tang. The most gifted scholars cultivated the art of the short story. Tales of the fantastic were much enjoyed and the writers gave free rein to their imagination. Romanticized biographies and love-stories were written too, whose heroes asserted their right of free choice in the face of society. These works all benefited from an energetic reform of prose style; great writers such as Han Yu freed prose writing from the constraints of the "parallel style" and instilled now vigour into it by going back to the old models. Unfortunately culmination was followed by a long decline. The scholars of succeeding dynasties lost the freedom of inspiration and the vigour of the Tang; not until the Qing was there a last awakening, "in extremis", of the short story in the written language.

One of the glories of the Song dynasty was the discovery of a remedy for the deficiencies of the scholars, allowing for the appearance of the novel. This period, which was famous for its paintings, its delicate vases and refined poetry, was also the age of public story-tellers. Ancient China was certainly not lacking in mountebanks and story-tellers who plied their trade in the streets. But the scanty information available concerns those who lived under the Song and flourished in the prosperous towns of South China; their repertoire was specialised in tales of the fantastic, historical narratives, legends, love stories, pious anecdotes, etc... These storytellers—and this is an all-important detail—used memoranda to help them, written in everyday language, which provided the basic substance of the great novels which came later on. Only a few stages in the fascinating and obscure history of these artists of the people are known to us, and the information is meagre. As far as their origins are concerned, the famous manuscripts found at the beginning of this century in the Dun huang caves (Gan su) reveal that at the end of the Tang, the Buddhist missionaries, who were working among illiterate people, decided to popularize their message, and the sacred Buddhist texts were adapted in everyday language. When they preached, they used prose and verse, speeches and songs, alternately. Not only do the manuscripts give the text of some of these sermons; they also give some secular imitations which were written as pure entertainment, as the technique had met with resounding success. Whether the art of the Buddhist preachers gave rise to or simply stimulated that of the secular story-tellers, it was so fashionable under the Song that it appears that memoranda were printed and then imitated by the men of letters who found them amusing, from that time onwards. The subject matter was expanded a little, the style was polished slightly, and the result was the first novels written in the spoken language.

Only the most famous of the novels, which have been translated once or several times in the West, will be mentioned here. Some of them have maintained an extraordinary instability as a legacy of their origins: the storytellers improvised round the basic substance which guided the narrative, and the works themselves have been re-arranged over and over again to please their successive editors. It is sometimes impossible to find out the author's or principal compiler's name, or to decide which was the original text. At the same time, they should be considered as the temporary, more or less finished crystallisation of novelistic "cycles", rather than as polished works. The cycles were not written by any one author. They belonged to the people, who may not have created them, but they modified them constantly by oral transmission.

Several of the great novels are based on historical events; the most famous, if not the best of them, the *Romance of the Three Kingdoms (San guo yan yi)*, follows one of the dynastic histories closely. Countless story-tellers and dramatists have enriched the exploits of the Three Kingdoms little by little. The work itself is attributed to a 14th century author, but it has been rearranged considerably since then. It is a great novel of wars and adventures, telling of the struggles waged by the heroes of the time, the valiant and the false, the strategists and the dare-devils. Each character enshrines simple virtues or vices, with no subtleties. A picaresque novel dating from the same period, called *The Water Margin* or *All Men are Brothers (Shui hu zhuan)* contains a mixture of countless legends and traditions. The historians recorded the existence in the 12th century of a band of brigands: popular imagination, helped by the novel, turned them into brilliant outlaws, knights errant, righters of wrongs. At the end of the Tang, lovers of accounts of the fantastic, supernatural tests and magic, had included the pilgrim Xuan Zang in the realms of legend, after his journey to India in the 7th century in search of the Buddhist holy writings. The *Record of a Journey to the West* or *Monkey (Xi you ji)* is a 16th century novel, a dazzling sequence of wonderful episodes, metamorphoses and fights against demons, which the monk experiences, emerging safe and sound with the help of his companions, one of whom is a famous monkey. The *Jin bing mei* (16th century?) joins the other two titles to form a famous triad. The hero of it appears in the *Shui hu zhuan* as well; he gradually sinks into a life of pleasure, debauch and illegality, bringing bad luck to the women with whom he associates, and finally dies of an over-dose of aphrodisiac. It is a sombre but outstanding study of the private life and corruption of the upper class, and deserves its high reputation for other, better reasons than its pornographic descriptions, which were fashionable under the Ming. No less remarkable and original is the *Dream of the Red Chamber (Hong lou meng)*, written in the 18th century by two authors, the second of whom claimed to finish the work of the first. The hero, the son of a great family whose fortune is on the decline, grows up among a crowd of young women, his sisters, cousins and their servant girls. The author analyses the joys and torments, impulses and manœuvres of these adolescents living in a large, luxurious house, with a degree of subtlety unknown in China until then. The book was appreciated, but surprised its readers so much that they looked for some sort of key in it, or at least an allegorical meaning or a satirical aim to explain such a new approach. In a different vein, *An Unofficial History of the Literati (Ru lin wai shi)*, written in the 18th century, seems to be the greatest novel of social satire; it is a bitter denunciation of the hypocrisy and dishonesty of the scholar officals.

Although it arrived late, the novel developed in several directions in China, and, it would seem, with as much variety as in the West. Narrative is however to be found more often than analysis. Poetic descriptions, satire on manners, and most of all, the working out of intrigues and the power of dramatic invention, interest the authors more than detailed study of character. It should not be forgotten that the novel originated in popular art, and that until the end of the empire it was considered as a minor form, outside literature as a whole.

Poetry

Poetry, more than any other literary form, gives some idea of the genius of China. For once, the whole nation shares the same enthusiasm; singing comes as naturally as breathing to most people and throughout the country, poetry punctuates work and the days themselves. The least distinguished scholars indulged in poetry as though it were a refined pastime. Children are steeped in poetic rhythms from a very early age. The old refrain and saying have given way, in schools, to revolutionary and patriotic songs, and picture books, even stories about animals for the very small, are often written in verse. Couplets and quatrains line up beside the doors of shops, in houses, on advertisements and instructions for use... The tourist can ask for the translation of the short passages which decorate beauty spots, monuments, gardens, or hermitages. At Hang zhou or Su zhou his guide may quote recent poems composed by the leaders of new China in memory of a trip to a famous spot. Although everyone knows that Chairman Mao, like many Chinese heads of State in the past, is a poet, people are surprised to find poems or calligraphy by other political figures, generals or officials everywhere, even on the front page of the newspaper. Constant exchanges take place between popular and learned poetry. Although a modern film depicts singers from a village of old gathered on the bank of one of the most beautiful rivers in Jiang xi engaged in a poetry competition with the local men of letters, who arrive in a boat laden with old books, to throw their opponents into confusion — and as was to be expected, the ardour of the improvisors wins easily over the learning of the pedants — ; in spite of this, the scene cannot disguise the fact that scholars loved popular rhythms and often used them, and that popular singers often took back from the intellectuals much of what had been borrowed, though it returned in a more elaborate form. From earliest times, the philosophers advised the sovereign to listen to the songs in the streets to find out whether the people lived well, if the government was doing its duty, and if the monarch himself retained the people's and therefore Heaven's, favour. Under the Han dynasty, the Emperors used to send out searchers into the countryside to travel about *incognito* collecting the popular songs and the children's rhymes. At the same time, the court had such a passion for popular music that a new imperial service was formed to collect popular melodies and their words, and to adapt them for use at festivals and to entertain the great. The *jongleurs* worked on this fairly rough material, and created a new poetic language which was soon discovered by the scholars, who cultivated its resources. This was the birth of classical poetry, whose career was to last twenty centuries. The process which formed it also rejuvenated it at several points in its history.

The nature of the language explains this flowering of poetry to some extent. Chinese contains no inflexions. The word is all-important; it is an invariable monosyllable evoking the thing or the idea like an absolute, remote from all relationships with other things apart from that created by its insertion in the sentence. The noun can become a verb, the verb can become a noun. If the writer so wishes, he may omit all indications of number, person or time, and the character retains its general aspect. The essence of the object is given, an action is kept free from any particularization. The language therefore allows for ambiguities, lack of precision or word-combinations which have only been rendered possible in the West by the daring of modern poets. The syntax is simple. Few "empty words" are used, and rhythmic grouping of words is preferred to the articulation of prepositions round these grammatical tools. Even in prose, rhythm determines the dividing of the sentence into meaningful sections. This rhythmic formation of speech can still be felt now in popular speech, although modern syntax tends to bind more and to juxtapose less. In any case, syntax never imposed a restraint on the poets of ancient China as it did, for instance, on French poets. Chinese poets know nothing of this difficulty; in fact, writers of prose were constantly concerned with avoiding the influence of poetry.

The musical aspect of the language constituted another disposition towards poetry. The tone system, which consists of equal inflexions, rising or falling, causing words to be pronounced at different pitches, has been in use since the late Middle Ages, alongside rhyme and metre, as one of the elements of poetic emotion. In poems of a fixed form, the arrangement of tones has to follow strict rules. Finally, the evocative properties of the script itself must not be forgotten, for a poem appeals to the eye as well as to the ear. Choice of words sometimes depends on considerations of shape: for instance, in a descriptive passage, a poet may use characters which contain the image of mountains or water.

Two currents animate classical poetry. One springs from a "classic" which was one of the most highly respected, the *Classic of Songs*. This heterogeneous collection of about three hundred pieces, most of them anonymous, includes hymns, didactic or moralising poems and popular songs, which come no doubt from all over China. The freshness and vivacity of the latter, and their naturalness and realism, and, it must be admitted, the expositions written by philosophers determined at all costs to read lessons of political wisdom into the text, as their compiler of sacred memory, Confucius, did, have won for them a passionate interest which lasted all through the centuries. A large proportion of the themes of classical lyric poetry, particularly those of separation, war, injustice, and many forms of prosody or methods of expression appear from the *Classic of Songs* onwards. In contrast to this collection, compiled in North China, on either side of the Yellow River, there exists another anthology, whose oldest pieces were written in the South, on the territory of the powerful kingdom of Chu where an original civilisation had developed. The first and most famous piece in the *Elegies of Chu (Chu ci)*, the *Li sao*, is the work of a famous poet, Qu Yuan (end of the 4th century B.C.), who has become a legendary figure. He was a loyal minister, but misunderstood, for his sovereign, misled by calumniators, banished him; Qu Yuan threw himself into a river. A yearly water festival commemorated his sacrifice right up until our own day. The passion and brilliance of the 374 lines of the *Li sao* stand out in contrast to the simplicity and humour of the sentimental songs from the North, and to the moralising, rather formal odes of the House of Zhou. The poem is a confession, but allegory blurs the image of the hero all the way through. The speech in defence and the appeal to the sovereign are metamorphosed into a mystic search. The splendour of the floral similes and the strangeness of the journeys in space submerge and disguise the truth. An art which was more complex and wider in scope than that of the *Classic of Songs* grew up out of the *Li sao* and the other poems written by Qu Yuan. But its chief qualities, its powerful imagination and the exuberant use of verbs, were quickly extinguished, giving way to cold rhetoric. Not until the Han was a new vocation discovered for poetry: description, first of all of the displays of the court and the town, and later of the beauties of nature. The two currents in ancient poetry met, even if they did not fuse, under the Han. The first pieces of classical poetry, which date from this period, mingle the simplicity and conciseness of the first with the dreamy, nostalgic inspiration of the second. Fed by these two sources and cultivated by countless gifted people, poetry grew steadily in richness until the era of the Tang. The most famous poets of all shed their lustre on this dynasty: Li Bai, a free and powerful artist, a brilliant meteor who was thought by some to be a god; Du Fu, not a god, but a man whose genius grew to maturity through suffering, who by means of his own misfortune acquired a deep understanding of the unhappiness of the times; and Bai Ju yi, inferior to the other two, but rendered great by the fertility of his work, which reflected all his own time in its diversity.

Two great dynasties followed the Tang: under the Song and the Yuan two new forms of poems to be sung grew up as a result of the exhausting of traditional forms. The lines were of different lengths from then on; the ruling governing the arrangement of tones became even more exacting. When a poet works in co-operation with the musician, as often happens when a renewal occurs in the history of poetry, he finds himself in competition with him, and the musical quality of his poetry becomes his chief concern.

Although each of the true poets created original work, although each period had its favourite themes, and although Chinese poetry can appear as varied as our own, the foreign reader may well tire of these slight works, reproaching them with poverty and monotony. This impression is not due only to the inevitable weakness of translations. Chinese poetry is even more difficult to approach than our own classical works would be for a foreigner. Nobody who does not know the rules can penetrate this world. The rules consist of a system of conventions of thought and expression, of themes and language which come not from the esoteric research of a privileged class, but from the nation's heritage. Mastery of the rules alone cannot replace sincerity. But new ideas and strong sentiments cannot be expressed as they come. They generally produce variations on a small number of themes, and the novelty of the variations can be appreciated by the initiated; the themes are separation and solitude, war, nature and the pleasures of life, the passage of time and death. As for situations which are common to every man, the aim of the variations is not to arouse curiosity but to attain a more general truth. The truth itself is not expressed. It is left to the reader to discover it, and the poet himself tries to bring the reader into a state of grace.

The Theatre

Chinese theatre is not a literary form; it is an art in itself. The text of a play is no more than a sketch of the final production. Chinese theatre needs to be seen—or "heard", as the Chinese themselves put it. This does not mean that it belongs to the domain of music rather than literature. The poet, the story-teller, the mime, the singer, the musician, the dancer, the acrobat, and the designer all take part in the creation of these spectacular plays. Just as poetry calls on singing, music and dancing, and painting asks for the help of poetry and calligraphy in China, the theatre too is a synthesis, a complete art.

The origins of the theatre are uncertain. Bas-relief carvings and stamped bricks found in Han tombs often depict the pastimes of high society; three themes which are closely linked, cooking, feasting and play-acting, appear again and again. Among the court entertainers in these compositions are musicians, singers, dancers, jugglers, acrobats, buffoons and masked actors. Perhaps all these artists combined their talents even then in some sort of coherent spectacle, a first rough outline of opera. A thousand years, more or less, had to go by before the appearance of trustworthy documents proving the existence of the theatre; the earliest ones date from the Song. It began to develop at the end of the Song dynasty, and above all under the Yuan. The techniques used by the Buddhist preachers and the public story-tellers probably had considerable influence on the maturing process, just as they influenced the origins of the novel. As the public story-teller was a solo performer, a singer and a narrator at the same time, this may account for the fact that in old Yuan opera, one actor alone, the hero of the play, had the privilege of singing certain parts of his role. It is as though the story-teller, representing the chief character, were helped by mere walkers-on. The history of dramatic forms over the centuries which followed is complex: the two schools which existed under the Yuan, a stricter one in the North and a less rigid one in the South, were followed under the Ming by a brilliant development of the southern school, which produced long plays of high musical and literary value, dominating the theatre until the Tai ping rebellion destroyed Hang zhou in the 19th century and precipitated its decline. The main school at the moment is that of the capital, Peking, but all kinds of local opera exist, differing in tone and style of acting, and above all in the composition of the orchestra and the style of music.

Although the reform of the opera, which began in 1964, has made it difficult, if not impossible, to see performances of the most famous operas in the repertoire, such as the *Romance of the Western Chamber (Xi jiang ji)*, the *Lute (Pi pa ji)*, both Yuan operas, the *Peony Pavilion (Mu dan ting)*, a Ming opera, or the *Peach Blossom Fan (Tao hua shan)*, which dates from the Qing, revolutionary opera has not however eliminated the classical theatre completely. If he is lucky, the foreign visitor will be able to see extracts from old plays or even complete operas, considered patriotic or progressive enough to be acted still today; they are put on during the festivities which accompany May Day and October 1st. Even modern opera, which takes its inspiration from the epic of the Chinese revolution, has so far been presented in the mould of classical opera. The workers, peasants and soldiers who now fill the stage no doubt act with more realism; but although the actors are encouraged to spend a long time mixing with the workers, that they may understand them better, it is obvious that they draw their dramatic energy and their powers of suggestion as much if not more from the acting of the nobles of long ago, than from the lives of revolutionary heroes. Nothing could be more natural. It would be hard to reproach modern theatre for its fidelity to an artistic tradition as long as this one, from which the masses derive such keen enjoyment.

Chinese theatre, like Chinese poetry and painting, is an enchanted world. When seen from outside, it is baroque and cacophonous, with sounds, colours and gesticulations which mystify the uninitiated, who is reduced to enjoying the magnificent costumes or the virtuosity of the somersaults to stifle his disappointment. Once the first step has been taken, however, once the spectator has realised that he must forget the voice, appearance and gestures, which are those of human beings, and all the other objects which surround them, forming part of the "reality" which our normal senses convey to us, he is lost: he is on the way to becoming a dreamer, with a wild enthusiasm for the theatre, who knows all the operas by heart, and like our music-lovers, can never tire of comparing interpretations of them. The plots, often full of dramatic situations, may be reduced in the simpler plays, which are often the most appealing, to a short argument, or a single situation, such as a meeting, a misunderstanding, a plot, a quarrel and a reconciliation. The themes belong to the same historical and legendary cycles as the themes of the novels. No separation of *genres* exists between the grotesque and the wonderful, or the everyday and the fantastic. One of the most outstanding features, which has been mentioned already with reference to the novel, is the flexibility of the text. A successful play is never static. It is a possession held in common, which is altered, re-written, lengthened or abridged without the slightest hesitation. Often only one section is performed, if the play is a long one, and some plays are no more than an anthology of great scenes. The theatre-lovers, who have come to judge the abilities of new performers in well-known pieces, never complain.

The art of the actor does not lie in giving a faithful reproduction of reality as he has observed it, but in translating reality into the conventional language which generations of artists have handed down to him. Actors are divided into well-defined categories, according to sex, age and the type of character which they are playing. There exist series of *dan*, or feminine roles, *sheng*, or chief masculine roles, *jing*, or heroic characters with painted faces, and *zhou* or fools. Each type is recognisable by details of costume, which are checked with infinite care, and in some cases by his make-up. Each of the patterns and the brilliant colours on the "painted faces" have a symbolic meaning: when red is the main colour it suggests loyalty, blue suggests cruelty, yellow suggests cunning, white suggests perversity, etc... Everything which the actor does, his entrances, exists, the gestures he makes with his hands, the way he walks, obey conventions which make each position a sign. Even the long, flowing sleeves and the pheasant feathers which sometimes decorate the head-dresses have their language. They can be used in several dozen different figures which have meaning for the initiated alone. One gesture with the sleeve indicates that the character is in disguise; the feathers can be manipulated to show that he is furious or astonished, proud or happy. The actors in their gorgeous costumes stand out against a stage which is virtually empty. At most, a chair is used to represent a mountain, two squares of material with a wheel on them on either side of a traveller suggest a chariot, a large piece of stuff with bricks painted on it and a hole cut out of it for a gate does duty for a town wall. In the latter case, the gate is too low for people to go in and out easily, so the whole wall has to be lifted up each time... The actor has few other properties. He relies on his four limbs, with the help of traditional gestures, to show that he is opening a door, stepping over a threshold, mounting a horse.

Berthold Brecht, who was greatly impressed by the acting of Mei Lan fang, the greatest modern Chinese exponent of female roles, wrote on the *Fisherman's Revenge* in 1936: "A young woman, a fisherman's daughter, stands rowing an imaginary boat. She steers it with a little oar which barely reaches her knees. The current grows faster; she has difficulty in keeping her balance, and steers the boat into a creek where she can row more easily. This is obviously the way to manage a boat; but this scene is like a picture, it is as though this method of steering had been described in countless ballads, as though everyone knew it. Each of the young woman's movements is as familiar as a picture; each bend in the river is well known to us; as for the next bend in the river, we know it even before it comes into view. The actress's interpretation of the scene creates this impression for the audience; she alone renders what we are watching so unforgettable." A contemporary Chinese critic recently recalled how Stanislavski produced *Othello:* "His notes on the production show how he overcame the problem of the Venetian gondola. Wheels with thick rubber tyres were fixed underneath the gondola so that it would move smoothly... Like the two boats in *The Ghost Ship*, the gondola was pushed by twelve men and electric fans and canvas were used to produce a wave effect... Stanislavski gave detailed instructions about the oars: they were made of tin, and had hollow blades which were half-filled with water, to imitate the sound of lapping waves which is one of the chief characteristics of Venice".[1] This comparison provides much food for thought, and is particularly well-suited to reveal the spirit and technique of the Chinese theatre.

The 1920 Literary Revolution

The beginning of the 20th century marks a break in the history of Chinese literature. The 1920 literary revolution

---

Littérature Chinoise, a magazine published in French in Peking, 1964, I, p. 139.

made a more radical break with the past than any of the movements which occurred in the history of French literature, such as Romanticism, for instance, whose promoters treated the question of language with the utmost care, or even the Renaissance, when writers remained faithful to classical models while creating a new national literature. The 1920 generation in China abandoned the written language, the very instrument of literary expression; they turned their backs on all national traditions, condemned the old society and thought that salvation was to be found in the foreign school. The literary movement was closely bound up with the history of the political and social revolution. The literary reformers, when not taking part in the struggles going on round them, observed them and wrote agonising descriptions of them. As writers, they were feeling their way, and reflect the country itself in this.

During the First World War, the magazine *New Youth* advocated the adoption of the common language in teaching and literature, and the abandoning of the written language, which was inaccessible to the people and ill-adapted to modern needs. As early as 1919, four hundred newspapers were published in the common language and the movement finally triumphed in 1920, when the government decided to apply teaching in the common language troughout all schools. The historians sometimes attribute this success to the tenacity and talent of the writers of polemics, one of whom was the famous Hu Shi, sometimes to the revolutionary May the Fourth Movement, 1919, which provoked a widespread patriotic movement throughout the whole country.

The revolution was not one of form alone. The spoken language became the vehicle for new ideas, for Western doctrines and systems. The intellectuals were passionately interested in European or American philosophers and made countless translations of literary works. Russian or Soviet novels, and the novels and short stories of the French realist school exerted great influence. The writers formed rival societies, some of whom upheld art for art's sake, whereas most of them denounced the vices of the regime and society, and threw in their lot with politics. The Literary Association, founded in 1921, of which Mao Dun and Lu Xun were prominent members, held that literature was the mirror of social life and not a mere pastime; the Creative Society, to which Guo Mo ruo and Yu Da fu belonged, gradually gave up the pessimistic romanticism and the aestheticism to which it had subscribed at first to rally to the slogan: "from the literary revolution to the literature of the revolution"; in 1930, Lu Xun, Mao Dun, Yu Da fu, Tian Han created a League of Leftist Writers in Shanghai, which was to serve the rising proletariat, and which was persecuted by the government; it was decided to disband it in 1936, to allow for the founding of an Anti-Japanese Federation of Writers and Artists in 1938, in which men of all tendencies were grouped together in patriotic resistance. Although Marxism had gained ground in literary circles during the thirty years which preceded the founding of the People's Republic, most of these bourgeois intellectuals were still feeling their way. They were individualists, inspired by a romantic cult of the revolutionary hero; they joined forces in the revolt, but since they could hold out little hope for the future, they often gave way to despair or to an incoherent search for personal happiness. Two torches blaze through their impassioned writings: love and the revolution.

Poets, dramatists and novelists all looked for their models abroad. The poets were influenced above all by the English Romantics or the French Symbolists and tried without much success to adapt *vers libre* to China. The dramatists introduced spoken plays. The greatest of them all, Cao Yu, took his inspiration from the Greek plays and Ibsen. Several of his sombre, yet burning plays, such as *Thunder and Rain (Lei yu)* or *The Sunrise (Ri chu)* were received enthusiastically by the bourgeoisie in the big cities. The most successful works of the period, however, were the short stories and novels. Four authors of different temperaments, all of them interesting, will be mentioned out of the many who were active. Lao She, a native of Peking, was born in 1899, a man full of humour, delicacy and tenderness for the rickshaw coolie whose honest life and pitiful fate is described in *Rickshaw Boy (Luo tuo xiang zi)*, (trans. by Evan King, Reynal and Hitchcock, New York 1945). Ba Jin, born in 1904, began writing in Paris to combat his loneliness and boredom. He won the hearts of the sentimental youth of his time with his trilogy *The Family (Jia)*, *Spring (Chun)*, *Autumn (Qiu)*, written in a limpid but wordy style. His tearful heroes deplore the defects and restraints of traditional society. Mao Dun, born in 1896, a severe writer of short stories and a sombre and turbulent novelist achieved a masterpiece in his novel *Midnight (Zi ye)*, in which he describes the city of Shang hai, with its capitalists and industrialists, its workers and revolutionaries. It is a fresco whose breadth of scope is unprecedented in China. The greatest writer of the 20th century, Lu Xun (1881-1936), is acclaimed in People's China as the precursor of revolutionary literature and a national hero. He is the "Chinese Gorki". At the end of his spiritual evolution, he did in fact turn to Marxism and fought valiantly for the cause of the proletariat. He is an essayist and short story writer of great genius; his prose alternately wounds or enchants the reader. It is hard to imagine a more skilful writer of polemics, and yet this master of irony is a poet as well. His two best known short stories are probably the *Diary of a Madman (Kuang ren ri ji)*, adapted from the work by Gogol — Lu Xun translated numerous Russian and Japanese works — and the *True Story of Ah Q (A Q zheng zhuan)*, written in 1921, in which the penetrating portrait of a simple peasant comes to represent a type and sheds ruthless light on the misery and weakness of the people.

Contemporary Literature

The literature of New China took shape in 1942, at Yan an, in the Shan xi mountains. The anti-Japanese war was at its height. Yan an was the capital of a liberated area, controlled by the Communist Party and the Red Army. The talks given by Chairman Mao at the forum on literature and art which took place during that spring constituted the charter of the "intellectual workers" of People's China. Writers of literary criticism and polemics have referred back to this document for over twenty years. It stated the all-important role of literature and art in the revolution: "If we had no literature and art even in the broadest and most ordinary sense, we could not carry on the revolutionary movement and win victory". The modern press devotes a good quarter of the space in its columns to culture every day. Another fundamental rule applying to the policy of the Communist Party was also formulated at Yan an: literature and art must serve the people. But to touch the broad masses of the workers and peasants, revolutionary writers and artists must begin by identifying themselves with the workers. In spite of their revolutionary ideas, no intellectuals brought up on bourgeois culture can fully understand and describe the people unless they have lived and worked with them. The writers were invited to partake in the struggles, hardships, and sufferings of the workers, and above all the peasants, for long periods at a time. Several modern novelists write of the hard experiences through which they lived in this school, isolated in the country. They acquired an intimate knowledge of a world which was virtually unexplored, the Chinese peasantry.

For several years now this movement of intellectuals towards the peasantry has taken on quite astonishing proportions. Not only artists and writers, but all students, teachers and cadres go and stay in the country. There can be no doubt that this mixing of classes which used to be such strangers to one another does gradually breath new life into them, in spite of the sterilizing effects imposed by politics on all the manifestations of cultural life. The Party and the Government, for their part, are constantly encouraging the workers and the peasants to collaborate in the development of the new literature. Workers who were formerly illiterate, young enthusiasts from all circles, write and publish their war memoirs, tell of their struggles, or, for the edification of their compatriots, compare the sufferings of the past with the blessings of socialism. The popular arts are given energetic stimulus: local forms of opera which were nearly extinct have been revived, public story-tellers and musicians are encouraged to develop or transform their repertoire, ballads or stories which were handed down by word of mouth among the minorities are being collected, adapted and published.

The famous "Hundred Flowers" campaign in 1956 and 1957 threw intellectual circles into a ferment. "Let a hundred flowers bloom together, let the hundred schools of thought contend": this new slogan, whatever the motives of its author, the Chairman himself, may have been, started a sharp battle. A shower of attacks was launched against the intellectual and artistic leadership of the Party, and even, rasher still, against the regime itself. To quote some of the reproaches collected by the official spokesmen: one "right-wing writer" stated "that the standard of soviet literature over the last twenty years was far lower than that of the twenty years before, and that Chinese literature had also declined during the fifteen years which had followed the Talks at the Yan an Forum on Literature and Art." Another said "that the authenticity of our literary and artistic work is of an extremely low standard". Writers were said to have to "look furtively to left and right before doing the slightest thing", that they might "think of a most moving, important and contraversial subject, but they did not dare treat it in any but the most down to earth way". The government reacted violently, and the "class enemies", right-wing bourgeois and revisionists who had given themselves away like this were silenced. The watchwords of "a hundred flowers" and "the hundred schools" were not dropped, but a series of commentaries were added which proved to be of great interest, stating the relationship between art and politics and the limits of liberty for writers. Those in charge of official propaganda were no doubt happy to recall the flowering of the philosophical schools during the Chun qiu and the Warring States periods, "the golden age of intellectual progress", but they immediately added that during the dictatorship of the proletariat, the "hundred flowers" policy could not take on the form of this anarchic development. They denounced the danger of dogmatism and sectarianism, and then recalled that in the Yan an days, Chairman Mao stated that literature and art are "an indispensable part of the entire revolutionary cause": they are "cogs and wheels in the whole machine" and must be "subordinated to the revolutionary tasks set by the Party". In this case, artists should place "the political criterion first and the artistic criterion second". One may well ask which flowers and which schools should be encouraged to bloom under these conditions. "On condition that they do not oppose socialism or the leadership of the Communist Party, artistic works can take on any form, treat any subject, in any style whatsoever". As for counter-revolutionaries, they obviously must be allowed no liberty at all. Counter-revolutionaries? The distinction between declared enemies of the regime and bourgeois intellectuals whose individualism cannot be reconciled with official ideology is not always clear. For "individualism has never been tolerated in the Party. There is no place for it today in any sector of our society, because our present society is socialist, collectivist." "In socialist society, individualism is the root of all evil." "Once delivered of this burden, a man feels light-hearted: he can then identify himself with the masses, be at one with the Party and derive infinite strength from the collectivity". In other words, "the flowers which must bloom are socialist flowers"; that the hundred schools should rival each other means competition under the leadership of Marxist-Leninist ideology, it means the spread and development of Marxist dialectic materialism, it means free debates to combat bourgeois idealism and bourgeois metaphysics". As for the "poisonous weeds", such as "contemporary works by reactionary bourgeois authors, full of characters who are obsessed with sex, morally degenerate, schizophrenic and misanthropic, hooligans, crooks, gangsters, assassins, raised to the position of heroes by the bourgeoisie, which is going downhill fast," they must obviously be rooted out mercilessly.

Since 1957, the new literature has continued on these lines. Songs, operas, novels, every work contributes to the struggle to build socialism. The revolutionary epic is a source of stirring themes: the great strikes of the period between the two wars, the war of resistance against Japan, the war of Liberation. the Long March, all abound in episodes of heroism which are brought up again and again. The comparison, in black and white, of the past and the present, is as widespread and efficient as the cult of revolutionary martyrs and heroes. "Before the liberation... after the liberation...", countless autobiographies, expositions and songs alternate the horror and the felicity of the two, helped by dramatic contrasts. China's international policy, particularly in Vietnam. inspires many artists, not only painters and poster designers. but story-tellers and dramatists as well.

This literature. although still young, is already encumbered with stereotyped situations and clichés. It is monotonous. It is often based simply on political slogans, illustrated with little or no inspiration. Authors who create "average" characters who are neither good nor bad, or who hold that "even the sun has spots on it" are disgraced. The new literature holds a trump card, however: skilful use of traditional techniques. The writers who preceded it were passionate supporters of the Western school, but they never made satisfactory adaptations of verse or drama forms. Modern theatre, however, is considered the heir of classical opera or its countless local varieties. Poetry is based on the rhythms of the popular story-tellers. In the eyes of the leaders, this nationalism is a guarantee of success in the opinion of the masses. It also means that contemporary works benefit from invaluable artistic experience. Mediocre plays are saved by the acting, for the actors draw on the accumulated skill of centuries. In spite of the flatness of their subjects, the sketches performed by amateurs in the parks on feast days attract and hold one's attention by the indefinable magic of their diction and rhythmic accompaniment. The task of modern writers is not exactly that of fitting new ideas into old moulds. They experiment with new forms too, anxious above all, faithful to the recommendations of Chairman Mao, "to cut away the dead wood to make room for the new". The qualities of hard work, faith in the country's future, a thoroughly Chinese mixture of self-confidence and the will to progress, may not be able to replace creative genius. But it would be surprising if the enormous effort to spread culture and awaken literary vocations in the very heart of the masses did not awaken the genius of the ancient masters once more.

CHINESE ART

Part 1: The Chronological Development

The Neolithic Era

The remains of Sinanthropus Pekinensis, the oldest inhabitant of China, were discovered at Zhou kou dian, not far from Peking. Up till now, excavations have revealed no traces of a transitional culture between the Paleolithic, and a Neolithic era covering, so it seems, the 4th, 3rd and 2nd millenaries B.C., and already well-developed.

At that time, three cultures can be distinguished, all using grey pottery with a stamped design on it:

1. The Gobi culture (north of the Great Wall, from Manchuria to Xin jiang) produced a series of stone tools in the microlithic tradition, and coarse brown pottery decorated with geometric motifs which were cut into the pots.

2. The Painted Pottery or Yang shao culture (called after the name of the village in He nan where it was discovered in 1921). Their fields were laid out on terraces on either side of the great river valleys; their puddled clay dwellings were round or rectangular; the cemetery was outside the village.

These sites have yielded stone and polished bone tools, ordinary grey pottery, and red pottery with a polychrome design. The shapes include bowls with flat edges, urns and globular jars with two little handles towards the top and a narrow, high neck. The decoration is painted in black or red on a burnished surface, and consists of straight and wavy lines, spirals, triangles, trellis patterns and sometimes schematized human figures.

The geographical area covered by the Painted Pottery culture stretches over north He nan (Miao di gou site), Shan xi, Shân xi (Ban po cun site), and Gan su (Ma jia yao site, with its cemetery at Ban shan, the Ma chang site, the Qi jia ping site). The Gan su culture seems to be a little later than that of He nan.

3. The Black Pottery or Long shan (Shan dong) culture has several affinities with the Yang shao culture; it developed a little later, and lasted well into the Bronze Age, until about 500 B.C. (sites at Xin dian, Jia jing and Si wa). The most important sites are in He nan, Shân xi and Shan dong. The Cheng zi yai site (Shan dong) has revealed a city surrounded by a

pounded earth wall, with dwellings built round a hearth in the centre, and pottery kilns. The dead were buried in the middle of the town. The stone and bone work shows a more advanced technique than that used at Yang shao. Divinatory bones and jade rings were found there too. The walls of the black pottery, which is wheel-turned, are extremely thin (4 to 2 mm.), and the shapes are plain: three-legged *ding* or cauldrons, narrow-necked jars, goblets with handles, jugs, *li* or hollow-legged tripods, wine-cups... They foreshadow the shapes of the first bronze ritual vessels. The burnished surface has an incised pattern of nets, dots and triangles. Polished red pottery and unornamented, delicate white ware were found alongside the black pottery.

In the Yang zi jiang basin, from Hu bei to Jiang su (Qin lian gang site) and in north Zhe jiang and An hui, all the archaeological remains show influence of the Neolithic cultures of the Huang he basin. Many sites also contain Long shan pottery.

The representatives of the Long shan culture, who were in contact with painted pottery centres and with the Baikal cultures, were perhaps the first people in China to use bronze and develop a culture based on metal.

The Shang Dynasty (about 18th to 11th century B.C.)

Until recently, little was known about the beginnings of the dynasty apart from a list of rulers. The Zheng zhou excavations (Lou da miao, Er li gang sites) in He nan enable this gap to be bridged to a certain extent. The Shang capital at Zheng zhou covered an area of 1½ square miles. The town was surrounded by a pounded earth wall, and contained dwellings of several different types. The rectangular or circular pits had steps or a sloping ramp leading down into them: the rectangular or square houses had pounded earth floors. Wooden pillars resting on stone or bronze disks held up the roof. Drainage trenches, bronze foundries, bone workshops and pottery kilns have also been uncovered at Zheng zhou. The bronzes found at Er li gang (the site was discovered in 1953) include large numbers of arrow heads, fish-hooks, awls, knives and vases *(li, ding,...)*. The bronzes, like other examples dating from the beginning of the Shang period, are small and often have flat bases. Compared with pieces dating from the end of the Shang period, the alloy is of mediocre quality, the walls are thin, the proportions are disappointing, the casting technique is fairly rough, the design clumsy, and only slightly incised. The motives consist of plain *tao tie* maks, concentric circles, triangles, ox heads and *lei wen*. These excavations at Zheng zhou go a long way to fill in the blank between the Neolithic culture and the wonderful flowering of art at An yang.

The Shang king moved to An yang, in He nan, in about 1400 B.C. This capital has been continuously excavated since 1928; it dates from the 14th to 11th century, and bears witness to a civilisation which had reached the height of its development, covering the middle and lower Yellow River basin and extending tis influence to the neighbouring provinces, as far as the Yang zi jiang basin. The rest of the Chinese territory was in the hands of unconquered tribes with whom the Shang traded and fought.

The site of An yang stretches over the north and south banks of the River Huan. The town itself occupied the south bank, and the north bank was reserved for graveyards. The rulers were buried in royal tombs, accompanied by elaborate tomb furnishings and numerous faithful servants. The finest pieces found in Shang tombs are of bronze, which was still rare and reserved for the king and for religious purposes. Besides the vases, covered with a patina ranging in colour from grey-green to emerald green, which is a marvel in itself, the articles consist of beautiful ceremonial weapons, heavy axes encrusted with turquoise and malachite, halbards and daggers with jade blades.

The art of sculpture in the round, which is to be found on some bronzes alongside infinitely delicate engraving, was applied to other materials as well, such as marble and jade. Marble was used as an architectural ornament: carvings of birds, oxen or human figures, in massive style, are to be found. More examples of sculpture exist in marble, mainly small pieces, remarkable for their strength and sense of volume.

Jade (particularly nephrite), known in China as early as the Neolithic era, was used by the Shang. The emblems, ornaments and weapons are carved with designs similar to those used on bronzes.

Two new techniques appeared alongside the grey pottery: glazed earthenware and white pottery. This luxurious pottery, which was wheel-turned, was made of a fine, hard clay not unlike kaolin, and was perhaps reserved for religious purposes and funeral rites, in imitation of the bronze vessels. It is usually decorated with a geometric design, which sometimes includes three ox heads in high relief.

The Zhou Era

This brilliant art did not lose its unity of inspiration with the invasion of the Zhou who conquered the Shang kingdom in 1028. The Zhou rulers, natives of Shân xi, adopted the customs and refinements of the An yang court. The former Western Zhou capital, Feng hao, seems to have been found on the Chang jia po site which was excavated in 1955–56. These diggings show that the standard of production and social life was much the same as at the end of the Shang Dynasty. As far as art was concerned, the old traditions continued without a break through the 10th and 9th centuries. The shapes and décor of the sacrificial vessels closely resembled their Shang models. The décor, however, which often consists of a band of varying width running all the way round the vessel, grew poorer and lost in content and intensity. Under the dislocated old designs, a new feeling was at work, stressing power and massiveness rather than concentrating on balance and elegance. This tendency grew more marked in the 8th and 7th centuries. The Zhou power then began to wane; the feudal princes' power increased, as is borne out by an appreciable decline in the number of vessels used by the Zhou royal house and the appearance of bronzes produced by the feudal states, whose standard was high enough to rival the royal bronzes.

The designs used during the Chun qiu era (770-475) are less varied, and arranged in parallel bands; the *tao tie* mask disappeared, the dragons became more elongated and were interwoven in long strips, losing all resemblance to an animal, and becoming simply an element in the design, like the scales and waves. New techniques made their appearance during this period, however, and developed over the centuries that followed. Iron seems to have been used from the 8th century onwards; glass and cornaline beads and a bronze mirror were found in tombs in the principality of Guo, dating from the 8th-7th century B.C., and are the oldest examples of their kind to be found in China.

The Warring States Era (475–221)

During this period, China went through an upheaval which affected every domain of her civilisation. The appearance of the plough, towards the 5th century, resulted in permanent, irrigated fields being made, and tools were improved by using iron. The population grew because of the new means of survival at its disposal and colonised new lands to the north and south, beyond the Yang zi jiang. Large states grew up in the outlying areas: Qin to the west, Chu, Wu and Yue to the south. As the principalities grew larger, new economic circuits grew up.

The rivalry, both in war and diplomacy, between these great states was accompanied by exaggerated riches and luxury. Each court included its workshops and artists. Art, which under the Shang had been essentially religious, became more and more profane, with a taste for finery and ornaments, keen powers of observation and a sense of movement. This aesthetic renewal found expression in a language based on borrowings from the past, the art of the nomads and the spirit of the times. The *tao tie* mask re-appeared on bronzes of high technical perfection, alongside animal designs of astonishing elegance and realism: ducks or cows on the lids of the vessels, fish or tortoises moulded on the bottoms of them. The interlaced dragons, lighter than in the 8th century, became a purely decorative motive whose flowing lines intertwined in one continuous movement. The decor of the vases consists of belts of spiral or lozenge designs, dots, comma-shaped hooks and scales separated by plait designs, which may have been borrowed from the art of the northern Asian nomads. These designs, which are either incised or in bas-relief, show astonishing imagination, impetuosity of line, and sense of harmony: each curve is matched by another, each stroke, each animal is balanced by and related to those round it and to the shape of the vessel.

Incrustations of gold, silver, turquoise and malachite were used to throw the flexibility of this decor into relief, on table legs, rings, hooks, weapons and vases.

Human and animal figures also appear on vases with scenes depicting hunting, shooting, mulberry-picking, or in the bronze figurines representing a kneeling human figure with a tube in each hand, such as those found at Jin cun, He nan.

The powerful state of Chu in central China went through an age of great splendour at this time. Graves at Chang sha (Hu nan) have yielded large numbers of bronzes, wooden figurines and pottery. The lacquer boxes, tools and ornaments are of particular interest. The exacting and refined art of lacquerware appeared at this time, if not earlier. Lacquer is obtained from the juice of a tree peculiar to the Far East, which is purified by repeated filtering and applied to wood, in several successive layers. Each layer, which may be coloured, has to be dried in a dust-free place, and is then rubbed down to give it a smooth, shining surface. Once this process is finished, the article is ready to be carved, painted or engraved.

The use of the mirror seems to have come from Eastern Asia. The Chinese mirror is round or square and has a knob in the middle of the back of it so that it may be hung up, forming the centre of the decor at the same time. Here again, geometrical patterns are combined with mythical beasts engraved in low relief.

Clasps, which were also borrowed from the peoples of the steppes, were fashionable too; they were useful and often precious at the same time, made of bronze to which gold, silver, turquoise or jade was often added.

The art of carving developed considerably during the same period, and the motives used for bronzes are to be found carved on jade too: spiral and hook shapes cover the surface of the *bi*, jade disks with a hole in the middle, symbolising the Heavens, used in sacrifices alongside the *zong*, a cylinder set into a cube, symbolising the Earth.

In 1949, the oldest known Chinese painting on silk was discovered in a tomb at Chang sha, Hu nan. It depicts a slender woman with her hands in an attitude of prayer; above her are a phoenix and a mythical beast.

The Han Dynasty (3rd century B.C.–3rd century A.D.)

The state of Qin unified China in 221 B.C., by means of a solid political structure and military experience acquired fighting the barbarian tribes. Qin despotism was short-lived and collapsed in scenes of violence and bloodshed. In 206 B.C., a peasant, Liu Bang, founded the Han Dynasty, one of the most brilliant in Chinese history. This new dynasty, which was to rule China until 220 A.D., is traditionally divided into the Former and the Later Han, with capitals at Chang an (Shân xi) and Luo yang (He nan) respectively.

Under the Han, art appealed to a larger and more eclectic public. The examples which have survived until now are objects connected mainly with funeral rites. A study of the tombs, their décor and furnishings enables the background of Chinese life at that time to be studied. It was customary for a man to be buried in a tomb which more or less resembled his earthly home.

With the statues of the animals in front of the tombs and the carving in the Ho qu ping tomb (Shân xi, c. 117 B.C.), a type of Chinese monumental sculpture stressing vigour and correct volume proportions, and executed with great economy of means, emerges for the first time. In He nan and Shan dong a little hall built of stone blocks and used for offerings stood at the end of the funeral way. The blocks were carved with everyday or mythical scenes, reproduced from the mural paintings decorating the palaces. The day to day scenes give a picture of the life of the times: historic events or events in the dead man's life, processions of chariots or horsemen, banquets and gatherings in pavilions. In bas-relief carvings from Wu liang zi (Shan dong), which date from 147–167 A.D., the scenes are placed one above the other. The stress is on line and movement; the silhouettes stand out against the streaky background of the stone. The third dimension is unknown in the world represented here, and the places where the scenes take place are shown only when it is indispensable, and then in a rudimentary way. A view from above appears in scenes from everyday life at Zhu wei (Shan dong), dating from the 1st century A.D. This search for construction in space is to be found again on stamped bricks from the province of Si chuan (1st-2nd centuries A.D.). Here the scenes often depict country life: workers in the salt mines, mountain scenery, hunters, market or harvest scenes portrayed with great skill and verve, and astonishing fidelity to nature.

The tomb furnishings reveal the standards of luxury and the taste of the times. Jade ornaments, numerous articles in coloured lacquer with delicate patterns of fluting or triangles are good examples of this. The bronze mirrors are different from the earlier ones. The carvings, slightly in relief, are arranged in concentric bands round the knob in the middle. The central zone, which is surrounded by an inscription, and animals symbolising the points of the compass, alternate with geometric patterns made up of T's, L's and V's. Clasps are numerous and varied. They are made of bronze or gilded bronze encrusted with turquoise and lapis lazuli, silver, jade or glass paste. The main decorations used are animal masks or fights between wild beasts. This theme of fighting wild beasts comes from steppe art and is also to be found on belt plaques and all kinds of bronze ornaments.

The custom of sacrificing human beings and animals that they might accompany the dead person into the next life had almost entirely disappeared in China by the Warring States period. The sacrificial victims were replaced by wooden, metal or pottery substitutes, called *ming qi*. These figurines, many of them painted, breathe life into the picture of Han China with its customs and its fashions. They include round-faced young women, with starched dresses disguising their slender bodies, dancing girls, craftsmen, horses like the ones which the emperor had sent from beyond the Oxus, teams of animals, models of houses, farms, boats: everything is reproduced with astonishing attention to detail.

Few Han paintings have survived. Contemporary writings praise the palace murals, however. The frescoes in the tomb at Wang du (He bei) dating from 182 A.D., and painted bricks from various places, depict hunting scenes or friezes of people walking and talking. The figures are drawn in black on a white ground, while colours are used inside the outline (light green, bright red, light brown); the brush is used with a freedom which recalls calligraphic style, giving a brief, witty sketch which foreshadows the conciseness and masterly use of the brush which the Chinese artists later developed over the centuries.

Apart from the tomb figurines, Han pottery is represented by vases whose shapes and décor imitate bronzes. Most of them are covered with a green lead glaze whose colour is obtained from copper oxide. A few new shapes appear both in bronze and pottery: the *lian* or toilet box, which is cylindrical and supported by three crouching bears, and the *bo shan lu* or incense-burner with a conical lid suggesting the rocks on the island where the Taoist Immortals lived. The most beautiful things which the Han potters made were the porcelain prototypes, however. They were stoneware pots fired at a high temperature, with slip which reddened in the firing. The technique was known before the Han, but seems to have been perfected at this time. The *hu* vases with their vigorous curves are coloured olive-brown or a sort of yellow on the bulge, and a décor of wavy lines and stylised birds is arranged in concentric zones on the coloured part. Finally, in the Yue area (Zhe jiang) kilns dating from the end of the Han era have yielded celadon prototypes of light coloured stoneware with a greenish glaze based on vegetable ash and feldspath.

The Three Kingdoms and the Six Dynasties Period (221–589), the Sui Dynasty (590–617)

The Han Dynasty fell in 220, weakened by court intrigues and peasant uprisings; it was succeeded by a troubled period which lasted until 589, during which Chinese society changed completely. As soon as the Han disappeared, the feudal system was re-instituted, accentuating the contrast between the luxury of the local courts and the misery of the peasants living under the constant menace of invasions, civil wars and famine. The aristocracy took refuge in the south, and devoted its time to dialectic competitions, poetry, calligraphy and painting.

Gu Kai zhi (344–406) lived at Nanking, enjoying the patronage of princes; it was said of him that he was outstanding for his intelligence, and also as a painter, and jester. Under the influence of Taoist teachings, he tried to penetrate the inner essence of beings and landscapes. The scroll "Admonitions of the Imperial Instructress" is no doubt a Tang copy (618-907) of one of his works. It is a set of illustrations accompanying a text by the poet Zhang Hua (c. 232–300), and falls into nine pictures (British Museum, London). The grouping is harmonious, the drawing flexible and sensitive. It has a feeling of spaciousness about it, and the empty areas lend serenity and elegance to the whole. This painting is closely related to the art of calligraphy, and also to the edifying poem which it illustrates: both the union with calligraphy and the moralising aspect of the work are characteristic of painting under the Six Dynasties.

Towards 500, the painter Xie He wrote his *Six Principles* on painting, also at Nanking; he paved the way for artistic criticism in China.

The Nanking emperors encouraged painting, and also retained the tradition of monumental sculpture under the form of animals guarding tombs. The winged lions with arched backs and swelling chests show a sense of rhythm and of power in movement which finds its true expression in this work.

Once Buddhism was introduced into China, rock shrines were made from Gan su, Si chuan, Shan xi and He nan as far as Shan dong to the east and Jiang su to the south. The Dun huang caves were begun in the 4th century; the place was originally a military post on the borders and a market at the same time, founded at the end of the 1st century B.C. at the entrance to the Gobi desert, the starting and finishing point for the silk roads. The main stream of ideas coming to Dun huang from India was enriched on the way through Afghanistan and Central Asia. The sanctuary was founded in 366 and developed unceasingly until the 10th century; it was inspired by the rock shrines which lay scattered along the caravan route through north Xin jiang, from Bâmyiân to Toum-chouq and Qyzyl. The earliest frescoes in the caves show this clearly. Many of them depict scenes from the former lives of the Buddha, arranged diagonally below a frieze of flying deities; the spontaneous movements and the naive attention to detail suggest a storyteller's art, with people from Central Asia and China supplying the characters.

Towards the middle of the 5th century, the Wei rulers wanted to favour Buddhism, and had the first caves cut at Yun gang, in north Shan xi. The largest caves at Long men (He nan) were preceded by buildings used as living-quarters by the monks attached to the place. The cave itself was in this case used as the shrine.

Western elements which are to be found in Buddhist sculpture, are present in the art of the *ming qi* who still filled the tombs. Warriors dressed in Iranian style and turbaned camel-drivers like those who frequented the silk route appear alongside the elegant ladies and domestic animals.

The development of pottery at the end of the Six Dynasties and under the Sui paves the way for the brilliant richness of shape and technique of the Tang era. The first celadon ware in porcelainous stoneware appeared in Zhe jiang as early as the 3rd century, in fact; it is known as Yue celadon ware. In the 6th century, and at the beginning of the 7th century, the Ju yan zhou (Zhe jiang) kilns produced vessels of varying shapes: goblets, jars, bottles, jugs in the shape of crouching lions, ewers with a cock's head for a spout. The main body of the vase is in light grey stoneware, covered with a thick layer of transparent crackled glaze, which is green. The décor is restrained and consists of stars, circles, and lotus leaves either stamped or in relief. Pottery with a lead glaze was also produced at the same time; the shapes heralded those made under the Tang.

The Tang Dynasty (618–907)

The Tang dynasty, founded in 618, restored unity to China and re-instated Chinese hegemony in Central Asia and Korea. This represented a large-scale military and political operation, and China was for two centuries afterwards, in the 7th and 8th centuries, the most powerful and widely-feared country in Asia. Chang an, the capital, with its two million inhabitants, was the largest and most cosmopolitan city in the world. Merchants and ambassadors went there from all countries in the world to take presents to the Chinese court, and the streets were thronged with foreigners, Syrians, Persians, Arabs, Jews, Turks, Japanese, and Tibetans.

Buddhism flourished as never before; China contained no fewer than four thousand large monasteries, and pious foundations constantly increased. The greatest painters, such as Wu Dao zi, concentrated on religious themes, and executed paintings

on the walls of Buddhist establishments in the capital. The
civil wars and the persecution in 845 destroyed all these, and
the Dun huang caves alone survived. The frescoes and banners
there bear witness to the progress of Buddhist painting. The
composition is conceived as a whole, without division into
separate parts, from a point giving a view from above which
was to remain a constant feature of Chinese narrative painting.

Intellectual life was not concentrated in the monasteries only.
Emperor Xuan zong (713–755) attracted the greatest poets
and the most famous painters of his time to his court. These
men of genius were often poets, scholars, musicians, calligraphers
and painters as well. Wang Wei is an example of this type of
person; he created the monochrome landscape and the poetic
emotion for which all later Chinese landscape painters searched.
Nothing is left now of his art, save copies of his works and
poems written by his own hand.

Wu Dao zi, a contemporary of Wang Wei and a pupil of the
great calligrapher Zhang Xu, used large ink strokes in his
paintings, and often left his disciples to finish his frescoes by
applying the colours. His genius extended to Buddhist scenes
and landscapes, but nothing has survived, unfortunately, beyond
a few later rubbings. One work by Li Zhao dao, another painter
at the court of Xuang zong, still exists; it is a landscape with
tortuous rocks cut up by clouds which reveal an art full of
minute detail, using light accurate strokes emphasised by bright
colours. This type of art, which carried on the traditions of
6th century works, was extremely different from the less accurate
but more vigorous style of Wang Wei. From the 8th century,
two different tendencies became apparent among landscape
painters: one, the style of Li Zhao dao, was "detailed"; the
other, the style of Wang Wei, was influenced by cursive calligraphy and knowledge of Chan Buddhism, and was known as
"abbreviated".

The Tang emperors adored horses; six huge carvings of the
Emperor's chargers stood before the tomb of Emperor Tai
zong (627–649). These powerful horses with their thick-set
necks and withers are depicted in haut-relief carvings (Xi an
Museum, Shân xi). In the 8th century, the great painter Han Gan
painted portraits of all the chargers in the royal stable. He studied
the peculiarities of each animal with accurate, sensitive realism,
combining the delicacy and vigour of the shaded outlines with
the elegant patches of colour.

Finally, the frescoes in the tomb of Princess Yong tai, in
Shân xi, provide a magnificent example of Tang mural painting:

they illustrate two court ladies speaking to each other, each surrounded by her servant girls.

Only the works of art can recall the luxury which reigned at the court. Jewellery, mirrors and vases reveal exotic techniques and ornaments. Apart from the rich tributes of silver ware and fabrics which were sent to the court, artisans from Sassanid Persia arrived, fleeing from the Moslem hordes. They brought with them new shapes and designs, as well as the technique of beating metal. Some of the mirrors are encrusted with gold and silver on a base of lacquer over bronze. Their décor of stylised plants with birds flying among them have a wonderful exotic charm. The large floral designs, the ducks or phoenixes in the centre of gold or silver cups, or on ornaments and toilet boxes, are much more Chinese in spirit.

A new technique appeared in the art of textile-making: chain stitch which had been used up till then was replaced by satin stitch, which became the basis of all later developments in Chinese embroidery.

The tomb figurines, with their exquisite vivacity and charm also reflect the sumptuous court. Horsemen, guards, servants, jesters, polo-players, slim or plump ladies from the Palace, musicians and dancing girls with their long loops of hair, take their places alongside the guardian spirits and animals whose duty it was to protect the dead man. The grey earthenware statues covered with white slip are often enhanced with black, green, brown or red colouring. From the 8th century onwards, some have yellow, brown or green glazes.

These brilliantly coloured glazes are one of the charms of Tang pottery. They are applied to the white slip in blobs or formed into compartments by deep incisions into the pot. Their varied shapes are sometimes Chinese in origin, or sometimes borrowed from Sassanid Persia, as in the case of the ewers or amphora vases with dragon handles climbing up from the shoulders to the rim of the vase. Certain designs, using rosettes, moulded leaves, foliage and engraved circles recall patterns used by goldsmiths and silversmiths.

White porcelain appears at this time, in several different shapes and types. Some small pieces (pots with lids, lobed bowls) are of a pure and lustrous white. Others are made in the shape of a little ewer with a handle consisting of a feline animal climbing up the side and plunging its head into the vase. The white glaze, which is more milky here, stops before the foot and reveals the beige body underneath.

The Five Dynasties Period (907-960)

The Tang dynasty collapsed at the beginning of the 10th century, leaving China exhausted by military and economic disasters. For a century the empire was a prey to anarchy, divided into independent kingdoms where one brief dynasty followed on another. The local courts were still active centres where the art of painting developed, following the example set by Wang Wei under the Tang. Dong Yuan (he was active in about 937–975), director of the Imperial Parks at Nanking, introduced a new poetic range into the art of landscape painting with his pictures of the damp and wooded southern Chinese countryside, and its mountain-tops disappearing into the mist. His research into the technical aspects and the universe which he conveys had considerable influence on the Song painters. He was the first to produce landscapes of immeasurable distances peopled with blurred shapes, compositions built up round mists and emptiness. His treatment of hills and trees, using large patches of more or rivers and waterfalls. The gnarled, jagged trees give rhythm to the glimpses of wild mountains dominating the foreground.

A northern painter, Li Cheng (active about 940–967), a Confucian scholar who divided his attentions between painting and the bottle, is more faithful to the exact value of outline. His strict compositions are balanced by successive planes joined by paths, rivers and waterfalls. The gnarled, jagged trees give rhythm to the glimpses of wild mountains dominating the foreground.

The Song Dynasty (960-1279)

Under the Song, China was surrounded by barbarians on all sides, and for three centuries the country turned its attention to its own riches, and studied the attainments of its fantastic heritage. The highest achievements of this period belong to the domains of painting and pottery.

Emperor Hui zong (1082–1135) was a collector, calligrapher, aesthete and painter. His paintings of flowers and birds with their clear outlines and fresh colours set the example for the artists of the Academy which he had reshaped. A court style grew up, which was realist and decorative, completely opposed in spirit to the group research carried out by the scholars of the day. The works of Hui zong give elegant expression to a precise and delicate form of art which combines with the Emperor's supple, light, somewhat feminine calligraphy.

Li Tang (1050–after 1130) retains the monumental style of the
Five Dynasties, but at the same time, instils into his work a
lyricism peculiar to the Southern Song artists. He often uses an
assymetrical composition, attracting the eye to one corner, and
progressing by successive disconnected steps. The rocks drawn
by facets and the violence of the strokes accentuate the powerful,
vertical rhythm, constantly broken by water.

Mi Fu (1051–1107), a great calligrapher, took up painting at
the end of his life, and used his experience as a calligrapher to
help him portray nature. He managed to convey the feeling of
the mountains and water of Jiang nan (a region south of the
Yang zi) by building up his landscapes with dots suggesting
mountains, and the trees and woods clinging to their slopes. His
son Mi You ren carried on in the same style (makemono in the
Imperial Palace Museum in Peking). Both painters were influenced by Dong Yuan, but their technique shows progress towards
evanescence: they have retained nothing more than the clouds
from the damp landscape portrayed by Dong Yuan.

Far away from the romanticism which reigned at the court of
Hang zhou in the 12th century, with its painters like Ma Yuan
(see scroll depicting waves, Imperial Palace Museum at Peking)
and Xia Gui, the painters living in the retirement of the Chan
Buddhist monasteries developed a spontaneous and independent
style of their own. Two great painters gave expression to the
spiritual experiences of this sect, at the end of the Southern Song
dynasty. Liang Kai (c. 1140–1210), who deserted the Hang zhou
academy, created an expressive, abstract style. His imaginary
portrait of Li Tai bo evokes the proud silhouette of the Tang
poet in a few rapid, decisive strokes and contrasts in ink. This
art of portraying the essential, making no concessions and
with no unnecessary repetition, attains completeness straight
away (National Museum, Tokyo).

Mu Qi, who lived in retirement in a hermitage near Hang zhou
(active c. 1240–1270), looked tenderly on the world. His favourite
themes are simple ones: persimmons, boats coming back to the
village, or a monkey and its young crouching on a gnarled pine
branch.

Like the painting of the time, Song pottery evokes a refined
civilisation of dilettantes, feeding on its own dreams. Its technical
perfection, improved by faster methods for turning and better
control of firing, will never be equalled. The preparation was
still empiric at times, and accidents in its making or firing give a
peculiar, mysterious charm to some pieces. The shapes are sober
and pure: bowls, cups, jugs, narrow-necked bottles known as

mei ping. Flowers, birds, fish are incised or moulded under the monochrome glaze. Sometimes the tonalities of the material and its velvety touch replace all ornamentation.

Several famous kilns existed at this time, some of which, like the ones at Ding zhou (He bei) were placed under the direct patronage of the Song emperors. Ding ware has a translucent, close-grained white body, covered with an ivory-coloured glaze; the naked rim is bound by a metal band, and the décor incised under the glaze is inspired by free floral compositions as found in paintings. A group of fine white porcelain ware resembles Ding in shape and décor: Ying qing or Qing bai (bluish white). The walls are thin, the glaze bluish in colour, and the décor is moulded or incised.

Under the Northern Song, celadon ware with an olive-green glaze decorated with a cut out pattern of foliage and flowers, was produced at Ru zhou (He nan). The kilns there worked for the court from 1107 to 1127; they then produced pink stoneware with a thick, finely crackled glaze, ranging from bluish grey to lavender blue. The shapes are extremely pure, and the beauty of these rare pieces lies in the material, so pleasing to the touch, with its deep, delicate and mysterious colour tones. Other pieces from the north include Jun ware, stoneware with a lavender-blue glaze, sometimes plain, sometimes splashed with purple, guan ware, heavy pieces again of a lavender blue, with a more coarsely crackled glaze, and Ge ware, which is greyish white, with a crackled glaze.

Yue celadon ware was made in Zhe jiang as before, but the kilns at Long quan, in the south of the province, became more important. They produced pottery of a brighter green than the Yue ware, which was exported all over Asia and as far as Europe.

The Jian ning district in Fu jian produced tea bowls with a dark stoneware body and shining brown glaze with metallic reflections. These bowls, with a mottled pattern known as "hare's fur" were extremely popular among Japanese collectors at the time; their Japanese name is "temmoku".

The Song scholar, who was sensitive to the power of the brush and to the delicacy of porcelain, was passionately interested in the past. Emperor Hui zong himself set the example, for he had excavations carried out at An yang and collected old bronzes and jade ware. The craftsmen took up old themes again, without always understanding the original meaning, and the minor arts (bronze, jade) suffered from this. The art of lacquer ware developed considerably, however, and several new techniques seem to have been put into use, particularly one in which the décor is cut out of thick layers of lacquer, a process which is at the origin of the so-called Peking lacquer ware.

The Yuan Dynasty (1280-1367)

Hang zhou fell to the Mongols in 1276 and for the first time, the whole of China was taken by the invader.

A few scholars went over to the new regime. The most famous of these was Zhao Meng fu (1254-1322), who agreed to serve Khubilai Khan in 1286 and held several different administrative posts. He was an excellent calligrapher and landscape painter; his pictures of horses are the best known of his works.

Painters living and working far from the Mongol court, such as Qian Xuan (1235-c. 1290), who painted flowers, birds and insects, kept the style of the Academy going.

The greatest painter of the period is perhaps Ni Zan (1301-1374), a solitary, bohemian soul of great sensitivity. His bare landscapes are usually small; his favourite themes are a few slender trees, a kiosk perched on a rocky shore, or a stretch of water with naked hills in the distance. His dry, sloping brush heightens the effect of the terse strokes by giving full play to the background of white; the empty spaces take on meaning, and seem to be bathed in calm, transparent light.

Huang Gong wang (1269-1354) who with Ni Zan, Wang Meng and Wu Zhen belonged to the group of landscape painters who retired to South China, bases his work on the rich, detailed compositions and solid structures of the 10th century painters. His free technique consists in using short, horizontal strokes, flattening the tree-tops, simplifying architectural details and stressing the rhythm of the steep mountainsides.

Most of the Song pottery kilns went on working under the reign of the Yuan, and exports rose, both to Persia and Indo-China and India. Cobalt blue, imported from Persia, probably appeared in China in the 13th century. The technique used to produce this new type of pottery with a blue décor under the glaze progressed, and the result was pieces with complex patterns using dragons, phoenixes and floral designs.

The Ming Dynasty (1368-1643)

The new Chinese dynasty which took the name of Ming wanted to carry on the tradition of the Tang. The third Emperor, Yong le (1403-1424) established his capital at Peking, embellishing the town with palaces, marble terraces, viewpoints and gardens.

Painting was still a privilege reserved to a few. Some of these, like Shen Zhou (1427–1509), founder of the Su zhou school (Jiang su) were amateurs for whom painting was an expression of their personality. The main characteristic of their eclectic style is perfection of technique and a combination of brush and ink which has affinities with poetry and calligraphy. Shen Zhou uses a wide, sloping brush for contours and vegetation which he conveys by spots of different sizes. His ink, sometimes silvery-grey, sometimes shiny black, enhances the light and shade effects.

Wen Zheng ming (1470–1559), the most gifted of Shen Zhou's pupils, devoted himself to painting, literature and calligraphy. Towards the end of his life, he returned to the austerity of the Yuan masters and painted gnarled old trees with their roots gripping the rocks. The drawing is clean, often brushed on with dry ink. The trunks and boughs of the trees, drawn with a double outline, stand out in white against the mottled, darker background of their leaves (Imperial Palace Museum, Peking).

Dai Jin (active between 1430 and 1450) gave expression to another characteristic of Ming painting: interest for all the different aspects of human activity. His works (Imperial Palace Museum, Peking) show a taste for narrative, and a subtle knowledge of wash tints.

At the end of the 14th century and in the 15th century, the minor arts went through a period of renewal which extended to the field of creative inspiration and that of working precious materials. The cloisonné enamel ware made in the 15th century is decorated with lotus leaves and cloud borders in turquoise blue, lapis-lazuli, dark red, white, yellow and dark green. The shapes (incense-burners...) show that they were pieces intended for religious purposes. Carved lacquer ware, which first appeared under the Song, attained a rare peak of perfection. The wooden body of each article was covered with layer after layer of lacquer, coloured with cinnabar. The successive layers produced a smooth, close-grained material, ready for the sculptor's chisel. The basis of the décor was formed by a layer of yellow lacquer usually worked in a floral pattern. The design is broad and vigorous, full of careful details, and the material is of exceptionally high quality.

Lacquer was also used to cover valuable furniture. Cupboards and trunks were engraved and the incisions were filled with red, black or brown lacquer. The principal elements of this rich, yet soberly elegant design were lozenges, swastikas, imperial five-clawed dragons, *shou*, the character for longevity, mountains and waves.

Pottery gained from this development of craftsmanship in art as well. The use of cobalt blue, which had appeared under the Yuan, gave birth to the "blue and white" designs. This delicate technique was increasingly fashionable. The most perfect blue and white pieces were perhaps those produced during the Xuan de period (1426–1435). The shapes are pure, the porcelain of fine quality and the blue is applied in mottled washes.

Ming potters combined under-glaze blue with coloured enamel. The *wu cai* or "five colours" pieces, which used more than five colours in fact, heralded the "famille verte" creations of the end of the 18th century. Iron red, brown and pale green combine with blue under the glaze. The round, robust shapes show an anxiety for stability characteristic of the Ming.

Stoneware with lead glazes, known as *san cai* or "three colours" often has a raised floral décor. The colours: dark blue, turquoise, aubergine and opaque white, are separated by incisions into the surface or by raised threads of clay.

A group of very fine blue and white pieces appeared during the so-called "transition period" at the end of the Ming, made, no doubt, in a private kiln. The shapes were new, the clay fine, and the different tones of blue beautifully luminous. Instead of the floral patterns or dragons used in preceding centuries, the décor consisted of landscapes, historical or legendary scenes, everyday objects, or gardens which combined with rigid leaves surrounding the neck of the vase. These pieces were exported to Europe in large quantities, and there they inspired the "Chinese" designs made in the Delft, Nevers, and Rouen potteries, among others.

The Qing Dynasty (1644–1911)

The Manchu managed to maintain their power in China for nearly three centuries; their dynastic name was Qing. Three great rulers followed each other from the second half of the 17th century to the end of the 18th century: Kang xi (1662–1722), Yong zheng (1723–1735) and Qian long (1736–1796).

The Imperial Palace in Peking, created by Yong le from 1409 to 1424 was burned when the Ming dynasty fell in 1644. The Manchu emperors restored and enlarged it. They had summer palaces built north-west of Peking, surrounded by gardens, water and pavilions, all showing a taste for over-ornamentation. Qian long restored the altar of Heaven, which Yong le had had built to the south-west of Peking. It contains five altars and palaces altogether. The Temple of Heaven stands on a triple marble terrace, with eight flights of steps leading up to it. The brilliant whiteness of the three horizontal terraces balance the building, which is red, with a blue tiled roof. Three rows of cylindrical pillars form the framework of the building, and hold up the three parts of the roof, a monumental framework of considerable daring. The beams and brackets are painted in blue, green, white and gold, on a red background.

The Qing period was the age of great encyclopedias, literary collections, of a taste for archaeology and compilations. Consequently many of the painters continued the ideals adopted by late Ming scholars, who were imbued with tradition. The four masters called Wang directed their energies to studying and copying old models, and acquiring technical perfection; Wang Hui was the most eclectic of them and Wang Yuan qi the most original. Wang Yuan qi (1632–1718) painted landscapes in which light colours add roundness and depth to different aspects of nature. His solid compositions have both grandeur and spontaneity.

Wang Hui (1632–1717) also worked at the court of Kang xi. His perfect technique, his delicate use of the brush, and the freshness of his colour notations constitute the chief charm of his works; he draws inspiration from the style of an old master.

Isolated artists carried on more personal work alongside these orthodox painters. Hong Ren (died 1663) became a Buddhist monk when the Ming dynasty fell. The genius of Ni Zan can be found perpetuated in his stark landscapes, in his dry ink techniques and in the luminosity and nobility of his compositions.

At the same time, two individualists retired to live in solitude, and showed their contempt for foreign rule and the eclectic research carried out by official painters. Shi tao (1630–c. 1707), who had retired to a Buddhist monastery, claimed complete freedom for the artist. He produced large, violent compositions, with strong contrasts, but alongside them, he also painted albums of sketches. Here free strokes of liquid ink were used, enhanced by transparent coulours among which green predominated. The veiled distances and thick shadows of the fore-ground, the atmosphere of heat which emanates from them, both reveal a convincing, overall understanding of nature (Shanghai Museum).

Ba da shan ren (1626–c. 1705) was also a Buddhist monk, who painted landscapes and animals with equal spontaneity. He uses a wide or contracted brush, with dry or free-flowing ink like a dialogue in vigorous, rapid and witty sketches.

Under the reign of Kang xi, the minor arts went through a last period of harmony before being spoiled by virtuosity and exaggerated ornamentation in the 18th and 19th centuries. Lacquer, incrusted with mother-of-pearl, metal, semi-precious stones, or sprinkled with gold or silver, was the chief ornament used in the elegant, simple furniture made at that time.

The Qing potters had reached such a high standard of technical perfection that they were able to invent new sorts of decoration, and monstrous products of virtuosity, at the same time. A highly developed system of division of labour, and the fact that the Imperial Potteries at Jing de zhen (Jiang xi), created under the Ming, were placed under the control of a director and the Academy of Painting, combined to stifle all personal initiative in the craftsmen, and eliminate all chances of any renewal taking place in the art of pottery making. The taste for archaism, and orders from the West, hurried the decline of pottery in the 18th century.

Under the reign of Kang xi, large amounts of pottery were produced, including blue and white, and plain colours with monochrome glazes or with glazes of a deeper colour. The main innovation was the "famille verte". The blue under-glaze was replaced by purplish-blue enamel. The range of enamel colours was enlarged by several tones of green, often iridescent. The décors were infinitely varied, and took their inspiration from the theatre, history, painting and silks.

The "family verte" enamels were used on un-glazed pieces, producing a more muted tone-range, in imitation of the Ming *san cai* (three colours). On some vases, the green, yellow, aubergine and white enamel stands out against a dark green background, so dark that is almost black. The black vases have a rich floral décor which combine with the vigorous curve of the vase.

The more powerful shapes grew lighter and slighter under the reigns of Yong zheng and Qian long. The "famille verte" and its brilliant colours gave way to the "famille rose" range, dominated by a pink based on gold chloride imported from the West. Although the ware made for export was characterised by overcomplicated design and clashing colours, the imperial porcelain, which was highly vitrified and translucent, retained all its freshness and charm. The floral designs, used assymetrically, still kept their full symbolic meanings: a branch of a peach-tree, the symbol of longevity, is linked, for example, with bats, the symbol of happiness. These delicate pieces of porcelain are the last balanced creations of the Chinese pottery kilns. Under Qian long and in the 19th century, the complicated shapes and countless ornaments lacking all harmony give clear proof of the decadence of taste in general, which left no field of art untouched.

Chinese Painting from 1850 to 1950

Three currents are apparent in the painting of this period: a traditional current, a current which might be described as a synthesis, and a current of renewal within the framework of purely Chinese painting, represented by Qi Bai shi.

The traditional current can be felt from the middle of the 19th century. The landscapes, flower and bird paintings carry on the experiments made by independent painters at the end of the 18th century, or try to discern the spirit of the old masters through the works of scholars of the 17th and 18th centuries.

Zhao Ji qian belonged to this current in the 19th century (1825–1884); he was a famous flower painter. His contemporary, the monk Xu gu (1824–1896), a specialist in flower and animal paintings, belonged to it too. Ni Mo geng (1853–1919) and Yao Meng fu (1876–1930), gifted exponents of every type of painting, remained loyal to old teachings, with their painstaking technique. Wu Jin nong (1848–1903) falls into the same category.

Ren Bo nian (1840–1896) is considered one of the important figures of 19th century Chinese painting. His varied talent is shown to its best advantage in his paintings of people. He combines acute powers of observation with an accurate, vigorous use of the brush in rapid strokes, using abundant ink.

The last member of this group, Huang Bin hong (1863–1954) was a teacher, art historian and landscape painter.

Numerous centres of painting were founded after the 1911 revolution. At the same time, the Imperial Palace at Peking was transformed into a museum and its collections made accessible to the public. Painters went abroad to study, some to Japan, some to Europe. Some brought back a taste for research into modern methods and for oil painting. Others wanted to renew national art by using Western elements, anxious to introduce realism, but retaining their respect for traditional principles at the same time. Gao Jian fu (1879–1951) belongs to this group; he studied art in Tokyo and then founded the Ling an school. His work is outstanding for its decorative realism, in which the search for colour plays a leading part. Zhen Shi zheng (1876–1923) also studied European art, but his work remained stamped with the spirit of Chinese classical painting.

Xu Bei hong (1895–1953) went to France to study painting in 1918. When he returned to China, he founded the "Central

Fine Arts Society" of Nanking in 1929. His horses combine an acute sense of movement with a firm brush and a terse, evocative stylisation.

Qi Bai shi (1863–1957) represents the third current. Born in Hu nan, he was a painter, a poet and an engraver. He was originally influenced by the innovations introduced by an 18th century painter called Li shan, and managed to create a profoundly original style, free of all convention, and yet closely linked with traditional painting. He is at his best when painting flowers and animals. His shrimps and fish reveal the painter's love for the humblest things in creation. His originality lies in the daring composition, with its intersecting lines, and in the richness of his brushwork. One of the most profound charms of his paintings is to be found in the luminosity of the splashes of colour, particularly carmine.

Part II

I. Architecture

General Principles

Every building in China is considered as an integral part of the countryside surrounding it. The architect takes the site into consideration as well; a much closer relationship exists between the architecture and the natural context than in Europe. Taking this as the basic principle, the architect plans his building on a north-south axis. The chief buildings lie one behind the other along the axis, separated by courtyards which are themselves flanked by buildings of minor importance to the east and west. The courtyard is the unit of construction; this is true for towns, palaces, temples and private houses.

The fundamental elements of this style of architecture are simple: a stone or brick terrace carries wooden pillars on stone bases. The pillars are attached to each other in both directions by beams which are let into them. The roof framework consists of beams of diminishing lengths placed one above the other, with the purlins placed at the end of them. This system allowed for great liberty in roof design. The outer walls and inner dividing walls have no structural function, but are merely screen walls. The most important elements in buildings of this kind are the terrace and the roof; the building itself is of wood, supported by pillars, or walls.

Another characteristic of Chinese architecture is that it lays particular stress on the roof, by means of the cantilever brackets used to support the overhanging eaves. The roof, its eaves and brackets, developed under the Tang and Song dynasties. Roof shapes were at their most varied and complex at that point. Later on, under the Ming, the overhang became less pronounced, and the system of brackets took on a purely decorative rôle (for example: the halls in the Imperial Palace and the gate towers in Peking).

The tiles covering the roofs were alternately concave and convex. On ordinary buildings, the tiles are only slightly fired, and are grey, whereas on important buildings they are coloured and glazed (yellow, blue or green). Terra-cotta figurines and ornaments called *kui long zi* decorated the ridges and ribs of the roof, which ended in dragons' heads.

Town Planning

Town life set the Chinese apart very early on from the other peoples (nomads or mountain peoples) who also lived on Chinese territory.

The basic principles of a Chinese town are: 1. the surrounding wall; 2. the axis and the symmetry; 3. the orientation, from south to north. Chinese towns have always been built after the manner of a former model, and consequently their unity is due to the traditional system on which their plan is based. Another source of unity lies in the fact that the whole town, not only a few buildings in it, was conceived as a monument. The heart of the town was not a centre from which everything fanned outwards, but a long progression along a fixed axis with elements arranged on either side of it: the axis in Peking, for instance, begins at Yong ding men to the south, and progresses northwards through Tian an men, Coal Hill, and ends at the Bell Tower, with the most important buildings in the capital arranged round it.

The Development of the Chinese Town

The Shang town, which was usually built near a water course, was above all a palace with a rammed earth wall all round it. The town was small. A market-place lay north of the prince's residence, and south of it were districts inhabited by craftsmen who worked for the nobility, bailiffs, scribes and diviners. This principle, attested by the Zhou li, of building the imperial palace so that it faced south and turned its back on the market was to influence all the capitals throughout Chinese history (except for

Chang an, built under the Tang, which was governed by questions of topography and water).

During the Warring States period, the city-palace, which in the old days had been the military, political and religious centre, underwent a transformation. The towns enlarged their ramparts as their population grew. An urban class of free-lance craftsmen and small tradesmen appeared. The development resulted in the highly organised urban system of the Han. The towns were surrounded by walls with gates on each of the four sides; inside, they were divided into several districts separated by streets or avenues. Each district, containing about a hundred houses, was also walled, with one gate opening into it. Little streets led to the doors of the houses from the single gate. All the gates were guarded and closed at night. The administrative centres were in the middle of the town; one district was reserved for the market place, with the merchants and craftsmen living nearby, while the farmers were grouped round the town gates.

This system of confining people to one district made supervision and recruitment easier.

The system became more flexible under the Tang. Each district had four gates leading into it, making communications much easier. The town grew larger still. Luo yang covered an area of 19 square miles under the Tang. These enormous towns with their broad avenues (the widest thoroughfares in Chang an were nearly 500 feet across, and the streets measured 140 feet) enclosed areas which were more or less empty: they were used for fields, parade grounds or polo fields, monasteries, or parks belonging to the nobility.

At the same time, the temporary markets, held at crossroads, grew more and more important, until they formed permanent towns, and developed into the new business towns (without walls round each district) which appeared under the Song. The formation of the great modern Song cities resulted from a combination of new features (pressure exerted by the barbarians, progress in agricultural and maritime techniques, the introduction of the monetary economy) which were to transform the economic life of the country, and consequently change the appearance of the Chinese towns: population density, growth of markets and suburban districts, the formation of trade corporations or guilds, development of trade and local crafts and of distribution, growth of the entertainment industry (cabarets, restaurants, theatres...); all of these factors were linked with the development of the urban working class.

These characteristics carried on throughout the dynasties which followed without any major changes. The arrangement of the Ming towns, the best example of which is probably Peking, is based on the old town planning traditions adapted to suit new economic conditions.

At this point a few elements should be mentioned, whose origins go back a long way, but whose present shape dates from the Ming and the Qing. The most important of these are the Drum and Bell Towers. They are two or three storey buildings, whose principal storey has a balcony running round it, overhanging the rest, and supported by cantilever brackets. The Drum Tower at Xi an (early Ming) is one of the finest of its kind.

The gates of Peking, and those of most of the large towns of North China are built in early Ming style. They consist of two towers: the outer one is of bare bricks, with battered walls pierced by four rows of square loop-holes, built on a wide base. The inner tower stands on the ramparts and is built in the style of a large pavilion with two or three roofs placed one above the other, and galleries running round the two main floors. Long sloping ramps lead up to the terrace.

Private Architecture and Gardens

From ancient times, private houses, like palaces, have consisted of a walled enclosure with one courtyard or more flanked by buildings.

The Han terra-cotta models yield information on country houses above all. Most of them had two stories with a walled courtyard, and the owner lived on the upper storey. Some models show fortified dwellings with walls and watch-towers at the corners. The house with more than one storey appears to have been common under the Han, and it has become widespread in Central and South China; single storey houses are the rule in the North. The traditional plan is similar in both cases. The main door is made in two halves and painted red; inside it, a brick screen, *ying bi* or *zhao bi*, protects the house from evil spirits. The spirit screens are often decorated with terra-cotta bas-relief carvings (which are coloured and glazed in large houses or important buildings, like the Nine Dragon Wall at the Bei hai in Peking). Another doorway behind the screen leads into the courtyard-garden flanked by the main building which contains the reception rooms. Covered ways link the other buildings. The central courtyard lies beyond the main building, with rooms on

Cross-section of a *dian*, showing framework and cantilever **brackets.**

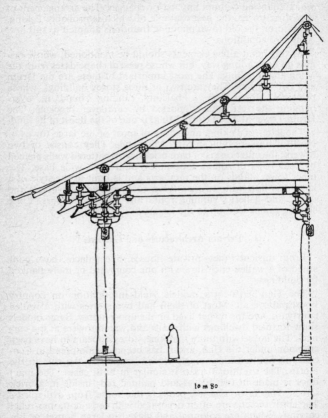

10 m 80

either side of it, and the rooms belonging to the master of the
house at the far end. Finally, the kitchens and the servants'
quarters give on to the courtyard behind that. This lay-out may
be doubled or tripled or varied according to the rank and wealth
of the owner.

All the pavilions are made of wood; the type most often found is the *dian*, a rectangular pavilion as a rule, divided by cylindrical pillars into three or more bays running crosswise. The lighting comes from the facade. The most magnificent example of this type is the *Tai huo dian* in the Imperial Palace in Peking. When the base of the building is a high one, it is known as a *tai*, a smaller pavilion than the *dian;* it often has two stories and may look like a tower. A pavilion with several stories is called *lou*, an open kiosk is a *ting;* the *lang* is the covered way, open on both sides, linking two pavilions.

These are the main elements of the Chinese house (or palace). The fairly strict conventions governing it are based on light, symmetry and straight lines.

The Chinese garden was the natural extension of the rooms; unlike the house, it was full of irregularities, asymmetry, curves, mystery, originality and imitation of nature. The garden was a work of imagination; it was created by and for an individual, and copied a walk in a much larger landscape, staying closer to nature than a Western garden.

Like the landscape painting *(shan shui)* to which it was closely linked, the essential elements of the garden were water and mountains. Added to this were trees and flowers, garden architecture, winding paths, walls, bridges and balustrades. Paths and stretches of water gave movement and variety, while mountains, buildings, plants and trees, gave roundness, light and shade.

Another characteristic feature of the Chinese garden is that no one point gives an overall view of the garden. It is made up of more or less isolated sections which have to be discovered gradually. As the composition is never entirely revealed, it retains some of the charm of the unknown.

The variety among Chinese gardens is due to differences in climate, vegetation and place. A Su zhou garden cannot resemble one in Peking. City gardens are different from gardens in the country, or mountains retreats as illustrated by the painters. The rocks used show profound interest in the beauty of minerals. From the Song dynasty onwards, people began to collect stones with strange shapes. They are generally placed so that they stand out against a white-washed wall, or are framed in the opening (shaped like a vase, a gourd, a petal or a full moon) of a window or a door in the white wall.

Funerary Architecture

Durable materials were reserved in China for utilitarian pieces of work (ramparts, terraces, bridges), a few religious buildings and for the resting-places of the dead.

Graves began to be elaborate as early on as the Shang era. The tomb, built of rammed earth, was usually rectangular. A sloping passage-way led from the surface down into the funeral chamber; the coffin was placed in the middle, surrounded by platforms where the funerary objects and sacrificial victims were arranged. The royal tombs dating from the end of the Shang era, such as the one excavated at Wu guan cun (An yang, He nan), which is 147 feet long, had two passages (one at each end of the short sides).

From the Han era onwards, the funerary chamber was surmounted by a tumulus with a way leading up to it (*shen dao* or way of souls) lined with a double row of statues, steles and pillars. The inner chamber was large or small, depending on the wealth of the family, but the general plan was always the same and continued so through the centuries, as did the strict observation of the laws of *feng shui* which determined the exact placing of the tomb. The tombs of the Ming and Qing emperors were built in the same tradition; the only variations are to be found in the dimensions, the buildings in honour of the dead, and the ornamental details added to stress the monumental air of the whole.

The *pai lou* comes into the category of buildings in honour of the dead; it was a memorial or honorary building, standing at the entrance to tombs, temples and some public buildings. Inscriptions were placed on the lintel of the central opening. It usually had three or five openings. The white marble *pai lou* standing in front of tombs and imperial sanctuaries often had uprights with winglike projections at the top, carved with clouds, a theme which also appears on the columns known as *hua biao* standing in front of palaces.

Religious Architecture

The pagoda, based on the Indian stupa and a Chinese pavilion with several stories *(lou)*, is supposed to house Buddhist relics or to mark the site of a holy place.

The oldest Chinese pagoda is the one at the Song yue temple on the Song shan (He nan). It is said to have been built in about 523, and is an octagonal brick pagoda. Large wooden pagodas were being built in China at that time, but no wooden buildings dating from the Six Dynasties or the Tang have survived. One example in Japan, the Hôryûji Temple near Nara, and an engraving of a pavilion on the lintel of one of the doors of the Da yan ta at Xi an, give an idea of what the architecture of that period must have been like.

Brick and wooden pagodas exist, such as the Rui guang si and the Bei si da ta at Su zhou. They are octagonal towers with a brick core; the brackets, roofs and balustrades are of wood, giving them a lighter appearance and making them resemble wooden pagodas fairly closely.

One of the chief types of old brick pagodas is the square brick tower with corbels of thin bricks dividing it into stories. The most famous example of this kind is the Da yan ta at Xi an (Shân xi), which was founded in 652 and partly rebuilt in 701. The pagoda now consists of seven stories standing on a terrace 15 feet high. Each storey has a wide cornice with six to eight layers of corbelled bricks. The walls consists of a main body of rammed earth faced with lightly fired yellowish bricks; they have no ornaments apart from slender pillars, arranged ten, eight, six and four to each storey, and an arched opening on each side.

The Xiao yan ta (707–709) is also at Xi an; it too is built on a square plan and originally had fifteen stories. Another example of the Tang type is the pagoda attached to the Bai ma si Temple, near Luo yang, which was built in 1175. It has a square plan, and its thirteen stories have brick cornices.

Octagonal pagodas, more or less conical in shape, appeared from the Five Dynasties period onwards, and under the Song. The octagonal brick pagodas at Su zhou (the Hu qiu pagoda) and Hang zhou date from this period. The Tie ta Pagoda at Kai feng belongs to this type as well (963–967).

Under the Song, external ornaments consisting of terra cotta figures and foliage were extremely important. In the case of the octagonal pagodas with their numerous false stories to be found in North China, the lower part is decorated with large bas-relief carvings of human figures; two pagodas in Peking are examples of this: the Tian ning si Pagoda and the Zu shou si Pagoda (Ba li zhuang). The former dates from the Liao, the latter from the Yuan.

No new shapes were invented under the Ming; they merely tended to become more monumental in character. Under the first Qing emperors, a special shape came into fashion: the Indian dagoba, or bottle-shaped pagoda mounted on a high cube-shaped base. Several instances of this exist at Peking: the Bai ta at the Miao ying si, built entirely in brick, the white

pagoda in the Bei hai, built in 1652, and the pagodas at the Bi yun
si and the Huang si, both in white marble.

Stone was often preferred to brick as a building material
for pagodas in South China. The stone pagodas, which are
imitations of wooden buildings, are particularly interesting
for their sculpture: three 10th century octagonal pagodas at
the Ling yin si at Hang zhou and at the Qi xia si at Nanking
are decorated with high relief carvings and mouldings.

No temples or monasteries earlier than the Ming era survive
today, except for a few buildings at the Fo guang si near the
Wu tai shan (Shan xi). Even the ones which were founded under
the Tang were rebuilt several times over. Their characteristics,
as far as lay-out and construction are concerned, are those
of Chinese architecture in general. Ming and Qing architects
often did no more than copy traditional shapes, reserving their
creative energies for ornaments, and in some cases, overdoing
the decorations. A few extremely fine groups of buildings
appeared, however, such as the Temple of Heaven in Peking,
begun in the 15th century, and used for imperial sacrifices

II. Buddhist Sculpture

The Mahayana or Greater Vehicle form of Buddhism began
to gain a foothold in China in the 2nd century A.D., brought
in by the caravans using the Silk Route. This origin explains
the influence of the Greco-Buddhist art of Gandhara, clearly
discernible in some of the earliest representations of the Buddha
in China; the same influence was felt throughout North India,
from the Punjab to Sogdiana. The earliest example of Buddhist
sculpture, a gilded bronze Buddha dating from 338, shows
clear traces of this influence. He is portrayed sitting cross-
legged in a position of meditation, on a pedestal, with the
Buddha's round chignon on the crown of his head. His monk's
clothing is arranged in rounded, regular and symmetric folds,
reflecting the Gandhara style.

The first great artistic centre of Chinese Buddhism appeared
at Dun huang (Gan su) in the 4th century. The new religion
did not triumph until the following century, however; at the
same time, Chinese craftsmen abandoned their foreign models.

For three centuries, Buddhist sculpture dominated artistic
creation as a whole, using mainly stone or bronze, and sometimes
clay or wood. The designs, symbols, ritual and Buddhist
attributes originated in India, and gradually changed once
introduced into China.

In Chinese sculpture, the Buddha is portrayed either standing or sitting on a lotus throne, or guarded by a pair of lions. When he is shown standing, the Buddha has one hand raised, with the palm turned outwards (freedom from fear or *abhaya mudra*), while the other hand is left pendent (giving or *varada mudra*). When he is seated, the ritual gestures are more varied: his hands may be joined together in meditation *(dyhana mudra)*, or one hand may be raised with the index finger touching the thumb, in the "discussion" position *(vitarka mudra)*. Both hands raised to the breast, one turned outwards, the other towards the body, with the fingers pretending to turn a little wheel, represent the Wheel of the Law *(dharma-cakra mudra)*. Finally, the *bhumisparsa mudra* is the "earth-touching" position, by which he calls the earth to witness his resistance to the temptation of Mara.

Bodhisattvas, merciful beings who renounce Nirvana in order to help men to wait for deliverance, are even more common than portrayals of the Buddha in Chinese iconography. They are shown wearing princes' clothing, with diadems on their heads. They gradually become transformed into a feminine deity, known as Guan yin. From the Song dynasty onwards, she is depicted sitting on a rock amidst waves (she helps those who cross the ocean of changes). She is also shown with several pairs of arms and with nine to eleven heads.

The Development of Buddhist Sculpture

During the Six Dynasties Period, the development is to be seen in the folds, the plasticity and the facial expressions.

The first phase, which corresponds to the Northern Wei, witnessed the growth of a Chinese style from the Indian models (Gandhara and Mathura style). The Northern Wei style was put into action in the Yun gang Caves (Shan xi), which were cut out of soft sandstone, from 460 onwards. The first caves (nos. 16 to 20) shows the eclectism of the art when it began; the great Buddha in cave 19 with his scarf with rounded folds recalls the colossal Buddhas at Bamiyan (Afghanistan). The one in cave 20 suggests the Mathura type (heavy folds of clothing leave the shoulder bare). The Chinese element is present in the halo with its design of flames and Buddhas in relief. The fusion of Chinese aesthetics and foreign themes can be seen in the rounded niches (the blind arcade used in Gandhara transferred to China), in the ornamental motives, where acanthus foliage is used alongside curtains held back by beading, and in the Chinese style roofs.

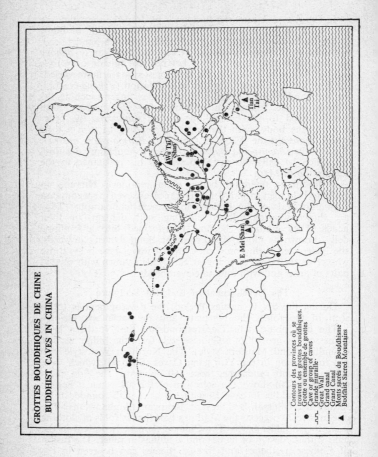

GROTTES BOUDDHIQUES DE CHINE
BUDDHIST CAVES IN CHINA

Tian Tai

Wu Tai Shan

E Mei Shan

Contours des provinces où se
trouvent des grottes bouddhiques.
Grotte ou ensemble de grottes
Cave or group of caves
Grande muraille.
Great Wall
Grand canal
Grand Canal
Monts sacrés du Bouddhisme
Buddhist Sacred Mountains

The human figures at Yun gang are fairly thin and flattened;
their faces are rectangular, rather flat, with pointed noses,
and mouths which turn up at the corners in an archaic smile
which is still relatively impersonal.

The imitation of Greco-Buddhist clothing reduced to folds ending in points resulted in the angular style which was the dominant feature of the sculpture at Long men, in He nan. The Long men shrines were founded in 494. The niches at Gu yang dong, where the same sharp style prevails, were cut from 508–515. The Buddha's face becomes thinner, the bodies grow longer and flatter under the mass of tubular folds of clothing. This alongated, sharp style resulted in a flamboyant type, when applied to gilded bronze sculpture, which was conceived symmetrically round a medial axis; the delicate folds take on the shape of wings, with a flexible rhythm and sense of line which are entirely Chinese in inspiration. A feeling of pure spirituality emanates from the long-necked, emaciated faces at Long men, corresponding to a stricter conception of religion, in which mystic thought was stripped of everything irrelevant.

The Shi gu si carvings at Gong xian were also begun at the end of the Northern Wei; they were continued after 534, and work went on there until the Sui dynasty. Large numbers of steles were carved at this time as well, sometimes with human figures on them, sometimes with niches containing Buddhas framed by bas-relief carvings of figures or ornamental motives.

From 536, the activity at Long men slowed down, and this lasted throughout the 6th century. From 534, a reaction occurred against the vertical lines which limited the portrayal of the human body in the angular style. At Yun gang and Long men, the arrangement of the clothing was far more important than the body beneath it, and the facial expression more important still. The composition was built up like a pyramid crowned with a head. New ideas appeared, bringing with them a search for greater suppleness, and a tendency towards plasticity and massiveness, all of which dominated the years from 534 to 550, a transitional period heralding the rich Bei qi era (550–577).

The second half of the 6th century was in fact an era of renewal. The new art of statuary was developed in the Tian long shan Caves (Shan xi); from 560–570 onwards, the Bei qi had about twenty large caves hollowed out (see caves 1, 2, 3, 10 and 16). The main features of the Bei qi style as far as clothing is concerned are the use of the scarf and the development of the drapery spreading to cover the pedestal in the case of seated statues. Plain folds with horizontal lines are softened to curves. The weight and suppleness of the fabric itself is conveyed (statues in cave 16 at Tian long shan). The folds follow the lines of the body and come into their own as they hang over the pedestal, where the gathering effect seems to be concentrated. Jewellery takes on great importance, thanks to Central Asian influence. Ideas from Central Asia, combined with others bringing the Gupta style from India, transformed the portrayal of Bodhisattvas, who are shown decked in jewellery, their clothing vanishing under chain ornaments caught by a wide buckle at the waist. The effort to attain more convincing roundness in the carving foreshadows the plasticity in the 7th century statues. Traces of *déhanchement*, which like the *drapé mouillé*, came from Indian Gupta style, are already to be found on a few bas-relief carvings. Finally, in caves 10 and 16 at Tian long shan, the statues, although meant to be seen from the front, stand out from the wall, foreshadowing the technique of volume and movement used under the Tang. The Bei qi replaced the vertical tension of the Wei by fullness. Supple clothing reveals the curves of the bodies; from 540, the faces are rounder and softer; the drawing of the lips, nose and eye-brows often shows that an effort was made to achieve some sort of individuality. The faces, although less spiritual, become more human.

Buddhist art produced still more under the Sui; gilded bronze statues for private altars appeared in large quantities. A still greater effort towards plasticity can be felt in the statues; the generous clothing with its broad vertical folds stresses the nobility of these deities, whose bearing suggests pillars.

Under the Tang, production was greatest and the artistic level highest between 627 and 712; from the middle of the 8th century, a decline set in.

The rulers still contributed monuments to Long men, and the huge Buddha there was completed in 676. The mystic gentleness of the Wei faces gives way to calm majesty and a condescending air which has something of the Emperor himself.

The pedestal, which is partly covered with long folds of drapery, takes on a new importance. The tendencies which developed during the second half of the 6th century come into their own at this point in a tense and supple technique, which is to be found above all in the portrayal of the Bodhisattvas. A tall head-dress, making the figures appear more feminine, replaces the traditional diadem. The upper part of the body is naked, with a small jewelled chain, and a narrow scarf round the shoulders. The clothing falls over the legs in a *drapé mouillé* from a slender, well-accentuated waist. A fairly large head and short neck convey an impression of power. The feeling for power is illustrated by the Dvârapâla, or guardians who are always to be found in pairs at the entrance to the shrines, as protectors against evil influences. Their terrifying faces, taut muscles and defiant attitudes testify to the interest in the study of the human body and the sense of realism which characterised the Tang.

The technique of clay sculpture reached its peak at this time too. This type of statuary, characteristic of the caves at Dun huang and Mai ji shan, in Gan su, developed in these places from the 5th century onwards, and followed the same development as stone carving, though retaining some local differences which have not been adequately studied as yet. With the end of the Tang dynasty, this technique (which was used at Dun huang until the Qing and at Mai ji shan until the Ming) fell into a gradual decay, like the rest of Chinese sculpture. The craftsmen still used Tang examples as their models, but the religious fervour evaporated and the style grew heavier. Under the Song, however, some statues of Guan yin, in painted wood, retain a certain supple grace and a calm expression under the high elaborate head-dresses.

III. Ritual Bronzes (shapes and designs used)

The art of bronze casting may have been a local invention, or it may have been introduced into China from the steppes at the beginning of the second millenium B.C.; whatever the case may be, the art was at its height under the Shang dynasty (c. 17th–11th century B.C.). The technical perfection, balanced proportions and elaborate designs of these vessels place them along the finest examples of metal work in the world.

The Shang bronze workers used moulds made in two parts for simple objects (knives, arrow-heads); the ones used for casting hollow vessels were made up of several pieces, held together by tenons and mortises. As time went on, both techniques improved in skill and accuracy.

When the Shang civilisation was at its height, between the 14th and 11th centuries B.C., vessels were made in different shapes to fulfil different functions:

1) Some were used for offerings of meat and grain: the *ding* or cauldron with solid legs, the *li*, a three-legged vessel with hollow legs, the *xian* or *yan*, vessels with a perforated base which rested on a tripod, the *gui*, which was a bowl mounted on a base, and the *dou*, a bowl with a stem and a lid. 2) Others were used for drink-offerings: the *zun*, which is round or square, the *gu*, a chalice-shaped wine beaker, the *you*, a globe-shaped vessel with a lid and an arched handle, the *hu*, or bottle, the *jue*, a

SHAPES OF ANCIENT BRONZES

HU

GU

ZUN

LEI

LI

JIA

JUE

HUANG

DING

GUI

YOU

FU

XU

PAN

ZHI

CLOCHE ZHONG

YI

drinking cup mounted on three legs with tapering ends, and two mushroom-shaped projections mounted on the rim, one on each side, the *jia*, a round three-legged vessel with mushroom-shaped projections, the *huang* (or *guang*) shaped like a jug with a lid in the shape of an animal's head, the *lei*, a globular vessel, and the *zhi*.

Under the western Zhou, from the 10th century onwards, some shapes disappeared or were transformed (*jue, gu, zhi, jia*). The legs of the *ding* gradually curved inwards, and had a definite curve to them by the 8th century. The bulge of the *gui* became more pronounced, the opening smaller, and the base square. New shapes appeared, such as the *xu*, a food vessel, the *pan*, used for water (a shallow bowl mounted on a rounded foot) and the *yi*, a vessel mounted on four feet, whose spout often has an animal's head as an ornament, and the sets of bells, *bian zhong*.

The most common shapes in the 6th century, during the Spring and Autumn period (*chun qiu*), were the *lu*, the *zun*, the *jian* (a bowl) and a rectangular vessel, the *fu*, with a cover in four pieces; the *ding* was also still in use.

These precious vessels, used when sacrifices were made to the ancestors or to natural deities, all had a magic meaning. The designs, based on a few fundamental motives, are infinitely varied. Fantastic animals haunt the vessels, and particularly a mask with round staring eyes, no lower jaw, and a cow's horns. This animal, known as a *tao tie*, which is sometimes highly stylised, sometimes naturalistic, is probably the representation of a sorcerer's mask. Other animals are portrayed as well: snakes, dragons, which are either stretched out full length or curled up, elephants, tigers, owls, crested birds, cicadas (often surrounded by a triangular frame), fish, tortoises and silk-worms.

Geometrical patterns are used alongside these animals, which are themselves used both as a main feature of the design and as an element in it: circles, spirals (*lei wen*, or thunder motive), wavy lines, lozenge shapes, all belonging to a highly inventive, though strict system.

The full symbolic meaning of these patterns is unknown; they are still shrouded in mystery. The popularity of hunting under the Shang, attested by short inscriptions engraved on some bronzes, may partly explain the rich animal designs, which are sometimes accompanied by human figures.

IV. Calligraphy and Painting (basic principles and technique). The Chinese Script

The Chinese script probably came into being at the beginning of the second millenium B.C. Excavations have shown that writing was used as early as the ancient period of the Shang dynasty. The script was pictographic to start with, and developed fairly rapidly into an ideographic writing. From the 14th to 11th centuries it was already stylised and abounded in abstract forms and characters made up of a combination of simpler signs. The Shang divinatory texts deal with sacrificial ceremonies, natural phenomena, military expeditions, the ruler's private affairs (hunting, travelling, etc...). The texts were written from the top downwards and from right to left; they were outlined on the bone with a brush first of all, and then incised more deeply into it, so that documents could be kept for a considerable time. Modern knowledge of archaic script is increased by inscriptions found on the bronze ritual vessels; under the Zhou, they were more numerous and longer. The Shang style is usually pointed and lacking in fixed standards, whereas under the Western Zhou it tended to become rounder, and the parallel lines were respected. From the 8th century onwards, it becomes more delicate, freer and less constricted.

Ancient writing earlier than the 3rd century B.C. are known as *gu wen;* the *da zhuan* or great curly script, used on the Zhou bronzes, was simplified and made uniform; the result was *xiao zhuan* or small curly script, which developed at the beginning of the Qin dynasty. Another step was taken towards simplification when the *li* script, used by clerks, was invented, also under the Qin, known as *li shu.* "Official" writing, or *kai shu,* was evolved from this clerical script; the oldest existing examples date from the Wei, and the script developed under the Jin. *Xing shu* or moving writing appeared under the Later Han. Both scripts were used for inscriptions on steles during the centuries which followed. The Han period also saw the origin of *cao shu* or cursive writing, which was rapid, and used at first for making rough copies.

For centuries, wooden and bamboo slips were the most widely used writing materials in China. Even after the invention of paper in the second century A.D., wood and bamboo were used alongside it for three centuries. Bamboo slips dating from the Warring States period have been found at Chang sha (Hu nan). They are inscribed with characters written in black ink, dating from the 4th century B.C. The Ju yan site, in north-west China has yielded the largest number of Han wooden slips. Some of them are bound together to form a book: the oldest Chinese book in existence (93-95 A.D.). Slips bound to form a book could take on two forms; they were either rolled or folded one on top of each other accordeon-wise. They were bound with strings of silk, hemp or leather.

Silk seems to have been used for writing as early as the 7th or 6th century B.C. It appears to have been reserved for extremely important or religious documents during the Warring States period. It was put to a much wider use under the Han, as it was easier to carry about than the slips; it was used for letters, illustrations and maps. Books made of silk were probably in the shape of scrolls.

Paper is traditionally held to have been invented in 105 A.D. by Cai Lun. Fragments of paper have in fact been found, made of vegetable fibres, and dating from the end of the Western and the beginning of the Eastern Han. Cai Lun made a synthesis of all previous experiments. The new material was made chiefly of hemp and rags. It rapidly improved and spread throughout the country by the end of the 2nd century A.D.

The brush has a long history, as it was already in use under the Shang. A brush made of bamboo and goats' hair, dating from the Warring States period, was found at Chang sha, Hu nan. In the 3rd century B.C., Meng Tian improved the brush, probably replacing the bamboo by wood, and the rabbits' hair by deer hair.

Such are the materials used for Chinese calligraphy, and later on for wash tints. Ink was made of soot mixed with resin, dried and made into sticks. It was crushed on to the ink-stone, which had been dampened to receive it. The tone of the ink, ranging from deepest black to silvery grey, depends on the amount of water used.

Spontaneity was the guiding principle when the art of calligraphy was born. "The calligrapher, impelled by creative power, naturally transmits the breath of life into his writing". Every character written must above all be natural and vigorous. Several great calligraphers lived from the 3rd to the 6th century A.D. Su jing, under the Western Jin, was the forerunner of the northern school with its strong, concise characters whereas Wang Xi zhi (303-361) and his son Wang Xian zhi (344-388), who lived under the Eastern Jin, were the creators of a school stressing grace and elegance.

At this time, calligraphy was considered as a way of communicating the ineffable through symbols, and of giving material reality to individual reactions and emotion. Art and magic were one and the same for the masters, constituting a life which was mobile, elaborate and yet so vigorous that it influenced Chinese aesthetics all the way through its history.

The Tang calligraphers continued the traditions of the northern school. The best representatives of it are Yan Zhen qing (708-784), Liu Gong quan (778-865) and Chu Sui liang (596-658). Their style is above all sober, solid and full of inner vigour. Zhang Xu (died in 740), a friend of the poet Du Fu and a specialist in the art of *cao shu*, created a style of his own known as "mad" *cao*.

The Song calligraphers were in search of elegance; they aimed at a synthesis of the styles of the two Wang (Wang Xi zhi and Wang Xian zhi) and Yan Zhen qing. The greatest of them were Su Dong po (1036-1101), Mi Fu (1051-1107) and Huang Ting jian (1047-1105), as well as Emperor Hui zong (1082-1135). Numerous works on the principles and methods of calligraphy appeared at this time.

The influence of Wang Xi zhi was even greater under the Yuan dynasty; his work inspired the painter and calligrapher, Zhao Meng fu (1254-1322), through the great calligrapher Sui Yu Shi nan (558-638). On the other hand, Xian Yu shu puts all the energy of the Tang into his characters. Under the Ming, Xing Tong, Wen Zheng ming (1470-1559) and Dong Qi chang (1555-1636) re-introduced the ancient calligraphy of the northern school. This renaissance continued under the Qing, with masters like Wu Wei ye (17th century) and Liu Yong (18th century).

Painting

The relationship between calligraphy and painting is obvious, first of all in the technique: both arts use the same materials (paper or silk, brush and ink). Both of them require a similar apprenticeship and skill. The aims and effects produced are similar: a flowing line, the importance of the stroke or dot, infinite variations achieved through combining the intensity of the ink, the speed of the stroke and the suppleness of the brush.

Chinese paintings exist in three forms: vertical paintings (kakemono) intended to be hung, horizontal scrolls (makemono) or, on a much smaller scale, paintings intended for albums or fans. The makemono is unrolled from right to left, introducing an element which is peculiar to it alone: progression in time. The theme develops and unfolds like music or poetry; the spectator moves forward in the painting as it gradually unrolls.

These works, painted on paper or silk, are never put permanently on show; they are kept in wooden boxes or brocade bags, to be looked at on suitable occasions.

The Western geometric perspective is unknown. Each part is considered from the viewpoint which sets it off to the best advantage. The spectator is not left outside the painting, but invited into it as though it were a living, changing landscape. The painter uses an aerial view to render perspective and distance, softening the washes and eliminating details as things fade into the background.

Ink, with its wealth of shades ranging from light grey to black, conveys the modulations in values better than any colour. Colours may be used, however, to heighten the effect of the painting; they are applied flat, rarely mixed, and made of mineral or vegetable substances, with water or glue added.

The brush-work defines the artist's style, revealing his personality and mastery of his subjects. Each stroke is rapid, allowing for no second thoughts, and may be long or short, supple or tense, summary or descriptive.

Nature inspires most of the works. Man is not excluded from them, but he is modestly made to take his place in the general scheme of things. This concept, typical of Chinese landscape painting, indicates a vision which is directly opposed to the European approach, with its landscapes adapted to fit in with the human scale. What is more, Chinese painters never used models for their painting; their works are the product of a lucid visual memory combined with an elaborate technique.

Two attitudes to painting appeared in the Six Dynasties period. The first considered painting as the creation of images, a way of understanding and interpreting the phenomena of nature. The second held that the artist became involved emotionally with the subject which he painted. In fact, the two conceptions are inseparable. The artist can express his personal vision and understanding of the world by the way in which he translates his visual impressions into pictures. The idea of communion between the artist and his subject perhaps gave rise to the painting of landscapes entirely for themselves which appeared under the Tang. At that time, brush techniques which had up till then been used in calligraphy only were introduced into painting, because they were suitable for painting too, and because they rendered the artist's temperament. This stylistic development probably contributed to the evolution of painting by scholars *(wen ren hua)*. The theory was formulated at the end of the 11th and beginning of the 12th centuries by

a group of artists and critics whose central figure was Su
Dong po (1036-1101). The fundamental idea was that a painting
reflects the nature of the artist, as well as the sentiments and
humours which he experienced as he painted. A noble painting
implies a noble artist. Painting became a way of conveying the
true nature of a great man, and thus contributed to the spiritual
enrichment of those who looked at it. The art of painting was
a way to improve and refine oneself; it used all a man's powers
in a desire for liberation, and was itself pure liberty. In the ideal
creative act, the painter creates as Heaven creates, with no
preconceived ideas; the inner quality of creative activity is
perfect spontaneity. This contains traces of Taoist teaching
and of the practice of emptiness in Chan meditation, perhaps,
as well. The love of simplicity and gentleness, the horror of
showiness were the chief characteristics of these scholar-painters
who considered that perfection of self and a knowledge of
classical culture were the best assets of technical skill. Their
art was completely devoid of all motives of interest, for painting
was not their profession. Nearly all of them were officials in
the Emperor's service. They lived in the true sense of the word
when they laid aside their worries, took up their brushes and
painted for their own pleasure and for those who understood
them, in a society closed to all vulgar elements, given over to the
worship of beauty.

The great achievement of painters of ink washes was their
ability to throw light on inner qualities by creating a living,
moving scene, full of light, around them. Faced with nature's
perpetual transformations, they did not attempt to crystallise
the fleeting aspect of things, but to touch on the guiding principle
which made them what they were. The vocation of painting
was to establish direct contact and by means of art to unveil
the reality which lies beyond the realm of speech.

Rubbings and Prints

Although the oldest existing documents mentioning rubbings
date from the beginning of the 6th century A.D., the technique
is traditionally supposed to date from the 2nd century A.D.

The most common method used to obtain a rubbing is as
follows: a sheet of tough white paper is cut to the size of the
area to be reproduced and lightly damped. It is then applied
to the surface and worked into place with a leather-covered
mallet or a hard brush. Once it is dry, thick ink is a applied to
it, using a wad of wool wrapped in silk. When the ink is dry,
the paper is peeled off.

This technique, which was widely used under the Tang, enables inscriptions or engravings on stone to be reproduced on paper. The oldest surviving specimens come from Dun huang (Gan su). As time went on, the methods used and the effects obtained were perfected and varied; rubbings were considered as works of art, and mounted on scrolls, panels, in books or albums.

The oldest example of a wood-cut is an illustration in a *sutra*, dated 868 and found at Dun huang. Figurative engravings dating from the 10th century have also been found at Dun huang. They are little Buddhist pictures printed in black and often coloured with a brush. Engraving seems to have been used for religious purposes at first. It was used fairly early on for illustrations to canonical books, or historical or literary works. From the 17th century onwards, engravings were used to reproduce pictures from private collections, either separately or collected in an album.

Coloured prints were coloured by hand at first. Towards the end of the 16th century, when colour printing existed in one colour only, experiments were made with the use of several coloured blocks. Colouring by hand and colour printing were often combined in the same print.

The collection known as the "Studio of the Ten Bamboos" seems to have been begun in 1619. It is an album of flowers, fruit, bamboos, stones, birds, etc. compiled by a group of artists to please people of good taste. As well as this collection, Hu Yue cong, the engraver, brought out the collection of the "Ten Bamboos Writing Paper" in 1644; the one surviving copy has been beautifully reproduced by the People's Republic of China. Other 17th century prints depict birds, branches of flowers, sometimes in a vase or else in a basket, and a scholar's equipment. The delicate outlines are printed in black; the colours are fresh, some of them printed and shading off, others added afterwards by hand. Some details, such as flower petals, are embossed.

The Mustard Seed Garden, the first part of which appeared in 1679, is a course in drawing. The second and third parts, which appeared in 1701, contain the last good Chinese coloured prints.

V. Music

Musical Theory

The set of chromatic intervals, called the twelve *liu*, which were invented, based on the first, the *huang zhong*, have no musical meaning on their own. A few of them have to be picked out to form a melodic progression.

The scales are based on rising progressions of fifths, starting from the *huang zhong* (the equivalent of F). Four progressions of fifths give five notes: F (*gong*: palace), G (*shang*: deliberation), A (*jiao*: horn), C (*zhi*: manifestation), D (*yu*: wings). These five notes placed in their positions in the octave form the first pentatonic scale. The five intervals of this, the first scale, gave five modes:

gong mode: F G A C D
shang mode: G A C D F
jiao mode: A C D F G
zhi mode: C D F G A
yu mode: D F G A C

The intervals in the arrangement of the notes in each mode differ from one to another; each of the twelve *liu*, giving the absolute pitch, can be used as the first note of one of the modes. The 12 *liu* combined with the 5 modes produce sixty different tones. Then two extra notes were added to the pentatonic scale, and were designated by referring them to the note immediately above them: *bian zhi* (altered or flattened *zhi*) and *bian gong* (altered or flattened *gong*). These two complementary intervals were used as passing notes in Chinese music.

Temperament

The twelve tempered *liu* were invented under the Ming and officially adopted in 1596, a century before the adoption of the tempered chromatic scale in Europe (c. 1700).

Musical Notation

In the old days, music was often taught orally, and handed down from one generation to another. The oldest Chinese musical notation in existence dates from the 8th century. It consists of small characters giving the abbreviated forms of the names of the *liu*, with no indication of measure. Popular notation is mentioned for the first time in the work *Meng qi bi tan*, which dates from the 11th century. Except for a few improvements, it has been retained as it was in scores of songs and popular music.

Musical Instruments

Stringed Instruments: the *qin*, the *se*, the *zheng* and the *pi pa* are all instruments which are plucked, whereas the *hu qin* and its variations are the only ones played with a bow.

The *qin:* a seven-stringed lute, and one of the oldest instruments. It looks like a flat, narrow wooden box, about 4 feet long, covered with black lacquer, with seven silk strings.

The *se* and the *zheng:* different varieties of the *qin.* They had different numbers of strings from one period to another. The *se* has from 16 to 50 strings, and the *zheng* from 13 to 16. A little bridge under each string regulates its pitch. The *zheng* is popular today.

The *pi pa,* which was introduced from abroad, was in use under the Qin. It is a wooden instrument about 3 feet long, not unlike the guitar.

The *hu qin* (foreign lute) is better known by its other name: Chinese violin. Several varieties exist: the *er hu* has two strings, the *si hu* has four; the *jing hu* is a small, shrill violin which accompanies Peking opera, and there exists yet another kind, the *ban hu.*

Wind Instruments: four instruments are made of bamboo: the *chi,* the *di,* the *xiao* and the *sheng.*

The transversal flute, which used to have five holes, is called *chi.* The *xiao,* another type of flute, played like a recorder, has a much sweeter sound. The *sheng* or mouth organ is an instrument composed of 13 or 17 little bamboo pipes, with reeds at the lower end, fixed in a sort of holder made of a gourd or of wood; it has a mouthpiece for blowing through, and the pipes are pierced with holes to be stopped by the fingers of both hands.

Two other instruments are made of wood: the *guan* and the *suo na.*

The *guan* is an instrument with a double reed; it is a pipe with 8 or 9 holes.

The *suo na* or Chinese oboe also has a double reed.

Percussion Instruments, which exist in great variety, are made of bronze, jade or wood, and play an important part in ritual music, as well as in popular music.

The single bronze bell is known as *bo zhong. Bian zhong* are sets of bells, usually numbering 16 and each giving a different note, hanging in a heavy wooden frame.

The *luo* and *bo* are known as gong and cymbals respectively in Europe.

The *te qing, bian qing* and *fang xiang* are made of jade. The *te qing* is single stone, shaped like a right angle, while *bian qing* are usually in sets of 16, hanging in a wooden frame. *Fang xiang*, a variety of *bian qing*, are rectangular.

The wooden instruments supply the rhythm: *po ban* (strips of wood which are hit) mark the strong rhythms, and the *mu yu*, of Buddhist origin, is used in popular music.

The drum, *gu*, is made in different shapes and materials.

VI. POTTERY (MATERIALS AND TECHNIQUES)

The term "pottery" covers everything made by craftsmen who work with clay, from earthenware to porcelain. The Chinese have been masters in this field since the Neolithic age. Their technical achievements, the skill and variety of their inventions have never been equalled.

The Chinese craftsman was familiar with stoneware, produced by firing clay at a high temperature, making it vitrify and rendering it impermeable, at a very early date, as well as with earthenware fired at a relatively low temperature. Porcelain is a variety of stoneware, vitrified so that it is translucent, made of a refractory clay called kaolin, which becomes white at about 1350ºC. This clay is mixed with a fusible white stone, petuntse, which, like it, is based on feldspath.

Slip is thin clay used either to mask the colour or imperfections of the body, or to act as a background for a painted design; glazes often cover the slip.

Treatment of the Surface

Low-fired lead-silicate glazes, based on silica (sand or quartz) and a fusing element (soda, potash or lead oxide) are coloured with metal oxides: copper (giving green or turquoise), cobalt (blue), antimony (yellow), manganese (purple). They are applied to earthenware (in the case of Han and Tang pottery, for instance) or to biscuit-ware (from the Ming onwards).

High-fired glazes, based on highly refined petuntse mixed with a fusing element (potash and lime), and let down with water, are applied to porcelain ware. Their composition is similar to that of the bodies on which they are used, they are fired at a high temperature at the same time, and they mingle with the body. As they are fired at a high temperature, the colouring matter used is limited to iron oxides (which give the range of celadons if fired in a reducing atmosphere), copper and cobalt oxides. The effects produced are infinitely varied, depending on the conditions of firing. The glaze is often crackled, which was originally due to accidents in the firing, and then achieved deliberately by using the right proportions of ingredients such as pegmatite, or by rapid cooling processes.

Enamel is a vitrified product, with a composition similar to that of lead glazes, but more fusible. It is achieved at a low temperature (800° C.), and is suitable for designs painted on a glaze which has already been fired. It appeared under the Song, and gave rise to the Ming "five colours" *(wu cai)*, and to the "famille verte" and the "famille rose" made under the Qing. Porcelain decorated with an under-glaze design using high temperature colours is fired once only, whereas porcelain with a design painted on to the glaze in enamel is fired a second time. Biscuit-ware also has to be fired twice in the case of pieces which have been fired unglazed, then glazed or painted with enamel, and fired once more at a low temperature or at a reduced high temperature.

Shapes of kilns and methods of firing (in a reducing or oxidising atmosphere) vary considerably.

Decor

Chinese craftsmen used coloured or painted decors, or decors in the body itself.

The designs applied directly to the body itself included engravings, incisions and incrustations, impressions made with baskets or fabrics. Decorations in relief have always been used, either by applying more clay, or by using slip in thicker layers, resulting in the open work which needed considerable skill (white porcelain, "three colours", made under the Ming). The latter technique was greatly used in the 18th century, alongside the "rice grain" technique, which consisted in making small oval perforations which formed a regular translucent pattern once the glaze had been applied.

The coloured decors included the marbled effects obtained by the juxtaposition of pugged clay and coloured coatings (glazes of both kinds, and enamel). Polychrome effects are obtained either by working on the unstable quality of the glazes, or by dividing them off from each other (Tang pottery, Ming "three colours", biscuit-ware).

Mingled tones or decorative marks in the glazes are achieved by variations in the composition or density, or by using special methods for firing (partial oxidisation, rapid cooling); the lavender-coloured *jun* splashed with purple, the *jian* with a metallic sheen, and the *flambés*, are all achieved like this.

When monochromes are used as a background for painted designs, the reserve process is generally employed: a piece of paper stuck on to the body before it is steeped leaves the surface to be decorated intact.

Painted designs tended to eclipse all other processes from the 14th century onwards. The method was already used under the Song, in the form of black paint applied to white slip and then glazed. Under-glaze painting ("blue and white", "red and white") uses high temperature colours: reds obtained from copper oxide and above all cobalt blues. The colour is applied with a brush directly on to the body before it is fired; the body absorbs it like blotting-paper. Painting on the glaze itself, using enamel, was sometimes combined with under-glaze blue ("five colours", *wu cai*, dating from the Ming, *dou cai*, where the enamel is enclosed within outlines drawn in blue under the glaze). On the other hand, the decor in "famille verte" and "famille rose" ware is painted entirely with enamel.

GLOSSARY (Historical, architectural
and archaeological terms which
have no exact equivalent)

Ban hu	A sort of Chinese violin, whose sounding box is covered with a thin board.
Bi	Flat jade ring found in the tombs of the first dynasties. Symbol of the sky?
Bian qing	*Te qing* hanging on a support.
Bian zhong	Set of hanging bells.
Bo	Cymbals
Bodhisattva	Merciful being who renounces Nirvana of his own accord in order to help men to attain delivrance.
Bo shan lu	Bronze or pottery incense-burner, with a conical lid recalling the Island of the Taoist Immortals.
Bo zhong	Single bell
Cao shu	Running hand script.

Chan	Buddhist sect, the "contemplation" sect (Japanese: Zen).
Chi	Transversal flute.
Chi wen (Chi shou)	Architectural term; ornamental pottery figurine placed at each end of the roof ridge.
Chuang	Buddhist pillar, several stories high, covered with inscriptions and bas-relief carvings. Found in temple courtyards.
Chun qiu	Spring and Autumn period, 770-485 B.C.
Dagoba	See *stupa*.
Dagoba	A late form of stupa, usually consisting of three parts: base, curved central part, and a spire surmounted by a metal ornament.
Dian	Hall: part of every Chinese architectural *ensemble;* both temples and palaces usually consist of a series of *dian* arranged on a north-south axis, separated by courtyards. A *dian* is therefore an independent building in itself.
Dvârapâla	(Sanscrit) guardian of the gate.
Er hu	Two-stringed Chinese violin.
Fang xiang	Jade percussion instruments hanging in a frame.
Feng huang	Mythical bird, wrongly assimilated to the phoenix. *Feng* is the male and *huang* the female.
Feng shui	A set of geomantic specifications which used to determine the placing of dwellings, temples and tombs. The direction of the winds *(feng)* and the orientation of water *(shui)* were the main considerations.
Fu	An insignia made in two parts; a figurine whose two halves fit into each other; a superior would give half of it to his subordinate, in token of delegated power, while keeping the other half himself.

Ge	Ancient weapon; a bronze hook mounted on a long handle.
Gu	Drum
Guan	Wooden wind instrument.
Guan	Taoist Monastery
Guan yin	Avalokitesvara (Sanscrit); Buddha of light.
Gui long zi	Architectural term; ornamental pottery figurines found at the end of the ribs of the roof, at the point where they turn upwards at the corners.
Hua biao	A pair of white stone pillars with bas-relief carvings and a wing at the top standing on either side of an alley, or a triumphal way, or an entrance.
Huang zhong	The first of the twelve chromatic intervals in Chinese music.
Hui	Name given to Chinese Moslems from the 13th century onwards, whether they are of Han or Western origin (central Asia, Persia); the Hui are now considered as one of China's minorities.
Hu qin	Chinese violin.
Jia gu wen	Inscription on bone or tortoiseshell; see An yang, p. 823
Jian	Intercolumniation or bay; it means basically the distance between two columns in a building; for instance, a temple facade is said to have 9 *jian*, meaning that it has 10 pillars; it also means the area lying between four columns in a building; in practice it is used as a rough measurement for indicating the area covered by the interior of a building: a "monastery of a hundred *jian*", for example.
Jing hu	Small, shrill violin used in Peking opera.
Kai shu	Official writing.

Kakemono	Scroll design, spirals decorating ancient bronzes.
Ke tou	Prostration which used to be performed as a mark of respect to a superior, in a kneeling position with the forehead touching the ground.
Lang	Covered way, open on both sides, joining two pavilions.
Lei wen	Thunder design, spirals decorating ancient bronzes.
Lian	Toilet box made of bronze or pottery, cylindrical in shape and supported by three crouching bears.
Li shu	Clerical script
Liu	Chromatic interval in Chinese music.
Liu li wa (zhuan)	Glazed tile (or brick).
Lou	Pavilion with two stories or more.
Luo	Gong.
Mahâyâna	(Sanscrit) Buddhism of the Greater Vehicle
Makemono	Scroll painting to be hung vertically.
Mâra (Sanscrit)	Demon which tried to tempt the Buddha before his Illumination.
Mei ping	Narrow-necked bottle made to take one branch of plum blossom.
Miao	Temple: used for the temple of the ancestors the temple of Confucius (e.g. Kong miao, Wen miao); also used for other temples, either Lamaist (La ma miao) or others (Guan di miao.)
Miao hui	Fair held in a temple courtyard.
Ming qi	Wooden, metal or pottery substitutes for the sacrificial victims.

Mudrâ	(Sanscrit) ritual gesture (Buddhism)
Mu yu	Wooden percussion instrument used by Buddhists, in the shape of a bell; they exist in different sizes; they are hit with a hammer.
Nan bei chao	Northern and Southern Dynasty, 420–589 A.D.
Nian hao	Dynastic year period, see p. 330.
Ni ren	Pottery figurine; see Tian jin, p. 655
Pai lou	Archway or portico: a sort of triumphal arch with 3 or 5 arches, made of stone or wood.
Pi pa	Stringed instrument, played by plucking.
Po ban	Wooden boards, designed to be hit.
Qi lin	Mythical beast, wrongly assimilated to the unicorn. *Qi* is the male and *lin* the female.
Qin	Seven-stringed lute.
Qi wen	Roof motive.
Ru yi	An object which brought good luck; it was long and slightly curved, often carved out of ivory or jade. The name means "in accordance with (one's) wishes".
San cai	"Three colours" technique for decorating stoneware.
San guo	The Three Kingdoms period, 220–280 A.D.
Se	Stringed instrument, played by plucking.
Shan shui	«Mountains and waters»; landscape painting.
Sheng	Mouth organ.
Si	Buddhist monastery; in some cases it also means mosque (e.g.: Qing Zhen si, Li bai si).

Si hu	Four-stringed Chinese violin
Stupa	Reliquary; a Buddhist monument of Indian origin, to house relics of the Buddha.
Suo na	Chinese oboe.
Sutra	Buddhist canon.
Tai	Pavilion with two stories resting on a high base.
Tai ping	Name given to the large-scale rebellion which broke out in Guang xi in 1851 and nearly overthrew the Manchu dynasty. Tai ping ("Great Peace") was the name which the leaders of the rebellion had chosen for the dynastic year period.
Tanka	Vertical scroll of painting, depicting deities from the Lamaist pantheon, in Tibetan tradition.
Tao tie	Glutton; the name of a legendary figure banished by the mythical emperor Shun; a mythical beast consisting of a head without a body; a design which appears on Shang bronzes (an animal's face with no lower jaw).
Te qing	Jade percussion instrument
Ting	Small open kiosk.
Wen ren hua	Painting by a scholar.
Wu cai	"Five colours" technique for decorating porcelain.
Xiao	Flute played like recorder.
Xing gong	Palace used for short stays; a temporary residence where the emperor stayed when travelling, often built near a temple.
Xing shu	Moving script.

Yin and yang	Two fundamental concepts of Chinese thought, which are opposites, and yet complement each other at the same time. See Philosophy and Religion, p. 131.
Ying bi or Zhao bi	Screen wall; wall built in front of or behind an entrance so as to hide the interior.
Yong	Tomb figurine; made in wood *(mu yong)* or pottery *(tao yong)*, representing people or animals; it used to be buried with the dead person.
Zao jing	Architectural term; it is used to indicate a type of decorated ceiling, either carved in stone (in Buddhist caves) or made of painted wood (in temples or palaces). In the second case, it can be translated by "coffered ceiling".
Zhan guo	The Warring States period, 485–221 B.C.
Zheng	Stringed instrument, played by plucking.
Zhuan shu	Curly script.
Zong	Cylinder set in a tube, usually of jade, symbolising the earth.

THE ECONOMY

The economy, its structure and its development, occupy a vital position in Chinese politics and are of the utmost importance for the future.

The aim of the country's leaders is to transform it from the poor, backward country which it remained until well into the 20th century into a modern and powerful nation.

To achieve this, they rely on the adaptability of a people which already has a magnificent civilisation behind it, and on the efficiency of an ideology which they think capable of bringing about a radical change in mankind and instituting a new social order.

The new regime has obtained impressive results and the production figures, in so far as they can be found out or guessed at, illustrate the progress made. But as Chairman Mao himself has said, "the country is still poor", the standard of living low, and formidable obstacles lie in the way of rapid improvement. The difficulties which need to be solved are on a scale corresponding to the vast country. However, the efforts made so far, particularly those aimed at spreading education and modern technical skills among a people unusually well-prepared to accept and cultivate them, have already resulted in astonishing progress and give promise of future success. As the Chinese repeat constantly to their foreign visitors, progress has been made, but much has still to be done and several decades will have to pass before the country can "catch up with the industrialised countries" which have been expanding continuously for the last twenty years.

Even if the results are inadequate, as the Chinese leaders themselves say, compared with the large tasks which still remain to be completed, it should not be forgotten that everything accomplished so far is the product of a very few years, and that since 1960, China has been entirely independent of foreign help, both financial and technical. Furthermore, the Chinese leaders probably want to be judged for the moment on the originality and value of their experiment rather than on results in terms of figures. A study of the Chinese economy should therefore give pride of place to the economic system and structure set up by the Communist regime.

The Vicissitudes of the Economic Policy

Since 1949, the Chinese economic policy has gone through many ups and downs, which fall in with the doctrine of the

Party stating that progress should be carried out in a "succession of waves". For the first three years of the new regime, the aim was to re-build the economy. Industrial production, which in 1949 was only 56% of the highest figure reached before that date, had caught up again, generally speaking, after three years.

The Chinese leaders then launched out on a planning policy. The first five-year plan, published in 1955 only, covered the years from 1953–1957. It was drawn up on the same lines as the Soviet plans, giving priority to heavy industry. Help given by the U.S.S.R., which was free only as far as the engineering and know-how were concerned, was the determining factor in the completion of the plan, as the Soviet Government granted credit facilities and also sent thousands of experts and technicians to China between 1950 and 1960. As well as this, Chinese students were sent in large numbers to be educated in the U.S.S.R. and other socialist countries.

Almost all heavy industry was socialised over this period, and agricultural workers were grouped into socialist co-operatives, where private ownership of land was abolished, and peasants retained no more than their houses and the plots close by them.

The Great Leap Forward, inaugurated in 1958, was an attempt, unlike any other in the history of developing countries, to reach a higher rate of growth than any so far recorded in the whole world, and to begin the building of a wholly communist society. After giving rise to the publication of exaggerated production figures which were admitted to be false even by the Chinese themselves later on, the Great Leap, which had originally benefited from exceptionally good harvests, stopped short and resulted in serious disturbances in the country's economy. It was an important factor in the ideological differences between China and the U.S.S.R., as the Soviet Union had questioned the heterodoxy of the whole plan from the beginning.

Some positive results of the Great Leap remained, however: large-scale collective work had been carried out in the countryside and numbers of factories were begun thanks to the mobilisation of the energy of a whole people. An experiment such as that of the blast-furnaces in the country districts had at least the merit of making millions of peasants familiar with industrial techniques, even if the products themselves were often unusable.

The Chinese economy, however, affected by the departure of the Soviet experts and by three bad harvests in a row, due to natural calamities, was disorganised. The attempt to create industry in country areas had led to neglect of agricultural work and a lack of man-power, a strange situation in this country, just when it was needed for the harvest.

The economy had to be put in order. The policy of "re-adjustment" adopted in 1961 was to achieve this.

As they realised that if agriculture were not in a prosperous and stable condition, the growth of the economy as a whole would be at the mercy of climatic hazards, the leaders announced that agriculture should be given priority over light industry, and light industry was to have priority over heavy industry. As the new watchword said: "agriculture is the basis of the economy and industry the managerial factor". Thirty million town-dwellers left their homes for the country. The percentage of savings compared with the gross national product, which had reached 30%, fell considerably, large-scale investments in industry were suspended and industry was called upon to give priority to agricultural supplies —fertilizers and equipment— which were essential for the advance of agriculture. Instructions given to industrial sectors advocated a policy intended to turn out more diversified products, improve quality and push down manufacturing costs, to comply with the slogan: "quantity, quality, economy, rapidity", instead of making rapid increases in quantity, as the Great Leap had revealed the disadvantages of this.

No more statistics were published in any field whatsoever, and observers were reduced from then on to guessing at pro-duction levels.

At the same time as the economy entered on its phase of re-adjustment, great stress was laid on a new doctrine: self reliance, a convenient though rather brief translation of a phrase meaning "renewal by relying on one's own efforts".

This doctrine, born as it was of the necessity to keep industry going which faced the Chinese after the sudden, mass departure of the Soviet experts, illustrated the Chinese leaders' determination to make their country into a modern power by drawing on its own resources to supply the elements of its pro-gress.

China has now renounced all foreign help; the trade debts to the Soviet Union were paid off in advance in 1964, and al-though she still buys complete factories from abroad, with all the most modern techniques, China has not one foreign expert living permanently on her territory, though a few engineers and technicians come periodically to set up the imported factories and get them going.

At the same time as she rejected all outside help, China extended aid to a growing number of developing countries which had not so far acquired the same advantages in the field of technical and industrial ability. Fulfilling what she considers to be her duty to "proletarian internationalism", China sent experts and financial help to large numbers of African and Asian countries. The modest standard of living of the Chinese experts, and the exceptionally favourable credit conditions with their low terms of interest, combined to make this help thoroughly appreciated in countries where it was directed mainly towards agricultural development and the building of factories.

The Chinese economy was severely dislocated by the Cultural Revolution, although it is hard to say exactly how each particular branch was affected. Industrial production seems to have stagnated from 1966 to 1970. Since then it has picked up again, helped by the discovery of large deposits of oil and natural gas; coal and iron production have increased considerably over the last few years, and in agriculture, harvests have been good, apart from that of 1977 which was affected by drought. New five year plans have taken over from that of 1966-1970, which was never put into action, owing to the circumstances.

Since Mao's death the new leaders have advocated a new economic line based on necessary technical modernization, determination to improve the people's standard of living, increased productivity and recourse to socialist competition; free markets have been allowed, enabling "subsidiary and family activities in the countryside" to become profitable (rather like the Kolkhozian markets in the Soviet Union). Foreign trade is being encouraged, and advanced technology is being bought from the West and Japan. Planning has been reviewed and long term targets fixed for 1985 and 2000. The country has been divided into six large economic regions, each of which has partial autonomy, and the Scientific and Technical Commission, which was suppressed during the Cultural Revolution, has been brought to life again. China seems to be making a new start on the road to development.

**

All Chinese economic policy has to be founded on basic geographical data: the low individual income, the rate of increase of the population and the technical level of the inhabitants, all have to be taken into account as well.

Area and Natural Resources

China covers an area of 3,657,765 square miles; it is larger than the United States, but only a third of the size of the U.S.S.R. 266 million acres of this are under cultivation, amounting to 12% of the total area; this represents 27% of the old China "of the 18 provinces", as it used to be called. A third or half of these lands produce two or even three crops per year.

Differences in climate are considerable, ranging from the Siberian climate in the north to the sub-tropical climate of Hai nan Island, where the oil-palm, rubber, coffee and cocoa are grown. Great varieties of altitude exist as well, as China shares Mount Everest (Mount Zhu mu lang ma) with Nepal. The climate is often extreme; drought and floods can follow on after each other in the same region in a short space of time. Erosion and saline soils present serious problems in certain areas, particularly in the north.

The vast distances and the complicated relief, which meant that the provinces used to be cut off from each other economically, make communications difficult. The railway lines are limited as yet (24,500 miles of track), and many of them are single track; river or canal traffic is heavy, but is confined to a few river basins.

The country possesses abundant natural resources, with considerable reserves for some products, though some essential raw materials are missing or in short supply: nickel, copper, wood and rubber, for instance. Prospecting is going on in many places and many discoveries have no doubt still to be made, as has recently been proved by the discovery of oil in the Northeast, at Da qing.

National Product

Chinese statistics gave the total national product for 1957 as 124 thousand million yuan, or roughly $ 80 per head. In 1966, Western sources extimated that it was roughly $ 150, and $ 300 in 1978.

The yuan is undervalued, however, at least from the point of view of its spending power in terms of basic necessities or services, and the calculation in dollars probably leads to the product per head being under-estimated.

Whatever the case may be, its low price is a serious handicap for China. This will be appreciated when the income per head in the U.S.S.R. in 1928, on the eve of the Five-year Plans period, is compared with that of China: it was three times as high as the figure stated for China in 1952.

Population

The Chinese population may be estimated at 885 million inhabitants (see p. 54) with a margin of error of 20 or 30 million. Two Chinese out of five are under fifteen, and the average expectation of life is sixty... Four fifths of the population live in the countryside, in spite of the vast size of a few cities like Peking (6 million inhabitants), Shanghai (10 million inhabitants) and Tian Jin (Tien Tsin, 4 million inhabitants).

In 1948, Chairman Mao declared that "a large population is a good thing, although it creates difficulties". Since then, the policy of the Chinese Communist Party in this respect has altered several times.

A campaign for the spread of birth control was launched in 1957, led by the Minister of Health, who came straight to the point when he admitted that "with a rate of increase of 2.5%, the country could not overcome poverty". Although no more was heard of this during the Great Leap, when China seemed short of man-power, the aim is now to lower the birth-rate and reduce the increase rate to 1% per year. The justification for this is put less crudely than in 1957, as the main aim is now said to be to make life easier for the mother of the family. The Party encourages young people to marry late, 25 being the right age for a girl and 30 for a man, while a family of not more than 2 or 3 children is the ideal; this policy has apparently met with some success in the towns, but it is extremely difficult to impose it in country areas, among the remaining 80% of the population.

It seems obvious, however, as Professor Ma, Dean of Peking University, wrote in 1957, that economic development will be hampered as long as the increase rate remains as high as it now is. With the low product per head, it represents one of the basic handicaps of the Chinese economy.

Another handicap which China is overcoming with remarkable rapidity is that of backwardness in the technological field and shortage of technicians.

Technical Progress

In 1949, the students in higher educational institutions amounted to a mere 150,000, and only 1,600 qualified engineers were turned out each year; the country as a whole cut a poor figure compared with other nations which base their power on the knowledge and use of modern techniques.

In 30 years, the numbers of engineers and technicians have been rapidly increased, thanks to help from other socialist countries, and latterly as a result of the country's own efforts. Better and still better equipment is now being designed in the research sections and made in the factories. Not a day passes without an announcement in the newspapers to the effect that new material and equipment has been made from Chinese designs by entirely Chinese labour. These successful undertakings, which arouse justifiable pride among the Chinese, are attributed to the joint efforts of the workers, technicians and administrative cadres, and the application of the slogan "three in one". A strong campaign in favour of technical innovations has been launched throughout the country, and the results obtained in the field of industrial production are said to be the consequence of this.

Chinese factories are now capable of producing machinery such as a 12,000 ton hydraulic press, an electric microscope which enlarges 200,000 times, 70,000 kw. turbo-generators, 2,000 h.p. diesel engines, 6,000 kw. gas turbines, electric engines, oscillographs and spectographs, as well as many kinds of measuring apparatus and precision machines. The permanent industrial exhibitions at Shang hai and Shen yang show the progress which has been made, and the standard reached. In fact these successes seem hardly surprising, coming as they do from a people which has a large series of inventions of vital importance to mankind to its credit already, such as printing, the rocket, fire-arms, the magnetic compass, the wheelbarrow, the stirrup, the rudder, deep drilling and the suspension bridge.

Little information is available on the scope of scientific and industrial research and on the financial means at its disposal, but the few scientific institutes and laboratories which foreigners have visited are well equipped and create an excellent impression. They are reported to be using techniques and obtaining results which are remarkable considering that the laboratories are all recent.

China has made no effort to replace the Soviet experts; the country is relying on its own resources to produce the scientists and technicians needed.   Teachers and engineers keep up with scientific and technical developments in the rest of the world by reading foreign publications, as they have few opportunities to travel outside their own country.

As yet only about a million students are enrolled in institutes of higher education—which must be understood in the broadest sense in this country—as many as in Japan, whose population is six or seven times less. The figures are increasing rapidly, however, and the enormous efforts being made at the moment to develop technical ability will, without any doubt, bear fruit very soon.

Financial Policy

The steady continuity of the financial policy stands out in contrast to the changes in the economic policy.

There is probably no other country which is able, as China is, thanks to the political background of the population and the precepts which are taught to it, to carry out as stringent a financial policy, and one which has proved as successful in keeping prices stable and maintaining a currency with such a constant purchasing power.

The Yuan—worth about U.S. $ 0.50—is under-valued from the point of view of its purchasing power in terms of basic necessities. The Chinese government has succeeded in keeping prices stable, in spite of the difficulties in 1959 and 1961 and the general strain which an expanding economy imposes on a currency. It has been able to exercise a strict control of the salaries paid, and therefore of the demand. Basic products are still rationed—cereals, fats, cotton fabrics—as are some industrial products. The cost of all services in a country where manpower is not only plentiful, but competent and skilful as well, is low as a rule.

The Economic System

The Chinese Communist Party, taking as its authority Marxism-Leninism, to which it claims to be more faithful than certain others, has, over the space of a few years, established a socialist system founded on democratic centralisation and on collective property, with as few concessions as possible to private property. The economy is directed by a state Plan, drawn up by the highest political authorities: the State Council, i.e. the government, the Central Committee of the Communist Party, the National Planning Committee, and the National Economic Committee.

The Central Committee lays down the general line and gives the instructions, the Government takes the decisions and the Committees draw up the Plan.

Apart from the Ministries specialised in technical questions and responsible for the chief industrial undertakings, other planning organisms exist at the level of the provinces and municipalities, in charge of local concerns.

As far as the drawing up of the Plan in concerned, it seems at the moment that the production units submit suggestions for production targets and investment forecasts to the upper ranks, and that the latter take them into acount when making their decisions, after some discussion.

The Chinese people, submitted to constant indoctrination which inculcates instructions for building socialism and increasing production, has made determined efforts to overcome the economic and technical handicaps which beset the country at the start. Before making any judgements on the measure of success shown by the results, it is essential to make a short study of the workings of the economic system set up by the Communist regime, particularly the organisation of agriculture and industry.

Agriculture

Organisation

In the China of the years before 1949, two thirds of the land was cultivated by land-owners, middle and rich peasants, while 70% of the agricultural workers had little or no land of their own. The Communists recruited their best troops and most ardent supporters among the latter. Even today, two thirds of the party members are peasants.

The agrarian reform of 1950 began by distributing the big land-owners' lands to the poor peasants. Collectivisation of agriculture was a gradual process, but was carried out more rapidly than in the U.S.S.R., for it was completed by 1958, 9 years after the Communist Party's assumption of power and 9 years before the final date set for completion. The peasants were asked to form into teams based on mutual help in 1951, then into semi-socialist co-operatives from 1953 onwards, and then from 1955, they were told to form a superior type of co-operative to which they contributed by giving their lands, while they were paid according to the work done. As these stages were completed without any serious crises, unlike what happened in the U.S.S.R. from 1928 onwards, the Chinese authorities decided, through the resolution passed at Bei dai he (Pei-ta-ho) on August 24th 1958, and revised by the Wu han resolution passed in December of the same year, to create a new unit of agricultural production: the people's commune, "of grandiose historical significance", "fresh as the rising sun appearing on the vast horizon of east Asia". It was to be the basic unit of social life in all its aspects—economic, cultural, administrative, military—and was the owner of all property, exercised complete power in economic matters and merged with the local administrative division—the *xian*. It was to be the testing-ground for a totally collective life, preparing the way for the development from the socialist system to the Communist system. The experiment was no doubt premature: some of the peasants jibbed at the excessive collectivisation which was extended to every sphere of activity, production suffered and the authorities had to confine their aims to the constituting of units which were allowed a large measure of autonomy in the choice and appointment of their organisation and structures. No uniform model of the commune exists: each one is a particular case and applies the measures which are considered most suitable for its own situation.

When the communes were created, there were 24,000 of them; this figure has risen to 74,000 now, which means that they contain less than 7,000 inhabitants on an average, though the largest have a population of up to 50,000. They retain ownership of industrial establishments and heavy material, and the management of medical and educational services. The basic cells of agrarian collectivisation are the brigade and the team for the moment. These units have most of the equipment at their disposal, are entirely responsible for the book-keeping and deal with most of the organisational difficulties arising out of their work by themselves. The contracts for delivery of agricultural produce to the State commercial organisations are usually negotiated at the team level, as well as those arranging the purchase of industrial products needed for agriculture, supplied by the same organisation. One commune contains about twenty brigades, and a brigade consists of about ten teams. Since 1960, brigades and teams have been allowed to take the initiative more and more often, but it is obvious, however, that the final target is to re-constitute the communes with the characteristics and attributions laid down by the Resolutions taken at Bei dai he and Wu han in 1958.

The collective income of the communes is used to cover taxes, expenses, investments and members' salaries.

Taxation, estimated in 1958 on a contractual income which is lower than the true income, accounts for 7 to 8% of the total revenue at the most. Taxes are usually paid in kind in the form of deliveries to the State commercial organisms.

The investments are financed by a special accumulation fund which varies in size with the results of the harvests. Unlike the industrial production units, whose investments are controlled by the State Plan, the people's communes are allowed to assign their profits to the work of their own choice. The authorities hand out the general directives of the economic policy through the party members in the commune itself. As they are allowed as high a degree of autonomy as this, it is easy to understand how the Chinese peasantry, who have always been forced by natural conditions to help each other out within the villages, find plenty of advantages in the people's commune system, especially as the State helps to finance some large-scale works, particularly in communes where natural conditions are hardest; when communes are hit by natural catastrophes, they are exonerated from taxation.

The funds for salaries, which represent 50 to 60% of the total income, are distributed to the peasants in proportion to the work done. Individual incomes vary according to the amount of work carried out and its quality and also according to the harvest, and therefore partly according to the fertility of the soil. The problem of the difference of income from one commune to another and one team to another is one which worries the authorities considerably; efforts are being made to try to find a solution.

In the communes shown to foreigners, each person who works earns an average income of 300 yuan per year. Payment is made according to various formulae: usually the "work points" are awarded on a system of norms fixed "on a basis of the quantity and quality of work contributed in one day by an average worker with a normal capacity for work". Next the peasants themselves meet, once the day or the task is over, to decide how many work points each completed job deserves.

Part of the income paid to the peasants is in kind, particularly in communes where food crops are produced.

The earnings from the private plot and handicrafts are over and above the income distributed to each family by the commune. The plots, used by each peasant to grow what he wants, represent at most 7% of the cultivated lands of a commune; the size of them, which varies between 78 and 240 square yards, depends on the density of the population. The income earned in this way by each family, mainly from raising pigs or chickens, seems to amount to 10% of the sum distributed by the collectivity on an average. The government encourages handicrafts, which are the peasants' traditional occupation during the dead season; the peasants keep them going, though certain basic work is now required of them, even in winter. These subsidiary activities may be carried out by the peasants individually for their own profit, or on a collective basis by the production brigades and teams.

Studies made in 1957 revealed that the peasants' standard of living was very much lower than that of workers in modern industry. The government policy is however to leave as much as possible of their revenue to the communes and to levy only a light tax; any increase in production, as Chairman Mao himself has stated clearly, should result in an increase in the peasants' income This policy, which is very different from the one adopted by Stalin after 1928, is designed to gain support for the regime from peasants who on the whole led precarious lives before 1949. On the other hand, it does not allow for much money to be collected from revenues from the countryside for use in industrial investment, and the assumption is that the authorities prefer to consolidate the agricultural basis of the country rather than step up the rhythm of industrialisation. The profits from the industries themselves provide most of their investments, for the moment. No doubt the authorities' aim is to claim more from the peasants to finance industrial development, once their incomes are high enough.

Results in Agriculture

Since it occupies over 80% of the population agriculture plays an important part in the country's economy and since 1960 has enjoyed top priority among targets for development. It is interesting to note that this percentage of 80% of the population employed in agriculture is about the same as it was 30 years ago, and that migrations to the towns comparable with those which marked the U.S.S.R. under Stalin have not occurred in China. During the Five-year Plan (1953–1957), in spite of the fact that agriculture was subordinated to industry, it registered considerable progress: 4.5% increase per year.

The chief aim of the Chinese economic policy since 1960 has again been to "consolidate" agriculture to feed a growing population and to stave off the danger of another food shortage like the one experienced during the years between 1959 and 1961, when it was caused by natural calamities.

The policy of importing cereals, begun in 1961, continues: over 2,500,000 tons are imported each year, which is enough grain to feed 30 million people at the present rate of rationing. The Chinese authorities justify this import by their intention of earning the maximum profit from their crops by exporting rice and importing grain, as the price of one ton of rice on the world market is twice that of one ton of wheat. Even so, the sales of Chinese rice abroad are still lower than the wheat purchases.

However skilful and industrious the Chinese peasant may be, the crop yield, depending as it does mainly on night-soil and animal manure for fertilizers, is lower than that of a county like Japan and could still be improved, although it has increased.

All the Chinese territories have not yet been fully developed. The area under cultivation amounts to 266 million acres, or 12% of the total area, which means that the peasants have claimed the most fertile lands, on the plains, neglecting land which could have been transformed into natural prairies.

Agricultural production could be improved in several ways: first of all, through the basic groundwork carried out in the communes, such as building dams and irrigation canals, levelling, afforestation. This lengthy work calls for the mobilisation of the peasant masses, and once completed, it should protect them from natural disasters. The Chinese leaders, unlike the Soviet leaders a few years ago, do not seem to consider the claiming of new land to be the best method of increasing agricultural production. Nevertheless new land is being brought under cultivation, particularly in frontier areas in Xin jiang, Hei long jiang and Hai nan Island, often by using the method of State farms employing ex-soldiers or volunteers from the eastern provinces, particularly Shang hai: 24 million acres have been turned into farming land since 1949.

Cultivation of virgin land calls for large investments, however, and substantial results in the field of increased agricultural production are expected in terms of better yield from land already being worked. The development of irrigation, which includes replacing norias worked by pedals by electric pumps, and the use of insecticides and fertilizers, are some of the chief methods used. Statements made by the Chinese leaders suggest that industries working for agriculture have borne fruit, after considerable effort towards investment: in 1957, not more than 631,000 tons of nitrate fertilizers were produced, whereas in 1965, the total figure for fertilizers of all kinds was 8 million tons. This figure rose to 39 million in 1977, and is still increasing. Thirteen modern fertilizer plants were ordered from Japan and the West in 1978. Mechanization is progressing more slowly. On the other hand, the area under irrigation (55 million hectares, representing half the total area under cultivation) is the largest in the world. 200,000 artesian wells have been dug since 1972. Villages have been moved to hillsides to make land available for cultivation, and even graveyards have been ploughed, making cremation of bodies compulsory from now on.

The regime has pledged itself to give top priority to the modernisation of agriculture, and various methods contribute towards this: the spread of agricultural knowledge and the growing numbers of demonstration farms, the encouragement of new methods introduced by the peasants, the creation of Agricultural Institutes and secondary schools specialising in agriculture, the system of sending officials and engineers from the towns to stay in the country, rivalry between poor and middle peasants—for the introduction of collectivisation has not yet eliminated class distinctions here—and the publicity given to advanced brigades, like the Da zhai brigade, who have worked wonders.

It is doubtful whether the results of an effort like this can be judged straight away, particularly as they become evident only gradually. The lack of all statistics over the last few years does not simplify the task. The most important datum in agricultural affairs is the cereal-production figure: the Chinese use the expression to cover wheat, maize, rice and other cereals, and also sweet potatoes, which count for a quarter of their weight. According to official figures, the production in 1957 was 185 million metric tons: 45% rice, 13% wheat, and 30% other cereals. The figure for the best year before 1949 was 140 million tons. It is estimated that during the bad years from 1959–1961 it fell to 160 or 170 million tons, and in 1971 it was 246 million tons, or twice what it was before the Revolution; in 1975, it was estimated at 295 million tons, almost half of which was rice. The North is more or less self-sufficient now, whereas it used to depend on imports from the South.

At the same time, it seems that more meat (particularly pork and poultry, which have been free of rationing since 1964) and fruit and vegetables are being produced now than before the bad years.

Industrial crops are encouraged by the authorities, especially in grain-growing areas where varied production seems advisable.

Cotton is the main industrial crop, as the textile industry needs large amounts, and it is also widely used for clothing, even in cold regions. Production is now approximately 2,400,000 tons, twice what it was in the 1950's.

The oil-bearing crops (soy-bean, peanuts, sesame, colza, castor oil, palm-oil, . . .) are not yet sufficient to meet the demand. The soy-bean production is estimated at about 13 million metric tons, and that of peanuts at over 2–8 million.

China produces tobacco (she is the world's foremost producer) and fibrebearing plants—jute, ramie, hemp.

The sugar production is now on the increase, but it is still low compared with the population figures (15 million tons). Most of the sugar produced is cane sugar grown in the south, but sugar-beet is being introduced in the North-East and Xin jiang.

Stock-raising as known in the West was unknown in the old China of the 18 provinces, where grasslands are virtually non-existant. On the other hand, it is practised on a large scale in Inner Mongolia, Qing hai and Xin jiang. The herds of cattle and sheep were estimated at 65 and 76 million head respectively altogether in 1978. Pigs (243 million) and poultry are the only stock raised on an intensive scale, partly privately and partly collectively; they are raised for the manure they produce as well as for their meat.

China has undergone de-forestation for centuries, and lacks timber, which is imported from Korea and the U.S.S.R. The timber-producing areas are remote (the North-East and the South), but the policy of intensive afforestation extended to the whole country since the liberation should eventually make more timber available.

Fresh-water fish are produced in large quantities, in fish-ponds in the peoples' communes. Sea-fishing also has considerable possibilities in a country such as this, with a coastline 8,500 miles long. With a harvest of 6,880,000 tons, China comes third in the world classification, after Japan and the U.S.S.R.

Industry and Commerce

Industrial Enterprises

Each industrial enterprise is headed by a manager appointed by the government. He is often a veteran of the revolution. His assistant is usually an engineer.

The real power lies with the committee of the Communist Party, elected by the members of the enterprise who are enrolled in the Party. The result is "the combination of collective management and personal responsibility". Although they condemn management by the workers, the Chinese claim that the "substructure" is consulted more often than in the U.S.S.R., but little information is available on the role of the workers and employees in the management of the undertaking.

Industrial concerns enjoy relative autonomy in questions of management, but none at all in the case of investments. All profits are paid directly to the State, after a certain amount has been claimed to go to the social fund. Profit-making is not considered their prime object; their first duty is to fulfil the State Plan. Lowering of manufacturing costs does however occupy an important place in the instructions given to the concerns.

The authority in charge of industry was de-centralised in 1957, and since then about 30% of the enterprises depend on local authorities; the others come under the directives of the Ministries specialised in technical questions, which number about thirty (there are eight ministries of machinery, for instance). All enterprises are controlled by the State Plan, as far as production targets and investments are concerned.

The enterprise is served by suppliers appointed for that purpose by the State. Finished goods are sold off through contracts made with wholesale distribution companies who may have their say as far as quality is concerned, and who in turn conclude agreements with the retailers.

Trade distribution works better at the retail stage than in any other countries with a State economy, and foreign visitors are surprised by the variety of consumer goods for sale in the countless large and small shops in the towns. Commercial establishments are divided into three categories: State shops, mixed shops where the State is the chief partner, and co-operatives. Private commerce is limited to a few pedlars and salesmen with very little scope. The Chinese authorities are trying to extend the commercial distribution and buying network as far as the most remote parts of the country, to stimulate economic activity there too. The success of the efforts to organise trade is an original feature of the Chinese economy.

Private capital still exists in industry; it is in partnership with the State, who is the senior partner, and brings a dividend of 5% of their share of the capital to the owners. The capitalists may be employed in the firm which they formerly owned and receive a salary.

The Workers

It is estimated that less than ten million people are employed by modern industry, but is must be remembered that handicrafts still ensure a large proportion of the supply of the country's consumer goods. Chinese workers are ingenious, hardworking and skilful. Most of those employed in modern industry are young, and the proportion of women employed is often high, even in heavy industry.

The basic salary in modern industry is 55 to 65 *yuan* a month for a 48 hour week on an average, according to statements made by factory managers. Paid holidays do not exist. The lowest salaries are 30 *yuan*, the highest 120 *yuan;* they may even reach 380 *yuan* for engineers of exceptional ability. It is considered normal for the factory manager to earn less than the best workers.

The managers, when they quote these figures to their visitors, point out that rents are extremely low (3 to 4 *yuan* per month per family); so is the cost of meals in the canteens (10 to 12 *yuan* per month for three meals a day, except on the weekly day off), as the food is almost entirely cereals. Medical care is free for the workers and half price for their families. Neither income nor salary are taxed. Many workers save through the People's Bank, placing their money for periods of 1, 2 or 3 years; the annual interest is about 4%. Bonus payments are made to the workers, although material stimulants are held to be incompatible with the spirit which should inspire a good socialist, and all managers, when asked about this, recall that the prime motive to work under a socialist regime should be ideology. The bonus payments may reach 15% of the total wages paid by the concern. Since the launching of the campaign for technical innovation, they have been granted above all to workers who contribute to the progress of production through their initiative and contributions to the improvement of productivity.

The visitor often has the impression, when going round a factory, that it abounds in personnel. It should not be forgotten that the main aim of the regime is to train workers and cadres in modern production methods, and that its policy in one of full employment. In this way, qualified manpower is trained and will later on play a vital part in the modernisation of the country in all fields.

Localisation of Industry

Before 1949, the two main industrial centres were the North-East, created by the Japanese, and Shang hai, where mainly foreign capital was invested. They have developed considerably since the liberation. Successful efforts have also been made to create new industries in the interior of the country: iron and steel factories at Wu han, Bao tou, Peking, Tian jin, Chong qing and Tai yuan, industry of all kinds at Nanking, Tian jin, Xi an and above all in Peking, which at the time of the liberation had little more than handicrafts to offer.

This de-centralisation has political as well as economic aims. The Chinese stress the fact that the socialist regime encourages the spread of industry in the most far-flung provinces, and that old factories should contribute to the creation of new ones by providing cadres and workers. Industrial ownership and manufacturing secrets do not exist; one of the virtues of socialism as the Chinese leaders see it is that all factories share in the technical progress made by one of them.

The new regime is particularly proud of the industrialisation of regions belonging to the Minorities, such as Tibet, or Xin jiang, neither of which had a single factory before 1949. Xin jiang is now self-sufficient as far as textiles, sugar and leather articles are concerned.

Under the influence of the U.S.S.R., and with its help, China built vast factories above all during the first two Five-year Plans.

The new policy, which has to take the limited investment possibilities into account, is to build smaller and less onerous production units.

As in the case of the other sectors, no figures have been published for industry since 1960, and the only trustworthy figures are those published in 1957. Outside observers trying to estimate the present level of production are reduced to making guesses founded on unofficial statements by this or that Chinese personality, or on the impressions garnered by foreign visitors.

Forms of Power and its Sources

Coal

Coal is by far the most important source of power. China possesses vast reserves, the anthracite production accounting for 25% and the lignite for 10% of the total. Present production is reckoned to be from 450 to 500 million metric tons. One of the chief difficulties, not yet overcome, is that of distribution, for the railway lines are already overcrowded.

Coal is exported to Japan and some other Asiatic countries. The mines are being brought up to date, and purchases are being made abroad to help with this; at the same time, the Chinese mining equipment industry is turning out more and more complicated machinery.

The chief centres of production are in the north: the North-East, with the famous open coal cut at Fu shun, among others, Shan xi, Shân xi, He bei, He nan and An hui. The biggest mines south of the Yang zi are those in Si chuan and Jiang xi.

Oil

This is one of the fields in which the most considerable and consistent progress has been registered. In 1957, the oil production was estimated at 1,430,000 metric tons; the probable figure for 1977 was 95 million metric tons. Until 1964, the oilfields were concentrated in the west and South-West—Xin jiang, Gan su, Qing hai, Si chuan and the North-East, where shale-oil is to be found at Fu xin. Since the discovery of oil deposits at Da qing, whose exact location has not been revealed, though it is thought to be in the North-East, near Ha er bin, China has become self-sufficient and exports crude. Prospection is still going on a large scale, for although China's needs are relatively modest at the moment, because motor transport is limited, the need for oil will certainly grow, and production is expected to increase. Prospecting, drilling and refining equipment has recently been bought in large quantities from abroad.

Nuclear Power

China has exploded atom bombs recently, showing that the country is capable of producing them, but nothing is known of the industrial use to which nuclear power is to be put. The only existing information is that four atomic reactors and a gaseous diffusion factory have been built at Lan zhou.

Electricity

Production is estimated at 150 thousand million kwh. 80% is thermal electricity. Potential hydro-electric reserves are considerable, particularly in the south-west and the Yellow River Basin (San men Gorges).

Steel

China has concentrated all efforts on the development of modern complexes since the abandoning of the experiment using small blast-furnaces. Production is estimated at 24 million metric tons.

An shan, in the North-East, is the centre of the steel industry: it includes 10 blast-furnaces, three steelworks, 15 heavy rolling-mills, and seamless steel tubing mills. The industry was created by the Japanese, expanded by means of Soviet help, and now produces about 4 million metric tons of steel per year. It is a few miles from iron deposits of a 30% ore content, and not far from the coal mines at Ben xi, Fu shun and Fu xin. The order of size of the other centres of the steel industry and their annual production are not known: Shang hai has three factories; near Wu han are the oldest steelworks in the country, built in 1891; the works at Bao tou in Inner Mongolia are said to be nearing completion; steelworks exist at Tai yuan, Shi jing shan in the Peking suburbs, Tang Shan, Qing dao; other smaller centres have been created since 1949 in provinces which until then had no heavy industry at all: Guang dong, Zhe jiang, Hu nan, He nan, Gui zhou.

China exports pig-iron and crude steel, but still imports special steel and sheet-metal.

Non-ferrous Minerals

China occupies an important place on the world market for antimony, molybdenum and tungsten. The country also has rich deposits of tin (19,000 metric tons per year) and manganese (300,000 metric tons). The supplies of aluminium are enough to meet the country's needs, but copper and nickel have to be imported. Most of the non-ferrous mineral mines are in the south. Xin jiang has rich uranium deposits.

Machine and Electrical Industries

Soviet help played a leading part in the creation of industries which did not exist in China before, such as the motor and the tractor industries. Numerous new centres have been founded all over the country. Since 1960, efforts have been concentrated above all on the industries providing supplies for agriculture, and the transport sector.

Transport Material

The chief lorry factory is at Chang chun, in the province of Ji lin; it turns out 160 per day, of two different kinds. It also produces the extremely luxurious "Red Flag" saloon cars, though these are made to order, and in small numbers. Taxis are imported. Nanking, Ji nan and Shang hai also have factories building vehicles. Tractor plants have been built at Luo yang, Shen yang, Shang hai and Tian jin.

China now makes electric and Diesel engines at Da lian. Jet planes and helicopters are also assembled. The Da lian, Shang hai and Huang pu shipyards build cargo boats of 10,000 tons and more.

Heavy Machinery

China produces heavy equipment for all her industries, including the steel and mining industries; hydraulic presses, of up to 12,000 metric tons; ball-bearings of all sizes, and textile processing machinery which is exported as well.

Machine Tools

The range of precision machine-tools produced at Shang hai, Wu han, Peking, Shen yang is becoming more and more varied. The machines reach a degree of accuracy of several microns.

Electrical Industries

The centres of this industry are in the North-East, Wu han and Shang hai. Among other equipment produced in China are 50,000 kW. generators, 72,500 kW. hydraulic generators, a steam turbo-generator with its stator and rotor directly cooled by water, electrostatic accelerators with a capacity of several million volts, 220,000 volt transformers, 5,000 h.p. steam turbine engines for merchant ships, ultrasonic spot-welding machines and resistance-heated vacuum furnaces.

The Shang hai electronic industry is expanding rapidly, and is capable of producing oscillographs. In November 1965, it was announced that the first Chinese electronic computer had been built in Tian jin. Transistor radio sets and television sets are being made in increasing numbers.

Chemical Industries

Chemical industries were virtually non-existent in 1949 and have been created mainly in the North-East and east: Da lian, Shang hai, Tian jin, which is near salt marshes, and Canton. Priority has been given to fertilizers. Plants with a production capacity of at least 100,000 metric tons a year have been built—such as the ones at Wu jing, in the Shang hai suburbs, Canton, Kai feng and Tai yuan—and also smaller ones with a capacity of 2,000 to 5,000 metric tons, which are scattered throughout the provinces. The first urea factory was begun in 1965 at Wu jing, using entirely Chinese equipment.

Chinese industry turns out many other products, but in small quantities compared with the demand for them: insecticides, synthetic rubber, dyes, synthetic fibres, antibiotics. The plastics industry, a recent creation, is developing rapidly, and turns out a wide range of products: the chief ones are polyvinyl chloride and polystyrene.

The rapid expansion of the oil production will contribute to the creation of a petro-chemical industry.

Light Industry

After suffering from the priority given to heavy industry and the agricultural crisis (80% of the raw materials come from agriculture), light industry has gone through a period of relative prosperity since it has taken the lead over heavy industry in the order of priority dictated by the Plan. "The duty to increase consumption", if the masses are not to be discouraged, recognised by the 8th Party congress in 1956, is one of the reasons for the renewed interest in light industry. This type of industry also needs much lower investments than are needed for heavy industry, and can be developed near the sources of raw materials and consumer areas.

The textile industry has retained its position as the most important branch of light industry, but Shang hai, where over half of it is concentrated, now has only a third of the 10 or 12 million spindles reckoned to be its full capacity. The textile machine industry has expanded and new factories have been built in the heart of the chief cotton-producing area, between Wu han and Peking, mainly in He bei, Hu bei, Shan xi and Gan su, and Peking, Han kou, Xi an and Lan zhou. The exporting of textiles, which the Chinese make as far as possible to appeal to foreign tastes, is on the increase.

The wish to complement the cotton supply has led to the development of artificial and synthetic textile production, but only small quantities are being produced so far. Rayon is being mixed with cotton more and more frequently, and China has just bought an acrylic fibre factory from Great Britain. A vinylon factory supplied by Japan has been built in the Peking suburbs, and it has been announced that the first totally Chinese vinylon factory has begun production.

Silk production and weaving have taken on their traditional importance once more. China exports raw silk and silk fabrics, the most famous of which come from Zhe jiang (Hang zhou).

The wool industry, which is concentrated in the north, uses mainly home produced raw materials, which exist in limited quantities, and some imported worsted yarns. Woollen fabrics are expensive, and the people living in the north wear sheepskin or padded cotton clothes to keep out the cold.

Leather shoes are still a luxury, but China produces sandals made of plastics, rubber shoes, and the hard-wearing and comfortable Chinese "slippers" which most townspeople wear.

Chinese light industry produces large varieties of articles, some of which are exported to many foreign countries: bicycles, sewing-machines, toys, watches, clocks and wireless-sets.

Transport and Communications

The enormous size of the country, the variety of the relief and its backwardness in this field in 1949, make the transport problem one of the most difficult to solve; what is more, good transport facilities are essential for the smooth development of the economy.

As river transport is possible in a few large river basins only (Yang zi, Zhu jiang and Song hua jiang — Sungari —), and lorries are still not plentiful, most commercial goods have to travel by rail. In 1913, China had 5,900 miles of track; this was increased to 16,000 by 1949, and the total mileage is now 23,000 which is the same as that of the Japanese railways. Wood and coal are the chief freight carried. The Ministry of Railways has a large development programme aimed mainly at extending the railways into mountainous areas and introducing diesel engines.

The roads are probably better than is generally thought. New roads built since 1949 often have great strategic importance, such as the ones in Tibet. The prime objectives of the plan are the increase in lorry production and improvement of existing models.

Most of the transport of goods in the towns is assured by vehicles drawn by animals, and above all people, or even by carrying or tracking.

Internal air transport is improving. The Chinese Civil Aviation Company (C.A.A.C.) uses Soviet and British planes. A few international lines have been opened; they go to Irkutsk, Rangoon, Pyong Yang and Dacca. Three international compan-

ies—Aeroflot, Pakistan International Airways and, Air France—
have regular services to Peking, Canton and Shang hai.

The merchant navy's total tonnage is estimated at 4,200 tons.

To ensure the transport of the products of her foreign trade,
which are bought f.o.b. and sold c.a.f. as a rule, China charters
foreign ships per year. As the Chinese are anxious to economise
foreign currency and lower the transport costs, while at the
same time gaining autonomy in a field where it is dangerous to
depend on foreign co-operation, a policy of buying foreign
cargo ships has been going on for some time—new and secondhand ships, and even liners, have been bought from France,
Great Britain, Holland, Japan, Rumania, Poland and Bulgaria.

The chief ports are: Da lian, Qin huang dao, Xin gang, Lian
yun gang, Shang hai, Huang pu and Zhan jiang; between them,
these seven handle 95% of China's international traffic.

Foreign Trade

The proportion of foreign trade to the national product is
only about 6%, which is roughly the same figure as in the case
of other "continent-states" such as the U.S.S.R. and the U.S.A.
The volume of this trade, which is low as yet, can be reckoned
at over eight and a half milliard dollars for either way.
The maximum figure before 1949 was 1 milliard dollars.

The variety of exportable products is already large. Heavy
products—such as iron ore, coal or salt—find a market in
Japan mainly; equipment, machines and textiles are sold chiefly
in south-east Asia and the "Third World" countries. Europe
buys non-ferrous minerals and metals (tin, wolfram, molybdenum, antimony, mercury), raw materials and foodstuffs, and
the traditional animal by-products—skins, feathers, hogs' bristle
—as well as wood oil, silk, textiles and handicrafts.

No consumer goods are imported, except for extremely rare
exceptions, such as watches. China's foreign currency is reserved
first of all for the purchase of raw materials (cereals, amounting
to over 2,500,000 tons—over 50,000,000 *quintaux*—per year,
cotton, rubber, wool, nickel, copper); semi-manufactured products (steel, textile fibres, paper pulp and manure) and equipment. The vital fact in this field was the substitution of western
countries for socialist countries as suppliers in 1963. Now that
China prefers to deal with capitalist countries rather than with
the U.S.S.R. and the socialist countries, the Chinese have

bought many complete factories (the orders covered the equipment, engineering and manufacturing licences, and the know-how) from European countries and Japan since autumn 1963 (fertilizer, textile fibres, chemical products, steel, bank-note paper factories).

The U.S.S.R. was China's chief partner until 1964. Their total exchanges amounted to 440 million dollars by then, as opposed to 1,497 million in 1956. The exchanges were to be equal, whereas in earlier years Chinese exports were much higher than her imports, to enable the Chinese debt to be cleared. Japan heads the list of China's customers and suppliers, and this position will probably be strengthened by the agreement concluded in 1978; trade with Japan represents two fifths of all China's foreign trade. Next comes Hong Kong, which buys a quarter of what China sells, but supplies very little: Hong Kong buys fresh meat, vegetables, and drinking water. China also owns factories, a shipyard, banks, garages, insurance companies, building societies, cinemas, newspapers, etc. there; the profits made by China in Hong Kong in 1978 were estimated at 2.2 billion dollars.

China's other trading partners, in order of importance, are: buyers of Chinese products:—Singapore, West Germany, France, Great Britain, North Korea, the Soviet Union, Rumania, the United States; suppliers:—the United States, West Germany, Canada, Australia, France, Great Britain, North Korea, the Soviet Union, Rumania, Singapore.

Australia and Canada are mainly suppliers; they sell most of the grain which China buys, but buy very little themselves.

Although it fell off during the years after 1958, the volume of foreign trade is now expanding, like the economy.

The Chinese are making determined efforts to gain a foothold on foreign markets, and to enlarge the openings.

Now that the quality of production is improving, China is becoming a serious rival for Japan in the fields of textiles and products of light industry, particularly on the Asiatic and African markets.

Chinese overseas trade is entirely in the hands of the government. Foreign companies negotiating with China, as in all socialist countries, deal with organisations authorised to do business with them, and not with the users of their products or with the producers of the products which they buy. The organisations are known as foreign trade "corporations"; they number a dozen altogether.

A fair is held in Canton twice a year, for a month beginning on October 15th and April 15th; representatives come from many countries to negotiate deals with the corporations, and to buy and sell.

Many foreign countries organise trade and technical fairs in the largest Chinese towns, to introduce their most modern equipment and techniques to a public composed chiefly of engineers, experts and students; these are the things which interest the Chinese most of all. The fairs give concrete proof of the attraction of this great country for the exporters from the more highly industrialised countries, anxious to find room for themselves on a market which they consider to have a great future.

Prices in Peking

(from J. Guiloineau, *Vivre á Pékin*, Plon 1978)

Average monthly salaries range between 50 and 60 yuan, or approximately US $ 25. This figure has little meaning for us, because rents are extremely low, transport is very cheap, and so is medical care; meals in factory canteens cost only 0.20 or 0.30 yuan; income tax does not exist.

Smoked pork (per pound) .	1.80 yuan per pound
Fresh pork (very fatty)	0.50 ,, ,, ,,
Beef	0.80 ,, ,, ,,
Mutton	0.60 ,, ,, ,,
Duck	1.05 ,, ,, ,,
Chicken	1.60 ,, ,, ,,
Fish	0.54 ,, ,, ,,
Apples	0.40 to 0.50 yuan per pound
Mandarines	0.42 yuan per pound
Tinned asparagus	2.58 yuan a litre
Green peas	1.20 ,, ,, ,,
Ordinary wine	2.10 ,, ,, ,,
Bottled beer	0.40 to 0.60 a half litre
Rice	0.05 yuan a pound (approx. price)
Leather shoes	5.45 yuan a pair
Cotton jacket	14 to 21 yuan
Cotton shirt	1.20 to 6.60 yuan
Padded cotton jacket	25 yuan
Filter-tip cigarettes	0.30 to 1.10 yuan a packet of 20
Alarm clock	10 to 35 yuan
Wrist watch	80 to 130 yuan
Transistor radio	15 to 60 yuan
Bicycle	170 to 200 yuan

Some products are still rationed: manual workers are entitled to an allowance of 52 lbs. of rice per month, clerical workers to an allowance varying between 26 and 32 lbs. a month; manual workers are allowed 350 gms. of oil a month, whereas others are entitled to 250 gms.; adults are entitled to 250 gms. of sugar a month, children to 750 gms. Meat, fish, milk, eggs and vegetables are not rationed.

Prices are extremely stable.

Production figures

(Figures for 1957 and earlier years are the official ones published by the Chinese; estimates are given for 1977)

	Best year before 1949	1952	1957	Estimates for 1977
Cereals¹ (millions of tons)	138.7	154.4	185	300
Cotton " " "	0.700	1.3	1.640	2.3
Coal " " "	61.880	66.490	130.000	490
Electricity (milliards of kwh.)	5.960	7.260	19.340	145
Steel (millions of tons)	0.923	1.349	5.350	24
Crude oil " " "	0.321	0.436	1.458	95
Fertilizer² " " "	—	0.181	0.631	39

¹ The Chinese group the following crops under this heading:
paddy-rice
wheat
secondary cereal crops (maize, sorghum, millet, rye)
sweet potatoes and potatoes, which count for a quarter of their weight.

² Until 1959, the figures published refer to nitrate fertilizers only.

GOVERNMENTAL AND ADMINISTRATIVE INSTITUTIONS

THE COMMUNIST PARTY

The Government

The first Chinese Communist Government was created on November 7th 1931 at Rui jin, a small town in Jiang xi. Its title was: "The Chinese Soviet Republic", and it had from ten to twenty million people under its control, scattered over different "bases".

After the Long March, when it was moved to north Shân xi in 1935–1936, the government controlled a million people only, and was dissolved in 1937, after an agreement made with the Nanking Central Government. During the war against Japan, the governmental duties were assumed by a "Revolutionary Military Committee".

In 1949, on the eve of its final triumph, the Communist Party called the "Chinese People's Political Consultative Conference", as it was anxious to be on a legal basis. The conference met from September 21st to 29th 1949, in Peking; it adopted a "Common Programme", which was a kind of Chinese National Charter, and passed a law on the organising of public authorities. This organic law (six chapters and thirty-one articles) and the organic law passed by the Political Consultative Council were to remain in force until the Constitution of September 20th 1954.

The Constitution of September 20th 1954 is preceded by a preamble recalling the history and aims of the regime, and contains four chapters and 106 articles; general principles, structure of the State, a citizen's rights and duties, the flag, the emblem and the capital. A new constitution appeared in 1975.

The National People's Congress and its Standing Committee and the State Council, all share the attributes of government.

The National People's Congress exercises legislative power, amends the Constitution, approves the choice of the Prime Minister, the budget and economic proposals. It is elected for five years and meets once a year for a single, short session. Out of session, the National People's Congress appoints a standing Committee. Theoretically at least, this committee (made up of a Chairman, 20 Vice-chairmen, and 175 ordinary members) is all-powerful, as it controls everything that the Prime Minister does and makes pronouncements on all that comes within the scope of the National People's Congress. It meets twice a year as a rule.

The State or Government Council is in fact the Cabinet (with about ten deputy prime ministers, about forty ministers and several committees); its duties are above all executive.

Other government organisms come directly under the National People's Congress or its Standing Committee: the Supreme Court of Justice, the Procurator General's office...

Regional and Local Administration

Three administrative levels exist in People's China today: Provinces, *xian*, which are districts or counties, and People's Communes.

The provinces correspond roughly to the traditional provinces (22 altogether now, with five autonomous regions inhabited by minorities in addition tot hem, and three independent municipalities: Peking and Shang hai).

The *xian*, which number a little over 2,000 (to which must be added about sixty autonomous *xian*) generally contain from 200,000 to 500,000 inhabitants; like the province it is an old administrative unit.

The People's Communes, which numbered about 25,000 when they were created in 1958, have since been reduced both in area and population. Over 70,000 exist today. On the whole, they correspond to the former *xiang* (cantons or village administrative units) and are divided into production brigades and production teams. The production teams correspond more or less to former villages (from ten to thirty families), and the brigades include ten to twenty teams. Thus a People's Commune may contain anything from 5,000 to 10,000 inhabitants, depending on the density of the population, communication facilities, and sometimes on the town which it supplies.

People's Congresses are elected at each of these three main levels, Provinces, *xian* and People's Communes; all citizens of 18 and over in possession of their citizen's rights, may vote. The People's Commune Congress elects the *xian* Congress, which in turn elects the Provincial Congress, which elects the National Congress.

All the above congresses sit for a few days only each year, and appoint People's Committees. These are their executive organisms, each one controlled by the level above, and ultimately by the State Council itself.

The Chinese Communist Party

Behind the façade of the State institutions, it is of course the Chinese Communist Party (28 million members) which takes on the true responsibility for government and administration [1].

Like its Western homologues, the C C.P. consists of: a National Congress elected for five years, a Central Committee (which at the moment has 20 regular members and 132 members in reserve), a Political Bureau (17 regular members and 6 substitutes), and within the Political Bureau itself, a standing committee consisting of the five most prominent members of the Bureau. Other offices under the general secretariat look after the internal administration of the Party.

The regional and local organisms correspond to the central organisms and follow the State administrative divisions more or less: Provincial Congresses and Committees, *xian* Congresses and Committees. Underlying all this, "primary party units" are formed, either within the enterprise (factory, People's Commune, administrative or military unit) or within the territorial organisation.

Interpenetration between Party and State institutions occurs in two ways:

1) the same men may belong to both (over 70% of the members of State organisations are Party members);

2) through provisions laid down by legal texts allowing for groups of Party members to be attached to all levels of State organisations (articles 34 and 59 of the Party's Statutes).

"Small Parties"

A few "small parties" still survive to justify the policy of the United Front (the role of the Political Congress is maintained in the same spirit). The parties appeal to bourgeois groups which are on the way out, and have no powers of decision.

---

[1] The Chinese Communist Party now has 28 million members, to whom should be added 23 million members of Communist youth organisations, not to mention various mass organisations and the pioneer movement.

It should be pointed out that an "Association for Foreign Relations" (Chairman: Zhang Xi ruo) exists alongside the Ministry of Foreign Affairs (Minister: Ji Peng fei), as well as a "China Council for the Development of International Trade" (Chairman: Nan Han chen), and several associations for the promotion of friendship between China and foreign countries. It goes without saying that large numbers of specialised associations exist (literary, artistic, scientific, technical, etc.). Their names and those of their office-bearers appear in the *Ren min Shou ce*, a directory written in Chinese, the last issue of which appeared in 1965.

National Defence

The law passed on July 30th 1955 enforced compulsory military service in the People's Liberation Army. However, as the service lasts for four or five years, depending on the branch of the armed forces, only a fraction of the contingent can be called up (about 700,000 men out of a total of 5 or 6 million).

The Army consists of thirty or forty armies, each with three divisions. The Air Force owns about 2,500 fighter planes, including about 1,500 Mig 15, Mig 17, Mig 19 and Mig 21, as well as some bombers. The Navy's total tonnage in surface craft amounts to nearly 250,000 tons, with about forty submarines.

A Police Force also exists.

The first three atom bombs were exploded by the Chinese, on October 16th 1964, May 14th 1965 and May 9th 1966. China exploded her first thermo-nuclear bomb on June 17th 1967.

DIAGRAM OF THE GOVERNMENTAL AND ADMINISTRATIVE ORGANISATIONS

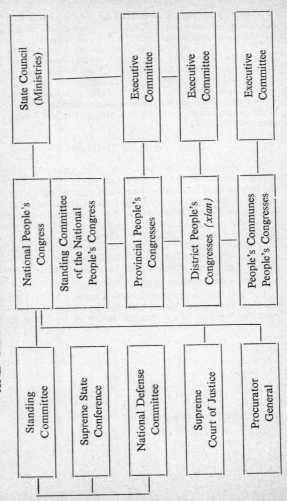

MODERN CULTURE

Maoism

Since the Communist Party's rise to power, Chinese culture has ceased all spontaneous development. It has nothing to compare with the somewhat anarchic profusion characteristic of the Western democracies. As in the case of all people's democracies, all works of the mind must be inspired by *ideology*.

The ideology in power today is *socialist realism*, as everybody knows. Modern China gives it its entire support. This variable system of dogmas and methods defined by Marx and Engels and taken up again by Lenin, Stalin, Jdanov and numerous theoreticians belonging to the Communist Party, officially colours all products of Chinese literature and art.

Shades of meaning have been introduced in China, however, which produce characteristics more or less peculiar to this country. Chinese theoreticians refer more and more to Mao Ze dong rather than to his forerunners. This has reached such a pitch that the term Maoism will be used to denote the rules which from now on are going to control the development of this civilisation, already several thousands of years old.

Mao Ze dong himself is not really a professional philosopher. He was born on December 26th 1893 at Shao shan, in the province of Hu nan, into a family of middle peasants; he received a solid primary school education and then went to the Teachers' Training College at Chang sha. Although he was to have been a primary school teacher, he abandoned this idea very soon to join in the revolutionary ferment which was rife in China between 1910 and 1920. His real discovery of Marxism dates from 1918, when he had the good luck to be taken on as library assistant in the Peking University Library, under the librarian, Li Da zhao (Li Ta chao), who was the first Chinese intellectual to be won over to Marxist ideas. After the May the Fourth Movement Li Da zhao became the founder of the Communist Party. When he was executed by a warlord in 1927, the Party lost its only theoretician. Mao Ze dong, who took up the torch, also took over the idea that the proletarian revolution could be accomplished by peasants, not workers, an idea which was not wholly Marxist, but was authentically Chinese. Being a man of action above all, Mao Ze dong did not have the possibility to enlarge at length on the doctrine. His voluminous works consist mainly of articles and speeches written as the circumstances dictated, and forming a collection of practical precepts. As far as literature and art are concerned, the line is based on the talks given by Mao at the Yan an Forum on Literature and Art, held in May 1942, during the Japanese occupation and the struggle with the Guo min dang, when the Communists had taken refuge in the caves of Shân xi.

Instead of rejecting it out of hand, Mao Ze dong begins by paying homage to the glorious culture of Ancient China. "We must take over all the fine things in our literary and artistic heritage, critically assimilate whatever is beneficial, and use them as examples when we create works out of the literary and artistic raw materials in the life of the people in our own time and place. It makes a difference whether or not we have such examples, the difference between crudeness and refinement, between roughness and polish, between a low and a high level, and between slower and faster work. Therefore, we must on no account reject the legacies of the ancients and the foreigners or refuse to learn from them, even though they are the works of the feudal or bourgeois classes." But he rectifies his thought at once: "Taking over legacies and using them as examples must never replace our own creative work; nothing can do that. Uncritical transplantation or copying from the ancients and the foreigners is the most sterile and harmful dogmatism in literature and art." [1]

The ancient past is therefore officially respected in China. Archaeology, prehistoric studies, paleontology have never enjoyed such respect ... Great pride was taken in the discovery of remains of "sinanthropus" which were older still than those found at Zhou kou dian by Teilhard de Chardin, all of which bear witness to the fact that China has pride of place in the history of the development of the human race. Museums emptied by the Guo min dang have been replenished. The ancient monuments have never been as carefully restored and maintained. Mao's revolutionary China turns to the cultural tradition for support in a way that the Soviet regime, which indulged willingly in iconaclasm at the beginning, never did.

---

[1] An excellent study of Maoism appeared in French in the magazine *Les Temps Modernes* (October 1964), signed by Isaac Deutscher; the English version appeared in *Socialist Register* (ed. Milliban and Saville, 1964). Stuart Schram's book *The Political Thought of Mao Tse-tung* (Pelican, 1969) contains the essential texts, with commentaries. See also, of course, the complete works of Mao published in Peking by the Foreign Languages Press.

Even so, the aim is the same: to struggle for the final liberation of the people. Although culture must be considered as "a cog-wheel in the whole revolutionary machine", it still has a political and social function: "If we had no literature and art even in the broadest and most ordinary sense, we could not carry on the revolutionary movement and win victory". Culture must be for the people, but it must spring from the people too.

For the people. All minds must be mobilised and convinced of the truth of Marxism, then put to serve the construction of socialism. All blurred feelings, tainted more or less with idealism or individualism, have no right to freedom. Some excellent writers such as Feng Xue feng, Hu Feng and Ding Ling ignored this, and were disgraced. Any effort to give aesthetic satisfaction is condemned as reactionary, because it diverts the attention of the public from the chief aim: the class struggle. Once, in 1956, Mao Ze dong thought the time had come to let artists and writers give free rein to their inspiration: "Let a hundred flowers bloom together, let the hundred schools of thought contend", as he said. Even romanticism was re-habilitated. But this growing individualism was rapidly nipped in the bud. In 1966, the existence of counter-revolutionary elements among the population, the "revisionist" policy of the U.S.S.R., threats from abroad too, accentuated by the war in Vietnam, all contribute to the tightening of discipline in literary and artistic creation. Every work which does not coincide exactly with the party line is rejected out of hand. It is in fact impossible for such a work even to be born.

For this reason, the authorities are cutting down the role of the intellectuals in the country today, and encouraging the people to produce the works it needs for itself. Apart from a few glorious figures like Guo Mo ruo, Chairman of the Academy of Science, it could be said that no other professional writers and artists exist. They are all amateurs, whose class-consciousness makes up for their lack of culture and craftsmanship. The ideal prototype of the new Chinese literature is Lei Feng, an exemplary character on whose life story a film has been based. He was the son of poor peasants, a peasant himself, and a victim of the Japanese and the big land-owners, who was initiated in the thought of Mao Ze dong by the Party. He worked until he became a tractor driver, then a soldier, and then an instructor of young pioneers. Throughout all the acts of his life he behaved like a true saint of Communism. Lei Feng wrote his diary without a thought for style, extolling work and faith in the revolution in the simplest terms of everyday language. This is the ideal type of writer, thinker and artist in new China. Of course the general opinion is that art will gradually improve until one day it will catch up on the forms used for all the most elaborate works in the past, but the moment for this has not yet come: nor will it, until the people as a whole are capable of understanding it. The intellectual whom the people cannot understand is an unnecessary luxury. Mao Ze dong calls for writers and artists who are on the same footing as the workers, peasants and soldiers, who speak the same language as them, who share the same life, who are at one with them. Never has spiritual asceticism been carried as far, except perhaps among a few religious communities.

Literature

The historians of the new revolutionary Chinese literature trace it back to its beginnings in the May the Fourth Movement, 1919. This was in fact the first time that Chinese intellectuals had united around one political idea: the struggle against feudalism and foreign imperialism. Certain literary consequences followed; writers abandoned the traditional forms, the formal system of aesthetics, and above all, the abstruse language used by scholars, which they replaced by the common language, bai hua. The influence exercised by foreign literature in translation on young Chinese intellectuals had paved the way for this emancipation for a long time, from the end of the 19th century onwards. In this field as in many others, China was brought nearer to the West by the opposition which arose against it.

Not all the writers followed the movement through to the logical end. Many of the most brilliant, such as Hong Shen, the poet and theoretician, like the supporters of the "Modern Review", like the "Crescent Moon Society", the nationalist school (Zhou Zuo ren), or the supporters of "liberty for art and literature", were to find themselves later on in Taiwan and in emigrant circles. Others were executed by the Guo min dang — Li Da zhao and Wen Yi duo — so that the ranks of the first generation have grown extremely thin. This does not alter the fact that the literature of the Peoples' Republic relied on and still gains support from the pioneers of the May the Fourth Movement.

The second important stage in this development was the formation, in February 1930, of the League of Leftist Writers in China. It was founded at Shang hai, a short time after the rupture between Chiang Kai-shek and the Communists, a tragic business which André Malraux describes in *La Condition*

Humaine. About fifty intellectuals, Mao Dun and Lu Xun among them, adopted a programme which was the charter of the new revolutionary literature. Emancipation of the proletariat; struggle against all diversion or reactionary movements; use of the experience gained by other peoples, and particularly the Soviet people; the promotion of workers and peasants to literary creation; the perfecting of a system of Marxist-inspired criticism; mass publication of periodicals and pamphlets: these were the chief targets of a plan of action which finally, after wars and massacres, achieved its ends.

One man dominated this era; he is sometimes known as "the Chinese Gorki": Lu Xun (Lou Hsün). He was born in Zhe jiang in 1881, and his real name was Zhou Shu ren; he was not an autodidact like Gorki, and although his family had come down in the world from a social point of view, they gave him a good education, which he continued by going to Japan. Although he had intended to be a doctor, he decided that it was absurd to try to heal bodies alone, when China's illness was in her mind. He went over to teaching, and held posts in Universities or Teachers' Training Colleges in Hang zhou, Amoy, Canton and Shang hai. At the same time, he wrote or translated, from Japanese or German, large numbers of novels and short stories denouncing despotism and social injustices. From the *Diary of a Madman* to the last *Old Tales Retold*, by way of his masterpiece, *The True Story of Ah Q*, his work is always that of a writer who is "committed" and whose life and liberty are often threatened. He came over to Marxist doctrines only towards the end of his life, under the influence of Qu Qiu bai and Lounatcharski, but the Communist Party recognise him, even so, as the great forerunner of proletarian literature.

Many other writers of the same period followed the same lines. Although brought up on classical literature, Guo Mo ruo (born in 1892) was won over to the service of the people and forced himself to write for them and like them, switching from the tradition of the humanities (he is an outstanding archaeologist and historian) to revolutionary literature, though he did not abandon his searches for new forms and style. He is Vice-Chairman of the State Council and Chairman of the Academy of Science, and has become the supreme authority on literature, art and education.

Mao Dun (born in 1896), whose real name is Shen Yan bing, also held a high post as Minister of Culture, but his attitude was questioned, and still is, for his powerful personality cannot be confined by the framework of ideology and overflows it. He is a "revolutionary" writer in the sense that he retains all the idealism and romanticism which the term sometimes conveys, rather than a strict Marxist. His novels gain universal appeal through this. The trilogy *Eclipse*, the novel *Agitation*, which describes the events of 1927, *Research*, which deals with the hesitations of the intellectuals in the 1930's, and finally *Midnight*, which is a long realist, socialist novel, written in 1932, and half-way between Tolstoy and Zola, are among the best examples of his literary genius.

Ba Jin (the pseudonym of Li Fei gan, born in Si chuan in 1904), was more romantic still, even anarchic, perhaps because he was influenced by French and Russian thinkers (he was a student in Paris in 1926). He centres his attacks on the traditional Chinese family, and his whole work is resumed in the long novel published in 1931 : *Jia (The Family)*, which is a bitter stab at the old social system and the restraints on individual freedom.

About ten other novels or collections of short stories can be found translated into English or French and published by the Foreign Languages Press in Peking. Some of the best are: *Harvest* (1935) by Ye Zi (who died young, in 1939), the first novel of a set of six illustrating above all the struggles between the peasants and the land-owners, and the nationalist army; *Schoolmaster Ni Huan-chih* (1929) by Ye Sheng tao. a novel on a more intimate, modest scale, with a penetrating psychological analysis; *Sanliwan Village* (1955), by Zhao Shu li (born in 1905), the last of a series of short novels on life in a village. *Changes in Li Village* also illustrated country life; it was written at Yan an before the victory of the revolution, and is a social and rural novel at the same time, poised between two worlds.

Literary life in China today is made up of constant discussions and controversies. As soon as a work appears, although it has been closely examined before reaching publication, it is examined and dissected from every possible angle by the official critics writing in the Party newspapers and magazines. None escape, not even traditional authors or foreigners. French novelists, in particular, are often held up for cross-examination. How far was Stendhal a progressive author ? Does the character of Julien Sorel, when looked at from the point of view of the class struggle, represent anything but bourgeois individualism ? Is the paternal love shown by "le père Goriot" a feeling which transcends class, or simply an example of the property instinct transferred ? Has Madame Bovary been shown clearly enough to be the victim of the society of the age? Does the right to describe average characters belong to capitalist countries only, or can it be practised by proletarian writers? All these questions give rise to interminable commentaries, with constant reference to Mao Ze dong's works and intervention from concepts of the new scholasticism, such as "the latent power of the classes", "the two in one", "the principle of limitation", etc. ... Few writers from the past find favour with the theoreticians. A long study of a famous collection of short stories which appeared under the Qing dynasty concluded that out of five hundred stories, only sixty are useful today. Literary talent is no excuse. It is a subjective idea which should be eliminated from our faculty of judgement.

Quantity has replaced quality, and China can outdo all other countries in this respect, except perhaps Soviet Russia. Official sources state that in the Shang hai area there are over 1,000 writers who do part-time work at the same time, working in the country districts. The number of amateur writers in He bei is reckoned at six hundred: they are workers, soldiers, employees in cultural centres ... In 1964, over 10,000 story-tellers gave accounts of events concerning the misfortunes and the resurrection of the Chinese nation. When a book measures up to the ideological requirements, it is immediately put on sale throughout the country, like the famous *Red Crag*, 4,400,000 copies of which were sold in two years. If all this were carried to its logical limits, China will soon allow one sort of writing only: anonymous literature, whose author is the whole people.

Individual genius has not disappeared in China even so. It is still to be found in poetry; a sensitive woman such as Bing Xin still makes herself heard from time to time, as do men of inspiration like Kang Bai qing, Wang Jing zhi, Feng Zhi, Ai Qing and many others whom the reader may discover for himself in the excellent collection edited by Patricia Guillermaz (Paris, Seghers, 1962).

Finally, by some extraordinary paradox, the guide of modern China, Mao Ze dong himself, in whose name all literature has been brought under control, is its greatest poet. Nor is he a popular or proletarian poet; he is a pure artist in the old tradition. Although "they should not be recommended to the young", as he said in his *Letter on Poetry* written in January 1957, his poems are published again and again. They are written in a style wgich is refined, scholarly, musical and often symbolical. If one day true poetry makes a re-appearance, the example of

Mao Ze dong, so unlike his precepts, will once more be able
to inspire the younger generations.

For the moment, each poet is but a tiny screw in a vast
machine. This is how Mu Ren expresses it, in a way rendered
more pathetic by his efforts to sound subdued. [1]

I would like to be a tiny screw
So that they can put me where they want and screw me in tightly
Whether on the arm of a powerful crane
Or in the simplest wheel.

Put me in place and screw me in tightly.
There, I shall stay firmly put, my heart at rest.
Perhaps people will not know that I exist
But I know that vibrating in the throbbing of a great machine
Is the life of a tiny screw.

Although I cannot be a machine all alone,
Although I can do nothing alone,
I can serve my country and the people even so.
I know that if I stay in the background, I shall soon
Be nothing but a piece of rusty metal.

I would like to be a tiny screw,
So that they can put me where they want and screw me in tightly.
I shall be happy, and in the choir of heroes
I shall tremble to hear my own passionate voice.

The Arts

The artists of New China founded the Union of Fine Arts
immediately after the revolution. Like the writers, they defined
their system of aesthetics in terms of the reigning ideology. In
this domain, as in all others, everyone "must serve socialism".

Some branches of art stand up better than others to the
restraints imposed on them by ideas. This is true in the case of
ARCHITECTURE, for here abstractions have to give way to
practical and technical necessities. To begin with, architects
based their work on the aesthetics of the Stalin era, influenced
as they were by the Soviet Union at that time. Peking, Shang

---

[1] Quoted in *Aspects de la Chine*, vol. III, p. 616 (P.U.F., Paris, 1962).

hai, Canton and other large towns each have a Radio Building, a Palace of Sino-Soviet Friendship or a Palace of Sport, whose Corinthian pillars and pseudo-Gothic spires bear an uncanny resemblance to the Moscow sky-scrapers. In the Soviet Union, this style did not outlive Stalin himself; it did not last long in China either. A taste for the monumental lingered on for some time, however, and buildings in Peking bear this out; the new station, which was finished in 1959, is a magnificent marble building with a steel-reinforced domed roof, matched in size by the immense buildings flanking Tian an men Square: the Museums to the east and the National People's Congress Building to the west. At the same time, they are relatively low and well placed with open spaces round them, so that they do not entirely overshadow the old houses and the Imperial Palace nearby. The Chinese sense of harmony which is one of their most characteristic features triumphed over the rest.

When building new living accommodation, the architects showed great modesty. They were ready to base their work on similar construction in Western Europe, and produced buildings which were rarely more than four of five stories high, and pleasantly arranged so as to avoid making them look like barracks. Quantities of trees and flowers brighten up the new districts, making them much more "human". The only concession to traditional style is to be found in the roofs of glazed tiles, with upturned eaves corners, decorated with mythical characters. New buildings like the Fine Arts Museum and the Cultural Palace of the Nationalities do not alter the venerable air of the capital, as the shape and colour of their roofs merge happily with the old houses round them.

SCULPTURE is virtually non-existent, except in monumental form: it complements town-planning and is used mainly for propaganda, for illustrating slogans in public places and on official buildings. The memorial to the Liberation Army soldier in the Pearl River Square at Canton sums up all the rest: a booted, helmeted figure 60 feet high, a machine gun in one hand and the other hand to his heart, dominating the crowd milling round his feet.

MODERN PAINTING has a great artistic heritage to draw on, but little is left. Few modern artists have remained faithful to the old technique of water colour painting on silk scrolls, or the paintings in ink, shading delicately from black to palest grey. A few works of this kind still appear at exhibitions. Reeds, ducks, flowers, unmistakably the work of a master hand, prove that the Chinese genius has not yet disappeared. The painter using traditional style has to make concessions to the official themes: a landscape is said to depict "the first bridge crossed on the Long March"; another, "orioles twittering among the willow-trees" by the great painter Fu Bao shi contains two little figures with an optimistic air about them. It is clear, in fact, that nature alone provides food for inspiration for the masters, just as before.

Oil painting lends itself better to propaganda themes. Artists from all provinces of China have taken up European techniques, learned from the Soviet Union. In other words, socialist-realism has carried the day. It is exactly like contemporary Russian painting: the same subjects in praise of work, the same perpetually smiling people, the same precision in the details, the same intense, violently contrasting colours. Some paintings reveal a slight trace of Impressionist influence, or even the influence of Bonnard or Matisse... It shows that Chinese artists are not entirely cut off from Western sources. The teaching of Xu Bei hong and Hu Hai su on their return from Europe is still bearing fruit.

Most artistic production is based on other techniques, however. Woodcuts receive higher approval than any other form, and the younger generation shows particular skill in this domain. Whatever the subject may be (the sorghum harvest, a factory interior, scenes from military or political life), the sheer technical ability cannot fail to win admiration. Both newcomers and veteran craftsmen alike bring consummate art even to propaganda. The same technique is used to make reproductions of Qi Bai shi's fascinating prawns and crabs.

Popular techniques still exist in large numbers and are given special support by the regime. Whether executing the naive "New Year pictures" or paper cut-outs, the Chinese always show the same incredible powers of invention; they use everything possible to help them create a work of art.

This art has its limitations however, and they are soon reached. A visit to the Arts and Crafts Research Institute at Shang hai is enough to illustrate this. The carvings using ivory or elaborate kinds of wood, the little statues made of bread, the carved grains of rice, the lacquer ware, marquetry, embroidery, tapestry work, are all the work of good craftsmen and no more. The Chinese today reserve all their talents for the applied arts, whether the subject is influenced by propaganda or not. High forms of Art are rarely attempted.

Entertainments

After the 1949 revolution, the theatre retained a large audience, drawn both from among the intellectuals and the masses. It is still the chief form of art in China, and the cinema and television only rival it in so far as they borrow subjects from it, as well as style. The figures, although they are incomplete, are revealing. In Shang hai alone, there were seven to eight million theatre-goers in 1964. Seventy professional companies, all specialised in different styles, presented nearly 500 plays, which ran into a total of 10,000 performances. Few of these plays were new creations, it is true, as in 1964 only 80 new plays were produced in the whole of China. This figure sheds light on the difficulties encountered by modern authors when trying to meet the requirements of the authorities.

Traditional forms of theatre have been discarded almost completely, at least officially. Classical Peking Opera is only to be seen during the festivities which accompany the 1st October, May Day or the Spring Festival, and then only as an exceptional concession to a taste which the masses have not yet thrown off. A few scenes from the *"White Snake"* are sometimes performed abroad, as an export product. The spirit of the old works is often changed to fit social history; the *"Red Pavilion"*, for example, has been interpreted in different ways, all of which were denounced by those judging on behalf of the party. *"The Boars' Forest"* has withstood the censors a little better. Most of these operas, constituting as they do the literary heritage, have been rejected out of hand: they are too influenced by feudalism with their emperors, ministers and generals dressed in sumptuous costumes, their princesses and concubines decked in sparkling jewels tripping across the stage with minute steps, living for love alone, with their servant girls who are constantly exploited, without a shred of class-consciousness, mere dramatic tools...

The new Peking Opera is based entirely on contemporary themes. The revolutionary struggles which took place before 1949 provide about a third of the subjects: the peasants' revolts in the 1920's (*The Red Guard on Lake Hong hu*, the *Azalea Mountain*, the *White-haired Girl*, etc.), the Long March (the *Crossing of the River Da du*), the anti-Japanese war of resistance (the *Red Crag*, the *Revolution Goes On*, the *Spark among the Reeds*, etc.), the struggle with the Guo min dang (*Door No 6*, the *Taking of the Bandit's Fortress*, etc...), the Korean War (*Raid against the White Tiger Regiment*), and will continue to do so until present-day events, wars and uprisings have provided new material. The building of socialism is a constantly-recurring, permanent subject. Everything is used as material for plays in order to convince the masses. *To Try the Chair* describes the struggle carried out by members of a people's commune against the old land-owners. *The Counter* deals with the problem of commerce under a socialist regime. *To Fight the Waves* extols seamen's solidarity. *A Bucket of Dung* is a dramatic portrayal of a long discussion between a man and a woman over a bucket of nightsoil: ought they to keep it for their own plot or hand it over to the commune? The idea of didactic and utilitarian art is carried very far indeed.

The subjects, costumes, sets and obviously the texts are new, but that is all. The music is borrowed from the old repertoire, and the audience can still pick out their favourite tunes, played by a traditional orchestra sitting on the right of the stage: little two or three-stringed violins, flutes, cymbals, drums. The acting itself is identical, as the pupils at the Peking opera school learn from the traditional operas: shrill singing, recitations in pathetic style, dancing steps, movements of hands and eyes, rapid walk using tiny steps, motionless attitudes, magnificent feats of acrobatics, elaborate use of make-up. The "back to back monologue" technique is widely used to show the dialectic opposition between two people from different social classes.

Peking Opera is the most popular of all, but other types of modern theatre exist in Peking and other Chinese towns. Differences between one *genre* and another are becoming more and more hard to define, and a real dramatic-lyric national theatre is evolving at the moment, which borrows elements from all existing schools. A play like the *Red Lantern*, which is one of the most successful on a purely dramatic level, contains borrowings from opera, tragedy, historical drama, comedy. In the case of works inspired by revolutionary deeds of foreign peoples who are still oppressed by the "imperialists", the style of Peking Opera is unsuitable and innovations have to be made. When dealing with Africa, for instance, the result is a sort of highly coloured, epic fresco with an astonishing sense of production, setting and expression. The amazing play *War Drums on the Equator*, describing the struggles waged by the Congolese against the American U.N.O. soldiers, or the countless plays on the Vietnamese war, are good examples of this.

True dramas in the strict sense of the word are rarely seen in Peking, though they are more frequent in Shang hai and Canton, where Western influence on the theatre is stronger.

Again their subjects are taken from current events or modern history. The play *Girls in the Air Force* produced by the Air Force Company shows five girls of different social origins who emerge from their training with brilliant results and carry out difficult missions: they include the daughter of a revolutionary hero who was killed during the Long March, a peasant who was a "child-wife" before the liberation, a student from a family of intellectuals, a worker's daughter, a general's daughter. The only point of the play is to throw differences in behaviour during training into relief.

Modern, or rather Western style ballet is not unknown in China either. Although it developed little outside the foreign concessions earlier on, it was given great encouragement during the period of Sino-Soviet friendship. Between 1950 and 1960, the Bolshoi and other famous companies came to dance purely classical ballets: *Swan Lake*, *Giselle*, the *Cordair*, the *Fountain of Bakhchisarai*, *Esmeralda*... Chinese companies put on the same ballets, sometimes with the help of some Cuban or Albanian dancer visiting the country. Here again these purely "formal" works are disappearing in the face of "revolutionary ballets", like *The Red Women's Detachment*. Productions like this one combine techniques of traditional dancing (points, pirouettes, leaps) with elements from folk-dancing, and especially with military drill movements, such as bayonet charges and rifle-shooting. Ballet-dancers dressed in military uniform, performing *entrechats* and dancing on their points with machine guns over their shoulders create an odd effect. The music is entirely new, played by a European style orchestra, with the addition of Chinese percussion instruments. The style, obviously, is war-like and revolutionary.

One of the chief aims of the present regime is to get the peasants and Minorities to play a part in the cultural life of the country as a whole. To help achieve this, actors and actresses from the big cities tour the countryside every year. Actors from Peking travelled thousands of miles in Inner Mongolia, living with the people whom they found there, helping them on occasions, and performing their usual repertoire in the evening, with the bare minimum in the way of stage sets and properties. Companies from outlying districts come to Peking every year to give performances as well. The Minorities' Dramatic Art Festival, usually held in October in the Nationalities' Cultural Palace (Min zu wen hua gong) is well worth seeing. It gives an idea of dramatic art all over China, and of costumes too.

A word must be said about *MUSIC* is modern China. Traditional music is totally unsuited to sweeping revolutionary sentiments, as the instruments make too thin a sound, and the composition technique is on the simple side. The official upholders of "folk music" cannot stem the growing popularity of Western music. Western music, however, has two serious faults: it is "foreign" in origin and "bourgeois" in inspiration. After examining the greatest German, French, Italian and Russian composers, the most radical critics' judgement of them is harsh: Debussy is decadent, Bach is formal, Chopin is neurotic, Tchaikowsky is sentimental, and Beethoven himself is guilty of having written a reactionary "Missa Solemnis" and a third symphony in praise of a tyrant. European music is very rarely heard in China in concert halls or on the wireless. It is limited more or less to a few recitals given by foreign artists and falling into the category of "cultural exchanges".

At the same time, however, the Chinese have to model their music on that produced in Europe. The Shang hai conservatoire produces excellent virtuoso performers on the piano and violin, such as Li Jie fan, and also composers whose technique is based on Western models, after a thorough study of Western music. The symphony orchestra, conducted by Xi De lun who was taught in Moscow, reaches an admirably high standard of playing. Unfortunately, the music which they play is as yet not up to their own high standards; it is comparable with the mediocre compositions in Europe at the end of the 19th century. It is intended to be dynamic and martial in style; it is usually emphatic or vaguely descriptive.

All these different elements—classical opera, modern drama, dancing and music—can be found synthesised in a few spectacular forms of entertainment which have been born of the revolution. Some take place in the open air, like the parades on May Day and October 1st in Tian an men Square, when a thousand performers combine to produce an extraordinarily colourful "festival", which is admirably directed and full of rhythm. Other, more elaborate, ones are held in the vast theatre in the National People's Congress Building (it seats 6,000); a thousand actors and a thousand singers act, sing and mime *The East is Red (Dong fang hong)* for example, a vast epic fresco of great technical perfection which depicts Chinese history over the last fifty years in the style of old coloured prints, like the French "images d'Epinal". Modern China has much in common with the artistic tradition of the French revolution, with its pompous festivals and ceremonies. In order to judge what it produces it should be remembered that it is contemporary with artists like David, composers like Méhul, and the melodramas.

Cinema

The Leaders of People's China take a particular interest in the cinema. It is after all the most important form of art in socialist countries. Lenin said that it has more power over the people than any other form of art. This field is therefore more strictly organised than any other branch of cultural activity.

The invention of the cinema was known to China from early on, as the first Pathé reels were shown in Shang hai in 1903. A classical opera was filmed in 1908. Then the Asian Motion Picture Company was created by the American Brovsky in 1913, after the highly successful documentary film of the Paris floods in 1910. Until 1949, the films produced had all the characteristics which those made in other capitalist countries in Asia such as Hong Kong and Japan still have today: they were commercial films showing strong American influence and apart from a few exceptions, lacking any great aesthetic originality or effort to produce high quality work. The exceptions include films by Cai Chu sheng *(The Lost Kids)*, Yuan Mu zhi *(Angels in the Street)* and *High Tide of Anger*. The greatest work on China was directed by a foreigner, Sidney Franklin: *Faces of the East*, with Paul Muni and Luise Rainer, made on the eve of the Japanese invasion.

Modern Chinese cinema was preceded by "progressive" cinema which came mainly from Shang hai and was influenced by Soviet films and realist Franco-Italian films. The *Tears of the Yang zi* (1948) was one of the films which prepared the population of China for the revolution. Its origin goes back to the years 1937–38, when the Dutchman Joris Ivens gave their first 16 mm. camera to the revolutionaries at Yan an, and the film grew out of the revolutionary armies. As early as the autumn of 1938, the Yan an Cinema Centre, attached to the political bureau of the Communist army, began to make news and propaganda films on the fights between the survivors of the Long March and the Japanese invaders, and later the Guo min dang troops. The conquest of Manchuria and the taking of the Japanese equipment and studios at Chang chun in 1946, followed by the taking of Shang hai and its studios in 1949 supplied the young Communist cinema with considerable means which enabled it to spread its action rapidly throughout the whole country.

From 1949 to 1957, the Chinese cinema industry produced about 170 full-length films, which amounts to about twenty per year. The "Great Leap" sent the numbers up to 103 in 1958 (45 of which were made in Shang hai), 77 in 1959 and 72 in 1960. From then on, the national production settled at about 50 films each year, plus large numbers of scientific films, cartoons, documentaries and newsreels. The chief studios are in Peking (including the August 1st Studios, which are connected with the army), Chang chun, Shang hai (two large units, not counting the cartoon studios and studios used solely for scientific and educational films), Xi an and Canton. The Ministry of Culture, or rather a specialised section, the "Cinema Office" is responsible for all material questions connected with productions, and gives ideological guidance. The Peking Cinema Institute trains most of the directors, actors and cameramen. The Institute of Research into Cinematographic Material at Shang hai is in charge of finding answers to technical difficulties which are peculiar to China.

Themes of films follow current political directives. The "building of socialism" is always the watchword, whether illustrated by praise of model workers or peasants, or by condemnation and ridiculing of the old land-owners who are unable to adapt themselves to it. Scientific or technical discoveries, sporting achievements also supply material for rudimentary plots. The Minorities are often figured, shown in such a way that they always appear to have retained their own culture, while reaping the benefits of the general progress at the same time. Other popular themes are furnished by the different wars against the Americans (Korea, Vietnam) or the fight against the Guo min dang. Love or passion is never used as the basis of a film. Each of these sentential didactic works, with its slow action and studied acting carries its own political lesson. At the same time they have a certain undeniable charm, arising from the quality of the photography, which is often expressionist, recalling old Soviet films, or from the singing, for many of the dialogues are interspersed with music and take their inspiration directly from Peking Opera. Now that the Sino-Soviet co-operation, which resulted in about 80 dubbed Soviet films being shown in China, is over, virtually no foreign productions reach China, apart from the occasional Albanian, Cuban or Korean film. One French film was seen in the big towns in 1964: *Tamango*, based on the anti-slavery story by Mérimée . . .

One branch of Chinese cinema is particularly refreshing and pleasant: cartoons. They are made at a special studio in Shang hai, using several different methods. Cartoons in the ordinary sense of the word—films of marionettes, based on an art which is itself several thousands of years old—are different from films based on paper cut-outs, another traditional speciality, or folded paper, or cartoons using the wash-tint technique, which owe much to traditional Chinese painting. Several of them have won prizes in international festivals, such as Locarno in 1960 *(Where is Mother?)* and Tours in 1964.

The numerous cinema magazines (*The Art of the Cinema, Cinematographic Literature, Cinema for the Masses*, whose publication figures run as high as 120,000 copies, *China's Screen* or *l'Ecran Chinois*, published in French and English) examine films solely to see how far they conform to current ideas. In 1964–65, for instance, several works such as *Spring in February*, based on the novel by Ru Shi, published posthumously though written thirty years earlier, *Northern Country, Southern Country, The Town that Knows No Night, The Shop of the Lin Family*, were criticised in countless articles and "readers' letters" because they might arouse sympathy for the old regime among young people. "The wheel of history moves on through the great era of socialist revolution and the building of socialism", according to the leader on the subject in the *People's Daily*. "Who are the people whom proletarian art and literature should illustrate? What ideas ought they to spread? Should they extol the *avant-garde* people who have joined resolutely in the revolutionary struggle, or the hesitant ones who stay outside the mainstream of the revolution? Should they propagate proletarian collectivism or bourgeois individualism? When considering the literary works of the past, should we adopt the proletarian point of view, condemning the old ideas of people in the past, and helping the audience to form a correct notion of times gone by, or should we adopt a bourgeois point of view, embellishing these figures and these ideas, so that they inspire nostalgia for the past"? And another paper adds: "The party has always stated that the theme of a film should be right, that it should spread Marxism-Leninism and the thought of Mao Ze dong, contribute to the elevation of the proletariat and the disappearance of the bourgeoisie. The conflict between characters in a film should reveal the substance of life, that is, it should reflect the class struggle." These quotations, chosen out of a thousand similar ones, are enough to reveal the inspiration of Modern Chinese cinema.

Sometimes a great sentiment or exceptional talent in one of the artists bursts through the framework of socialist-realism and produces a work which is deeply human and true, capable of appealing even to a European audience. This is true of the film *The Serfs*, which illustrated the liberation of the slaves in Tibet. A director: Li Jun, a great actor: Wang Tui, a cameraman: Wei Lin yue. The miracle happened somehow, one does not know how. Cinema goers should keep an eye open for Chinese films. It would be surprising if the next few years did not produce other successful films, intentional or otherwise.

A few figures:

Average production: 50 films per year.

Number of projection centres: about 20,000, of which 2,000 are public cinemas in towns (usually mediocre, though they are equiped with 35 mm. projectors), 4,000 club rooms (factories and schools, etc.), 4,000 halls in people's communes, 8,000 mobile units (usually 16 mm.). Peking has about 30 public cinemas.

Average cost price of a film: 200,000 yuan (£ 29,000).

Number of cinema-goers: about 4 thousand million per year.

Education

Modern China is like a vast school. The whole population is possessed with a frenzied desire for knowledge. Every citizen, whatever his trade or his age, devotes part of his time to learning and part to teaching, as each one hands on what he has learned to his neighbour, who may be younger or less well-informed than himself. This widespread movement is reminiscent of the impetus to learn in the Russia of the years after 1917, or the campaign organised by the "Ligue d'Enseignement" in France at the end of the 19th century. In China, however, it all takes place on a larger scale, as befitting a population of 900 million people...

The Chinese have always made brilliant use of their intelligence. The "mandarin", a veritable hothouse plant tested by grim competitions, earned the admiration of Voltaire and the European scholars of the Age of Enlightenment. At the beginning of the 20th century, a type of student more like their European equivalents appeared in the foreign universities in China, such as the famous Aurora University founded by the Jesuits at Shang hai, or the American University in Peking. Many young Chinese studied abroad with admirable success, particularly in

Western Europe, Japan and the United States. Several Nobel prize-winners are to be found among these "Returned Students".

These examples, bearing witness of the natural ability of one of the most able peoples in all History, must not however be misunderstood. It must be admitted that education was a privilege before 1949. Primary education, which is the foundation of all the rest, existed in exceptional circumstances, where a patron or a missionary had founded a school. 80% of the Chinese population could neither read nor write.

The figures which can be quoted now reveal the progress accomplished since 1949: one hundred million pupils in primary and secondary schools, a million in higher educational establishments, three million qualified teachers... These abstractions, which cannot be verified in any case, are less impressive than the sight of a people who seem to spend so much of their time reading in the libraries and the bookshops, and who know how to use a brush or a pen, it matters little which, to write the magnificent and difficult script which has come down to them through the ages. It is not uncommon to come across a notice at the entrance to a village in the country saying: "Everyone here can now read and write". Even if one takes the line that the Authorities have used this as a powerful weapon with which to stir up the masses, the intellectual benefits which the revolution has produced are enormous, when considered in terms of the future of humanity.

To attain these results, the Chinese authorities have modelled their system partly on those adopted by other great countries which are now more highly developed, and particularly the Soviet Union. A system like this is highly complicated and takes a long time to set in motion. Original methods have been invented at the same time to reconcile the needs of education and production This use of two methods simultaneously is known in China as "walking with both legs."

The Chinese Educational System includes more or less all the same levels and grades as Western schools. The progression of classes and examinations is similar too.

Nursery Schools for children from three to seven are essential, as nearly all the women work, both in country districts and in the towns. The old grandmothers with bound feet look after babies when they are small. The *crèches* which are unassuming but clean, open early in the morning and close late at night; the children are kept busy with activities which are recreational and educational at the same time, such as dancing and singing songs in praise of socialism or Chairman Mao. At the end of the day, the parents re-claim their offspring, well-fed and cared for. The children spend Sundays and holidays with their parents, just as in any other country.

Primary Schools take children from 7 to 13. For these six years, they learn little more than Chinese and arithmetic. Learning between three and four thousand characters is no easy matter, and other subjects suffer in consequence. A certain amount of Chinese geography and history is taught at the end, and sometimes basic notions of a foreign language as well. As in the Soviet Union, a few special schools in big towns are beginning to teach English, French and Russian to children of 10 upwards.

Primary education is free and compulsory. Only a small proportion of children, from 5 to 10%, do not go to school, and they live mainly in country districts. This will no doubt be dealt with fairly soon by some means or another, such as taking children into part-time schools, travelling schools, or schools collecting children from over a wide area.

The way in which the schools are financed varies considerably. The State supplies about half. Local collectivities, particularly people's communes, supply the rest. They often take their own decisions about putting up new buildings, recruiting teachers, and paying them from the proceeds of the sale of their agricultural produce.

Once they are thirteen, nine-tenths of the children start to work, but they rarely abandon school entirely. A flexible and skilfully-organised distribution of work and study hours, which varies from one profession to another, and from one region or season to another, enables them to go on attending classes in general subjects while following training for a trade or profession at the same time.

Secondary Education in the proper sense of the word also lasts six years. It is comparable to secondary education in Western European countries, but it exists almost solely in towns, and takes in about ten million pupils. Many schools still do not go beyond the first degree. The entrance examination is fairly stiff; another examination has to be passed to quality for admission to the second degree, at the age of sixteen or so. The certificate issued at the end of secondary education is given to almost all pupils who have attended school in a normal way, as in most other countries. Although recruitment is completely democratic, out 50%abof the pupils in secondary schools come from families who are relatively well-off; their parents are officials, engineers, doctors, etc., among whom a tradition of good education existed even before the revolution.

The curriculum is similar to that of Western schools as far as the teaching of science is concerned, but that is all; the standard of science as taught in the highest forms is high. General history and geography are hardly taught at all, and most Chinese know nothing about anything outside their own civilisation for almost all their lives. Foreign languages are taught somewhat unsatisfactorily by teachers who themselves have never been able to acquire any practice. Political instruction, on the other hand, has several hours devoted to it every week, apart from countless meetings and supervised discussions. Physical training is also encouraged.

Secondary Teachers' Training Schools train primary school teachers who are qualified to teach up to the end of the first degree in secondary schools. They are virtually the same as ordinary secondary schools, except that they give up several hours a week to classes in theoretical and practical pedagogy. It is said that five hundred schools like this exist, but they cannot produce all the teachers needed, and people with other training will have to be taken on as teachers for some time yet.

Specialised Technical Schools are much less clear in their structure. They often depend directly on firms, and not on the Ministry of Education; sometimes they are run by a technical ministry. Factories usually train their own senior technicians themselves. Courses may be spread over six years, as in secondary schools, but they may also vary in length according to their speciality. Manual work is always combined with theoretical teaching. From the age of sixteen onwards, it usually takes on more importance than the theoretical classes, which are reduced to a few hours in the evenings, and are often attended by adults as well. A wide range of such schools exists, from apprenticeship centres to specialised technical schools, and their methods are constantly being adjusted to try and resolve the fundamental problem facing China at the moment: how to build up modern industry when the available manpower consists of peasants alone.

It is tempting to think that in these conditions *higher education* in its traditional form is a luxury. This would be so, in fact, were it not for strict rules limiting the entry to it, and improving its output.

When they leave their secondary or technical schools at the age of 19, candidates for higher education have to sit a competitive examination which is held a few weeks after the school-leaving examination, and is based on the same syllabus as the latter, though a much higher standard is required. Successful candidates are sent to different places, depending on their own personal wishes, their placing in the examination lists, the needs of the State, the numbers of free places; naturally, their own record, their social origin and political activities and those of their family also play an important part in the choice. It should be pointed out that the sons of former "bourgeois" families or former "land-owners" are not systematically reject-ed. Only half of the students come from workers' or peasants' families. The others are admitted as long as they have behaved in a suitably "progressive" fashion.

Higher Educational Establishments include the universities in the strict sense of the word, the technical universities, and the specialised institutes, which include about fifty "Teachers' Training Colleges" which depend either on the State or the province, and train teachers of all subjects. A Ministry of Higher Education is in charge of about a thousand universities or university-type establishments.

About forty *Universities of the Traditional Type* exist; the most justifiably famous among them are those in Peking, Shang hai, Nanking, Canton and Wu han. Peking University originated mainly in Yan jing (Yenching) University which the Americans founded, using the indemnities paid after the Boxer Rebellion. Shang hai University owes a great deal to the Aurora University founded by the Jesuits. All of them have been modified and expanded on the Soviet pattern: they have been divided into numerous faculties, the teaching staff has grown in numbers and now includes a hierarchy of readers, lecturers, etc. ..., the courses have been lengthened to five or six years or even more, in the case of medical students. Although they have considerable prestige on an intellectual level, these Western type universities do not receive much help from the State. They are respected, but their numbers are kept relatively low by Chinese standards. More stress is laid on developing the technical universities and institutes.

The *Technical Universities* are in fact like polytechnic or engineering schools, and contain as many faculties as they do specialities. They exist in the large towns already mentioned, and two of the most famous ones are at Tian jin (Tientsin) and

Zhong qing (Chungking). The Qing hua (Tsinghua) University in Peking includes large workshops where the future engineers work at the benches like workmen, learning about the machines and sharing a little in production.

Specialised Institutes have grown more and more numerous and now number several hundreds, perhaps even a thousand. They are tending to replace the universities, as the teaching which they give is less theoretical and their turnover is more rapid. Students from traditional-type universities go on to do scientific research or become teachers at the higher educational level. Students from the institutes go straight into the ministries or specialised organisations. This is the case, for instance, for students from the Modern Language Institutes, which turn out interpreters and translators by the dozen; they are expected to make themselves useful immediately and have little general culture. Things have to move fast in China today. This involves heavy sacrifices in terms of classical humanism and university traditions.

No matter which category they belong to, the students live the life of a boarding-school. Two or four of them share small, almost entirely comfortless rooms. Their lodgings are free, but they pay for everything else: meals in the university canteen, clothes, books, all call for a contribution from their families, though the poorest of them are awarded grants which cover part if not all of their expenses. Discipline is strict; classes are numerous and attendance compulsory. Student life is more like life in one of the harder boarding-schools than university life as lived in the West. Almost all spare time is taken up by political lectures or physical training. Even holidays are devoted to civic work, particularly on the land, by means of which the young intellectual is supposed to renew his communist ideals through direct contact with the peasant masses. Finally, although most of the establishments take in girls and boys, they abstain from any kind of sensual or sentimental attachments until their studies are over. People are strongly advised not to marry before the age of 25, and this rule is rarely broken. Chinese higher education is considered as a machine to turn out "engineers of men", and like all other activities in the country, it serves the Revolution.

The expression "to walk on both legs" means that the system as it has just been described corresponds to the good leg but that the bad leg, which is unsure and weaker, must still be used, and is in fact indispensable. Present conditions in China prevent this methodical organisation, so satisfying on paper, from being widely applied. The difficulty is to find a way to found schools and universities modelled on this perfect pattern throughout the length and breadth of a country as large as the whole of Europe, some regions of which are virtually inaccessible, and to supply human ant-hills like Shang hai with adequate equipment and teachers.

In order to try to achieve this, the *"half work half study" method of teaching* has been introduced alongside full-time education. Millions of men and women study in the evening, thanks to the wireless or television, or during special hours set aside during their working days, without ever leaving their jobs. The "Spare Time Industrial University" at Shang hai, created in 1960, awards to engineers and highly skilled workers. The workers concerned take 16 hours off work and 8 hours from their free time each week, for four or five years. "Students trained by this method" ran the newspaper article, "will be new men, able to work with their hands and their brains. This new socialist-type education is infinitely better than capitalist education. To adopt it is to perform a revolutionary action, contributing to the training of men capable of carrying on the revolution, who will achieve one of mankind's great ideals: to efface little by little all the difference between intellectual and physical work".

It is not surprising, then, that this half work, half study education is acclaimed everywhere. Papers from the "New China" news agency announce increases in enrolment figures and diploma-holders as thought they were victories. At Shang hai alone, 24,000 people were enrolled in 63 colleges in 1964. In Peking, 10,000 factory workers attend classes outside working hours in 32 special colleges and 60 secondary technical schools. Tian jin has 38 schools of this kind and every year several thousand workers obtain technicians' or even engineers' diplomas. Thousands of young peasants in the people's communes attend special classes to enable them to qualify as mechanics, electricians, accountants, veterinary surgeons, agricultural experts... Classes are held on Saturday and Sunday, as well as in the evenings and throughout the dead season. A system of correspondence courses complements the direct teaching. Wireless broadcasts are also used, as well as the television, where possible, and public halls are set aside for the sessions.

A two-way movement is gathering strength in China: pupils from ordinary full-time schools are sent periodically to factories and into the country, not only to learn their future trades, but above all to develop a feeling of solidarity with the workers themselves; at the same time, workers attend school and go on studying all their lives long, so that they may reach the same level as the college-trained engineers, undergoing a sort of promotion in the social scale. Whatever their origins may be, the two categories merge rapidly and share the same patriotic and socialistic outlook. The ideology answers the country's material needs perfectly. Apart from a few rare exceptions, the whole population joins in the same effort. China, at once very old and very young, is moving at a good speed, walking on both legs.

CHINESE SCRIPT

(See plate page 337)

A few remarks have already been made elsewhere (see p. 65) on the relationship between the characteristics of the Chinese language and its writing (the relationship between the fact that the monosyllabic Chinese word cannot be decomposed into smaller parts, and the graphic unit which each written character represents). Ideographic writing is one of the elements which contribute to the originality of the Chinese civilisation, and which have confirmed its development in one particular direction. The use of this script still has a considerable influence on the everyday life of the Chinese. The foreigner visiting China for the first time may find some details on the subject helpful.

It is widely thought that it is far more difficult to learn Chinese characters than our own method of writing. Some people go so far as to say that it is indispensable to know 40,000 characters. This figure corresponds to the total number of characters in the most complete Chinese dictionary ever compiled: the Kang xi dictionary, compiled by order of the emperor in 1716. Out of these 40,000, at least 30,000 have never been in current use: they are variants, mistakes made by copyists, or aberrations which are catalogued there through philological mania. In fact, 2,000 to 3,000 characters are enough today to read most newspapers and current publications. Four to five thousand are needed to read literary works or learned publications. A complete printer's case contains 6,800 as a rule. If, as rarely happens, this is insufficient, the printer calls on a specialist who makes lead type to supply the missing characters.

Learning this limited number of characters is not the formidable hurdle which it seems to be at first, as the complete set of
characters is a coherent system, built out of a few hundred
simple elements. Some elements recur frequently, which helps
the memory (see p. 87). Taken all in all, the Chinese script
is not much more difficult to master than spelling in a language
like English. It has grave practical drawbacks, however: for
instance, it is impossible to guess the sound and meaning
of a character when seeing it for the first time. By extension,
it is impossible to note down a Chinese word if one knows
the sound and meaning, but not the character. The
Chinese themselves quite often forget a character momentarily.
This can mean that they cannot write what they want to for
the moment; in the case of our own languages, the result would
probably be a spelling mistake and no more.

The originality of Chinese script is not to be found at the
level of these practical difficulties. Each character is an entity,
a unique figure whose form cannot be confused with any other.
Each character on its own represents a word and an idea, and
consequently has its own independent existence, its value as a
means of expression, and an evocative power which the letters
of the alphabet do not possess; they are merely the elements,
devoid of meaning in themselves, of a limited collection of
phonetic signs. Letters only take on meaning when combined
with others, and cannot retain the reader's attention on their
own. Each character, however, is irreplaceable as the expression
of a single idea. The characters taken as a whole represent the
world of ideas to a certain extent. They represent it in a way
which is completely different from what we are accustomed to:
each character is an abstract figure which nothing (pronunciation which may vary from place to place or from one period to
another, the development of the language, different styles of
writing) can touch.

History reveals that the Chinese script originally had a
religious function. "... Between the era of inscriptions on bone
and tortoiseshell at the end of the Shang dynasty and the 7th
century B.C., writing seems to have been limited to colleges of
scribes who were versed in the sciences of divination—and in
some positive techniques which used numbers—and acted as
assistants to the princes during their religious ceremonies. At
that time the essential function of writing was doubtless to
serve as a vehicle of communication with the world of gods and
spirits during divination and religious practices." (J. Gernet,
L'Ecriture et la psychologie des peuples, Colin, Paris 1963). Over

the centuries preceding the foundation of the empire, when the various crafts and techniques, the trade networks, the arts of war and positive thought were all evolving in China, writing became a purely practical and profane means of communication, while retaining some of its former religious prestige at the same time. "... At that time writing began to become simply a means of communication, of recording and expressing thoughts. What is astonishing is that in spite of the radical transformations which took place in the Chinese world during the three centuries before the foundation of the Empire, writing did not become limited to that, but that in some of its uses it retained all its prestige, and that its dealings with magic, divination and religion still survived. Countless proofs exist right through the whole history of imperial China, showing that writing retained its powers for good or ill, while fulfilling the profane duties which seem to us to be inherent in it. (...) As the script was the complete set of the symbols representing and evoking all the beings in the universe, and because it was accepted that it was the Emperor's privilege and his main duty to give to each man his name and rank, the writing could not be modified by those who used it. The Emperors alone could forbid the use of certain signs or put new ones into circulation. Throughout the imperial period, from the Han until modern times, much of China's political activity was devoted to granting names, choosing propitious characters to designate eras, deities, official buildings, towns, duties..." The traveller will see these practices reflected in the innumerable steles and stone tablets, in the panels hanging above the entrances to temples and palaces, in the symmetrical parallel signs fixed on either side of the doorways of shops and houses. All the prestige and importance of the scholar-officials came from their knowledge of characters. It constituted a means of government, the monopoly of which they jealously kept for themselves, and at the same time it was the expression of the power of the civilising force which issued from the Emperor, whose representatives they were. The efficacy of the characters in writing is comparable with that which the Indian and Western traditions attribute to the Word.

Today, the special value of characters still lives in several different uses. Mao Ze dong opens political campaigns with slogans in his own hand-writing. This personal touch is highly appreciated by the Chinese. The title of the *People's Daily* is in his hand. Most of the signs on official buildings in Peking have illustrious authors. A calligraphy is a particularly personal present to give someone. At the same time, characters with

propitiatory powers such as *fu* (happiness), *shou* (longevity),
xi (joy) and double *xi* (shared joy) can be found everywhere on
all sorts of different things, and although they are weakened by
use, they still retain an evocative power. The Chinese are sensitive to the quality of writing, not only because it reflects the personality of its author, but also for any purely aesthetic qualities
it may have. The relationship between written characters and
the world of ideas is all the more appreciable when they come
nearer to an ideal form of beauty. The creation of a style represents long work; it is like a form of discipline, in the course
of which all the dross of ordinary hand-writing is gradually
eliminated. Although the modern Chinese have little time to
devote to calligraphy themselves, they still have a keen sense
of its value. Great calligraphers who create a style are rare: out
of the thousands of artists who have practised calligraphy over
the centuries, only a few dozen great names stand out and are
considered as creators of genius. But their work retains their
surge of life and power of inspiration; they are the sources to
which everyone still turns. The publication of rubbings and
reproductions of great works is a living proof of this. In all
Chinese bookshops amateurs are be to seen looking through
the collections of them, in search of such and such a work, or
discovering a new one. No one great style can be taken as the
final example, but each one constitutes an individual approach
to the abstract yet living reality which the characters express.

It is hard to convey the life which emanates from a calligraphy to anyone without a long acquaintance with Chinese
script. The appreciation of a calligraphy is a dialogue between
the conception of the ideal which has formed within the spectat-
or's mind after a long apprenticeship (study of the models and
practice) and the realisation before him. The dialogue may be
an agreement, a meeting, a surprise or a contradiction. The
reading of a calligraphy is a dynamic process in which the
mind tries to apprehend the forms which it knows and contains
under the forms which have come from another's brush. Obviously it is essential to know the order in which the strokes of a
character are written before the circulation of the movement
within them can be perceived. Each Chinese character can be
written in one way, and one only (which governs the order and
the direction of the strokes). When this has become automatic
for each character, the spectator is then capable of following
the development of a calligraphy. It is not an easy art to appreciate. It is to be hoped, however, that the examples given here
will help the reader to feel the difference in style, the individual

life in each one, and the original synthesis between conforming to the archetypes (legibility) and invention born of inspiration.

Fig. 1: Two characters (*de*, virtue; *huai*, to carry within oneself) from a calligraphy by Ou yang Xun, a senior official at the court of the Sui and later the Tang. The work is called *The Ambrosian Spring Inscription of the Nine Times Perfect Palace (Jiu cheng gong li quan ming)*; it is kept in the Imperial Palace at Peking. It is a magnificent example of the classical style known as *kai shu* ("official writing") which developed under the Northern and Southern Dynasties, and flourished under the Tang. This non-cursive, architectural, severe, even hieratic style was the most widely used type of writing on steles and inscriptions of all kinds. It has been used as the basic model for printed characters since the Song. It is the script taught in schools; students of calligraphy learn it before all else. Historically, it was formed out of the script known as *li shu* ("clerical writing"), created at the time of the unification of the empire by the Qin.

Fig. 2: Four characters (*jing lü*, to meditate motionless; *zi de*, fulfilled) from a calligraphy by Liu Gong quan (778–865), a scholar and senior official at the Tang court; his style is one of those most frequently taken as a model for the *kai shu* script.

Fig. 3: Four characters (*er, yi, you, xiang*) by Wang Xi zhi (303–379), the greatest of all Chinese calligraphers. He was general for a time under the Jin dynasty, but he spent most of his life as a hermit. It is said that he used to practise calligraphy tirelessly beside a pond. So great were his patience and perseverance that finally he blackened its waters through washing his brushes there. He is considered the greatest master of the *xing shu* ("moving writing") style. *xing shu* has no strict rules; it consists in linking the parts of a character written in another style, as the movement dictates. Wang Xi zhi created a style of writing, based on *li shu*, in which strict composition and freedom of movement are perfectly matched (the same characters in printed *kai shu* style are shown on the left). *xing shu* developed from the end of the Han onwards, and flourished under the Jin. Its most famous exponents are Wang Xi zhi and his son, Wang Xian zhi. The second column contains three characters representing Wang Xi zhi's name, in his own hand.

Fig. 4: The character *fei* (to fly) written by Wen Zheng ming (1470–1559) in *xing shu* style. Wen Zheng ming was a senior official under the Ming dynasty, and a famous painter, calligrapher and poet as well. The character *fei* is held to be one of the most difficult of all.

Fig. 5: A fragment of a poem by Mao Ze dong, written in *xing shu*, in his own hand. Beside it are the same characters in printed style: *shuang chen yue, ma ti sheng sui*, "moon on a frosty morning, horses' hooves ringing pellmell". *(Lou shan guan, Lou shan Pass)*.

Fig. 6: Four characters (*yan fu li nang*, the wild goose does not leave its bag) written by the Song Emperor Hui zong (1101–1126), a patron of the arts and at the same time one of the greatest painters and calligraphers of his time (Northern Song.) He created a highly personal style of writing, known as *shou jin shu*, "slender gold writing".

Fig. 7: Two characters written in *cao shu* style by Zhang Xu, a great Tang calligrapher: *yan xia*, under the cliff. They are an extract from a series of four poems signed by Zhang Xu. *cao shu* is a style in which the characters are abbreviated, giving free reign to the movement. The economy of style is often such that it is hard to read for all but the initiated. It gives incomparable liberty, however, to movement and invention, producing works of startling spontaneity. The printed characters alongside show to what extent liberties have been taken with the traditional shape of the characters.

CHINESE NAMES

Chinese names are made up of two elements, like ours: the surname *(xing)* and the Christian, or more logically here, given name *(ming);* unlike ours, however, the surname comes first, followed by the given name. Surnames usually consist of one syllable, though some exceptions consist of two. Given names may have one or two syllables. The complete length of a Chinese name may therefore vary from two to four syllables. In this guide book, the first syllable of the surname and the first syllable of the given name have capital letters, the rest small letters. For example: Du Fu (surname: Du), Mao Ze dong (surname: Mao), Si ma Qian (surname: Si ma), Ou yang Yu qian (surname: Ou yang).

About three hundred surnames are in common use in China, almost all of which are monosyllables: Zhang, Wang, Li... Some belong to particular provinces. Mao is found in Hu nan, Ma in the Moslem north-western provinces. Some names are extremely ancient: Kong, Confucius' name, is still to be found today. The names of the states of the Warring States period almost all survive as surnames now: Zhou, Zhao, Song, Chu, Wu, Wei, etc.... Other names are more recent. Zhu, Zhang, Gu, for instance all came into widespread use during the Five Dynasties period. Two-syllable names are rare: Si ma, Si tu, Ou yang, Zhu ge...

When a woman marries, she does not take on her husband's name. The wife of Sun Yat sen, for instance, has always been called Song Qing ling, and the wife of Mao Ze dong used her original name, Jiang Qing. Children may choose to bear either their mothers' or their father's name. Sometimes parents give the father's and the mother's name to the children alternately.

Although surnames are limited in number, the choice of given names is entirely free in China. The situation is the exact opposite of the prevailing situation in most European countries, where given names are limited in number, but surnames infinitely varied. The Chinese who wants to invent a given name has the entire vocabulary at his disposal, and often the name he finds is a masterpiece of imagination or allusion. The allusion may refer to a passage of the classics or some other literary text, or a saying of good omen or else a meaningful event connected with the birth of the child in the minds of those who name it. The given name must also sound well. In former times, countless superstitions linked with astrology and the theory of the five elements entered into the decision. It was hoped that the destiny of the child might be altered and good fortune obtained by a judicious choice. In old Chinese literature, innumerable stories exist, both tragic and comic, inspired by the choice of an unfortunate, or on the other hand well-chosen, name.

Although Chinese names are infinitely varied and constantly being created anew, it should not be forgotten, however, that the evocative element is ignored in daily life. Their real meaning is remembered in more pensive moments, or when teasing people. Many given names are formed without much thought, based on words frequently used for names.

The style of names develops differently in different periods and social classes. The mandarin class used to choose names recalling the Confucian virtues. The republican era also had its fashions. Since the liberation, names such as *Sheng li* (Victory), *Jian jun* (Creator of the army), *Guo zhong* (Faithful to the country) have made their appearance. In country districts, repeated names are often found: *Xing xing, Shuang shuang, Fei fei*...

In theory, girl's and boys' names cannot be distinguished from each other. Some characters are habitually reserved for boys', and others for girls' names, however. *zhi* (will), *shan* (mountain), *guo* (country), are usually given to boys, whereas *fang* (scented), *xiang* (scent), *lan* (lotus), *shu* (excellence, beauty) are usually girls' names. This separation is not an absolute rule, however.

The Chinese do not use surname and given names in the same way as we do in everyday life. When they do not know each other personally, they call each other by their surnames followed by *tong zhi* (comrade) or *xian sheng* (Mr.): *Wang tong zhi*, (Comrade Wang, which might be for a man or a woman); *Li xian sheng* (Mr. Li). *Xian sheng*, and its feminine equivalent, *tai tai* (Mrs.) are rarely used in the People's Republic, except among old people. *Xian sheng* has retained its meaning of "master", though, and is used when speaking to a writer or an older teacher. The official personalities are referred to by their surnames followed by their title: *Mao zhu xi* (Chairman Mao), *Zhou zong li* (Prime Minister Zhou). This usage is extended to other titles: *Huang xiao zhang* (Huang the Rector), *Ma zhu ren* (Ma, the man in charge), etc....

When people know each other, they usually call each other by their full names, surname and given name, with no other addition. Friends, colleagues or close acquaintances often use "Little Wang" (*Xiao Wang*) when talking to someone younger or "Old Zhang" (*lao Zhang*) when talking to someone their senior. Terms indicating relationships are far more numerous and precise than ours. The Chinese often use *er biao* when speaking to each other: it means "younger of the cousins older than the speaker", or *san biao mei*, for example: third of the cousins younger than the speaker, or *da mei mei*: the eldest of several younger sisters, etc.

A foreigner in China may well be addressed as *shu shu* or *a yi* by small children; *shu shu* is the equivalent of uncle, and *a yi* of aunt, and they are used by children when they do not know people's names.

Ni and *nin* are both used in Chinese for "you"; *ni* corresponds roughly to the French *tu* and *nin* to "*vous*". *Nin* is however much less often used than *vous*, and is limited to occasions when the speaker is adressing someone distinctly his superior in rank, or old people to whom he wishes to show respect, or people whom he is meeting for the first time. In everyday life, the Chinese use *ni* almost as generally as we use "you".

So much for the outline of the present system. The old system was further complicated, in the scholar—official class at least, by two other kinds of name: the zi and the hao. They are translated as "usual given name" *(zi)* and "nickname" or a literary name" *(hao)*. The given name *(ming)* was given shortly after birth, whereas the usual given name was given on the day each person came of age (20 for boys and 15 for girls). In Ancient China, coming of age was accompanied by a ceremony, the hat ceremony *(guan li)* for boys and the hairpin ceremony *(ji li)* for girls. The usual name was generally chosen so that it had some connection with the given name. It was then used among friends and in public, rather than the original given name, which was used by intimate friends or as a mark of familiarity. Later on, especially from the Ming onwards, it became customary to choose one's zi oneself. The hao was a literary name given to writers, poets, artists and mandarins. It often referred to the room where they worked or their place of retirement.

Anyone studying Chinese history and literature has to know the different names for the people whom he comes across. Some poets are often referred to by their zi, others by their hao, or sometimes one, sometimes the other. The poet known to us as Li Tai bai (or Li Tai bo) is called Li Bai by the Chinese. He is one and the same man, however: *Bai* is his given name, *Tai bai* his usual name. Take Su Shi, the Song dynasty writer, for instance, who is often called Su Dong po: *dong po* means "eastern slope" and is the literary name which Su Shi chose at the end of his life, after his chosen retreat, somewhere in Hu bei. Another, even better example is the philosopher Wang Fu zhi, who lived at the end of the Ming and the beginning of the Qing: his given name *(ming)* was Fu zhi, his usual name *(zi)* Er nong, and his literary name *(hao)* was Jiang zhai, meaning "ginger chamber", referring to the place where he worked. He is traditionally known by a fourth name, Wang *Chuan shan*, which was given to him because he retreated to live in a mountain in Hu nan called Shi chuan shan when the Qing came to power. The fourth name comes into the category of bie hao, "extra names".

It is never surprising, then, to find one person referred to by several different names. Things would have been relatively simple if the Chinese had had only given names, usual names and literary names. But, as has just been shown, they took other names as well as extra ones; furthermore, many writers and poets were also called after the place where they held an

official post, or after the rank they held at court, or by a posthumous name conferred on them by their admirers, not to
mention the religious names adopted by people who entered
Buddhist or Taoist orders. To put a stop to this endless and
useless multiplication of different names, an effort is being made
in China now to call people by their surnames and given names
only *(xing* and *ming)*. In the case of the examples given above,
the people referred to will be called Li Bai, Su Shi and Wang
Fu zhi in future.

· Emperors' names should be mentioned too. They had a
family name (e.g. Liu under the Han dynasty, Li under the Tang)
and a given name (e.g. Li *Shi min*, the second Tang Emperor).
As Emperor, they had a special name known as the "temple
name", *miao hao*: Li Shi min was given that of Tai zong. The
Emperors are often called by the temple name (or "reign name")
preceded by the dynasty: Tang Tai zong, or Emperor Tai zong
of the Tang. Each Emperor had a posthumous name conferred
on him as well *(si hao)*. Some of the emperors and princes of
the Warring States era are occasionally referred to by these
names.

The custom of giving *nian hao*, titles of dynastic year periods,
to whole reigns or parts of reigns, appeared under the Han, and
was used in ancient China as a method of dating. Thus the Kai
yuan year period was proclaimed by the Tang Emperor Xuan
zong in 713, and lasted until 742, when the next period, Tian
bao, was proclaimed. According to his method of counting,
the year 713 was "the first year of the Kai yuan era" *(Kai yuan
yuan nian)*, 714 was "the second year of the Kai yuan era"
(Kai yuan er nian), etc... Some eras are famous because they
coincided with particularly brilliant moments in China's history,
such as the Kai yuan and Tian bao periods, quoted above.
Until the end of the Yuan dynasty, most emperors changed
the name of their reign several times, so that there were more
nian hao than there were emperors. The Tang dynasty had 23
emperors but 78 *nian hao*, each of which lasted from 1 to 29
years. Under the Ming and the Qing, the habit of changing the
nian hao often was abandoned. From then on, a new *nian hao*
was adopted when a new emperor came to the throne. As the
length of the year period and the reign corresponded to each
other, the emperor is called either by his emperor's name or
by his year period title. Emperor Yong le, who is always referred
to as such, and who reigned from 1503 to 1425, was in fact
called Cheng zu. Yong le is strictly speaking the name of the
year period. The same is true for the Qing Emperor Sheng zu,

who is known by his year period title of Kang xi, and Emperor Gao zong, known as Qian long.

These fundamental ideas on ancient and modern Chinese names may be supplemented by reading *Der chinesische Personenname* by W. Bauer, Harrassowitz, Wiesbaden 1959, 406 p.

THE CALENDAR

The Old Chinese Calendar

Chinese society has been based on agriculture since the Zhou dynasty. As peasant life had to be regulated according to the seasons, the science of the calender developed early and has always been important in Chinese civilisation. At the same time, one of the basic concepts of this civilisation is that the natural order and the moral order are bound by an unbreakable link, and that there is constant interaction between the two. The natural extension to this was the belief that the sovereign was responsible for both the natural and the social orders. The science of the calender, which gives structure to the natural year and controls the peasants' activities, has therefore always been considered as one of the pillars of the government, and consequently surrounded with a semi-religious prestige. It was the Emperor's privilege to publish the calendar, and the court had the exclusive monopoly on the editing and selling of it. The prestige granted to the science of the calendar spread to astronomy and mathematics, which enabled them to attain a high level of development in Ancient China. For the history of these sciences, see *Science and Civilisation in China* by Joseph Needham, vol. 3, sections 19 and 20, Cambridge University Press, 1954–55; *Melanges posthumes* by Henri Maspéro, vol. III; *L'Astronomie dans la Chine ancienne* (19 p.), publ. by the Musée Guimet, Paris, 1950.

A calendar has to reconcile the two fundamental natural phenomena of the solar year and seasons on one hand, and the lunar months on the other. The solar year contains 365¼ days. Instead of making an arbitrary division of the solar year into twelve months as our calendar does, the traditional Chinese calendar builds the year up from the natural lunar months. 12 lunar months come to a total of 354 days only, however, or 11¼ days less than a solar year. Added up over three years, this represents a little more than a lunar month. Every three years, therefore, an "intercalary month" is added (*run yue*). This intercalary lunar month is not enough, though, so that every five years an extra one has to be added. This addition every five years is too much, however. After long research into the matter, the Chinese finally added 7 intercalary months for every period of 19 years. They were inserted at different times of year according to the era, though generally they came at the end of the year, after the 12th month, or after the 9th month (the 9th month was the last in the year under the Han).

The Shang and the Western Zhou divided the year into two seasons, spring (*chun*) and autumn (*qiu*). The expression *chun qiu* meant one year. This was the origin of the name "Spring and Autumn" which was given to the annals written during the period, and by extension to the era itself. These two seasons were then sub-divided into two, giving four seasons: spring (*chun*), summer (*xia*), autumn (*qiu*) and winter (*dong*). Each season was divided into three equal parts. Using the terms *meng*, *zhong* (*shu*), *ji*, which formed part of names, indicating the first-born, the second, etc., the first month was called *meng*, the second *zhong*, and the third *ji;* this applied to each one of the seasons. The expressions *meng chun*, *zhong chun*, *ji chun*, *meng xia*, etc. come from this custom. Each month was itself divided into three ten-day periods (*xun*).

The solar year of 365¼ days was divided into 24 equal sections (*qi jie*), corresponding to the different positions of the sun in the zodiac (for the names of the 24 sections see below).

Each month therefore had two of these sections: the first was called *chu qi* and the second *zhong qi*. But a *chu qi* and a *zhong qi* added together usually gave 30½ days, whereas the lunar month contained 29 or 30. The difference accumulated until a *zhong qi* had to be left out. Some months therefore had a *chu qi* only, and no *zhong qi*. These were the moments chosen for the insertion of the intercalary month.

From the very earliest days in China, there has existed a system of counting based on the combination of the two cycles: one cycle of 10 (called the 10 "heavenly stems", *tian gan*) and a cycle of 12 (called the 12 "earthly branches", *di zhi*). They are called *gan* and *zhi* for short. A Chinese character stands for each term of these two cycles, the pronunciation of which is as follows:

gan:	jia	yi	bing	ding	wu	ji	geng	xin	ren	gui
	I	II	III	IV	V	VI	VII	VIII	IX	X

zhi:	zi	chou	yin	mao	chen	si	wu	wei	shen	you	xu	hai
	1	2	3	4	5	6	7	8	9	10	11	12

When they are combined, these two cycles produce a large one of 60 units. The combination is made as follows: the two cycles begin at the same time (I/1, II/2, III/3, IV/4, etc.); when the cycle of 10 runs out, it begins again from I, whereas the cycle of 12 goes on (IX/9, X/10, I/11, II/12); when the cycle of 12 runs out, it begins again at 1, while the cycle of 10 carries on (III/1, IV/2, V/3, etc.); the two cycles go on overlapping like this until the 61st combination, which is the same as the first. Most Chinese dictionaries have a complete table of the 60 combined terms of the cycle at the end (*jia zi, yi chou, bing yin, ding mao*, etc.).

This system was used to number the days under the Zhou. From the Han until the end of the Qing, it was generally used to number the years. Take the year 1911, for example, the 48th of its cycle, with the title *xin hai*. This explains why the Chinese call the 1911 revolution *(ge ming)* "*xin hai ge ming*" (lit. the Revolution of the 48th Year). Some modern examples of this dating system will be given later on.

The *gan zhi* have been used in a large variety of different ways as a system of numbering. For a small set of objects, the cycle of 10 was used. This custom still survives in some cases in everyday life. In printed works, for instance, the characters in a dialogue are called *jia, yi, bing*, etc., if they have no proper names, just as in the West they would be A, B, C.

The cycle of 12 had a special use, as it was used to enumerate the 12 "hours" (of 2 hours each) which constituted a day in the calendar. This two hour unit was called *shi chen*. The expression *xiao shi*, used in modern Chinese for the 60 minute hour, is an abbreviated form of the term *xiao shi chen*, "small *shi chen*". The first *shi chen*, known as *zi*, began at 11 p.m. and lasted until 1 a.m. At two hourly intervals afterwards, *chou, yin*, etc. followed. Each *shi chen* was subdivided into two parts *(xiao shi chen)* called *chu* and *zheng*. The order of the day was as follows:

hours	zi		chou	yin	mao	chen	si		wu		wei		shen		you		xu		hai
chu	23		1	3	5	7	9		11		13		15		17		19		21	
zheng		24	2	4	6	8		10		12		14		16		18		20		22

A system of correspondence existed between the units of the cycle of 12 and twelve symbolic animals, twelve directions, etc.

1	zi	23– 1 o'clock (3rd watch)	shu	rat	North
3	chou	1– 3 o'clock (4th watch)	niu	ox	N.N.E.
3	yin	3– 5 o'clock (5th watch)	hu	tiger	E.N.E.
4	mao	5– 7 o'clock	tu	hare	East
5	chen	7– 9 o'clock	long	dragon	E.S.E.
6	si	9–11 o'clock	she	snake	S.S.E.
7	wu	12–13 o'clock	ma	horse	South
8	wei	13–15 o'clock	yang	goat	S.S.W.
9	shen	15–17 o'clock	hou	monkey	W.S.W.
10	you	17–19 o'clock	ji	cock	West
11	xu	19–21 o'clock (1st watch)	quan	dog	W.N.W.
12	hai	21–23 o'clock (2nd watch)	zhu	pig	N.N.W.

The set of symbolic animals generally indicated the years as well, in cycles of twelve. This system, which was linked with the practice of astrology, worked parallel with the cyclic numbering of the *gan zhi*. The corresponding titles and animals for several years are as follows:

year of the rat	geng zi	(37th)	e.g.	1900, 1972
ox	xin chou	(38th)		1901, 1973
tiger	ren yin	(39th)		1902, 1974
hare	gui mao	(40th)		1903, 1975
dragon	jia chen	(41st)		1904, 1976
snake	yi si	(42nd)		1905, 1977
horse	bing wu	(43rd)		1906, 1978
goat	ding wei	(44th)		1907, 1979
monkey	wu shen	(45th)		1908, 1980
cock	ji you	(46th)		1909, 1981
dog	geng xu	(47th)		1910, 1982
pig	xin hai	(48th)		1911, 1983
rat	ren zi	(49th)		1912, 1984

Another system has an even more important role in China than the cyclic systems: that of the reign titles *(nian hao)*. For details see p. 330.

Modern Usage

China adopted the European calendar (solar) in 1912. January 1st was declared' "January 1st of the 1st year of the Republic". From 1912 to 1949, the years were dated "the nth year of the

Republic" *(min guo n nian)*. It amounted in fact to adopting the system of dynastic eras once more ("the nth year of the reign of Qian long" ...). The Chinese government has brought the international system into use since 1949.

When a date is given, it begins by the year. In Chinese, years are not read as a number, but as single figures ("one nine six six" instead of "nineteen hundred and sixty-six": *yi jiu liu liu*). The month and then the day follow after the year. The months are not given names as ours are; they are numbered from one to twelve:

yi yue (1st month) January   *qi yue* (7th month) July
er yue (2nd month) February   *ba yue* (8th month) August
san yue (3rd month) March   *jiu yue* (9th month) September
si yue (4th month) April   *shi yue* (10th month) October
wu yue (5th month) May   *shi yi yue* (11th month) November
liu yue (6th month) June   *shi er yue* (12th month) December

Nian means year, *yue* means month, and *hao* (or *ri*) means day; a date is therefore given as follows: *yi jiu liu liu nian "shi yue" yi hao*, or October 1st 1966. The days of the week are also indicated by numbers:

xing qi yi (or: *li bai yi*)   Monday
xing qi er (or: *li bai er*)   Tuesday
xing qi san (or: *li bai san*)   Wednesday
xing qi si (or: *li bai si*)   Thursday
xing qi wu (or: *li bai wu*)   Friday
xing qi liu (or: *li bai liu*)   Saturday
xing qi tian (or: *li bai tian*) Sunday

The *tian* which appears in *xing qi tian* (Sunday) means "day". *Xing qi tian* is therefore the "day of the week". *Li bai* means "to pray"; *li bai tian* therefore means "prayer day", and is obviously a name with a Christian origin.

The solar calendar *(yang li)* and the lunar calendar *(yin li)* are still used simultaneously. The solar calendar is the official system, while the lunar calendar is used more widely in the country (the peasant almanachs which are published each year bear this out). The difference between the two varies from year to year. For 1966, the two were 21 days out of step with each other, that is to say, the Spring Festival for 1966, which marks the first day of the lunar year, was celebrated on the 21st January. The 1st October, 1966 was the 17th day of the 8th month of the year 1966 (or *bing wu*) in terms of the lunar calendar.

The almanachs published each year give tables of correspondences for the two calendars. All newspapers bear both kinds of dates.

An old method of dividing the year into 24 sections is still alive today; the table is given below. These 24 sections fix the framework of the peasant's year, and are known as *qi jie*. The dates vary slightly from year to year on the solar calendar. The dates below were valid for 1966:

li chun	Beginning of Spring	February 4th
yu shui	Rain Water	February 19th
jing zhe	Waking of Insects	March 6th
chun fen	Spring Equinox	March 21st
qing ming	Pure Brightness	April 5th
gu yu	Corn Rain	April 20th
li xia	Beginning of Summer	May 6th
xiao man	Grain Full	May 21st
mang zhong	Grain in the Ear	June 6th
xia zhi	Summer Solstice	June 22nd
xiao shu	Slight Heat	July 7th
da shu	Great Heat	July 23rd
li qiu	Beginning of Autumn	August 8th
chu shu	Stopping of Heat	August 23rd
bai lu	White Dew	September 8th
qiu fen	Autumn Equinox	September 23rd
han lu	Cold Dew	October 9th
shuang jiang	Frost's Descent	October 24th
li dong	Beginning of Winter	November 8th
xiao xue	Slight Snow	November 23rd
da xue	Great Snow	December 7th
dong zhi	Winter Solstice	December 22nd
xiao han	Slight Cold	January 6th 1967
da han	Great Cold	January 21st 1967

The dates of these 24 sections vary by 1 or 2 days only as a rule from year to year on the solar calendar.

Feast Days

The use of the two calendars simultaneously in Chinese public life is shown by the feast days, which are of two kinds: those which depend on the solar calendar and are therefore unchangeable, and the rest which are variable, because they are fixed by the lunar calendar. Although the traditional Chinese feast days were very numerous and spread over the whole year, only those celebrated officially or at least widely celebrated still will be mentioned here. For further details, the reader should consult *Annual Customs and Festivals in Peking* (see. p. 392) and other works which specialise in this subject.

Lunar Calendar Feast Days

Spring Festival (chun jie). It marks the beginning of the lunar year. The date varies from year to year from the end of January to the beginning of February. It is the most important feast day of the year for the Chinese, a day for large and noisy family parties. All the Chinese have four days' holiday and many take the opportunity to go back to their native town or village. The shops are usually open.

Countless customs and beliefs used to be connected with this feast day. (cf. for example, the study entitled *Spielgeräte und Spiele im chinesischen Neujahrsbrauchtum, mit Aufzeigung magischer Bedeutungen* published by M. Eder in the magazine *Folklore Studies*, vol. VI, Peking 1947, 202 p.). The superstitious side of the festival is now being eliminated as far as possible. It is still a great family occasion throughout China, however, celebrated with large meals and accompanied by noisy firecrackers. The houses are decorated with *nian hua* (New Year pictures). These are large coloured pictures, originally woodcuts which portrayed the kitchen gods and other things associated with popular beliefs. Both the manufacture and the subject matter have now been modernised.

Feast of the Dead. It falls on the 15th day of the 3rd month, or usually at the beginning of April. The name of the festival, *sao mu*, means "to sweep the tombs"; it was the day when people went and tidied up the tombs, and left offerings for the dead. The tradition of burning paper offerings (money, flowers) is still very much alive in the country districts. Processions of school-children come and leave wreaths of paper flowers at the foot of the memorials to revolutionary martyrs. The Feast of the Dead used to be a great Buddhist festival.

Dragon-boat Festival. In falls on the 15th day of the 5th lunar month, towards the end of May. The name of the festival, *duan wu* or *duan yang*, means "the beginning of the sunny season". Since earliest times, it has been widely celebrated throughout China and South-East Asia. Countless religious and folk traditions have become attached to it. In south China dragon-boat races used to be held. Triangular cakes *(zong zi)* used to be thrown into the River Mi lu (Mi lu jiang) in Hu nan in memory of the great poet Qu Yuan who threw himself into the river in 277 B.C. *zong zi* are still eaten on this day throughout China.

Autumn Festival (zhong jiu). It falls on the 9th day of the 8th lunar month, and as its Chinese name indicates, marks the middle of the autumn. It usually falls at the end of September, coinciding with the autumn equinox. People gather to admire the full moon and eat "moon cakes" *(yue bing).*

Solar Calendar Festivals

New Year (yuan dan). New Year's Day is a much less important event in Chinese life than the beginning of the lunar year (Spring Festival), but it is being celebrated more and more, especially in schools, factories and other organisations, with various festivites and 2 days' holiday.

Woman's Day (fu mu jie). An international festival, celebrated on March 8th.

May Day (Workers' Day) (lao dong jie, or wu yi). Everybody has 2 days' holiday throughout China, marked by widespread merrymaking. The military parade which used to be held in Peking has not happened for several years now. Extracts from operas, plays, pieces of dancing and music are performed in all the parks of the capital. The day ends with a fireworks' display at Tian an men.

Chinese Youth Festival. (Zhong guo qing nian jie). It is celebrated on May 4th in memory of the movement started by Peking students on May 4th 1919 for national independence and cultural renewal. This movement, of the greatest importance in modern Chinese history, is called *Wu si yun dong* in Chinese.

Children's Festival (er tong jie). International festival celebrated on June 1st.

National Liberation Army Festival (Zhong guo ren min jie fang jun jian jun jie). The anniversary of the founding of the National Liberation Army is celebrated on August 1st.

National Day (guo qing jie). It is celebrated on October 1st in memory of the proclamation of the People's Republic of China on October 1st 1949, at Tian an men. A huge parade representing industry, agriculture, education, the arts, the people's militia and sports takes place every year at Tian an men. Mao Ze dong and the other leaders watch from the balcony high up on the gate. The evening is an occasion for more general merrymaking in Tian an men Square, with a large fireworks' display.

December 9th (yi er jiu). Anniversary of the patriotic demonstration led by the Shang hai students in 1935.

THE ABACUS

The abacus *(suan pan)* which is to be seen in use throughout the whole of China, has a long history behind it; in its modern form, it is a development of the old *"chou suan"*, a method for calculating by means of movable elements, in which little bamboo counters were used. According to the oldest work on the subject, the *Zhou bi suan jing*, it seems safe to say that the method using little counters was in current use as early as the Spring and Autumn Period (770-221 B.C.). Under the Western Han (about the first century B.C.), it was used for the four basic operations of addition, subtraction, division and multiplication and even for relatively complicated ones like area and volume calculations: the *Jiu zhang suan jing* dates from this period and gives clear proof of it.

Later on, under the Sui and the Tang dynasties, the main manual used was the *Suan jing shi shu*, the *Ten Canons of Calculation:* the bamboo counters were still in use; at the end of the Tang dynasty, however, the system was considered inadequate and impractical; multiplication methods were improved, and new formulae were found to speed up operations. At that time, the *Shu shu ji yi (Miscellaneous Information on Calculation)* mentions "beads" *(zhu):* under the Song, the *Suan jing, (Canon of Calculation)* mentions the abacus *(suan pan)*, but it is not known exactly what the object used was.

In any case, at the end of the Yuan dynasty, the *Nan cun chuo geng lu* (1311) by Tao Zong yi mentions the abacus with movable elements. Later on a treatise on the abacus appeared, under the Ming, called the *Shu xue tong gui:* the abacus with thirteen rows of beads which it describes is exactly the same as the modern abacus.

At the end of the Ming and the beginning of the Qing dynasties the Chinese abacus spread, reaching Korea, Japan, Vietnam, Thailand and even Europe, in the 18th century.

Description

The modern abacus *(zhu suan pan)* consists of a wooden frame *(kuang)* with rods set vertically into it *(dang)*; two sets of beads *(zhu)* are threaded on to the rods, separated by a bar across the middle. They are referred to as *shang zhu*, the upper set of *beads*, and *xia zhu*, the lower set of beads.

The abacus exists in several varieties, but two are more important than the rest:
– the large abacus with 7 beads on each rod, with a total of 11, 13 or 17 rods of them: the top set are worth 5 units a bead; the ones in the lower set are worth one unit each.
– the small abacus with 6 (sometimes 5) beads to a rod, with a total of 21, 25 or even 27 rods of beads. The bead at the top of each rod is worth 5 units; the bottom ones are worth one unit each.

In the short description which follows, the model used is the large abacus.

Preliminary Instructions

The essential principle is this: the only beads which count in the calculation are the ones touching the cross bar *(liang)* mentioned above. In other words, the frame is registering nothing when the beads at the top are pushed up towards the top, and those at the bottom are pushed down to the bottom.

Each of the beads in the top part of the frame is worth *five units;* each bead at the bottom is worth *one unit.* The fourth rod from the right serves as the basis for all operations (the rod is made of metal, whereas the others are wooden): it represents the units; when a bead from the bottom set on this rod is touching the cross bar, it represents one unit; when the five beads in the bottom set have all been moved up towards the bar, they are moved down again and replaced by one bead from the top set; if the two beads from the top set are moved down, they are pushed back and replaced by one bead from the bottom set in the next row, i.e. a bead from the lower set of the fifth rod from the right. As the numbers grow larger, the calculation moves over from right to left.

The system is therefore a decimal one: left of the metal rod will be the tens, the hundreds, the thousands, etc. Right of the rod will be the fractions, the tenths, the hundredths, the thousandths, etc... Should six numbers be needed after the decimal point, the basic rod used for the units can be moved to the left to make more space to the right.

Lastly, the thumb is usually used to slide the beads from the bottom upwards; the first finger is used to move the lower set of beads downwards; the middle finger is used to move the top set of beads both ways. It is better to use this system of fingering from the beginning, as it avoids mistakes through clumsy movements which mean that the whole operation has to be begun all over again.

Fig. 1: Some examples of numbers recorded on the abacus: 15; 3,270 ; 2,470, 575, 35.

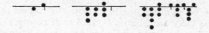

(Figure 1)

N.B. The little mark indicates the units column in each figure.

Addition

When adding two numbers, the first step is to divide them into units, tens, hundreds, etc. ...; then the rest is carried out step by step, starting with the highest and working downwards, hundreds + hundreds, tens + tens, units + units, etc.
Example: 23 + 26
23 is marked up on the frame; then 23 is added to 20, and lastly 43 is added to 6.

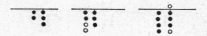

(Figure 2)

22 + 43
22 is marked up on the frame. Next step: 22 + 43. The beads in the lower set are not enough to add four tens, so 5 tens have to be brought down (1 bead from the top set) and one has to be taken away (lower one bead from the bottom set of tens). Next step: 62 + 2. Three beads from the lower set on the units rod have to be moved up, making a total of five against the cross bar; they are moved down again and one bead from the top set of units is brought down. The frame reads 65.

(Figure 3)

96 + 35

The same method is used: 96 + 30 (or 9 + 3 = 9 + 5 – 2);
then the two beads from the top set on the tens rod will be
converted into 1 bead from the lower set on the hundreds rod,
to the left of the one before. Next step: 126 + 5; all that is
needed is to bring down one bead from the top set on the units
rod: then, as there are 2 beads worth 5 each against the bar, they
must be pushed up again and a ten (one bead from the bottom
set) is brought up from the next rod to the left. The frame reads
131.

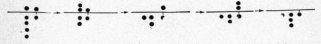

(Figure 4)

77 + 67 = 144 (figure 5) can be done immediately, by reducing
each group of two beads from the top set of a rod to one bead
of the bottom set of the next rod to the left.

(Figure 5)

967 + 85 can also be done immediately; then the result obtained
(figure 6) has to be reduced to something easily readable: 1,052

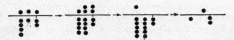

(Figure 6)

Lastly, 4,784 + 3,041 + 25,690
By working gradually through the "reductions", the total 33,515 (figure 7) can be obtained in a few seconds.

(Figure 7)

Subtraction

Here again, the operations are performed step by step: the tens are subtracted from the tens, the units from the units, etc. 89 – 35. 89 is marked up on the frame straight away. Then the next step is 89 – 30 = 59; and 59 – 5 = 54. Two simple movements are enough to complete the operation (figure 1).

(Figure 1)

Next: 56 – 24
56 is marked up on the frame. 56 – 20 = 56 – 50 + 30 (i.e. the bead from the top set, worth 5 tens, is moved up again, and three from below worth 3 tens are brought up the bar). Last step: 36 – 4 = 36 – 5 + 1 (the bead worth 5 units is pushed up, and 1 bead of 1 unit is moved up). The frame reads: 32 (figure 2).

(Figure 2)

It will be noticed that to calculate 47 – 8, 47 – 5 has to be be done first (by moving up the top bead on the units rod again): then a bead in the lower set on the tens rod has to be moved down, and transferred to the next rod to the right, by lowering two beads from the top (twice 5 units); then the operation goes on: two take away three units, one bead in the top set is moved up again (i.e.–5 is recorded) and + 2 is added (two beads from the bottom set on the units rod are moved up). As Chinese novels say, "The action was short, but the narration is leisurely" ... The operation which is simplicity itself in practice (figure 3) must become an automatic action if the complicated calculations yet to come are to be carried out.

(Figure 3)

576 − 132
444 is obtained straight away (figure 4): with practice, it can be done in under 5 seconds.

(Figure 4)

4,132 − 758
The steps can be written as (figure 5) first of all: 4 . 1 . 3 . 2

(Figure 5)

Then:
    3 . 1 . 3 . 2 then, subtracting 7 tens: 3 . 4 . 3 . 2 .

Multiplication

When multiplying, it is easier to have a paper and pencil at hand: this is not because the sum has to be done in the western way, but because it is quicker if the numbers to be multiplied are not marked up on the frame. One could of course merely memorize the figures, but this might be awkward when they have more than 5 digits...

Once more, everything is done step by step, the hundreds, then the tens, etc. ....

53 × 5

First step: 50 × 5.5 × 5 = 25 is done mentally and 25 is marked on the frame, to the left of the units, as the figure belongs to the tens. Next: 3 × 5 = 15; 15 is marked on the frame: one bead from the bottom of the tens rod, one from the top of the units rod. The frame reads 265. Only four movements were needed (figure 1).

(Figure 1)

6,283 × 2

In this type of sum, the number to be multiplied can be marked up on the extreme left of the abacus, to help remember it. The first steps are done mentally: 2 × 6 = 12; 2 × 2 = 4; 2 × 8 = 16; 2 × 3 = 6; each result is marked up on the frame. For 2 × 8 = 16,6 tens (one bead from the top and one from the bottom set on the tens rod) and 10 tens (one bead from the bottom set of the next rod to the left) are marked; the result is 5 hundreds (5 beads from the lower set) which are immediately converted by moving them down and replacing them by one bead from the top set on the same rod which is moved down to the bar.

Result: 12,566 (figure 2)

(Figure 2)

The next sum is 67 × 28
The operation is broken down as follows (figure 3):

(Figure 3)

$$67 \times 28 \begin{cases} 60 \times 28 = \begin{cases} 6 \times 2 = & 12 \\ 6 \times 8 = + 48 \end{cases} = 1680 \\\\ 07 \times 28 = \begin{cases} 7 \times 2 = & 14 \\ 7 \times 8 = + 56 \end{cases} = 0196 \\ = 1876 \end{cases}$$

5,832 × 316

The rod to be used first for marking the results must be carefully worked out; the number to be multiplied has four digits and the other one has three, making a total of 7: there must be seven columns to the right starting from the units column.

The operation is broken down as follows:

$$5,382 \times 316 = 5000 \times 316 \quad \text{(i.e.} \quad \begin{aligned} 5 \times 3 &= 1\,5 \\ +5 \times 1 &= 0\,5 \\ +5 \times 6 &= 3\,0 \end{aligned}$$

$$+ \quad 300 \times 316 \quad \text{(i.e.} \quad \begin{aligned} 3 \times 3 &= 0\,9 \\ +3 \times 1 &= 0\,3 \\ +3 \times 6 &= 1\,8 \end{aligned}$$

$$+ \quad 80 \times 316 \quad \text{(same operation)}$$

$$+ \quad 2 \times 316 \quad \text{(same operation)}$$

All this gives a total of 1,700,712 without involving too much effort (figure 4).

(Figure 4)

Division

For this, it is essential to choose the correct row for the dividend.

The number of digits in the dividend are counted, and 1 is subtracted. Then the number of digits in the divisor is subtracted from this. The units column is kept as usual (i.e. the rod fourth from the right of the frame), unless the number requires to be moved further over to the left.

Figure 1 shows how to mark up the dividend correctly in these operations:

$$1,128 \div 3; \ 18 \div 3; \ 11,429,600 \div 700$$

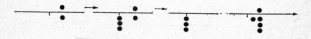

(Figure 1)

As usual, the method to be followed proceeds step by step from the highest downwards. The operation falls into several parts: the dividend is marked up; the number of times the divisor "goes into" it is worked out; the quotient is marked up; multiplication/subtraction is carried out.

The method used for marking up the quotient is unusual:

– if the divisor is lower than or equal to the dividend, the quotient will be marked on the second rod to the left of the dividend (in other words, the rod immediately to the left of the dividend is passed over);

– if the divisor is higher than the dividend, the quotient will be marked on the rod immediately to the left of the dividend.

Once the quotient is marked up, the multiplication/subtraction begins: the divisor is multiplied by the quotient, and the result is subtracted from the dividend. The same operation is repeated for each part of the dividend, moving from left to right.

Example (figure 2): $6 \div 2$

(Figure 2)

1) the correct rod is chosen for the dividend: $1 - 1 - 1 = -2$, so 6 is marked on the second rod to the right of the units column.

2) the calculation: 2 into 6 goes three times; the quotient 3 is lower than the dividend 6: it is marked on the second rod to the left of the dividend, i.e. the units rod.

3) the divisor 2 is multiplied by the quotient 3; two threes are six: 6 is subtracted from the dividend 6 — 6 = 0. All that is left on the abacus is the quotient 3, in the right column.

In the same way (figure 3) 18 ÷ 3 = 6

(Figure 3)

To take a better example: 9,144 ÷ 6

9,144 is marked up correctly (figure 4); the quotient of 9 ÷ 6 is worked out, which is 1; it is marked on the second column to the left of 9; then 1 × 6 = 6; 6 is subtracted from 9; the next step is 31 ÷ 6; the quotient is 5; it is marked on the second rod to the left of 31; 5 × 6 = 30, which is subtracted; the next step is 14 ÷ 6, with a quotient of 2, marked on the second rod to the left of 14; then 2 × 6 = 12, 12 is subtracted from 14, leaving 2; the last step is 24 ÷ 6 = 4. 4 is marked up; then 4 × 6 = 26; 24 is subtracted. The final result is marked up: 1,524.

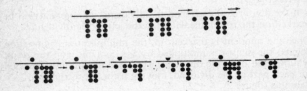

(Figure 4)

The last example with a simple divisor is 11,429,600 ÷ 700 = 16,328 (fig. 5).

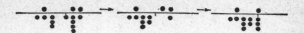

(Figure 5)

Next sum: 96 ÷ 48

96 is marked up correctly. Next 9 ÷ 4 = 2; 2 is marked up on the second rod to the left of 96. To multiply the quotient 2 by the divisor 48, 2 is multiplied by 40 first, giving 80. 8 tens are taken away; then 2 is multiplied by 8, giving 16. 16 is subtracted. The result on the abacus is 2 (figure 6).

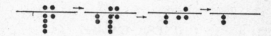

(Figure 6)

Next sum: 296,784 ÷ 687

The operation is arranged first of all (figure 7); 1st step: 29 ÷ 6 = 4, and the quotient is marked up; then 4 is multiplied by 6, then 8 and then 7 and the results are marked up, and subtracted from the dividend; then, 2nd step: 21 ÷ 6 = 3; the quotient is marked up; then 3 is multiplied by 6, then 8, then 7, and the results are subtracted from the dividend. 3rd step: 13 ÷ 6 = 2; 6 is multiplied by 6, then 8, then 7, and the results are subtracted. No remainder; the quotient reads 432.

(Figure 7)

Lastly, 94,386 ÷ 124

(figure 8) 1st step: the quotient is marked up correctly: it is 7, so it is multiplied by 1, then 2, then 4 and the results are subtracted; 2nd step: quotient is 6; multiplication and subtraction; 3rd step: quotient is 1: subtract 124 from the dividend.
Result: 761, remainder 22.

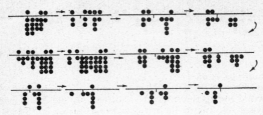

(Figure 8)

CHINESE GAMES

TIAO QI

This is a game widely played in China and relatively easier than *wei qi* and *xiang qi*. It is played on a board shaped like a star of David, with lines on it parallel to the edges of each point of the star. The men are placed at the intersection of the lines, in squares: they are usually glass marbles made in different colours which are put into hollows in a heavy draughts board. The lines are arranged on the board so that each point of the star has ten squares; each point represents a camp with a special colour (red, green, blue, yellow, orange, black). At the beginning of the game, the marbles are put in their own camps, according to their colour, and the hexagon in the middle is left empty. (figure 1 see Atlas, pl. 17).

Two people can play (each person can take one camp, or even three), or else three (each player takes two camps) or as many as six, and the combinations can be arranged to suit the circumstances. Six people can divide into two teams of three people each, or into three teams of two.

The aim of the game is for each player to move the men from his camp into the one on the opposite side of the board, across the centre of the star. The first person to achieve this wins. The game can be made longer by deciding that the men must all be moved across and then back again to the same camp. Again, the first person to finish is the winner.

Each person moves one man forward in turn. When there is nothing in its way, each man can be moved in any direction whatsoever, as long as it moves along the lines traced on the board. Each time a man comes up against an obstacle, in the shape of another man, whether one from his own camp or from his adversary's camp, he can be jumped over it, as in draughts, though without taking it. If after the jump, another man is to be found in a next door square, the first one may be jumped over him too, and so on (figure 2 see Atlas, pl. 18). Single obstacles enable a man to move on more quickly; on the other hand, if two or more men stand in his way, he can move no further.

The tactics consist therefore in:

– forming chains with one's own men or one's adversary's, in which each man has an empty space after him, and making them as long as possible: when a chain is cleverly made, a man can be made to hop over the whole board in one move, and reach the opposite camp.

– spotting the chains made by the other players with their own men: this needs a quick eye, as when the game is moving fast, the mixture of chains and colours is almost impossible to sort out.

– moving one's own men so that they hamper one's opponent's moves as far as possible, and making chains which can be used once only, by ensuring that once the move is over, the man is placed in a position which prevents the opponent's men from crossing the board by using the same chain, and invading one's own camp.

In practice, it is often more amusing to form broken chains rather than straight ones. As the Arab proverb goes, "The easiest way to cross a square is by going round three sides of it" ... It is often possible to cross the central hexagon by working almost all the way round it, using a succession of broken chains.

"BLITZ", ANOTHER WAY TO PLAY

The rules explained above are more or less the most basic ones of all. The Chinese have invented another one, for the use of the true experts. The other method can be used as a whole or in part, at the same time as the rest:

1. When a straight chain contains two men or more, with an empty square at each end, the pieces can be hopped over the whole length of the chain (figure 3 see Atlas, pl. 19).

2. When similar sets of two men or more occur, with an empty space between them, the pieces can again be hopped over them all. (Figure 4 see Atlas, pl. 19).

3. When two or more than two similar sets occur, with empty spaces between them, the men can be made to hop over the whole series. (Figure 5 see Atlas, pl. 19).

4. Each time sequences of men or empty spaces which resemble each other occur, the pieces can be hopped over them all. (Figure 6 see Atlas, pl. 19).

Games played according to these rules, by experienced players, can move at tremendous speed.

CHESS: "XIANG QI"

Although some people claim extremely ancient origins for this game, the oldest document which refers beyond all doubt to *xiang qi* dates from the Bao ying era (762 A.D.) of the Tang dynasty; a chapter of *Xuan guai lu*, the "Chronicle of Strange Mysteries" by Niu Seng ru contains this passage: "Cen Shen of Ru nan lived in the Lü family house in the mountains. One night, he dreamed that two armies were confronting each other: each one had generals, chargers, chariots and soldiers... When he woke up, he dug up the floor (of his house) and came upon an old tomb. He found a gold chess board in the tomb, with a game under way; the chargers were lined up on the board just as they would be for a game of chess". This makes it seem reasonable to suppose that the game was often played during that period. Other accounts which have been found suggest that the rules were not unlike the modern ones, although the nember of pieces was not the same. The *Bo qi li*, a Japanese history of chess, states that at the end of the 8th century, *jiang qi*, which was the ancestor of modern *xiang qi*, already included the following pieces: golden general, jade general, cinnamon charger, scented chariots and foot-soldiers; the pieces from these luxurious armies have come down to the present game, which is known in Japan as "Bao ying (Tang) Chess".

The game developed considerably under the Northern Song dynasty: the *pian* and the *bi* appeared, which correspond to the *shi* and *xiang* (officers and ministers) in the modern game. As early on as this, the general was surrounded by a special area (the general holds roughly the same position as the king in Western chess); a frontier zone, or no man's land was established between the two camps; thirty-two pieces were used, etc.... All these characteristics still survive today.

At the end of the dynasty, the great Chinese poetess Li Qing zhao mentions chess, and makes the laconic comment: "Games of chess, whether *xiang qi* or *wei qi*, large or small, can be played by two people only".

Liu Ke zhuang, writing under the Southern Song dynasty (1201–1276) devoted a poem of 240 characters to the game of *xiang qi;* whatever the poetic value of the poem may be, it reveals that changes had been introduced: the cannon *(pao)* had appeared, an extremely important man which marks an essential difference between the Chinese and Western games.

Xiang qi has remained the same from that period onwards.

Description

The board (which is often no more than a piece of paper with a chess board outlined on it, or even a chalk outline on the pavement) consists of vertical and horizontal lines giving a total of 90 points of intersection. The men are moved along the lines, not from square to square. The general's domain is marked out by two diagonal lines. An empty strip in the middle, drawn horizontally, denotes the river (Han jie, Chu he) which is the frontier between the two camps (figure 1 see Atlas, pl. 20).

The men amount to 32 altogether, and are usually round, made of wood, with the characters "general, soldier, etc...." engraved on them. They consist of:

- 2 *ju*, chariots (marked C)
- 2 *ma*, chargers (marked CH)
- 2 *pao*, cannons (marked CA)
- 5 *zu* (or *bing*), pawns (marked P)
- 2 *xiang*, ministers (marked M)
- 2 *shi*, officers (marked O)
- 1 *jiang* (or *shuai*), general (marked G)
to each side.

Each colour, red and black, has 16 pieces. They are all the same size. Some pieces (ministers, officers, generals, soldiers) can be told apart by their colour and by their names:

RED PIECES		BLACK PIECES
shuai	general	*jiang*
shi	officer	*shi*
xiang	minister	*xiang*
bing	pawn	*zu*

The homophones *shi* and *xiang* are written with different ideograms which unfortunately cannot be conveyed by the transcriptions.

The placing of the pieces is shown in figure 2.

The special domain surrounding the general in each camp is known as Jiu gong, "the nine palaces".

Movements

1. The Chariot

Like the castle in Western chess, it can be moved horizontally or vertically, with no limit on the distance. It cannot hop over another piece: it can take another, however, by taking its place (figure 3).

2. The Cannon

It moves in the same way as the chariot. It is a powerful piece, used in a special way: when it takes another piece, a third must be placed between the cannon and its victim (figure 4).

The cannon may take up all the positions marked by a black dot in figure 4; the red pawn is an insurmountable obstacle. The red officer is threatened: to save it, either it or the minister between it and the cannon must be moved.

3. The Charger

The Chinese charger moves in a different way from our "Western knights". It moves one square, either vertically or horizontally, and then another square diagonally from there. It may not, as might have been expected, hop over other pieces; on the other hand, it may take an opponent's piece by taking its place (figure 5).

The red charger on the figure (marked I) can take up all the positions marked by a black dot; it may also take the black chariot. The black charger, marked 2, may only take up two positions (black dots); the others, marked with a cross, are inaccessible.

4. Pawns

As long as they have not crossed the river, they move one square at a time, vertically. Once they have crossed the frontier, they can move as they like, either vertically or horizontally, though never diagonally. They move one square at a time. They are the only pieces which may not move backwards.

The red pawn *(bing)* on figure 6 has one possible position, which is marked by a black dot. The black pawn *(zu)* has crossed the river: it may either take the red chariot or occupy any of the horizontal positions marked by a black dot.

5. *The Minister*

If the two camps were each divided into two equal squares, two more squares could be drawn diagonally within the others: these diagonal lines are the movements which the ministers are allowed to make: they fly from one corner to another, as long as another piece does not stand in the way.

The arrows on figure 7 show how the red ministers can move; either of them may take the black charger. On the other hand, the ministers in the black camp each have only one possible position.

6. *The Officer*

As often happens, they do not join in with the fight, but stay in their quarters inside the Nine Palaces, where they move backwards or forwards diagonally, one square at a time (figure 8).

The red officer on the figure has only one possible opening (black dot). The black officer has three possibilities, and he could also take the red charger.

7. *The General*

The general is also confined to the Nine Palaces; he can move backwards or forwards, to right or left, one square at a time; he never moves diagonally.

The red general on figure 9 *(shuai)* may take up positions 4 and 3 only. The black general *(jiang)* may move to position 2 only (if he goes to 1, he will be checked).

The aim of the game is "to corner" your opponent's general and "threaten him with death" *(kun bi)*, or to check him (saying "*Jiang!*", check); if he cannot escape, he is checkmated *(jiang si!)*. One last word: the black camp usually begins.

CHESS: "WEI QI"

Whereas *xiang qi* has something in common with Western chess (known in China as "international chess"), *wei qi* is completely different from our ideas of chess. It also exists in Japan, where it is called *go*. It gives rise to tournaments which excite the same passionate interest as other forms of chess, but China and Japan seem to be the only two countries to play *wei qi* at the moment. *Wei qi* was played in Korea in times gone by (another form of *xiang qi* exists there too, with some pieces— pawns, officers, generals—which move according to rules which are different from the Chinese ones) but does not seem to be particularly popular today.

Wei qi (*wei* means to surround, to encircle), or *yi*, as it used to be called, is a very ancient Chinese invention. The *Bo wu zhi* by Zhang Hua, written under the Western Jin Dynasty (265– 316) mentions it, saying that it originated under Emperor Yao "or perhaps" as it amusingly adds "under Emperor Shun" ... The philosopher Meng zi, who was born in 372 A.D., also mentions *wei qi* in a famous parable. There was once, he says, a chess champion called Qiu who was superior to everyone else in this domain. He had two disciples. One of them thought of nothing beyond what the Master said. The other listened too, of course, but could not help thinking that all at once a flock of wild geese might fly across the sky: and he was perpetually on the watch, bow and arrows in hand, ready to shoot. Although the two pupils studied under the same master, the results which they obtained in their work were totally different.

Wei qi has been extremely popular for two thousand years, and was one of the four sublime pastimes alongside the lute, calligraphy and painting *(qin, qi, shu, hua)*. The first treatises on it date from the Warring States period (they were burned by Qin shi Huang di, with numbers of other books). After these vast holocausts, the game almost disappeared at one point. Under the Eastern Han, the great author Ban Gu (32–92 A.D.), a writer of mythological or fantastic stories, devoted one chapter *(yi zhi)* to *wei qi*. The game was enormously popular under the Three Kingdoms and during the period which followed. The Liang Emperor Wu (502–549) even organised nation-wide competitions so that at one point, the Masters of various different categories numbered no fewer than 278. Under the Tang, the poet Du Fu mentions *wei qi* in nine different poems; Emperor Xuan zong instituted officials who were put in charge of this game of chess, the *qi dai zhao*, who came under the Academy of the Forest of Brushes, like the *shu dai zhao* and the *hua dai zhao* for calligraphy and painting. Nearer our own day, in the Kang xi and Qian long eras (1662–1723 and 1736–1776), *wei qi* was all the rage. The names of a few great Masters have survived (Huang Long shi, Fan Xi ping, Xu Xing you, Shi Xiang xia, etc....), as have numerous treatises, such as the *Yi li zhi gui*, *Wei qi Rules*, the *Tao hua quan*, or *Peach Flower Spring*, etc.

The present regime encourages young people to play the game, as it is considered "a rich cultural heritage, helpful in training the mind in intelligence, will, perspicacity, etc." Judging by the number of modern treatises on the subject, it must be difficult to play *wei qi* correctly; the Chinese themselves reckon that it takes forty years of practice to play well. The forewords to the brochures and treatises claim that this is far from the case, and Marshal Chen Yi himself, Chairman of the Chinese *Wei qi* Society has declared: "It is easy to learn *wei qi*, but very hard to reach its quintessence: however, the further one gets into the spirit of the game, the more fascinating it becomes!"... In 1963, a 19 year-old Chinese, Chen Zu de, won a brilliant victory over five Japanese champions.

Description

The game is played on a large chess-board with 19 vertical and 19 horizontal lines, giving a total (sides included) of 361 intersections *(lu)*: the pieces use the intersections, not the squares. Nine of these points are particularly important: they are called *xing* (stars); they fall one at each corner, one in the middle of each side, and one in the middle of the board, called the *tian yuan*. They divide the board into nine zones: upper left corner, lower left corner, upper right corner, lower right corner, upper side, lower side, left side, right side and "belly" (in the middle). When stating the exact position of a pawn, the Chinese use Arabic numerals for the x-axis and Chinese figures for the y-axis; as Arabic numerals, only, for obvious reasons, can be

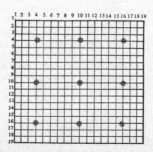

Fig. 1

used here, the first numeral given will always indicate the x-axis. *(Figure 1)*. The pawns, or pieces, which are generally little porcelain cones, one set black and the other white, are heavy and voluminous: there are 180 white pieces and 181 black.

Two players play at the same time: one takes the black, and the other, obviously, the white pieces; "and then", as the Chinese rule puts it, inadvertantly copying Lewis Carroll, "each one plays in turn until the last move, and then the game stops".

The aim of the game is simple: the pieces have first of all to be placed carefully on the board; once a piece has been played, it stays where it is and does not move about the board. This promises a somewhat static game: but under certain circumstances the opponent's pieces can be eaten *(chi)* when they are correctly surrounded. The player who has achieved this then takes over the territory occupied by his opponent's pieces; the whole game consists in planning in such a way as to claim as much territory as possible. Once all the pieces have been played, the amount of territory has to be calculated: he who has the most wins.

Elementary moves will be described here: the opening, strong lines, encircling, taking, etc....

Opening of the game

Two ways of opening the game exist: *dui zi qi* and *rang zi qi*. 1. *dui zi qi:* two players of the same standard will use this method. Black begins. The least able of the two plays black. 2. *rang zi qi:* the "courteous" openings, used when the two players are of different standards. White begins and the weaker player plays black (it should be remembered that there 181 black pieces as against 180 white). The stronger player of the two may also play under a handicap and let his opponent make from 2 to 9 moves and take up all the strategic positions on the board; then the game begins, with white making the first move.

At the beginning of the game, the players usually take up the strategic positions: the four corners (xing).

Strong lines

Figure 2.

When two (or more) pieces from the same camp are in line, it is known as a liaison *(lian jie)*; in figure 2, there is a liaison

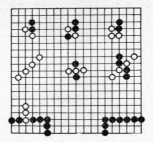

Fig. 2

of 3 whites in the centre (belly); the liaison breaks up two blacks, and cannot itself be broken up by the opposing camp.

Upper left corner: two blacks have formed a liaison; the two whites are not linked.

Upper side: a black (9–5) has split up two whites.

Upper right corner: a white (15–5) makes a double liaison.

Left side: the four whites can be considered as a liaison; two possibilities for a liaison exist, (4–10) and (3–9); if the blacks take up these positions, the whites are split up.

Right side: the four whites arranged in a diagonal line have been broken up by the blacks; this shows that diagonal liaisons are less certain than horizontal or vertical ones.

Lower right corner: 8 linked blacks occupy 10 intersecting points altogether; these ten points are what is known as a "territory" *(di)*; this technique of sealing off an area is the essential principle of the game, and may enclose empty squares, or pieces from the opposing camp, either temporarily or permanently.

Lower left corner: a situation resembling the one just described, though the three whites (3–17) prevent the area from being sealed off completely, so the points encircled by the blacks cannot be considered as a territory.

Routes: "Dan Guan"

As soon as a liaison has been built up, wherever it may be on the board, the next step is to encircle a territory. The zones linking territories belonging to the two opponents are known as *dan guan*.

Figure 3

Upper right corner: the blacks have sealed off a territory of 10 intersecting points: the expressions used are 10 "routes" *(lu)* or 10 eyes *(mu)*.

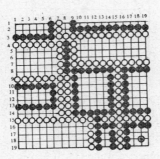

Fig. 3

In the upper left corner, the blacks have encircled a territory with 10 routes (2×5); in the belly in the centre, they enclose 20 routes (4×5); on the lower side they have 3 routes; on the left side they have 15 (3×5); in the lower right corner they have 8 routes, making a total of 76. The piece at (18–18) is black (marked by a black dot): this territory counts as 8 routes, not 9.

The whites have 30 routes on the right side (3×10), 24 on the left side (4×6), 40 in the lower left corner, making a total of 94 routes.

This figure shows a situation which would arise towards the end of the game, where the whites are leading by 18 routes (or 18 points: see later on for the methods for counting points).

As far as zones of contact between enemy territory are concerned, it will be noticed that there are two points on the upper side, 6 on the left side (8–1 and 8–2; 1–14, 2–14, 3–14, 4–14, 5–14, 6–14 respectively): these are not territories, but *dan guan*, which could be translated as public property. As they cannot be used either to enlarge one's own territory, or to limit the enemy's, they are usually left as they are until the end of the game, when each player places pieces there in turn.

TAKING THE ENEMY'S PIECES - BREATH

Figure 4

Upper left corner: the black piece on 4–4 (star) commands four lines: routes 4–3, 4–5, 3–4, 5–4, which represent the four possibilities of combination open to it; it is said to have four "breaths" *(qi)*, four sources of energy; if the opponent takes the four points surrounding the black piece, it will lose all its "breaths" and will be dead (see below), at which point the opponent can take it and remove it from the board.

Upper side: a black piece has taken over the star (10–4), and is already surrounded on three sides by whites (9–4; 10–5; 11–4); once the whites take over 10–3 (the piece marked) the black piece will be dead and can be taken (*ti:* to pick up).

Upper right corner: four whites have encircled a black piece and taken it.

Left side: as the piece on 1–10 is on the edge of the board, it has only three "breaths": three whites only would be needed to take it.

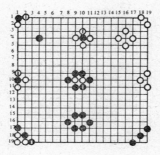

Fig. 4

Right side: 3 whites have just taken a black.

Upper left corner: the piece on 1–1 has only two "breaths", because of its position: two other pieces could take it, once the whites have taken over 2–1.

Upper right corner: two whites have just taken a black piece.

Generally speaking, once the pieces have had all their sources of breath cut off and are dead, they are no further use on the board, and are removed.

In the centre: black plays 10–11 and takes two whites.

Lower side: two whites have just been taken.

Lower left corner: if black plays 3–19, he can take three whites.

Lower right corner: three whites have just been taken.

The elementary tactics revealed by all this are as follows: to win, one must take over as much territory as possible; in order to do this, the open spaces must be encircled and sealed off; as well as this, the enemy's pieces must also be surrounded, for as soon as this has been achieved, they are dead, so they are taken, and the taker claims the territory which they occupied.

A FEW POSSIBILITIES

Figure 5.

Upper left corner: the intersection 4–4 is surrounded by white pieces: a black piece must not be put there, for it would be killed immediately.

Upper side: the same is true for 11–4.

Upper right corner: the same is true again for 17–3.

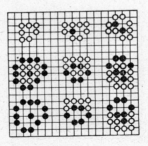

Fig. 5

Left side: the black piece marked 1 takes over 4–10: although all sources of breath *(qi)* are cut off, it must be placed there, because the white pieces round it are themselves encircled by another ring of black pieces. At this point the black pieces take the 7 white ones.

Lower left corner: the white pieces have just been taken.

Centre: once black has played 11–9 (piece marked 1), the two white pieces will be taken. If black does not play 11–9, white will play, take over 11–9 and take a black piece (10–9),

Lower side: two white pieces have just been taken.

Right side: black piece 1 plays 17–10 and takes two whites. If the black piece had not been played there, white could have done so and would have taken two black pieces (16–10 and 17–11).

Lower right corner: two white pieces have just been taken.

STRIKE – UNITE – EXTEND – RECOVER

Figure 6

Upper side: once the white piece 1 has been played, another white one must be played (9–3) to take the black one: this tactic is known as striking *(da)*. In this case, black 2 is played and takes over 9–3 to save the threatened piece (10–3) and at the same time to link it with the other vertically placed black pieces. This is known as *nian*, to unite.

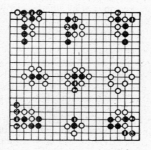

Fig. 6

Lower side: a black piece is surrounded by three white ones; black must then play 10–16, and complete what is known as an "extension" *(chang)*. This manœuvre gives three sources of breath to the black pieces instead of one.

Left side: although the two black pieces still have breath available, they are already surrounded and cannot escape.

Centre: if black is not careful, he will play piece 1 and place it on 10–11, in the hopes of saving the two black pieces which have already been encircled; the white piece 2 would then be able to take 3 black pieces.

Right side: the three pieces just mentioned have been taken.

Upper left corner: the black pieces are threatened, so one makes a diversion by taking over 4–1; this move is known as a "recovery" *(li)*. The white piece 2 strikes; the black 3 creates a diversion (3–1), a move described as "sinuous" *(qu);* it has achieved nothing which could change the source of breath for the black pieces which are now sealed off by the white pieces (piece 4). The manœuvre made by black, aimed at saving one piece, lost three.

Upper right corner: black 1 strikes; the only course left to white is to play piece 2. Both adversaries have played well: black has managed to cut down the losses and take part of the corner of the board.

Lower left corner: black 1 carries out an extension (2–16); white 2 makes a recovery; the sinuous move made by black 3 cannot prevent white 4 completing the encircling move; black's tactics have done no more than increase his losses.

Lower right corner: black 1 strikes, leaving white 2 to take a black piece. This is sound tactics: if black 3 makes an extension, it could result in sealing off the territory at the corner of the board.

EYE – FALSE EYE – INNER BREATH

When several pieces surround an intersection, it is known as an "eye" *(yan:* eye, hole, eyelet). This is done to prevent the the opponent from taking certain pieces. As will now be seen, however, dangerous "false eyes" may occur.

Upper left corner: 7 black pieces have surrounded a point, which is now in their possession, and its breathing capacity is indicated by the expression *nei qi*, meaning "inner breath". White will not dare play into this territory, for it is a true eye.

Upper side: 5 black pieces outline an eye.

Upper right corner: three black pieces form an eye.

Left side: six black pieces (three of them marked) surround a point which looks like an eye; in fact it is nothing of the sort! Two dangerous white pieces (marked in the figure, on 5–9 and 3–11) are going to strike the 3 marked black pieces; if white then plays on 4–10, the three marked black pieces will be taken.

Centre: white 1 isolates three black pieces and takes them.

Right side: situation once the pieces have been taken.

Lower right corner: to save the three black pieces which are likely to be encircled, black must place the piece with a mark on it on 4–16, and unite them.

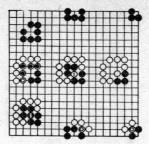

Fig. 7

Lower side: the four black pieces (because of the white piece with a mark on it) form a false eye.

Lower right corner: the two black pieces also form a false eye, because of a white piece (with a mark on it).

MOVABLE EYE – HALF–EYE

When a piece is surrounded, all source of breath is cut off and it can be taken, as has already been said. The method for forming defensive "eyes" on the board has also been described. But if an enemy piece is placed in the middle of an eye which has already been surrounded all the pieces are lost. A way of avoiding this must be found: the technique is to form *two* "*eyes*"; it is known as *huo qi*: "movable arrangement". It is also called "movable eye" (*huo yan*).

Figure 8

Upper left corner: although the white pieces have pushed the black pieces into a tight corner, they cannot take them because of their "movable arrangement": white cannot play on 5–5 or 5–7.

Right side: the black pieces have created a movable arrangement.

Upper right corner: although 6 black pieces are surrounded by numerous enemies, they are in no danger, because of the two eyes, (19–1 and 18–2).

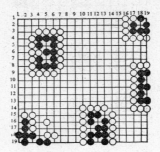

Fig. 8

Lower side: the black pieces have been placed in a movable arrangement; if white plays on 11–17, the black pieces can form two eyes (13–15); if white plays on 13–15, black plays on 11–17 and forms two eyes.

Lower left corner: the black pieces have again been placed in a movable arrangement. If white plays on 4–18, changing 3–19 into a false eye for black, black plays on 1–16 and forms an eye; if white breaks up this eye from 1–16, black can still make one on 4–18. As black already has an eye on 1–19, as well as two unfinished ones, it is more accurate to speak in terms of a "half-eye": whatever attack white makes, whichever black eye is broken up, black can always make up another one and still have a total of two.

DEATH

When a group of pieces is surrounded by the enemy and when it has *not got two eyes*, it is said to be "dead".

Figure 9

Left side: two black pieces are almost surrounded by white pieces; although they can still breathe, they cannot create any diversions: they are dead.

Upper left corner: the black pieces have formed only one real eye; the other one is a false eye, as two white pieces with marks on them are close by; the black pieces are dead.

Upper right corner: the black pieces are arranged in such a way that they are dead. In fact if the pieces marked 1, 2, 3 play, they can take three black pieces by moving on to 15–5, and then six black pieces from 14–4.

Lower side: the black pieces have formed one eye only; the eyes at the edge of the formation are false ones. White plays on 12–19 and takes 3 black pieces, then on 9–19 and takes one black piece.

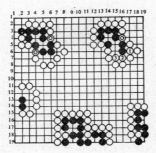

Fig. 9

Lower right corner: the black pieces form one eye only; as a white piece with a mark on it is present in the other, it is a false eye.

In all these cases, pieces were arranged in such a way that they were dead: this is important when counting the points.

It is impossible to explain many of the basic moves and opening or battle tactics in detail here. One useful piece of strategy will be described, before an account of the points system is given.

"TO STRIKE LIGHTLY"

Figure 10

Nine white pieces are encircled by black pieces; they form one eye only, and the black pieces are particularly well-arranged round the outside: the white pieces seem to be in a dangerous position.

They may be saved in this way:

The white piece 1 "strikes lightly" *(pu)* on 5–19; this manœuvre allows the white piece 3 to prevent the black pieces from
uniting. If the black pieces do unite by using 5–19, white plays
on 7–19 with piece 5 and takes all the black pieces. In no time
at all, white has created a movable arrangement.

Fig. 10

The three black pieces at the bottom are under attack from
the white pieces, but to take them, white has to risk three
pieces. If white moves in to attack, black replies immediately:
a special trick is needed to take the three black pieces. The tactic
known as "striking lightly" forces black to obstruct his own
position. White continues and strikes with piece 3, making
black unite by playing on 5–19, which means that he gets even
more tied up. White has won; he takes three pieces and loses
only one.

COUNTING THE POINTS

The Chinese method will be described (the Japanese use a
different one).

The board contains 361 intersections, or 180½ for each side,
if they are counted as equal; consequently it is a waste of time
to count the results for one camp and then for the other, and
it is quite enough to count up one player's points only. The
number of points of intersection occupied by one player will
be counted, including the empty territories belonging to him,
and the positions occupied by his pieces: the player who has
a total of over 180½ points is the winner.

Several steps are followed:

1. First of all, all the dead pieces are removed from the board.
Figure 11 shows the state of the battlefield at the end of the
game. *Figure 12* shows it cleared of the bodies.

2. The large numbers are counted first of all, such as those of the white player on this figure. To make this easier, the small territories are filled with white pieces; figure 12 shows 8 sets of 10, i.e. 80.

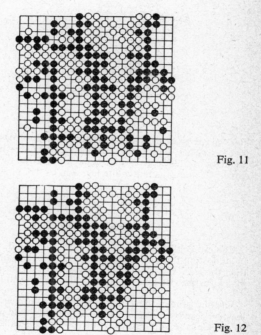

Fig. 11

Fig. 12

3. The rest are counted. Once all the small territories have been counted *(figure 13)* the result is 102 for white, giving a total of 182; the white player has therefore won by 1½ points.

4. When the game is a "courteous" one between opponents of different standards, when the white player has for instance accepted a handicap of, say, 9 pieces, it is customary for the

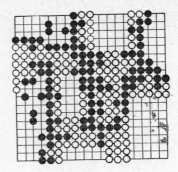

Fig. 13

black player to give back half of this, in this case, 4½. Supposing that white has accepted a handicap of 4 pieces in the above calculations: black gives him back 2 points at the end of the game, which means that white has won by 3½ points.

CHINESE COOKING

Chinese cooking is famous all over the world, and enjoyed by almost all those who know it; its traditions go back further than those of French cooking and are just as varied. It is a fit match for the rich and powerful civilisation which has produced it.

Various studies have been written in China itself on its history, development and wealth. The last to date was published by the Chinese administration in 1963, and is called *Zhong guo ming cai pu, A Treatise on Chinese Cooking*.

Recipe books in foreign languages are fairly numerous, but treatises on Chinese gastronomy are extremely rare. *Musings of a Chinese Gourmet* (pub. in London) by F. T. Cheng, once Chinese ambassador to Great Britain, provides a pleasant insight into the subject.

The rich vocabulary associated with cooking gives some idea of the enormous variety of recipes and the countless dishes. Over 20 terms exist to describe methods to be used, and even more deal with the appearance or consistency of a dish: anything crisp is called *su*, peeled food is known as *ren*, rolls are *juan*, anything in threads is *si*, cubes are *ding*, pieces are *kuai*, finely chopped food is *mo*, powder is *fen*, little balls are *qiu*, larger ones are *wan zi*, egg fritters are *gao li*, fritters are *ruan sha*, anything in sections is *duan*, anything long is *tiao*, anything with caramel round it is *ba si*, etc. etc. ...

Chinese cooking is extremely versatile and most of the meat, fish and vegetables known in Europe are used. As well as these, and partly, it seems, thanks to the lively imagination of the Cantonese, other products unknown in Europe and America or viewed by foreigners with prejudice or even disguest, are used. This category includes, for instance, what is known as "bird's nest", and which is in fact mucus from the salivary gland of the salangane, "sharks' fins", "sea-slugs", snake, dog, bears' paws, and fish stomach. One's taste papillae are a more reliable guide to these than one's imagination.

The foreign traveller should not make a mistake here however — the dishes which appear in everyday life are not rarities such as these: dog and bears' paws are not often to be found. The Chinese do not make up their ordinary fare according to the menus of the great restaurants. Until the last few years, the Chinese peasant ate much more frugally than the bourgeoisie; the situation was comparable with that in 18th century France.

Although the cooking is refined in the extreme, the surroundings are almost wholly neglected as a rule. The table is rarely decorated, and the dining-room summarily so. The table cloth, when it exists, is of rough cotton; napkins are exceptional. The glass ware is of the most undistinguished, and the chairs are uncomfortable: the food is all important. Other striking differences occur in the drinks: those found most frequently are spirits, yellow wine, beer or sparkling fruit juice. Beer and sparkling fruit juice are both recent innovations, and partly due to the taste of foreigners; the Chinese themselves seem to enjoy them, however. Cheese is unknown, and "puddings" are outstanding, but few in number compared with the other dishes. Bread as we know it does not exist, but each meal is accompanied by different kinds of biscuits or pancakes, or rolls which are steamed or baked.

As chopsticks are used, knives are not, and every dish has to be cut up beforehand into pieces which are small enough to pick up easily. Consequently the food is often unrecognisable: the intricate preparation and subtle sauces often mask the taste, disguising the true nature of the dish.

A meal consists of many courses, but each one is small in quantity: everything to appeal to the gourmet. It should be added that here, as in everything else, the general tendency is now towards simplification, and elimination of methods of preparation which are particularly long and recipes which involved cruelty, such as donkey scalded alive. Other dishes are becoming rare because the animal concerned is disappearing: this is the case as far as bears' paws are concerned. They are said to be delicious, but have now almost completely vanished.

Foreign influence has also left its mark: a Chinese table used not to have any glasses on it; china bowls of different sizes were used, which fitted into each other. Ordinary glasses have now replaced the bowls. Even yellow wine, which above all is usually considered to require a china bowl, is sometimes served in little glasses with stems. A spare pair of chopsticks is now provided for the host to help his guests, whereas before he would always use his own. Table decorations often receive more attention in official banquets, to vie with those abroad, whereas in the south more than the north, both the room and the furniture are becoming less makeshift.

The Customs and the Setting

Meals are usually early. Breakfast is between 6 and 8 a.m.; lunch is between 11 and 1 o'clock; and dinner from 5.30 to 7.30 p.m. When invited to a meal, it is polite to arrive slightly early. The invitation is sent to you on a card, which may be engraved with bamboos, either on the day before or even the day itself. Characters written in red (festive) are only to be seen on official invitations extended by the Government. Courteous Chinese formulae such as the one requesting your "luminous presence" (guang lin) are used.

Whether you are received — though this is exceptional — in a drawing-room near the dining-room, or as is usually the case, in the dining-room itself, green tea will be offered on a low table surrounded by sofas and arm-chairs, and hot towels will be handed round for guests to wipe their hands or, if they like, their faces as well. An extremely general conversation lasting at least ten minutes or at most half an hour precedes the meal.

Your hosts will be wearing the classic Chinese jacket which buttons up to the neck in winter; in summer they will be in short sleeved, open-necked shirts.

Protocol

The table is round; the ideal figure is considered to be eight people.

According to classic protocol, the place of honour was opposite the door leading into the room; the other guests were placed in order to the left and right of this place, the host taking the last place. This rule is still in use, but Western protocol has made its influence felt. The hosts themselves often preside, in fact, the most important of them sitting opposite the door, and the guests taking their places on the right and left, in that order, of each of them. Women are rarely present, and the presence of foreigners makes interpreters necessary, which disrupts the normal order.

The Individual Place

Each person usually has a little plate in front of him; in front of it to the left is a little saucer, for mixing sauces, with a china spoon; beside it are a bowl and a pair of chopsticks.

In banquets, also as a result of foreign influence, three wine glasses are to be found in front of each place: the one to the right is for spirits, the one in the middle for white wine and the one on the left for red wine. A large glass accompanies them, for beer or sparkling orange juice. Green tea is always available when asked for. Yellow wine is served in a little bowl to the right of the glass for spirits.

Chopsticks, which are usually eight inches long, may be of many different kinds. The plainest of all are made of bamboo or wood, the most elaborate are of lacquered wood, bone or ebony. They may also be made of tin (though this is rare), ivory and silver. Plastics are coming in here too, and chopsticks are sometimes made of this.

The longer wooden chopsticks, which foreigners usually call "Mongolian" chopsticks, are used only when a Mongolian stew is on the menu, when each person cooks his own food in a communal pot, or over charcoal, in the middle of the table.

The host gives the signal to begin at the opening of the meal by helping the guests on either side of him with a pair of chopsticks placed specially for this in front of him.

It is customary to make speeches at a banquet, and they are given after the hors d'œuvre, and always before a main dish. The host may either reply straight away, or wait until the next dish arrives. Toasts are drunk before speeches, after speeches and all through the meal, in spirits or *mao tai*. If the spirits are thought to be too strong, it is no longer considered discourteous to decline to drink them, and to prefer to drink wine, or even beer or orange juice instead, if one is forbidden to drink alcohol. Incidentally, it is forbidden to drive in China after drinking even the smallest amount of alcohol, including beer. It is the custom to reply to each toast which may be proposed to you by raising your glass in turn.

The meal ends with fruit, served either at the table or at the low tables in front of the arm-chairs where the guests are received at first. Hot towels are again distributed for wiping one's fingers. Neither coffee, cigars, nor liqueurs are served. The evening ends soon afterwards; dinners finish early in China, at about eight or nine o'clock.

Regional Differences

In China, as in France, for example, provincial styles of cooking exist, each with their peculiarities and specialities (*zhuan men cai*). The Chinese divide them mainly into southern (*nan fang cai*) and northern (*bei fang cai*) cooking; the former is usually more highly spiced and therefore hotter than the latter, no doubt because of the damper southern climate, in which, according to the Chinese, spices are needed to stimulate the appetite, and the dry climate in the north. A touch of sugar is also used in southern dishes. Sausages (*xiang chang*) from Canton are sweetened, whereas the ones from Peking are not.

Canton may be considered as the capital of southern cooking. It is well known for its numerous restaurants, and many restaurants abroad have Cantonese specialities on their menus. Dishes from there are known all over south China, but they are still at their best in the town itself. Some of the most well known are: beef cooked with oyster oil (*hao you niu rou*), boned fish (*song su tuo gu yu*), snake (*she*) either fried or in a soup, goose (*shao e*), turtle (*yuan yu*), eel (*shan yu*), white chicken (*bai zhan ji*), and sweet cutlets (*tang pai gu*) as part of the hors d'œuvre.

Si chuan is known for the abundant use of pimento and spices. The dishes are extremely hot; Si chuan noodles are one of the most characteristic ones from this rich province.

The *Jiang huai* area in Jiang su, near the Yang zi, is famous for its steamed shad, its rolls filled with stuffing and eaten with soup, its rolls stuffed with crabs' eggs, and its vegetables (broad beans and peas) fried in chicken fat. The cooking here is essentially much lighter than that to be found in central China.

Jiang xi is famous for a speciality known as "three glass (soya sauce, water and wine) chicken" *(san bei ji)*, and also for steamed meat or duck with crushed rice.

Hu nan and *Hu bei* are both known for chicken and pimento *(la zi ji)*, soy-bean omelettes *(dou pi)* and bread with stuffing.

Yun nan is best known for its steamed chicken, cooked in a special steamer *(qi juo ji)* and ground rice vermicelli, soaked in hot sauce *(guo qiao mi xian)*.

The northern style of cooking includes that of *Shan xi*, famous for its use of noodles.

Shan dong is the native province of many Pekingese cooks, and its specialities have gradually spread throughout north China, so that it is now hard to tell Shan dong and Pekingese cooking apart. The province has produced many great dishes, to be found on the menus of all big restaurants in Peking. Roast ducks and stews are specialities of the capital itself.

PLAIN COOKING

Breakfast *(zao dian)* is eaten early, and naturally earlier in the country then in town.

In the towns and villages, at least, it consists of dry biscuits, fried food, and unleavened rolls stuffed with bean paste *(bao zi)* or coated with sesame seeds *(zhi ma)*, eaten with salted vegetables. The Chinese are particularly fond of a crisp fried form of food known as *you zha gui*, or "devils fried in oil". Thick noodle soup is often eaten as well. In the North, soy—bean milk *(dou fu jiang)* is drunk, and in the south, they drink a sort of clear soup made from rice, which takes a long time to cook *(da mi zhou)* *(conjee)*.

Breakfast is therefore a substantial meal, entirely Chinese in its composition: coffee and tea, whether China or Ceylon tea, are of course unknown. Green tea is drunk very rarely.

Rice is the basic food in the south, and noodles form that of the north.

"Pasta" *(mian shi)* include other types apart from noodles and vermicelli: *shui jiao* or ravioli, and *bao zi*, or stuffed steamed rolls, *bing*, or pancakes and dry biscuits, and a type of bread *(man tou)*.

Noodles of all kinds are to be found *(mian tiao)*, ranging from rice noodles *(mi xian)* and noodles of wheat flour and eggs *(yu fu mian)*, a Shang hai speciality, to vermicelli made of flour *(gua mian)*. They are made in several different ways: sometimes the dough is cut up with a knife over the cooking-pot *(dao xiao mian)*, sometimes a more liquid dough is cut round the edge of a bowl with a chopstick *(bo yu)*.

They may appear in a soup, with other ingredients *(tang mian)*: with chicken *(ji si tang mian)*, meat *(rou si tang mian)*, shrimps *(xia ren tang mian)*, with eel *(shan yu tang mian)* or with various different things *(shi jin tang mian)* or with pimentos *(dan dan mian)*, a Si chuan speciality.

They may also be grilled or fried *(chao mian)* with the same ingredients as in the list of soups, and with others too. Or they may be eaten cold with pimento *(la zi leng mian)* or hot in a stew accompanied by various cereals *(za mian)*, which is a Pekingese speciality.

Ravioli exists in many forms too: in soup *(hun dun)*, in water *(shui jiao)*, steamed *(zheng jiao)*, lightly fried *(guo tier)*, etc....

The same variety of preparation is to be found in the different sorts of *bao zi*, or rolls stuffed with vegetables and meat *(cai rou bao zi)*, or meat alone *(tian jin bao zi)*, a Tian jin speciality to be found at the *Gou bu li* restaurant "even dogs cannot see" (the secret of the recipe), or with medlars or aromatic herbs *(tang bao zi)*, with a sweet, dark brown stuffing *(dou sha bao zi)*, or with soup *(tang bao zi)*. They may also be stuffed, but open *(shao mai)*.

Pancakes also exist in as many different varieties *(bing)*: they may be very thin *(bao bing)* —to eat with roast duck—; they may be "spring" *(chun bing)*, or "family" *(jia chang bing)* pancakes (the latter are large floury ones), or stuffed with meat *(rou bing)*, or sesame *(shao bing)*, or without sesame *(huo shao)*, with leeks *(cong huar bing)*, spiral-shaped *(luo si zhuan)*, in the shape of a donkey's hoof *(lu ti)* or a horse's hoof *(ma ti)*, both of which are a sort of dry biscuit with sesame, or crisp and brittle *(yi wo si qing you bing)*.

Finally, the bread may be made into round loaves *(man tou)*, rolls *(hua juanr)*, or threads *(yin si juanr)*.

The Principle of Chinese Gastronomy

Three senses have to be satisfied in order to comply with the conception of Chinese gastronomy: sight, taste and smell.

Dishes have to fulfill special criteria as far as their colour, smell and taste are concerned.

The colour of a dish has to be satisfying to the eye, and the balance of colours is kept in mind during its composition. Bamboo shoots, which are much the same colour as an eggshell, are combined with the green leaves of a type of fried cabbage. Green or red peppers are used to contrast with the white part of a chicken. Sea-slugs are also combined with bamboo shoots.

The sense of smell is satisfied by avoiding all unpleasant smells, as well as all strong ones which might dominate the rest. Different tastes should balance each other as the colours do. The Chinese base their cooking on five tastes: acid *(suan)*, hot *(la)*, bitter *(ku)*, sweet *(tian)*, salt *(xian)*.

A balanced meal should contain alternating crisp and juicy, dry and sticky dishes. Sugar and vinegar are mingled in a famous sauce *(tang cu)*, used either with fish or meat, usually pork.

The taste may be unadulterated, but in this case it should be backed up in some way. At the same time, the china used is theoretically extremely important, and should be as delicate as the dishes it contains. Its colour may be chosen to match the occasion: red or pink for a wedding (red is the symbol of happiness in China), yellow decorated with the character for longevity, or with symbols standing for it (peaches, for instance) is used for celebrations marking a birth in the family; blue and white are the colours for everyday use.

According to tradition, there should be as many dishes as there are guests, not counting the hors d'œuvre and the soups. This custom has been simplified, although each meal still consists of a large number of dishes. The composition of the menu requires the greatest care, as might be expected. It consists of hors d'œuvre, lesser dishes, great dishes, soups and dessert. The hors d'œuvre *(leng cai)* may be arranged in a single dish divided into four or eight sections, when it is called "butterfly" hors d'œuvre *(ku die pin pan)*, or in four, six or eight different plates.

The "lesser dishes" should balance the "great" dishes, and the former should outnumber the latter. Furthermore, the fundamental principle of balanced taste and texture should be observed within the main framework, so that a crisp dish is followed by a smooth, creamy one, and a salted dish is followed by a sweet one.

The same principle must apply to the great dishes. Duck, for instance, cannot be preceded or followed by chicken; it is better followed by sea-slugs *(hai shen)* or sharks' fins. The last of the great dishes is often fish; it precedes the soup, which marks the end of the meal. Sometimes, though not always, soup is accompanied by sweet dishes.

The most sumptuous banquets may contain the same pattern of dishes repeated twice over: the hors d'œuvre is followed by a first series of "lesser dishes", "great dishes", soup and dessert, and then by a second series of lesser dishes, great dishes, soup and dessert, all in the same order as the first one.

It should be pointed out that generally speaking, the dishes are not arranged in the strict order which they should traditionally follow.

The dishes forming the hors d'œuvre are all cold. They usually contain: the famous "rotten" eggs *(song hua)*, usually black or orange, which are eggs cooked slowly by chemical reaction induced by a bath of lime; they cheat the imagination, for they are not 100 years old, but only one or two months; ham *(huo tui)* from Yun nan or Jin hua, a town in Zhe jiang, both well up the standard of the best foreign ham; duck of various kinds, either the feet, or sliced duck, or liver; lotus roots *(ou)*; mushrooms *(mo gu)*, either fresh or dried—the best dried mushrooms come from the north east; dried jelly-fish mixed with cucumber; shrimps *(xia)*; dried oysters, or smoked or salt oysters *(ge li)* ormers or haliotides *(bao yu)*; and more rarely, crab preserved in white spirits; sweet fish in vinegar *(su yu)*; scalded chicken *(bai zhan ji)*; little sausages from the south; and finally, a selection of cooked vegetables, which may include beans, peppers, bamboo shoots and sometimes tomatoes, in honour of foreign guests. Jujubes in honey *(mi zao)* sometimes appear too.

Too many "lesser dishes" exist to allow them to be listed, even only partially. Crayfish in sauce *(da xia)*, shrimp rissoles *(gao li xia ren)*, and fried duck liver *(zha ya gan)* are the best known.

Among the "great dishes", bird's nest soup is one of the best known *(yan wo tang*, literally: swallow's nest), which does not at first, at least, appear to be a special dish; it is nevertheless a soup with a remarkably subtle flavour. Sea slugs, the very thought of which generally provokes disgust in foreigners, are caught off the south coast of China, or imported from Japan. They are dried in the sun and soaked for seven days. They are cleaned on the second day, to make them dilate, and in summer they are boiled once a day to prevent them from rotting. They should be soaked in spring, not tap water. They are often mixed with "fish stomach" *(yu du)*, and the whole is served in a sauce based on the soy-bean, which to a Chinese palate gives an infinite subtlety to the dish. Sea-slugs are considered as a strong tonic in China.

Sharks' fins need lengthy preparation, because they are bought dried. They have to be cleaned several times with the greatest care. They are a speciality of Peking and Shang hai, and are served mixed either with chicken or pork fillet in a sauce based on the soy-bean.

Roast duck, the most famous Peking speciality, is a white Peking duck, forcibly fed and killed young (from 3 to 6 months). The ducks are killed and eaten at the restaurant; before cooking, they are emptied through a hole pierced under the wing, and air is pumped under the skin. The inside of the bird is half filled with water through the rump, and the opening plugged with a section of sorghum stem. It is then hung up in the oven by its head. The water inside is converted into steam, so that the flesh is cooked from the inside, and the fire, for which jujube-tree wood or sometimes pear wood or apricot-tree wood is used (because they produce the least smoke) roasts the outside skin until it is crisp. It takes three quarters of an hour to cook, in an open or a closed oven (the open oven is most widely used), and it is basted with its own fat while it is cooking. When done, it is cut into thin slices which are eaten rolled in pancakes made of wheat flour, or in rolls covered with sesame seeds, cut in two. Each slice is dipped into a thick brown sauce made from wheat flour fermented for a month *(mian jiang)* before the pancake is wrapped round it. Leeks, cucumber or sometimes turnips, finely sliced, are served with the sauce. Roast duck may be included in the menu for a banquet.

Ormers *(bao yu)* are considered an excellent dish; they usually appear as ivory-coloured slices.

Bears' paws have for centuries—Confucius himself shared this opinion—been considered as the rarest delicacy of all. They grow more and more rare as the years go by.

Stews

Stews, another speciality of the north, and usually known as "Mongolian", are served in winter in a limited number of restaurants (in Peking these are: "Dong Lai Shun", "Hong Bing Lou", "Kao Rou Wan", "Kao Rou Ji").

A copper pot, with red-hot charcoal in a compartment at the base of it to keep the water, and later the soup, at boiling-point, is placed in the middle of the table. Plates are arranged round the pot, in front of the guests, containing finely sliced mutton, liver, kidneys, vermicelli, noodles, cabbage, parsley, onion and ravioli.

While the ingredients are cooking in the pot, each person makes up his own sauce in his bowl from a tray of seven different ones which are offered to him (*jiang you:* soy sauce; *lü xia you:* shrimp sauce; *jiu cai hua:* chive-flower sauce; *zhi ma jiang:* sesame-seed puree sauce; *la jiao you:* pimento sauce; *jiang dou you:* bean-curd sauce; *pao jiu:* old wine sauce). Then each person helps himself to meat, vegetables and noodles and makes up his own mixture, adding sweet cloves of garlic; rolls covered with sesame seeds are eaten at the same time.

At the end, the soup left from the cooking of the ingredients is drunk.

In October and November, an added touch of subtlety may be given by using chrysanthemum petals *(ju hua)* as well; the variety thus created, which originated in the south, is then called after the flower.

The same type of ingredients may be cooked on a heated metal plaque instead of in water. In this case, it is placed outside, instead of on the table, and the guests prepare their food round it, and eat it standing up. Beef may be used as well as mutton, and is also cooked by each person as he wants, using the so-called Mongolian chopsticks, and adding eggs and vegetables. This method cuts out the use of vermicelli and noodles. The seven sauces used in the stew are replaced by soy sauce, into which the meat is dipped before being cooked on the plaque.

Lastly, it should be pointed out that the Moslem restaurants specialise in mutton cooked on the spit, and coated with sesame seeds *(yang rou chuan)*.

Soups

A meal without at least one clear soup is unthinkable. An enormous variety of soups exists; most of them are of a highly subtle flavour. The ingredients of some soups may vary from one restaurant to another, and obviously from one town to another. This is the case with, for instance, "three fresh ingredients" soup *(san xian tang)*, which is always delicious, but which varies from one place to another.

The masterpiece among soups is bird's nest soup, which has already been mentioned in the paragraph on "great dishes". Another delicately flavoured soup is the *chun cai tang*, made from water plants gathered in the famous Western Lake at Hang zhou. *zhu sun tang* is a soup made from bamboo marrow. *suan la tang* is made of peppers and vinegar, to which chicken blood and bean-curd are added in the north. "All fish" soup *(chuan yu tang)* is a kind of bouillabaisse. *zha cai tang* is a vegetable soup using vegetables from Si chuan, *bai cai tang*, a cabbage soup, is more delicate than its name suggests; *ji dan tang* is made of eggs and vinegar, *za huo guo ze* or "the pot of different goods" is a pleasant surprise, like *quan jia fu*, or "the whole family's happiness", which comes under the heading of a great dish, or again *shi jing huo guo* "ten brocade stew". This is but a glimpse of what may be found.

Cheeses

Cheese does not exist in China. Bean curd, translated as "fromage de soja" in French, is not a cheese, but a form of vegetable. A milk cheese made for foreigners can be found, with some difficulty; it is like Gouda, though a little drier. It is known as *ji si*, a transcription of "cheese". Excellent yoghourt is made *(suan niu nai)*.

Fruit

The vast differences in latitude in China gives birth to a great variety of fruit: apples *(ping guo)*, oranges *(guang gan)* and bananas *(xiang jiao)* from the south, mainly from Fu jian, are available all the year round. Oranges are said to have been brought to China from Europe by the Portuguese in the 16th century; it is also said that mandarins *(ju zi)* were so called because they were particularly appreciated by Mandarins.

Most fruit found in the northern hemisphere is available in China, depending on the season: pears *(li)*, peaches *(tao)*, apricots *(xing)*, strawberries *(yang mei)*, cherries *(ying tao)*, grapes *(pu tao)*, melons *(xiang gua)*, water melons *(xi gua)*, plums *(li zi)*, nuts *(he tao)*, chestnuts *(li zi)*, figs *(wu hua guo)*, olives *(qing guo)*, etc...., as well as fruit which grows in hot countries: grapefruit *(you zi)*, pineapples *(bo luo)*, guavas *(ji shi guo*, "chicken manure") mangoes *(mang guo)*, lemons *(li meng* or *xiang tao)*.

Lichees are to be found in China more easily than elsewhere, and are among the most delicately flavoured of all fruit: "the dry, crackling skin reveals a pale amber-coloured fruit, full of juice, with a lazy flavour which gradually steals over the mouth like an after-thought" (quoted by Claude Roy).

The curious may also taste longans *(long yan)*, *pi pa*, which is a sort of yellow loquat from the province of Guang dong, and *jin ju*, a kind of tiny clementine which is eaten skin and all. Azerolas *(shan zha* or *shan li hong)* "red mountain fruit" are a kind of small apple, which are sold in the street in winter, coated with caramel and threaded on little sticks. Lady-apples *(hai tang)*, physalis or "love in a cage" *(dou gu niang)*, and arbutus berries *(yang mei)* can also be found.

Suan mei are sour plums which are dried and then cooked, to make a refreshing drink, mixed with sweetened water.

The persimmon *(shi zi)* is the glory of the late autumn in China. Two kinds exist: one is like a large, flattened apple, and the other, held to be superior, is about the size of a lemon. They are eaten over-ripe, but they can be made to ripen overnight once they have been soaked in hot water.

Cakes

The Chinese love cakes, and at least a hundred different kinds exist. The moon cake *(yue bing)* is eaten at the moon festival (the 15th day of the 8th lunar month).

The imperial kitchens were famous for the countless sweet-meats which accompanied the main dishes.

A Few Words of Advice

First of all, lay all prejudices aside. Do not allow yourself to be put off either by the name, the appearance or the price of a dish... The cheapest dishes are often as good as the most expensive.

Breakfast: *zao dian*: "black" tea *(hong cha)*, green tea *(lü cha)*, coffee *(ka fei)*, milk *(niu nai)*, sugar *(bai tang)*, bread *(mian bao)*, butter *(huang you)*, jam *(guo zi jiang)*, eggs *(ji dan)*... are to be had in all large hotels. Or a Chinese breakfast *(zhong guo zao dian)* may be preferred (see the section of Plain Cooking).

Lunch and dinner: the following are examples of menus for:

Two people: 1. *Pin pan* (hors d'œuvre)
2. *Kao li xian ren* (shrimp rissoles)
3. *La zi ji* (chicken and pepper)
4. *Wu yu dan tang* (cuttle-fish eggs soup)
5. *Ba si ping guo* (apples fritters coated in caramel)

Four people: 1. *Pin pan* (hors d'œuvre)
             2. *Da xia* (crayfish)
             3. *Fu rong ji pian* (chicken with white of egg)
             4. *Zhu rou sun si* (shredded pork with bamboo shoots)
             5. *Chun juanr* (spring rolls) (eight rolls: *ba ge*)
             6. *Sha guo shi jing* (soup: "ten brocade stew")
             7. *San bu zhan* (pudding: mixture based on egg yolks)

Eight people: 1. *Shi jing leng pan* (ten kinds of hors d'œuvre)
             2. *Zha ya gan* (grilled duck liver)
             3. *Gong bao ji ding* (fried diced chicken)
             4. *Chao ou* (lotus roots)
             5. *Kao ya* (roast duck)
             6. *Bai cai tang* (cabbage soup)
             7. *Xiang ren lao* (cream of almonds)

Suggested menu for a banquet:

1. *Leng cai*   *Song hua dan* (Chinese eggs)
(hors d'œuvre) *Jin hua huo tui* (Jin hua ham)
               Ban hai zhe (dried jellyfish)
               Xiang gu (black mushrooms)
               Yu juanr (fish rolls)
               Leng bao yu (ormers)
               Ya zhang (duck's feet)
               Bai shan ji (white chicken)
               Long xu cai (asparagus)
               La niu rou (beef with pimento)
2. *Zhu sun tang* (bamboo marrow soup)
   or *Yan wo tang* (bird's nest soup)
3. *Chao xia ren* (shelled shrimps)
   or *Hui sheng ji si* (shredded chicken)
4. *Liang zuo yu* (two recipe fish)
   or *Hai shen* (sea slugs)
5. *Bao yu bai cai* (cabbage hearts and ormers)
6. *Chao zi zhu* (roast sucking-pig) (found at Canton particularly)
   or *Xiang su ya* (crisp scented duck)
7. *Chun cai tang* (soup made of water plants from the Western Lake, Hang zhou)
8. *He tao lao* (cream of walnuts)

It is also possible to order a meal costing 8, 9 or 10 yuans; a meal for 15 yuans will produce the best available.

If an aperitif is required, it is worth trying *wei mei si*, a kind of red vermouth. *Gan bai pu tao jiu* is a dry white wine; *zhang yu hong pu tao jiu* is a rather sweet red wine. *Mao tai* is the name for the white spirit drunk during the meal; *ying tao bai lan di* is a liqueur which could be drunk after a meal, though this is not a Chinese custom. Beer is *pi jiu; wu xing pi jiu* and *Qing dao pi jiu* are both a kind of lager, whereas *wu xing gao ji hei pi jiu* is a dark beer. For smokers: *tai shan* are miniature cigars; *hong xing* is a make of cigars; for pipe tobacco, try *yan tou feng huang* or "Phoenix"; *zhong hua xiang yan* are roughly like British or American cigarettes, and *tian shan* are made of black tobacco.

Tea, and green tea mainly, is however the most widely drunk of all, since this is the country where tea is grown: *long jing* or "Dragon Well" tea is drunk in summer, and *hua cha* or jasmine tea in winter. The best black tea of all, and also the most expensive, is *tie guan yin* or Iron Buddha, which is less easy to find than *wu long hong cha*, or Black Dragon Tea, which comes from Fu jian.

Mineral water from *Lao shan* is to be had if required. Bottles of fizzy fruit juice, mainly orange, can be bought almost everywhere *(ju zi shui)*.

A SHORT BIBLIOGRAPHY

I. Introduction

Aspects de la Chine (3 vol.), P.U.F., Paris, 1959.
   (Sections on Geography, History, Religion, Literature and Art).
H. Franke: *Sinologie* (in German), A. Franke, Bern, 1953.
   (An introduction to the study of Chinese, possible methods and difficulties).

II. General Reading

Mao Dun: *Midnight* (difficulties experienced by the Shang hai bourgeoisie during the 1930's economic crisis). Foreign Languages Press, Peking, 1962.
A. Malraux: *La condition humaine*, Gallimard
A. Malraux: *Les conquérants*, Gallimard
S. de Beauvoir: *La longue marche*, Gallimard
S. de Beauvoir: *Les mandarins*, Gallimard

III. Geography and Population

A. Herman :: *Historical and Commercial Atlas of China*, Harvard, 1 35.

Ding Wen jiang and others: *New Atlas of the Chinese Republic (Zhong hua min guo xin di tu)*, Shang hai, 1934.

Atlas of the Provinces of the Chinese People's Republic (Zhong guo fen shang di tu) Peking, 1st edition 1956, 2nd edition 1963, 3rd edition 1965.

Bartholomew's *China, Mongolia and Korea*, Edinburgh, 1962.

Père L. Richard: *Géographie de l'empire de Chine*, Shang hai, 1905 (several re-editions).

J. Sion: *La Chine*, in *Géographie universelle*, *Vol. V*, by Vidal de la Blache and Gallois, Paris, 1929.

G.B. Cressey: *Land of 500 millions, a geography of China*, New York, 1955.

P. Gourou: *L'Asie*, pp. 1–220, Paris, 1953.

Jen Yu-ti: *A Geography of China*, Foreign Languages Press, Peking, 1965.

Chi chao-ting: *Key Economic Areas in Chinese History, as revealed in the development of public works for water control*, London, 1936.

R. Guillain: *600 millions de Chinois*, Paris, 1956.

R. Dumont: *Révolution dans les campagnes chinoises*, Paris, 1957.

J. Kessel: *Hong kong et Macao;* Paris, 1957.

V. Purcell: *The Chinese in Southeast Asia*, London, 1951, re-ed. 1965.

T.R. Tregear: *A Geography of China*, University of London Press, 1965.

CHINA: Esselte Map Service, Stockholm, Sweden and Cartographia, Budapest, Hungary, 1965.

IV. Language

B. Karlgren: *Sound and Symbol in Chinese*, Hong Kong, re-ed. 1962.

B. Karlgren: *The Chinese Language*, New York, 1949.

P. Demiéville: *Matériaux pour l'enseignement élémentaire du chinois*, Paris, 1963.

J. Gernet: *La Chine, aspects et fonctions psychologiques de l'écriture* in *L'écriture et la psychologie des peuples*, Paris, 1963.

Modern Chinese Reader, 2 vols., Peking, 1st. edition 1958.

English-Chinese Conversation, Foreign Languages Press, Peking 1958/9

Paul Kratochvil: *The Chinese Language Today*, London, Hutchinson University Library, 1968.

Elementary Chinese (English Edition), Vol. I and II, Commercial Press, Peking.

V. History

General works:

E. Eberhard: *Chinas Geschichte*, Francke, Berne, 1948.
English translation: *A History of China from the Earliest Times to the Present Day*, Routledge and Kegan Paul, London, 1950.

Geschichte Chinas vom Urbeginn bis auf die Gegenwart, in Geschichte Asiens. Weltgeschichte in Einzeldarstellungen, pp. 361–542, München, 1950.

Topics in Chinese History. Harvard-Yenching Institute Studies, Vol. 4, Cambridge (Mass.), 1950.

C.P. Fitzgerald: *China, a Cultural History*, London, 1935. Revised edition, 1950.

L.C. Goodrich: *A Short History of the Chinese People*, 3rd edition, New York, 1959.

W. Francke: *China und das Abendland*, 140 p., Vandenhoeck & Ruprecht, Göttingen, 1962.

J. Gernet: *Le Monde chinois*, Paris, Armand Colin, coll. Destins du monde, 1972.

J. Spence: *The China Helpers, Western Advisers in China, 1620-1960*, London, The Bodley Head, 1968.

Specialised works:

1. Classical China

J. Gernet: *La Chine ancienne, des origines à l'empire*, Que sais-je? P.U.F., 1964.

M. Granet: *Danses et légendes de la Chine ancienne*, 2 vol., 5re-ed. P.U.F. Paris. 1959.

H. Maspéro: *La Chine antique*, revised edition, Paris, 1955.

E. Chavannes: *Les Mémoires historiques de Sse ma Ts'ien*, vol., Paris, 1895–1905.

H.H. Dubs: *The History of the Former Han Dynasty*, 3 vol., Baltimore, 1938–1955.

W. Eberhard: *Das Toba-Reich Nordchinas*, Leiden, 1949.

J. Gernet: *Les aspects économiques du bouddhisme dans la société chinoise du V au Xème siècle*, Publ. de l'Ecole française d'Extrême Orient, Saigon, 1956.

E. Balazs: *Beiträge zur Wirtschaftsgeschichte des Tang* – Zeit, Berlin, 1931–1933.

E. Balazs: *Le traité économique du "Souei chou"*, Leiden, 1953.

E. Balazs: *Le Traité juridique du "Souei chou"*, Leiden, 1954.

E.C. Pulleyblank: *The Background of the Rebellion of An Lu-shan*, London, 1955.

D.C. Twitchett: *Financial Administration under the T'ang Dynasty*, Cambridge University Press, 1963.

J. Gernet: *La vie quotidienne en Chine à la veille de l'invasion mongole, 1250-1270*, Hachette, Paris, 1959.
Trans. into English by N.M. Wright: *Daily Life in China on the Eve of the Mongol Invasion, 1250-1270*, pub. 1962.

K.A. Wittfogel, Feng Chia-sheng et al: *History of Chinese Society* (Liao) TAPS, 1948, pp. 1–650.

L. Hambis: *Marco Polo, La description du monde*, 1 vol., Paris, 1955.

Moule and Pelliot: *Marco Polo — the Description of the World*, 4 vol., Routledge, London, 1938.

C. D'Ohsson: *Histoire des Mongols*, 4 vol., Amsterdam, 1852.

L. Hambis: *La Haute Asie*, coll. "Que sais-je?" P.U.F., 1953.

A.C. Moule: *Christians in China before the year 1550*, London 1930.

H. Bernard-Maitre: *Le P. Mathieu Ricci et la société chinoise de son temps (1552-1610)*, Tientsin, 1937.

C. Commeaux: *De Kang hi à Kien long*, Paris, 1957.

A.W. Hummel, ed.: *Eminent Chinese of the Ch'ing period*, 2 vol., Washington, 1943–1944.

Lindley: *The Ti ping Revolution*, London, 1866.

J. Chesneaux: *La révolution Taiping d'après quelques travaux récents*, in *La Revue historique*, Paris, Janvier–mars 1953.

Edwin O. Reischauer and John K. Fairbank: *East Asia the Great Tradition*, Boston, Houghton Mifflin Co., Tokyo, Charles E. Tuttle, Inc., 1962.

2. Modern China

J. Chesneaux and J. Lust: *Introduction aux études d'histoire contemporaine de Chine*, Mouton, Paris, 1964.

W. Francke: *Das Jahrhundert der Chinesischen Revolution 1851-1949*, Munich, 1958.

Li Chien nung: *The Political History of China, 1840–1928*, Van Nostrand Co. Inc., Princeton, 1959.

S.Y. Teng and J.K. Fairbank: *China's Response to the West*, Cambridge, Mass., 1954.

Ho Kan shih: *A History of the Modern Chinese Revolution*, Foreign Languages Press, Peking, 1959.

R. Pelissier: *La Chine entre en scène*, Julliard, Paris, 1963.

F. Farjenel: *A travers la révolution chinoise*, Plon, Paris, 1914.

Wu Yu-tchang: *La révolution de 1911*, Foreign Languages Press, Peking, 1963.

J. Chesneaux: *Sun Yat sen*, Paris, 1959.

W. Francke: *Chinas Kulturelle Revolution. Die Bewegung vom 4 mai 1919*, Munich, 1957.

H.K. Fairbank, A.O. Reischauer, A.M. Craig: *East Asia, the Modern Transformation*. Houghton Mifflin Co. Boston, 1965.

J. Chesneaux: *Le Mouvement ouvrier chinois de 1919–1927*, Mouton, La Haye, 1962.

E. Snow: *Red Star Over China*, New York Modern Library, 1954. Revised and enlarged edition 1968.

A. Smedley: *The Great Road: the Life and Times of Chu Teh*, New York.

J. Guillermaz: *La Chine populaire*, coll. "Que sais-je?" P.U.F., 1959.

J. Guillermaz: *A History of the Chinese Communist Party*, London, Methuen, 1972.

J. Guillermaz: *Le Parti communiste chinois au pouvoir*, Paris, Payot, 1972.

Lucien Bianco: *Origins of the Chinese Revolution, 1915–1949*, 1971.

J. Etienne: *La voie chinoise*, P.U.F., 1962.

E. Snow: *The Other Side of the River, Red China Today*, Random House, New York, 1961.

VI. Religion and Philosophy

H. Doré: *Manuel des Superstitions chinoises,* introduction by M. Soymié, Paris and Hong Kong, Centre de Publication de l'Unité d'Enseignement et de Recherche Extrême-Orient–Asie du Sud-Est de l'Université de Paris, 1970.

A.T.C. Verner: *A Dictionary of Chinese Mythology*, Kelly and Walsh, Shang hai, 1932, re-pub. New York, 1961.

A. Forke: *Geschichte der alten chinesischen Philosophie*, 3 Bd., Kommissionverlag L. Friedderischen & Co, Hambourg, 1937–1938.

R.A. Stein: *Les religions de la Chine*, in l'*Encyclopédie française*, vol. XIX, Paris, 1957.

Bi Yän Lu: *Meister Yüan wu's Niederschrift von der smaragdenen Felswand*, verdeutscht und erläutert von Wilhelm Gundest, Karl Hanser Verlag, Munich, 1960, 580 p.

P. Demiéville: *Le concile de Lhassa*, P.U.F., Paris, 1952, 398 p.

Feng You lan: *A History of Chinese Philosophy*, 2 vol., trans. from the Chinese by D. Bodde, Princeton, 1952–1953.

Hou Wai lu and others: *Zhong guo si xiang tong shi*, a history of Chinese philosophy, 5 vol., Peking, 1956.

E.S. Needham: *Science and Civilisation in China*, vol. II, *History of Scientific Thought*, Cambridge, 1955.

M. Granet: *La Pensée chinoise*, La Renaissance du Livre, 1934, Albin Michel, 1968.

M. Granet: *La Civilisation chinoise*, Paris, La Renaissance du Livre, 1929, Albin Michel, 1968.

H. Maspéro: *Le Taoïsme et les religions chinoises*, Paris, Gallimard (Bibliothèque des histoires), 1971.

A. Rygaloff: *Confucius*, Paris, 1946.

A. Waley: *The Analects of Confucius*, London, 1938.

A. Forke, Lun Heng: *Philosophical and Miscellaneous Essays of Wang ch'ung*, Leipzig, London, Shang hai, 1907, 1911.

VII. Literature

P. Demiéville: *Letteratura cinese* in *La civiltà del Oriente*, vol. II, p. 861–997, Rome, 1957.

P.A. Feifel: *Geschichte der chinesischen Literatur und ihrer gedanklichen Grundlagen*, Peking, 1945, (trans. of book by Nagasawa Kikuya in Japanese).

O. Kaltenmark-Ghéquier: *La littérature chinoise*, coll. "Que sais-je?", no. 296, P.U.F., Paris, 2nd edit. 1961.

M. Kaltenmark: *La Littérature chinoise* in *Histoire des littératures*, vol. I, p. 1067–1300, *Encyclopédie de la Pléiade*, Gallimard, Paris, 1955.

Lai Ming: *A History of Chinese Literature*, London, 1964.

Lu Hsun: *A Brief History of Chinese Fiction*, Foreign Languages Press, Peking, 1959.

Lu Hsun: *Selected Works*, Vol. I, Peking, Foreign Languages Press, 1956.

Ting Yi: *A Short History of Modern Chinese Literature*, Peking, 1959.

J.R. Hightower: *Topics in Chinese Literature*, Harvard University Press, 1950.

M. Davidson: *A List of Published Translations from Chinese into English, French and German. Part I: Literature, exclusive of Poetry*, Ann Arbor, Michigan 1952. Part II: *Poetry*, Newhaven, Conn., 1957.

L.C. Arlington: *The Chinese Drama*, Shang hai, 1930.

Anthologie de la poésie chinoise classique, sous la direction de Paul Demiéville, Gallimard, Paris, 1962.

C.S.L. Zung: *Secrets of the Chinese Drama*, New York, 1937, 1964.

W.J.F. Jenner: *Modern Chinese Short Stories*, London, Oxford University Press, 1970.

C.T. Hsia: *A History of Modern Chinese Fiction, 1917-1957*, New Haven and London, Yale University Press, 1961.

M.A.C. Scott: *The Classical Theatre of China*, London, George Allen and Unwin, 1957.

VIII. Art

General works:

M. Paul-David: *Arts et styles de la Chine*, Larousse, Paris, 1953.

W. Willetts: *Chinese Art*, 2 vol. Harmondsworth, Middlesex, 1958.

R. Grousset: *La Chine et son art*, Plon, Paris, 1951.

W. Speiser: *Chine*, collection l'Art dans le Monde, Albin Michel, Paris, 1960.

L. Sickman, A. Soper: *The Art and Architecture of China*, Penguin books, London, 1965.

New Archaeological Finds in China, Peking, Foreign Languages Press, 1972.

Architecture:

O. Siren: *Les arts anciens de la Chine*, vol. IV, Paris and Brussels, 1930.

O. Siren: *The Walls and Gates of Peking*, London, 1924.

O. Siren: *Les palais impériaux de Pékin*, Paris and Brussels, 1930.

A. Boyd: *Chinese Architecture and Town Planning*, London, 1962.

Sculpture:

V. Segalen, G. de Voisin and J. Lartigue: *L'art funéraire à l'époque des Han*, Paris, 1935.

O. Siren: *Histoire de la sculpture chinoise*, 4 vol., Paris, 1925–1926.

Painting:

P. Swann: *Chinese Painting*, ed. Tisné, Paris, 1958.

O. Siren: *Chinese Painting*, 7 vol., London, 1956–1958.

J. Cahill: *La peinture chinoise*, ed. Skira, Geneva, 1960.

W. Speiser, R. Goepper and J. Fribourg: *Arts de la Chine (peinture, calligraphie, estampages, estampes)*, Office du Livre, Fribourg, 1964.

Pottery:

B. Gray: *Early Chinese Pottery and Porcelain*, London, 1953.

D. Lion-Goldschmidt: *Les poteries et porcelaines chinoises*, Paris, Presses Universitaires de France, 1957.

Music:

Ma Hiao-tsiun: *La Musique chinoise* in *Histoire de la musique*, Vol. I: *Des origines à J.S. Bach*, Encyclopédie de la Pléiade, Gallimard, Paris.

IX. Economy

M. Menguy: *L'économie de la Chine populaire*, coll. "Que sais-je?", P.U.F., 1964.

C. Bettelheim, J. Charrière, H. Marchisio: *La construction du socialisme en Chine*, Economie et socialisme, Maspero, 1965.

S. Adler: *The Chinese Economy*, Monthly Review Press, 1957.

Lavallé, Noirot, Dominique: *Economie de la Chine socialiste*, Genève, 1957.
Ten Great Years, Foreign Languages Press, Peking, 1960.
Wu Yuan li: *An Economic Survey of Communist China*, New York Bookman Associates, 1956.
Li Cho-ming: *Economic Development of Communist China*, University of California, 1960.

X. Peking

General Works:

De l'Isle: *Description de la ville de Pékin*, Paris, Hérissant, 1765.
E. Bretschneider: *Recherches archéologiques sur Pékin et les environs*, French trans. by Collin de Plancy, Leroux, Paris, 1879.
Mgr. A. Favier: *Pékin: histoire et description*, Peking, Imprimerie des Lazaristes au Pé-t'ang, 1897.
C. Madrolle: *Peking and its environs*, Hachette, Paris, 1912.
Capt. M. Fabre: *Pékin, ses palais, ses temples et ses environs*, Tien tsin, 1937.
L.C. Arlington and W. Lewisohn: *In Search of Old Peking;* Vetch, 1935.
Peking, a Tourist Guide: Foreign Languages Press, Peking, 1960.
Nigel Cameron and Brian Brake: *Peking, a Tale of Three Cities*, New York and Evanston, Harper and Row, 1965.

Specialised Works:

G. Bouillard: Over ten articles on Peking and its environs, published in several sets by Nachbaur at Peking, from 1921.
Hsiang shan, ou Parc de chasse, 1923.
Le temple des Lamas, 1931.
Tombeaux impériaux, 1931.
Le temple du ciel, 1923.
M. Adam: *Yuan ming yuan. L'œuvre architecturale des anciens Jésuites au XVIIIe siècle.* Imprimerie Lazariste, Pei p'ing, 1936.
O. Siren: *The Walls and Gates of Peking*, Lane, London, 1924.
O. Siren: *The Imperial Palace of Peking*, 274 plates after photographs by the author, 12 architectural drawings and 2 maps, with a short historical account. 3 vol., Paris and Brussels. G. van Oest, 1926.

H. Hildebrand: *Der Tempel Da-chüh-sy (Tempel des grossen Erkennens)*, Berlin 1897. Re-pub. 1943.

Devine: *The Four Churches at Peking*, Burns, London, 1930.

W. Grube: *Zum Pekinger Volkskunde*, Berlin, Spemann 1901.

D. Bodde: *Annual Customs and Festivals in Peking (as recorded in the yen-ching sui shi chi, by Tun Li-chen)*. Translated and fully annotated, fully illustrated, Vetch, Peking, 1936.

H.Y. Lowe: *The Adventures of Wu: the Life Cycle of Peking Man*, 2 vol., The Peking Chronicle Press, Peking, 1940–1941.

G. Douin: *Cérémonial de la cour et coutumes du peuple de Pékin*, in Bull. de l'Association amic. Franco-chinoise (Vol. II p. 105 .. 215, 347, vol. III p. 134, 209, vol. IV p. 66).

Works in Chinese:

Sources: Numerous old descriptive works and travel books, dating from the Ming and the Qing, re-published from 1961 onwards in Peking. The most interesting are:

Di jing jing wu lüe (Brief account of the capital's landscapes) by Liu Tong and Yu Yi zheng (1634), re-pub. 1963.

Chen yuan shi lüe (A brief account of the Imperial City) by Wu Zhang yuan (1788), re-pub. 1964 (includes an old map).

Studies: among many recent works:

Bei jing you lan shou ce (Guide to Peking) 1957.

Bei jing jie dao de gu shi (anecdotes on streets in Peking) 1959.

Hou Ren zhi: *Li shi shang de bei jing cheng* (History of the City of Peking) 1962.

Hou Ren zhi: *Bu fang ji*, a collection of articles on the history of Peking, 1962.

Luo Zhi wen: *Wu ta si* (the Wu ta si Temple), 1957.

Dan Shi yuan: *Gu gong shi hua* (A History of the Imperial Palace), 1962.

Bei jing fa hai si ming dai bi hua (The Ming Wall-paintings in the Fa hai si Temple near Peking) 1958 (with colour reprocductions).

Suggested Reading:

P. Loti: *Les derniers jours de Pékin*, Calman-Lévy, Paris, 1925.

E. Backhouse and J.O.P. Bland: *Annals and Memoirs of the Court of Peking*, London, Heinemann, 1914.

V. Segalen: *René Leys*, Plon, 1922, 1950, Rencontre 1962.

P. Tillard: *Le montreur de marionnettes*, Julliard.

Description

NOTE ON THE DESCRIPTION SECTION
OF THE GUIDE

The writers of the descriptive part of the guide were inevitably faced with several problems of size. China is one of the largest countries in the world, and her history is one of the longest of all. The Chinese have always been conscious of the fact that they are the creators of a unique civilisation, and consequently have studied and recorded their own history with great care. Everything in China happens on a large scale, whether in time or space; it is absurd to write a description of a few hundred pages on this vast country. At the same time, it is a worthwhile undertaking. No guide books have appeared since the 1930's, and although politicians and journalists are constantly writing on China, a complete and practical introduction to the country has for some time been a conspicuous lack. The aim of this book is to supply the reader or traveller with the information which has hitherto been missing.

It has been no easy task. For one thing, large areas of China are about of bounds to foreigners for the moment, and for another, adequate information on all aspects of Chinese life is unobtainable. Different methods have been used in this book to suit the different cases. Detailed descriptions have been given of the big towns which are open to tourists. The authors have tried to describe them as other guide books would handle towns in Spain or Italy, for instance, giving as many accurate details as possible, an account of their history, and explanations; when necessary, information has been taken from old or modern books in Chinese. These towns amount to about twenty at the most, and represent a fraction of China as a whole. The question was whether to stop there, ignoring countless things which are inaccessible to tourists for the moment, but which exist nonetheless. This would have been impossible. It would have given far too limited a vision of China. A brief description of each Chinese province has been given, mentioning the most important monuments, in the hope that the information will some day prove of use to other travellers luckier than ourselves. Old European and Chinese handbooks, travel books, and also various reviews and other publications (guide books, monographs), which have been written over the last few years, were used to provide information on places which the authors were unable to visit themselves. It is to be hoped that the tourist will not use the same criteria to judge the passages based on first hand information and those based on other sources.

This work is intended to be a catalogue of the chief historical and artistic monuments in China, as well as a guide book for tourists. Its main aim is to impart as much information as possible, and convey to the reader some idea of the immense riches contained in this great country. A constant effort has been made to provide explanations and historical notes to help the reader towards a better understanding of these riches, and to place them in their true historical setting, while at the same time pointing out the connections between them. At first sight, it may appear that the historical aspect has been over-emphasised. In our view it is of the utmost importance, for no-one can hope to get to know China through the present alone, and unless he has acquired some basic knowledge, the visitor will glimpse only part of the reality which lies before him; the aspects of the present to which the past provides the key will be hidden from him, completely inaccessible, and he will be aware of the superficial aspect alone. All that many readers demand of a guide book is that it should be up to date, and give an accurate account of the present state of affairs without lingering too long over the past. This book was written in a different spirit: instead of describing China today, isolated from the rest, the authors have preferred to try to link the past with the present, indicating the historical continuity, and to point out the forces at work in a development process in which the present is but a fleeting moment. In some places, out of date information has been given, things have been described as they no longer are, and monuments which have now vanished have been included. Dates and sources have been given in these cases, and the reader is invited to make his own comparisions. In other cases, the only available information refers to the condition of monuments in the past; the visitor can then correct the mistakes himself, criticising where necessary, and should he be willing to do so, he is welcome to hand on the information to the authors themselves. On the whole, however, the information given is up to date and complete.

Other, more technical difficulties arose from the work. Take the case of translations, for instance: should names of places, temples, monasteries, palaces, etc. be given in their Chinese form or translated into English? An approximate translation has been given as far as possible, so that those who read Chinese can find the characters used, and not merely to add an exotic touch. Some common nouns present almost indissoluble difficulties, either because they have no English equivalent, or because they have several. The Chinese word si, meaning a Buddhist temple and the buildings attached to it, has been translated sometimes by temple and sometimes by monastery. In this case, as in many others, the lack of accepted English translations results in inaccuracies. Some archaeological and architectural terms referring to things belonging to Ancient China have no equivalent and have been left in Chinese in the text. The reader will find explanations of them in the glossary (p. 256). It should be remembered, in order to reduce possibilities of misunderstandings, that the Chinese, when counting the floors of a building, refer to the ground floor as the first floor, the first as the second, etc. The same method has been used here in several cases. It should also be noted that the dates given after an emperor's name are those of his reign, and those following the name of an ordinary person indicate the years of his birth and death.

The writers' chief source were: 1) Wen wu, a monthly artistic and archaeological review, founded in 1950 in Peking, in Chinese; 2) The list of historical monuments in China published in Wen wu (No 4–5, 1961); 3) The atlas of the provinces of China, Zhong guo fen sheng di tu, 3rd edition, Peking 1963; 4) Numerous handbooks, monographs and studies published in China over the last years; 5) A few old tourist handbooks in European languages (published before the 2nd World War). Other works, both in Chinese and in other languages, some old and some new, were also used from time to time; they are generally mentioned in the text.

Note to the third edition

Many things have changed since this guide was written in 1965–66. As far as Peking is concerned, up to date information is obtainable through tourists and other visitors; accurate information about monuments and places of interest in the provincial towns is almost impossible to get without going there onself.

Several districts in Peking have been or are being entirely rebuilt and modernised. The Cultural Revolution brought changes with it too; some historical monuments or old buildings such as the temples in Peking are now closed to visitors, while others have re-opened after extensive restoration work, or with new exhibits, in the case of museums. This has been indicated briefly where possible in the description of Peking; at the same time, since this book is intended to be a catalogue of the chief monuments and places of interest as well as a guide book for tourists, descriptions *of the temples and other places now closed have been left in the hope that some day they will be accessible once more. For the same reason, the description of the Historical Museum has also been left intact, although the museum is closed at the moment. Most changes in names, particularly names of streets, appear to have been short-lived, and the old ones seem to be still in use.*

THE CITY OF PEKING

INTRODUCTION

I. POSITION AND CLIMATE

Position

Peking is on a latitude of 39º 54' north (roughly the same as Constantinople and Southern Italy), and on a longitude of 116º 25' east. It is in the south-west of a little plain, the further-most part of the great North China plain which covers He bei and most of He nan, Shan dong and An hui. This northern stretch is enclosed by mountains to the north, west and north-west, which rise little by little (1,300–1,500 feet, then 3,100–4,800 feet) to join the high Mongolian plateau. It is at an average altitude of 441 feet above sea level, and is chiefly made up of deposits which the rivers bring down from the north-western mountains. Its history is closely linked with that of the river Yong ding, which rises on the Mongolian plateau, flows down through the mountains and enters the plain from the west, at San jia dian (about 12 miles from Peking). The river has altered its course more than once, changing the face of the plain, and sometimes causing widespread damage.

The alluvial plain is extremely fertile; the mountains nearby contain deposits of coal, iron ore, copper, aluminium, wolfram, lead and zinc. The stone is quarried, to provide building material.

Climate

The region of Peking has an exceptionally high rainfall (annual average of 24 ins.); the north-western mountains form a natural barrier for the monsoon winds coming from the south-east in summer. This is unusual, as the north China plain is extremely dry in general. The temperature is warmer (average: 52º F), and the summers less hot (average temperature: 79.5º F) than in the centre of the great plain. The widest differences in temperature recorded over the last few years are: 110º F on June 15th 1942, –6.2º F on January 13th 1951. The winter is long (about 80 days) and relatively cold, but rain is rare (2% of the total for the year in December, January and February);

TEMPÉRATURES ET PRÉCIPITATIONS
ANNUELLES À PÉKIN
TEMPERATURES AND ANNUAL
RAINFALL AT PEKING

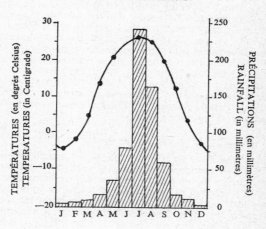

apart from a few days of snow, the weather is always sunny.
The spring is short, the sun grows rapidly hotter, causing
even greater evaporation, and as the moisture is so rare, all
this gives an impression of extreme dryness. At the same time,
strong winds bring clouds of dust with them (the yellow wind).
The summer lasts about three months, and the monsoon winds
bring the rain (75% of the rainfall occurs in June, July and
August). The heat and rain combined are good for the harvest,
though violent thunderstorms are not so favourable. The autumn
is fairly short; the rainfall is slight and the temperatures mild;
it is generally considered the pleasantest of the seasons. The
climate of Peking is extremely healthy; even in the 18th century,
the Jesuits spoke highly of its "goodness", and found it hard to
understand how it was that the town was relatively "free of
epidemics".

II. HISTORY
(See plate p. 433)

The Beginnings

The remains of Peking man found at Zhou kou dian (south
west of Peking, cf. p. 647) prove that the area was inhabited at
an extremely early date. Since the beginning of the historic age,
the Peking area seems to have been on the route linking the
Yellow River plain with the mountainous regions in the north-
east; remains of a first settlement have been found close to the
present Marco Polo bridge (cf. p. 643). The north-south route
had to cross the Yong ding river, and this spot, downstream
of the western mountains and above the eastern marshes, was
clearly the most practicable. The settlement was probably
formed near a bridge or a ferry.

The Town of Ji

Under the Zhou (it is impossible to say exactly when) the
first site was abandoned, and a new settlement was formed,
roughly where the south-east districts of the present town now
stand. It is referred to as the town of Ji (the reeds) in contemporary texts, and for a time it was the capital of the state of
Yan, one of the seven "hegemons" of the Warring States period
(403–221). When Qin shi Huang di founded the empire, Ji
remained a busy trading centre: under the Han, the historian
Si ma Qian wrote: "Ji is one of the large northern towns; it is
in touch with Qi (present Shan dong) and Chao (south of
present He bei) in the south, and with the northern barbarians
in the north-east...; it is rich, and fish, salt, jujubes and chestnuts can be found there; it receives merchandise from the
northern barbarian regions and from Korea". (*Historical
Records*, chap. 129); under the Wei, work was begun on a plan
to divert part of the river Yong ding to the town; under the
Tang, the town prospered, and was used as a base for expeditions
against Korea. It was known as Yu zhou.

The town of Yan jing

After the end of the Tang dynasty, the Great Wall lost its
strategic importance for a time, and the Peking area was no
longer the "frontier province" which it had been up till then.
Instead it became part of a northern empire, which was to

expand southwards, under the pressure of the non-Han elements
of the population (Khitan, Jürched and Mongol). When the
Khitan, the founders of the Liao dynasty, took Ji in 936, they
used it as their secondary capital and called it Nan jing (the
southern capital), or Yan jing (after the former state of Yan).
Yan jing was roughly where the western part of the southern
half of the town now stands; it was square, with two gates on
each side; the Fa yuan si Temple stood in the south-
east corner. The imperial palace was in the south-west and the
market-place was in the north-eastern corner; the town was
divided into districts, each one enclosed by a wall.

The town of Zhong du

At the beginning of the 12th century, the Jürched took over
from the Khitan and founded the Jin dynasty; they took Yan
jing, renamed it Zhong du (central capital) and enlarged it to
the east, west and south. It was still square; each side had
three gates. The north-west gate, Hui cheng men, gave its name
to the village of Hui cheng men cun, west of the present Bai
yun guan (cf. p. 567). The imperial palace was in the middle
of the town, slightly to the south of the present Guang an men
Gate (Gate of Endless Peace). The Lian hua chi pool, which
irrigated the imperial gardens, emptied into a little river, which
ran south-west of the town (outside the southern part of the
present town). To the south of the palace, it was spanned by a
beautiful bridge leading to the main south gate. The buildings
were on a generous scale; we are told that it cost 200,000 pieces
of money to move one piece of wood alone, and that one chariot
was hauled by 500 men". Gold and the five colours were used
to decorate the interior; "one palace alone cost a hundred
million pieces of money..." The Jin also brought trophies
taken from the Song at Bian jing (Kai feng) in 1127 to their
new capital: astronomical instruments (cf. p. 521), stone drums
(cf. p. 477).

The town of Da du

The town of Zhong du was rased to the ground during the
struggles between the Jürched and the Mongols in the 13th
century. When Khubilai decided to make Peking his capital in
1261, nothing was left of the Jin palace for him to take over.
It is almost certain that he settled in a palace which had survived
in the north-east of the town, where the Bei hai now is (cf. p.

485, the description of the round town, where there is still a carved basin, given to Khubilai). The new Mongol capital, Da du (the great capital) was centred round this. The town stretched as far south as the present Chang an jie; the observatory was at one of the corners (cf. p. 521). The northern wall was beyond the Yellow Temple, and remains of it can still be seen. There were ten gates. The palace was roughly where the Imperial Palace now is; the Temple of the Ancestors was to the east, and the Altar of Earth and Harvests to the west. The business districts were to the north, round the Drum and Bell Towers. Canals supplied the town with water and carried barges which brought grain to the capital; they unloaded at a wharf near the market, on the banks of Shi sha hai (cf. p. 498).

Marco Polo, who visited the town towards the end of the 13th century, left a long description of it (he calls it "Cambaluc", from the Mongol "Khan baliq", the Khan's town): "Moreover I tell you that in this city of Cambaluc there is so great a number of houses and of people, between inside the town and outside; for you may know that there are as many suburbs as gates (these are twelve), which are very large so that the suburb of each gate touches the suburbs of the gates on either side, and they extend for three or four miles; that there is no man who could tell the number. For there are many more people in those suburbs than in the town. And in these suburbs... stay and lodge the merchants and the travelling foreigners, of whom there are many from all parts to bring things as presents to the lord and to sell to the court... Moreover I tell you that there are as beautiful houses and as beautiful palaces in the suburbs as in the town, except those of the great lord. And you may know that no man who dies is... buried in the town. But if he is an idolater then he is carried to the place where the body must be burnt, which is outside the town and outside all the suburbs. And so it happens with the other dead (if he is of another faith when it is right to bury him, as a Christian and Saracen and other manner of person), who are also carried to be buried far outside all the suburbs in an appointed place, so that the land is more valuable and healthy in consequence. And again I tell you another thing, that inside the town dare live no sinful woman (unless it is secretly) as is said before, these are women of the world who do service to men for money, but I tell you that they all live outside in the suburbs. And you may know that there are so great a multitude of them for the foreigners that no man could believe it, for I dare tell you in truth that they are quite twenty thousand ..... who all serve men for money, and they all find a living. ... Then you can see if there is great abundance of people in Cambaluc since the worldly women there are as many as I have told. And again you may know quite truly that I believe there is not a place in the world to which so many merchants come and that dearer things and of greater value and more strange come into this town of Cambaluc from all sides than into any city of the world, and greater quantity of all things... And this happens because everyone from everywhere brings there for the lord who lives there and for his court and for the city which is so great and for the ladies and for the barons and the knights of whom there are so many and for the great abundance of the people of the armies of the lord, which stay round about as well for the court as for the city. And for this reason which I have told you more dear things and of greater value come to this town and greater quantities than into any town in the world, ... so that so much of everything comes there that it is without end. For you may know in truth that ... almost each day in the year there come into this town more than a thousand carts loaded with silk alone, for many cloths of gold and silk are made there and many other things. ... And yet it is true that they have cotton and hemp in some places, but not enough to satisfy them; but they do not make much of it, because of the great quantity which they have of silk, and cheap, which is better than flax or cotton. And again this city of Cambaluc has round it infinite villages and more than two hundred other cities both far and near which come, the people of these towns, ... to buy many things in this city ... and live for the most part while the court is here by selling the things needful to the city. And so it is not a great thing if as many things as I have told you come into this city of Cambaluc so that it is a city of great trade...

"And in this town he has his great palace and I will describe its likeness to you... there is first of all a great four-sided wall which is for each side one mile long, that is to say that it is four miles all round. It is very thick, and of height they have quite ten paces, and they are white and embattled. And each corner of his wall has again a great tower, very beautiful and very rich, in which are kept the great Kaan's equipments, these are bows, and quivers, saddles and bridles for horses, bowstrings and all things needful for an army. And again between one palace and the second there is also a palace in the middle like those of the corners, so that all round the walls there are eight very beautiful palaces, and all and eight are full of the equipments of the great lord. And you may know that in each palace there is only one thing, that is that in one are bows and nothing else, and the second had saddles and nothing else, and so it goes all round that in each is all one manner of thing. And this wall has five gates on the quarter towards midday, in the middle a great gate which is never opened except only when the great Kaan comes out of it to make war... And beside this great gate are two small ones, one on each side, ... And then there is towards the corner another very large one, and towards the other corner another, by which again the other people enter, so that they are five, and the large one is in the middle, and by those four smaller gates enter all the other people... And inside this wall is another wall which is rather more long than broad. There are also eight palaces on this wall all in the same way as the eight others outside... And again the equipments of the great lord are kept there inside. There are also five gates in the side towards midday all like the other wall in front... And in the middle of the space which is inside these two walls is the great palace of the great lord, which is made in such a way as I shall tell you. Know that it is the greatest and most wonderful that ever was seen. It has no upper floor, but is on a level base in such a way that the pavement is about ten palms higher than the other ground around. And the roof covering is extremely high. The walls of the halls and of the rooms are all covered with gold and silver and there are portrayed dragons and beasts and birds and knights and other different kinds of things; and the roof also is so made that nothing else is seen there but gold and silver and paintings. The hall is so great and broad that more than six thousand men would well feed there at once. And in that palace there are rooms, so many that it is a marvel to see them... And the roofs above, that is outside, are all red and green and azure and peacock-blue and yellow and of all colours, and all glazed so well and so cleverly that they are bright like crystal ... And you may know that roof is so strong and so firmly put together that it lasts many years... And between the one wall and the other of those of which I have told you are lawns and trees in which are many kinds of strange beasts; these are white stags, the animals that make the musk, roe-deer, fallow-deer, and squirrels and ermines and many kinds of other strange and beautiful animals in great abundance. And all the grounds inside the walls are full of so many of these beautiful animals that there is no way, except the roads along which men walk to and fro. And at one corner... is a very large and deep and beautiful lake... in which are many kinds of fish and plenty, for the great lord has made them put many kinds of fish there... and every time the great lord wishes some of those fish he has them at his will and at his pleasure. Moreover I tell you that a great river flows in there and flows out... but it is so planned that no fish can escape, and this is done with nets of iron and of brass...

"And again I tell you that towards transmontaine, about one crossbow-shot distant from the palace, he has had a mound made by hand... It is a hill which is quite a hundred paces high, and it is more than a mile round; the which hill is all full and all covered with most beautiful trees which at no time lose their leaves... but are always green. And I tell you that the great lord, wherever one tells him that there was a beautiful tree in those regions, he made them take it up with all the roots and with much earth round it and made them carry it with elephants to plant on that hill. And the tree might be as great as it pleased, but he would have this done with it. And in this way there were the most beautiful trees in the world there, and always green. And I tell you that the great lord has had all that hill covered with azure-stone which is very green, so that the trees are all green and the hill all green. So that nothing is seen except green things and therefore it is called the Green Hill; and truly it has a good right to its name. And on the top of the hill in the middle of the summit is a palace very fair and great, and it is all green within and without. And I tell you that this hill and the trees and the palace are so beautiful to see for the verdure all of one kind that it is a wonder; for all those who see them have delight and joy from them, and all people go there. And therefore has the great lord had them made, to have the fair sight and because it gives him comfort and enjoyment and gladness in his heart..." (from *Marco Polo: The Description of the World*, by A.C. Moule and Paul Pelliot, Routledge, London, 1938).

Peking under the Ming Dynasty

When Zhu Yuan zhang overthrew the Yuan and founded the Ming dynasty (1368), Nanking became the capital for a short time. Da du was renamed Bei ping (northern peace) and fell to one of the victor's sons, who was enfeoffed as the "King of Yan". When he came to power in 1403 (taking Yong le as his reign-title) he decided to make what had been the Yuan capital the capital of the empire, and he called his fief Bei jing: "the northern capital" (which Europeans adapted to Pékin and Peking). The town changed considerably under the Ming. New walls were built to the north, well inside the old ramparts, so that a large section of the Yuan town was left outside the walls; to the south, the process was reversed, and the walls were carried much further south than the walls of the Mongolian town. The suburbs south of the new walls were enclosed within an earth wall (1524) later built in brick (1543). This gave the town its appearance of a double town, which it still has today: the inner city to the north, roughly square; and the outer city to the south, rectangular in shape. In Yong le's reign, the Imperial Palace was re-arranged, and the result was much the same as the present one; the Temple of Heaven and the Altar of Agriculture were built in the outer city.

Peking under the Qing Dynasty

Li Zi cheng reached Peking at the head of his army, drawn from the people, in 1644; the last Ming emperor committed suicide (see p. 484). He in turn was soon overcome by the Manchu, founders of the Qing dynasty which was to last until 1911. They did nothing to change the shape of the town; they merely improved the Forbidden City, as the Imperial Palace is often called, and built a sumptuous Summer Palace in the north-western suburbs (see p. 586). Most of the building was done under Kang xi (1662–1732) and Qian long (1736–1796).

At the end of the 18th century, European travellers estimated the population at two or three million. One of the greatest difficulties for the administration was the supplying of the town; according to Grosier, granaries were built in both towns and in the suburbs, and enormous stocks of rice were stored there against times of famine; more were built at Tong zhou, a town a quarter of a league from Peking. "All these public granaries are faithfully administered, carefully stocked and kept always full: they contain enough rice to feed the capital for eight years; as well as these granaries for rice, the emperor has others which he has filled with corn, small grain, vegetables and all kinds of cheese" (*Description de la Chine* I, chap. 1, p. 17).

Travellers were also impressed by the orderliness of a town as vast as this one: "The Governor of Peking, a Manchu Tartar, called the General of the Five Gates, is responsible for the maintenance of public order as well as for the soldiers; the police force is an extremely active one, and it is astonishing to see how it is possible to move unmolested among such countless crowds of Chinese and Tartars... Each main thoroughfare has its permanent guard of soldiers who patrol night and day, wearing sabres at their belts and carrying whips... The side streets are also guarded by soldiers and have gates made of trellis work, so that a watch may be kept over them more easily; the gates are closed at night, and are rarely opened, except to people who are well known, and only then, if they are carrying a lantern and have a valid reason for going out, such as calling for a doctor... A police force which prevents all nocturnal meetings would no doubt seem extraordinary in Europe, and would probably not appeal to our elegant young men and our mistresses; but the Chinese presumably think like this: they believe that a town's magistrates must prefer a peaceful, orderly situation to vain pleasures which usually result in attempts being made to steal the possessions or even to take the lives of citizens". (*Desc. de la Chine* I, chap. 1, p. 21).

Many provincials and even foreigners came to Peking to do business or simply as tourists. "Foreigners are amazingly well received; they ride in sedan chairs or on horseback, which is more ordinary, but they are always accompanied by a guide to show them the way and point out the houses belonging to great people or leaders. There is even a book on sale which gives information on each district, the squares, places of interest and the houses of the great. In summer, iced water is sold to the people from little huts scattered through the town; there are refreshments, fruit, tea, and houses selling food everywhere..." (*Desc. de la Chine* I, chap. 1, p. 16).

When the Europeans arrived in force in Peking after the Opium War, the consequences for the town were serious. The Summer Palaces were burned down, and the emperor was obliged to cede land to the Powers, south-east of his palace, where legations, protected by exterritoriality, could be built (see p. 531). The Europeans were besieged here in 1900, during the Boxer Rebellion. At the end of the dynasty, the Dowager Empress Ci Xi (Tseu Hsi), known as "Old Buddha", attempted some restoration work.

The Republic

After the Revolution of 1911, Peking remained one of the new republic's political centres. Yuan Shi kai, who was appointed President of the Republic after Sun Yat sen's retirement, signed the 21 Demands there and tried to have the empire restored, with himself as emperor. When, in 1919, the Treaty

of Versailles granted the defeated Germany's possessions to
Japan (in spite of the fact that China had entered the war on the
Allies' side), the Peking University students organised a demonstration in front of Tian an men. This was the famous May 4th
Movement *(Wu si yun dong)*, which was the first stage in the
slow process of evolution towards independence, socialism and
democracy. For years the patriotic element of the population,
becoming gradually more and more Communist, opposed first
the armed troops of the warlords (particularly Zhang Zuo lin)
and then, after the Marco Polo Bridge Incident (July 7th 1937),
the Japanese troops, who occupied the town until 1945. When
the capital was established at Nanking, Peking was once more
renamed Peiping until 1949. After the end of the world war,
resistance to the Guo min dang forces continued (underground
network in Peking, guerillas in the hills to the west of Ba da
chu).

Peking and the Communist Victory

The old residents still remember the Communists' entry into
Peking on January 31st 1949; the enemy had withdrawn several
days before, and the town, its electricity supply cut off, was
living in a state of expectation. One evening, the lights suddenly
went on, and the Liberation Army, headed by its band, made
its entry, in a general atmosphere of gaiety. On October 1st, the
same year, Chairman Mao Ze dong proclaimed the foundation
of the Chinese People's Republic and hoisted the red flag of
New China in Tian an men Square. The constitution of the new
state lays down "that the capital of the People's Republic is
Peking".

III. PEKING TODAY

Peking was handed over without a fight, but one army after
another had been quartered there for about thirty years, and
next to nothing had been done in the way of town planning.
The houses were almost all one storey and buildings with several
floors were very rare indeed. The new leaders drew up a building and restoration plan, which is still in operation, though its
results are already obvious. The old walled town became the
centre of a vast autonomous administrative area: the Municipality of Peking (Bei jing shi), an enclave within the province
of He bei. It covers an area of 9,500 square miles, and has a
population of seven million. It is divided into twelve districts
(four *qu* and eight *xian*).

Town Planning

Building was begun straight away; in 1960, the area available was 29,788,000 square yards, 1.3 times that of the old town. Large public buildings appeared in the old districts: the National People's Congress Building and the Revolutionary and Historical Museums (near Tian an men), the central Station, the Wang fu jing Department Store, the Art Gallery, The Natural History Museum, the Minorities' Palace, several large hotels (Xin jiao, the Minorities' Hotel, the Hotel for Overseas Chinese). New districts have been built outside the walls: industrial and residential districts and large public buildings; to the west: the Ministries of Building Construction and Foreign Trade, the State Planning Commission and the Museum of the Revolutionary Army; to the east: the Agricultural Exhibition Centre, the Workers' Stadium, the new embassies' quarter. The 170 miles of tarred roads in Peking dating from before the liberation have been repaired and 350 miles more have been tarred. It has been decided to knock down the walls little by little, to make communications easier. At the same time, tree-planting has been undertaken on a large scale, to help soften the extremes of climate: the plan includes the Western Hills, Coal Hill, many of the parks, and the lines of trees along all the avenues.

The earthquake of 28 July 1976 caused considerable damage and many old houses fell down. The population is so well disciplined that repairs were carried out in record time.

Agriculture

The south-west of the Municipality of Peking is a fertile plain, on which cereals and vegetables have been grown for a long time. The growth of the town market has triggered off new agricultural expansion. The creation of reservoirs and canals enables large areas of land to be irrigated; one third of the land under cultivation is irrigated today, as opposed to 2.8% before the liberation. Other improvements include better communications, which allow for swifter transport tp Peking, and mechanication. Collective farming enables produce to be systematized to a certain extent (the large model commune, „Red Star", lies to the south of Peking).

As before, the Peking region produces cereals: wheat, rice, maize, sorghum (which often grow side by side). The most important branch is now market gardening: Chinese cabbage *(bai cai)*, turnips, spinach, tomatoes, cucumbers, aubergines, sweet potatoes, beans, soya-beans, peas, lotus roots, onions, garlic; after the harvest (November), the cabbages are stored in vast "clamps" *(bai cai jiao)*, half underground, which are one of the most characteristic features of the Peking country-side (they are covered in earth, sometimes tarred, and have ventilators to air them). The "Evergreen" People's Commune is famous for its greenhouses, where vegetables are grown all the year round. Fruit trees and even grapevines (grown in private gardens) flourish here, because of the mildness of the climate. Orchards were planted after 1958, chiefly to the nort-east (on the road to the airport), and to the west (near Ba da chu); apples, pears, apricots, peaches, nuts, persimmons (which ripen in October and November), water-melons, medlars *(hong guo)*, chestnuts, jujubes *(zao)*, and lotus seeds *(lian zi)* are grown. Many of these are made into crystallised fruit, which is a tra-ditional Peking speciality (a medal was won at the International Competition at Panama in 1913). Groundnuts are also grown on a large scale: grilled or boiled peanuts are eaten with tea or wine; as well as oil, a sort of cream is made from them, and used as a condiment. Cotton is produced in the regions of Da xing, to the south, and Ping gu, to the west.

Stock-breeding was very limited at the beginning of the 20th century. The horses and mules used as draught animals all came from Mongolia; there were scarcely any milk-cows. Pig and sheep-rearing have been expanded and a people's commune supplies the milk for the capital. Peking duck are reared as well; they are a white breed, similar to geese, of delic-ate flavour, used for the famous "roast duck" *(kao ya)*, and fish are bred in ponds near the town.

Horticulture was highly developed owing to the presence of the court, both in the town itself and the suburbs (hothouses in the Long fu si Temple and the Hu guo si Temple); the tradit-ion has survived, and throughout the year magnificent exhib-itions of flowers can be seen (chrysanthemums, peonies) in several of the parks (Coal Hill, Bei Hai, the Sun Yat sen Park, Yi he yuan).

Industry and Handicrafts

Industry scarcely existed in the Peking region in the first half of the century; apart from the Men tou gou coal mines and the Shi jing shan ironworks, the rest can be classed only as handicrafts. A 1923 guide book gives this brief list for Peking itself: a carpet works (300 workmen), a match works, a cigar-ette works and a small electricity works (the actions were held by high-ranking civil servants). Just before 1949, the total annual production amounted to 170 million *yuan;* the workers number-ed about 70,000.

In 1958, production rose to 4,600 million *yuan* and the work-ers numbered 870,000. Priority was given to modernising the Men tou gou coal mines and the Shi jing shan ironworks; the latter were transformed into steel works. Coal production quadrupled between 1949 and 1958, and cast iron production increased twenty times; steel production rose to 60,000 tons in 1958. Light industry was created as well: weaving, chemicals, pharmaceutics, food, agricultural tools, machine tools, electric motors, wireless valves. These new industries are grouped in the eastern suburbs mainly.

Luxury handicrafts were highly developed under the empire. Large numbers of private enterprises existed alongside the imperial workshops, which were near the Forbidden City. Glass, lacquer ware, cloisonné ware, jade ware, ivory ware, embroidery, silks, and carpets (particularly famous) were all made. Under the Republic, a state workshop was organised, employing five hundred workmen (south-west of Liu li chang). The present government has collected the craftsmen in a new workshop, north of the town. Some products of this workshop are sold in shops in Wang fu jing. A few independent workshops still exist apart from the principal one (toys made of terra cotta and silk thread, lanterns, little pictures in wrought iron, etc.)

Communications

(City bus lines, see p. 529)
(Suburban bus lines, see p. 561)
(Trolleybus lines, see Atlas, pl. 6/7)

Peking and large sections of the suburbs now have both a bus and trolleybus service. Goods are carried more often now by motor transport, but animals are still used (carts drawn by a horse with a mule or a donkey tied alongside it and the human element has not yet disappeared (many pedicabs, or *san lun che*).

Peking became the centre of the North China railways when they were first built at the beginning of the 20th century. It is now the centre of the national network; direct trains go from Peking to Shang hai, Qing dao, Bao tou, Tai yuan, Canton, Nan ning, Zhong qing, Lan zhou, Da lian, Harbin, as well as to Pyong yang, Hanoi, Ulan Bator and Moscow. Airlines also exist to all these places, and to others which as yet have no railways, such as parts of Yun nan, and Tibet. The Chinese Air company (C.A.A.C.) runs regular services to Moscow (via Irkutsk), Ulan Bator, Pyong yang, Phnom Penh (via Hanoi), Rangoon (via Kunming and Mandalay), and Dakka (from Canton).

The Political and Cultural Centre of the Country

Since 1949, Peking has become the political and cultural centre of the country once more. The National Assembly meets there (in the National People's Congress Building, near Tian an men); the Council of State (south of the Bei hai), the ministries, the two Higher Courts of Justice and the Central Committee of the Communist Party are all there (the last three are southeast of Tian an men, in the old "legation quarter").

Peking already had famous universities before 1949: Peking University (Bei jing da xue), founded in 1898, famous for its teaching of literature, and Qing hua University (Qing hua da xue), known for its technical and scientific teaching, among others. Many more higher educational establishments have been founded since the liberation. The following are some of the most important: the People's University (Ren min da xue) which produces cadres and economics specialists mainly; the Peking Teachers' Training College (Bei jing shi fan da xue); the Central Institute of Minorities (Zhong yang min zu xue yuan) where part of the students come from national minority races; several foreign languages institutes; the Peking Institute of Medecine (Bei jing yi xue yuan); the Peking Institute of Foreign Trade (Bei jing dui wai mao yi xue yuan); the Peking Cinema Institute (Bei jing dian ying xue yuan); the Central Drama Institute (Zhong yang xi ju xue yuan); the Peking Agricultural University (Bei jing nong ye da xue); the Peking Agricultural Mechanisation Institute (Bei jing nong ye ji xie xue yuan); the Peking Forestry Institute (Bei jing lin xue yuan); the Peking Institute of Metallurgy (Bei jing gang tie xue yuan); the Peking Geological Institute (Bei jing di zhi ran tan xue yuan); the Peking Petroleum Research Institute (Bei jing shi you xue yuan); the Peking Mining Institute (Bei jing kuang ye xue yuan); the Peking Railway Institute (Bei jing tie dao xue yuan); the Peking Post and Telecommunications Institute (Bei jing you dian xue yuan); etc.

When the Chinese Academy of Science was founded in 1949 (the "Academia Sinica", Zhong guo ke xue yuan), the managing committee and most of the research centres were set up in Peking (some other towns, such as Nanking and Shang hai have branches). The centres fall into four main sections: 1) mathematics, physics and chemistry; 2) biology; 3) technology; 4) philosophical studies. The National Institute of Agricultural Research, which is strictly speaking outside the Academy, (Zhong guo nong ye ke xue yuan), supervises the agricultural institutes in each province.

The largest library in the country is in Peking; the Peking Library (Bei jing tu shu guan); the Record Office, the Film Library, the National Historical Museum, many of the publishing and press houses: the *People's Daily (Ren min ri bao)*, the *Workmen's Daily (Gong ren ri bao)*, and the foreign languages press, etc., are all in Peking.

Peking also has over twenty-five theatres and a large number of cinemas.

IV. NOTE ON THE WATER SUPPLY

Considering how extremely dry the Peking climate is between autumn and spring, it is astonishing to see that the vegetation still stays green, and the supply of market gardening products is seemingly endless. During periods of dryness, the town gardeners water each tree in the avenues individually, filling the little hollow made specially at its foot; the visitor may well wonder where this abundant supply comes from. Peking is not on a river, and all the water has to be brought from elsewhere.

Some of it comes from deposits about 30 feet below the ground, which occur over much of the region; artesian wells are frequent, and they are still being drilled, by means of an electric drill, or in the old fashioned way, using a hand-driven drill.

This enables some villages to be supplied with drinking water, and provides water for irrigation, but it is insufficient.

From the earliest history of the town, the question has been how to make use of the rivers and springs in the neighbourhood. The Bai he flows to the east; it comes from the north, fed

by the Sha he ("sandy river"), through Tong xian, and flows
on southwards. The tumultuous Yong ding he ("calmed for
ever", by contrast) flows to the west; it is also called Hun he,
the "muddy river", and is a large river flowing down from the
Shan xi plateau and the north-west of He bei. After a twisting
course through the mountains, it reaches the Peking plain not
far from San ji dian, flows under the Marco Polo Bridge and
then on south-eastwards to meet the Hai he north of Tian jin.
Its flow is irregular: in the rainy season, it rises rapidly, carrying with it large quantities of alluvium (a phenomenon which
is accentuated by the intensive deforestation). The force of the
current as it flows down through the mountains brings it down
to the plain, where it is deposited, raising the level of the river
bed considerably. At Marco Polo Bridge, it flows 50 feet above
the level of Peking, and only 9 miles away, a difference in level
which is extremely dangerous when the river is high, but which
can be used for canalisation. Several springs rise at the foot of
Fragrant Hills, and on the little Jade Fountain Hill.

The Supply under the Jin

When the Jin decided to make Peking their capital, they
realised that the water of the Lian hua Pool (west of the present
Chinese Town), which had supplied the Liao town, was no
longer adequate. They also hoped to build a canal linking
Zhong du to Tong xian, enabling barges carrying grain from
the south up the Bai he to Tong xian to come as far as the
capital (the Bai he was the northern section of the Grand
Canal). The first part of the plan was completed; water was
diverted from the Yong ding he to the north of the capital
(slightly south of the present Chang an jie Avenue), and was
made to flow towards Tong xian. In 1171, the Lu kou canal
was opened; but in 1175 the Yong ding he rose, burst the dykes
and drowned a village, and the engineers were forced to block
the canal.

The Supply under the Yuan

When his capital, Da du, was under way, Khubilai commissioned the famous engineer Guo Shou jing to find a new answer
to the problem. In 1262, he suggested that the waters of the
Jade Spring should be brought to the town, by means of a
little river, the Gao liang he, and made to flow into the eastern
section of the old Jin canal, which was then south of the town.

PÉKIN, RÉGIME DES EAUX 1° — RÉGIME ANCIEN
PEKING, WATERCOURSES 1° — FORMER SYSTEM

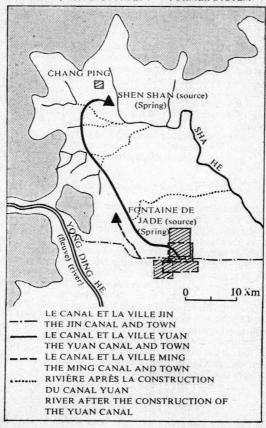

CHANG PING

SHEN SHAN (source)
(Spring)

SHA HE

FONTAINE DE
JADE (source)
(Spring)

YONG DING HE
(Fleuve) (river)

0   10 Km

LE CANAL ET LA VILLE JIN
THE JIN CANAL AND TOWN
LE CANAL ET LA VILLE YUAN
THE YUAN CANAL AND TOWN
LE CANAL ET LA VILLE MING
THE MING CANAL AND TOWN
RIVIÈRE APRÈS LA CONSTRUCTION
DU CANAL YUAN
RIVER AFTER THE CONSTRUCTION OF
THE YUAN CANAL

This was done; unfortunately the water, though it provided drinking water for the whole capital, was not sufficient to maintain the level hoped for in the canal. After a three-year stay with the Xia xi (north-east of the Yellow River as it now is), Guo Shou jing drew up a new plan; the Jin canal was to be re-opened, and the danger of floods lessened by digging a channel to lead surplus water back to the Yong ding river. This was completed in 1276; part of the countryside could then be irrigated, and timber from the hills could be brought as far as Peking; but the problem of navigation still remained, apparently, as work was soon under way on another solution. Guo Shou jing completed his third plan: he tried once more to use the waters of the Jade Spring, adding at the same time water from a spring to the north (Bai fu quan), south of Chang ping, and the waters of the Sha he. The new canal was called the Tong hui he; it was 50 miles long, and was opened in the autumn of 1293. Barges could then come as far as the capital of Da du. The northern part of the canal was abandoned, however, in 1368.

The Supply under the Ming and the Qing

Under the Ming and the Qing, the difficulty was to supply water to the Summer Palaces being built north-west of the town; the plentiful waters of the Jade Spring were used once more, as they were near at hand, and also those of Fragrant Hills, which were brought by means of an aqueduct. After flowing through the Yi he yuan and the Yuan ming yuan, most of the water ran out through the Gao liang, (now canalised and called the Chang he, to the north of Peking), to the Shi sha hai lakes, and after that, either to the three lakes (north, south and central) or the Yu he canal (inside the eastern wall of the Forbidden City; it has since disappeared); the Yu he canal flowed through the Legations Quarter and ended in the moat separating the inner town from the outer town; in this way, the waters joined the Tong xian canal. At the beginning of the 20th century, the development of the railway removed most of the traffic from the Tong xian canal.

The Present Supply

The need for electricity has now been added to the age-old difficulties of flood-control and irrigation of crops. Towards 1925, the Yong ding river was used to generate electricity in a

PÉKIN, RÉGIME DES EAUX 2° — RÉGIME ACTUEL
PEKING, WATERCOURSES 2° — PRESENT SYSTEM

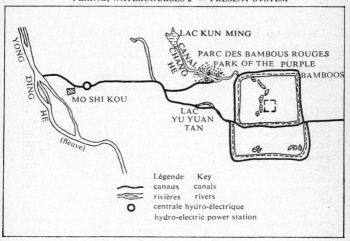

small electricity works near the town of Ma yu, not far from
where the Jin canal had begun. After 1949, work was begun
on a final answer to the problem. Two large artificial lakes have
been made: the Mi yun reservoir, north-east of the city (in the
Mi yun district) and the Guan ting reservoir in the north-western
mountains, beyond the Great Wall. They regulate the Bai he
and the Yong ding he upstream, draining off the water when
it rises, and re-distributing it when the rivers are low. Two
other lesser projects have also been carried out: 1) the construction of the Ming Tombs Reservoir (south of the Tombs, on
the Wen yu he, an affluent of the Sha he); the water feeds a
hydro-electric power station and irrigates the neighbouring
countryside; 2) the building of a hydro-electric power station
near Mo shi kou, which uses the waters of the Yong ding he
and feeds them back into the river through a channel which
follows roughly the same course as the Jin canal, dividing
downstream to join the former Chang he (in the Purple Bamboo
Court), to the north, and to the south, the canal which separates
the inner and outer cities.

PEKING

(See plan p. 465)

Peking has changed so much over the last thirty years that those who knew it before 1949 will soon find it unrecognisable. The lay-out of the old town is still clear, however, and although the walls have disappeared, the best way to describe it is still as the "walled town" as opposed to the suburbs.

The old guide books usually divided the walled town into four separate towns: 1) in the middle, the "Purple Forbidden City" *(zi jin cheng)*, which was the Imperial Palace itself; 2) the Imperial City *(huang cheng)* surrounding it, also enclosed within a wall, which contained the court, the ministries and their dependencies; 3) round this, the "inner city" *(nei cheng)*, also called the "Tartar city" because the Manchu lived here during the Qing dynasty (it was divided into eight districts, each belonging to one of the eight banners); 4) the "outer city" *(wai cheng)*, south of the inner city, also known as the "southern city" or "Chinese city" (as opposed to the Tartar city).

The northern part of the town will be described first, followed by the southern part. The northern town is almost square: 4 miles from east to west and 3½ miles from north to south, and the southern town is rectangular: 5 miles from east to west and 1¾ miles from north to south.

I.   The northern part of the walled town

When Yong le decided to establish his capital at Peking, he had the walls of the inner city built. In 1437, they were faced in brick; as time went on, they were restored and reinforced several times. A way ran along the top, wide enough to take a man on horseback; at intervals, the walls were either reinforced by towers (particularly at the corners) or pierced by "gates" *(men)*. De Lisle described them in 1765: "They are tall and well curved (arched); they support nine-storey pavilions with windows or loopholes; the ground floor is a sort of hall used by officers and men when they are about to mount the guard, or have just finished. In front of each gate lies a stretch of open ground, like a parade-ground, over 360 feet long, shut in by a circular wall of the same design as the walls of the town; this has a pavilion like the first to defend it, and whereas the gun in the gate covers the enclosure, the one in the outer pavilion covers the surrounding countryside and suburbs".

There were only nine gates at first; each one was used for specialised traffic. Two opened to the north: to the west, the Gate of Virtue and Victory (De sheng men), used by armies when they left to begin a campaign; to the east, the Gate of Certain Peace (An ding men), through which night-soil was taken (on its way to three sewage farms, near the Altar of the Earth, where it was treated before being used as fertilizer). Two opened to the east: to the north, the Due East Gate (Dong zhi men), through which the wood was brought from the canal (even now, there are more carpenters in the north-east of the town than elsewhere); to the south, the Gate of the Rising Sun (Chao yang men), through which grain transported by water from Tong xian was brought; it was stored in numerous granaries inside the walls, between Chao yang men and Dong zhi men (the largest, like the "Officials' salaries Granary", can be traced in the toponymy). Three gates opened into the outer city, to the south: to the east, the Gate of Sublime Learning (Chong wen men), through which loads of wine were brought (made in the eastern and southern suburbs); in the middle was the Gate which faces the Sun (Zheng yang men), which was used by the Emperor; to the west, the Gate of the Majesty of Arms (Xuan wu men), through which those condemned to death were led (they were executed at the Vegetable Market, in the west of the southern city). Two gates opened to the west: to the south, the Gate of Abundance (Fu cheng men), through which coal was brought, from the Men tou gou mines; to the north, the Due West Gate (Xi zhi men), through which water for the Emperor's table was brought (it came from the Jade Fountain springs and was transported at night, so that it would arrive cool, in containers covered with yellow cloth, embroidered with the imperial dragon, and carried by mules). Later on, other gates were built, such as the Renaissance Gate (Fu xing men) to the west, the Construction of the Country Gate (Jian guo men), to the east, and the Peace Gate (He ping men) to the south. The gates have either been destroyed or are now out of use; the road no longer passes through the few which still survive, but makes a detour round them.

The main thoroughfares within the walls are laid out like a chessboard, and the rectangular areas between them are covered with a network of little winding streets, or *hu tong*. Some of the main streets have always been wide, to help prevent the spread of fires. In theory, the geometrical plan made communications easier; in practice, as the Imperial City was in the centre, surrounded by an area on a north-south axis reserved for the court and officials (from north of Coal Hill to Zheng yang men), this interfered with east-west traffic. While the palace was the living centre of the town, this seemed natural enough, but once it had turned into a museum, it was very inconvenient.

Improvements have been made since 1911, and most of all, since 1949; two roads cut through the north-south axis: a new throughfare south of Coal Hill runs almost directly between Fu cheng men Gate to the west and Chao yang men to the east, and Chang an jie Avenue, south of the Imperial City, links Fu xing men Gate, to the west, with Jian guo men Gate, to the east.

Tian an men Square, which is now both the topographical and the emotional centre of the city, will be described first; then the group of buildings which were once the Imperial Palace, which still retain their unity (the former palaces and parks are now museums and public gardens); and finally, the northern districts, the western market-places and surrounding area, the eastern market-places and surrounding area, and the southern districts.

A. TIAN AN MEN SQUARE

Any visit to Peking must begin with Tian an men Square (the Gate of Heavenly Peace Square). It is easily the most enormous in the town (about 98 acres), and lies south of the Imperial City, in the centre of Peking.

History: The square did not exist under the empire. Ministries and other offices stood here, on either side of a way going from north to south, leading from Tian an men Gate to Zheng yang men Gate. The Ministries of Rites, Works and War, and the Astronomical Office stood on the eastern side; the Ministry of Justice, the Office of Sacrifices and the Court of Censors stood on the western side. These were all enclosed within a wall with three gates, to the south, east and west. Chang an jie Avenue, which now runs north of the square, did not exist, and to go from one side of the town to the other, people had to go all the way round Qian men, to the south.

When the Emperor went to the Temple of Heaven (in the southern city), he passed, with great pomp, through Tian an men. Before leaving on a journey, he made a sacrifice in front of the gate; and on great occasions, imperial edicts were let down from the top of the gate in a sort of gilded box in the shape of a phoenix (the edict was put into the mouth of the phoenix). High-ranking officials, kneeling at the foot of the gate, facing north, would receive the message in a wooden tray decorated with a cloud design and take it to the Ministry of Rites, where it was copied several times over and sent throughout the empire. From this custom came the expression: "the imperial orders given by the gilded phoenix".

The buildings were damaged in 1860 and 1900. Some of them were destroyed, and the north-south way was widened, till it almost became a square. After the fall of the empire in 1912, the government of the Republic used the former Imperial Palace for a short time. Each time that the inhabitants of Peking wanted to demonstrate against the official policy, which they considered over-timid, they would gather in front of Tian an men. Several large mass demonstrations which were landmarks in the evolution of modern China took place here: the demonstration on the 4th of May, 1919, in protest against the Treaty of Versailles which handed the former German possessions over to Japan, instead of giving them back to China, the patriotic march on the 18th of March 1926, the anti-Japanese demonstration on December 9th 1935 (the starting point of the war of resistance against Japan). On October 1st 1949, Chairman Mao Ze dong hoisted the red flag with its five stars here and proclaimed the People's Republic of China. The Gate of Heavenly Peace is represented in the arms of the new Republic, on its banknotes and on its coins; the square is, as it were, the navel of the country as a whole. Vast changes were carried out in 1958 and 1959. Parades take place here on important days, such as the rally on May 1st and the parade on October 1st. The leaders and their important guests take their places in the upper gallery of the gate; the delegations crowd on to the stands, which can take 20,000 people; the crowd faces them In the evening, firework displays are given all round the square.

Description. To the north, the square is bounded by a long red wall going from east to west: the southern wall of the Imperial City, with the imposing mass of Tian an men in the middle. Chang an jie (Perpetual peace) Avenue runs alongside the wall; it cuts through the northern part of the town from one end to the

other, from east to west, roughly following the line of
the walls of the Yuan town. To the south, beyond
Mao Ze dong's Mausoleum, the square end at Qian
men (formerly Zheng yang men), the double gate
which connected the north and south towns. It is
flanked on either side by huge modern buildings: the
National People's Congress Building to the west and
the Museums to the east. A mausoleum containing
the embalmed body of Mao Ze dong was built on
Tian an men square in 1976-77.

1. Tian an men Gate

Tian an men is a massive stone building, painted
"purple", with five passages leading through it at its
base, surmounted by a wooden edifice with a double
yellow roof. The Golden Waters Spring (Jin shui)
flows through the palace, and runs along the foot of
the gate. Five marble bridges, with balustrades, lead
over it, one for each of the five openings. Two *hua biao*
stand in front of the bridges; they are sculpted white
marble pillars (some say that they are symbols of pillars where each man could formerly record his petition
or request).

The five passages used to be closed, and were used only on
great occasions; the Emperor alone had the right to use the central
corridor. The gates stayed shut even after 1912, but now they
stand open and lead into the palace. The wall carries two inscriptions: to the west, "Long live the People's Republic of
China" *(Zhong hua ren min gong he guo wan sui);* to the east:
"Long live the great union between the peoples of the world"
(Shi jie ren min da tuan jie wan sui). Stands have been built on
either side of the gate, to accommodate delegations at parades.

2. The Monument to the People's Heroes and Mao Ze dong's Mausoleum

The monument is in the middle of the square.
The work was finished in 1958 (it was unveiled on

May 1st). It is a massive granite obelisk, on a double terrace with marble balustrades, 120 feet high. Two inscriptions in gilded characters decorate it: to the north, in Chairman Mao Ze dong's calligraphy, "The People's heroes are immortal", and to the south, a longer text by the Prime Minister, Zhou En lai. Ten bas-relief carvings decorate the base of the obelisk, forming a white marble frieze 6 feet high and 130 feet long. Most of them show episodes from the revolution.

East side: 1. The patriotic mandarin Lin Zi xu destroys crates of opium (Canton, 1842); 2. The beginning of the Tai ping rebellion (Jin tian, in Guang xi, 1851); *South side:* 3. The rising led by Wu chang against the Manchu (1911); 4. The May 4th demonstration against the terms of the Treaty of Versailles (Peking, 1919); 5. The May 30th demonstration against the Japanese and the English (Shang hai, 1925); *West side:* 6. Nan chang military rising (Jiang xi, 1927); 7. Scene from the guerilla war against the Japanese (1937–1945). *North side:* in the centre; crossing of the Yang zi by the Communist troops (1949); to the right; "grain for the front"; to the left, "long live the liberation army".

The Mao Ze dong Mausoleum was built in the square lying between the Monument to the People's Heroes and Qian Men Gate; the buildings at the southwestern and southeastern corners were demolished, almost doubling the area of the square. The Mausoleum was built in national style, by over 700,000 Chinese volunteers who relayed each other at the task from October 1976 to August 1977, when it was inaugurated. It is 33 metres high and covers an area of over 20,000 square metres; the materials come from every region of China; the base is of red granite, and the thirteen pine trees planted round the building were brought from Yan an, in memory of the thirteen years that Mao spent there (1936-1949).

3. The National People's Congress Building
(Ren min da hui tang)

This building, on the west side of Tian an men Square, covers an area of 561,786 square feet (it has been pointed out that even the buildings of the former Imperial Palace cover a smaller area than this). It contains a banqueting hall (which can accommodate 5,000), and a large theatre (to seat 10,000). The People's Congress sits here when it is summoned; the big political meetings are also held here. Plays are sometimes put on here ("The East is Red" in 1964).

4. The Museums

(Both these museums were closed during the Cultural Revolution and had not re-opened in March 1972.)

The Museums are opposite the National People's Congress Building, on the east side of Tian an men Square. The building was put up in 1959, and houses two museums: the Historical Museum (in the right wing) and the Revolutionary Museum (in the left wing). They were opened in 1961.

a) The Museum of Chinese History (Zhong guo li shi bo wu guan). It occupies the right wing of the building. The subject of the museum is Chinese history from the beginnings up to the Opium War (1840). It is divided into three main sections: 1. Primitive society, 2. Slave society, 3. Feudal society. The various stages in the evolution of history are shown by exhibits in glass cases and pictures on one side of each hall; larger exhibits and models are on the other side, either in cases or on separate pedestals. The museum is essentially didactic; copies or replicas of things belonging to other museums are included without hesitation, when they are needed to clarify the rest. The visitor should bear in mind that a) most of the portraits of famous men are later works (sometimes as late as the 20th century) and as such have no value as historical documents; b) the models of agricultural tools and astronomical instruments are mainly copies made with reference to later texts. The Han mill, or noria, for instance is a reconstruction, based on treatises dating from the Yuan or the Ming. It is assumed that the authors of the treatises were simply describing devices which had been in use for centuries. The museum consists of a ground floor and a first floor.

Ground Floor

Entrance hall. On the walls: large relief map of China, quotation from Mao Ze dong's works and a chronological table of the dynasties; reconstructions of astronomical instruments built by the engineer Su Song in 1088: an armillary sphere to the right, and a celestial globe to the left.

Primitive Society (500,000–4,000 B.C.)

First Section: Paleolithic Era (500,000–15,000 B.C.)

Statue of primitive man in the centre; on the right wall: *chronological table of primitive society:* lower Paleolithic (500,000-150,000 B.C.), Zhou kou dian culture; middle Paleolithic (150,000–50,000 B.C.), Ma ba (Guang dong), Chang yang (Yang zi valley), Ding cun (Shan xi) and He tao (Ordos bend) cultures; upper Paleolithic (50,000–15,000 B.C.), Liu jiang (Guang xi), Zi yang (Si chuan), Shan ding dong (Zhou kou dian site) cultures; Mesolithic (15,000–10,000 B.C.), Zha lai nou er culture (Inner Mongolia); Neolithic (10,000–4,000 B.C.), Yang shao and Long shan cultures; map showing distribution of Paleolithic sites. On the left: reconstruction of a stratographical cross-section showing the level of Paleolithic remains.

1. Lower Paleolithic (500,000–150,000 B.C.), *Zhou kou dian Culture.* Right-hand wall: map showing site of Zhou kou dian in relation to Peking; to the left, case 1, photograph of site number 13 (500,000 B.C.); replicas of bones of Peking Man (skulls, femurs, jawbones); cases 2 and 3, collections of Chellean picks and blades; case 4, use of fire (photograph of marks of ashes, blackened bones and stones); samples of grain; cases 5 and 6, fauna (fragments of bones belonging to wild boar, deer, buffalo, elephant, rhinoceros, wolf, tiger); to the right, model of Long gu shan cave, near Zhou kou dian, where remains of Peking Man were found.

HISTORY MUSEUM

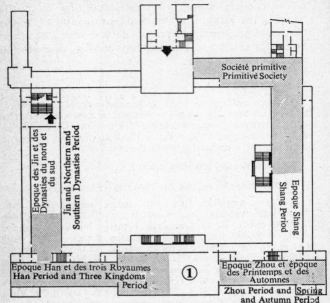

Société primitive
Primitive Society

Epoque des Jin et des Dynasties du nord et du sud
Jin and Northern and Southern Dynasties Period

Epoque Shang
Shang Period

Epoque Han et des trois Royaumes
Han Period and Three Kingdoms Period

①

Epoque Zhou et époque des Printemps et des Automnes
Zhou Period and Spring and Autumn Period

REZ-DE-CHAUSSÉE — GROUND-FLOOR

① Epoque des Royaumes combattants
— fondation de l'empire par Qin Shi Huang di

Warring States Period — foundation of the empire by Qin Shi Huang di

◄ Flèche indiquant le sens de la visite
Arrow showing the direction to follow during the visit

---

2. Middle Paleolithic (150,000–50,000 B.C.). *a) Ma ba and Chang yang Cultures:* case 8, map showing the two sites of Ma ba (in Guang dong, near Yao guan) and Chang yang (in Hu bei, west of Wu han); photograph of the Shi zi yan cave at Ma ba, near Shao yang (left); fragment of human skull discovered in

1958; photograph of the Long dong cave at Xia zhong jia wan near Chang yang (right); fragments of human jawbone discovered in 1957; fragments of animal bones (buffalo, rhinoceros). *b) Ding cun Culture (Shan xi, south of Tai yuan, near the town of Li cun):* right, reconstruction of a stratographical cross-section at Ding cun, showing the different levels; cases 9 and 10, map of the Ding cun site and photographs; tools found in 1957 (axes, two-edged tools); case 11, fauna (horns of aurochs, elephants', horses', and woolly rhinoceros' teeth). *c) Ordos Bend Culture* (He tao): case 12, map of a site on the banks of the river Sa la wu su; fragments of human bones and skulls found in 1956; two human teeth found beside the river; tools found in Gan su (Chellean picks, blades, flakes); case 13, fauna (fragments of bone belonging to horses, buffalo, elephants, camels, wild donkeys, boars, woolly rhinoceros and deer).

3. Upper Paleolithic (50,000–15,000 B.C.) *a) Shan ding dong Culture* (on the Zhou kou dian site): case 15, fragments of human bones found in 1933; necklaces of bones and shells, bone needles; fauna (fragments of deer, rabbit, wolf, fox, tiger and bear bones). *b) Liu jiang (Guang xi) and Yu shu (Hei long jiang) Cultures:* case 16, map showing distribution of Upper Paleolithic sites; map of the Zi yang site (south of Cheng du); photograph of the Qi lin shan cave (Guang xi); skull and fragments of human bones found in 1958 at Liu jiang; human skull found at Qi lin shan in 1956; human skull found in 1951 at Zi yang.

N.B. No mention has yet been included in the Paleolithic section of the site at Lan tian in Shân xi, where remains of sinanthropus no doubt as old as those found at Zhou kou dian have recently been discovered.

Second Section: Mesolithic (15,000–10,000 B.C.)

Zha lai nuo er culture (Inner Mongolia): case 17, map of the Zha lai nuo er site; two human skulls; tools from the Sha yuan region in Shân xi (microliths: arrowheads, flakes, awls).

Third Section: Neolithic (10,000–4,000 B.C.).

1. Early Neolithic (10,000–6,000 B.C.). Map showing distribution of Neolithic sites (in blue and brown, the Yang shao and Long shan cultures; in green, the microlithic cultures; in red, all other sites); case 19, Lower Yellow River culture (polished axes, made in several shapes, blades with holes in them, a little pottery ware, cultivation of grain); case 20, Yang zi culture: axes; large collection of Si chuan pottery ware (beautiful flask with design in black), Jiang su and Zhe jiang pottery ware (large tripod); spindle (Jiang xi); weights for fishing nets; case 21, north-eastern culture: grey pottery ware, large blades with holes in them, stone mortar (Liao ning), arrowheads; case 22, western cultures (Tibet, Xin jiang, Gan su): microliths, arrowheads, axes, blades, scrapers, polishing stones, stone ploughshare (?); case 23, southern cultures: spades, axes, shouldered and quadrangular axes, spearheads, awls, spindles, knives, black painted pottery ware.

2. *Middle Neolithic (6,000-5,000 B.C.), Yang shao culture.* On the right, model of the Ban po site near Xi an; in the left-hand corner, remains of the floor of a hut from the Bao ji shi site (Shân xi) excavated in 1959; the village was made up of twenty huts, all of the same type; the circular base covered 57 square feet; the hearth was in the middle, with a hollow in the ground next to it to catch the cinders; the door was on the north-west side; cases 24 and 25, improvement in the quality of tools: fine polished axes, spades, Chellean picks; borers, gravers and blades in bone; stone blades and knives; pottery case 26, hunting and fishing: awls, arrows, fish-hooks, harpoons, pebbles to stretch the nets, shells; case 27, weaving: spindles found at Ban po and in He nan; marks left by fabric and woven mats on the bottom of pottery ware; bone needles; cases 28 and 29, pottery ware: jars, urns, cooking pots from He nan and Shân xi; case 30, decorative art: animal designs from Ban po (fish, fourfooted animals); geometric designs; a kind of pictogram; pottery ware in the shape of animals and rings; in a case on the right, a pottery kiln from Hua xian in Shân xi.

3. *Late Neolithic (5,000-4,000 B.C.), development of the Long shan culture.* Case 31, map of the San li qiao and Miao di gou sites, near Shan xian in He nan; black pottery ware (tripods, amphora); bone knives, needles, comb; case 32, improvement in quality of agricultural implements: stone sickle, a sort of wooden fork (marks left by the implement in the earth), shell knives; case 33, domestic animals (fragments of dog, pig, ox, goat, deer bones); fishing and hunting (arrowheads, spearheads, fish-hooks); case 34, the invention of the potter's wheel, the beginning of handicrafts (good collection of beautiful black pottery, from Shan dong and Zhe jiang); case 35, various cooking utensils (large collection of tripods from Shan dong and He nan; stone from He nan; fragments of basket ware); case 36, the arts (bone necklaces, jade bracelets; several square axe

heads with a hole in them, made of precious stones, fragments of clay figures, and a clay bell, a human face carved in bone); on the right, full scale model of a hut found at San li qiao near Shan xian in He nan (the circular base is 9 feet across, the walls are 3ft. 9 inches high, the door is to the east, the fire-place against the west wall).

4. Transitional Period. a) The appearance of bronze in Gan su: case 37, finds from the Huang niang niang tai site, near Wu wei in Gan su: bronze knives and rings, table of the chemical analysis of bronze, bone fork, animal's scapula used for divination (with small round marks on it), pottery ware, some with geometric designs, some plain. *b) The appearance of a different kind of society in Shan dong:* cases 38 and 39, models of graves found in 1959 in a communal cemetry, near Ning yang in Shan dong, which contained one hundred graves altogether, of three main types: articles found in a small grave (grey pottery ware, spindles), articles from a middle-sized grave (fine collection of grey, red, and painted pottery ware, polished stone axe, bone needles and ornaments, awls and knives), photograph of a large grave (rich collection of pottery ware, including a set of large, white pieces, jade bracelet, necklaces and rectangular blades, stone axe). *c) Ancient China, according to traditional history.* Map showing the traditional idea of ancient China, table of inventions attributed to the Yellow Emperor (Huang di).

Slave Society (2,100–475 B.C.)

First Section: the semi-mythical Xia dynasty. In the centre, a statue of Da yu, the founder of the dynasty, and subduer of the waters; on the walls: map of China under the Xia; copy of the design of a Han brick found in Shan dong, depicting Jie, the last emperor of the dynasty, known for his bad government, sitting on the bodies of two women; table of the Xia emperors.

On the right, a dug-out canoe stretches the length of the wall (33 feet long and 2 ft. 11 inches wide in the central part); it was found in 1958 in a river near Wu jin xian, in Jiang su, with twenty pieces of pottery, all with designs; they are presumed to be very old (?).

Second Section: the Shang dynasty (16th century–11th century B.C.).

Map of China under the Shang (with a sketch in the corner showing the sites which have been found); table of the hierarchy; case 1, weapons, which have been fitted with new handles according to old pictograms (knife, spear, axe, *ge*, bronze arrows, 16th–11th century) and photograph of a set of spears found in a noble's tomb at An yang (He nan).

1. Agriculture. On the wall, a table of the calendar in use at that time; case 2, the importance of agriculture: list of different sorts of grain, drawn up from characters found in inscriptions, bronze spade found at An yang in 1953 (14th–11th century ?), stone knives and hoes, plain axe, stone and shell sickles.

2. Silk-worm rearing and weaving. Case 3, photograph of pieces of silk found at An yang; jade silk-worms, found in large quantities at An yang (14th–11th century ?); table of different characters used, referring to silk, found in contemporary inscriptions; remains of fabric on a bronze plaque, found at An yang in 1953; bone needles; stone spindles.

3. Animal rearing, hunting and fishing. Case 3 (continued), bronze fish-hook, found at Zheng zhou in He nan (14th–11th century ?); bone and stone spearheads; round clay balls, for use with a bow; dog, pig bones, goat and ox horns.

4. Bronze. Cases 4 and 5, casting of bronze: table of chemical analysis of Shang bronze; sample of modern copper ore; charcoal and slag found at An yang; three melting-pots of different shapes, two found at Zheng zhou, one at An yang (14th–11th century); sketch showing vertical cross-section of the two types of melting-pots; models showing different stages in making moulds; case 6, magnificent *zun* (bronze sacrificial vessel used for wine) from An hui; in the middle: case 7, large *ding* (rectangular cauldron) 4 feet high, weighing 143 stone, from An yang (14th–11th century ?), one of the largest bronzes found; it shows that the technique must have been very advanced, and the work extremely well organised, as judging by the melting-pots that have been found, it has been estimated that 80, all ready at the same time, must have been needed to cast it; on the left, two small cases: moulds found at Zheng zhou (beginning and end of the dynasty); bronze implements (knives, among them one very large one found at Hui xian in He nan in 1951, gravers from Shan xi, axes); in a case to itself, a fine *zun* decorated with rams, from He nan (14th–11th century); cases 9, 10, 11, and 12, bronzes: two fine specimens of *yan* (vessel with three feet, made in two parts, for steaming food) found at An yang (14th–11th century); in the middle: large bell, decorated with four elephants (14th–11th century); magnificent musical stone, found at An yang in 1951 (14th–11th century).

5. Pottery ware. Case 12, map showing where kilns were found at Zheng zhou; model of a kiln; failures found in a kiln at Zheng zhou; tools used to make pottery (little clay mallets, moulds to make the design); case 13, striped grey pottery ware from Zheng zhou and An yang; figurines in the shape of fish and tortoises, from Zheng zhou; clay whistles (Hui xian in He nan, 14th–11th century); interesting pot with a pierced bottom for steaming from Zheng zhou (16th–14th century).

6. Bone, jade and stone work. Case 14, bone ornaments (hairpins, necklaces); bone tools (borers, combs, arrowheads); raw materials (boars' teeth, fragments of bone, deer horn); stone carving: bird, ox head, sitting animal from An yang 14th–11th century); jade implements: *ge* and axe inlaid with turquoise (14th–11th century).

7. Bone inscriptions (jia gu wen) and divination. Cases 15 and 16, picture showing how bone was perforated; bronze borer used for this; collection of inscriptions on bone (the oldest date from the Wu ding period, 16th–14th century); photographs of texts inscribed on bone.

8. Trade and communications. To the right: case with map showing where jade, cowries, tortoises, horses, and whales came from, all of which were used in long-distance trade; whale bones and sea shells found at An yang; cowries from Zheng zhou; sketch of a chariot with the skeletons of two horses found in a tomb at An yang; pieces of a chariot, and chariot ornaments, made of bronze; small bell.

9. Tombs. In the middle, model of a dignitary's tomb, of a late date (14th–11th century), discovered at An yang in 1950; it consists of a central pit with two long corridors leading to it; inside, there were grave furnishings (bronzes, pottery, musical stone...), horses, remains of 45 bodies and 34 heads buried at the same time as the dead man; on the left wall, photograph of a very rudimentary tomb, that of slave (one jar only beside the body).

In a small case to the right: model of a pile of bone inscriptions found in a pit at An yang in 1936.

Third Section: the Western Zhou (11th century–7th century B.C.).

1. Founding of the new dynasty. Case 18, drawings of the first three Zhou kings (Wen wang, Wu wang, Zhou gong) taken from a Han brick, and a set of bronzes found in Shân xi and near Luo yang; in the centre of the case, a *gui*, a sacrificial vessel used for grain, with an inscription recording Wu wang's victory over the Shang in the 11th century; on the wall, map of the chief fiefs at the beginning of the dynasty and table of the administrative hierarchy under the Western Zhou; in a case by itself, a large *ding* with an inscription recording the success-ful campaign of a certain Yu who was sent to subdue the people of the south-east, who had come to attack the Zhou (9th cen-tury); case 19, map showing sites where bronzes have been found (northern limit: Liao ning, eastern limit: Jiang su and An hui, southern limit; Hu bei, western limit: Shân xi); interesting collection of bronzes: to the right: 10th century *gui*, with ins-cription recording the military successes of a dignitary; to the left: *gui* with an inscription recording the granting of a fief to a noble by King Kang; 11th century bronze shaped like a horn, from Jiang su; two interesting *zun*, one shaped like a horse, with inscription, dating from the 9th century, found in Shân xi, the other shaped like a duck (11th–8th century ?) found in Liao ning.

2. *Zhou society*. Case 20, from right to left: 9th century *gui* with inscription about tribute to be paid to the Zhou king by his vassals; 9th century *gui* with inscriptions telling how a dignitary had received land and slaves from the king, in return for a successful military expedition against the Zhou clan's enemies; 10th century *hu* (sacrificial vessel for alcohol) with inscription recording the king of Zhou's gift of twenty slaves to a dignitary, with the order to build a palace near Luo yang; 9th century *gui* with inscription about the inheriting of offices; two rubbings on the back wall of the case concern the sale of slaves: the first states that five slaves are worth one horse and eleven rolls of silk; the second (taken from an inscription on the bottom of the large *ding* in the central case) records how King Kang made a present to a dignitary of chariots, horses and 1,709 slaves; in the two central cases, large 11th century *ding* (with the inscription reproduced on the rubbing in case 20) and a very interesting rectangular basin over three feet long, with an inscription recording rewards given by King Xuan to a dignitary who had distinguished himself in combat (9th cen-tury).

3. *The agricultural system*. Case 21, table recording the appearance of the system known as *jing tian* (the land was divi-ded into nine farms, and the tenants of the eight farms round the boundaries worked by turns on the farm in the centre,

which belonged to the landlord), collection of bronzes: from right to left: *gui* (11th–9th century ?) with inscription recording a judgement pronounced by King Li in a case about renting of land; 9th century *gui* with inscription recording a grant of land by King Xuan to a noble.

4. Agricultural techniques. Case 22, table of the system supposed to have been used to distribute land according to the quality of the soil, and collection of agricultural implements (six spades: two of bone, two of bronze and two of stone; nine axes: six in bronze and three in stone: several shell knives, some with holes in them).

⌊*5. Handicrafts.* Case 23, grey pottery ware from Shân xi, He nan and Jiang su (three fine specimens of *dou*, sacrificial vessels, found in Jiang su in 1955); case 24, five lead vessels found at Luo yang in 1955; bone hairpins and jade ornaments; bronze chamfrons and knives; in the centre of the hall, chariot reconstructed using some found in a tomb at Xun xian, He nan, as models.

6. Differences in social rank. Photograph of an extremely simple grave in Shân xi (several pieces of rustic pottery beside the body); case 25, grave furnishings from the grave of a dignitary of middling rank in Shân xi (bronze and clay vessels, bone and jade ornaments, bronze bells).

Fourth Section: Spring and Autumn Period (Chun qiu Period) (770–475 B.C.).

⌊*1. The rise of the Hegemons.* Drawing depicting Duke Xuan of Qi with his political adviser Guan zhong, taken from a Han brick; in the case below: text of the *Guan zi* (collection of Guan zhong's conversations with his ruler); text of the *Guo yu (Conversations of the States);* on the wall, map of the chief states, and scenes of important oaths and battles; in the case below, collection of weapons: five swords, four from He nan (770–655 B.C. ?) and one from An hui (493–447 B.C. ?), arrow and spear heads, set of *ge*, some with inscriptions and one with a human head depicted on it; on the wall: table showing the evolution of society from the Western Zhou period to the Chun qiu period.

2. Bronzes and the conception of riches. Cases 26 and 27, some of the hundred bronzes found in a tomb at Xin zheng xian in He nan in 1923 (magnificent set of eleven bells); cases 28,

29, and 30, bronzes from several different places (*zun* in the shape of a rabbit found at Shan xian in He nan in 1957, *ge* with an inscription in gilded characters, chariot-wheel hub); in the two cases on the left, a large round basin, three feet in diameter with a tiger design (770–475 B.C. ?); two bells (the smallest, on the left, bears an inscription saying that Zhu gong had it cast in honour of his officers); sword belonging to the king of Wu (5th century B.C.).

3. *Changes in agriculture.*   Table stating the lapse of the *jing tian* system, the beginning of privately owned fields, all connected with the use of iron, and the creation of a tax based on landed property in the state of Lu, in 594 B.C.; in the case below, agricultural implements (shell blades, bronze and bone spades, bronze knife and axes).

4. *Handicrafts, the development of trade and the first use of money.* Table with quotations from contemporary texts which mention iron; list of famous merchants, drawn up from texts; in the case below, set of coins shaped like spades, cowries from Shan xian in He nan (770–655 B.C. ?).

5. *Culture during the Chun qiu period.* On the wall, portrait of Lao zi; below it, a copy of the *Way and Power Classic;* modern picture of Confucius and his disciples; beside it, a portrait of Confucius after a painting by Wu Dao zi; in the cases below, copies of the six classics: *Classic of Songs (Book of Poetry), Classic of Documents (Book of History), Classic of Changes (Book of Divination), Record of Rituals (Book of Rites), The Spring and Autumn Annals, The Analects;* rubbing (after a Song painting) showing Confucius and his disciples; table showing the evolution of the concept of the divine *(shen)* and the people *(min);* in a case in the middle, collection of jade jewellery, stone necklaces and articles in bronze from Shan xian in He nan; little bronze mirrors, about two inches across; bronze sword, with engraved ivory sheath, found at Luo yang in 1954.

6. *Technical ability and Astronomy.* Portraits of Sun Zi and copy of his military treatise; copy of *Lu Ban jing (Classic of Lu Ban),* a Ming dynasty treatise on carpentry (Lu Ban, who lived in the 5th century B.C., in Lu, was considered the patron of carpenters); copies of two commentaries on the *Spring and Autumn Annals (Gong yang zhuan* and *Gu liang zhuan)* opened at the page where eclipses are mentioned (eclipses are mentioned thirty-seven times in the *Annals);* on the left wall, models of military contrivances supposed to have been used during the

Chun qiu period: "cloud ladder", "perched hut" (taken from a Song treatise).

7. *Local culture.* Two cases on the left: the first contains bronzes and implements from Zhe jiang, Guang dong, Jiang su, Fu jian (among them is a beautiful bronze vessel mounted on three wheels); the second contains a map showing the areas controlled by the hegemons, and objects from the north-eastern, southern and south-western regions (among them a fine polished stone *ge*, from Guang xi).

8. *Transitional period, decadence of the slave society.* On the wall: a quotation from a contemporary text, showing the beginning of private property; clay measure from the state of Qi (presumed to have been used to reckon taxes); map showing artisans' risings (according to the *Spring and Autumn Annals)*; in a case, rustic pottery ware found in the graves of the poor in He nan; on the wall, picture showing the beginning of new classes in society.

Feudal Society (ten sections)

First Section: The Warring States and the Founding of the Empire by Qin (475–206 B.C.).

1. *How Feudal Society was formed.* To the right: map of the states under the Warring States period; 4th century B.C. reformers (Shang Yang of Qin, Wu Qi of Chu, Li Kui of Wu); one of Shang Yang's measures; rubbing from a *ge* bearing the characters for the name "Shang Yang"; pass in use in the state of Chu (gold characters on a black background); insignia made in two parts *(fu)*, shaped like a horse or a tiger (the sovereign kept one part and gave the other to the official whom he entrusted with his authority); set of *ge* in bronze and jade; case 1, pottery ware and small implements used by peasants (He bei); first use of iron: case 2, good collection of moulds; case 3, ploughshares and spades; case 4, irrigation: well-sweep system, well with pulley, irrigation work commissioned by Xi men Bao in He nan (photograph of its present state, memorial stele and statue); case 5, towns: ruins of Xia du, one of the capitals of the state of Yan (plan, sections of water-pipes and stamped bricks); case 6, fragments of fabrics and silk (Hu nan), lacquer ware (found at Chang sha in Hu nan); case 7, different types of coins: map with specimens of the type used (round coins with a hole in the middle used in the state of Qin; "spade"

used in Chao, Wei and Han; "ant's nose" used in Chu; "knife" used in Qi and in the state of Yan); various measuring devices: set of weights, scales consisting of two trays with ring-shaped weights; in the centre: large measure (said to come from Shan dong).

Central cases: 1) some of the eight hundred objects found in 1957 at Xin yang, in He nan, in a set of tombs dating from the Warring States: lacquer ware (copies), iron and bronze instruments; 2) model of the irrigation work carried out by the engineer Li Bing, on the Du jiang River in Si chuan.

To the left: *ge*, jade ware and mirrors (one made of lacquered copper); photographs of inscriptions on bamboo; set of thirteen bells found at Xin yang; lacquered wood bed (in the middle), large drum (on the wall) and *se* (musical instrument with horizontal strings), all found at Xin yang; mirrors, bells, little jade figures, very fine buckles, beads; lip of a well and the end of a water-pipe in the shape of a gargoyle, in clay, from the site of Xia du; cases devoted to the culture of the so-called "national minorities" (marginal regions): inlays, necklaces, lancehead (found in Liao ning in 1958); sword blades, bells, cooking-pots, buckle shaped like a rhinoceros (from Si chuan); things found in the so-called "boat coffin" tombs in Si chuan (each body was buried in the owner's skiff): bronzes, with rubbings of the original pictograms on some of them; articles found in tomb No. 172 on the Yang zi shan Mountain, near Cheng du, in 1955; large *ding*, vessels with chains, fourteen little silver cylinders, jade ware, parts of a crossbow.

2. Cultural Development during the Warring States period: in the middle: statue of the poet and patriot Qu Yuan (from the state of Chu); to the right: photograph of the temple dedicated to Qu Yuan at Xiang Yang, in Hu nan; later scroll painting illustrating a theme dear to Qu Yuan, the Taoist way (a celestial journey which is a means of consolation for those wearied by the difficulties of life); "portraits" and works of the philosophers Mencius, Xun Zi, Mo Zi, Han Fei Zi, Zhuang Zi and the doctor Bian Que; copy of the oldest painting on silk found so far, depicting a woman and two imaginary animals (from a tomb in Hu nan); inscriptions on bamboo.

3. Unification by Qin and the Founding of the Empire: collection of swords; map of Qin shi Huang di's campaigns; *ge;* parts of crossbows; on the wall, drawing of a battle-scene (taken from a bas-relief), interesting for the weapons, boats, war machines, drums; table of the administrative system intro-

duced by Qin shi Huang di; specimens of insignia in two parts
(fu); table showing the standardisation of writing (by the
minister Li Si); "portrait" of Qin shi Huang di (259–210);
standardisation of the coinage: specimens of Qin coins (round
with a square hole) which were distributed throughout the
empire; two little round gold plaques, with their weight engraved
on them (found at Lin tong, Shân xi, near Xi an, in 1963);
map of the Great Wall built by Qin shi Huang di (showing
earlier walls, built by the Warring States); photograph of a
section of the Great Wall in Shân xi, in its original state (the
Great Wall to the north-west of Peking was rebuilt under the
Ming); official weights and measures. In the middle: replica
of the famous Lang ya shan Mountain stele (Shan dong),
which is the only one which remains from the Qin dynasty (the
first line is said to date from Qin shi Huang di, and the rest
from his son, Er Huang di; the original is in the Ji nan museum)}

Second Section: The Han and the Three Kingdoms (206 B.C.-265 A.D.).

*1. Risings at the end of the Qin dynasty and the arrival of
the Han:* the extensive public works undertaken by Qin shi
Huang di and the resulting social disturbances; the great tumulus (photograph of it as it is today; large round brick with a
decorative pattern, piping, parallelepiped shaped brick, all
found near the tumulus); the A fang gong Palace (photograph
of the mound on its site); large scroll painting of the palace,
in imaginative style, dating from the Ming; quotation from a
poem by the Tang poet Du Mu, with a description of the palace);
passage from the *Historical Records* of Si ma Qian describing
the misery of the people; map of risings under the Qin; passage
from the *Historical Records* on the rising led by Chen Sheng
and Wu Guang ("the first popular rising in the history of
China"); in the middle: statues of the two heroes, Chen Sheng
and Wu Guang; on the wall: "portraits" of the rival generals,
Xiang Yu and Liu Bang (founder of the Han dynasty).

2. Economic development under the Western Han: table of
the measures taken by the first Han rulers to pacify the people;
case 10, five "silo-urns", found in tombs, with the grain that
they contained; string of sapekes; clay figurines of a sow and
her three piglets; stone millstone (Shan dong); on the wall:
diagram of the *dai tian* method, a sort of strip crop-rotation,
which first appears at this time (the second year, the furrows
between the preceding year's crop were planted); iron plough-

shares and implements; photographs of the Shân xi country-side, where Han dynasty water engineering can still be seen; full-scale model of a "plough-seed-drill" *(lou che)*, rebuilt after a later text; small-scale model of a well with a pulley (from a tomb); in the middle, model of the strip crop-rotation method perfected by Fan Sheng shi (eight strips); models of the water engineering in the "land of the passes" under the Western Han (remarkable "hanging canal" bringing water into the capital, Chang an); model of a sixteen-oar boat (copied from a model found at Chang sha); fine set of pottery ware (eleven pieces) with polychrome designs; bronzes and mirrors; map of the towns and roads under the Han; weights, measures, coins; metal work; case 11, plan and vertical cross-section of blast-furnaces found at Gong xian (He nan), slag, melted objects; case 13, articles made in cast iron from He nan, Shân xi, Shan dong, Si chuan, Liao ning; fabrics: silk and wool found in Xin jiang (little bags for perfume with "cloud shape" pattern); "portrait" of Emperor Wu di of the Han; introduction of salt and steel monopolies: treatises written on this in 81 B.C.; map showing the distribution of officials in charge of the mono-polies (they are noticeably more numerous in the northern regions of the empire); plan of Chang an, the Western Han capital; funerary "coins" made in clay, like the coins in circu-lation in Chu under the Warring States; case 14, lacquer ware, beautiful red dish (found in Gui zhou), lacquer boxes (found in Guang dong); war and conquests, photographs of the tombs of the generals Huo Qu bing and Wei Qing (near Xing ping, in Shân xi); swords and parts of crossbows.

3. *Social Unrest at the end of the Western Han dynasty:* luxurious lives of the privileged: small gold plaques (found at Chang sha); mirrors; small models of houses (found in tombs at Canton), some built on piling ; jewellery found in Hu nan and Canton; a photograph of a poor man's tomb by way of comparison; the reforms carried out by the usurper Wang Mang (beginning of the Christian era): measures, large bushel measure, with rubbing of the inscription to the right; specimens of various coins put into circulation under Wang Mang; peasant uprisings: map of the "Green Mountains" and the "Red Eye-brows" uprising.

4. *Economic development under the Eastern Han:* iron plough-shares; remains of a statue of a peasant holding an agricultural implement; two engraved bricks from Si chuan, with their rubb-ings, one depicting a hunting and harvest scene, the other

showing grain pestles, worked with the feet; large triangular ploughshare (about 18 inches across) found in Shan dong; sickles; map of water engineering work carried out under the Eastern Han; central case, fine set of iron ware: large cooking-pots, thirteen-branch candlestick (from Luo yang), hammer (from Cheng du), large swords (from Chang sha and Xi an), three-pronged fork (from Si chuan); next hall, on the right: two bas-reliefs, found in Jiang su, with their rubbings, one depicting a plough drawn by two oxen, the other, a house with a weaving-loom; a model of the work done in the San men Straits on the Yellow river, and a photograph of it as it is today (a towing path was cut out of the cliff, so that barges could be brought up); stone engraving of the making of a chariot (from the Shan dong museum); case 18: jade and pottery ware; jade rings *(bi)*; large silver-plated urn with lid, found in Shan dong; bronzes: four mirrors, measure, cooking-pots, cylindrical box (Guang xi) and bowl with a stylised sheep design (Shan dong); in the middle, models of bellows for use in a forge and a set of grain pestles (with wobbler-shaft), built according to a later text; on the left, bas-relief from Shan dong showing the working of iron (left: bellows); means of transport: boat (Canton), model of a wheel-barrow, beautiful clay group from Si chuan showing a cart and horse (about 6 feet long).

5. Strengthening of the land-owners' power: set of carved bricks from Si chuan: a kitchen, the courtyard of a landlord's house, with a keep to the right, the snail harvest (?), wine-making, a rock-salt mine, dancers and jugglers; on the wall: two large rubbings of farming work and a scene of general merry-making; on the left wall: lintels and side-posts from a tomb in Shan xi, found in 1953 (the design depicts a plough, oxen, various plants); in the two large central cases, clay grave furnishings from several places: models of houses (including a large keep, from He bei), animals, vehicles, pestles; fine set of figurines: musicians (Si chuan), dancers, cooks (some with interesting head-dresses). Reproduction of wall-paintings from Wang du's tomb (He bei); fine set of six carved bricks from Si chuan, with chariots and horsemen (interesting carving of a bridge).

6. Social unrest at the end of the Eastern Han and the Yellow Turbans Rising: map of the risings between 109 and 184 A.D.; Eastern Han weapons (parts of crossbows, traps, small shield with metal points); case 20, copy of a wall-painting of a land-lord's granary (He nan) and six stones with rough inscriptions,

found at Luo yang ("grave steles" erected to men condemned
to forced labour; the inscriptions give their names, the date of
death, their punishments: to have their heads shaved, to work
on the walls); large map of the Yellow Turbans rising; case 21,
funerary vases with inscriptions in red characters, revealing
social unrest; table of the social system under the Yellow Turbans; long swords (one from He nan, one from Hu nan, one
from Shân xi and two from Guang xi).

7. *Economic Renewal under the Three Kingdoms:* "portrait"
of Cao Cao (155–220), founder of the Wei kingdom (photograph of a later drawing); copy of a political treatise by Cao
Cao; seals belonging to Wei dignitaries; table of pacifying
measures carried out by Cao Cao (introduction of a sort of
system of military colonies, restoration of the dykes and water
works, tax reform); map of the forty-one "colonies" *(tun tian)*
created, and of the water works (the Yang zi and Huai regions
were particularly important); mirrors and coins from the
kingdom of Wu; coins from the kingdom of Shu (Si chuan);
Zhu ge Liang (181–234), minister and strategist of the kingdom
of Shu, who afterwards became a popular hero, ("portrait",
works, photograph of the temple dedicated to him at Cheng
du); in the centre: wooden model of a hand-powered machine
for drawing water; to the left: pottery found in a tomb near
Nanking (kingdom of Wu, 265), which is one of the earliest
examples of bistre pottery *(qing).*

8. *Dealings with the Minorities and Foreign States under the
Han and the Three Kingdoms:* case 23, culture of the Xiong nu
(northern frontier): photograph of a tomb, one of those supposed
to be the tomb of the Chinese princess Wang chao jun, who
married the chief of the Xiong nu in 33 B.C. (there are at least
ten in what is now Inner Mongolia; the photograph is of the
one at Khara Khoto); pottery objects (little stove, figurines);
square brick with inscription, round brick; small bronze objects;
case 24, small inlays of gold and silver (origin not
stated); grey and black pottery; examples of animal carving,
known as "steppe art"; case 25, north-eastern cultures (Manchuria): glass trinkets, iron swords, small bronze plaques, very
fine damascene "heart-shaped" plaque, with arabesque design
(about 6 ins. across); case 30, south-western cultures (Gui
zhou, Si chuan, Guang xi): set of bronze musical instruments,
shaped like upturned urns (found in Si chuan and Hu nan):
large sword (found in Gui zhou), axes (western Hu nan); gold
seal (Si chuan); the exhibits in the centre of the hall also come

from the south-west: two large bronze drums with a frog design, and a star-shaped design in the centre (one was found in Guang xi; the origin of the other is not stated), and two large cases with exhibits found in several tombs at Jin ning (south-west of Lake Kun ming, in Yun nan): a kind of bronze drum whose upper part consists in a group of figurines (bulls, people, houses etc....); lanceheads with two prisoners hanging by their hands; two squatting human figures, each holding a large stick; golden seal, bearing four characters which mean "The King of Dian's seal" (which suggests that the local chief was invested with his insignia of office at the Han court); jewellery, little bells, *ge*, axes, daggers, bits, ploughshares, all in bronze; five bronze standards, made to be mounted on staves (one in the shape of a fish); case 27, southern and south-eastern cultures (Fu jian, Guang dong): pottery with cord markings, bronzes; case 26, cultures of the far western regions (Xin jiang): fragments of silk; wooden weapons (modern copies), scraper; slag, rough-hewn stone tools from iron-mining sites (Mount Aai, near Kutcha); seal belonging to a Qiang minority chief: case 28, Zhang Qian's journey in Central Asia (he died in 114 B.C.): copy of a fresco at Dun Huang which depicts him, photograph of his tomb (at Cheng gu in Shân xi), brick and clay seal from his tomb, map of his journey across Central Asia, passage in the *History of Earlier Han* referring to his journey; case 29, map of the "silk route", articles made in China under the Han, found in the west or in south-east Asia (fabrics, bronzes, mirrors); list of foreign embassies sent to China between 108 B.C. and 231 A.D.

9. Cultural Development under the Han and the Three King-doms:

a) Philosophy and literature: bust of the philosopher Wang Chong (27–96) and a copy of his treatise, the *Lun Heng;* left, in the passage, two fragments of the classics, on stone, which were kept in the Imperial College at Luo yang (175 A.D.); to the right, principal anthologies of poetry (poems by Si ma Xiang ru, by Cao Cao, *Nineteen Ancient Poems,* etc.); *b) Astronomy:* in the middle, statue of the astronomer Zhang Heng, wooden model of the seismograph he invented (the faintest vibration set the central axis in motion: one of the dragon's mouths opened and dropped a ball into the mouth of the frog below; this revealed roughly where the earthquake was); model of a water-powered celestial globe, also invented by Zhang Heng (it showed the part of the heavens visible above

Luo yang at any given time; the fifteen blades on the right represented the days of the fortnight; one blade rose each day, indicating the date); to the left: Han sun-dial; study of sun-spots (28 B.C.); first mention of a new star (in 134 B.C.); *c) History:* the great historian Si ma Qian ("portrait" depicting him talking to two peasants, his tomb and the temple dedicated to him at Han cheng in Shân xi, copies of his monumental work, *The Historical Records*, or *Shi ji*); copies of the *History of the Han*, by Ban Gu (23–92 A.D.); *d) Medecine:* "portraits" of the surgeon Hua Tuo (c. 141–208 A.D.) and the doctor, Zhang Zhong jing (alive in 170 A.D.); bronze pestle and mortar; photograph of prescriptions written on bamboo slips; e) *The Invention of Paper:* inscriptions on wooden slips (used before paper); fragments of paper found at Xi an in 1957; photographs of the tomb of the eunuch Cai Lun (traditionally held to be the inventor of paper) and of the house in Lei yang, Hu nan, where he was born; *f) The Arts:* copies of bas-reliefs; model of a house; tomb figurines of jugglers, acrobats, musicians (one holding a drum is particularly life-like; it comes from Si chuan); animals: duck, goose, a fine bronze rhinoceros found in Shân xi in 1962.

In the cases in the centre: one of the steles on which the classics were engraved (in the Kingdom of Wei in the 3rd century), with each line of the text written three times, using a different script each time: great and small curly script, *li* script; very fine clay horse (Si chuan); *bi xie* (imaginary animal, not unlike a leopard), from Luo yang; stone horseman with remains of paint on him (He bei); model of the tomb at Yi nan (Shan dong), which was opened in 1954 (interesting arrangement of rooms, and bas-relief carvings); very fine clay dog (Si chuan).

Third Section: "The Great Melting-pot", the Northern and Southern Dynasties (265–589).

1. The Western Jin: bronze measures and coins; contract for the sale of land on a metal plaque (with rubbing); case 33, set of clay tomb figurines of warriors and horsemen; officials' seals; map showing shifts in population under the Western Jin.

2. The Eastern Jin and the Southern Dynasties: case 34, exhibits found at Nanking, clay tomb figurines, bistre pottery, metal coffin nails, parts of crossbow; map of the Sun En rising (c. 400); case 35, table of the measures carried out by the Song dynasty; pottery from Fu zhou; coins; the battle of Fei Shui (383), which checked the attacks from the northern armies and fused the empire for two centuries (imaginary battle-scene and map of the battle); central case, objects found in a tomb in Jiang su, dated 297 (bronze, pottery, gold jewellery, bricks).

3. The Mixing of the Different "Nationalities" in the Yellow River Valley and the Wei Dynasty: map of the "sixteen kingdoms" (the sphere of influence of each one is shown by a different colour for each "nationality": blue for the Han, green for the Xian bei, orange for the Qiang he, dark brown for the Qiang, light brown for the Di, red for the Xiong nu); coins; rubbings of a stele commemorating the restoring of a temple (mentioning several "nationalities" by name); case 36, insignia in two parts; bronzes; small stove; table of the measures carried out by the Wei, who were from the north, from 483 to 496 (many tended to force Chinese customs on the northern families); "portrait" of the emperor Xiao wen (467–499) and his suite; round brick; coins; square slab with a funerary inscription to a member of the imperial family (it is pointed out that the dead man bore the name "Yuan", chosen by the emperors for their clan); case 37, set of clay tomb figurines (mixture of Chinese and Northern costumes); case 38, horses and horsemen in terra cotta; Wei measuring rod (the unit of measure was longer than that used by the Han, and a Han rod lies beside it); photograph of a large column erected at Ding xing (He bei) in 562, under the Northern Qi, in memory of the extinction of a popular uprising; very fine set of thirty bricks with relief carving and paintings from a tomb opened at Deng xian in He nan (beautiful designs: soldiers, imaginary animals, etc.); in the cases in the centre: terra cotta tomb figurines, from Xi an (ox-cart, servant, horseman) and Tai yuan, in Shan xi (animals found in a tomb dating from 559); alongside the right hand wall: three models of mills (rebuilt according to later descriptions); funerary inscription of a man called Xian bei, whose daughter married a Han (proof of the "fusion" under way at that time).

4. The Culture of the Northern and Southern Dynasties: a) Technical ability: case 39, bistre pottery *(qing)* from the south (map of the places where it was made in the lower Yang zi region, several examples); case 40, bistre pottery from the north; metal work: hardened steel technique, iron ware and bronze mirrors; copy of the *Gu jin dao jian lu (Treatise on Ancient and Modern Blades and Swords)*, by Tao Hong jing (452–536); *b) The Sciences:* Zu Zhong zhi (429–500), astronomer and mathematician; model of a paddle-boat which he designed;

table of contents of an agricultural treatise, the *Qi min yao shu;* the alchemist Ge Hong (author of the *Bao pu zi*) and the cartographer Pei Xiu (223–271); *c) Dealings with Foreign Countries:* map of the Buddhist pilgrim Fa Xian's journeys through Central Asia, India and South Eastern Asia (4th century); copy of a work by another pilgrim, the monk Song yun (end of the Northern Wei); two monks from Fu nan (modern Cambodia) who visited Nanking; Persian coins found in Canton; *d) "Buddhism and Rationalism":* in the same case, Buddhist statuettes and canons and Wang Zhen, the author of *The Destructibility of the Soul. e) Art and Literature:* on the far wall, photographs of a fluted column (from a Liang tomb near Nanking, clear Indo-Grecian influence), the Song yue si Pagoda (He nan), the great Buddha at the Yun gang caves (Shan xi), the Mai ji shan Buddha (Gan su); in the cases, copies of the *Ballad of Mu lan* and the treatise on literary critism, then *Wen xin diao long;* Ming rubbing of calligraphy by Wang Xi zhi; text by Xie He on the art of painting; photograph of a scroll painting by Gu Kai zhi (341–402): *Admonitions of the Imperial Instructress;* on the right wall, Northern Qi sculpture (555); in the middle, full scale reproductions of two chariots which work machines: in the first one, the wheels set in motion two wooden figures which beat a big drum in the middle: in the second, a complicated system of cog-wheels, linked to the axle, worked a little figure standing on the top and kept its arms always pointing in the same direction, whatever the direction of the chariot; it was known as "the chariot which points to the south".

First Floor

Landing: replicas of three bas-relief carvings of chargers, from the tomb of the emperor Li Shi min, near Xi an (Tang); there were originally six; four are in the museum at Xi an, and two are in the United States.

Fourth Section: Sui, Tang, Five Dynasties and Ten Kingdoms (581–960).

1. The Re-unification of the Empire under the Sui: "portrait" of the emperor Wen Di (541–604), the founder of the Sui Dynasty (modern replica of a picture attributed to Yan Li ben); map showing the course of the Grand Canal which linked the middle Yellow River capitals with the lower Yang zi agricultural region (notice the granaries indicated alongside the canal);

HISTORY MUSEUM

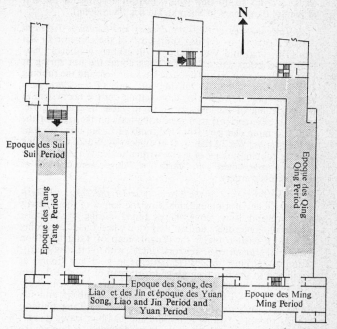

PREMIER ÉTAGE – FIRST FLOOR

Sui coins; pottery found in Shan xi and Hu nan; little glass flask (from the western suburbs of Xi an); pottery tomb figurines *(tao yong)*, some from Hu bei (figures with ox and monkey heads, from a set of twelve cyclical animals); in a case in the middle, a model of the Chao zhou bridge in He bei, built under the Sui; against the right wall, a section of the decoration from the bridge (bas-relief carving of a dragon), and one of the iron tenons which supported the stone blocks; in the second central case, model of a Sui tomb (608) found in the suburbs of Xi an in 1957 (the tomb of a little princess who died at the age of nine; several clay figurines, and jewellery in the inner chamber);

brick from a state granary, mentioning the amount of grain claimed in tax (from Luo yang); map of uprisings at the end of the Sui (large ones in Shan xi, He bei, Shan dong).

2. *The Founding of the Tang dynasty and Measures Taken to Set the Economy to Rights:* "portraits" of the emperor Li Shi min (Tai zong) and Wei Zheng, a 7th century politician (580–643); inscription written by Tai zong about the hot spring at Hua qing chi, near Xi an (the stele has vanished, and the rubbing exhibited was found at Dun huang); copy of the *Zhen guan zheng yao* (legislative work); table setting out the tax system at the beginning of the dynasty (taxes payable in grain, fabric, hemp or silk, *corvée*); iron measuring-rod; on the right of the hall, two more chargers from the tomb of Li Shi min; portrait of the empress Wu Ze tian; text of a poem by Wu Ze tian (Ming dynasty rubbing); copy of a text written under Wu Ze tian (the characters *ren*, "man", *di*, "earth", *ri*, "day", were changed at the empress's order).

3. *The Prosperity of the Economy under the Tang: a) Agriculture:* model of a plough, marking the names of the different parts; several iron ploughshares found during excavations; models of stone rollers and an irrigation wheel (made according to a work written under the Yuan); map of Tang irrigation works; *b) Handicrafts:* mirrors (inlaid with mother-of-pearl); beautiful hairpins; decorative patterns in gold leaf (found at Xi an and in the San men gorge area); map of the distribution of handicrafts under the Tang: textiles (Si chuan was extremely important), metal work, pottery; examples of fabrics and silk found in Xin jiang; magnificent collection of Tang pottery: "three colours", "white", "flowers and bamboo leaves glaze"; silver-gilt vessel from Xi an (a large dish with a lion in the middle); *yang sui* found at Chang sha (little metal mirror, with one concave side to catch the sun's rays and light a fire; *c) Development of trade:* in a case in the middle, model of the San men gorges area (middle Yellow river), with a towing-path hacked out of the side of the cliffs to enable grain convoys to be brought as far as the capital; rubbings of inscriptions found at Long men containing the character *Hang*, meaning "*guild*", which proves that trade associations existed; coins and strings of coins; map of Asian trade in 7th and 8th centuries; pottery figurines of camels and merchants from Central Asia (recognisable as such because of their pointed caps and their long noses); *d) The greatness of the capital, Chang an (modern Xi an):* shards of jars, with traces of seals, found in the Da ming

gong Palace, north of Xi an (the provincial officials sent their tribute to the court in jars sealed with clay, bearing inscriptions giving their names, provinces, the date and the contents: these shards enable the system of tribute and the official hierarchy to be studied); small oval plaques used as passes to each of the palace gates; bricks from the Da ming gong Palace; plan of Chang an under the Tang; in a case in the middle: metal grid for a sewer.

4. *Dealings between the Tang and the Regions Neighbouring on the Empire, which are now part of the People's Republic: a) Xin jiang:* fragments of the classics, frescoes, statuettes found in the oasis region; coins found in Xin jiang; *b) Tibet:* marriage between the Tibetan king Strong tsan gam po and the princess Wen Cheng; scroll attributed to Yan Li ben depicting the Tibetan embassy to the emperor Tai zong; photographs of two statues of the Tibetan king and the Chinese princess (the statue are in the Potala at Lhassa); copy of a Song scroll depicting a game of polo — the game is said to have been imported from Tibet (?) — (the scroll is in the provincial museum of Liao ning); in the middle: rubbings of the four sides of a large stele with the text in Tibetan and in Chinese, mentioning an alliance concluded in 821 between Tibet and China (three copies of this stele exist: one at Chang an, one at Lhassa and one at the frontier; the one at Lhassa is the only one to survive today); photograph of the Da Zhao si Temple at Lhassa (said still to contain musical instruments brought by the princess); copy of a history of Tibet, written in Tibetan, by the fifth Dalaï Lama (1643); *c) North-east:* various Tang dynasty exhibits found in the north-eastern provinces: metal fibulae, fragments of bricks, brick and iron architectural elements; pieces of sculpture (head of a monster in the central case); *d) South-west:* (then the independent state of Nan chao): photograph of the great Qian xun ta Pagoda; rubbing of a stele dated 794; carved bricks.

5. *Cultural Development under the Tang: a) The Sciences:* bust of the great astronomer Zhang Yi ving; map showing how he made his approximate calculation of the meridian; in the middle: model of a water-driven celestial sphere (invented and built by Zhang Yi xing); first use of printing: Buddhist pictures; portrait of the doctor Sun Si miao (died in 682); medical dictionary compiled by order of the emperor in 659 (found at Dun huang); *b) Literature:* "portraits" and works of the chief poets and philosophers: Li Bai, Du Fu, Bai Ju yi, Han Yu, Liu Zong yuan; *c) Architecture:* copy of the cave number 159 at Dun

huang (niche with wall-painting); wooden model of the temples
Fo guang si (869) and Nan zhan si (782), both near Wu tai in
Shan xi; d) Music: fresco from Dun huang showing an orchestra;
copy, with little figures, of a show of dancing at the court;
musical instruments (five-stringed pi pa, cymbals, little gong);
e) Painting: Dun huang frescoes depicting landscapes; examples
of painting on silk: court ladies, The Scholars' Garden, by Han
Guang; in the middle, fragments of funerary wall-paintings
from tombs in the Xian yang and Xi an area.

6. Dealings with foreign countries: a) Korea: table showing
exchanges in the fields of medecine and music; photograph of
sticks of ink from China and Korea (of identical make); Korean
travellers' accounts of their journeys in China; b) Vietnam:
tomb of the Vietnamese writer Qiang Gong fu, who died in
Fu jian; rock called after him; products which came from Vietnam during the first few centuries A.D.: the ge plant (its bark
was used for making fabrics), rice giving a double harvest,
sugar cane, various medecines; c) Burma: frescoes from the
shrines at Pagan; quotation from a work by the poet Bai Ju yi
on the music of the Piao (who then occupied what is now
Burma); d) Japan: photographs of a statue of the Japanese
monk Jian zhen (688-763) who came to China six times in
twelve years, of the tomb of one of his two disciples, who died
near Canton, and of the temple which he had built in Japan
when he went back; the plans of Chang an and of Kyoto side
by side, showing the influence of Chinese town-planning;
Chinese lacquer ware found in Japan; a list of the twelve embassies sent by Japan to China between 630 and 838, and of the
six Chinese embassies which went to Japan between 632 and
778; e) India: map of the journey made by the Chinese monk
Xuan zang in India; photographs of several sites which he
visited and described as they now are (Nalanda, Bamiyan,
Lambini); in the middle of the hall, a plinth in the shape of a
lotus flower, with an inscription dating from 662, bearing the
name of Xuan zang (found in Shân xi in 1957); text proving
that an Indian doctor practised at Chang an; f) The Persian
and Moslem West, and the Sunda Isles: map of the distribution
of Persian coins found in China; the pilgrim Yi jing's journey;
photograph of a Moslem tomb at Quan zhou (Fu jian); Tang
pottery found in Indonesia; little tomb statues of Western
people; photograph of the minaret of the Canton Mosque;
inscription from a funerary stele found at Xi an in 1955 (tomb
of a man and a woman, with a text in Chinese and Middle

Persian); 6th century Byzantine coins, found at Xian yang, and 8th century Arabian coins found at Xi an; rubbing of the famous "Si Ngan Fou Stele", dating from 781, showing that Nestorian Christianity had been introduced into China (texts in Chinese and Syriac; note the cross on the top).

7. *The Huang Chao Rising and the end of the Tang:* map showing the semi-independent commanderies which appeared under the late Tang; bars of silver given to the emperor by local officials; several contracts found at Dun huang (showing how large estates were formed); map of the Huang Chao rising, and the route followed by his troops across China; bust of Huang Chao; photograph of the Chang an palace where Huang Chao established his headquarters when he had taken the town; photograph of the defile of Xian jia ling (between Zhe jiang and Fu jian) and of traces of the road built by Huang Chao's army, on its way through, in 878; funeral slab mentioning Huang Chao's success (found at An yang in He nan).

8. *The Five Dynasties and the Ten Kingdoms:* map of the political divisions; coins from different areas; copies of two flat trunks found in the tomb of a king of Shu who died in 918 (near Cheng du, in Si chuan); model of the improvements in the Lake Tai hu region; *qing* pottery; figurines from a Southern Tang tomb (near Nanking); metal hinge-pin (the king of Shu's tomb).

Fifth Section: The Song, the Liao, the Xi xia and the Jin (690-1279).

1. *The Northern Song:* "portrait" of the founder, Tai zu; imperial seals; map showing the migration of certain sorts of cultivation; small mill-stone: grain found in Gan su; model of a *wei tian* (flooded field); recent copy of a wooden float (used for transplanting rice in Hu bei); map of mines (considerable development in mining in the south); iron agricultural implements (found in He nan, Shan xi, Shan dong); small iron statue of an ox; model of a water-driven forge bellows and a set of water-driven mill-stones; pottery ware (black and white, celadon); map of textiles; map of salt and tea; scrolls of paintings showing everyday life at Kai feng under the Song; cross-section of a rich tomb discovered in 1951 at Bai sha zhen in He nan; portrait of the reformer Wang An shi (11th century); table of his reforms; map of the chief risings under the Song: Wang Xiao po in Si chuan (993-995), Song Jiang in Shan dong and

Fang La in Zhe jiang (1120–1121); statue of Fang La; model of a paddle-boat used during the suppression of one of the rebellions, on Lake Dong ting.

2. *The Liao and the Xi xia Cultures:* photographs of the remains of the walls of Shang jing, the Liao capital (in what is now Inner Mongolia) and of the pagoda at Zhong jing, another Liao capital (1007); scroll depicting the king of the Khitan and his horsemen; rubbing of the funerary stele erected to the Liao emperor, Dao zong, who died in 1101 (the stele is in Shen yang museum; the inscription is in Chinese and Liao characters); very fine pottery found at Da tong in Shan xi; tools, mirrors, melting-pot found in Shan xi and Liao ning; in the middle of the hall, a large model of the Fo gong si wooden pagoda, in Shan xi (1056; 120 feet high); cases with some exhibits from the thousand objects found in 1954 in a Liao tomb in Inner Mongolia: fragments of silk, little bells, white pottery, silver saddle ornaments; Qing map of the Xi xia territory; several round bronze plaques with Xi xia characters; text of a Xi xia — Han lexicon, written in 1190; coins; little knives; rubbings of a 1094 stele in Xi xia and Han characters, found in the Wu wei district in Gan su.

3. *The Conflict between the Southern Song and the Jin, and later the Yuan:* photograph of part of the walls of the Jin town of Zhong du (now Peking); seals, mirrors, coins and vases, all Jin; rubbing of a 1224 stele in Jürched characters, now in the He nan museum; photograph of Yue Fei's tomb at Hang zhou; iron statue of Qin Gui, the traitor responsible for the loss of Yue Fei (he is kneeling, with his hands tied behind his back; the statue comes from the Jing zhong miao Temple, which used to be in the Southern Town in Peking); handicrafts under the Southern Song: mirrors, lacquer ware; first examples of paper money; portrait of Wen Tian xiang (1238–1282), who fought the Yuan in Jiang xi and Fu jian; copy of his works; silver ingots and contracts for the sale of land.

4. *Maritime Trade under the Song:* map; various contemporary works on the southern seas; small bronze mirror with reproduction of a sea-going ship; plan of the port of Quan zhou under the Song; photographs of steles proving that merchants from the southern seas came to China at that time; in a case in the middle, Song pottery found overseas (Japan, Korea, Malaya, the Sunda Isles), or near the kilns in Fu jian where it was made for export; specimes of products imported from the southern seas (medecine, ambergris).

5. *Cultural Development under the Song. a) The Sciences:*
"portraits" of two scholars, Su Song (1020–1101) and Shen
Kua, (1030–1094), various scientific works; model of a water-
powered celestial globe invented by Su Song; rubbing of a
map of the heavens dating from 1247 (the stele is in the Temple
of Confucius at Su zhou); life-size human figure used to teach
acupuncture; the "three great inventions" (gunpowder, printing and the compass); in the centre, statue of Bi Sheng (active
between 1041 and 1048) who is said to have invented printing;
models of various machines (chariots with automatic figures);
statue of Huang Dao po (he lived in Song jiang, in the mid-
13th century) who learned how to make cotton while staying in
Hai nan, and introduced the technique into his own province;
b) Literature: "portraits" and works of Zhang Zai (1020–1077),
Zhu Xi (1130–1200), Su Shi (1036–1101), the poetess Li Qing
zhao (1084–1151), the poet Lu You (1125–1210); *c) The Arts:*
funerary wall-paintings of shepherds and their flocks (He bei);
fan paintings; photograph of statues in a temple at Tai yuan.

Sixth Section: Unification under the Yuan (1271–1368).

1. *The Arrival of the Mongols and the Founding of the Yuan
Dynasty:* portaits of Genghis Khan and Khubilai; set of seals,
some with 'Phags-pa writing; photograph of the tomb of a
Moslem official, Sai dian chi (1211–1280), who distinguished
himself by his administration of Yun nan (the tomb is at Kun
ming); photograph of a statue of the prince Ye Lü chu cai
(1190–1244) who was Genghis Khan's adviser (the statue is in
a temple at the Yi he yuan); photograph of a fresco in the
temple of Tashilumpo (at Shigatse) depicting 'Phags-pa before
Khubilai; gold seal sent to the king of Bai lan, with a camel
on the top; reproduction of a portrait of 'Phags-pa (1239–1279).

2. *The Yuan Economy:* reproduction of an illustration from
Wang Zhen's *Book of Agriculture* (showing several handicrafts:
smith's work, weaving); leather boots found near Da tong,
Shan xi; photograph of a painting in the Nanking museum of
the Marco Polo Bridge (showing wood being floated down the
river); map of north China trade routes (the sea route, the
Grand Canal); coins, silver ingots, metal plaque used to print
paper money; map of Da du, the Mongol capital (on the site
of modern Peking); exhibits found during excavations, north
of De sheng men (brick architectural ornaments); texts telling
how an Iranian, Ye hei tie er, helped to build the capital, and
how a Nepalese, A ni ge (1243–1306), worked on the Bai ta si

Temple; map of maritime trade with the southern seas; texts
referring to trade, among them Marco Polo's book; Moslem
influence under the Mongols: small iron astrological square
found at Xi an in 1956 (it has 66 figures, arranged so that each
line adds up to 111); various works by Moslems on medecine,
arithmetic, irrigation.

3. *Cultural Development:* "portrait" of Guo Shou jing, the
astronomer and hydraulic engineer; photograph of an astronomical instrument built by him, now in the Nanking observatory; copy of Wang Zhen's *Book of Agriculture;* fresco of a
play (in the Guang sheng si Temple, in the Hong chao xian
district in Shan xi); scroll painting of horses, by Ren Ren fa,
who died in 1327; plays and novels: *The Romance of the Western
Chamber, The Story of the Water Margin, The Romance of the
Three Kingdoms;* "portrait" of Shi Nai an, author of *The Story
of the Water Margin;* photograph of the inscriptions on the
Ju yong guan Gate (see p. 620); copy of the *Secret History of
the Mongols;* in the middle: Yuan pottery (dish with grey and
pink pattern), brown lamp (with a snake and a monkey);
bronzes (note re-appearance of old designs, three-legged vessels,
etc.) two pieces of pig-iron found in a tomb in An hui; large
clepsydra, made up of four superposed bronze vases, from
Canton, and the oldest in existence (1361); wooden model of
a clock worked by sand, with two small clockwork, figures which
beat drums.

4. *Risings at the end of the Yuan dynasty and the founding of
the Ming Dynasty:* some of the three hundred things found in
the tomb of a rich land-owner in An hui (large jade belt, ewers,
ladle, jewellery); map of rebellions in the 14th century; portrait
of Zhu Yuan zhang, the founder of the Ming dynasty; order
signed by him in 1363 (before his accession); view of Peking, in
particular Tian an men (original Ming painting); reproduction of two maps of Nanking; copy of the *Da ming hui dian*
(legislative anthology); seals; copy of a 1387 register known as
the "fish scale register" *(Yu lin ce)* (large cadastral survey, so
called because of the shape of the plots of land); in a case in
the centre: some of the 174 things found in a military boat
which sank in the river Song jin, near Liang shan, in Shan
dong: weapons, helmets, bits (for horses), farming implements,
anchor (dated "Hong wu period"), cauldrons; the boat belonged
to a military colony *(jun tun)* whose members were soldiers
and peasants at the same time (a system which was widespread
under the Ming),

Seventh Section: Rapid Economic Development under the Ming (1368-1644).

1. Economic development: a) Agriculture: table of measures carried out at the beginning of the dynasty; census form (1371); tax exemption certificate, granted to peasants who had brought new land under cultivation (dated 1425 and 1446); rubbing of a stele dating from 1391, recording the migration of a group of peasants (110 families) from Shan xi to He nan; map showing the spread of the cultivation of cotton and the sweet potato; table showing the progress of irrigation work; map showing improvements made in the course of the Yellow River; *b) Handicrafts and Industry:* drawing of an anchor being cast (illustration taken from the *Tian gong kai wu*): photograph of the great bell from the Da zhong si Temple in Peking; long straight sword and sheath; table of iron production under the Ming (1,197,000 lbs, in 1403, 8,329,000 lbs, in 1434); silk: drawing of a loom and samples found in a tomb near Shang hai and in Jiang su; cotton: map showing the export of cotton made at Song jiang; samples of linen (from a tomb near Canton); in two cases in the centre: pottery; model of a Jing de zhen kiln (in Jiang xi); alongside the right wall: wooden model of a water-mill from An hui; bronze incense-burner of the Xuan de period (1426-1436): model of a loom in which the threads of the woof are moved by a mechanism worked by a rope round the weaver's back (*yao ji*, "back" loom). *c) Towns and Trade:* copy of a scroll painting of Peking in the 16th century (interesting portrayal of shops); abacus and scales dating from the Wan li period (1573-1620); large bank note dating from the Hong wu period (1368-1399); weights.

2. Dealings between the Han and the Minority Races under the Mings: photographs of Tibetan architecture; red, blue and yellow scroll, sent by the Ming court in 1379 to confirm a Tibetan dignitary in office, as he had been promoted under the Mongols; small bell and *zhu* given by the Ming to a Tibetan dignitary and given back to Qian long by the Dalaï Lama in the 18th century: several scrolls with the text in Chinese and Tibetan; portrait of Yu Qian, who defended Peking against the Mongol invaders in about 1450.

3. Dealings between China and Foreign Countries under the Ming: The voyages made by the eunuch Zheng He in the southern seas; rubbing of a stele which he had engraved in 1431 before his seventh voyage (the stele is in Fu jian); copy of a map made during the expedition (Ormuz can be seen to the left and Ceylon to the right of the part exhibited); map of the route taken by the expeditions; rubbing of a stele which the eunuch had put up in Ceylon in 1409 (text in Chinese, Tamil and Arabic; the stele is in Colombo museum); three works on the voyage; lance heads made in Indonesia, with the three characters "*San bao gong*" (the name by which Zheng He became known as a legendary figure among the Chinese communities in the southern seas); along the right wall, enormous rudder 35 feet long, found at Nanking, on the site of the old shipyards; samples of various products introduced into China from the Tang to the Ming (pepper, cloves, etc.); in a case in the middle, Chinese pottery found overseas; resistance of Japanese pirates *(wo kou):* photograph of a defense tower near Su zhou; portrait of Qi Duan guang, who put up a valiant resistance to the pirates (1528–1587); his sabre; his military writings; photograph of a temple dedicated to him at Fu zhou; large painting of a town in Zhe jiang attacked by the *wo kou;* large mirror, made in Japan, found in 1947 in a temple at Quan zhou (possibly brought to China under the Ming?); Japanese paintings inspired by Chinese techniques; porcelain made by a Japanese craftsman who came to study the craft at Jing de zhen; Sino-Korean alliance against the Japanese (end of the 16th century); in the centre: model of a "tortoise boat" (a sort of battleship invented by the Koreans, and used against the Japanese); medical treatise written by a Korean; Japanese stirrups (taken by Chinese soldiers); on the right wall, painting of a giraffe, introduced into China in the 15th century (copy made under the Qing).

4. *Social Unrest at the End of the Ming: a) The Appearance of a privileged class:* texts of contracts for the sale of land; silver ingots used for paying taxes; officials' possessions (large belt, brushes, ink-stones, stirrups); steles with texts relating the misery of the peasants in He nan (1639 and 1641); works of Hai Rui, a Moslem from Guang dong (1515–1587), describing the faults of the regime; in the middle, tomb furnishings from the tombs of rich landowners (model of a house found in He nan and beautiful set of 500 *Yong* dating from 1557, found in 1958 in a tomb in Jiang xi: sedan chair, horsemen, servants etc.); jewellery, bracelets and crowns found in the tomb of the Ming Emperor, Wan li (he died in 1620), with large numbers of contracts for the sale of land and slaves in the same case (a deliberate contrast); *b) Workers' Movements:* map of urban

uprisings, chiefly workers' uprisings, between 1596 and 1608 in China (opposition to the eunuchs responsible for collecting taxes or administering the imperial mines and workshops); documents referring to the uprising led by Ge Cheng at Su zhou in 1601 (passages from the *True Accounts of the Ming* and the *History of Su zhou*, photograph of the tomb of Ge Cheng at Su zhou, which has been restored since the liberation, rubbing of a stele erected to his memory in 1673, by the people of Su zhou); *c) Peasant uprisings:* map of peasant uprisings under the Ming (note the 1628 uprising in the Yan an area, Shân xi); the beginning of the Li Zi cheng uprising (map, photograph of the cave where he lived for a time, map of the town of Rong yang, in He nan, where the rebel leaders are said to have met to invest him with the supreme command); in the next hall, spread of the Li Zi cheng uprising and the Zhang Xian zhong revolt in Si chuan; in the middle, large statue of Li Zi cheng, on the walls, modern pictures of Li Zi cheng entering Peking and Zhang Xian zhong passing sentence on dishonest officials; large map showing the spread of the revolt; photographs of one of the halls of the Peking palace, where Li Zi cheng set himself up when he had taken the town, and of the tree from which the last Ming Emperor is said to have hanged himself (on Coal Hill); weapon belonging to Li Zi cheng; photograph of the palace where Zhang Xian zhong settled, in Cheng du; copy of a stele forbidding soldiers and officials to molest the people of Cheng du (1645); small cannon used during the Li Ding guo uprising in Yun nan (1647–1662).

Eighth Section: the Progress of a Multi-national State under the Qing (1644–1840).

1. Various Movements of Resistance to the Manchu, at the beginning of the Qing Dynasty: Overall map; the Li Ding guo uprising in Yun nan (photograph of the temple dedicated to his memory at Meng la, in the southernmost part of the province); the Shi`Ke fa uprising in Jiang su (photograph of his tomb at Yang zhou, his seal); the Zheng Cheng gong (Koxinga) rising in Fu jian: photograph of the spot where he trained his troops at Amoy; copy of a manuscript referring to the uprising, kept in Fu jian; chronological table showing the relations between China and Formosa from 230 to 1684; grenades used by Zheng Cheng gong's troops against the Dutch in Formosa; photograph of a European engraving of the surrender of the Dutch; biography of Zheng Cheng gong (written by a member of his family); poems by Zheng Cheng gong and his son; a fine scroll depicting Zheng Cheng gong playing chess with a friend (given to the museum by one of his descendants).

2. *The Founding of Manchu Power:* photographs of the palaces at Shen yang and Peking; drawing of the Manchu chief Nurhachi attacking a city wall; seals and coins (with Manchu characters); copy of a portrait of the Emperor Kang xi (1662-1722); table of the agricultural measures taken by the Qing; census registers *(huang ce)* and cadastral registers *(yu lin ce)*.

3. *Agriculture, Handicrafts and Trade:* interesting set of drawings of agricultural work (1696), weaving (1696), preparation of cotton (1765); scrolls depicting work on the dykes; to the right: wooden noria wheel from the neighbourhood of Luo yang (19th century); samples of cotton and silk, from the Imperial Palace reserves; very large silk loom from Cheng du (Si chuan), used in the 19th century (two men were needed to work it); Qian long period cupboard (decorated with dragons and waves); fine sets of pottery and porcelain ("five colours", cloisonné ware); in two separate cases: a "five colours" urn with a scene from the *Xi xiang ji* (the separation of two lovers) and a large vase with gilded flowers, birds and additions (both pieces date from the Kang xi period); photographs of the illustrations to a work on the Jing de zhen pottery kilns, in Jiang xi; model of a Shi wan kiln (in Guang dong); to the right: model (old) of a boat used for transporting grain on the Grand Canal, and a set of old signs (rice-merchant, goldsmith); measure for public use from the Shang hai neighbourhood (1813); to the left, large abacus (from the Canton museum); measures and coins; strings of coins, small scales, set of copper parallelepiped shaped weights which fit into each other (from Su zhou); various rights granted to tradesmen; view of a Peking street; four drawings of shop-fronts; scroll depicting the traffic on the Grand Canal; several plates from the *Book of the Three Hundred and Six Corporations*.

4. *Life and Economy of the Minorities. a) Life:* left-hand cases: Tibet (butter churn, ewer, pottery, votive plaque with Tibetan characters); Mongolia (fabrics, embroidered bag, case for chopsticks and knife); Xin jiang (materials, silver ewers, bellows, embroidered jacket, leather holsters); long scroll dated 1798, showing the different racial minorities in the empire (a man and a woman for each one); on the wall: Uighur carpets; central cases: 1) Yi armour; Yi pottery (with black, red and

yellow design); Wa drinking-horn and weaving materials; Miao, Ha ni, Yao, Na xi clothes; Tai silver and pottery; 2) Gao shan bow and carved plaque (Formosan minority); Li weaving materials; Zhuang yellow fabric; Kazak saddle and large round box; 3) Long Kazak leather belt; Gao shan basket; E lun chun bag and fur; red Kazak robe; left hand case: *b) Administrative Dealings with the Minorities:* copy of the seal granted by Qian long to the Dalaï Lama; little gold plaques (copies) with inscriptions in Manchu, investing the eleventh Dalaï Lama (1841) and the seventh Panchen Erdeni (1845) with their offices; Tibetan copy of the *Twenty-nine Statues* concerning Tibet, issued by the Qing government in 1753; photograph of the golden urn given by Qian long to the Dalaï Lama in 1793; view of the Potala; copy of the great five-language dictionary *(Wu ti Qing wen jian)* compiled under the Qing; *c) Trade Dealings with the Minorities:* Samples of imports: furs and materials from Central Asia; products used in pharmacopoeia: ginseng, crab fossils, tiger bones, bezoars (all from the Imperial Palace reserves); to the right, terra cotta figurines, representing the south-western minorities (1959).

5. *Social Unrest under the Qing:* table showing the total area of land confiscated by the Manchu banners, after 1644; contracts for the sale of land; privileges granted to merchants; stele forbidding Su zhou workers to go on strike; table of the strikes in Jiang xi (fourteen between 1670 and 1837); map of peasant uprisings under the Qing; old drawings of the Miao population resisting the Manchu armies (1703); modern drawing of the Lin Shuang wen rising in Tai wan (1786); text of one of his declarations and a bamboo helmet which belonged to him (copy of the original, which was kept in the Imperial Palace). In the centre: stele (with rubbing) forbiding the Su zhou workers to go on strike (1822); tax measure (from Su zhou); hospice sign from Shan xi.

6. *Dealings with Abroad:* in the middle, large cast iron vats made at Fo shan (near Canton) for export to the southern seas; left-hand case: map of China with the chief trading ports; passages from texts on foreign trade; views of the harbours of Canton, Ning bo, Amoy; products for export (raw silk, silk fabrics, pottery). *a) "Friendly dealings with Asia":* first case: Korean fans, elephants' tusks given to the Emperor of China by Vietnam, Vietnamese vase, Korean silk; second case: casket with Arabic characters, Indian vase, Nepalese dagger, Cambodian silver mug, cylindrical red box imported from Burma

through Yun nan; third case: dealings with Japan and Indonesia (photograph of a Chinese district in Indonesia); *b) "Friendly dealings with Africa and Latin America":* photographs of Chinese pottery found at Zanzibar, samples of plants imported from Africa; 19th century geographical treatises with maps of Africa and America; table of the plants imported from America since the 16th century (maize, sweet potato, potato, peanut, sunflower, tomato, tobacco); *c) "Trade dealings with Europe":* Chinese articles imported by Europe or made in Europe after Chinese models; products imported from Europe (French clock, English watch, English sheets, French leather, Western snuff); photograph of silk made in Lyons; central case: China tea as an export: tin boxes, tea leaves, tea brick, and large bale of tea in the middle; to the right; works of Korean painters and poets who came to China to study "Chinese style".

Ninth Section: Cultural Development under the Ming and Qing Dynasties.

1. Philosophy: "portraits" and chief works of Wang Yang ming (or Wang Shou ren, 1472-1528), Li Zhi (1527-1602), Wang Fu zhi (1619-1692), Huang Zong yi (1610-1695), Gu Yan wu (1613-1682); *2. The Sciences:* portrait of Xu Guang qi (1562-1633), author of the *Complete Treatise on Agriculture;* table of the chapters, reproductions of illustrations and copy of the *Tian gong kai wu,* sort of summary of the different techniques (17th century); portrait, works and map of the journeys of the traveller and geographer Xu Xia ke (1586-1641); photograph of the village where the great botanist Li Shi zhen was born, in Hu bei, copy of his *Catalogue of Plants (Ben cao gang mu);* in the centre, a wooden statue of him; in cases on the right: copies of war machines ("fire arrows"); clock and celestial spheres made in China; excellent collection of pharmaceutical instruments (pestle and mortar, little stove, precision scales, funnel, cauldron, little chopper (for herbs) wooden moulds for making pastilles and pills); *3. Learning:* the three biggest works compiled during this period: the *Yong le da dian* (early Ming, 22,877 volumes), the encyclopedia *Gu jin tu shu ji cheng* (Kang xi period, 10,004 volumes) and the *Si ku quan shu* collection (Qian long period, 79,070 volumes); in the latter collection, the classics, the histories, the philosophical works and the "miscellaneous" works were indicated by the colour of the cover (green, red, blue and brown respectively); photographs of the big Qing librairies: then Wen Yuan ge and the imperial archives (in Peking, in the Forbidden City), the Tian yi ge (at Ning bo), the Hai yuan ge (at Liu cheng, in Shan dong); *4. Music:* a Qing *pi pa*, a Ming lute, a big Tibetan horn, a Miao mouth organ; *5. Literature:* "portrait" of Pu Song ling, author of the *Strange Tales from Liao zhai*, and of Wu Qing zi, author of the *Scholars;* ink-stone which belonged to Pu Song ling; copy of the *Journey to the West* (illustrated); re-edition of the *Dream of the Red Chamber;* "portrait" of Tang Xian zu (1550–1617), a playwright, author of *The Peony Pavilion;* old painting of a play; *6. The Decorative Arts:* in the cases in the centre: lacquer ware, jade and porcelain; along the right wall, large panels inlaid with ivory; *7. Drawing and Painting: nian hua* depicting children; wood engravings; illustration from the *Mustard Seed Garden Painting Manual* (1679); nine vertical Ming and Qing scrolls; *8. Architecture:* plan of a Qing house; view of the north-western suburbs of Peking (the Xiang shan area); varnished terra cotta elephant (part of a group from the Ming palace at Nanking); wooden model of a Ming temple in Peking (the Zhi hua si).

Tenth Section: The Arrival of the Europeans and the Reaction of the Chinese.

Several scientific instruments brought to China by the missionaries; works by Chinese authors against the Christian religion; the opium trade (oil painting of Canton harbour, an opium warehouse in India, table showing how the trade increased between 1821 and 1839); opposition by the mandarin Lin Ze xu, who had cases of opium destroyed at Canton (portrait, works, manuscripts, large modern bas-relief of the case being destroyed); map of anti-English risings, during the Opium War; photograph of a letter writen from an Englishman to Lord Palmerston; cannon and weapons used in the San yuan li rising (north of Canton) in 1841; "three-starred" flag (black with three white spots), adopted by the rebels; British uniform. In the cases on the right: the embassy led by Lord Macartney in 1793 (reproductions of contemporary English drawings, ceremonial sabre, given by Macartney to Qian long); documents on two zenophobic societies founded at Canton, in about 1840: the "Xi hu shi xue" and the "Dong ping gong shi" (memorial steles, photographs of houses in Canton where the members met).

b) The Museum of the Chinese Revolution (Zhong guo ge ming bo wu guan)

It occupies the left wing of the museum building. Its aim is to trace the history of China over the last hundred years, laying particular stress on the revolutionary movement and the part played by the Communist Party. There are three main sections: 1. The first democratic revolution (1840-1911); 2. The new democratic revolution (1911-1949); 3. Triumph of the revolution and the establishment of socialism (from 1949 onwards).

First Section: The First Democratic Revolution.

The Opium War: photograph of an opium warehouse in India; portrait of the mandarin and patriot, Lin Ze xu (1785-1850) who tried to prevent the import of opium; photographs of the ruins of the Summer Palace, destroyed by Anglo-French troops; cannon dating from 1836; map of military operations. *The Tai ping Rebellion* (1851-1864): seal which belonged to Tai ping leader, Hong Xiu quan, the founder of the "Celestial Empire of Lasting Peace"; table of the new social hierarchy; coins struck by the Tai ping (one very large one); souvenirs of the Miao rebellions and of the secret society known as the "Little Swords", at Shang hai (1853). *Franco-Chinese War (at Tonking)* and the *Sino-Japanese War:* a Korean artist's drawing of a fight between the French and the Black Banners (1884); naval battles with the Japanese (1894). *The Hundred Days of Reform* (1898): list of the newspapers which appeared; photographs of the "reformers", Kang You wei and Liang Qi chao; the panel which used to hang at the entrance to the College (Da xue tang) founded by the Emperor in 1898. *The Unequal Treaties:* metal plaque, with a text in English and Chinese, which was placed at the entrance of the International Concession at Shang hai in 1899; drawing of the "break-up" of China (each power is represented by an animal); copies of treaties signed with the Europeans Powers. *The Boxer Rebellion* (Yi he tuan): photographs of Bei tang Church before and after the rebellion, several European army divisions, the execution of the insurgents; engraving of the participants at the Congress of Peking (which ordered China to pay indemnities, 1901). *Tibetan Resistance to the British:* weapons. *The 1911 Revolution:* photographs taken during the uprisings at Wu chang, Canton, Shang hai, Yan an; cannons cast by the Emperor's supporters in 1903 and used by the rebels; red flags with black stars and white circles (used by the Wu chang rebels); photographs taken at the meeting of the Nanking Assembly and of the election of Sun Yat sen as President; the new Republican flag (five horizontal stripes of red, yellow, blue, black and white, one stripe for each of the five main nationalities in the new state); text of the Emperor's abdication, signed by the ministers and the Regent (February 2nd, 1912); robes worn by Yuan Shi kai when he performed the sacrificial ceremony at the Temple of Heaven in December 1914 (he hoped to restore the empire and ascend the throne himself).

Section Second: The New Democratic Revolution.

The May 4th movement, 1919: photographs of demonstrations, tracts, copies of the review *Youth* (1915). *Founding of the Communist Party* (1921): model of the house at Shang hai where the first general meeting was held, July 1st, 1921; model of the boat where the delegates fled to escape the police; photographs of five of the principal founder members (one of whom is Mao Ze dong). *First Civil War* (1924-1927)*:* founding of the united front; first national meeting of the Guo min dang; copy of *Analysis of the Classes in Chinese Society* written by Mao Ze dong in 1923; the northern expedition; copy of *Investigation of Peasant Movement in Hu nan*, written by Mao Ze dong in 1927; break between the Communists and the Guo min dang (gallows where Li Da zhao was hanged). *Second Civil War* (1927-1937)*:* documents of the Nan chang rising (1927); map showing the progress of the revolution throughout China; maps and souvenirs of the Long March (1934-1935). *Anti-Japanese War* (1937-1949): opposition by the eighth route army, the new fourth army, guerillas in the south and the north-east allied army; life in the revolutionary bases; several cases devoted to heroes who died in action, including the Canadian doctor, Béthune (Chinese name: Bai Qiu en), who went to Yan an to help look after the Communist wounded, and died there. *Third Civil War* (1945-1949): defeats suffered by the Guo min dang: the flag which Mao Ze dong hoisted in Tian an men Square, October 1st 1949,

Third Section: Triumph of the Revolution and the Establishment of Socialism. The Korean War; the rectification campaign, 1957; the Great Leap Forward in 1958.

B. THE IMPERIAL PALACE AND ITS SURROUNDINGS

The parts of the town which constituted the old Imperial City (the Huang Cheng) will be described first. The city used to be enclosed within walls; the only part to remain is the southern section, flanking Chang an jie Avenue (from the south-western corner of the Nan hai to the Peking Hotel). To the west, the walls followed roughly the same direction as the present Fu you jie and Huang cheng gen Streets; to the north, they followed the long thoroughfare running from Ping an li, north of Lake Bei hai, past the Di an men cross-roads; to the east, they were flanked by Huang cheng gen.

This area was cut up by walls within it dividing off the Western Lakes, Coal Hill, and the eastern districts. The central part was the Imperial Palace, which was called the "Purple Forbidden City" (Zi jin cheng). The colour purple was symbolically attributed to the North Star, and it was used here to show that the Imperial Residence was a cosmic centre. The "Forbidden City" was gradually opened to the public after the Republic was founded in 1912. The palace is now called Gu gong, "the old palace".

1. The Imperial Palace (Gu gong)

(Plan, p. 497)

The Imperial Palace covers a rectangle 1,050 yards by 820 yards, an area of 250 acres. It is surrounded by

a moat, still full of water, 54 yards wide, and walls over
35 feet high. Four towers stand at the corners, each
surmounted by a pavilion with an elaborate yellow
roof. Four gates lead into the city, one on each side:
the Wu men (Meridian Gate) to the south; the Shen
wu men (Gate of Divine Military Genius) to the north;
and the Dong hua men and Xi hua men (the East and
West Flowery Gates) on the other two sides. The road
leads through Tian an men, across two enclosures, to
Wu men.

History: The Imperial Palace has stood in roughly the same
place since the Yuan. When the third Ming Emperor, Yong le,
decided to establish the capital of the Empire at Peking (1403),
the palace was entirely rebuilt on a new plan, and the general
outline of this has survived until the present day. The work
lasted from 1407 to 1420, and over 200,000 workmen were
employed. The stone came from quarries near Peking, and the
wood for the great columns and beams came from the forests
of Yun nan and Si chuan. The palace was constantly re-
furbished and re-arranged over the reigns which followed. Most
of the buildings are 18th century.

The outer buildings became a museum from 1914 (furniture
from the Jehol palaces was used). The imperial family, however, lived in the private apartments until as late as 1924 (for
the description of this life of imprisonment, see the memoirs of
the last Emperor, Aisin-Gioro Pu Yi (d. 1967), *From Emperor
to Citizen*, Peking, 1964, vol. I, p. 77 to 149). Extensive restoration work is going on, and most of the buildings can already
be visited.

Description. The courtyards and buildings are centred round three parallel axes, running from north to
south; the central axis is the chief one: the buildings
for official occasions are to the south (San da dian),
and the main private apartments are to the north (Nei
chao). The side axes consist of secondary apartments
and annexes.

a) The Wu men Gate and the Outer Courtyard

The Wu men Gate is the largest one of the Palace;
it was built in 1420, restored in 1647 and 1801; after
victories, the Emperor would preside over military
ceremonies here, and it was here that he announced
the new calendar.

The plan is unusual; the south façade, 302 feet long, is
flanked by two wings; the north façade is 408 feet long; the
whole building is surmounted by five pavilions, a large rectangular one in the middle and two square ones on each side (they
have been nick-named "the five phoenix", Wu feng lou); the
roofs are of yellow tiles, like those of all the rest of the Palace
(yellow was the colour reserved for the Emperor).

The Wu men gives on to a vast paved courtyard, with
he Golden Water River (Jin shui he) running across it
from east to west, spanned by five marble bridges
(symbols of the five virtues). Two gates (Xie he men and
Xi he men) lead off on either side to the lateral axes.
Opposite the Wu men three gates lead into the next
courtyard; the Tai he men in the middle (the Gate of
Supreme Harmony) was rebuilt in 1890 (it has nine
ntercolumniations and a double roof).

b) The Three Great Halls (San da dian)

This courtyard is the largest in the Palace. A gallery
runs round it; the imperial shops used to be here.

Grosier describes them at the end of the 18th century (Description, Livre I, chap. 1): "The first shop is full of vases and
other work in different kinds of metal; the second contains the
finest samples of skins and furs; the third has clothes lined with
squirrel, fox, ermine, zibeline, which the Emperor sometimes
gives to his officials; the fourth is a depot for precious stones,
rare pieces of marble and pearls fished in Tartary; the fifth,
which has two stories, is full of cupboards and chests of silks
for the use of the Emperor and his family; other shops contain
arrows, bows and other weapons taken from the enemy or given
by various princes",

In the centre of the courtyard, on a triple marble terrace about 25 feet high shaped like a capital I, stand the Three Great Halls, on the north-south axis.

1. The Hall of Supreme Harmony (Tai he dian) was built in 1669, repaired in 1765, repainted under Yuan Shi kai and restored very recently. Three flights of marble steps lead up to the terrace; in the middle of the central flight is a carved marble ramp, over which the Emperor's chair was carried. On the terrace, to the west, stands a little miniature temple where a grain measure was kept, and to the east was a sun-dial (the measure and the sun-dial symbolised the imperial justice and rectitude). The Hall of Supreme Harmony is 87 feet high, 210 feet long and 115 feet wide; twenty-four columns support the roof; the six central ones are gilded and carved with dragons; the rest are painted red. The ceiling is very fine (particularly the central motive). On a platform 6 feet high in the middle of the hall stands the Emperor's throne, surrounded by precious furniture (screens, cloisonné incense-burners).

The hall was used for ceremonies which marked great occasions, at the winter solstice, the new year, on the Emperor's birthday, at the publication of the list of successful candidates in the imperial examinations, or at the nomination of the generals at the beginning of a campaign. The setting was sumptuous; standards and pennants streamed in the wind from the foot of the terrace as far as Tian an men; orchestras were grouped near the galleries, mainly sets of musical stones and golden bells (hence another name for the hall, Golden Bell Hall, Jin luan dian); some of the bells are now exhibited in the Treasure Hall (see below p. 476). An armistice ceremony was held here as late as 1918. It was proposed that Parliament should sit here under the Republic.

2. The Hall of Perfect Harmony (Zhong he dian). This can be reached by going round behind the Hall of Supreme Harmony, without leaving the terrace.

It was restored in 1627 and in 1765. It is square, with windows on all sides. In the middle stands a throne, with sedan-chairs on either side. The Emperor came here to make his last preparations before going into the Hall of Supreme Harmony; final touches were given to the message to be read in the Temple of the Ancestors, and once a year, the seed intended for the new harvest was examined here.

3. The Hall of the Preservation of Harmony (Bao he dian). It was restored in 1627 and in 1765.

An imperial throne stands in the middle. Under the Qing, the great banquets given in honour of ambassadors or vassals were held here, and also the examinations for the title of "doctor" (jin shi).

An excellent collection of works of art is now on show in this hall and in the galleries on either side (where the shops used to be); many of them come from among the imperial treasures. Everything is exhibited in chronological order. a) Bao he dian: from the Neolithic age to the end of the Spring and Autumn period (bronzes, terra cotta ware, inscriptions on bone, jade, horn and shells); b) eastern gallery: from the Warring States to the end of the Song: belt buckles; glass beads from the Warring States period; bas-reliefs; two sheep carved in stone; instruments used for divination; fragments of Han fabrics; tomb furnishings (from the 3rd to 9th centuries); paintings (copies of originals kept in the reserves) and pottery dating from the Song; c) western gallery: from the Yuan to the end of the Qing; in the entrance to the gallery, large Yuan fresco of five sitting Buddhas, from the Xing hua si Temple, in Shan xi (47 feet long; it was cut up by merchants who wanted to sell it in 1928, and saved by the Peking University Research Centre); paintings, statuettes, fabrics and porcelain (from the 13th to the 19th centuries); art of the minorities (Miao batik, Yi armour, Tibetan gold jewellery); some 19th century groups of terra cotta figures (ni ren).

A flight of steps behind the Bao he dian leads down from the terrace into the further part of the central courtyard (the grey bricks used for paving it have just been renewed).

Three gates give on to the private apartments: to the west (on the left) Long zong men leads into the western axis (it is closed at the moment; the two arrows still to be seen sticking out of the upper woodwork are relics of the Lin Qing rising in 1813); to the east (on the right) Jing yun men leads into the eastern axis (Feng xian dian and the Palace of Peace and Longevity); opposite, in the centre, Qian qing men gives on to the Inner Court (Nei chao) and to the Three Rear Palaces (Hou san gong) which are in the Inner Court; opposite, on either side, two corridors lead to the Six Western Palaces (Xi liu gong) and the Palace of Culture of the Mind, to the west (Yang xin dian); to the east lie the Six Eastern Palaces (Dong liu gong).

c) The Three Rear Palaces (Hou san gong) and the Imperial Garden (Yu hua yuan)

The Qian qing men (Gate of Heavenly Purity) leads to the Inner Court; under the Ming, the Emperor came to this gate to hear his ministers' reports. The Three Rear Palaces stand in the centre, on a stone terrace, placed on a north-south axis, like the three great halls for official ceremonies.

1. The Palace of Heavenly Purity (Qian qing gong) is the largest of the three; it was built in 1420, but was burned down several times; the present building dates from 1798.

Four gilt incense-burners stand on the terrace before it, with bronze tortoises and cranes (symbols of immortality) and a grain measure and a sun-dial, symbols, like the ones in front of the Tai he dian. Two small miniature temples stand one on either side of the terrace, each one surmounted by a sort of gilded tabernacle; their meaning is not clear; a little door led in from the courtyard. Originally the Emperor's bedroom was in the Palace of Heavenly Purity (under the Ming and the early Qing, until Kang xi moved further to the west, to the Yang xin dian, see below, p. 472). Later on the Palace was used as an audience chamber; foreign ambassadors were received here, and the Empress was sometimes present at the receptions. The imperial throne stands in the middle, surrounded by cloisonné incense-burners; notice the four large mirrors and the carved wooden cupboards.

2. *The Hall of Union (Jiao tai dian)*: it was built in 1420 and restored in 1655. It is smaller than the rest, and corresponds to the Zhong he dian in the large courtyard.

It used to be the Empress's throne-room. From the reign of Qian long onwards, the imperial seals came to be kept here *(bao xi)*. The twenty-five caskets which contained them are still here, on stands, with covers over them; the seals have been taken out of their caskets to be put on show in glass cases on either side of the door. The large chiming clock on the left hand side was built in the palace under Qian long; the clypsedra on the right was built under Jia qing (c. 1800); a white tablet at the far end bears the two characters *wu wei*, which resume the political ideals of ancient China; they are often translated as "laissez faire", "to refrain from action".

3. *Palace of Earthly Tranquillity (Kun ning gong)*: like the Hall of Union, it was built in 1420 and restored in 1655.

Under the Ming, the Empress lived here. Under the Qing, the Emperor and Empress spent no more than their wedding night here. The Palace is divided into two unequal parts by a partition. The table and the big vats used for sacrifices to the god of the kitchen (1,300 pigs a year) are to the left; the little room at the side was the wedding chamber; it is entirely painted in red, and decorated with the "double *xi*" (repetition of the character *xi*, meaning "joy", symbol of happiness and fertility). Pu yi, the last Emperor of the Manchu dynasty, tells how disconcerted he felt when he entered the room on his wedding night: "This was rather a peculiar room: it was unfurnished except for the bed-platform which filled a quarter of it, and everything about it except the floor was red. When we had drunk the nuptial cup... and entered this dark red room I felt stifled. The bridge sat on the bed, her head bent down. I looked around me and saw that everything was red: red bed-curtains, red pillows, a red dress, a red skirt, red flowers and a red face... it all looked like a melted red wax candle. I did not known whether to stand or sit, decided that I preferred the Mind Nurture Palace, and went back there." (*From Emperor to Citizen*, Peking 1964, p. 121).

Large numbers of clocks and clockwork figures are now exhibited in the north-eastern gallery behind the Palace of Earthly Tranquillity; they date from the 18th and 19th centuries, and used to be part of the imperial collection. (The exhibition of clocks and clockwork figures was closed in 1972.)

They are either of Chinese make (from Canton, Su zhou and Peking) or European (from France and England). At the hour, the mechanism sets little figures and a musical box in motion. Several birds in cages recall the famous "Emperor of China's nightingale". Groups of people are taken round at specified times, and the guide winds each clock in turn.

The Gate of Earthly Tranquillity (Kun ning men) leads from the Inner Court to the *Imperial Garden* (Yu hua yuan).

It was laid out under the Ming, and some of the trees are said to date from then. The Hall of Imperial Peace stands in the middle (Qin an dian), surrounded by a rectangular wall; it dates from the beginning of the 15th century. Two gilded bronze unicorns guard the door *(qi lin)*. It stands in a setting of large trees, natural rocks mounted on pedestals, bronze incense-burners, alleys paved with stones laid out in patterns, or in pictures. To the east is the Pavilion of Ten Thousand Springs (Wan chun ting) built in 1535 and restored under Xian feng; the round roof contains an interesting lantern tower. A little artificial mountain with a cave lies to the north-east (the cave is closed for the moment); fountains play round it and a pavilion stands on the top; it is known as the Dui xiu shan, and dates from 1583. The Qing Empresses used to climb it at the double nine feast.

The Cheng guang men (a plain gate with two gilded bronze elephants flanking it) and the Shun zhen men lead out of the Imperial Garden, to the massive Gate of Divine Pride (Shen wu men), which used to be the main gate of the Palace.

It was built in 1420 and restored under Kang xi. The upper part used to house a drum and a bell which told the time to the people living in the Palace. The Empress Ci xi (Tz'u Hsi) fled through this gate with the Emperor in 1900, and it was guarded by Manchu soldiers until 1924. A square north of Shen wu men used to lead directly to the foot of Coal Hill; it was walled on the east and west sides. The walls have now disappeared and a large street now separates the Palace from Coal Hill.

d) The Palace of the Culture of the Mind (Yang xin dian) and the Six Western Palaces (Xi liu gong)

A corridor west of the Qian qing men gate leads here.

1. The Palace of the Culture of the Mind:

It was built under the Ming and restored in 1723. Kang xi used it for his private apartments, and the last three Manchu Emperors spent most of their time here. Tong zhi lived here during his minority, Guang xu spent the last years of his life here and died here in 1908, Xuan tong lived here from 1912 to 1924. Most of the furniture dates from the 19th century.

2. The Six Western Palaces: they are north of the Palace of the Culture of the Mind, three on each side of an alley going from north to south.

The Empress, secondary wives and widows used to live here. Ci xi lived in the Palace of Eternal Spring (Chang chun gong) during the reign of Tong zhi. The last Emperor's wife lived in the Palace of Accumulated Elegance (Chu xiu gong) until 1924. The apartments still contain the original 18th and 19th century furniture. There are some fine paintings illustrating the famous novel *The Dream of the Red Chamber*, and some *trompe l'œil* views in the Chang chun gong courtyard.

e) The Palace of Abstinence (Zhai gong), the Six Eastern Palaces (Dong liu gong) and the Hall for the Worship of the Ancestors (Feng xian dian)

A corridor east of the Qian qing men Gate leads to the Palace of Abstinence and the Six Eastern Palaces.

The Jing yun men Gate leads to the Hall for the Worship of the Ancestors.

1. The Palace of Abstinence: it is the first hall on the right of the corridor.

It was built under Yong zheng in 1731, and now houses an exhibition of bronze ritual vessels. The first room: the development of the *ding* (cauldron) from the Shang to the Han; specimens of *li* and *yan* (vessel in two parts, separated by a grid, for steaming the offerings). The second room: some fine specimens of *gui* (round, with handles), *dou* (sort of goblet), *pu* (rectangular dish), *xu* (oval), etc. ... The Yu qing gong lies east of the Palace of Abstinence; the court used to assemble here to offer their congratulations when a son was born, and Qian long handed over his office to Jia qing here, when he abdicated (it is closed).

2. The Six Eastern Palaces: like the Western Palaces, they stand on either side of a north-south alley.

Most of them were restored in the 17th century. The Jing ren gong and the Yan xi gong are to the south; the Cheng qian gong and the Yong he gong are in the centre; and the Zhong cui gong and the Jing yang gong lie to the north. Some of the women of the Palace lived here. The aquariums and the birdcages were kept in the Cheng qian gong in winter. All the palaces except the Yan xi gong, which is closed for the moment, house collections from what was the Imperial treasure (the exhibitions are opened in turn).

The Jing ren gong contains the second part of the exhibitions of bronzes begun in the Palace of Abstinence: *hu* (shaped like flagons), *jia* (tripods), *zun* (widening at the top) etc. Pottery, ceramics and porcelains are exhibited in the Cheng qian gong and the Yong he gong; the first room of the first palace: Neolithic pottery, Han, Jin, Sui, Tang, Song and Liao ceramics; to the right: good collection of Yuan ceramics; the second room of the first palace: Ming ceramics; in both rooms of the second palace: Qing ceramics and porcelain. Fabrics and silks are exhibited in the Zhong cui gong and the Jing yang gong (beautiful samples of Ming and Qing work).

East of the Six Palaces lay the store-houses for tea and some of the brocades. The Five Northern Kitchens (Bei wu chu) to the north fed everyone living in the eastern part of the Palace.

3. The Hall for the Worship of the Ancestors was dedicated to the ancestors of the imperial family. A side door leads into a fore-court followed by a large courtyard, with the Hall in the middle of it; a short covered way links the back of the building with an annex.

It now contains sculpture (visited by appointment); Zhou clay figures; tomb figurines (5th century B.C. to 9th century A.D.); a gilded head of the Buddha (Song); two *chuang* bases, dating from the Liao (from Tong xian, east of Peking); an effigy of Guan Yu (Ming, from Tai yuan); Qing statues of the Buddha and terra cotta figurines *(ni ren);* alongside these originals: casts of Han statues and Buddhist bas-reliefs (from Yun gang, Long men, Gong xian, Mai ji shan, the Qi xia si Temple, near Nanking).

f) The Palace of Peace and Longevity (Ning shou gong) and its annexes

It lies in the north-east corner of the Imperial Palace. A long blind corridor separates it from the group of buildings just described. Jing yun men, followed by Xi qing men, lead to it.

The palace was first built in 1689, then embellished and refitted from 1772 to 1776 by Qian long, who hoped to be able to retire there after his abdication. He retired there in 1795, when he had handed over the government to Jia qing, and lived there for four years until his death. Afterwards the buildings stood empty for almost a century, until 1889, when the Emperor Guang xu came to power, and the dowager Empress Ci xi went to live there. It was here that she decided to leave Peking, in 1900, with her court, when the Europeans were about to enter the city.

Xi qing men leads into a fore-court full of beautiful trees; on the right (facing north) is a magnificent nine dragon screen (Jiu long bi) in polychrome glazed tiles not unlike the one at the Bei hai (see p. 489). The

Gate of Imperial Supremacy (Huang ji men) on the left gives on to the big courtyard of the Palace of Peace and Longevity, a name particularly well-chosen for the place where the old Emperor Qian long hoped to end his days.

The Gate of Peace and Longevity (Ning shou men) leads into a smaller enclosure, surrounded by galleries, where the Hall of Imperial Supremacy (Huang ji dian) stands; it is a replica, on a smaller scale, of the Palace of Heavenly Purity (Qian qing gong, in the Inner Court).

The Dowager Empress Ci xi held her last council here before deciding to flee in 1900, and later her coffin lay here for over a year, waiting for a propitious day for the funeral.

The Palace of Peace and Longevity stands behind the Huang ji dian; it is a replica of the Palace of Earthly Tranquillity, where sacrifices were performed.

The precious original paintings kept in the Gu gong are shown here, in rotation, in a side gallery of the enclosure (they form only a part of the old imperial collections; the rest are at Tai wan).

North of the Ning shou gong, the Gate of the Culture of Character (Yang xing men) gives on to another enclosure containing three halls, on a north-south axis.

The private apartments of Qian long and Ci xi were here. The old Emperor died here on February 17th 1799, and it is said that the Dowager hid her casket of jewellery here in 1900, and found it intact when she returned. The first hall is the chief one; its name, the Hall of the Culture of Character (Yang xing dian), must have reminded the old Emperor of the Hall of the Culture of the Mind (Yang xin dian), where he lived for a long time, in the west of the Palace; the second hall was used by Qian long as a library (Le shou tang), and the third (Yi he xuan), was for repose.

Part of the old imperial treasures are exhibited in these three halls.

First Hall (which has a beautiful coffered ceiling): *the central section,* boat-shaped silver ingots; silver-gilt perfume-burners; set of sixteen golden bells, cast in 1715 under Kang xi (931 lbs. of gold), and another set of sixteen bells, also made of gold, cast in 1790 under Qian long (853 lbs. of gold); each bell is marked with the note it gives when struck; set of musical stones (of the same shape as those used under the Shang) dating from the 18th century; imperial seals; *in the right hand section:* some of the three thousand pieces which made up the imperial table-ware (4,600 ounces of gold, and 40,000 ounces of silver were needed): ewers, gold and silver bowls, crystal and jade ware, chopsticks; on the wall: a picture which consists of gold leaf on a blue background; *in the left hand section:* set of *ru yi* (sort of sceptre) made of gold; forty-nine sacrificial tripods (their shape is taken from that of old *jue* bronze vessels); gold bowls from the temples at the imperial tomb, the Dong ling; cloisonné reliquary, shaped like a stupa, made in 1777 to receive Qian long's mother's hair when she died. *Second room* (with a fine glass chandelier): *the central section:* large jade basins; magnificent set of jewellery and ornaments used by Empresses (among them a copy of the famous "phoenix head-dress" made of kingfishers' feathers, found in the tomb of the Emperor Wan li cf. 629); ceremonial saddles; large coat of mail made under Qian long (each one of the six hundred thousand links is either gilded, silvered, or lacquered black; it weighs over 30 lbs.); *in the right hand section:* Qing religious objects: reliquaries shaped like pagodas or stupas, one set of the seven and another of the eight "Buddhist treasures" (symbols placed in front of statues of the Buddha); *behind the screen:* elephant's tusks (no indication of origin) and an enormous block of carved jade (the stone comes from Xin jiang). *Third room:* green jade basins (made under the Ming); block of brown stone (worked under the Qing); set of vases of artificial flowers, their petals made of semi-precious stones; fine collection of jade *ru yi;* other things made of jade and coral.

The Chang yin ge (Pavilion of Pleasant Sounds) lies east of the Yang xing dian, with a raised stage and mechanical devices; the audience sat opposite (to the north) in the Yue shi lou (the Tower of Inspection of Truth). Under Qian long, a garden was laid out in the space west of the Yang xing dian; like the southern gardens, it has rockeries, and artificial hills, one of which has a gazebo on the top, where the Emperor, so it is said, liked to sit.

The way out to the north of the Yang xing dian enclosure passes close by the well known as the "concubine Zhen fei's well";

In 1900, the Dowager Empress pushed the unhappy concubine into the well, because she had criticised the plan to leave the Palace, and proposed to stay there (another version says that she committed suicide).

g) The southern part of the eastern lateral axis

Jing yun men leads into this part; the first building is a small pavilion which stands by itself, the Arrow Pavilion (Jian ting), which was restored in 1965. The famous stone drums are exhibited there for the moment.

The stone drums are ten roughly drum-shaped blocks, of stone (hence their name). Each one carries an inscription in great curly script *(da zhuan)*, one stanza each of a ten-stanza poem describing a hunting expedition led by the Duke of Qin, along a river bank. They are the oldest existing Chinese epigraphs on stone.

The "drums" were discovered in the Tang dynasty, in the 7th century, in the Feng xiang district in Shân xi; generations of scholars have worked on them since then. Under the Song, they were taken to the seat of local government of Feng xiang, and from there to Bian zhou (Kai feng), then the capital. When the Jin took Bian zhou in 1127, they took the "drums" to Zhong du (now Peking). The Yuan had them kept in the Temple of Confucius, where they stayed until the beginning of the 20th century. During the Civil War, they were carried about to several different place (they went as far as Si chuan).

The venerable stones are now in glass cases, to the right and left inside the Arrow Pavilion. One of them disappeared very early on, and was replaced by an old copy. Rubbings of the inscriptions, which are now very faint, have been put beside the "drums". The texts were fortunately copied and studied when they were much more legible than they are now (in the centre of the hall stands a more recent stele giving the texts in modern characters). It is now thought that the person mentioned is a certain Duke of Qin to whom references are made in other texts, where he is said to have lived round about 375 B.C.

The Kitchens: the outside wall of one of the three Palace kitchens is on the left (east) a little further to the south (it is closed for the moment).

The Palace of Culture (Wen hua dian) and its annexes: A small enclosure lies further south, containing several buildings devoted to culture or the veneration of culture.

The Gate of Culture (Wen hua men) leads into it; the building in the centre is the Hall of Culture (Wen hua dian), where the feast of the classics was celebrated in the second month of each year (it is now used for temporary exhibitions); the further part of the enclosure is filled by a two-storey library, the famous Wen yuan ge, built under Qian long to house the collection *Si ku quan shu* (the books are now in the Peking National Library); in the Zhuan xin dian pavilion to the east, sacrifices were made to great men and imperial tutors. A stele which was recently found in the south of the enclosure revealed that the Nei ge offices (an important organ of administration created by the dynasty) were here in the Ming dynasty.

h) The Western Lateral Axis

These buildings have recently been opened to the public after being restored (1972).

The West Flower Garden (Xi hua yuan) lies to the north; several palaces used to stand here, until they were burned down on the night of June 26th 1923 (the fire was probably started deliberately, to hide the fact that for several months the treasures they contained had been steadily disappearing). A tennis court was laid there for the last Emperor. The Rain Flower Pavilion (Yu hua ge), a Lama temple several stories high, built under the Ming and restored under Qian long, stands in the south of the garden. Its rooftops, with their golden dragons, can be seen from the other courtyards and from the top of Coal Hill.

The biggest of the western palaces is the Palace of Peace and Tranquillity (Ci ning gong), improved round about 1650; it lies to the south. The Dowager Empress Niuluku, Qian long's mother, lived and died here; the "Eastern Empress", Ci an, who, with Ci xi, was co-Regent during the Emperor Tong zhi's minority, also lived here. The Hall of the Great Buddha (Da fo tang), with statues of the eighteen *luo han*, stands behind the Ci ning gong. An enormous garden with several small Lama temples in it stretches to the south.

Still further to the south stands the Hall of Military Prowess (Wu ying dian), where the imperial printing presses used to be. The anthologies of imperial poems (chiefly those of Qian long), the great encyclopedias and other collections commissioned by the Emperor, were all printed here. The building was burned down in 1869 and in 1900, and was rebuilt in 1903. The Xian an gong, a school founded by Qian long, stood to the west of the Wu ying dian; the pupils were Tibetans and Turks about to take up administrative posts in the Western Marches, who came to absorb Chinese culture.

1972: New archaeological finds, discovered during the Cultural Revolution, are now on show in the west of the Imperial Palace (entrance at Xi hua men Gate). The permanent exhibitions in the Palace have been reduced in size, and temporary exhibitions of paintings are held in some of the eastern pavilions.

2. The Surroundings of the Imperial Palace

The Imperial Palace used to be surrounded by another, much larger, rectangular enclosure (it covered an area about six times that of the Palace), which was known as the Imperial City (Huang cheng). Once the empire had fallen, the walls lost their meaning, and as by this time they were beginning seriously to inconvenience east-west communications in the town, they were removed entirely on three sides, north, east and west; three thoroughfares were built on the site of them: Dong huang cheng gen, Xi huang cheng gen, and Bei huang cheng gen, whose names recall the old walls ("streets at the foot of the Imperial City"). The southern walls have been partly preserved; they stretch

on either side of Tian an men, as far as the end of the
People's Cultural Park to the east, and as far as the
south-western corner of the Nan hai to the west. The
walls were pierced by four gates, one on each side.

All the guilds which worked on the upkeep of the Palace
used to be lodged within the Imperial City (stone-masons,
carpenters, brick-makers, joiners, painters), as well as those in
charge of the supplies for the court (food, clothes, various
handicrafts), and the administrative bodies who supervised all
the craftsmen. It also contained granaries, storehouses for
goods in everyday use and for rare products, the imperial
stables, parks (used for rearing sheep, cows... and rare animals), vegetable gardens and orchards. High officials, princes and
even sometimes the Emperors themselves had houses there,
each shut in behind its enclosing walls.

Some of the temples linked with the imperial office were here
too: the Altar of Earth and Harvests, the Temple of the Ancestors, the Temple of the Thunder God, the Wind God and the
Cloud God, several large Buddhist and Taoist temples, and a
Roman Catholic Church, founded in 1693. The staff responsible
for running the internal affairs of the court, and the Palace
guard, all lived there too.

Some of the residences and temples have vanished; others
have been taken over by sections of the administration, but the
toponymy still recalls what once existed. The old Altar of Earth
and Harvests, now the Sun Yat sen Park, to the south, will
be described first, followed by the old Temple of the Ancestors,
now the People's Cultural Park; then Coal Hill, to the north,
and lastly, the east and west sections of the Imperial City.

a) The Sun Yat sen Park (Zhong shan gong yuan)

It has two entrances, one giving on to Chang an jie,
just west of Tian an men, and the other inside the
Imperial Palace, to the left, in front of the Wu men
(when approaching it from the south).

Under the Liao and the Jin, this area lay to the north-east of
the town as it then was, and the Temple of the Re-birth of the
Country (Xing guo si) stood there; under the Yuan, it was
known as the Temple of Longevity and Re-birth of the Country.

The Ming Emperor Yong le moved the the Altar of Earth and Harvests (She ji tan) here in 1421, from the site used by the Yuan, further north, and west of the Palace. It became a public garden as early as 1914; in 1928, it was called the Zhong shan Park, after Dr. Sun Yat sen (known as Sun Zhong shan in China). Several pavilions and rocks were brought here from other places (particularly from the Yuan ming yuan).

A large white marble *pai lou*, with blue ceramic superstructure, is visible from the entrance.

It was built by the European Powers, in memory of Baron Kettler, who was killed by the Boxers in 1900; it originally stood in "Ha ta men" (now Chong wen men da jie); it was brought here in 1918. The pediment now bears two characters only, meaning "defend the peace". The alley which starts at the entrance soon takes a right angle turn to the left; the large rock on the right comes from the Yuan ming yuan (the inscription is by Qian long). The alley goes on to the left among magnificent cypress trees, some of which are said to have been planted under the Liao.

The enclosure of the Altar of the Earth and Harvests is on the right of the alley; a path going from north to south leads up to the altar itself; east of the path stands a modern theatre, which is used in the summer.

The altar itself is a square white stone terrace, surrounded by low walls faced with tiles, with four gates; it is divided into five sections, each filled with earth of a different colour (white to the west, green to the east, black to the north, red to the south and yellow in the middle); the earth, which was brought from the four corners of the empire, symbolised the principle according to which all the earth under the sun belonged to the Emperor. The sacrifices took place twice a year (in spring, during the second lunar month, to obtain a good crop, and in the autumn, after the harvest) and the Emperor himself performed them. The Hall of Prayer (Ba i dian), built at the beginning of the Ming dynasty, and probably one of the best-preserved old buildings in the town, stands north of the altar. It was dedicated to Sun Yat sen in 1928. It is now used for funeral ceremonies of distinguished members of the party or the government. The Hall of Halberds is north of the Prayer Hall; the sacrificial instruments used to be kept there, along with seventy-two halberds meant to protect the altar; a chamber of commerce uses the building now. A wide alley runs from east to west, north of the enclosure, lined with beautiful cypress trees; the moat of the Imperial Palace forms the northern boundary; to the east, a large gate gives on to the fore-court of the Palace, on a level with the Wu men.

To visit the south-west corner of the park, it is best to start from the southern entrance to the altar enclosure.

The first pavilion, the Xi li ting, the Pavilion where ceremonies were practised, was moved here in 1921, from the Ministry of Rites; next comes the Tang hua wu, a hot-house where flowers are exhibited; then the Lan ting pei ting, a pavilion housing an 18th century stele, from the Yuan ming yuan; and to the south lies a little lake, with an island and a pavilion. Right of the wall and the altar enclosure several pavilions still stand, one of which, the Tou hu ting (built in the form of a cross) takes its name from an old game which consisted in throwing arrows into a vase.

b) The People's Cultural Park
(Ren min wen hua gong)

It has two entrances, one east of Tian an men giving on to Chang an jie, and the other inside the Imperial Palace, on the right of the Wu men (when approaching it from the south).

The Temple of the Imperial Ancestors was east of the Imperial Palace under the Yuan; it was moved here in 1420, in the Ming dynasty, under Yong le, and then rebuilt in 1544. The Ming and Qing Emperors paid homage to their ancestors here at their coronations, their weddings, and on New Year's Day. After 1949, the buildings were restored and it is now a park, with a theatre, where people come to play chess, ping pong etc.

The entrance opens into a wide alley with beautiful cypress trees all round on either side (in the 18th century, there was a heronry on the right hand side). North of the alley, a three-arched gate gives on to the first enclosure; then steps lead up to the Da ji men

Gate, leading into the second courtyard. The Front Hall (Qian dian) stands on the first terrace, with the Middle Hall (Zhong dian) behind it; the Front Hall was used for the ceremonies which took place five times a year; on each occasion, the tablets of the ancestors were placed there. For the rest of the year, the tablets were kept in the Middle Hall, which has been converted into a games room, with a ping pong table. Both halls have very fine ceilings. The third and last hall (also converted into a games room) stands on the second terrace. The north gate of the enclosure gives on to a large alley, with the moat of the Imperial Palace to the north, and a gate leading into the forecourt of the Palace, on a level with the Wu men.

c) Coal Hill (Mei shan)

Coal Hill lies due north of the Palace, with a gate opposite the north gate of the Palace (Shen wu men) and two more in the west and east walls of the rectangular enclosure which surrounds it. Another name for it is Jing shan (Prospect Hill).

The area was a private park for the Emperor and his court from the Yuan dynasty onwards. It was improved under the Ming, and the five hills were made, using unwanted earth from the moat round the Imperial City. A story says that the Emperor had supplies of coal hidden under the middle hill (hence the name, Coal Hill), but recent searches have revealed nothing at all, and the legend seems to have scant support. Qian long had pavilions built on each of the hills, and the hills planted with fruit trees; the place was called the Garden of a Hundred Fruit Trees (Bai guo yuan). It was stocked with "hares, rabbits, deer and other similar animals" and "thousands of birds in the trees made the air resound with their melodious songs" (De Lisle, Description de Pékin, p. 17). In the 19th and 20th centuries, the park fell more or less into ruin; the hills have recently been replanted with trees, to restore them to what they once were.

The Beautiful View Tower (Qi wang lou) stands opposite the south gate; it was dedicated to Confucius, but is now used for exhibitions of flowers and fish. A path climbs up the hillside to the top of the middle hill and the Pavilion of Ten Thousand Springs (Wan chun ting) which stands there. It contains a large recent statue of the Buddha. The view from the top is magnificent; to the south lie the yellow roofs and the courtyards of the Imperial Palace; to the north, the northern districts of the town punctuated by the Bell and Drum Towers; to the west, at the foot of the hill, the Da gao dian, a palace built under the Ming Emperor Jia jing. The palace used to contain a Taoist temple, where the Emperors came to pray to the Yellow Emperor, god of rain, and a school for eunuchs and future Palace servants; the modern buildings in the enclosure and the old ones are now used as administrative offices, though there is still a pretty round pavilion with a blue tiled roof in the north of the enclosure.

At the foot of the hill, on the east side, stands the tree from which the last Ming Emperor, Chong zhen, is said to have hanged himself on March 17th, 1644, after being forced to commit suicide.

Although the story is no doubt fiction, it is still told. A German Jesuit priest, Adam Schall, was living in Peking at that time, and left his own account of what happened when Li Zi cheng's troops entered Peking and overthrew the last Ming Emperor *(Relatio Historica)*, taken from the French translation by P. Bornet, 1942, p. 106): "So mounting his horse, (the emperor) wanted, with his little escort of horsemen, to go into the outer city through the gate nearest our residence (the modern Xuan wu men), but the eunuchs would not let him... Therefore, forced to go back into the palace, he told his wife, the Empress, to strangle herself, and the three sons which he had had were to escape from the capital as best they could... Finally, he did not know what to do himself, so he left the palace once more, but on foot; he went straight to the hill which is behind the palace *(ad montem qui est post ipsum palatium)* to the place where once he had examined the cannons which I had cast... He took off his boots and threw back his imperial head-dress, then he hanged himself from a beam at the entrance to the above mentioned place *(e trabe porticus eiusdem loci)*."

North of the hill stands the old Hall of Imperial Longevity (Shou huang dian), built under Qian long, where the portraits of past Emperors used to be kept (they disappeared during the Guo min dang period); the two central buildings are now the Peking Children's Palace. Three fine wooden *pai lou* stand in front of the entrance, with stone lions' heads all round them, which seem to grow up out of the ground.

d) The Western Side of the old Imperial City

Three large lakes, known as the north, south and central lakes, fill part of this area; the court used to come and stay in the pavilions and summer-houses which are dotted about their shores. Princes' houses, granaries, workshops and temples covered the rest of the area. The State Council is at the moment housed in the buildings round the central and southern lakes, and they are closed to visitors. The district north of Xi an men da jie will be described first, followed by the southern district.

1. The Northern Lake (Bei hai). It lies north-west of the Imperial Palace and west of Coal Hill; it is the most northerly of the three lakes belonging to the Imperial City.

It is almost certain that the Liao Emperors built a pleasure palace on the area corresponding to Qiong hua Island and the Round Town. Under the Jin, the lake was dug and the palace enlarged. Khubilai Khan settled here when he had decided to establish his capital at Da du. The palace, which stood on Qiong hua Island, was embellished and renamed Guang han dian; the lay-out of the lake was changed slightly and a new city was planned with this as its focal point. At the beginning of the 15th century, the Ming had the lake divided into two; the Bei hai to the north and the present Central Lake (Zhong hai) to the south. The palace was in ruins by the end of the 16th century, and in 1651 the White Dagoba (Bai ta), which is still standing, was built on the old site. The neighbourhood was improved under Qian long (the Ten Thousand Buddha Pavilion was built), etc.). The buildings were damaged in 1900. The lake was re-dug in 1951, and the great marble bridge separating the Bei hai from the Zhong hai was built in 1956.

The lake and its surroundings are enclosed within walls which are pierced by three gates (south, east and north).

The Round Town (or, more accurately the Round Fort, Tuan cheng)

It is south of the lake near the marble bridge; it used to be an island. A temple was built here under the Jin, and rebuilt several times in the later dynasties; the present buildings date from 1746. The walls of the Round Town were built in 1417 (they are 870 feet in diameter, and 14 feet high).

A gate opens in the south-east of the walls (outside the walls surrounding the northern lake).

The beautiful white pines in the courtyard are said to date from the Liao or the Jin; in the middle, the little pavilion (built under Qian long, in 1745) contains an enormous black jade bowl (over 15 feet round), which was given to Khubilai in

1 Tuan Cheng (the Round Town)	8 Tie Bi (Iron Screen)
2 Cheng Guang Dian (Hall which Receives the Light)	9 Children's museum of Science and Technology
3 Yong An Si (Temple of Eternal Tranquillity)	10 Wu Long Ting (the Five Dragon Pavilion)
4 Yi Lan Tang (Restaurant)	11 Da Xi Tian (Great Eastern Sky)
5 Yue Gu Lou (Pavilion for Reading Ancient Manuscripts)	12 Pavilion of the Ten Thousand Buddhas
6 Xiao Xi Tian (Small Western Sky)	13 Open-air Cinema
7 Jiu Long Bi (Nine Dragon Screen)	14 Great Marble Bridge
	15 Children's playground
	16 Northern gate
	17 Southern gate

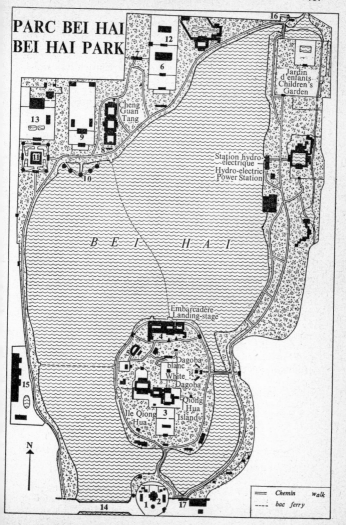

PARC BEI HAI
BEI HAI PARK

Jardin
d'enfants
Children's
Garden

Cheng
Guan
Tang

13

9

8

11

10

12

6

Station hydro-
électrique
Hydro-electric
Power Station

B E I   H A I

Embarcadère
Landing-stage

Dagoba
blanc
White
Dagoba

Qiong
Hua
Island

Ile Qiong
Hua

3

15

N

14   1 2   17

Chemin   walk
bac   ferry

1265; the carving on the outside (sea monsters) is very fine. It used to be in the Guang han dian Palace, on Qiong hua Island; under Qian long it was brought here. The Cheng Guang dian is the chief building in the Round Town (the Hall which receives the Light); it is a large square building. The richly clothed white jade Buddha inside (just under 5 feet high) was brought from Burma under Guang xu (1875–1908). Temporary exhibitions are now held in the central buildings and the annexes.

Qiong hua Island. Two bridges lead on to the island from the south and the east, each one preceded by a *pai lou*. The southern bridge ends almost at the entrance of the Yong an si (Temple of Everlasting Peace); its buildings climb up the hillside to the foot of the Dagoba.

Both were built in 1651, when the Dalaï Lama first came to Peking. Long flights of steps lead up the hill, beside rocks symbolising the cosmic mountain (Sanskrit: Sumeru, Chinese: Kun lun) and steles in memory of Qian long (engraved in four languages). The White Dagoba is a block of masonry in four parts: a square terrace; a base several stories high; a central part, slightly onion-shaped, with a niche on the southern side with an inscription in superposed Sanskrit characters (this niche, the *yan guang men*, "door of the light of the eyes", is not found on dagobas before the Qing); and a spire on the top, ending in a motive (*tian di pan*, "disc of heaven and earth"). South of the Dagoba stands a pretty little miniature temple made of glazed tiles (the colours of the little statues of the Buddha are particularly good). The view over Peking from the top of it is superb: the north-south axis (the Bell and Drum Towers, Coal Hill, the Imperial Palace, Tian an men, the Monument to the People's Heroes, Qian men); the southern and central lakes, and the west of the town.

Numerous other buildings cover the northern and western banks of the island (covered ways, pavilions, summer-houses).

The covered way known as Yi lan tang (restaurant and jetty) lies to the north; south-west of that is the Yue gu lou (Pavilion where the old texts are read), a crescent-shaped building, where

495 samples of famous calligraphy were collected in 1747. On the top of the hill, behind the Yue gu lou stands a curious little octagonal pavilion with stone columns covered with inscriptions. Beside the Yue gu lou, another pavilion houses an exhibition of contemporary calligraphy.

The Eastern Shore of the Bei hai. A walk lined with flowers leads to the north gate; the little hydraulic power station beside the lake was built in 1956, to emphasise the importance of electrification to the young pioneers. A nursery school has taken over the site of the old Altar of Silk-worms (Can tan); it consisted of two stone terraces surrounded by mulberry trees (on the eastern one sacrifices were made to the god of silk-worms, on the western one to the god of mulberry trees), a hall where the Empress offered sacrifices to the goddess of silk-worms and finally buildings where the silk-worms were reared.

The Northern Shore of the Bei hai. (Going from east to west.) A large glazed tile *pai lou* marks the entrance to the Xiao xi tian (Small Western Heavens), which was built under Qian long (the first building, now standing empty, is the only one which can be visited). The Ten Thousand Buddha Pavilion is north of the Xiao xi tian; it was built by Qian long for his mother's eightieth birthday.

It is a three-storey building with a yellow tiled roof, and ten thousand niches which used to hold the Buddhas; they were stolen in 1900. The courtyard is now an open-air cinema. The Nine Dragon Screen (Jiu long bi) stands back slightly, to the south west; it is 87 feet long and over 15 feet high, built in 1417, to protect the temple which used to stand just north of it, and which no longer exists; it is made of glazed tiles, and on each side nine dragons, all in different colours, are portrayed playing with balls (so it appears) among the waves.

The Chen guan tang is to the south-west; the "Iron Screen" (Tie ying bi) stands in front of it (10 feet high, and 6 feet wide).

It is in fact made of volcanic stone, and the bas-relief carvings, also of dragons, date from the Yuan; it used to be in a lane, near the De sheng men Gate, and was brought here in 1947. The Chan fu si Temple (Temple of Happy Meditation) was to the west of this point; it has been destroyed. A science museum for children has been built on the site of it; in front, beyond a pool full of lotus plants, stand five pavilions which form a jetty as well; they date from the 16th century, and are known as the Five Dragon Pavilions (Wu long ting), because the line of the bases suggests a dragon's spine.

Still further to the south-west, near the outer wall, stands the Da xi tian (Great Western Heaven), which is still called the Guan yin dian (Hall of Guan yin).

Built under Kang xi, it is a large square wooden building, enclosed within walls, with a pavilion at each corner, a *pai lou* on each of the four sides, and surrounded by a moat. The roof-frame, which is enormous, is supported by four sets of columns: 36 columns round the outside, then 28, 18, and 4 in the centre. In 1930, an artificial mound still existed in the middle, with a flight of steps leading up to the top, and a hundred stucco statues illustrating the various stages of the re-incarnation. It now contains several ping-pong tables.

2. The Peking Library (Bei jing tu shu guan). It is in Wen jin jie Street, west of the Bei hai, just beyond the bridge.

The library was founded at the end of the empire (1910) and opened to the public in 1912. In 1931, it was moved to its present building, built on the site of the ruins of a Ming temple dating from 1513. The library has expanded considerably since the liberation (it receives a copy of every book which appears in China). In 1962, it contained 7,200,000 books. The staff of 500 is divided into six departments: 1) Lending service for the use of social organisations (900 in Peking alone) and private individuals; 2) Buying department; 3) Cataloguing department (each book is entered under three headings: subject, title, author); 4) Bibliography department; 5) Reserves; 6) Central office of administration, also in charge of the Restoration Service and the Service responsible for exchanges with other countries (3,200 organisations in 126 different countries).

The library possesses old manuscripts (the oldest come from Dun huang, and date from the 5th century); *incunabula* (Song and Yuan); most of the surviving volumes of the *Encyclopedia of Yong le* (which was scattered in 1900); 2,970,000 works in 57 foreign languages, including some very fine 15th century European *incunabula* from the old library belonging to the Jesuits; 50,000 works in languages of the minority races; several rare editions of Marxist Leninist works; copies of Mao Ze dong's works in Chinese, the minority languages, and in 18 foreign languages; manuscripts of Lu Xun and Wen Yi duo; a copy of the *Si ku quan shu* (from the imperial collection belonging to Qian long).

The visit includes the reading rooms (public reading room, reading room reserved for research students, periodicals room, microfilm room; the 500 seats enable 700 readers to be admitted each day on an average, and 1,000 at the most), and the workshop (restoration of old manuscripts).

A little street runs parallel to Wen jin jie, to the north of the library, whose name, Red Sandalwood Buddha Temple Street, (Zhan tan si jie), recalls that the temple used to stand here.

It was built under the Ming and restored under the reign of Kang xi; it was one of the largest and richest temples in the town. The main hall contained a large sandalwood statue of the Buddha, about 5 feet high, no doubt of ancient origin, which was said to have come from the West. Every year, on the eighth of the first lunar month, the Living Buddha of Peking performed a ceremony similar to the one performed at the Yong he gong (see p. 501). In 1900, the Boxers established their headquarters there (with the consent of the Lamas, as they supported the rebellion, it seems). After the victory of the Powers, the temple was destroyed by way of reprisal.

3. The Former Bei Tang (Northern Cathedral): On the right hand side of Xi an men da jie (when going westwards), is a little lane, usually full of people selling fruit and vegetables. Through a grille at the end can be seen the impressive façade of what was once the third Bei tang.

History. *The First Bei tang:* A small group of French Jesuits, sent to China by Louis XIV, arrived in Peking in 1688: Fathers Gerbillon, Bouvet, Fontaney and Visdelou. They rendered innumerable services to the Emperor Kang xi (astronomical calculations, interpreting during the signing of the Treaty of Nertchinsk with the Russians), were soon favoured by him, and persuaded him first of all to pass the edict of tolerance. Then, in 1693, when they had cured the Emperor of a serious illness, using quinine sent from Pondichéry by Father Doulu, they were granted a piece of land on which they had permission to build a church. The site was exceptionally well-situated, near the Palace, within the Imperial City, west of the Central Lake (Zhong hai). The first Bei tang was accordingly built there; it was dedicated to "Christ on the Cross", and it was seventy-five feet long, consisting of a nave and side chapels. "The end wall of the church was painted in *trompe-l'œil*, to make the church appear to carry on further". The tower was used as a library and observatory. A five-character inscription on the pediment protected the church from sacrilege and added to the prestige of the missionaries: "Church built by Imperial command".

For the first years of the 18th century, the little community lived fairly peacefully, but then came difficulties, hostility on the part of the Emperor Yong zheng and finally the suppression of the Jesuit order. Louis XVI sent a group of Lazarists to take over, but the French Revolution put a stop to all financial help. Under the reign of Jia qing, the Bei tang was sold to a mandarin, Yu, for five thousand taels, by order of the Emperor. The famous inscription on the pediment was taken down, carefully wrapped in yellow silk, and put away in the Palace reserves; then the church itself was destroyed, in 1827.

The Second Bei tang: In 1860, the Powers insisted that the land be given back. All that the Lazarists (Mgr. Mouly) could find of the old church amongst the ruins and later buildings on the site was a wrought iron grill dating from Louis XV; they built a chapel straight away, and gradually built a larger church in Gothic style, which was to be a cathedral (they had bitter arguments about the height of the towers with the Chinese authorities). The new church was barely finished, when it was abandoned. The marriage of the Emperor Guang xu was going to mean that the Dowager Empress Ci xi (Tz'u Hsi) had to hand over her apartments in the Imperial Palace to the new Empress. Ci xi wanted to live on the far shore of the Central

Lake, near the Bei tang, and she disliked the proximity of foreigners.

The Third Bei tang: After long discussions between Li Hong zhang, representing the Chinese, and Mgr. Favier, a Frenchman, representing the Europeans, an agreement was reached to build a new cathedral, on a site further to the north, but still within the Imperial City. The chosen site was occupied by store-houses (the Ten Western Store-rooms, Xi shi ku), where confiscated treasures where kept; a Buddhist temple, the Ci yun si, lay to the north. The store-houses and the temple were handed over to the missionaries, with an indemnity of 350,000 taels. The third Bei tang, Saint Saviour's Cathedral, was then built, and consecrated in 1889. The buildings round the second Bei tang were destroyed, and the church transformed into a depot.

During the 1900 rebellion, the Bei tang had to withstand a long and difficult siege; Mgr. Favier, the bishop, and sub-lieutenant Henry both distinguished themselves by their gallantry. Four hundred of the Christians who took part in the fighting alongside the Italian and French soldiers were killed; finally, they were relieved by a detachment of Japanese soldiers.

In the *Derniers jours de Pékin*, Pierre Loti tells how he visited the second Bei tang, then used as a store-house for all the treasures which Ci xi had received as presents. The Boxers had been defeated, and the soldiers were about to plunder the city: "The church was full of pagan riches, but the organ was still in place, although it had been silent for thirty years. My companion and I climbed up to the loft to fill the place once more with strains of Bach and Handel, while below us, our cavalry-men, knee-deep in ivory, silk, and ceremonial robes, went on with their clearance work."

The second Bei tang was destroyed in 1911; the third, which in spite of the fighting, had been damaged surprisingly little, was restored early in the 20th century. An orphanage was founded in the Buddhist temple and a European cemetery was laid out to the north to receive the bodies of those killed in 1900.

The church has been transformed into a school (a red star now decorates the pediment). The yellow roofs of the pavilions built to house steles given by the Emperor can still be seen from the grille. The cemetery has been moved to the eastern suburbs.

4. The Central and Southern Lakes (Zhong hai and Nan hai). At the beginning of the Ming dynasty, the

Central Lake was separated from the Bei hai and the Nan hai was dug to the south. As time went on, several palaces and lesser buildings were built on their shores, for members of the Imperial family and their suites.

The main entrance used to be the Xin hua men Gate which gives on to Chang an jie Avenue. The gate was originally a tower, built by Qian long for his favourite, the Moslem Xiang fei, so that she could gaze at the Moslem district on the other side of Chang an jie Avenue; the tower no longer exists.

The Ocean Terrace (Ying tai), the residence where the Emperor Guang xu was held prisoner by the Empress Ci xi, was on an island in the middle of the Nan hai. On the western shore of the Zhong hai, to the south, stood first of all, the Ju ren tang (Palace where Goodwill lives), built in 1912 by Yuan Shi kai, then to the north, the Xing ren tang (Palace of Prosperity and Goodwill), which Ci xi had done up for her when she was forced to leave her Palace apartments on the marriage of her son. Further north stood the former Bei tang (see p. 491), the Zi guang ge (Hall of Purple Effulgence) where military examinations were held, and where the Emperor received ambassadors (the walls were covered with paintings depicting the exploits of Qian long). On an island in the Zhong hai stood a pretty pavilion, from which "eight views of Peking" were to be had.

All these buildings have been adapted to house the State Council; they are closed to all visitors and it is impossible to know what state they are now in. All that can be seen of them is the little pavilion in the Central Lake, which can be glimpsed from the great marble bridge south of the Bei hai.

West of the Zhong hai and opposite the Peking Library stands the Hundred Birds Palace (Bai niao tang), built under the Ming; there used to be an aviary there. During the Republic, it was taken over to be used as offices dealing with the administration of the town; it is still used as offices now, and no visitors are allowed.

e) The Eastern Side of the old Imperial City

It covered a smaller area than the western part, and contained buildings and parks. North of Sha tan were: 1) the head offices of several administrative services, the service in charge of the upkeep of the Palace (in Gong jian hu tong Lane), the service of rites (in Huang hua men da jie Street); and 2) the dye-works, the forges, the stores of wax, all of which can still be traced in the toponymy.

A little further south was the Temple to the God of Horses, which was originally next to the Imperial stables (under the reign of Qian long, they were moved south of Sha tan, to the lane still known as the Horses' Park Lane, Ma juan hu tong).

In 1898, the Imperial University, later to become *Peking University* (Bei jing da xue), was built on the site of the Temple to the God of Horses; the university stayed there until 1953, when it was moved out to the western suburbs, into the buildings which formerly belonged to Yen ching University. The large red-brick buildings along the north side of Sha tan can still be seen today. They now house a museum devoted to Mao Ze dong (who was once employed by the library there) and Li Da zhao.

A large throughfare running from north to south, called Bei chi zi to the north and Nan chi zi to the south, leads into the part south of Sha tan. To the east of Nan chi zi was a garden with a vineyard and a shop where porcelain was stored (they can still be traced in the toponymy).

The Former Imperial Archives (Huang shi cheng). They are at the southern end of Nan chi zi.

The building was put up under the Ming, in 1534, rebuilt under the Qing and restored in 1956. The *Shi lu* ("True notes", written for use in compiling the dynastic histories) and the

Imperial edicts were kept here. The hall has an arched stone roof, to guard against fire. 153 chests, made of wood overlaid with copper, stand on a stone platform 5 feet high, 138 feet long and 26 feet wide; the archives were kept in the chests.

In 1900, the Emperors' Private Oratory (Tang zi) was rebuilt in the south-eastern corner of the Forbidden City. Before that, it was in the Legation Quarter; it was one of the biggest temples in the city (it was destroyed by the Allies). The Emperors came here to celebrate a private cult to the Imperial family; one of the special occasions was New Year's Day; the temple also contained a picture of the god of horses, to whom a sacrifice was made before each campaign.

C. THE NORTHERN DISTRICTS

Under the Yuan, much of the commercial activity of the town was concentrated in the northern districts, especially near the Bell Tower and on the shores of Lake Shi Sha hai; under the Ming, the court officials, attracted by the cool waters of the lake, built houses round it; several monasteries were built here as well. Under the Qing, several princes had palaces built here: Prince Kong's Palace, famous for its gardens (west of the Front Lake), the Palace belonging to the second Prince Chun, where Pu yi was born (near the northern walls, north of Guo zi shi da jie), Prince Qing's Palace (near the Hu guo si Temple); they are now transformed into schools or offices. The district will be described from west to east.

1. Xi zhi men Gate

It used to be called Kai men, the open gate, because as it leads to the Summer Palace, it was open night and day when the Empress Ci xi was living there. It was entirely rebuilt in 1894. At the moment, it is in a better state of repair than most of the other gates; the two towers are still standing, as well as the crescent-shaped wall round the inner courtyard (now used for parking buses). This gate has recently been demolished (1972).

2. The Western Church (Xi tang)

It is on the south side of Xi zhi men Street, a few hundred yards from the gate itself.

History: When the Papal Legate, Mgr. de Tournon, was preparing to come to China in 1705, an Italian Lazarist, M. Pedrini, known for his musical ability, was sent to join him. M. Pedrini arrived in China after a six-year journey via Chile and Manilla. He gradually worked himself into the Emperor's favour, in spite of the Bull of 1716, whose attitude to the question of rites was not what the Chinese had hoped for. In 1723, he bought a Chinese house, near the Xi zhi men Gate. This was the beginning of the first Xi tang. This is how he described it himself in a letter to his brother: "I have bought a beautiful house, with seventy rooms, both big and small, and about ten courtyards", and in another letter, to the Prefect of Propaganda, he says: "Our house is at some distance from the Jesuit Southern and Western Churches. It cost 1,850 taels. I have added twenty taels for various expenses which do not appear in the contract and twenty more for the servants, as is the custom in this country .. I have planted flowers in the garden, and even vines, which produced several bunches of grapes this year". As M. Pedrini had been tutor to Yong zheng, his church escaped the severe measures which the Emperor meted out to the Jesuits. When he died, the church reverted to the Propaganda. During Jia qing's persecutions in 1811, the last four Lazarists were expelled and the church destroyed. The site was given back in 1860, and a new church (Our Lady of the Seven Sorrows) was consecrated in 1867. It was demolished in 1900 during the Boxer Rebellion, and rebuilt once more at the beginning of the 20th century.

The last building has survived to this day; the little garden in front of it is still open.

3. The Protect the Country Temple (Hu guo si)

It is on the north side of Hu guo si jie Street.

Under the Yuan, the site was occupied by a Mongol prince's Palace. He fell into disgrace and committed suicide; several years after his death he was rehabilitated and his palace was transformed into a temple dedicated to him. Under the Qing, the temple was famous for its large fairs (held several times a month) at which mainly flowers and shrubs were sold. The temple is now out of use, and the buildings in a poor state of repair; a large bazaar has been built in front of it, as at Long fu si; shrubs and flowers are still sold there.

4. The Northern Lakes

There are three of them altogether: from north-west to south-east: the Lake of the Ten Western Monasteries (Shi sha xi hai), the Lake of the Ten Back Monasteries (Shi sha hou hai), the Lake of the Ten Front Monasteries (Shi sha qian hai).

Under the Yuan, the barges coming up through the various canals from Tong zhou used to stop along the shores of Xi hai, which was then called Ji shui tan; the neighbourhood of the lake (particularly Drum Tower Street and Silver Ingots Bridge Street near by) was the busiest part of the capital. Under the Ming, the barges no longer came as far as the lake, and it no longer acted as a harbour; the only boats on its waters were pleasure boats. The court dignitaries had houses built on its shores. The Temple of Upright Conduct (Jing ye si), on the north shore of the Xi hai, famous for its gardens, was frequented by high officials of the court. Festivals were held on the shores of the lake each year: on the sixth day of the sixth month, the grooms from the Imperial stables came and washed the horses here (there was a "terrace where the horses were dried" Liang ma tai); on the evening of the fifteenth day of the seventh month, many-coloured lanterns were floated on the water to mingle with the lotus flowers, and the spectators spent the whole night in merry-making. In the winter, children came to slide on the ice.

The neighbouring monasteries made the first rice fields in this low-lying, damp area. In 1467, the Long hua si Temple (on the northern shore of the Hou hai) owned 800 *mou* of rice-fields, and contemporary writings say that homesick travellers from the south would come here to enjoy the scent of the rice flowers. A stele inside the Temple of the Great Transformation (Guang hua si), which stands just east of the Long hua si, says that the temple was built by a monk, who for a long time had amassed savings from the rice given him in alms.

Under the Qing, the princes had houses built round the lakes, and the whole district was popular among the court dignitaries as it was always cool in summer.

The temples are either non-existent or out of use (converted into factories); the lakes are surrounded by modern buildings; the waters are used as fish-ponds (fishing is allowed in a certain spot). A little temple still stands on the mound on the island in the Western Lake; it used to be dedicated to Guan yin, and under the reign of Qian long it was called Hui tong ci (a stele inscribed with the Emperor's calligraphy stands in front of the temple). On the northern slope of the mound stands a meteorite; just below it, a fine stone lion watches over the water coming from the Western Hills.

5. The Drum and Bell Towers

a) The Drum Tower (Gu lou). It stands at the north end of Di an men da jie.

The present building dates from the Ming (1420); the geometrical centre of the Yuan capital, Da du, was near there, and the first tower was built on the central spot in 1272. The tower contained several drums which were beaten to mark the hours, night and day, and a large clepsydra. The building was restored under the Qing; it now houses the cultural centre of the eastern district of Peking.

It consists of a brick base, a first story in red brick, and a double roof of green tiles.

b) The Bell Tower *(Zhong lou)*. It is north of the Drum Tower. Under the Yuan, the main hall of the Temple of Ten Thousand Tranquillities (Wan ning si) stood on its site.

It was built under the reign of the Ming Emperor, Yong le, but was later burned down; the present building dates from the reign of Qian long. The great iron bell which used to hang there has been taken down and put against the northern wall of the Drum Tower. A children's library uses the buildings now.

The architecture of the Bell Tower is not the same as that of the Drum Tower; the base is higher, with less sloping walls, and the bricks are grey.

6. The Former Imperial College (Guo zi jian)

It is in the north-east of the town, south-east of the An ding men Gate, near the former Temple of Confucius.

Under the Yuan, it was a private school. The Ming enlarged the buildings and used them for an official college; the sons of high-ranking families went there to improve their knowledge of the Confucian classics. Qian long had it considerably restored in 1783; he had the thirteen classics engraved on stone tablets, so that this one should be the standard version (80,000 characters altogether); the tablets were put in the central courtyard ("classics engraved on stone" had existed since the Han dynasty see p. 784). The Emperor himself would sometimes come to expound the words of Confucius. The College has been transformed into the Municipal Library (Shou du tu shu guan).

The gate leads into a forecourt; at the far end four steles with inscriptions referring to the building and restoration of the Guo zi jian (one has a plan) stand near the door leading into the inner courtyard, which has a large portico of green and yellow glazed tiles. In the middle of a square pond, once famous for its carp, is a large two-storey square pavilion, built under Qian long; it was here that the Emperor would come to expound the classics. The former Yi lun tang, where the masters gave their lessons (now a reading room) stands at the far end of the courtyard. The side galleries, where the classics used to be exhibited, are now reserves. The tablets have been stored in an annex for the moment, and can no longer be seen.

7. The Former Temple of Confucius (Kong miao or Wen miao)

It is due east of the Guo zi jian.

It was founded under the Yuan, and carefully kept up under the Ming and the Qing. It was used for the worship of Confucius and his disciples. The most important ceremony was held on the twenty-seventh of the eighth month, the anniversary of the sage's birth. Near the great Da cheng men Gate used to stand the "stone drums", now kept in the Imperial Palace (see p. 477); in the courtyard stood 190 steles bearing the names of scholars who had been successful in the examinations held in the capital (since the Yuan); in the central hall (Da cheng dian) was the tablet of the sage, in front of which services were held. The buildings are now occupied by a school of printing and a drama school. It is closed to all visitors.

8. The Lama Temple (Yong he gong)

It is in the north-east of the town, near the Temple of Confucius and the Guo zi jian. It is one of the largest, best-preserved temples in Peking. The Chinese name, Yong he gong, means Palace of Eternal Harmony.

History: The site was originally that of a palace inhabited by the Emperor Kang xi's fourth son, who succeeded his father in 1722, and became Emperor Yong zheng. In accordance with an old tradition, the palace where a prince who later succeeded to the throne had lived had to be converted into a temple. The palace stood empty during the reign of Yong zheng, but under the reign of Qian long (fourth son and successor of Yong zheng), it was transformed. Part of it became a Lamaist monastery, and three hundred Tibetan Lamas settled there, as well as two hundred Chinese and Tartar disciples, "who learned Tibetan or Tangut from them, as well as Buddhism, mathematics, medecine, and rhetoric" (De Lisle, *Description de Pékin*, 1765, p. 25). Sculptors and painters were also attached to the monastery. In another part of the temple, the tablet of Yong zheng was exhibited in a hall set aside for it alone, and an apartment *(xing gong)* was reserved for the use of the Emperor, when he came to pay homage to his father. This part was burned down.

Each day, the Lamas gathered at fixed times to chant sacred texts in Tibetan. On certain occasions, the ceremony was more elaborate. The festival fell on the last day of the first month in the Chinese calendar: an enormous crowd would assemble to watch the "devil dance" (in Chinese: *song gui*, "send the spirits away", or *da gui*, "to beat the spirits"). It was a savage rite, which came from Tibet; in its original form, the performers tore to pieces and chewed a doll made of dough, in human form, a custom which was originally a human sacrifice (the dough contained red liquid to represent blood). The Chinese version was very much watered down, and was little more than a pantomime performed by Lamas dressed as devils. It continued until about 1930, but was then abandoned. Now it is sometimes possible to be present at recitations performed by groups of Lamas, accompanied by very a simple ritual; one of the Lamas pours rice mixed with small coins into a large dish held for him by an assistant; he builds a sort of pile supported by crowns (symbolising the construction of the world). At the end of the 19th century and the beginning of the 20th, the temple was in a very poor state; the buildings were dilapidated and the Lamas had lost much of their old prestige (some of them lived by begging, and tried to get tips from visitors by unveiling for them the famous so-called "obscene" statues, see below). The temple has been restored since the liberation; a small community of Han and Tibetan Lamas still lives there.

Description. A side door leads in through the western wall. It opens into an *inner court* containing two pavilions housing memorial steles, the Bell and Drum Towers, and two pagoda masts. To the south (on the right), a gate gives on to a vast forecourt, which is now an orchard, at the far end of which three large arches can be seen. The main entrance used to be there. Small

YONG HE GONG
(Temple des lamas)
(Lama Temple)

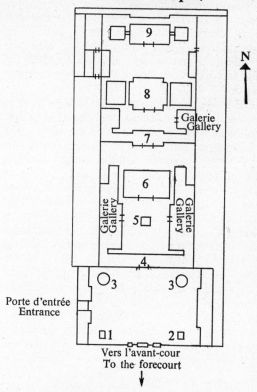

1 Drum tower
2 Bell Tower
3 Stele Pavilion
4 Tian Wang Dian (Hall of the Celestial Guardians)
5 Great Stele Pavilion
6 Yong He Dian (Hall of Eternal Harmony)
7 Yong You Dian (Hall of Eternal Protection)
8 Fa Lun Dian (Hall of the Wheel of the Law)
9 Wan Fu Ge (Pavilion of the 10,000 Blessings)

cells line the forecourt, formerly inhabited by monks or rented to private individuals.

To the north (left) a door leads into the first hall (Tian wang dian); in the centre stands a beaming statue of Maitreya, the Coming Buddha, with two celestial guardians on either side, and behind the screen, facing north, the statue of Wei tuo, the defender of Buddhism.

Behind this lies the *second courtyard*. A pavilion in the centre houses a large square stele, inscribed in four languages, which tells the history of Lamaism (1792). Galleries run along both sides; on the right: very fine equestrian statues, in sombre colours and an excellent collection of tankas (scroll paintings, Lamaistic in inspiration); on the left: countless figures of Tsong Kapa, the founder of a reformed Lamaist sect, in the early 15th century, who can be recognised by his yellow cap; a model symbolising the cosmic order *(mandala)*. At the far end of the courtyard stands the Hall of Eternal Harmony (Yong he dian); in the centre stand three figures of the Buddha (past, present and future); against the side walls, statues of the eighteen *luo han*.

At the end of the *third courtyard* stands the Hall of Eternal Protection (Yong you dian); in the centre, a statue of the Buddha of Longevity; on his left, the Buddha of Medecine.

Behind this lies the *fourth courtyard*. The gallery on the right hand side contains some interesting and characteristic samples of Lamaistic carving: the goddess Lamo riding a mule covered with a human skin (that of her son, whom she has just sacrificed), masculine and feminine deities in a close embrace (several of them have been covered with a yellow veil); the origin of the two large wooden statues of four-footed animals is unknown. At the far end of the courtyard stands the Hall of the Wheel of the Law (Fa lun dian), built on the plan of a Greek cross, with an elaborate roof. A large sitting statue of Tsong Kapa is placed in the centre, under the lantern tower; the tiny statue of the Buddha in front of him is the most venerated of all the Buddhas in the temple; frescoes illustrating the life of Tsong Kapa stretch round the walls; alongside the right hand wall stand bookcases holding long-shaped books, wrapped in silk; behind the screen is a large coloured stucco carving, showing the *luo han*. The monks gather here for study and prayer.

At the far end of the *fifth and last courtyard* stands the Pavilion of Ten Thousand Happinesses (Wan fu ge): it is three stories high, and linked to two side pavilions by hanging galleries; the monumental statue of Maitreya (in his Tibetan form) stands in the middle; it is about seventy-five feet high, and said to be carved out of a single trunk of sandal-wood. All the woodwork in the pavilion used to be covered with paintings, traces of which can still be seen.

North-west of the fifth courtyard there used to stand a hall dedicated to Guan Yin and a little temple dedicated to Guan yu, the god of war. East of the temple was an Imperial library; and to the south-east was a Buddhist temple, the Bai lin si, founded in 1347, and now used as a reserve for a library.

9. The Soviet Embassy

It covers a vast area, in the north-eastern corner of the walls.

Towards the end of the 17th century (the exact date is un known) the Chinese planted a small colony of Orthodox prisoners there, mainly Russians, taken at the siege of Albazin. They were accompanied by a priest, Maxim Leontiev, who converted a small pagoda into a church dedicated to St. Nichol as. The little community grew when the Treaty of Kiachta (1728) allowed the Russians to send a permanent Orthodox mission to Peking. The Archimandrite, his assistants and the student interpreters who accompanied them settled in the south of the inner city (in what later became the "legation quarter", cf p. 531), but they naturally remained in touch with those in the north-eastern corner of the town. The two settlements were known as the Nan guan, "southern residence", and the Bei guan, "northern residence". The Orthodox mission retained some of the characteristics of a diplomatic mission until 1858, when an official embassy was created at Peking. The religious community then handed over the "southern residence" to the newcomers and retired to the "northern residence". The little St. Nicholas Chapel became a large Russian church. In 1900, the whole place was sacked and several hundred Christians were killed, among them many Chinese converts. At the be ginning of the 20th century, the area was considerably enlarged and everything was rebuilt; the monks had their mills, bee hives, and printing-press. After 1949, the church was destroyed and the mission's land was handed over to the Soviet Embassy, which has rebuilt the area on a large scale.

South-west of the Embassy lie a small Buddhist temple (Zhen wu miao) and an Orthodox chapel (built recently).

10. Fu xue hu tong Lane

It runs west from Dong si bei da jie. Under the Yuan, it was a firewood market; under the Ming, a school was founded there, hence the name, Imperial School Lane. It is interesting to notice that even today, the site of the former Imperial school is now a primary and nursery school.

The lane is also famous because the name of Wen Tian xiang, the great patriot, is connected with it. Under the Song, he fought heroically against the Yuan, until he was finally captured by the Mongols in 1278 they imprisoned him here, where he later died. In 1407, under the Ming, a temple was built to his memory on the very spot where he was imprisoned (inside the Imperial School). The temple has now been destroyed, but the two trees which Wen Tian xiang planted, now in the courtyard of the school, are still pointed out to the visitor; in one of the rooms, a set of stone tablets still remain, set into the walls, telling about the hero.

D. THE WESTERN MARKETS AND THE SURROUNDING NEIGHBOURHOOD

The western corner of the northern town used to contain various reserves (of wood, skins, clothes...), centres of handicrafts (bows and saddles were made, hog-bristle was prepared, brocade was made), numerous temples (dedicated to Guan yin, to the Buddha, the God of the Kitchen, to Taoist deities), and market-places (for sheep, horses, sheepskins, jars), which can still be traced in the toponymy. Two main thoroughfares cross the district at the moment: Sheep Street (Yang shi da jie), which continues eastwards as Fu cheng men da jie, and Xi dan da jie Street. The sheep market has disappeared without trace, but the street is still a busy one. To the west, it ends at Fu cheng men Gate (like Xi zhi men, this gate is in good repair); to the east, it ends at Xi dan da jie. A succession of interesting monuments line the north side of the street: from east to west, the house where Lu Xun lived and the museum devoted to his memory, the White Dagoba Temple, the Di wang miao and the Guang ji si, seat of the Peking Buddhist Association.

1. The Lu Xun Museum

A little beyond Fu cheng men, a lane leads off to the left (indicated by a poster with the silhouette of Lu Xun and an arrow)..

The Museum is a large modern building, east of the house where the writer lived from 1924 to 1926. It was opened in 1956, on the twentieth anniversary of his death, and traces the story of his life and his literary career with the help of manuscripts, photographs and personal belongings. In the entrance hall are a large bust of Lu Xun and a quotation from Chairman Mao.

First Section: Childhood and education (Shao xing, Nanking, Japan, 1881–1909). Views of the town of Shao xing where he was born in 1881 (Zhe jiang); portraits of his father, Zhou Po yi and his mother Lu Tuan (Lu Xun, whose real name was Zhou Shu ren, took his mother's surname as the first part of his pen-name); picture *(nian hua)* of a procession of rats (which he liked as a child); reading-book with which he learned to read; illustrated copy of the *Mountain and Sea Classic (Shan hai jing)* which belonged to him; books and exercise-books which he used at the Mining and Railway Engineering School at Nanking (1898–1903); souvenirs of his stay in Japan (he studied medecine from 1903–1909); copies of two novels by Jules Verne which he translated into Chinese *(Autour de la lune* and *Voyage au centre de la terre); copy of Les Misérables;* works of Russian authors (in German); Russian manual; anatomy exercise-books; contemporary literary reviews; Tang statuettes and Ming mirrors which belonged to him.

Second Section: his travels (Hang zhou, Shao xing, Peking, Amoy, Canton, 1909–1927). Herbarium and notes for botany classes which he gave at Hang zhou; rubbings which he used for researches into epigraphs; copy of the *New Youth Magazine (Xin qing nian)*, founded in 1915, where his first short story, *Diary of a Madman* was published; copies of collections of his short stories, *Wanderings* and *Wild Grass,* among others, and of his short story *The True Story of Ah Q.;* illustrations of these works; documents referring to the political struggle waged by the Peking students (Lu Xun joined in when teaching at the Teachers' Training School for Girls); model of his house in Peking (next to the museum), which he found it wiser to leave in 1926; notes for his classes given at Amoy and Canton.

Third Section: stay in Shang hai (1927–1936; see p. 1058, Lu Xun Museum in Shang hai). Model of his house there; documents referring to the League of the Leftist Writers of China (to which he belonged) and his friendship with the Communist writer, Qu Qiu bai; translations of Russian works, with prefaces by Lu Xun; decorative motives which he collected (for use in his

MAISON DE LU XUN
HOUSE OF LU XUN

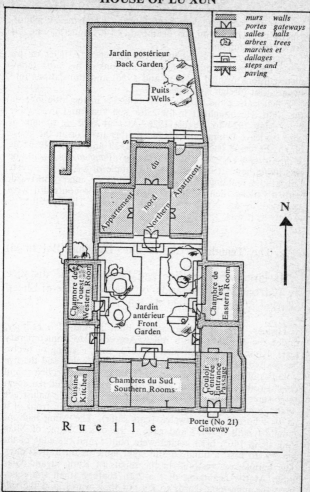

murs — walls
portes — gateways
salles — halls
arbres — trees
marches et dallages — steps and paving

Jardin postérieur
Back Garden

Puits
Wells

N

Appartement du nord
Northern Apartment

Chambre de l'ouest
Western Room

Jardin antérieur
Front Garden

Chambre de l'est
Eastern Room

Cuisine
Kitchen

Chambres du Sud
Southern Rooms

Couloir d'entrée
Entrance Passage

R u e l l e

Porte (No 21)
Gateway

(d'après la revue «Wen Wu»)
(after the magazine "Wen Wu")

books); the complete works of Gorki (in Japanese); photographs of Lu Xun on his deathbed, of his funeral, and his graves (in Shang hai).

Fourth Section: the extent of his influence. Articles on his work; memorial meetings; Chinese editions of his work (complete editions printed in 1938 and 1956) and translations into twenty-four foreign languages.

When leaving the museum, his house is in the little lane on the right. He bought it in 1932 for 800 yuan and lived there from May 1924 to August 1926. At that time he thought it wiser to leave Peking, and his old mother lived on in the house alone; he came back to see her in 1929 and 1932. He wrote *Wild Grass (Ye cao)* and *Wandering (Pang huang)* while he was living here. It is an excellent example of a Chinese private house; the buildings are grouped round an inner courtyard, with a little garden behind. Two trees in the courtyard were "planted by Lu Xun" (replanted in 1956). The furniture is exactly as it was.

2. The Temple of the White Dagoba (Bai ta si)

Its large white outline can be seen some distance away from where it stands, on the north side of Sheep Market Street (Yang shi da jie).

History. The first dagoba was built in the 11th century, under the Liao, to house relics. According to contemporary texts, Khubilai had it opened in 1272, and "a string of twelve beads, two thousand little pagodas of scented clay and the five volumes of the *Book of Formulae* (Dharanipitaka), rolled round crystal rods", were found inside. The Emperor Khubilai spent large sums of money on having it restored; he had a balustrade added, and ordered a Lamaist temple to be built in front of it (it was burned down twelve years later). The Ming had the temple rebuilt in 1457 and gave it the official name of Miao ying si; in 1465, brick niches were built round the edge of the gallery, to hold a hundred and eight lanterns on festival days. The temple was restored in the reigns of Kang xi and Qian long. At the beginning of the 20th century small tradesmen used the inner courtyards to lay out their wares, and the side annexes were rented to private individuals. On the 5th and the 6th of each month, a large fair was held. The tradesmen have disappeared, but the tenants are still there. The dagoba is now being entirely restored.

Description. The visitor is taken through the outer courtyards to the third hall, which contains some interesting sculpture; the doors are very finely carved as well. A little door behind this hall leads into the fourth hall which in turn gives on to the dagoba. The fourth hall contains some good examples of Lamaist sculpture: statues of the three Buddhas and the two disciples (in glass cases, surmounted by canopies); fine collection of *tankas* (paintings of Tibetan inspiration); notice the offerings, also in glass cases, and the ceiling decoration. Two flights of stairs lead up to the gallery of the dagoba; on the second flight is a fine sculpture of a group, carved from painted marble: the wheel of the law (with a characteristically Chinese motive in the middle, the *yin* and *yang* interwoven) between two gazelles (symbol of the Buddha's sermon at Benares). The dagoba is about 90 feet round; the upper part is protected by a horizontal carved copper plaque.

The Chao tian gong was built in 1424 (on the same lines as the Chao tian gong at Nanking) just east of the Bai ta si; it was one of the largest Taoist temples in the town. To the north, it stretched beyond the present Jade Emperor's Lane (Yu huang ge hu tong) and included a vast vegetable garden. To the south, it had a vine, which left its name to a street. In 1626 it was burned down; it was commonly believed that the fire was due to two streets nearby intersecting in the shape of a cross (the character *huo*, "fire", is vaguely like a St. Andrew's cross). This unlucky arrangement of buildings was changed afterwards by putting up new houses in the lanes.

3. The Temple of Universal Rescue (Guang ji si)

It is a little east of the Xi si crossroads, on the dısnorth e of Yang shi da jie (Sheep Market Street).

History. Under the Jin, a temple called Xi liu cun si (the Temple of the Village of the Western Liu) stood on this site. It was enlarged in 1457 (by the Emperor Tian shun, who had just regained his throne after several years' captivity in Mongolia); it was repaired under Kang xi. It used to possess a large library and a statue of the Buddha, 10 feet high, carved out of a trunk of sandalwood. The buildings were badly damaged by fire in 1932. It is now the head office of the Chinese Buddhist Association.

Description. The façade of the temple is striking, as it has four yellow diamond shapes let into it, each one carrying a character. Read from right to left and beginning at the top, the inscription means "the wheel of the Law turns, eternal" *(Fa lun chang zhuan)*. A vast forecourt lies behind the façade, and a little gate in the far corner, to the right, leads into the second courtyard. A large hall stands at the far end of the courtyard, with some very fine sculpture: three statues of the Buddha (past, present and future); statue of the eighteen *luo han* stand round the walls; a handsome bell hangs from the ceiling, on the right, with a wooden clapper in the shape of a fish; on the left hangs a drum; in front of the altar are a *mu yu* (percussion instrument, made of wood, in the shape of a little bell) and a *qing* (copper percussion instrument shaped like a mortar); two fine Ming *chuang* (with little sculpted columns carved out of a single sandalwood trunk, about 11 inches across); behind the screen is an original "finger painting", 30 feet by 19 feet, showing the Buddha expounding the Law, by Chuan Wen (an 18th century painter who specialised in this technique; the Imperial Palace Museum is said to own several more rare examples of his work).

The hall in the third courtyard is devoted to Guan yin.

It contains three most remarkable statues: in the centre, a large gilded statue of Guan yin "with a thousand eyes and a thousand arms" dating from the Qing; on the left, a copper statue of Guan yin, which used to be gilded, dating from the Ming; to the right, a copper statue of Guan yin mounted on a lotus flower (Ming); in front of the central statue, a little modern statue of Guan yin (in a lacquer box), given by the Japanese Buddhist Association in 1960. North of the fourth courtyard stands the last hall, where presents from foreign Buddhist Associations are exhibited (Korea, Vietnam, Mongolia, Nepal, Japan, Burma, Cambodia, Thailand, Indonesia, Ceylon, India). The remains of the once famous library are on the first floor (among other things, three rare volumes of sutras in Tibetan, printed under the Ming).

Further east along Yang shi da jie, on the north side of the street, stands the former **Temple of the Succeeding Generations of Emperors (Li dai di wang miao).**

It was built under the Ming Emperor Jia qing in 1523; the tablets of all dead Emperors were put there, except for tyrants, usurpers and enemies of learning. Judgements varied from one dynasty to the next (Khubilai's tablet was put there, then removed by Jia qing, and put back by the Qing Emperor Kang xi). The temple fell out of use under the Republic; it is now a school, and no visitors are admitted.

4. Xi dan da jie Street and its northern extension, Xi si bei da jie

All the commercial activities which used to be spread over the neighbouring area are now centred in this long street. The four western *pai lou* (arches), *Xi si pai lou*, which used to stand at the crossroads of Xi si da jie and Yang shi da jie and Ma shi da jie had to be removed, as they were too much of a hindrance to traffic. In the north of Xi si da jie, on the east side of the street, a small pagoda can still be seen. It was built to shelter the remains of

Wang Song, who lived at Da du under the Yuan,
and was for three years tutor to Ye lü Chu cai (Ghengis
Khan's adviser).

On both sides of the southern stretch of Xi dan da
jie are shops and bazaars: on the east side, book
shops (scientific works, books in minority languages,
(scientific works, books in minority languages,
secondhand books...), department stores; on the
west side, markets and restaurants...

E. THE EASTERN MARKETS AND THE SURROUNDING NEIGHBOURHOOD

The east of the town used to contain the granaries,
which stretched from inside the Chao yang men
Gate (grain brought from Tong zhou by water was
brought through here) as far north as Dong zhi men
Gate and as far south as Officials' Salaries Rice
Granaries Lane (Lu mi cang hu tong). These granaries
played a vital part in the economy of the town.
They were built in accordance with clearly defined
rules, in order to protect the precious grain from the
attacks of both nature and men. After 1930, they
either fell down or were used for other purposes.

From the Ming dynasty onwards, princes and high court
officials also lived in this area. Several residences can be traced
in the toponymy (Chinese *fu*, residence): Wang fu da jie (Street
of the Princes' Residences), Wang fu jing (Well of the Princes'
Residences); under the Qing, Prince Duan had a palace built
there, known as Wu ye fu (Fifth Prince's Palace); Prince Yi
also lived there (both palaces were a little to the south of Chao
yang men).

It was also important as a commercial centre, like its western
counterpart. The lantern market, the rice, pig, horse and pid-
geon markets were all held here, and streets are still named
after them.

Wang fu jing and its northern extension, Wang fu da jie will
be described first, then Dong si da jie and Chong wen men da

jie and finally Lu mi cang hu tong lane and the Zhi hua si Temple (the "Growth of the Intellect" Temple).

1. Wang fu jing and Wang fu da jie Streets

Wang fu jing, formerly Morrison Street, is a large thoroughfare starting slightly east of the Peking Hotel and running due north from Dong Chang an jie Street as far as Zhu shi da iie (Pig market Street), on a level with the Exhibition Centre of the Chinese Artists' Association; the northern section is called Wang fu da jie.

Under the Ming and the Qing, Wang fu jing was the centre of a district full of princely residences; over ten were built in the Yong le period alone under the Ming. It is said that the street had only one well (where the offices of the *People's Daily*, *Ren min ri bao*, now stand), and this is how it got its name, Wang fu jing: Well of the Princes' Residences. When, at the end of the Qing dynasty, the Legation Quarter was formed and the Eastern Peace Bazaar (Dong an shi chang) built in 1903, on a former military parade ground, Wang fu jing gradually became a busy shopping street.

A convent of Franciscan nuns existed in a street running eastwards in the south of Wang fu jing. They ran a school attended by children of the diplomatic corps, and Mass was celebrated there every Sunday. The convent was closed in 1966.

The **Dong an shi chang Bazaar** lay further north, on the east side of the street; it has now been completely changed and has become a modern department store, known as Dong feng shi chang. It has three entrances, two in Wang fu jing itself, one at its northern end and one at its southern end, and a third in the street to the north, Goldfish Lane (Jin yu hu tong).

The Eastern Church (Dong tang). It is on the east side of Wang fu jing, just south of Chun shu hu tong (Ailanthus Tree Lane), at the far end of a vast courtyard.

The church stands on the site which Father Adam Schall's house once occupied. He died there on August 15th, 1666. His disciple and successor, Father Verbiest, took it over for the Portuguese Jesuits; part of the house was converted into a church (known as St. Joseph's). Little is known about the first church, except that it was small, built in ionic style, and very beautiful (the most beautiful in Peking). After the suppression of the Jesuits, the Portuguese Lazarists took over the church. In 1811, the library was burned down, and Jia qing seized the opportunity to expell the missionaries (who had to take refuge in the Nan tang) and destroy what was left of the buildings. The Chinese gave the land back to the Lazarists in 1860 and between 1880 and 1896, the second Dong tang was built (it was 228 feet long, and had 16 red sandstone pillars with gilded capitals, and an altar in Naples marble, with cloisonné enamel decorations). This in turn was destroyed by the Boxers in 1900, and the present building dates from the beginning of this century.

A little further north along Wang fu jing, Deng shi kou da jie leads off to the right. Its name means "Lantern Market Street".

Under the Ming and the Qing, both sides of the street were lined with little shops selling lanterns; the street was at its busiest at the time of the lantern festival, which lasted from the 13th to the 18th of the first lunar month. Crowds would gather here to admire the lanterns, which were extremely varied in shape and decoration.

On the left, on a level with Deng shi kou da jie, Nai zi fu Lane (Nurses' Office) runs off to the west.

Under the Ming, in the second, fourth, eighth and eleventh lunar months, the court used to send out an appeal for wet-nurses to suckle the palace babies. Several conditions were required (applicants had to be over fifteen and under twenty). Twenty women were chosen each time: ten with boy babies and ten with girls, and they were lodged here; from that moment, on, they no longer brought up their own babies. When a prince was born, he was given to a woman who had just given birth to a girl, and a princess was given to one who had just had a son.

Further north, to the east, is the Eastern Factory Lane (Dong chang hu tong).

The headquarters of the secret police organised by the Ming, known as the Dong chang, was in this lane.

The next street is Pig Market Street (Zhu shi da jie). South of it, on the east side of Wang fu da jie, stands the Hotel for Overseas Chinese, a large white building.

Slightly west of the crossroads of Wang fu da jie and Zhu shi da jie, on the north side of the latter street, is the **Exhibition Centre of the Chinese Artists' Association** (**Mei shu zhan lan guan**). It is a fine modern building, with a roof of yellow glazed tiles. It has no permanent exhibition, but temporary ones are often held there (ancient and modern art, Chinese and foreign, photographs, *nian hua*).

A little lane going westwards from Wang fu da jie (just north of the Exhibition Centre) leads to Big Buddha Temple Lane (Da fo si hu tong), where there is a bookshop which specialises in works on Buddhism.

2. Dong si da jie and Chong wen men da jie Streets.

Like Xi si da jie, Dong si da jie (Street of the Four Eastern arches) has lost its four beautiful arches of painted wood. It is still the centre of a busy shopping district.

The People's Market (Ren min shi chang) and the Temple of Prosperity and Happiness (Long fu si). They are in Long fu si hu tong, which runs west

out of Dong si da jie, just north of the Pig Market
Street. The lane itself is a busy one, full of little
shops (secondhand bookshops, artificial flower sellers,
little restaurants, cinemas, marionette theatres...).

The market is in what was the compound of the old Long fu
si. The temple was founded in about 1450, by the Ming Emperor
Dai zong. It had five courtyards and five halls. Each one was
surrounded by balustrades brought from a palace in the south
of the town. It was put in the charge of some Lamas, who
collected a number of statues which were considered unorthodox;
the minister of rites, when he discovered this, reported it to the
Emperor and dissuaded him from inaugurating the temple.
Soon afterwards, a Moslem from the west burst into the temple
one day and killed several of the monks; when he was asked
why he had done it, he replied that some of the statues resembled
his own people, and he wanted to avenge such a sacrilege.

From the reign of Yong zheng onwards, (1723–1736) a large
fair was held in the temple courtyards on the 9th and 10th, the
19th and 20th, and the 29th and 30th of each month. The temple
was partly burned down in 1901, and by 1913 no monks were
left. After the liberation, the huge buildings of the People's
Market were built on the site.

Behind the market halls, full of extremely varied
goods, lies one of old courtyards, where parts of
the old temple still stand, among them a large hall
with a coffered ceiling. The old People's Market (Ren
min shi chang) no longer exists, though a large shop
is still to be found there.

A short way south along Dong si da jie, beyond
Pig Market Street, a narrow lane leads off to the
west to the Bows and Arrows Courtyard (Gong jian
da yuan). Over fifty families lived there under the
last dynasty, all craftsmen specialised in the making
of bows and arrows, to meet the demands of the
soldiers who came to town to sit their examinations.
Only a few years ago several old craftsmen still
lived there.

The Dong si Mosque. It is on the same side of the street as Gong jian da yuan, to the south.

It was founded under the Ming, and has several times been badly damaged. Most of the present buildings are modern. Three cupolas still survive at the far end of the prayer hall, but the mihrab has disappeared; remains of old carvings can be seen in some of the arcades. A porch leads into the hall: beneath it, on the right, can still be seen the metal ball which used to top the minaret, an inscription dating from the Wan li period (1573–1620) in praise of Islam, and an incense-burner dating from 1518, inscribed in Arabic and Chinese. The library still contains manuscripts of the Koran dating from the Ming and the Qing.

On the east side of the street, on a level with Deng shi kou da jie stands a little miniature temple of grey brick; it is a temple which was dedicated to Er lang, usually called the Dog Temple.

In Taoist mythology Er lang is the son of Li Bing, a master of irrigation work. His dog was almost more famous than Er lang himself, and a clay effigy of him stood in the temple. He was thought to have remarkable healing powers. The temple is unused now and the entry has been walled up.

Still further south, the Foreign Ministry Street leads off to the east (Wai jiao bu jie).

The first Zong li ya men was created here in 1860; it became the Wai wu bu in 1900, and then the Wai jiao bu in 1911. In 1860, the Tong wen guan (College of Universal Education) was founded behind the Zong li ya men; interpreters for the ministry were trained there.

3. The Officials' Salaries Rice Granaries Lane (Lu mi cang hu tong)

It runs eastwards from Chong wen men da jie, and is the extension of Qian mian hu tong.

Between 1644 and 1654, granaries were built here to store the rice which the officials received in payment. They were enlarged in 1683, and the total number was 81. Some of the buildings to the north of the street still survive today.

The "Growth of the Intellect" Temple (Zhi hua si). It stands at the eastern end of Lu mi cang hu tong, on the north side.

Wang zhen the eunuch had it built in 1443; a statue of him and a stele praising him used to stand in the temple, but they were removed in 1742, under the Qing. The temple is now used by a service in charge of restoring historical monuments.

The temple, with its dark blue tiles, is one of the most beautiful in the town; it contains four halls. The third one, the Ten Thousand Buddha Pavilion (Wan fo ge) is a magnificent example of Ming architecture. It is a two-storey building with wooden galleries round the outside. Its fine coffered ceiling has been taken down and is now in the United States. All that now remains is the decoration on the partition walls. Some valuable manuscripts of religious music were found here, which only a few monks still knew how to interpret.

F. CHANG AN JIE AVENUE AND THE SOUTHERN DISTRICTS

1. Chang an jie Avenue

This spacious, new avenue cuts straight through the whole of the northern town, from east to west. It was formerly no more than two short sections, one on either side of Tian an men Square. After the liberation, it was decided to lengthen it on either side as far as the ramparts, and then beyond them. Several sacrifices had to be made to the plan: the Two Pagoda Temple had to be pulled down, to the west. Many of the new buildings which have been put up since 1949 stand along the avenue. The description will begin with the eastern end.

At this end, the avenue entered the town through the Gate of the Construction of the Country (Jian guo men), which was nothing more than a break in the walls, as it was cut recently and never had a tower to protect it; the massive Observatory stands due south of this point; north of the avenue, flanking it for a short way, is the former site of the old Examination Hall.

The Old Observatory (Guan xiang tai). It stands at the south-eastern corner of the walls of the Yuan capital, Da du (Chang an jie follows the site of the walls of the Yuan town).

When they had taken Bian zhou (Kai feng), the Jin took several astronomical instruments which they had found in the Northern Song capital north with them to Peking (Zhong du, as it was then called). Under the Yuan, Khubilai commissioned two astronomers, Wang Xun and Guo Shou jing to set up a new observatory in the south-eastern corner of his capital, to reform the calendar, which was faulty. The two scholars had new instruments cast, among them a sundial *(gui biao)* and an armillary sphere *(hun yi)*. Later on, Moslems were put in charge of the observatory. The arrival of the European missionaries, Fathers Matteo Ricci, Adam Schall, Ferdinand Verbiest, in the 17th century, caused a minor revolution. When their forecasts had proved exact on several occasions, they were put in charge of the Observatory, replacing the Chinese astronomers (for an account of part of the controversy, see the memoirs of Father Adam Schall, *Relation Historique*, Tientsin, 1942). In 1674, the Emperor Kang xi commissioned Father Verbiest to build a set of instruments, which were put on the observatory terrace. Missionaries were still in charge of the Board of Astronomy at the beginning of the 19th century (the last one was Mgr. Pires, who died in 1838). After the intervention of the Allied Powers in 1900, Germany had some of the instruments removed to Potsdam, but gave them back in 1919. The instruments built by Guo Shou jing (or rather, copies of them built under the Ming), were moved to the Nanking Observatory in 1933 (see p. 997). The observatory now looks like an enormous cube of masonry; the superstructure disappeared a long time ago. The instruments made by the missionaries are kept on the terrace.

The Site of the Examination Hall (Gong yuan)

The hall was built under the Ming Emperor Yong le, on the site of the Yuan Ministry of Rites. Every three years, in the third month of the lunar calendar, the great national examinations were held there. Several hundred "graduates" *(ju ren)* gathered in the capital from all over the empire to take part in them in the hopes of winning the title of "doctor" *(Jin shi)*. The enclosure round the hall contained about 8,500 small narrow cells, 10 feet high. When he arrived, each candidate had to change into special clothes (to avoid all possibilities of hiding papers in his own), and find the cell which had been assigned to him; each cell bore a different character, with which the candidates marked their papers. The doors were carefully sealed, and on no pretext whatsoever were they opened before the end. The test lasted three days and two nights. The passages between the cells were constantly patrolled to make sure that nothing was handed in to the candidates. These examinations were no longer held after 1900; the buildings began to fall down, and were finally destroyed completely in 1913. Carp Street (Li yu hu tong) was near the examination hall; it was called after the carp (symbol of success), which served as a sign for a travel agency where candidates who had come from southern provinces by boat used to buy their tickets home.

West of this site stands a modern building housing several research centres grouped under the Academy of Science (philosophy, history, literature); then comes the Dong dan crossroads. The glacis which protected the Legation Quarter used to begin south of this point. Several theatres and cinemas line the avenue on its north side, and the next crossroads is that of Wang fu jing and Chang an jie.

West of Wang fu jing, still on the north side of the avenue, stands the Peking Hotel (Bei jing fan dian), once under French direction; official guests and diplomats stay there now. To the south lies the Ministry of Fuel. The Imperial City began immediately west of the Peking Hotel. The southern wall still exists today; the yellow roofs of the Tang zi can be seen above it at the corner (see p. 496). Next comes Tian an men Square; on the north side, gates lead into the Cultural Palace, the Imperial Palace and the Sun Yat sen Park; to the south, the square is flanked by the massive Museum Building and the National People's Congress Building.

Beyond the square, the next gate to the north leads into the enclosure surrounding the Central and Southern Lakes; the palaces round them are now used by the State Council. In the 18th century, the Moslem camp, Hui hui ying, built by Emperor Qian long for his Moslem soldiers, used to lie to the south.

It consisted of 147 little rooms, built round a square; the officers lodged in a tower in the middle, called Xi yang lou (Pavilion of the Western Ocean), an allusion to the western origins of Islam. The tower was slightly foreign in style; four bronze tortoises stood on top of it, each pointing to one of the points of the compass. It is said the beautiful and unhappy Xiang fei used often to gaze at the tower from the windows of her apartments near the Southern Lake; it reminded her of her native country (she came from Aksu). The tower, which was sometimes mistaken for a mosque, was destroyed in 1914, as Yuan Shi kai no doubt feared an attempt on his life (a magnificent view was to be had over the Palace from the top of the tower).

The site of the Two Pagoda Temple (Shuang ta si) was a little further west; it was founded under the Jin, restored several times, and then knocked down to give way to Chang an jie Avenue. The Xi dan crossroads beyond is one of the busiest (theatre, cinemas, shops); west of it stands the Minorities' Cultural Palace.

The Minorities' Cultural Palace (Min zu wen hua gong). Founded in 1959, the building consists of a central tower, 13 stories (195 feet) high, and two side wings; a lift goes up to the top of the tower, from which there is a good view over the town. The façades are faced with white glazed bricks, and the roofs are of turquoise blue glazed tiles. It is said to cover an area of 9,567 square feet.

The Palace consists of four sections: 1) cultural centre; 2) theatre, in the east wing; 3) library of over 600,000 books (rich collection of books written in the languages of the Minorities: Mongol, Tibetan, Uighur, Kazak, Zhuang, Manchu, Korean, Miao, Bu yi, Jing po, Tai, Wa, La gu, Li su, Ha ni, Tong, etc...); 4) museum, with eighteen exhibition halls.

The museum falls into two sections: the first, general, section gives an overall picture of the difficulties presented by the Minorities, their liberation and rise to autonomy, and the second, much larger, section illustrates the regions where Minorities live; in some cases, they are so numerous that autonomous regions have been created (for instance the Uighurs in Xin jiang, the Tibetans in Tibet, the Hui in Ning xia, the Mongols in Inner Mongolia, the Zhuang in Guang xi); in other cases, when they are fewer, several are grouped under the same administrative unit.

Each geographical region illustrated is presented in exactly the same way, to give the impression that all the Minorities have evolved in the same way, and are moving on towards the same aim. A large map of the region is shown first, showing areas inhabited by the Minorities and autonomous regions. Statistics are given alongside the map (based on the 1957 census). Next follow documents concerning the liberation (photographs of the first public meetings and the first votes, texts of official statements, the red flag); sometimes details about the history of the Minorities are given, with heavy insistence on the opposition between the privileged and the proletariat (cases exhibiting the gaudy clothes of one group and the rags worn by the other; contracts for the sale of land and children; instruments of torture; measures used for levying loans); then follow the economic achievements accomplished since 1949; distribution of land, nationalisation of production, creation of industry (samples of ore, cultivated plants, precious wood, stock animals, models of dams and irrigation works, agricultural machinery or machinery parts produced in the region); and finally the cultural achievements (school exercise-books, works published in the Minorities' languages, studies in Chinese on the culture of the Minorities); sometimes the local pharmacopeia and handicrafts are also shown.

The large entrance hall leads into the *great presentation hall*. A big picture depicts the 54 Minorities of China, each symbolised by a man or a woman in national dress, standing round Chairman Mao. A large map of China on the left shows where they all come from.

To the left of the entrance hall: *Tibet and Guang xi*. a) *Tibet:* main resources (furs, deer antlers used in pharmacopeia); history: marriage (under the Tang dynasty) between a Chinese princess and a Tibetan king (Chinese musical instruments introduced at that time); good relations between China and Tibet under the Qing; Tibetan resistance to the English (weapons and shields); the new Tibet (creation of industry); instruments of torture formerly used by the privileged (skins of their victims); western arms used by reactionaries. b) *Guang xi* (principal Minority: the Zhuang): model of a school for cadres built at Nan ning; text of the agricultural reform; model of a people's commune in karst country (each field is at the bottom of a sink-hole); samples of the main products: maize, rice, sugar-cane, pine-apples, citrus fruits, silk-worms (fed on leaves from a special tree, the *mu shu*), oily aniseed, precious wood; water-buffalo-rearing; model of the Xi jin hydro-electric power station on the Yu jiang; gold and aluminium ore; crafts: silver jewellery, embroidered fabrics (geometric pattern); local pharmacopeia; bronze drum (in the corner); books in Zhuang and Chinese; musical instruments.

Right of the entrance hall, Inner Mongolia and the north-eastern provinces. a) *Inner Mongolia:* founding of the Mongolian Communist party in 1924; creation of the Inner Mongolian Autonomous Region in 1947; agricultural reform; resources (furs, stock-breeding, forests); shearing-machines and creamers. b) *Province of Hei long jiang:* skins; fauna (tiger, sturgeon); samples of coal, copper and iron ore; ginseng roots. c) *Province of Ji lin:* (Korean Minority). d) *Province of Liao ning:* open-cast coal mining.

First floor, to the left, Si chuan, Yun nan, Gan su and Qing hai. a) *Si chuan* (Yi and Tibetan Minorities): red flag with Yi,

Tibetan and Chinese characters on it; resources: coal, asbestos, mica, gold, furs, deer antlers. musk; model of the modern buildings of the administrative centre of the autonomous Yi district of Liang shan; wool-producing sheep reared in the west of the province; creamer; forestry. b) *Yun nan:* large map showing the distribution of the 22 Minorities, the eight autonomous zones and the fifteen autonomous districts (gradually created between 1953 and 1964; the first autonomous zone was that of the Tai Sip song pan na); small Mongolian community near Tong hai, dating from the 13th century; model of the Kun ming Minorities Institute; improvement in roads; former Tai society: local code written in Tai; model of lands owned by a local chief, with specialised villages; his riches (his wife's ornaments, silver table ware); texts of agricultural reforms; economic development: tea, textiles (embroidered ribbons and printed fabrics with Minorities' designs); interesting section on superstitions (sacrifice of a hen to cure a sick person, practised by the Jing po, sacrifice of a water-buffalo in front of carved poles, practised by the Wa; skulls of human sacrifices stored away by the Wa; contract in two parts, with notches, used by the Wa; numerous publications in Minority languages. d) *Gan su:* notice the large percentage of Han inhabitants along the "corridor" where the road and railway run; model of irrigation works. e) *Qing hai:* large goose from the Tsaidam region; use of horse-hair.

To the right, *Xin jiang* and *Ning xia.*

Exhibition halls fill four stories of the tower. On the third floor: special questions; the place of the Minorities in urban life; on the fourth floor: Hu nan; on the fifth floor: Guang dong and He bei; on the sixth floor: *Gui zhou:* rock crystal, natural sulphur, coal, copper, lead and iron ore; a Miao family before and after liberation; copies of the *Gui zhou Newspaper;* cereals (hemp, millet, wheat, floating rice); forestry; development of road communications; problem of salt (formerly exchanged against cereals); a tiger skin (a few still remain in the reserves); regional pharmocopeia; some Miao, Bu yi and Dong dictionaries; beautiful example of a Bu yi batik (wax printing on fabric). The Minorities' Hotel stands next to the Minorities' Cultural Palace, to the west. Chang an jie Avenue continues westwards towards the Renaissance Gate (Fu xing men, which is a recent breach in the walls, like Jian guo men); there are no more buildings of interest.

2. The South Western Districts

This area has changed considerably over the years. Under the empire it was relatively calm. The palace of the first Prince Chun (the last Emperor's grandfather) stood in the south-west corner of the walls. Behind the palace was a little altar, highly revered by the people of the district, dedicated to the god of the town; to the north-east, opposite the Southern Lake, was a Moslem quarter (see above, p. 554); to the south, beside the walls, stood the Southern Cathedral (Nan tang) and the Imperial Elephant Stables (Xiang fang).

Great changes were made under the Republic; several organisations were created there, which bore witness to the modernisation of China: banks, institutes of higher education (the Teachers' Training School for Girls, and the College of Law and Political Studies). From 1912 onwards, the new Chinese parliament sat there. It became, in short, the counterpart of the Legation Quarter on the other side of Qian men. Even now, several banks and insurance offices in Xi jiao min xiang still occupy buildings in the style of European buildings of the 20's. Few of them are really worth a visit in the strict sense of the word, but the quiet streets are full of historical memories.

a) The Southern Cathedral (Nan tang)

It stands near the walls, next to Xuan wu men Gate (the tower of which has now disappeared); its façade (large pediment with a crucifix above it) makes it easy to recognise. On sunny days, chess players often gather in front of the walls.

History. In the 17th century, the house where Father Matteo Ricci lived and died stood here. After his death in 1610, the German Jesuit, Father Adam Schall, took over the place; and it was here that he lived through the uneasy times at the end of the Ming dynasty, when Li Zi cheng's armies occupied Peking, and the Manchu finally entered the town (see the account of all this in his *Relation Historique*, Tientsin, 1942). He defended his house from being sacked and burned, and then, when he had won the confidence of the new Emperor through his knowledge of astronomy, he obtained his permission to build a church in 1650. It was the first one to be built in Peking, after the disappearance of the Archbishopric of Khanbaliq, created under the Mongols. At first the church was called Tian zhu tang, Temple of the Lord of the Heavens; later on it was known as the Southern Cathedral, to distinguish it from the others. The Emperors gave 10,000 taels to have it built. It had a high altar and two others; the side walls were decorated with religious texts written in Chinese; next to the sanctuary was a little chapel dedicated to the Virgin, where the women met (two more centuries were to pass before men and women would meet in the same church).

The church was built in 1703 and for three quarters of a century, its annexes were used by the Portuguese Jesuit college. In 1775, the buildings were burned down; the Emperor Qian long granted the money needed to rebuild them, but the suppression of the Jesuit order then under way had impaired its authority. When Jia qing passed his measures against the Church at the beginning of the 19th century, the Southern Cathedral sheltered the Portuguese Lazarists for a time, after their expulsion from the Eastern Cathedral (see p. 515). The last missionary, Mgr. Pires, who was tolerated because of his invaluable services to the observatory, died there alone in 1838. After that, no European Roman Catholic priests were left in Peking. The Archimandrite of the Russian mission took it upon himself to look after the excellent library and to safeguard the church from demolition. In 1861, everything was given back to the French Lazarists (Mgr. Mouly), who had restored the church by 1862; it was then dedicated to the Immaculate Conception (the dogma of the Immaculate Conception had just been introduced by Pope Pious IX). The church was destroyed in 1900, at the same time as the Western and Eastern Churches. The present building dates from early in the century (the fourth Nan tang).

The church is now used by national Catholics, who have rallied to the new régime and are almost entirely independent of Rome. Mass is celebrated every Sunday (passages in Chinese alternate with passages in Latin); there is no sermon. The interior is lacking in interest (panels of false marble); the crucifix in the choir has been replaced by an inscription in Chinese.

b) *The Former Imperial Elephant Stables (Xiang fang)*

They were near the Southern Cathedral, next to the Xuan wu men Gate.

They were built in 1495, as several elephants had been sent as presents from Annam and Burma; the animals were used in ceremonious parades, and pulled the Emperor's chariot when he went to sacrifice at the Temple of Heaven. They were badly treated, however; by 1860, they had all died, and the stables stood empty. In 1873, Annam sent two presents of six elephants; their keepers would admit people to see them, for a consideration, and on the sixth day of the sixth month, they were washed with great ceremony in the moat of the ramparts, attracting large crowds of spectators. In 1884, one of them went beserk and seriously injured a passer-by; it was decided not to use them any more for Imperial ceremonies, and they were not replaced. In 1897, Mgr. Favier saw the chariot which they used to draw still standing in the empty stables. Nothing is left of the buildings now.

c) *The Former Chamber of Parliament*

The hall where the first Chinese Parliament sat from 1912 to 1924 was near the Elephant Stables. It met for the first time on May 13th 1912.

The French sinologue Fernand Farjenel was present on that memorable occasion, and has left an account of it *(A travers la révolution chinoise*, Paris, Plon, 1914, p. 197 sqq.):
"It takes place in the morning. We therefore leave our lane (in the east of the town) early, and amid clouds of dust, we start out along the red walls of the Imperial City to witness the beginning of the Chinese parliamentary régime. We have to skirt the whole of the southern part of the Palace and the red town by a series of short cuts through twisting streets which bring us to the central Gate, Qian men (Chang an jie had not then been cut through); it is a long detour, as the Assembly meets in the west, in the Law School... The building where the Assembly is sitting has an imposing door opening on to the dusty street which follows the line of the city walls; as we reach our goal, we come upon a string of camels from Mongolia, linked together by a rope...

"A few foreign cars, some guards: we are in front of the Assembly. We show our invitation cards, which are carefully examined and we are shown into the passages of this House of Parliament, where places are reserved for the public and the press. The chamber is rectangular, with the Speaker's chair at the far end, decorated with two Republican flags against the white wall; little tables are arranged in a half-moon for the 126 members. The public galleries line three sides of the room; the balustrades are very plain, painted grey, as velvet, gilt and carvings have no place here, where the representatives of the people meet. The public attendance is large; the galleries, provided with chairs, are full. We notice a big group of suffragettes; one, a stout woman wearing gold-rimmed spectacles... only half a dozen foreigners. Nearly all the members are in their places in the chamber, leaning on their tables or wielding the brush.

"The Speaker... declares the session open; he wields the bell like M. Deschanel himself. It is just like a western session. If the members were not almost all wearing silk robes, one could think oneself in some congress meeting in Europe. Only one or two wear pigtails; they are Mongol princes. Now the Cabinet ministers make their entry, amid polite applause from members; they take their places, sitting with their backs to the far wall, on either side of the Speaker's chair, facing the chamber. Unlike the members, the ministers wear European frock-coats, except for the ministers of war and of the navy, who are in uniform... The prime minister goes up to the rostrum, which like ours, is placed in front of the Speaker's chair, and sets out his programme... Once the applause at the end of this speech is over, each minister in turn comes to set out his ministry's programme... It is long past lunch-time and this first meeting of the government and the provisional Chamber ends at two o'clock".

From 1935 onwards, the buildings were taken over by a school.

3. The South Eastern Districts

Chong wen men Street, which ends at Chong wen men Gate (formerly known as Ha Ta men Gate, because a Mongol prince, Ha Ta had a palace in the area), divides the south-eastern district into two rectangular parts, roughly equal in size. To the west is the former Legation Quarter, and to the east, the district round the new railway station.

a) The Former Legation Quarter

East of Tian an men Square, bordered by Dong chang an jie to the north, Chong wen men jie Street (which ends at Hata men) to the east and by the ancient Tartar city wall to the south, lies a large area of a style contrasting sharply with the rest of the town. It was once the Legation Quarter, where the diplomatic missions, the services dependent on them, and the foreign troops who guarded them, were concentrated until 1949. It has nothing Chinese about it. The European houses combine all the styles in fashion at the beginning of the 20th century: mock gothic, mock baroque, mock Empire, modern style, with all the bad taste of the European nations and America put together. Even the two large buildings which have appeared since the Revolution,—the central office of the Communist Party and the Xin Qiao Hotel—are redolent of Soviet architecture during the Stalin era. In spite of the medley, the shady streets and large gardens hidden behind the walls make it a delightful district to take a stroll in or to live in.

History: The district south-east of Tian an men seems to have sheltered foreigners for several centuries. The Russians were the first to come; according to Chinese historians, they—Slavs and Sarmatians—have been here since the 14th century. The terms of Treaty of Kiachta (1728) granted the Russians permission to send a permanent ecclesiastic mission, commercial missions and six students. A small colony was founded near the former Russian Embassy, at the corner of the Jade Canal and Legation Street. The English and the French, who were the first, after them, to open diplomatic relations with the Middle Kingdom, in about 1860, settled nearby, and then other powers came to join them. It is easy to see why the armies of the *Society of Patriotic Fists* (known, absurdly, as the Boxers), an organisation of nationalists and zenophobes supported on the side by the Empress Ci xi (Tz'u Hsi), attacked the Legation Quarter in 1900.

After the events in which nearly all the buildings were destroyed, the eight powers who had occupied Peking (Britain, the U.S.A., Japan, Russia, Germany, France, Austria-Hungary, Italy) claimed exterritorial rights for the whole quarter, and after the Protocol of September 7th 1901, it became a sort of international concession. The Legation Quarter "Administrative Committee" was completely independent of the City of Peking. China lost all sovereignty over the area. No Chinese had the right to live or even to own a house there. Chinese soldiers and the Peking police were forbidden to enter. Each evening, the foreigners would gather there, with a strict minimum of Chinese servants, protected by high walls and an international guard of about 1,400 soldiers. A glacis stretched alongside Chang an jie, used by the troops for exercise each morning, which enabled the surrounding neighbourhood to be covered by gunfire in case of insurrections. This status lasted until 1949, even after the seat of the Chinese government, and consequently the embassies also, had been transferred to Nanking.

The Chinese authorities have now reclaimed the whole area. The fortifications have been demolished, the glacis has been transformed into a pleasant public garden, and in the heart of the area, Tai ji chang Street, a large brick and cement building has been put up to house the central committee of the Communist Party. The Embassies of countries who did not recognise the new Chinese government in 1949 have been taken over by government services: the former French, British, American, Italian, Japanese Embassies... Some have remained as they were: Rumania, Burma, East Germany, India, all of them in Dong jiao min xiang Street, (formerly Legation Street), and especially the magnificent former Austro-Hungarian Embassy, which fell to Hungary in 1919 (Austria was granted the one at Berne, which is identical), and which the Hungarian Republic still holds, standing in old gardens, in Tai ji chang er tiao.

Description: The former Legation Quarter has a wide main street, running from east to west, from the Xin qiao Hotel to Qian men, parallel with the city walls, at the foot of which runs another dusty, deserted street. "Legation Street", now Dong jiao min xiang, begins almost at Ha ta men Gate, where the Xin qiao Hotel has replaced the former German barracks. A modern hospital has replaced the German hospital which used to stand opposite. Further on, on the right, stands the former Rumanian Embassy, opposite the former Belgian Legation, later the Burmese Embassy. The two gothic towers of Saint Michael's Church mark the corner of Taj ji chang Street.

It was founded in 1902 by the Lazarists, and has a magnificent organ which has not been touched since 1949.

At the other corner of Tai ji chang, is the large compound of the former French Embassy. The high red gate with its two stone lions gives on to Legation Street, and several pleasant buildings with balconies can still be seen; today they are used by official guests of the government or the Party. Westwards along Legation Street, the next building was the former French post office, the hôtel Chamot, which played an important rôle in the fighting in 1900; then came the former Spanish Embassy, which was taken over by a bank, and is now the Service Bureau, which exists to meet the needs of the Diplomatic Corps at Peking. On the left stands the former German Embassy, which East Germany has taken over, just as it was; the former Wagon-lits Hotel stands on the corner, going back as far as the walls. For a long time this was the largest hotel in Peking, and several novels have immortalised its famous dance floor and reception rooms, where the writer Blaise Cendrars worked in about 1905.

The avenue crossing Legation Street used to be a canal, known as the "Jade Canal", although it was little more than an open sewer. It ended at an opening in the walls, known as the Water gate. In 1925 it was filled in, and a garden laid out in its stead.

Beyond the avenue, the Russian Embassy, later to become the Soviet Embassy, had a large compound on the right, bordered to the north by the British Embassy, which stretched as far as the glacis. The French hospital—Saint Michael's Hospital—was the last building on the right. On the left, several buildings with imposing columns surmounted by corinthian capitals housed foreign banks: the Bank of China has taken over one of them; another is now headquarters of the organisation for Public Safety. Next comes the former Dutch Embassy, a delightful place with a tennis court and swimming-pool, and a replica of a little Dutch castle. The American Embassy and barracks were next to it. The High Courts of Justice stand in the road which is opposite them.

The foreign tourist, who, for better or for worse, wants to search this quarter for traces of where his forbears lived, can still find, in the Avenue of the former Jade Canal, the old Japanese Embassy, on the right hand side; and the impressive gate of the former Italian Embassy, the last on the left in Tai ji chang. Opposite it the International Club still stands, unchanged, with its tennis courts, swimming-pool and its restaurant, offering shelter to foreigners looking for innocent distractions. The Hungarian Embassy is east of it, and the former Voyron Barracks were to the south; they used to house a detachment of the French colonial infantry. The barracks gate opened on to rue Labrousse, now San tiao Street, which was once almost entirely French, with its Centre of Chinese Studies and the Institute of Geo-biology founded by Father Teilhard de Chardin.

The former "Legation Quarter" holds little meaning now for anyone except for tourists stirred by old memories. As far as the Chinese are concerned, this somewhat inelegant mixture of so many Western styles, a symbol of foreign sovereignty in the very heart of their capital, is destined to disappear before long. Even so, its out-of-date residences, its slightly neglected gardens and its streets lined with pink mimosas still cannot fail to charm the nostalgic visitor. The last surviving embassies had all been moved to new buildings in the new legation quarter by 1972.

b) The Neighbourhood round the New Station

Before the liberation, a labyrinth of tiny streets covered the south-east corner of the northern town, with names which reflected the old trades plied here: Hemp and Cotton Lane, Big and Small Wool Lane, the Smiths' District, Bean-curd Lane, Pipe Lane, Shield Workshop. Now that the Central Station has been moved to this area (it used to be near Qian men, in the southern town) the whole district has changed. Two large ways have been opened out among the old houses. The first goes from east to west, to enable the railway line to cut through the walls and run into the station itself. The second runs south from the main road, and ends in an enormous square in front of the station, used as a car-park and bus terminus (the buses no. 10 and 20 and the trolley-buses no. 8 and 11 all start and end here). The new station has an area of 262,467 square feet (8 times that of the old) and can handle 200,000 passengers a day, so it is said. It was built in the space of ten months; the plan was drawn up by students of the Qing hua Technical University.

A few streets east of the station have remained untouched by the change, and apart from a few modern buildings, such as the new Ministry of Agriculture, they are as they were. A walk in this

peaceful area might well end with a visit to the Xu
Bei hong Museum, at number 16, Dong shou lu street.
(Demolished in 1967.)

II.   The southern town

The walls of the southern town dated from the middle
of the 16th century. Their circumference was about
9 miles and they were pierced by ten gates, three
of which opened into the northern town. Only part
of the town was built on; large areas were covered
by parks, lakes, fields, or were simply waste ground.

In 1765, a French writer described the northern district, which
was the busiest: "Large hotels accommodate the Chinese who
come to Peking from the southern provinces. There is a fine
workshop making porcelain, and a flourishing trade in gold
cloth, jewellery, varnished furniture, tea, precious fabrics, ginseng... It is also the Chinese town which has the most book-
sho" (De Lisle, *Description de la ville de Péking*, 1765, p. 28).
Some of the names of the streets show where the market-places
used to be: Flower market (Hua shi), Vegetable Market (Cai
shi), Garlic market (Suan shi), Rice market (Mi shi), Horse and
Mule market (Luo ma shi), Meat market (Rou shi), Jewel
market (Zhu bao shi), Pearl market (Zhu shi)...

The walls have now disappeared almost completely;
one of the gates to the north has been left standing
(Qian men). Some of railway lines leading to the old
central station near Qian men have been diverted,
now that the station has been moved to its new site,
in the south-east corner of the Northern City. The
canal still surrounds the town, following the line of
the walls.

The main thoroughfare is still the avenue which
runs due south from Qian men, linking it with Yong
ding men, dividing the Chinese town into two roughly
equal parts; to the north, it is called Qian men da
jie, and in the south, Tian qiao nan da jie. The northern

districts are the most thickly populated; several streets are full of shops (Chong wen men da jie, Da zha lan, Liu li chang jie) and one area, the Bridge of Heaven district (Tian qiao), is reserved as an amusement quarter. Many little workshops still exist, employing only ten or twenty people (knitting, handsewn soles, barrels, little silk figures, etc...). The southern districts still have several open spaces: from east to west, the Tao ran ting Park, the Temple of Agriculture Stadium, the Temple of Heaven, the Dragon Lakes.

The north-south axis will be described first, with the Temple of Heaven, and the districts west of the axis, then those to the east.

A. THE NORTH-SOUTH AXIS

The large central avenue begins north of Qian men Gate and ends south of Yong ding men Gate.

1. Qian men Gate (Front Gate)

It was the largest and most important of the three gates which led from the Northern town to the Southern town.

It was built in the reign of Yong le, at the beginning of the 15th century; its official name was Zheng yang men (the "gate which faces the sun"). It was made up of two lofty towers, one behind the other, linked by a wall shaped like a halfmoon, which enclosed an inner courtyard. Three gates led into the courtyard from the south, one in the middle (under the tower) and one on each side. The Central Gate was supposed to be opened only twice a year, when the Emperor went to the Temple of Heaven. Normal traffic used the two side gates. Two little yellow-roofed temples stood within the half-moon wall; the eastern one was dedicated to Guan yin, and the other to Guan di, the god of war, and special patron of the Manchu dynasty;

when the Empress Ci xi (Tz'u Hsi) came back from Xi an in
1901, she made a halt in front of the little temple. The super-
structures of both towers were burned in 1900, but they were
restored soon afterwards. During the 1911 revolution, the
Europeans, who feared another wave of zenophobia, occupied
the tower, as it could have been used to attack the Legation
Quarter, had an insurrection occurred. The double gate was a
serious inconvenience for modern vehicles, and in 1916, two
breaches were made in the walls to ease the traffic.

The half-moon wall has now disappeared, and the two little
temples can be seen, built up against the walls.

Peking's Central Station was east of Qian men
Gate before; now that it has been transferred to the
northern town, the old buildings have been converted
into a club for railwaymen.

An underground railway has been built south fy the
northern town. The entrance to it is near Qian men.

2. Two shopping streets:
Da zha lan and Zheng yang men da jie

Da zha lan is a little street which runs east-west,
starting from the main street, Zheng yang men da jie
(about a hundred yards south of Qian men), on the
right; it goes through to Liu li chang (see p. 547).
Its name, Da zha lan, means "big barrier", and it
dates from the time when a barrier was put down
across the street every evening (to control the traffic
and insure public safety).

From the early years of the Qing dynasty, Da zha lan has
been a street known for its shops and entertainments, particularly its theatres. Several old shops survive, among them a
chemist's shop which was opened in 1669. In 1900, a long stretch
of the street was burned, but it was soon rebuilt and became
as active as before; the first cinema to be built in Peking was
opened here in 1913. It is still an extremely busy street full of
little shops (some have many-coloured stucco façades).

Zheng yang men da jie is also a lively shopping street, at its busiest to the north. Some of the old façades still survive. It has food shops, a few bookshops, restaurants (Si chuan regional cooking, Peking duck, milk foods), chemist's shops selling traditional Chinese medecines (ginseng roots, deer antlers, etc...).

3. The Bridge of Heaven Quarter (Tian qiao)

It is east of the main street, south of the Pearl Market Crossroads (Zhu shi kou).

It used to be a low-lying, marshy area; to make it easier to reach the Temple of Heaven, the Emperors had a stone bridge built, known as the Bridge of Heaven (Tian qiao); later the the level of the ground was raised and the bridge disappeared in 1934; the name survives, however, and has been applied to a whole quarter. It has been an amusement quarter since the Ming dynasty. At the beginning of the 20th century, it was frequented by vagrants, in organised bands, who used to hold the artists to ransom; it was also the haunt of pick-pockets and prostitutes. All that has changed since 1949. The big Tian qiao Theatre has been built, and several small ones, where a variety of shows can be seen: films, plays or operas, acrobats and jugglers, story-tellers, musicians, Chinese shadow puppets.

4. The Natural History Museum (Zhong yang zi ran bo wu guan)

It used to be inside the Imperial Palace, and has now been moved to a large modern building, opposite the Bridge of Heaven quarter (just north of the entrance to the Temple of Heaven). It was opened to the public in January 1959. The ground floor contains the paleontology (central hall) and zoology (side wings) sections; the botany section is on the first floor.

Paleontology. The imposing skeleton of Tsintaosaurus Spino-rhinus Young, found in 1951, near Qing dao, in Shan dong (15 feet high, 21 feet long, 135 million years old) is in the centre. The enormous skeleton of Mamenchisaurus Constructus Young stands out against the far wall; it was found in 1952, in Si chuan (42 feet long, 165 million years old). Among other exhibits, some of the most interesting are: Parakannemeyeria Youngi Sun, found in Shan xi, and a skeleton of Elaphrurus found at Tong zhou, east of Peking (Elaphurus was reared from the Shang era onwards; the last known living specimens were in the Nan yuan Hunting Park, south of Peking, in 1900 or so). The glass cases contain an interesting collection of fossils, animal and vegetable, from all over China.

Zoology. Left hand hall: old works in Chinese on animals; map of the distribution of all the various species in China; the invertebrates (diatoms, molluscs, etc.) and fish. Specimens of a Chinese sea turtle, a cobra from Guang xi, a salmon from the Yang zi, etc.... In the right hand hall: higher vertebrates. Map of their distribution (it is interesting to note that natural fauna is rarest in regions which have been under cultivation for a long time, and at its most plentiful in the north-eastern provinces, and in Si chuan and Yun nan). Collection of naturalised animals.

Botany. Left hand hall: the world's flora. Right hand hall: Chinese flora, divided into zones according to climate and vegetation. This is the most useful section for the traveller, who will find examples of plants whose names he knows, but which he has never seen: soya bean, gao liang, ginseng, Ha mi melon, different sorts of rice, bamboo, tea plants, and all the species of trees.

5. The Temple of Heaven (Tian tan)

It lies to the east of the main avenue. The enclosure, which is nearly 4 miles long, is square to the south and round to the north. Two entries lead into it, on the north and west sides (it is best to take the western entrance). A second enclosure lies inside the first one, the same shape, but smaller (2½ miles round), with a wall cutting across it from east to west (see plan). This inner enclosure surrounds three main elements built once more on a north-south axis. The Round Mound (Huan qiu tan) and the Imperial Heavenly Vault (Huang qiong yu) lie to the south; the Hall of Prayer for Good Harvests stands to the north (Qi nian dian).

History. Most of the buildings were built for the first time in the 15th century, and then repaired (particularly in the 18th century, under the reign of Qian long). The Emperor carried out two sorts of ceremonies here. At the winter solstice, he went to the Round Mound (after a time of preparation spent in the Hall of Abstinence) to "speak with the heavens" *(jiao tian)* and impart to them all the important events of the last year. In the first month, he went to the Qi nian dian, to render homage to the heavens and to "gain their confidence" *(de xin)*; in more recent times, he prayed for a good harvest as well. After 1911, the Emperor or his representative no longer performed the ceremonies, and the Republican government tried for a time to carry on the traditions. On October 10th 1912, the first Chinese National Day, "the Temple of Heaven was thrown open to all, and a minister performed a sacrifice to the Supreme Lord, on behalf of the President of the Republic... The people had never been allowed to enter the Temple of Heaven. On the 10th of October and on the next two days, its vast precincts were opened to all and for the first time, they trod the sacred ground". (Farjenel, *A travers la révolution chinoise*, Paris, 1914, p. 303). At the 1914 winter solstice, President Yuan Shi kai, who hoped to restore the Empire and win the throne for himself, went in person to the Temple of Heaven (the clothes which he wore for the ceremony are now in the Museum of the Chinese Revolution (see p. 463). The whole place is now a public park.

Description. The western gate gives on to an avenue (several buildings on the right used to comprise the lodging for the staff attached to the Temple, the department which supplied the sacred music and the park for the sacrificial animals). Another red gate leads into the second enclosure. A way leaving the

central avenue to the right through a grove of evergreens leads up to the *Hall of Abstinence* (Zhai gong),
which is a group of buildings surrounded by a square
enclosure and a moat. It now holds an exhibition of
specialised material (no visitors allowed).

Slightly south of the Hall of Abstinence a red
gate leads into the southern part of the second
enclosure; the Emperor's cortege used to take the
same route. A diagonal path goes off towards the
Round Mound, to the left. Two enclosures encircle
the Mound, both painted red and surmounted by
blue tiles; the outer one is square and the inner one
round. Both enclosures have triple marble porticos
facing the four cardinal points of the compass. In
the outer one stand a large furnace made of green
porcelain (in which the sacrificial victim was burned),
iron cressets, and stones which held poles for banners.
In the inner enclosure is the Round Mound (Huan
qiu tan), built in 1530 and enlarged in 1749.

It consists of three round white marble terraces; each one is
edged with a marble balustrade. The number nine, symbol of
the sky and the Emperor, recurs several times in the arrangement of the blocks of stone and the flagstones (particularly on
the upper terrace, where the flagstones are arranged in concentric circles round the central stone, itself round: nine in the
first circle, eighteen in the second, twenty-seven in the third,
and so on, up to eighty-one). The terrace produces a curious
accoustic effect: someone crouching on the central stone,
speaking softly, will hear his voice coming back to him, considerably louder. The Emperor arrived from the south, halted
in a tent put up outside the first enclosure and signed the declaration which was to be read to the heavens, then proceeded to
the terrace. The victims were prepared in the sacred kitchens,
east of the Mound (the buildings still exist).

The first building north of the Round Mound is the
Imperial Heavenly Vault, standing in its own enclosure
(Huang qing yu). The surrounding wall is grey, with a

TIAN TAN (Temple du ciel)
TIAN TAN (Temple of Heaven)

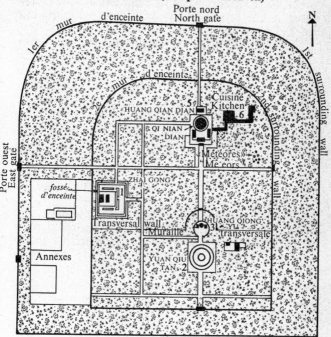

roofing of blue tiles. Three gates to the south lead into the inner courtyard (white marble arcade carved with foliage, surmounted by green and yellow glazed tiles, and blue tile roofing). The courtyard contains two side buildings (used to store vessels, implements etc.) and a little circular temple in the middle, built entirely of wood (it dates from 1530, and was restored in

1752). The cone-shaped roof of blue tiles is topped by
a gilded ball. The temple is 51 feet across and 63 feet
high; the roof-beams rest on eight pillars. The tablets
used in the ceremonies were kept here for the rest
of the year, on pedestals which can still be seen,
and only taken up to the Mound for the ceremonies
themselves. Here too curious accoustic phenomena
occur: 1) two people standing on opposite sides
of the courtyard, near the wall, can hear each other
speaking without raising their voices; 2) three large
rectangular stones lie in the central alley leading to the
temple, known as the San yin shi ("the three echoing
stones" or "the triple echo stones"): a single shout
or hand-clap given on the first (starting from the
bottom of the steps) produces a single echo, on the
second stone it produces a double echo, and on
the third, three echos.

A large red gate leads through the east-west wall
into the north part of the inner enclosure. Here, a
wide paved way leads straight to the entrance to the
Qi nian dian, 78 feet wide and nearly 500 yards
long. About 300 yards along, a square terrace with
a balustrade round it juts out to the east (to the right);
the Emperor used to stop here to change his robes
in a tent put up for the occasion.

At the far end of the way stands another red gate
like the southern one, followed by another, smaller,
one at the top of a flight of steps. This is the Gate
of Prayer for Good Harvests (Qi nian men). The
Hall of Prayer for Good Harvests stands in the middle
of a large courtyard (Qi nian dian).

It was built in 1420 (at that time it was called the Da qi dian,
Hall of great Sacrifices); it was restored in 1751, and was then
given its present name. It was struck by lightning and burned
down in 1889, and rebuilt soon afterwards, on the original

plans. It has been restored since 1949. It stands on a triple round marble terrace, each layer encircled by a balustrade, which is 36 feet high and 195 feet across at its widest point. Eight flights of steps lead up to the terrace. The hall itself is round (96 feet across) and topped by a triple cone-shaped roof of blue tiles, surmounted at the highest point of all by a gilded ball (123 feet high altogether).

A door opens to the south. Not one nail was used to build the hall, which is entirely in wood, supported by twenty-eight wooden columns made from trees brought from the forests of Yun nan. The four large pillars in the middle, each 60 feet high, symbolise the four seasons of the year (they are known as the "dragon's well pillars", *long jing zhu*, in books); twenty-four other columns are arranged in a double circle round the four central ones: the first circle of twelve stands for the twelve months of the year; the second represents the twelve hours of the day (the ancient Chinese divided the day into twelve instead of twenty-four). The roof-framework is extremely intricate; the first (lowest) roof rests on a circular framework, supported by the twenty-four outer pillars; the structure of the second is the most daring, as it rests partly on the twelve inner columns and partly on a circle itself supported by four cross-beams linking the four "dragon's well pillars"; the third and highest rests on the top of the four central pillars and on eight shorter ones built on the circular framework already mentioned. The whole framework is painted in brilliant colours. A circular stone lies in the middle of the floor, with most unusual natural veining, called the "Phoenix and dragon stone" *(long feng shi)*. On the platforms stand thrones; the tablets of dead Emperors and of the heavens were placed on them, when the Emperor came to "ask for confidence" or to pray for good harvests.

Two rectangular blue-roofed buildings stand on either side of the courtyard, and were formerly used as annexes. On a lower level behind the Qi nian dian stands the Temple of the August Heavens (Huang qian dian), a rectangular hall, with a roof of blue tiles, where the tablets were kept normally. It is not open to visitors.

A door leads eastwards out of the Qi nian dian enclosure into a covered way (72 bays) which goes to the annexes: the former slaughter-houses, shops, wells, kitchens. As it sometimes rained during the ceremonies, the offerings could reach their destination still dry. South-west of the way lie the Seven Meteorites (Qi yun shi); in fact they are not meteorites, but blocks of rough-hewn stone, of unknown origin. It is said that rites to obtain rain used to be performed in front of them.

6. The Former Temple of Agriculture (Xian nong tan)

It used to stand in a vast enclosure, over 2½ miles round, west of the Temple of Heaven, on the other side of the north-south avenue.

Each year the Emperor used to perform the rite of ploughing the first furrow there, and would sacrifice to obtain rain. The enclosure contained a field for the ploughing, a mound for the sacrifices, a temple dedicated to the planet Jupiter *(Sui xing)* and various other buildings where the tablets were stored and the sacrifices prepared. It was built under Jia jing in 1530 and restored under Qian long. Under the Republic, it was used to station police and troops, and as offices; the buildings gradually fell down. Not much of it was left by 1949, and the new régime decided to transform it into a sports ground. It now contains a stadium big enough to seat 30,000 people, and a swimming-pool, the Tao ran ting, which is the finest in China (six pools which can hold 4,000 swimmers).

B. THE WESTERN DISTRICTS

The area roughly corresponds to the site of the Jin town; a few remains, and place-names, still survive. Under the Ming this was an extremely important area economically speaking; it contained the biggest glazed tile works, and an ordinary brick works. Later on, the Imperial gunpowder works were founded in the south-west corner of the walls. It was also full of inns and the hostels of regional organisations, as travellers from the south crossed Marco Polo Bridge and entered the town through the Guang an men Gate; inns and hotels grew up in the surrounding district to accommodate them.

The Glazed Tile Works Street (Liu li chang jie) will be described first, then the Tiger District Bridge Street (Hu fang qiao jie), the neighbourhood of the Vegetable Market Crossroads (Cai shi kou), the north-western district, Ox Street (Niu jie) and the Mosque, the Temple of the Source of the Law (Fa yuan si) and the district round it, and lastly the Joyous Pavilion Park (Tao ran ting gong yuan)

1. Glazed Tile Works Street (Liu li chang jie)

It is south of the Peace Gate (He ping men) and runs eastwards and westwards from the main street, Nan xin hua jie.

This area was part of the eastern suburbs of the capital under the Liao and the Jin. A Liao tomb found here in 1770 gives the name of the village which was then on the site as Hai wang cun. When the Ming decided to establish their capital at Peking, and work on the palaces began, the one and only glazed tile works which then existed could not hope to meet the demand (it was in the eastern suburbs, at Liu li qu cun, and it was managed by a man called Chao, from Shan xi). It was decided to set up another works, south of the town, in the area between Xuan wu men and Qian men. Officials were put in charge of it and it was known as the Inner Works, (Nei chang) as opposed to the Outer Works, (Wai chang) as Liu li qu cun was then called. The Inner Works have left their name to the present Liu li chang Street.

The factory covered a large area, stretching over both sides of the present Nan xin hua jie (which was built in 1927, when the He ping men Gate was opened in the southern walls). The whole district is now full of teaching institutions; when they were being put up, large amounts of pottery remains were found, and the factory's sign, with the five characters *Guan liu li yao chang*, "Imperial Glazed Tile Works". The area surrounding the works was not a densely populated one, and four parks encircled it: the North-East Park (Dong bei yuan), the South-East Park (Dong nan yuan), the North-west Park (Xi bei yuan) and the South-West Park (Xi nan yuan), which are recalled in the place-names. A canal linked the works to the western mountains, so that raw materials could be brought by water. Several things were produced by the factory: glazed bricks and tiles, decorations for roofs, and windows, jars, toys and whistles.

At the end of the Ming and the beginning of the Qing, small tradesmen began to cluster round the factory gates (toy and sweet sellers, for instance). At the beginning of the Qing dynasty, the bookshops, which before were almost all near the Lantern Market, moved to this area. The names Factory Market (Chang shi or si), Factory Shop (Chang dian), both recalled in the name Chang dian Street (north of Liu li chang and east of Nan xing hua jie), date from this period. During the new year festivities the book market, which stretched to include stalls selling everything which a scholar could need (paper, brushes, ink and ink-stones, calligraphies...), became a meeting place for intellectuals. Under Qian Long, Liu li chang became busier than ever; over thirty bookshops and secondhand book stalls were in business there. Well-known printers set up workshops there (in 1792, the first edition of *Man Meng Han san he bian lan*, the tri-lingual dictionary in Manchu, Mongol and Han, was printed there). Finally antique-dealers opened shops there.

The glazed tile works were destroyed at the end of the Qing; in 1917, a public park (Hai wang cun gong yuan) was laid out on the site east of Nan xing hua jie, and north of the park a large hall was built to house industrial and handicrafts exhibitions under the Republic. All that was left was Liu li chang, as in the past, with its book shops, antique dealers, its sellers of calligraphies and rubbings, of seals, paper and ink, and its famous new year fairs.

Now, the four bookshops, the book-binders, the antique-dealers, the shops selling rubbings, calligraphies and paintings, the seal engravers all share a clientele made up of intellectuals and foreigners.

The most famous is **Rong bao zhai (Studio of Glorious Treasures),** where reproductions of traditional paint-ings are still made. The colours to be reproduced are chosen first of all; then a block (pear wood) is made for each colour; then the reproduction is applied to each block in turn, coated with its appointed colour.

The Long Life Temple Street (Yan shou si jie)

It leads north from the east end of Liu li chang Street. When, in 1441, under the Ming, a sewer was being dug there, a fragment of a stele was found, bearing the five characters *Da jin yan shou si*, which mean the Jin Dynasty Temple of Long Life. It was then decided to build a temple with the same name on the spot where the stele was discovered. The roofs of the temple can still be seen from the street; it is now out of use.

2. Tiger District Bridge Street (Hu fang qiao jie)

It runs from east to west, beginning at the southern end of Nan xin hua jie.

At number 45, the door of the "house where little plants are contemplated" can still be seen (Yue wei cao tang), where Ji Xiao feng, a writer who lived under the reign of Qian long, used to live (he wrote a short story there, and called it after his house: *Yue wei cao tang wu zhong*). At the beginning of the 20th century, one of the courtyards still contained a large "lake stone" from one of Emperor Yong zheng's gardens. In 1931, the great actor and exponent of classical opera, Mei Lan fang, lived there, and it was there that he founded the National Theatre Study Group (Guo ju xue hui). The buildings are now a restaurant, the Jin yang fan zhuang. They have changed considerably since the 18th century; at that time, one of the rooms was shaped like a boat.

3. The Vegetable Market Crossroads (Cai shi kou) and district

The road running from Guang an men Gate westwards to Zheng yang men da jie (it is called Guang an men da jie at first, and then the western part is known as Luo ma shi da jie, Mule and Horse Market Street) crosses the avenue leading north to Xuan wu men Gate (Xuan wu men da jie) at Cai shi kou.

Until 1901, executions were held on the Vegetable Market. The victims came south from the inner city through Xuan wu men Gate and were executed at dawn, before the market opened.

South-west of the crossroads, Bei ban cai hu tong Lane runs into the main street.

In a little house on the west side of its southern end lived the poet and reformer Tan Ci tong (he and Kang You wei took part in the Hundred Days of Reform); he called his house Mang cang cang zhai (the Green Groves Pavilion). When he was thirty, he collected all the poems written during his youth and called them *Poems of the Green Groves Pavilion*. When the Hundred Days of Reform movement was squashed in 1898 he and six other reformers were executed at the Vegetable Market Crossroads.

Rice Market Lane (Mi shi hu tong) is south-east of the crossroads; the Inn of the Southern Seas Association (Nan hai hui guan) used to be there in the 19th century.

Kang You wei, a native of Guang dong, lived there when he stayed in Peking. It was there that he founded the Canton study group, Yue xue hui, in 1897; later on it became the

Economic Study Group, Jing ji xue hui, and then the Society of Those Who Recognise Shame, Zhi chi hui, whose principal aim was to win the Emperor round to a policy of reform.

4. The North-western District

This used to include a relatively open area, with few buildings, between Xuan wu men wai jie to the east and Guang an men jie to the south. Numerous temples were built there; the most famous of them gave their names to the streets where they were, such as the Temple of Everlasting Spring (Chang chun si) and the Recompense the State Temple (Bao guo si).

The Temple of Everlasting Spring (Chang chun si)

The first street to the west (Shang xie jie) in Xuan wu men wai da jie leads to Chang chun si jie, which is perpendicular to Shang xie jie.

The temple was built in 1560, by Emperor Wan li's mother. One day when her son was ill, she vowed that she would make him enter a monastery if he recovered. The child got better; his mother, however, found someone to go into a monastery instead of him, and had a magnificent temple built for the new monk, worthy of the imperial offspring whom he was replacing. The roofs of the temple can still be admired from the first courtyard, but as part of the temple is now a factory, and the rest lived in by private individuals, a visit is out of the question

The Recompense the State Temple (Bao guo si).

A lane leads northwards from Guang an men da jie to the temple (leaving the main street at the "Bao guo si" bus stop).

It was built under the Liao or the Jin (at the beginning of the 20th century, two pine trees still stood in the courtyard, said to have been planted under the Jin). Under the Ming, the temple was dedicated to Guan yin, and a porcelain statue stood in one of the halls. During the second half of the 19th century, the Bao guo si was famous for its carpet-making, an art much appreciated by the Manchu. A monk from the west arrived with about twenty disciples, all from Gan su and Tibet, who were skilled carpet-makers. The temple has now been converted into a factory, and visiting is forbidden.

The Temple dedicated to Gu Yan wu (Gu xian sheng si)

Just west of the Bao guo si stands the door of the temple which was built in 1843 in memory of Gu Yan wu, the 18th century historian and philosopher, who stayed here when he visited Peking under the reign of Kang xi. He was interested in the history of Peking and the surrounding area, and among other things, he left an account of his visit to the Ming tombs. The temple itself has been destroyed, and the site is now occupied by administrative offices.

5. Ox Street (Niu jie) and the Mosque

Ox Street (or Cow Street or Oxen Street, the Chinese title does not specify) is a fairly narrow street, going from north to south. The northern end runs into Guang an men da jie Street, at the Niu jie bei kou crossroads.

Ever since Peking has been a capital, all Moslems, whether Chinese or foreign, have always converged on this street and the lanes around it. The street was apparently given its name because the inhabitants ate beef instead of pork, like the other Chinese. They went in for small trades, and were mainly pastry-cooks, pedlars, or rickshaw boys. Their Han neighbours often disliked them heartily, and the annals of the street are rich in stories, some more easily credible than others, about episodes rising from this latent hostility. The lives of these people have certainly been easier since the liberation; they are now said to belong to the "Hui Minority". Arabic characters can still be seen above the doors of some of the houses in the district; some of the Hui have physical characteristics revealing their non-Han origins (Central Asian mainly).

The Mosque. It is half way along Ox Street, on the left, when facing the south. In Chinese it is known as Li bai si, Temple of Prayer, or Qing zhen si, Temple of Purity.

It used to be the spiritual centre of the whole district. It was founded under the Song (probably in the 12th century); the buildings were restored under the Ming and the Qing, and in 1955.

The observation tower (Wang yue lou) is just behind the entrance; it was used for making the astronomical observations needed for drawing up the calendar. It is a hexagonal tower, entirely Chinese in style. A side door leads in to the right, to an alleyway running alongside the hall of prayer, which gives on to the delightful inner courtyard, full of flowering oleander bushes in the summer. The minaret stands in the centre of the courtyard (on the ground floor is a large copper cauldron, which was used to prepare communal meals); to the right and left of the tower stand pavilions housing memorial steles, inscribed in Arabic and Chinese, and now almost illegible.

The façade of the prayer hall is west of the courtyard. Three doors lead into a narthex, and then into the hall itself, which consists of five naves. The three central naves going longways (from east to west) are divided into five bays, some narrow, with coffered ceilings, and some wide, with high beam ceilings. The side naves have plain ceilings of beams laid lengthwise.

The mihrab is in the far wall; its beautiful wood carvings are probably Ming. The decoration of the hall shows an interesting mixture of eastern and western influences; Chinese flowers and clouds are mingled with Arabic inscriptions on the coffered ceiling, and the glass chandeliers are slightly reminiscent of Venetian glass. Two Moslems who came from the West in the 13th century to preach the faith are buried in another courtyard alongside; Ali the Iranian, and Achmed Burdani, from Bokhara. The tombstones have been set into the wall. In the Imam's library are manuscripts of the Koran and old wooden printing blocks (the Mosque used to be a printing-house as well).

In the south-east of the district stands a large building put up after the liberation, and easily recognisable, with its large green cupolas: the headquarters of the Islamic Society (Yi san lan jiao xie hui).

6. The Temple of the Source of the Law (Fa yuan si)

It is in a lane (Fa yuan si hu tong) slightly to the north of the Islamic Society Headquarters. It is one of the most interesting Buddhist temples in Peking, and now houses the Buddhist College. It can be visited by appointment. (Closed in 1972.)

History. When the Tang Emperor, Tai zong, came back from a disastrous campaign in Korea in 645, he wanted to render homage to the shades of the soldiers who had been killed in battle, and founded the first temple here, the Min zhong si (Temple for Grieving over the Faithful). The temple consisted of a little brick pagoda and a two-storey pavilion, and it was in the south-east corner of the Tang town. In the 12th century, Hui zong, the unfortunate Song Emperor, was imprisoned here by the Jin, after being captured by them at the fall of Bian zhou (Kai feng). Under the Yuan, the buildings were used as examination halls for Mongol candidates. The Ming renamed the temple Chong fu si and restored it several times (1443 and 1608).

In the 17th and early 18th centuries, a famous fair was held in the temple courtyards on the eighth day of the fourth lunar month; it was suppressed by Qian long. In 1734, under the reign of Yong zheng, the temple was restored and given its present name, Fa yuan si. In the first half of the 20th century, the buildings were used to billet soldiers and were pillaged several times. After the liberation, it was decided to put the Buddhist College here.

The Buddhist College. At the moment it consists of about ten teachers and over seventy pupils (Han, Mongol and Tibetan), divided into two different sections: Chinese section (four year course) and Tibetan section (five year course). Theravadin Buddhism, practised in south-east Asia and Ceylon, is taught, as well as Mahayanism (the "Great Vehicle"), which is the Buddhism traditionally practised in China. Classes are given on the doctrine and history of Buddhism and its sects, as well as on sections of texts from the canons. Languages are also taught (Pali, Japanese, English, but not Sanskrit).

Description. The first courtyard contains pagoda masts, and the Drum and Bell Towers. The Hall of the Celestial Guardians (Tian wang dian) stands at the end, with statues of the four guardians, Maitreya and Wei tuo (the protector of Buddhism). In the second courtyard stands the Da xiong bao dian (statues of the three Buddhas, with the eighteen *luo han* round the walls; on the floor are yellow cushions for the pupils to sit on).

In the middle of the central alleyway which crosses the third courtyard is a stone reliquary, shaped like a cubic house, with a pyramid roof. Under the Liao, it was buried under the pagoda which then stood in the centre of the courtyard (on the site of the present Guan yin Pavilion). It was dug up under the Qing and placed where it can now be seen. The Guan yin Pavilion is modern. It contains a gilded wooden statue of Guan yin with eleven faces and thirty-two arms, which is said to be Ming (it is almost certainly a copy). Several pieces of steles with inscriptions on the history of the temple (8th, 10th, 12th, and 18th centuries) have been set in the outside wall of the Pavilion, to the east. The Hall of Universal Illumination (Da bian jie tang) stands at the far end of the third courtyard. Several things referring to the Chinese pilgrim Xuan zang, who went to India under the Tang to bring back sutras, have been collected there.

The finest piece of all is a beautiful pagoda-shaped blue cloisonné reliquary, dating from the reign of Qian long; the

curators of the Imperial Palace made a present of it in 1950,
so that a piece of the pilgrim's skull might be kept in it. The
skull has a long history. Xuan zang died in Xi. an and was
buried in the Xing jiao si Temple, in the south of the town (see
p. 951). During the Huang Chao rebellion in the 9th century,
his tomb was violated and a piece of the skull was taken to
Nanking. At the beginning of the Song dynasty, this precious
relic was put in a stone casket and buried under one of the
pagodas of the Bao en si (on the Yu hua tai Hill, south of Nanking, see p. 985). The Bao en si was destroyed during the Tai
ping rebellion, and the casket stayed hidden until 1943, when
it was found during some excavations led by the Japanese. The
skull was then divided and shared between several centres of
Buddhism. One piece stayed at Nanking, another was sent to
Peking, to a temple near the Bei hai. It did not reach the Fa
yuan si until 1950. On the walls are: a map of Xuan zang's
route in India; a view of the Da yan ta Pagoda, where he translated the sutras from Sanskrit into Chinese; copies of his translations; rubbings of inscriptions at Xi an (one is in praise of
the monk); view of the Xing jiao si at Xi an, old picture of the
Bao en si at Nanking; rubbing of the inscriptions on the stone
casket, said still to exist at Nanking; Western works on the
life and travels of the monk. A side courtyard leads into the
fourth courtyard, with a large two-storey building at the end
of it. The ground floor is a class-room. A staircase leads up the
side to the first floor, which is divided into several rooms, constituting a sort of a museum of Buddhism.

First Room: Manuscripts. Original fragments of manuscripts
from Dun huang (one has some music on it); two Japanese
manuscripts dating from the Song period; Ming Chinese and
Tibetan manuscripts, Burmese and Mongolian manuscripts
dating from the Qing period; two little lacquered bookshelves
with Ming sutras.

Second Room: Painting. Four beautiful Ming paintings, one
of them by Tai Jin (on the far wall, on the right); several Qing
scrolls.

Third Room. (above the class-room). Five large Qing statues
of the Buddha, mounted on very fine carved pedestals (they
represent the Buddhist hell); in front of these statues is an
altar, with three beautiful Ming bronzes (Buddha with a beard);
at the end, a large case with a fine collection of statues of the
Buddha (the oldest date from the Northern Wei; interesting
"Buddha of Sorrows", dating from the Qing, a rare piece from

the iconographic point of view); the side walls are lined with bookshelves; examples of works kept in the temple are exhibited, for instance, several volumes of a Buddhist canon printed under the Ming (the cover still has its original silk on it); there is no catalogue as yet.

Fourth Room: statues and accessories. Strings of beads and sceptres *(ru yi)* dating from the Qing; little statuettes of the infant Buddha (Ming) and the ritual vessels in which they were washed on the eighth day of the fourth month

Fifth Room: Musical instruments (bells, drums); a monk's robes; book cover; staff used by the superior of the monastery; alms bowl; altar laid out as for the Lamaist rite.

7. The Joyous Pavilion Park (Tao ran ting gong yuan)

It is due west of the old Temple of Agriculture. There are two entrances, one to the east, the other to the north. It is one of the rare spots in Peking where hills can be seen, though they are very small.

History. The site has been inhabited since the Warring States period (remains were discovered in 1939); in the 11th century, it was east of the town; under the Yuan, the Temple of Mercy was built here (Ci bei si); under the Ming and the Qing, several brick kilns were built. In 1695, Jiang Zao, secretary at the Ministry of Works, had a pavilion built near the temple and called it the Joyous Pavilion (Tao ran ting), recalling two lines written by the Tang poet, Bai Ju yi: "Let us wait until the chrysanthemums are golden and our wine brewed, then with you, all shall be intoxication and joy". It rapidly became famous; scholars and officials used to meet here to drink and write poetry together. In the 19th century, much of the charm had already been lost; at the beginning of the 20th century, Li Da zhao, one of the pioneers of Chinese Communism, hired several of the temple annexes to hold political meetings there. The lakes have been re-dug since the liberation, and a park has been laid out on their shores.

Description. The park contains three things of particular interest: a) two large porticos in coloured wood *(pai lou)*, which used to be in the Chang an jie Avenue, where they interfered with the traffic, so they were moved here; b) the Joyous Pavilion and the Temple of Mercy, which are side by side on a little mound between the two lakes; the *chuang* (Buddhist pillar) in the inner courtyard of the temple probably dates from the Jin; the little hall on the right still contains a few statues; to the left is the entrance to the Joyous Pavilion (tea room with a terrace); c) to the south-west lies a double pavilion built in southern style, dating from the 18th century, which was moved here in 1954 from the eastern shore of the Southern Lake (Nan hai). The park also has an open-air theatre, a reading room and a children's playground; boats can be hired on the lakes.

C. THE EASTERN DISTRICTS

Under the Qing, the area north of the Temple of Heaven was thickly populated, but the south-east corner of the town was much less so; lakes and marshes filled most of it, and there were no streets at all. The eastern districts have nothing of particular interest which calls for a special visit; a few historical details will be given however.

1. The Northern Districts

a) The Markets

Several markets can still be traced in the place-names (garlic, herbs, horsehair, brush markets...). One of the best known was the Flower Market (Hua shi), held in the north-east of the southern town, in a street perpendicular to Chong wen men wai da jie.

The flowers were artificial ones. It is said that under the Ming, one of the Palace ladies had a scar on her face, which she used to hide with a flower. A workshop making artificial flowers was created here, so that even in winter, she should always have flowers. Under the Qing, over two hundred families were employed to make flowers or little people of silk and paper. They were sold in winter, until the Spring Festival. Merchants bought them and redistributed them throughout the rest of the empire. Even today a little workshop still survives in Hua shi da jie Street, where little velvet birds *(rong niao)* are made.

Two other important markets were the Little Market (Xiao shi), in a street running perpendicular to Flower Market Street, and the Morning Market (Xiao shi), slightly north of the Temple of Heaven. They were much the same as our Flea Markets; people who were hard up came to sell off what they no longer needed. It is said that the Morning Market was so called because people of good family who preferred to go unrecognised used to come at day break.

b) The Temples

There used to be many of them in this part of the town; all of them are now either out of use or no longer standing. The best-known were, from west to east:

The Yue fei Temple or Jing Zhong miao
(the Loyal to the Last Temple)

It is in the Jing zhong miao jie Street, north-west of the Temple of Heaven.

It was built by Qian long, in honour of the famous Song general who distinguished himself against the Jin and was treacherously executed at the promptings of his rival, the minister Qin Kui. Like the one at Hang zhou (see p. 1080), the temple contained statues of Qin Kui and his wife; the visitors would spit in their faces. The statue of Qin Kui is now in the Historical Museum.

The Temple of the Kings of Medecine (Yao wang miao). It is in Yao wang miao qian jie Street, north east of the Temple of Heaven.

It was built under the Ming; it was dedicated to Fu xi, Shen nong Huang di, and all other doctors who made themselves famous throughout Chinese history.

The Temple of Peaches (Pan tao gong). It is in the north-east of the town, south of the former Dong bian men Gate.

It was dedicated to the Western Queen Mother (Xi wang mu), an important Taoist deity. A fair was held from the first to the fifth of the third lunar month. The buildings are now lived in.

2. The South-eastern Districts

a) The Lakes

Under the Qing, private gardens and brick kilns were built round the lakes and marshes in the south-east of the town. In the 20th century, the area of the lakes was cut down, and their boundaries were fixed. A walk is being built round them at the moment. A road runs between the two largest ones and goes on towards the Zuo an men Gate.

A small grey-brick modern building (1952) stands on the northern shore of the lake, slightly east of the road; several old steles have been set into the walls, commemorating Yuan Chong huan, the national hero who defended Peking against the attacks of the Jürched Nurhachi (ancestor of the Qing dynasty) under the

reign of Wan li; he once had his headquarters here.
West of the lake stands the parachute tower.

b) The Temples

Large numbers of temples grew up in this empty
space, as there was room for orchards and vegetable
gardens. The chief ones, from north to south, were:
the An hua si, the Xi zhao si, the Nian hua si, the Yu
qing guan. Most of them have disappeared without
trace; the only really noticeable remains of them all is
the Fa ta si Temple Pagoda, which stands at the crossroads formed by Long tan lu and Xing fu jie. The
temple is said to have been built under the Jin and
repaired in 1451. The six-storey hexagonal pagoda
dates from the Ming; the base has been restored; each
storey contains niches where 58 little statues of the
Buddha used to stand; the top ends in a bulb-shaped
piece of masonry. According to a Ming text; on new
year's eve "the monks put little lamps in the niches, on
either side of the statues, and played music all round
the pagoda".

c) The built-up areas

Only a very small proportion of this large area had
houses built on it; a Manchu district grew up east of
the Temple of Heaven, and north-east of the Fa ta si
Pagoda; it was called the Western camp (Xi ying
fang); it consisted of fourteen lanes and blue banner
families lived there. Half the population of the area
is still Manchu today.

New buildings have been put up everywhere where
there is space for them, particularly north of the Dragon Lakes, where vast numbers of new buildings have
grown up.

III. Outside the walls

A. THE WESTERN SUBURBS

The Zoo (Dong wu yuan) would be a good place to begin a visit to the western suburbs; it is west of Xi zhi men Gate, and a large bus terminus lies opposite it. The developments over the last few years (the building of the Exhibition Centre and the Planetarium, the renovation of the Zoo, a new bazaar, new restaurants) have made this into a centre which attracts large numbers of people, particularly on Sundays and holidays.

Parts of the western walls of the town are still standing (the 19 bus route runs alongside them). Going from north to south, the bus passes close to the site of the former Chala cemetery (south-west of Fu cheng men Gate), where the Jesuits of the Peking mission were buried (the first one was Matteo Ricci, who died in 1610); it was sacked by the rebels in 1900 and nothing remains today. Next comes the former Altar to the Moon (Yue tan), now a public park; then the Bai yun guan, a Taoist temple still in use, near the north-west corner of the walls of the Chinese City, and finally, slightly to the south of the temple, the Tian ning si Pagoda.

1. The Zoo (Dong wu yuan)

The southern entrance is opposite the bus terminus.

History. Under the Ming, the area was an imperial park; under the Qing, the park belonged to one of the Emperor Kang xi's sons for a time, and was called the "Third Son's Garden" (San bei zi yuan). Qian long had it renovated for his mother's sixtieth birthday. It was improved again under Ci xi; in 1902, Duan Fang, the viceroy of Shan xi, came back to China after a trip to seventeen different foreign countries; he brought back a fine collection of animals and birds from Germany, as a present for the Empress. It was put in the park, which was renamed the Wan shou yuan (Park of ten thousand animals). In 1906, a botanical garden was laid out there, and in 1908 it was opened to the public. The gardens were badly neglected during the civil wars; according to a Chinese handbook, only "twelve monkeys, three old parrots and a one-eyed ostrich" were left by the end of them. After the liberation, the zoo was re-stocked, and now possesses nearly 4,000 animals. Many were caught on Chinese territory, in outlying areas of the Republic to which the original fauna has gradually retreated (Manchuria, Tibet and particularly the south-western provinces); others are presents from friendly countries or have been acquired through exchanges.

The most striking animals are the tigers from Manchuria, the pandas from west Si chuan, the yaks from Tibet, the big sea-turtles from the Chinese seas, and, among the animals from other countries: the tiger from Sumatra, the big anthropoid apes, the Asian and African rhinoceroses, and four elephants, from Vietnam, Burma, Pakistan and India.

2. The Five Pagoda Temple (Wu ta si)

It is behind the Zoo, on the other side of the canal which used to link the town moats with the Yi he yuan. It can be reached either through the Zoo or by getting off the 32 bus at the White Stone Bridge stop (Bai Shi qiao), and taking the path which leads off to the right of the road, along the canal just mentioned.

History. Under the reign of the Ming Emperor Yong le — famous for the expeditions which he sent to the southern seas (see history, p. 119) — Pandida, an Indian monk, presented "five golden statues of the Buddha and a model of the Diamond Temple (at Boddhgaya)" to the court at Peking. The Emperor ordered the Temple of the True Awakening (Zhen jue si) to be built to receive the precious objects. In 1473, the Emperor Xian zong had a building with five pagodas, copied from the model from India, constructed in the middle of the temple. The Yong le temple was restored under Qian long (1761), but it was damaged in 1860 and again in 1900, this time by the European armies, and finally it was sold piece by piece by the warlords after 1927. Nothing is left of it now, except the building with its five pagodas, which has been restored since the liberation.

Description. The enclosing wall still stands; inside it lies a stone base with three little walls decorated with Sanskrit characters still standing on it (possibly the podium of a former building?). The façade of the Wu ta si is partly hidden by two enormous trees.

The most interesting part of the building is the decoration on the outside (bas-relief carvings). The five upper rows consist of a set of statues of the Buddha; he is portrayed sitting, in a sort of niche, but his attitudes (mudras) are different from one niche to another. The lowest row is the most striking, and the carving is more delicate: two bands of lotus petals and Sanskrit characters, and between them, a set of Buddhist symbols: animals (lion, horse, elephant, peacock, garuda—bird with a human head—), celestial guardians, the wheel of the law, motives depicting interlocked claws, vases of flowers. The arch in the south face is also covered with beautiful bas-relief carvings, said to be reminiscent of the carvings on the Ju yong men Gate (see p. 620) and those at the Bi yun si Temple (see p. 607).

The key can be obtained at the south gate of the Zoo. Most of the statues are missing from the inside. Two flights of stairs lead up to the terrace, right and left of the door. The bas-relief carving on the bases of the little pagodas echoes the carving on the lower part of the buildings; the south face of the little central pagoda bears the Buddha's footprints on its base.

Two steles, one on either side of the Wu ta si, commemorate the restoration work carried out under Qian long (the one to the left is inscribed in Mongol and Tibetan, the one on the right in Chinese and Manchu).

3. The Planetarium (Tian wen guan)

It is opposite the Zoo, and its large dome makes it unmistakable.

It was opened in 1957. In the entrance hall: a Foucault clock; to the left: lecture hall, where films are also shown; to the right: permanent exhibitions, with models and photographs of the skies (solar system, Milky Way, nebulae); at the far end, round hall (80 feet in diameter, 600 seats) with the projector in the middle. The circular passage round the hall has photographs

WU TA SI (Temple aux cinq pagodes)
WU TA SI (Five Pagoda Temple)

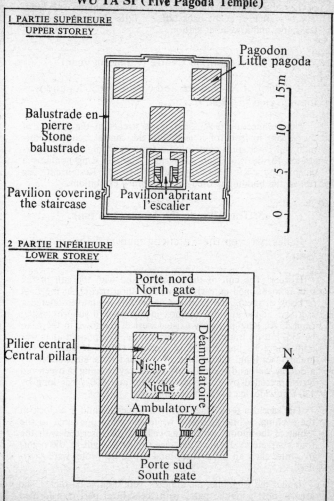

1 PARTIE SUPÉRIEURE
UPPER STOREY

Pagodon
Little pagoda

Balustrade en pierre
Stone balustrade

Pavilion covering the staircase

Pavillon abritant l'escalier

15 m

10

5

0

2 PARTIE INFÉRIEURE
LOWER STOREY

Porte nord
North gate

Pilier central
Central pillar

Déambulatoire

Niche
Niche

Ambulatory

N.

Porte sud
South gate

of the old astronomical instruments, now in Nanking or Peking. The two annexes at the back house a little observatory, with a telescope, and a weather station.

4. The Exhibition Centre (Zhan lan guan)

It is west of Xi zhi men and east of the Zoo, and was inaugurated in 1954.

The architecture is Russian; three arches at the far end of the square in front of it lead into the central buildings, surmounted by a spire containing a light lit at night; two wings stretch forwards, one on each side. The left wing contains a cinema and a Russian restaurant, the Moscow Restaurant. The rest of the building is used for temporary exhibitions.

5. The Altar to the Moon (Yue tan)

It lies between the Fu cheng men and Fu xing men Gates.

History. The cult of the moon, linked with the cult of the sun, is mentioned as early on as the Zhou period, in the *Li ji* (a book of rites). The Emperor or his representatives offered a sacrifice at the autumn equinox in the western suburbs of the capital. An altar probably existed west of the town in the Liao period, but no trace of it has been found. The present altar was built under Jia jing, the Ming Emperor (1531). It was restored under Qian long. It consisted of a plain terrace surrounded by a double wall and several annexes. A way running between red walls, preceded by a wooden pavilion, and 600 yards long by 130 feet wide, led to the north entrance.

The sacrifice took place between 6 o'clock and 8 o'clock in the evening. White jade and white silk were presented to the tablet of the moon, which was yellow, and inscribed with the four characters: *Ye ming zhi shen* (Spirit of light of the night) in white; then an ox, a sheep and a pig, all white, were sacrificed.

Under the Republic, the annexes were used as barracks. The area is now a public park, with the central part transformed into a sports ground. The annexes cannot be visited, as they are used as a school and as administrative offices.

Description. The long entrance way and the *pai lou* have vanished without trace; the street runs along the site where they once were. The entrance to the gardens is the old east gate; on the other side of the street the trees which stood in the outer enclosure can still be seen. Opposite, to the west, stands a three-arch marble portico giving on to the central enclosure where the sacrificial terrace stands. The enclosure is about 330 yards round; it used to be shut in by a wall surmounted by a green tiled roof. The four stone porticos leading into it are still standing (single ones to the north, west and south, a triple one to the east). The terrace in the middle is square (42 feet along each side), and 5 feet high (four flights of steps lead up to it).

North of the central enclosure stand the Bell Tower (it still contains the bell which was rung at sacrifices), and the massive North Gate; the *Ju fu dian* buildings, with green tiled roofs, are to the north-east; they were used by whoever performed the sacrifice, as robing-rooms (they have been transformed into a school); the shops, slaughterhouses and the kitchen stood to the south-west.

6. The White Cloud Taoist Temple (Bai yun guan)

The inhabitants of Peking usually call it the Bo yun guan.

A little way beyond the north-west corner of the southern town a path to the right leads, after a few minutes' walk, to the entrance of the Bai yun guan: the White Cloud Taoist Temple (a screen wall and a tall wooden portico mark the entrance). It is near the site of the northern wall of the old Jin town.

History. The first temple, the Tian chang guan, was founded under the Tang. Under the Jin, it was known as the Tai ji gong. Under the Yuan, it was enlarged, and became the centre of Taoism for North China. A famous Taoist monk, Chang chun, from Shan dong, retired there and later died there. The present name, Bai yun guan, dates from the early 15th century. The word *guan*, whose primary meaning is "observatory", is often used for Taoist temples. The buildings date mainly from the Qing.

Until recently, a large fair was held in the temple from the first to the twentieth of the first lunar month *(zheng yue)*. People came from far away to venerate the statues of Chang chun and other deities and to do business and enjoy themselves at the same time. In 1965, the fair lasted one day only (the first day of the first month) but several thousand people still came to it. The temple possessed an extremely rich library, famous for its Taoist texts. The rarest manuscripts have now been put in the National Library.

Now that the Dong yue miao (see p. 576) has been converted into a secondary school, the Bai yun guan is the only Taoist temple in Peking which is still in use. Over twenty *dao shi* (Taoist monks) still live there; they are easily recognisable because they wear their hair long, gathered into a knot on the top of the head and kept in place with a silver or jade pin. Some of them also wear a head-band.

Description. A low opening in a gate leads into the fore-court. The main entrance at the far end opens into the first courtyard. As in Buddhist temples, the Bell and Drum Towers stand to the right and left of the first courtyard; at the far end is the Ling guan dian, restored under the reign of Kang xi: the tormented statue of the temple guardian, Wang shan (cf. the Buddhist *Tian wang*) is in this hall.

The Hall of the Jade Emperor (Yu huang dian) stands at the end of the second courtyard; it was built under Kang xi, and restored and furnished in the 18th century. A large bronze incense-burner dating from the Wan li period (about 1600) stands in front of the door. The Jade Emperor (Yu huang), the supreme Taoist divinity ever since the Song dynasty, stands in a niche in the middle of the hall; one servant *(zhan tong)* stands on each side of him. Notice the head-dress, with the bead fringe, the offering of artificial peaches, and the long streamers embroidered with cranes. The peach and the crane are Taoist symbols of longevity. Statues of the four *sheng* and the twenty-eight *su* (Taoist spirits, forming the thirty-two *tian di* altogether, or with Yu huang, the thirty-three *tian*) used to line the walls on either side. The statues have disappeared and rather disappointing modern paintings now replace them (two *sheng* and fourteen *su* on each side).

The bell and the bronze horse on the terrace in the third courtyard were brought here from the Dong yue miao in 1961. Beyond them is the **Lao lü tang**; two porcelain tiles in front of the entrance bear the characters *qing* and *gui*: "purity" and "rule" (the same thing is sometimes to be found in Buddhist temples); inside on the right is a drum dating from the Ming, with a dragon painted on the hide (it also comes from the Dong yue miao); in the centre stand four tables of offerings with musical instruments, and sacred books wrapped in yellow; at the far end are seven statues of Taoist saints.

The **Hall of the Ancestor Qiu (Qiu zu dian)** in the fourth courtyard is dedicated to Qiu Chu ji or Chang chun (who died here under the Yuan dynasty). The statues, some of which represent Chang chun, date from Qian long; the wooden basin in the middle comes from Xin jiang and was given in offering by Qian long. The faithful still throw money into it.

In the fifth courtyard stands a two-storey pavilion built under the reign of Kang xi. The ground floor is the **Si yu dian** (Hall of the four *yu*, Taoist deities); it contains some fine statues. A staircase on the right leads up to the first floor, where there are statues of three more Taoist divinities, the three *qing*; the one on the right and the one on the left hold intertwined symbols of the *yin* and *yang*; at the end: old book cases and branches of false coral arranged in vases; to the left, on the wall, a modern scroll, with the conventional Taoist figures in red, representing the symbols of the five sacred mountains (Song shan, Tai shan, Hua shan, and the two Heng shan). These five figures together constitute a talisman with remarkable powers of preservation; they are often reproduced on metal amulets, or engraved on steles, rubbings of which had the same powers of preservation as the amulets (see E. Chavannes, *Le T'ai chan*, p. 415 onwards).

A way through the annex buildings to the west (near the library) leads to the gardens just north of the Si yu dian. They contain some interesting rocks and, in the middle, the **Jie tai** and its annexes; it is a sort of square platform with a roof over it, linked by a double covered way to the pavilion opposite it on the other side of the courtyard. The Taoist monks of the neighbourhood would come here periodically to be taught by one of the older ones. The teacher spent a time of preparation in the pavilion, and then came along one of the covered ways to the platform, to address the disciples who had gathered in the courtyard. In the base of the pavilion and under the terraces can be seen the niches where ascetics came to meditate. They fasted all day and ate only at night. People came from far away to seem them. *Jie tai* like this one are rare; they only existed in large temples. They are sometimes to be found in Buddhist temples like the Jie tai si, for instance, in the western suburbs of Peking (see p. 645).

7. The Temple of Celestial Peace (Tian ning si)

The pagoda of the Tian ning si can be seen far off to the south of the Bai yun guan. A little path across the fields leads to it.

History. The exact origin of the pagoda is not known, though it is certainly one of the oldest in Peking. Some texts attribute the founding of the temple to the Northern Wei, others to the Sui Emperor Wen di. The present pagoda dates no doubt from the Liao (early 13th century); at that time, it was inside the city walls (see passage on the history of Peking). It does not look as though it has been restored very often since that date. The temple which stood beside it was restored in the 15th century, when it was named the Tian ning si; the name has now been transferred to the pagoda. Under the Ming and the Qing it was famous for a curious phenomenon: when it was looked at through the different interstices of one of the temple walls, the pagoda seemed to be upside down and multiplied (dark room). The temple has disappeared completely; a little factory has been built on the site and entry is forbidden.

Description. The pagoda is 190 feet high, and made up of three sections: 1. an octagonal podium resting on a square base, with two rows of niches, a false balustrade, and then three sets of "lotus petals"; 2. the central part, with interesting bas-relief carvings; the facets facing the cardinal points have a door with a celestial guardian on either side; 3. the upper part made up of 13 superposed roofs; the understructure of each roof is made to look like wood; a little bell hangs at each corner.

B. THE NORTHERN SUBURBS

Under the Yuan, the northern suburbs were part of the city of Da du, as the walls were nearly a mile and a half north of the Ming city walls (their foundations can still be seen in some places). In the 18th century, the ruins of one of the Mongol city gates were still standing, north of the De sheng men Gate. Qian long, who was interested in archaeology, thought it was the remains of the former town of Ji (see p. 402) and had a stele erected on the ruins, with a little pavilion to shelter it, and his mistake was thus perpetuated for some time (even the first European historians believed it). The Ming abandoned the northern part of the town, for reasons unknown, and moved the walls further south. When the Emperor Jia jing built the Altar to the Earth, the area already had become the suburbs of the city. Under the Qing it became busy once more; several new temples were built in the open spaces, some Buddhist, like the Jue sheng si (now the Great Bell Temple), some Lamaist, like the two Black Temples (so called because of their black tiled roofs) which have vanished, and the Yellow Temple, part of which still survives. As trade with the north of the empire, Mongolia and Manchuria increased, several caravanserais, inns, and customs offices grew up. Today the area is once more developing; large brick buildings several stories high are going up in what otherwise is still an agricultural area: factories, workmen's living quarters, higher educational establishments (the Post and Telecommunications Institute, the Medical School), hospitals, scientific research centres (the Institute of Music).

The following may be visited, from east to west: the Museum of the Institute of Music, the Great Bell Temple, the Yellow Temple, the Altar to the Earth, the Handicrafts Centre.

1. The Museum of the Institute of Music

The National Museum of Music (Min zu yin yue chen lie guan) is attached to the National Institute o Music (Min zu yin yue yan jiu suo), itself attached to the Chinese Conservatoire of Music (Zhong guo yin yue xue yuan). For the moment, it is near the Xue yuan Avenue, in Peking's north-western suburbs. The 31 bus route goes there (the "Shi jian fang" stop).

The National Institute of Music was founded in 1954. It specialises in research, not teaching, and over a hundred research workers study the history of music in China (difficulties of old musical notation, collection of old instruments); they also gather material on popular music and the music of the national Minority Races (instruments and documents), and help New China's musicians to create a style of "national music". It contains laboratories, a library of 60,000 books and an extremely interesting museum which can be seen by appointment. Only part of the collection is exhibited.

First Section. Method of research used and its results (one room). Map showing the present state of the research, by province (He bei and Hu nan have been studied in great detail). Exhibition of some of the Institute's numerous publications, some of which are reserved for its own use only *(nei bu)*.

Second Section. History of music from its origins up to the Qing dynasty. *First room:* from the origins up to the Six Dynasties: terra cotta ocarina found on a Neolithic site in Shan xi; whistle from Ban po (see p. 944); Shang era musical stones (from a tomb in An yang); set of thirteen bells dating from the Warring States (He nan). Maps showing the origin of *guo feng* (poems intended to be sung, which occur in the *Shi jing* or *Classic of Songs*) and *yue fu* (popular poems collected by an office of music under the Han). Remarks of ancient authors on the subject of "music and society". Bronze drums from Yun nan; a lute *(gu qin)*.

Second room: Sui, Tang and Song periods: Tang and Song documents *(qu zi* and *bian wen,* both types of poems which were sung, from Dun huang); Tang tomb figurines of an orchestra; photographs of bas-relief carvings of musicians on the base of the tomb of King Qian Wang of Shu (Si chuan, 10th century); copies of Song instruments *(pi pa)*.

Third room: Ming and Qing dynasties: orchestras and musicians (Tu jia and Miao Minorities, a Shang hai theatre); manuscript with characters to indicate the notes. Han, Mongol, Uighur, Miao and Yao musical instruments.

Fourth room: Contemporary music (an enormous hall). The invasion of Western music (Church music, Maurice Chevalier); Chinese reaction (popular songs of the Tai ping period). The two great Communist composers: Nie Er (1912–1935) and Xian Xing hai (1905–1945). Musical renewal since 1945. Documents given by friendly countries.

Fourth Section. Restoration of instruments (one room). Forty-four specimens of old instruments restored for use in modern music (set of bells and gongs etc.).

Fifth Section. Han and Minority instruments: Yao double drums, Han cymbals, large range of Tibetan instruments (long horn, drum etc....), string instruments, Han *sheng* (mouth organ) and a fine set of *lu sheng* (some of impressive size) from the Dong and Miao Minorities.

2. The Great Bell Temple (Da zhong si)

It is a little under a mile north-west of Xi zhi men Gate, on the north circular road. It is on the No 16 bus route, a few minutes' walk north of the stop "Da zhong si".

History. The temple was built comparatively recently, in 1733, under the Qing Emperor Yong zheng. It was called Jue sheng si. Then the famous bell was brought there from the Wan shou si in 1743, under Qian long; from then on, the temple was known by its present name.

Description. Little is left of the buildings in front of the temple (they are now used by a small crystallised fruit works). A little side door leads through the right hand wall into the last courtyard. The pavilions are being restored (1965). The Bell Tower, 52 feet high, stands to the north; it is possible to have the door unlocked to see the bell.

The bell is enormous. It was cast in 1406, under the Ming Emperor Yong le, with five others like it; they were to be hung at the six corners of the city walls to strike the hours. This is the only one left now. It is 22 feet high, 10 feet across and 8 inches thick at the thickest point in its wall. It weighs 84,000 Chinese pounds, or 116,000 avoirdupois pounds. Complete passages of Buddhist texts (the Lotus and Diamond Sutras) are inscribed on its sides, making a total of 200,000 characters. It has no clapper, but remained in a fixed position and was hit on the outside. The quality of the work gives some idea of the technical perfection of Ming craftsmen. A legend tells how the master craftsman only achieved such perfection through the sacrifice of his daughter, who threw herself into the molten metal. It is also said that the Chinese of the neighbourhood used to throw coins through the openings in the roof, hoping that they would be transformed into gold.

3. The Yellow Temple (Huang si)

The No. 8 bus terminus (northern) is at the Huang si. To reach the temple, turn to the left (west) round a large area of military territory; the remains of the temple are just behind it.

History. A temple has existed on this site since the Liao. In 1651, under the Emperor Shun zhi, the western part of the temple was converted into a residence for the fifth Panchen Lama, who came on an official visit to Peking in 1652. The temple was restored under Kang xi and devoted entirely to the Lamaist sect. Tibetan dignitaries stayed here when they came to Peking. Under Qian long, the Panchen Lama died here of small-pox; in 1780, the Emperor had a magnificent mausoleum built for him in one of the temple courtyards. The thirteenth Dalai Lama stayed at the Huang si in 1908.

The temple consisted of two parts: the temple itself to the east (Dong huang si); and the residence to the west (Xi huang si), only part of which remains. At the beginning of the 20th century, the buildings were still used as a caravanserai by Mongol merchants passing through Peking. The monks used to make things of copper (vases later covered with cloisonné enamel, idols of gilded metal). A little building used to stand north east of the temple, containing boxes with the bodies of dead lamas waiting to be taken back to Tibet. On the 23rd and the 25th of the first lunar month dances like those at the Yong he gong (see p. 501) used to take place here.

The temple was badly damaged during the twenty years just before the liberation. The monks have all disappeared now; the temple is in ruins, and the annexes of the residence are used to billet soldiers.

Description. The Hall of the Temple Guardians still has four fine statues of celestial guardians; a second hall, in the middle of the second courtyard, has a photograph of the present Panchen Lama on the altar. The white marble stupa built by Qian long to house the remains of the Panchen Lama who died in Peking stands behind them. A flight of steps leads to a gallery which runs round the stupa. The base is covered with beautiful bas-relief carvings (damaged in 1900 and badly restored) depicting scenes from the life of the Buddha: departure from the town of Kapilavastu, the sermon at Benares, the struggle with the demons sent by Mara, parinirvana... Little pagodas stand at the four corners. The ruins of the old Dong huang si (bases of pillars, steles mounted on tortoises) are on the right.

4. The Altar to the Earth (Di tan)

The site of the former Altar to the Earth, which is now a public park, is about 800 yards from the An ding men Gate.

History. Originally, the cult of the earth was closely associa- ted with the cult of heaven, and the sacrifices were made on the same mound. Under the Han, a distinction began to be made. Later on the two were mingled once more, and were not finally separated until the Ming dynasty.

In 1530, the Emperor Jia jing built the first altar, north of Peking, and called it Fang zi tan, which he changed to Di tan in 1534. Qian long had it rebuilt in 1748, and the size of the mound was almost doubled.

The ceremonies took place once a year, at the summer solstice. The tablet of the earth (painted vermilion) was placed on the mound, with the tablets of the five sacred mountains, the four seas, the four rivers... and those of the dead Emperors, which were brought from the Palace. The Emperor spent the night in preparation in the Hall of Abstinence (Zhai gong) and proceeded up to the altar (seven quarters of an hour before sunrise). He made several offerings (the meat of a yellow bull, a cup of wine, silk) and prostrated himself nine times. An assistant read a prayer; each stage in the rites was accompanied by appropriate music. Finally the offerings were buried in a special pit.

The altar fell out of use in 1911 and has been badly pillaged. Several parts of it (which could still be visited in 1923) were used as soldiers' billets and still are.

The plan is much the same as that of the Altar to the Moon: two square enclosures, one inside the other, surrounded the Hall of Abstinence, the mound, the slaughter-house, the shops, and, to the south, the room where the tablets were normally kept. As a whole it is disappointing now. All that is left is the wide way running from east to west, the remains of the Zhai gong to the north, and to the south, the enclosure round the mound where the sacrifices took place.

5. The Handicrafts Centre

It is a fair way north of the Altar to the Earth, east of the main road, An ding men wai da jie Avenue.

Under the Republic, a state workshop already existed, near Liu li chang, where objects were made in glass, cane, lacquer, silk and wool. A printing press and museum were attached to it, and engineers specialised in sinking artesian wells were trained there. In 1923, 500 workmen were employed there.

After the liberation, a new handicrafts centre was created here, in new buildings. The craftsmen are grouped under several sections: cloisonné ware, lacquered furniture, lacquer ware, silver jewellery; jade and ivory ware; little vases painted on the inside with a very fine brush.

C. THE EASTERN SUBURBS

The eastern suburbs fall into three clearly defined districts: a new quarter to the north, with tree-lined roads crossing at right angles; in the centre, the quarter just outside the former Chao yang men Gate, with old houses, and busy shopping streets; and to the south, an area which is still sparsely populated, dotted with old single storey houses, with little trace of modern urbanisation.

The northern district embraces the new diplomatic quarter (San li tun, "the Village three li away", i.e. a mile from the city), the huge Workers' Stadium (it was opened in 1959 and can seat 80,000), the Gymnasium and the Agricultural Exhibition Centre (Nong ye zhan lan guan) where temporary exhibitions are put on.

The European cemetery is to the north-east, near the road to the airport; it is in the middle of the fields and difficult to find without the help of someone who knows the way. The European cemetery which used to lie north of the Bei tang (cf. see p. 493) has been entirely transferred here. The graves are those of French, English, German, Italian, Dutch residents or soldiers killed in the campaigns of 1860 and 1900.

Chao yang men wai jie is the main street in the central part, and it has some old shop fronts still; the Tai shan Temple was here; nearby are the remains of the Altar to the Sun.

1. The Former Tai shan Temple
(Dong yue miao: Eastern Peak Temple)

It is about half a mile from the site of the Chao yang men Gate on the north side of Chao yang men wai jie Street.

The worship of the god of Mount Tai shan, Tian qi, and of his daughter, the princess of coloured clouds (Bi xia yuan jun) was extremely widespread in China. Almost every town had a Dong yue miao (Eastern Peak Temple) in its eastern suburbs, where they were both worshipped (the cult was connected with Taoism, see E. Chavannes: *Le T'ai chan, essai de monographie d'un culte chinois*, Paris 1910). The temple in Peking was one of the richest of all; it was founded under the Yuan, at the beginning of the 14th century, and enlarged under the Ming; when in 1698 it was destroyed by fire, it was instantly rebuilt, and then done up under Qian long. The statues of Tian qi, who was in charge of the fate of spirits in the after world, and Yue fei, the god of vengeance, were worshipped here; the women came to pray to the princess of the coloured clouds, and her eight attendants, known collectively as Niang niang, to grant them sons, and to protect their children from disease in general. There used to be a statue of a mule famous for its healing powers: "he who had a sore ear touched its ear, he who had sore eyes touched its eyes". The temple was open to the faithful on the first and the fifteenth of each month, and during the second fortnight of the third lunar month (crowds of people would come on the 28th of the month, as it was the birthday of the king of the underworld). One of the annex buildings contained stucco groups showing the various courts of justice before which human beings passed after death (depicting the tortures which awaited them in the after life); H. A. Giles, at the end of his book: *Strange Stories of a Chinese Studio*, describes the groups.

The temple has been a school since 1949 and no visits are allowed. All that can be seen is the beautiful *pai lou*, with its green and yellow glazed tiles (on the south side of the street) and the two stone lions in front of the door.

2. The Altar to the Sun (Ri tan)

Almost opposite the Dong yu miao a wide street leads south to the Altar of the Sun. The eastern suburbs market used to be held permanently in this street.

History. The worship of the sun, linked with the worship of the moon, is mentioned as early as the Zhou period, in the *Li ji*, a book of rites; it consisted in a sacrifice offered by the Emperor at the spring equinox, in the eastern suburbs of the capital (the side nearest the rising sun). It is thought that an altar has existed east of the town since the Liao, but no traces have yet been found; the present altar was built under the Ming Emperor Jia jing, in 1531; it was restored and enlarged under Qian long. It consisted of a square terrace encircled by a round enclosure and various annex buildings; a long avenue heralded by a wooden *pai lou*, with red walls on either side, led to the northern entrance. The sacrifice took place between 6 o'clock and 8 o'clock in the morning; several ritual presents, all coloured red, were offered, and an ox, a sheep and a pig were sacrificed, before the tablet of the sun, which was gold, inscribed with four characters in vermilion: *Da ming zhi shen* (Spirit of Great Light). The annex buildings were converted into billets for soldiers in 1927, and into a hospital in 1937. The whole area is now a park.

The eastern entrance gate is still standing, as are the annex buildings with their green roofs (the room used by the Emperor as a robing room, the sacred kitchens and shops); the altar in the middle of its round enclosure (270 yards round) is 50 feet long each side.

D. THE SOUTHERN SUBURBS

From the Ming dynasty onwards, almost all this area was a huge park reserved for the Emperor's use, surrounded by a wall 37 miles round, with nine gates. 1,600 sailors were settled there; land had been granted them and they studied the military arts at the same time. The estate produced flowers and fruit. The court used to come to take the air and to hunt (in winter and spring particularly). Rare animals were bred there, among them the famous *si bu xiang* (elaphurus, see p. 540). The allied troops breached the walls in 1900 and most of the animals escaped; the park ran wild; towards 1920, barracks and a flying school were built there.

Most of the park walls have disappeared by now and the area is occupied by fields or factories; built up areas occur at intervals.

THE SURROUNDINGS OF PEKING

(Map, see Atlas pl. 2 and 3)

I. The north-west greater suburbs

The first foot-hills of the mountains rise out of the plain about 12 miles north-west of the city: Longevity Hill, Jade Fountain Hill, and the Western Hills (Xi shan), some of which are known as the Fragrant Hills. Several natural springs rise here (such as the Jade Fountain), freshening the countryside and watering the fields.

As early as the 10th century, the Emperors began to have their summer residences built here; temples, monasteries and mandarins' houses grew up round the imperial palaces until under the Ming and the Qing it became one of the most attractive and popular of the suburbs of the capital.

The area took on a new character at the beginning of the 20th century; educational establishments were founded here in the green countryside (Qing hua University, Yan jing University, the latter founded by the Americans, in a former mandarin's garden). Almost all the new higher educational establishments built since 1949 are here, and the area is now the university quarter of the capital.

Agriculture had already been stimulated by the proximity of the palaces, and the monasteries were well-known for their skill in silviculture and horticulture; all the residences, whether lay or religious, were surrounded by vast estates with offices, outbuildings and tenant farms. Agriculture has been developed still further to meet the needs of Peking, and also as a result of collectivisation: rice is grown near the Yi he yuan and in what used to be the estate round the Yuan ming yuan, vegetables, grapes and fruit are grown east of the Western Hills (the "Evergreen Commune" on the road to Ba da chu), the hills have been replanted with trees (the Forestry Institute now occupies the annex buildings of the Wo fo si Temple).

Finally, this has always been an area used for military exercises. Under the Emperors, garrisons guarded the palaces, and

Qian long trained his troops in the Western Hills (see training towers, p. 610); under the Republic, the Xi yuan Park was a barracks (south east of Yi he yuan); the Western Hills were of great strategic importance during the civil wars (communist resistance); and now, many camps have been built near the hills, and there are many military zones to which entry is forbidden.

A. THE ROAD TO THE SUMMER PALACE

Two different ways led to the summer palace before: 1. the road from Xi zhi men Gate to the town of Hai dian (the No 16 bus now follows part of this road); 2. the canal, the Chang he, which started at the north-west corner of the city walls, ran behind the present Zoo, south of the Wu ta si (see p. 563), and the Wan shou si (see below), then alongside the town of Lan dian, and finally ended at the southern tip of Lake Kun ming. The canal (about five and a half miles long) still exists; the old paved road still runs alongside it, though it is in poor condition now. Six bridges spanned the canal, and six locks regulated the water, as the level changed by about 40 feet over the whole of the canal. Starting from Xi zhi men Gate, the bridges were a) the **Sorgho Bridge** (gao liang qiao), which recalls the old name of the canal: Gao liang he (sorgho river). Under the Ming, the ceremony of bathing the Buddha took place here, on the eight day of the fourth month; his statue was dipped into the canal and it was followed by general merry-making; b) the **White Stone Bridge** (Bai shi qiao), west of the Wu ta si Temple; c) the **Bridge of the Great Spring** (Guang yuan qiao); the biggest lock was here, and it was here that one changed boats, to go either to the Summer Palace or back to the capital.

The Emperor and his train used to stop here for a short time; in 1577, the eunuch Feng pao, the favourite of Wan li,

had the Temple of Ten Thousand Ages (Wan shou si) built on
the north bank of the canal. Qian long had it rebuilt in 1752,
and in 1862, the Dowager Empress Ci xi, who was fond of this
spot, had a palace built to the left of the temple, where she
could rest on her journey. The bridge (with fine balustrades),
the stone uprights used for hauling up the sluice gates, and the
outside of the temple, now a nursery school, can all still be seen
today.

d) the **Corn Farm Bridge** (Mai zhuang qiao), between the Wan shou si Temple and the village of Lan
dian; e) the **Bridge of Eternal Spring** (Chang chun
qiao), at the entrance to the village of Lan dian; f) the
Bridge of the Embroidered Waves (Xiu yi qiao), at the
southernmost tip of Lake Kun ming, inside the Yi he
yuan enclosure (it is a beautiful hump-backed marble
bridge).

These two routes can be covered on foot, but cars
take a new road (the 32 bus route) which will now be
described. It runs alongside the south wall of the Zoo,
then turns north and crosses the Chang he canal by a
new bridge beside the old White Stone Bridge (Bai shi
qiao).

The entrance to the **Purple Bamboo Park (Zi zhu
yuan),** a public park of 56 acres, is just before the
bridge, on the left.

Under the Yuan, the engineer Guo Shou jing had lakes dug
here to regulate the flow of the water, and the canal which he
built to bring the waters of the Jade Fountain and the Bai he
to Peking (the first canalisation of the Chang he) ran through
here. Under the Ming, the Wan shou si Temple (see above) and
the Purple Bamboo Park Temple (which left its name to the
area) were built north of the lakes. The Emperor Qian long
had a "Su zhou street" built to the east, to remind him of his
travels in the south; it was destroyed in 1860. The three lakes
have now been re-dug, and regulate the water in the new western
canal, which brings water from the River Yong ding to the
Chang he; the lakes are now used for rearing fish. All the old
buildings have disappeared, except for a pretty nine-storey,
octagonal brick pagoda, dating from the Ming dynasty.

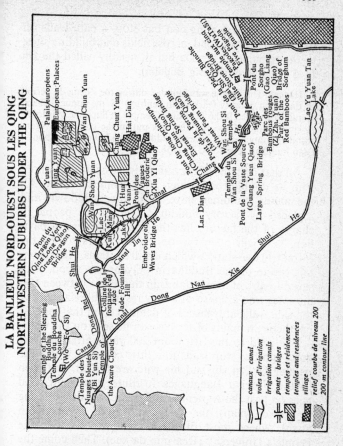

After the White Stone Bridge, the road passes the Social Science Institute (on the left), then the Central Institute of Minorities (Zhong yang min zu xue yuan), which contains a small museum on the Minorities, and the village of Wei gong cun.

Before the Wei gong cun bus stop, a path leads off
to the right of the road, across fields and building sites,
to the remains of the Da hui si, usually called the **Da
fo si (Temple of the Big Buddha)**.

History. The temple was founded during the Zheng de period
of the Ming dynasty (early 16th century) by the eunuch Zhang
xiong, who called it the Da hui si (Temple of Supreme Wisdom).
A large statue of the Buddha was put in the central pavilion.
Another eunuch made several additions in 1550 or thereabouts;
Qian long had it restored in 1758.

All that remains of the temple is the central pavilion,
with its double roof, which dates from the Ming. All
the annex buildings have been knocked down and
replaced by factory buildings. One of the people in
charge of the factory has the key of the central pavilion, and will open the door for visitors to see the
extremely fine statues which it still contains. An enormous statue of the Buddha in polychrome wood, with
several pairs of arms, stands in the centre between two
disciples who are also of a very respectable size. Along
the side walls are statues of demons from the Lamaist
pantheon; remains of frescos can be seen on the walls.

The road to the left about 200 yards after the Wei
gong cun bus stop leads to a little cemetery where the
painter Qi Bai shi and his wife are buried, and then
to the Foreign Languages Institute; the main road
goes on past the Agricultural Research Institute (Nong
ye ke xue yuan), the Friendship Hotel (You yi bin
guan), where most of the foreign experts live, the
People's University (Ren min da xue). Then come the
outskirts of the village of Hai dian.

Hai dian was so called because there were numerous
ponds here under the Ming dynasty. It was an important stage on the road to the Summer Palace; high
officials used to have houses built here. It is now no

more than a little shopping centre, with an attractive main street, where peasants from the neighbouring countryside come to do their shopping.

After the Zhong guan cun stop, the road takes a right angle turn to the left, and continues between Hai dian (to the left) and the south wall of Peking University (on the right), then it takes the right hand road at a fork junction and goes on past the east wall of the University (right) and the site of the former Chang chun yuan Park (on the left). All that remains of the park are the two little pavilions at the entrance (red with yellow roofs). The entrance to Peking University is on the right; it is easy to recognise, with its great red gate and the two stone lions flanking it.

Peking University (Bei jing da xue). The University is in a huge park, which was owned by He Shen, the favourite of Qian long, at the end of the 18th century; this powerful man had had a magnificent house built there, where he kept part of his treasures (an enormous list of them, drawn up at the end of the century, when he fell into disgrace, still survives). Several spots in the grounds were reminiscent of the Yi he yuan gardens, and a stone boat, a replica of the one which Qian long had built, still stands in one of the lakes.

❚ When Macartney came to Peking, he was received here by the great mandarin in 1792. At the beginning of the 20th century, the Americans founded Yan jing University (Yenching University) here, to give an education in English to a limited number of Chinese students. Towards the end, Leighton Stewart, an American who was born in China, and who was also the last American ambassador to China, was the principal of the University. In 1953, it was decided to move Peking University (founded in 1898) here, as the old buildings east of Coal hill (see p. 495) were too small.

New buildings have been added to those left by the Americans; the University is divided into 18 sections, eight of them devoted to scientific subjects (mathematics, physics, chemistry, geography, biology, geology, telecommunications, atomic science) and ten to arts subjects (Chinese language and literature, history, economics, administration, law, librarianship, Oriental languages, Western languages, Russian). 76% of the students are entirely financed by the State. There are 10,000 students.

The road runs alongside the western wall of the University, then turns to the left once more, through rice-fields, and reaches the Yi he yuan in a short time.

B. THE SUMMER PALACE (YI HE YUAN) AND THE RUINS OF THE YUAN MING YUAN

1. The Summer Palace (Yi he yuan)

It is about 6 miles from Xi zhi men Gate, to the north-west (No 32 bus route). The grounds cover 659 acres altogether; Longevity Hill (Wan shou shan) to the north, on which the palaces are, takes up a quarter of it; the Lake Kun ming to the south covers the other three-quarters. Walls surround the whole area, with a few gates.

History. In 1153, the Jin Emperor Wan yan liang built the first palace of all here; it was called the "Garden of Golden Waters" (Jin shui yuan); under the Yuan, the engineer Guo Shou jing enlarged the lake considerably and made the Jade Fountain and the Chang ping springs flow into it from the north. The Ming built the Temple of Perfect Calm (Yuan jing si) and several pavilions, and called the whole place the "Garden of the Wonderful Hills" (Hao shan yuan). The lake was renamed several times: the Big Lake, the West Lake, the Western Sea. Emperor Qian long undertook the most extensive work. For his mother's sixtieth birthday, he transformed several spots to look like some of the places which she

LE LAC KUN MING SOUS LES MING ET SOUS LES QING
LAKE KUN MING UNDER THE MING AND THE QING

A) LE XI HU SOUS LES MING
A) THE XI YU UNDER THE MING

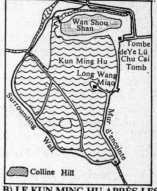

B) LE KUN MING HU APRÈS LES
AMÉNAGEMENTS DU XVIIIe S.
B) THE KUN MING HU AFTER
THE CHANGES OF THE 18th C.

had particularly admired at Hang zhou, and called the hill by its present name of Longevity Hill. The park was then called the "Garden of Clear Waves" (Qing yi yuan); it was part of a vast sweep of imperial gardens: the Yuan ming yuan, the Chang chun yuan and the Wan chun yuan stretched away to the east, all of them laid out by Kang xi or Qian long. As the court came here to avoid the heat, all the residences were known as the Summer Palace. The most magnificent of all was certainly the Yuan ming yuan (see p. 595). In 1860, the European troops sacked all the palaces, and the Qing yi yuan suffered like the rest. It was in ruins when the Dowager Empress Ci xi (Tz'u Hsi) decided in 1888 to spend the money meant for the improvement of the navy on rebuilding it. She herself gave it its present name of Yi he yuan (the Garden where Peace is Cultivated). She liked to stay there and had it restored after it was damaged anew in 1900. She kept the Emperor Guang xu prisoner there after the "hundred days" affair in 1898, until his death in 1908. The gardens were opened to the public for the first time in 1924. Large-scale restoration work has been carried out since

1949. It is now one of the parks which is most frequented by the inhabitants of Peking (skating in winter, bathing and boating in summer).

Description. A large wooden *pai lou* stands in front of the main entrance to the Yi he yuan, followed by a screen wall *(ying bi);* these lead into the forecourt, with the Eastern Palace Gate (Dong gong men) at the far end, which is the entrance (tickets are shown here). It is impossible to describe each palace and pavilion in detail, so the most interesting ones will be grouped under four headings.

a) The Eastern Palaces

1. North and south of the first courtyard stretch the former outhouses and offices; in the centre of the second one stand a bronze unicorn from the Yuan ming yuan and four incense-burners shaped like animals; temporary exhibitions are put on in the buildings to right and left; at the far end: *Hall of Goodwill and Longevity (Ren shou dian)*, where the Emperor gave audience (rebuilt in 1888). The throne and the nineteenth century furniture are still there. 2. On the right stands the *Palace of Virtue and Harmony (De he yuan);* a *three-storey theatre* occupies the middle of it, rather like an Elizabethan theatre; the stage and ceiling have trap-doors, to enable actors to appear and disappear; a well supplied water effects. Ci xi watched the play from the *Yi le dian* (opposite the stage); sometimes she would take part, disguised as Guan yin (goddess of mercy). The Yi le dian contains a good collection of clocks and clockwork figures (a bird in a cage, clocks in railway engines) and some terra cotta figures *(niren from Tian jin, see p. 657)* depicting Mu lan, scenes from the *Xi xiang ji* and the *Hong lou meng.* 3. To the south-west, the *Jade Waves Palace (Yu lan tang)* stands on the shore of the lake. For ten years it was the Emperor Guang xu's prison; on the right hand side of the courtyard, a brick wall has been put up behind the wooden partition wall. The Emperor's furniture, his table and bed, can be seen inside. 4. Going westwards along the lake, the next building is the *Palace of Joy and Longevity (Le shou tang)*, which was Ci xi's residence: dining-room (four peach-shaped incense-burners), bed-room.

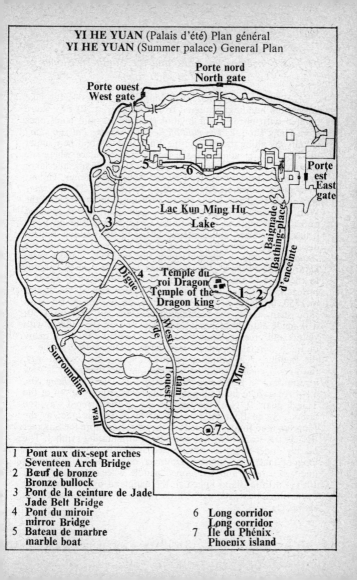

YI HE YUAN (Palais d'été) Plan général
YI HE YUAN (Summer palace) General Plan

Porte nord
North gate

Porte ouest
West gate

5

6

Porte
est
East
gate

Lac Kun Ming Hu
Lake

Baignade
Bathing-place

3

Digue

4

Temple du
roi Dragon
Temple of the
Dragon king

1 2

West dam

Mur d'enceinte

Surrounding wall

7

1 Pont aux dix-sept arches
   Seventeen Arch Bridge
2 Bœuf de bronze
   Bronze bullock
3 Pont de la ceinture de Jade
   Jade Belt Bridge
4 Pont du miroir
   mirror Bridge
5 Bateau de marbre
   marble boat

6 Long corridor
   Long corridor
7 Île du Phénix
   Phoenix island

b) The Shores of the Lake and the Southern Slopes of the Wan shou shan

1. A covered way, 900 yards long, runs alongside the lake linking the buildings scattered from east to west. Its beams are painted with historical or mythological scenes, and landscapes from Hang zhou. 2. *The Hall of Regular Clouds (Pai yun dian)* is half-way along the gallery; the Yuan jing si stood here under the Ming. Ci xi converted the temple into a palace where she celebrated her birthdays; a tall *pai lou* stands beside the lake; inside are a portrait of Ci xi by the American painter, Hubert Vos, and a collection of 19th century furniture. 3. The *Fo xiang ge Pagoda* (150 feet high) stands on the southern slope of the Wan shou shan, just above the Pai yun dian; it was founded under the Ming and rebuilt under Ci xi; ramps lead up to it; it has four stories, and contains statues of the Buddha and his disciples (19th century). 4. East of the Fo xiang ge stands the *Zhuan lun cang*, a library where the Buddhist classics were kept. 5. *The Pavilion of the Precious Cloud (Bao yun ge)* stands to the west of the Fo xiang ge; in the middle of it stands a bronze kiosk (Tong ting) said to have been cast by the Jesuits in 1750. 6. North of the Fo xiang ge, on the top of the Wan shou shan stands the rectangular *Zhi hui hai*, built in 1750; it is made entirely of brick, and decorated on the outside with yellow and green ceramic figures (statues of the Buddha, many of them mutilated); inside is a large gilded seated statue of the Buddha. 7. Continuing westwards along the covered way, the *Ting li guan* is the next building; an old theatre, it is now a restaurant (it had a two-storey stage). 8. The *Hua zhang you*, a sort of gazebo built up against the rocks, stands north of the Ting li guan. 9. Near the western end of the covered way, the famous Stone Boat built by Ci xi stands in the lake; as the Empress used funds intended for the navy to restore the Summer Palace, the stone boat was considered an amusing symbol. The marble under-structure which acted as a jetty dates from Qian long in fact; the Empress Dowager only added the wooden under-structures and the stone "paddle wheels" on the sides. 10. On a little island linked to the mainland by a bridge, west of the stone boat, stands the little *Temple of the Five Sages (Wu sheng si)*.

c) The Back Lakes and the Northern Slopes of the Wan shou shan

A chain of lakes stretches north of the Wan shou shan which can be reached either from the east, by leaving the De he yuan to the north, or from the west, going on from the Stone Boat; the second route is the one described. 1. North of the Stone Boat, a little metal paddle boat was found; it is the *Yong he* (Eternal Peace) which Japan presented to the Empress Ci xi; she used to go for "cruises" in it on the Kun ming hu; it has recently been brought up from the bottom of the lake. 2. The Imperial Boat-houses were a little further on, on the left; the boats were laid up here. 3. A right hand turn along the banks of the little lakes leads to landscapes which are meant to recall Southern China. Near the big three-arch bridge, Qian long had little shops built on both sides of the water-course to remind him of the canals of Su zhou and their lively trade. It was known as the "Su zhou Street"; nothing is left of it now. The north entrance to the park is north of the bridge. To the south, a Buddhist temple, the *Xu mi ling jing*, founded under Qian long, clings to the northern slopes of the Wan shou shan; the ground floor hall has statues of the Buddha and the *luo han;* above them, massed rocks, square towers and stupas symbolise the cosmic mountain (Mount Sumeru, *Xu mi* in Chinese). 4. The *Many Treasures Pagoda (Duo bao ta)* is to the east, on the slopes of the hill; it used to be the central building of a group which was destroyed in 1860. It is built in brick, decorated with multicoloured tiles; the seven stories are unequal in height, and some have little niches with statues of the Buddha. 5. Close together, to the south-east, stand the *Jing fu ge* (a gazebo), the *Yi shou tang* (a private

YI HE YUAN
LES PALAIS DE LA RIVE NORD DU LAC KUN MING

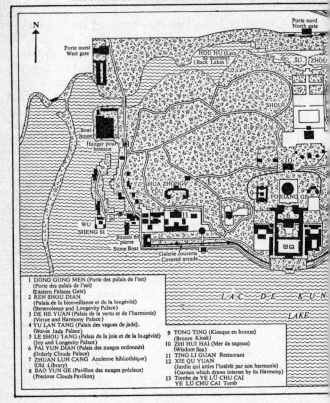

1 DONG GONG MEN (Porte des palais de l'est)
  (Porte des palais de l'est)
  (Eastern Palaces Gate)
2 REN SHOU DIAN
  (Palais de la bienveillance et de la longévité)
  (Benevolence and Longevity Palace)
3 DE HE YUAN (Palais de la vertu et de l'harmonie)
  (Virtue and Harmony Palace)
4 YU LAN TANG (Palais des vagues de jade).
  (Waves Jade Palace)
5 LE SHOU TANG (Palais de la joie et de la longévité)
  (Joy and Longevity Palace)
6 PAI YUN DIAN (Palais des nuages ordonnés)
  (Orderly Clouds Palace)
7 ZHUAN LUN CANG Ancienne bibliothèque)
  (Old Library)
8 BAO YUN GE (Pavillon des nuages précieux)
  (Precious Clouds Pavilion)
9 TONG TING (Kiosque en bronze)
  (Bronze Kiosk)
10 ZHI HUI HAI (Mer de sagesse)
   (Wisdom Sea)
11 TING LI GUAN Restaurant
12 XIE QU YUAN
   (Jardin qui attire l'intérêt par son harmonie)
   (Garden which draws interest by its Harmony)
13 Tombe de YE LÜ CHU CAI
   YE LÜ CHU CAI Tomb

house), the *Le nong xuan (Pavilion of Joy and Agriculture)*, built to look like a peasant farm. 6. The western
slope of the hill reveals the *Xie qu yuan (the Garden
which attracts Interest by its Harmony)*; a dozen little

YI HE YUAN
THE PALACES ON THE NORTHERN SHORE OF LAKE KUN MING

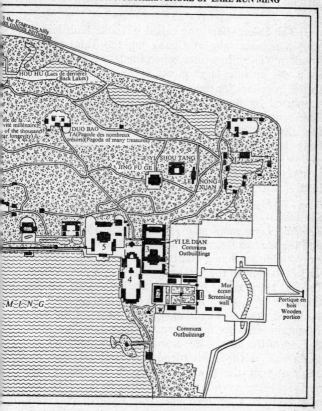

the Fragrance hills
les collines parfumées

HOU HU (Lacs de derrière
Back Lakes)

DUO BAO
TA(Pagode des nombreux
trésors)(Pagoda of many treasures)

ifle de
vité millénaire)
of the thousand
ar longevity)

YI SHOU TANG

JING FU GE

LE NONG
XIAN

YI LE DIAN
Communs
Outbuildings

Mur écran
Screening
wall

Portique en
bois
Wooden
portico

M~I~N~G

Communs
Outbuildings

pavilions cluster round a pool of lotus plants (they
were built in 1750 and afterwards restored). It is meant
to imitate a celebrated spot at Wu xi (Jiang su); Ci xi
is supposed to have come to fish here. It is an enchant-

ing spot, and has been nick-named the "garden of gardens".

d) **The Lake.** Qian long called it "Lake Kun ming" after a famous lake at Chang an, the Tang capital (modern Xi an). In winter, when the lake is frozen, the ice is cut up into large pieces to be taken away and stored in cellars for use in summer (a custom which is supported by documentary evidence as early as the 18th century). 1. The *Long wang miao Island*. When the lake was enlarged to the east, under the reign of Qian long, a promontory was left isolated in the middle; a magnificent seventeen-arch bridge was built to link it with dry land; a bronze ox stands near the bridge, with a poem by Qian long inscribed on his back; it is supposed to represent the oxen used to clear the lake. On the island itself stand the *Dragon King Temple (Long wang miao)*, built in the 18th century, and the *Han xu tang*, from which, it is said, the Emperor Qian long watched boating contests. 2. The *Western Dyke* is a copy of the Su Dong po Dyke on the Western Lake at Hang zhou; six bridges are built along it; one, a stone bridge, has a high hump back and is called the *Jade Belt Bridge (Yu dai qiao)*; the waters of the Jade Fountain used to flow through here into the lake. 3. East of the lake, a tree-lined way runs alongside the outer wall; to the south it leads to a large gate near the beginning of the canal which goes to Peking (see p. 581); there is a fine arched bridge; to the north, the way ends at a fortified gate: the *Gate of Flowering Culture (Wen chang ge)*, which leads to the Eastern Palaces; the Emperor came by this route when he came by land. North of the gate the *Tomb of Ye lü chu cai* (1190–1244) can still be seen; he was adviser to Genghis Khan.

2. The Ruins of the Yuan ming yuan

Another group of palaces stretched north-east and east of the Yi he yuan. The Emperor Kang xi lived for a long time in the Chang chun yuan (Garden of Everlasting Spring), west of the present Peking university (the two entrance pavilions can still be seen, almost opposite the red gate of the University itself). The Emperor Yong zheng laid out the Yuan ming yuan (Garden of Perfection and Light, not "Garden of Round Light", as it is sometimes translated); the Emperor Qian long carried out an even more ambitious plan; he had two new gardens, the Chang chun yuan (Garden of Eternal Spring) and the Wan shou yuan (Garden of Ten Thousand Ages) laid out to the east of the Yuan ming yuan.

Father Attiret, a Jesuit and court painter to Qian long, describes Chinese gardens in a letter dated September 1st, 1743 (published in the *Lettres édifiantes)*: "Hillocks have been built, 20 to 60 feet high, forming endless little valleys. Channels of clear water, brought from the mountains which dominate the area, water the valleys, and divide, to meet again in several places to form pools, ponds and lakes.

"The slopes of the mountains and hills are covered with the flowering shrubs and trees so frequent in China. The channels do not follow straight lines; the rough stones along their banks are placed with such consummate art that ti seems to be none other than the work of nature. Sometimes the channel widens, sometimes it is narrow, then it winds; the banks are starred with flowers growing out from among the rocks, different ones for each season.

"The buildings are to be seen on entering the valley. The façade is composed of pillars and windows; the beams are gilded, painted and varnished; the walls of grey brick, carefully cut and polished. The roofs are covered with glazed tiles, red, yellow, blue, violet, mingled and arranged so that they form a pleasant variety of divisions and patterns.

"Every valley has its house, which is small, if one considers the enclosure as a whole, but big enough to lodge the greatest of our lords and his train. Several houses are built in cedarwood, brought from five hundred leagues away, and in this vast area, there are over two hundred of these palaces, not counting the eunuchs' pavilions.

"Bridges of all kinds span the channels. Some of them have white marble balustrades, wonderfully worked, with bas-relief carvings. In the middle of the big lake, a little palace stands on a rock, in the very centre, in a spot carefully chosen by the architect so that it commands views of all that is beautiful in the park. Magnificent boats carry people across the lakes; they are often as big and as spacious as a fine house.

"The Emperor's appartments contain all the most beautiful objects possible (according to Chinese taste of course) in the way of furniture, ornaments, paintings, precious wood, lacquer from China and Japan, old vases, porcelain, silk, cloth of gold and silver. Everything which art and good taste can add to the riches of nature has been collected here".

One of the curiosities of these gardens was the set of "European palaces" which Qian long had built between 1740 and 1747. The architects and foremen were all Jesuits (Castiglione, Sichelbarth, Benoist). The palaces covered the north part of the Garden of Eternal Spring; from east to west they were: first a pavilion, with music rooms and ornamental pools, then a labyrinth, an aviary, a little gazebo (later transformed into a mosque for Xiang fei, the beautiful Uighur favourite, in 1760), five bamboo kiosks inlaid with glass and shells, the Palace of the Calm Sea, with beautiful fountains... and finally, an imitation of the Aksu countryside, using stage scenery, made to please Xiang fei.

The Jesuits themselves described the palaces:

"Beautiful pieces of water adorn the second European building in the Emperor's garden. Some of them are in very good taste, and the large one could stand up to comparison with the ones at Versailles and St. Cloud. When the Emperor is on his throne, he sees on each side of him a large pyramid of water standing in the centre of a group, and in front of him, several fountains arranged with the utmost skill so that when playing they represent the war supposed to be waged by the fish, birds and different kinds of animals in the pool, round the edge, and amongst the rocks, placed with seeming carelessness, and forming a hemicycle which is all the more delightful because it is rustic and wild. The part which Father Benoist found most difficult of all was the piece of water at the foot of the house,

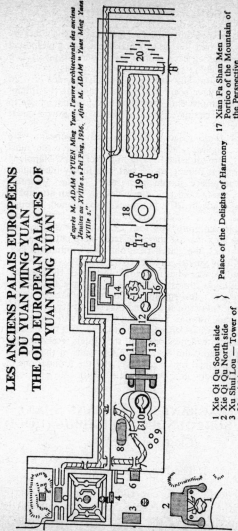

LES ANCIENS PALAIS EUROPÉENS
DU YUAN MING YUAN
THE OLD EUROPEAN PALACES OF
YUAN MING YUAN

d'après M. ADAM «YUEN Ming Yuen, l'œuvre architecturale des anciens
Jésuites au XVIIIe s.» Pei Ping, 1936. After M. ADAM "Yuen Ming Yuen
XVIIe s."

1 Xie Qi Qu South side
2 Xie Qi Qu North side
3 Xu Shui Lou — Tower of
  Nourishing Water (cistern)
4 Hua Yuan Men —
  Flower Garden Gate
5 Hua Yuan — Flower Garden
  (Maze)
6 Yang Qiao Long (Aviary)
7 Monumental Gateway
8 Fang Wai Guan — Belvedere
  (Xiang Fei Mosque)

Palace of the Delights of Harmony

9 Zhu Ting — Bamboo Kiosks
10 11 12 13 Hai Yan Tang —
  Palace of the Calm Sea
14 Yuan Ying Guan (Observatory)
15 Da Shui Fa — «Fountains
  Playing»
16 Guan Shui Fa — View of the
  fountains playing

17 Xian Fa Shan Men —
  Portico of the Mountain of
  the Perspective
18 Xian Fa Shan — Mountain.
  the Perspective
19 Xian Fa Shan Dong Men —
  Eastern Portico of the
  Mountain of the Perspective
20 Hu Dong Xian Fa Hua —
  Painting in perspective to the
  east of the lake

for as the Chinese personify the twelve hours of their day by twelve animals, he had the idea of making it into a perpetual water clock, by making each animal spit water during its two hours..." (Lettres édifiantes, vol. 13 p. 469 onwards).

The Jesuits sent drawings to Paris giving a good idea of what the buildings must have been: "forty views" now at the Bibliothèque Nationale, and twenty copper-plate engravings, made in China in the 18th century, prints of which are now a great rarity.

In 1860, all these palaces, Chinese and European, were sacked by the English and French troops. "First the most valuable things were set aside for Queen Victoria and Napoleon III, then the soldiers plundered the rest, and finally the English decided that the palace should be burned" (*Guide Madrolle*, 1904). Even so, the fire did not utterly destroy it; an attempt at restoration was made in 1879, but quickly abandoned, through lack of funds. "After that, everything disappeared... the beautiful marble sculpture was torn apart to get at the iron which held the sections together, the trees were cut down for firewood, the bricks, the glazed tiles, almost everything in fact, was sold..." (Mgr. Favier, *Peking*, 1897).

Rice fields now cover what used to be the site of the gardens; the Chinese buildings, almost entirely of wood, have disappeared leaving not a trace; a few ruins of the European palaces are all that now remain (north-west of Qing hua University, across the fields). The façade of the Yuan ying guan is still there (the southern side, with traces of the fountain), and so is the massive block of masonry which supported the water reservoir (the former Palace of the Calm Sea), and a few walls of the gazebo which was transformed into a mosque, and the foundations of the Palace of Harmony and Delights (Jie qi qu).

C. THE FRAGRANT HILLS (XIANG SHAN) AND THE SURROUNDING NEIGHBOURHOOD
(Closed in 1972.)

1. The Fragrant Hills

The road leads off to the right out of the square in front of the Summer Palace, and runs westwards along the north wall of the park (No. 33 bus route).

Due west of the Yi he yuan, and south of the barrier of mountains which dominates the plain at this point, rise the twin hills of the **Jade Fountain,** visible from some way away because of their shape and their two pagodas.

The Jade Fountain Hill (Yu quan shan) is the result of a geographical phenomenon, a violent flexure, accompanied by faults, which pushed a particularly hard layer of upper sinian limestone to the surface. The limestone has been partly transformed into marble, and is excellent material for sculpture. Several plentiful springs rise in the area, which have been used since very early days to supply Peking and its neighbourhood with water.

The Jin were the first to use this magnificent site; they built a palace here. Kang xi laid out a park, known as the Jing ming yuan; then Qian long had several pavilions, palaces, Buddhist and Taoist temples built, and also had some beautiful rock shrines cut in the marble. The area is a military zone now, unfortunately, and no visitors are allowed. All that can be seen are an octagonal tower, seven stories (100 feet) high, and a small tower (Miao gao ta), of Indian inspiration.

A yellow-roofed pavilion with a little round red brick enclosure behind it stands on the other side of the road, north of the double hill.

It is the **Tomb of Tai zong,** the seventh Ming Emperor (Jing tai period, 1450–1457); when the sixth Emperor, Ying zong, was captured by the Mongols in 1450, his brother took over the throne; several years later, Ying zong was set free and managed to get it back (1457). His brother died soon after; Ying zong, who did not want him to be considered as legal Emperor, had him buried in this modest tomb, instead of letting him take his place in the valley where the other imperial tombs are. A memorial stele stands in the pavilion, with a plain stone tumulus in the enclosure behind it.

The road goes on towards the west, with cemeteries, sometimes large ones, on either side. At the crossroads, the road to the right leads to the Temple of the Sleeping Buddha (Wo fo si) and the one to the left goes to the Round Fortress (see p. 610); straight on, it soon ends in a vast square. A paved alley leads off to the north to the Temple of the Azure Clouds (Bi yun si); a road to the south-west goes to the entrance of the Fragrant Hills Park.

2. The Temple of the Sleeping Buddha (Wo fo si)

The temple is built up against the side of the Shou an Hill; it is one of the oldest foundations of the Peking area. It was chiefly famous for the prostrate statue or statues of the Buddha, and for the rare trees growing in its courtyards. This last tradition has survived, and a modern School of Forestry has been founded in the annex buildings.

History. The temple was founded under the Tang; it was called the Dou shuai si, and it is thought that it already possessed a recumbent statue of the Buddha, in sandalwood. The buildings were enlarged under the Yuan in 1321, and the *History of the Yuan* states that "500,000 pounds of copper" were used to cast an enormous recumbent statue of the Buddha; 7,000 workmen carried out the operation, which succeeded at the second attempt only, in 1331. In 1452, under the Ming, it was repaired and renamed the Yong an si; several contemporary texts refer to the two recumbent statues of the Buddha and two Boddhi trees "brought from India under the Tang dynasty", as well as magnificent peonies. The temple was rebuilt in 1734 and renamed the Temple of Universal Spiritual Awakening (Shi fang pu jue si); it was still known by its easier name of the Temple of the Sleeping Buddha (Wo fo si), however. From the 18th century onwards, only one recumbent statue of the Buddha is mentioned. The temple was restored in 1955.

Description. A beautiful avenue of ancient evergreens *(bo shu)* leads up to an 18th century three arched portico (green, yellow tiles). The portico is instead of a gate, which is unusual.

In the first courtyard, an arched bridge spans a little pool. To the right and left stand the Bell and Drum Towers (the instruments are still on the first floor); the first hall contains statues of the Celestial Guardians.

Amongst the beautiful trees in the second courtyard stand the two *sala (shorea robusta)* trees said to be the ones brought from India; in front of the second hall: bronze incense-burner dating from Qian long; in the second hall: Maitreya in the centre, with the four Tian wang grouped round about; behind the screen: Wei tuo.

The third hall stands on a terrace at the far end of the third courtyard, with statues of Sakyamuni (in the centre, between the two disciples, Amitabha (on the left) and the Buddha of Medecine (on the right). The eighteen *luo han* are round the sides; behind the screen is a statue of Guan yin in a cave of greenish rocks.

The fourth hall, at the end of the fourth courtyard, is also on a terrace; it has two stories and five bays; the recumbent statue of the Buddha (the Sleeping Buddha) is inside it. His right arm is bent to support his head, and his left arm lies along his side. The statue is in lacquered bronze, and it is most unlikely that it weighs 500,000 pounds, as reported in the *History of the Yuan;* it is probably a later copy, substituted for the other at an unknown date. Statues of the twelve Bodhisattva stand round it. In about 1920, a pile of shoes could still be seen in a corner of the hall, offerings from the faithful for the Buddha's bare feet.

Galleries flank the courtyards on both sides; they contain a few statues. The living quarters for the

superior and the monks were to the east of the central
axial buildings, with the refectory, kitchens and guest-
rooms; to the west was a palace used by the Emperor
when he came here *(Xing gong)*; a Taoist temple used
to stand south-west of the palace; it was founded by
three eunuchs who used to let out rooms during the
summer. None of these side buildings can be visited
now (they are now used as offices and a school); the
Cherry Vale Garden (Ying tao gou yuan) is open to
visitors, however; it is a most attractive valley, north-
west of the temple, where cherry trees once grew. The
cave where a hermit stopped to enjoy the scene is still
there; the garden contains bamboo groves and various
different kinds of trees.

3. The Temple of the Azure Clouds (Bi yun si)

The buildings of the Bi yun si are spread out on an
east-west axis on a slope of the Fragrant Hills (north-
east of the Xiang shan Park). They fall into two groups:
the temple itself, and behind it, the Jin gang bao zuo ta
(Diamond Throne Pagoda), a building in Indian style,
which can be seen from far away rising out of the trees,
and from which there is a magnificent view over the
whole plain round Peking. It is one of the finest spots
in the whole area.

History. A convent was founded here in about 1330. At the
beginning of the 16th century, some rich eunuchs had the
temple enlarged, thinking that they would be buried there, but
the work was abandoned. Several attempts were made to carry
on, particularly under Qian long in the 18th century. In 1748
the Hall of the *luo han* was built (imitating the one at the Ling
yin Temple at Hang zhou) and the Diamond Throne Pagoda.
The temple fell into a very poor state and was restored in 1954.

Sun Yat sen's body lay in the pagoda from 1925—when he
died— until 1929, when it was transferred to Nanking. A little
museum devoted to him was founded in the furthermost halls
of the temple; it has been renovated since the liberation.

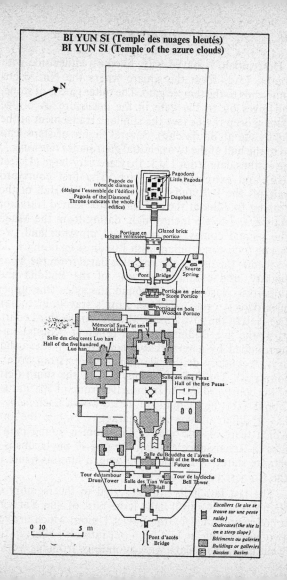

BI YUN SI (Temple des nuages bleutés)
BI YUN SI (Temple of the azure clouds)

N

Pagodons
Little Pagodas

Pagode du
trône de diamant
(désigne l'ensemble de l'édifice)
Pagoda of the Diamond
Throne (indicates the whole
edifice)

Dagobas

Portique en
briques vernissées

Glazed brick
portico

Source
Spring

Pont   Bridge

Portique en pierre
Stone Portico

Portique en bois
Wooden Portico

Mémorial Sun Yat sen
Memorial Hall

Salle des cinq cents Luo han
Hall of the five hundred
Luo han

Salle des cinq Pusas
Hall of the five Pusas

Chuang

Salle du Bouddha de l'avenir
Hall of the Buddha of the
Future

Tour du tambour
Drum Tower

Tour de la cloche
Bell Tower

Salle des Tian Wang
Hall

0   10   5 m

Pont d'accès
Bridge

Escaliers (le site se
trouve sur une pente
raide)
Staircases (the site is
on a steep slope)
Bâtiments ou galeries
Buildings or galleries
Bassins Basins

Description. A paved way, lined on either side with houses, leads from the square where the No. 33 bus route ends to the temple gate. The outer gate is of stone, and gives on to the gate in the enclosure. A bridge spans a deep ravine (see the similar arrangement at the eighth site at Ba da chu). Several flights of steps lead up to the hall of the two celestial guardians *(tian wang);* the statues date from 1513; they are very large (15 feet high) and extremely expressive. The first courtyard contains the Bell and Drum Towers; the Hall of the Coming Buddha at the end has a fine seated statue of Maitreya, 7 feet 6 inches high, dating from the Ming. The second courtyard has a pool of water and two *chuang* (octagonal pillars with Buddhist texts engraved on them); the hall at the end also dates from the Ming dynasty, and contains a statue of the Buddha and numerous plaster statues round the sides (the upper ones depict scenes of Xuan zang's travels in India). The Hall of the Five Pusas (Ming) is in the third courtyard: the five Bodhisattvas on different pedestals are surrounded by a remarkable collection of stucco figures (secondary deities, demons, donors from distant countries). The hall of the *luo han* to the south (left) of the courtyard has an impressive group of 508 statues (about 5 feet high), made of gilded wood. Each *luo han* has a different face and character. Notice the one which tears his old man's skin from a young man's face (a Renaissance theme). On one of the beams is a minute statue of the monk Ji gong, a famous figure in the Chinese pantheon.

The last few halls are dedicated to the memory of Sun Yat sen. Central hall: large bust of Sun Yat sen; a coffin presented by the Soviet Union, which arrived two weeks after he had been put into his coffin; in the walls are marble slabs with quotations from his works.

Side halls: photographs of his youth, his travels, and his political life as the first President of the Chinese Republic.

Several flights of steps lead westwards and upwards, through three porticos (the first of wood, the second made of stone—with some fine bas-relief carvings—, the third made of glazed bricks), to the white marble Diamond Throne Pagoda. It is 117 feet high altogether, and its overall shape is strikingly similar to that of the Wu ta si (see p. 563). The base is of rough-hewn stone; two flights of steps lead to the main entrance, with bas-relief carvings again reminiscent of the Wu ta si. The outside of the upper gallery is decorated with monsters' heads (a late development of the *tao tie*). Inside, the former sanctuary has been walled up (an inscription states that "Sun Yat sen's clothes and hat" are still there). His body lay there from 1925 to 1929. Two inner staircases lead up to the terrace; a many-storied tower stands in the middle, surrounded by four little square pagodas and two small round pagodas. A small pavilion, with a vaulted dome, different from the rest, has been built over the top of the staircase; the eastern part is a little oratory, and the walls are covered with extremely delicate engravings. A spring runs past the foot of the monument, to the north; it used to supply the Emperor's lakes and palaces with water.

4. The Fragrant Hills Park (Xiang shan)

The Jing yi yuan Park lies in a valley in the Fragrant Hills, hence its more frequent name: the Xiang shan Park. It used also to be called the "Hunting Park". The largest stream which runs through it rises to the west, on Mount Gui jian chou (1,962 feet) and runs eastwards; when it leaves the park to flow into water

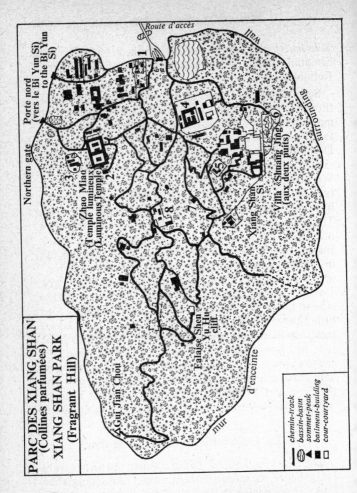

PARC DES XIANG SHAN
(Collines parfumées)
XIANG SHAN PARK
(Fragrant Hill)

chemin-track
bassin-basin
sommet-peak
bâtiment-building
cour-courtyard

Route d'accès
to the Bi Yun Si
Porte nord
(vers le Bi Yun Si)
Northern gate
Temple lumineux
(Luminous Temple)
Zhao Miao
Xiang Shan Si
Villa «Shuang Jing»
(aux deux puits)
Falaise Shen Yu Hu cliff
A Gui Jian Choù
mur d'enceinte
wall

1 Mian Gate
2 The Glazed Tile Pagoda
3 Jian Xin Zhai (Pavilion of Introspection)
4 Hotel Xiang Shan (former palace used for short stays)
5 Hong Guang Si
6 «Shuang Jing» Villa (of the two wells)
7 Jade Milk Spring
8 Jade Flower Villa

courses which used to supply the city, it is 330 feet above sea level. A wall surrounds the park. It used to be famous for its flora and fauna (one of the "eight Views" of Peking). Much of its old splendour has vanished, but its woods are still delightful, especially in autumn.

History. The park abounded in game in the 12th century and the Emperors used to hunt there. The *History of the Jin* records that the Xiang shan Temple was built in 1186. The Jin Emperor Xiang Shi zong, who particulraly liked the place, had a palace built there, and planted some chestnut trees. The *History of the Yuan* states that the Emperor Ren zong presented paper money to the value of ten thousand ingots to the temple in 1312, and ordered restorations to be made. In 1436, a powerful eunuch, Fan hong, gave a present of gold fish and seventy thousand strings of coins towards the enlarging of the buildings. He had his tomb built there, but was never buried there, as he died in exile, and only his cap and his robes were put there (nothing is left now of the tomb). At about the same time, another eunuch, from Korea, had another temple built, north-west of the Jin temple: the Hong guang si, which had a round hall, with a thousand statues of the Buddha sitting on lotus flowers (after a Korean model); it has completely vanished. The Pavilion of Introspection (Jian xin zhai) was also built under the Ming.

The park was at the height of its splendour in the 18th century, under the reign of Qian long. Game by that time was scarce, and hunting stopped. The Emperor had a wall built round it and had special deer brought from Manchuria (*ma lu* or "horse-deer", cervus elaphurus). He had twenty-eight "sites" created: pavilions, terraces or summer-houses, erected steles bearing his calligraphy, ordered the Luminous Temple (Zhao miao) to be built, in the style of Tibetan temples, as well as the glazed tile pagoda beside it. It was one of the most beautiful parks in China.

The court later deserted the place and it fell into decay. The European armies damaged it in 1860 and 1900; under the warlords and Guo min dang, those in power had summer villas built there. The palace was transformed into a hotel and the Zhao miao into a hospital. By 1923, "it lay in ruins and a great effort of imagination was needed to reconstruct the Xiang shan as it must once have been" (Bouillard). Recent restoration work has done something towards remedying this.

Description. The No 33 bus stops in the square; in the south-west corner (at the far end, on the left) a path leads off, turning to the right, to join the main entrance way (760 yards long), formerly lined with shops (its old name was Mai mai jie, the Tradesmen's Street). Two bronze lions guard the main entrance. A path leads north inside the walls (to the right) to the Zhao miao and the Pavilion of Introspection (the most well preserved of all the "sites"). Another leads south (left) to the remains of the Xiang shan Temple, and goes on westwards among ruins and modern villas towards the cliff known as Shen yu hu. Energetic walkers can climb the Gui jian chou, at the furthermost western point.

The Zhao miao (Luminous Temple). It was built in 1780, as the Panchen Lama's residence, whenever he came to Peking. The style is imitation Tibetan (a copy of a temple at Tashilumpo). The Xu mi fu shou Temple at Cheng de (Jehol) was built at the same time, on a similar plan (see p. 669). The Zhao miao consists of two enclosures, one beside the other. The east façade is the best preserved; two flights of stairs lead to the upper part, and two low gates with triangular pediments give on to the inner courtyard. A building with five bays stands on the surrounding wall. Square false windows break the monotony of the façade (a feature of Tibetan architecture). A fine polychrome portico stands in front of the façade bearing inscriptions in four languages (Manchu, Chinese, Tibetan, Mongol), with four large pedestals near it (bases of flag staffs).

The **Glazed Tile Pagoda** stands on a natural hillock west of the temple (it closely resembles the pagoda of the Xu mi fu shou at Cheng de). The base is in stone, with badly-damaged bas-relief carvings, and inside is a vaulted ambulatory; a covered way made of wood (rebuilt in the 20th century) runs round it; the seven upper stories of yellow and green glazed tiles were restored recently; bronze bells hang from each storey and sound in the wind. From the foot of the pagoda there is a view straight down into the inner precincts of the Zhao miao, transformed into a hospital under the Republic and still not opened to visitors.

The **Pavilion of Introspection (Jian xin zhai)** is due north of the Zhao miao; it was built under the Ming, but has been considerably modified since (it was restored in 1958 and in 1965). It contains a large semi-circular pool surrounded by a covered way, which is not unlike the long covered way at the Yi he yuan. From the Jian xin zhai it is only a short way to the north gate of the Park, and from there to the Bi yun si.

The Xiang shan Temple (Xiang shan si). It was once a temple built on an enormous scale; it stretched over five consecutive terraces built into a steep hillside. Nothing is left but the terraces, the bases of a few halls and a fine wooden screen dating from the 18th century at the top, standing in front of a modern building. A pagoda and two stupas are carved on the eastern facet, inscribed with Buddhist texts; on the western facet are carvings of the Buddha and two people. The balustrade at the top and the capitals reveal the influence of Western art.

The ruins of the **Villa with Two Wells (Shuang jing)** lie south of the Xiang shan si; they still contain pools and a spring, and a well, covered by iron roofing. The enclosure east of the villa was for tame deer to spend the night in. The annex buildings north of the Xiang

shan si have been converted into houses and are now
unrecognisable. The Hong huang si once stood north
east of the temple (influenced by Korean art) but has
been entirely destroyed.

5. South-west of the Fragrant Hills Park

On the No. 33 bus route is a crossroads, one fork
of which leads to the Wo fo si; the other half opposite
it runs southwards past several interesting places, and
finally goes on to Ba da chu.

a) The Round Fortress (Tuan cheng)

This is an enormous oval fort, built by Qian long as an
observation tower from which to watch his troops'
manœuvres in the plain below (hence its other name,
Yue wu lou: "the tower from which the troops are
inspected"). It is a type of military architecture which
is rare in China. The walls are about 15 feet thick, and
used to be crenellated; a path for the watch runs round
the top, with two rectangular two-storey pavilions on
it. The inner courtyard is paved, and two flights of
steps lead up to the battlements. Three terraces are
built into the slope below the main entrance, which is
to the south. A large pavilion with a covered way round
it still stands on the middle terrace. Nearby, next to
road, stand the remains of a stone watch tower, with
staircases up the sides. The site is now used by horti-
cultural services.

b) The Training Towers (Diao)

Rough stone buildings, about 30 to 45 feet high, are
scattered all over the Xiang shan area; they are plain,
square towers, with terraced roofs and false windows.

Some can be found to the north as well, near the Wo fo si. Several can be seen from the Round Fortress, dotted over the slopes of the Xiang shan. The Emperor had them built before setting out on his famous campaigns against the south-western Minority races (the Jin chuan war, in what is now Si chuan), and used them for training his troops in a new art of siege.

c) The Remains of the Temple of True Victory (Shi sheng si)

A little further on, on the left, stands a large yellow-roofed pavilion, containing an impressive square stele, with inscriptions in four languages (Manchu, Chinese, Mongol and Tibetan). This, and the remains of a gate, on the right of the road, are all that survives of a temple built in 1749. It is interesting to notice that it was called after a victory won with the greatest difficulty against the little principalities of Jin chuan (the "south-western barbarians" as the stele says).

d) The Remains of the Fan xiang si and the Bao xiang si

Further on, on the right, one of the gates of the former Fan xiang si, founded in 1749, can still be seen (built in stone, imitating wooden architecture); at the foot of the hill stands a beautiful square building, red with yellow tiles: the remains of the Bao xiang si, built in 1762 under the reign of Qian long. The most interesting feature of the hall is its vaulted stone roof, with the tiles laid directly on it, with no beams. (No visitors allowed.)

e) Buddhist Cemetery

Still further on, to the right, the tombs of an ancient Buddhist community lie spread beneath fine old trees. Several are in the shape of stupas.

D. THE EIGHT GREAT SITES (BA DA CHU)
(Closed in 1972.)

They are south of the Western Hills (at the terminus of the No 47 bus route). Three hills, the Cui wei shan to the west, the Ping po shan in the middle and the Lu shi shan to the east, are divided by two short mountain streams which merge at the foot of the Lu shi shan. The eight "sites" are scattered among the steep wooded valleys, with a rough stone path leading from one to the other; they are eight temples or monasteries, out of use now, but still visited by tourists and even by some of the faithful. During the anti-Japanese war and the third civil war, the liberation army occupied the area and used it as a base for their operations against the Japanese and the Guo min dang. The eight sites will be described in the order in which they are numbered.

(First Site Yi chu). Temple of Eternal Peace (Chang an si). It stands on the plain, at the foot of the Cui wei shan Hill; the southern bridge leads to it. It was first built under the Ming, in 1504; it was then called Tian xi zhan si. The many beautiful trees growing in its courtyards are said to have been planted under the Yuan; the orchards are of course more recent. The entrance gate is not in line with the rest of the temple. The first hall contains a very fine bronze statue of Guan yu, the hero of the Three Kingdoms period, who later became the god of war; the statue has traces of gilding on it still, and slits in the face where the beard and moustache were put. It dates no doubt from the Ming. In the covered way behind the hall are to the left, a bronze bell dating from 1600, and to the right, an iron gong made in the Kang xi period. The second hall, the

BA DA CHU (The Eight Great Sites)
BA DA CHU (Les huit grands sites)

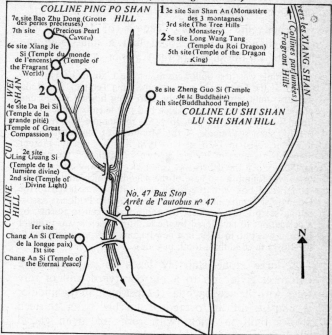

Hall of Sakyamuni, contains three statues of the Buddha which are not particularly interesting ones, and an iron "mortar" which is late 15th century (a musical instrument). The third hall is dedicated to Niang niang, a female Taoist deity known for her powers of granting children; her statue in the middle is flanked by four other minor female deities, whose duty it was to protect children from illness;

the attributes of each statue have now almost all disappeared (one carried a child, one a pair of eyes, one a box of medecine).

Second Site (Er chu), Temple of Divine Light (Ling guang si). It is about half a mile from the first site, on the slopes of the Cui wei shan.

A temple was first built here under the Liao, in 1071; it was known as the Long quan si (Dragon Spring Temple). A pagoda was also built, and the Emperor Dao zong himself placed one of the Buddha's teeth here, which had just been brought to him from India. Under the Jin, in 1162, the temple was renamed the Jue shan si (Temple of the Mountain of the Awakening); it was restored in 1428, and in 1478 it was given its present name. The armies of the eight powers demolished the pagoda in 1900. When the debris was being cleared away an engraved brick was found in the base of the pagoda, which contained the sandalwood box with the tooth inside it; it was taken to the Guang ji si Temple in Peking (the centre of the Buddhist Association, see p. 511); in 1955, the tooth was taken to Burma, by a delegation, to be adored by the faithful; when it was brought back, it was put, in 1959, in a new pagoda built especially for it, the Fo ya ta (Buddha's tooth pagoda).

A large stone stairway leads to an impressive entrance, giving on to a big courtyard, full of rare trees, with the new pagoda, 162 feet high, in the middle; it consists of an octagonal marble base, thirteen stories built in brick (with roofs of green glazed tiles), the whole topped by a gilded apex.

Modern annex buildings (including a restaurant) are on the left, and at the foot of the cliff the stone base of the old Liao pagoda can still be seen (traces of fine bas-relief carvings), with a little pond near it, which is covered with water-lilies in the summer, and contains some enormous goldfish, some of which are said to be over a hundred years old.

Third Site (San chu), the Three Hills Monastery (San shan an). It is north of the second site, and is said to be called after the three hills standing near it. The date of building is unknown; it was restored under the reign of Qian long (it was in fact a nunnery). The entrance hall contains three polychrome wooden statues of the Buddha; the far hall contains a Buddha in the centre, surrounded by the eighteen *luo han*, in gilded wood; from a terrace on the left, a pleasant view can be had over the valley and the plain.

Fourth Site (Si chu), Temple of Great Pity (Da bei si). It is north of the third one. The date of building is unknown. The entrance gate has some interesting bas-relief carvings: animals arranged above each other (elephant, lion, winged horse), and a sort of garuda between two apsaras at the top; fine bamboos grow in the little entrance courtyard; the gilded wood statues of the eighteen *luo han* in the first hall are attributed to Liu Yuan (also called Liu Lan), a famous Yuan dynasty sculptor; each *luo han* is on a rock, and is accompanied by a disciple, on a smaller scale. Two fine gingko trees *(yin xing)* growing in the next courtyard are said to be several centuries old. A drum, with an elephant-shaped stand, and a bronze bell, stand in the covered way, just in front of the far hall; the hall contains four bookcases, which used to be covered with lacquer.

Fifth Site (Wu chu), Dragon King Temple (Long wang tang). It is north-west of the fourth site, and the path to it leads past some tombs (left hand side). It is also known as Long quan an (Dragon Spring Nunnery).

It was founded under the Qing. The spring which gives the temple its name rises opposite the gate; a flight of steps leads to a small hall with statues of spirits in painted plaster. The chief hall is to the right: it contains fine gilded wood statues of the three Buddhas with their disciples; notice the four lanterns of storied glass.

A terrace south of the temple gives a fine view over the plain.

Sixth Site (Liu chu), Temple of the Fragrant World (Xiang jie si). It is north of the one before.

It was founded under the Tang, in the 10th century (the name was then Ping po si); it was rebuilt in 1425, and again under Kang xi (a very old statue of Guan yin was found in the process); in 1748, Qian long had a palace and a library built and gave the temple its present name. It is now used as a rest home for primary school teachers. It is the biggest of the eight sites, and is built on a north-south axis, on the slopes of the hill; the statues are not particularly interesting.

Seventh Site (Qi chu), Precious Pearl Cavern (Bao zhu dong). It is the highest of the eight sites. A wooden *pai lou* heralds it. It is said that a monk called Hai Shan you lived for forty years in the little cave behind the flight of steps going up to the temple (his statue stands inside it). The finest view over Peking and the area is to be had from the seventh site.

Eighth Site (Ba chu), Buddhahood Temple (Zheng guo si). It is half-way up the Lu shi shan, down hill from the seventh site and across the ravine.

A legend says that a hermit, Lu shi, lived in a cave in the hill under the Tang dynasty; the rock above the cave was called the Mi mo ya (Rock of the Mysterious Demon); under the Yuan, a temple dedicated to Lu shi (Lu shi si) was built, of which nothing now remains; it was renamed several times. Steep steps lead up to it, with a memorial stele on either side; the bell on the right in the first courtyard dates from 1470. Behind the temple (to the left) is the Rock of the Mysterious Demon (there is a small cave in which the monk Lu shi is supposed to have lived; statues of the Buddha stand inside).

E. THE TEMPLE
OF THE GREAT SPIRITUAL AWAKENING
(DA JUE SI)
AND THE WONDERFUL MOUNTAINS
(MIAO FENG SHAN)

The Temple of the Great Spiritual Awakening (Da jue si) is twenty-four miles north-west of Peking (bus No 46), at the foot of the Yang tai shan Hills.

The Vulture's Peak (Jiu feng), so called because of the shape of the two great pines on the top of it, and the Wonderful Mountains (Miao feng shan), well worth a visit, rise north of the Da jue si.

II. The Great Wall and the Ming Tombs

A. FROM PEKING TO THE GREAT WALL

At the beginning of the 20th century, visitors to the Great Wall travelled in horse-drawn carriages or rode mules. "A trip to the Great Wall has to be arranged with great care, especially when ladies are included. It can be quite expensive as supplies have to be taken too, tins, bread, wine, mineral water...; those unused to travelling in China are advised to join a group making the excursion" (*Guide Madrolle*, 1904, p. 32). Once the Peking—Kalgan railway had been opened (September 19th 1909) it was easier to go by train (getting off at Qing long qiao station, in the Nan kou pass). Nowadays, the tourist goes by car, by a delightful road, leaving Peking by De sheng men (it is not necessary to ask permission to make the trip).

The road runs through the villages of **Qing he** (Clear river), named after a stream from the Jade Fountain, **Sha he** (Sand river), and **Chang ping,** a name which has existed since the Han dynasty; when the Mongol hordes led by Genghis Khan broke unexpectedly through the Great Wall, they took Chang ping, while the Chinese armies were waiting for them at the Nan kou Pass; the town was fortified under the Ming. It used to be possible to go from Chang ping to Tang shan, to the east, a little town where a hot spring rises (hence its name, "Hot Spring Hill"); it was a watering-place under the Qing (the road there is closed to foreigners for the moment). A crossroads on the other side of Chang ping has a sign pointing to the Ming Tombs (to the right) and the Great Wall (to the left).

To the left, the road leads to Nan kou (the Southern Pass). It was a walled and fortified town which made its living from the caravans passing through on their way from Mongolia. Horses, camels and porters jostled one another, hurrying over the enormous slippery paving stones of the one street; they used to spend the night in the inns. In 1895, the traffic included "bales of wool and skins from Mongolia, on their way to Peking, bricks of tea from Tian jin destined for Kiakhta, on the Siberian frontier" (Monnier, *L'Empire du milieu,* Paris, Plon, 1903). The town is calm now and the camels which use the pass are few and far between.

The road runs into steep hills soon after Nan kou, near the Peking to Bao tou railway, and soon reaches the **Ju yong guan Pass** (the name has been found in documents dating from as early as the 3rd century B.C.). It is famous for the magnificent gateway which the modern road leaves on the right hand side; the old road passed underneath it, hence the name: Guo jie ta, the "Tower which Bestrides the Road".

It is built in stone, and dates from the Mongol period (1345). The plan is square, and the upper part, which today is simply a flat roof with a balustrade round it, was meant to have a stupa on it. The most interesting part is the passageway itself; the shape of the vaulted archway is unusual for that period; bas-relief carvings depict the Buddha with four very lively celestial guardians; on the right and left walls are inscriptions in six languages.

The inscriptions attracted the attention of European sinologues at the end of the last century; in the 1894 *Journal asiatique*, E. Chavannes gave a list of the languages: "Sanskrit, Tibetan, Mongolian, written in 'Phags-pa script, Uighur Turkish, Chinese, and finally an entirely unknown language". In 1895, Prince Roland Bonaparte financed the editing of the epigraphs (Paris, gr. in fol, 15 plates). In 1898/99, Devéria recognised the sixth language as that of the "kingdom of Xi xia or Tangut" (a little state which was autonomous between 1032 and 1226, between the Ordos bend of the Yellow River and the Koukounor region, now Gan su). The texts are several *dharani* (incantations).

A little beyond Ju yong guan, several sections of walls can be seen (the remains of minor fortifications). The road passes close by Qing long qiao station (which has a statue of the engineer Chan tian yu, 1860–1919, who was in charge of the building of the Peking to Bao tou railway), and then winds upwards until it reaches the fort of Ba da ling, on the Great Wall, about 6 miles beyond Ju yong guan.

B. THE GREAT WALL

The Great Wall of China (Wan li chang cheng: "the long wall of 10 000 *li*) has for a long time fired the imagination of Europeans ("the only building visible from the moon") and excited the enthusiasm of travellers.

In his *Voyage autour du Monde*, the Comte de Beauvoir wrote in 1867: "It is a supremely wonderful sight! To think that these walls, built in apparently inaccessible places, as though to balance the Milky Way in the sky, a walled way over the mountain tops, are the work of men, makes it seem like a dream... This fantastic serpent of stone, its battlements devoid of cannons, its loopholes empty of rifles... will be stored in my mind like a magic vision. But if one stops to think after admiring such a magnificent view, how easy it is to see in it the work of a people of overgrown children, led by despots..." The "dream" evaporates after a look at its history.

History. From as early on as the Warring States period, about the 5th century B.C., the rival states in Central China built walls to protect themselves from each other and from the "barbarians". They were built in the states of Yan, Chao, Wei and Qin. When Qin shi Huang di had unified the empire, he linked up the existing fortifications on the northern frontier to ward off the attacks of the Xiong nu. Contemporary texts record that 300,000 men worked for ten years, led by General Meng Qian, to carry out his plans. Under the Han (threatened by invasion by the Xiong nu), the Northern Wei, the Northern Qi, the Sui (threatened by the Tu jue, the Ruan ruan, the Khitans), the wall was kept up and new sections were built.

From the end of the 6th century onwards, the Great Wall ceased to be the northern frontier for a time. It lost its strategic importance and was abandoned. Under the Tang, the Tu jue were conquered and the frontier pushed further north. Under the Song, on the other hand, the frontier was moved further south and both sides of the wall were under the same government: the Liao, the Jin and the Yuan. This probably explains why Marco Polo never mentions the Wall, although he lived in Peking for a long time.

Once the Ming had thrown the Mongols out, one of the first things they did was to rebuild the Great Wall, to keep the enemy in his place. As early as 1368, Emperor Tai zu put General Xu Da de in charge of beginning the work; it went on until 1500, and restoration work was still being done in the 16th century. The second Great Wall stretched from the Ya lu River in the east to the Jia yu guan Pass, in Gan su; over 2,484 miles, divided into nine administrative sections or commanderies *(jiu bian)*: Liao dong, Ji zhou, Xuan fu, Da tong, Tai yuan, Yu lin, Ning xia, Gu yuan, Gan zhou. The furthest eastern section was a rammed earth construction with a hedge of "willow branches" *(liu jiao bian)* which has completely disappeared, but from the Shan hai guan Pass onwards (the present boundary between the provinces of He bei and Liao ning), as far as Gan su, it was built of stone.

The average height of the wall was 22 to 26 feet; it was 21 feet thick at the base and 18 feet wide on the top. It was faced with stone, and the inside was filled with earth and rubble. The top was faced with three or four layers of brick, carefully pointed, to prevent water seeping through (brick used as a material for the Wall was introduced by the Ming). Arched gateways were built at intervals along it, ramps led up to the top, and watch towers with observation terraces for signaling were spaced along it. At some particularly vulnerable points, as many as five, six or even nine, successive walls were built.

The chief purpose of the Great Wall was certainly a defensive one. It had other uses, however. It acted as means of communication along which news, men or even food could travel rapidly through mountainous regions where otherwise movement was difficult. Most of the way which ran along the top of it was wide enough to take five horses abreast. "Such is its breadth", says Father Ripa, who was in Peking under Kang xi, "that carriages can drive along the top with ease. I was informed... that it was built of that breadth not only for convenience in time of war, but also to facilitate the transport of materials while it was building, as it would otherwise have been impossible to carry it over steep and precipitous spots." *(Memoirs of Father Ripa*, Naples, 1832, reprinted Peking, 1939, p. 69.) This raised roadway enabled colonies of soldiers and their families to be settled great distances away (extension of Chinese influence into non-Han regions)—cf. the role of the Trans-Siberian railway. A permanent barrier was also the best way of controlling the nomadic population, stock-breeding people who were constantly on the move. It is possible, too, that the Great Wall helped farming by breaking the force of the winds from the Steppes (cf. "the great green wall" which New China is trying to plant along her northern frontier).

Although the Great Wall has caught many people's imagination, it has never been studied in its socio-geographical context. A thorough analysis using aerial photography would help towards an understanding of its real significance (cf. the study of the *limes* in Syria).

Under the Qing, the Wall was abandoned and gradually fell into decay. The present régime has had it restored at three famous points: the Shan hai guan Pass, the Ba da ling Fort and the Jia yu guan Pass (far to the west).

Description. From Ba da ling, an arched gateway leads through the wall towards Kalgan (from the Mongolian Kalgha: "pass"; the Chinese name is Zhang jia kou). A flight of steps on the left leads up to the top; one may walk in either direction (along sections which have been restored).

It is a fine example of Ming military architecture: there is a two-storey watch-tower (guard room below and observation platform above it); the pathway is sometimes broken by extremely steep steps; the battlements give a glimpse of the Guan ting reservoir (recent construction) to the north.

C. THE MING TOMBS

The road leaves from the De sheng men Gate, and until the village of Chang ping, it is the same as the road to the Great Wall (see p. 619). On the other side of Chang ping is a crossroads; the right hand turning (as indicated by the sign post) goes to the Ming tombs. The road soon leads past a huge stone portico *(pai fang)*, standing on the right, marking the beginning of the "sacred way" which leads to the tombs of the Emperors of the Ming dynasty (Chinese: Shi san ling, "the thirteen tombs").

History. From a very early date, Chinese sovereigns had tombs built, generally during their lifetimes, near the capital, where they were later buried. The tumuli of the Zhou kings and the enormous tomb of the first Emperor, Qin shi Huang di, can still be seen near Xi an (see p. 949). The tombs of the Tang Emperors are also near Xi an; the Song tombs are south of Gong xian (He nan).

Hong wu, the founder of the Ming dynasty, had his tomb built east of Nanking, the town which he had chosen for his capital (see p. 991). The third Ming Emperor, Yong le, ousted the second one, who fled and was lost track of completely; he then transferred his capital to Peking (early 15th century) and chose this valley in which to build his tomb, the Chang ling. All his successors except one, who was dethroned (see p. 599), followed his example and had their tombs built near the Chang ling. Out of the sixteen Emperors of the Ming dynasty which lasted from 1368 to 1644, thirteen lie here with their Empresses and their second wives. Hence the Chinese name: Shi san ling, the thirteen tombs.

The site was chosen with the greatest care, taking the *feng shui* (a collection of rules for avoiding evil influences) into account. The semi-circular range of the Tian shou shan Hills to the north acted as a barrier against the harmful emanations brought by the winds *(feng)* from the steppes and the topography of the region enabled water *(shui)* to run gently in front of the tombs. It is one of the most beautiful places in the Peking region; the forests which used to clothe all the neighbouring hills have dwindled to a few copses round the tombs, but it is planned to re-plant the whole area.

The Shi san ling necropolis lies in a vast natural arena covering 3 miles from north to south and 2 miles from east to west, which used to be bounded by a red wall (in the valley) or by posts (on the hilltops). This space was forbidden ground for every living being apart from those who were officially in charge of its upkeep. It was forbidden to cultivate it, to cut down wood there, and to take stones from it. No one could enter it on horseback; even the Emperor himself dismounted at the gate. A garrison with a headquarters at Chang ping mounted the guard; a large administrative body and an impressive number of employees, whose duties were inherited, were in charge of the upkeep.

The "sacred way" led from the *pai fang* to the entrance to the chief tomb, which was Yong le's; the others were built round it, one by one. Each one was in three parts: 1) buildings where sacrifices were prepared and offered; 2) the tower for the the stele; 3) the tumulus itself, covering the underground vault containing the body. Until 1956, when the Ding ling was excavated, (see below), the arrangement of these "underground palaces" was known only from a few vague descriptions. Once the Emperor had been buried, the passage leading to the vault was sealed, theoretically for ever. It was only re-opened on most exceptional occasions, when the Empress or even a second wife died after the Emperor and was buried at his side. The Qing abandoned this custom and never re-opened their tombs.

Sacrifices were offered (oxen, sheep, rice, etc.) at the *qing ming* (Chinese equivalent of All Saints' Day), the *zhong yuan* (the 15th of the seventh month), at the winter solstice and the last day of the year, as well as on the first and the fifteenth of each month and on the anniversary of the death of the people who were buried.

The following quotation comes from a report written in 1644 by the official ordered to bury the last Ming Emperor (he had committed suicide by hanging himself from a tree on Coal Hill) in the tomb of Tian the Concubine. Peking was occupied by the troops of Li Zi cheng and the Emperor was buried with a very simple funeral. When the Manchu came to power, they ordered a tomb to be built (the thirteenth and last) and the remains of the last Ming were moved from the tomb of the concubine to the new one. The account is quoted in Backhouse and Bland, *Annals and Memoirs of the Court of Peking* (London, 1914, p. 105 and onwards).

"On the 25th day of the 3rd Moon (that is, seven days after the capture of Peking) I received orders from Li Hsi-Chang, styling himself Prefect of the city, that we were to inter their late Majesties in the grave chamber of the late concubine, the Lady T'ien, and that I was to engage labourers to open up the passage leading thereto, whose wages would be paid out of public funds. On the first day of the fourth Moon I therefore engaged thirty bearers for the Imperial coffin and sixteen for that of the Empress, and arranged for their conveyance to Ch'ang P'ing-Chou. The preliminary obsequies were fixed for three days later, and the actual interment took place on the fifth. The departmental treasury was quite empty, and as the Secretary of Li Tzu-Ch'eng's Board of Ceremonies (responsible for the due performance of the ceremony) refused to provide any funds, I was obliged to collect subscriptions from charitable persons. Thanks to the generosity of two worthies, I obtained the sum of 340 tiao. So I set to work to open up the grave-tunnel, which was 135 feet long by 20 feet wide and 35 feet high. We worked for three days and nights, and early on the morning of the fourth day we came upon the stone gate opening into a grave ante-chamber. The workmen were obliged to force the lock before we could enter. Inside we found a lofty hall

SHI SAN LING (tombeaux Ming) PLAN GÉNÉRAL
SHI SAN LING (Ming tombs) GENERAL MAP

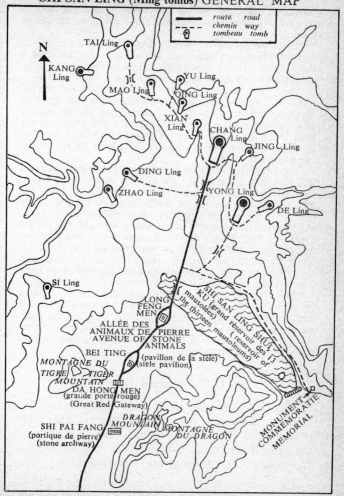

route   road
chemin   way
tombeau   tomb

N

TAI Ling

KANG Ling

MAO Ling

YU Ling

QING Ling

XIAN Ling

CHANG Ling

JING Ling

DING Ling

ZHAO Ling

YONG Ling

DE Ling

SI Ling

LONG FENG MEN

SHI SAN LING SHUI KU (grand réservoir des 13 mausolées)
(reservoir of the thirteen mausoleums)

ALLÉE DES ANIMAUX DE PIERRE
AVENUE OF STONE ANIMALS

BEI TING
(pavillon de la stèle)
(stele pavilion)

MONTAGNE DU TIGRE
TIGER MOUNTAIN

DA HONG MEN
(grande porte rouge)
(Great Red Gateway)

DRAGON MOUNTAIN

MONTAGNE DU DRAGON

SHI PAI FANG
(portique de pierre)
(stone archway)

MONUMENT COMMÉMORATIF
MEMORIAL

containing sacrificial vessels and many ornaments. In the centre was a stone vessel, whereon stood enormous candles of walrus fat.

"Next, we opened the central tunnel gate, and found ourselves within a much larger hall, in the centre of which stood a stone couch 1 foot 5 inches high and 10 feet broad. On it lay the coffin of the Lady T'ien, covered with silk drapery.

"At 3 p.m. the coffins of their Majesties arrived at the entrance to the mausoleum, and were sheltered for the night in a temporary mat-shed which I had erected. We offered sacrifice of a bullock, gold and silver paper, grain and fruits. At the head of the few officials present I proceeded to pay homage to our departed Sovereign and we wept bitterly at the foot of the Imperial biers.

"Next day, the two coffins were borne through the tunnel and into the grave chamber. We placed them on the stone couch, from which we had first removed the coffin of Lady T'ien. We then deposited the coffin of the Empress on the left of the couch, the Lady T'ien's remains were replaced on the right, and lastly, His Majesty's coffin was lifted into the central place. The Lady T'ien's death had occurred at a time of peace, and her coffin had consequently been provided with the customary outer shell, but that had been no means of preparing in the present case for His Majesty. So I had the shell of the Lady T'ien's coffin removed and used to cover that of the Emperor.

"The obsequies having ended, we refilled the tunnel, banking up the earth so as to conceal the approach to the door leading into the grave chamber. On the following morning, the sixth, we offered libations of wine, and I had a mound erected over the grave by the peasants from neighbouring hamlets (concubines' tombs had no tumuli)."

1. The "Sacred Way"

This is a somewhat innaccurate translation of the Chinese: *shen dao* (way of the spirit). The body of the dead person was carried over this route at the funeral ceremony. It is nearly 4 miles long, from the stone portico to the gate of the chief tomb.

The *stone portico (shi pai fang)* was built in 1540. It is a monumental construction, built in white marble, with five arches. Six rectangular pillars support it, each one rising out of a base of plaques of blue-grey stone, covered with beautiful bas-relief carvings (lions, dragons, lotus flowers). Double lintels, each one a single block of stone, link the six pillars; the roofing, like Chinese roofs, is made of round marble tiles, with up-turned corners. The way used to pass beneath the portico.

About half a mile further on stands the *Great Red Gate (Da hong men)*, which is the entrance to the necropolis properly speaking. It is a massive building with three archways through it, 120 feet high and 35 feet wide. It used to have three huge wooden doors. The central opening was used by the body of the dead Emperor alone; living sovereigns had to use one of the side openings when they came to pay homage to their ancestors. The walls which closed the mouth of the valley started from either side of the gate. Stone steles stood in front of the gate, ordering horsemen to dismount.

The *Stele Pavilion (Pei ting)* stands about 500 yards from the Great Red Gate. It used to consist of a double roof supported by twelve large wooden pillars. A huge stele stands in the middle on the back of a tortoise. It was erected in 1426, and is 30 feet high; one side bears an inscription by the fourth Ming Emperor, Hong xi, and the other, an inscription by the Emperor Qian long. A marble column *(hua biao)* stands at each corner of the pavilion.

The famous *avenue of animals* begins about 300 yards from the stele pavilion. Stone animals are found at the entrances to tombs from the Han dynasty onwards (cf. the famous horses at the tomb of General Huo Qu bing, in Shân xi). The Xi an museum (see

p. 936) has some examples of this type of funeral statues. No other group is as famous as that of the Ming tombs, however.

Two columns *(wang zhu)*, one on either side, begin the avenue. They are hexagonal, carved with a cloud design, and the top of each shaped like a rounded cylinder. Then follow, one on each side; a kneeling lion, a standing lion, a kneeling *xie chi*, a standing *xie chi* (a *xie chi* was a mythical beast of the feline family, with a mane and a horn on its head), a kneeling camel and a standing camel, a kneeling elephant and a standing elephant, a kneeling *qi lin* and a standing *qi lin* (a *qi lin* was a sort of imaginary animal with a scaly body, a cow's tail, deer's hooves and, here, horns on its head), a kneeling horse and a standing horse; twelve animals on each side and twenty-four in all.

Then the "sacred way" turns slightly (in accordance with the demands of *feng shui*) and the human statues appear (only Emperors or *wang* "kings" had a right to them); on each side stand: two military mandarins *(wu chen)* wearing sabres, two civil mandarins *(wen chen)*, two "retired" mandarins *(xun chen);* six on each side, and twelve in all.

These statues all date from the 15th century. It is interesting to compare them with the statues at the tomb of Hong wu at Nanking (see p. 991) which are scarcely any older and yet much less fine. The meaning of the figures is still not clear; the *qi lin* and *xie chi* are supposed to be animals of good omen; the men and some of the other animals (horses, elephants) are meant to serve the dead in the next world (cf. the wooden and pottery tomb figurines buried with the bodies).

The avenue of animals ends at *Ling xing men* (or Long feng men), a portico with three openings, surrounded with vegetation, with the road running on either side of it.

The sacred way goes on beyond the portico towards the chief tomb, Yong le's tomb. It runs over a modern bridge; at that point the Thirteen Tombs Dam (Shi san ling shui ku, see "Note on the Water Supply", p. 415) can be seen on the right. The dam was built in six months, in 1958; (the principal members of the Communist Party and Chairman Mao himself came to join in with the work); it provides water for irrigation works in the Peking plain and works the turbines of a hydro-electric power station. A path to the right leads to the dam, after a long walk; a memorial has been erected east of the dam.

A little further north along the "sacred way" a path goes off to the right to the Yong ling and De ling tombs, then further on still, another leads off to the left to the Ding ling tomb. The way itself leads straight on to the Chang ling, the chief tomb.

It is perhaps a good idea to see the Ding ling first, as its vault has been excavated and can be seen, and then the Chang ling, the biggest of all, whose buildings are in the best state of repair. Then, if time allows, some of the others can be visited; they are less well preserved, but the sites are all delightful.

Much of the area which was the old necropolis is now farmed by the "Thirteen Tombs People's Commune".

2. The Tomb of Emperor Wan li (Ding ling)

The Excavation of the Tomb. The Ding ling contained the bodies of Emperor Shen zong (*nian hao:* Wan li) who reigned for 46 years, from 1573 to 1620, his wife, the Empress Xiao duan, who died in 1620, only a few months before the Emperor, and his secondary wife, the Empress Xiao jing, who died in 1612. Xiao duan, who became Empress in 1578 had no sons, Xiao jing had two. The elder of the two, Guang zong (*nian hao:* Tai chang) succeeded Wan li in 1620 for a very short time, as he died 29 days after his accession and left the throne to his son, Xi zong (*nian hao:* Tian qi). As Xiao jing was only the second wife, theoretically she was not entitled to the privilege of sharing the Emperor's tomb. In 1612, her body was laid in the "eastern well" *(dong jing,)* the tomb reserved for second wives. When her son became Emperor, she was raised to the rank of Empress Dowager, and it was decided to move her body to the Ding ling.

In 1583, the young Emperor Wan li, then only 22, chose the site for his tomb. Work was begun on it in 1584 and it was finished four years later; it cost eight million ounces of silver. The bricks were brought from Shan dong, the stone from the Fang shan, and from He nan, the wood from Si chuan and Hu guang. In 1644, the Manchu damaged the buildings, which were not restored until the reign of Qian long, when the sacrifices were re-instated in the Ming tombs. The buildings were knocked down again at the beginning of the 20th century.

In 1956, it was decided that the tomb should be excavated. It was the first time that the scientific excavation of an imperial tomb had been undertaken in China. The main difficulty was to find the opening of the entrance corridor by which the coffins were taken in, so as to enter the vault without having to damage it. It had been noticed that at one point in the wall round the tumulus (*bao cheng*, precious wall), to the south, left of the stele tower, the bricks were showing signs of weakening; a few were removed and revealed an archway through the wall; it was the opening of the entrance corridor. The mound was dug into on the other side of the wall, and the beginning of the corridor was found (two brick side walls with no ceiling, and filled up with earth). Near the arch a stele was found which gave details of the length and direction of the corridor. Borings were made and the corridor was followed some way towards the north-east. However, near the stele tower, the brick walls which had been guiding the searchers stopped abruptly. It was thought that the vault must be lower down, and so they dug down from there.

At that point they discovered a second little stele, which said that "the diamond wall was 16 *zhang* away, and 3.5 *zhang* down". Like the first stele found, this one was meant to guide those who re-opened the tomb; it is understandable that the builders who had worked on the tomb in 1590 should have left them for those who might need them later on, but it is hard to see why, in 1620, when the tomb was closed for the last time, they should still have been left. The instructions were followed and a second passage with walls of rough hewn stone (but no ceiling, and consequently full of earth) was found. This led to the "diamond wall", the outside wall of the underground palace.

Theoretically, this wall should have been a carefully-pointed brick wall, and in this case it would have been difficult to know where to attack it. In fact, some of the bricks had been put back in a hurry and revealed exactly where the entrance was. One by one they were removed, and an ante-chamber was found, whose far wall was an enormous marble door, in two parts. According to old texts, the doors of tombs were sealed from the inside by a block of stone which swung into place as the doors were closed, and prevented the two halves from being opened again. An iron rod was slid through the crack between the two doors and the stone was manoeuvred aside without damaging the doors themselves. They opened on to the first chamber of the vault. A second chamber was opened in the same way, and three altars laden with ritual objects were found; then a third chamber was found, with the three coffins, and 26 chests full of precious objects placed beside the dead.

The wood of the coffins and the chests had partly disintegrated and their contents were in complete confusion. Photographs were taken and the contents removed piece by piece. Some of the originals and several copies are now exhibited in the modern buildings in front of the tumulus. The excavation work begun in 1956 went on until 1958; a fascinating colour film has been made, tracing all the various stages.

Description. Just beyond a little bridge stands a stele mounted on a tortoise (the pavilion which housed it has disappeared, and the stele is unusual in that it has no inscription). The way leads from here to the great entrance gate into the first courtyard, where the kitchen and sacred shop used to be; at the far end, a flight of stone steps leads on to a terrace where once a hall stood; in the second courtyard is another terrace, where the Ling en dian (the hall where sacrifices were made) used to stand; the third courtyard now contains two exhibition rooms.

First Room (to the right): **the excavation work and the Empresses' possessions.** Model showing how the entrance to the vault was found; two little steles found during the diggings (the inscriptions helped the search); a brick from the entrance passage (engraved: the inscription shows that it was made in Shan dong); on the walls: photographs of various stages in the diggings.

A set of metal hairpins and jewellery found in the Empresses' head-dresses (photographs of the skulls when they were found); skirt and jackets of precious fabrics; interesting jacket with embroidered figures of little boys playing (worn by the Empress Xiao duan, who longed to have a son); coins sewn into the shrouds; jade pendants (worn at the belt); dressing-case (brushes, mirror, lacquer boxes); Buddhist rosary made of amber; rolls of fabrics; funerary inscriptions on wooden plaques *(yi ce);* double square stone slab with an inscription about Xiao jing's life history (the slabs used to be held together by iron fittings which have now disappeared, leaving rust marks). In the central cases: gold and silver vessels; porcelain vases; copies of the two "phoenix crowns" (worn by the Empresses at ceremonial occasions); one has twelve dragons and nine phoenixes, the other six dragons and three phoenixes; the upper part was made of king-fisher feathers mounted on paper (which made them extremely light); they are copies of the originals, which were in poor condition; fragments of scented wood (jia nan xiang), from the south, or perhaps from south-east Asia.

b) **Second Room** (to the left): **the Emperor's possessions.** Set of wooden tomb figurines (people and horses) of much less fine workmanship than the rest of the objects; set of twelve embroidered silk kneelers; tin funerary objects; rolls of brocade; silver and gold ingots, cast in Wan li's reign; boots and trousers, imperial robe; head-dresses worn when giving audiences: jade belt; funerary inscription *(yi ce);* jewellery; on the walls: copy of a portrait of the Emperor; photograph of the chignon of Wan li, as it was when the tomb was opened; view of the Ming Tombs seen from above (date not given). In the central cases: gold vessels; ewers and large vases known as *mei ping* or "plum-blossom vases" (others have been found in the tomb of a concubine, recently excavated; it seems to have been a Ming custom to put vases like these in tombs; the blue is produced by a special colouring matter brought from the southern seas); gold filigree crown, plumed war head-dress and ceremonial sword.

At the far end of the third courtyard stands the massive cube-shaped **Square Tower (Fang cheng),** built in brick and surmounted by the Stele Tower (Ming lou); as it is in stone, it survived the fire. The Square Tower is built up against the Precious Wall (Bao cheng) which encircles the base of the tumulus. Flights of steps lead up the sides to the top of the Bao cheng; more steps go up to the top of the Square Tower, where the stele can be seen, and from the top of the Bao cheng, it is possible to walk directly on to the tumulus itself.

The opening of the entrance passage leading to the underground palace is near this point. The archway through the encircling wall has been cleared of earth (and is sealed by a door for the moment); the first little stele was found here. The passage has been only partly cleared, but the brick walls can be seen. The corridor which has been built down to the staircase leading into the vault is towards the central axis of the tomb, in front of the Stele Tower. A notice shows the spot where the second stele was found (several yards below ground level). The present passageway is on a much higher level than the original one; the decoration on the door at the entrance is modern. The staircase gives some idea of the depth of the trench which had to be cleared.

The ante-chamber at the bottom of the staircase is modern; the "diamond wall" now contains an opening, triangular at the top. The vault itself begins only after the brick wall; all the rest was full of earth. A little ante-chamber precedes the marble door giving on to the first chamber. The bricks blocking the opening in the "diamond wall" have been re-mounted in a wooden frame which stands agains the left wall of the ante-chamber.

The two great doors now stand against the walls, each behind a sheet of glass (note the beautiful bas-relief carvings of lions' heads). The block of stone which swung down from within to act as a locking device stands against the wall. The bottom end fitted into a socket in the ground, and each door has a similar socket which received the top.

The first chamber is no more than a long entrance corridor, and nothing was found there. The elaborate vaulted ceiling is the same here as in the other chambers. A second door like the first leads into the central chamber, where the three altars stand one behind the other (they were found in slightly different positions). The first two were dedicated to the Empresses, the last one to the Emperor. They are all three iden-

MAUSOLÉE DE L'EMPEREUR WAN LI (DING LING)

MAUSOLEUM OF EMPEROR WAN LI.

Vue perspective   Bird's eye view

Salle du fond
Far Hall

Cercueils
Coffins

Salle latérale
Side Hall

Salle centrale
Central Hall

Autels
Altars

Salle latérale
Side Hall

Salle antérieure.
Outer Hall

Mur de Diamant
Diamond Wall

Petite antichambre
Small antechamber

d'après Hou Ren Zhi «Bu Jang ji». Pékin, 1963.
after Hou Ren Zhi "Bu Jang ji. Peking, 1963.

tical. The "eternal lamp" stands in front of them on a round base; it is a large vase with a blue design on it, full of oil which was meant to feed the eternal flame. In fact, the lack of air probably prevented the flame from burning for long and the vase is still full of solidified oil with the remains of a wick in it. Five ritual vessels in yellow pottery stand behind the lamp, on smaller bases; and behind them is a sort of altar (or throne), with some very fine carving on it.

A third door leads into the third and last chamber, larger and higher than the others. A stone dais, about 18 inches high stands in the middle. Most of what it contains now are copies. In the centre stood the Emperor's coffin, with the Empresses one on each side of him; 26 chests containing the treasures buried with them stood round them; among the chests were large porcelain vases *(mei ping)* and pieces of stone, chosen for their beautiful shapes. At the left end of the dais is a double stone slab bound with iron, a replica of the one in the first room of the museum (the funerary inscription of the Empress Xiao jing). The explanation of some of the things which were found is still not clear, for example the little lances standing on the Emperor's coffin, and the bits of rotten wood lying in front of the dais.

The two side chambers at the end of narrow corridors with stone doors, one on each side of the central chamber, are equally mysterious. They both contain a dais obviously intended for a coffin, like the end chambers. What is more, each one has a corridor leading out of the tumulus, like the main entrance corridor, only narrower and steeper, with brick walls. The rooms were both found completely empty. One possible explanation exists: when work was begun on the tomb in 1584, it could not be foreseen that both Empresses would die before the Emperor; should they have outlived him, their coffins would have been placed in the two annex chambers, and there would have been no need to re-open the main vault. As they died before Wan li, they were buried with him, and the need to open the annex corridors never arose. This does not, however, explain why the Empresses were not laid in the annex chambers in 1620 when they were all buried together. Perhaps the corridors leading from the central chamber to the annex chambers were too narrow to let the coffins through.

In 1960, new excavations were begun to try to find the answer to the question of the corridor to the right hand chamber. A new staircase was built leading down into it, which can be used to leave the underground palace.

3. The Tomb of Emperor Yong le (Chang ling)

The Chang ling contains the remains of Emperor Cheng zu (*nian hao* Yong le), the third Emperor of the Ming dynasty, who reigned for 22 years, from 1403 to 1424, and those of his wife, the Empress Ren Xiao ci, who died in 1407.

A massive three-arched gate gives on to the first courtyard, 150 feet long, which ends with the Ling en men (Gate of Eminent Favours), a large hall with a yellow tiled roof; in the south east corner of the courtyard stands a pavilion with a Qing stele. The Ling en men leads into an enormous courtyard 500 feet long, planted with big pine trees, with the Ling en dian (Hall of Eminent Favours) at the end of it. It is a superb building on a triple terrace of white marble, bordered with balustrades. Three flights of steps lead up to it; the middle one has a central ramp of three large stone slabs carved with a phoenix and dragon motif, and steps on either side. Four stoves covered in porcelain, used for burning the offerings, stand in front of the steps. Three flights of steps lead down from the terrace on the north side; the building reaches to the edge of the terrace on this side. The hall itself is 220 feet long and 105 feet wide. Its double roof of yellow glazed tiles is supported by 32 colossal wooden pillars, three feet thick, linked by horizontal beams, and by 28 smaller pillars 2 feet 6 inches thick, arranged round the outside of the large pillars, and supporting the lower roof. The side and back façades are built in such a way that the pillars are partly embedded

MAUSOLÉE DE L'EMPEREUR YONG LE (CHANG LING) — COUPE SUPPOSÉE
MAUSOLEUM OF EMPEROR YONG LE (CHANG LING) — HYPOTHETICAL CROSS-SECTION

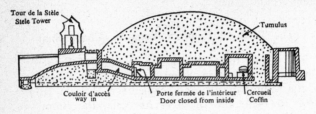

Tour de la Stèle
Stele Tower

Tumulus

Couloir d'accès
way in

Porte fermée de l'intérieur
Door closed from inside

Cercueil
Coffin

in the wall; the front façade has windows and double
doors; a screen wall stands about 7 feet inside the
north door; the coffered ceiling, which has recently
been restored, is painted in green, white and red.
The funeral tablet used to lie on the wooden altar
in the middle of the hall; sacrifices used to be made
in front of it. The wooden pillars are each made of
one single trunk and the wood (from Yun nan)
is magnificent.

Another massive three-arched gate leads out of
the second into the third and last courtyard, which
is nearly 300 feet long up to the foot of the Square
Tower. About 60 feet from the gate stands a little
portico, and 120 feet or so further on is a marble
altar, with the five ritual objects, also of marble.
The massive Square Tower (Fang cheng) is 70 feet
further on, with the Stele Tower (Ming lou) on top
of it. A tunnel 60 feet long runs through the Square
Tower, sloping upwards, and then branches off and
comes out the other side. The stele, 7 feet high,
has the two characters *Da Ming* (Great Ming) inscribed in curly script on the top, and the middle
part bears the inscription: "Tomb of the Emperor
Cheng zu". The terrace gives access to the top of the

MAUSOLÉE DE L'EMPEREUR YONG LE
(CHANG LING)—PLAN
MAUSOLEUM OF EMPEROR YONG LE

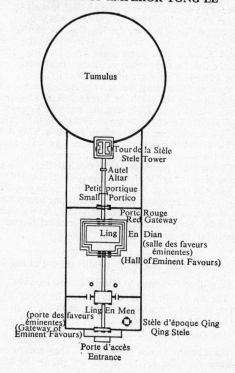

Tumulus

Tour de la Stèle
Stele Tower

Autel
Altar

Petit portique
Small Portico

Porte Rouge
Red Gateway

Ling — En Dian
(salle des faveurs
éminentes)
(Hall of Eminent Favours)

(porte des faveurs
éminentes)
(Gateway of
Eminent Favours)

Ling En Men

Stèle d'époque Qing
Qing Stele

Porte d'accès
Entrance

"Precious Wall" encircling the tumulus (330 yards
across). It is proposed to excavate the tomb of Yong
le soon; it would probably yield even more than that
of Wan li.

4. The Other Tombs

South of the Ding ling are the **Zhao ling**, tomb of Emperor Mu zong (*nian hao:* Long qing, 1567–1572), and the **Si ling**, the tomb of the last Emperor, who killed himself in 1644; his tomb was built by the Qing (see above, p. 624).

East of the Chang ling are the **Jing ling**, the tomb of Emperor Xuan zong (*nian hao:* Xuan de, 1426–1435), the **Yong ling**, tomb of Emperor Shi zong (*nian hao:* Jia jing, 1522–1566) and lastly the **De ling**, tomb of Emperor Xi zong (*nian hao:* Tian qi, 1621–1627), the grandson of Wan li.

West of the Chang ling, the order of the tombs is as follows: 1) the **Xian ling**, the tomb of Emperor Ren zong (*nian hao:* Hong xi, 1425); 2) the **Qing ling**, the tomb of Emperor Guang zong (*nian hao:* Tai chang, reign of 29 days in 1620), the son of Wan li; 3) the **Yu ling**, the tomb of Emperor Ying zong (*nian hao:* Zheng tong from 1436–1449, then Tian shun from 1457–1464) 4) the **Mao ling**, the tomb of Emperor Xian zong (*nian hao:* Cheng hua, 1465–1487); 5) the **Tai ling**, the tomb of Emperor Xiao zong (*nian hao:* Hong zhi, 1488–1505); 6) the **Kang ling**, the tomb of Emperor Wu zong (*nian hao:* Zheng de, 1506–1521). The buildings which preceded the tombs have fallen down in most cases, and the square tower and the stele are all that remain. Some tombs have been restored recently, others have been left as they were.

5. Other Imperial Tombs near Peking

None of them are open to visitors for the moment.

a) **The Jin Tombs (12th century)** They lie north of the Fang shan (see p. 648). They were violated under the reign of Wan li and are in very bad condition.

b) **The Qing Tombs.**

1. The Eastern Tombs (Dong ling). They are 74 miles east of Peking, near the village of Ma lan yu, at the foot of the Chang rui Hills, on the right bank of the River Wei jia. The first Manchu Emperors were buried here, after the dynasty had settled in Peking. When the Emperor Yong zheng was about to choose the site for his tomb, geomancers are said to have suggested a far more favourable site to him, 86 miles west of Peking, about 12 miles west of Yi xian. This was to become the Xi ling (Western Tombs). Some of the later Emperors chose the Dong ling, some the Xi ling.

The eastern cemetery covered an immense arena 21 miles wide, enclosed by walls, fences or hill-tops. The thirteen tombs there include those of Shun zhi (1644–1662), Kang xi (1662–1723), Qian long (1736–1796), Xian feng (1861–1862), Tong zhi (1862–1875), and Empress Ci xi (who died in 1908).

In 1928, a warlord, Sun Tian ying, closed the tombs under the pretext of using the ground for manoeuvres, and with the help of his troops, opened the tombs of Qian long and Ci xi to steal the treasures. Aisin-Gioro Pu yi, the last Manchu Emperor, tells of the horror with which this violation was received, and of his own personal sorrow at it in his memoirs (*From Emperor to Citizen*, Peking 1964, p. 194).

2. The Western Tombs (Xi ling). They lie in an arena up against the Xi shan, surrounded by a wall nearly 18 miles round. The design of the tombs, like the Dong ling tombs, show the influence of the Ming Tombs. Among the ten Emperors buried here are Yong zheng (1723–1736), Jia qing (1796–1821), Dao guang (1821–1851), and Guang xu (1875–1908).

III.   The Western and South-western Suburbs

The western and south-western suburbs are relatively uninteresting; the plain is almost entirely under cultivation and apart from one or two ancient monuments (the Ba li zhuang Pagoda and the Marco Polo Bridge), a modern museum (The Military Museum of the Chinese People's Revolution), and a park (Yu yuan tan), the contrast between farming land and new dormitory areas is the only thing which attracts the attention.

Several old temples (Fa hai si, Jie tai si, Tan zhe si, Xi yu si), the prehistoric site at Zhou kou dian and several recent industrial centres (the Men tou gou coal mines and the Shi jing shan steel works) lie in the foot-hills of the mountains. These places are all out of bounds as far as foreigners are concerned at the moment, unfortunately, and it is extremely difficult to obtain permission to see them.

The Jade Abyss Pool (Yu yuan tan)

It is also called the Fishing Terrace (Diao yu tai). It is west of the north-south road, San li he lu, on a level with the trolley bus stop "San li he" (bus No. 2), slightly north of the Military Museum of the Revolution.

An imperial residence was built here as early as the Jin dynasty. In 1773, Qian long had the lake enlarged and built a palace on its shores, which was destined to fall into ruins soon afterwards. The lake has recently been re-dug.

Water is brought from upstream from the River Yong ding, through a canal; a hydro-electric power station has been built downstream; the overfall flows into the moat of the town eventually. The shores of the lake have been re-wooded and it is now popular for bathing and boating.

The Military Museum of the Chinese People's Revolution (Zhong guo ren min ge ming jun shi buo wu guan).

It is a few miles west of the Fu xing men Gate (No. 1 bus, the Jun shi buo wu guan stop).

The museum was opened in 1959 and covers an area of 65,000 square yards. It is a large white stone building, with spire topped by a red star. The two figures "8–1" in the star commemorate the Nan chang military rising (the 1st of the eighth month — August 1st, 1927), which led to the founding of the revolutionary army.

It is divided into five main sections: 1) the second civil war (1927–1937); 2) the war of resistance against the Japanese (1937–1945); 3) the third civil war (1946–1949); 4) the protection of the building of socialism; 5) the Korean war (1950–1958); each section contains large numbers of maps, documents and other exhibits (weapons, flags...), illustrating the progress of the Communist Party towards its final victory. It is an interesting complement to the revolutionary museum at Tian an men Square. An enormous collection of weapons, nearly all of Western make, captured during the civil wars, are exhibited in a vast annex building.

The Ba li zhuang Pagoda.

The buses No. 35 and 36 (from Fu cheng men Gate) both go past the Ba li zhuang stop; the name means the village eight li—two and a half miles—from the town walls. The pagoda stands all alone amongst the fields.

History. The Ci shou si (Temple of Compassion and Longevity) was founded in 1576 under Wan li of the Ming dynasty, by Empress Ci sheng, who dedicated it to Guan yin. The temple contained a solid gold statue of Guan yin with lotus flowers, one foot high. In 1937, the monks were short of money, and made an agreement with the authorities to demolish the temple and sell the contents and materials.

Description. The elegant octagonal pagoda is all that remains; the stone base is carved with scenes from the Diamond Sutra, and a double row of lotus petals; the middle section has some stucco figures which are interesting because their dilapidated state reveals the technique used to make them (wooden and iron frameworks); the upper part consists of thirteen stories built in brick, but imitating the style of wooden buildings. Two steles, engraved with portraits, stand at the foot of the pagoda; they date from the Wan li period.

The Marco Polo Bridge (Lu gou qiao: "the River Lu gou Bridge").

The Marco Polo Bridge, as the Europeans call it, is indeed a famous one; it spans the River Yong ding, which used to be called Lu gou (black moat), south-west of Peking. The 39 bus stops at "Lu gou qiao", and the bridge is at the end of the main street. The little village of Wan ping stands on the left bank of the river; it is a walled village, full of inns. It was the scene of the "Marco Polo Bridge Incident" (Qi qi shi bian), on July 7th 1937, which began the resistance movement against the Japanese.

History. From a very early period, the great north-south route linking the Yellow River provinces with the north-eastern regions crossed the River Yong ding at this point (see introduction to Peking). At first there was only a pontoon bridge, which was often washed away when the river rose, or burned (the 1123 fire). In 1189, the 29th year of the Da deng era, the Jin Emperor Shi zong ordered the first stone bridge to be built. The work was completed three years later, in 1192, and the bridge was officially called the Guang li qiao.

This was the bridge that Marco Polo saw when he stayed at Khanbaliq towards 1276, and afterwards described in *"The Book of Marco Polo"*. calling it Pulisangin (from the Persian: *pul*, bridge and *sang*, stone): "And over this river is a very great stone bridge... For you may know that there are few of them in the world so beautiful, nor its equal... It is made like this. I tell you that it is quite three hundred paces long and quite eight paces wide, for ten horsemen can well go there the one beside the other... it... is all of grey marble very well worked and well founded. There is above each side of the bridge a beautiful curtain or wall of flags of marble and of pillars made so as I shall tell you... And there is fixed at the head of the bridge a marble pillar, and below the pillar a marble lion... very beautiful and large and well made." (*Marco Polo, The Description of the world*, Moule and Pelliot, Routledge, London, 1938). This famous description earned the bridge its name, which is still used by Europeans. It was restored under the Ming in 1444, and under the Qing in 1698, after two arches had been washed away by flood waters.

Description. It is 768 feet long, and consists of eleven stone arches built on cypress-wood piling. Parapets run along both sides of the roadway; each one has 140 little columns with lions on the top of them, all different. At the end of each parapet are stone elephants, which look as though they are supporting the bridge. Pavilions at either end (once covered with yellow tiles) house imperial steles, one in memory of the restoration work of 1698 (Kang xi), the other describing "morning moonlight on the Lu gou qiao" as one of the eight "views" of Peking (Qian long). An iron railway bridge now spans the Yong ding, parallel to the Lu gou qiao, and at night the glow from the Shi jing shan iron works lights up the river. The Guang ting reservoir has been built up river; it regulates the flow of the Yong ding, irrigates farming land, and supplies water for Peking.

The Temple of the Sea and the Law (Fa hai si)

It is south-west of Ba da chu, near the village of Mo shi kou (No 36 bus).

It was built between 1439 and 1444 and included several buildings at that time. One hall only (Da xiong bao dian) remains now, with magnificent Ming frescoes on the walls. The far wall (adoration of the Buddha) has no fewer than thirty-five figures. Peking Art Publications have brought out an excellent volume of reproductions in colour (see bibliography, p. 390).

The Ordination Terrace Temple (Jie tai si).

It is 5 miles north of Tan zhe si, at the foot of the Man an shan hills (hill paths lead to it).

It was founded under the Tang in 622. Under the Liao, a monk, Fa chun, built the first terrace *(jie tai)*; the temple was restored under the Ming, and the last restoration work dates from 1891. On an appointed day each year, all the monks from the neighbouring area used to gather there to hear their elders preach from the terrace.

The main features of the temple are: 1) the terrace, over 10 feet high; 2) the Qian fo ge (the Thousand Buddha Pavilion); 3) to the north-east, two pagodas in good condition, one dating from the Liao (1091) and one dating from the Ming (1448); two steles and three *chuang* date from the Liao and the Yuan respectively. Magnificent pine trees grow all round the temple.

The Temple of the Pool and the zhe Tree (Tan zhe si).

The *zhe* tree has two uses: it feeds silk-worms and its bark gives yellow dye.

The temple is a little way south of Men tou gou; its origins date back to the 3rd century A.D. Under the Tang it was particularly famous and prosperous; people used to come to listen to the Classics being expounded. It was restored under the Liao and the Jin. A legend says that the Emperor Khubilai's daughter went into retreat here. Under the Ming and the Qing it was restored and enlarged; a palace was added.

It is the largest of all the temples in the Peking district; the buildings are grouped round three separate north-south axes. The pagoda dates from the Liao or the Jin.

The Western Valley Temple (Xi yu si)

It lies south-west of Men tou gou, in the Fang shan Hills.

Its history goes back to the 6th century, when some monks decided to engrave Buddhist canons on stone, and to collect the tablets here. In the 12th century, this library on stone was still being compiled.

Over two thousand inscribed stone slabs are still there, in natural caves in the side of the Shi jing shan Hill (Hill of the Sutras written on Stone).

The Xi yu si, south-west of the Shi jing shan, is a large temple with extensive buildings. It is famous above all for its two pagodas: the *Luo han* Pagoda, which dates from the Tang, and the Pagoda "which crushes the Buddhist canons" (Ya jing ta), said to date from the 12th century (so called, apparently, because large quantities of engraved stone tablets, over four thousand, it is said, are buried beneath it). The temple is surrounded by *chuang* and monks' tombs.

The Jin Tombs (12th century) were north of the Fang shan Hills. When Nurhachi, a Jürched like the Jin, was threatening the northern frontier in the 16th century, the Chinese sacked the Jin Emperor's tombs, as a measure of reprisal.

Zhou kou dian---the Sinanthropus Museum

The village of Zhou kou dian (better known in the West transcribed as Tcheou kou tien or Chou kou tien) is 30 miles south-west of Peking, at the foot of the Fang shan Hills.

This is where Father Teilhard de Chardin discovered the first fragment of the skull of Peking Man, sinanthropus pekinensis, on December 2nd, 1929, a discovery of primordial importance, which was to revolutionise research into the origins of man. Later excavations revealed 180 fragments of animal bones, and over 40 fragments of human bones, as well as stone tools. It was also proved beyond all doubt that Peking Man (500,000 B.C., approximately) used fire. Most of the discoveries were taken to Tai wan and the United States before 1949. In 1958, a lower jawbone was found.

In 1953, the Laboratory of Paleontology founded a prehistoric museum at Long gu shan ("the dragon bone mountain"), near the site of the excavations. Part of it is devoted to Peking Man and the Zhou kou dian Culture, and the rest deals with the evolution of man in general, and Peking Man in relation to the other hominids.

IV.   The Eastern Suburbs

The Road to Pa li kao Bridge (Ba li qiao) and Tong xian

The eastern suburbs of Peking now include a large industrial area (workshops producing spare parts for cars, small ironworks, textile mills, knitwear factories, a brewery, flour mills, wireless valves workshops etc...). The large brick buildings of the new workers' living quarters are much in evidence.

The bus No 42 goes as far as the **Eight li Bridge (Ba li qiao),** one of the limits of the prescribed area. It is a fine three-arch bridge, famous chiefly for the victory which the Anglo-French troops won there over the Imperial armies in 1860. The Frenchman Cousin-Montauban was given the title of "Count of Pa li kao" after the battle.

The road goes on to **Tong xian,** a village which used to be important because it stood at the point where the Bai he met the canal which flowed on to Peking. Boats which came up from the south via the Grand Canal would unload there, and numerous warehouses were built. The largest granaries of all stood in there the 18th century: "enough rice for over eight years was stored there, as well as wheat, vegetables and animal fodder" (De Lisle).

In the enclosure of the former Zou sheng jiao Convent stands a pagoda 100 feet high, known as the "tower of the lighted lamps" (Rao deng ta). It is traditionally said to date from the Northern Zhou. The style is rather that of the Jin period, however. It is an octagonal brick tower, whose style imitates that of wooden buildings. The base has some beautiful bas-relief carvings, and higher up, each of the eight facets on each storey is separated from the next by a column. One unusual thing about is is that over two thousand small bronze bells hang from the beams of its thirteen roofs and sound in the wind. The thirteen roofs are built very close to each other.

The Village of Jiao zhuang hu

It is easy to obtain permission to visit the village of Jiao zhuang hu, which was was an important centre of resistance to the Japanese. It is near the village of Shun yi, in the north-east of the Peking area. During the anti-Japanese war, the peasants dug a network of underground passages below the village, and took refuge there when the enemy approached. The passages were built so that a watch could be kept over the main streets, and the enemy could be shot at. A little museum has been founded there.

HE BEI

(Map see Atlas pl. 1)

The province of He bei is bounded by the Bo hai sea, the province of Liao ning, the Inner Mongolia Autonomous Region, Shan xi and He nan. Its 48 million inhabitants include over 500,000 Hui people (autonomous districts east of Peking and south of Cang zhou) and over 10,000 Mongols in the north. *He bei* means "north of the river"—the Yellow River. The Peking district forms an independent enclave in the centre of the province.

It falls naturally into two roughly equal parts: the mountainous tableland to the north and the vast southern plain. The plateau and its foot-hills furrowed with valleys and basins form part of the Mongolian tableland (over 3,000 feet above sea level); the foot-hills, with the Great Wall winding through them, begin just north of Peking. To the east they form a chain of hills (the Yan shan Hills). West of Peking rise the Tai hang Mountains, a chain forming a barrier over 250 miles long between the plains of He bei and the Shan xi tableland. The highest point is 11,448 feet, at the northern end of the formation; they slope downwards as they run south. The plain encircled by these mountains is vast and monotonous, with cultivated fields stretching as far as the eye can see, broken here and there by weeping willows or poplars, little villages or muddy rivers. Although the sea is not far away, the climate is continental; it rarely snows in winter, the air is extremely dry, and the temperature often falls below 14° F. In summer, it often rises to over 104° F, and there is heavy rainfall in July and August (30 or 40 days of rain or snow each year). Until recently, the climate had severe disadvantages, although healthy in itself: droughts were frequent when the summer rainfall was inadequate, heavy flooding followed over-plentiful rainfall, and violent winds from Mongolia brought with them dust-storms in the spring.

Although it has been inhabited since the very earliest days (Peking Man dates from the Paleolithic era), He bei was for a long time of only marginal importance in the history of China. Two kingdoms were formed there under the Zhou; the Yan in the north and the Zhao in the south, but both of them played a minor role in the Chinese world of the Warring States period. Under the Han, with the building of the Great Wall, He bei became a frontier province where the Chinese and nomad Hun armies confronted each other. Under the Tang, the position was much the same; He bei was the jumping off point for the conquest of Korea. The feats of arms performed by the Emperor's soldiers in the hostile countries beyond the Great Wall constitute a theme which recurs again and again in the poetry of the time. The strength of the Tang garrisons quartered in He bei turned out to the disadvantage of the Emperor, however, for in 745, An Lu shan, the commander of the Peking garrison, took the capital and led a revolt lasting for several years, which shook the empire to its very foundations. From the 11th century onwards, things changed. He bei was controlled by the Liao, then the Jin took over in the 12th century, and finally the Mongols in the 13th century. Paradoxically, it flourished during this period of non-Chinese domination, and became one of the most important provinces of modern China. The Liao made Peking their capital; the Jin took it over and developed it further; the Yuan made it into a great metropolis, linking it to South China by the building of the Grand Canal (which the Jin had begun). When the Ming dynasty was founded at Nanking, it seemed for a time that the south would once more become the economic and political centre of the Empire; Yong le, the third Ming Emperor, re-established Peking as the capital, however, in 1421, and set the final seal on the political supremacy of the north over the south. It lasted as long as the empire, and was then contested at the beginning of the 20th century (Sun Yat sen's government at Canton, Chiang Kai shek's government at Nanking); it has been re-affirmed since the founding of the Chinese People's Republic. From the Yuan onwards, and especially under the Ming and the Qing, it led to the development of trade and handicrafts in He bei. From the middle of the 19th century, the Western influence (Tian jin) could be felt, though it was much weaker than in Shan dong, in the Yang zi River Valley, in Shang hai or in South China. This comparatively weak influence, which can be explained by the presence of the imperial court in Peking, enabled Li Hong zhang, the viceroy of Zhi Li (the old name for He bei) to carry out economic and military reforms aimed at helping China to resist the encroachments of the Western Powers and Japan. The attempts ended in the Allies' occupation of Peking in 1900 and the fall of the empire in 1911. Foreign economic influences attracted the political centre of gravity towards south China for half a century (Shang hai, Canton, Nanking). One of the factors which led the government of the People's Republic to make Peking its capital in 1949 and to continue the development of He bei was no doubt its wish to repudiate the bourgeoisie of these towns, who had gained considerable importance over the last few decades.

The foundations for industrial development had already been laid during the second half of the 19th century (the Kai lan mines were founded near Tang shan in 1877, Tian jin had become an industrial city); furthermore the province is a rich mining area (iron, coal). The Tang shan mines, in the east of the province, and the Han dan (Feng feng) mines in the south were mechanised and enlarged. An iron industry was created at Tang shan, Tian jin, Peking, Han dan. The machine industry has developed considerably as well, helping the development of a modern textile industry with large centres at Shi jia zhuang and Han dan. The centre and south of the He bei plain is China's best cotton producing area (a quarter of the total annual production). Wheat is also grown in large quantities. To ensure a regular increase in cotton and wheat production, a permanent solution had to be found to the two problems of the droughts and floods which used to ravage the plain of He bei in turn. The River Hai he, into which most of the rivers and streams of the province flow near Tian jin, and which used to overflow its banks almost every year, often with catastrophic results, has been brought under control by large-scale work carried out on the river itself and its tributaries. In 1965, further work was begun in the south of the province, between Han dan and Cang zhou. All this irrigation and drainage work will protect a quarter of the total area of the He bei plain from natural calamities.

On 28 July 1976 the Tang shan region was badly hit by an earthquake, reported to have killed 700,000 people at Tang shan, Tian jin and Peking.

Rice, millet, maize, gaoliang, tobacco, oil-yielding plants etc., are also grown in He bei, as well as cotton and wheat. Millet and maize are the main crops in the northern, mountainous district. Great stress is laid on stock-breeding. Fruit is also produced in great variety (Xuan hua grapes, Tian jin pears, Liang xiang nuts, etc.). Along the coast, and particularly in the Tian jin region, fishing and salt extraction are extremely important.

Tian jin and its neighbourhood will be described first, followed by: east He bei and the Bo hai coast, the area bordering on Shan xi and Mongolia, the north of the plain, the centre and south of the plain.

TIAN JIN
(Map see p. 689)

Tian jin is a little over 60 miles south-east of Peking. It stretches along the banks of the Hai he, just south of the point where the Bei yun he (north section of the Grand Canal), the Yong ding he and the Zi ya he meet. As capital of the province of He bei, the town has developed considerably over the 20th century, until it is now second only to Shang hai among China's industrial and commercial towns, and is the largest port in the north. It has a population of 4,000,000.

1. The origins of the town. The first mention of a settlement on the site of the present town occurs under the Song. Under the Jin, the town was called Zhi gu ("buying and selling") and as its name suggests, it was an important trading post; all the grain brought up to the capital by the Grand Canal was stored at Tian jin. Under the Yuan, the name was changed to Hai jin zhen (the sea ford town). The volume of trade grew; the main business district was on the right bank of the Hai he as it now is, on a level with the Shi zi lin qiao Bridge.

2. Under the Ming and the Qing. In 1404, rectangular walls were built round the town, with four gates opening in them, and it became a garrison town. It was renamed Tian jin wei (Guardian of the Celestial Ford). Emigrants arrived in large numbers from the provinces of Fu jian, Jiang su and Shan dong (many Hui people were among them). Under the Qing, in the 18th century, the town was extremely prosperous. A member of the first Dutch Embassy which arrived in China in 1655, led by Peter de Goyer and Jacob de Keyzer, described what he saw: "On July 15th, we arrived at the port of Tien cien wey, one of the most famous of all the ports in China... it is in the east of the province of Peking, at the meeting of three rivers, where an imposing fort has been built. The countryside round it is a low-lying, marshy plain. The town of Tien cien wey is 30 miles from the mouth; it is surrounded by sturdy walls over 25 feet high with watch-towers and other defence works built at intervals along them; the town has many temples; it is thickly populated and trade is very brisk — it would be hard to find another town as busy as this in China—because all the boats which go to Peking, whatever their port of origin, call here, and the traffic is astonishingly heavy.., all sorts of goods can be found here; it is a free port, and no tax is levied on imports or exports. The fort, which stands at the meeting of the three rivers, has high battlements and towers, so that it can command both the town and the surrounding countryside." Salt production, which had been begun here under the Yuan, increased at the same time as the trade. The salt-pans were south of the town, where they still are today.

The large numbers of sailors at Tian jin gave birth to the worship of Tian hou (Celestial Queen), popularly known as Niang niang ("the good mother"). A legend dating from the Yuan says that she was a sailor's daughter, and that she saved her father from a ship-wreck, from afar; a magnificent temple was built to her, outside the east gate of the town, on the quayside. Sailors came to ask for her protection and burned incense; in spring, pilgrimages were made to the temple, and each crew brought a model of their ship (the temple still existed in 1936, but it has now disappeared).

3. The Arrival of the Europeans. On June 26th and 27th 1858, the Chinese signed treaties with Britain and France at Tian jin; among other advantages, the two powers were given the right to have a concession in the town. Anglo-French troops occupied the area in 1860 and a European town rapidly grew up round it (Japanese concession in 1895, German concession in 1896, enlarging of the British concession in 1897, Russian, Austro-Hungarian, Italian and Belgian concessions in 1900).

They were all south-east of the Chinese town, on either side of the Hai he; on the right bank, from north to south, were the Japanese, French, British and German (until 1914) concessions; on the left bank, from north to south, were the Austro-Hungarian (until 1914), Italian, Russian (enormous), and Belgian concessions. The toponymy was varied to say the least (Rue du Baron Gros, Victoria Park, Baron Czekam Strasse, Via Vittorio Emanuele, Pokotilova, Asahi gai...); the architecture was mixture of all the European styles (it still is today).

The Europeans did more than build a new town south of the old one; they stimulated trade by their presence.

4. The Reaction of the Chinese. The Chinese themselves reacted to the impact of the Europeans and their ideas. Li Hong zhang (1823-1901) is an excellent example of a member

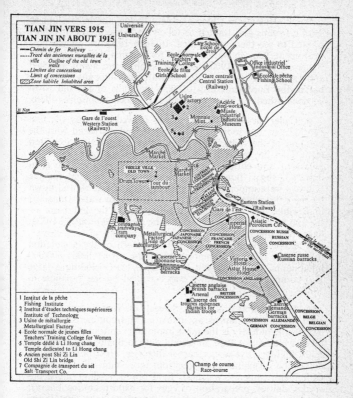

TIAN JIN VERS 1915
TIAN JIN IN ABOUT 1915

— Chemin de fer Railway
---- Tracé des anciennes murailles de la ville Outline of the old town walls
--- Limites des concessions Limit of concessions
░░ Zone habitée Inhabited area

1 Institut de la pêche
  Fishing Institute
2 Institut d'études techniques supérieures
  Institute of Technology
3 Usine de métallurgie
  Metallurgical Factory
4 Ecole normale de jeunes filles
  Teachers' Training College for Women
5 Temple dédié à Li Hong chang
  Temple dedicated to Li Hong chang
6 Ancien pont Shi Zi Lin
  Old Shi Zi Lin bridge
7 Compagnie de transport du sel
  Salt Transport Co.

of the section of high officials who were interested in Europe and anxious to introduce reforms inspired by the West into their own country. He was from the province of An hui, and became viceroy of the province of Zhi li; he wanted above all to strengthen his country, and introduced improvements (in industry, schools and the army) which gave Tian jin the reputation of being one of the most "advanced" towns of the empire. His protégé Yuan Shi kai reaped the benefit of these reforms. In 1905, the Emperor had a temple built at Tian jin in honour of Li Hong zhang; Duke Li's Temple (Li gong si),

Some elements in Chinese society looked for inspiration to the Europeans and wanted to follow their example, but others wanted to see them annihilated. In June 1870 the French possessions at Tian jin were attacked for the first time. During the Boxer rebellion in 1900, the concessions were again attacked and the agressors were warded off with great difficulty. After the battle, the Europeans insisted that the walls of the old town be demolished, as the rebels had entrenched themselves there.

5. Under the Republic. Trade was slowed down by the first World War, but soon picked up again and increased with the building of the railway. Raw cotton and wool were exported form Tian jin, as well as minor products (peanuts, skins, jujubes...) and cotton fabric (which formed 40% of the total imports), sugar, flour, cigarettes, wood and material for the railways were imported. In winter everything was slowed down by the cold, which froze the canals and made water transport impossible. The salt industry developed, on the left bank of the Hai he between Tian jin and Tang gu (19,000 tons in 1923); light iron industry, soap factories, match and glass factories, and textile mills also grew up. The growth of the population reflects the increasing importance of the town; 1908: 600,000 inhabitants, 1920: 850,000, 1936: 1,200,000 (including a large Hui community). The town was occupied by the Japanese in 1937.

6. The Town as it is Today. Since 1949, Tian jin has become even more important as an industrial and commercial centre. The textile industry is the most important: cotton, wool, hemp, all of which make Tian jin second only to Shang hai; there are mills, filatures, dye-works, carpet factories. Next in importance come the machine and precision tool industries (scientific equipment, cameras, watches); food products (flour mills, oil-works, dairies, preparation of eggs for export, confectionery); cigarettes. The chemical industry (based on salt), metallurgy (rolling mills) and the rubber industry (Tian jin comes third, after Shang hai and Canton) are also important.

As far as trade is concerned, Tian jin is first of all the centre of the northern region, where products from He bei, He nan, Shan dong, Shan xi, Shân xi, Gan su and Inner Mongolia are collected, and the centre of distribution for goods from the south (Shang hai, Canton); it is also an international port, handling exchanges with Japan and Europe.

It is also a university centre.

Note on the terra cotta figures made at Tian jin

Tian jin has been famous for its terra cotta figures since the 19th century *(ni ren)*. They originated from the work of a craftsman of the town, Zhang, nick-named Ni ren Zhang (Zhang of the terra cotta figures), who used to make little figures (5 to 10 inches high) representing characters from mythology, literature or everyday life. Some of the museums in Peking (particularly the Summer Palace and the Imperial Palace) still have groups of them. The tradition was handed down in the family, and the son, and later the grandson carried on. In *Les derniers jours de Pékin*, (p. 335), P. Loti tells how after the allied troops had passed through Tian jin, in 1900, figures of Western warriors, correct down to the smallest detail of their uniforms, were sold in the town and its neighbourhood. Some nations were given "ferocious expressions", so he says, but the French, on the other hand, with their berets, and yellow or brown silk moustaches, had more kindly expressions. Some even carried Chinese babies in their arms; and carried away by a wave of patriotism, Loti exclaims: "if only copies of the figures could be distributed in Europe, it would be a glorious war trophy for us, by comparison, and would silence a good many fools in the country itself". Orders from officers in command caused the accusing figures to be removed rapidly from the circulation! A descendant of the same Zhang family is still alive today; his statuettes take their inspiration from new ideas. The town Fine Arts Museum owns some examples.

Gastronomical Specialities

The Tian jin restaurants are known for their sea food: crabs *(pang xie)* and prawns *(xia)*. Another speciality is pâté, known as *gou bu li* (dogs, i.e. fools; will not touch it), which can be sampled in a restaurant at 97, Shan dong Street.

Description

The Town Centre

It is on the right bank of the Hai he and corresponds roughly to the former Japanese, French and British concessions. From the central station (on the left bank), a metal bridge, the Liberation Bridge (built in 1903 by French engineers to replace the old pontoon bridge) leads over the river to the centre. Most of the buildings lining its wide streets date from the era of the concessions. The two main streets are Peace Street (He ping lu) and Liberation Street (Jie fang lu). The first one is the chief shopping street; the department stores, the bookshops, the Communica-ations Hotel (Jiao tong lü guan) are all there. The other is the administrative centre; the Tian jin Hotel (Tian jin fan dian), the former Astor Hotel, and the Fine Arts Museum (founded in 1928) are there; the museum has an excellent collection of Yuan, Ming and Qing paintings, as well as modern paintings and handicrafts. In the streets nearby are the People's Library and the Provincial Assembly building.

The Old Town

The former "Chinese town", built on a rectangular plan, is north-west of the town centre. It used to be surrounded by walls, re-built in the 19th century and demolished in 1900. Boulevards have been laid out on the site of the old walls. The main streets in the old town (two of them only) cross at right angles in the middle; they used to end at the town gates. The four districts lying between them are crossed and re-crossed by a network of tiny lanes. The market-places used to be north-east of the walls; the names of the streets show where they were (Needle Market Street, Grain Market Street, Donkey Market Street...). Another market, which was less organised, used to be held south-west of the town: the Devils' Market (Gui shi), where old things and stolen goods used to be sold. The amusement quarter, with its theatres, jugglers, acrobats etc., was to the south.

The temples were in and round the old town. The Temple of Confucius (Wen miao) was within the walls; east of the walls stood the temple to Niang niang (see history, p. 654); north-west lay the Great Mosque (in 1936 fifteen mosques were still in existence).

The Northern Districts.

The Nan yun he, the Zi ya he, the Bei yun he and the Xin kai he all flow through this part of the town, into the Hai he. It contains numerous new dormitory areas, the Western Market Park, and the Historical Museum (founded in 1915, and entirely re-arranged since the liberation; some good collections), which is closed for the moment (1965).

The Western and Southern Districts

Before the liberation, the south-western part of the town was a low-lying, partly marshy area. The Europeans built a race-course and the International Club here (the latter is now a workmen's club). After 1949, the new university centre was built to the west (the He bei University, the Tian jin University, the Nan kai University); to the south lie the Shui shang gong yuan (Park on the water), with a stadium and an exhibition centre near it, and a smaller park, the Jian shan gong yuan (the Pointed Mountain Park).

The Eastern Districts

The industrial centres are now east and south of the River Hai he, with their workers' dormitory areas and other facilities (stadium, hospitals, and a Cultural Palace).

The Surrounding Area

1. Xin gang (the "new port")

Trains from Tian jin station go to Tang gu, a small modern village on the left bank of the River Hai he; a bus to Xin gang leaves from near the station square. The road goes through the salt-pans, known since the Yuan dynasty as Chang lu ("the long reeds"). They are arranged round five centres, Da gu, Tang gu, Han gu, Da qing he and Huang hua, which provide 27% of the national salt output. Work on the harbour at Xin gang was begun by the Japanese in 1939, but it was interrupted by the war; the Chinese began work again in 1951 and finished it in 1952. The visitor is allowed to look round the docks and ships. Two small pavilions with green tiled roofs in the distance mark the great Hai he lock; the harbour is on the left bank of the Hai he, several miles from the mouth of the river; Da gu, a lively fishing port, lies between it and the Gulf of Bo hai. The famous forts which resisted the Europeans fleets were at Da gu, or Ta kou.

2. The Village of Yang liu qing

It is nine miles west of Tian jin; a train service links it with the town. It is famous for its printing works which reproduce a type of popular posters, known as *nian hua* ("annual" pictures), because they are not kept beyond a year; new ones come out at each new year, and they are bought to stick on doors or inside houses, to replace the last year's, which are often sadly tattered. Yang liu qing, like Yang zhou and Su zhou (Jiang su), Chu nan tan (Hu nan), Feng zhen (Shan xi), and Liu cheng (Shan dong), was a centre which produced very popular posters.

Little is known of the history of these printing works before the 19th century. Some Yang liu qing posters, when analysed, suggest that some printing shops existed as early as the end of the Ming dynasty, but the earliest reliable information about them goes back no further than 1851. In 1854, the workshops, which were in a temple, were burned down, and rebuilt in another place in the village. At the end of the 19th century and the beginning of the 20th century, production flourished and over twenty-three neighbouring villages had workshops as well. Large numbers of little shops sold *nian hua* at Yang liu qing round about 1900, and the annual production was as high as a million pictures. The best craftsmen from the neighbouring villages came to set up in Yang liu qing, which then had several hundreds of master craftsmen and apprentices. The war hampered production during the first half of the 20th century. After the liberation the workshops were re-organised and old wood-blocks were collected all over the country. In 1960, a museum of wood-blocks and posters was opened in the village. Modern posters printed there can be bought at a shop in Tian jin, at 136 Zhang chun Street (in the shopping centre).

EAST HE BEI AND THE BO HAI SEA COAST

Ji xian

The little town of Ji xian is about 55 miles east of Peking. Two very fine old temples stand there, forming part of the *Monastery of Solitary Joy (Du le si)*.

A Buddhist Monastery, it was probably founded under the Tang, but the two temples as they are today were built in 984 (Liao dynasty).

The larger of the two, which stands in the middle of the monastery and is known as the Guan yin Temple (Guan yin ge), is an architectural masterpiece. Above the first roof, with its upturned eaves corners reaching far out into space beyond the walls, a gallery runs round the main body of the temple. The upper roof above the gallery follows the same lines as the first; between them they seem to carry the whole weight of the building. At its four corners, each one is supported by four slender wooden pillars. Inside the temple, two galleries—the upper one gives on to the outer gallery—encircle a central well, which contains a clay statue of the goddess Guan yin, nearly 50 feet high, dating from the Liao dynasty, with an accolyte on each side of her. The statue is a masterpiece which matches the temple itself. A magnificent coffered ceiling spreads over its head; the upper part and the head are lit by light from the opening in the upper storey. The architecture, sculpture and decoration are in complete harmony; from a purely architectural point of view, technical perfection is allied with beauty of proportion. Both temples are classed as historical monuments.

The Qing Dynasty Imperial Tombs (Dong ling)

They are about 25 miles north east of Ji xian, near Ma lan yu, in the district of Zun hua.

Tang shan

Tang shan is an industrial town with 800,000 inhabitants on the railway line from Tian jin to Shen yang, about 60 miles from Tian jin. It has grown up largely because of the rich coal mines in the area.

The first mining company was founded in 1878, to supply coal for the arsenals of the province and for the newly-created Chinese merchant navy. An English company bought it up in 1900, and from 1912 on it was called Kai luan (Kai-lan) Mining Company. Tang shan has been developed even further since 1949; the mining industry is still the most important, but metal, machine and textile industries have developed alongside it. It produces reinforced concrete and electricity. The town is also well known for its porcelain. It was severely damaged by the earthquake of 1976.

About two miles north of the town, two Buddhist temples used to stand on **Tang shan Hill,** one of which masked the entrance to a deep cave. The hill is surrounded by a wall which the Tang Emperor Tai zong (627–650) had built during an expedition to the region. Two Tang generals lie buried at the foot of the hill, and two more temples stand to the west. The present condition of these monuments is not known.

Feng run

About 12 miles north of Tang shan, in the Feng run area, three Liao era buildings stand grouped on a hill. They are part of a former monastery known as the *Monastery of the Long Life Summit (Shou feng si)* and they include an octagonal pagoda, 87 feet high, somewhat squat in appearance, rounded off at the top, built between 1032 and 1055, and partly rebuilt in 1480 under the Ming; a 90 feet high square pagoda, two stories of which were added under the Ming, in 1598; and a Buddhist pillar *(chuang)* in front of the second pagoda. The square pagoda, massive and severe, commands a good view of the surrounding countryside. Another building stands nearby, surmounted by a belfry; it is of a much later date.

Chang li

It is on the railway line from Tang shan to Qin huang dao, and it is a small town chiefly known for its vineyards and orchards, where pears, peaches, chestnuts and other fruit is grown. The famous Tang writer, Han yu (768-824), who inspired Chinese prose with new vigour held an official post here; this explains his other name of Han Chang li. Even after the first World War, his descendants still lived at Chang li.

A tall pagoda over 150 feet high stands near the north-west corner of the walls; it is thought to date from the Liao or the Jin, but its exact age is unknown. It used to be part of the Yuan ying si, a monastery which has now disappeared. An inscription explains that it was built to ward off an evil wind which carried off stones, killed men and beasts and laid the country-side to waste. Once the pagoda had been built, the wind ceased.

Bei dai he

Bei dai he is a large seaside resort, stretching alongside a sandy beach on the Bo hai coast, south-west of Qin huang dao. It grew up at the beginning of the century, when it was used as a holiday resort by missionaries and Western diplomats stationed at Tian jin and Peking. Foreigners from Peking still go there for the summer. Its most important function is that of a resort to which cadres and work-men are sent to rest, and a children's holiday camp. The surrounding hills contain several monuments which used to be pointed out as worth a visit; they are unfortunately in areas which are now closed to the public. The neighbourhood specialises in orchards and fishing. Mao Ze dong describes the place in the first lines of a poem, *Bei dai he:*

> It is raining over You yan
> The waves overlap one another
> Towards Qin huang dao, fishing boats

On the waters stretching to infinity
Disappear
But where?

(N. *You yan* is one of the old names for the province).

Qing huang dao

Qin huáng dao is important because it has an **excellent harbour,** which is fairly deep, and which does not freeze in winter. The harbour is linked directly with the railway, and has a leading role in the economy of the province.

Since the last century, much of the coal from Tang Shan destined for Shang hai, Hong Kong and Japan has been shipped from Qin huang dao. Between the two wars, 15,000 tons of coal were loaded there every day all the year round. It is the chief coal-exporting port of the whole of the Far East (see Richard, *Géog. de la Chine*). In 1898, the Chinese government decided to open the port to foreign trade; the decision took effect in 1901. The foreign powers used the port to land troops going to relieve the foreigners besieged by the Boxers in Peking in 1900. The South African Colonization Company used Qin huang dao for a long time to ship whole boatloads of Chinese workers to South Africa to work in the gold mines. The harbour can take boats of up to 10,000 tons.

The town also has a metal industry.

Shan hai guan

Shan hai guan is the gate of ancient China; it is here that the Great Wall reaches the sea. It comes winding down through the mountains to block the narrow coastal plain alongside the **Bo** hai sea which links north-east China with ancient China (only small sections of it still stand on the plain. Shan hai guan itself means the "gate between the mountains and the sea". It is the name of the great gate which guarded the road from China to Manchuria, and of the town which grew up near it. It is the boundary between the provinces of He bei and Liao ning.

For a long time, Shan hai guan played an important strategic role and savage battles were fought there over the centuries when, from the Sui to the Northern Song, China was constantly threatened by the warlike north-eastern peoples. A gate was built at Shan hai guan in the first year of the Tang dynasty, in 618. The place was called Yu guan at that time. The present gate was built under the Ming, in 1639, at the same time as the two other most important gates in the Great Wall: the Ba da ling Gate, near Peking (see p. 622) and the Jia yu guan Gate, near Jiu quan in Gan su (see p. 387).

For the Manchu Emperors, when they lived in Peking, Shan hai guan became a stage on the road which they took regularly to go to Shen yang where the ancestors' tombs were. The allied powers occupied the place in 1900 during the Boxer rebellion. Later on, Britain, France, Italy and Japan took advantage of the 1911 revolution to send more troops there, and each power manned one of the four forts on the Great Wall near Shan hai guan. They stayed there until the twenties.

The town is built inside (west of) the wall. It used to have four gates, north, south, east and west, linked by two streets crossing at right angles in the middle of the town; a tower was built at the crossroads. The northern gate has disappeared, and the finest remaining one is the east gate. Five characters are inscribed on the outer side: tian xia di yi guan, **the first gate in the world.** The government had it restored entirely in 1952.

A **little temple dedicated to Meng qiang nu,** a popular heroine whose story is known by every Chinese, stands outside the east gate. The story goes that her husband was sent to work on the Great Wall, under the Qin, and she lived alone for several years. Her family threatened to marry her again, so she left home to look for her husband. When she reached the Great

Wall, she was told that he had died at his work. Her tears of anguish made the wall fall down.

Cheng de

The town is in the north-west of the province, and a railway line now links it with Peking. It used to be called Jehol (Chinese: Re he, "warm river", from the name of the tributary of the Luan he near which the town stands).

History

In 1703, the Emperor Kang xi had a summer palace built at Jehol, and called it Bi hu shan zhuang (Mountain hamlet to flee the heat). The plan was much the same as the palace at Peking; it was in a vast park surrounded by a battlemented wall fifteen and half miles round. Father Ripa, who visited the palace at the end of Kang xi's reign (1662) describes the palace: "The residence of Je-hol is in Tartary, about one hundred and fifty miles distant from Peking. It is situated in a plain surrounded with mountains, whence flows a torrent, which, though usually dry, swells fearfully in time of rain or thaw... A hill rises gently from the plain, its side studded with buildings destined for the Emperor's followers, and a copious spring of water... forms a noble lake containing a remarkable quantity of fish. To an admirable disposition of the ground, nature has here added the charms of a luxuriant vegetation. Throughout the vast extent of those regions of Tartary a tree is rarely seen. At Je-hol, however, the plain, the slopes, and the hill are thickly covered with foliage; and the filberts, corianders, pears and apples, though growing wild, have so delicious a flavour that they are served on the Emperor's table. The plain, slopes, and hill are so extensive that it took me an hour to make the tour of the inclosure on horseback... There are many cottages and summer-houses... provided with silk curtains on all sides so as to prevent observation from without; and have seats all around, with a table or bed in the centre. (They)... are for the service of the Emperor, who retires thither with his queens and concubines; for at Je-hol he rarely sees anyone except his ladies and eunuchs." *(Memoirs of Father Ripa,* Naples 1832, reprinted Peking 1939, p. 72).)

From 1767 onwards, Emperor Qian long had Lamaist temples and halls built, copied from Tibetan buildings; one was a copy of the Potala at Lhassa. These plans coincided

RÉSIDENCE IMPÉRIALE ET TEMPLES DE CHFNG DE
IMPERIAL RESIDENCE AND TEMPLES OF CHENG DE

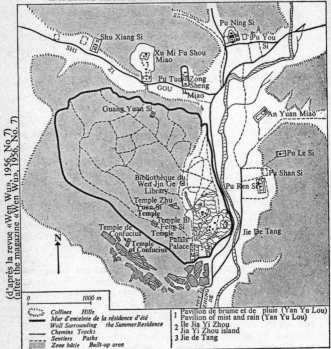

(d'après la revue «Wen Wu», 1956, No. 7)
(after the magazine «Wen Wu», 1956, No. 7)

Shu Xiang Si

SHI
ZI
GOU

Pu Ning Si
Pu You Si

Xu Mi Fu Shou Miao

Pu Tuo Zong Sheng Miao

An Yuan Miao

Guang Yuan Si

Pu Le Si

Pu Shan Si

Bibliothèque du Wen Jin Ge Library

Pu Ren Si

Temple Zhu Yuan Si
Temple
Temple Bi
Feng Si
Temple

Temple de Confucius
Temple
of Confucius

Palais
Palace

Jie De Tang

N

0   1000 m

Collines   Hills
Mur d'enceinte de la résidence d'été
Wall Surrounding   the Summer Residence
Chemins Tracks
Sentiers Paths
Zone bâtie Built-up area

1 Pavillon de brume et de pluie (Yan Yu Lou)
   Pavilion of mist and rain (Yan Yu Lou)
2 Ile Jia Yi Zhou
   Jia Yi Zhou island
3 Jie de Tang

exactly with Qian long's hopes of closer understanding with the Lamaist clergy. In 1779, he received the Panchen Lama at Jehol.

The libraries at Jehol were famous, particularly the Wen jin ge library, which received a copy of the *Si ku quan shu* in 1773. Lord Macartney had an audience with Emperor Qian long on September 14th, 1793, at Jehol.

Emperor Jia qing was struck by lightning near Jehol in August, 1820. After this bad omen, the court abandoned Jehol for a time, but Emperor Xian feng fled there in 1860 when the Peking palaces were occupied by the Anglo-French troops, and died there a year later.

Cheng de shi is now a distribution centre for forestry products, medecinal plants and fruit.

Some of the temples and palaces can still be seen a few miles north-west of the town. What used to be the palaces and gardens are now a large public park, surrounded by walls, lying to the west of the River Re he. East and north of the park nine temples dating from the 18th century can be seen in the hills.

1. The first group of four temples is east of the park, on the other bank of the Re he; from north to south they are: the *Pu ren si* (Temple of Universal Love) built in 1713, on a north-south axis; it is built in Chinese style; the *Pu shan si* (Temple of Universal Goodness) built in 1713, in Tibetan style; only part of it is left; the *Pu le si* (Temple of Universal Joy), built in 1766, in Chinese style, though it includes an interesting round building (Xu guang ge, the "Pavilion of the Light of the Rising Sun") built on a square, double terrace; it has a double roof, with yellow tiles; the *An yuan miao*, also called the Ili Valley Temple, because it resembles a temple in that region (Xin jiang); it was built in 1764.

2. The second group of five temples is north of the park; from east to west they are: the *Pu you si* (Temple of Universal Help), built in 1760, in Chinese style, though the statues are in Tibetan style; the *Pu ning si* (Temple of General Peace), just west of the former one; it is a copy of a Tibetan temple, built in 1775; the *Pu tuo zong sheng miao*, built in 1767; the buildings are like those of the Potala, and it is the biggest temple at Cheng de, covering an area of 239,000 square yards; the *Xu mi fu shou miao*, built in 1780, in Tibetan style; a little glazed tile pagoda stands inside the enclosure, like the Xiang shan pagoda at Peking (see p. 608); the *Shu xiang si*, built in 1774; it resembles the Shu Xiang si Temple on the Wu tai shan Mountain in Shan xi.

TOWARDS SHAN XI AND MONGOLIA

The valley of the River Yang he, a tributary of
the Yong ding he, constitutes a corridor linking
Peking with the tablelands of Shan xi and Mongolia.
It has always been an important trade route, used by
horse breeders, hunters and gold prospectors from
Mongolia, and at the same time it has great strategic
importance. Invaders from the steppe could use
it too. This mountainous area of He bei is in complete
contrast to the vast open plains with their wide muddy
rivers in the south of the province. Rugged mountains
and plateaux are broken up by steep valleys and ravines.
"Yellow, fertile loess covers it here and there. Then
it gives way to volcanic rock of different colours,
or pasture land with flocks grazing on it... The winter
is long and severe, even more so than on the plains,
and all the houses have *kangs*, on which the family
lives all through the winter... "(Richard, *Géogr. de la
Chine I*, p. 172). For several hundreds of years, the
region has been systematically stripped of its trees.
Efforts are being made now to replant it, to help stop
the erosion.

The railway line through the valley was built
at the beginning of the century by Chinese engineers,
without foreign help. A French journalist visited
the area just before first World War and describes
his impressions: "(the engineers) determined to
show the whites that they were capable of working
alone; they managed it; at one place, at a pass, the
slope is too steep and the engine can haul only a
few waggons. The Europeans, convinced of their
own superiority, spare no irony in reproaching them
for their mistake. For myself, when I took the train,
I thought that only a few years ago the builders,

administrators, telegraphists, and all the staff employed on the intense civilising process which this railway represents, were all in the mental and social state which the European societies were in thousands of years ago, and I was far more impressed by the speed of the progress than by any imperfections of the work itself". (F. Farjenel, *A travers la révolution chinoise*, Plon 1914, p. 268).

Protestant and Roman Catholic European missionaries, and particularly the French Lazarists, were very active in this remote part of He bei. In the Jia qing period (1796–1821) the missions in Peking lost the Emperor's favour and were persecuted; "large numbers of Christians, fleeing the Chinese authorities, moved north beyond the Great Wall, to seek peace and liberty in the deserts of Tartary, and lived here and there off little plots of land which the Mongols allowed them to cultivate. The missionaries persevered until they had gathered these scattered Christians together, then settled among them and ran the former Peking mission there." Xi wan zi, north east of Zhang jia kou, was one of the centres. In 1844, Father Huc started out from here on his long trip through Mongolia and Tibet (the above quotation is taken from the book he wrote afterwards, *Souvenirs d'un voyage dans la Tartarie et le Tibet*, Gallimard 1962, vol. I, p. 35). The missionaries went on with their work in the area throughout the first half on the 20th century, and have produced some valuable books on the folkore and languages of the region.

Xuan hua

This town is about 15 miles from Zhang jia kou, in a loess region. Its fertility has enabled it to be turned into a market gardening area and Xuan hua is a centre of market gardening and vineyards which helps to feed Peking. Its pears and grapes are famous. Sheep-rearing has given rise to a large trade in sheepskins. Iron and coal mines help industrialisation. Xuan hua used to have both a Protestant and a Roman Catholic mission.

Zhang jia kou

Zhang jia kou is an important trading centre on the Great Wall, on the edge of the Mongolian plateau, at an altitude of 2,697 feet. Caravans of camels used to converge here, and still do, though by now modern transport has replaced most of them, bringing wool, and furs for China from Mongolia, Gan su, and Tibet. They take back fabrics, paper and tea. Tea from south China, loose or in bricks, is stored in the warehouses of Zhang jia kou, to be taken by other caravans to Siberia and Russia. "Nearly half a million camels were used for transport" (Richard, *Géogr. de la Chine*). The building of the railway line from Peking to Da tong has made the town more important still.

Zhang jia kou is better known in Europe by its Mongolian name, Kalgan, "pass". The town grew up round a stretch of the Great Wall. Even now, the wall runs almost through the town itself. Under the Qing and the Republic, Zhang jia kou was the seat of the government of the special district of Chahar. The administrative buildings were in the higher part of the town, the banks and market-places were below. The station is separated from the town by a river which flows into the Yang he further downstream.

"The town is not a pleasant one to live in. Encircled by arid rocks, it suffers from heat in summer, and from dust and wind at all times of the year" (Richard, *Géogr. de la Chine*). The town has been developed systematically since the liberation. It now boasts a machine industry, a food industry, tanneries and other industry. There are 200,000 inhabitants.

A group of old red buildings with ochre roofs, surrounded with trees, can be seen on the mountainside from the town itself: the **Cloud Spring Monastery (Yun quan si)**, 3,294 feet up; it was built under the Ming in 1393. It commands a good view over the town and the neighbourhood. It has been made into a place for walking and resting. Behind a **temple** (miao) which is independent of the convent, two spring rise in the rocks, very close to each other. One is frozen all the year round, the other never freezes, even in the depths of winter.

THE NORTHERN STRETCH OF THE HE BEI PLAIN

Zhuo xian

This is the first large station on the Peking—Zheng zhou line, outside the Peking municipal area. The town walls date from the 15th century; just outside them is a **stone bridge** built under the reign of Qian long. A stele near it bears an inscription of Qian long's account of the building of the bridge. One of the neighbouring villages is supposed to be the birth-place of a famous historical character: Liu Bei. He played an important part in the fall of the Han dynasty and became the first Emperor of the kingdom of Shu (221–263, the Three Kingdoms period). A **temple** used to stand in the village (it may be there still?), dedicated to him and his three faithful lieutenants, Guan yu, Zhang Fei and Zhu ge Liang, whose heroic deeds fill the *Romance of the Three Kingdoms (San guo yan yi)*, a famous and extremely popular work written under the Ming dynasty. From then on, right up to modern times, Zhu ge Liang was traditionally considered the prototype of the ever-resourceful, infinitely capable general and minister. Guan yu was transformed from a historical character to the god of war, and was worshipped as such until recent times. Countless temples were dedicated to him all over China.

Gao bei dian, Yi xian, the Western Tombs and Lai yuan

Gao bei dian is on the railway line south of Zhuo xian. Its name means "inn of the tall stele". A stele used to stand here marking the frontier of the states of Yan (to the north) and Zhao (to the south). A train used to run from Gao bei dian west along the River Yi (Yi shui) to Yi xian and the "Western Tombs"; it has been replaced by a road.

A famous story is linked with the *River Yi*, told by Si ma Qian in the *Historical Records*. During the Warring States period, the prince of Yan decided to send Jing Ke, one of his faithful companions, to assassinate the prince of Qin, who reigned over present Shân xi. It was a dangerous mission. "*...the prince and the court dressed in mourning to accompany (Jing Ke). When they reached the banks of the Yi, they made a sacrifice to the god of the road, Gao Jian li played his instrument, Jing Ke sang to accompany him, and began to dance. First he sang in a minor key, and all the heroes sobbed. Then he moved forward, singing: 'The wind blows, the waters of the Yi are frozen: the hero goes away, never to come back.' He sang once more, in a major key, pathetically. The heroes opened their eyes wide, their hair stood on end and lifted up their head-dresses. Then Jing Ke climbed into his chariot and left without looking back.*" (*Shi ji, Ci ke lie zhuan.*) Jing perished on his mission, but became the traditional prototype of a loyal and valiant man.

The village of Yi xian is about 25 miles west of Gao bei dian. It contains the **Kai yuan Period Monastery (Kai yuan si),** built in 1105, under the Liao (it has a magnificent coffered ceiling). The remains of the **ancient capital of the state of Yan (Yan du xia)** are about 2 miles from the present village. It was between two branches of the River Yi. The ramparts were over 14 miles round. Sections of them still stand, several hundred yards long at a time, and up to 22 feet high.

The state of Yan and its capital had an important part to play during the Zhou dynasty and during the Warring States period. Excavations have uncovered large amounts of pottery remains dating from the Eastern Zhou (1066–770 B.C.), and from later periods. The town was at the crossroads of several routes, going to Lai yuan and Shan xi to the west and to Qu yang and Han dan, capital of the state of Zhao, to the south. The remains have all been classed as historical monuments. In the Warring States section of the Peking museum, several things are exhibited which were uncovered during the excavations, beside the plan of the remains of the capital.

The **Western Tombs of the Qing Dynasty** are further west along the Yi. The Qing tombs are grouped in two sites in He bei: the "Eastern Tombs" (Dong ling) are 84 miles east of Peking as the crow flies, north-east of Ji xian, near the Great Wall and the village of Ma lan yu, in the Zun hua district, and the "Western Tombs" (Xi ling) are near Yi xian (see p. 622 on the imperial tombs).

The Manchu court had a railway line built from Gao bei dian to a point beyond Yi xian, **Liang ge zhuang,** from which the tombs could be reached easily. The line was reserved for the use of the court at first, but was opened to the public in 1906. It is no longer in use now. The valley chosen for the tombs is a vast natural arena surrounded by mountains. The oldest tomb is built on the central axis, with a wide paved way and a marble bridge leading up to it. Statues of animals, and civil and military officials,

line it on either side. The cemetery includes numerous
tombs, temples and other buildings, all relatively
well preserved even now. Both temples and tombs
are on a magnificent scale, and represent the summit
of achievement of Qing architecture; they compare
very favourably with the palaces of the Imperial
City in Peking.

A route leads west from Yi xian into the Tai hang
mountains which has for generations been a much
frequented passage through to the Shan xi plateau.
The little town of **Lai yuan** was formerly a stronghold
on the frontier of the state of Yan. A very fine **wooden
temple** dating from the Liao still stands there. It
contains a set of clay statues, on and around the
altar, dating from the same period, though partially
restored under the Ming. The central statue depicts
the Buddhist deity Wen shu (Manjusri) riding a lion.
The temple is known as Wen shu da dian, or "Great
Wen shu Temple"; it was part of a monastery, said
to have been founded at an even earlier date (late
Han?). A Buddhist pillar *(chuang)* dating from
960 (Liao) and a large bell dating from 1114 stand
in front of the temple. The other monastery buildings
were rebuilt under the Qing.

Xin cheng

Xin cheng is about 9 miles south-east of Gao bei
dian. At the north-east corner of the town stands the
main **temple** of an old monastery, which has now
disappeared, the **Kai shan Monastery (Kai shan si):**
the temple is surrounded by water on three sides.
The monastery dated from the Tang or the Song,
and was said to be older than the town round it.

The existing temple dates from the Liao, and must have been built between 1004 and 1123, when the Liao, who came from Manchuria, held the north of China as far as Xin cheng, and a little further south. The Song empire paid them a regular tribute, which explains the wealth of the region at that time, and the existence of a large monastery with a magnificent temple.

Its style is sober; the roof is gently curved and reaches far out beyond the walls. The overhang is almost 6 feet. It is a building of great beauty; a detailed study of it, written in Chinese, can by found in the review *Wen wu* (1957, no. 10). The other old buildings surrounding it are of later date.

Ding xing

Ding xing is on the railway line, several miles south of Gao bei dian. About 6 miles west of the town, the stone column known as the **Yi ci hui Column**, about 22 feet high, stands in the village of Shi zhu cun ("the village of the stone column").

Under the northern Wei dynasty a large scale peasant revolt took place in He bei between 525 and 527. The peasant armies were led by Du Luo zhou, Ge Rong and others; they were several hundred thousand strong. The imperial armies were sent from Luo yang, the capital, to crush them. The people living in the region erected a large wooden column in memory of the rebels who fell on the battlefield; in the next dynasty, however, between 567 and 670, the officials replaced it by the present stone column, and at the same time took the opportunity to have a passage in praise of the imperial armies engraved on it.

The column has over 3,000 characters on it, telling the story of the "disorders", the repression of them and the erecting of the column. It is the only one of its kind, both because it is a memorial to a group of people, and because its style is most unusual.

The base is square, surmounted by a crown shaped like a lotus flower, and the body of the column is square as well. Instead of a capital, it carries an enormous stone platform, apparently very heavy, with a little stone temple on top of it. The roof of the temple is wider than the base on which it stands, so that from below all the architectural details can be seen, faithfully reproduced (beams, tiles etc.). It gives invaluable information about architecture before the Tang, and is classed as a historical monument. The section on the Wei dynasty in the Peking historical museum includes a photograph of it. In Ding xing itself, there used to be a Yuan dynasty monastery, which may still be there, whose main building was called **Ci yun ge, Temple of the Merciful Cloud.**

Bao ding

Bao ding was important under the Qing dynasty, because it was the provincial capital *(fu)*; the province was then called Zhi li. It faded into second place when the seat of provincial government was moved to Tian jin by Li Hong zhang (1823-1901), who was governor of the province, and at the same time one of China's greatest politicians, during the second half of the 19th century. A university was founded here in 1901; it also had a medical school and a school for officers.

Bao ding has now regained some of its importance, as it handles a brisk water traffic of junks travelling to Tian jin. It is a centre for several industries: textiles, food and electricity are produced there. The people's council for the province of He bei sat there for a time before it could be moved finally to Tian jin.

The town walls date from the Ming. It used to contain several temples and monasteries, one of which was a temple dedicated to General Lian Po; Si ma Qian describes his differences with the minister Lin

Xiang ru in the *Historical Records*, and they were both famous for long afterwards. The temple may still be standing today. In the middle of the town is the **Lotus Pond (Lian hua chi),** which used to be known as the "Lotus Academy" (Lian hua shu yuan); it was made under the Tang during the Shang yuan period (674–676), and was a place much frequented by scholars and high officials of the province. The pool lies amidst artificial hills and beautiful trees, with pavilions, summer-houses and terraces scattered among them, linked by paths, covered ways and twisting bridges. In the eastern covered way a collection of steles record the history of the garden. Several of them bear texts originally written by Emperors Qian long, Jia qing and Dao guang (1736–1851). The northern covered way has 88 stones with calligraphy on them set into the wall, all dating from the Ming and the Qing. A Tang dynasty stele stands beside the pool. The garden was restored in 1951.

The Bai yang dian Lakes

In the centre of the He bei plain, east of Bao ding, lies a large area covered with shallow lakes, known as the "the white pools" (Bai yang dian). They cover an area of 186 square miles. Several rivers rising to the west empty into them, and the water flows on towards Tian jin. The river traffic from Bao ding and Tian jin crosses the lakes, and as parts of them are full of reeds, it often seems as though the sails of the junks are moving through a pale green or golden sea. In summer, lotus flowers bloom in profusion. The inhabitants live in a different way from those of the rest of He bei: the men fish, while the women make reed matting well known for its excellent quality. Ducks are raised as well.

During the **war of resistance against the Japanese,** the lakes were as impregnable as the strongest fortress; the inhabitants with their infallible knowledge of the area kept the upper hand over the Japanese and waged a merciless guerilla war against them. The author Sun Li has written many widely-read short stories about the region and the guerilla war.

Wang du

The little town of Wang du is on the railway line from Bao ding to Ding xian. On the way into town from the station are two large tumuli; it was discovered in 1952 that they contained **Han dynasty tombs,** which were excavated in 1954-55. The first tomb consists of three chambers arranged on an axis 125 feet long; four side vaults lie two on each side of the central part. The walls and vaulted ceilings are made of brick, and the walls of the first chamber are covered with Han frescoes depicting officials, other people and animals, all drawn with great realism; each element bears its title in large characters. The second tomb, made up of five successive chambers flanked by eight side vaults, is built in the same style as the first. Remains of frescoes were found, together with a large collection of objects: stone carvings and coffin, pottery, clay, jade and bronze tools, a clay model of a three-storey Han house (now in the Peking Historical Museum), and a contract for the sale of land. All are of great historic and artistic interest. Two Taoist temples used to stand on the tumuli; one was dedicated to the god of medecine (Yao wang), the other to the "Princess of the Coloured Clouds" (Bi xia yuan jun).

The **Tomb of Yao's Mother** is also at Wang du. Yao was a legendary Emperor, supposed to have lived between 4000 and 3000 B.C., considered by the followers of Confucius as the model of all civic virtues. The tomb is outside the east gate of the town. Two temples were built outside the town, dedicated to Yao himself and to his son. It is not known whether they still exist or not.

Ding xian

Ding xian is half way between Bao ding and Shi jia zhuang. A little pagoda stands near the south gate of the town, known as the **Watch Tower (Liao di ta).** It once belonged to the Kai yuan Period Monastery (Kai yuan si), which no longer exists. It earned its name under the Song dynasty, when it was used as a watch tower, as Ding xian was then a post on the frontier between China and the Liao invaders. It gives a wide view over the He bei plain, and can be seen from 9 miles away. It was built between 1001 and 1055 (Song), and is one of the highest of the old towers in China: it has eleven stories, and is over 250 feet high. It is built in brick, which is an innovation for that period; no wood has been used even for the staircases and the flooring inside. It is an architectural masterpiece. The severity of its style, the harmony of the eleven stories tapering off towards the top, the dignified symmetry of the square windows and doors as they are repeated on each facet of each storey, all combine to make it a building of great beauty. It is classed as a historical monument.

Other ancient monuments at Ding xian included a building dating from 1512 (Ming), no longer standing,

which was the main hall of the Da dao guan convent,
and an enormous **examination hall** dating from the
Qing, with four roofs one above the other, and a
line of windows running round the building between
each one, to give light to the inside.

Qu yang

**The Temple of the Northern Sacred Mountain (Bei
yue miao),** where from the Han dynasty to the beginning of the Qing dynasty, the Emperors of China
offered great sacrifices to the Northern Sacred Mountain, is at Qu yang, west of Ding xian. The Northern
Sacred Mountain is one of the five sacred mountains
of ancient China (cf. the Tai shan, p. 715). The
mountain is the Heng shan, north-west of Qu yang
in the province of Shan xi (altitude 6,726 feet).

According to ancient chronicles, the temple
precincts were large, and stretched from the west
gate of the town as far as the south-west gate. A
general plan, dating from the Ming, engraved on
stone inside the temple, shows the layout of the
former temple, with the main buildings, the summer-
houses and the secondary temples, and the ways leading
to them, spanned by porticos and triumphal arches,
or by the great entrance gates. The precincts are now
much smaller, and only two of the main buildings
survive: one of the great temples used for ceremonies,
and an octagonal pagoda with a triple roof which
stands outside the present temple area. It dates from
the Ming.

The present temple building, known as the **Temple
of Tranquil Virtue (De ning dian),** dates from the
Yuan, and was built in 1270. It is an imposing hall
with a double roof, like the great palaces of the

Imperial City in Peking. The roofs reach far into
space and are supported by clusters of cantilever
brackets *(dou gong)*, a characteristic feature of
Chinese traditional architecture. The inside of the
building is 4 bays deep and 7 bays wide. Like the
Peking palaces, the De ning dian stands on a marble
terrace about 6 feet high. A beautiful parapet carved
with a lotus motive runs round the edge. The capitals
are decorated with designs which are typical of the
Yuan era (hai tang qu xian).

The temple contains some old frescoes traditionally
supposed to be by Wu Dao zi, the famous Tang
painter, but they are more likely to date from 1270,
when the temple was restored. The east wall has a
procession of richly dressed court ladies, whose airs
of boredom and varied attitudes are most realistically
depicted. The western wall has demons brandishing
pikes, their clothes flying in the wind, with menacing
expressions on their faces. The paintings recall the
powerful realism of Tang works. The demons have
inspired several local legends, and a saying referring to
the work of Wu Dao zi is still in use now: "the Qu
yang demons and the waters of Zhao zhou" (Qu
yang gui, Zhao zhou shui). The "waters of Zhao
zhou" are also frescoes attributed to Wu Dao zi
(see Zhao zhou, p. 689).

A large collection of **steles** stand round the temple;
the oldest of them dates from the Northern Qi dynasty
(574), and the most impressive, from the Ming (1371).
Others date from the Tang, Song, Yuan, Ming,
and Qing dynasties. They record details of sacrifices
offered in the temple and of the important people who
attended them. As a collection, it is as important
as the collection of ancient steles at the Temple of
Confucius at Qu fu.

Near the temple, to the south-west, stands a
five-storey octagonal pagoda, whose unusual proportions give it rather a strange air. Its plain base takes
up a quarter of the total height; the lower part has
no opening at all. The top part is more in accordance
with this type of building: five roofs succeed each
other rapidly. On the first floor of the tower, parts
of frescoes were found, in the same style as the ones
in the neighbouring temple.

THE CENTRE AND SOUTH
OF THE HE BEI PLAIN

Zheng ding

Zheng ding, a town of many temples and monasteries,
is north of Shi jia zhuang. The oldest and largest
is the **Long xing Monastery (Long xing si)**, which
covers an area of 2 square miles. Although its history
goes back to the 586 (Sui dynasty), the general disposition of the present buildings dates from 971 (Song
dynasty). The temples themselves are Song and Jin
dynasty. The Long xing si is therefore the oldest
of the five monasteries still existing in China, completely or partially preserved, and dating from before
the Ming dynasty. The other four are: the Du le si
at Ji xian (see p. 661), the Jin ci at Tai yuan (see p. 852),
the Shan hua si at Da tong (see p. 874), and the Yong
le gong at Rui cheng (see p. 910).

The chief temple of the monastery, the **Temple
of Great Mercy (Da bei ge)**, is conspicuous from some
way away. The sumptuous arrangement of the alternating red and yellow galleries and roofs dominates
all the surroundings with its massive proportions.
It is built on a square plan; a huge gallery of red pillars

travels round the building below the first roof. Two
more roofs follow and then, high up, a second gallery
of red pillars surrounds all four sides. The last
double roof rises to 100 feet above the ground. Two
of its sections are sloping; the side pieces are vertical
pediments. A bronze **statue of Guan yin** stands inside,
71 feet high, dating from the Song dynasty, like
the temple (Kai bao period 963–976). It is traditionally
included in the four marvels of He bei (see the bridge
at Zhao zhou, p. 689). The town chronicles for Zheng
ding tell how hundreds, if not thousands, of craftsmen
worked on the statue, and that the process was
divided into seven stages, first the lotus-shaped
plinth, then the parts up to the knees, up to the
navel, up to below the shoulders, then the shoulders
and the head. The goddess' 42 arms were added
later. The art and knowledge of the Song craftsmen
can never be admired enough. The stone base supporting the statue is covered with magnificent carving;
Mount Sumeru, the Buddhist sacred mountain,
is represented by symbols, and a series of celestial
musicians carved in bas-relief.

**The Pavilion of the Rotating Library (Zhuan lun
zang dian)** is another superb piece of Song architecture in the same monastery. It houses a rotating
octagonal library where the monastery's sutras
were kept. To enable the library to turn freely inside
the building, the architects had to abandon traditional
methods and invent a special beam framework
to support the roof. The outside of the pavilion is
surrounded by an overhanging gallery. The style
is austere, like the Temple of Great Mercy (the eaves
corners are only upturned), and the subtlety lies
in the arrangement and proportions of the various
elements. The arrangement in tiers of the roofs and

galleries is calculated so that it gives an overall impression of life.

In 1949, the buildings were in a sad state and some were even on the point of falling down. After two years spent in preparation, the Chinese government has restored them completely (1954–1956). The Pavilion of the Rotating Library was almost entirely rebuilt. Not all the damage was reparable however: the terra cotta bas-relief decorations on the walls of the Temple of Great Mercy were destroyed during the Japanese occupation, when an attempt was made to restore the temple.

The monastery also includes three other Jin (12th and 13th centuries) buildings: a **Temple of Mouni (Mou ni dian)**, a **Temple of the Merciful One (Ci shi ge)** and a portico *(shan men)*. There is also a Qing preaching dais *(jie tai)* in the enclosure. One of the many steles round the temples is particularly interesting: it is nearly 8 feet high, and stands in front of the main temple. It dates from 586 (Sui) and is the oldest thing in the whole of the monastery. Its characters are very fine.

The town of Zheng ding boasts another old building: the **Flowered Tower (Hua ta)**. It was originally part of the Monastery of Far-reaching Wisdom (Guang hui si), and its full name is the Guang hui si hua ta. Nothing remains of the monastery now. The tower (pagoda) was built between 1161 and 1189, under the Jin dynasty. Its plan and its baroque air are most unusual; it is built of brick, on an octagonal base, with doors with semi-circular arches on each of the four most important facets. Four hexagonal turrets, each ending in a pointed roof, one to each of the other four facets, are built up against it. The first storey, also octagonal, rises among the roofs of the turrets, with a square door on each of the four main facets. The second storey

is the same shape, but as it is smaller than the first,
it gives the effect of being built on a terrace. The
upper part of the tower tapers away to the top,
following a curve, and ending in a huge pointed
capital. The upper part used to be covered with
countless carvings of lions, elephants and towers.
Unfortunately the pagoda is in a sadly dilapidated
state: large sections of the cornices and carvings
are missing. It is possible that after being classed as
a historical monument in 1961, it has been partly
restored.

Another interesting pagoda at Zheng ding is the
**Brick Tower of the Kai yuan period Monastery (Kai
yuan si zhuan ta).** It is as sober and classic in style
as the other is baroque. It is completely plain, and
square; a series of rectangular facades, each one
smaller than the last, with a window in each one,
follow one another to the top. It stands at the water's
edge.

Zheng ding includes more monuments dating
from the Tang, Song and Jin dynasties: the **Great
Temple of Confucius (Wen miao da cheng dian),**
the **Green Tower of the Lin ji Monastery (Lin ji si
qing ta),** the **Wooden Tower of the Monastery of
Celestial Tranquility (Tian ning si mu ta),** and others.

Shi jia zhuang

At the beginning of this century, Shi jia zhuang
was a little village of five or six hundred inhabitants.
With the building of the Peking to Han kou (Wu
han) and Shi jia zhuang to Tai yuan railway lines,
it has developed into a town.

The first of the two lines was built between 1897 and 1905,
and was financed by a Belgian syndicate; the Chinese government

bought it afterwards. The second was built by a Russian company, using French capital, between 1903 and 1907. It too was sold to the Chinese government, but was run by a French company for some time. In the twenties, the town already had 10,000 inhabitants, including 25 Frenchmen who were working on the line.

A third railway line runs from Shi jia zhuang to De zhou, in Shan dong. The town is therefore an important railway junction. It is also the centre of the He bei cotton production, and one of the largest centres of the Chinese textile industry. It also produces metal, machines and electricity; the factories are run on coal from the mines in the Jing xing region, which are conveniently near, to the west. It has a population of 400,000.

The one monument of artistic value which it possesses is a pair of beautiful **bronze lions** dating from 1185 (Jin dynasty) which stand in the central alley of the military cemetery (Lie shi ling yuan).

The **tomb of General Wu Lu zhen** is in the town; he advocated constitutional reform of the empire under the Qing, and was assassinated in Shi jia zhuang station in 1912.

Jing xing

Jing xing is in the picturesque valley which leads from Shi jia zhuang to the province of Shan xi. As a corridor between two important provinces, it has been a strategic point throughout the history of China. (Cf. the Battle of Jing xing described by Si ma Qian in the *Historical Records*, in the chapter *Huai yin hou lie zhuan.*) It is a rich coal-producing area.

North of the town, a pagoda stands on the banks of the river Mian he. It dates from the Liao or the

Jin, and is built of brick, imitating the style of wooden buildings. False windows and doors are carved on the four facades of the base; one of the doors is half open, and a figure has been added, just about to come out. The second storey is octagonal; the upper part, which rounds off to the top, is covered with carvings inspired by religious subjects: immortals, legendary animals, etc...

About 18 miles south-east of Jing xing, in a rocky and mountainous area, is the **Hanging Palace of the Green Cliff** (Cang yan shan qiao lou dian), a strange building constructed several hundred feet up on a single stone arch spanning a narrow gorge. Stone steps lead up to it. It was built under the Sui and rebuilt under the Qing. The palace is 5 bays wide, and has a double roof. Several other old buildings stand nearby among the trees. It used to be a place of worship to which pilgrimages were made; poems were written in praise of the hanging palace, which "seemed to fly with the clouds and the light". During the anti-Japanese war, it was used as a base for guerilla warfare.

Zhao xian

The town of Zhao xian (formerly Zhao zhou) is about 25 miles south-east of Shi jia zhuang. 2 miles south of the town, the **Zhao zhou Bridge (Zhao zhou qiao),** also called the Great Stone Bridge (Da shi qiao) or the Safe Passage Bridge (An ji qiao) spans the River Xiao shui.

The bridge is remarkable for its daring conception, its technique and its elegance. According to a popular saying, it ranks as one of the three marvels of He bei, with the lion of Cang zhou (see p. 692), and the statue of Guan yin at Zheng ding (see p. 685); another version claims that there are four marvels. According to the legend, Lu Ban, the craftsman and genius of the Warring States period, built the bridge in a single night. In the morning, one of the eight immortals (Lu Ban and the eight immortals: see p. 161-171) arrived with an acolyte to test the bridge; he was riding a mule, and had the sun and the moon hidden in his bag, to add extra weight, while his acolyte was pushing the five sacred mountains (see p. 715) in a cart. Even today, the marks left by the mule's hooves and one of the wheels of the cart are pointed out on the bridge. It stood up to the test, but Lu Ban had to support it, and the prints of his hands can still be seen on the arch.

In fact, the bridge was built under the Sui dynasty, between 605 and 617. It was a period when much work was done to improve communications in the empire, to make its recent political re-unification a reality. Nothing is known of the builder of the bridge but his name: Li Chun. His knowledge enabled him to reconcile two contradictory needs: the bridge had to be as flat as possible, so that the chariots of the imperial army could cross it without difficulty, but it could not be built so low that it risked being carried away by the frequent floods; it had also to be light, because of the shape of the banks, and yet strong enough to take the slow, heavy trade and military convoys. Li Chun solved both difficulties by building a single, flattened arch with a span of 122 feet 10 inches, and a rise of 23 feet. The two pairs of spandrel arches (one at each end) acted as an overflow for flood water and gave the whole structure a consummate grace. The main arch consists of 38 parallel lines of archstones, fixed together by a system of iron cramps and bars. In building the Zhao zhou bridges, Li chun created a type of flat bridge which was frequently imitated later on, as it was particularly well adapted to the needs of life in North China, a flat country where road transport was used, as opposed to south China, where water transport was more usual, which meant that bridges had to be arched to allow junks to pass underneath.

The Zhao zhou bridge has been in constant use from the day it was finished until now. It has been repaired five times, once in 1900 or so and later on from 1955 to 1958, when it was done with the utmost care. In 1952, several pieces of the original parapet, with beautiful bas-relief carvings of the Sui period, were found at the bottom of the river. They depict stylised dragons and other animals; one section is now in the Peking Historical Museum, where there is also a model of the bridge (in the section on the Sui). The bridge is classed as a historical monument.

Several more beautiful **old stone bridges** exist in the Zhao zhou region: the Gu ding qiao and the Ling kong qiao at Luan cheng, the Ji mei qiao and the Yong tong qiao near Zhao xian. The **Yong tong qiao (Bridge of Eternal Passage)** is a copy of the Zhao zhou bridge, on a smaller scale, and probably dates from the Song.

A **stone pillar** 52 feet high, erected under the Song in 1038, stands in Zhao xian. It is a *chuang*, or dhâranî pillar, a special type of Buddhist monument bearing religious inscriptions, or formulae used as prayers (dhâranî). The Zhao xian *chuang* is the tallest in China, and one of the most beautiful. It consists of six sections, each one separated from the next by a circular frieze. The three sections which make up the base and the friezes are carved with themes

from Buddhist iconography: various people, animals
(lions) and lotus flowers. They are portrayed with
delightful freshness.

The Cypress Monastery (Bo lin si) stands inside
the town, near the east gate. According to the local
chronicles, the monastery dates from the end of the
Han dynasty, but its present name dates from the
Qing only. The main building is in the style of the
Ming period. The famous Tang painter Wu Dao zi is
said to have painted frescoes of flowing water there;
they no longer exist now. An octagonal pagoda
with a seven-storey roof, dating from the Yuan,
stands near the temple, with several steles, dating
from the Jin, the Song and the Yuan.

On the site of the Temple of Confucius, which no
longer exists today, a large Tang stele was found,
dating from 775.

Near the town, west of a spot known as Song cun,
are the remains of the **Monastery of the Stone Buddha
(Shi fo si):** a hexagonal pagoda and bits of columns
and stone Buddhas dating from the Ming. An inscription on the pagoda gives the year it was built: 1275
(Yuan). This type of hexagonal pagoda is rare. A
chuang dating from 1349 stands in front of it. The
tomb of Li Zhou che, the Qin dynasty strategist, is
nearby (cf. *Historical Records*, chapter *Huai yin
hou lie zhuan*).

Cang zhou

In the former Cang zhou (Jiu cang zhou), about
12 miles south-east of the town of Cang zhou, stands
one of the "three wonders of He bei" ("The three
Wonders, see p. 689, Zhao zhou): an iron lion,
16 feet high and 16 feet long. It is an impressive

sight: its neck is stretched as though it is roaring, and it is in a walking position. A large round lotus-shaped plinth on its back used to carry a statue of a bodhisattva. Three characters can still be read on the plinth: Shi zi wang (King of lions). It has inscriptions on its stomach, but they are illegible now. On the right side of its neck, a seven-character inscription says that it was cast in 954 (Northern Zhou dynasty). The craftsman's name is on the left shoulder: Li Yun, from Shan dong. It is one of the oldest and largest iron statues known in China.

Jing xian

A few miles from the Grand Canal, in the southeast of He bei, stands a beautiful tower, the **Tower of the Abandon of Profits (She li ta).** It is octagonal, built in brick, and nearly 200 feet high. It forms part of the old buildings of the Kai fu Period Monastery (Kai fu si), and it is reflected in a large stretch of water nearby. It is said to be one of the finest sights in the province. A spiral staircase leads up to the top, which commands a wide view over the little town of Jing xian, the Grand Canal, and the endless plain of He bei. The tower is devoid of all ornamentation, and its beauty lies in the harmony of the progression and the proportions of the thirteen stories and cornices. Legends exist which say that it was built by a supernatural craftsman; it is said to date from the Sui, but is probably later than that.

Xing tai

This town in the south of He bei has been well known for generations; under the Yuan, the Ming and the Qing, it lay on the route leading from their capital towards central China. From the Jin until the Qin, the town was called Shun de (or Shun de fu).

The **Kai yuan Period Monastery (Kai yuan si)** stands in the north-east corner of the walls, founded under the Tang in the Kai yuan period (713–742). Under the Yuan, the monastery was protected and favoured by the court. Its reputation and its riches grew rapidly, until the day when the monks "took advantage of the name of religion to commit large numbers of injustices and crimes". They were condemned to death, and the monastery was burned. Later on, it was partly rebuilt under the Ming and the Qing.

Now, a few monuments which used to stand within the enclosure are outside it. West of the monastery stand **two large Buddhist pillars,** or *chuang*, covered with delicate carving. One of them, with a fluted column, dates from the end of the Tang dynasty. The other, which is damaged (only 22 feet of it remain), dates from the Later Liao (907–923).

Beyond the present monastery stands a **pagoda** dating from the Yuan. The upper part consists of eight roofs, built close together, and a slender spire. It was built by order and favour of the Emperor in 1215.

The monastery contains about fifteen steles, the oldest of which dates from the Jin. They record the history of the town and the monastery. In the last hall but one stands a bell over 10 feet high, cast in 1184. It is inscribed with "Long live the Emperor, long live the Empress" *(Huang di wan sui, huang hou wan sui)*. The last temple of the monastery is probably Ming.

In the north-west corner of the town stands the **Monastery of Celestial Tranquility (Tian ning si),** founded under the Tang, and rebuilt during the Wan li period (1573–1620) of the Ming. Two temples remain; their style is that of the Yuan, though parts of them date from the Qing. Nearby stands a **Buddhist column** of the *chuang* type, dating from the end of the Tang, and a pagoda erected under the Yuan, in 1313, in memory of a Buddhist preacher called Xu Zhao ming.

North-west of the Kai yuan Period Monastery, on the site of an old Taoist monastery, Long xing guan, now no longer in existence, stands a **Taoist column (Dao de jing shi tai)**, with a simple carved capital. Inscriptions cover all eight facets of the column. At the top of the south facet is written: "Inscription of the commentaries (on the *Dao de jing*) made by the Emperor, a genius in the arts as in war, under the Tang dynasty, in the Kai yuan period." The two parts of the *Dao de jing* follow, covering three and four facets respectively. The text is engraved in large characters, the commentaries in small characters. The eighth facet bears inscriptions written in 739 and 988 (Song).

This is an invaluable monument, because it bears a version of the *Dao de jing*, and also because it is proof of the esteem in which this work was held under the Tang, when it was raised to the ranks of a classic *(jing)* and included in the syllabus for the imperial examinations, on the same footing as the Confucian classics. The *Dao de jing* is a short work (5,000 characters altogether), written in the 4th century B.C., which the Taoists afterwards considered as a sort of sacred writing. The only information about its author, Lao zi, takes the form of several legends, all impossible to verify.

Another Buddhist column stands on the site of the former **Pure Land Monastery (Jing tu chan yuan)**. It was erected in 1282 in memory of a great preacher

who died in 1246, called Wan Song. A stele was found
there dating from 962, with a text of over 4,000 characters, describing the history of the monastery, from
878 (Tang) to 962 (Song). It has been transferred to
the courtyard of the local government offices.

Han dan

During the Warring States Period, Han dan was the
capital of the principality of Zhao. Remains of the
ancient capital can still be seen, about 3 miles south-
west of the modern town. Known as the **King of Zhao's
Town (Zhao Wang chang),** they are classed as a
historical monument. About half a mile west of the
town, at Wang lang cun, over fifty **Han dynasty
tombs** have been found.

The present town has a population of 300,000 and
specialises in the production of textiles.

An enormous raised **terrace** still exists in the north-
east corner of the town walls, called the **Cong tai.** It is
said to have been built towards 400 B.C. by Wu ling,
the King of Zhao, for the pleasure of the citizens of
his capital. It may originally have been intended as a
stand for reviewing troops; it is certainly old, and has
been regularly repaired over the centuries. A pavilion
with red columns stands on it. A wide view is to be
had from there, over the town and the undulating Tai
hang Mountains in the distance. After 1949 it was
converted into a park (Cong tai gong yuan).

The **Great Military Cemetery of the Provinces of He
bei, He nan, Shan xi and Shan dong (Jin Ji Lu Yu lie
shi ling yuan)** is at Han dan. It was begun in March 1949
and finished in October 1950. Its name is inscribed
over the entrance, in eight characters written by Zhu
De. An avenue leads up to the principal monument,
which is surmounted by a red star, and bears inscrip-

tions on three sides, written by Mao Ze dong (east side), Zhu De (west side) and Liu Shao qi (north side). The dome of the People's Heroes' Mausoleum is further on. General Zou Quan is buried to the right of it. The six characters on his tomb were written by Zhou En lai. A little museum in memory of him stands just beyond his tomb. At the other end of the cemetery is another small museum.

Feng feng

On the railway line, south-west of Han dan, is the mining district of Feng feng, where there are two large areas of Buddhist rock carvings about nine miles from each other, known as the **Mount Xiang tang Caves (Xiang tang shan shi ku).** The earliest carvings date from the reign of the Northern Qi Emperor Wen xuan, between 550 and 560. Some may even date from the dynasty before. Carvings were constantly added right up to the Ming. The result is a magnificent collection of statues and bas-relief carvings, like an open air museum. Unfortunately most of the statues were badly damaged during the first half of the century (under the Japanese occupation) and perhaps earlier still. Nearly all of them have lost their heads. The caves are classed as a historical monument. They are in two groups, north and south.

The **south group** is at the southern end of Mount Gu shan, near the village of Peng cheng, not far from the **Monastery of the Echoing Hall (Xiang tang si).** The monastery buildings date from the Qing. The largest group of carvings are behind the east buildings. A path leading east up the mountain passes others; still more, smaller ones, can be seen west of the monastery and on the hillside opposite.

The main group consists of seven caves spread over
two levels, two below and five above, all cut out of the
rock. The five upper ones open on to a terrace with a
path going up to it. The caves are square and measure
7 to 11 feet along the side. Each one contains damaged
statues and beautiful mural decorations, giving a
planned architectural effect. Bas-relief carvings decorate the rock alongside the path east of the monastery,
one of them, a large Guan yin, dating from the
Northern Qi, judging from the style. The cliffs opposite
the monastery are carved with over thirty figures of all
sizes, depicting Buddhist saints and deities, probably
dating from the Song and the Yuan. An old seven-
storey octagonal pagoda stands south-east of the
monastery.

The **northern group** is on the western slopes of
Mount Gu shan, about nine miles from the first
group, near the village of Hu cun. The **Monastery of
Eternal Joy (Chang le si)** stood at the foot of the mountain. Nothing remains of it now but a nine-storey
pagoda and several ancient steles. The caves are a little
higher up the mountain side, divided into three different groups, all of them interesting. The south group
consists of three caves. The eastern group is mainly a
large chamber 23 feet by 26 feet containing numerous
statues dating from before the Tang dynasty. Most of
the heads were re-made later on. The northern group
is the largest: five caves on two different levels, three
above and two below. One of them contains an inscription saying that the work dates from 1524 (Ming).
Another cave contains an inscription dating from 1042
(Song). The largest cave of all is here: it is 40 feet
square. Fourteen niches along the walls contain bodhisattvas. The middle of the chamber is a solid piece of
rock going up to the ceiling, with niches hollowed out

of three sides of it, each containing three statues of the Buddha. The walls and the niches are covered with bas-relief carvings. The strong lines of the statues and carvings produce an even, architectural effect. A well at the far end has been covered over.

The Mount Xiang tang carvings include several masterpieces of Chinese Buddhist carving. The affected style of the Northern Wei has vanished. The stiff, immobile figures have become more lifelike, closer to reality. The movement of the draped clothing is more generous and flowing than in the earlier periods. The Mount Xiang tang Caves show how the north China artists took over the Buddhist forms imported from India, made them their own and gradually created a truly Chinese realist Buddhist art. They foreshadow what was to be the summit of the art of sculpture under the Tang and the Sui.

SHAN DONG

(Map see Atlas pl. 8)

Shan dong is bordered by Hei bei to the north-west, He nan to the west, An hui and Jiang su to the south. The east of the province is a peninsula with the Bo hai Gulf to the north and the Yellow Sea to the south. It used to be a rocky island, but little by title the alluvium deposited by the Yellow River (which sometimes flowed into the sea to the north, sometimes to the south of the peninsula) has joined it to the mainland. This explains why the province falls naturally into two parts: the peninsula and a mountainous region to the east, and a plain to the west, which is in fact part of the north China plain. The mountainous region has given its name to the province: "the mountainous east". It includes the Tai shan massif (several peaks over 5,900 feet and the Tai shan itself, 5,060 feet), and the hills on the peninsula, with the valley of the River Jiao he lying between them. Shan dong has a longer coastline than any other Chinese province. On the peninsula it is sharply indented and provides excellent natural harbours; as the hills are rich in coal and iron ore, lying close to the surface, the peninsula lives mainly by mining and fishing, while the plain is mainly agricultural. In 1933 the Yellow River changed its course, and now flows into the Bo hai. To the south of it, in the south-west of the province, lies a large marshy area which for a long time was not cultivated at all. The climate of the western part is almost exactly the same as that of the rest of the north China plain, but the rainfall is slightly more abundant. The Yellow River, although liable to flooding, is drawn on for irrigation at all other times. The hills have rich underground water supplies and efforts are being made to use the spring water for irrigation as well. The peninsula has a maritime climate.

These dual characteristics have made themselves felt all through the history of the province. Two currents can be traced: an attraction towards the sea and a tendency towards autonomy, and the link with the rest of the empire, particularly when the building of the Grand Canal made the north-south traffic pass through the province. Some of the earliest Neolithic remains were found in Shan dong: the Long shan Culture, called after the place 21 miles east of Ji nan where the excavations were carried out. In the turbulent centuries before the formation of the empire (the Warring States period), several important states were founded in Shan dong. The strongest was the state of Qi, whose capital was Lin zi; part of its force was due to its use of products of the sea (fish and salt); it was one of the last to stand up to Qin shi Huang di. The most widely known was the little state of Lu where Confucius was born in 551 B.C. Mencius was born in 372 B.C. in the little state of Zou, in south Shan dong.

One consequence of this early development was intensive deforestation, as in the middle Yellow River provinces. The construction of the Grand Canal and its extension to Peking under the Yuan made the west of the province into a main trade route. Big trading towns like De zhou, Lin qing, Liao cheng and Ji ning grew up all along the route under the Ming and the Qing. Economic development was accompanied by constant social unrest; several peasant risings are recorded, the most famous of which was the rebellion led by Song Jiang under the Song dynasty, in the marshy area round Mount Liang shan. It is described in the novel *Story of the Water Margin (Shui hu zhuan)*, written by Shi Nai an under the Ming (see p. 194). A new phase in the history of Shan dong began in the second half of the 19th century. The Germans, and later the English, obtained leased territories (Qing dao, Wei hai wei) and extended their sphere of influence from there. The Germans founded the town of Qing dao, then built the railway line from Qing dao to Ji nan, and developed the coal mines. Their territories and their privileges were taken over by the Japanese in 1915, and given back to China in 1923.

Industry has developed enormously since the liberation, from the foundations laid by the Germans and the Japanese (see p. 702 and 773, Ji nan and Qing dao). A new railway line has been built from Qing dao to Yan tai. At the same time, new land has been brought under cultivation, and over half of the total area of the province is now farming land.

The principal food crops are: wheat, sweet potatoes, maize, and the main cash crops are: cotton, peanuts and tobacco. This is the chief peanut producing area in China; they are grown mainly in the east. Cotton is grown in the north-west plain and tobacco in the Yi du and Wei fang regions. Shan dong is well known for its fruit: peaches, pears, apples, grapes. All these varied agricultural products provide raw materials for light industry: flour-milling, oil extracting, textiles, cigarette making. The population is now 54 million.

Ji nan and the towns in the west of the province, on the Grand Canal, will be described first, followed by two centres of great historical and artistic interest in the south of the province: Mount Tai shan and Qu fu, and finally the east of the province from Ji nan to Qing dao and Yan tai, at the furthest point of the peninsula.

JI NAN

Ji nan is the capital of Shan dong. It is a town of 1,200,000 inhabitants, and as well as being the political centre of the province, it is a communications centre, an industrial town and a university town. It has a long history.

It is three miles south of the Yellow River, at the foot of the Li shan Mountains, a chain which forms the foot-hills of the Shan dong massif; it is a delightful place to stay in, as **seventy-two springs** rise in the town, providing water for the numerous canals and lakes all the year round. Few Chinese towns have such a good and plentiful water supply.

Ji nan has had an arms factory, an electrical parts factory, and flour mills since the beginning of the century. It was famous for its silks and imitation precious stones. **Industry** has developed considerably since the liberation: the town now produces lorries, machine tools, precision instruments, fertilizers and other chemicals, and high quality paper, as well as textiles, flour and light industry products. Handicrafts from Shan dong are sold there, such as embroidery, basket work, stone carvings and objects in wood plated with silver.

The town has three theatres and several cinemas. The most important of its higher educational establishments are: Shan dong University, the Shan dong Medical School, the Shan dong Teachers' Training College and the Shan dong Polytechnic Institute. The **Shan**

dong Library and the **Shan dong Provincial Museum** are also there; other institutions can be seen marked on the map of the town.

History

The site of Ji nan has been inhabited since the prehistoric era; so-called Neolithic black pottery, known as Long shan pottery, has been found here (see p.106, Long shan Culture).

Excavations in the north-east of the town have uncovered objects dating from the Shang dynasty (1711-1066 B.C.). Under the Zhou, Ji nan was a walled town belonging to the kingdom of Qi. It was a flourishing commercial town under the Tang and the Song. At the beginning of the Ming, in 1371, the town walls, which had up till then been earth ramparts, were faced with stone and brick. Under the Ming and the Qing, Ji nan, as the capital of Shan dong, was an important political centre. A succession of enterprising provincial governors at the end of the Qing and the beginning of the Republic did much to improve the town.

After the Sino-German treaty of 1898, which gave Germany certain rights in the Qing dao area and permission to built mines and a railway in Shan dong, the line between Qing dao and Ji nan was begun. Prince Henry of Germany witnessed the start of the work in 1899; it was carried out by a company called the Schantung Eisenbahn Gesellschaft. Up till then, Ji nan's only link with the sea had been a navigable river running east between the town and the Yellow River to the Bo hai; the Xiao qing he. The opening of the line to Qing dao in 1904, followed by others going to Tian jin and the centre of China in 1912, made Ji nan the communications centre for the whole province. Furthermore, the Chinese government themselves opened Ji nan to foreign trade in 1906; it was the first time that the Chinese had offered a concession to foreigners without being forced to do so either by arms or unequal treaties. The concession was near the station, in the business districts in the west of the town, which were kept under strict control by the Chinese government. The town soon had tidy modern streets, electric lighting and trams. Several foreign missions were founded: an American Presbyterian Mission, an English Baptist Mission; Ji nan was also the centre of the North Shan dong Diocese (Roman Catholic).

The town has always had a large Moslem population.

Description

The main places worth visiting inside the town are the Fountain Spring, the Black Tiger Spring and the Lake; south of the town, the Thousand Buddha Mountain.

The **Fountain Spring (Ba duo quan)** is one of the most attractive spots in the town. Little paths lead from one stretch of water to the next, round pools, over bridges. Three natural springs gush up through the water, a rare sight in China, and one which attracts constant visitors. The temple close by used to hold several fairs and markets each month, drawing large crowds to take part. The pavilions and other old buildings round the pools have been restored.

The little **Li Qing zhao Museum (Li Qing zhao ji nian guan)** stands nearby, in a delightful courtyard. It contains portraits and old editions of the works of Li Qing zhao, the most famous of all China's poetesses, who was born in Ji nan in 1084.

JI NAN

1 Shan Dong Hotel
2 Tourist Office
3 Handicraft Shop
4 Zhu Fang De Restaurant
5 «Hors d'œuvre» Restaurant
6 Qing Er Street Department Store
7 Da Guan Yuan Market
8 New Market
9 People's Market
10 Department Store
11 Workers' Theatre
12 Da Dong Theatre
13 Shan Dong Theatre
14 Cultural Palace
15 Ji Nan Workers' Club
16 Ming Xing Cinema
17 Shan Dong Medical School
18 Shan Dong Polytechnic Institute
19 Shan Dong Provincial Library
20 Shan Dong Provincial Museum
21 Shang Dynasty diggings
22 Fountain Spring (Bao Duo Quan)
23 Black Tiger Spring (Hei Hu Quan)
24 Pearl Spring
25 Ji nan Lake (Da Ming Hu)
26 People's Park
27 Industrial Exhibition Hall
28 Youth Club
29 Five Dragon Pool
30 Zhuan Zheng Street Stadium
31 Shan Dong Provincial Stadium
32 National Defense Athletics Club
33 Monument to the Martyrs of the Revolution
34 Cemetery of the Martyrs o the Revolution

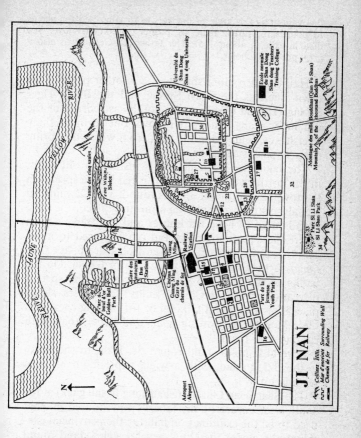

She married Zhao Ming cheng, a poet and scholar like herself. When the north of China was invaded by the Jin, they both fled to the south, taking with them their large collection of old and new works of art. Zhao Ming cheng died in 1129, and after his death, Li Qing zhao wrote *ci* (poems intended to be sung) of poignant sadness, which became famous; they were an innovation, as this style of poetry was usually used for poems to courtisans, rather than for poems on conjugal love. She died in exile in about 1151. Her father, Li Ge fei was also a great poet and scholar.

Half a dozen more springs rise in other parts of the town, such as the **Pearl Spring** and the **Black Tiger Spring (Hei hu quan),** at the south-east corner of the old inner walls. The water flows out through three tiger heads, sculpted in the rock from which the spring rises. A park surrounds it.

The lake, the **Da ming hu,** is inside the old walls, in the north-east of the town. It is fed by the springs in the town, and is about 3 miles round. The Da ming hu has always been popular as a meeting place; the little islands used to have tea houses and theatres on them where merchants, scholars and officials used to meet. The rich gave banquets on board pleasure boats *(hun fang)* as they used to do elsewhere in China. On the banks of the lake are various places for the sort of recreation which the Chinese enjoy: tea houses, shady places for sitting and talking, or for playing chess. On the lake itself are rowing boats and larger boats with roofing over them.

Several temples stand round the lake; to the north is the **Bai ji miao,** with a wide, triple flight of steps leading up to it.

The **Shan dong Library (Shan dong tu shu guan)** at the south-west corner of the lake is now housed in what used to be the examination hall for the provincial examinations, under the Qing. Several steles stand round it. At the water's edge, a little temple was built at the beginning of the century to the memory of Li Hong zhang, the statesman (see p. 654).

From Ji nan, a pleasant trip can be made to the **Thousand Buddha Mountain (Qian fo shan),** south of the town. The top of the mountain gives a splendid view over Ji nan and the Huang he plain. The first and second parts of the temple are a little way from each other; behind the second part rises a great wall of rock, where hundred of statues of the Buddha and other people have been carved, all of different sizes. A spring rises nearby, in a huge cave, about 480 feet deep, called the Dragon Spring Cave (Long quan dong). The sculpture in the cave dates from the Northern Wei. The bas-relief carvings elsewhere on the rock date from the Sui dynasty. They were executed between 581 and 601, one after the other, in no particular order. They were done at the request of believers who often would join in a group to finance the work. In many cases, it was an act of devotion to insure the welfare of their dead parents.

This group of religious carvings is not the only one in the area. Others exist in the mountains south of Ji nan, of which the most interesting are: the **Yellow Stone Cliff (Huang shi ya),** on the north-west point of Mount Li shan, where the carvings date from the Northern Wei (from 524); the group on the **Jade Casket Mountain (Yu han shan),** which date from the Sui (between 584 and 600); the group on the **Mountain of the Wisdom of the Buddha (Fo hui shan),** near a Kai yuan Period Monastery, which dates from the Tang. All these carvings scattered in the mountains round Ji nan enable the evolution of religion and Buddhist art in the region to be traced in detail (many are accompanied by inscriptions) from the Northern Wei (6th century) to the Tang (9th century) and in some cases, up to the Northern Song (10th century). The custom of having pious images carved in the rocks was first of all restricted to the nobility (Wei), but gradually it became a general one (Sui and Tang). The Wei and Siu

sculpture is the finest; the art of Long men has clearly
influenced it.

In 1964, more carvings, dating from the beginning
of the Tang dynasty, were found 15 miles south-east of
Ji nan, on the **Bronze Mountain (Qing tong shan),** on
the site of the former **Big Buddha Monastery (Da fo si).**
A cave contains a Buddha 29 feet high.

THE TOWNS SOUTH OF JI NAN
AND ON THE GRAND CANAL

Zhong gong

Zhong gong is about 12 miles south of Ji nan, in a
valley of the northern foot-hills of the Tai shan. In the
chain of hills (Chang cheng ling) between Zhong gong
and the Tai shan, remains of the **Great Wall of Lu** can
still be seen. It was built in the 5th century B.C., and
is the oldest of the great walls.

Near the village of Liu bu, which can be reached by
following the course of the River Jin yang chuan eastwards from Zhong gong for about 9 miles, are some of
the oldest Buddhist remains in Shan dong. They are
in two groups, one a few miles north-east of the village,
the other a few miles to the south.

The first group are the remains of the **Shen tong
Monastery (Shen tong si).**

The founding of the monastery, in the mid-4th century A.D.,
is a landmark in the early history of Chinese Buddhism. Its
founder, called Lang gong by the Chinese, lived there himself
from 351 to 420. The present name of the monastery dates
from 583.

Parts of it are still standing. 1. The **Four Door Tower
(Si men ta)** is a fine square building, built of stone, dating from the Eastern Wei (544); the four beautiful
seated statues of the Buddha (and the standing statues

of the bodhisattvas) inside date from the same period.
The plan of the monastery can still be traced from the
ruins. 2. The **Pagoda of the Dragon and the Tiger (Long
hu ta)** dates from the Tang; it stands above the ruins,
surrounded by about forty **stupas,** most of them dating
from the Yuan and the Ming; the monastery's cemetery was here. Higher up still is the **Thousand Buddha
Cliff (Qian fo ya),** covered with statues of the Buddha
and of people of every degree in life, whose pious descendants had them immortalised in stone. The carvings are cut out of the rock itself, and date from the
beginning of the Tang; seven of them are over 6 feet
tall, and there over 200 small ones.

(For the history of the monastery, see *The Shên-t'ung monastery and the beginning of Buddhism in Shantung,* by F.S. Drake,
in *Monumenta serica,* vol. 4, Peking, 1939/40, and an article
in Chinese in *Wen wu* 1956, No 10).

The second group of remains includes two important ones: 1. the **Nine Point Pagoda (Jiu ding ta)** dates
from the Tang; it is built of grey brick. It consists of an
octagonal tower of slightly concave design, completely
bare of any ornamentation, except for nine little
square pagodas each with three roofs (one in the middle
and eight round it) on the top. It was restored with the
greatest care in 1962. It once belonged to the **Guan yin
Monastery (Guan yin si),** also known as the Nine
Towers Monastery (Jiu ta si), which was founded
under the Tang. 2. Above the old monastery is another
group of **Tang carvings,** carved out of the rock, divided
into three sets. There are about fifty carvings, some in
almost entirely inaccessible places.

Ling yan

The **Monastery of the Magic Cliff (Ling yan si)**
stands on the Ling yan, or Ling yan shan, in the north-

western foot-hills of the Tai shan. It is about 6 miles
by road from Wan de station, south of Ji nan.

According to the *Tai shan Chronicle (Tai shan zhi)*,
the monastery was named after a miracle which occurred each time the monk Lang gong, founder of the
Shen tong Monastery (see above), passed nearby: "the
wild beasts knelt down, the rocks bowed. This is why
the cliff was called the *magic cliff*". The monastery
was founded under the Eastern Jin (357), but was
demolished under the Northern Wei (446) when the
Northern Wei Emperor Dao wu carried out a systematic persecution of Buddhism. From the Tang to the
Ming, the monastery was a large one. Parts of it can
be visited today.

1. The **forest of stupas (ta lin).** The stupas were
erected to the memory of over a hundred priests who
directed the monastery under the Tang, the Song, the
Yuan, the Ming and the Qing. The oldest one in the
shape of a tower, called Hui chong ta, dates from the
Tang (Zhen guan period, 627–650).

2. A slender nine-storey octagonal **pagoda,** known
as the Bi zhi ta, dates from the beginning of the Song.

3. **The Thousand Buddha Temple (Qian fo dian)** was
built under the Tang and often restored afterwards.
It is seven bays wide, and has kept its Tang style in its
general lines; the carved bases to the pillars are also
Tang. The temple contains an unusual set of **forty luo
han** which date from the Song; the statues line the side
walls, and are extremely realistic in their expressions,
positions, and clothing; no two are alike. The only set
which can be compared with them is the set of statues
(female) of the Jin ci at Tai yuan (see p. 852). A detailed
description of them is given in the *Wen wu*, 1959, No 11
in Chinese).

4. East of the Thousand Buddhas Temple is the stone base of the **Five Flowers Temple (Wu hua si)**. The bases of the columns have Song style carvings on them.

Xiao li pu

A monument of the greatest historical, archaeological and artistic interest still stands near the village of Xiao li pu, in the district of Li cheng (formerly the districts of Fei cheng and Chang qing), at a place known as the Mountain of the Chapel of Filial Piety (Xiao tang shan): the **Funerary Chapel of Guo Ju (Guo ju ci,** or Guo shi mu shi ci). It is a small stone building with two bays, dating from the beginning of the Eastern Han dynasty (1st century A.D.). It is the oldest surviving example of domestic architecture in China. On the walls inside are Han frescoes and inscriptions of war scenes and social life. A building was put up in 1954 to protect the chapel, and it is classed as a historical monument.

De zhou

De zhou is an industrial and trade centre in the north of Shan dong, on the Grand Canal. Its wealth in the past was due to the key position which it held in the economy of the province: for centuries all the products from Shan dong for Tian jin and Peking were loaded, and all the products imported from the north unloaded, at De zhou. Another great trading centre on the Grand Canal, the town of Lin qing, (about 50 miles south-west), was taken by the Tai ping in 1855, and never recovered; De zhou, however, regained its importance when it became the junction of two railway lines. The town has had a large arsenal since the beginning of the century.

MAISON DE GUILDE MARCHANDE DE LIAO CHENG
LIAO CHENG MERCHANTS' GUILD HOUSE

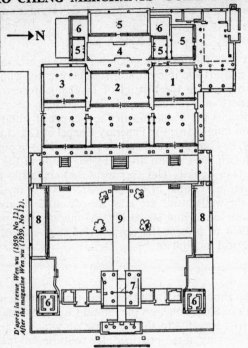

D'après la revue Wen wu (1959, No. 12).
After the magazine Wen wu (1959, No. 12).

Les numéros se réfèrent à la description donnée dans le texte.
The numbers refer to the description given in the text.

Liao cheng

This is another trading town on the Grand Canal, in the west of Shan dong. It used to be extremely prosperous, particularly under the Qing. The **Shân xi and**

Shan xi Merchant Guilds Hotel (Shan shan hui guan), which was begun in 1744, bears witness of this. It is about half a mile from the east gate of the town, and was built to fulfil several functions. It contained three temples, one dedicated to the god of wealth (Cai shen da wang) (1), another to the god of war (Guan di) (2), and a third to the god of literature Wen chang, (Wen chang huo shen) (3). The living quarters (5) were grouped round the north courtyard (4). Summer-houses (wang lou) of baroque design stood at the four corners of the hotel (6). A pavilion which served as a stage (xi lou) (7) and two galleries (8) (kan lou), enabled the large main courtyard (9) to be transformed into an open air theatre. The plan of the hotel and the lively style of the buildings are both equally remarkable.

Ji ning

Ji ning is in the south-west of Shan dong, on the Grand Canal. Like De zhou, Lin qing and Liao cheng (see above) it was a flourishing trading centre. In the 20th century it has become one of the big industrial cities of the province. It produces foodstuffs and agricultural instruments. It is also well known for its handicrafts, which are exported in large quantities: wood, bamboo, iron and copper ware.

TAI AN AND MOUNT TAI SHAN

Tai shan is the highest peak of the massif in the centre of Shan dong. From the earliest times, it was worshipped as the greatest of China's sacred mountains, and as such it has been the object of countless beliefs and the centre of an intense religious life, as its many temples and monuments show. The mountain can be climbed in a day, and it is a fascinating expedition from every point of view. There are magnificent views over the province below, and the sunrise seen from the peak of Tai shan is an unforgettable sight.

The town of Tai an lies at the foot of the mountain, to the south; a regular train service runs between there and Ji nan. Several hotels have been built since the liberation to accommodate tourists, some in the town and some on the mountain itself. The government has had the principal temples and the paths leading to the summit restored, and restaurants and tea rooms have been built on the way up. In 1949, everything had been allowed to fall into disrepair; the Tai shan Temple had been transformed by the Guo min dang into a sort of municipal bath house, with showers and hairdressers' saloons; other temples were used as soldiers' billets, as happened elsewhere in China.

Tai an does not live by tourism alone; a sanatorium has been built, an Agricultural Institute founded, and the orchards round it produce apples and other fruit. Over a hundred species of medecinal herbs are to be found on Tai shan. The mountainsides have been replanted with trees (finished in 1959), and two artificial lakes have been dug, one in 1944 (the Dragon Lake, Long tan shui ku), the other in 1956 (the Tiger Lake, Hu tan shui ku).

The **tomb of Feng Yu xiang,** a large monument built in stone from Tai shan in 1952, lies at the foot of the mountain, near Tai an. The inscription was written by Guo Mo rou. Feng Yu xiang, the "Christian general", was a famous warlord, who possessed armies in northwest China, which he sometimes used in support of Tchiang Kai-chek, sometimes against him. He was drowned in a shipwreck after the Second World War.

History

The French sinologist, Edouard Chavannes, wrote an exhaustive study of Tai shan called *Le T'ai chan, Essai de monographie d'un culte chinois (Annales du Musée Guimet*, vol. 21, Paris, Leroux, 1910; pirated edition, Peking, 1941); the following quotations all come from chapters I and II. The modern transcription of the Chinese names has been added in brackets.

"Mountains are deities in China. They are considered to be naturalistic powers which act like living beings, and can therefore be won by sacrifices or moved by prayers. They vary in importance: some are little local spirits whose sphere of influence is small; others are majestic sovereigns wielding power over a vast area. Five are more famous than the rest: *Song Kao* (Song gao) or Central Peak, *T'ai chan* (Tai shan) or Eastern Peak, *Heng chan* (Heng shan) or Southern Peak, *Houa chan* (Hua shan) or Western Peak, *Heng chan* (Heng shan) or Northern Peak.[1] One of the five is more famous than the rest: *T'ai chan* or Eastern Peak."

"*T'ai chan*, which rises, bulky and steep, to the north of the prefectural town of *T'ai-gnan fou* (Tai an), is not an impressive mountain; it is only 8,064 feet high.[2] As it is higher than the other mountains in East China, it is considered to govern the rest; it is the president of the East.

"This belief that high places are suitable for supernatural revelations is not peculiar to China. Sinai and Olympus show that in all countries and at all times mountains have been the haunts of gods.

"But the mountain is not only the place where gods and immortals appear; it is itself a deity. The official honours heaped on T'ai shan are proof of this; from the *Tcheou* (Zhou) dynasty onwards, if *Sseu-ma Ts'ien* (Si ma Qian) is to be believed (see p. 190), the gods of the five peaks were treated as the equals of the court, the three dukes. In 725, the *T'ang* (Tang) Emperor *Hiuan tsong* (Xuan song) raised the *T'ai chan* god to the rank above by granting him the title of "King equal to the Sky" (tian qi wang). In 1008, the *Song* dynasty Emperor *Tchen tsong* (Zhen zong) added a new element to the title, which became: "Good and holy King, equal to the Sky" (ren sheng tian qi wang); in 1011 he was promoted again, this time to the rank of Emperor;

---

[1] These are in Henan (p. 810), Shan dong, Hu nan (p. 1148), Shân xi (p. 966) and Shan xi (p. 682) respectively.

[2] 8,024 feet in fact.

the *T'ai chan* god is called "the Emperor equal to the Sky, good and holy" (tian qi ren sheng di). The title was elaborated again in 1291, under the Mongol dynasty: "Emperor equal to the Sky, great giver of life, good and holy" (tian qi da sheng ren sheng di). In 1370, however, the Ming Emperor *T'ai tsou* (Tai zu) put an end to the out-bidding of one dynasty by the next in their efforts to win the deity's favour; he declared that human honours, whatever they might be, must always be powerless to express the full veneration due to a god; the highest respect that man could show would therefore be to give him the simplest possible title; and to address the god of *T'ai chan*, the name "Eastern Peak, *T'ai chan*" (dong yue tai shan) with no other additions was to be used.

"A mountain deity has two kinds of general attributions: first of all, it influences the surrounding countryside by sheer weight and acts as a stabilising force; it prevents the ground from moving and the rivers from overflowing; it opposes earthquakes and floods. Secondly, clouds gather round the mountain top, which seems to produce them, and which earns the homeric epithet of "gatherer of clouds" (xing yun); the mountain deity therefore has life-giving clouds at his command which can enrich the world and he makes the harvest grow."

Countless prayers addressed to Tai shan by Emperors of different dynasties were engraved on steles which were then erected on the mountain, and Chavannes has translated and analysed them. "When rain is scarce, when the corn wilts in the fields and the peasants begin to fear famine, the sovereign of men appeals to the majestic Peak who can and should put an end to misfortune. In times of earthquake or flood appropriate prayers are made to remind *T'ai chan* of his duties as the lord of the region, inviting him to restore it to order."

One of the fundamental concepts of the ancient Chinese civilisation was that moral and natural order work in with each other and act on each other. In the case of physical catastrophes, the main cause was looked for in the moral order of things. The Emperor accused himself of lacking in virtue. But the *T'ai shan* god had to be made aware of his share in the responsibility. "The *T'ai chan* god is not the cause of the people's misfortunes; but as his duty is to collaborate with the Sky to ensure the prosperity of living creatures, he is reprehensible when he fails to bring prompt relief to distress which is pointed out to him. 'If I have attracted calamities through my own faults,' says an Emperor to him in 1455, 'I certainly accept the personal responsibility; but as far as transforming misfortune into happiness is concerned, it is you, O god, in truth, who has the duty to undertake that'...."

"Thus the Emperor and the *T'ai chan* god seem like two high-ranking dignitaries, more or less equal, whom the Sky has appointed to ensure the people's happiness; one through his wise government creates harmony and virtue among men, the other uses his controlling influence to maintain order in the physical world.

"The religious attributions mentioned up till now are shared by *T'ai chan* with the other mountain gods in China; some are peculiar to *T'ai chan* alone; *T'ai chan* is the Eastern Peak; he therefore presides over the East, over the origin of all life. All existence begins at the east, as does the sun. The concept of *yang*, which makes the sap rise in plants, takes its life-giving breath from the Eastern Peak. In 1532, when an Emperor prays for a son, he addresses his prayer to *T'ai chan*, for the mountain is an never-failing source of births.

"As *T'ai chan* is the source of all future lives, it is consequently the meeting-place for those whose lives have ended. During the first two centuries of the Christian era, it was widely believed in China that the souls of the dead returned to *T'ai chan*. Popular literature contains countless anecdotes full of information on the Elysian Fields where the dead go on acting and talking as they did during their lifetimes; official posts are much sought after, recommendations from influential people are most useful; another subterranean China blossoms beneath the sacred mountain." Chavannes gives several examples of these anecdotes in the chapter on *Croyances populaires*.

"It was traditionally believed that the souls of the dead gathered at a special place at the foot of *T'ai chan*: on a little hill, called *Hao li chan* (Hao li shan), about a mile south-west of the town of *T'ai ngan fou*;... The *Hao-li* emple has some magnificent buildings, and like other large temples elsewhere dedicated to the *T'ai chan* god, it has a large inner courtyard with seventy-five chambers round the walls; they are judgement seats, with clay figures showing the judgements of hell. The cult of *T'ai chan* is shown here associated with rewards and above all punishments meted out in the after world, which gives rise to a problem of religious history: up till now, the *T'ai chan* god has appeared as a naturalistic deity, watching over the rain and stability of the earth, or presiding over life and death, all natural phenomena where no moral element intervenes; for this reason, the cult is a Taoist cult, for Taoism is above all a naturalistic religion, unlike Buddhism which is mainly a moral religion; throughout the Chinese empire, Taoist priests look after the shrines dedicated to deities symbolising forces of nature. If this is so, how is it that in the cult of *T'ai chan* a moral element intervenes, the idea of the judgement of souls who are punished or rewarded in the other world according to their conduct in this one?

"It is perfectly certain that this idea is not inherent to the cult and that it was introduced under the *T'ang*, that is, in the 7th or 8th century A.D. This intrusion can be attributed to a Buddhist influence on Taoism; in Buddhism, the idea of retribution for actions is a primitive and an essential one; it may even be called the foundation of the religion, for it neglects nature and concentrates only on morals (......). Taoism has therefore borrowed the moral theory of punishments and rewards from Buddhism, and its hell is closely copied from the Buddhist hell; once the addition had been made, a cult had to be found to which to attach it." It was attached to the cult of Tai shan, who gradually became the great judge.

Chavannes also wrote, at the beginning of this century: "The cult of T'ai chan is one of the most popular in China. Every town of some size has a *T'ai chan* temple," generally called the 'Eastern Peak Temple' (Dong yue miao). "The seventy-five courts of justice lining the walls of the main courtyard in the Eastern Peak Temples, the appalling tortures reserved for wrong-doers after death, both strike religious terror into the hearts of those unfortunate enough to have some minor wrongdoing on their minds; consequently they come in their crowds to the temples, where they are promised by cunning monks that with some money and a great deal of incense they can win the favour of the awful judge of their destiny in the after life."

The most popular of all, especially among women, was not the Tai shan god himself, but the female deities who shared his temple. The most important one was the Princess of the Coloured Clouds, Bi xia yuan jun. "She is the goddess of the dawn and considered as the daughter of *T'ai chan*, the god of the orient".

The Princess of the Coloured Clouds appeared under the Song dynasty. She "...rapidly attracted large numbers of worshippers; the shrine dedicated to her grew larger and larger; it is now the most magnificent of all the temples on *T'ai chan* (see p. 733). The cult of the goddess was particularly flourishing under the Ming; it became, for the north, the equivalent of the cult of *Kouan-yin* (Guan yin) in the south." "She is usually accompanied by two other goddesses: one holds a symbolic eye in her hands; she is the lady of good eyesight (yan jing niang niang, *or* zi sun niang niang)." Chavannes goes on to say: "The group of the *Pi hia yuan kiun* (Bi xia yuan jun) and her acolytes, which plays an important part in the religious life of the women of north

China, is now the centre of attraction of the cult attached to *T'ai chan;* it is this group which attracts the crowds of pilgrims who flock to the sacred mountain in the first four months of each year."

Another important aspect of the cult of Tai shan must be mentioned: the *feng* and *shan* sacrifices offered with great ceremony at the foot and on the summit of Tai shan by the Emperors. The first was to the Earth, the second to the Sky. The historian Si ma Qian, who devoted a whole book of his *Historical Records* to the sacrifices, says that Qin shi Huang di, the unifier of China, climbed Tai shan in 219 B.C. "When he reached the top, he had an inscription made on a tablet, praising his own virtues, and declaring that he had been able to accomplish the *fong* (feng) sacrifice; on the way down, he was overtaken by a violent storm and took refuge under a tree; in his gratitude, he conferred the title of grand officer of the fifth degree (wu da fu) on the tree."

In fact, the sacrifices were first celebrated in 110 B.C. The first Eastern Han Emperor performed them again in 56 A.D., and later they were performed by Emperor Gao zong in 666, the Tang Emperor Huan zong in 725, and the Song Emperor Zhen zong in 1008. In 695, Empress Wu Ze tian performed the same *feng* and *shan* sacrifices on Song gao, the Central Peak. The sacrifices were only celebrated five times in the whole of China's history. Chavannes describes them and says: "The chief object of the *fong* and *chan* sacrifices was to proclaim the success of a dynasty to the Earth and the Sky; at the summit of his power, the Emperor recalled the merits of his predecessors and thanked the Earth and the Sky for the support they had given to his line." Two inscriptions still remain on Tai shan describing the sacrifices, dating from 726 and 1008. "(they) are irrefutable witnesses to the pomp of these solemn and magnificent occasions. It may even have been the elaborate display involved which caused their disappearance; the religious ardour which transported the Emperor, followed by his train of civil and military officials, the foreign ambassadors, even his wives, to the sacred mountain, encouraged all sorts of abuses; large amounts of money were spent, which a number of clever people knew how turn to their own advantage; it was an excellent opportunity for schemers seeking a gullible Emperor's favour to invent all kinds of miracles to make him believe that he was favoured by the supernatural powers; on the other hand, it was a cause of suffering for the people, who had to pay a high price for the glory of having a sovereign who was loved by the gods. These inconveniences were

never more obvious than during the ceremonies of 1008; this is
no doubt why they were never repeated after this date; but even
though they have been abolished now for nine hundred years, the
memory of them has remained alive in men's minds, and when
the traveller visits *T'ai chan* several monuments summon up for
him the entrancing spectacle of the sumptuous processions which
once wound from the foot of the mountain right up to its topmost
peak."

Even today, Tai shan is still a fascinating place; but the world
of superstition and obscurantism which surrounded it has been
swept away for ever.

Description

In the work which is quoted above, Chavannes mentions 252 temples and monuments in the town of Tai
an, at the foot of Tai shan, and on the way up to the
top. Apart from the temples, every ravine, rock and
section of the path has its name and its string of anecdotes. To make things easier, only the chief monuments will be described, starting from the bottom and
going up to the top; the climb will be divided into four
sections: the Tai shan Temple, the mountain itself, the
summit, and finally the temples at the foot of the
mountain, outside the walls of Tai an. Anything in
inverted commas is a quotation from Edouard Chavannes' work, Chapter II.

Three ways lead up to the summit: the western path
(xi lu), the central path (zhong lu) and the eastern path
(dong lu). The central path will be described, as it is
the richest in views and monuments. A good walker
can cover the path in an hour, if he does not stop on
the way. At certain times of the year it is possible to
spend the night on the top of the mountain in a hotel,
and to watch the sunrise next morning. As it is cold at
night, even in the summer, padded jackets can be hired
at the hotel.

LE TEMPLE DU TAI SHAN
THE TAI SHAN TEMPLE

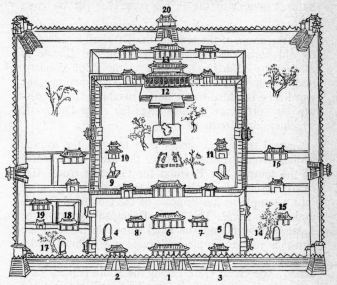

D'après le T'ai chan, Essai de monographie d'un culte chinois, par Edouard Chavannes (Paris, Leroux 1910).
Les numéros se réfèrent à la description donnée dans le texte.
After The T'ai chan, Monograph on a Chinese cult by Edouard Chavannes (Paris, Leroux 1910).
The numbers refer to the description given in the text.

1. The Tai shan Temple (Dai miao)

The temple, which is a large one, covers about a quarter of the area within the old walls of the town of Tai an. At the beginning of the century, Chavannes wrote: "Most of the rest of the town is full of public or religious buildings; even so, large empty spaces still exist within the walls. The crowds of pilgrims who come in the first months of the year are all that enliven this town, which has no other reason for its existence than to receive the multitudes attracted by the supernatural powers of the *Pi hia yuan kiun* (Bi xia yuan jun)."

In the name of the temple, the Tai shan is called by its old name, *Dai*, which is used in the *Classic of Documents (Shu jing)*, written in the Zhou dynasty, and which is often used in poetry. Sometimes the word *zong* is added to the name, meaning "first ancestor" or "protector", which gives the name Dai zong, which is fairly frequent.

Several triumphal arches used to span the avenue leading from the south gate of the town to the entry of the temple; the Pavilion for Greeting from Afar (Yao can ting) which also stood there, was transformed into a temple to the Princess of the Coloured Clouds under the Ming. The great **Triumphal Arch of the Eastern Peak (Dong yue fang)** stands in front of the entrance to the temple enclosure; it was built under Kang xi in 1672. The three gates into the enclosure are called: The Great Gate Facing the South (Zheng yang men) (1), the Gate where Grandeur is Glimpsed (Jian da men) (2), and the Gate for Admiring the Height (Yang gao men) (3).

Of the many steles in the first courtyard, two are especially impressive. The one to the west (4), "about 22 feet high, dates from 1013; it commemorates the statute passed by the Song Emperor *Tchen tsong* (Zhen zong) to raise the god of *T'ai chan* to the rank of Emperor, calling him "Emperor equal to the Sky, good and holy" (Tian qi ren sheng di)." The one to the east, called the Xuan he period Stele (Xuan he bei) (5), "a little over 19 feet high, dates from 1124; it records the restoration of the temple and praises *T'ai chan*," The four characters on the back were carved in 1588: *wan dai shan yang, ten thousand generations look there.*

Three large buildings stand in the first courtyard. The middle one is called the Gate of He who is Associated with the Sky (Pei tian men) (6). "This phrase indicates the god of *T'ai chan,* who unites with the Sky to direct the universe." Two bronze lions (Ming) stand in front of it. The east building is called the Hall of the Three Divine Marquises (San ling hou dian) (7), in honour of the three censors of the Zhou dynasty who appeared here miraculously in 1008. The west hall is the Hall of the Military Commander (Tai wei dian) (8).

"The second courtyard is vaster than the first. The walls used to be lined with cubicles (...) which must have been the seventy-five judgement seats. The courtyard is full of beautiful evergreens, against which the whiteness of the many steles stands out." There are numbers of curiously-shaped stones. A large stone pillar *(chuang),* (9) whose date is not known, stands in the south-west corner of the courtyard. The characters of the Buddhist inscriptions which it once bore have been effaced by time. Nearby, housed by a pavilion, stands a large stele dating from the beginning of the Ming (1370) (10). On the other side of the court, another pavilion houses an inscription dating from the 35th year of the Qian long period (1780), written in Chinese and Manchu (11). Like many other steles, it bears a prayer to Tai shan.

Three terraces lead up to **the temple** itself (12), known as the Temple of the Celestial Gift (Tian kuang dian) or the Temple of He Who is Higher than the Rest (Jun ji dian). It is a beautiful building with nine bays, and a double roof of yellow tiles. It was built under the Han, then enlarged under the Song, and has often been restored. The government had it completely restored in 1956. Two little pavilions, to the right and left of the temple, contain poems written by Emperor Qian long, engraved on stone.

"Inside the hall, the visitor finds himself in the presence of the god of *T'ai chan*, enthroned in a niche dressed in flowing yellow robes and holding the oblong tablet which is the insignia of his authority; he looks like an Emperor. The five sacrificial vessels laid out before him bear the symbols of the five peaks." The sacrificial vessels, delicately worked in various precious materials, date from the Ming and the Qing. The complex symbolism on them refers to the great imperial sacrifices in which they were used. "A long fresco on the walls, now slightly damaged, depicts the Emperor's journey from his palace to *T'ai chan;* on the western wall, the sovereign is shown leaving, his yellow chair placed on a four-wheeled chariot; the procession unfolds along the south wall and reaches *T'ai chan* on the east wall." These realistic, highly detailed paintings are extremely lifelike and invaluable as a document.

In the north of the Temple, beyond a little courtyard, stands the Temple of the Bed-room (Qin gong) (13). "It is the building devoted to the wife of the *T'ai chan* god; it contains the statues of the god and of his wife; paintings on the walls show the other women who people this gynaeceum." The wife of the god is a deity who appeared much later than her husband. Her title, the Perfect and Intelligent Empress (Shu ming hou), was conferred on her in 1011, when the god was raised to the rank of Emperor.

The first side courtyard contains six ancient evergreens *(bo)*, said to have been planted under the Han Emperor Wu in 110 B.C. (14). "Poets have vied in praising these venerables witnesses of the past." The little temple nearby is dedicated to Duke Bing ling, the third son of Tai shan (Bing ling gong) (15). The ornamental pool dates from 1956. In the next courtyard (16) stands another little temple called the Hall of the Three Mao Brothers (San Mao dian). On the other side of the main temple buildings stands a beautiful acacia tree, dating from the Tang, in the first courtyard (17). North of this courtyard is the Temple of Yan xi (Yan xi dian) (18). It was dedicated to the True Man Yan xi (Yan xi zhen ren), a Taoist saint who lived in a cave on the mountainside. His cult was linked with the cult of Tai shan in the Kai yuan period (713–741), under the Tang. "The walls (of the courtyard) (19), are full of engraved stones which have been set into them; scholars spend delicious hours reading poems composed and sometimes even signed by famous authors belonging to several different dynasties. The pavilion in this courtyard bears the symbolic name of the Pavilion Encircled by Songs (Huan yong ting)." In the next courtyard, a niche has been built into the wall for a reproduction of a stele dating from the end of the Qin dynasty (209 B.C.). The original stood in the Temple of the Princess of the Coloured Clouds, on the top of Tai shan. It was destroyed when the temple caught fire in 1740, but in 1815, a fragment with seven characters written in the *xiao zhuan* style of the Qin dynasty was discovered.

The north gate of the temple enclosure is called the Lu zhan men, the Gate which is seen from Lu (20). The name refers to two lines from the *Classic of Songs (Shi jing)*: "Tai shan is high, the whole of the country of Lu contemplates it" (Tai shan yan yan, Lu bang suo zhan).

2. Taï shan

The path begins at a stone triumphal arch (Dai zong fang) (1) which was built in 1730 and restored in 1956, 500 yards north of the temple. About ten temples stand at the foot of the mountain, dedicated to all kinds of deities (see Chavannes).

A group of temples stand on the right of the path, a little way from the beginning. The first is the **Hall of Lao jun (Lao jun tang)** (2), which is dedicated to Lao zi, the ancestor of Taoism. His statue stands there, flanked by two acolytes, one of whom is perhaps the famous frontier guard for whom Lao zi wrote the *Dao de jing*, according to Chavannes. Legend has it that the old philosopher, tired of this world, set off on a buffalo to look for a peaceful retreat. At the frontier, a guard asked him to go back to his philosophy, and then disappeared. This is said to be the origin of the *Dao de jing*. In the temple courtyard stand two steles joined under the same capital, known as the **Mandarin Duck Steles (Yuan yang bei)**. "The two facets bear twenty-five dedications, poems or lists of names, whose dates vary from 661 to 698. It is an interesting monument, both from the point of view of the history of writing and of the history of Taoism under the *T'ang*."

The **Western Queen Mother's Pool (Wang mu chi)** (3) lies a little further on, in the forecourt of a temple dating from the Tang. "It is called the Jewel Pool (Yao chi) and the name of the famous Western Queen Mother (Xi wang mu) is added; she reigns in the mysterious western mountains amid dazzling riches". The temple above it is dedicated to a few female deities. Above that stands the **Patriarch Lü's Tower (Lü zu lou)** (4). The building is dedicated to Lü Dong bin, who lived under the Tang and was taken into the Taoist pantheon (see the eight immortals, p. 161 and p. 911). The temple dedicated to him dates from the Ming. His statue stands inside.

A little way on, lower down in a small valley, the **Patriarch Lü's Cave (Lü zu dong)** (5), where the immortal lived, is pointed out. The **Cave of the Hornless Dragon who became Immortal (Qiu xian dong)** (6) is up hill from it. "The legend says that a hornless dragon used to come and prostrate himself in front of the poems which *Lu Tong-pin* (Lü Dong bin) wrote on the rock; one day, when the master magician touched him with his brush, he turned into a horned and winged dragon and vanished."

Once back on the path again, the next temple on the left is the **Temple of Guan di (Guan di miao)** (7), or the Temple of Emperor Guan, the god of war. "The Emperor *Kouan* (Guan) is the name given to the deity who, when mortal, was *Kouan Yu* (Guan Yu), who died in 219 A.D.; he was famous for his devotion to the founder of the Han dynasty and became the prototype of loyalty to the sovereign. Temples to *Kouan ti* are usually used as meeting-places by people from *Chan-si* (Shan xi), because Kouan Yu was a native of that province; the custom exists here and this temple at the foot of *T'ai chan* is a club for people from *Chan-si* (Shan xi hui guan)." Chavannes goes on to say: "When I was there, a play was about to be performed; the secondary statue of the god had been taken out of the temple so that he could see the play, and he had been put on the veranda, so that he had the best seat."

The climb begins properly at the **First Celestial Gate (Yi tian men)** (8), an austere stone arch, built in 1717. Just above it, **another stone portico** inscribed with the five characters *Kong zi deng lin chu* marks "the spot where Confucius began to climb the mountain" (9). Perhaps it was from here that Confucius found that the country of Lu looked small, while he found that the whole empire was small when he arrived at the top (see below). The arch dates from 1560. A **third arch** similar to the other, and dating from 1563, bears the two characters: *tian jie*, "staircase of the sky" (10). Several other buildings stand here, among them the **Red Gate Palace (Hong men gong)** (11), a temple dedicated to the Princess of the Coloured Clouds, and founded in 1626. The building on the right was used by officials of the imperial train for changing their clothes.

The path leads on upwards through a large arched gateway. Up on the right is the **Tomb of the White Mule (Bai luo zhong)** (12). In 726, Emperor Xuan zong rode up to the top of Tai shan and down again, without feeling the slightest fatigue. His mount, a white mule, died mysteriously a few minutes after accomplishing its work; the Emperor gave it the title of general, and ordered a solemn burial. Next comes the **Tower of the Ten Thousand Immortals (Wan xian lou)** (13), which spans the path, built in 1620 and restored in 1953. Higher up on the right stands a former Taoist convent, called the **Temple of the Goddess of the Great Bear (Dou mu gong)** (14), which has also been restored. Statues of the goddess and a train of forty constellations, all deities, used to stand inside it. Another hall contained a Buddha. After the arch known as the **Taoist Gao's Bridge (Gao lao qiao)** (15), the path goes to the right.

At a fork a little further on (16), a little path leads to the **Valley of the Stone Sutra** (Shi jing yu) (17) on the right. The **Diamond Sutra (Jin gang jing)** is engraved in beautiful characters on the rocky side of the valley.

The inscription dates from the Wu ping period (570–576) of the Northern Qi dynasty. An unknown scholar of the Ming dynasty carved a paragraph from the Confucian treatise *Great Learning (Da xue)* beneath the Buddhist text.

On the right hand side of the main path is a rock called the **Cliff where the Horses are left to Rest (Xie ma ya)** (18), as the rock used to form a shelter under which the horses could be led. Higher up, alongside some stone steps, a stone archway marks the place where the Song Emperor Zhen zong had to dismount from his horse. Three characters on the pediment: *hui ma ling* mean the "summit from which the horses turn back" (19). The **Second Celestial Gate** above it **(Er tian men)** (20) is the half-way mark. Several temples stand round about, among them the **Temple of He Who Heightens Happiness (Zeng fu miao)** (21). "Among the deities who form the court of *T'ai chan*, one is responsible for increasing happiness and the other for lessening it. The temple is no doubt dedicated to the first of the two". The path then turns west round the mountainside; this stretch is called the *kuai huo san li*, "the three *li* full of pleasure" (22). A large pointed rock on the left is inscribed with the three words *Zhan yun jian*, "the sword which cuts through the cloud".

A bridge, the **Step over the Clouds Bridge (Yun bu qiao)** spans a stream flowing down from a waterfall (23), and the path begins to climb once more. To the right is the **Esplanade of the Imperial Tent (Yu zhang ping)** (24), where Emperor Zhen zong is said to have broken his climb. Then, above the Rock which came from the Air (Fei lai shi) (25), is the Five Pine Pavilion (Wu song ting) (26), restored and enlarged in 1956.

The terrace, in the shade of three big pine trees, is a delightful resting-place. "The five pine trees which received the title of 'grand official' must have been there, as the triumphal arch a little lower down recalls; it is inscribed with the characters *Wou ta fou song* (wu da fu song), and popular belief has interpreted this as meaning 'the five pines which received the title of grand official' since the *T'ang* at least. This is based on a mistranslation, however; the only possible translation is 'the pine tree which received the title of fifth degree officer'. In the *Historical Records* by *Sseu-ma Ts'ien* (Si ma Qian), the author tells how, in 219 B.C., when Emperor *Ts'in che houang ti* (Qin shi Huang di) climbed *T'ai chan*, he was overtaken by a violent storm; he sheltered under a tree, and to show his gratitude, he conferred on it the title of *wou ta fou*, 'grand officer of the fifth degree'."

The **Cave Facing the South (Chao yang dong)** (27) is to the left, a little higher up, with a little shrine dedicated to the Princess of the Coloured Clouds, known as the Hall of the Princess (Yuan jun dian) (28). Two poems by Emperor Qian long in praise of the cave are engraved on a rock on the other side of the path, and as the characters are colossal, at least three feet across, the rock is called the **Stele a Hundred Thousand Feet High (Wan zhang bei)** (29).

On a level with the Pine Tree Mountain opposite (Dui song shan) (30), a turning in the path suddenly

After The *Tai shan*, Monograph on a Chinese cult, by Edouard Chavannes (Paris, Leroux 1910). The numbers refer to the description given in the text.

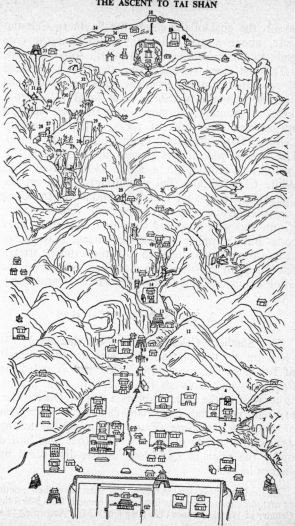

reveals the goal of the climb, the Southern Celestial
Gate, above a dry and rocky landscape; the gate
leads to the mountain top. It is still some way off.

The last steep stretch before the top is heralded
by an little triumphal arch, the **Arch from which one
rises to Immortality (Sheng xian fang)** (31). From
there, a monumental stone staircase rises straight
up between two walls of rocks, with the **Southern
Celestial Gate** silhouetted against the sky at the top.
The tourist was always carried up and down this
precipitous last lap in a sedan chair before. The
White Clouds Cave (Bai yun dong) (32) is on the
right of the steps; the clouds mentioned in the *Gong
yang* commentary on the *Spring and Autumn Annals*
(Chun qiu) were supposed to come from here: "They
come out, bumping against the stones; they gather
in less time than it takes to turn the hand or stretch
the finger; in less than two mornings, they cover the
whole empire with rain" (from Chavannes' translation).

3. The Summit of Tai shan

The **Southern Celestial Gate (Nan tian men)** (33)
gives on to the plateau stretching to the summit
of Tai shan. The upper storey of the gate is called the
Pavilion which Touches the Sky (Mo tian ge). A
stone west of the building bears a text by Du Ren jie,
a Yuan poet and statesman, called the *Inscription
of the Celestial Gate* (Tian men ming), protesting
against the society of his day. The stone was buried
under the reign of Qian long and re-discovered by
chance in 1956.

All the lesser peaks on the top of Tai shan have their poetic
or mythological names. One is called the **Summit from which the
Country of Wu can be seen (Wu guan feng)** (34). "According to a

traditional story which *Wang Tch'ong* (Wang Chong, 27–97 A.D.) tells in the *chou hiu* section (shu xu, Chapter IV) of his work *Louen heng* (Lun heng), Confucius climbed *T'ai chan* (Tai shan) with *Yen Yuan* (Yan Yuan); when he was looking south-east from the top of the mountain, Confucius caught sight of a white horse tied up at the Tch'ang gate (Chang) of the capital of *Wou* (Wu); he called *Yen Yuan* to him and pointing out what he wanted to show him, he asked: 'Can you see the *Tch'ang* gate of the capital of *Wou* (Wu)?' 'Yes, I can,' replied Yen Yuan. Confucius then asked: 'What is there outside the gate?' The other replied: 'Something that looks like a piece of silk tied to it.' Confucius touched his eyes and made him see it clearly. But, as they both went down the mountain, Yen Yuan's hair turned grey, his teeth fell out, and he died an early death as a result of the effort, which had been too much for him. *Wang Tch'ong* makes fun of the story and gives abundant proof of the absurdity of claiming to see the capital of *Wou*, which was then *Sou-tcheou-sou* (Su zhou), in *Kiang-fou* (Jiang su), from the top of *T'ai chan*."

A stone path and steps lead to the **Temple of the Princess of the Coloured Clouds (Bi xia gong, or Bi xia ci)** (35). The **Temple of Confucius (Kong zi miao)** (36) is on the left before the path to the temple. "The scholars did not think of building a temple to Confucius on *T'ai chan* before the *wan-li* period (1573–1619) of the Ming dynasty; the temple was rebuilt in 1714." A square terrace below it, used as an observatory, was also built during the Wan li period (37). The Temple of the Princess of the Coloured Clouds is below the highest peak; it is the largest shrine to this deity on Tai shan. "The goddess' temple on the top of *T'ai chan* is still the centre of attraction for all those who come to make the pilgrimage to the top of the sacred mountain every year; the Emperors themselves share in this devotion, and from 1759 until our own day it has been the custom for the Emperor to send an envoy on the eighteenth day of the fourth month to make an offering to the princess." The foundation of the shrine dates from the Song.

All the buildings have been carefully restored since 1949. The entrance gives on to the lower courtyard, surrounded by high walls to shield it from the wind, containing five halls. The southernmost one used to be a stage. The northern building leads to the upper courtyard. The three temples here were used for the worship of the princess and her two acolytes. A four-sided pavilion stands in the middle of the courtyard, with a double roof of yellow glazed tiles. It used to contain a richly dressed statue of the goddess, before which the pilgrims used to prostrate themselves and present their offerings. The main temple was the hall at the far end. Two bronze steles dating from 1615 and 1626 stand one on each side of the central pavilion. They were damaged by the fire of 1740. All the buildings except three pavilions in the upper courtyard of the temple are covered with iron tiles, as they stand up better than ordinary tiles to the high winds on the mountain top.

The **peak of Tai shan** is called the Summit of the Celestial Pillar or the Celestial Pillar (Tian zhu feng) (38). The summit itself is enclosed in a temple dedicated to the Taoist deity known as the Jade Emperor (Yu huang ding). An octagonal balustrade in the courtyard surrounds the highest point of the mountain. A little shrine stands behind it, with iron tiles to stand up to the wind. It contains a magnicent gilded statue of the god, with his insignia of rank in his hands (gui). "He wears a drooping moustache, a little goatee beard and long, thin black side whiskers. His hat is of the *mien* (mian) kind, a sort of rectangular board with thirteen red threads hanging from it, before and behind, with green, red and blue balls on them; in front, the fringe hangs down to the wearer's eyes. A tablet in front of the statue bears the inscription: "image of the great god, jade sovereign, Emperor of the Heavens (Yu huang shang di da tian zun)." Four other deities stood round the walls, on which were frescoes portraying the eight immortals (to the east) and five old men contemplating mystic diagrams (to the west).

A four-sided column of stone stands in front of the entrance to the temple; it is nearly 15 feet high, ends in a capital, and is called the **Stele with No Inscription (Wu zi bei).** "It is traditionally supposed that this is the stele erected in 219 B.C. by *T'sin Che huang ti* (Qin shi Huang di); the inscription, the text of which was recorded by *Seu-ma Ts'ien* (Si ma Qian), is said to have been effaced completely by the inclemencies of the weather during its two thousand years on the mountain-top." Modern Chinese historians say that even if the stele was not erected by Qin shi Huang di, it is not later than the Eastern Han. It is now classed as a historical monument.

Below the summit to the east, a wall of rock covered with characters can be seen; it is the **Stele Engraved on the Rock (Mo ya bei)** (39). The inscription was composed and written by the Tang Emperor Xuan zong, when he performed the great *feng* sacrifice on the peak of the mountain in 726. It was later engraved on a rectangle of rock measuring 29 feet by 16 feet, in characters 7 inches high and 8 inches wide. They used to be gilded, but the gold has been worn away by weather and time.

The four characters *ji tai shan ming* head the inscription: "Eulogy in memory of Tai shan". Edouard Chavannes translated the text into French (loc. cit., p. 318). It begins as follows: "For fourteen years I have occupied the high position of Emperor. I am however troubled by my lack of virtue; I am ignorant of perfect reason. The duties which I have to fulfil are hard to fulfil; the calm which I should preserve is hard to preserve. Now I know not whether I have committed an offence against the gods or the people and my heart is tossed on the floods as though I were crossing a great river. Thanks to the protection granted to me by the Emperor above and thanks to the riches accumulated by the sovereigns who preceded me, my chief ministers and the crowd of my officials combine their efforts to achieve imperial perfection (.....). My officers of all ranks have deliberated together and as one man they have exhorted me to perform the *fong* (feng) and *chan* (shan) sacrifices, saying that to pay one's respect to one's father is the highest of all acts of filial piety, saying that to address a declaration to the Sky is the most august of all ceremonies. As celestial tokens had arrived and as men's hopes were at their height, the urgent prayers (of my officials) were unending and my constant refusals could not be maintained. So with a few of my ministers, I examined the *Yu tien* (Yu dian) chapter and I explained the rules of the *Han*. Then I deployed the power of my six imperial armies; I made the nine regions tremble with fear; the colours and standards were drawn up; horses and soldiers were in silence; and what majesty! what a beautiful sight! what pomp! Thus I arrived at *T'ai tsong* (Tai zong, i.e. Tai shan), all was as it should be." The inscription—a long one—ends with an eight-stanza eulogy, the last line of which is as follows: "I have engraved my sentiments on this steep rock—to announce them publicly to the multitude of the mountain's peaks."

The **sacrifice known as feng,** which played such an important role in the history of Tai shan, consisted of a solemn message, in which the Emperor thanked the Sky for the continued existence of his dynasty and for the glory of his reign. It was engraved on five jade tablets. During the ceremony the tablets were carefully covered with a skilful arrangement of stones to protect them from the assaults of nature. Chavannes concludes that as the tablets were neither buried nor burned, as usually happened in the worship of the deities of the earth and the sky, Tai shan was considered here as a messenger to whom the tablets were entrusted so that he could transmit them to the Sky.

When Chavannes visited the place in 1907, the huge inscription (39) was partly hidden by a temple which used to stand in front of it, but which no longer exists today: the Eastern Peak Temple (Dong yue miao).

A little to the east, behind the ruins of an old temple (40) a stele used to stand (it may still be there) which bore the characters *Kong zi xiao tian xia chu*, "the place where Confucius found the world small" A passage in Mencius says: "When Confucius climbed Tai shan, he found that the world looked small. In the same way, he who has contemplated the sea finds it hard to think much of other waters; he who has frequented the stage finds it hard to think much of the words of other people."

Nearby is the **Summit for Contemplating the Sun (Ri guan feng)** (41). "From this peak, with its view down the valley, which cleaves a way down the side of T'ai chan to the north-east, the sunrise is at its most spectacular." It is a little lower than the Summit of the Celestial Pillar (38). "Here, in 1008, Emperor *Tchen tsong* (Zhen zong) performed the *fong* ceremony, as was proved by the discovery, in 1747, of two jade boxes on the same spot, one of which contained 17 slips of jade; each slip has one line of characters on it, forming the text of one of the prayers addressed to the deity in 1008. In 1482, jade slips dating from 1008 had already been found, but the Emperor had ordered them to be re-buried."

4. Monuments at the Foot of Mount Tai shan, outside the Walls of Tai an

The only ones mentioned here are those round **Hao li shan** (Hao li Hill), just over a mile south-west

24

of the town of Tai an. The *shan* sacrifice to the earth
used to be performed near this hill; the ritual was the
same as for the *feng* sacrifice on the top of Tai
shan. The entrance to the lower world was supposed
to be here, connected with the sacrifice to the earth. It
was traditionally believed that the souls of the dead
gathered here before going on to the kingdom of the
dead.

Chavannes gives a detailed description of the monuments which he visited when he was here in 1907. The
Temple of Supernatural Fulfilment (Ling ying gong)
stands near the hill; it was built in 1611, and dedicated to the Princess of the Coloured Clouds. "A colossal statue of the Princess of the Coloured Clouds
stands in the main building; her head-dress is that of
the three birds with outstretched wings; a lacquered
statue in front of her acts as a reflection. In front of
her stand two groups of two standing statues, depicting the young man and the young woman, both vir-
gins, who are her servants; two Bodhisattvas, one on
each side of the room, sitting on lotus flowers, have
standing statues of the young man and the young
woman in front of them; all the statues are in bronze,
and beautifully made; the standing ones are between
eight and a half and nine feet high." The two Bodhisattvas, unusual in a Taoist shrine, represent the mother
of the Ming Emperor Shen zong, Empress Xiao ding,
who died in 1614, and Empress Xiao zhun, who gave
birth to the future Emperor Zhuang lie in 1610, and
died soon afterwards. The building behind the main
hall is used for "the worship of the goddess of *T'ai
chan*, under the name of the Holy Mother (Sheng mu);
she is shown with the goddess of good eyesight on one
side of her and the goddess who promotes childbirht
on the other. Against the eastern wall stands a beauti-

ful bronze statue of the Princess of the Coloured Clouds which, during the *wan-li* period (1573–1619), was erected in the *Kin k'iue Pavilion* (Jin que) on the top of the mountain by Emperor *Chen tsong* (Shen zong); this pious act was intended to save his mother from blindness. The statue was then moved down to the foot of the mountain and the one which can be seen today is the same one."

The foot of the hill itself is enclosed within a vast wall. The hill is in two parts, called She shou shan and Hao li shan; the second used to be called Gao li. The *History of the Western Han (Qian han shu)* tells how the Han Emperor Wu performed the *shan* sacrifice there in 104 B.C. At the beginning of this century, Chavannes wrote: "The popular belief that the souls of the dead live in *Hao-li* is still alive; it is noticeable as soon as one enters the enclosure through the gate bearing the words *Hao-li-chan;* immediately after the stage used for plays a veritable forest of funerary steles rises on either side, and particularly along the two avenues, marking the place where offerings are made to the parents of three dead generations (xi gu san dai zong qin xiang ji zhi chu); most of them are erected by all the inhabitants of one or several villages joined in a religious association, who pool their resources.

"At the end of the southernmost alley among the steles, a path leads north through a door guarded by two fierce guardians, one green and the other blue, to a fine, spacious building." It is the **Sen luo Hall (Sen luo dian).** "A colossal god sits there in a red niche; he has an air of awful majesty about him which is really moving; his face and hands are gilded: he holds a green *kouei* (gui) with a triangular constellation on it; two assistants stand before him, one on each side, a civil one and a military one; the western civil official holds a brush and a book entitled 'General Register of Births and Deaths'; the eastern one carries a scroll; the two soldiers are armed, one with a lance, the other with a halberd; the ten hells are depicted round the walls (...). Seventy-five judgement seats line the walls of the courtyard, with portrayals of the sufferings inflicted."

Two other shrines nearby are dedicated to other deities who judge of merits and defects: the **Pavilion of the Iron General (Tie jiang jun lou)** and the **Hall of Yan luo (Yan luo dian)**.

A last enclosure, higher up on the hill, contains the **Hall of the Ten Kings (Shi wang dian)**. The ten kings, whose statues are in the hall, are the kings of hell. Other deities are there as well. Leaving the courtyard, the highest point, to the north-east, is She shou shan Hill, which gives an excellent view over the Tai an plain and Tai shan. The *shan* sacrifice was celebrated here in 666 and 725, under the Tang dynasty, and in 1008, under the Song.

QU FU

Qu fu is the town of Confucius. It is built on the spot where he lived and taught; all its temples and its monuments are dedicated to him, or were built in memory of him or his disciples. Throughout the history of the Chinese Empire, from the Han to the Qing, Qu fu was protected like a holy place; the direct descendants of the master were its guardians and administrators, from one generation to the next right up to the 20th century. Apart from all the memories linked with Confucius himself as a historic person, which fill the town, Qu fu

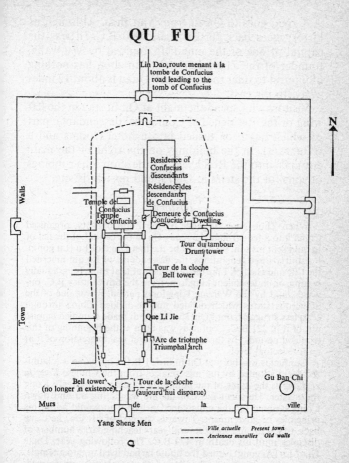

QU FU

Lin Dao, route menant à la
tombe de Confucius
road leading to the
tomb of Confucius

N

Walls

Residence of
Confucius
descendants

Résidence des
descendants
de Confucius

Temple de
Confucius
Temple
of Confucius

Demeure de Confucius
Confucius Dwelling

Tour du tambour
Drum tower

Tour de la cloche
Bell tower

Town

Que Li Jie

Arc de triomphe
Triumphal arch

Bell tower
(no longer in existence)

Tour de la cloche
(aujourd'hui disparue)

Gu Ban Chi

Murs   de   la   ville

Yang Sheng Men

—————— Ville actuelle   Present town
- - - - - - Anciennes murailles Old walls

also represents the expression of what the cult of Confucius meant to imperial China.

A road goes to Qu fu from **Yan zhou.** Although its history goes back further than 1000 B.C. (it was the capital of one of the nine fiefs founded by Wu wang, founder of the Zhou dynasty), Yan zhou has nothing of interest to offer to the tourist. Qu fu is about 12 miles away, to the east.

Visitors who spend the night at Qu fu stay in the left wing of the Residence of Confucius' descendants, part of which has been turned into a hotel (rooms and a restaurant). In the buildings on the right of the main entrance into the Residence, a little shop sells rubbings of some of the steles at Qu fu, and postcards, etc.

History

When Zhou gong, founder of the Zhou dynasty, organised China into a feudal state, he made Qu fu the capital of the fief of Lu and sent his son, Bo qin, to be the first Duke of Lu (Lu gong). For thirty-three generations, the descendants of Bo qin inherited the title and the fief. Like the other fiefs at that time, Lu gradually became an independent kingdom, from the 6th century B.C. onwards, and by the Warring Kingdoms period, it was one of the numerous states which divided and re-divided China through ceaseless struggles, until Qin shi Huang di made a unified empire out of it in 221 B.C. Confucius was born at the beginning of this troubled period. His thought was the first real expression of it at an intellectual level.

Confucius was born at Qu fu in 551 B.C.; his name is a latinized form adopted by the missionaries from the Chinese *Kong fu zi*. *Kong* is the name of the family; *fu zi* means "master": Kong the master. He spent most of his life wandering up and down China looking for the enlightened prince who would adopt his principles of government. Towards the end of his life, he came back to Qu fu, and spent several years teaching large numbers of disciples until his death in 479 B.C. The following year, Duke Ai of Lu (Ai gong) turned the house he had lived in into a temple. During the centuries which followed, the temple was transformed, enlarged, surrounded by several others, and rebuilt or restored several times.

In 154 B.C., the Han Emperor Jing di made his son Liu Yu prince of Lu, granting him the title of Prince Gong of Lu (Lu gong wang). A spacious palace was built at Qu fu, the Lu ling guang dian, which was very well known; a few remains of it can be seen today. Under the Song the name of the town was changed to Xian yuan, "Source of Immortals". It regained its former name under the Jin, in 1129.

In its present form, Qu fu dates from the Ming. Armed bands attacked and sacked the temple of Confucius and the residence of the Kong family in 1513, so walls were built to encircle it; the work lasted from 1522 to 1567. Even today, it is obvious that the town was built round the temple and the residence. The temple enclosure (it covers nearly 49 acres) cuts through almost the whole town, from north to south.

A teachers' training college was founded at Qu fu after the liberation, in memory of Confucius, called Qu fu shi fan xue yuan.

Description

The most important monuments at Qu fu are the **Temple of Confucius,** the **Residence of Confucius' Descendants** and **Confucius' Tomb.** All three are classed as historical monuments. The first two are worth a visit of at least two or three hours. The tomb is outside the town, and can be reached on foot or by car. Other monuments in the area are not easy to see: the Tomb of the Emperor Shao hao, the Tomb of Confucius' Father and Mother, the sculpture on the Nine Dragon Mountain and the Temple of Confucius on Mount Ni shan. Visitors interested in archaeology will be anxious to see the **Remains of the Ancient Capital of Lu (Jiu lu cheng yi zhi)** which date from the Warring States period and are classed as a historical monument, and the remains of the Lu ling guang dian Palace, which are Han.

A. Inside the Town

The **Temple of Confucius (Kong miao** or **Zhi sheng miao)** is the finest, most famous and richest of the monuments at Qu fu, from every point of view. The enclosure covers a large area of the western part of the town. Several gates lead into it: the western one is inscribed *dao guan gu jin*, "the *dao* (principle) dominates the past and the future"; the eastern one bears the characters *de mou tian di*, "virtue equals heaven and earth"; the southern one is called Ling xing men. *Ling xing* is the old name for a star in the Great Bear, which symbolises the highest literary virtues; the genius of Confucius is compared with it here. This is the main gate of the temple; it stands due north of the south gate of the town, known as the "Gate of looking towards the Stage" (Yang sheng men).

The temple enclosure is full of old evergreens, some of which are said to date from the Han dynasty; a stream runs between marble parapets, spanned by three gently rounded bridges. On the left, a little way further inside, stands a pavilion containing two great **stone men** dating from the Eastern Han (1st and 2nd centuries A.D.). They were discovered south of Qu fu, and were brought to the temple in 1953. Each one bears the title of the person portrayed, in *zhuan* characters: an official to the left, a guard to the right.

The central alley crosses the stream and goes through three gateways with pottery, sculpture and **bas-relief carvings** dating from the Han, on either side, all found in the region of Qu fu. Some of the bas-relief carvings are extremely interesting. An impressive **collection of steles** stands near the third gateway; it contains more Han steles than exist anywhere else in China—there are 16 all together, and the oldest one dates from 56 B.C. (the stele of Prince Xiao of Lu, Lu xiao wang bei). Another dates from the Huang chu period (220–227) of the Wei. Others date from the Northern Wei and the Sui. They have great artistic as well as historical value; some of them are housed in little shelters built exactly to measure. The Cheng hua period stele (1465–1488) is nearly 20 feet high, and stands on the back of a tortoise. It was built in 1468, by order of the Emperor, to commemorate the restoration of the temple. The temple enclosure contains over 1000 steles altogether, most of them engraved in memory of a restoration of the temple, a great ceremony or the planting of a tree. Visitors have also left their impressions engraved on some of them.

The first large temple after the three gateways is the **Gui wen ge: Great Pavilion of the Constellation of Scholars,** a beautiful wooden building dating from 1190 (Jin dynasty). It has other names: the Pavilion of Libraries (Cang shu lou) or the Palace for practising Ceremonies (Xi yi dian). It contains some magnificent old editions. It was used by the priests belonging to the temple for practising the complicated ceremonies performed in spring and autumn in honour of Confucius. A poem *(fu)* engraved in the stone at the foot of the pavilion was written by the great Ming calligrapher, Li Dong yang, in praise of its beauty *(Gui wen ge fu)*. It is about 85 feet high, and has three roofs; a gallery with pillars runs round the whole building between the first and second roofs.

Behind the Gui wen ge stand 13 identical pavilions, all with double roofs of glazed tiles. They were built to house **imperial steles (yu bei).** The oldest of them date from the Jin and the Yuan. The steles themselves date from the Tang, Song, Jin, Yuan, Ming and Qing dynasties. An avenue runs across the width of the enclosure between the pavilions; it is one of the busiest streets in the town, and is always open to the public. To the left is the Gate of the Spectacle of the Virtues (Guan de men); to the right is the Gate of the Search after Purity (Yu cui men), which leads out of the enclosure, just beside the Residence of Confucius' Descendants.

North of the avenue, the temples are arranged on three parallel and independent axes. The Gate of He who Heralds the Sage (Qi sheng men) leads into the western part. "The King who Heralds the Sage" (Qi sheng wang) was the title conferred on Confucius' father in 1330. The first hall after the gate used to house the musical instruments used during the ceremonies, hence its name of the Hall of Silks and Metals (Jin si tang), which means "stringed and percussion instruments". The temple dedicated to Confucius' father is further north: the Temple of He who Heralds the Sage (Qi sheng dian). Two white marble columns with dragons twined round them, like the ones in front of the Great Temple of Confucius, stand in front of it. A little shrine behind the temple, called the Hall of Private Appartments (Qin dian), is dedicated to Confucius' mother.

The central axis is the most important of the three. The Gate of Great Perfection (Da cheng men) and several side gates lead into it, into a vast courtyard surrounded by galleries. On the right, just inside, stands **Confucius' tree,** which he is supposed to have planted, now sheltered by a little pavilion. The Chinese name for the species is *kuai*, and it resembles a juniper-tree. A Ming stele next to it bears the words *xian shi shou zhi kuai*, "kuai planted with his own hands by the old sage". It is said that the roots of the tree have never ceased to live, and that they produced the present trunk from 1732 onwards.

The pavilion in the centre of the courtyard is an unusual one (the upper roof has triangular pediments on all four sides); it stands on the spot where Confucius

TEMPLE DE CONFUCIUS
TEMPLE OF CONFUCIUS

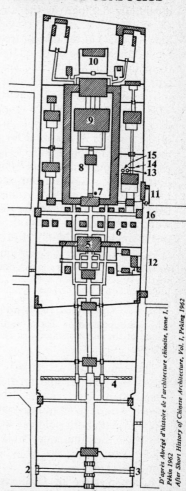

1 Main gateway
2 West gateway
3 East gateway
4 Brook
5 Gui Wen Ge
6 Imperial steles
7 Confucius' Tree
8 Xing Tan
9 Great Temple of Confucius
10 Sheng Ji Dian
11 Confucius' Dwelling
12 Que Li Jie
13 Confucius' Well
14 Lu wall
15 Pavilion
16 Yu Cui Men (Gateway)

D'après Abrégé d'histoire de l'architecture chinoise, tome I, Pékin 1962

After Short History of Chinese Architecture, Vol. I, Peking 1962 taught his disciples in the shade of an apricot tree *(xing)*, and it bears the two characters **Xing tan: Terrace (or altar) of the apricot tree.** The legend that Confucius taught in the shade of an apricot tree comes from the philosophic and polemical work *Zhuang zi* (Chuang tzu), probably written in about 300 B.C.

The **Great Temple of Confucius** stands in this courtyard **(Da cheng dian).** A vast terrace with a marble parapet, built on two levels, stretches along the front of the temple; it was used for ceremonies (dance and music). The temple is 84 feet high and 153 feet (9 bays) wide. The roof is double. Ten big marble columns support the lower roof in front, each hewn out of a single block of stone, with magnificent bas-relief dragons twisting round them. Inside the hall, 12 pillars of *nan* wood (a highly prized wood peculiar to China), each one a single trunk, support the roof structure.

The first Temple of Confucius, built a few years after his death, was only three bays wide and was near the Terrace of the Apricot tree. A large temple was built under the Tang, in 739. In 1018, under the Song, another new temple was built, this time on the site of the present one. It was 7 bays wide. Two more were added under the Ming in 1499. Under the Qing, it was struck by lightning and burned down. The present temple was built in 1724; it is one of the finest examples of classic architecture under the Manchu.

The temple is particularly interesting because it shows the cultural and religious aspect of Confucianism, often neglected for the moral and intellectual aspect. Although Confucianism was first and foremost a philosophy, both political and social, the philosophy was backed or illustrated by a solemn, elaborate cult, whose high priest was the Emperor himself, dating from the Han.

A large **statue of Confucius** stands under a rich canopy inside the temple; he carries the insignia of "scholarly duties". This term is used to indicate everything connected with "culture", *wen*, in the Chinese state, which included writing, the study of the classics, historiography, diplomacy, etiquette and rites; its traditional opposite was *wu*, used to indicate the other category of duties equally essential to the state: military duties. The two categories, *wen* and *wu*, were an indivisible pair in Chinese thought, both complementary and contradictory. This statue of Confucius was used as a model for all other statues of him. A tablet in front of it bears the characters *zhi sheng xian shi kong zi shen wei (the sacred tablet of the very wise master Kong)*. It is the type of tablet used in the worship of the ancestors. The characters are meant to suggest the presence of the departed person. Under the Ming and the Qing, each prefecture or sub-prefecture had a temple of Confucius (Wen miao) containing a similar tablet. The temples had no priests; the officials performed the ceremonies. All this reflects the extremely close ties between Confucianism and the politico-administrative system of imperial China.

Statues of the four companions (si pei) stand right and left of the central statue, under two other canopies. To the left are Kong Ji, Confucius' grandson and the author of two of the four great Confucian classics (see Tomb of Kong Ji, p. 768) and Mencius. Mencius was born in the little kingdom of Zou, where the little town of Zou xian now stands, south of Qu fu; he lived from 372 to 289 B.C. He continued Confucius' teaching, and after him became the first great philosopher of the Confucian line. His philosophical dialogues constitute the fourth of the four classics, after the *Analects (Lun Yu)* and the two treatises by Kong Ji. Mencius is the latinized form taken from *Meng zi* by the European missionaries; the Chinese means

"Meng the master" (Meng is the name of his family)
On the right stand Yan Hui and Zeng Sen, the two
disciples whom Confucius loved best of all, and who
appear frequently in the *Analects*. **Statues of the twelve
disciples** are lined up further on. They represent eleven
of Confucius' disciples and the great philosopher Zhu
Xi (1130–1200), who created a richer and more orderly
system of Confucianism under the Song, which was
later taken up and adopted by orthodox Confucians
under the Ming and the Qing.

The principal hall of the temple and the galleries
contain **altars** dedicated to Confucius, his disciples,
and to all those who won the right to be worshipped in
such a high place, either through their outstanding
qualities or by their commentaries on the classics. The
richly carved wooden altar in front of Confucius'
statue dates from the Qing; it was used by the Emperor
when he came to offer sacrifices, and the five sacrificial
vases for wine (wu gong) date from 85 A.D. (Han).
Four are of bronze, one of porcelain; two of the bronze
ones represent animals, a bull and an elephant, and
the third and fourth ones are called "vase of clouds and
thunderbolt" and "vase of the mountains". Another
set of sacrificial vessels is kept in the temple, a set of
ten (shi gong) dating from the Shang and Zhou dynasties. One of them is in the shape of an animal, and five
have inscriptions on them. The yellow sunshade (?)
with dragons on it was given by a Qing Emperor.

The **musical instruments** are perhaps the most interesting of all the exhibits in the temple. All the great
ceremonies, performed on the fourth day *(ding ri)* of
the second, fifth, eighth and eleventh months to mark
the beginning of the seasons, and known as the *si da
ding*, and on Confucius' birthday each year, were
accompanied by dancing and music. Dozens of people

took part, dressed in magnificent robes, with hats rather like mortarboards; the sacred dances were executed on the terrace in front of the temple. Each person played an instrument, either percussion, wind or string. On each side, others played the heavy instruments, the great *sheng*, the bells, the musical stones. Some of the instruments in the temple were traditionally reserved for the cult of Confucius alone and are rarely to be seen elsewhere (the mouth organs, the *sheng* of various shapes, with a long, vertical mouthpiece, elegantly curved at the top, the pan-pipes set in wood, etc.). The bronze bells and musical stones *(qing)*, of which there are several sets, are all extremely old, like the rest of the instruments in the collection. The *Analects* and other ancient works dealing with Confucius' era show that they played an important part in the life of the court and in religious ceremonies. Confucius himself played the lute *(se)*. It is a flat instrument with 25 cords, which were plucked in various different ways; with the *qin*, another form of lute, it is the noblest of all instruments in Chinese classical music. The Japanese *koto* is a descendant of it. A *se* is on show among the other instruments.

The Confucian ceremonies lost much of their splendour after the fall of the empire, and were soon abandoned. They were revived briefly during the Japanese occupation, and some could still be seen after the war. The following passage from *Origins and Development of the State Cult of Confucius*, by J.K. Shryock (New York, 1932) quoted by Needham in *Science and Civilisation in China*, vol. 2, p. 32 (Cambridge University Press, 1956), gives some idea of what they were like up to the beginning of this century:

"The account of the rubrics of the service, as it existed in the 14th century A.D., is largely devoid of colour, whereas it is in

reality one of the most impressive rituals that has ever been devised. The silence of the dark hour, the magnificent sweep of the
temple lines, with eaves curving up towards the stars, the aged
trees standing in the courtyard, and the deep note of the bell,
make the scene unforgettable to one who has seen it even in its
decay. In the days of Khubilai the magnificence and solemnity
of the sacrifice would have required the pen of a Coleridge to do
it justice. The great drum boomed upon the night, the twisted
torches of the attendants threw uncertain shadows across the
lattice scrolls, and the silk embroideries on the robes of the officials gleamed from the darkness... Within the hall, the ox lay
with its head towards the image of Confucius. The altar was
ablaze with dancing lights, which were reflected from the gilded
carving of the enormous canopy above. Figures moved slowly
through the hall, the celebrant entered, and the vessels were presented towards the silent statue of the Sage, the 'Teacher of Ten
Thousand Generations'. The music was grave and dignified...
Outside in the court the dancers struck their attitudes, moving
their wands tipped with pheasant feathers in unison as the chant
rose and fell. It would be hard to imagine a more solemn or
beautiful ceremonial." "Shryock adds, however, his conviction
that no one would have been more surprised at it, and perhaps
even shocked, than Master Khung himself." (J. Needham).

The eastern side gallery, on the right of the temple
courtyard, contains a rich collection of steles, calligraphy and other things. The temple to the north of
the Temple of Confucius is dedicated to his wife; it is
five bays wide. It has no statue, only a tablet; it houses
a collection of works of art now (porcelain, statuettes,
etc.).

The last building on the central axis is the **Hall of
Memories of the Sage (Sheng ji dian).** Four great
blocks of stone bearing one character each stand at the
entrance: *wan shi shi biao.* They mean "master (shi)
and model (biao) of 10,000 (wan) generations (shi)";
Kang xi paid this tribute to Confucius in 1687. The
characters are engraved to reproduce the exact brush-
strokes which the Emperor made when he wrote them.
The hall contains the **legend of Confucius:** a series of

150 pictures engraved on stone, each one accompanied
by a short text, tracing the events of his life, his wanderings throughout China, and countless marvellous tales
about him which have been accumulated through the
ages. These pictures, which are often reproduced in
China and abroad, are in fact copies of an older set
(they date from 1592 only); the oldest known series
dates from the 14th century. Other engravings on show
there are reproductions of pictures whose originals
disappeared some time ago: a portrait of Confucius
with his disciple Yan zi, engraved in 1118 from a painting by Wu Dao zi (Tang, 8th century); Confucius and
his disciples, after a painting by Gu Kai zhi (Eastern
Jin, 4th century), engraved in 1095; a Ming portrait
of Confucius in his official robes of minister of justice.

To see round the eastern axis of the temple, the visit-
or returns to the avenue cutting through the enclosure,
the Succession of the Sage Gate (Cheng sheng men) to
the right of the gate to the central axis. Inside the gate
on the right stands a building known as the **Dwelling
of Confucius (Kong zi zhu zhai),** because the philosopher
lived on a house on the same site 25 centuries ago. It
was then called the "tower district" *(que li)* after an
old tower *(que)* which stood there. The road running
alongside the east of the temple enclosure is called the
Tower District Street (Que li jie), and a triumphal arch
bears the characters *que li.*

Next comes a hall 5 bays wide called the **Hall of
Rites and Poetry (Shi li tang).** The name comes from
an anecdote recorded in the *Analects.* When someone
asked Confucius' son whether his father had ever
given him any special teaching, he replied: "No, never.
One day, he was standing there, alone, and I was
crossing the courtyard with short, rapid steps (a sign
of respect). He said to me: 'Have you studied poetry

(the *Shi jing*)?' I replied: 'Not yet.' He then said: 'Without studying poetry, it is impossible to learn to express oneself.' I therefore retired to study poetry. Another time, he was again standing there when I was crossing the courtyard with short, rapid steps. He asked me: 'Have you studied the rites?' I replied: 'Not yet.' He then said: 'Without studying the rites, it is impossible to strengthen one's character.' I therefore retired to study the rites." (16,3). The scene is said to have taken place where the temple now stands.

Confucius' Well is behind the Hall of Rites and Poetry, with a stele bearing the characters **Kong zi gu jing** beside it; it is surrounded by a parapet dating from the Ming, which gives out a clear sound when the east side is hit. Nearby, a stele commemorates an important event in the history of Chinese thought. It has two characters on it: **Lu bi: the Wall of Lu.** When Qin shi Huang di, the unifier of the empire, persecuted the followers of Confucius and burned their writings, Kong fu, the ninth descendant of Confucius, hid the Confucian books in a wall there. The texts were re-discovered by chance under the Han, when prince Gong of Lu had the wall knocked down to enlarge his palace. According to the legend, this is how the sacred texts were saved and handed down to posterity. It is a fact that the Confucian heritage was recovered in two ways after the fires to which Qin shi Huang di consigned the books: first through what the scholars who escaped the persecutions could remember of the texts, and later on by the discovery of texts which had been hidden to escape the disaster. The supporters of the two different ways formed rival schools (Gu wen and Jin wen), who remained at odds with each other until the Qing dynasty and carried on one of the most lasting scholastic disputes in the history of China,

Two other temples stand beyond the Wall of Lu: the first is dedicated to the five ancestors of Confucius (their statues are inside it); the second is a family temple (jia miao) where the tablets of all the members of the Kong family who distinguished themselves in one way or another are kept.

The **Residence of the Descendants of Confucius** is usually called **Kong fu,** residence of the Kong family, or Yan sheng gong fu, residence (fu) of the princes who are the Sage's heirs (yan sheng gong), or else Sheng fu, residence (of the descendants) of the sage. It is in the centre of the town, east of the Temple of Confucius. The main entrance gives on to the street going from the east gate of the temple to the drum tower (see the map of the town). It leads into a magnificent patrician mansion, a perfect example of traditional Chinese architecture, and of the great houses of the mandarins of ancient China; it gives a good idea of the immense power and wealth of the families of officials who were the pillars of the social and political structure of imperial China. The Kong family lived there until very recently. The 76th direct descendant of Confucius, Duke Kong De cheng, lived there before the war, and would receive people who came with a letter of introduction.

After the liberation, a curator was put in charge of the upkeep and study of the residence and everything in it: archives, paintings, works of art and objects used in the worship of Confucius, furniture and clothes. The parts of the residence open to visitors contain pictures, furniture, dinner services etc., all left in place, reconstituting the surroundings in which the great family lived at the end of the Qing dynasty. Clothes belonging to former members of the family are on show in several of the rooms.

History

Ever since the Han dynasty, when the leaders of China first looked to the teachings of Confucius to provide them with a system to form the basis of their power, to strengthen the state, and unify the country both morally and intellectually, they have honoured the sage's descendants with special treatment. Throughout all the dynasties from the Han to the Qing, the imperial favour shown them never failed and consequently the Kong family survived all the troubles which shook the rest of China over the two thousand years.

The family was ennobled under the Han, and new titles were added by each dynasty. When in the Kai yuan period (713–742) of the Tang dynasty, the title of Wen xuan wang was conferred posthumously on Confucius himself (it means "king of letters" or less literally "king who spreads culture"), his descendants bore the title of Wen xuan gong ("princes of letters"). Under the Song, they were given the title of Yan sheng gong ("princes and heirs of the sage"), which they kept through the centuries that followed. During the Tai ding period (1324–1328) of the Yuan dynasty, several ministries were created in the Kong fu. From then on, members of the Kong family presided over the temple ceremonies and administered their estates as the Emperor's officials. After the Ming dynasty came to power in 1368, orthodox Confucianism had more influence than ever before; the power of the Kong family was consequently strengthened and new privileges were granted. They were responsible for the civil, economic and financial administration of a vast estate, controlled the rites and ceremonies of the temple, kept the local archives, etc.... All the religious and civil duties arising from the running of the shrine and the offices connected with it fell to them: master of the rites, of the writings, of the seals, etc.... The Kong family residence became a sort of seat of local government, different from other local seats of government in that it was a direct dependancy of the court and owed it no taxes.

Miraculously sheltered from the vicissitudes of history, countless treasures were kept in the Kong fu and have survived to this day unharmed. Over 8,000 **sets of clothes** were found, stored in more than 100 trunks, dating from different periods, the oldest of them belonging to the Yuan dynasty (officials' head-dresses). Ceremonial robes worn by men and women under the Ming dynasty were found, alongside costumes worn by those taking part in the ceremonial dances of the cult of Confucius under the Qing, and those worn under Yuan Shi kai, when, anxious to prove his desire to restore the empire, he encouraged the cult of Confucius, which by this time was on the way out. Rich collections of ancient embroidery, silks and works of art of all kinds were also found.

The most precious treasure of all in the Kong fu, however, was without any doubt the **archives**. Elsewhere in China the records of the old houses dating from the imperial era were burned, scattered or sold off by weight to paper merchants; the records of the Kong family are almost completely intact, and the local history can be traced as far back as the Ming dynasty, over more than 500 years. They are divided into eight sections: 1. list and description of the temples and academies; restoration work done; list of the rites, musical instruments, etc. 2. administration of the estate, tenant farms, taxes due; 3. history of the Kong family and of about twenty families linked with it, several of whom claimed descent from Confucius' disciples (Yan, Hui); members of the family who were successful in the imperial examinations, transmission of the titles from one generation to the next, ceremonies performed in honour of Confucius; 4. civil administration of the estate and office, various trials; 5. several chronicles on the lives of the officials; 6. accounts of the profits realised from the Qu fu market, or from trade carried out directly by the Kong family; 7. chronicle of the events at court and in the empire; 8. genealogical questions, cases of exemption from *corvée*. These archives are full of information on the society and politics of Ming and Qing China, on the economy and development of Qu fu, and the tenant farming system; they contain information on the history of the local population, the evolution of the climate, floods, or changes in the course of rivers; they give details on the history of temples dedicated to Confucius, and of the life of the Kong family. They describe trials, marriages, sales of land. As they give a complete and concrete picture of Chinese life in a limited area, they are entirely different from the imperial archives preserved at Peking or the local chronicles compiled by provincial governors under the empire. They are unique in every respect. Just before the liberation of Qu fu, an official tried to flee with several hundred-weight of archives, but luckily he was caught before he could get far away.

Under the Song, the town was called Xian yuan, "Source of Immortals", and was outside the present town. No traces remain of the Song town and the first house of the Kong family. When the first Ming Emperor, Zhu Yuan zhang, came to the throne, Kong Ke jian, the 55th descendant of Confucius, went to see him at Nanking to obtain his favours. In 1378, a house was built by order of the Emperor on the site of the present Kong fu. In 1488, the temple and the residence were burned down, and rebuilt in 1504, again by order of the Emperor. But the ambition of the sage's descendants was not to be satisfied as easily as that, and between 1522 and 1567, they rebuilt their palace, giving an "imposing and orderly" air to the "countless buildings". The style and arrangement of the buildings have changed little since them. The buildings were restored under the Qing; the work was completed in 1844. Seven pavilions were burned down in 1884 and rebuilt in 1886. After that, the family's power declined; parts of the house deteriorated, and even fell down, as the family lacked the enormous sums of money needed to restore so large a house. When Duke Kong De cheng was married in 1935, however, it was repaired throughout and re-painted. Most of the paint inside the buildings dates from this time.

Description

All the buildings are centred round a north-south axis in the middle, about 360 yards long. A close study of the plan of the residence is most rewarding from the point of view of the history of Chinese architecture. The pavilions and buildings of a house like this were laid out according to elaborate rules, drawn up with reference to the *yin* and *yang* theory, the symbolism of the five elements and the five cardinal points, and points arising from the worship of the ancestors. Several peculiarities of the Kong residence pose thorny problems to experts on the subject. It is not known, for instance, why the central axis which runs throughout the whole residence is interrupted at several points. On the other hand, it is known that the position of the temple of the ancestors, south-east of the living quarters, which is against all normal rules, was to ensure the perpetual renewal of literary talent in the family (the south-east symbolises renewal and spring).

The whole town of Qu fu grew up because of the residence, whose offices spread outside the house itself.

Little streets containing services ran round the four
sides of the buildings. To the west of the walls lay the
western granary (1). Valets, servants and guards used
to live to the north of the house (2). To the east were
the orchards, the vegetable gardens, the stables and
other offices (3). This whole area was itself surrounded
by walls, which have disappeared now, but they are
shown on the map of the town given above. The present **Drum Tower (Gu lou)** was one of the gates in the
old walls. It is clear from the plan that as they held the
Bell Tower (no longer in existence) and the Drum
Tower, the Kong family controlled the main street of
the town. The walls also had a north gate. The south-
east area of the old town belonged to the family as well,
and was used to lodge guests and the troops of musicians and actors employed by them.

The Drum Tower which stands to the east of the
gate of the residence dates from the Ming, but was
restored under the Qing. The drum, still there, was
used to strike the hours. West of the entrance, at the
northern end of Que li jie street, stands a **Bell Tower
(Zhong lou)** dating from the Yuan.

To make the tour of the house easier, it can be
divided into five sections: the first central part, or
yamen; the second central part, where the living quarters were; the western part, for study and leisure; the
eastern part; the gardens.

1. The First Part (yamen)

Two stone lions stand at the gate, with two mounting blocks nearby. An inscription above the great
entrance gate (4) bears the characters *sheng fu.* Side
buildings line the first courtyard, which used to house
the guards and the couriers (5). The one on the right
was transformed in about 1931, into the "Classical

Music Conservatoire" used by the priests of the Temple of Confucius. The entrance gate also gives on to a second gate beyond the courtyard (6), inscribed with the characters *sheng ren zhi men (gate of the sage)*, which was opened only on great occasions. Two little passages went round on either side for normal use. This leads into the main courtyard, in the middle of which stands a ceremonial gateway, elaborately decorated with paintings and glazed tiles (yi men, 7). Offices occupied the buildings flanking the courtyard: the seals department (8) (jurisdiction, edicts); the rites department (9) (temple ceremonies); sacrifice department (10) (extended to include grain supply etc.); department of letters and archives (11); department of music (12) (for ceremonies); civil administration department (13) (tenant farms, *corvée* and registration office for other estates under the same jurisdiction). The great hall *(da tang)* (14), where the members of the Kong family carried out their official duties, occupies the north of the courtyard. A dais used to have the insignia of their duties, and a desk had on it all the attributes of a magistrate, such as seals, brushes, etc. A gong at the side marked the hours and the openings of the court sessions. The public collected at the sides, separated from these taking part in the hearing itself by balustrades which are still there today. At the back of the great hall, a covered way led to the second hall *(hou ting)* (15). Official examinations used to be held there, to enable the family to recruit the officials who served in the temple of Confucius. Candidates sat examinations in rites and music. Right and left of the examination hall were two secretarial offices (16). Two little courtyards (17) lie one on each side of the passageway linking the great hall to the second hall, planted with pomegranate trees and lilac bushes, with paintings

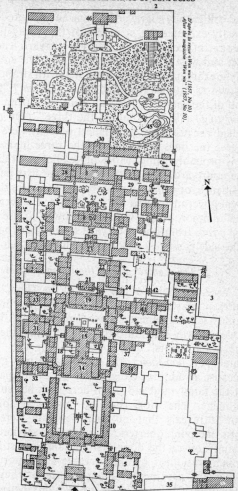

D'après la revue «Wen wu» (1957, No 10).
After the magazine "Wen wu" (1957, No 10).

N

Les numéros se réfèrent à la description donnée dans le texte.
The numbers refer to the description given in the text.

0 1 20 30 40 50 m

and calligraphy engraved in stone and set into the walls, mostly executed by members of the Kong family. A passage at the end of each little courtyard leads to the east and west parts of the house (18). The court north of the examination hall is decorated with strange stones, known as "stones from the lake" *(hu shi)*. The third hall of the *yamen* is the "hall built back from the rest" *(tui ting)* (19), or "hall of the three" *(san tang)*, so called because only the highest officials were received there: the ones belonging to the three highest ranks. It is probably Ming. More offices lie on either side of the courtyard. This is the end of the first part of the residence, or *yamen*, which was more or less the seat of local government and the law courts. The servants and the common people were not allowed to use the halls for going from one courtyard to another, but had to take side passages, which were built for their use.

2. The Central Part (the living quarters)

A passage north of the "Hall of the Three" links the different parts of the residence (20). Beyond it, the family's living quarters *(nei zhai)* begin. A low Ming style gateway leads into them (21), called the "gate of the appartments" *(nei zhai men)* or the "eunuchs' gate" *(tai jian men);* the latter name was given to it because an adopted daughter of Qian long married one of the family and moved in here with her suite of ten eunuchs. The story has no historical foundation, but it reveals that no men servants were allowed into the living quarters; only women servants entered them. Left of the door a stone tank can still be seen which was filled by the servants each morning with water for use in the living quarters. They filled it from outside, and the maids would then draw the water which they needed from the inside. The gate

leads into a large courtyard where friends used to
be entertained, and parties held. At the end of the
Qing, Kong Ling yi, the 72nd descendant of Confucius,
a great lover of the theatre, had two little buildings
put up in the east of the courtyard to serve as actors'
dressing-rooms (22), which destroy the original
symmetry of the courtyard. At the end of the courtyard
stands the first building of the living quarters themselves, a two-storey building (23), of a style characteristic of the end of the Ming and the beginning
of the Qing dynasties. At the south-east corner of the
buildings on the east side is a three-storey one, set
back slightly from the rest, and solidly built (24);
it is a "tower of refuge" (bi nan lou) to enable the
family to stand up to attacks and looting when
bandits or rebellious peasants threatened the house.
It is extremely well-conceived: the staircase leading
up to the first floor is movable, and the ceiling of
the ground floor is lined with iron to prevent fire from
spreading to the stories above. Beyond the first
house, and still on the central axis, lies another,
smaller courtyard (25) surrounded with rooms on all
four sides. Yet another courtyard lies beyond that
one, this time more spacious and planted with various
kinds of trees. Another two-storey building stands
at the end of it (26) with a gallery at first floor level
round the outside. This is perhaps the best illustration
of how Chinese traditional architecture was perfectly
adapted to all seasons of the year. The architects
have contrived it so that fresh air blows into the courtyard even during the heavy summer heat. In front of
the severe northern façade of the first two-storey
building, a most decorative two-storey pavilion was
built to hide it (27), which was cool in summer and
warm in winter. In the left hand corner of the courtyard,

a passage leads to the Buddhist chapel *(fo tang lou)* (28). From the far right hand corner, another passage leads to the servants' quarters (29). North of the second two-storey building stands another pavilion, still on the central axis, which was transformed into a granary under the Qing (30). Another stood to the north, traces of which can still be seen. Counting the one that has disappeared, ten buildings lie on the north-south axis which runs through the whole residence. The kitchens and other offices were on the right of the granary.

3. The Western Part (rooms for study and leisure)

The architecture is freer and more imaginative in this part. Scholars retired here for quiet study or for the pleasures of conversation, and it has been built in such a way as to create a peaceful world, detached from the rest. When coming from the centre of the residence by the entrance mentioned before (18), the "hall of loyalty and indulgence" (zhong shu tang) (31) is to the right, and the "pavilion of the red chalice" (hong e xuan) (32) is on the left. Northwards, to the right, is the "hall of inner peace" (an huai tang, 33), often called the "hall of nine partitions" (jiu tao tang), because of its unusual design. Nine partitions divide the interior, making a sort of small labyrinth, and multiplying the restricted area of the hall. The principles used in laying out gardens have been applied to the inside. An inscription on an inner wall in one of the previous pavilions shows that the scholars of the family used to meet here to recite poetry and hear others reciting. To the north lies a succession of gardens, courtyards, pavilions, guest-rooms, studios and libraries, rooms for historical or literary study. Some of these buildings have been restored in a modern style, influenced by the West.

4. The Eastern Part

In its present state it no longer has any unity. To the south, there used to be pavilions, used for leisure pursuits and for study, built under the reign of Qian long (1736–1796) Remains of them still exist (34). There is still a large terrace, made of earth, called "the terrace for watching what is going on" *(guan jin tai)* (35). On feast days, people used to gather there to watch the streets, which were full of tradesmen and activity. Further away, at the corner of the residence, were several buildings used by the guards in charge of protecting the house (36). Two more buildings were used as a kitchen (37) and wine cellar (38). Among the remains of old buildings are those of the pavilion of imperial writings *(yu shou lou)* (39), where works of several Qing Emperors were kept, in original manuscript form, several of which were by Qian long. Later on, the manuscripts were engraved on steles, some of which are still there. The three temples to the ancestors of the family are nearby (40), with the altars on which the sacrifices were offered. Towards the level of the centre of the residence stand some buildings grouped round a courtyard; the principal one is called the "hall of favours received" (mu en tang) (41), which refers to sacrifices offered by the Emperor in 1826 (the inscriptions hanging in the central part prove that they happened). North of the hall, a gateway with the inscription "gate where favours are received" (ying en men) (42) leads to a separate set of appartments where other branches of the family used to live. It originally included three courtyards and three buil-

dings, one behind the other, with side buildings
round the two further courtyards; the first one of
the three has disappeared. A little family temple
stands in this part (43), with two buildings which
used to be kitchens (44).

5. The Gardens

The northern part of the residence consists of
spacious gardens, with pools of lotus flowers, arbours
and pavilions. As far as one can judge from the
age of the trees growing there, the artificial hill
overlooking the pool dates from the Ming. The big
pavilion at the end of the central alley dates from
the Republic, as does the distressingly inappropriate
wooden bridge spanning the pool; the pool itself is a
deep one, fed by an underground spring, which explains the difficulty of cleaning it.

Near the Temple of Confucius, to the north-east,
stands the **Temple of Yan hui (Yan miao),** also called
the Temple of the Second Sage (Fu sheng miao).
Yan hui is the name of Confucius' favourite disciple,
the wisest and most virtuous of them all, tireless
in his search after perfection. He came of humble
origin. When he died at the age of 32, Confucius
was deeply distressed.

A stone gateway leads into the temple; inside it,
a pavilion marks the well of Yan Hui, known as the
Well of the Narrow Street (Lou xiang jing). A passage
in the *Analects* says, in fact, that Yan Hui lived in
the "narrow street" *(lou xiang)*. Nearby stand trees
planted by Yan Hui, and the Pavilion of Joy (Le
ting), which is on the spot where Yan Hui liked to
play the lute. The temple is built in exactly the same
style as the Temple of Confucius, but is only 7 bays
wide. The double roof is the same, so are the columns,

and there is a terrace in front, like the one at the temple of Confucius. Yan Hui's statue stands inside, with that of his son, among others.

A stretch of water at the south-east corner of the town, called the **Old Semi-circular Pond (Gu ban chi)** is said to be the place where Bo Qin, the first duke of Lu, came to study. Qian long built a little palace here. Nothing remains of it today.

B. Outside the Town

Confucius' Tomb.

A road lined with evergreens over 800 years old (planted under the Jin and the Yuan) leads from the north gate of the town towards the tomb of Confucius. About a mile from the town, it passes through a stone gateway dating from the Ming (1594) bearing the inscription *eternal spring (wan gu chang chun)*. A wooden gateway stands a little further on, also dating from the Ming: it is the entry to the graveyard of Confucius' family, called the "great sage's forest" (zhi sheng lin) or the "Kong forest" (Kong lin). Confucius, and nearly all his descendants, right up to the present day, are buried here. As the name suggests, this ancient graveyard is full of trees as old as the graves. It is surrounded and protected by a wall 7 feet high. After the second gateway (permission used to have to be asked of the guardian before he would open the gate), a long way leads to the second gate of the graveyard, which is built on the same lines as a gate in a fortified town. It stands on the site of one of the gates of the ancient capital of Lu, the kingdom of the Warring States period, of which Confucius himself was a citizen. At the foot of the gate, inscriptions ask the visitor to dismount from his horse. After the gate, a little Ming gateway heralds the Bridge over the River Zhu (zhu shui qiao), an old stone bridge of a classical shape. From there, the red walls surrounding the sacred place can be seen through the trees, and the gate, beyond which the avenue of honour begins. The avenue, which is paved, is lined with stone statues, two panthers, two griffins, and two guardians, symbols of the highest funerary honours. It ends at the Temple of Offerings (Xiang dian). **Confucius' Tomb** is behind the temple: it is a grassy mound, 12 or 15 feet high and 21 or 24 feet across, with a little brick wall round it. A stele erected in 1443 stands in front of it, with the characters: *tomb of the prince Wen xuan, very accomplished and very holy (da cheng zhi sheng wen xuan wang mu)* written in old-fashioned *zhuan* style. *Wen xuan* is the posthumous title given to Confucius under the Tang. The trunk of a tree planted by Zi gong stands between the temple and the tomb; a disciple of Confucius, he spent six years in mourning for him, whereas the others spent only three. A little brick tower has been built to shelter the remains of the tree. A pavilion nearby marks the spot where Emperor Sheng zu (Kang xi, 1663–1723) put his foot to the ground when he got out of his palanquin to see the tomb. The tomb of Zi gong is in an austere building west of Confucius' tomb, on the spot where Zi gong built a hut in which to spend the six years during which he mourned Confucius. East of the main tomb is another mound sheltering the remains of Confucius' son, Bo yu. Near that is the tomb of the latter's son, Kong ji, known under the name of Zi zi, because he wrote the *Doctrine of the Mean (Zhong yong)*, a short text which became one of the four clas-

sics of Confucianism under the Han (with the *Great
Learning*, and the *Analects* of Confucius and Mencius'
philosophical dialogues). Another illustrious member
of Confucius' family buried nearby is Kong Shan
ren (1648–1718), a great dramatist who wrote at the
beginning of the Qing dynasty, author of the *Peach
Flower (Tao hua shan)*, in which he tells the story
of the Southern Ming dynasty's fate, and vain attempts
to resist the arrival of the Qing, under the guise of
a love story. Kong Shang ren was also a great scholar:
when Kang xi, on his way home after a tour of inspection in the south, went through Qu fu to offer sacrifices
before Confucius' tomb in 1685, he heard Kong
Shang ren expounding the *Analects* of Confucius
and appointed him a doctor of the imperial academy
in return.

On the site of the Han palace, Lu ling guang dian,
(see above), stands a **Temple of the Duke of Zhou
(Zhou gong miao).** The Duke of Zhou, who is traditionally supposed by the followers of Confucius
to have drawn up the rites of the cult of the ancestors
and to have written the *Classic of Changes (Yi jing)*,
one of the Confucian classics, was the brother of
Wu wang, founder of the Zhou dynasty. His statue
stands in the temple, under an impressive carved
canopy. The temple stands a little way east of Confucius' tomb.

Tomb of the Legendary Emperor Shao hao
(Shao hao ling)

The tomb of Shao hao is two and a half miles
east of Qu fu, in a little round grove of cypress trees.
He is one of the five legendary emperors supposed
to have ruled China in the prehistoric era, and later
venerated as the deities of the five cardinal points.

The tomb is also called the Mountain of a Thousand Stones (Wan shi shan). It is a pyramid, made of large blocks of stone, 80 feet wide at the base and 20 feet high, dating from the Song dynasty. A little temple on the top contains an image of the emperor (Song carving).

Tomb of Confucius' Father and Mother (Liang gong lin)

The tomb is hidden among old pines and cypress trees, about 7 miles east of Qu fu, in a pleasant place near the river Si shui. Old trees grow on the mound, and in front of it stand an altar and two plain steles, very close to one another. The parents of Confucius were called Shu Liang ge and Yan shi.

Ni shan Hill

The Ni shan Hill rises about 15 miles south-east of Qu fu. Confucius was born here in 551 B.C. Today several monuments have grown up there: Confucius' Cave (Kong zi dong), the Temple of Perfection (Da cheng dian), the Pavilion with a view of the river (Guan chuan ting), a pavilion kept for study (Ni shan shu yuan), a temple in memory of Confucius' mother (Yan mu si) and the well where she drew her water. Here, as in other revered places, a grove of old trees stands in the midst of a countryside which was robbed of its trees a long time ago.

The Carvings on the Nine Dragon Mountain (Jiu long shan)

These are some Buddhist rock carvings dating from the Tang, 6 miles south of Qu fu, near the village of Wu jia cun. They are classed as a historical monument. There are not many carvings, but they are of the greatest beauty. They are divided among six niches; marks in the rock near them show that they were once sheltered by a wooden building.

THE PENINSULA

Bo fu

Bo fu is the most important coal mining centre in Shan dong, about 18 miles east of Ji nan; it is also an industrial town. It is on the railway line which serves other mining centres, further south, in the mountains, of which Bo shan, a town well known for its coal mines, glass works and pottery kilns, is one. The mines in this area were equipped and run by the Germans during the first twenty years of the century; Bo shan was known by its old name, Zhang dian, at that time.

The small mining town of Zi chuan (Zi bo) is about 12 miles south of Bo fu. The great writer, **Pu Song ling** (1640–1715) was born near there in 1640; he is best known for his collection of supernatural stories, *The Strange Tales of Liao zhai (Liao zhai zhi yi)*. His birthplace is open to the public; it is about two and a half miles east of the town, north of the Pu family Estate (Pu jia zhuang). The manor, damaged during the Japanese invasion, has been partly restored and kept up by the government since 1954. Systematic research carried out in the village and surrounding neighbourhood has brought to light several things which belonged to the writer, such as manuscripts, a portrait, a stele written by him.

Lin zi

Lin zi (its name means "on the river Zi") is east of Bo fu, a few miles north of the railway (nearest station: Xin dian). During the Warring States period, it was the capital of the kingdom of Qi, which held the north of Shan dong and played an important part in the affairs of the country during the centuries before the unification. The kings of Qi appear in the philosophical dialogues of Mencius (372–289 B.C.), where they take the part of interlocutor. Lin zi was one of the most important towns in China at this point. In an old chronicle, the *Yan zi chun qiu*, one of the characters says that "in its three hundred districts, if the people only lifted their sleeves, they would cover the sky, if they shook the sweat from them, it would appear to rain; it is thronged with people, the crowds are dense there". **Remains of the walls of the former capital of the kingdom of Qi (Qi guo cheng)** can still be seen there, and are classed as a historical monument.

In a mountain about 2 miles south-east of **Yi du,** south-east of Lin zi, near the village of Wang jia zhuang, some Buddhist caves and carvings have been found cut out of the rock. North-east of the village, in the Cloud Gate Mountain (Yun men shan), there are two groups of bas-reliefs carvings, and three little caves. South-west of the village, on the Camel Mountain (Tuo shan), four caves, some small and some slightly larger, and two groups of bas-relief carvings, have been cut out of the rock. The work dates from the Northern Zhou (557–581), the Sui (581–618) and the beginning of the Tang (618–907). It is the finest example of Buddhist sculpture in eastern Shan dong.

Wei fang

It is a commercial centre and a flourishing industrial town in the central Shan dong plain; it has coal mines, and a textile and food industry. The town is famous for its handicrafts: embroidery, things made of wood plated with silver, copies of ancient bronze vases, new year pictures printed on wood *(mu ban nian hua)*. It is a trading centre for local products (silk, tobacco). Like Ji nan, it was opened to foreign trade in 1906.

Qing dao

Qing dao has over 800,000 inhabitants; it is the second largest town in Shan dong, and the most important industrial town in the province. Its spacious harbour, which is deep enough to take large ships, is sheltered and never freezes in winter, and is one of the best harbours in China. Qing dao is also the most pleasant seaside resort in northern China; cold currents flowing past its beaches help to diminish the heat in summer.

The town (Qing dao means "green island") is built on the peninsula which encloses the bay of Jiao zhou, on the south-east coast of Shan dong. The town faces the bay on one side, and the open sea on the other. A lighthouse marks the entrance to the bay. The harbour is on the inside. The bay is called after the former prefectural town of Jiao zhou, now Jiao xian, about 6 miles to the north-west.

History

The history of the town begins in 1898; before then, a small, unimportant village stood on the site of Qing dao.

During the last decade of the 19th century, the European powers were in close rivalry, each trying to secure its zone of exclusive influence in China. Germany was perturbed by Russian ambitions in north-eastern China and Korea. "The German government was determined to act as soon as any of the other powers tried to gain exclusive advantages. William II had warned the Tsar on July 30th 1895 that if Russia acquired a 'territorial establishment' in China or Korea, Germany would make certain 'at least' of a 'coal depot'. But why should Germany have to depend on previous initiative taken by another State before it could act? As early as September 1st 1895, Chancellor Hohenlohe felt that something should be done, 'even if Russia does not acquire territory'. He had sounded the opinion of the Imperial Court ... saying that to safeguard her trading interests in the Far East, Germany needed to keep a fleet of warships in the Chinese seas, and therefore needed a naval base there. (....) Richthofen the geographer and Admiral von Tirpitz, in command of the Far Eastern squadron, suggested the bay of Kiao-Tcheou (Jiao zhou), in the Chantoung peninsula (Shan dong), a region rich in economic resources. After sending a specialist in harbour engineering, Georg Franzius, to look into the various suggestions, the German government, with Tirpitz who was now Secretary of State for the Navy, decided, in the summer of 1897, that they required Kiao-Tcheou.

"The assassination of two German Roman Catholic missionaries in Chantoung on November 1st 1897 gave them the chance to carry out their plan. German troops landed and occupied the town of Kiao-Tcheou on December 3rd, 1897. William II said that 'the Chinese had to be shown in the sternest way possible, if necessary with brutal severity, that the Emperor of Germany was not to be trifled with'. The Chinese government protested, but gave way and agreed to enter into negotiations." A treaty was signed on March 6th 1898. "China ceded to Germany, for ninety-nine years, the two entries to the bay of Kiao-Tcheou, and the islands in the bay, with the right to build a fortified naval base (the port of Tsing-Tao)." China also conceded the right to build and run railways in Shan dong and to work the mines in an area of 9 miles on either side of the railway line. (The quotations are from *La question d'Extrême-Orient* 1840–1940 by Pierre Renouvin, Paris, 1946, p. 164–166).

Within a few years Germany had built a modern, up-to-date town, and harbour, with electric lighting, divided into a business district, a residential district and a Chinese district. A Chinese customs office levied duty on merchandise destined for Chinese territory. The German garrison consisted of 2,000 men. Qing dao quickly became a trading centre and even rivaled Tian jin; Europeans from Shang hai went to spend their holidays there, and the Germans founded missions and a university.

In 1905, a railway line was built from Qing dao to Ji nan. During the 1911 revolution, countless Chinese came to take shelter there, and the town developed still further. As soon as war was declared, the Japanese occupied Qing dao (November 7th, 1914), and in 1915, Japan made China give official recognition to their taking over all the rights which had belonged to Germany. Not until 1922, after the Washington Congress, did the Chinese regain control over the territory.

Before the liberation, Qing dao possessed filatures, breweries and groundnut oil works.

An ambitious development plan has been applied to the town since 1949. It has become an important centre of the Chinese textile industry, like Tian jin and Shang hai. The Qing dao engine works produced the first engine of entirely Chinese make. It now has factories producing weaving looms, machine tools, groundnut oil, tobacco, flour and wine. It is also still a well known seaside resort, with holiday camps, and sanatoria.

Description

Qing dao has no historical monuments or works of art, unless the former German governor's residence in the east of the town can be considered as such. Even so, four pieces of sculpture dating from the Northern Wei were found there, probably from Zi chuan.

It possesses a *"Sea Museum" (Hai chan bo wu guan)*, with modern aquariums etc. Over 600 different species of sea plants, fish and other creatures are on show there. It also owns over 3,000 species which are kept for research purpose only. A **Town Museum (Qing dao shi bo wu guan)** was begun in 1959, and has probably been opened by now.

Qing dao is said to be one of the most beautifully situated of all the Far Eastern coastal towns. Other beautiful places can be visited from there: **Lao shan,** a mountain 3,702 feet high which rises out of the sea east of the town, **Zhan shan,** and the islands nearby, among them **Swallow Island (Yan er dao).**

Yan tai

Yan tai means "smoke terrace": terrace where beacon fires used to be lit. It is an important port, which controls, like Dairen to the north, the straits linking the Yellow Sea to the Gulf of Bo hai. It is the biggest fishing port in Shan dong.

The town has over 100,000 inhabitants, and is better known abroad by the name **Zhi fu,** as the peninsula which stretches into the sea north of the town is called. The town has grown considerably since it was opened to foreign trade in 1862. Several European powers, Japan and the United States, had trading establishments there, but no concessions.

After the liberation, the Yan tai—Lan cun railway line was built, linking Yan tai to the centre of the province (the line meets the Ji nan-Qing dao line at Lan cun). Yan tai does not live only by fishing; the neighbourhood contains some of the most fertile orchards in China, where apples, pears, peaches and grapes are grown. Wine is made there from grapes *(pu tao jiu),* brandy is also made there *(ba lan di)* and rose-petal wine *(mei gui jiu).*

Wei hai

Wei hai is another excellent port, on the tip of the Shan dong peninsula, about 45 miles east of Yan tai. In the last century, China spent enormous amounts of money on building a naval port here, which was taken by the Japanese fleet during the Sino-Japanese war of 1894–1895. Japan kept the town until the Chinese had paid their war indemnity in full, then handed it over to England to whom it had just been ceded by the Chinese. "On February 25th the Chinese government itself, in its anxiety to gain support against Russian expansion, offered, through Sir Robert Hart, to cede the lease on the port of Wei-Hai-Wei, at the southern entrance to the Gulf of Pei Chihli (Bei zhi li, i.e. He bei), opposite Port Arthur, to the British Cabinet. The British government finally came round to this suggestion. On July 1st 1898, the act of cession was signed by the Chinese government. It was similar to the Sino-German agreement of March 6th 1898: the bay of Wei-hai-wei became British military territory; a zone 10 miles wide round the bay was part of the concession, but remained under Chinese administration; a 'zone of influence' was added to the 'leased territory', including the whole of the eastern peninsula of Shantung. The agreement was to hold good as long as Port Arthur is occupied by the Russians'." (Renouvin, *La question d'Extrême-Orient*, p. 170).

HE NAN

(Map see Atlas pl. 10)

The province of He nan is bordered by He bei, Shan xi, Shân xi, Hu bei and An hui. As it name shows, most of it is south of the river—the Yellow River. The Peking–Canton railway line divides the province into two more or less equal parts. Mountains and hills, the extension of the Qin ling range, in Shân xi, fill the western part. Several large rivers rise there. Some of them flow into the Yellow River, some flow the length of the province from west to east and join the Huai, others meet in the Nan yang basin, in the south of the province, and flow into the Han, in Hu bei. The east of the province is an immense plain, formed mainly of alluvium brought down by the Yellow River. The hydrographic pattern of the plain has changed considerably over the centuries, as the Yellow River has sometimes flowed south-west to empty into the sea to the south of the Shan dong penin-sula, sometimes north-west into the Bo hai sea, off the north of Shan dong, as it does now. The history of He nan is a long record of disastrous floods and constant efforts to dominate the whims of the river. The sand and loess which cover the plain are fertile if well-irrigated. As rain is scarce in He nan (heavy rain in June and July, but otherwise eight months can go by with no rain at all), agriculture depends entirely on irrigation, using water drawn from the Yellow River and the other water courses. The control of the waters is therefore essential for two reasons. The climate, which is fairly severe in the north (north winds in winter) grows milder towards the south, where it is more like the climate of the Yang zi valley.

The province of He nan is the heart of classical China. Excavat-ions have shown that the north, near the Yellow River, the Luo river valley (Luo yang) and the foot of the Shan xi plateau were the most thickly populated areas in China during the Neolithic Era. At An yang, also in this area, remains of Yin, the last capital of the Shang dynasty (bronze age) were found. When the Zhou moved from the west to settle near present Luo yang where they founded the Eastern Zhou dynasty (770 B.C.), the countryside had already been brought under cultivation and worked for some time. In the centuries which followed, the first Chinese states known today by written records were formed there: the states of the Chun qiu period (770–481 B.C.). As time went on, the states on the borders spread in towards the centre and grew more powerful. The result was that during the Warring States period (475–221 B.C.), several powerful kingdoms on the borders quarrelled over the little states in the middle, which could not spread and grow stronger (several of them were in what is now He nan). The large states used them as a chessboard, constantly making war on them, either directly or by means of another country. This situation went on until the unification of China by Qin shi Huang di in 221 B.C. The Han, who first of all established Chang an as their capital (Shân xi) moved to Luo yang in 25 A.D. (Eastern Han.) Until the end of the Tang, Chang an and Luo yang were capital turn and turn about, or at the same time. Luo yang was important because it is near the He nan plain, the chief grain growing area in the empire. The role played by this grain producing area in the economic life of the state became increasingly important under the Han and during the periods which followed. At the same time, its centre of gravity moved further and further towards the south and the south-east (lower Yang zi region). To drain off some of its riches towards Chang an, the Sui (581–618) had a canal built, starting at Hang zhou, leaving the Yang zi at Yang zhou, running through central China, which joined the Yellow River west of present Zheng zhou. The convoys then followed the Yang zi upstream to Shân xi. The great southern agricultural regions supplied Luo yang and Chang an via this canal under the Tang. From the Song, China began to withdraw into herself. One sign of this was that Chang an was abandoned, and the capital was transferred to Kai feng. The Liao invasion and the sack of Kai feng in 1126 put a sudden end to the power of the Northern Song and He nan lost the central position which it had held since the beginnings of Chinese history. The conquerors retired to the north and the conquered to the south (Southern Song). From the Yuan dynasty onwards, the north predominated and Peking became the political centre of the empire. He nan was un-important in the history of China until, with the advent of the railway in the early 20th century, the Peking–Han kou (Wu han) and the Xu zhou–Luo yang lines were built. The town of Zheng zhou grew up at their intersection. On February 7th 1923, the railwaymen started a strike there which was to go down in the annals of the Chinese revolution.

In order to develop its economic potentialities, He nan had to be protected from possible flooding of the Yellow River or the other rivers, and it had to be adequately irrigated. Considerable work has been done on this since the liberation: the "People's Victory Canal" now drains off water from the Yellow River towards Xin xiang, the sandy areas on the banks of the river have been planted with trees, reservoirs have been created in the hills to the west (Bai sha), irrigation and drainage canals have been dug in the eastern plain. In the space of a few years, the region was made into the best grain-producing province of all China. Large amounts of cotton are produced in the north (Zheng zhou, Luo yang, Xin xiang and An yang are all textile industry centres), as well as tobacco (centred round Xu chang); sesame and peanuts are grown (modern oil-presses have been built at Zheng zhou, Kai feng and Shang qiu). He nan has mineral resources as well as agricultural possibilities, and several large mining centres have been created since 1949: He bi (the newest) and Jiao zuo (an older one) in the north, Ping ding shan and other smaller mines in the centre of the province, producing iron and coal. A medium sized iron and steel works has been created at An yang, and several other factories on a smaller scale have been built elsewhere. Both rich and well-placed in the centre of the country, He nan is on the way to becoming one of the pillars of the Chinese economy.

It is also a province which is exceptionally rich in historical monuments; the town of Luo yang and its neighbourhood will be described first, followed by the west of the province, Zheng zhou, Kai feng, the north of the province, and the south of the province.

LUO YANG

Luo Yang is in the north-west of the province of He nan, to the north of the river Luo (altitude 444 ft). To the south are the foothills of the Song shan Hill and the Xiong er shan Hill (the Bear's Ear Hill); to the north is the Bei mang shan plateau. The site has been inhabited since Chinese history began; during the 20th century, the town has developed at remarkable speed (20,000 inhabitants in the 1920's, 100,000 in 1953, 400,000 in 1963).

1. From its beginnings up to the Han dynasty. The site was inhabited in the neolithic era; remains have been found dating back to the Yang shao and the Long shan cultures. When the

Zhou king Wu overcame the Yin in the 11th century B.C., he founded a temporary capital *(xing du)* here, and called it Luo yi. To strengthen his authority in the east, the Zhou king Cheng built two settlements surrounded by ramparts and moats at Luo yi: Wang cheng, north-west of the existing old town, and Cheng zhou, also called Xia du, east of the Temple of the White Horse; traces of the fortifications have been found. In 770 B.C., under King Ping, the Zhou made Luo yang their chief capital, and it remained the king's residence until 205 B.C. (The court spent 252 years at Weng Cheng, then 205 years at Cheng zhou, and then moved back to Wang cheng for 50 years.) Excavations have revealed the sites of the royal palace, the temple of the ancestors (to the left), the altar of earth and harvests (to the right), and the market place (behind). The texts tell us that the people of Luo yi preferred crafts and trade to administrative duties. Tradition has it that the philosopher Su Qin was born here, that Lao Zi lived here and worked on the archives, and the Confucius came here to study music.

When Qin shi Huang di had unified the empire, he made Luo yi the *jun* of the three rivers (San chuan jun) and gave it to Lü Bu wei, his supposed father, to govern as a fief. He enlarged the boundaries of Cheng zhou and built palaces to the north and south, which were originally the Han and Wei palaces. The settlement contained 100,000 families. Liu Bang, the founder of the Han dynasty, only spent three months at Luo yang before making Chang an his capital (see p. 925). Under the Western Han dynasty, Luo yang became a capital of secondary importance; the Red Eyebrows took the town before going on the Chang an.

Under the Eastern Han dynasty (25–220) Luo yang once more became the chief capital, and was greatly expanded. The ramparts can still be traced: they cover 4,218 yards to the east, 4,162 yards to the west, and 2,740 yards to the north; in some places, the wall is still over 30 feet high. West of the walls, and south of the Temple of the White Horse, was the great imperial college, to which over 30,000 students came from all over the empire; there were 240 buildings, containing 1,800 dormitories. Confucian classics were inscribed on steles at the entrance. The library was a large one; when the Han fled from Luo yang, 7,000 chariots were needed to move it. Ban Gu, the historian, author of the *History of the Han*, lived here during this period, as did the "novelist" Yu Chu, Chang Heng, the astronomer who built a hydraulic armillary sphere, the eunuch Cai Lun, who is traditionally said to have invented paper, the surgeon Hua Tuo, who

is said to have made up an analgesic drink; Buddhism was also
introduced at this time: according to the tradition, a white horse
entered the town, carrying the Buddhist canons, and a temple
was built on the spot where he stopped (68 A.D.). This is pure
legend, but the date is correct.

2. The Three Kingdoms and the Six Dynasties. The Wei (220–
265 A.D.) and the Jin (265–316) used Luo yang as their capital.
The Wei had the classics inscribed once more on 28 stone steles;
the text was written three times over, using a different kind of
writing each time (large and small "curly" script, and *li* calligraphy); two pieces of the steles can be seen in the museum. Luo
yang was an important centre of learning at this time: the poet
Xi Kang and his friends (the Seven Sages of the Bamboo Grove)
lived here; so did the poet Zuo Si, whose work *Fu of the three
capitals* met with resounding success (so many people wanted to
copy the text that the town's paper reserves were rapidly exhausted); the historian Chen Shou, who wrote the *History of the
Three Kingdoms*, lived here, and so did the scholar Ma Jun, who
invented the "chariot which points to the south".

At the end of the 5th century, the Northern Wei, who had
settled at Da tong, occupied the middle of the Yellow River
valley, and made Luo yang their capital; they stayed there from
494 to 534. Emperor Xiao wen di wanted to order some new
buildings, so he sent the architect Jiang Shao you to Jian ye
(present day Nanking), which was the Qi capital, to look for
inspiration. A contemporary text, the *Luo yang jia lan ji*, describes
the town: it had twelve gates, each one surmounted by a tower;
wide avenues were laid out; the palace was at the centre,
with the administrative part of the town to the south; the population was divided among 220 *li* or districts, both within and
outside the walls; each district was surrounded by walls, with
four gates, and had an officially appointed administrator.
To the west of the walls was the big market place, where each
street specialised in one branch of trade; in the little market,
to the east, grain, cattle and horses were sold; in the Market
of the Bridge of Eternity (Yong qiao shi), to the south, fish,
and foreign goods imported from Central Asia, were sold;
the foreign merchants stayed nearby, in an inn reserved for
them, called the *Si yi guan*. There were 1,367 Buddhist temples
in the town. Some rich men used to pay a "substitute" *(ti
shen)* to go into retreat for them. At the same time, work was
begun on the first of the Long men Caves. According to the
History of the Wei, the population was "109,000 families."

LUO YANG SOUS LES WEI DU NORD (Ve — VIe siècle)
LUO YANG UNDER THE NORTHERN WEI (5th — 6th centuries)

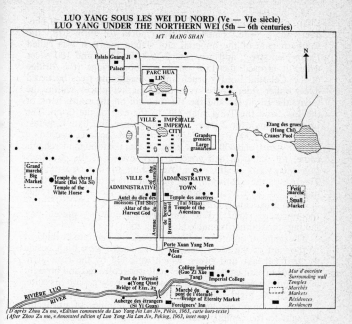

(D'après Zhou Zu mo, «Edition commentée du Luo Yang Jia Lan Ji», Pékin, 1963, carte hors-texte)
(After Zhou Zu mo, «Annotated edition of Luo Yang Jia Lan Ji», Peking, 1963, inset map)

3. The Sui and the Tang. When the Wei fell from power, the town which they had built was completely destroyed, and the Sui emperor Yang di (606-617) chose a new site for his capital. Yu Wen kai, the engineer of the Grand Canal, was commissioned to lay the foundations of the new city, west of the Temple of the White Horse, on the plain where the existing old town still is, near where the rivers Jian and Chan flow into the Luo. The ramparts can be traced; their circumference was over 16 ½ miles, and the walls were faced with brick. The imperial city, in the north-west of the town, had a perimeter of 5 ½ miles; it was fortified by a triple wall to the north, and by a double wall on the other three sides. The palace was in the centre of the imperial city, surrounded by administrative offices. There were 30 districts north of the Luo, on both banks of the river

Chan, and 96 south of the Luo. The streets were laid out chequerwise; a wide avenue ran from north to south from the southern gate of the imperial city (Duan men); it was called Duan men street, and was over 2 ½ miles long, and 100 paces wide; it crossed the Luo on a pontoon bridge (the Bridge of the Celestial Ford); peach and pomegranate trees bordered it on either side. There were three market places within the town: the Li du shi and the Da tong shi on the south bank of the Luo, and the Tong yuan shi, to the east of the Chan. The Li du shi was over 2 miles in circumference and had 12 gates; it contained 3,000 shops, divided into 120 sections, according to their wares, and 400 inns. It was here that the foreign merchants came, for Yang di had concentrated several of the country's rich merchants in this area. According to the *Geographical Treatise* of the *History of the Sui*, the town had "202,230 families", or nearly a million inhabitants. Newly-made roads and two great canals linked the capital to the rest of the empire: the northern canal led to the area surrounding present-day Peking; the southern canal led to Hang zhou.

The emperor ordered the Western Park (Xi yuan) to be laid out to the west of the town; sixteen little palaces were built beside an artificial lake and rivers, which were fed by the river Jian. All kinds of exotic plants and animals were collected and brought here, and the emperor liked to come and ride here, with his suite, especially at night. He loved music and literature, and was himself a composer; he had over 3,000 families of musicians brought to the capital, where they were given lodgings in two districts south of the Luo; he himself used to adapt popular songs *(su qu)*. Liu Gu yan was given the task of drawing up the catalogue of his library, which contained over 370,000 books. He lived surrounded by scholars and engineers, (Yu Wen kai, He Chou, Yuan Pi), who built him portable palaces and paddle boats. The first fortnight of each new year was a holiday for the whole town: the inhabitants, and the foreign ambassadors who came to pay tribute at that time, could watch troupes of acrobats and musicians from the four corners of the empire performing along the whole length of the great Avenue of the Celestial Ford; when night fell, torches were lit, and the festivities went on.

The Tang had two official capitals, Chang an and Luo yang, but they lived chiefly in the former. Only six sovereigns came to live at Luo yang, representing about forty years out of the two hundred and eighty covered by the dynasty. The town changed its name five times during this time. Empress Wu Ze tian (684-

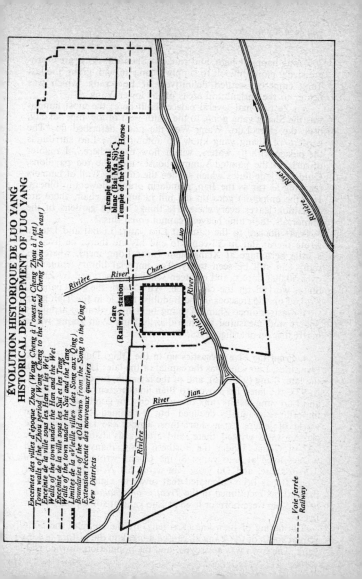

ÉVOLUTION HISTORIQUE DE LUO YANG
HISTORICAL DEVELOPMENT OF LUO YANG

Enceintes des villes d'époque Zhou (Wang Cheng à l'ouest et Cheng Zhou à l'est)
Town walls of the Zhou period (Wang Cheng to the west and Cheng Zhou to the east)

Enceinte de la ville sous les Han et les Wei
Walls of the town under the Han and the Wei

Enceinte de la ville sous les Sui et les Tang
Walls of the town under the Sui and the Tang

Limites de la «Vieille ville» (des Song aux Qing)
Boundaries of the «Old town» (from the Song to the Qing)

Extension récente des nouveaux quartiers
New Districts

Voie ferrée
Railway

Temple du cheval blanc (Bai Ma Si)
Temple of the White Horse

Gare
(Railway) station

Rivière — River Chan

Rivière — River Luo

Rivière — River Jian

Rivière — River Yi

705) was happiest here, and called it Shen du. As it grew progressively more difficult to supply Chang an with grain, the last Tang emperors settled definitively at Luo yang, which was nearer to the agricultural areas of the lower Yang zi.

Wu Ze tian had several palaces built here; the most famous was the Shang yang gong, to the south-west of the imperial city, near the river Luo. Wang Wei, the poet, described it: "The gardens of Shang yang know no autumn. The Luo surrounds the palace with its waters, which flow everywhere... Laughter of girls in the painted summer-houses and the red pavilions, Gold and jade flutes which sadden the stroller, Wall of banners reaching as far as the Jian, mandarin orange flowers in bloom. He (the emperor) goes up the hill in his jade chair, there are cinnamon leaves everywhere, He thinks of the gardens of the immortals, their nine heavens cannot equal this."

Poets flocked to the court at Luo yang; Li Bai and Du Fu wrote there; Bai Ju Yi came to end his life there; he lived in a little hermitage at Xiang shan (near Long men), where his tomb can still be seen today. The imperial library contained over 50,000 books, and eighteen scholars, supervised by Zhang Shuo, worked on the catalogue. Wu Dao zi, the great painter, worked on the frescoes in the Buddhist temple in the Tian gong si; the astronomer Zhang Yi xing built his hydraulic armillary Sphere and measured the meridian; Zhang Wen zhong wrote his treatise on pharmaceutics.

4. From the Five Dynasties up to the Qing.

During the Five Dynasties, Luo yang was the capital of the later Liang (907-923), the later Tang (923-936), and of the later Jin, for eleven months. In 937, the later Jin moved to Bian jing (present day Kai feng), and Luo yang lost its rank of capital city for good. Its economic importance gradually declined, but it retained its place in the world of letters for a short time. Under the later Tang, the classics were printed there, and afterwards distributed to the rest of China. Under the northern Song, many scholars and writers lived at Luo yang: Si ma Guang wrote his *Historical Mirror* there, and Ou yang Xiu wrote his *New History of the Tang*. It has been calculated that seven or eight out of ten of the authors mentioned in the *Treatise on scholars* in the *History of the Song* were born or lived at Luo yang at some time in their lives.

The taking of Bian jing (Kai feng) by the Jin, and the Song retreat south of the Yang zi, caused a break in the history of Luo yang. The town was destroyed, and the population, now considerably diminished, took refuge behind new fortifications (just under 3 miles in circumference), on the site of the existing old town.

Under the Yuan, the Ming and the Qing, the town was merely the capital of He nan (He nan fu).

5. After the Liberation. Since 1949, and particularly since 1954, the town has developed once more. A tractor plant has been built (the first one to be built in China), as well as machinery works, ball bearings factories, and glass works. A new town has been built to house them some distance to the west of the old one; the two are linked by a regular bus service.

Description

1. The new town. The hotel where foreigners stay is in the new town, which is built round the confluence of the river Luo and the river Jian. The main factories with their workers' living quarters are here; there are still some agricultural areas, though they are receding gradually as the new buildings advance.

The tractor plant. (Di yi tuo la ji zhi zao chang) is to the north of the new town, south of the river Jian. It was built in four years, from 1955 to 1959, with Soviet aid. 20,000 workers (1,000 of them women) are employed in its seventeen workshops. It is pointed out that it covers as large an area as the old town. The factory has its own hospital, a club, seventeen day-nurseries, five primary schools, and a technical school to train workers and cadres.

The **Wang cheng park** has kept the name of the old Zhou town (it means "Royal Town"), as it occupies the same site. An exhibition of lanterns is held here for the first fortnight of the Chinese year, as lantern-making is one of the town's traditional crafts. A long suspension bridge across the Jian leads to two subterranean Han dynasty tombs, in which modern staircases have been built.

a) *Western Han tomb:* to the right and left of the entrance are two small, low niches, where pottery was found: opposite is a room with wall-paintings, where the coffin was.

b) *Eastern Han tomb:* similar antechamber, with niches; notice the stone doors with their bas-relief carving. Then follows a higher rectangular room, with a fine vaulted ceiling, built of brick; to the left at the end are two vaults where the nails from the coffin can still be seen.

2. The old town. The old town is between the river Luo and the river Chan; this is the site of the town under the Yuan, Ming and Qing dynasties. The ramparts were knocked down in 1939. The roofs of several temples can be seen, including that of the temple to the Gods of the Town (in the north-west, near the old ramparts), none of which can now be visited. Attractive old streets (earthenware shops, lantern makers...)

3. The Temple of the White Horse or the White Horses (Bai ma si) is 8 miles to the east, west of the Han town. It is built on the site of one the very first Buddhist temples to be built in China, under the Western Han. According to a work written by a Buddhist at the end of the Han dynasty: "Emperor Ming di (58-76) dreamed that a spirit entered his palace; the next day, he asked his ministers to explain this to him, and they replied that it was Buddha. It was then that Wang Zun and Cai Yin, who had been to

BAI MA SI (Temple du cheval blanc)
BAI MA SI (Temple of the White Horse)

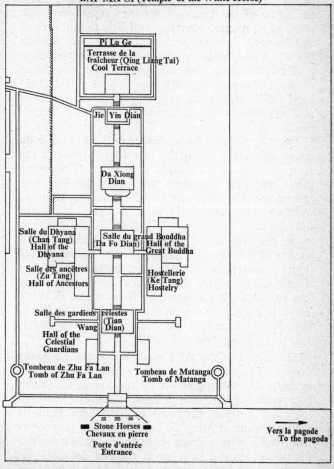

Pi Lu Ge

Terrasse de la fraîcheur (Qing Liang Tai)
Cool Terrace

Jie Yin Dian

Da Xiong Dian

Salle du Dhyana (Chan Tang)
Hall of the Dhyana

Salle du grand Bouddha (Da Fo Dian)
Hall of the Great Buddha

Salle des ancêtres (Zu Tang)
Hall of Ancestors

Hostellerie (Ke Tang)
Hostelry

Salle des gardiens célestes (Tian Dian)
Wang
Hall of the Celestial Guardians

Tombeau de Zhu Fa Lan
Tomb of Zhu Fa Lan

Tombeau de Matanga
Tomb of Matanga

Stone Horses
Chevaux en pierre

Porte d'entrée
Entrance

Vers la pagode
To the pagoda

the country of the Yue shi, to copy the *Forty-two article Sutra*, came back riding white horses; hence the name of the temple." Another legend says that two Indian monks, Matanga and Zhu fa lan, arrived at Luo yang, bringing with them sutras, "on a white horse". The temple has been rebuilt several times, and the buildings are not earlier than the Ming dynasty. Restoration work was done in 1952, 1954 and 1957. Monks of the Dhyana *(chan)* school still live there; it is an important centre of Chinese Buddhism.

Two stone "white horses" stand in front of the main door. This gives on to the first courtyard, with the Hall of Celestial Guardians at the end (Tian wang dian); the four guardians are Qing; the Wei tuo, behind the screen, is said to be Ming; the Maitreya in the middle dates from 1935. A second courtyard follows.

On the left is the Hall of the Ancestors, with statues of the first six masters of the Dhyana school (Qing dynasty), and north of this, the Hall of Dhyana (Chan tang), where the monks gather for study (the jade Buddha was a present from Burma in 1935). There is a Tang *chuang* in the courtyard. The Da fo dian is at the end of the courtyard; the carving is said to be Ming, restored in 1935.

At the end of the third courtyard is the Da xiong dian, with eighteen *luo han* said to date from the Yuan dynasty. The carving of the Jie yin dian in the fourth courtyard is Qing. At the back, a staircase leads to the Cool Terrace, supposed to have been built by the Han emperor Ming di. Tradition has it that sutras from India were brought here to be translated. The inscription on the Pi lu ge at the end describes the arrival of the sutras. East and west of the Pi lu ge are rooms with statues of the two monks, Matanga and Zhu fa lan; the stele "with the fragmented text" (Duan wen pai) on the terrace is so called because the characters are written horizontally, and not vertically (it was written by a monk, Ju Xiu, under Kang xi).

The visitor returns to the first courtyard by way of vegetable gardens to the west, to look at the tombs in the western and eastern corners, traditionally supposed to be those of Zhu fa lan and Matanga.

The Qi gong ta Pagoda lies to the east of the temple; the date of its foundation is unknown. The lower stories were restored in 989 (under the northern Song), and the upper stories in 1125 under the Jin; steles beside the pagoda commemorate both restorations. The pagoda is square, about 60ft high, with 13 stories.

4. The Mang shan Hills rise north of the town. The Chinese who lived in the area considered them a pleasant last resting-place. A saying claimed that one should be born and live at Su zhou and Hang zhou, but die and be buried in the Mang shan Hills ("Sheng ju Su Hang, si sang Bei mang"). There are many tombs to be seen, and from the summit, there is an excellent view of the town.

5. The Town Museum dates from 1958; it is housed in the old Guan di Temple, south of the town, east of the Long men road.

Guan di, or Guan Yu, was a hero, belonging to the Three Kingdoms era; he was a Shu kingdom general who remained faithful to his sovereign, Liu Bei, until death; he was made a god of war, and many towns dedicated temples to him; the temple at Luo yang (Guan lin, or Guan di miao) was built during the Ming dynasty, under Wan li, and restored under Qian long and Ci xi (Tz'u Hsi). At the beginning of the century, the three main buildings contained several statues of the hero (seated, reading the *Spring and Autumn Annals*, lying down...). Today the statues have vanished, but behind the temple can still be seen a little mound, supposed to contain the skull of Guan di. How this precious relic was handed down, from the 3rd century, when the general died, to the 16th century, when the temple was built, is a question to which the legend gives no answer... Two magnificent iron lions, dated 1597, stand at the entrance.

Most of the things found since the liberation have been collected here. Luo yang's economic rebirth provoked extensive terracing work, and consequently discoveries have been made. Over sixty people work in the town's archeological section. The richest collections are those representing the periods when Luo yang was the capital.

First section. Historical evolution: quaternary fossils, (elephants' tusks, large numbers of ostrich eggs found in the Bei mang shan Hills); neolithic pottery; a fine collection of Shang bronzes; a Shang pottery kiln discovered in 1955 in the village of Sun qi tun; Zhou pottery and kiln, from the site of the town of Wang cheng, found in 1957; Han dynasty: tomb figurines—figures with animal heads, a troupe of jugglers; very fine examples of painted pottery; seven different kinds of grain found in the tombs; fragments of the classics inscribed on stone; stele dating from 278, with the names and origins of the students attending the Luo yang college at that time; a map showing where they came from, drawn up according to the stele; Tang tomb figurines and ceramics.

Second section. Special items: separate rooms devoted to bronzes, mirrors, ceramics, weapons, jade and sculpture.

6. The Long men Caves. These are about nine miles south of Luo yang, at a spot where the river Yi, on its way north-west towards the Luo, flows for about 600 yards between high cliffs (hence the name Yi que, "the gate of the Yi", and the more frequent one of Long men, "the dragon gate". A bridge crosses the Yi at this point.

When the Northern Wei made Dai jing (modern Da tong) their capital, work had already begun on the famous Buddhist caves at Yun gang (see p. 876) east of the town. When Emperor Xiao wen di moved his capital to Luo yang in 494, he commissioned similar work, to be done in the Long men cliffs. The work did not end with the Northern Wei; it was carried on by the Eastern Wei, the Western Wei, the Northern Zhou, the Northern Qi, the Sui and the Tang (particularly under Wu Ze tian, who lived for a long time at Luo yang); a few pieces of sculpture date from the Five Dynasties and the beginning of the Song, but not many. Altogether there are 1,352 caves, 750 niches, 39 small carved pagodas, 97,306 statues and 3,608 inscriptions.

All this was sacked by 19th and 20th century antiquarians. The heads of nine-tenths of the statues have been damaged or removed; marks left by saws are clearly visible in several places. The Chinese lay particular stress on an adoration scene, which was in the Ping yang Cave in the middle, and is now in the United States. The main groups on the side of the western cliff will be described first, going from north to south. It is best to go there in the mor-

GROTTES DE LONG MEN (FALAISE OUEST)
LONG MEN CAVES (WEST CLIFF)

← S Ouest   N Est →

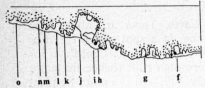
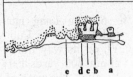

o   nm l k   j   ih   g   f   e d c b   a

a   Qian Qi Si Cave
b   Northern Ping Yang Cave
c   Central Ping Yang Cave
d   Southern Ping Yang Cave
e   Jing Shan Si Cave
f   Cave of the ten thousand
     Buddhas (Wan Fo Dong)
g   Lotus flower Cave
     (Lian Hua Dong)
h   Wei characters Cave
     (Wei Zi Dong)

i   Tang characters Cave
    (Tang Zi Dong)
j   Ju Xian Si Cave
k   Medical prescriptions
    Cave (Yao Fang Dong)
l   Gu Yang Cave
m   Cave burnt by fire
     (Huo Shao Dong)
n   Shi Ku Si Cave
o   Lu Dong Cave

ning, when the slanting rays of the morning sun
bring the contours to life. Sometimes the Yi overflows
slightly and floods the base of the cliff; this makes
visiting difficult.

a) The Qian qi si Cave. In 1913, a temple, still
inhabited by monks, led into the cave, which is
30 ft. high, just over 30 ft. wide and 21 ft. deep.
A stele outside the Ping yang cave says that it was
hollowed out in 641, at the beginning of the Tang
dynasty. A Buddha, seated on a draped platform,
is in the middle, with his two disciples, Ananda and
Kaçyapa, one on each side; two large Bodhisattvas
and two celestial guardians, with most expressive
faces, are on the side walls.

b) The northern Ping yang Cave. This is the first
of a group of three caves; the name, Ping yang

means: "which greets the sun", and the caves face east. The sculpture, which was begun under the Northern Wei, was not finished until the beginning of the Tang dynasty (641-650). There is a large seated Buddha, about 24 ft. high, on a platform apparently supported by smaller figures, in the middle; to the right and left are *luo han* and Bodhisattvas; small niches in the walls contain statues of the Buddha; there are two celestial guardians at the entrance.

c) *The Central Ping yang Cave.* This is one of the two first caves begun by the Northern Wei emperor Xiao wen di. An inscription says that the work on the cave lasted from 500 to 523, and that it needed 802,366 workmen. The cave contains eleven large statues of the Buddha; the one in the centre is the most striking: it is 26 ft high; the Buddha is seated, with legs crossed, and one hand raised, the other pointing towards the ground; a circular halo surrounds his face, which is smiling; his robe is draped round him in masterly folds. Like the two Buddhas at the side, he stands out against his background of a flame-shaped halo, carved in bas-relief on the wall. The ceiling should be noticed. This is one of the richest of the Long men caves; the adoration scenes removed to the United States in 1935 used to be here.

d) *The southern Ping yang Cave* was begun under the Northern Wei and finished under the Sui (595-616). Two techniques of sculpture can be seen: "flat relief", used by the Wei, and high relief, later used by the Tang. The Buddha in the centre, heavy-faced and dull-eyed, is very different from the one in the cave before. There are several niches and inscriptions round the walls.

e) The Jing shan si Cave was hollowed out between 627 and 663. The head of the Buddha in the middle has been damaged; there are two Bodhisattvas inside, and two guardians outside.

f) The Cave of Ten Thousand Buddhas. (Wan fo dong.) This cave, hollowed out in 680, under the Tang, is further away, to the south. It is square; the ceiling consists of an enormous lotus flower, with an inscription giving the date. On the side walls are 15,000 small Buddhas (hence the name of the cave). Four followers stand round the Buddha. 54 lotus flowers cover the back wall, with a little Bodhisattva emerging from each one. The musicians below the 10,000 Buddhas should be noticed, and the Guan yin, now headless, at the entrance to the cave.

g) The Lotus Flower Cave (Lian hua dong) was hollowed out round about 527, on a rectangular plan. The large lotus flower on the ceiling gives it its name. The central figure is a standing Buddha, whose head and fore-arms have been removed. To the right, a relief carving depicts Kaçyapa; the face has disappeared, but the folds in the robe should be noticed. Very fine apsaras decorate the ceiling, and the niches in the south wall contain small relief carvings of scenes of adoration of the Buddha.

h) The Wei Character Cave (Wei zi dong) is so called because it contains epigraphs dating from the Wei. The Buddha in the centre, which dates from the same time, still retains some of its facial expression, although damaged.

i) The Tang Character Cave (Tang zi dong) was begun in the Wei dynasty and continued in the Tang; an inscription is dated 661. The outside is Wei; the sculpture inside is Tang.

j) The Ju xian si Cave. This is by far the biggest cave of them all. From east to west it measures 115 ft., and from north to south, over 100ft. The huge Buddha in the middle is 56ft. tall; his head measures 12ft., and his ear 3ft 3ins. The lower part of the statue has disintegrated. Right and left of him stand the two disciples, Ananda and Kaçyapa (the latter almost completely destroyed), and two Bodhisattvas wearing crowns; against the side walls are, on each side, a Tian wang (celestial guardian) and a Li shi (a defender of the Buddha). The Tian wang on the north wall is most striking; his left hand is on his hip, and he carries a pagoda in his right hand, while with his right foot, he tramples on an evil spirit. In Wu Ze Tian's time, this was approached through a vast wooden temple, built up against the cliff; the temple disappeared long ago, but the holes for the supporting beams can still be seen.

k) The Medical Prescription Cave (Yao fang dong) is so called because under the Northern Qi, recipes for a hundred and twenty remedies (for fever, madness, vomiting, heart diseases, diabetes, skin diseases), were carved round the entrance. The sculpture was begun under the Wei, continued under the Northern Qi, and touched up under the Tang. The style is uneven.

l) The Gu yang Cave was begun under the Northern Wei, in 495, and completed under the Northern Qi, in 575. It is one of the oldest and finest of the caves. The statue of the Buddha, in the centre, was restored under Guang xu; the statue's new face reminded people of Lao Zi, so it was nicknamed "Lao jun" (hence the name Lao jun dong, by which the cave is sometimes known). The statue has two lions at its feet. The carving of the niches is particularly detailed; *tao tie* heads, holding streamers in their mouths; there are also numerous carvings in low relief, showing religious scenes or scenes from everyday life (houses etc.). Nineteen of the "twenty calligraphies" of Long men *(er shi pin)* are in this cave; most of them date from the northern Wei.

m) The Cave Burned by Fire (Huo shao dong) is probably so called because the cave was struck by lightning, unless it refers to the design on the tympanum. The cave dates from the Northern Wei; there are two inscriptions of 522 and 523. The central statue bears a close resemblance to that in the previous cave.

n) The Shi ku si Cave dates from the Northern Wei. It is known above all for its adoration scenes, the finest at Long men now that the Ping yang cave scenes are no longer there.

o) The Lu dong Cave dates from the Northern Wei. Four inscriptions inside date from 539, 549, 550 and 572. The tympanum is of flame design; a Jataka is depicted on the south wall (Buddha's previous incarnation), a rare thing at Long men; interesting carvings of houses with staircases leading up to them decorate the northern wall.

More caves have been dug in the cliff on the opposite bank of the river Yi. They are fewer in number and more recent than those in the western cliff. They all date from the Tang. Three are larger than the rest.

a) The cave of the temple where the sutras are read (Kan jing si) was hollowed out during the reign of Wu Ze tian (700–720). The ceiling, decorated with a lotus in the centre, and apsaras, is 30 ft. high.

Twenty-nine *luo han* decorate the lower part of the walls; their faces are extremely expressive, sometimes almost like caricatures. There is a seated figure of the Buddha on a pedestal in the centre; his bloated face, plunging nose and gaze fixed on the ground leave a strange impression.

b) The Three Caves on the Terrace where the Drum is Beaten. There is a striking Buddha in the southern cave, with tiara and breast-plate, seated on a rectangular pedestal.

c) The Cave of Ten Thousand Buddhas (Wan fo gou). A lotus stalk carries five flowers, arranged horizontally: the biggest one, in the middle, contains a seated Buddha, and the ones on each side carry standing Buddhas; the bas-relief carvings on the western wall are traditionally attributed to Bai Ju yi.

The eastern and western caves contain inscriptions and several well-known steles: the Long men countryside, Guan di on horseback, figures based on characters. Rubbings of these can usually be bought.

On the Pipa Hill (Pi pa feng), east of the Yi, the tomb of Bai Ju yi, who died at Luo yang in 846, at seventy-eight, can still be seen. It is known that he liked to retire to this spot.

THE AREA WEST OF LUO YANG

Mian chi

It is a district headquarters on the railway line about 43 miles west of Luo yang, in the Jian valley (Jian shui). It contains some curious houses with carvings on them. The village of Yang shao (Yang shao cun), where extensive **Neolithic remains** have

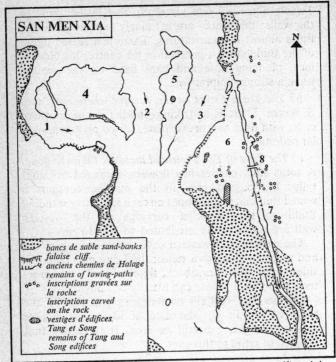

D'après le rapport de l'Académie des sciences de Chine. Les numéros se réfèrent à la description donnée dans le texte.
After the report by the Chinese Academy of Sciences. The numbers refer to the description given in the text.

been found, is about 4 miles north of the town. This discovery, made in 1921, proved that a Neolithic culture once existed in China. Remains of a whole settlement were found at Yang shao, with large numbers of tools and implements made of polished stone, bone and clay, particularly numerous vases, bowls, goblets, amphora, all made of smooth clay decorated with figurative or purely ornamental paintings (see Peking Historical Museum, p. 429). The discoveries at Yang shao gave their name to a type of culture, remains of which have now been found in over a thousand sites in northern China: the **Yang shao culture,** which is thought to date from roughly 4,000 B.C. It extended mainly over He nan, Shân xi, Shan xi, and outposts have been found in Gan su, Hu nan, He bei and Inner Mongolia. The Chinese people was born during this era; their history began at this time.

About 15 miles before it reaches Mian chi, on the way from Luo yang, the railway goes through a town called the "Iron Gate" (Tie men zhen). About a mile and a half to the south-west lie the Village of the stone Buddhas (Shi fo xiang) and the **Hong qing Monastery (Hong qing si).** Six caves have been hollowed out in the rocks behind the monastery, and decorated with bas-relief carvings, depicting scenes from the life of the Buddha. The carvings include a rare element: armies of flying demons, with bows and arrows. Judging by the style, it is thought that the carvings date from the Northern Wei.

San men xia

San men xia is a town in the west of He nan, on the line going to Shân xi. It is the headquarters of the Shân xian district, and has become an industrial town since the liberation. Its name means the "Three Gates Gorges", referring to the Yellow River gorges not far away, called the *San men* ("Three Gates"; *xia* means gorge).

From the point where it enters He nan as far as the Luo yang neighbourhood, the Yellow River flows through a narrow valley. About 12 miles downstream from the town, it cuts through a great rocky barrier. Then it takes a sharp turn to the south, and divides into three. The three passages are called the Demon Gate (Gui men) (1), the Gate of the Gods (Shen men) (2), and the Gate of Men (Ren men) (3). The rocky islands in the middle of the river are called the Demon Gate Island (Gui men dao) (4), the Gate of the Gods Islands (Shen men dao) (5), and the Gate of Men Island (Ren men dao) (6). Yu the Great, the legendary founder of the Xia dynasty (towards 2,000 B.C.) and the mythical inventor of techniques for controlling the waters, is traditionally meant to have cut out the three passages for the Yellow River. This feat gave rise to the expression *gui fu shen gong*, *"from the axe of a demon, a divine work"*..

The rapid current, whirlpools and reefs made the San men Gorges a formidable obstacle to navigation. A way to overcome it had to be found under the Han, to convey supplies from the northern plains to the capital, Chang an. Wooden, overhanging towpaths were built into the rock face. Most of the traffic went through the Ren men. When research was done on the site in 1955, remains of pathways built as towpaths under the Han were found all along the cliffs (traces in the rock itself). In the Kai yuan period (713–742) under the Tang, work was begun on an artificial canal through the mountain which was to avoid the rapids. The canal, called the New Canal of the Kai Yuan period (Kai yuan xin he) (7) ran east of the Gate of Men Island, which was not a real island up till then. It was 300 yards long, 20 to 26 feet

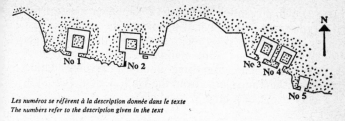

No 1   No 2   No 3 No 4   No 5   N

Les numéros se réfèrent à la description donnée dans le texte
The numbers refer to the description given in the text

wide, and 16 to 32 feet deep. A towpath ran alongside
it and a bamboo bridge spanned it (8).

From the Han to the Tang, the gorges were always
busy. The towing made all sorts of other equipment
necessary. Granaries and temples were built nearby,
among them a temple to Yu the Great (Yu wang miao).
For centuries, travellers used to engrave texts of
various kinds on the rocks, often choosing almost
inaccessible places.

Since the liberation, work has been going on to
close up the passage which Yu the Great made and
make the San men Gorges into a hydro-electric
station. As this will change the area considerably, an
archaeological team was sent there before work was
begun, to make a close study of the place (see the
report published in Chinese by the Academy of
Science: *The traces of the San men Gorges Canal,
San men xia cao yun yi ji*, Peking 1959, 129 p., 43 p.
of plates). Zhou dynasty tombs were found near
the pass, containing bronze objects (cauldron,
mirror, weapons) and remains were found on the
islands dating from the Yin and from the Neolithic
cultures of Long shan and Yang shao.

Qi li pu station lies east of San men xia, on the
railway line. About half a mile to the south, amidst
a landscape of steep rocks, known as the Battlements
of Wang mang (Wang mang zhai), near the village of
Wen tang cun, are some Buddhist carvings, dating
from the Tang (some from the Da li period, 766–780),
carved out of a huge vertical cliff.

THE AREA EAST OF LUO YANG

Gong xian

The town of Gong xian is south of the confluence
of the River Luo and the Yellow River, half way
along the railway line from Luo yang to Zheng zhou.

1. Iron work under the Han. The sites of several
forges were found at Tie cheng kou, near Gong xian,
in 1958, dating from the 2nd century B.C. Excavations
uncovered the remains of seventeen furnaces, pig-
iron (containing 33% carbon), and cinders which
prove that coal was already in use.

2. Northern Wei Buddhist Caves. The five Shi ku
si caves are nearly 2 miles north-west of Gong xian,
on the north bank of the River Luo, at the east end
of the Mang shan Hills. They were hollowed out
between 517 and 534, under the Northern Wei, which
earned them the name of Xi xuan si; the present
name, which means "Temple of the Caves" dates
from the Qing.

The outside of the cliff has three large statues of
Bodhisattva (the biggest is 17 feet high) and 238 little
niches. The caves are numbered from 1 to 5, beginning
from the west (left). *Cave No 1* has scenes of adoration
of the Buddha (unfortunately very badly lit); *Cave*

No 3 has a set of musicians carved along the bottom of the walls; *Cave No 5* has lotus flowers and apsaras on the ceiling. The style is extremely even; some details foreshadow the art of the Sui.

3. Tang Pottery kilns. Large quantities of pottery shards dating from the Tang (bowls, plates, figures) have been found south-west of Gong xian, on the banks of the River Luo (near the railway bridge). This may possibly be the site of the "Gong xian pottery kilns" mentioned in contemporary texts. Similar shards have been found even in the ruins of the Da ming gong Palace north of Xi an.

4. Song Dynasty Imperial Tombs. Eight Northern Song dynasty imperial tombs lie south-west of Gong xian, on the plain between the River Luo and the Song shan, near the town of Zhi tian zhen. They contain the remains of the seven first Emperors of the dynasty and one of their ancestors, Chao Hong yin. Small annex tombs, usually north of the main tomb, house the remains of the Empresses and other members of the imperial family. The general layout of the tombs is based on the Tang tombs (north-south orientation, a square tumulus enclosed in a square wall, with a door on each side, and an alley of statues leading up to it from the south). The Emperors themselves did not build their tombs during their lifetimes, but each tomb was built by the successor, who had to see that the work was completed in the seven months which followed the Emperor's death (this is one reason why the tombs are less elaborate than the Tang tombs). The tombs were damaged by the Jin armies, but even so, all eight of them are still in good condition. The statues on either side of the sacred way are particularly impressive (the way is

ENVIRONS DE LUO YANG — ENVIRONS OF LUO YANG

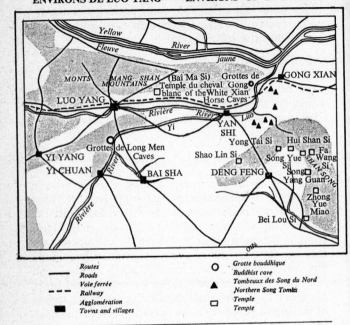

——	Routes	
	Roads	
- - -	Voie ferrée	
	Railway	
■	Agglomération	
	Towns and villages	

○	Grotte bouddhique
	Buddhist cave
▲	Tombeaux des Song du Nord
	Northern Song Tombs
□	Temple
	Temple

unusually broad): animals (sheep, lions, tigers, elephants with their keepers, horses and riders) and men (civil and military officials, and envoys from tributary states, wearing their national costume, and carrying an offering).

Yan shi

Yan shi is a district headquarters on the railway line from Zheng zhou to Luo yang, about 18 miles from Luo yang. Eu Fu (712-770), considered with

Li Bai (701–762) to be the greatest Tang poet, is buried two and a half miles to the west of the town. His tomb is a little mound encircled by a hexagonal brick wall, with a stele in front of it.

Deng feng

Deng feng is the same distance from Zheng zhou and Luo yang, south of Song shan Hill, about 37 miles as the crow flies from Luo yang. A road leads there from Yan shi. Several extremely interesting historical monuments lie round Deng feng (see map, p. 806).

The **Little Forest Monastery (Shao lin si)**, about 12 miles north-west of Deng feng, was one of the greatest centres of Chinese Buddhism. It was founded under the Northern Wei in 496, and later on became the residence of an illustrious Indian monk, Boddhidarma. Da mo, as he is called in Chinese, landed in Guang dong in about 520 and went to Jian kang (present Nanking) to see the Liang Emperor Wu, the protector of Buddhism. Coming straight to the point, he explained to the Emperor that in spite of all his good actions in the past, he had not yet acquired even a shadow of merit, as the only conceivable merit was the mystic knowledge of the nothingness of everything. Disappointed by the Emperor's inability to understand him, Boddhidarma is then said to have crossed the Yellow River on a reed and to have settled at Shao lin si, where he spent 9 years sitting motionless in front of a wall, his eyes fixed on it, in a state of illumination. He died in 535, was buried in the area, and is supposed to have gone back to India on foot, wearing only one sandal, as the other stayed in his grave. He is considered as the first patriarch and founder of Chinese *Chan* (*chan* is an abbreviated translation of a sanskrit word meaning "meditation"; the Chan sect, called Zen in Japanese, teaches the rejection of books, doctrines and reflection, and is founded on introspection alone, see p. 152). The historical existence of Boddhidarma has but scant support. However, he is constantly present in the Chinese Buddhist tradition. He is often represented sailing on his reed, sitting in front of a wall, or in other anecdotes which are told about him.

The Shao lin si was enlarged under the Sui, burned down in 617, rebuilt under the Tang 10 years later, and enlarged again under the Song, the Yuan and the Ming. Ancient frescoes, in excellent condition, in the main temple (Temple of the Thousand Buddhas, Qian fo dian), depict 500 *luo han* (arhats). The temple is a fine building 7 bays wide; the façade is unusually tall and the roof is extremely plain, with no overhang. The monastery has given its name to a type of wrestling (shao lin quan), which is still practised in China and Japan. The spot in the main temple which was used for training can still be seen.

The **Forest of Stupas (Ta lin)** is a few hundred yards south-west of the monastery. 220 little towers stand on the side of the hill, built in memory of heads of the monastery.

A little Buddhist temple, called the **Chu zu an** (the First Ancestor's Monastery) stands on the hillside about half a mile away. The main temple dates from the Song (1125). It is the oldest wooden temple in He nan. The stone pillars inside are covered with bas-relief carvings which are most important in the history of art.

The **Yong tai Monastery (Yong tai si)** and the **United Virtues Monastery (Hui shan si)** are both north of Deng feng. The second was founded under the Northern Wei, between 471 and 475, and was originally intended to be a leisure palace for the Emperor. Under the Tang, many distinguished people were priests there, among them the astronomer, mathematician, and scholar Zhang Yi xing (682–727). All that now remains is a large hall 9 bays wide, a Tang pagoda, a stele dating from 576 and another dating from 549. The second one, which dates from the Eastern Wei, has two bas-relief Bodhisattvas on one side and 92 little niches containing 106 Bodhisattvas, all delicately carved in bas-relief, on the back.

The **Song shan Monastery (Song yue si)** is in a valley on the slopes of the Song shan, about 3 miles north-west of Deng feng. It was founded under the Northern Wei in 508 and finished in 512, and was used at first as a leisure palace by Emperor Xuan wu. In 520, he had 15 pagodas and palaces built, with a total of over 1,000 intercolumniations. One of the pagodas is still standing today; it is the oldest pagoda in China, and one of the few twelve-sided ones. The base consists of twelve sides, completely plain, followed by twelve sides with carvings, separated by little half columns. Fifteen cornices above taper off to the top, describing a parabolic curve. It is built entirely in brick, and is 130 feet high. It is classed as a historical monument.

To the east lies another monastery, known as the **Monastery of the King of the Law (Fa wang si)**.

The **Song yang Academy (Song yang shu yuan)** is east of Deng feng: the academy "south of Song shan" *(Song yang)*. It was founded as an imperial academy in 484 under the Northern Wei, transformed into a Taoist academy under the Sui *(dao yuan)*, and into a Taoist Monastery under the Tang *(guan)*, hence its name: **Song yuan guan**. It was one of the four great imperial academies under the Song. It was abandoned under the Jin, the Yuan and the Ming, and rebuilt under Kang xi (1662-1723). Two evergreens in the courtyard date from the Han; the trunk of the largest one is 45 feet in circumference. A Tang stele, erected in 744, 28 feet high, stands outside.

The **Central Peak Temple (Zhong yue miao),** about 2 miles outside the town, at the foot of the Song shan, is the most interesting monument at Deng feng. Song shan, also called Gao shan, is one of the five sacred mountains of ancient China: the central mountain. It is therefore called the Central Peak as well (Zhong yue). Like the four other sacred mountains, the Central Peak had its own special worship, and was a religious centre (see Tai shan, p. 736). The temple and the enclosure date in their general outline from the Kai yuan era (713-741) of the Tang. Most of the buildings were restored and rebuilt under the Song and the Jin, and then again under the Qing during the Kang xi and Qian long eras. The buildings as a whole probably covered about 6 square miles. Under the Song, they included 850 pavilions housing steles and 470 frescoes. The main temple where the Emperors offered sacrifices to the sacred mountain is beyond a series of courtyards and gateways, surrounded by ancient evergreens. Bronze statues of armed guards rise straight out of the ground in one of the courtyards. The oldest thing of all near the temple is a pair of *que* dating from the reign of the Han Emperor Wu, or to be more precise, from 118 B.C. They are small stone buildings, 15 feet high, originally placed one on each side of a way leading to the temple. They now stand surrounded by fields, to the south of it. They contain engravings of considerable archaeological interest. In 110 B.C. Emperor Wu climbed Song shan and gave

it the name of Tai shi, hence the name of the two buildings *(Tai shi que)*. With two other similar buildings in
the area, they are classed as historical monuments (the
others are the Qu mu que, one and a half miles north
of Deng feng, and the Shao shi que, 3 miles west of
Deng feng).

The **Stele Tower Monastery (Bei lou si)** lies south of
the temple.

9 miles south-east of Deng feng, north of the town
of Gao cheng zhen, an **observatory (guan xing tai)**
stands in the enclosure of the Duke of Zhou's Temple
(Zhou gong miao). It is a brick tower, over 30 feet
high, with four trapezium-shaped sides which are
slightly sloping, making it look rather like a pyramid.
Flights of stairs lead up to the top on two sides. A vertical corridor which used to contain bronze guide marks
divides the north façade into two equal parts. At the
bottom of it, a flat wall one and a half feet wide runs
for 96 feet perpendicular to the façade. It used to have
marks on it to measure the shadow thrown by the top
of the vertical corridor. This contraption, called *shi gui*
or *liang tian chi* ("sky measurer") enabled the winter
and summer solstices to be calculated. The observatory, which includes other things as well, was built
under the Yuan, in 1279, by Guo Shou jing (1231–1314)
(see p. 416), the astronomer, hydrographer and mathematician. It is the oldest astronomical observatory in
China to survive in its complete state. A small covered
building was built on the top of it later on; it was
repaired under the Ming in 1542. The observatory is
classed as a historical monument.

ZHENG ZHOU

The town is 15 miles south of the Yellow River, at
the junction of the Peking-Canton and Long hai rail-

ÉVOLUTION HISTORIQUE DE ZHENG ZHOU
d'après la revue «Wen Wu» (1961, No 4–5)

HISTORICAL EVOLUTION OF ZHENG ZHOU
after the magazine "Wen Wu" (1961, Nos. 4–5)

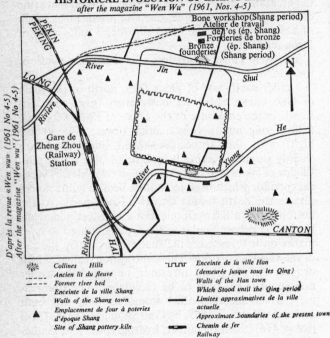

⠿ Collines Hills	⊐⊓⊔ Enceinte de la ville Han (demeurée jusque sous les Qing)
– – – Ancien lit du fleuve *Former river bed*	Walls of the Han town Which Stood until the Qing period
—— Enceinte de la ville Shang *Walls of the Shang town*	—— Limites approximatives de la ville actuelle
▲ Emplacement de four à poteries d'époque Shang *Site of Shang pottery kiln*	Approximate boundaries of the present town
	▬ Chemin de fer *Railway*

way lines (from Gan su to the sea). It has undergone
spectacular development over the last few years; it is
the capital of He nan, and has a population of 700,000.

History

Zheng zhou is at the same time one of the oldest and newest
towns in China. Under the Shang dynasty, and particularly from
2100 to 1400 B.C., a large settlement occupied the present site

of Zheng zhou; it was roughly rectangular in shape, and surrounded by earth ramparts, parts of which have been discovered recently. It is thought, judging by the sections found, that the ramparts must have been 4 to 5 miles round. The foundations of several houses, storage pits, bronze foundries, pottery kilns, bone workshops have all been found, as well as several graves. It ranks with An yang as one of the largest Shang sites in He nan.

After its brilliant beginnings, however, the town soon waned in importance; it was too near Luo yang, the Han, Wei and Tang capital, and Kai feng, the Northern Song capital until 1127. From the 13th century onwards, the economic centre of gravity was transferred to the lower Yang zi region, and then later to the Peking region, and conditions did not favour the development of the Yellow River towns. In the 17th century, brick walls were built round the town, which was then only about 2 miles round (a third smaller than the area of the Shang town).

The town began to expand once more after the building of the Peking—Canton and Long hai railway lines, whose junction was just over half a mile south-west of the old town. A large metal bridge which was built to the north of the town improved communications with the north of the country. In 1923, the railwaymen working on the Peking—Han kou line came out on strike in protest against the administration of the warlord Wu Pei fu. The strike was later to be known as the "February 7th Strike" (one of the streets in Zheng zhou is called "February 7th Avenue"). Another strike in 1926 was severely suppressed.

The town has developed enormously since 1950. Before the revolution, the population was 100,000; now it is 700,000. The town then had five factories and 700 workers (not counting 2,000 railwaymen); today it includes 149 factories and over 100,000 workers. It is the chief centre of the textile industry in He nan, and a specialised factory has been created to supply equipment for it. Agricultural tools and electrical equipment are also made. The town now contains 175 primary schools, against 38 before 1949, 42 secondary schools as opposed to 9, 13 technical schools as opposed to one, and six university faculties. There are 13 cinemas and 8 theatres.

Description

Most of the town is completely modern, consisting of red brick workers' living quarters and factories

After 1949, the new districts grew up between the old town and the railway line; now they are spreading beyond that. Visitors are generally taken to see some of the textile mills and the machine tool factory, and a little workshop specialised in working jade (electric and pedal-operated grinding and buffing wheels; the jade comes mainly from the north-eastern provinces, but a certain kind comes from He nan).

The He nan provincial museum is at Zheng zhou; it contains most of the things which have been found recently, during excavations. It is in two parts: ancient history and revolutionary history.

a) The Ancient History Section

Ground floor

Neolithic Era: Yang shao and Long shan Culture tools; *Shang Era:* good collection of things from sites at An yang, Zheng zhou, Tang yin, Luo yang, Nan yang and Xin xiang; map of the Shang settlement at Zheng zhou; *Zhou Era;* things from a tomb of the Warring States period found at Xin yang in 1956 (excellent collection of lacquer ware, wooden tomb figurines, pottery, bronzes, texts on bamboo slips); *Han Era:* rich collection of tomb figurines.

First Floor

The Six Dynasties Era: map of the division of the province of He nan during the Northern and Southern Dynasties; carved bricks from a Southern Dynasties' tomb (showing two episodes from a set of 24 examples of filial piety); photograph of the Pagoda of the *Song yue si Temple* (Wei) on Mount Song shan, south-west of Zheng zhou; *The Sui Era:* tomb of a general buried in 595 near An yang (excavated in 1958), with some beautiful tomb figurines; *Tang Era:* bronzes; photographs of the tombs of Bai Ju yi (near Long men), Du Fu, born at Gong xian, Han Yu, born at Nan yang; map of the Huang Chao rising; *Song Era:* map of the unification of the empire; map of Kai feng; iron tools; pottery "pillow"; map of the kilns under the Song; photograph of four iron statues, 10 feet high, at the Zhong yue miao Temple on the south slopes of Song shan; anchor found at Kai feng; bas-relief carvings from Song tombs (fish-wives, acrobats); photograph of an imperial tomb at Gong xian; reproduction of wall-paintings found in 1951 in a tomb at Bai sha zhen (north-west of Yu xian); copy of the works of Wang An shi; photograph of the Yue Fei Temple at Huai yang (east He nan), iron statues of the traitors who had Yue Fei condemned to death; *Yuan Era:* specimens of paper money; photographs of an observatory 30 *li* south-east of Deng feng xian, and of the Tian wang si Pagoda (at Hui xian); the agronomist Wang zhen, author of a treatise on agriculture; the Red Turbans rising, led by Liu Fu tong; *Ming Era:* Hong wu period coins; steles recording shifts in population; pottery, among other things three large pieces with design in brown; large bronze mirror; photograph of the Shao lin Temple at Deng feng; the technical encyclopaedia of *Tian gong kai wu;* photographs of stone animals from a Ming tomb at Xin xiang, south of An yang; model of a house from a tomb.

b) History of the Revolution

Railwaymen's strike in Zheng zhou in 1923; map of peasant associations (along the railway line); map of damage done by the 1938 floods (the Yellow River flooded 9,360,000 *mu* of land and caused the death of

470,000 people); map showing the comparative strength of forces in the Zheng zhou region just before 1945 (the Japanese held the railway lines, the Communists held the rest of the countryside).

KAI FENG

Kai feng is a town of 300,000 inhabitants east of Zheng zhou, a few miles south of the Yellow River. It was capital of China several times, for instance under the Northern Song (960–1127). It is still a cultural centre, but it has little industry and plays only a minor part in the economy of the province. Handicrafts still flourish there, however, and the town acts as the commercial centre for agriculture in the east He nan plain.

History

Kai feng, then called Da liang, was the capital of the Wei dynasty (220–265) during the Warring States period. It remained an administrative centre and became the capital of China during the Five Dynasties period (907–960). Under the later Liang (907-923), it was known as the Eastern Capital (Dong du), and at the same time, it became the headquarters of the province, under the name of Kai feng fu. Under the later Tang (923–936), it was called Bian zhou. It became the capital again under the later Jin (936–946) and remained the capital under the Han (947–950) and the later Zhou (951–960), when it was called the Eastern Capital (Dong jing) because it was the imperial capital and Kai feng fu because it was the headquarters of the province. It kept its two names through the Northern Song dynasty (960–1127), and at the same time became a magnificent metropolis, also called Bian jing or Bian liang. The Song town was divided into three concentric parts, as the Yuan capital at Peking was later: imperial city, inner city and outer city. The Dragon Pavilion in Kai feng shows where the Song imperial city was.

Meng Yuan lao, a Song author, left a description of the town, called *Flowery Account of the Dream of the Eastern Capital (Dong jing meng hua lu)*. "There (Kai feng), the Imperial Way was 300 yards wide! On each side there were covered-in arcades where the merchants, up to the years 1111-1117, were authorized to trade. Barriers, painted black, and a double barrier painted red partitioned the route from north to south, leaving a central passage which was reserved for the emperor and prohibited to people and horses. Traffic was confined to the arcades, beyond the barriers. Two narrow canals ran alongside the arcades. They had lotuses planted in them, and were bordered by flowering trees: plum, peach, pear, and apricot; so that in spring one got the impression of a brilliantly-coloured embroidery." (see J. Gernet: *Daily Life in China on the Eve of the Mongol Invasion 1250-1276*, trans. H.M. Wright, George Allen and Unwin, 1962, p. 41-42) Another document bears witness to the splendour and prosperity of Kai feng under the Song: a painting by the painter Zhang Ze duan, kept in the Imperial Palace at Peking. It is a horizontal scroll painting over 15 feet long full of minute details of the everyday life in the town, the harbour, the shopping districts, general merry-making, the arrival of a caravan of camels, etc. The painting is called *Qing ming Festival on the River (Qing ming shang he tu)*. The Wen wu publishing house (Peking) published a reproduction of it in black and white on 20 separate sheets in 1959.

The Nu zhen armies (Jürched) took Kai feng in 1126 and all this splendour came to a sudden end. The invaders captured Emperor Hui, his son, Emperor Qin, all their court, over 3,000 people altogether, and took them as prisoners to north-east China. At the same time, they sacked the palace, removed everything which they could find of value in the capital and took with them the Chinese craftsmen, artists and musicians who worked there. One prince alone escaped the disaster, and proclaimed himself Emperor in Nanking in 1127. He later established the Southern Song capital at Hang zhou. As for the town of Kai feng, it never recovered. The Nu zhen (Jin) called the town Bian jing, then Nan jing when they established their capital there in the Zhen you period (1213-1217). It was called Nan jing, then Bian liang under the Yuan, Bei jing under the reign of the first Ming Emperor, and then finally was given the name of Kai feng. Under the Ming and the Qing it was the capital of He nan.

The position of Kai feng, in the middle of the great plain of north China, has several times made it the centre of violent struggles. When the Mongols attacked the Jin in their capital in 1232, the Jin used grenades against them, an important event in the history of fire arms. In 1644, the defenders of the town,

faithful to the Ming dynasty, put up a frantic resistance against
the Manchu invasion; they opened the dykes of the Yellow
River to flood the area. 300,000 people are said to have died
as a result. The proximity of the Yellow River has always been
dangerous for the town, even in peace time. If the dykes were
not kept in good repair, or if the river rose suddenly, floods
could sweep though the town. This may well have been one
of the reasons why Kai feng never became an important industrial
city at the end of the 19th and the beginning of the 20th centuries.
For a long time, the town remained extremely conservative,
closed to foreign influence, and relatively slow to develop
(it had 280,000 inhabitants in 1923 and has 300,000 today).
A Jewish colony which settled there should be mentioned here;
they came, probably from Hang zhou, under the Jin. They were
mostly money changers, bankers or brokers, and held influential
positions in the town, and in the 14th and 15th centuries, their
community numbered about a thousand. In 1489, it included
70 families. In 1904, only 6 families remained. Three steles,
dating from 1489, 1512 and 1619 record details of the history of
the community. (See *Inscriptions Juives de Kai feng fou* by
J. Tobar, Imprimerie de la Mission Catholique, Shang hai,
1912.)

Before the liberation, the town possessed flour mills, oil
presses, and a factory making electrical parts. Since the liberation,
modern factories have been built (agricultural machinery factory,
chemicals factory).

Description

The **Dragon Pavilion (Long ting)** is in the north-west
corner of the old town walls, where the imperial
palaces stood under the Song. Under the Ming, the
King of Zhou's Palace (Zhou wang fu) was built here
in 1378, and destroyed in 1642 when the Yellow River
burst its banks. In 1659 (beginning of the Qing dynasty)
an examination hall was built on the same spot. It was
rebuilt under Kang xi (1662–1723) and was called the
Palace of the Life of Ten Thousand Years (wan shou
gong). It is an impressive building, five bays wide, with
a double roof, built on a pyramid made up of several
massive terraces. It is usually called the Dragon Pavi-

lion, because a cube-shaped stone inside, about 6 feet on each side, is carved with dragons on four sides. It was probably the pedestal of a throne originally. Lakes surrounded with vegetation lie on two sides of the pavilion.

The **Xiang guo si Monastery** is in the south of the town. It was founded under the Northern Qi in 555, and rebuilt under the Tang in 712. Under the Tang, and even more under the Song, it was one of the foremost Buddhist monasteries in China; under the Northern Song, it was the centre of the activity of the capital. It was rebuilt under the Ming in 1484, then completely destroyed when Kai feng was swept by floods in 1642. The present buildings date from 1766 (Qian long). They include: the Great Treasure Temple (Da xiong bao dian), the Octagonal Palace with Glazed Tiles (Ba jiao liu li dian) and the Palace of the Sutras (cang jing dian). These magnificent buildings have been restored by the government, and now contain an exhibition, a nursery school, a library and the Palace of Youth (Qing nian gong). Before the liberation, it was a market.

For the history of the monastery, see *Study on the Xiang guo si (Xiang guo si kao)*, by Xiong Bo lü, Zheng zhou 1963, 269 p.

In the north-east of the town stands a slender, tall pagoda, entirely covered with brown glazed tiles: the **Iron Pagoda (Tie ta),** so called because of its colour. The wooden pagoda belonging to the Shang fang si Monastery was burned down in 1044, and this one was built to replace it in 1049; it is a thirteen storey octagonal brick pagoda, 175 feet high, entirely covered with glazed tiles, decorated with apsaras, dragons, unicorns and Bodhisattvas. It was badly damaged when the Japanese bombed the town in 1938, but it has recently been carefully restored and classed as a historical monument. It is sometimes called by the last name given to the monastery to which it was attached, although the monastery no longer exists: You guo si.

The **Old Music Terrace (Gu chui tai)** is in the south-east of the town, in a beautiful park; it is said to have been built during the Chun qiu period by the musician Shi Kuang. Under the Tang, great poets like Du Fu, Li Bai and Gao Shi recited their poems and drank wine there. Under the Ming, a temple dedicated to Yu the Great (Yu wang miao) was built on the terrace, and since then it has often been called King Yu's Terrace (Yu wang tai).

The Monastery of Celestial Purity (Tian qing si) used to stand in the south-east suburbs of the town. It was burned down in 1841; all that remains is a pagoda dating from the Northern Song (977). It had 9 stories when it was built, but 6 were demolished under the Yuan. The remains of it are still 99 feet high, and a little bell-tower has been built on the top. It is hexagonal, and a sutra is engraved near the south door; the bricks are carved in low relief. The pagoda is known as the **Fan ta.**

THE NORTH OF THE PROVINCE

Xin xiang

This is the largest of the towns north of the Yellow River. Xin xiang is at the junction of the Peking—Zheng zhou and the Xin xiang—Jiao zuo railway lines; the latter is going to be extended northwards into Shan xi, as far as Tai yuan. It is also the terminus for the river traffic coming from Tian jin by the Grand Canal and the River Wei, the Wei he (from Lin qing). A canal, the People's Victory Canal (Ren min sheng li qu), drains off some of the water from the Yellow River and transfers it to the Wei he at Xin xiang, thus regulating the Yellow River and irrigating the Grand Canal region in north Shan dong and south He bei.

Xin xiang is an important cotton and textile industry centre.

Jiao zuo

Jiao zuo is an industrial town west of Xin xiang, at the foot of the Tai hang Mountains. The Jiao zuo coal mines, which were small before the liberation, have been developed since 1949; Jiao zuo is now one of the most important mining towns in China.

Qin yang

Qin yang is a district headquarters north of the Yellow River beside the River Qin (Qin he), southwest of Jiao zuo. A **wooden temple** dating from the Yuan lies 3½ miles to the south-east; it used to be the Central Temple (Zhong fo dian) of the Monastery of Great Light (Da ming si).

The Buddhist **bas-relief carvings** on Mount Xuan gu shan are in the neighbourhood of Qin yang, near the village of Zi ling xiang; they consist of six groups of carvings spread along the side of a cliff. The carvings seem to date from before the Song, and to have been re-touched under the Ming and the Qing.

Bai quan

Bai quan means "a hundred springs". It is nearly 2 miles north-west of Hui xian, and it is a district headquarters, about 12 miles north of Xin xiang. The springs rising at the foot of the Tai hang Mountains flow into four little artificial lakes, dug out under the Tang to control the irrigation of the surrounding plain, and remade or repaired over the centuries which followed. Round the lakes are 43 ancient monuments altogether: bridges, archways, pavilions, halls. One of the most interesting is the terrace known as Xiao tai, where Sun Deng (209–241), a hermit, lived under the Jin dynasty, and studied the *Classic of Changes (Yi jing);* he was also a poet and musician, and was much admired by the two best-known poets of the time, Ruan ji (210–263) and Ji Kang (223–262); nearby is the study of the philosopher Shao Yong (1011–1077), who was one of the Song philosophers; the academy run by the Confucianist Sun Qi feng (1584–1675) is there as well. Other scholars and philosophers had houses and taught there too, particularly under the Song and the Ming. In 1952, an Office for the Upkeep of Ancient Monuments was created at Bai quan.

Tang yang

It is a district headquarters on the railway line, about 12 miles south of An yang. Another line goes from Tang yang to the town of He bi, to the west, which has become a coal mining centre since the liberation.

Tang yang is the birthplace of **Yue Fei** (1103–1142), the general who fought heroically to defend the China of the Song against the Jin invaders. Under the Ming, in 1450, a temple was built in memory of him in the south-west of the town (Yue Fei miao). It consists of three archways and four temples, all in excellent condition (they were repaired several times under the Qing). Over 100 steles stand in the enclosure; some of them are engraved with poems and other passages written by Yue Fei.

Near the village of Miao kou xiang, about 18 miles west of the town, a small cave has been hollowed out of the base of a high cliff, with carvings in it dating probably from the end of the Six Dynasties period (6th century?).

Xun xian

It is a district headquarters south-east of Tang yang, on the banks of the Wei he. The Monastery of the Thousand Buddhas (Qian fo si) is about half a mile south-west of the town, on Mount Fu qiu shan. Two small caves have been cut out of the rock, with carvings of Buddhas and Bodhisattvas covering the walls. Under the Ming, a **Temple of the Princess of the Coloured Clouds (Bi xia gong)** was built nearby. It was repaired under the Qing, and is in good condition.

The **Monastery of Celestial Tranquillity (Tian ning si)** stood north-east of the mountain, on Mount Da pei shan; it was founded under the Northern Wei. All that remains of it now is a stone Buddha, about 80 feet high. Under the Qing, several other buildings appeared here; the **Temple to Lu Dong bin (Lu zu miao)**, dedicated to the Taoist immortal, the **Temple to Yu the Great (Yu wang miao)**. The Yang ming Academy (Yang ming shu yuan) and the Eight Dragon Cave are nearby.

An yang

An yang is in the north of He nan, on the railway line going to He bei. It used to be a busy trading centre, but not a production centre; it has become an industrial town since the liberation.

In 1899, an important discovery was made near the village of Xiao tun cun, about one and a half miles north-west of the town, on the south bank of the River Huan (Huan he), about half a mile west of the railway bridge over the river. The **remains of Yin** (Yin xu), the Shang dynasty capital (1711–1066 B.C.) were found. Wan Yi rong, the epigraphist and archaeologist (1845–1900), noticed some unusual writing on a bone which he had bought from a chemist to be used as medicine. He went into the matter immediately, and found that the bone, sold as a "dragon bone", came from the neighbourhood of An yang, from a place on the banks of the River Huan. In his *Historical Records*, Si ma Qian states that the ruins of Yin were on the banks of this river. Excavations proved him to be right. The characters dated from the Shang period; they still resemble pictograms fairly closely, but are already developing into an ideographic style of writing. As they were engraved on tortoise shells and the shoulder blades of oxen, they were called *jia gu wen*, "writing on tortoise shell and bone". Several thousand fragments of bone and tortoise shell were found at An yang; they were originally used for divination. Questions to be asked of the oracle were engraved on them, and they were thrown into the fire. The pattern of the cracks caused by the fire gave the answer. In the *Classic of Changes (Yi jing)*, one of the oldest books in existence in China, information can be found about this ancient method of divination.

The documentary value of the *jia gu wen* found at An yang even surpassed all hopes. They enable studies of various aspects of the Shang civilisation to be made, give the names of some of the kings, and afford definite proof of the historical reality of this dynasty which many scholars were inclined to accept only as legend.

At first, the excavations were conducted in somewhat haphazard fashion. Many foreigners removed the *jia gu wen*, so that now they are scattered all over the world, and imitations were made. From 1928 onwards, they were organised more systematically. Nearly all the *jia gu wen* which the Chinese still possessed were taken to Tai wan by the Guo min dang in 1945.

Many other things were found apart from the inscriptions on the site of the Shang capital. Large numbers of tools, and different kinds of utensils, were uncovered. Some of them are now exhibited in the Peking Historical Museum (see p. 432); among the most interesting are a magnificent bronze vessel decorated with tigers and dragons, a large musical stone *(qing)*, pottery, and some superb pieces of jade. Several remains of palaces, communal houses and workshops were found. The most spectacular discovery of all was probably a tomb which proved that the Shang kings were accompanied in death by an impressive train of slaves, domestic animals, chariots, and horses (see the reproduction of the tomb in the Peking Historical Museum).

The first Shang dynasty capital was Yan, near the present town of Qu fu, in Shan dong. In about 1300 B.C., King Pan geng moved his court north of the Yellow River and founded Yin, the new capital. The period from the founding of the dynasty until the transfer of the capital is usually called the "Shang dynasty", and the period from the founding of Yin to 1066 B.C. the "Yin dynasty". Often, instead of using the term Shang, "the Shang and the Yin" is used.

Xu chang

Xu chang is in the centre of He nan, south of Zheng
zhou, on the railway line to Wu han. It is an important
tobacco growing centre.

An old bridge called the **Eight League Bridge (Ba li
qiao)** is west of the town. It is said to have been built
at the end of the Han dynasty, in 200 A.D., and to have
witnessed a memorable scene at the fall of the dynasty.
The rebel General Cao Cao, who was preparing to
found the Wei dynasty, took the Han general, Guan
Yu, prisoner, but treated him with generosity and appointed him general under his command. Guan Yu,
however, faithful to the Han cause, escaped. Cao Cao
pursued him to the Eight League Bridge, and when he
caught up with him, offered him a cotton robe. Guan
Yu took it with the point of his sword, put it on his
shoulders, and galloped off. A stele marks *the spot
where Guan di picked up the robe with the point of his
sword (Han Guan di tiao pao chu)*. Guan Yu is ref-
ered to as Guan di, "Emperor Guan" in the inscription; he received this title when he was transformed by
popular belief into the god of war. His feats of arms
and his loyalty to the Han between them earned him
the honour of deification. He appears in the *Romance
of the Three Kingdoms* (San Guo Yan yi).

The region west of Xu chang contains many historical monuments worth pointing out. The most important of them are at Bai sha zhen, Jia xian and Lin ru.

Bai sha zhen

"The town of white sands" is north-west of Xu
cheng, about 18 miles south-east of Deng feng, in the
valley of the River Ying (Ying he), a tributary of the
Huai. When work was begun in 1951–1952 on a reser-

voir on the River Ying, three underground Song tombs
were found near Bai sha zhen. They contained some
beautiful frescoes depicting domestic scenes, merry-
making and music. They are now in the Zheng zhou
museum (see p. 815). A detailed archaeological report
was published in Chinese on the tombs: the *Bai sha
Song Tombs (Bei sha Song mu)*, (pub. Wen wu, Peking
1957, 102 p. 49 p. of plates).

Jia xian

Jia xian is a district headquarters over 30 miles west
of Xu chang, in the valley of the river Ru (Ru he).
A little village, **Su fen si cun, the Su Tomb Monastery
Village,** lies about 13 miles north-west of it.

The "three Su", Su Xun, Su Shi and Su Zhe, all
great Song writers and poets, are buried here. Su Shi
(1037–1101), the son of Su Xun and the elder brother
of Su Zhe, is the most famous of the three, and best
known under his literary name of Su Dong po. He
lived at Xu chang at the end of his life. The tombs
stand grouped together in a little wood of 600 evergreens. The monastery buildings contain numerous
Ming and Qing steles, and a statue of Su Dong po.

Lin ru

Lin ru is on the River Ru; hence its name, which
means "which gives on to the Ru". Roads go to it from
Luo yang and Deng feng, which is about 21 miles
north. The White Clouds Monastery (Bai yun si) is
about 5 miles north-east of the town; it is more often
called the **Wind Hollow Monastery (Feng xue si)** from
the name of the valley in which it stands. It was founded
under the Tang, partly rebuilt under the Five Dynasties, in 950, and restored under the Ming and the

Qing. Most of it is in excellent condition. In the centre
stands a square pagoda built during the Kai yuan
period (713–742) of the Tang dynasty. The Zhong fo
dian is probably the most striking of the halls of the
temple; it stands in the middle of the central courtyard
of the monastery. Judging from its style, it was probably built under the Jin dynasty. The sculpture inside
is of the same period, or perhaps a little later (Song?).

Ping ding shan

Ping ding shan is about 46 miles west of Luo he, and
linked to it by the railway. It is the centre of a coal-
bearing area which has been developed since the liberation, and its coal industry is expanding rapidly. The
town is on the edge of the great He nan plain, where
it meets the foothills of the western He nan mountains.

Huai yang

Huai yang is a district headquarters about 46 or
more miles east of the town of Luo he, in the eastern He
nan plain. A large mound of earth about 30 feet high
rises north of the town, near the River Cai: the **tomb of
Tai hao.** Tai hao, or as he is more often called, **Fu xi,**
is one of the mythical emperors of classical China.
Tradition has it that it was he who taught men the art
of hunting and fishing, the art of animal-rearing and
net-making. He invented the lyre, and from the designs
on a tortoise shell, he took the eight trigrams *(ba gua),*
symbols which each consisted of three complete or
broken lines. They are the basis of the *Classic of
Changes (Yi jing),* an old treatise on divination which
is one of the Confucian classics. Fu xi is also said to
have invented the calendar and to have drawn up rules
for matrimony.

Several buildings stand round the mound, dating from the Ming, and restored or rebuilt under the Qing (three large gateways, two temples). Pilgrimages used to be made here each spring. Since the liberation, the buildings have been repaired and the whole place converted into a public park.

Xin yang

Xin yang is a town in the south of He nan, about 11 miles from the border of Hu bei, on the line from Zheng zhou to Wu han. Until the beginning of this century, Xing yang was the furthest point which could be reached by carriages coming from the north; south of it began the road through the mountains separating He nan from Hu bei, which was unsuitable for carriage traffic. Xin yang is the economic centre of south He nan.

Chang tai guan is about 12 miles north of Xin yang, on the railway line. In 1956, one of the most important archaeological discoveries of the last few years was made about 2 miles north-west of the town. Some people digging a well came across the underground tomb of a **great personage** (a prince?) **of the kingdom of Chu.** This large kingdom which held the south of China (Hu bei, Hu nan) during the Warring States period had a culture of its own, completely different from the northern Chinese kingdoms. The tomb contained large numbers of things whose archaeological and artistic value is so great as to be inestimable: musical instruments (among them a complete set of bronze bells, a wooden lute), bronze cauldrons and other vessels, lacquer ware, jade, wooden carvings of men, carvings depicting grinning monsters (deities?), painted black, with long red tongues. A wooden bed covered with lacquer ornaments, and texts written on bamboo slips, were also found. Some of these things or copies

of them are on show in the Peking Historical Museum
(see p. 437) and in the Zheng zhou Museum (see p. 814).

Mount Ji gong shan is south of Xin yang, near the
Hu bei border; it is a delightful place to spend a holiday, and is well known for its landscapes and its climate. Hotels, sanatoria and a swimming-pool have
been built there.

Nan yang

Nan yang is in the south-west of He nan, in the centre
of the Nan yang Basin (Nan yang pan di), drained by
rivers flowing south into the Han, in north Hu bei.
It is the economic and administrative centre for all the
surrounding area. Until the building of the Zheng zhou-
Wu han line (1897–1905), Nan yang was an important
stage for traffic travelling between northern China and
the China of the Yang zi. The boats sailed up the Han
to north Hu bei, and then up the White River (Bai he)
as far as Nan yang. From there onwards, the travellers
took to the road to go north, through a pass 1,470 feet
above sea level, to the capitals of Luo yang or Kai
feng, where they could use the canals once more to go
on to Peking or Tian jin.

The **tomb of Zhang Heng** (78–139 A.D.), the poet and
scholar of the Han dynasty, is about 12 miles to the
north, in the Stone Bridge Town (Shi qiao zhen). His
most famous poem is *Er jing fu (Fu of the Two Capitals)*, which describes the two Han capitals, Chang an
and Luo yang, in prose poetry; his greatest invention
was his seismograph, a life size model of which is on
show in the Peking Historical Museum (see p. 443).
He was also the first person to use a source of power
to rotate his astronomical instruments. He became president of the Imperial Chancellery. His tomb is a plain
earth mound, with several steles in front of it.

The **tomb of Zhang Zhong jing** (150–219 A.D.), the great Han doctor who was also governor of Chang shan, is east of the town. Two works of his are still extant: the *Treatise on Chills (Shang han lun)* and the *Silver Casket Treatise (Jin kui gui yao lue)*. A temple (Zhang Zhong jing ci) was built near the tomb under the Yuan. It was restored after the liberation.

The **Recumbent Dragon Peak Park (Wo long gang)** is west of the town. It contains several Ming and Qing buildings. The Nan yang Historical Museum has been founded there.

Zhen ping

It is a district headquarters about 18 miles west of Nan yang. The **Pu ti Monastery (Pu ti si,** i.e. "Boddhi Monastery") is about 7 miles north of the town, on the northern slopes of Mount Xing shan. The Monastery stands near a spring, in a beautiful landscape of mountains and forest; it was first built under the Tang, and rebuilt under the reign of Kang xi in 1681. It contains precious collections of sutras.

SHAN XI

(Map see Atlas pl. 9)

The province is bordered by He bei to the east, He nan to the south, Shân xi to the west (they are separated by the Yellow River) and the Inner Mongolian Autonomous Region to the north (the other side of the Great Wall). The name *Shan xi* means "the mountainous west".

Shan xi is made up of a large mountainous plateau, whose average altitude is over 3,300 feet, separated from the He bei plain by the Tai hang and the Wu tai Mountains. The Lü liang mountains to the west include some peaks 8,500 feet high. In the north, the range curves north-eastwards to join up with other ranges, which form the foot-hills of the Mongolian plateau. Geographically speaking, therefore, Shan xi is a separate unit, like a well-fortified stronghold overlooking the plains of He bei and He nan. The plateau is covered with loess, furrowed by deep ravines. In some places, the erosion has exposed the limestone underlying the loess, and the coal deposits running through the limestone itself. In the middle of the province lies a series of depressions, each one separated from the others; the highest lies to the north, and they grow lower to the south. They were formed by lakes, which have now disappeared, leaving behind them a thick layer of alluvium which is much more fertile than the yellow loess around it. The largest ones are the Tai yuan, Lin fen and Yun cheng basins. The River Fen runs through the first two. The Shan xi climate is harder than that of the north China plain, partly because of the altitude, and partly because the winds from Mongolia bring cold in winter and heat in summer from the high continental tablelands. Snow often falls and lies for months in winter, and the temperature often drops below 5°F. The summers are hot (77° F. at Tai yuan), and droughts are not unusual.

The fertile plains of Central Shan xi, rich in mineral deposits, have been inhabited since the beginning of Chinese civilisation, during the bronze age. The Western Zhou (who had settled in Shân xi, on the other side of the Yellow River) created the fief of Jin there, with its capital near present-day Hou ma. This fief became a powerful kingdom during the Chun qiu period (770–481 B.C.), then divided into three kingdoms (Han, Wei, Zhao) during the Warring States period. When the empire was founded, and under the Han, Shan xi acted as a bulwark between the Chinese and the growing danger which the northern peoples represented (building of the Great Wall). Later on, it was to assume this role each time a strong and united Chinese empire had to defend its northern frontiers against invasion from the northern steppes (under the Sui, Tang, Northern Song and Ming dynasties).

Whenever the unity of the empire showed signs of breaking up, and the central power weakened, Shan xi became a powerful, semi-autonomous area, like a wedge driven into the heart of the empire.

During the Northern and Southern Dynasties (420–589 A.D.), non-Chinese peoples settled there. One of them, the Tobas, who founded the Wei dynasty in the Da tong area in 386, conquered the whole of northern China in half a century (439) and brought Buddhism with them. One of the dynasties which followed, the Northern Qi (550–577) was founded from Tai yuan (then called Jin yang). Li Yuan, who overthrew the Sui dynasty in 618 to found the Tang, was also based on Tai yuan (Jin yang). The same pattern repeated itself when the Tang dynasty fell, at the time of the Five Dynasties (907–960): the Tang had made Tai yuan into such a powerful military base that the generals were able to found several brief dynasties, (Later Tang, Later Jin), an independent kingdom (Later Han), and to put up strong resistance to the re-unification of the empire by the Song. The Song finally managed to bring the province to heel and check its tendencies to autonomy, but only briefly: the Liao took it soon afterwards, and were then able to march down on the Northern Song capital, Kai feng, in 1125–1126.

In the first half of the 20th century, China was again broken up into several parts and once more Shan xi became semi-independent (the warlord Yan Xi shan set up a military dictatorship there).

From a military and political point of view, the history of the province shows it was used alternately as a bulwark to defend the empire or to turn against it. From the point of view of social and economic history, it was dominated by handicrafts (mines, arsenals) and trade. Its relations with Mongolia have always been frequent, and they produced the most active merchants in all China, and the first bankers (with those at Ning po in Zhe jiang). As their province was relatively poor, they extended their sphere of activity outside it. Under the Ming and the Qing, they had guilds in every town in China. As com-

munications with Mongolia, and therefore with all Central
Asia were easy, Shan xi was one of the areas in which Buddhism
flourished particularly (see Da tong, p. 869 Wu tai shan, p. 892).
A Buddhist monk, Fa xian, set out from Ping yang, in the
modern Lin fen area, in 399 A.D. to look for a complete set
of the Buddhist canons in India. He came back by sea in 414 A.D.
The account of this journey, one of vital importance for the
history of Buddhism in China, is given in the *Fo guo ji* (*Memoir
on the Buddha's country*).

One of the main aims behind the first five year plan was
to develop industry in Shan xi, so that its iron and coal deposits,
among the most plentiful in the world, might be used for the
benefit of the whole country. Tai yuan has become one of the
foremost industrial towns in China (for steel). The Da tong
and Yang quan mines have been brought up to date and fully
equipped. Agriculture was threatened with complete failure
owing to erosion resulting from centuries of felling trees without
replanting in many areas, particularly in the north and the
west of the province. To improve this situation and prevent
further erosion of the soil (loess), extensive work has been
carried out since the liberation (replanting trees, terracing the
land, digging canals). The mountainous areas are now producing
more and more millet, maize and barley, and are tending to
develop an economy combining agriculture, stock-breeding
and forestry. The main agricultural districts are the fertile,
well-irrigated plains in the centre of the province, however.
Cotton is grown on the southern plains, particularly round Lin
fen (it is sent to the Tai yuan mills or out to other provinces),
and up to three crops of wheat have been grown over a period
of two years. Millet, gaoliang and maize are the staple crops
in the area north of Tai yuan. The Da tong area produces
only one crop of wheat per year. Fruit is grown in great variety
on the Tai yuan plain; grapes furnish the biggest crop.

The province will be described beginning with Tai yuan, and
followed by north Shan xi (Da tong, Yun gong), central Shan xi
and south Shan xi.

TAI YUAN

Tai yuan, the capital of Shan xi, is a town of a million inhabitants. It lies in the heart of the province,
4,250 feet above sea level, at the northern end of a vast
plain called the Tai yuan Basin (Tai yuan pan di).

This fertile, thickly populated plain of yellow loess is watered by the River Fen (Fen he) and numerous tributaries. It is about 95 miles from north to south. The Tai yuan Basin has some of the richest deposits of coal and iron ore in the world.

So many natural resources concentrated in a small space would have been enough to lend interest to the history of Tai yuan. But the strategic element has been just as important. Tai yuan guards the northern entrance to the central plain of Shan xi, predestined to be used as a way into China by invaders from the north. Tai yuan has had a troubled history, full of dramatic episodes, bitter struggles and outstanding people.

From the end of the 19th century, it began to develop into an industrial town and since then, its economic potentialities have never ceased to grow. Before the First World War, the population was 60,000; in 1923 it was 230,000. It is rapidly increasing at the moment.

History

East of Tai yuan, a mountain called Ji zhou shan: "Mountain where the boat was moored" stretches north-eastwards. According to the legend, Yu the Great, the mythical hero said to have founded the Xia dynasty in 2140 B.C., came to visit the area, and as the whole of the Tai yuan plain was covered with water at that time, he tied his boat up at the foot of the mountain. Numerous fossils found all over the plain prove that the lake existed until about 3000 B.C. At the end of the Neolithic Era, the waters withdrew and some drainage work may possibly have been carried out. In all events, the Tai yuan area was fairly well populated. Extensive remains dating from this period have been discovered, mainly at the foot of the hills (weapons and tools of polished stone, fragments of pottery of various kinds, among which the "Painted Pottery", *cai tao*, 2000–1500 B.C., is the most common). Numerous finds are exhibited in the Tai yuan Museum. The most unusual ones come from the sites at Yi jing cun (found in 1953, 6 miles south-west of the town), Yan jia gou (5 miles west of the town) and Dong tai bao zhuang (found in 1954, 3 miles south-east of the town). The last of these three contained skeletons of horses and pigs and some objects made of bone.

Soon after the foundation of the Zhou dynasty (1066 B.C.), the Fen valley became a fief of that kingdom; it was called Tang at first, and later Jin. The first prince to rule it was Shu yu, the younger brother of Cheng wang, the second king of the dynasty. The King of Jin's Temple (Jin wang ci), usually called Jin ci (see below, p. 852) was founded to honour the first ruler, considered as the ancestor of the country (the date of foundation is uncertain). Near the Jin ci two ancient tombs are said to be those of Prince Shu yu and his son. They have not yet been excavated. The town of Jin yang ("to the north of the River Jin"), the forerunner of Tai yuan, was probably founded under the Western Zhou; under the Chun qiu it became a fortified town. It is described as such in the *Zuo zhuan* (a chronicle going back to the Chun qiu period, written during the Warring States era) referring to an incident in 497 B.C. Clearly visible remains of the walls of this period exist south of Tai yuan, on the left of the road to the Jin ci, just before the little fortified town of Jin yuan. From the time when its walls were built in 497 B.C. up to its savage destruction under the Song in 979 A.D., Jin yang grew and pushed out its walls, but did not move from that site. Judging from the remains still visible today, near the Jin ci road, the western wall of the town must have been nearly 3 miles long at the end of the Han and under the Jin. The Jin ci stood at its gates. The poem by Li Bai, where he talks of his rides on horseback near the temple "close to the pools west of the town" bears this out.

In 588 B.C. a regime was introduced in the principality of Jin which placed the responsibility for ruling the state in the hands of six ministers. The fact that the posts were hereditary brought six families to power, and it was not long before they disagreed. Once two of them had been removed from the scene, three more, the Zhi, the Han and the Wei joined forces against the Zhao, who took refuge at Jin yang. Zhi Bo, the head of the coalition, laid siege to the town and resorted to a stratagem which seemed certain of success: he diverted the waters of the River Jin in so as to drown the town little by little. The story goes that the water had almost reached the walls when the Zhao, the Han and the Wei conspired against Zhi Bo and assassinated him, in 453 B.C. The canal he had dug still exists (see p. 854). Yu Rang, a minister in the service of Zhi Bo decided to avenge his master. He hid under a bridge and waited for Zhao Xiang zi, head of the Zhao family, to pass by. But Zhao Xiang zi discovered the plot and Yu Rang committed suicide. Remains of the bridge which witnessed the drama can still be seen near the village of Chi qiao cun ("Village of the Red Bridge"), east of the Jin ci. A little temple dedicated to Yu Rang commemorates the incident. After the death of Zhi Bo, the Han, the Wei and the Zhao divided up the territory of the principality of Jin between them and created three kingdoms. Jin yang fell to the Zhao.

Under Qin shi Huang di, the Jin yang region was called the Great Plain District (Tai yuan jun) and Jin yang became Tai yuan cheng, "Great Plain (District) Town", or simply "Great Plain". As the threat of a Hun invasion grew more real, Tai yuan became a stronghold of the utmost strategic importance under the Han. The southern stretch of the Great Wall passed (it still does) 93 miles to the north. In 200 B.C., a Chinese general's treachery nearly put Jin yang at the mercy of the Huns. Their horsemen reached the walls of Jin yang, but Liu Bang, the founder of the Han, came to the rescue with his armies and beat them back after 7 days' fighting (the final victory was won near Da tong).

As long as the empire was strong enough to resist the advance of the Huns, Jin yang was marked out for special attention from the court. The Emperor was careful to appoint members of his own family as governors there and to make visits of inspection there. But with the divisions of the Three Kingdoms Period and under the Jin, the control was relaxed. In 304, the Huns founded a dynasty (Han) and set out to take Chinese towns, led by their chief, Liu Yuan. In 312, the successor of Liu Yuan attacked Jin yang, which was guarded by Liu Kun. Liu Kun had built powerful fortifications, but all to no avail. The Chinese predominance in that area of China was at an end. The Huns were not the only ones to move in. Other peoples, such as the *Jie*, the *Xian bei*, the *Tobas* also made their growing power felt and constant wars were fought there. To defend themselves from the barbarian armies who were perpetually on the move, the peasants made their villages into fortified camps. Some names of villages round Tai yuan ("stronghold", "little fort") may well date from this period. In 396, Jin yang was conquered by the Tobas, who had founded the Wei dynasty three years earlier, and established their capital at Da tong (see p. 869). When, at the beginning of the 6th century, their power began to wane, a general, Gao Huan, took power at Jin yang (532) and brought about the division of the Wei empire into two parts. One had its capital at Ye, north He nan, and a secondary capital at Jin yang: Gao Yang, the son of Gao Huan, proclaimed a new dynasty there in 550, the Qi dynasty (Northern Qi, 550–577). Jin yang was the capital under this dynasty, almost on an equal with Ye. Spacious palaces were built there, the Jin ci was transformed into imperial gardens, Buddhist rock shrines and temples appeared in the mountains west of the town (see p. 868). In 576, the town fell into the hands of the Zhou (Northern Zhou) in spite of spirited resistance (the women and children pelted the enemy with stones from the house-tops).

When the Sui re-united the empire and restored its military power, Jin yang once more became an important frontier town, as it had been under the Han. The Sui Emperor Yang enlarged the town, encircled it with walls 40 feet high and built a military road over the Tai hang Mountains linking Jin yang with the He bei plain. He also had a luxurious palace built for himself at Jin yang. But the load on the peasants was too heavy and they rebelled. The Emperor sent Li Yuan to suppress the movement and defend Jin yang, which they were threatening. Instead of that, he took command of the rebel armies, overthrew the Sui and founded the Tang dynasty (618). He chose this name because, before marching on the capital, he went to the Jin ci to ask aid and protection of Shu yu, Prince of Tang. It was a testimony of his gratitude.

Under the Tang, the Turkish peoples who lived to the north of the frontiers began to menace the empire. To help guard the frontier, the Empress Wu Ze tian decided in 690 to raise Jin yang to the rank of "northern capital" *(bei du)*. This was the beginning of an era of splendour and power such as the town had never known before. It was made up of three different towns at that time, one built in 637 and the other under the reign of We Ze tian. The last part was east of the Fen. The *History of the Tang (Xin Tang shu)* describes Jin yang as it was then: a town of great strategic importance, great military power, but also a town of great wealth, both economically and in the field of literature and the arts. The town was rased to the ground under the Song, and little or nothing of all this splendour has survived.

Turkish armies crossed the Great Wall several times and tried to take Jin yang, but always in vain. The military power which the Tang conferred on Jin yang became a serious threat to the dynasty when the central power began to fail in the 9th century: whoever held the town could well take over the empire sooner or later. Jin yang gave no signs of revolt, however, and stood up to all the attacks of Zhu wen, the overthrower of the Tang dynasty, who founded the Liang in 907 (Later Liang). The governor of Jin yang, Li Yong ke, of Turkish origin *(Sha tuo)* remained faithful to the Tang for 15 years after their fall. His son, Li Cun xu, left Jin yang with his armies, overthrew the Later Liang and proclaimed himself Emperor at Luo yang in 923, taking the name of Tang once more for the dynasty which he founded (Later Tang). Jin yang became the "western capital" *(xi jing)*, then the "northen capital" *(bei du)*. In 936, the dynasty of the Later Jin succeeded the Later Tang, founded at Jin yang by another Turk *(Sha tuo)* called Shi Jing tang. His rise to power boded ill for the future, as he had the support of the Khitan *(Qi dan)*, future invaders of China, who were already making their presence felt in the north-east and north of China (they founded the Liao dynasty in 907). The next dynasty, the Later Han (947–950), was again founded at Jin yang, by another Turk, a general called Liu Zhi yuan. He defended the town against the assaults of the Liao armies and earned himself the rank of a popular hero because of this. He appears more than two centuries later in a Yuan period opera (in *Bai tu ji*). In 951, yet another dynasty was founded at Jin yang: the Northern Han; it was no more than a small kingdom, however, encircled by the Liao, dependent on them and paying them heavy tribute. The tribute was in fact paid by the Wu tai shan Monastery (see p. 892). The Later Zhou dynasty who meanwhile had taken over the power in North China tried several times to overcome the kingdom of the Northern Han, but never succeeded. Jin yang was an almost impregnable fortress, all the more formidable because of the bellicose spirit of its inhabitants.

This strength and pride brought misfortune to the town. Nine years after the founding of the Song dynasty (960), the Emperor Tai zu himself led his armies to overcome the little kingdom of the Northern Han; he reached Jin yang with no difficulty, but could not take the town. The walls were too solidly built, the archers too well-trained (the inhabitants of the kingdom were grouped into "archery societies"; everyone underwent training). The Emperor resorted to the stratagem which had succeeded once before in the past: the town was to be flooded out, and the Emperor himself, stripped to the waist, organised the work. The heat was overpowering; soldiers died of sunstroke, and the imperial armies retreated, carrying off with them all the peasants in the neighbourhood by force

(they were moved to Shan dong). In 976, another expedition
failed as the first one had done. When it retreated, tens of
thousands of peasants were removed by force and settled in
He nan. In 979, the second Song Emperor took up the battle
with four armies which attacked from each point of the compass,
while a fifth was responsible for blocking the way for any Liao
reinforcements who might come from the north. The Emperor
himself was in command, and finally overcame the rebel town,
which was defended by Liu Ji yuan. When the town surrendered,
the order was given for it to be set alight and rased completely
to the ground. No trace was to remain. So that the ashes themselves should be removed, the waters of the Jin and the Fen
were diverted to wash away the debris. And so Jin yang met
its end.

When he led his expedition against Jin yang, the Emperor
stayed in a nearby monastery. After his victory, he had his
portrait put there and had a new town built there, called Ping
jin, "pacified Jin". When he left, the inhabitants persistently set
fire to the monastery until the sacrifices in honour of the Emperor
were abandoned, and for 70 years they refused to live in a town
whose very name humiliated them. Like Li shi min before
him (see p. 862), the Emperor had a memorial stele put up
inside the Jin ci. The inhabitants destroyed the inscription with
hammers. The steles is said still to be standing in the Jin ci.
It was originally called the Tai ping xing guo period Stele (Tai
ping xing guo bei), but is now called the Stele with no Characters
(Wu zi bei).

The inhabitants of Jin yang gradually settled round a little
village called Tang ming zhen. As it expanded rapidly, they
decided to built walls round it and make it more like a town.
The Emperor demanded that all the street intersections should
be T-shaped inside the town, like the Chinese character pronounced *ding*, which is like a T. If the radical meaning "metal"
is added, it forms a new character, still pronounced *ding*, but
meaning "to nail". This decree was intended to symbolise
that the townsmen of the old Jin yang were *nailed down* once
and for all, and to suppress all wishes for independence. Some
of the T junctions built as a result still survive in Tai yuan,
and are quite easy to find.

The history of Tai yuan was brutally interrupted in 979,
but from the Song until now, it has continued without a break.
A town of merchants and artisans gradually grew up once more,
on the site of the south-west district of the present town. Many
of the names there, irrelevant to the life of today, refer to the

trades or markets once centred there (rice, wood, vegetable markets, etc.). From 1913 to 1949, two large monasteries founded under the Song in the 11th century acted as markets: the Great Central Market, Da zhong shi, and the Kai hua Market, Kai hua shi. The Tai yuan of the Song and the Yuan was born of the economic force represented by its trade and its handicrafts; it was a town of narrow streets, little shops crowding one against the other, busy markets, totally different from the town built by the Emperor's strategists and architects that Jin yang had been. Amusements and entertainments flourished, particularly opera. It may well be that the people of the region first acquired their taste for the theatre under the northern Qi, when the Emperor had his own companies of actors at Jin yang. Gao yang, the founder of the dynasty, was particularly fond of the theatre and acted himsel. So did Li Cun xu, the first Emperor of the Later Tang dynasty, who took the name Li Tian xia as his stage name. He was an accomplished musician and composed music for operas. One of his compositions was still being sung at Tai yuan under the Song. Several interesting documents have been found in the last few years on Shan xi opera and the theatre under the Yuan (see Zhao cheng, p. 904).

The military history of Tai yuan did not end in 979 either. The Liao brought still more pressure to bear on the northern frontiers in the 10th and 11th centuries. In 986, Emperor Zhao Guang zi, who had had Jin yang destroyed, sent General Fan Mei on an expedition north of the Great Wall to re-conquer the territories lost to the Liao. With him was sent Yang Ye, who had shown incomparable courage when defending Jin yang against the Emperor himself. Yang Ye left first and was to retreat before the Liao, thus enticing them into an ambush where Fan Mei's army awaited them. But Fan Mei, who had heard that Yang Ye was to be unlucky in arms this time, retreated and left him to fight it out alone. His army fought gallantly, but was wiped out by the Liao. Yang Ye was taken prisoner, but refused to eat and died in three days' time. In novels and classical opera, he has become the prototype of unhappy loyalty. One of the operas most frequently put on by the Peking Opera, "The Lady General", tells how, when all the men in the family had perished in the struggle against the Liao, the women took over and were victorious.

The Northern Song were too weak to resist the invader for long. In 1115, the *Nu zhen* had founded the Jin dynasty. In 1122, they took Peking (Yan jing), the Liao capital. In 1125, two armies started from there to march on Kai feng, one going through the He bei plain, the other through Da tong and Tai yuan. The head of the Tai yuan garrison in charge of the defence of Shan xi fled even before the enemy arrived, and once more the townsmen were left to defend their own town. Led by Zhang Xiao chun and Wang Bing, they put up a fight which lasted for eight months. But the Jin finally got the upper hand, by surrounding the town with walls, so that they could fight on a level with the adversaries (1126). Wang Bing committed suicide, Zhang Xiao chun was executed by the conquerors.

Although it was now cut off from the Chinese empire, which had retreated south of the Yang zi River, Tai yuan recovered from the defeat. As a trading centre, it was not affected by the change of masters, except for the better: trade with the north was made easier by the fact that the Jin, and then the Mongols, held both sides of the Great Wall. Tai yuan was handed over to the Mongols in 1218. From 1348, violent peasant revolts broke out in almost every part of China, and like other regions, the Tai yuan area was ravaged by wars. The population fell in Tai yuan and round it. It is said that all the old families in the town settled there under the Ming, and that one only, the Chen, dates back to the Yuan.

In 1368, the Ming founded a national dynasty and took the Great Wall in hand once more. From 1376, the walls of Tai yuan, still threatened by the Mongols, were enlarged and rebuilt. They were repaired regularly until the 19th century, and large sections of them still survived in 1949. They hindered the development of the town, however, and were knocked down from 1950 onwards. They were originally 7 miles round, about 40 feet high, with a tower at each corner and 92 turrets. There were eight gates. Zhu Yuan zhang, founder of the Ming, appointed one of his sons, Zhu Gang, to be viceroy of the province of Shan xi (Jin wang). A viceroy's palace (Jin wang fu) was built from 1378 at Tai yuan. Nothing is left of it now, except the names of about a dozen streets which ran along various parts of it. Broadly speaking, the arrangement of the streets has changed little since the Ming.

In 1644, the peasant leader Li Zi cheng proclaimed a new dynasty at Xi an and started out to conquer the empire. He marched on Tai yuan first of all, whose garrison declared that it would fight to the last man. But the viceroy's hard rule had inspired so much discontent in the country that the town of Tai yuan put up no resistance at all. The Ming officials fled or gave banquets in honour of the usurper, while in the streets, the people chanted: "Open the great gate and let Chuang wang

in; when Chuang wang is there, we won't pay taxes any more"
*(Kai le da men ying Chuang wang, Chuang wang lai shi bu na
liang)*. "*Chuang wang*" means more or less "the king who
enters everywhere", "to whom all gates are open". It was the
peasants' name for Li Zi cheng. He went on to take Peking
a month later. He was thrown out almost immediately, however,
by the Manchu armies, who had seized the opportunity offered
by the change in dynasty to cross the Great Wall and seize power
in China (Qing dynasty). Li Zi cheng retreated to Tai yuan,
then to Shân xi, entrusting the defence of Tai yuan to Chen
Yong fu. Cheng Yong fu had defended Kai feng against Li Zi
cheng and had put out his left eye with an arrow. Li Zi cheng
had won him over after the victory however, breaking an
arrow in front of him as a sign of pardon. Chen Yong fu began
by putting the town of Tai yuan in order and killing all the
remaining members of the viceroy's household, as the Ming,
opposing Li Zi cheng, had collaborated with the Manchu
invaders. The first assault made by the Qing armies was resisted.
The second time they used cannons, and Tai yuan fell to them
(1644). Even so, the town was for a long time the centre of
resistance against the Qing. The resistance was mainly political, patriotically led by the scholar and official class. It
had no support from the peasants and resulted in no great
feats of arms (though there was a brief episode of resistance
based on the Jin ci).

One of the members of the viceroy's family, itself a branch
of the Ming imperial family (Zhu family) escaped the massacre
in 1644. His descendants still live near Tai yuan, in the village
of Huang ling cun. The memory of Li Zi cheng was kept green
right into the 20th century, through a feast day held at Tai
yuan on the eighteenth of the sixth month. It was called *duo
chuang* "resistance to Chuang wang", in order not to displease
the Qing, but it was in fact directed against them: the hairdressers
took the day off. When the Manchu took over power in China,
they forced all Chinese to wear the pigtail, and the corporation
of hairdressers grew correspondingly in importance. This
explains this way of protesting against the Manchu power.

The White Lotus secret society was formed under the Mongols
(Bai lian jiao). Under the Ming and the Qing, it was continued;
at the end of the 19th century, one of its branches, called the
Yi he tuan ("League of Justice and Fidelity") took over the
leadership of an anti-Western movement known abroad as the
"Boxer Movement". In the evening of June 1st, 1900, the
Boxers set fire to the English mission church. A missionary

(a woman), was killed in the fire. As the movement was rapidly growing, the provincial governor thought it advisable to lend his support to it. If he tried to protect the missionaries and the converted, he ran the risk of exposing himself to the anger of the crowd. Under the pretext of giving them his protection, he got the missionaries and the Chinese converts to assemble on June 30th, in the afternoon, and had them killed while the crowd looked on. 44 foreigners and 17 Chinese converts perished.

By picking on the missionaries, the movement attacked first and foremost the growing economic and financial power of the Western powers in Shan xi. In 1898, the governor, Hu Pin zhi, had ceded the working of the Ping ding, Yu xian, Lu an and Ze zhou (east Shan xi) mines for 60 years. Other plans appeared likely to disturb the province's economy. Hu Pin zhi himself founded a powder factory in 1892, a mill, a machine workshop and a soap factory in 1898. When the European powers occupied Peking in 1900, the Qing court, which had supported the Boxers at one stage, withdrew its support and gave way to the Europeans. Western influence increased. In 1902 it was decided to build a railway line from Tai yuan to Zheng ding (He bei). The capital used was half Russian and half Chinese; the building contract went to a French firm. The line, a narrow gauge one, was opened to traffic in 1907, four years after work began on it in 1903.

When the line reached the area where the English owned mines (Yang quan), the mining company began to annex small mines owned by the Chinese, by illegal purchase of land. A new movement took shape against the foreigners: the Mines Movement (Zheng kuang yun dong). Li Pei ren, a Shan xi student who was in Japan at the time, wrote a pathetic appeal to his compatriots and threw himself into the sea. When his coffin was brought back to Tai yuan, his appeal was read in public and inspired the inhabitants of Shan xi to raise enough money to buy back all the English mines.

The telegraph was introduced in Tai yuan in 1896. The post office followed in 1901 (partly run by the French), and the telephone in 1902. The first newspaper *(Jin bao)*, printed in lead moveable characters, appeared in 1902. Electricity was introduced in 1909. Zhu Yi wen, the first photographer in Tai yuan, was famous in the town because he was the first person to ride a bicycle there in 1901.

Education was modernised too. A military academy was founded in 1898, at much the same time as the Shan xi University (Shan xi da xue tang). The university developed considerably from 1902 onwards, under the direction of an English missionary, Timothy Richard. He was a man of wide influence, who had acted as adviser to the Chinese government during the negotiations which took place after the Boxer Movement and the Allies' arrival in Peking. He proposed that the indemnities paid by Shan xi should be put towards the founding of a university at Tai yuan. "It would eliminate ignorance, which is the cause of massacres", and would be handed over to the Chinese government after 10 years. The new university was specialised in Western teaching *(yang xue:* law, medecine, science, litterature, etc.), the old university went on giving a Chinese education *(zhong xue)*. Although the first one was administered by the Chinese, they both formed one establishment. The policy of Timothy Richard ensured that Westerners stayed in Shan xi long after the retreat of 1900. Modern Chinese historians reproach him with this, and make him into one of those responsible for the "cultural invasion" *(wen hua qin lue)* of China by the foreign powers (his name is pronounced Li ti mo tai in Chinese). Other schools were founded at Tai yuan between 1902 and 1906: a School of Agriculture and Forestry, a Teachers' Training School, a Secondary School, and primary schools. The first theatre was built in 1902. Up till then, operas were performed in temples and monasteries in the town. Under the Qing, the five big temples in Tai yuan (Guan di miao, Temple to the god of War; Cheng huang miao, Temple to the god of the Town; Nai nai miao, Temple to the Mother; Lü zu miao, Temple of Lü Dong bin; Tai shan miao, Tai shan Temple) put on operas each month, on certain days. Four other temples gave one each year. In the 27 temples to the god of War, Guan di miao, performances were held almost daily. Four different kinds of opera had grown up at Tai yuan and in the neighbouring area under the Ming and the Qing. At the turn of the century, Peking Opera and *Kun qu* were given there too. The Tai yuan area operas are still popular now, particularly the *pu ju* and *zhong lu xi* kinds.

When the 1911 revolution took place, Shan xi was the fourth province to rise against the Qing, on October 29th 1911. After a short fight, the revolutionaries won the day and proclaimed a military government in the province of Shan xi, with Yan Xi shan at the head of it. The court ordered General Wu Lu zhen, whose troops were stationed at Shi jia zhuang, to march on Tai yuan. But Wu Lu zhen, who sympathised with the republicans, did not move. Yuan Shi kai, whose influence was growing at Peking, had him assassinated (November 16th) and replaced him by a general known to be faithful to the Manchus. When the imperial army was near, Yan Xi shan made certain of a thousand supporters and fled, riding on a mule. When he saw that the revolution was gaining power, and that a new balance was about to be established between the revolution and Yuan Shi kai, he declared his allegiance to the latter and came back to Tai yuan in March 1912. He ruled Shan xi as an absolute dictator until the eve of the liberation.

The tradition of **handicrafts** in Tai yuan is a long-established one. It is likely that forges have existed there ever since the art of working metal was first discovered. Several recent finds have proved that bronze coins were struck there during the Warring States period (coins found in 1950 and 1954 bear *Jin yang* stamped on them). Under the Northern Song, the Tai yuan arsenals were the most famous in the empire, and the Emperor had coins struck there. At the Jin ci, iron statues bear witness to the art of the Song craftsmen (see p. 854). The historical records give no information on the coal mines before the Sui dynasty, but it is possible that they were worked as early as the Western Han, like others in China. They were important under the Tang and the Song, as the documents prove: the Song put a tax on the mining of coal. Pottery kilns have existed at Tai yuan since the Tang dynasty (countless fragments have been found at Tai yuan, in the Jin ci). Under the Song, the imperial court administered "state kilns". In 1936, a pottery storehouse was found (about a hundred pieces) with a bronze seal inscribed *"state pottery workshop, He dong province* (Shan xi), *Song* (dynasty)."* Another craft which flourished at Tai yuan was that of making glazed tiles (*liu li wa*). Although no definite proof has yet been found, it is possible that the tradition goes back to the Tang. It is certain, on the other hand, that the art was invented in Shan xi, and that glazed tiles were widely used in the province under the Yuan (they did not appear in Peking until the Ming dynasty). The roof of the old Temple of the god of War (Gu guan di miao) in Tai yuan has tiles and lions dating from the Yuan. The art of making glazed tiles includes all the figures which traditionally decorate the roof corners and ridges (spirits, guardians, lions, dragons, other animals). The genius of the Shan xi craftsmen transformed these figures into masterpieces of baroque art. (Zhao cheng has some excellent examples, see p. 904.)

The most famous of the craftsmen are the Su family, who live in the village of Ma zhuang cun, south of Tai yuan. The Fan lin Temple (Fan lin si) in the village is a striking example of their work.

Tai yuan has its specialities in the fields of pharmacopoeia and cookery (a delicious soup called *tou nao*, flavoured with local herbs, is eaten round about the time of the spring festival). The Tai yuan area wine, known as *Fen jiu* ("Fen wine") is said to be the best in China. It was already thought to be so under the Tang, when it was referred to as *Fen qing*, "clear Fen wine". The tribute paid by the Northern Han to the Liao included wine. When the Song conquered the Northern Han, the secret of making it was taken to Kai feng. Under the Tang and the Yuan, it was offered among the foods presented at sacrifices. Marco Polo tasted it and declared it to be excellent.

Since the liberation, a systematic programme has been put into action to make Tai yuan into a modern industrial town. It now produces textiles, machine tools, chemicals, and building materials. Mining and iron smelting are the most important industries.

Description

Although it has a rich history and has for centuries been the economic, political and cultural centre of the province, Tai yuan presents a modest air to the stranger. The only monuments to be seen inside the town are a temple and the Shan xi Museum. Five temples in the suburbs are worth a visit. The Jin ci is the most interesting of all; it is about 15 miles away, and will be described here in detail.

The two biggest monasteries in existence under the Song, the Kai hua si and the Shou ning si, which played an important part in the life of the town until the end of the Qing, were partly burned, and then were transformed into market-places in 1913. Other temples were neglected in the time of Yan Xi shan and have now disappeared. The only one to remain today is the **Temple where Goodness is Worshipped (Chong shan si),** in the south-east corner of the town. In the same spot, outside the walls, stood a monastery called the White Horse Monastery (Bai ma si) under the Song, later renamed the Prolonged Life Monastery (Yan shou si). When Zhu Gang, the son of the first Ming

Emperor, came to Tai yuan as viceroy, he enlarged the
walls of the town. The monastery was then inside the
walls and in 1381 when the Empress, his mother, died,
he made it into a large temple, with an enclosure
176 paces wide and 343 paces long, containing several
dozen buildings (the temple still contains a detailed
plan). The main temple, which was 9 bays wide and
nearly 100 feet high, was dedicated to Zhu Yuan zhang,
the founder of the dynasty and the first Ming Emperor.
Behind it, in a separate courtyard, a secondary temple,
7 bays wide, was dedicated to the memory of the
Empress. The monastery was called the Monastery of
Imperial Goodness (Zong shan si), and later the Monastery where Goodness is worshipped (Chong shan si).
The character for *zong* ("imperial ancestor") becomes
chong ("to worship") when the character for "mountain" is added on the top. When the number of monks
grew smaller, the townspeople tried to keep them from
leaving, by placing a mountain on them, ironically,
which then became part of the name. In 1864, a fire
broke out and destroyed the main temple and three
quarters of the other buildings. The present street
beside it used to be the passage through it separating
the great courtyard of the main temple from the secondary temple courtyard. The only building which survived south of the street was later transformed (1882)
into a Temple of Confucius (Wen miao). A brick gateway north of the street has three semi-circular arches,
with a pair of bronze lions cast in 1391 in front of it.
A beautiful wooden temple stands inside, 7 bays wide
and 4 bays deep, with a double roof; the upper roof
is held up by pillars on the outside. It is one of the
purest examples of early Ming architecture to be seen
in China. Its lively style bears no resemblance to the
academic formalism which prevailed under the

Qing. The temple, known as Temple of Great Mercy (Da bei dian), contains three statues about 16 feet high, representing "Bodhisattvas with a thousand eyes and a thousand hands". A little temple in one of the eastern side courtyards contains another Ming statue, which is reminiscent of the Yuan style. It portrays Bin tou lu (Pindola), a Buddhist saint and a disciple of the Buddha, who was severely reprimanded by his master one day when he was showing off his magical powers by flying over a crowd of believers, standing on his wooden alms bowl. He is worshipped as one of the great defenders of the faith. A fine bronze vase stands on a pedestal in the Da bei dian, dating from 1460. The two miniature pagodas in front of the temple date from 1586. The large bell hanging near the entrance gateway was cast in 1449. The temple possesses a **valuable collection of sutras** comprising large numbers of volumes, some of them illustrated, dating from the Song, the Yuan, and the Ming. The Song sutras are wood engraved editions, made at Fu zhou in 1085, 1208 and 1268. The Yuan editions come from Su zhou and date from 1306 and 1315. The Ming editions were printed in Peking in 1440. The temple also possesses 32 leaves of the *Da cang jing* sutra, engraved by order of the Emperor at Cheng du in 973 (this one was printed in 1108) and most of the *Taoist Canons (Dao cang)* printed under the Ming in 1446. Some of these precious editions are now kept in the library of the Shan xi Museum.

The **Shan xi Museum (Shan xi sheng bo wu guan)** possesses another collection of sutras engraved and printed under the Jin (152 scrolls). Each scroll bears the name of the translator, and often that of the donor who financed the printing of the sutra. The collection come from the Guang sheng si Monastery at Zhao cheng (see p. 904). The museum contains a collection of stone carvings, with some beautiful pieces among them, mostly of Buddhist inspiration, dating from the Western Han to the end of the Qing. Some of them were uncovered during excavations on the site of Jin yang, where, so the archaeologists think, many Qi, Sui and Tang carvings probably still lie hidden. The museum also contains stone and clay animals from a Han tomb found in 1953 in the northern suburbs of Tai yuan. In the same year, the tomb of a Tang official buried in 696 was found in the village of Dong ru cun, 9 miles south-west of the town. The tomb contained some beautiful frescoes, divided into ten parts by painted columns, and depicting 2 officials, 4 people presenting offerings and several scenes of walks and games out of doors. Other tombs, dating from the Song or earlier are constantly being found in the neighbourhood of the town, as much work is under way.

Several temples in the suburbs or surroundings of Tai yuan are well worth mentioning.

The **Temple of the Jin Minister (Jin dai fu ci)** is in the village of Lan cun, 3 miles north-west of the town; it was built in memory of Dou Chou, a minister whom Confucius greatly respected, who was assassinated by Zhao Jian zi, prince of Jin. Its date is uncertain. The shrine existed already under the Tang, and people used to come to it under the Song and the Jin to pray for rain. The present buildings date from the Yuan (1343).

An **Old Temple to the god of War (Gu Guan di miao)** stands in the village of Xiao wei ying, west of the town; it dates from the Song or even earlier. It was rebuilt under the Yuan, but in Song architectural

style. The temple, frequently restored under the Ming
and the Qing, contained a statue of Guan di which
was removed in 1951. The Temple of the Private
Appartments stands behind the temple (Hou qin
gong), the domain of the wife of Guan di. The statue
dates from the Yuan, and like the one at the Jin
ci (see p. 857), it is surrounded by 20 ladies-in-waiting.
Another temple to Guan di stood outside the east
gate of Tai yuan. It contained a rare statue of the god
of war standing brandishing a sword, and holding his
horse's bridle. The statue is 10 feet high, in bronze,
and is now exhibited in the Shan xi Museum; it
dates from the Song or the Yuan.

The **Monastery of Endless Happiness (Yong zuo si)**
is south of the village of Hao zhuang cun, near the
town. It is famous for its two pagodas (shuang ta)
which appear on the flag of Tai yuan. They were built
under the Ming, during the Wan li period (1573–1620),
at a time when the monk Fo deng was thinking of
settling to preach at the monastery. Fo deng left
soon after and settled at Wu tai shan (see p. 892).

Three large Buddhist monasteries were founded near
Tai yuan under the Ming and the Qing: the **Monastery of the White Cloud (Bai yun si)** was the largest
(it was founded during the reign of Kang xi, 1662–
1723). It is perched high on the rocks near a spot
known as Hong tu gou, south of the town, and is
one of the most popular walks for the townspeople.
The life history of Tian te, its founder, is engraved
on a stele now in the Shan xi Museum. The passage
on the stele was composed and written out by Fu
shan (see p. 864).

The **Monastery of the Scented Forest (Fang lin si)** is
north of the village of Ma zhuang, 4 or 5 miles south-
east of Tai yuan. It was founded under the Song in

1069, almost destroyed under the Yuan, and rebuilt under the Ming in 1477. In 1948, Yan Xi shan's soldiers destroyed several of the buildings. The gatewag (shan men), the main temple (Da xiong bao dian) and a large square pavilion dating from the beginniny of the Qing are all that survive today. The roofs of the first two are covered with glazed tiles and decorated with magnificent lions and dragons, made by local craftsmen (see p. 846).

The Jin ci

The Jin ci is the most famous temple in Tai yuan. It is 15 miles south-east of the town, and the journey takes an hour by bus. Temple is a misleading term here, for there are several of them, grouped round a spring at the foot of Mount Xuan weng shan; the most interesting of all is the Sheng mu dian, the Temple of the Holy Mother, which contains 44 famous Song statues.

History

When Wu wang, who founded the Zhou dynasty in 1066 B.C. died two years later, he was succeeded by his son Song, still a child, under the name of Cheng wang (1063 B.C.). One day, when he was playing with his little brother, Yu, he took a leaf from a *tong* (Eloecocca) tree, made it into the shape of a *gui*, the jade tablet which was the insignia of power in feudal society, and gave it to his brother, appointing him Prince of Tang (Tang hou: *tang* and *tong* were homophones in classical Chinese). The ministers, who had noticed this, immediately asked the king to fix a suitable day for the ceremony; the king replied that it was only a game, but the ministers insisted that his brother be appointed Prince Shu yu of Tang (Tang Shu yu) with all the correct rites. He ruled over the area round present Tai yuan. After his death, his son, Xie, changed the name of the principality from Tang to Jin, as the River Jin (Jin shui) rose near the capital of his fief, Jin yang. Jin, the name of the river, then became the name of the province of Shan xi, and still is the literary name for he province. Later on, a temple was built in memory of Tang Shu yu, the first prince, near the source of the Jin: the Jin ci. *Ci* is translated here as "temple", though the exact meaning of the word is a temple where an ancestor is worshipped.

It is not known exactly when the first Jin ci was founded. The temple is mentioned in the *Shui jing zhu*, a geographical work dating from the end of the 5th century (Northern Wei). Under the Northern Qi dynasty (550–577), Jin yang was more or less the capital, though its status was that of secondary capital, *bie du*, as the dynasty's capital was Ye, in north He nan; the Emperors built large palaces there, and Jin ci, near Jin yang, became their leisure palace; halls and pavilions were built there, surrounded by gardens watered by the plentiful spring. A few pavilions dating from this period still survive (see below). In 569, the Jin ci was named the Da chong huang si.

Under the Northern Dynasties, the monastery was extremely rich and flourishing, reflecting the economical and political development of province of Shan xi as a whole as relations and exchanges with the northern peoples were particularly good at this time. Li yuan, when he attacked the Sui dynasty and founded the Tang in 618, started out from Jin yang. In 646, his son, Li Shi min, the second Tang Emperor, known as Tai zong, came back to the area and stopped at the Jin ci; he composed, and himself wrote out, a *Jin ci Inscription, with a preface (Jin ci zhi ming bing xu)*, which was engraved on a stele (see below). In 941, the former Prince Shu yu of Tang was honoured by the Emperor with the posthumous title of "King who extends the peace", Xing an wang, and the Jin ci was called the Xing an wang miao. In 979, the second Song Emperor sent a military expedition to Jin yang to destroy the Northern Han, a local dynasty, who still held the area. Jin yang and its palaces were burned; the town of Tai yuan was built a little to the north (see p. 835). The Jin ci temples escaped the destruction, and were restored, a work which lasted five years; they were then called once more by their former name, Jin ci. During the Tian sheng period (1023–1032), Emperor Ren zong conferred the title of "King east of the Fen" (Fen dong wang) on Prince Shu yu, and had the Sheng mu dian, the Temple of the Holy Mother, built in honour of his mother Yi jiang, King Wu's wife. The temple as a whole and its religious significance were changed by this. The Sheng mu dian and the buildings surrounding it became the chief centre of attraction, and the cult of Prince Shu yu faded into the background, if not into complete oblivion. The Holy Mother (Sheng mu) who was worshipped there was held to possess magic

powers; prayers for rain and requests to know the future were
addressed to her. In the Xi ning period of the Song dynasty
(1068–1078) she was given the title of "Holy Mother, illuminating
and helpful" (Zhao ji sheng mu); new buildings were added to
the temple, and the "flying bridge" leading into it was built.

After the liberation, the Sheng mu dian and the other temples
at the Jin ci were completely restored, and a new way leading to
them was built. The Jin ci is classed as a historical monument.

Description

A large gateway built in 1955 leads into the enclosure
of the Jin ci (1). The old gate (2), the Gate of the
Pure Landscape (Jing qing men) is on the left.

The first building to be seen, the **Water Mirror
Terrace (Shui jing tai)** (3), probably dates from the
Ming. The sharply upturned corners on the double
roof, the pillars and the round windows are all
typical of the Shan xi style of architecture. It used
to be used as a theatre on temple feast days. Tea is
now served here for visitors.

A little further on, the **Bridge where the Immortals
meet (Hui xian qiao)** (4) spans a branch of the Jin,
called the **Canal of Zhi bo** (5) **(Zhi bo qu)**. During
the Chun qiu period, Zhi bo was a minister in the
Jin principality which had its capital at Jin yang;
three big families, the Zhao, the Wei and the Han
were fighting for power (eventually the principality
was split into three separate kingdoms of Zhao,
Wei and Han). To flood out the Zhao family, who
were entrenched in the capital, Zhi bo had a canal
built to divert the Jin from its normal course. The
canal afterwards helped to irrigate the region but
it has kept the name of its builder.

The **Metal Men Terrace (Jin ren tai)** is on the
other side of the bridge (6): the men are four iron
statues of ferocious warriors, which originally carried

weapons, one at each corner of a little, low terrace. The one at the south-east corner (first on the left) dates from 1089 (Song); its head, which was missing, was remade in 1926. The one at the north-east corner was entirely remade in 1913. The north-western one dates from 1098, though its head was remade under the Ming. The south-western one was cast in 1097 and has needed no restoration. The little building in the middle probably dates from the Ming. Next comes a large gateway (7) called the Dui yue pai fang; the two characters *dui yue* on the pediment, *face (the country of?) Yue*, were written by the Ming calligrapher Gao Ying yuan. The gateway and the two little towers which stand one on each side of it, the Bell Tower (Zhong lou) (8) and the Drum Tower (Gu lou) (9) were all built during the Wan li period (1573–1620) of the Ming dynasty. The **Temple of the Offerings (Xian dian)** (10), where the faithful prayed to the Holy Mother and presented offerings to her, stands beyond the gateway. This small temple (it is only 3 bays wide) is a good example of old wooden architecture; it dates from 1168 (Jin dynasty) and the lower part has not been touched since then. The roof was remade under the Ming, during the Wan li period, in a heavy style which is out of tune with the rather austere Jin architectural style. A mixture of masonry and wood was used in the lower part which is rarely seen in later buildings. The beams and the cantilever brackets supporting the roof on the outside are worth a close look. Two fine bronze lions of uncertain age stand in front of the temple; they probably date from the Northern Song.

From the Temple of the Offerings, the **Flying Bridge (Fei liang)** (11), a most striking piece of architecture, unique in China, leads over to the Temple of

the Holy Mother (12). A spring rising under the
temple flows into a large pool *(yu zhao)* with fish in it.
A stone platform stands in the middle of the pool,
linked to the sides by four wide footbridges, also
in stone. Two of them, on the same axis as the temple,
are horizontal and on a level with the temple; the
others spring up from the side of the pool to meet
the central platform. 34 octagonal stone columns
carry the structure. The balustrades used to be in
brick, but were replaced by marble ones in 1953.
No written record has ever been found referring to
the bridge, but everything suggests that it dates
from the Northern Song, in its present form. The
two lions at the foot of the east footbridge date from
1119.

The **Temple of the Holy Mother (Sheng mu dian)** (12)
rises above the white marble of the Flying Bridge.
It was built under the Song, during the Tian sheng
period (1023–1032), and rebuilt in the first year of
the Chong ning period (1102). It is one of the most
beautiful examples of Song architecture which has
survived until now, and the most imposing of all
the buildings in the Jin ci. It has a double roof,
without an upper gallery; it is 7 bays wide and 6 bays
deep. The eight columns supporting the roof produce
a magnificent effect; they are red, with gilded dragons
twisting round them, thrown into relief by the deep
shadow behind them. The façade of the temple is
two bays further back than the pillars, so that they
appear to carry the whole building alone, as the rest
is apparently hidden in the shadows. A vertical panel
between the two roofs bears the characters: **sheng
mu dian,** the name of the temple. The first thing which
meets the eye inside is a central niche with the goddess
herself, Yi jiang, known as the Holy Mother, against

a background of paintings of seas and mountains.
She is seated, in ceremonial dress, with a large diadem
(feng guang) on her head, of intricate baroque design,
in sharp contrast to her rather severe, dignified features.
She is surrounded by **44 statues of women** arranged
along the far, right and left walls. They are life size
terra cotta statues of the ladies-in-waiting and others
who form the Holy Mother's train. Four of them
are wearing officials' head-dresses and robes, and
are depicted in a conventional attitude of respect.
The others look as though they were caught as they
were about to hold something out to someone, or
lean towards their neighbours, or are simply waiting,
dreaming, looking into space. The positions of their
bodies, the hang of their clothes, their gestures, the
expressions and their eloquent looks, all make each
one of them appear to belong to a moment of reality,
and to be a member of the group, each with her
own position with regard to the rest. No two are
alike: dress, duty, size, bearing, all differ from one
to another; elegant young women stand alongside
elderly matrons; some look as though they are talking,
or about to reply, and others are lost in thought.

The carving dates from the Song; the statues are
clearly contemporary with the building. Although they
stand in a temple, the art they represent is secular; the
psychological realism with which they are portrayed
is characteristic of the refined civilisation bred by
urban life under the Song. They date from the 12th
century, but they are a perfect illustration of the type
of man whom J. Gernet describes in *Daily Life in
China on the Eve of the Mongol Invasion 1250-1276*
(George Allen and Unwin Ltd. 1962, p. 247): "The
Chinese of the thirteenth century seems to have been
much more sentimental and romantic than his fore-

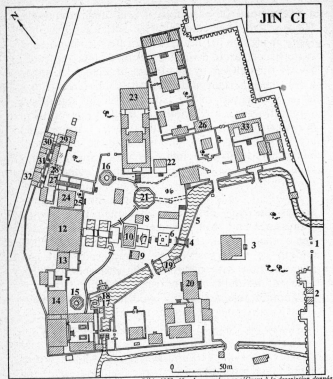

d'après Jin ci, par Chai Ze jun, éd. Wen wu, Pékin 1958, 46 p. Les numéros se réfèrent à la description donnée dans le texte
after Jin ci, by Chai Ze jun, pub. Wen wu, Peking 1958, 46 p. The numbers refer to the description given in the text.

bears. He seems to have been consumed by a sense of the sadness of life, to have suffered from the depths of despair, which found expression in his works of art. The passing of time, failure, disgrace, the pain of parting, were frequent themes in his poetry; but he did not, as did the Chinese of T'ang times, find a counterbalance to this profound melancholy in action. On the other hand, he showed a sense of curiosity and an enlargement of outlook unknown a few centuries earlier. His free way of life would have scandalized his T'ang forebears. Because of his courteousness, his sense of humour, and his taste for social life and the art of conversation, he is one of the subtlest and most highly cultured types of human being that Chinese civilization has ever produced. From the history of his daily life emerges a general impression of natural self-discipline, of gaiety and charm. He had an extraordinarily keen sense for the finer shades... The Chinese of the thirteenth century seems to have been more free and easy of manner, less stilted than his counterpart in T'ang times. His politeness was not artificial, did not consist merely of a formal code of etiquette and prescribed behaviour; on the contrary, his entire social life, which was founded on exchanges of presents and services, was permeated by human warmth and sympathy."

The statues also give valuable information on the clothes, head-dresses and hair-styles under the Northern Song. Unfortunately they have been badly painted, at a later date, with garish colours: red, green and a little ochre for the clothes, chalky white for the faces and hands, black for the hair, eyebrows and eyes, red for the lips. The colours mask the elegant outlines and the effect of the sculpture itself. The temple where the statues stand is also very dark; it is planned to build a special hall to show the statues off properly.

Two imposing statues of generals stand in front of the temple, each one over 12 feet high. The left-hand one dates from the Song; the one on the right was re-made in 1950.

The **Tai tai Temple (Tai tai miao)** (13) is left of the
Sheng mu dian; it contains a wooden statue of Tai tai,
a legendary hero who is said to have drained the
waters of the River Fen and created land fit for cultivation and safe from floods in the plain of Tai yuan. This
feat is supposed to have been performed even before
Yu the Great, founder of the Xia dynasty, got the
Yellow River under control.

A temple with two roofs, and a gallery running
under each one, stands a little further on: the **Shui mu
Temple,** "water mother" **(Shui mu lou)** (14), built under
the Ming in 1545, and rebuilt in 1844 under the Qing.
A bronze statue on the ground floor depicts Shui mu
with her hair knotted on the top of her head (Shui mu
shu fa), and on the first floor, she is shown, in a statue
and frescoes, with her hair normally done. The temple
was built in memory of a young peasant called Liu
who, according to a legend very popular in the area,
was extremely ill-treated by her mother-in-law. Her
mother-in-law forced her to spend all day drawing
water for the needs of the household at a well a long
way away. One day, she met an old man who asked
her for water for his horse; the girl generously gave
him all the water in her pots. In return, the old man
gave her a magic whip which she had only to wave
inside her water-pots for them to fill with clear water.
After a time, the mother-in-law, surprised to see that
she no longer went to the well, sent one of the children
to see what was happening. The child waved the whip,
water gushed out and almost flooded the house. The
daughter-in-law was doing her hair at that moment,
so she quickly knotted it on top of her head, ran and
covered the water-pot and then sat on it. From then
on, the spring never failed: it became the source of the
River Jin. The statue shows the young peasant

girl, the "water mother", enthroned on the spring.

The octagonal pavilion in front of the Shui mu Temple, built under the Northern Qi (550–559), and rebuilt under the Ming, stands over the **Spring for ever Young (Nan lao quan)** (15), the chief source of the Jin. The water gushes out from a depth of 16 feet or so, with a flow of 1.8 cu.m. per second. It never varies through drought or rain, and the temperature is always 63° F. The water provides drinking water, irrigates the fields, and further on is harnessed to provide electricity for the town of Tai yuan. The pavilion is built in Ming style; inside hang several panels with calligraphy on them.

The Jin has three sources, but the Source for ever Young is the most abundant. The others are under the Sheng mu dian (11, 12) and a little further off (Shan li quan) (16). Below the pavilion, surrounded by water and covered with a pretty roof, stands the **Boat which is not Moored (Bu ji zhou)** (17). The Chinese take photographs of each other there. A little column rises out of the water near the boat called the **Stone Pillar in the middle of the Stream (Zhong liu di zhu)** (18). It is said to be the tomb of Zhang lang, to whom another legend is attached: the Jin splits at its source into two branches which run separately towards the middle of the plain; bitter quarrels used to go on between the peasants of the area about the sharing out of the water in the two streams; finally, the authorities thought of a way to put an end to the matter, and put a pot of boiling oil near the source, containing ten strings of sapekes; whoever managed to take out a certain number of the ten would ensure the same proportion of water for his party. Zhang lang came forward and took seven out of the pot, but died from the burns he received. Ever since then, seven tenths of the water has flowed along the northern course and three tenths along the southern course, and Zhang lang lies buried at the point where the waters divide. Many poets, particularly Li Bai, have praised the coolness of the spot.

The **White Crane Pavilion (Bai he ting)** (19) is a little way back along the bank, at the water's edge, with a little courtyard leading into it. The bridge upstream from it is called the **Hanging Snow Bridge (Gua xue qiao)** because in winter, when the water still rises at a temperature of 63° F., it evaporates and hoar frost forms under the low arches of the bridge, and is reflected in the water. From the first floor of the pavilion nearby (Sheng ying lou) (20), there is a good view of the Jin ci as a whole.

To the right, beyond the octagonal Lotus Pool (Ba jiao lian chi) (21) dating from the Ming, is the **Tang Stele Pavilion (Tang bei ting)** (22), which houses two almost identical steles 10 feet high called the *Jin ci Inscription (Jin ci ming)*. The right hand one dates from 647; the text is a reproduction of the one written by Li Shi min, or Tai zong, the second Tang Emperor, himself, when he came here to thank Prince Shu yu for the protection he granted him and his father when the Sui dynasty was overthrown; both father (Emperor Gao zu, founder of the Tang dynasty) and son had come to ask his help before going to war. 9 large characters at the top of the stele give the date of the imperial visit: the 26th day of the first month of the 20th year of the Zhen guan era (647). The inscription is in four parts: a passage praising the merits and virtues of Prince Shu yu; another praising the Jin ci countryside; a third deploring the disorder and moral decay of the empire under the reign of the Sui Emperor Yang (Sui Yang di); finally a passage expressing gratitude to Prince Shu yu, asking for his protection for the dynasty in future. As the characters seemed likely to be effaced completely by the weather, a calligrapher called Yang Yu made a copy of the stele in 1773, which now stands on the left of the original.

Steps lead up left of the steles to the **Prince Shu yu of Tang's Temple** (Tang Shu yu ci) (23). A gateway and two courtyards lead to the temple, which is 5 bays wide and 4 deep. The exact history of the temple is unknown; it was probably built at the foot of the mountain, near the spring (15) at first; it may have been transferred to its present site under the Northern Song; the buildings date from the Ming, and must have been rebuilt under the Qing; it was enlarged in 1771. The hall between the two courtyards is the "hall of sacrifices" *(xiang tang)*; 7 poems by Mao Ze dong and 4 by Zhu De have been engraved on stone and set into the walls. Mao Ze dong's poems are: *The Long March (Chang zheng); Mount Jing gang shan (Jing gang shan); Mount Liu pan (Liu pan shan); New Year's Day (Yuan dan); Reply to Liu Ya zi (Wan xi sha)* and *Snow (Xue)*. The poems by Zhu De are entitled: *To the Elders of Si chuan (Ji yu shu zhong fu lao); On Leaving the Tai hang Mountains (Chu tai hang); A State of War (Zhan ju shi ju); To the Generals who Fight in the South (Ji nan zheng shu jiang)*. Under the covered ways on either side of the first courtyard, about 120 four-sided pillars are exhibited, engraved with Buddhist sutras *(Hua yuan jing, Avatams'aka sutra)*; they date from 700. Certain parts disappeared and were re-engraved under the Northern Han (947–950). They were originally at Feng dong li, 2½ miles north of the Jin ci. The Japanese tried to remove them during the occupation, but they were forestalled by the local inhabitants. In 1952, the pillars were restored and put in the temple courtyard.

A path leads to the right outside the temple towards the Sheng mu dian, beside which stands a little temple called the **Descendants' Temple (Miao yi tang)** (24). The date of its foundation is not known; it was rebuilt under the Yuan in 1328 and in 1511 under the Ming. It contains Ming sculpture. An evergreen *(bo)* (25) in front of the temple is said to have been planted when the Zhou dynasty was founded (1066 B.C.). The tree is now almost lying on the one beside it, which is another evergreen of the same age. A third one used to stand there, but it was cut down in the last century. In the Eastern Peak Temple (Dong yue ci) (26) courtyard (behind the Tang steles, 22) stands another magnificent evergreen, dating from the Eastern Zhou (770–256 B.C.). Several *kuai* trees in the Jin ci enclosure (Chinese juniper?) date from the Tang.

A long flight of stone steps right of the Descendants' Temple leads to the **Cave which faces the Sunrise (Chao yang dong)** (27). It is a natural cave, and is heralded by pillars; inside is a statue of Ling guan (The Magician Official, a popular deity), who holds a gold whip in his hand; portraits and autographs of famous men decorate the walls.

Another cave, the **Stay in the Clouds (Yun tao dong)** (28) is to the right of it; it is about 30 feet deep, and **Fu Shan** (1608–1684) used to live in it. Fu Shan is one of the most famous historical figures in Shan xi, known and respected by all the inhabitants in the province. He was a calligrapher (the two characters *yun tao* above the entrance to the cave are his), a poet, a painter, a philosopher and doctor (he wrote a treatise on gynaecology, *Fu shi nu ke*). When the Qing dynasty came to power in 1644, he became a Taoist and spent his life travelling through various provinces in China, working as a doctor and plotting against the Qing. In 1654 he was suspected of being in league with Ming supporters in the south; he was thrown into prison in Tai yuan and tortured, but would reveal nothing, so finally he was released. He became a friend of another implacable enemy of the Qing, Gu Yan wu (1613–1682), a distinguished scholar and philosopher; they often used to meet at the "stay in the clouds", where Fu Shan lived, away from the world. In 1678, Emperor Kang xi invited Fu Shan to sit the imperial examinations in Peking. He refused. The next year, the Emperor was so insistent that he went as far as Peking, but on the day of the examination, he pretended to be ill and did not appear. Kang xi excused him from sitting the examination and offered him a high post. Etiquette required that he should go and prostrate himself before the Emperor as a sign of gratitude; he did not go, and when people were sent to fetch him and put him in a sedan chair to take him there, he stood motionless; when he was asked to prostrate himself before the Emperor, he lay flat out on the floor to show that he would never collaborate with the Qing usurpers. He was 73 at the time. His unswerving loyalty to the Ming nationalist cause made him a hero; popular legends, drawing on accounts of his numerous talents, particularly his medical knowledge, turned him into a sort of friendly magician. As far as the history of thought is concerned, he belongs, like Gu Yan wu, to a generation of rationalist thinkers and sceptics, who approached the study of the classics in a new, critical spirit, drawing inspiration at the same time from Buddhism, Taoism and Confucianism.

The former Wen chang Palace (Wen chang gong) has been turned into a **Fu Shan Museum (Fu Shan ji nian guan)** (33); it is in the east of the Jin ci enclosure. It contains examples of his work as a calligrapher, painter, poet and doctor, and various documents referring to his life. His poetry is collected under the title of *Xia hong kan quan ji*.

Further along the Stay in the Clouds Terrace is a building three bays wide called the **Small House for Waiting for the Wind (Dai feng xuan)** (29), which contains various things found in the neighbourhood of the Jin ci (stone and pottery objects belonging to the Yang shao Culture, Song and pre-Song pottery and porcelain). A flight of steps leads up to three more buildings, dating from the Qing, on another terrace: the Pavilion of the Three Terraces (San tai ge) (30), the Reading Terrace (Du shu tai) (31) and the Lü Zu Pavilion (32). They contain photographs of several historical monuments in the neighbourhood of the Jin ci and of sculptures in the Tian Long shan and Long shan Mountains (see below). The third building houses a statue of Lü Zu, or Lü Dong bin, one of the Eight Immortals (see p. 163). The terrace overlooks the Jin ci and the Fen plain. A seven-storey pagoda, 120 feet high, can be seen in the distance; the first one was built under the Sui, but the present one dates from the Qian long era (1736–1796). It belongs to the Feng sheng si, a monastery which has been converted into a sanatorium.

Monuments in the Jin ci Neighbourhood

Several monuments still exist in **the mountains round the Jin ci,** or rather, round the former town of Jin yang; although tourists do not generally visit them, they are worth mentioning. As most of them are in bad condition, or were plundered during the first half of the century, they are of archaeological or historical, rather than artistic interest.

Buddhism spread throughout China under the Northern and Southern dynasties. The breaking up of the empire weakened the scholar class and created the right climate for a great wave of religious feeling, which extended everywhere. Under the Northern Qi (550–577), Jin yang was a capital, and countless monasteries grew up in the mountains nearby. In 556, the founder of the dynasty had a Buddha over 160 feet high carved out of the rock in the **Long shan (Dragon Mountain)** and the Tong zi si monastery was built nearby. The Buddha was re-carved under the Ming, but it has now disappeared; the position is still clear from the low relief carvings which surrounded it, which can still be seen. Two 16 ft. high carved stone lanterns are all that remains of the temple. They are the oldest in China. A few hundred yards to the north-east are the remains of the Stone Gate Monastery (Shi men si), sometimes called Long quan si: two rock shrines, with sculpture probably dating from the Sui or the beginning of the Tang. To the west on the other side of the mountain is another cave know as the Nun's Cave (Gu gu dong). It used to contain some beautiful sculpture, but it was all stolen in 1929. A head of the Buddha, too large to take away, sticks up out of the ground. About half a mile south of the former Tong zi si, a **Taoist monastery,** the Hao tian guan, Endless Sky Monastery, was founded on the top of the Long shan under the Tang, in 1295. Its founder was the Taoist Song De fang, a native of Su zhou, whose name for religious purposes was Pi yun zi, "clothed in clouds". He made **eight shrines,** which are still in fairly good condition. A large recumbent statue lies in the third one, in which he died. These shrines, of a kind rare in China, are as triking example of the influence of Taoism on Buddhism. The Long shan is 3 miles west of the Jin ci; it is approached from the village of Xi zhen.

The **Meng shan,** north of the Long shan, can be reached from the village of Luo cheng, or from the road from the Jin ci. In 551, the Empress had a statue of the Buddha 200 feet high carved there, lit up at night by 10,000 oil lamps, and visible from the palace at Jin yang. The Fa hua si Monastery was founded at the foot of the statue, later renamed the Kai hua si. Both the monastery and the Buddha have been destroyed. All that remains are two pagodas about 20 feet high, which are interesting because they combine Tang and Song styles. The lower part is square, and the upper part is octagonal, and fairly elaborate.

The **Celestial Dragon Mountain (Tian long shan)** is about 14 miles south-west of the Jin ci, called after a monastery which was founded there under the Northern Qi (Tian long si). The monastery was in use until 1948, when it was burned down. Near the two peaks of the mountain are 25 Buddhist rock-cut shrines dating from the Northern Qi, the Sui and the Tang. They contain a group of carvings in excellent condition (only slightly eroded) which show the evolution of Buddhist carving from the hieratic style of the Northern Qi to the powerful, realistic style of the Tang. (The folds of the clothing are a good example to take: they begin as concave, and end with a more natural, convex representation). Some of the heads of the Buddhas and the bas-relief carvings have been taken to the United States or Japan. The Monastery of the Immortals' Cliff (Xian yan si) used to stand near the eastern peak. 12 caves in the rock can still be seen there (4 date from the Northern Qi, 2 from the Sui, 6 from the Tang). Part of the Pavilion of the Big Buddha (Da fo ge) can still be seen near the western summit; it was built up against the mountain in 560. The upper part contains a large seated Buddha, the lower part a standing Buddha. 13 caves are grouped round it (2 date from the Northern Qi, 11 date from the Tang). One of them has a stone porch supported by two columns at the entrance, which represents a valuable piece of documentation on Northern Qi architecture. Remains of the Northern Qi Emperors' Summer Palace (Bi shu gong) can be seen near the shrines at the eastern summit.

NORTH SHAN XI

Da tong

Da tong is the largest town in north Shan xi. It lies in a long, rather infertile plain, 3,900 feet above sea level. Since the liberation, Da tong has been developed into an industrial town, as there are large deposits of coal and soda to the south-west. It is also an important railway junction for lines between He bei, Shan xi and Mongolia.

Da tong was important in the past as a centre of cultural and trade exchanges with Mongolia, and as a garrison town. It lies in a strategic position between two sections of the Great Wall (the northern stretch follows the northern boundary of Shan xi, and the southern stretch, which only exists in part now, is about 60 miles to the south). Da tong belonged to the kingdom of Zhao during the Warring States period. Under the Han, it was called Ping cheng. The Tobas, a non-Chinese people whose origins are uncertain, established their capital there when they founded the Wei dynasty in 386 (Northern Wei). The town was the centre of political, cultural and religious (Buddhist) life of the dynasty until the 6th Emperor, Xiao wen, moved the capital to Luo yang, in 494. The shrines at Yun gang, 9 miles west of the town, bear witness to this past age of splendour (see below, p. 878). Once the imperial court had left, Da tong waned in importance. From the Sui onwards, however, the empire, now re-united, had to defend its northern frontiers against the invader, and Da tong came into its own again as a frontier town and

DA TONG ET YUN GANG
DA TONG AND YUN GANG

1	Paroi des 9 dragons Nine Dragon Screen	3	Couvent d'en bas Lower Monastery
2	Couvent d'en haut Upper Monastery	4	Couvent du sud Southern Monastery

═══ Voie de chemin de fer
━━━ Route
▫◦ Village

⠿⠿ Falaise dans laquelle
sont creusées les grottes
de Yun gang

🪨 Collines

D'après Yun gang shi ku, ed. Wen wu, Pékin 1957, 80 p.
After Yun gang shi ku, ed. Wen wu, Pekin 1957, 80 p.

Gare de Da Tong (railway) station

Ville/Old town ancienne

Temple de Guan Yin

Route de Yun Gang

Grottes de Yun Gang
Yuan Gang Caves

Rivière Wu Zhou He River

N

0 1 2 Km

fort. In the 10th century, the unity of the empire was broken by the Liao invasion from the north-east. In 960, they took over Da tong and made it one of their secondary capitals *(pei du)*, giving it the name which it has held ever since *(Da tong* means "great harmony"). The town underwent a second period of expansion, as the monasteries to be mentioned later bear out. It remained a secondary capital under the Jin (1115–1234).

Under the Ming, it was one of the forts which were scattered along the length of the Great Wall. General Xu Da (1332–1385) had walls built round the town in 1372; they still stand there today, and their circumference is almost 4 miles. To the north, east and south of the walls were fortified encampments.

Description

Da tong is 7 or 8 hours from Peking by train; the Trans-Siberian (via Mongolia) goes through it. Tourists stay in the hotel built to lodge the Soviet experts. The town itself has four monuments worth a visit, but the Yun gang caves are the chief attraction for the tourist. They can be reached by bus or taxi without difficulty. A special section will be devoted to them further on. The Guan Yin Temple is half-way to them.

The **Nine Dragon Screen (Jiu long bi)** is near the centre of the town. It was built early in the Ming dynasty, and is said to have stood in front of the viceroy's palace at Da tong. It is 147 feet long, 6 feet thick and 18 feet high, covered with glazed tiles of 5 different colours, and portrays 9 dragons rising out of the waves to fight over several suns, which are symbols of immortality. It is a masterpiece of imaginative art. The screen was moved 90 feet in 1954 to fit in with building plans.

Two monasteries stand close to each other in the west of the town: they are both called the **Hua yan**

Monastery (Hua yan si). To distinguish between them, they are referred to as the Shang si, or Shang hua yan si, Upper Monastery, and the Xia si, or Xia hua yan si, Lower Monastery. *Hua yan* is the name of a Buddhist sect, founded in China under the Tang. The name comes from a sutra, the *Hua yan jing (Avatams'aka sutra)*, which it adopted as its chief canon. This sutra was particularly popular in Chinese Buddhism; it contains highly imaginative accounts of the miracles performed by the Buddha before he appeared on earth.

The **Upper Monastery** was founded under the Liao. It was almost entirely destroyed during the disturbances which heralded the fall of the dynasty and was rebuilt under the Jin in 1140. One unusual feature about it, extremely rare in China, and probably explainable by the fact that it was built by the Liao, is its orientation: it faces east instead of south. The main temple, the **Da xiong bao dian** (Great Temple of Powerful Treasure) dates from 1140. The other buildings—about ten of them—date from the Qing, but they are arranged in the same way as the Liao and Jin monastery was.

The Da xiong bao dian and the Yi xian Temple (in Liao ning) are the two biggest Buddhist temples still standing in China. The Da xiong bao dian is 176 feet wide (9 bays) and 94 feet deep (5 bays); the edge of the roof is 30 feet above the ground. The style is entirely different from the usual temples built in China by the Song, the Ming or the Qing: the roof is straight, and the main façade has three wooden doors each of which fills one bay; apart from them, the main façade and the three others are bare walls, with no ornaments whatsoever; a single roof with an overhang of 11 feet, supported by clusters of cantilever brackets, completes these severe lines. The temple is important as an example of old architecture, and is classed as an ancient monument.

Above the central entrance hangs a panel with the four characters: da xiong bao dian. The richness of the interior decoration, with its coffered ceiling, frescoes and sculpture, presents a striking contrast with the austerity of the outside. 5 Buddhas stand on enormous pediments in the centre. The middle ones are carved in wood, the ones at each end in terra cotta. All of them are gilded. They, and the small statues at their feet, as well as the statues round the walls, all date from the Ming (1426–1465). The frescoes were repainted under the Qing. Two Ming steles, dating from 1465 and 1582, are also kept in the temple. The copy of one of the corner towers of the Da tong town walls is by Li Yan gui, a sculptor who lived at the end of the Qing dynasty.

The two Buddhist pillars *(chuang)* in front of the temple date from 1077 (Liao). Four steles bearing texts written by the Song philosopher Zhu Xi (1130–1200) are set into one of the walls of the monastery.

The **Lower Monastery** was also founded under the Liao. Most of the present buildings date from the Ming and the Qing. One old one has survived as it was when it was built in 1038: the monastery **library** (Jiao cang), called the **Bo jia jiao cang dian.** It is behind the first hall after the entrance (Temple of the Celestial Guardians, Tian wang dian); it is a fairly small building, 80 feet (5 bays) wide and 32 feet (4 bays) deep, of great beauty. The decoration, frescoes and sculpture are all of the highest artistic value, and date from the Liao. About thirty little edifices line the walls, made to house the monastery's sutras, like little two-storey buildings; he one in the middle of the far wall is above thet

ground, like a little hanging palace. Two flights of
steps against the wall lead up to it. The building is
classed as a historical monument.

A third monastery still stands in the south of the
town, known by the townspeople as the "south monastery" *(nan si)*. Its real name is the **Shan hua Monastery (Shan hua si)** or the Kai yuan period Monastery
(Kai yuan si). As its name suggests, the monastery was
founded under the Kai yuan period of the Tang
dynasty (713–742). When the Liao dynasty fell, it was
completely destroyed, to be rebuilt under the Jin from
1128 to 1143. Its ten temples and galleries covered then
a total area of over 80 intercolumniations. In 1446,
under the Ming, a large library of sutras was created
there, and a sort of college, a "school of ceremonies"
was installed there.

The old buildings have now dwindled to four. An
entrance hall *(shan men)* 5 bays wide, built under the
Jin, between 1135 and 1149, leads into the temple. The
four large statues inside show that it is in fact a
"temple of the celestial guardians" *(tian wang miao)*
and that the gateway properly speaking must have
been outside. To the right stands a stele describing
how the monastery was restored in 1177. The second
temple, also 5 bays wide, dates from the same time as
the first one and is called the Three Saints' Temple
(San sheng dian). Next came two square, two-storey,
matching pavilions on the right and the left, on the
enclosure walls. One has disappeared, and the surviving one was carefully rebuilt in 1953, and is a faithful
copy of an example of Liao architecture, with a double
roof and a circular gallery. The last building is the
Great Temple of the Powerful Treasure (Da xiong bao
dian). It is 130 feet wide (7 bays) and 80 feet (5 bays)
deep. The large statues of the Buddha in the centre and

the 24 other figures lining the left and right hand walls
are probably Liao sculpture. One of the best pieces is
the Guan yin with six arms on the right. The fine
frescoes date from the Ming.

The **Temple of Confucius (Wen miao),** dating from
1398 (Ming), stands in the south-east corner of the
town. It is not open to visitors.

About 5 miles from the town, on the road to the Yun
gang Caves, is a **Guan yin Temple (Guan yin tang).** It
was first built in 1038 under the Liao, then it was burned
at the beginning of the Qing dynasty and was rebuilt
in 1652. The stone carvings in it are mainly Liao. The
screen in front of the temple is covered with glazed
tiles and depicts 3 dragons; it is in the same style as the
9 Dragon Screen in Da tong, and must therefore date
from the beginning of the Ming.

At You yu (a little fortified town about 50 miles
west of Da tong as the crow flies, near the Great Wall)
a magnificent collection of 136 **scroll paintings** was
found, dating from the beginning of the Ming dynasty,
and perhaps even from the Yuan. They were kept in
the Bao ning Monastery (Bao ning si) and were brought
out for the inhabitants of the town on the 8th day of
the 4th month every year (a Buddhist feast day known
as the "Buddha's Bath"). 61 of the scrolls are paintings
on Buddhist themes, 47 depict popular deities, 12 portray historical characters, and 13 are paintings of
scenes from everyday life. They are vertical scrolls.
The background is a soft brown, the drawing delicate
and detailed, and the colours are sober. The office
responsible for the monuments at Da tong and Yun
gang (Da tong Yun gang gu ji bao yang suo) has taken
charge of the collection; it is not certain if it is usually
available for the public to see.

Yun gang

The Yun gang Buddhist Caves rank with the ones at
Long men (see p. 793), Mai ji shan (see p. 1369), and
Dun huang (see p. 1322) as one of the greatest monuments of Chinese religious art. They are 10 miles west
of Da tong, in a valley running from west to east, dug
out of a stretch of hillside over half a mile long; the
hill is low, and ends just above the caves, which face
south. The buildings of the Old Monastery of the
Stone Buddhas (Shi fo gu si) stand in front of three of
the largest ones.

The name Yun gang means "cloud hillock". It is a
dry, deserted spot; for centuries, the wind has been
eroding the sandstone of the cliff, threatening the
caves as well, whose rows of openings now look like a
deserted hive. A two-fold plan has been put under
way: the valley is to be re-planted with trees, and protecting walls are to be built up against the cliff in front
of the caves. Galleries will be built to give access to the
higher ones. The plan includes various facilities for
tourists. Yun gang is classed as a historical monument.

History

The Yun gang rock temples were carved under the Northern
Wei (386–534 A.D.). They are mentioned in the geographical
work, Shui jing zhu, which dates from the end of the 5th century;
the History of the Wei (Wei shu) also mentions them in the chapter headed Chronicle of Buddhism and Taoism (Shi lao zhi).
After that, Yun gang appears to have been forgotten completely.
Not until a Japanese scholar, Isoto Chuta, went there in 1903,
did people remember this sanctuary of Buddhist art and begin
to make a study of it.

In fact, it was not so much forgotten as consigned to oblivion
by the Confucian scholar class. The Wei were a non-Chinese,
Buddhist dynasty, considered by orthodox tradition as "barbarians". Zhu Yi zun (1629–1709), an early Qing philologist and
historian, wrote of the Yun gang carvings: "They (the Wei)
were afraid that the statues were too small, and that they would

*not be noticed; as a diametre of one cubit was not enough, they
wanted to make it several cubits; as several cubits did not always
answer their needs, they did all they could to make diametres of
several dozen cubits, and to produce a work which would last, they
carved Buddhas by hundreds and thousands in the rock. The people
whom they sent to look at the carvings were impressed; they therefore thought that they had reached the heights of wisdom, little
thinking that they had reached the heights of folly. The way of the
Duke of Zhou and Confucius has been followed for thousands of
years, but does it need illustrations such as these?" (Memoir on
the Buddhist Carvings at Yun gang. Yun gang shi fo ji).* In the
eyes of this Confucian scholar, the art of Yun gang was merely
contemptible idolatry, foreign to Chinese civilisation. In fact,
Yun gang is the majestic expression of a moment of vital importance in Chinese history.

At the beginning of the 4th century, numerous warlike peoples
from Central Asia burst upon the north of China and set up
small transitory kingdoms there. In 386, the Tobas, a people
whose origins are still uncertain, founded a state in northern
Shan xi; not long afterwards, they had conquered and unified the
whole of North China (386–439). In 398, they established their
capital at Da tong (then called Ping cheng). Their chieftain
declared himself Emperor and created the Wei dynasty (Northern Wei). In 493, the Northern Wei moved their capital to Luo
yang. Under their reign, north China gradually emerged from
the state of anarchy it had been in before, and it emerged profoundly changed. A widespread fusion had taken place, blending
countless races and people, Han and barbarian, in the same melting-pot. This fusion, which was a determining factor in the making
of the China of the Tang and later dynasties, was deliberately
and intelligently brought about by the Wei leaders, through
their laws on the distribution of land, on marriage, and on the
assimilation of the Tobas to the Chinese population.

Tang China, energetic, creative, open to foreign influences,
was in the making under their reign. Their reign also saw the
triumph of Buddhism in China, brought from India via Central
Asia. This triumph can be explained in several ways: a century
and a half of perpetual disturbances and wars, widespread poverty and insecurity, gave rise to the need for a religion of redemp-
tion, for a faith in the after-life; the Wei also used Buddhism as
a powerful weapon in their struggle against Confucianism and
Taoism, both Chinese religions, and therefore strongholds of
resistance against the Wei conquest. The Wei made Buddhism
the state religion, identifying the Emperor with a living Buddha,

and introducing the worship of the Emperor. Even so, Emperor Tai wu (424–452), the third of the dynasty, was converted to Taoism under the influence of his minister Cui Hao and a great Taoist called Kou Qian zhi. He forbade Buddhism, had monasteries burned and forced the monks to return to the secular life. Later on he fell dangerously ill. Convinced that his illness was a punishment for his persecution of Buddhism, he had Cui Hao and all his clan killed and returned to Buddhism. His successor, Emperor Wen cheng (452–466), had the monasteries rebuilt and the Buddhist canon reconstituted. In 460, he appointed the monk Tan Hao head of the church and ordered him to have five monumental statues built, under the form of Buddhas, to represent his five predecessors; it was to be a majestic illustration of the regained authority of Buddhism and the glory of the dynasty. Tan Hao carried out his mission and had five gigantic statues carved in the cliffs at Yun gang (see below, 16–20). From 460 to 494, numerous other shrines were carved in the same place in honour of court nobles and monks. After 494, the year in which the court was moved to Luo yang from Da tong, the work went on for some time longer, until 525 or so, probably, but on a lesser scale. The work begun and abandoned at Yun gang was continued at Long men. One of the caves at Yun gang seems to have been carved under the Sui (581–618).

A legend tells how, before moving to Luo yang, the Wei court had the shrines walled up; they were afraid that the Han inhabitants of the area would give vent to their hatred of the Toba oppressor by desecrating the sacred monuments left behind at Yun gang. The Tobas were considered as invaders and their art was probably thought of as foreign as well. When they brought Buddhism with them from Central Asia, they brought Buddhist art too; the Hellenistic Buddhist carving of Gandhara, which developed in North India from the 1st century onwards, and spread throughout all Central Asia in the centuries which followed. The *History of the Wei* records that in 455, five Indian monks came to Da tong, and that they were excellent sculptors and painters. It is tempting to relate this to the beginning of the work on Yun gang five years later, but the exact part played by the monks in the creation of the Yun gang carvings is not known.

The art of carved rock temples originated in India and penetrated to China from the west (see map, p. 240). The Dun huang caves are one of the earliest examples; they were begun about a hundred years before the Yun gang caves. The Dun huang sculpture was in terra cotta. The Yun gang carvings are the earliest stone carvings of this type in China. They were clearly influenced by several different sources: the Indian influence can be seen in the folds of the clothes, the head-dresses, the appearance of the elephant, the Iranian and Byzantine influence in the wearing of beards, the weapons and the lions, the Greek influence in the trident and the acanthus leaves. Broadly speaking, the iconography is taken from Indian Buddhism, and the strongest influence is that of Graeco-Buddhist style. But in the interpretation given by the Wei sculptors to this heritage, the vigorous realism which was to blossom later on in Tang carving can already be felt. The large Buddhas at Yun gang are hieratic, immobile; the Bodhisattvas are more lively, nearer to reality, and their attitudes are less stiff; and the disciples, monks and other people depicted have none of the archaic rigidity of the monumental Buddhas. Numerous designs show how the artists moved beyond their Indian models. The towers in the centre of several of the shrines (caves no. 1, 2, 21) come from India; here they have become square buildings, purely Chinese in style; the same thing is traceable in the bas-relief carvings. In Graeco-Buddhist art, the aureoles are usually extremely plain; at Yun gang they are decorated with scrolls, flames, lotus petals, apsaras and little Buddhas. Dragons, phoenix birds, *tao tie*, tigers and other animals from the Chinese tradition appear elsewhere. Among the apsaras which recur everywhere, some are Indian, with short robes and feet appearing beneath them; others are Chinese, of a more aerial build, their robes ending in long trains flying out behind them. The designs taken from plants, lotus or other flowers, reached China at the end of the Han. They can be seen used to full advantage at Yun gang (see description of the pillars of the doorway separating the two parts of cave no 9).

Yun gang marks a crucial moment in the history of Chinese art. Countless fertile influences were brought to China by the Central Asian people, inspiring a great renewal in the creative spirit at a time of social and political upheaval. There are 21 shrines altogether. Their exact dates are not known, but their chronology can be judged roughly from the evolution of the style: the shrines from 16 to 20 are the oldest; then numbers 7 and 8 (2nd period), 9, 10 and 12 (3rd period), 5, 6, 11, and 13 (4th period), 4, 14, and 15 (5th period), 1 and 21 (6th period). The third one seems to date from the Sui.

The visitor will notice that large numbers of the statues have lost their heads. 680 heads of Buddhas, Bodhisattvas and apsaras are missing altogether; 24 bas-relief carvings have been taken away or mutilated; several statues have been removed completely. Nearly all these works of art are now in European, Japanese, or

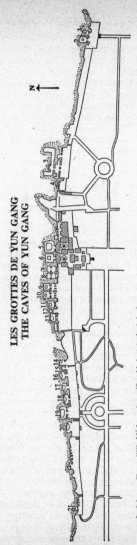

LES GROTTES DE YUN GANG
THE CAVES OF YUN GANG

N ←

d'après la revue «Wen wua» (1959, n° 8). Les numéros se réfèrent à la description donnée dans le texte.
after the magazine «Wen wu» (1959, n° 8). The numbers refer to the description given in the text.

American museums. During the first half of the century, count-less foreigners came to see the shrines and used to mark the carvings which they liked most with chalk; afterwards they came to an arrangement with the Chinese, who went and cut away the piece of their choice and sold it to them at the accepted price. In 1930, a Shang hai newspaper reported that over 90 pieces of sculpture had disappeared like this between April and May, nearly all of them sold to foreign learned societies. It is impos-sible not to be distressed by the unscrupulousness of these art-lovers, and the carelessness of the Chinese authorities at the time; however, in spite of the losses, Yun gang is still one of the finest examples of Chinese sculpture.

Description

The 21 caves are usually numbered from east to west. They fall naturally into three groups: 1 to 4, 5 to 13, 14 to 21. The first ones, beginning at the east end, are slightly disappointing, as they are the least interest-ing; however, as this is the usual order, they will be described beginning from the east. No. 1: It is a little over 16 feet high, and 30 feet deep, growing wider towards the end. The entrance is decorated with dra-gons in bas-relief. Other bas-relief carvings on the walls depict various scenes from the life of the Buddha. No. 2: It is the same shape as the first one, but larger. In the middle stands a two-storey tower, very delica-tely carved; the corners of the two stories are linked by little columns, some of which are missing. Bas-relief carvings cover the tower and the side walls. Three characters are engraved in the rock outside: *yun shen chu, place where the clouds are thick*. No. 3: This is the biggest of all the shrines, although the outside does not show it at all. The cliff, which is 80 feet high at this point, has traces of buildings on it; a legend exists which claims that a monastery, the Monastery of the En-chanted Cliff (Ling yan si), used to stand there, and that the monk Tan Hao taught there. The outer part of the cave is 35 feet wide; the inner part is 135 feet

wide, 48 feet deep and 43½ feet high. It contains three
Buddhas, carved in high relief; the middle one is
seated, with both hands raised, and is about 30 feet
high; the other two stand one on either side of the
central figure, like companions; they have one hand
raised to their chests, and are 20 feet high. All three,
but particularly the central figure, are extremely satisfying; the folds of their garments and their features
are carved with great restraint and elegance. They are
unique among the statues at Yun gang, and many
people have thought that they may date from the Sui.
It is possible that they were carved by order of the Sui
Emperor Yang, to expiate the crime he committed
when he assassinated his father, Emperor Wen, founder of the dynasty. Others have thought that these three
statues date from the beginning of the Tang, or the end
of the Northern Wei. Whatever the answer may be,
they are certainly later than the rest of the statuary at
Yun gang. The eastern part of the cave is unfinished; it
was probably begun under the Wei and abandoned
when the court was moved to Luo yang. No. 4: A small
cave. The column in the middle, the walls and the
little cave adjoining it are all decorated with bas-relief
carvings.

A ravine breaks into the mountainside after the
fourth cave. The **Old Monastery of the Stone Buddhas
(Shi fo gu si),** which dates from 1652 (beginning of the
Qing dynasty), stands just beyond it; it consists of several temples with annex buildings, and three towers
with wooden balconies built up against the mountainside, which act as a protection for caves Nos. 5, 6 and 7
and give access to the upper part of them. It is not
known whether other buildings like these ones stood
there before 1652. The Indian Buddhist caves are
shrines which are sufficient in themselves, and are not

usually completed by monasteries. The builders of the Yun gang Caves probably wanted originally to follow the Indian pattern. The *Shui jing zhu*, however, a geographical work written under the Northern Wei, during the Tai he period (477–500) says of Yun gang: "*...the stone was hollowed out, the mountainside was opened and buildings were made from the sandstone of the cliff*" and "*halls, pavilions and monasteries alternated among the water, the mountain and the mist*". It may have developed like this because it was near the capital. It is not certain what became of the monasteries later on. 10 monasteries are mentioned by name in a local chronicle dating from the Yong zheng period (1723–1736). The chronicle *(Shuo ping fang zhi)* says: "*Since the Sui and the Tang, under the Song and the Yuan, buildings of all sorts have been laid out there, one above the other; trees spread their branches there; it is a magnificent, ordered landscape. The mountain top is called the Cloud hill (Yun gang); three summer-houses stand on the hillside, with five characters in front of them, written by Emperor Zhi zu (1644–1662): xi lai di yu shan, the first among the mountains which come from the west*". It goes on to mention the cold spring which rose in the second shrine and a visit from Emperor Kang xi in the winter of 1697, when he wrote the four characters: *zhuang yan fa xiang, the great unity of all the doctrines*, still to be seen at the entrance to the 6th cave. According to this chronicle, Yun gang was never abandoned, from the Sui until the Yuan, and was held in honour under the Qing. Only one of the ten monasteries remains now, and only three caves (5, 6 and 7) still have their façades. A pavilion with a double roof and 5 bays still stands on the cliff above the 6th shrine: it is the highest point at Yun gang.

The buildings east of the monastery are a summer villa built by Zhao Cheng shou, who commanded the cavalry under Yan Xi shan (Yan Xi shan was the warlord who ruled Shan xi between the two world wars). Zhao Cheng shou also had the village of Yun gang built. According to the inhabitants, this was the only good thing he ever did all his life.

No. 5: This is the first cave belonging to the central group, and one of the most interesting; it is in good condition, thanks to the monastery buildings which shelter it. It is rounded, and about 60 feet high. A large wooden building stands at the entrance, 5 bays wide, three stories high, with balconies round the outside of it, and four roofs. A seated statue of the Buddha, 55½ feet high, and 50 feet wide at the base, stands just inside the entrance to the cave. It is the biggest statue at Yun gang and one of the biggest in China. It is traditionally said to have been made by Xiao wen (471–500), the most outstanding of the Northern Wei Emperors, in honour of his father, Emperor Xian wen (466–471). Its air of indomitable power and calm self-confidence gives a good idea of what the Northern Wei were like, and of the extent of their creative energy. The art of Yun gang reaches its summit in this Buddha. The walls round it are covered with bas-relief carving. On the side walls of the entrance, the fig-tree under which the Buddha received his illumination can be seen. The most delicate carvings in this shrine are probably the high relief carvings on either side of the opening on the floor above, over the entrance.

No. 6: This cave and the preceding one represent the highest point of achievement in the work at Yun gang. The statues and the bas-relief carvings are in good condition, as a three-storey building in front of the cave gives shelter. It forms a pair with the building in front of the 5th cave: they resemble two towers built up against the mountainside. A passage runs between the third stories, and another one leads left to the gallery above the 7th cave. The 6th cave is square, with a square tower in the middle, 49 feet high, covered with bas-relief carvings. At the bottom of each side are niches containing one or two Buddhas. The next storey has standing Buddhas against each facet; columns supporting the corners are carved in the shape of nine-storey pagodas. A wooden flight of steps leads to the upper storey of the tower, and it is possible to walk all round it. The facets of the tower and the walls of the shrine are covered with bas-relief carvings which relate scenes from the life of the Buddha, from his birth to his death, with never-failing vigour. The cave, a treasure of religious imagery, is said to have been made by Emperor Xiao wen (Wei) in memory of his mother.

No. 7: It is smaller than the 5th and 6th caves and like them has wooden balconies in front of it. It contains some fine bas-relief carvings, particularly six praying Bodhisattvas above the doorway between the two parts of the cave, on the inside. Two fine lions carved in high relief lie at the feet of the Buddha at the far end of the cave. Like the 5th and 6th caves, this one was restored in 1955.

No. 8: The 7th and 8th caves form a symmetric pair. The right door post has carvings of a guardian carrying a trident, and a Vichnou above him with three faces and eight arms, sitting on a bull. On the left doorpost is another guardian with a trident, and above him, a Shiva with five faces and six arms sitting on an eagle. These two carvings and others in the same cave are

excellent illustrations of the fusion of Chinese and
Indian art (the bull and the eagle are straight from the
Han tradition of sculpture). The trident carried by the
guardians is a Greek motive.

No. 9: The 9th and 10th caves are another pair. The
doorway leading into the further part of the cave is
surmounted by a lintel and roof delicately carved in
bas-relief. The doorposts are covered with plant designs. A rich universe peoples the inner part of the
cave, where withdrawn Bodhisattvas sitting peacefully
in their niches are surrounded by countless apsaras
whirling about them. A large Buddha is enthroned at
the far end, one hand raised, and guarded by two lions.
In spite of the countless figures all over them, the walls
of the cave are beautifully constructed; they represent
two-storey buildings with roofs; the vaulted ceiling is
the sky. Some of the finest pieces of bas-relief carving
are to be found beside the opening above the entrance
(a Bodhisattva riding an elephant, another sitting on
a lotus flower).

No. 10: The doorway leading into the inner part of
the cave is particularly fine, like the one in the preceding cave (the lintel and the doorposts are covered with
plant designs). A guardian stands on each side of the
doorway, brandishing the symbol of the thunderbolt.
They are each wearing winged helmets which like the
thunderbolts could easily be a borrowing from Greek
art. The inner cave is another little world, on the same
lines as the one in the 9th cave, but the effect is more
static. Bas-relief carvings below the niches with the
Bodhisattvas depict scenes from the life of the Buddha.
The sky is again full of whirling apsaras. The large
Buddha at the far end of the cave is a modern terra
cotta statue, of no artistic value.

No. 11: At the top of the outer part of the shrine a large cave opens out, shaped like a hemisphere, with a large Buddha enthroned in the middle. A square tower stands inside, with a bas-relief carving of the Buddha, 17 feet high, on each side. These graceful, gentle figures are the product of an art at the summit of its development. Some of the statues lined up alongside the walls were painted at a much later date. An inscription dating from 483 is engraved at the top of the eastern wall, and gives valuable information on the carving of the shrine, and the reason for it: it was made to ensure happiness for the Emperor and his family. This pious work was executed by monks and others: over 50 people altogether. The inscription says that the cave contains 95 carvings, without counting the innumerable little Bodhisattvas which fill up all the spaces in between them.

No. 12: It is in two parts. Palaces decorate the walls of the first part, and like other similar carvings at Yun gang, they give precious information on contemporary Chinese architecture. Buddhas and Bodhisattvas sit in different parts of them. The most interesting sequence of all in this part of the cave is the set of celestial musicians which runs round three of the walls, accompanying the Buddha's entry into a state of illumination. They are playing flutes, lutes, drums and other instruments. The large central statue in the second part of the cave looks as though it has been restored or changed at some later date.

No. 13: This shrine contains a statue of the Buddha Amitaba, 42 feet high, portrayed sitting cross-legged, with one hand raised. The raised hand is held up by a figure with four arms standing on the Buddha's leg, new to Chinese sculpture and unique at Yun gang. The wall behind the majestic statue is rounded, but not decorated, so that it forms a sort of enormous aureole for the deity. The other walls are decorated with countless bas-relief carvings of all sizes, as usual. Parts of them are painted. A stele inside the cave tells how at the end of the Qing dynasty, Wang Yong chang, a rich land-owner living in the area, spent large sums of money on having the statues in the 9th, 10th, 11th, 12th, and 13th Caves painted. The stele was erected by his son in memory of his devotion.

No. 14: A small cave, the first in the western group (14–21). As the front has fallen in, the interior has been eroded by the wind. A column inside it has a round base and square shaft, and is covered with Bodhisattvas sitting in little niches.

No. 15: This square cave, 32 feet high, had also suffered from erosion. A large Buddha in a niche decorates the far wall. The other walls are covered with over 10,000 Bodhisattvas, only a few inches high, carved in little niches, arranged in rows.

No. 16: This oval cave is one of the five which were carved from 460 onwards, by order of Emperor Wen chang; the monk Tan Hao was put in charge of the work. All five are made on the same lines, and take the form of an enlarged niche, to protect one monumental statue. They are different from the Indian rock temples and from the style of caves which evolved at Yun gang later on, ornamented with statues and bas-relief combining to give the impression of a small scale universe. The 16th cave contains one huge Buddha, 43 feet high, in a walking position, with one hand raised. The style is more archaic and massive than in the other caves preceding it.

No. 17: The ground level in this cave is slightly lower than the outside level. The central figure is a Buddha

50 feet high, sitting cross-legged, flanked by two accompanying figures, one sitting, the other standing. These three statues give an impression of great strength and grandeur; the style is different from the rest of the caves. Bas-relief carvings decorate the side walls. An inscription near the opening above the entrance says that the cave was made in 480.

No. 18: This is the most impressive and complete of the five early caves. It is oval like the others. A Buddha 50 feet high stands in the middle, on a lotus flower pedestal, his left hand on his chest. Although the carving is in simple style, the whole figure is full of intense life. Its garments are decorated with little bas-relief carvings of Bodhisattvas, arranged in processions, following the lines of the folds. The four Bodhisattvas grouped around the central figure (especially the ones on the right) are among the finest masterpieces at Yun gang and of Chinese Buddhist art as a whole.

No. 19: It consists of three caves, forming a triptych. The two side parts are 16 feet above the ground and each contains a Bodhisattva 26 feet high, which stands out in high relief against an enormous ornamented aureole. The Buddha in the centre is 55 feet high. The side walls are covered with little Bodhisattvas in meditation in little niches; they look like the cells of a vast honeycomb. The central Buddha and the sculptures on the right hand wall are all in the same severe style, whereas those on the left-hand wall are in a gentler, more graceful style; they seem later than the rest, and herald the sculpture of Long men. It may be that the shrine was carved shortly before the transfer of the court from Da tong to Luo yang, and the replacement of the Yun gang caves by those at Long men.

No. 20: As the building above the shrine has fallen down, the Buddha inside it now stands under the open sky, and can be seen from a long way off. It is 35 feet high, and is a perfect example of the style of the first period of the Northern Wei: severe and immobile. The features are strong and geometric (large mouth, protruding nose, colossal ears); the shoulders are of immense width, almost two thirds of the total height. The Buddha is portrayed seated, cross-legged with his hands on his legs; but the legs look like the pediment, so that at first the statue seems to consist only of the upper part. As it is easy to photograph, this is the most famous of the Yun gang statues.

Several smaller caves west of the 20th one also contain bas-relief carvings, with some fine apsaras and scenes from the life of the Buddha. The style is more ornate, and suggests that they belong to the Long men period (after 494).

No. 21: This square cave is different from all the rest. A five-storey pagoda stands in the middle, each storey separated from the next by a roof in traditional Chinese style, and the whole tapering off towards the top. The top ends in a lotus flower which seems to support the ceiling. Each facet of each storey is divided into 5 niches, each containing a Bodhisattva carved in low relief. Twelve rows of niches round the walls of the shrine also contain Bodhisattvas. The sculpture is clearly of a later date than the other caves and may date from the end of the Northern Wei.

Ying xian

Ying xian is a district headquarters about 40 miles south of Da tong as the crow flies. It was once a large town, under the Liao, with a Buddha's Palace Monastery (Fo gong si); the **large wooden pagoda (Shi jia ta)** is still standing. It was built in 1056 and is the only old wooden pagoda still existing in China. It is octagonal, with 6 roofs, the first of which is carried by 24 pillars, and is larger than the rest. The topmost roof ends in a slender spire. The pagoda has nine stories, only four of which open on to the outside (they have circular balconies); the others are on a level with the roofs and have no windows or doors. It is 216 feet high, and is built entirely of wood. A stretch of water lying beside it reflects it.

A model of the pagoda is exhibited in the Historical Museum at Peking (see p. 452). Wen wu publications of Peking are preparing a detailed study of it, which will appear under the title of *Fo gong si shi jia ta*. It is classed as a historical monument.

The pure Land Monastery (Jing tu si) stands in the north-east corner of the town. The main temple dates from the Jin (1124).

Shuo xian

Shuo xian is a district headquarters on the railway line, about 70 miles south-west of Da tong as the crow flies. A **monastery** there, the **Chong fu si,** was founded under the Tang and rebuilt under the Jin. The main temple, called Mi to dian, dates from 1143 (Jin) and contains some fine Jin sculpture and decoration.

CENTRAL SHAN XI

Central Shan xi stretches north as far as the southern section of the Great Wall, and includes the River Hu tuo basin, with the towns of Xin xian, Ding xiang and Yuan ping; the Yang quan region, west of Tai yuan; the Tai yuan basin. It is full of places of historic interest. The most important monuments will be briefly described.

Wu tai

Wu tai is a district headquarters about 70 miles
north-east of Tai yuan as the crow flies. It can be
reached by train as far as Ding xian or Jiang cun
(via Xin xian) and by road from there. The name of the
place means "five terraces"; it is about 3,000 feet above
sea level. The **Guang ji si Monastery** stands in the west
of the town, inside the walls; the main temple is a fine
example of Yuan architecture. The road from Jiang
cun to Wu tai goes through a little town called Dong
ye zhen; the **Nan chan si Monastery** is 5 miles to the
north. It includes a temple dating from the Tang (782)
which was forgotten during the destruction of Buddhist
temples ordered by the Emperor in 845, and is now
one of the few temples belonging to that period which
still survive. It is classed as a historical monument. The
temple is 3 bays wide; a door and two windows, all
surmounted by semi-circular arches, open in the façade, which is of masonry. The gently sloping roof is
supported by wooden cantilever brackets. It contains
a fine collection of Tang statues. The **Yan qing si
Monastery,** dating from the Jin, is about 7 miles north
of Dong ye zhen.

Wu tai shan

The Wu tai shan, "Five Terrace Mountain", is
about 30 miles north-east of Wu tai, not far from the
He bei boundary. It rises to 9,483 feet above sea level.
Its summit is made up of four terraces encircling a
depression, in the middle of which rises a fifth terrace.
The name Wu tai shan comes from this, and has been
extended to include all the mountains round it. Its
cool climate, and several clear springs which rise on

it, have earned the mountain its other name of Qing liang shan, Pure and Fresh Mountain. A road leads to it from Wu tai.

The Wu tai shan used to be one of the most important centres of Chinese Buddhism; pilgrims flocked there from all over China. The Bodhisattva Manjusrî (Wen shu in Chinese) was worshipped there, for he was traditionally supposed to have lived and taught there. Several rich monasteries flourished there under the Wei and the Tang. Ennin, the Japanese pilgrim who travelled about China from 837 to 847, under the Tang, described it with the greatest admiration (see *Ennin's Diary*, translated by E.O. Reischauer, Ronald Press Co., New York 1959).

A road led there from the capital, Changan. Hostels run by Buddhist priests were scattered at intervals along the way. Three other roads led there from He bei and Mongolia. The monasteries had great temporal as well as spiritual power; they supplied a large proportion of the tribute which the transitory Northern Han dynasty (951–979), whose capital was Tai yuan (see p. 839), paid to the Liao. Every year, they presented the court with the gifts left by the pilgrims (fabrics, gold) and made a further present of several hundred horses. They also had silver mines, forges and other workshops in the Fan shi valley to the north, and these products were given to the Liao as well. The Wu tai shan was the high place of Mongolian Buddhism; a large lamasery stood on the top with several Mongolian burial-places round it, and right up till the 20th century, Mongols used to bring their parents here to bury them, spending a year over the journey if necessary. The French sinologist, Edouard Chavannes, visited the place at the beginning of this century. It was possible, he said "to watch the Mongols at close quarters as they perform their devotions, as they take the ritual walk round the great stupa, turning the prayer wheels at the corners, or when the hour for prayer came, prostrating themselves countless times on the wooden planks arranged there for the purpose." (See *Chine du nord*, Guides Madrolle, Hachette, Paris 1913, p. 166.)

The richest, most frequented monasteries were the ones in the centre, built between the five terraces, and on the middle terrace. One of them contained a revolving library, described by Chavannes: "It takes up the whole building, from floor to roof; it is octagonal, and wider at the top than at the bottom. A trap-door opens in the floor, giving access to two levers at the base of the axis used to turn the heavy contraption. No books are left in it now; when it housed the complete collection of the sacred books, four men were needed to move it." (loc. cit.) The richer, more flourishing monasteries in the centre were perpetually showered with presents by officials and merchants and were often changed, enlarged, or rebuilt under the Ming and the Qing, so that they contain little or nothing earlier than the Ming dynasty. The more isolated monasteries were poorer and have stayed much as they were. One of them is particularly interesting.

The **Monastery of the Light of the Buddha (Fo guang si)** is south-west of the five peaks, 3 miles north of the village of Dou cun zhen, in the bottom of a wild valley with terraced fields built into the sides. The monastery faces west like the valley, and is built on two levels. The lower part contains the **Temple of Manjusri (Wen shu dian),** a hall 7 bays wide and 4 bays deep, facing south. The **Main Temple (Zheng dian)** stands on the upper level, dominating the whole of the monastery;

it is 7 bays wide and 4 bays deep as well. Both temples—
the first dates from the Jin and the second from the
Tang—are extremely precious buildings and are classed as historical monuments.

The monastery was founded under the Northern
Wei, in the reign of Emperor Xiao wen, between 471
and 499. It was burned to the ground during the Buddhist persecutions in 845 and rebuilt several years later.
The Main Temple dates from 847. Its style is of the
utmost simplicity; it stands on a slightly raised base,
and 5 out of the 7 bays are filled with solid square
doors. The lower halves of both the end bays are of
masonry, but the top halves are wooden grills. The
roof spreads far beyond the pillars, and is supported
by a powerful system of eaves clusters. The curve is
a slight one. The only decorations are the two ridge-
ornaments, one at each end ("pheasant tails"). The
inside is as beautiful as the outside. Tang frescoes and
inscriptions cover the walls. A long dais, stretching the
width of 5 bays, one and a half bays deep, and shut in
on three sides by partition walls, has about 30 Tang
statues standing on it. Other, smaller statues are scattered round it, outside the partitions. They are all in
excellent condition. A detailed description appeared
(in Chinese) in Wen wu (1953, No 5/6, p. 76–121).

The Temple of Manjusrî closely resembles the Main
Temple, although it was rebuilt under the Jin in 1137,
except that it has only three doors, taking up the three
central bays in the façade. Two other bays are of
masonry and wood, and the end bays are entirely of
masonry. The dais is square, roughly one bay's width
each way. Seven statues stand there: Manjusrî riding
a lion, two Bodhisattvas, two officials, a guardian and
a worshipper. The style is Tang, but a few details suggest that they may well date from the Jin.

FO GUANG SI (WU TAI SHAN)

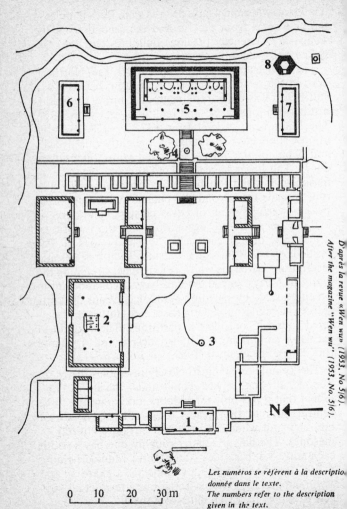

D'après la revue «Wen wu» (1953, No 5/6).
After the magazine "Wen wu" (1953, No. 5/6).

Les numéros se réfèrent à la description
donnée dans le texte.
The numbers refer to the description
given in the text.

0   10   20   30 m

Inside the monastery and in the area round it stand 6 pagodas and 2 Buddhist pillars *(chuang)*, all of them of great interest to the student of art history.

Ping xing guan

North-east of the Wu tai shan, the Shan xi-He bei road goes through the Ping xing guan pass. This was the scene, on September 25th 1937, of the first battle between the Communists and the invading Japanese army; the Communists' victory was a decisive one, politically at least, even if it was not entirely decisive from a military point of view. The 115th divison, led by Lin Biao, the main force of the 8th route army, routed the Japanese army which was marching on Tai yuan.

Yu ci

Yu ci is a town 15 miles south-east of Tai yuan, at the junction of the railway lines from He bei (Shi jia zhuang) to Tai yuan and south Shan xi, and from He bei to Xi an. Yu ci has become a centre of the cotton industry since the liberation. It also produces machines, particularly weaving looms, and acts as a commercial centre for the Tai yuan basin agricultural area.

Yang quan

This is the third most important town in Shan xi after Tai yuan and Da tong; it is on the railway line from Tai yuan to He bei, about 18 miles from the provincial boundary. It is the centre of an extremely rich mining basin producing coal, iron, sulphur, bauxite and other minerals. The town has possessed a metal industry for centuries; it has recently been brought up to date. The town has for years furnished supplies to the neighbouring province of He bei, by means of the road from Yang quan to Shi jia zhuang and Zheng ding, which was once the capital of He bei.

In 1923 it was described like this: "The volume of traffic on this road is enormous. Anthracite, pig-iron, cast-iron cooking pots, lime, skins, pottery is taken down, both by train and by almost never-ending strings of mules, donkeys, porters, and camels during the night only. Fabrics, oil, grain, flour, tea and European goods come in the other direction. Up to two or three thousand mules and donkeys, and two or three hundred camels a day have been counted in the past as they travelled down, laden, to the plain." (See Richard, *Géographie de la Chine*, vol. I, p. 114.)

In 1954, a Yuan tomb was found near **Ping ding**, a few miles south-east of Yang quan. It contained some beautiful frescoes (portrait of the dead, domestic scenes, and domestic animals).

Qing xu

Qing xu is a district headquarters about 9 miles south-west of the Jin ci, on the Tai yuan plain. The **Temple of the Perfumed Cliff (Xiang yan si)**, built in 1190, under the Jin, is about 2 miles west of the town. As it is built entirely in stone, it is often called Wu liang dian, "temple without beams". It contains 16 wooden statues of *luo han*, dating from the Ming.

Wen shui

It is a district headquarters on the edge of the Tai yuan plain, about 18 miles north-east of Fen yang, on the road to Tai yuan. It contains several old temples. 3 miles north-east of the town stands a temple, probably Song, dedicated to the Tang Empress Wu Ze tian (Ze tian miao).

The village of Yun zhou xi cun is about 13 miles east of Wen shui, on a fertile plain between the Fen (Fen shui) and the River Wen yu (Wen yu he).

In 1946, a 16 year-old peasant girl, **Liu Hu lan,** was beheaded south of the village because she refused to give information on the National Liberation Army to the soldiers of Yan Xi shan, the Shan xi warlord. The execution took place near an old temple dedicated to Guan yin (Guan yin miao). In 1959, the temple was transformed into the Liu Hu lan Museum.

A large stele erected in front of it bears eight characters written by Mao Ze dong in honour of the heroine: *sheng de wei da, si de guang rong,* "an admirable life and a glorious end". Behind the temple are a statue of Liu Hu lan and her tomb.

Tai gu

It is a district headquarters about 30 miles south of Tai yuan, on the railway line. Under the Ming and the Qing, it was full of rich merchants and bankers. Unlike Tai yuan, the town has hardly changed at all since the end of the Qing. Its massive square walls date from the Ming. A drum tower *(gu lou)* stands in the middle of the town, on an east-west axis lying between the east and west gates. The local government offices are just north of it. The south gate of the town was moved to the west, so that it no longer lay in a line with the drum tower and the government offices. The reason for this is said to be that the governor was afraid his good fortune *(fu qi)* would escape. Several old houses still survive; they have as many as ten courtyards, and are decorated with glazed tiles and bricks. A few old shops are still standing too; they lie perpendicular to the street, with the shop, the offices, the store-rooms and the living quarters all built on the same axis. High walls, solid enough to discourage most thieves and looters, surrounded them (they still do), with a watch tower at the far end. The town contains a Temple to Confucius *(Wen miao)*, a temple to the earth *(tu di miao)*, a temple to the god of the town *(cheng huang miao)* and four Buddhist monasteries. The **Zi fu si** in the south-east district of the town still has one beautiful building which survived the Japanese occupation (the rest of the monastery was burned), a library *(cang jing lou)* which is a large building 5 bays wide with four roofs. A balcony with pillars runs round it between the 2nd and 3rd roofs. The building dates from the Qing, but it is much lighter in style than most of the architecture of that dynasty.

Ping yao

It is a district headquarters on the railway line about 30 miles south-west of Tai gu. Like Tai gu, it was a rich town under the Ming and the Qing; its bankers were known all over China. As it was never a political centre or a military garrison, but a peaceful little town, it has kept most of its ancient monuments, which have accumulated over the centuries. The temples in the town and the surrounding area contain an exceptionally rich collection of statues.

The **Temple of Confucius (Wen miao)** is in the south-east of the town. The main temple is a handsome square hall, 5 bays deep. It was rebuilt under the Jin in 1163, but in Song style. It was restored at the end of

the Qing dynasty and again in 1953. The stone lion
dates from the Jin. The **Market Tower (Shi lou)** bestrides the north-south avenue in the centre of the
town; it was built under the Qing. Its roof of yellow
glazed tiles bears the double character *xi* (happiness)
drawn on it in green. The **Imperial Temple (Tai zi
miao)** and the Taoist Monastery **Qing xu guan** both
contain some good sculpture, and the **Nine Dragon
Screen (Jiu long bi)** has bas-relief carvings in glazed
tiles dating from the Ming dynasty.

Outside the town, the village of Bu yi cun, to the
south, contains steles, bas-relief carving and sculpture
dating from the Northern and Southern Dynasties,
the Sui and the Tang. The **Qing liang si Monastery**
contains Ming statues. The **Temple of Ye lu's Wife (Ye
lu fu ren miao)** is at Gan keng (Ye lu was the surname
of the Liao ruling house). A Ming pagoda, covered
with glazed tiles, is decorated with the incredible adventures of Sun Wu kong, the monkey king, and hero
of the satirical novel written in the 16th century by
Wu Cheng en, entitled the *Xi you ji (Journey to the
West)*.

About 6 miles north of Ping yao, near Hong shan
railway station and a village called Hao dong cun,
stands a monastery: the **Zhen guo zi,** "which protects
the empire by exorcising evil spirits". It can be seen
from the train. The central temple is the only surviving
example of Northern Han architecture, and was built
in 936, at a time when the Northern Song had not
finally subdued the rebellious dynasty (see p. 839), and
their architecture had not replaced the former style.
The temple still shows several characteristics of Tang
architecture. It contains 11 painted statues also dating
from the Northern Han. Other parts of the monastery
contain Yuan statues.

The **Ci xiang si** monastery stands in the village of Ji guo cun, 5 miles east of Ping yao. Its octagonal pagoda, which has nine roofs, dates from the Jin; the temple and the other buildings date from the Qing.

The **Two Forests Monastery (Shuang lin si)** is 3½ miles south-west of the town, in a village called Qiao tou cun; it has a collection of Ming and Qing sculpture which is unique in China. The monastery was founded under the Northern Wei (386–534) and was called the Monastery of the Middle Capital (Zhong du si) at first. Its present name dates from the Northern Qi (550–577). It was restored or rebuilt several times under the Song, the Ming and the Qing. The present buildings all date from the Dao guang period (1821–1851). They consist of 4 temples lying on the central axis, 5, 5, 7 and 5 bays wide respectively, with three courtyards between them. The second temple is flanked by the drum tower and the bell tower. On either side of the second courtyard, which is the biggest, stand two temples, each 7 bays wide: the 1,000 Buddha Temple (Qian fo dian) and the Bodhisattvas' Temple (Pu sa dian).

Four colossal "celestial kings" (tian wang) stand at the entrance to the temple, to protect it from evil spirits, all visible from a long way off. They are different from most of the stereotyped, scowling monsters brandishing weapons at the doors of countless Chinese temples; keen psychological observation is united with complete control of mass and movement to make them a great work of art. They date from the Ming, or possibly from the end of the Yuan dynasty.

Several thousand other pieces of sculpture, in high relief, or in *ronde bosse*, modelled in clay, and painted, can be seen in the other temples of the monastery. Like the frescoes in the Fa hai si near Peking, they are

a magnificent expression of the creative upsurge in
China at the beginning of the Ming dynasty. Some of
them seem to have been remade or added under the
Qing, but they are not out of harmony with the rest.
In some cases, it is clear that a Ming model has been
used several times, and repeated. Several scenes with
groups of people line the side walls of the second
temple, illustrating legends (a unicorn, *qi lin*, watching
over a sleeping woman) or scenes from real life (an
official casting aside the world and its honours to enter
a religious life). The groups are composed with the
same assurance as the individual statues. Some fine
statues of Buddhas and Bodhisattvas stand in the
middle.

The 1,000 Buddha Temple, on the right of the second
courtyard, is a museum in itself. It reveals a whole world
of masculine and feminine deities, and statues of men
and women praying. The theme of the believer praying
to the deity appeared in Chinese art under the Northern Wei. At that point, he was shown as very small,
praying at the feet of the deity. Under the Ming, the
two worlds, human and divine, became more balanced:
the sculptor portrayed his life-size men with as much
realism as the deities. The building on the opposite side
of the courtyard is full of hundreds of statues of *luo
han* (arhats, hermits), every one of them different from
the rest, the fruit of an inexhaustable imagination.
One of the most striking is the figure who is taming
a tiger by sheer force of will. The tiger seems to have
lost all his violence before his new master.

Fen yang

Fen yang is a district headquarters in the south-
western tip of the Tai yuan plain. Roads lead there

from Ping yao and from Tai yuan (via the Jin ci, Jiao cheng, Wen shui). The town is famous for its vineyards which yield "Fen wine", *Fen jiu*. The name of the town means "on the sunny banks of the Fen". There are several old temples there.

SOUTH SHAN XI

This area covers the Lin fen basin, the lower reaches of the River Fen and the Yun cheng basin, in the far south-west of the province. The Chang zhi area in the south-east of the province will not be mentioned here. It has numerous historical monuments, but on the whole they are less interesting than those in other regions.

Zhao cheng

Zhao cheng is a small town on the railway line from Hong dong to Huo xian, in the north of the Lin fen plain. This plain, with Mount Huo shan (8,361 feet) overlooking it to the east, has always been used by commercial and military traffic on its way to Tai yuan, and it was a stage in the pilgrimage to the Wu tai shan. One of the most interesting monuments lies 12 miles south-east of Zhao cheng, near a spring, at the foot of Mount Huo shan: the **Monastery of Widespread Victory (Guang sheng si)**. It is classed as a historical monument, by virtue of the frescoes inside. There are three different parts: the Lower Monastery (Guang sheng xia si), the Dragon King Temple (Ming ying wang dian) and the Upper Monastery (Guang sheng shang si). The monastery is famous because a **collection of sutras comprising over 4,300 scrolls** was found in one of the halls in the Lower Monastery before the war. The scrolls date from the Jin dynasty and were engraved and printed between 1148 and 1173 by Lin fen craftsment. In 1942, the National Liberation Army (8th route army) saved the scrolls from the Japanese, who had laid hands on them. They are now in the National Library at Peking. A few scrolls are in the Shan xi Museum at Tai yuan (see p. 849).

The first monastery on this spot was founded under the Western Han in 147 B.C. It was rebuilt under the Tang. On the night of the 6th of the 8th month in 1303, the temples were burned down. They were rebuilt from 1305 onwards. Most of the buildings which can be seen today date from the Yuan; some of them date from the Ming or the Qing.

The temples of the **Lower Monastery** reveal great inventiveness and at the same time great simplicity. The first temple *(qian dian)* is 5 bays wide and dates from 1472 (Ming); the second *(da fo dian)* dates from 1309 (Yuan) and is 7 bays wide. No ornaments break up the strong proportions of the building or the handsome wood-work. The roof is plain as well. A ridge as wide as the temple itself crowns it, and the two sides curve gently down from there. The temple contains statues.

The enclosure of the **Dragon King Temple** (Long wang miao, or Ming ying wang miao), on a lower level than the monastery enclosure, is next to it. Two large gateways lead into the temple, whose architecture is much more advanced, although it dates from 1319. The double roof has sharply upturned corners, whose effect is heightened by the daring overhang; the main body of the building covers 3 bays, but the lower roof spreads over 5 bays; it forms a sort of arcade, supported by 6 pillars on each side of the temple. The façade of the temple stands back and the roofs give the main outline of the building. The walls inside the temple are covered by **Yuan frescoes** of inestimable value, both as a work of art and as a document; they date from 1325. Instead of representing religious scenes or legends, they show episodes from social life under the Yuan, and in particular scenes from operas. They constitute one of the most precious documents in existence for the study of production and costumes in this golden age of Chinese opera.

The Dragon King (Long wang, or Ming ying wang), to whom the temple is dedicated, is the sovereign of the dragon world, that is, the world of water, whether springs (as here), clouds, rain, river, lake or ocean.

The Upper Monastery is on a flattened hill top, about 500 yards from the Lower Monastery. A winding path leads up to it. The magnificent **glazed tile tower (lui li ta),** known as the Flying Rainbow Pagoda (Fei hong ta) can be seen from some way away. It is octagonal, 168 feet high, and entirely covered with glazed tiles. It has 13 richly decorated cornices; between them, each facet of each storey has a little balcony in the middle, with carvings on either side. The pagoda has an unusual profile, because each storey is much smaller in diameter than the one below. The diameter of the top storey is not more than a third of the base. The tapering is carried out according to a mathematical progression, however, and the lines are straight. The building dates from the Tang, but it was re-covered with glazed tiles and re-decorated under the Ming, from 1525–1527. It is the finest example of this type of work in China. A steep staircase (60°) gives access to the top. As no openings let in light from outside, there are candlesticks on each landing. The base of the pagoda is surrounded by an arcade with wooden pillars.

The pagoda stands in the first courtyard of the monastery. Three temples follow: the first, 5 bays

wide, dates from the Yuan and contains some handsome bronze Buddhist statues. The style is Song; the
most striking of them are two Bodhisattvas standing
on imaginary animals. The second temple, also 5 bays
wide, contains other unusual statues. A large statue
of the Buddha stands in the centre; he is depicted sitting on a lotus throne, with two Bodhisattvas beside
him, one riding a lion, the other an elephant. The statues are in wood and appear to date from the Ming.
Open-work wooden partitions stand in front, acting
as a balustrade. The third temple was built under the
Ming in 1497; it is 5 bays wide, with one doorway, in
the central bay. The other four have no openings.
The hall has a slightly strange air about it, because the
ridge of the roof is no wider than the central bay, giving the roof, as it curves down to the four corners, an
unusually long, flowing line.

Note: In 1954, the districts of Zhao cheng and Hong dong
were combined under the name of "Hong zhao district" (Hong
zhao xian). Anything written before 1954 places the monastery
in the Zhao cheng district, whereas later sources put it in Hong
zhao. There is in fact one monastery only, not two.

Lin fen

The town of Lin fen, "on the banks of the Fen" as
its name implies, is the centre of the most fertile area
in the province. The plain is well-irrigated and produces large amounts of wheat and cotton.

Lin fen used to be called Ping yang, and under this
name it was a governor's residence under the Ming
and the Qing. It is traditionally supposed to be one of
the oldest capitals in China: Yao, the fourth of the
five legendary emperors who reigned between 2550 and
2140 B.C. is supposed to have lived there, and his
tomb is supposed to be to the east of the plain. The

mountain east of the town is called the Mountain of the Ancestor of Man (Ren zu shan). A discovery made in 1954 near the village of Ding cun proves that the area was inhabited at an extremely early date. Fossilized human teeth belonging to the Paleolithic era were found, suggesting that a **Ding cun Man** must have existed. It is thought that he lived in 300,000 or 400,000 B.C. Other things have been found on the same site: over 2,000 stone tools etc. and fossils of at least 26 kinds of vertebrate animals (rhinoceros, elephant, water-buffalo, horse, etc.). The site is classed as a historical monument.

A six-storey glazed tile pagoda, built in 1719, under the Qing, stands in the town of Lin fen. The base is square. The rest is composed of five cubes, one on top of each other, each one smaller than the one before. The pagoda is an excellent example of the art of glazed tiles, which was particularly highly developed in Shan xi (see p. 846 and 906). It is part of a monastery founded under the Tang: the Great Cloud Monastery (Da yun si).

Hou ma

This town lies in the area where the Fen runs westwards to flow into the Yellow River about 50 miles away. A railway line is planned for the area, starting at Hou ma, following the lower reaches of the Fen and crossing the Yellow River at the Long men pass ("Dragon Gate"), and going on to Xi an, via Xian yang. Hou ma has been developing into an industrial town since the liberation.

The Hou ma area is one of the oldest inhabited areas in China. Countless archaeological discoveries have been made there, particularly since 1956. The most extensive discoveries relate to the Eastern Zhou era (770–256 B.C.). In 1957, the remains of a town were found, which was probably the capital of the principality of Jin during the Chun qiu period (770–481 B.C.); they are classed as a historical monument. In 1959, a tomb was found, with remains of four slaves who had been buried with their masters; it contained clay moulds, delicately engraved, for casting bronzes, and other tools. Other finds include remains of dwellings, pottery kilns, ditches used for hunting, hundreds of graves, bronzes, etc., Han, Tang, Song, Jin and Yuan tombs. The Jin tombs, dating from 1210, were covered with bas-relief carvings depicting the interior of a house in minute detail.

Xin jiang

Xin jiang is a district headquarters west of Hou ma, inside the bend formed by the river Fen. In 1923, it was described as a "picturesque town on the slopes of the right bank of the Fen ho (Fen he), a river-traffic terminus and the largest market town in south Chan-si (Shan xi). It lies on a fertile plain, near coal mines. In winter the trading boats are immobilised by ice and form a little town. The volume of trade is not due only to the position of the town; it is swelled by the varied produce of the whole area: coal, iron, cotton, tobacco, rice. Silk, cotton fabrics, tea and salted foods are brought up from the south." (Richard, *Géographie de la Chine*, vol. I, p. 118).

Wan rong (Wan quan)

Wan rong is a district headquarters, known as Wan quan up to 1954, now called Wan rong, about 30 miles south-west of Hou ma as the crow flies, north-west of Mount Ji shan (4,197 feet). The Eastern Peak Temple

(Dong yue miao) is now used as government offices;
it dates from the Qing. One of the buildings is a most
unusual one: the **Tower which Flies in the Clouds (Fei
yun lou),** which is 100 feet high, and one of the rare
examples of a tall building in Chinese traditional style
which has survived until now (with the exception of
pagodas, which are strictly Buddhist in inspiration).
The Fei yun lou probably dates from the Ming, but it
was rebuilt during the Qian long period (1736–1796)
and is classed as a Qing monument. The alternating
balconies and sharply upturned roofs produce a most
striking effect.

Rui cheng

Before it enters the Yellow River valley and Shân xi,
the railway line from Tai yuan runs alongside a salt
lake, on the banks of which lies the town of Yun cheng;
12 miles or so beyond that, it goes through Xie zhou.
25 miles south of there by road, over a little range of
hills, lies Rui cheng, a district headquarters in the
Yellow River valley. The journey can easily be made
by coach. A little to the north of the town stands the
Yong le gong, one of the most interesting monuments
in Shan xi. The three main temples and the gateway
are all covered with magnificent **Taoist murals, dating
from the Yuan.**

The Yong le gong, or the "Yong le Palace (gong)"
was near the village of the same name, on the banks of
the Yellow River. As the San men xia Dam (see p. 801)
was eventually to submerge the whole area, including
the village of Yong le, it was decided to move the
temples and their paintings north of Rui cheng. The
work was carried out with the utmost care, using all
the most up to date methods; it was begun in 1959 and

finished in the following year. The Yong le gong is in a sense a "discovery" made since the liberation; it lay abandoned and completely forgotten during the first half of the century. It was not noticed again by the public, art-lovers and specialists until the 1950's.

In 1964, Art Publications for the People (Ren min mei shu chu ban she) of Peking brought out a volume of reproductions of the Yong le gong with 206 pages of photographs, black and white and colour, and 18 pages of introduction, entitled *Yong le gong*. In 1958, Wen wu publications had already published a selection of black and white reproductions *(Yong le gong bi hua xuan ji)*.

Lü Dong bin was born into a family of high officials living in the village of Yong le under the Tang dynasty, in 755. When he was 20, he went to Lu shan, in Jiang xi, and there he met a fire dragon who gave him a magic sword which enabled him to fly. Later on, when he visited the capital, Chang an, Lü Dong bin met Zhong Li quan (also called Han Zhong li), who had been a general under the Zhou dynasty and had discovered the secret of immortality; he was staying on earth for a time. When Zhong Li quan told him the secret of immortality, Lü Dong bin expressed an ardent desire to spread the true doctrine of alchemy among men. He emerged successful from the test of the ten temptations, and found that he possessed magic powers, which he used for the next 400 years to do innumerable good deeds. His feats are described in countless legends. Several contradictory accounts exist of his meeting with Zhong Li quan.

Another legend claims that after his death, under the Tang, Lü Dong bin's house was transformed into a temple and that sacrifices were made to him each year. This story is supported by a stele dating from 1262 at the Yong le gong, which bears the inscription: "*Ever since the Tang, the inhabitants have called his house "The Temple of Mr Lü", and every time that the season when the corn ripens comes round, people gather there from far and near, both dignitaries and commoners: there is music and wine, and it goes on until evening*". At the end of the Jin dynasty, the temple was enlarged and converted into a *guan*, or Taoist monastery.

Taoism was becoming more and more widespread at this time; the upward movement began under the Song and under the Yuan it was to flourish as never before. The group of the Eight Immortals *(ba xian,* see p. 161) gradually formed during this period, out of several dissimilar elements. Some of these highly coloured characters were worshipped among the Taoist deities, others were born of popular imagination. Three of them, Zhang Guo lao, Zhong Li quan and Lü Dong bin, seem to have been historical characters. Under the Yuan dynasty, they were formed into a group of inseparable companions, at the centre of the Taoist pantheon. Lü Dong bin and Zhong Li quan had pride of place among them.

The temple dedicated to Lü Dong bin was burned down in 1244. The heads of the Taoist church took the opportunity of asking the Emperor, the defender of their religion, to promote the Yong le monastery from the rank of monastery *(guan)* to that of palace *(gong)*, and to have a sanctuary built, which was to be one of the three most important ones in the empire, with two others, one at Peking, the other south of Chang an. Work was begun in 1247 and lasted until 1262. The great gateway (Wu ji men) was not built until 1294. Most of the paintings were finished in the 14th century. The last touches were put to the ones in the Lü Dong bin Temple (Chun yang dian) in 1358. The creation of the Yong le gong went on throughout almost the whole of the Yuan dynasty (1280–1368). (Note: in 1244, the Mongols already held north China; 1280 saw the end of the Southern Song and the extension of their power throughout the whole of China).

The four most important buildings are all still standing, all lying on the same axis. They are: the gateway, Gate of the Unfathomable (Wu ji men); the main temple, the Temple of the Three Pure Ones (San qing dian); the temple dedicated to Lü Dong bin, called the Chun yang dian (Note: *Chun yang* is one of Lü Dong bin's names); the temple dedicated to Wang Zhong yang (Zhong yang dian). A Qing gateway leads into these four. The Yong le gong originally had one more temple on the central axis, and to the east of the main axis lay seven groups of other buildings, all smaller (temples, monastery, library). They have now disappeared. The four surviving buildings were restored reveral times under the Ming and the Qing. Extensive sestoration work was carried out in 1559, 1689, and 1890. The 1689 restoration work lasted for three years. In 1890, parts of the paintings were restored as well.

The buildings and the paintings will be described briefly. In August 1963, the Chinese review *Wen wu* devoted a whole issue to the Yong le gong (description of the buildings, analysis of the iconography of the frescoes, reproduction of inscriptions on them, etc. The issue is sold out).

The **Gate of the Unfathomable (Wu ji men)** (1) is also called the Tiger and Dragon Gate (Long hu men). It is 5 bays wide, and built on the same lines as a temple, except that it is open; its sole function is to provide a frame for the three doors. The side sections each contain two lodges. Two out of the four have murals (the two inside ones). The paintings share the same symbolism as the paintings inside the main temple, and they illustrate: Shen tu, the god of doors (a), Yu lei, the god of doors (b), celestial generals and their armies (c, d), celestial scribes and grooms (e), local deities, both military and civil (f).

The **Temple of the Three Pure Ones (San qing dian)** is a large building, 7 bays wide, standing fairly high off the ground, with a flight of steps leading up to a terrace round it. Two big glazed tile dragons decorate the ridge-ends. Five doors fill five bays of the façade. An altar three bays wide inside is enclosed on three sides by partition walls. Statues of the Three Pure Ones used to stand on it (San qing). They are the three highest deities of the Taoist pantheon, in honour of whom the temple was built: the Jade Pure One (Yu qing), the High Pure One (Shang qing) and the Supreme Pure One (Tai qing). The paintings should be related to the deities; they represent **all the Taoist gods,** assembled round the central deities. The idea of painting the complete pantheon is a borrowing from Buddhist habits. Pictures of the Buddha preaching *(shuo fa tu)* became "pictures of the supreme court" *(chao yuan tu)*. Buddhism, and reaction against its influence, led the Taoist leaders, from the Tang onwards, to create a carefully graded hierarchy of deities, by searching through the traditions of the autochthonic religions. The Taoist pantheon as illustrated at Yong le gong had been drawn up by Song theologians, and was taken up without many changes by the schools in north China under the Jin and the Yuan.

286 gods altogether cover the walls of the temple, grouped round eight principal figures, dressed as emperors. The chief of these is the Great Emperor of the South Pole (a). His train of 13 attendants includes 5 philosophers who were deified by the Taoist tradi-

tion, among them Lie zi and Zhuang zi (see p. 145).
5 other philosophers can be recognised among the followers of the Great Emperor of the East Pole (b). A
college of second rank deities (32 of them) decorates
the width of the altar, facing outwards (c): the celestial
Princes who reign over the 32 skies of the universe.
Next comes the Great Emperor of the North Pole (d),
surrounded by a train of 44 dignitaries, among whom
are 14 of the gods of the 28 constellations in the Chinese
sky, the gods of the 7 stars of the Great Bear, the
5 planets, the sun and the moon. Three fathers of the
Taoist church are to be found among them. Three
more fathers and 14 gods of constellations form part
of the train of the Great Emperor of the Stars (e). It
consists of 40 people altogether, and includes the Administrator of the Sky, and the Administrators of the
Earth and the Waters. The Jade Emperor and the
Empress of the Earth are enthroned on the east wall
of the temple (f), amidst 134 celestial dignitaries. Opposite them (g) are Mu gong, the patron of the immortals
and the Western Queen Mother (Xi wang mu). The
deities of the eight trigrammes *(ba gua)* and Confucius are among the 75 people in their train. The last
two figures are the two fearsome guardians, to be found
in every Taoist temple: the Blue Dragon Lord (h) and
the White Tiger Lord (i).

Each of these supernatural characters portrayed is
over 6 feet high. They are massed, one behind the
other, in four rows. The paintings themselves are
15½ feet high. Every figure is full of character and life.
The rich colours, among which bronze, brown, red,
pink and light blues and greens predominate, are controlled by firm, sure linear drawing. This Assembly of
the Gods recalls the greatest masterpieces of the Italian
renaissance.

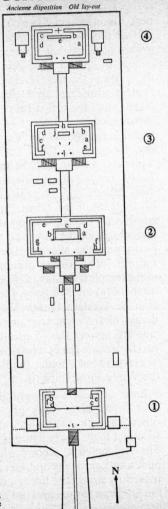

YONG LE GONG

Ancienne disposition   Old lay-out

N.B. – The staircases with a diagonal stroke through them represent ramps.

After the magazine *Wen wu* (1963, no 8). The letters refer to the description given in the text.

The second temple, dedicated to Lü Dong bin, is called the **Chun yang dian** (3). Like the main temple, it stands on a fairly high plinth. It is five bays wide. Nearly all the inside walls are covered with paintings telling the story of Lü Dong bin's life and the many feats attributed to him. There are 52 pictures altogether, and each one depicts an episode in his life. An inscription explains each one, and the transition from one picture to the next is managed by a skilful use of landscape. The real and the supernatural mingle throughout. Many of the pictures show twenty or more people involved in different things and bird's eye views of towns, palaces and monasteries. The realistic interpretation makes them a valuable source of information on daily life under the Yuan. Other subjects are illustrated, apart from the Lü Dong bin's life (a, b, c, d). The frescoes to the right and left of the entrance (e, f) show scenes in the life of a Taoist monastery. On the north wall of the partition (g) **Lü Dong bin and Zhong Li quan** are shown sitting under an old pine tree, in a wild valley with a little stream flowing through it. Zhong Li quan is speaking to his pupil, who listens to him pensively, with his joined hands hidden in the sleeves of his scholar's gown. The whole countryside is brown, save the green pine needles and moss. Zhong Li quan is dark-skinned, dressed in a gown tied negligently about him, which is of a slightly brighter green than the pine-needles. He seems to be the personification of nature itself. Lü Dong bin is dressed in a white gown with black borders which stands out in contrast to the landscape. Were it not for his meditative expression, he would seem a complete stranger to all around him. The Taoist inspiration reaches heights which the great celestial scenes in the San qing dian do not aspire to, making it perhaps the peak of the art of the Yong le gong. Above the north door (g) the Eight Immortals are shown crossing the sea (see p. 161); paintings on either side of the door show other Taoist figures (i, j).

The third temple, the **Zhong yang dian,** is dedicated to Wang Zhong yang (1112–1170), the founder of a Taoist sect called the Quan zhen jiao, "Teaching of True Integrity". It played an active part in the Chinese resistance to Jin domination and under the Yuan, it held a strong position in north China. The Yong le gong is its creation. The frescoes in the third temple include 49 pictures (a, b, c, d) describing the turbulent life which Wang Zhong yang and his 7 disciples led. Esthetically speaking, they are less interesting than the paintings in the Chun yang dian, but they are a source of precious information on the period. They appear to have been finished in 1368. An inscription explains each picture. On the north side of the partition wall (e) a painting represents the Three Pure Ones.

For other information on the Yong le gong and its paintings, and especially for questions concerning the identity of the painters, or the architecture of the temples, see the works quoted above.

SHÂN XI

The province of Shân xi borders on Shan xi (the Yellow River forms the boundary), He nan and Hu bei to the west, Si chuan to the south, Gan su and the Hui Autonomous Region of Ning xia to the east, and the Inner Mongolian Autonomous Region to the north. It falls into three distinct regions: the northern Shân xi plateau; the valley of the Wei (a tributary of the Yellow River) in the middle; the Qin ling Mountains and the Han valley to the south The northern loess plateau is lowest in the south-east (2,600 feet above sea level) and the highest point is reached in the north-west and north (3,900 feet above sea level); the higher regions are cut up by deep ravines. To the north, the plateau ends in chains of mountains which form the foothills of the Ordos plateau (Inner Mongolia). The plateau is rich in coal and oil, particularly in the south, which is known as the "black belt". The Wei valley is about 186 miles long, and stretches from Bao ji (in the west) to Tong guan (in the east); at Bao ji it is deep and narrow but it widens out towards the west, and from Xi an on- wards, it forms a plain stretching as far as the Yellow River, of which the River Wei is a tributary. The Yellow River flows out of the province through the Tong guan Pass, which at the same time gives access to the Wei basin. The old name for the basin, *guan zhong*, "inside the pass", and the present name for the province, Shân xi, "west of the pass", both come from this geographical feature. N.B.: the only difference between the names *Shân xi* and *Shan xi* as far as pronunciation is concerned is the tone of the first syllable; the first European writers spelled Shân xi with an "e", Shen xi, to mark the distinction; a circum- flex accent is used here instead, as it is nearer the correct pron- unciation, and falls in with *pin yin* romanisation.

South of the Wei plain are the Qin ling Mountains, which are mainly over 6,000 feet. The most well-known peak is the Hua shan (see p. 966), and the highest is the Tai bai shan (11,418 feet). Further south, the upper reaches of the River Han separate the Qin ling Mountains and the Da ba shan Mountains. The Qin ling Mountains screen the Han valley from the cold coming from the north, so that its climate is sub-tropical.

The Wei valley and the middle Yellow River area were the cradle of Chinese civilisation during the bronze age, and remain- ed the most highly developed area in China right up to the

Tang. From the founding of the Zhou dynasty (1066 B.C.) until the end of the Tang (907 A.D.), the capital of the empire was first in one area, then in the other. The Wei valley was the centre of the Chinese world under the Western Zhou (capital: Hao), the Qin (capital: Xian yang), the Western Han, the Sui and the Tang (capital: Chang an). It is also one of the areas of China which has been inhabited longest of all (the Lan cun culture dates from the Paleolithic era).

Towards the end of the second millenium B.C., nomads from the east settled there and founded the Zhou dynasty. In the 3rd century B.C. a strong military state, Qin, was formed on the northern plateau of Shân xi; its fifth sovereign, Qin shi Huang di, unified China by force of arms and proclaimed himself emperor in 221 B.C. The Han took over the new empire and extended it southwards and westwards. Great military expeditions left from Chang an towards what is now Gan su, and discovered Central Asia (the Silk Route). Under the Han, and even more so under the Tang, Chang an was a cross-roads between east and west, the biggest military, economic and cultural centre in Asia. From the 10th century onwards, the centre of gravity of Chinese life moved southwards. Shân xi was no longer the centre, and became instead a border province. From the Ming dynasty until modern times, the poor regions in the north of the province became a strong-hold of revolutionary tradition. Li Zi cheng led his peasant armies from north Shân xi to overthrow the Ming dynasty on the eve of the Manchu invasion. Towards 1930, a peasant soviet was formed in north Shân xi; the Communist Party and the National Libe-ration Army were based there from 1935 onwards (Yan an). This poverty-stricken region once more took up the role which it had played at the time of Qin shi Huang di, that of a well-defended base from which the reconquest of China could be organised.

During the hundred years or so of foreign influence, the fo-reign powers concentrated the centres of the Chinese economy on the coastline, in places like Shang hai, Qing dao and Tian jin. Now that China is once more in control of her own economy, the main centres are gradually being moved to the interior of the country. Shân xi is naturally regaining the key position which it used to hold, especially since the building of the new railway line from Bao ji to Cheng du (linking Shân xi and Si chuan) and the extension of the Xi an to Tian shui (Gan su) line as far as Lan zhou, and from there to Xin jiang. The textile industry has been developed in the Wei plain, so that the finished cloth is now distributed throughout western China, and cotton is no longer sent from Shân xi to the Shang hai mills as used to be the case before the liberation. This was made possible by expanding the machine tools industry first of all, and by developing the metal, chemical and building industries as well. It was a fairly rapid process, thanks to the rich natural resources of the province, and most of all because of its many sources of power.

The coal deposits in the "black belt" on the southern edge of the plateau are the richest in China, after the Shan xi coal-fields. The largest mining centres are in the Tong chuan area, which is on the railway line to Xian yang and Xi an. Oil is produced at Yan chang, east of Yan an. Research institutes and higher educational establishments have been founded at Xi an as a result of this economic development, and the Shang hai Communications Institute has been transferred there.

Agriculture varies from one part of the province to another. The Han valley, in the south, produces rice, tea, and vegetable oil among other things. The Wei plain in the centre produces mainly wheat and cotton. Cotton is the main industrial crop in Shân xi. Wheat is grown on 20% of the land under cultivation and represents 42% of the cereal production of the province (maize and goaliang come after it). Orchards have been planted on the northern slopes of the Qin ling Mountains. Since the liberation, tremendous efforts have been made to combat the two evils of drought and erosion on the northern plateau; the countryside is gradually being transformed by the new tree plantations and the terraced fields on the hillsides, all of which is made easier by the fact that the loess soil is naturally fertile. The work carried out by the population of the village of Nan ni wan is famous throughout China as an example of the triumph of man over nature. Stock-breeding is the main activity on the northern pasturelands (cattle, donkeys, mules, horses).

The town of Xi an and its neighbourhood will be described first, followed by the road from Xi an to Yan an, and then the towns west of Xi an and in the south and east of the province

XI AN

Xi an is in a fertile basin, which produces both cotton and grain, several miles south of the River Wei, between two other rivers which flow into it: the Feng shui, to the west, and the Ba shui, to the east. The Qin ling Hills, rich in wood and minerals, are to the south; a plateau to the north, though not as high as the hills,

LA RÉGION DE XI AN

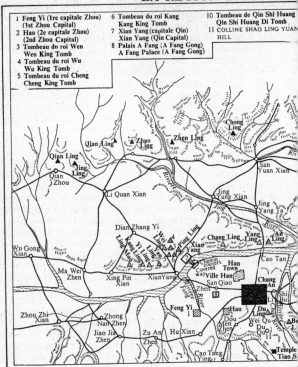

1 Feng Yi (1re capitale Zhou)
  (1st Zhou Capital)
2 Hao (2e capitale Zhou)
  (2nd Zhou Capital)
3 Tombeau du roi Wen
  Wen King Tomb
4 Tombeau du roi Wu
  Wu King Tomb
5 Tombeau du roi Cheng
  Cheng King Tomb
6 Tombeau du roi Kang
  Kang King Tomb
7 Xian Yang (capitale Qin)
  Xian Yang (Qin Capital)
8 Palais A Fang (A Fang Gong)
  A Fang Palace (A Fang Gong)
10 Tombeau de Qin Shi Huang
   Qin Shi Huang Di Tomb
11 COLLINE SHAO LING YUAN
   HILL

shelters the town from the north winds in winter, and
the temperature does not fall much below 23° F. Xi an
was once the capital of the empire, and is now the capital of the province of Shân xi (Chen Si). Since the liberation, the town has undergone a new phase of development; it is now the most important centre in the
north-west. It has a population of 1,600,000.

THE REGION OF XI AN

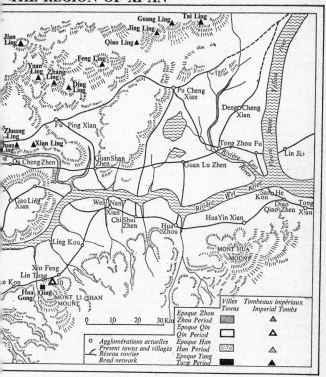

Guang Ling •   Tai Ling ▲
Jing Ling •
Jian Ling
Qiao Ling ▲
Feng Ling ▲
Yuan Ling ▲ Zhang Ling ▲
Ding Ling ▲
Pu Cheng Xian
Dengo Cheng Xian
Zhuang Ling
Fu Ping Xian
Xian Ling ▲
Tong Zhou Fu
Lin Ji
Quan Ling
Da Cheng Zhen
Guan Shan Zhen
Guan Lu Zhen
Gao Ling Xian
Wei Nan
San He Kou
Diao Qiao Zhen
Tong Xian
Xian Chi Shui Zhen
Hua Zhou
Hua Yin Xian
Ling Kou
MONT HUA MOUNT
Xin Feng
Lin Tong
An
Hua Gong
Qing
MONT LI SHAN MOUNT

0   10   20   30 Km

Villes   Tombeaux impériaux
Towns   Imperial Tombs

Epoque Zhou / Zhou Period   ▲
Epoque Qin / Qin Period   △
Epoque Han / Han Period   ◿
Epoque Tang / Tang Period   ▲

○ Agglomérations actuelles / Present towns and villages
⌐ Réseau routier / Road network

History

1. From its origins up to the Qin. Remains of several Neolithic settlements have been found near the village of Ban po, 6 miles east of the town. Excavations have revealed that the site belongs to the so-called Yang shao culture, about 6000 B.C. Other information about the origins of the town comes from old texts. The Zhou dynasty, who at first ruled over western Shân xi (the Jing valley), were constantly harried by the "western barbarians"

and several times moved their capital further east. The Zhou
king Wen moved his capital to Feng yi (south-west of modern
Xi an, 3 miles north of the village of Hu xian, on the left bank of
the River Feng shui); no traces of it are left. In 1122 B.C., when
the Zhou king Wu had annihilated the Yin dynasty, he made Hao
his capital (east of the Feng shui). It remained the Zhou capital
until 770 B.C., when they finally established their capital at
Luo yang.

Qin shi Huang di had a park laid out near Hao; later on,
the Han emperor Wu di had a lake dug, which was supplied with
water from the Feng shui; no trace of all this remains, beyond
the name of a marshy area, Hao chi, "Hao pond", about 18 miles
south-west of Xi an, east of the Feng shui. The only remains
which survive are the tumuli, said to be those of the four Zhou
kings (Wen, Wu, Cheng and Kang), on the north bank of the
Wei, 6 miles from Xian yang. The walls which still encircled the
tombs at the beginning of the 20th century, the gates, the sacrificial halls and the steles, all date from the Ming and Qing
dynasties; and as the texts do not agree as to the site of the
tombs, it is uncertain whether the tradition is correct.

The principality of Qin, a vassal of the Zhou, was granted
a fief north of the upper part of the river Wei, and grew up
among the "barbarians". Later on, they moved their capital
further east; in the reign of Xiao gong (361–338), the capital
was transferred to Xian yang, on the left bank of the Wei
(12 miles east of modern Xian yang). Qin shi Huang di enlarged
the town after the unification of the empire. According to Si ma
Qian, "Qin shi Huang moved as many as one hundred and
twenty families to Xian yang, rich and powerful men from all
over the empire. The various ancestral temples and the Shang
terrace and the Shang lin park were all south of the river Wei.
Every time Qin overcame a prince, he copied the plan of his
palace and had it rebuilt at Xian yang, on the north bank; the
palaces looked on to the Wei to the south. From Yong men
(modern Feng xiang) going east as far as the rivers Jing and Wei,
the buildings, dwellings, covered ways and arcades touched each
other. Everything that Qin shi Huang di took from the lords, such
as beautiful women, bells and drums, he ordered to be put in his
palaces, which were full of them... then (in 212) as Shi Huang
considered that the population of Xian yang was large and the
palaces of his predecessors (the kings) were small, he began to
have a palace built, for audiences, south of the river Wei, in the
Shang lin park; the first part to be built was the anterior hall;
it measured a hundred paces from east to west; fifty *zhang* from

north to south; ten thousand men could sit upstairs and standards five *zhang* high could be raised below. A raised track encircled it. A straight line went from the foot of the pavilion as far as the southern hill, on whose summit a triumphal arch was built for a gate. A covered way, going from the A fang palace, across the river Wei, as far as Xian yang symbolised Tian ji which rises to cross the Milky Way and ends at the constellation of Ying shi. When the A fang palace was still unfinished, people wanted to choose a more honourable name for it when it was completed, but as the palace had been built next to the capital, everybody called the palace A fang ("near" in Chinese)." *(The Historical Records of Si ma Qian,* translated by E. Chavannes). The work was continued by Er shi Huang di, but when the Qin fell, everything was destroyed by the troops of Liu Bang.

2. **The Han and the Northern Dynasties.** When Liu Bang became Emperor Gao zu of the Han in 206 B.C., he followed the example of the Qin, and placed his capital Chang an (everlasting peace) "within the passes" (in Chinese: *Guan zhong*), in an area which can be reached only by mountain passes, east of Xian yang and slightly north of modern Xi an. He had the Palace of Prosperity and Joy restored (it had been a temporary palace under the Qin) and renamed it the Palace of Great Joy (Chang le gong). In 200 B.C., he commissioned the architect Xiao He to build him a new and larger residence: the Wei yang gong (west of the former one). The town remained fairly small until Emperor Hui di (194–187) decided to enlarge it and to build a wall round the palaces. The wall followed the arrangement of the buildings, and the resulting irregular shape is unusual; it was 12 miles round and had 12 gates. The palaces occupied all the south of the town, and two thirds of the northern part. The market-places and the craftsmen were in the eastern and western suburbs. Later on, a palace in a large park was built in the west suburbs, and a palace for short stays in the east suburbs.

At the end of the Western Han, the suburbs increased in size, to match the increase in population. In 129 B.C., a canal was built linking the town to the river Feng and the area round the upper reaches of the Wei to the west, and to the river Chan and the lower reaches of the Wei to the east (the canal was used until the beginning of the Tang). At the end of Wang Mang's reign, the town suffered some upheavals and the Wei yang gong was burned. The imperial tombs of the Western Han were built round the town: nine in the hills on the north bank of the river Wei (the furthest east, the An ling, is slightly north-east of the town of Cao tan, and the furthest west, the Rong ling, is north-

LA VILLE DE CHANG AN SOUS LES TANG
THE TOWN OF CHANG AN UNDER THE TANG

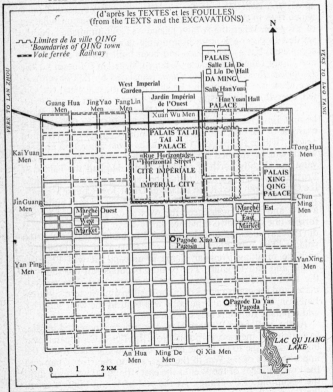

(d'après les TEXTES et les FOUILLES)
(from the TEXTS and the EXCAVATIONS)

N

⌐⌐ Limites de la ville QING
'Boundaries of QING town
▬▬ Voie ferrée   Railway

VERS TO LAN ZHOU

VERS TO LUO YANG

PALAIS
Salle Lin De
☐ Lin De Hall
DA MING
Salle Han Yuan
Han Yuan Hall
PALACE

West Imperial Garden
Jardin Impérial de l'Ouest

Guang Hua Men   Jing Yao Men   Fang Lin Men

Xuan Wu Men

PALAIS TAI JI
TAI JI PALACE

Kai Yuan Men

«Rue Horizontale»
"Horizontal Street"
CITÉ IMPÉRIALE
IMPERIAL CITY

Tong Hua Men

PALAIS
XING QING
PALACE

Jin Guang Men

Marché Ouest
West Market

Marché Est
East Market

Chun Ming Men

○ Pagode Xiao Yan Pagoda

Yan Ping Men

YanXing Men

○ Pagode Da Yan Pagoda

LAC QU JIANG LAKE

An Hua Men   Ming De Men   Qi Xia Men

0   1   2 KM

ast of the town of Xing ping), two in the south-eastern hills on either side of the river Chan shui. The town became less important under the Eastern Han and the Northern Dynasties and faded into the background.

3. The Sui and the Tang. The Sui Emperor Wen di founded his new capital, Da xing cheng ("town of great prosperity") south-east of the old Chang an of the Han, in 582. The architect Yu Wen kai (555–612) was put in charge of the work. When the Tang came to power, they took over their predecessors' capital, gave it its old name of Chang an, and enlarged it. The town then had a million inhabitants and formed a vast rectangle, 6 miles long and 5½ miles wide; an earth fortification was built round it, with eight gates to the north and three on each of the other sides. The city was divided into three parts: the palace *(Gong cheng)*, the imperial town *(Huang cheng)*, and the outer town *(Jing cheng)*.

a) **The palace:** it was the Emperor's residence; the central part of the outer town's north wall separated it from the imperial park. It was enclosed within a wall 1½ miles long, just under 1 mile wide, which was 58½ feet thick at the base; there were seven gates (only two have been found). The Palace of the Lofty Summit stood in the centre (Tai ji gong).

b) **The imperial city:** this was the seat of the administration. It was 1½ miles long and 1 mile wide, and had walls on three sides; east, west and south; a wide avenue called Horizontal Street (Heng jie) divided it from the palace on the north side. There were five gates, three to the south, one to the east, and one to the west (traces of their sites have been found).

c) **The Outer Town:** this was the residential area; a long avenue, running from north to south, from the northern gate (Xuan wu men) to the southern gate (Ming de men), cut it in two; eleven streets running from east to west and fourteen from north to south divided the town into 108 districts *(fang)*; each district was walled; the smallest had two gates (east and west) and the largest had four (one on each side). The gates were closed at night.

The busiest areas at this time were the large central street and the districts of the two market-places, east and west (each one occupied the area of two districts). Two streets running from north to south and two from east to west divided each market-place into nine districts; the central one contained the administrative body, under the "Head of the Market". The shops and stalls specialised in over two hundred different things. The stewern market-place has recently been excavated (it was half a mile south-west of the Ming walls) and Chinese, Arabian, Persian, and Byzantine coins were found, as well as pearls and ornaments; the merchants from Central Asia lived in this area. All the temples in the town (over a hundred: Taoist, Buddhist, Nestorian or Moslem) were in the Outer Town. Some of the Emperors settled there; Xuan zong, for instance, moved, with all his court, to the Xing qing gong palace (south of the Ming town, just to the north of the present University of Communications) in 728; the site is now a public park, called the Xing qing Park, after the old palace.

The Tang Emperors had residences built outside the town to escape from the heat of summer. The largest one was the **Da ming gong** (the Palace of Brilliant light), built in 634, on a hill to the north-east of Chang an; it was enlarged in 662, and became the permanent residence of the Emperors for a time. Five gates linked the palace to the town, to the south, and the other three sides were walled. It was made up of gardens, ornamental pools and about thirty buildings; two were larger than the rest. The Han yuan dian was the throne room (in the south of the palace) and was used on ceremonial occasions, or when civil and military officials came to greet the Emperor, at the new year and at the winter solstice. The Lin de dian (north of the other) was the largest (249 feet wide and 341 feet long); it had 164 pillars (whose bases can still be seen) and was divided into three rooms. The Emperor received his ministers here, and gave his banquets (such as the one given by the Emperor Xian zong in 819, attended by over two thousand officials, including military ones). The Western Park (Xi yuan), west of the Da ming gong, contained several polo grounds.

The Tang Emperors had their tombs built on the hills north of the Wei (except for the last two, who are buried in He nan). The furthest east, the Tai ling, is north of the town of Pu cheng xian; the furthest to the west, the Qian ling, is north of Qian zhou. The tumuli are built on a square base, with a surrounding wall; an altar generally stands to the south, with an avenue of stone animals leading up to it (some of these can be seen in the provincial museum). The town had already suffered during the An Lu shan rising, and was largely destroyed when the Tang dynasty fell.

4.The Song, the Yuan, the Ming and the Qing. After the fall of the Tang, the town went into a long decline, from which it emerged at the beginning of the Ming dynasty. In 1370, Emperor Hong wu gave Chang an in fee to his son Zhu Shuang; the town was then called Qin wang fu ("the king of Qin's town"). Ren Chi wan (later to become one of the king of Qin's ministers) was commissioned straight away to build a palace for the king, and to rebuild the town (which occupied only a sixth of the area covered by the Tang town). New walls were built, with three gates to the south and one on each of the other three sides.

The Ming palace was abandoned under the Qing, and an area between the north and east walls and the bell tower was taken over by the Manchu as their district (it was enclosed by walls which were knocked down at the beginning of the Republic). Here is the description that Grosier gives of the town in the 18th century: "Xi an fu, the capital of the province, is one of the largest and most beautiful towns in China; its wide, high walls are four leagues round; they are flanked by large numbers of towers each one an arrow's flight from the next, and encircled by a deep moat. Some of the gates are magnificent and remarkably tall. An old palace can still be seen in the town, in which the former kings of Shân xi used to live. The rest of the buildings are no finer than those to be seen elsewhere, the houses are built after the Chinese style, and are very low and rather badly built, the furniture is less clean than in the southern provinces, the varnish is coarser, the porcelain rarer... The main Tartar forces, responsible for defending the north of the empire, are stationed in a garrison at Xi an fu, with one of their generals in command, and they occupy a district of the town, walled off from the rest."

At the end of the Qing dynasty, the town experienced several upheavals: Moslem risings, and worst of all, the massacre of the Manchu during the 1911 revolution. The following passage is taken from an eye witness' account (J. C. Keyte, *The Passing of the Dragon*, 1913, quoted by Backhouse and Bland, *Annals and Memoirs of the Court of Peking*, 1914, p. 209): "The Tartar General, old, hopeless, cut off from his people at the critical juncture, was unable to face the situation. The safety he had won for the moment he felt not worth the keeping; he ended his life by throwing himself down a well. Houses were plundered and then burnt... The revolutionaries, protected by a parapet of the wall, poured a heavy, unceasing, relentless fire into the doomed Tartar city... In despair, many Manchus themselves set fire to their houses... Into the English hospital, days afterwards, when the first fury was passed, men were brought in a shocking condition; men who had attempted to cut their throats. Asked why they had done so they answered simply: 'The wells were full.' And the Shensi wells are not the shallow ones of some parts of

China; they are thirty-six feet deep... When the Manchus found that further resistance was useless, they in many cases knelt on the ground, laying down their weapons and begged the soldiers for life. They were shot as they knelt."

5. The Republic and the Present Regime. The building of the railway (1930) made the town less isolated. First steps were taken towards industrialisation, but this was soon hindered by the war.

Its development dates from after the liberation. Xi an was one of the towns to benefit most of all from the changes made during the first five-year plan (1953-1957). People moved in from the neighbouring countryside to work in the new factories (1949: 490,000 inhabitants; 1953: 730,000; 1965: 1,600,000). Large numbers of new cotton mills fed by the cotton produced in the area have made Xi an into the biggest textile centre in the north-west. The new electrical equipment industry now sends its products all over the country. Since 1958, small and medium-sized factories have been started in the western suburbs, to produce nitrate fertilizers, plastics, boilers, machine tools and electric motors for agricultural use.

At the same time, town-planning work has been going on: in the old town, sanitation has been improved in the old houses, sewers have been built, running water has been laid on, roads have been tarred, and modern buildings have been put up: the People's Hotel (Ren min da sha), department stores, administrative buildings; in the suburbs, residential districts have grown up near the factories, with shops, restaurants, nursery schools, welfare centres, cinemas, sports grounds, parks (a bus service, started in 1959, now links the suburbs with the old town).

This development has also been extended to the cultural field. The two higher educational establishments already in existence in 1949 have been enlarged since the liberation (one was the University of the North West); a district given over entirely to educational establishments, in the southern suburbs, has 17 institutes and universities (one of which is the University of Communications, Jiao tong xue xiao, transferred here from Shang hai in 1956), and 23 secondary technical schools.

Description

The contrast between the area covered by the Qing and the Tang towns respectively is still striking (the

ÉVOLUTION HISTORIQUE DE XI AN   HISTORICAL DEVELOPMENT OF XI AN

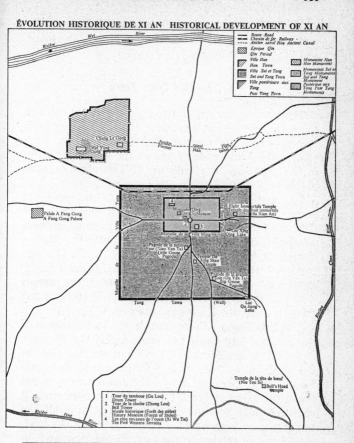

	Route - Road
	Chemin de fer Railway
	Ancien canal Han Ancient Canal

	Epoque Qin Qin Period		Monument Han Han Monument
	Ville Han Han Town		Monuments Sui et Tang Monuments Sui and Tang Monument
	Ville Sui et Tang Sui and Tang Town		Posterieur aux Tang Post Tang Monuments
	Ville posterieure aux Tang Post Tang Town		

1   Tour du tambour (Gu Lou) Drum Tower
2   Tour de la cloche (Zhong Lou) Bell Tower
3   Musée historique (Forêt des stèles) History Museum (Forest of Steles)
4   Les cinq terrasses de l'ouest (Xi Wu Tai) The Five Western Terraces

former covered a narrow rectangle about a sixth of the
size of the Tang town, as a glance at the map will show).
Since the liberation, however, building campaigns have
been started and the former Tang town is being built

up again. The Qing town will be described first, followed by the monuments still standing in the Tang town, and finally the suburbs.

1. The Old Qing Town

The plan is symmetrical: two main streets cut through the town, meeting at a crossroads, which is the town centre, where the massive Bell Tower stands. Each street begins and ends at one of the four main gates of the old town. The walls are still standing in some places.

The station is north-east of the north gate; the People's Hotel (Ren min da sha) is in the north-east district, a little to the east of the north-south avenue. The Bell Tower will be described first, then the western districts (the Drum Tower, the Temple to the Gods of the Town, the Great Mosque, the Five Terrace Temple, the Temple of Great Goodwill), and lastly the eastern districts (the Historical Museum, the Temple of the Eastern Peak, the Kai yuan year period Temple).

The Bell Tower (Zhong lou). It was in the centre of the imperial city under the Tang, facing the Zhu que men Gate to the south and the Xuan wu men Gate to the north (at the crossroads of the present Xi da jie and Guang ji jie Streets). When the town was restored under the Ming, in the 14th century, the northern and southern gates were moved to the east; as a result, the tower was no longer on the north-south axis. In 1582, it was rebuilt further to the east, on the new axis; in 1740 it was restored. The Guo min dang, realising its strategic importance, put guns on the balconies which could cover each of the four main streets which converged at the foot of the tower. It has been restored since the liberation.

The tower is 68 feet high, and consists of two parts:
the square base, with four arched doorways (each side
measures 104 feet), and the three upper stories, to
which two flights of stairs lead on the northern side.
On the north side of the balcony on the first storey
there is a fine 15th century iron bell. From the second
storey, the view over the town is excellent.

The Drum Tower (Gu lou). It is north-west of the
Bell Tower, in the southern part of Bei yuan men da
jie Street. It was built under the Ming in 1370 and
restored in 1669, 1739, and after the liberation. Its
height is 90 feet and like the other tower, it consists of
two parts: a rectangular base (170 feet by 120 feet) built
in brick, with an archway through it, and three upper
stories, supported by wooden pillars.

The Temple to the Town Gods (Cheng huang miao).
It is slightly west of the intersection of Xi da jie and
Guang ji jie Streets. The first temple was founded in
1367, in the east of the town; in 1432, it was rebuilt on
its present site. A five-arched portico in sculpted wood,
the top section covered with glazed tiles, stands in
front of the entrance. A paved way lined with shops
leads to the temple. The pavilion in the first courtyard
is surrounded by little shops; it has a two-storey roof,
with eaves sharply upturned at the corners (fine wood-
work). Two iron lions (15th century) stand at the far
end of the second courtyard in front of a central hall,
built in 1723, with material from the King of Qin's
palace (built under the Ming, cf. below, History of the
town). The building is encircled by an arcade, supported on wooden pillars; the two-storey roof is
covered with turquoise blue glazed tiles. The doors are
very finely carved, with geometrical motives and dragons undulating among a sea of clouds. The hall contains statues, but it is not open to visitors.

The Great Mosque (Qing zhen si). It is in Hua jue gang Street, in the middle of a district chiefly inhabited by Hui Minority people (bounded by Xi da jie Street to the south and Bei men da jie Street to the east). It is the largest of fourteen mosques said still to be in use in Xi an. It was founded under the Tang, in 742. The present buildings date mainly from the end of the 14th century (the Hong wu era). It has been restored several times (1606, 1768), and futher restoration work is planned.

The entrance pavilion contains several Ming and Qing steles, with inscriptions in Arabic (calendar, memorials). Next comes a minaret (in Chinese style) and then the main courtyard. The Phoenix Pavilion (Feng huang ting) stands in the middle; it is a resting place, in Chinese style; the prayer hall opens off the far end; it is a large building, with a large six-pillar portico leading into it. Five doors open into the hall, each giving on to one of the five central aisles; there are two side aisles as well. It has a coffered ceiling, decorated with Arabic letters: each panel is different (one is said to date from the Tang). On the right of the entrance stands the old imperial altar, which used to be in the centre, for the faithful used to render homage to the Emperor, before praying to Allah. An old painting on one wall shows a map of Mecca (with the Kaaba in the centre); it was used for teaching. The *mihrab* and the *minbar* (pulpit) at the far end of the hall may date from the Ming dynasty. The library is in an annex (it contains manuscripts in Arabic, written in China; thirty books date from the Qing); one wall is decorated with Arabic characters, arranged like Chinese characters, and forming an inscription; the stele commemorating the founding of the Mosque is here (the date is given as "the first year of the Tian bao era", that is to say, 742). The authenticity of the stele has been doubted; it is possibly a Ming copy.

The Five Western Terraces (Xi wu tai). They are north-west of the Qing town, in the district known as the Lotus Pond district (Lian hu), and they constitute the An Qing Temple, which was founded under the Song, on the ruins of the southern wall of the old Tai ji Palace, built under the Tang. The terraces rise out of each other, starting from the east; originally they each supported a building, but the fourth, the last but one, has been destroyed, so the series is now incomplete. The central one is said to date from the Ming only. The temple was inhabited by nuns. A fair was held each year, in the sixth month of the lunar calendar. The central building contains some fine Ming sculpture.

The Temple of Great Goodwill (Guang ren si). It stands in the north-west corner of the present town, near the walls, and is also known as the Lama Temple.

It consists of a vast series of buildings, built in 1705, for Tibetan monks. The area covers a hundred intercolumniations. It was restored at the beginning of the Republic and again in 1952. The central hall contains some fine gold-leaf statues (brought from the Kai yuan Si under Kang xi) and a large marble jar with a lotus flower design. The library contains Buddhist manuscripts, some of which date from 1700.

The Historical Museum. The Museum is housed in the former Temple of Confucius (Kong miao), near where the famous "forest of steles" (Pei lin) was founded in 1090. The Pei lin was a somewhat curious form of archives: under the Tang, the twelve classics were engraved on stone and collected there (in 837). The "forest" grew larger as later steles were added to it. The museum was begun under the Republic; excavations over the last few years have enriched it considerably, and it now contains nearly 3,000 exhibits. It is in three parts: the Shân xi provincial museum, three additional halls, and the forest of steles.

a) The Shân xi provincial museum. *First courtyard:* to the left: a fine stone horse, from the state of Xia (north Shân xi, 424 A.D.), brought here in 1955; note the figure at the horse's hindquarters; to the right: a Tang bronze bell (711) from the Xing xiang guan, the Taoist temple. *First room: from the beginnings up to the Northern and Southern Dynasties:* photograph of the temple dedicated to Yu the Great, at Han cheng (north Shân xi); a large bronze *ding* weighing 193 pounds, with two inscriptions, one Shang and one Zhou. *Zhou era:* chamfron; pottery; tiles; some magnificent bronzes. *The Warring States:* a copy of one of the ten "stone drums" (the originals are at Peking); a sort of stone stele (one of the earliest ones), with a hunting-song engraved on it; gold coins found at Lin tong (east of Xi an) in 1963 (about an inch across; rare). *The Qin era:* engraved iron weights, found about 3½ miles south of Xi an in 1964; small metal plaques engraved with an imperial order, found at Xian yang; photographs of the ruins of the A fang gong Palace (east of Xi an): three specimens of *yong* (tomb figures representing the dead person); section of a stone sewer. *Han era:* beautiful "peacock" lamp, made in two parts, with a peacock on the top; bronze rhinoceros; iron tools; fragments of paper; cog wheel; photographs of Si ma Qian's tomb at Han cheng. *The Six Dynasties:* collection of *yong*.

Second Room: from the Sui to the Qing. The Sui era: map of the new capital (Da xing cheng), made under the Sui; white porcelain; vase dedicated to Guan yin; jewelry; a girl's coffin, found west of Xi an (a sort of stone reliquary, with the four characters *Kai zhi ji si:* "Death to the desecrator" on the top). *Tang era:* fragments of stone water pipes; bricks, with their maker's marks; passes, granting entrance to the different gates of the palace (shaped like a fish, and a tortoise); agricultural tools; engraved bronze measuring-rod; things found during the excavation of the Western Marketplace (dice, small objects in ivory); things found during the excavation of the palaces (embossed silver plates, two silver bars given to the Emperor by noblemen); documents referring to the presence of foreign merchants in the town (Persian, Arab and Byzantine coins, a stele commemorating the death of a Persian, inscribed in Pahlavi); square stone in memory of the founding of a polo ground (the game was introduced from Central Asia under the Tang); five statuettes of poloplayers; wall paintings from the tomb of Wu Ze tian's daughter-in-law (710); fine collections of tomb figurines (horses, camels). *Song era:* iron tools; Tong chuan celadon ware and other porcelain (north of Xi an); a little wooden cannon (2 feet long); clay *yong* of a child; photographs of sculpture in a temple at Fu xian (north of Yan an), showing the Buddha in a trance; paintings from a noble's tomb discovered at Bao ji (west of Xi an, on the Wei). *Yuan era:* astrological square, with Arabic figures (found in the foundations of a house in Xi an). *Ming and Qing Eras:* large straight sword; Southern Ming cannon (1655); map of Tai wan; signatures of the mandarin Lin Zi xu, who had the cases of opium imported by the English destroyed.

b) The Three Annex Halls. The first contains bronzes, the second porcelain and pottery. The last one is the largest, and it contains a fine collection of statues, mainly originals; it was opened in 1963. All the exhibits come from Shân xi, and most of them date from the Han, the Wei or the Tang. The most striking are:

a copy of a horse in front of the tomb of Huo Qu bing, the general who overcame the Xiong nu, under the Han; two *bi xie*, rather like leopards (from a Western Han tomb, near Xian yang); animals from Tang imperial tombs: rhinoceroses, ostriches (ambassadors from the South Seas brought these animals as presents for the Emperor), tigers, horses (four of the six famous chargers from the tomb of Li Shi min; the two others are in the United States).

c) **The Forest of Steles.** This is the oldest and richest collection of steles in China (1,095 pieces). There are some Han fragments; the best date from the Tang, and comprise: 1. a hundred and fourteen steles with the text of the twelve classics (560,000 characters); they were engraved in 837 and given to the imperial college, where they were used for teaching; they were brought here in 1090; 2. several memorial steles, the most famous of which is the one recording the arrival of the Nestorian priest A lo pen at Chang an, and the foundation, in 781, of a Christian chapel in the Tang capital; it is the famous "Si Ngan Fou stele", discovered in 1627, and quoted by the Jesuits as early as the 17th century as evidence of an early "conversion to Christianity" of China (the text and a first translation appeared in the *China illustrata* by Father Kircher); the text is in Chinese, with some passages in Syriac; it is surmounted by a cross. 3. a large stele, mounted on a three-storey stone base, inscribed with the *Classic of Filial Piety;* the gloss and the calligraphy are by the emperor Xuan zong (8th century); the stele is called the "Classic of Filial Piety on stone" (Shi tai xiao jing). There is also a fine set of Song steles (some are engraved with maps of China, the oldest in existence), and some Yuan, Ming and Qing steles, with calligraphy and drawings.

The Temple of the Recumbent Dragon (Wo long si).
It is in Bo shu ling jie Street, near the Historical Museum. It is said to have been built under the Sui. Under the Tang, it was called the Guan yin Temple. In the Song dynasty, the monk Wei guo liked to come and lie inside the temple, and as he was called the "recumbent dragon", the temple took its name from him. It was restored under the Ming (in 1521), under the Qing, and in 1952. It is one of the most well-known temples in Xi an, and possesses a rich library (texts in Pali, and a sutra dating from the Southern Song, which has been put into the Provincial Library).

The door has a fine three-arch portico. Beyond the second door there are a bell, cast in the Song dynasty (1003), and a series of *chuang*, dating from the Tang. The central hall contains a stone engraving of Guan yin, attributed to Wu Dao zi, and a delicately-carved marble incense-burner (Qing dynasty). The statues of the Buddha in the far hall and the refectory are all made in white clay, covered with five layers of hemp and lacquered.

The Bao Qing Temple Pagoda is east of the Historical Museum, in the south of Shu yuan men jie Street. The temple is said to have been founded in about 705, near the Little Goose Pagoda, much further south. In 730, a pagoda in glazed bricks is supposed to have been added, which explains the most frequent name for the temple: the Multi-coloured Pagoda Temple (Hua ta si). At the beginning of the 10th century, when the town shrank after the fall of the Tang, the temple is said to have been rebuilt on its present site. The pagoda is all that is left; the glazed bricks have vanished without trace, but it is still called "Hua ta".

The pagoda is octagonal, built in brick and has seven stories. Each of the eight facets of the lower stories contains an arched niche with a stone effigy of the Buddha. The top storey has only one niche, with an unfinished statue of the Buddha.

The former Tai shan Temple (Dong yue miao: the Eastern Peak Temple) is inside the east gate of the Qing town, to the north. It was founded in 1116 and restored under the Ming and the Qing (1724 and 1843). It is now used as a school. Two carved pillars *(hua biao)* stand in front of the temple portico. Another stone portico, with beautiful sculpture dating from 1582, leads into the central hall, where sacrifices were made to Tai shan (the screen at the far end of the hall has some fine paintings); behind the room at the end, which also has some murals, lies a terrace with a little pavilion probably dating from the beginning of the Qing. The Palace of the Three Religions (San jiao gong) was in the east wing of the temple; Ming statues of Lao Zi, the Buddha and Confucius are grouped there, as if to unite the three doctrines.

The Kai yuan year period Temple (Kai yuan si). It is south-west of Dong da jie. It was founded in the first year of the Kai yuan year period (713) during the Tang dynasty, hence its name; its original site is unknown, as the temple was destroyed at the end of the Tang, leaving no trace. The present site must have been chosen after the town had grown smaller at the end of the Tang dynasty. A two-storey pavilion is all that now remains of the old temple; it used to be the library, though the books have been moved to the Provincial Library. The foundations of the old central hall can still be seen in front of the pavilion; it is now a market-place.

2. The Area Covered by the old Tang Town

Most of the temples founded under the Sui and the Tang were here. The Little Goose Pagoda, the Da xing shan Temple, the Big Goose Pagoda, all three of which are outside the Qing town, to the south, will be described first, followed by the Taoist Temple of the Eight Immortals, east of the Qing town.

The Little Goose Pagoda (Xiao yan ta). It is just under two miles from the South Gate (Nan men), slightly west of the north-south axis of the Tang town. It is all that remains of the Da qing fu Temple.

Empress Wu Ze tian founded the Da xian fu Temple in honour of Emperor Gao zong in 684, the year of his death. It was slightly to the north of the present pagoda. It was restored in 690, and given the name of Da qing fu; two hundred monks lived there, and it became a well-known temple. In 705, the pilgrim Yi jing settled there to translate into Chinese the Sanskrit Buddhist texts which he had brought back with him after his travels. The pagoda was built in 706; the name, the Little Goose Pagoda, appeared later on (several legends provide explanations of the name, all equally unconvincing). Towards the end of the Tang, the temple was destroyed and rebuilt just beside the pagoda, but it was destroyed a second time, and the pagoda alone survives, although it too was damaged by two earthquakes, in 1555 and 1563 (it was cracked, and the two top stories fell down).

The pagoda now has only thirteen stories, and is 140 feet high; it is square, and the north and south faces of the base have arched doorways (the Tang engraving on the upper part recalls the engraving of the Big Goose Pagoda). Two large bells stand in what was the first courtyard of the temple, dating from 1192 and 1507.

The Da xing shan Temple (Da xing shan si). It is just over three miles from the South Gate, east of the old north-south axis. It is said to have been founded in the

3rd century, and to have been called the Temple where goodness is venerated (Zun shan si). When the town became the Sui capital in 582 and changed its name to *Da xing cheng* ("Town of great prosperity"), the temple, which was in the *Qing shan* district, was called the Da xing shan si.

The temple was a large one, with a large community of monks. Several Indian monks came to teach there (Jing gang zhi, Shan wu wei and Bu kong are mentioned) under the Tang, and particularly during the Kai yuan year period (713-742). In 807, the temple was restored and two pavilions were added. At the end of the Tang and during the Five Dynasties period, the temple was badly damaged, and finally destroyed. In 1403, a monk had it rebuilt on the same site; in 1648, another monk, Mai qi, restored it, enlarged it and had a wall built round it. Again restored in 1685, it was almost completely destroyed at the end of the Qing. It was rebuilt in 1956, and now houses a community of lamas. The temple possesses a fine collection of Tibetan paintings (tankas).

The Big Goose Pagoda (Da yan ta) and the Temple of Great Goodwill (Da ci en si). These are five miles south of the Qing town, well to the east of the north-south axis. The pagoda was called the Pagoda of the Classics (Jing ta) under the Tang; the popular name which it now bears appeared fairly late; several elaborate hypotheses try to give the reason for it.

The first temple, the Temple of Celestial Manna (Tian lu si), was founded under the Sui; it had already disappeared by the beginning of the 7th century. In 647, Emperor Gao zong had the Temple of Great Goodwill built in honour of his mother, Empress Wen de. It is said that every morning and evening he would turn in the direction of the temple, in his northern palace, to fulfill his filial devotions. Xuan Zang the pilgrim settled in the temple to translate the Buddhist canons. In 652, he had a large five-storey pagoda built to house the precious texts which he had brought back with him. The pagoda soon cracked, so it was restored, and two more stories were built on to it, at the beginning of the 8th century. Under the Tang, as nowadays, there were few houses near the pagoda. The western stream of the Qu jiang ("the winding river") flowed to the south; its meanderings took up the south-eastern corner of the town (roughly where the village of Qu jiang cun now is). It was widely known as a beautiful spot; numerous pavilions were built there, and people would come to take the air. Twice a year, the townspeople were allowed to come here to feast. Everybody used to climb the pagoda to admire the view from the top.

At the end of the Tang, the buildings fell into ruins and the canal which brought water from the river Ba to the Qu jiang became blocked. In about 1070, the inside of the pagoda caught fire, and in 1227, the temple was largely destroyed by fire. It was restored in 1580. After the liberation, the staircases of the pagoda were repaired and the temple was restored; it is still in use.

In the recent outer buildings, various documents on the life and work of the Buddhist pilgrim Xuan Zang are exhibited (map of his journey across Central Asia and India, steles, photographs of places which he visited).

The pagoda is square, with seven stories (240 feet high). Each side of the base is 148 feet long, and it is 13½ feet high, with four arched doors; a fine engraving on the pediment of the western door shows the Buddha preaching the Law, in a Chinese setting (interesting examples of Tang architecture). Steles set into the wall flank the south door; the inscriptions are by the calligrapher Chu Sui liang (Tang dynasty). A large wooden staircase fills the centre of the pagoda and leads up to the top. On the outside, the stories are separated by a system similar to weather-boarding, but built in brick. Each storey has openings on each of the four sides, with a vaulted passage leading to them. The view over the surrounding countryside and the town is excellent; it gives an idea of the extent of the Tang town, whose southern boundary was nearly 2 miles south of the pagoda.

The Taoist Temple of the Eight Immortals (Ba xian an). This temple is just over a mile outside the East Gate (Dong men) of the Qing town. Founded under the Song, it was enlarged by order of the emperor, and by private individuals, under the Yuan, the Ming and the Qing. It was restored in 1952. It was one of the biggest Taoist temples in Xi an, with the Tai shan Temple. A large fair was held here every year, from the 14th to the 16th of the fourth lunar month, with stalls, sideshows, and travelling players. The temple is still in use. A fine three-arch brick portico stands in front of the entrance, with a carved frieze at the top.

3. The East Suburbs

The Bridge on the River Ba (Ba qiao). The famous Bridge on the River Ba is 6 miles north-east of the town. Its foundations date from the Han; it was rebuilt under Wang mang (after a fire in 22 B.C.) and later under the emperor Wen di of the Sui in 582. The present bridge dates from 1833. It is over 330 yards long; the flooring, made of wood and bricks, is supported by sixty-eight sets of six stone pillars (408 pillars altogether). The distance between each set varies; sometimes it is 13 feet, sometimes 23 feet. Another bridge whose foundations date from the Han spans the river Chan (Chan qiao), 3 miles from Ba qiao.

The Neolithic Site at Ban po Village. The site is 6 miles from Xi an, on the left bank of the river Chan, on a hillock north of the village of Ban po. It is one of the largest Neolithic sites, and belongs to the Yang shao culture (6000 B.C.). It was discovered in 1953, when the foundations of a factory were being laid. About a fifth of the total area was excavated between 1953 and 1957. Considerable finds were uncovered:

a) a village (45 houses, with foundations still in good condition, 200 storage pits, pottery, tools, animal bones); b) east of this: a pottery-making centre (remains of six kilns); c) to the north: a graveyard (174 adults' graves, 76 children's graves, 37 funerary urns). The site was opened to the public in 1958; the visitor looks round the museum first, then the site itself, now covered with roofing to shelter it.

The museum has four rooms. *First and second rooms:* dwellings and way of life; map showing Ban po in relation to the other centres of Yang shao and Long shan culture; reconstruction of the three types of dwellings which were found in the village (the foundations showed twelve huts with a passage-way leading into them, thirty-one circular ones and two square ones); stone, bone, and mother-of-pearl tools; pottery with geometric and animal designs (fish); spindles and needles; remains of domestic animals. *Third room:* graves; collective burial (some bones, which were found dis-arranged, suggest that the bodies were sometimes moved, then re-buried). *Fourth room:* pottery kilns.

The village was built on high ground, to escape the floods which were frequent in this region; a ditch encircled it. The foundations of the huts can still clearly be seen (they make it possible to reconstruct the three types of huts mentioned above), as well as the storage pits.

Li shan Hill and the Site of the Hua qing gong Palace. Li shan Hill ("Black Horse Hill") lies 35 miles east of Xi an, south of the town of Lin tong. Several legends and historical anecdotes are attached to it.

The oldest story dates from the 8th century B.C. The Zhou king You (781-770 B.C.) had a concubine, the beautiful Pao si, whose fault was that she rarely laughed. The king was in despair, and tried everything he could think of to make her laugh, but in vain. One day it occurred to him to light the beacon fire on the top of Li shan which was used to call his vassals in time of danger (on the Feng huo tai: the Terrace of the Visible Signal). The vassals hurried to their king and were astonished to find they had been called unnecessarily; Pao si was amused to see them mortified and laughed. King You was pleased with his success, and the joke was repeated several times; but the day came when a real danger threatened him. The vassals stayed at home, and the king was killed at the foot of the hill. The story was handed down as an illustration of the danger run by the prince who ranks his own pleasure higher than politics, and Pao si became the prototype of the "fatal beauty".

A hot spring rises in the hill (107° F.) and the kings who lived at Xi an always liked to come and bathe in it. Qin shi Huang di had a residence built there, which was restored under Wu di of the Han (140–87 B.C.), and under the Northern Wei (5th and 6th centuries); a Wei stele still survives, praising the hot spring.

In 583, under the Sui, the buildings were repaired and trees were planted. In 644, the Tang Emperor Tai zong had a palace built there, called the Hot Spring Palace (Tang quan gong); in 747, Emperor Xuan zong had it enlarged and called it the Palace of Glorious Purity (Hua qing gong), the name which has been kept until now. Xuan zong was particularly fond of the place; it is said that at the end of his life, he would come and spend the last two months of the year here with the beautiful Yang Gui fei, and only went back to Chang an for New Year's Day. When he was dead, the court came here less and less often, and once the capital was moved to Luo yang, they never came back. The buildings gradually fell down.

In 936, a Taoist community built a monastery from the ruins. The Song, the Jin and the Yuan founded several temples and had the pools re-dug. Six pools were left at the end of the Qing. Under the Republic, some of the buildings were converted into a watering-place, and Chiang Kai-shek was staying here when he was arrested by General Zhang Xue liang ("the Xi an incident", December 1936). Repairs have been carried out since the liberation; the watering-place still exists, and it is possible to have a bath.

Nothing is left of the Tang dynasty buildings here, though the "pool where the beautiful Yang Gui fei

used to bathe" is still pointed out. The most interesting
remains are the little Taoist temples on the slopes
and at the foot of the hill: below the buildings of the
watering-place, to the right, a little sanctuary dedicated to Yu the Great (interesting sculpture) still
stands, and is still inhabited by some hermits; on the
western peak of the hill (Xi xiu ling) stands a temple
dedicated to Lao Zi, with a marble statue of him, possibly Tang; several other hermitages, all still lived in,
are scattered on the slopes of the hill. The bed room
which Chiang Kai-Shek left hurriedly when told he
was about to be arrested can be seen, and higher up
the hill, a little pavilion (in "classical" style) marks the
spot where he was caught.

The Tumulus of Qin shi Huang di. It is several miles
east of Lin tong; its size is impressive and it can be seen
from a long way off.

Qin shi Huang di, the first Emperor of China, began
to build his tomb at the beginning of his reign (he reigned from 221–209 B.C.). Si ma Qian, the historian, has
left an excellent description, no doubt true, of this
gigantic undertaking: "The workmen sent there numbered over seven hundred thousand. They dug down
as far as the water; bronze was poured in and the sar-
cophagus brought; ...marvellous tools, jewels and
rare objects were brought there and buried... Artisans
were ordered to make automatic crossbows and arrows; if anyone had tried to make a hole and enter the
tomb, they would immediately have fired on him. The
hundred water courses, the Jiang, the He and the vast
sea were represented by quicksilver; machines made it
run and carried it from one to another. All the signs
of the heavens were above, and the geographical arrangement below. Fish grease was used to make torches
calculated to burn for a long time... The emperor

ordained that all his wives should follow him when he died... When the work was over and the central passage leading to the tomb had been disguised and blocked, the outer door to it was dropped into place, shutting in all those who had been employed as workmen or craftsmen... Plants and grass were planted so that the tomb looked like a hill." *(Historical Records,* Chapter 6, Trans. E. Chavannes). When the Qin dynasty fell, General Xiang Yu is said to have opened the tomb and removed all it contained. No archaeological excavations have been undertaken yet. The tumulus was used as a fortified camp during the last civil war.

It is about 260 feet high, and about 520 yards from east to west, and 480 yards from north to south. The remains of the walls that encircled it can still be seen, as well as traces of the trenches dug during the civil war. The mound is approached from the north, starting from the road (two modern steles). Many small modern tumuli have been made round it.

4. The North Suburbs

The Remains of the Palace of Brilliant Light (Da ming gong). The palace was built on a level with Long shou yuan, just over ½ mile north of the Qing town. It was one of the largest palaces of the Tang town. The plans were drawn up in 662. It was originally a vast enclosure, surrounded by walls, containing at least thirty buildings and independent halls, with no symmetrical order. Excavations carried out from March 1957 to May 1959 revealed the foundations of the surrounding walls and about twenty buildings.

The enclosure fell into two parts: the southern part was rectangular and the northern trapeze-shaped. It was 2,467 yards long from north to south; the south-

ern wall was 1,827 yards long, and the northern wall
only 1,239 yards. The north, east and west walls of the
northern part were double; the walls were 174 yards
from each other to the north, and 59 yards from each
other to the east and west. The palace guard was
stationed between the two. The southern part, bordered on either side by the east and west imperial parks
(Dong nei yuan and Xi nei yuan) had a single wall.
Ten of the numerous gates mentioned in the records
have been discovered (for instance the Xuan wu men
gate, in the middle of the north wall, which measured
108 feet by 51 feet at its base).

The remains of the great hall Lin de dian have been
found, slightly west of the centre of the palace. It was
built on a rectangular platform 423 feet by 83 feet
(over 4,380 square yards) and divided into three parts;
the bases of 192 pillars which supported the roof have
been found.

Large numbers of stamped bricks and terra cotta
ornaments have been found during the excavations, as
well as an interesting set of clay seals (the provincial
civil servants used to send their tribute in sealed clay
jars, with their name, address and the date, during the
Tang dynasty). Some of these are in the museum.

The excavations have been filled in, and all that can
be seen are the terraces which carried the Lin de dian
and the Han yuan dian, and the hollow left by the ornamental lake to the north-east.

The Remains of the Han Town. The Han town was
about 2 miles north-west of the Qing town. Parts of the
earth ramparts can still be seen, as well as the sites of
several of the gates and the terrace of the Wei yang
gong palace; a memorial stele (1740) stands on the
terrace.

5. The West Suburbs

The Remains of the A fang gong Palace. The A fang
gong palace stood about 7 miles east of the Qing town,
south of the village of San qiao. Little is left of the
magnificent palace built by the emperor Qin shi Huang
di near his capital Xian yang. All that can be seen is a
large, roughly triangular mound, about 25 feet high,
which was perhaps the base of a building.

6. The South Suburbs

The high-ranking officials and nobles of the Tang
dynasty had villas built here, monks founded temples
here (the valley of the river Pan chuan, renowned for
its beauty, had at least eight temples: the eight temples
of the river Pan chuan, Pan chuan ba si), for the
countryside is beautiful. Even now, people come for
walks here from Xi an, to enjoy the scenery.

The Bull's Head Temple (Niu tou si) The temple is
15 miles south of the town, north-east of Wei qu, on
the Xun yin po slope of the Shao ling yuan Hill. It was
founded in 632; contemporary poets praised the magnificent scenery. The present name dates from 1086. It
was later restored several times, particularly under the
Ming.

The temple owns some *chuang* dating from 849,
with inscriptions on all eight facets, a stele dated 1169,
with a text and engravings, and some well-preserved
Ming sculpture.

The Temple Dedicated to Du Fu (Du Fu ci). It is just
to the east of the Bull's Head Temple. It was built
under the Ming, in 1526, and dedicated to Du Fu, the
famous Tang poet (712–770). The buildings were
restored in the 17th century, and then burned at the
end of the same century, but later on they were rebuilt.
A statue of Du Fu, seated, stands in the central hall.

The Temple of Flourishing Teaching (Xing jiao si).
The temple is 24 miles from Xi an, south-east of Du qu
(facing the river Pan chuan to the south).

It was founded in 669, at the same time as a pagoda built
to house the remains of the famous pilgrim Xuan zang (his
remains had up till then been on the White Stag Plain, Bai lu
yuan, south-east of Xi an). The temple flourished at first, but
fell into decay two centuries after its foundation; an inscription
on the pagoda deplores the state of it: "The pagoda has no
guardian, the temple no monk, the traveller is sad to see it so".
The temple had been damaged several times, and finally was
destroyed at the end of the Qing. In 1922, a monk managed
to rebuild it which the help of subscriptions, and new buildings
were added (a library was built in 1939).

The main hall contains a white jade statue of the
Buddha, which came from Burma. The pagoda dedicated to Xuan Zang is east of the temple; built on a
square base, it has five stories. The pilgrim's statue
stands in the lower part. Two small three storey pagodas stand on either side of the pagoda, dedicated to his
two disciples (Gui mo and Yuan zi).

The Hua yan si is 18 miles south of Wei an, on the
slopes of the Shao ling yuan. It was built during the
Zhen guan period (627–650). In the 17th century, a
landslide carried away the temple, and the two pagodas are all that survives today. In 1937, three little
temples were built near them. The large pagoda, seven
stories high, and square, recalls the style of the Big
Goose Pagoda; the small one is hexagonal, and only
four stories high.

The Cao Tang si. This temple is 36 miles south of the
town, at the foot of the Gui feng Hills, in the village of
Cao tang ying. In the 5th century, a palace built by the
Later Qin King Tao xing stood on the present temple's
site; the Indian monk Kumaradjiva came to teach
Buddhism here. The Tang Emperor Wu zong used
the ruins of the palace to have a temple built. All that

now remains is a little stone pagoda, certainly very old
(Tang or Song), dedicated to Kumaradjiva. It is just
over six feet high, and consists of a square plinth, a
round base, and the pagoda itself, which is octagonal.

THE ROAD FROM XI AN TO YAN AN

Xian yang

Xian yang, the second most important town in the
province and the centre of its textile industry, is north
of the Wei, about 12 miles from Xi an. Before the liberation, most of the cotton produced in Shân xi was
sent to the mills in Shang hai or in other coastal
towns. Since the liberation, Xian yang has become a
well-equipped industrial town which supplies cotton
material for the whole of north-western China. It is
also a trade and communications centre. Barges with
cargoes of coal and salt from Shan xi used to be towed
up the River Wei as far as Xian yang.

In about 250 B.C., King Xiao (Xiao gong or Xiao wen wang)
established the capital of the kingdom of Qin at Xian yang.
When his descendent Qin shi Huang di unified China, the town
was the capital of the empire for a short time. Qin shi Huang
di collected there the prisoners and weapons captured from the
armies which he conquered. A few years later, however, he
moved his capital to the other side of the Wei and founded
Chang an. From then onwards, Xian yang took second place
and its history is closely bound up which that of Chang an
(for the history of Chang an, see Xi an.

As it was near the former town of Chang an, the
neighbourhood of Xian yang is full of historical and
archaeological monuments. One of the most interesting is the great stone lion guarding the tomb of Yang
shi, the mother of Empress Wu Ze tian (Tang). Both
the lion and the tomb, known as the **Shun ling,** have

been classed as historical monuments. At the end of 1965, a collection of 3,000 coloured terra cotta statues were found at Yang jia wan, about 2 miles from the tombs of the Han Emperors Gao zu and Hui (for details of their tombs, see Xi an). The statues date from the Han; they vary between 1 foot 3 inches and 2 feet in height, and represent soldiers, horsemen, officers, musicians and dancers. They were arranged in a magnificent procession. No other such discovery has ever been made in the history of Chinese archaeology.

Yao xian

Yao xian is a district headquarters about 18 miles north of Xi an as the crow flies, on the railway line to Tong chuan. It contains a **superb collection of over two hundred steles,** the oldest of which date from the Northern Wei (5th century B.C.); the most recent date from the Qing. The Northern Wei steles (14 altogether) have bas-relief portraits carved on the upper part, and are of the greatest historical interest. They have been classed as historical monuments, and 76 out of the collection have been put into a museum which has been built specially for them (the Yao xian Museum, Yao xian bo wu guan).

Three Buddhist cave-temples can be seen cut in the rock on the side of the **Mountain of the King of Medecine (Yao wang shan),** a mile east of Yao xian. The mountain used to be called the Five Terrace Mountain (Wu tai shan); its present name derives from the memory of the Taoist doctor, Sun Si miao, who retired under the Tang to live a hermit's life in a cave there, the Cave of the Great Mystery (Tai xuan dong). A little temple near the cave is dedicated to him (Sun zhen ren ci), and a small museum has been built nearby: the **Sun Si miao Museum (Sun Si miao ji nian guan).**

Sun Si miao (581–682) was the greatest doctor of the Tang era. He was a hermit and a scholar, with a detailed knowledge of the Taoist canon and Buddhist texts. His reputation was such that the Sui Emperor Wen offered him a post of academician, which he refused several times over, preferring to devote his life to the study of drugs. He accepted a high post at the court of the Tang Emperor Gao zong, but went into retirement soon afterwards, pretending to be ill. His main work, the *Qian jin yao fang (Recipes of inestimable value)*, which dates from 652, gives over 5,000 prescriptions. A supplement followed later on (682), the *Qian jin yi fang*, in which about 800 medecines were analysed. Another work, the *Yin hai jing wei, Exhaustive Knowledge of the Silver Sea*, was attributed to him as well (the *silver sea* is a Buddhist term for the white of the eye). This treatise, which may in fact have been written at a later date, is the earliest ophthalmological monograph in Chinese. Sun Si miao is not only well known as a hermit, doctor, pharmacologist, encyclopaedist and alchemist; he is also venerated as the prototype of the man who helps his neighbour with a complete disregard for all selfish ends. Taoist legends have grown up about him, attributing to him all sorts of supernatural powers. A stamp was issued in memory of him in 1963. (Some of this information comes from: *La Médecine chinoise*, P. Huard and M. Wong, in the Que sais-je? collection, Paris 1964, p. 35.)

The cave-temples are about 200 yards east of the temple. There are three of them, cut into the mountainside; they contain several pieces of Buddhist sculpture dating from the Tang. The right hand one contains a standing statue of Guan yin; it is clear from this that Guan yin had not yet become a female deity at this time. The middle one contains four large statues, several small ones and some inscriptions. The left hand one contains a seated Buddha. Several of the inscriptions date from the Northern Zhou, and some of the small statues from the Song and the Jin.

Tong chuan

Visitors going from Xi an to Yan an go as far as Tong chuan by train and then go on northwards by coach. The name of the town means "copper river". It is a coal mining town.

In 1959, remains of 9 pottery kilns dating from the Tang and the Song were excavated in the little town of Huang bao (Huang bao zhen), half way along the road from Yao xian to Tong chuan. Others have been uncovered in the villages of Li di po, Shang dian and Chen lu zhen, further to the east. They are all usually referred to as the **Yao zhou Kilns (Yao zhou yao)**. Under the Tang, they produced black and white pottery, or occasionally yellow, green or light blue, and then under the Song they became specialised in the production of famous celadons (particularly the Huang bao zhen kilns). The eastern kilns are later, and mainly at work under the Jin and the Yuan. The craftsmen used local coal to feed their furnaces.

Huang ling

Huang ling is a district headquarters about half way along the road from Xi an to Yan an. It used to be one of the fortresses built to protect Xi an from the invasions of northern peoples, the Huns, the Mongols and the Turks. Visitors going by coach from Xi an to Yan an spend the night at an inn here, built round an inner courtyard, in the style typical of the houses in Shân xi.

Huang ling means "the yellow tomb"; about 200 yards north of the inn, above the town, lies the **Tomb of the Yellow Emperor (Huang di ling)**. The path up the mountainside leads past a temple dedicated to him, which has recently been restored. At the top of the hill is a mound covered with greenery; according to a very ancient legend, the Yellow Emperor (Huang di), the mythical ancestor and first sovereign of the Han race, said to have reigned at some time during the third

millenium B.C., lies buried there. This legendary figure
is also regarded as a hero who taught men civilisation;
he is said to have invented the working of metal, the
wheel, weapons and pottery. His exemplary reign is
the age of gold. A stele erected in 1959 bears the calligraphy of Guo Mo ruo, and describes him as the *father
of the Han people*. Another stele standing there dates
from the Qing. The tomb is classed as a historical
monument.

At the **Town of the Two Dragons (Shuang long zhen)**
a cave can be seen, cut out of the rock, with Buddhist
statues and bas-relief carvings. It was originally part of
a monastery, the **Monastery of the Ten Thousand Buddhas (Wan Fo si)**. A passage about 12 feet long leads
through the rock into a large square chamber, about
28 feet square. A large concave altar in the middle sup-
ports several seated statues of the Buddha, joined at
the top and the bottom to the rock from which they
were carved. The outer walls and the walls of the passage are carved in bas-relief with scenes of the life of
the Buddha and Bodhisattvas. The cave, sculpture and
several inscriptions on the walls date from the Northern Song (1094–1106).

Fu xian

Fu xian is a district headquarters on the road from
Huang ling to Yan an, in the River Luo valley. Two
groups of Buddhist sculpture in the neighbourhood
are worth a visit, although they are not easy to get at.
The first group is south-east of the village of **Duan jia
zhuang,** 9 miles south of Fu xian; it consists of one
cave cut out of the rock, with five statues and pillars
covered with bas-relief carvings. It dates from the
Northern Song, and used to be part of a monastery,

the Ge zi tou si. The second group is 40 miles west of Fu xian, behind the **Stone Cavity Monastery (Shi kong si,** also called the Shi hong si). One of the buildings is still there, leaning up against the rock face. Seven caves have been cut out of the rock, all of elaborate shapes, and all containing several statues and pieces of bas-relief carving. The largest has 28 statues; the oldest date from the Tang (the Jing long period, 707–710), and the latest from the Ming. Several inscriptions tell the history of the place.

Yan an

The town is on the south bank of the River Yan shui, at a point where it takes a right angle turn to the north-east. It is completely surrounded by loess hills, with cave dwellings hollowed out of the cliffs. The town has for a long time been the market town where the peasants from the countryside around come to buy their supplies.

It already had a long revolutionary tradition behind it (risings at the end of the Ming dynasty and in 1911) when the Communist armies arrived there in October 1935, after the Long March, and established their headquarters there. The town was bombed by the Japanese and even abandoned for a short time (when the Guo min dang threat became too pressing, Chairman Mao launched the famous slogan: "To keep Yan an is to lose Yan an, to lose Yan an is to keep Yan an", meaning that a tactical retreat would allow the true revolutionary spirit to come into its own within a short time). In spite of numerous difficulties the Communists won back the town and triumphed.

The Yan an pagoda has come to be the symbol of the revolution. Today, Yan an is the cultural and economic centre of north Shân xi, with several factories and a university. It is linked by road to Tong chuan and an airline operates between Xi an and Yan an. It has about thirty thousand inhabitants.

1. Historical remains

a) Buddhist caves. Three Buddhist caves can be seen at the foot of Qing lian shan Hill; they contain some interesting Song and Jin statues.

b) The Yan an Pagoda. It stands on an isolated hill overlooking the south-east of the town; it was built under the Song, and has been restored several times.

c) The Ming Tomb. It is on the left bank of the Yan shui, north of the town. The stone animals lining the "sacred way" are still there, but no trace of the tumulus can be seen.

d) The Buddhist Cemetery. A number of little carved pagodas (false doors, niches, animals) grouped on the slopes of Qing liang shan Hill can be seen from the road which runs alongside the left bank of the Yan shui: they are the graves of a Buddhist community. One of them is dated 1515 and most of them appear to date from the Ming.

e) The Taoist Hermitage. It stands on a magnificent site, on the peak of an outcrop of rock overlooking the bend in the Yan shui, to the north. It consists of a small temple, now out of use.

2. Souvenirs of the Revolution

The visitor is taken to see several buildings in and round the town which once housed revolutionary organisations, as well as the cave dwellings where the leaders lived from 1935 onwards.

a) In Yan an itself: the house in which Chairman Mao lived (with its air-raid shelter) and the Museum of the Revolution (opened in 1958).

b) At Yang jia ling: The Assembly Hall (Zhong yang da li tang), which has been rebuilt as it was, and the caves where Chairman Mao, Liu Shao qi, Zhou En lai and Zhu De lived for a time.

c) At Wang jia ping: The headquarters of the Eighth Route Army.

d) On Qing lian shan Hill: the head office of the *Ren min ri bao* (People's Daily).

e) At Zao yuan ("the jujube garden"): the leaders' houses.

Yu lin

Yu lin is in the far north of the province, near the Great Wall, and for several centuries it served a double purpose. Under the Tang, the Song and the Ming, it was a garrison of great strategic importance in defending China against the northern invaders, and at the same time, it was a market town where the Mongols came to barter horses, furs, leather and camel hair for tea, salt and other products which they needed. The town played an important part in the relations between the empire and the Xi xia under the Northern Song. It is now a district headquarters and the centre of trade between Shân xi and western Inner Mongolia. The name means "elm tree forest".

Heng shan

Heng shan is a district headquarters south-west of Yu lin; it too was a frontier town near the Great Wall. The **Ruins of the town of Tong wan (Tong wan cheng yi zhi)** are about 30 miles to the north-west, on the frontier of Shân xi and Inner Mongolia, in a stretch of desert-like countryside. They are the remains of the capital built there by He lian bo bo, king of the Xian xia. From 407 to 431 A.D., the Xia were one of the five barbarian states which shared Northern China with 16 other kingdoms, until the Northern Wei managed to unify it (439). The town was begun in 413; several things of archaeological interest have been uncovered there.

WEST OF XI AN

Xing ping

Xing ping is a district headquarters lying on the railway line west of Xi an. The **Tomb of Han Wu di,** the Han Emperor Wu, who reigned from 140 to 86 B.C., is just over half a mile from there. The tomb is called Mao ling, and has given its name to the neighbouring village: Mao ling zhen. The tomb is classed as a historical monument.

Another tomb near Mao ling zhen is also classed as a historical monument: the tomb of Huo Qu bing, a great general who distinguished himself several times in battles against the Huns (Xiong nu) under the reign of Han Wu di. One of his greatest feats was performed in 119 B.C.; he brought 80 enemy chiefs back as prisoners and won a large stretch of what is now northern He bei for China. Han Wu di honoured him by having a magnificent tomb built for him. The great earth mound can still be seen today, with a little brick gateway in front of it, and a brick funerary shrine on the top. Six very handsome stone statues and three bas-relief carvings were found buried there: a horse trampling on a man, two horses lying down, a tiger, a bull and a boar, also lying down. The bas-relief carvings depict a large scowling monkey, a bear and another wild animal which is shown leaping. They date from the Western Han and are among the finest masterpieces of ancient Chinese sculpture. They are in the Xi an Museum.

In 1957, 6 other statues were discovered: a man, two unidentifiable wild animals, two fish and a frog.

Qian xian

It is about 30 miles north-west of Xian yang, on a tributary of the Wei. The tomb of Li Shi min, Emperor Tai zong, son and successor of the founder of the Tang dynasty, is near there. The six bas-relief carvings considered one of the masterpieces of Tang sculpture came from this tomb, which is called **Zhao ling.** They depict six standing or galloping horses. Two of them were taken to the United States; the other four are in the Xi an Museum, with reproductions of the missing two. Other reproductions can be seen in the Peking Historical Museum, on the stairs leading up to the first floor. The remains of the tomb are classed as a historical monument.

The **Qian ling** tomb is nearby; it contains the remains of Gao zong, the third Tang Emperor, and of his wife, Empress Wu Ze tian. Wu Ze tian became a Buddhist nun, and returned to politics later on. When the Emperor died, she seized power and reigned for 21 years. Her reign (684–705) was famous for a long series of political murders, accompanied by systematic encouragement of Buddhism. Emperor Gao zong was buried in 684. The tomb was re-opened at vast expense to receive the body of Wu Ze tian in 705.

The tomb is inside a hill, the Lian shan, about 3 miles north of Qian xian. A mile outside Qian xian, remains of two towers *(que)* herald the beginning of the way leading to it *(yu dao)*, which is over 1½ miles

long, on a north-south axis. On either side of it are two
hills with 48 foot towers *(que)* on the top of them, and
two obelisks *(hua biao)*, each 25 feet high, followed
by two monumental stone winged horses. Then come
two ostriches (they are in fact "scarlet birds", *zhu que*,
which symbolised the south in ancient Chinese astronomy), five pairs of horses and ten pairs of large standing statues of men. Next come two steles, each measuring 20½ feet. The left hand one bears a passage in
praise of the reign of Gao zong, composed by Wu Ze
tian, and written out by Zhong zong, the rightful successor of Gao zong, whom she de-throned to take over
power. The right hand one, called the Stele with no
Inscription (Wu zi bei) has bas-relief dragons and several Song and Jin inscriptions, one of which is written
in the language of the Nu zhen, the founders of the
Jin dynasty. It has a Chinese translation beside it.
After these come the remains of two towers *(que)* and
large groups of stone statues representing the people
who went to the Emperor's funeral. There are 29 on
one side and 31 on the other, arranged in rows. Each
one originally had the name of the person engraved
on the back. None of the heads are left now. They are
about 5 feet high. Two colossal stone lions follow the
statues, and the ruins of the Hall of Offerings (Xian
dian) lie at the bottom of the hill, with a stele erected
by Qian long. The bare hillside rises behind. The
entrance to the tomb was found in 1958, but it has not
yet been opened. It does not seem to have been sacked.
The hill used to be enclosed by a square wall, a mile
long on each side, with four gates, north, south, east
and west. Stone statues of lions and horses still stand
where the gates used to be. Many of the statues have
been repaired since 1957; the ones which had fallen
down have been righted.

Lin you

Lin you is a district headquarters about 25 miles upstream, in the same valley as Qian xian. A few miles west of the town, remains of the summer palace used by the Sui and Tang Emperors can be seen; they used to come to the **Palace which is Nine Times Perfect (Jiu cheng gong)** to escape the heat of Chang an. The palace is often mentioned in Tang poetry. The Emperor caught a white unicorn there once, and the name of the town means "unicorn walk".

Several examples of **Buddhist sculpture** were found nearby in 1958. On the Lama's Cap Mountain (La ma mao shan) 9 miles south west of Lin you, three Buddhas and hundreds of Bodhisattvas, arranged in long rows, were found carved in bas-relief on an almost inaccessible cliff. Another cliff, a few yards west of the town near an old bridge, has large niches with about fifteen Buddhas on it. Both groups date from the Tang. Finally, about one and a half miles south-west of the town are two caves, about 500 yards from each other, cut out of the rock, containing a set of beautiful statues of the Buddha, also dating from the Tang. The largest is 14 feet high, and they are in good condition. They are usually called by the name of the monastery to which they belong, the Monastery of Merciful Goodness (Ci shan si).

Bin xian

Bin xian is a small district headquarters near the Gan su frontier, in the Jing valley, about 60 miles north-west of Xian yang as the crow flies. 6 miles north-west of the town, on the banks of the Jing, is a group of **colossal Buddhist statues,** which are part of the **Big Buddha Monastery (Da Fo si)**. The statues are in eight caves carved out of the rock, the biggest of which is 96 feet high. It contains three large seated statues of the Buddha; the middle one is 75 feet high. Altogether, the caves contain over 800 statues, in bas-relief, haut-relief and ronde bosse. They all date from the Tang, and the oldest date from 629. The style of the statues, and the ornaments round them are magnificent. Some of the faces are enhanced by paint.

Bao ji

Bao ji is in the west of the province, on the north bank of the Wei, at the junction of the railway lines from Gan su and Xin jiang and from Si chuan via the Qin ling Mountains. It is an industrial town, the third most important in the province, and still developing rapidly. The neighbourhood is known for the Cha ping ling waterfalls (Cha ping ling pu bu) and the Wei gorges, called the Bao ji Gorges (Bao ji xia).

THE SOUTH AND EAST OF THE PROVINCE

HAN ZHONG

Han zhong, whose name means "on the Han", is in south-west Shân xi, near Si chuan, at an altitude of 1,536 feet above sea level. It is the most important administrative and economic centre in south Shân xi (the Han valley). The upper reaches of the Han flow through a fertile basin about 90 miles long, enclosed on either side by high mountain ridges.

The climate is hot and damp, and almost the same as that of south China. The whole area, often referred to as Han nan, is like a miniature Si chuan; its country-side is almost exactly the same, as well as the climate.

It used to be part of Si chuan. "No roads, only paths, and they are sometimes impassable by beasts of burden. The hills are full of streams and mountain rivers, navigable by small boats when they are low lying, but dangerous in the rainy season—the bridges have to be removed, or else they would be swept away. It is a region rich in minerals and vegetation, full of waterfalls ready to be used for generating power when industry is developed. The area is thickly populated, particularly along the Han-ho (River Han)." (Richard *Géographie de la Chine*, vol. I, p. 96.)

The town of Han zhong used to be a stage on the road from north China to Cheng du, in Si chuan. This function has disappeared since the building of the Shân xi–Si chuan railway line, but it is still the commercial and industrial centre of the whole area.

Cheng gu

The town of Cheng gu is about 18 miles west of Han zhong. **Zhang Qian,** the diplomat sent by the Han Emperor Wu to Central Asia, who reached Tashgent and the Province of Bactria after a long series of adventures, is buried there. The news which he brought back after his twelve years' absence did much to widen knowledge of the outside world in China.

Han cheng

Han cheng is a district headquarters in east Shân xi, near the Yellow River. The **Tomb of Si ma Qian** is a few miles south of the town, near the village of Zhi chuan zhen. Si ma Qian lived under the Han dynasty, from 145-87 B.C. He began his career as an official at the court of Emperor Wu, but fell into disgrace and spent the end of his life in prison, where he wrote one of the greatest works in Chinese literature, the *Shi ji*. This book, which combines several literary forms, records the history of China from its beginnings up to the author's time, and became the model for all later Chinese historians. The first part of the *Shi ji* has been translated into French by Edouard Chavannes (*Les Mémoires historiques de Se-ma Ts'ien*, 6 vols, Leroux, Paris 1895; it has recently been re-issued). Unfortunately Chavannes did not translate the second part, which consists of biographies of the chief figures in ancient China, and whose literary value is greater than the first part.

Si ma Qian was born at Zhi chuan zhen and buried there too. His tomb is a plain, round monument, inside the enclosure of the Funerary Temple of the Great Chronicler (Tai shi ci), to which a long flight of stone steps gives access. "Great Chronicler" *(tai shi)* was Si ma Qian's title at court.

Six Yuan temples still survive in the neighbourhood of Han cheng: the Fa wang miao (Temple of the King of the Law) at Xi zhuang, the Yu wang miao (Temple of Yu the Great) at Zan cun, the San cheng miao (Three Sages' Temple) at Xue cun, the Guan di miao (Temple of the God of War) at Xiao yi cun, the Pu zhao si (Monastery of Omnipresent Light) at Wu cun and the Zi yun guan (Purple Cloud Monastery) northwest of Han cheng.

Hua shan

Hua shan, which rises 7,986 feet above sea level, overlooks the lower Shân xi plain, and the confluence of the Yellow River, the Luo and the Wei, and the He nan mountains to the east. Its name means "*flowery, glorious or splendid mountain*". It is the western sacred

mountain (Xi yue; for details on the five sacred mountains, see Tai shan, p. 715). Since very early on, it has
been the centre of a special cult, and pilgrimages used
to be made there.

The great temple used for the sacrifices was at the
foot of the mountain, to the north, in the town of **Hua
yin** (whose name means "the north slope of Hua
shan"). The temple used to be widely known; it is
impossible to say whether it can still be visited now.
Hua yin is a little less than 60 miles by train from Xi an;
the visitor begins the climb from there. The first part
of the way is easy and pleasant, but the second half
is up steep stone steps leading almost straight up to the
top without a break. A good walker could manage it
in half a day, but inexperienced walkers and children
might well find it difficult.

The mountain itself is magnificent and extremely
varied. It has three peaks altogether: the Lotus Peak
(Lian hua feng) in the middle, the Immortal's Peak to
the east (Xian ren feng) and the Peak where the Wild
Geese Land (Luo yan feng) to the south. A little valley
filled with old pine trees lies between the peaks; several
springs rise there, forming waterfalls down the mountainsides. Mist often hides part of the valley, making
it look like a dream of paradise.

The worship of Hua shan was Taoist in inspiration, and the mountainsides and the surroundings of
the peaks are dotted with temples and monasteries.
It is possible to spend the night in one of them; Taoist
monks are still in charge of it, and provide meals of
home-made noodles and tea for their guests. Another
rounded peak with a little bronze pavilion on it can
be seen below the main summit: the Game of Chess
Pavilion. A poet once had a memorable game of chess
with a Taoist immortal who happened to be there. A

cave in the wall of rock below the mountain-top has been made into a shrine, which is almost completely inaccessible now; a wooden bridge used to hang alongside the rock, leading to it.

Hua shan was the scene of an astonishing feat at the time of the liberation. Some Guo Min dang troops had taken refuge there, taking with them generous supplies of arms, ammunition and food, in what seemed to be an impregnable fortress. Eight Liberation Army soldiers managed to climb up the mountain behind them and take them by surprise. A film was later made about it.

JIANG SU

(Map see Atlas pl. 4/5)

The province of Jiang su is bordered by Shan dong to the north, An hui to the west, Zhe jiang and Shang hai to the south; the sea forms the eastern boundary. Except for a handful of hills in the west of the province (old rock with mineral deposits) most of it is low-lying land which has gradually been reclaimed from the sea. At the beginning of the Christian era, the coastline was at least 30 miles further inland than it is now. Two great rivers, the Yang zi to the south and the Huai to the north, have gradually brought down alluvium from the rest of the continent, which has helped to form countless lakes: the biggest are Lake Hong ze hu (north), Lake Gao bao hu (in the centre) and Lake Tai hu (south). An intricate network of natural and man-made waterways covers the province, so that it is often called the "water country"; they are a great help to agriculture, both for irrigation and transport purposes. As the sandy coastline is unsuitable for harbours, these are mainly built slightly up-river (Nanking). The climate of Jiang su is mild and wet; the growing period lasts for eight or nine months, so that there are usually two harvests each year.

As early as the Paleolithic era, and especially during the Neolithic era, several cultures grew up in this area (see Nanking, Historical Museum, p. 988). During the Warring States period, three states fought over the lower Yang zi region (the states of Wu, Yue and Chu), and the basic techniques of metal-working were discovered in the Nanking area. From the Han dynasty onwards, the region gradually came under Chinese influence; the highest point in its cultural development was reached when the Southern Dynasties chose the site of present Nanking for their capital. Contacts with the Yellow River area and with the south seas (arrival of Buddhism) speeded up the cultural development. The building of the Grand Canal at the beginning of the 7th century, under the Sui, was an important stage in the history of the province, for that, combined with the natural waterways in the north of the province, linked the grain-producing area of the lower Yang zi to the consumer centres of the middle Yellow River area. This set in motion the first stages of development under the Tang dynasty. Under the Southern Song, the Huai valley became a frontier region for a time and the traffic along the Grand Canal was interrupted, but the lower Yang zi towns gained enormously from the presence of the court at Hang zhou (Su zhou, for instance, developed because of this). Both the Yuan and the Ming, after establishing the capital of the newly re-united empire at Peking, quickly renewed the links with the lower Yang zi (by sea convoys, and then by re-opening the canal and extending it as far as Peking). Nanking, Su zhou and Yang zhou were important economic and cultural centres, and the Qing Emperors never failed to make a halt there while "travelling in the south". The importance of the lower Yang zi grew in the 19th and 20th centuries; the Tai ping made their headquarters there and set out to try to conquer the north; the development of Shang hai nearby stimulated the local bourgeoisie into laying the foundations for local industry (particularly at Wu xi); and finally Sun Yat sen was elected President of the Republic at Nanking itself, where the bourgeoisie provided strong support later on for the Guo min dang government.

The development of the region since the liberation has been carried out in two ways: 1) the already existing industries in the south of the province have been re-organised and improved: the textile industry has been developed (cottons, silk), and so has the chemical industry (particularly at Nanking); heavy industry has been introduced, and heavy machinery, steam turbine and tractor plants have been built (at Nanking and Wu xi); 2) agriculture has been considerably improved in the north of the province, which had always lagged slightly behind the south before; one of the most spectacular projects carried out was the work done on Lake Hong ze hu: a dyke 760 yards long was built along the western bank and an overflow was dug so that the water can flow directly into the sea to avoid flooding. Production has been increased by the use of nitrate fertilizers and by the elimination of excess salt in the alkaline soil along the coast. The main crops are rice, wheat, cotton, rape-seed and millet. The Lake Tai hu basin is famous for its raw silk (three or four crops of silk-worms per year). The population of the province is 50,000,000.

Nanking will be described first, followed by the other chief towns in the south, Su zhou and then a few northern towns.

NANKING

(Map see p. 977)

Nanking is on the south bank of the Yang zi, in the south-west of Jiang su. It is a historic city and has several times been the capital; its name in Chinese is Nan jing, "the southern capital", and it is still one of the most important economic and cultural centres of the country. It is the provincial capital, with a population of 1,500,000.

History

1. The beginnings. Prehistoric remains (polished stone blades) show that the site of Nanking has been inhabited since about 4000 B.C., and that bronze was used there from about 3000 B.C. The history of the town begins only with the Spring and Autumn period and the Warring States (771-221 B.C.). At this point, the town was on the borders of three states: Chu (to the west), Wu (to the north-east), and Yue (to the south-east); its strategic position on the heights overlooking the plain of the Yang zi aroused the jealousy of each in turn. In the 6th century B.C., the Wu king He Lü is said to have commissioned the blacksmith Gan jiang to make him two swords; the master craftsman is said to have executed the order on one of the hills of present Nanking, where the Chao tian gong now is; one sword was called Gan Jiang after him, and the other was called Mo xie, "the inflexible" or "the faithful". The existence of metal ore in the hills had resulted at that time in a small settlement of blacksmiths being formed: Ye cheng ("the metal founders' town").

In 473 B.C., King Gou Jian of Yue overcame Wu, with the help of his minister, Fan Li, and built a fort in the region of Nanking, as a base from which to attack Chu. The ruins of the fort, later called Yue Cheng ("the town of Yue"), have been found to the south of the existing town. At the end of the 4th century, the Chu king Wei conquered Yue, and he too settled in the same area; he chose Qing liang shan hill, and founded the town of Jin ling (the "golden mound") there. When Qin shi Huang di unified the empire, he made it the headquarters of one of his commands, and changed the name to Mo ling ("the hillock where the horses are fed").

2. The Three Kingdoms and the Southern Dynasties. From the 3rd century A.D. onwards, Nanking gradually developed into an important political, economic and artistic centre. The southern Dynasties all used it as their capital. In 229, during the Three Kingdoms period, the Sun, founders of the state of Wu, moved their capital from Wu chang to Mo ling, which they called Jian ye. Irrigation, canalisation and other measures to improve the economy stimulated agricultural development, and links were established by sea with foreign countries (Korea and the south seas). The Sun had a new town built, south of Lake Xuan wu; built on a rectangular plan, its circumference was over 6 miles. The palace was in the north of the city; water diverted from the lake was used to irrigate it. To the west, on the Qing liang shan hill, the site of the old Jing ling, a stone Fort (Shi tou cheng), was built, and south of the existing town, the first Buddhist temple was built, in 247, in honour of some monks who had arrived from the west. It was called the Jian chu si; the work of the Buddhist painter, Zao Bu xing, is mentioned in contemporary records.

In 317, Jian ye fell into the hands of the eastern Jin, who changed the name to Jian kang. After the Jin, the Song (420–479), the Qi (479–502), the Liang (502–557) and the Chen (557–589) all made Nanking the centre of their little empires. Jian kang was roughly the same size as Jian ye; the population consisted of "280,000 families". Under the Jin, the walls of the stone Fort were re-built, and a new quarter, Dong fu cheng, was built to the north-west, to house the civil servants. Under the Song these were both changed into palaces, and two parks were laid out south of Lake Xuan wu.

The town was very important as an economic centre, famous for its forges and foundries (ten workshops in all), which specialised in producing "steel tempered a hundred times" (bai lian gang) and "mixed steel" (in which pig iron was mixed with iron which had already been worked); it was also famous for its weaving (carried out in monasteries and nobles' houses), the speciality of which was a "veined" brocade (luo wen jin) which was exported overseas, and for its pottery kilns (a glaze known as qing; large amounts have been found in the course of excavations). There were four large market places and over ten small ones, each one specialised in various products (horses and cattle, materials, salt, herbs, etc...). The town had trading links with the south seas and many exotic products were sold there: ivory, pearls, coral, agate, rhinoceros horns. In 507, three elephants arrived in the town.

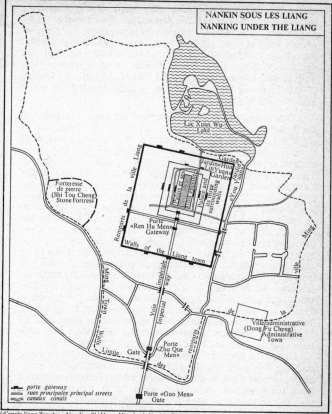

NANKIN SOUS LES LIANG
NANKING UNDER THE LIANG

Lac Xuan Wu Lake

Remparts de la ville Liang

Forteresse de pierre (Shi Tou Cheng) Stone Fortress

Garden
Jardine Hua Lin
Yuan Yuan Garden

Palais clos
cross enceintes
Palace and its three surrounding walls

(You Yuan)

Porte «Ren Hu Men» Gateway

Walls of the Liang town

Ming Town Walls

Voie impériale way
Voie Imperial

ville Ming

de la

Ville administrative (Dong Fu Cheng) Administrative Town

Limite Gate

Porte «Zhu Que Men» Gate

des remparts

Porte «Guo Men» Gate

porte gateway
rues principales principal streets
canaux canals

(d'après Jiang Zan chu, «Nan Jing Shi Hua», Histoire de Nankin, Pékin, 1963)
(after Jiang Zan chu, «Nan Jing Shi Hua», History of Nanking, Peking, 1963)

Jian kang was a flourishing artistic centre too: Fan Zhen, the philosopher famous for his essay, the *Destructability of the Soul*, Zu Chong zhi, the mathematician who made an approximately correct calculation of *pi*, Xie Ling yun, one of the first poets to write about landscape, Wang Xi zhi, the calligrapher, Gu Kai zhi, the painter, all lived there, to name only a few. The Buddhist pilgrim Fa Xian wrote his memoirs at Jian kang as well, after his long wanderings through Central Asia, India and Indonesia. Buddhism triumphed under the Liang emperor Wu, himself a devout Buddhist; many temples were built in and around the town. All that is now left at Nanking of this flowering are a few tombs of kings and the Thousand Buddha Cliff on Qi xia shan Hill.

3. The Tang, the Southern Tang and the Song. The name of the town was changed several times under the Tang, and it remained an important local centre. The poet Li Bai lived there for several years towards the end of his life, and wrote a famous poem there, entitled "On climbing the Phoenix Terrace" (south-west of Nanking). When, at the end of the Tang dynasty, the empire was broken up, the town was for some years (937–975) the capital of a local dynasty once more: the southern Tang, who governed the present-day provinces of Jiang su, An hui, Jiang xi, Hu nan, and Fu jian. The old name of Jin ling was re-adopted and the town was once more expanded; its circumference was over 10 ½ miles, and it covered approximately the same area as it was later to cover in the Ming and Qing dynasties. The intellectual and artistic life was still active, and included many painters and poets, among them the emperors Li Jing and Li Yu. Buddhism flourished; the five-storey octagonal stone pagoda still standing in the Qi xia si Temple was built at this stage. Since the liberation, two southern Tang imperial mausoleums (the emperors Li Bian and Li Jing) in the southern suburbs, near Niu shou shan hill, have been opened; both are large and magnificently decorated.

Under the northern Song, the name was changed to Jiang ning fu; Wang An shi, the well-known reformer, held an administrative post there, and died there in 1086. Under the southern Song the town was called Jian kang fu; it was an advance post in the resistance against the northern invaders. In 1130, the famous general Yue Fei won a great victory over the Jin on Niu tou shan Hill (today called Niu shou shan, "the Bull's Head Hill").

4. The Yuan and the Ming. The Yuan changed the name of the town to Ji qing. In 1356, Zhu Yuan zhang (who originally came from east An hui) took the town and re-named it Ying tian fu. When his supremacy was established in 1368, he decided to make it his capital. His son Yong le made Peking the capital of the empire, and it was he who called the town Nan jing, "the southern capital".

Nanking owes its present form and aspect to the Ming dynasty. In 1391, the population was estimated at 173,200 inhabitants. Zhu Yuan zhang had compelled nearly 20,000 rich families to come and settle there, in order to people his capital. He pledged them to give money for building, and rewarded them with official duties and honorific titles. Thus the records tell us that a third of the new rampart was "given" by Chen Wan san, a native of Wu xing in Zhe jiang.

The first wall was built in brick, and was over 35 miles round (whole sections still exist today). As well as the Song and the Yuan towns, it enclosed a large space to the north, between the Yang zi and Lake Xuan wu, and a smaller area to the south-east, round the new emperor's palace. The inhabitants of 152 districts of the middle Yang zi were responsible for making the bricks; they were all the same size (15½ inches long, 7½ inches wide, 4 inches thick); each one bore the workman's and his overseer's name. There were thirteen gates. A second, outer wall was then built, 71 miles round and made of earth, which followed the Yang zi to the north and encircled the hills to the west. The names of its seventeen gates still survive in the toponymy of the town. Broad avenues were opened out, paved with large marble slabs, often over 3ft. wide. The plan of the palace in the east of the town was later to inspire the architects of the imperial city in Peking. As in Peking, the ministeries were in the fore-court; there were five marble bridges, the great Wu men gate, the Altar of the Earth to the west, the Temple of the ancestors to the east, then the First and Second Courtyards, each with five successive halls. After Hong wu the palace was abandoned and gradually fell into ruins. Little is left now.

Industry developed considerably during the Ming dynasty. 45,000 families of workers and artisans were recorded. Northwest of the town, near the Yang zi were the San cha he shipyards, where sea-going boats were built (among others, those used for the eunuch Cheng He's expedition to the south seas at the beginning of the 15th century); the largest were 465 ft. long and 100ft. wide, and could carry a thousand men. The Ming government had various species of plants, trees etc. planted on Zi ji shan Hill to supply the raw materials (pitch, fibres for rope). Since the liberation, a 36ft rudder has been found (at present on view in the Historical Museum in Peking), and more recently still, a capstan. Weaving also became very important; some workshops were under the supervision of civil servants, others were private concerns. Trades were strictly separated, and the toponymy recalls this still: brocade district, watered silk district, dyers' district, etc. Several printers, from Hang zhou, Hui zhou (An hui), Jian yang (Fu jian), settled down to work in Nanking. The official printing works at the Guo zi jian College printed a valuable edition known as *Nan jian ben;* several private printing works also existed. The first edition of the *Ben cao gang mu,* Li Shi zhen's great pharmaco-poeia, appeared at Nanking. There were many pottery kilns; 72 are recorded on the slopes of Yu hua tai Hill, south of the town, alone. Near this hill stood the famous "China Pagoda" (built by Yong le, in honour of his mother), so often to be found reproduced in 17th and 18th century western works.

The town contained over ten market places. Outside the eastern ramparts, going from north to south, there were three: the Yi feng men Gate Market (wood and bamboo), the Qing liang men Gate market (fabrics, tea, salt, bamboo), the Jiang dong men market (grain and livestock). Within the walls, there were several more small markets dealing with redistri-bution and at least ten inns.

Nanking was an important artistic centre at this time. Many Chinese and foreign students came to study at the Imperial College, where a team of scholars were compiling the enormous *Yong le da dian* (Yong le Encyclopedia). In the Ji ming shan and the Ju bao shan observatories, Moslem astronomers worked on the official calendar, known as the "Moslem calendar", which was to remain in force until the 17th century. The Jesuit priest Matteo Ricci twice tried to obtain permission to enter the city, in 1595 and 1596, as he considered it the most important city in China; twice the permission was refused, and he had to stay on board his boat, west of the city; only after asking a third time, in 1599, was he granted leave to settle *intra muros*.

5. The Qing dynasty. The development of industry, parti-cularly weaving, continued. 30,000 looms and nearly 50,000 wor-kers are recorded. Nanking remained an important artistic centre; the action of Wu Jing zi's famous novel *The Scholars (Ru lin wai shi,* English version published in 1957 by the Foreign Languages Press, Peking) takes place here, and the novel contains a fascinating and penetrating analysis of Nanking society in the 18th century. The Manchu emperors, although they kept Peking as their capital, were always full of attentions for the southern town; Kang xi and Qian long stayed there while on journeys to the south. And on January 22nd, 1707, at Nanking. Monseigneur de Tournon, papal legate to China, published his famous edict of Nanking, Pope Clement XI's decree banning the exercise of Chinese rites. In 1842, the Treaty of Nanking was signed with England, on board an English ship tied up in the harbour. Nanking was declared an open port; it was the first of the "unequal treaties". In March 1853, the Tai ping armies attacked and took Nanking. The town was re-named Tian jing ("celestial capital") and was declared the capital of the new empire. The celestial emperor, Hong Xiu Quan and the various kings who attended him, had vast palaces built for them. The crafts were re-organised and given new encouragement; new industries, particularly armaments, were created (cannons, ammunition, warships). Trade was directed by the state, which gave its patronage to a series of guilds and struck a new coinage. Several books based on the new ideas held by the Tai ping were printed, and at the same time a new form of art came to light to a certain extent.

The Englishman Lindley, who visited Nanking at this time, gives the following description in his book, *The History of the Ti Ping Revolution*, published in London, in 1866, p. 235:

"The walls of Nanking cover an immense area... but for many years the greater part of the enclosed space has been destitute of houses and only used for gardens or to cultivate corn and other cereal produce... Passing through the high gates, under a tunnel at least 100 ft. long, we stood within the capital of the Ti ping. A sharp ride of more than half an hour brought us to the inhabited part of the city, in its southern quarter. Our way passed through fields of grain, interspersed with gardens, small villages and detached houses... The southern part of Nanking was thickly inhabited, and seemed altogether of a better and more handsome style than any Chinese city I had previously seen. Many large palaces and official buildings occupied prominent positions; the streets were very wide and particularly clean, a rare thing in China."

The town was to suffer considerably at the hands of the imperial armies, when it was re-taken in 1864. They in fact were responsible for the devastation which used to be attributed to the Tai ping rebels. Little remains today of the buildings put up by Hong Xiu quan's supporters. The new régime has published a large album of reproductions of some frescoes and various objects which have survived.

By the beginning of the 20th century, the town had partly recovered from the catastrophe; in 1908, the railway linking it to the great port of Shang hai was built. From June to November 1910, the Chinese put on an exhibition showing products of the empire and particularly of the three provinces forming the "vice-royalty" of which Nanking was the centre.

6. The Republic. In 1911, the town was occupied for a time by the troops of the reactionary general, Zhang Xun, then liberated by the revolutionary armies of Jiang su and Zhe jiang. The delegates of the seventeen provinces met at Nanking and elected Sun Yat sen president of the new Republic. The first of January, 1912 was declared the first day of the republican era *(Min guo)*. In the first months of 1912, the representatives approved the articles for a provisional constitution. But this democratic enthusiasm was short-lived; on the first of April, Sun Yat sen gave way to Yuan Shi kai; on April 5th, the assembly decided to transfer the capital to Peking. After the successes of the northern expedition, the Guo min dang decided to make Nanking its base once more; Chiang Kai-Shek's government took over the ancient palace of Hong Xiu quan. A magnificent mausoleum was built to Sun Yat sen, and his ashes were brought from Peking and placed there in 1929. The government fled to Zhong qing before the advance of the Japanese; they occupied the town until the end of the war.

7. Since the liberation. Industry has developed considerably since 1950: iron and steel, chemicals (fertilizers), machinery building, optical instruments, textiles, foodstuffs. The enlarged market has led to the development of agriculture in the suburbs (350,000 *mou* under cultivation); as well as grain, tea, vegetables, apples, cherries and water-melons are grown. Scientific, artistic and educational activities have developed as well; Nanking has eighteen institutes and colleges of higher education and several research centres. The Zi jin shan observatory is one of the largest in China; the Academy of Science has a botanical garden there, near the Sun Yat sen mausoleum, one of the largest in the country.

Description

The ramparts of Nanking follow no regular plan, unlike those of most other towns. To the north-west they are not far from the Yang zi; to the north, they follow the bank of Lake Xuan wu, which remains outside; to the east they encircle the area where the imperial palace of Hong wu once was; south and south-west they follow the irregular course of the Qin huai river, leaving the Rain of Flowers Hill (Yu hua tai) outside, but including the small Chao tian gong and Qing liang shan Hills; a space is left between the ramparts and the river to the west; the naval shipyards and the market places (Xi guan district) used to be here during the Ming dynasty.

The north-western districts, Lake Xuan wu, the centre, the southern district and its surroundings, the eastern district, the eastern hills, and the road to the Qi xia si will all be mentioned in turn.

1. The north-western districts and Lake Xuan wu

The traveller coming from Peking by train comes through Pu kou, north of the Yang zi first of all. Hong wu fortified the settlement at the same time as Nanking. It depends entirely on trade (transport of foodstuffs beyond the river) for its existence. Even before the railway was built, products from the neighbouring regions, particularly oxhides, would be brought there, in barrows or on mules; from there the caravans started north, with their southern merchandise, which included European goods from 1850 onwards. The coming of the railway has made it even more important as a transit depot. The river is crossed by ferry, from which there is a view of the port of Nanking. The station is just north of the old ramparts; the line passes north of the town and goes on to Shang hai.

The old Yi feng men Gate (now restored), once the haunt of pedlars, leads into the town; the Lion Hill (Shi zi shan), overlooking the river (a point of vantage, which used to be fortified), is on the left; the Flowering gardens Hills (Hua yuan gang) are on the right. From there, a broad, straight avenue, lined with plane trees (brought from France in the 1930's), the Sun Yat sen Avenue (Zhong shan lu) leads south-east towards the town centre. This area was built up comparatively recently. The British, American, German and Japanese consulates, and the race course, all used to be there. The Nanking Hotel has been built there. Next follows a roundabout (the left hand turning goes to Lake Xuan wu); then a second one; the massive **Drum Tower (Gu lou),** built under the Ming, stands near here; there is a good view of the town from the top. East of the Sun Yat sen Avenue stands the Great Bell Pavilion (Da zhong ting), which makes a pair with the Drum Tower.

Wooded hills, where there were once many temples, stretch south-east of the Sun Yat sen Avenue. The 18th century poet Yuan Mei retired to Xiao cang shan Hill here, near Qing liang shan Hill. He had acquired a little garden here, which once had belonged to a certain Sui, and then been abandoned. He moved his library there, and wrote poems about the surrounding countryside. Yuan Mei is sometimes called the Lord of Sui's Garden *(Sui yuan xian sheng)*. The southern Tang had a summer residence built on **Qing liang shan Hill,** to escape to from the heat; the buildings of a temple, the **Qing liang shan si,** can still be seen; it is an attractive walk, with a view over the Yang zi. Within Shui xi men, and south-east of Qing liang shan Hill, is another little hill, where the smith Gan Jiang is supposed to have forged King Wu's swords (the Ye cheng settlement). The Song had a palace built there, which was known as Chao tian gong at the beginning of the Ming dynasty.

The University of Nanking (near the Bell Tower) and the Wu tai shan stadium (further south) have recently been built among these hills.

South of the Chao tian gong Hill, in Tang zi jie Street (No 74) stands an old Tai ping residence. It was forgotten. It was only in 1952 that wall paintings dating from the Tai ping period were discovered in the house, after some information had been given by the Li family, who were the owners. The family had fled when the rebels arrived in the town, and the house was taken over by the new masters of the city. After the victory of the imperial armies, the Li family took back their house, and found it had been decorated with pictures, which they considered worthless (some were scraped off, others were covered over with paint). Restoration work begun in 1952 uncovered part of the paintings. At the same time, research was begun to try and discover who had owned the house, but in vain. As it is small, however, it probably could only have been lived in by a second grade civil servant. The surviving paintings (a five-storey watch-tower, a landscape, flowers and animals) are unmistakably of Tai ping origin; several contemporary texts speak of the Tai ping leaders' houses being decorated with paintings; and the watch-tower tallies exactly with descriptions of those used by the rebels.

Lake Xuan wu lies north-east of the northern ramparts; the characters *xuan* "black" and *wu* "war" represent a group of constellations, and here they mean "north". The lake has five islands, recently linked by dykes, each of which is called after one of the five continents. The imperial archives used to be housed on "Australia", where the water surrounding them protected them from fire. The lake is covered with magnificent lotus flowers in summer.

A chain of little hills runs south of the lake; there the Southern Dynasties used to have their palaces. The Bei ji ge Observatory (North Pole Pavilion), and on a lower level, to the west, the Imperial College (Guo zi jian), stood there during the Ming dynasty. The **Ji ming si** (Cock's Crow Temple), a convent where the nuns are still active, can be seen on one of these hills. Hong wu is said to have founded it to appease several ghosts which had been seen nearby (under the Yuan, executions took place here); in the 19th century, food was still left out to appease the souls of the dead. The temple contains some interesting Ming sculpture (particularly the large statue of Guan yin at the entrance). On the south slope of the hill, the Beauties' well is pointed out to the visitor; the last Chen sovereign is said to have hidden there, with two of his wives, to escape from the victorious Sui troops who were entering the town.

2. The town centre.

The centre corresponds roughly to the southern districts of the old Six Dynasties town. Today, the busiest cross-roads is **Xin jie kou** ("the new cross-roads"), which is a vast roundabout with the statue of Sun Yat sen in the middle. The buildings are modern; the district is a busy one, full of cinemas, department stores, shops and bazaars. The Town Library, the Workers' Cultural Palace, the Fu chang hotel and the **Former Seat of the Guo min dang government** are all near the centre.

The Guo min dang government sat in the ancient palace of the Tai ping emperor Hong Xiu quan (the buildings now house administrative offices). A long gallery leads through the halls of the old palace to an inner courtyard, where a modern building was put up under the Republic (the window of Chiang Kai-shek's office is pointed out). To the west are the gardens of the Tai ping palace (notice the gallery with inlaid calligraphy and the rockeries); it is said that Hong Xiu quan committed suicide on the terrace, and that the thousand ladies of his household all drowned themselves in the ornamental lake nearby, when the news of the emperor's victory reached Nanking; in fact, he probably died of an illness. A stone boat converted into a drawing-room stands in the middle of the lake; Zeng Guo fan rested there, apparently, when, after his victory, he was appointed viceroy of the region.

The Bi lu si Temple is to the west of the ancient palace.

3. The southern districts of the town and the suburbs

Under the Qing, this southern area was the "Chinese town", as opposed to the "Tartar town" (to the east, south of the imperial palace). It was rectangular, and confined to the space surrounded by Hong wu's stone ramparts at this point. Countless little canals fed by the moat crossed and re-crossed it (several still exist); a large straight road leads from the north to the Zhong hua men Gate (the old Ju bao men Gate) in the south; it is an old district, with ancient wooden houses, still inhabited by small craftsmen.

The palace of the eastern king (Hong Xiu quan's assistant) was in the east of this southern district. The three great halls and the garden to the west of them have all survived. The Ministry of the Interior was put here under the Republic, and it became the Police Head Office in 1944. Since 1959, it has housed the **Museum of the Heavenly Kingdom of Great Peace (Tai**

ping tian guo wu guan). *First room:* photograph of the village of Jin tian (Gui ping district, in Guang xi), where the first rising took place; the stone near which flew the flag, before which the rebels took their oath before leaving for their campaign; a map showing the extent of the movement, from Guang xi as far as Nanking (1851–1853); Hong Xiu quan's declaration, made when he entered Nanking (he branded the Manchu oppression as infamous and set out his new policy); seal belonging to Hong Xiu quan and to one of his four sons; text of the agrarian law; an example of tax forms (taxes were fairly low, and collected in spring and autumn); various kinds of coins: *da hua bi* (which was given as a present), *ku bi* (held in reserve), and *xiao qian* (put into circulation); a table of the military organisation; an appeal to the soldiers, asking them to avoid molesting the people; badges worn by the military civil servants on their belts; an appeal for peaceful collaboration, issued in each newly conquered town. *Second room:* cannons cast by the Tai ping (1853, 1855, 1857); a stele put up at Xia guan, north of Nanking, on the banks of the Yang zi, to fix the ferry boat tariffs (it was free for the poor); social laws (equality in marriage, abolition of the custom of buying secondary wives; a wife owed obedience to her husband, however); cultural policy: attempt at suppressing the study of the classics; passports giving permission to travel within the empire; examples of pictures distributed to the people at the New Year *(nian hua)*; map showing the other risings contemporary with the Tai ping rebellion (the Hui and Yi minorities in Yun nan, the Miao minority in Gui zhou, the Society of Little Swords at Shang hai); red and gold seal belonging to Du Wen xiu, a Hui chief from Yun nan inscribed with Arabic and Chinese characters (the original is in the Kun ming museum); standard and weapons belonging to Yun nan Moslems. *Third room:* internal divisions among the leaders; attacks by the Manchu and Europeans; the fall of Tian jing ("the celestial capital"), i.e. Nanking, in 1864.

In an annex: the history of the Tai ping movement shown in coloured pictures. The garden has a waterfall, rockeries, galleries and an example of fine calligraphy in the character *hu* ("tiger").

In the New Street of the Plum-tree garden, and in a street nearby, in the neighbourhood of the Tai ping museum, are the **two houses where the delegation from the Chinese Communist Party stayed** when, in May 1946 and March 1947, they opened negotiations for peace with the Guo min dang. The delegation was led by Zhou En lai and Dong Bi wu. It is pointed out to the visitor that the Guo min dang, who let the houses to the Communists, kept them under a strict watch, and the windows used by the spies are shown.

South of the Zhong hua men Gate, a road leads to the top of the Terrace of the Rain of Flowers Hill (Yu hua tai). It passes near the site of the famous "China Pagoda" (Bao en ta: "the pagoda of gratitude") built under Yong le, in the Bao en si Temple, itself a very ancient foundation. Both were destroyed during the Tai ping troubles; in about 1910, the bronze cupola which surmounted the pagoda could still be seen, lying upside down on the ground, like a basin. In 1943, Japanese archeologists found the stone casket containing the skull of Xuan zang (cf. Peking, Fa yuan si, p. 554) in the ruins of the Bao en si.

The **Yu hua tai** is said to take its name from the following anecdote: under the Liang emperor Wu di, the monk Yun guang is supposed to have settled on the hill, to preach the law of the Buddha; he preached

so well that a rain of flowers fell on his audience;
hence the name "the Terrace of the Rain of Flowers".
The hill was covered with temples (the most famous
were the Yong ning si, the Gao zuo si and the Gan
lu si); several tombs were found there, among them
that of General Deng Yu, who joined Zhu Yuan
zhang's army when he was sixteen, and fell ill and died
during a campaign in Central Asia. Two friends of Sun
Yat sen were also buried there. A special point of
interest today is the stele erected after the liberation
to the memory of 100,000 revolutionaries who were
shot here by order of the Guo min dang. A tea planta-
tion covers the southern slope. The spot is known for
its springs and for its pebbles of many colours, which
are sold to tourists (the monks used to sell them
before); they are sold in a container full of water,
which brings their colours to life.

West of Yu hua tai Hill, and south of An de men
Gate (old gate in the earth fortifications), is the
King of Borneo's Tomb; he died at Nanking in 1408,
when visiting the court of Yong le. Archaeologists
pointed out the little tumulus, with its alley of stone
statues leading to it, a long time ago. As the alley
contains two statues of men, a privilege reserved for a
wang (or king), endless conjectures were made as to
the identity of the dead man. Recently fragments of
the stele have been found, with inscriptions saying
that: "the king of Po ni (Brunei), Ma na ri jia na, died
at Nanking, and was buried outside An de men." The
stele can still be seen, now re-mounted on its tortoise,
as well as the alley of statues leading to the tomb.

The Bull's Head Hill (Niu shou shan). In 1130, Yue
Fei inflicted a resounding defeat on the Jin on this spot.
The hill was covered with temples. Since the liberation,
two southern Tang tombs have been excavated near

here; those of Emperor Li Bian, and his son, emperor Li Jing, the first and second emperors of the dynasty (10th century). Each tomb contains three main rooms and ten less important ones. The walls are decorated with paintings and sculpture. One room has a map of the heavens on the ceiling, and a map of the earth on the floor.

The next landmark to be seen outside the western ramparts, when going north, is the **Light-hearted Lake (Mo chou hu)**, outside the Shui xi men Gate. Mo chou, the "Light-hearted", is a heroine of the time of the Liang emperor Wu. She was a native of Luo yang, and was moved to Nanking with her father; from the age of 13, she had to work on an estate near the lake; at 16, she had a child, whose father was a noble's son. The memory of her misfortunes lasted until the Song dynasty, when the lake was called after her. At that time it was a pleasure-ground, famous for its lotus flowers. A pavilion whose foundations date from the Ming dynasty still stands by the lake: the Pavilion of the Victory at Chess (Sheng qi lou); Zhu Yuan zhang is said to have won a game of chess there, against his counsellor Xu Da. There are several steles, two of which refer to the heroine: one depicts the fair Light-hearted, and the other tells her story. The banks of the lake are now a public park.

4. The eastern district

Hong wu had his palace built here, and in the Qing dynasty, it was here that the Manchu liked to stay. The southern end of the Sun Yat sen avenue crosses the district from east to west. South of this can be seen the scanty remains of the palace.

The site of the **Ming palace** was originally a vast lake, which was filled in (a small pond still remains to the north-west). The buildings, abandoned under Yong le, gradually fell into ruins; little was left at the beginning of the 20th century. Nothing remains now beyond the bases of a few pillars, the flooring of the five bridges (cf. the five bridges spanning the golden waters, at the entrance to the Palace at Peking) and a massive main gate with five arches (Wu chao men).

Today, the visitor comes upon the ruins from the north, that is to say, through the "interior" of the old palace. A stele can be seen erected to the memory of the loyalty of Fang Xiao ru, who stoutly supported Emperor Jian wen against the king of the Yan (i.e. he supported the second Ming emperor against the third, Yong le). After the victory, Yong le asked Fang Xiao ru to draw up the proclamation of his accession to the throne. Fang Xiao ru refused, and then, when commanded to do so, merely wrote "the king of the Yan is an usurper"; he and several of his supporters were executed, and his body was buried secretly on Yu hua tai Hill. A century and a half later, he was rehabilitated, granted the posthumous title of Wen zhong, and the stele was erected.

The **Jiang su Provincial museum** is a little further east, north of Zhong shan nan lu. (The buildings are Chinese in style, but the framework is in reinforced concrete.) *First room:* map of the province; interesting *prehistoric section*, showing objects found during excavations from 1954–1956; the "Qian lian gang Culture" (circa 5000 B.C.): tools of polished stone (a handsome blade with seven holes), pig and dog rearing, hemp-weaving, grey and red pottery with geometrical designs, bone needles, jade jewellery. *Second room:* the four contemporary cultures of Liu lin, Long shan (both in the north), Liang zhu and Hu shu (to the south), during the period from 4000 to 2500 B.C. ; magnificent pottery with black and white designs, jade jewellery, tortoiseshells; the discovery of bronze, about 3000 B.C. (finds uncovered at Nanking, near the University); *Shang era:* some fifteen sites found near Xu Zhou; bronzes (not one single inscription on bone has been found in all the province); *Zhou era:* Founding of the state of Wu; tomb presumed to be that of its founder and ruler, near Wu xi; map of the wars between the Wu and the Yue; *Treaty on War*, by the philosopher Sun Zi, a Wu statesman; *Han era:* iron smelting and salt trade (map); very fine Han pottery with green glaze and arabesque designs. *Third room:* rubbing of a bas-relief carving of a weaving loom; fragments of material; lacquers from Si chuan; a fine niello cross, found in 1960; *Six Dynasties era:* map of Nanking; map of maritime trade with the south seas; several rubbings of great epigraphs; fine collection of tomb figurines; photographs of stone lions from Liang tombs in the Nanking area; cultural life under the Six Dynasties: the painter Gu Kai zhi (392–467); the mathematician Zu Chong zhi, who was born in He bei, but lived in Nanking (he calculated *pi*); the Taoist and alchemist Ge Hong (284–363), who spent his last years at Hang zhou. *Fourth room:* iron agricultural tools (Song); model of machines designed by Huang Dao po for weaving cotton (early Ming); photograph of a Moslem's tomb at Yang zhou (1275); rubbing of the map of the town of Su zhou (1247); replicas of two very expressive statues of *luo han* (from a temple near Su zhou, Song dynasty); copy of *Meng ji bi tan*, a scientific work written by Shen Gua in Jiang su, under the Song; objects found in the two southern Tang tombs (south of Nanking); wall-paintings from a Song tomb (1094); part of a Ming clepsydra from the observatory. *Fifth room: Ming and Qing eras:* chiefly an exhibition of the region's handicrafts; late Qing weaving loom; samples of material; iron basin for evaporating salt (late Qing); map of Jiang su's 23 salt-pans; scroll painting of the town of Su zhou (early Qing); the seven successive stages of a lacquered panel with mother of pearl inlay; jade and ivory work; clocks; embroidery frame; photographs of the pediments of the Su zhou Mosque (1802) and the Nanking Mosque (fine carved bricks); plan of the Yang zhou Mosque; map of the journey made by Xu Xia ke, a famous 16th century geographer, and a native of Jiang su; works by Moslem authors; copies of works printed at Nanking under the Ming emperor Jia jing (1522–1567); plans of Nanking; a brick from the wall (with the name of the maker and the overseer); photographs of a gate in the earth ramparts, and of the site of the naval shipyards; Spanish coin found in 1958, at Nanking; photograph of the Tomb of the King of Borneo who died at Nanking under the Ming; documents referring to the Nanking Imperial College (Guo zi jian). *Sixth room:* furniture belonging to a rich landowner, living at the end of the Qing dynasty; souvenirs of the Heavenly Kingdom of Great Peace; on the walls: enlarged photographs of the coloured illustrations of Lindley's work: *The Ti Ping Revolution* (London, 1866).

5. The Eastern Hills

The Zhong shan men Gate leads out towards the eastern hills, known as the Zi jin shan (Purple and Gold Mountains); the Jin emperor Yuan di (317–323) is said to have given them this name. There are three places to visit: Emperor Hong wu's Mausoleum, Sun Yat sen's tomb, and the Ling fu si Park.

a) Emperor Hong wu's Mausoleum. It is known as Xiao ling, or Huang ling (emperor's tomb). The emperor Tai zu, founder of the Ming dynasty, who died in 1398, at the age of 71, is buried there beside the empress Xiao xi, who died in 1382. (For general remarks on imperial tombs, see p. 622.)

As at the Ming tombs near Peking, the sacred way passed through a Great Gate (Da hong men) and beside a tall stele mounted on a tortoise; 21 yards further on, it turns sharply to the west and crosses a bridge over a little river; then stone animals line it on either side. The sacred way is narrow as it passes between the statues; it is barely 10 feet wide, whereas the one at Shi san ling is over 30 feet wide. At first, the animals are alternately standing and lying: lions, *qi lin* (imaginary animals), camels, elephants, horses, then two pillars, and last of all the military and civilian civil servants. The Ling xing men Gate, over 50 feet wide, was 65 feet beyond the last civilian civil servants. On the other side of the gate, the sacred way turns east, then continues on a north-south axis, which is that of the tomb.

A red gate leads through the surrounding wall (to right and left of it stand recent steles, with inscriptions in several European languages, urging people not to spoil the surroundings of the tomb). The gate opens on to the first courtyard; at the end, ruined steps lead up to a terrace, where the Long en men used to be; a more recent building stands in its place, and houses a series of steles, the largest of which date from Kang xi. On the southern side of the middle stele are inscribed the four characters *Zhi long Tang Song* ("His reign surpassed those of the Tang and the Song"), a tribute rendered by Kang xi to his predecessor. In the centre of the second courtyard stood the Ling en dian; only

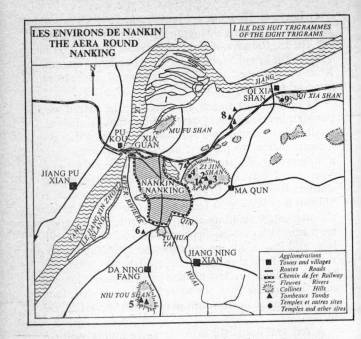

1 MAUSOLEUM OF HONG
 WU (14th C.)
2 TOMB OF SUN YAT SEN
 (20th C.)
3 GU LING SI TEMPLE
4 MOUNT ZI JIN SHAN
 OBSERVATORY

5 SOUTHERN TANG TOMBS
 (10th C.)
6 THE KING OF BORNEO'S
 TOMB (15th C.)
7 TOMBS OF XU DA AND
 LI WEN ZHONG (15th C.)
8 LIANG TOMBS (6th C.)
9 QI XIA SI TEMPLE

the terrace and the bases of the pillars remain; the
façade of the building was nine intercolumniations
long, and five deep (188 feet by 88 feet). The building
now standing on the terrace dates from the 20th century. A new gate (Ling qin men) leads into the third

and last courtyard, which is over 160 yards long. A fine marble bridge crosses a canal, which runs from the east past the foot of the tumulus; beyond it is a massive rectangular building in rough-hewn stone. It measures 210 feet by 118 feet at its base, and is 50 feet high. As the walls are oblique, it measures only 136 feet by 80 feet at the top. A door 10 feet wide leads into a passage travelling the length of the building. The passage slopes considerably; the level at the end is 20 feet higher than at the door. It gives on to a terrace which is bordered on the north by the wall surrounding the tumulus. Ramps at the side lead to a higher platform, surrounded by massive walls. The roofing has vanished. This building corresponds to the square towers in the Ming tombs at Peking, though it is uncertain whether a stele has even been found there. No traces of foundations have been found. The tumulus properly speaking occupies a spur of the hill, and the surrounding wall climbs the spur, taking on a slightly ovoid outline (360–390 yards in diameter).

b) **Sun Yat sen's Tomb (Sun zhong shan ling).** This is east of the Mausoleum, on the southern slope of Zi jin shan. It was built between 1926 and 1929, the year in which Sun Yat sen's body was brought from Peking (cf. Peking, Temple of the Azure Clouds, p. 602). The blue and white used in the building is meant to recall the Guo min dang flag (a white sun on a blue ground). The first three-arched gate has the two characters *Bo ai* ("universal love") on the lintel; from there, an alley of beautiful trees leads up a gentle slope to the main gate, which also has three arches. The four characters *Tian xia wei gong* ("the world belongs to everyone") are inscribed on the pediment. Behind the gate is the Stele Pavilion, a tall, blue-roofed building containing a colossal granite stele. A long flight of steps (eight sections in all) leads up to the mausoleum itself. There are three doors: the Guo min dang flag is on the ceiling; quotations from Sun Yat sen's work and extracts from the 1912 constitution cover the walls, and in the middle is a white marble seated statue of Sun Yat sen, on a pedestal carved in bas-relief, signed by the French sculptor Landowski ("Paris, 1930"). A door in the far wall opens into a circular, domed hall; in the centre, on a lower level, lies a recumbent, marble figure of Sun Yat sen.

c) **The Ling gu si Park** is east of Sun Yat sen's Tomb. A temple stood on the site that Hong wu chose for his tomb, so he had it rebuilt here, and called it the Temple of the Valley of Spirits (Ling gu si). When it was founded, in 1381, the temple was a large one; it gradually fell into ruins. A shaded walk leads to a recent gateway and on to the only surviving building, considerably restored, the **Wu liang dian**; it is so called because it used to house a statue of the Buddha "of immeasurable eternity" *(Wu liang shou fo);* afterwards, it was called by the first two words only, *Wu liang,* and the two characters used were no longer those meaning "without weight" but two others meaning "without beams". The Wu liang dian is in fact a rare example of architecture in which no wood is used (three cradle vaults joined lengthways). In this hall, the classics were read, and books were pressed (cf. the old archives at Peking, p. 495).

A round garden, once a fish-pond, lies behind the Wu liang dian. The surroundings are now a public garden; there is a large pagoda, with a central staircase of reinforced concrete, which was built under the Guo min dang (good view to be had from the top). Walking in the park, the visitor comes upon the Tomb of the monk Bao zhi of the Liang (6th century), with a modern tumulus (of cement!), and a famous Tang stele, with a poem by Li Bai and a design by Wu Dao zi.

Further east there is a recently-founded Buddhist temple, still in use.

6. The road to the Qi xia si

This starts at the Tai ping men Gate, north-east of the town. The main road goes to the Qi xia si, but a narrower one to the right leads up the side of the hill to the **Purple and Gold Hill Observatory (Zi jin shan tian wen tai).** It is one of the biggest in China, after the Peking and Shang hai observatories.

It was founded in 1934 and reorganised after the liberation. Over 200 research workers are attached to it. The telescope can be seen, and also a collection of ancient astronomical instruments arranged on the neighbouring terraces. The principle of some of the instruments was discovered by Zhang Heng of the Han, or by Guo Shou Jing of the Yuan, but the instruments themselves are Ming at the earliest. Most of them date from the Qing. There is a celestial sphere, two instruments used to draw up the map of the heavens, and a gnomon.

Just under two miles north of the Tai ping men Gate, immediately to the left of the Qi xia si road, are the tombs of the two great counsellors of the first Ming emperor, Zhu Yuan zhang; Xu Da and Li Wen zhong. Xu Da, a native of Yang zhou, was a much respected minister; he died in 1384. Li Wen zhong was the emperor's nephew; he distinguished himself by capturing the family and the seals of the last Yuan emperor. Their tombs are a few hundred yards from each other, both facing east. The large steles mounted on tortoises can still be seen (Li Wen zhong's is almost 24 feet high) as well as the stone statues before the tumuli (notice the horses and their riders).

Further north, the road passes through the area which was the **Liang Dynasty Burial Ground** (502–556). It used to be a marsh; now it is rice paddy; only a few statues have been found. The sites of four tombs have been determined; those of four younger brothers of Emperor Wu (he had eleven younger brothers, all of whom died before him; his tomb has not been found).

a) First tomb. A fluted pillar, with a lotus-shaped capital (pronounced Indo-Greek influence) and a *bi xie* (a sort of chimera) with a most expressive face, are all that remain.

b) Second tomb. A stele (now housed in a recently-built pavilion) with a remarkably well-preserved text, signed by a certain Bei, and a *bi xie* sheltering a smaller one are all that remain.

c) Third tomb. Only two *bi xie* are left.

d) Fourth tomb. This one is in the courtyard of the Gan jia xiang village school; the sculpture is the best preserved of all: four steles mounted on tortoises, a pillar *(hua biao)* and two *bi xie*.

The **Qi xia si** is twelve miles further on, hidden in the bottom of a valley, on a very fine site. It was founded in 487, restored under the Tang and the Yuan. The present buildings date from Guang xu (1875–1908). The temple is still in use, and the present Superior, the Rev. Guang Jian, who is also Director of the Buddhist Association of Jiang su, is a highly respected monk (1965).

To the left of the entrance, a pavilion houses a stele inscribed with the calligraphy of the Tang emperor Gao zong. The architecture is generous, with upturned corners to the eaves. The temple contains a beautiful little Tang statue of the Buddha, and a very fine library (7,200 books). Another hall is devoted to the Japanese monk Jian Zhen, who came to China under the Tang and stayed there for three years (a small re-mounted statue of Jian Zhen, given by the Japanese in the 20th century; a photograph of the Zhao ti si, the temple which Jian Zhen founded on his return to Japan, and where he is buried).

To the right of the temple is a fine six-storey pagoda founded by Wen di of the Sui (the octagonal base has bas-relief carvings of eight moments in the life of the Buddha; higher up there are four large, very expressive guardians). The Thousand Buddha Cliff (Qian fo ling), with sculpted rock shrines, the oldest of which date from the southern Qi, is beside the pagoda.

OTHER TOWNS SOUTH OF THE YANG ZI

Zhen jiang

Zhen jiang is on the south bank of the Yang zi, at the point where the Grand Canal flows into the river; it is on the Nanking–Shang hai railway line.

Under the Southern Dynasties the town was called Xu zhou; its development began with the opening of the Grand Canal under the Sui. Its present name dates from the Song. Marco Polo visited the town under the Yuan, and left the following description: "The inhabitants have large quantities of silk which they use for making gold fabrics and different kinds of silk; great and rich merchants are to be seen there. Game is plentiful and there are abundant supplies of everything needed from day to day." Judging by what Marco Polo says, trade was even brisker in the little town of Gua zhou on the opposite bank. But a European visitor, writing at the end of the 18th century, was struck by the number of junks and boats which came to tie up alongside the quay. Concessions were created there, and British and French consulates opened. The town is still an important lower Yang zi harbour, famous for its silk, vinegar and pickled vegetables. The population is 200,000.

The town, built partly on an outcrop of rock, is one of the most attractive in the lower Yang zi valley. **Golden Hill (Jin shan),** 105 feet high, is a few miles west of the town; the Jin shan si, a temple founded in 1021, stands there. **Jiao shan Hill** in the middle of the river is famous for its scenery.

Zhou yang

Zhou yang is a small town on the Shang hai–Nanking railway line, 15 miles south east of Zhen jiang. Several Qi (479–502) and Liang (502–557) dynasty tombs can still be seen in the neighbourhood of the town. Ten have been found altogether; only part of their sculpture still survives (bi xie, a sort of imaginary animal, pillars, steles).

The tombs can be divided into five groups: the *first group* is 9 miles north-east of the town, and includes the tomb of the Qi Emperor Gao di, the Tai an ling (dated 482), and that of Gao di's father, the Yong an ling (it is the oldest of all, and dates from 479); the *second group* is 10 miles north-east of the town, and includes one tomb only, that of a brother of the Qi Emperor Jing di, the Xiu an ling (dated 495); the *third group* is 12 miles from the town, on the northern slopes of the Shui jing shan, and includes two tombs which have not yet been identified; the *fourth group* is 9½ miles east of the town, north of the village of Rong jia cun; it includes one tomb, that of the Qi Emperor Wu di, the Jing an ling (dated 493); the *fifth group*, 7 miles east of the town, includes four tombs; 1. the tomb of the Qi Emperor Ming di, the Xing an ling (dated 498); 2. that of the Liang Emperor Wen di, the Jian ling, slightly north of the one before (dated 502?); 3. the tomb of the Liang Emperor Wu di, Wen di's son, the Xiu ling, near the Huang ye si Temple (early 6th century); 4. the tomb of the Liang Emperor Jian wen di, the Zhuang ling, north of the Xiu ling (dated 552).

Ju rong xian

Ju rong xian is a small town about 18 miles east of Zhou yang. The **tomb of Xiao ji** (502–557), a member of the Liang royal family, can still be seen there. The statues are in good condition (a pair of *bi xie*, two pillars, the stele).

Chang zhou

Chang zhou is on the Nanking–Shang hai railway line, half way between Zhen jiang and Su zhou. It was founded under the Sui, and owed its size to the fact that the Grand Canal washes its walls. It is now a centre for the textile and food industries. The **Tian ning si Temple,** the **Red Plum Pavilion** (Hong mei tang) and **Qu Qiu bai's house,** now converted into a museum, are all worth a visit.

Wu xi

Wu xi is Chinese for "without tin"; a legend says that tin *(xi)* was to be found in the hill nearby under the Zhou dynasty, but that the vein was exhausted under the Han dynasty, and the town earned the name of Wu xi.

It is on the Nanking–Shang hai railway line, 31 miles north-west of Su zhou, on the north bank of Lake Tai hu. It is one of the largest industrial towns in the province, and has a population of 600,000.

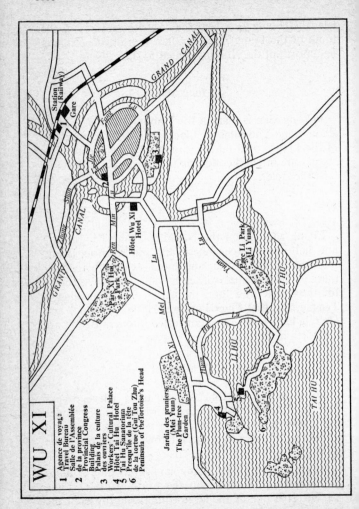

WU XI

1 Agence de voyages
  Travel Bureau
2 Salle de l'Assemblée
  de la province
  Provincial Congress
  Building
3 Palais de la culture
  des ouvriers
  Workers' Cultural Palace
4 Hôtel Tai Hu Hotel
5 Tai Hu Sanatorium
6 Presqu'île de la tête
  de la tortue (Gui Tou Zhu)
  Peninsula of the Tortoise's Head

Jardin des pruniers
(Mei Yuan)
The Plum-tree
Garden

Wu xi was founded under the Han, and like Su zhou, it was under the commandery of Gui ji. Over the years that followed, it never seems to have been more than a little country town. With the advent of modern industry at the beginning of the 20th century, the town suddenly expanded. In 1933, rich Chinese, with the help of foreign technicians, built 45 filatures, 5 flour mills, 9 cotton ginning factories, 18 oil-extracting plants and a soap factory. The population was 500,000 at that time. It soon supplanted Su zhou and became a lively commercial centre, where goods (cereals) from the surrounding area were collected before being sent on to Shang hai by water. The town was also famous for its municipal library, which contained 170,000 volumes. New industries have been developed since the liberation, particularly the machine-building industry.

Wu xi is also famous for little painted clay figurines which are made there, known as Hui shan ni ren, Hui shan figurines, after the name of the hill from which the clay to make them is dug, in the western suburbs of the town. They were made as early as the Ming dynasty, when peasants used to make them for sale at the market; under the Qing, the technique was taken over by specialised craftsmen who made statuettes of characters from operas and plays (particularly characters from Kun qu, the southern regional theatre). The names of several of the craftsmen are still remembered today: Zhou A sheng, Ding Tuo zi, and Ding A jin, who always made models of scenes for three characters. Several thousand people still work in the workshops where the statuettes are made; once completed, they are sent all over the country.

The town contains no old buildings or archaeological remains and is not very interesting in itself.

Some pleasant parks have been laid out, however, in the western suburbs, among them the **Xi hui gong yuan,** which still contains the remains of some old temples. The **Ji chang yuan,** the garden at the foot of the hill, was created at the beginning of the 16th century by a high-ranking official. The buildings are recent, but the lay-out of the garden is exactly as it was.

The **village where Xu Xia ke (1585–1641) was born.** Xu Xia ke, the famous geographer who wrote an account of his journey through south China, was born in Nan yang zhi cun, a village near Jiang yin xian, about 25 miles north of Wu xi. His tomb can still be seen there today, and the Qing shan tang, a little building put up in 1961, contains several steles referring to him; his memory is still fresh among the villagers.

Lake Tai hu

Lake Tai hu stretches south from Wu xi. After Lake Dong ting and Lake Po yang, it is one of the biggest lakes in the country; it covers an area of 1,397 square miles, and is fed by several rivers: the Zhao xi and the Jing xi to the south-west, the Liu he and the Wo song jiang to the east. Over 90 islands are scattered over its surface; the biggest are the Ma ji shan (in the north-west), the Dong ting xi shan and the Dong ting dong shan (in the south-east). Fish are reared in the lake, and water plants are grown there (lotus, water-chestnut). The shores of the lake are famous for their beautiful scenery and for their mulberry-trees; several convalescent homes have been built there recently.

The main hall of the **Zi jin an Temple** on the Dong ting dong shan island still contains some magnificent statues (among them a set of *luo han*) said to date from the Song.

Yi xing

It is about 9 miles west of Lake Tai hu; the town was founded under the Han. It is famous for its pottery kilns (south of the town, in a little village called Ding shu zhen). A beautiful white marble archway dating from 1627 stands in front of the **Temple of Confucius** (the temple contains some fine statues).

SU ZHOU

Su zhou is in the south of Jiang su, about 12 miles from Lake Tai hu, on the old imperial canal. A range of hills lies between it and the lake, the most famous of which is the Tiger Hill. It is a very ancient town, well-known for its silks since the Song dynasty. Since the liberation, many new industries have been started and it is pointed out to the visitor that numerous factory chimneys have now grown up beside the town's seven pagodas. The population is 600,000.

History

1. From its beginnings up to the Tang Dynasty. Su zhou, with Cheng du and Shao xing, is one of the oldest towns in the Yang zi basin. King He Lü of Wu founded it in the 6th century and made it his capital. According to later texts, (particularly the *Su zhou fu zhi*), the town was already about as big as it was later under the Song. It already had "eight gates and eight water gates". Parts of the walls were for a long time to retain the names given to them under the Wu; the north gate was known as Qi Gate (after an ally state); the north-west gate was the Gate of the Defeat of Chu (the Wu troops used to leave from here when going to attack their dangerous neighbour); the south-west gate was the Xu Gate (called after one of He Lü's ministers); the south gate was the Serpent Gate (the serpent was compared to the state of Yue, which finally conquered Wu). No evidence exists of the boundaries of the first settlement. A tradition still alive today holds that He Lü was buried on Tiger Hill, with large numbers of the swords which represented the strength of his kingdom. The kingdom gradually declined: in 473 B.C., the kingdom of Yue annexed its land, then in 315 B.C. Chu conquered Yue and the Su zhou area became part of the great western kingdom.

Qin shi Huang di attached the town to the "commandery of Gui ji". Liu Bang, the founder of the Han dynasty, made his younger brother, Liu Jia, king of Jing, and Liu Bi, king of Wu. At the death of Liu Bi (154), the town once more became part of the "commandery of Gui ji". When Si ma Qian came here, he was most struck by the beauty of the buildings *(Histo-*

rical Records, Biography of the Lord of Chun shen). At the beginning of the 3rd century B.C., Sun Quan, the founder of the kingdom of Wu, lived at Su zhou for a short time, before transferring his capital to Jian ye (Nanking), which was the economic and cultural centre of the lower Yang zi throughout the Southern Dynasties period. Su zhou had only a secondary rank; but it benefited, like the rest of the region, from the arrival of hosts of emigrants from the north, and became a base for the Han penetration of the south, towards the present province of Zhe jiang. The population of Su zhou took part in the Sun En rising, at the end of the 4th century.

Under the Sui, the town became more important once more, and it was given the name of Su zhou in 589; work was begun on the Grand Canal, which passed close by it. It continued to develop under the Tang (it is mentioned by name in poetry of the Tang period) and under the Five Dynasties. Some of the gardens (part of the Cang lang ting in particular) and temples (the Yuan yan si, on Tiger Hill, and the Kai yuan si) date from this period.

2. The Song and the Yuan. The Song and the "withdrawal" towards the south brought about a great development in Su zhou (then called Ping jiang fu). Two documents help to form an idea of the town at this time: a local history, the *Song Ping jiang cheng fang kao*, and a map of the town, carved in the 12th century (on a stele now in the Temple of Confucius). The town was the same size then as it is now. It was a rectangular shape, on a north-south axis, enclosed within walls and surrounded by canals. It had six gates: one to the north, one to the south, and two on the two other sides. Six canals ran from north to south, and fourteen from east to west. The administrative district was in the centre of the town. The Xuan miao guan and the Bei si were to the north; the Wan sui yuan (its "twin pagodas" still survive today) was to the east; the Can lang ting garden was to the south; and finally, the Kai yuan si was to the west. The town became a centre for silk-weaving; wood, floated there, was then sold, and so were flowers (particularly peonies, the best of which rivalled the best in Luo yang). Its development was twice hampered, once by the looting of the Jin armies in 1128, and later by the looting of the Mongol armies in 1275.

In 1276, the Yuan called the town Ping jiang lu. Marco Polo described it: "Sugui is a very noble city and great, the people of which are idolaters and are subject to the rule of the great Kaan, and have money of notes, and they have silk in very great quantities. And they live by trade and by crafts, and they make many cloths of golds and of silk for their clothing... The city is so large in its circuit that it is forty miles round. And it has so very great quantity of people in it that no one could know their number. Moreover I tell you that if they were men or arms, those of the province of Mangi, they would easily conquer... all the rest of the world. But they are... not men... used to the exercice of arms; but I tell you that they are clever... merchants and cunning men of all crafts, and also there are great very wise men called Sages, like our philosophers, and great natural physicians who know nature very well... Moreover I tell you quite truly that there are quite six thousand bridges of stone in this city, below the greater part of which one galley and two would well pass. And again I tell you that in those mountains of this town the rhubarb grows there... and ginger... in very great abundance."

In 1356, Zhang Shi cheng rebelled against the Mongols, took Su zhou, and declared himself "king of Zhou". He managed to stay there for ten years or so, but had to submit to Zhu Yuan zhang in 1367 (Zhu Yuan zhang founded the Ming Dynasty in the next year).

3. The Ming and the beginning of the Qing. In 1368, the town reverted to its old name, Su zhou. The silk industry was considerably developed at this time, and Su zhou became one of the most important centres in the whole empire. Some texts have enabled Chinese historians to say that silk production methods were already capitalistic. According to the *True Accounts of the reign of Shen zong* (1573–1620), production was very specialised, and most workmen hired themselves out by the day to one of the large contractors *(ji hu)*, as most of them did not own their own machines: "the population was wretched, living from day to day, unable to know each morning how the evening would find them; if there was work, they subsisted, if not, they died; all the unemployed would take up their stands on the bridge at dawn, and wait in their hundreds... craning their necks to watch... if the *ji hu* cut down the work, a whole crowd would be left without food or clothes". There was a rising by the workmen in 1626; as there were five leaders, it was known as the "rebellion of the five". Su zhou silk and embroidery were highly prized at court, and the Qing made the town into an autonomous administrative district, so that production could be more closely controlled. Steles dated 1715, 1734, 1822 have been found, with texts forbidding the workmen to go on strike.

The city was known for its pleasures as well as for its industry. Mr. Hüttner, a member of Lord Macartney's embassy, wrote at the end of the 18th century: "This town, which is the school of the greatest artists, the most well-known scholars, the richest merchants, the best actors, the most nimble acrobats, is also the home of delicately-made women with tiny feet. It rules Chinese tastes in matters of fashion and speech, and is the meeting-place of the richest pleasure-seekers and gentlemen of leisure in China. All these attributes demand that it be classed as one of the chief cities in China. It is so big that Lord Macartney covered only part of it, and he was over four hours on the road. Canals thronged with gondolas cross it in all directions; it is a delightful place to walk in, both inside and outside the walls."

For a whole class of people of leisure, Su zhou was an earthly paradise; as the proverb said: "In heaven there is paradise; on earth, Su zhou and Hang zhou" *(Shang you tian tang, xia you Su Hang).*

4. From 1850 to 1950. After they had taken Nanking, the Tai ping troops, commanded by their *Zhong wang* Li Xiu cheng, reached Su zhou, and entered it without striking a single blow (1860). In his *Memoirs,* Li Xiu cheng tells how the crowd ran to meet them, and that in the streets, the doors of the houses and shops carried posters saying: "We agree to exterminate the soldiers and civil servants of Chang and He" (two local officials). The king of the Tai ping settled in a palace in the north of the town, which now contains the Town Historical Museum.

When the movement failed, Su zhou gradually entered the economic orbit of Shang hai and was subjected to European influence. The city was officially opened to foreign trade on September 28th 1896, and a Japanese concession and an international concession were created (in the south of the town). Towards 1920, the population was 280,000, including 80 Japanese, 60 Americans, and about 40 other foreigners. Silk spinning and weaving were still the main industries; the raw materials came almost entirely from silk-worm rearing houses in the immediate vicinity. The spinning was mainly done in two large factories, and the weaving chiefly at home (4,000 hand looms).

5. Since the liberation. The economy has expanded since 1949; the textile industry is still the most important, but chemical industries have been started as well. Other lesser industries are paper-making, hand-embroidery, manufacture of sandalwood fans and parasols.

The Gardens of Su zhou. Su zhou has always been famous for its gardens, and still is; it is an ancient tradition which has been handed down by the successive dynasties. As early as the 10th century, a garden existed on the site of what is now the Cang lang ting; gardens were created under the Song, the Yuan, the Ming and the Qing; the most recent, the Xi yuan, dates from Guang xu (it is said to combine the styles of all the earlier ones). The names of fifteen parks are known, some of which have survived until now; six have been restored since the liberation and are now open to the public.

The history of the gardens sheds light on the people who owned them, who were mainly rich local officials, or sometimes high-ranking court officials (civil officials, like Wang Xian chen, the censor, or soldiers, like General Han Shi zhong). After a life spent surrounded by distinction and honour at the capital, they would retire to their native province, to finish their days in peace; there they would buy a plot of land and build a "garden" (*yuan lin*) which was in fact a villa. Next to the garden properly speaking there was usually a house, sometimes a large one (like the one in the Gang shi yuan).

Walking in these sumptuous surroundings, it is easy to imagine the life of their owners, full of small gatherings among scholarly friends, suppers with yellow wine to stimulate the intellect, well-chosen concerts. They would vie with each other in their knowledge of literature, write poems and dedicate them; later they would be engraved on stones, to be set in the walls of the galleries. These intellectual pleasures have austerity about them; for mandarins who had tasted the pomp of an active official life, their retirement amounted almost to a renunciation of the world. They affected to live a rustic life, to return to nature, "de cultiver son jardin" (see later on the etymology of the "Plain Man's Politics" Garden, Zhuo zheng yuan). All the gardens are carefully cut off from the rest of the world and the life of the surrounding town. A small door leads into them, sometimes at the end of a narrow lane, giving no hint of the existence of the oasis of peace behind it. The brilliant red doors flanked by stone lions denoting the *ya men* were very different.

The history of these domains also reveals the instability of Chinese society. Countless gardens were sold or gambled away, by incapable sons, sometimes as early as the second generation. It is impossible to quote the names of all the owners of each one, but one garden may have five or six different owners in three centuries. A competitive society, the Chinese society allowed large fortunes to be amassed, but not handed down.

To understand the significance of these gardens, they must be considered within their philosophic context. A garden is a microcosm, in which a man can construct his world; they contained minerals, plants and animals (they have vanished now, but used to be an important element; there are still fish, and caged birds at the Gang shi yuan). Buddhist ideas, particularly those of the Dhyana school, which inspired the famous Zen gardens in Japan, are connected with the creation of these microcosms. Often the gardens have been sold to a monastery at some time of their history, and annexed to a temple, so that monks would meditate there, as the scholar had done before them. The Garden of the Forest of Lions (Shi zi lin) is an example: it was created by the superior of a monastery.

The creator of a garden must be a person of extremely varied knowledge. The true master (the names of some are still known) must be an architect, a painter, a poet and more. The aim is to create as many perspectives as possible within a confined space. He has four main elements at his disposal: a) **buildings,** sometimes massive *(lou, tang, shi)*, sometimes on a smaller scale, or elongated, taking the form of galleries *(lang)* or isolated, summer-houses and pavilions *(ting, ge)*; b) **hillocks,** always artificial, as the town is built on a plain; sometimes carefully-chosen rocks are cemented one on top of another; sometimes they are covered with earth and vegetation, so that they seem natural; c) **water,** always available, as the land is marshy; still water, full of lotus plants and fish; little, irregularly-shaped lakes, with islets and bridges; a few springs, occasional waterfalls, but no fountains; d) **vegetation,** arranged in clumps: bamboo groves, tiny coppices of different kinds of scented trees, dotted about the hillocks; but few flowers (at least at the moment).

Several other things can be used by the landscape gardener: *bian e*, or tablets, inscribed, sometimes by the composer's own hand, with a name recalling a literary allusion, or suggesting a landscape; *hu shi*, "stones from the lake", carefully chosen and put at the bottom of the Lake Tai hu for several decades, to be washed and eroded by the waters; *lou chuang* or *hua chuang*, "lattice windows", square, round, rectangular or polygonal, with complicated latticework made in earthenware and afterwards painted with whitewash (the designs are sometimes geometrical, sometimes emblematic); *zhuan ke*, "carved bricks", little earthenware pictures, with scenes of everyday life (plays, banquets, fishing, games), animals (fables) or leaves; this kind of ornamentation appeared under the Ming.

Description

Although the walls have been knocked down recently, it is easy to trace the boundaries of the old Song town. It is still surrounded by canals, on which numerous flat-bottomed boats are still used. Streets and canals cut through the town at right angles to one another. Many houses have one street gate, and another giving directly on to the canal (hence the name "the Venice of China", sometimes given to Su zhou). Tourists can no longer be taken on the canals, and can only catch sight of them beneath the little hump-backed bridges. The streets are generally wide and straight, lined, like the ones at Nanking, with plane-trees imported from France. In summer, the shops have no fronts, and open directly on to the street. The northern, central and southern districts will be described, followed by the suburbs to the west, and finally the Protection of Sages Temple.

1. The northern districts

The railway line lies to the north of the town; the road to the centre crosses the northern canal, and then Ping men lu Street leads towards the south. The great pagoda of the **Temple of Gratitude (Bao en si)** also called the Northern Temple (Bei si), can soon be seen on the left. The pagoda has a long history. A temple was founded on this site in the reign of Sun Quan, the founder of the state of Wu, in the 3rd century. At the end of the 10th century, a new temple, known as the Bao en si, was built, with an eleven-storey pagoda; everything was destroyed by the Jin in 1130. Under the Southern Song, a temple and a nine-storey pagoda were built; they were restored several times, and finally burned in about 1570. Both were extensively repaired under Kang xi. The temple is now used as a depot, so all that can now be seen is the nine-storey pagoda, built in wood, with a covered gallery at its base.

Left after the pagoda, Xi bei Street leads to the **Historical Museum.** The building once belonged to Li Xiu cheng, the king of the Tai ping. A large section of the exhibits are on show in a big hall which used to be a private theatre (central stage). *Prehistoric Era:* Liang zhu neolithic civilisation (black pottery); *Zhou Era:* map of Zhou sites in the lower Yang zi River area; pottery with cord design; bronze and iron ware; a military treatise by the philosopher Sun Zi; bronze sword from the state of Wu (found south of Su zhou); map of the canals in the Chun qiu period (Su zhou was already linked by a canal to Lake Tai hu); *Han Dynasty:* map of the Gui ji commandery (note the advance towards the south from the old Wu area); objects found in tombs in the Su zhou neighbourhood; *the Six Dynasties:* map showing the thrust of population towards the south, with approximate figures; mining, photograph of an old copper mine at Tong jing shan ("the copper well hill") in the state of Wu; text on gold-mining at Jin shan ("gold hill"); *qing* pottery; map to show how Su zhou joined in with the Sun En rising (about 400); *The Sui and the Tang Dynasties:* map of the Grand Canal; texts on Su zhou's economy; map of the water-works near the Tai hu (28 locks); the Han shan si Temple trading centre (west of Su zhou, cf. later on), which dealt in rice, soya-beans, tea, bamboo, wood (several authors refer to it, among them Bai Ju yi); list of intellectuals who were natives of Su zhou under the Tang (nineteen names have survived); *The Song and the Yuan dynasties:* development of silk weaving as a craft (already in existence under the Five

Dynasties); pieces of silk (some of them found in the Tiger Hill Pagoda, cf. later on); articles from the tomb of a princess (the lady Cao) discovered in 1964, south-west of Su zhou: silk jacket, silver toilet articles (scissors, mirror, casket, brush, boxes for make-up, and a large box containing all these things); Song porcelain found at Su zhou; rubbings of three Song steles, kept in the Temple of Confucius: a map of Su zhou, a map of the heavens and a map of the earth: photographs of very expressive *luo han* statues, from Bao sheng si (a temple at Jiao zhu zhen, near Su zhou); *Ming and Qing Dynasties:* map of hydraulic engineering work at that period; ten Qing drawings showing various techniques for working silk; samples of Qing silk; stele with the plan of a factory; two hewn stones used for rolling fabrics (the lengths of silk were rolled round a cylinder placed between these two stones, the craftsman climbed on to the top one, and used his weight to swing it first one way, then the other); a carved brick; clocks made at Su zhou; map showing the provinces represented at Su zhou by "associations" *(hui guan);* photograph of the fortifications built to protect the town from Japanese pirates; portrait of Jen Huan, who defended Su zhou against the pirates; stele in memory of the workmen's rising in 1626 (known as the "rising of the five"); three steles forbidding the workmen to go on strike under the Qing.

The **"Plain Man's Politics" Garden (Zhuo zheng yuan)** is next to the museum (to the left on the way out). It was laid out in the 16th century by Wang Xian chen the censor, who retired here "to cultivate his garden" after a hard political life. The idea for its name came from a remark made by Fan Yue (Jin dynasty): "to cultivate one's garden to meet one's daily needs, that is what is known as the politics of a plain man".

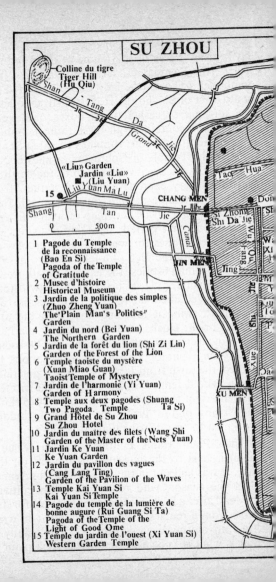

SU ZHOU

Colline du tigre
Tiger Hill
(Hu Qiu)

Hu Shan Tang

Da Grand Jie

«Liu» Garden
Jardin «Liu»
(Liu Yuan)

Liu Yuan Ma Lu

15

CHANG MEN

Tao Hua

Shang Tan Jie

Si Zhong Shi Da Jie

0   500m

JIN MEN

Jing

XU MEN

1 Pagode du Temple
   de la reconnaissance
   (Bao En Si)
   Pagoda of the Temple
   of Gratitude
2 Musee d'histoire
   Historical Museum
3 Jardin de la politique des simples
   (Zhuo Zheng Yuan)
   The"Plain Man's Politics"
   Garden
4 Jardin du nord (Bei Yuan)
   The Northern Garden
5 Jardin de la forêt du lion (Shi Zi Lin)
   Garden of the Forest of the Lion
6 Temple taoiste du mystère
   (Xuan Miao Guan)
   Taoist Temple of Mystery
7 Jardin de l'harmonie (Yi Yuan)
   Garden of Harmony
8 Temple aux deux pagodes (Shuang Ta Si)
   Two Pagoda Temple
9 Grand Hôtel de Su Zhou
   Su Zhou Hotel
10 Jardin du maître des filets (Wang Shi Yuan)
   Garden of the Master of the Nets
11 Jardin Ke Yuan
   Ke Yuan Garden
12 Jardin du pavillon des vagues
   (Cang Lang Ting)
   Garden of the Pavilion of the Waves
13 Temple Kai Yuan Si
   Kai Yuan Si Temple
14 Pagode du temple de la lumière de
   bonne augure (Rui Guang Si Ta)
   Pagoda of the Temple of the
   Light of Good Ome
15 Temple du jardin de l'ouest (Xi Yuan Si)
   Western Garden Temple

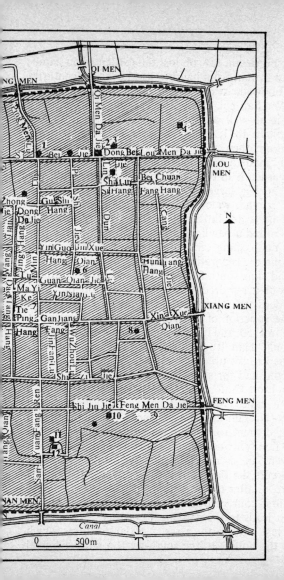

After his death, his son lost the garden when gambling, and it went from hand to hand over the centuries which followed. At one time it belonged to the son-in-law of Wu San gui. Under the Tai ping, Li Xiu cheng owned it as well as the house next to it (now the museum). In 1871, it became the seat of the Banners Association, then a school was started there, and it was only made a public garden in 1952.

The garden is in two parts, separated by a wall; the eastern part is larger. As the park was laid out on marshy ground, water occupies most of both gardens (several islets are linked by dykes). To the east, it is centred round a pavilion, the Pavilion of Distant Perfumes (Yuan xiang tang); to the west, a long gallery runs along the separating wall.

A road runs south from the entrance to the garden, and about a hundred yards further on, on the right hand side, is the **Garden of the Forest of Lions (Shi zi lin).** The superior of the Hua zhan si Temple had it laid out in 1350, and it was originally part of the temple. The monk, Tian Ru, belonged to the Dhyana school; he wanted to set up a memorial to his master, Zhong Feng, who had for some time lived in a place known as "the Lion Cliff" (hence the name of the garden). Tian Ru called together a galaxy of designers and painters (Ni Yun lin, Zhu De run, Chao Shan zhang) and asked them to lay out the gardens. Later on the Huang family owned them, under the Qing; by then they were in a much-deteriorated state. The last owners were the Bai family, who presented the garden to the town after the liberation.

The first courtyard is square and a passage on the far right leads to the garden. It consists of two parts: to the east and north, a series of large rooms which formed the house; to the south-west, a large artificial

JARDIN DE LA POLITIQUE DES SIMPLES
(ZHUO ZHENG YUAN)

« THE PLAIN MAN'S POLITICS » GARDEN

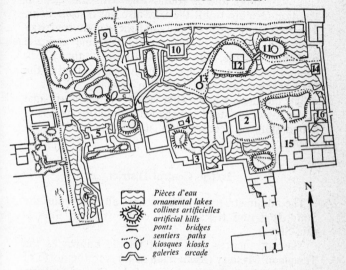

Pièces d'eau
ornamental lakes
collines artificielles
artificial hills
ponts   bridges
sentiers   paths
kiosques   kiosks
galeries   arcade

N

1 Entrance
2 Pavilion of Distant Perfumes
3 "The little Waves"
4 The land of Perfumes
5 Pavilion of the Thirty-six Mandarin Ducks
6 The Pavilion of the Pagoda's Shadow
7 Kiosk where one stops to listen
8 Fan Kiosk
9 Pavilion of the Inverted Shadow

10 Pavilion with a view of the mountain
11 Kiosk where one awaits the Hoar-Frost
12 Pavilion of the Perfumed Snow and of the Abundant Clouds
13 "The scent of the lotus flowers is everywhere"
14 Retreat among the Bamboos and the Sterculias
15 Pipa Tree Garden
16 Eastern Garden

lake surrounded by rocks and hillocks. The Hall of
the Spreading Cloud (Wo yun shi) and the approach
to it are perhaps the most charming, and certainly
very typical of their kind: the building stands on an
eminence, and a path winds up to it among caves and

over little suspension bridges. There are two islands in the lake, a square one with the Octagonal Pavilion (Liu jiao ting) and a round one with the Central Pavilion (Hu xin ting); the lake also has a stone boat. The west bank rises steeply, and there a covered way links the Pavilion of the Gentle Perfume and the Spreading Shade, the Waterfall Kiosk, the Kiosk where the Plum-tree is asked Questions, the Hall of the Two Scented Immortals, the Fan Pavilion.

The **Northern Garden (Bei yuan)** is in the north-east of the town; it dates from the Ming dynasty. As it is in a bad state of deterioration, it has not yet been re-opened to the public.

2. The Central District

The administrative buildings were all here under the Song. It is now the shopping centre (bazaar, Friendship Store).

The entrance to the Taoist temple known as the **Temple of Mystery (Xuan miao guan)** is to the north of Guan qian jie Street. It was founded in the 3rd century, then rebuilt and renamed under the Tang and later under the Northern Song. The Jin armies destroyed it in 1128. In 1146, Wang Huan, the prefect of Su zhou, had two galleries built, and decorated with pictures, but nothing remains of them. In 1181, the Hall of the Three Qing was built. In 1264, the temple was given its present name: Xuan miao guan. It was restored several times under the Ming and the Qing (particularly under Kang xi). It was burned in 1816, and considerably damaged during the Tai ping period.

The entrance pavilion (containing large statues of the celestial guardians) gives on to an enormous courtyard, with the Hall of the Three Qing at the far end.

JARDIN DE LA FORÊT DU LION
(SHI ZI LIN)
GARDEN OF THE FOREST OF THE LION

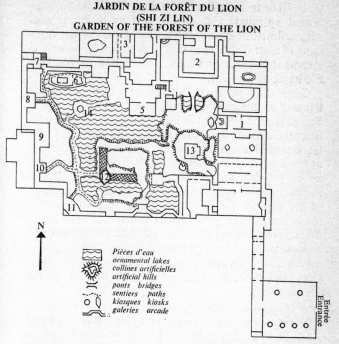

Pièces d'eau ornamental lakes
collines artificielles artificial hills
ponts bridges
sentiers paths
kiosques kiosks
galeries arcade

1 Small square room
2 Hall where the Thuya is shown
3 Garden of the Five Old Pines
4 Pavilion with a view of the mountain
5 Lotus Flower Chamber
6 Stone boat
7 Pavilion of the Gentle Perfume and of the Spreading Shade

8 Waterfall Kiosk
9 Kiosk where one questions the Plum-tree
10 Hall of the Two Scented Immortals
11 Fan Pavilion
12 Octagonal Pavilion
13 Hall of the Spreading Cloud
14 Central Pavilion

A market used to be held here, with travelling show-men and performances of plays; the small tradesmen took refuge in the arcades surrounding it. The San

Qing Dian is an enormous rectangular building, supported by pillars and surmounted by a double roof with upturned eaves corners. The statues of the three Qing (Taoist deities) can still be seen inside, as well as several steles, one of which is attributed to Wu Dao zi (depicting Lao Zi).

Guan qian jie street (the street which passes the temple) continues westwards, and meets Ren min lu Street. Here the visitor turns to the left; about 600 yards from the crossroads, on the right, is the entrance to the **Garden of Harmony (Yi yuan)**. This is the most recent of the gardens in Su zhou; it was laid out under Guang xu, by the official, Gu Wen bin, who spent 200,000 ounces of silver on it. The architect turned to the oldest of the gardens for inspiration, and borrowed several ideas from them. Three others which had been abandoned provided the rocks. It was said the garden was particularly rich in four things: stones from the lake, tablets above the entrance to the buildings, white pine-trees and animals. The garden was opened to the public in 1953.

A covered way running from north to south divides it into two; its windows open on to both sides, east and west. The Pavilion of Stones Listening to the Lute (Shi ting qin shi) lies in the eastern part; it contains a lute said to have belonged to the poet Su Dong po of the Song dynasty. The stele in the Jade Rainbow Pavilion (Yu hong ting) was inscribed by the Yuan painter, Wu Zhong gui. The artificial lakes and hillocks (with caves hollowed out in them) lie in the larger, western part.

The **Two Pagoda Temple (Shuang ta si)** is to the south-east, in a narrow little street called Ding hui si gang. The first temple was founded under the Tang in the 9th century; two brick pagodas were added under the Song, which inspired the name: the Two Pagoda

JARDIN DE L'HARMONIE
(YI YUAN)
GARDEN OF HARMONY

1 Pavillon des pierres qui
 écoutent le luth
 Pavillon of stones which
 listen to the lute
2 Pavillon qui retient le visiteur
 Pavilion which holds back
 the visitor
3 Pavillon de l'arc-en-ciel de
 jade
 Jade Rainbow Pavilion
4 Salle «du Bateau de pierre»
 Hall «of the stone boat»

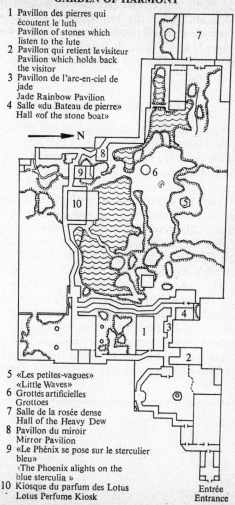

5 «Les petites-vagues»
 «Little Waves»
6 Grottés artificielles
 Grottoes
7 Salle de la rosée dense
 Hall of the Heavy Dew
8 Pavillon du miroir
 Mirror Pavilion
9 «Le Phénix se pose sur le sterculier
 bleu»
 ‹The Phoenix alights on the
 blue sterculia »
10 Kiosque du parfum des Lotus
 Lotus Perfume Kiosk

Entrée
Entrance

Temple. Both temple and pagodas have been burned several times. After the last fire, in 1860, the two pagodas were restored once again. The temple has now disappeared, and a school occupies the site; nothing can be seen but the two pagodas, which are visible from the street.

3. The Southern Districts

The southern part of the town was not entirely built up in the 19th and the beginning of the 20th centuries. Even now there are still patches under cultivation. The Su zhou Hotel was built here after the liberation, in Feng men da jie Street. The **Garden of the Master of the Nets (Wang shi yuan)** is a little to the west of the hotel; Shi jin jie Street leads to it. It was laid out in 1140 by Shi Zheng zhi, an official from Yang zhou, who settled here when he retired. He called it the Fisherman's Retreat (Yu yin). The garden was sold and then abandoned after his death, and was left untouched until 1770, when another retired official, Song Zong yuan, decided to restore it. He called it Wang shi yuan (the Garden of the Master of the Nets), perhaps because of its old name, or perhaps simply because the garden was near Wang si Street (at Su zhou, no distinction is made between shi and si). It passed from hand to hand in the 19th century, and was acquired by the town in 1958.

Pièces d'eau
ornamental lakes
collines artificielles
artificial hills
ponts   bridges
sentiers   paths
kiosques   kiosks
galeries   arcade

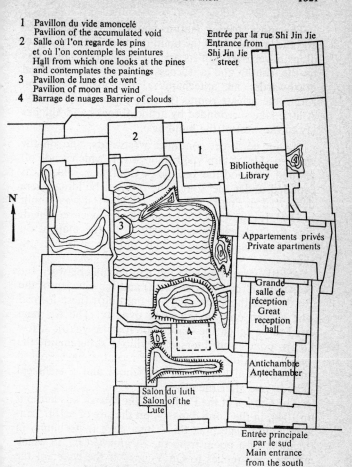

1 Pavillon du vide amoncelé
   Pavilion of the accumulated void
2 Salle où l'on regarde les pins
   et où l'on contemple les peintures
   Hall from which one looks at the pines
   and contemplates the paintings
3 Pavillon de lune et de vent
   Pavilion of moon and wind
4 Barrage de nuages Barrier of clouds

Entrée par la rue Shi Jin Jie
Entrance from
Shi Jin Jie
   street

Bibliothèque
Library

Appartements privés
Private apartments

Grande
salle de
réception
Great
reception
hall

Antichambre
Antechamber

Salon du luth
Salon of the
Lute

Entrée principale
par le sud
Main entrance
from the south

JARDIN DU MAÎTRE DES FILETS
(WANG SHI YUAN)
GARDEN OF THE MASTER OF THE NETS

The most striking feature about it is its small size and the large scale of the buildings in it. Halls and pavilions cover over half its area. The main entrance was to the south, and a succession of rooms stretched northwards: an antechamber, the main reception room, the private rooms (two floors), and the library. A little lake surrounded by artificial rocks and hillocks lay to the west of the buildings.

Shi jin jie Street continues westwards, and on the western side of San yuan fang Street, which leads off to the left, stood the Temple of Confucius, which was founded under the Song. The original buildings were destroyed during the Tai ping rebellion; it was rebuilt in 1864. It is now a school, and can no longer be visited. The three steles (Song dynasty) with the map of Su zhou and maps of the heavens and the earth are still there.

A little street opposite the temple runs between the Ke yuan Garden (to the north) and the Garden of the Pavilion of the Waves (Cang lang ting); these formed one garden only in the Song dynasty. The **Ke yuan** used to be called the Garden of Joy (Le yuan). A few rocks, ponds and floors of pavilions still remain; the present buildings, put up more recently, have housed the provincial library, an art school and a technical school, one after the other.

The **Garden of the Pavilion of the Waves** was laid out in 1044, in the Song dynasty, on the site of a 10th century house. The poet Su Zi mei gave it its name, in memory of a poem from the *Elegies of Chu,* in which a fisherman replies to Qu Yuan: "If the water of the river Cang lang is clean, I wash the ribbons of my hat in it, if it is dirty, I wash my feet in it." Cang lang, which also meant "wave", became a symbol of adaptation to the necessities of life and slight laziness

JARDIN DU PAVILLON DES VAGUES
(CANG LANG TING)
GARDEN OF THE PAVILION OF THE WAVES

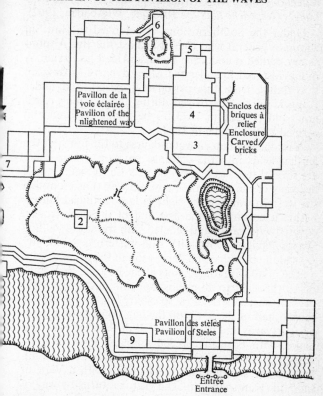

Pavillon de la voie éclairée
Pavilion of the Enlightened way

Enclos des briques à relief
Enclosure Carved bricks

Pavillon des stèles
Pavilion of Steles

Entrée
Entrance

Pavilion of the Imperial Stele
Pavilion of the Surging Waves
Pure Perfumes Chamber
Hall of the five Hundred Sages
«Charming Greenery»

6 Pavilion with a View of the Mountain
7 Hall where one Smells Marvellous Perfumes
8 Kiosk from which one Looks at the Fishes
9 Pavilion of the Water's Edge

Several scholars liked to use the symbol, particularly
Yan Yu, who, in the 12th century, wrote *Cang lang's
reflections on poetry* (trans. by G. Debon, *Ts'ang-
Lang's Gespräche über die Dichtung*, Wiesbaden, 1962).

Under the Southern Song, it belonged to Han Shi
zhong, a general who fought against the Jin. A monastery owned it under the Yuan, and let it go to ruin. A
monk restored it under the Ming dynasty (a description dating from this period still exists), and under
Kang xi; it was destroyed during the Tai ping rebellion, and remade in 1873, to be finally restored and
opened to the public in 1954.

A bridge spanning a water-course to the north of the
garden leads into the entrance pavilion, where there
are several steles (a text by the poet Su Zi mei, a bird's
eye view of the garden). A covered way runs alongside
the western wall, on the right; a large artificial hillock
beside it constitutes the first half of the park (rocks,
covered with earth, and planted with trees; the Rolling
Waves Pavilion crowns it). The western covered way
runs along the edge of a depression in the ground, with
a little pond with lotus plants at the bottom, then leads
off to the right to an enclosure containing large numbers of carved bricks (a speciality of Su zhou); the
second half of the park, on the left, consists of a series
of courtyards and pavilions (Hall of the Five Hundred
Sages, with portraits of 500 scholars, most of them
natives of Su zhou). On the top of a little artificial hillock to the south stands the Pavilion with a View of
the Hill (Kan shan lou). The visitor returns by way of
the eastern pavilions (Ming dao tang, "Pavilion of the
Enlightened Way"); a covered walk encircles the hillock, then comes the Kiosk for Watching the Fish
(Guan yu chu), the Waterside Pavilion (Mian shui
xuan), and then the entrance pavilion once more.

ENVIRONS DE SU ZHOU
AREA ROUND SU ZHOU

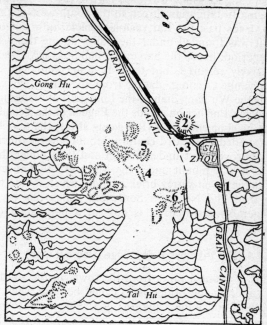

▬▬ ▬▬ *voie de chemin de fer*	1 Pont de la ceinture précieuse (Bao dai Qiao)
railway	Precious Belt Bridge
⍀⍀⍀ *collines*	2 Colline du Tigre (Hu Qiu)
hills	Tiger Hill
▬▬▬▬ *Grand Canal*	3 Temple de la montagne froide (Han Shan Si)
	Cold Mountain Temple
	4 Colline Ling Van
	Ling Yan Hill
	5 Colline Tian Ping
	Tian Ping Hill
	6 Colline Shang Fang
	Shang Fang Hill

The large Greco-Roman style building to the east of the Cang lang ting was once part of the art school.

Fu ma fu tang qian Street, in the south-west of the town, leads past the **Kai yuan si Temple,** now out of use (it was founded under the Tang, during the Kai yuan period, hence the name; the buildings have been extensively restored, but there is a fine hall with a stone vaulted ceiling, dating from the Ming, which recalls the Wu liang dian of the Ling gu si at Nanking, cf. p. 994). Further on stands the **Pagoda of the Temple of the good-omened light (Rui guang si ta)**; the temple was founded in the 3rd century, rebuilt several times, and destroyed first under the Jin and then under the Yuan; it was rebuilt under the Ming. All that is left now is the seven-storey brick pagoda, which is said to date from the Northern Song, but which has been considerably restored. It is now in a poor state of repair.

4. The Precious Belt Bridge (Bao dai qiao)

This is about 4 miles from the town, in the south-east suburbs; the bridge is so called because when it was built, under the Tang, the governor of the town, Wang Zhong xu, presented his ceremonial belt to help meet the expenses. The present bridge has been restored, particularly in 1872. It carries the road over Lake Yan tai hu, and measures over 100 yards from north to south; there are 53 arches, with three higher than the rest, in the centre, to allow boats through.

5. The Western Suburbs

a) Tiger Hill (Hu qiu). Tiger Hill is about 2 miles north-west of the town. The Wu king He Lü is traditionally supposed to have been buried on the top of

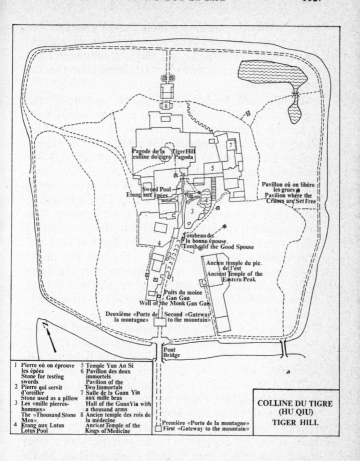

Pagode de la colline du tigre — Tiger Hill Pagoda

Sword Pool — Étang aux épées

Pavillon où on libère les grues — Pavilion where the Cranes are Set Free

Tombeau de la bonne épouse — Tomb of the Good Spouse

Ancien temple du pic de l'est — Ancient Temple of the Eastern Peak

Puits du moine Gan Gan — Well of the Monk Gan Gan

Deuxième «Porte de la montagne» — Second «Gateway to the mountain»

Pont — Bridge

1 Pierre où on éprouve les épées Stone for testing swords	5 Temple Yun An Si
2 Pierre qui servit d'oreiller Stone used as a pillow	6 Pavillon des deux immortels Pavilion of the Two Immortals
3 Les «mille pierres-hommes» The «Thousand Stone Men»	7 Salle de la Guan Yin aux mille bras Hall of the Guan Yin with a thousand arms
4 Étang aux Lotus Lotus Pool	8 Ancien temple des rois de la médecine Ancient Temple of the Kings of Medicine

COLLINE DU TIGRE (HU QIU)
TIGER HILL

Première «Porte de la montagne»
First «Gateway to the mountain»

the hill, and a tiger is said to have appeared, to guard his tomb: hence the name of the hill. Under the Six Dynasties, a local official had a villa built on the hill; two temples were built here under the Tang, but were soon destroyed; one was rebuilt on the summit. The big pagoda was built here under the Five Dynasties. Apart from the pagoda, all the old buildings have perished; the present temple was rebuilt after the Tai ping rebellion.

A wide walk leads over a bridge, and under the Second Gate of the Mountain (Er shan men), built under the Yuan dynasty, which has an unusual beam frame (the beam supporting the ridge is in two parts). A path leads up to the top of the hill; to the left is a well sunk under the Liang, by the monk Gan gan. Further on, to the right, lies the Stone where the Swords are Tried (Shi jian shi); the Wu king He Lü is said to have tried a sword here, which split the stone. The Pillow Stone is further on, on the left; the monk Sheng gong is said to have rested here. The **Tomb of the Good Wife** (**Zhen niang mu**) is here too; the lady Hu, of the Tang dynasty, was sold as a courtesan after the death of her husband; in her distress, she committed suicide, and was buried here, at the expense of people living in the neighbourhood; she was often referred to by poets. The path gives on to a little plateau, covered by scattered stones: the Thousand Stone Men (Qian ren shi); they are supposed to be the followers of King He Lü, who were killed during his funeral rites (the stones are said still to roar after rain); another legend says that they are the stones which, moved by the words of the monk Sheng Gong who had retired into the "desert", bowed their assent. To the east of the little plateau there is a slight depression in the ground, with a lotus pond, and beside this, a little Qing pavilion, which houses two steles with portraits on them. Higher up on the left is the Pond of the Swords (Jian chi); it is a long rift in the hillside, filled with water, and traditionsally aid to be the place where King He Lü was buried with 3,000 of his celebrated swords. Emperor Qin shi Huang di is supposed to have tried to find the entrance to the tomb, while travelling in the south, and the water gushed out to prevent him. The supposed entry is said to have been found in 1955. The Bridge with the Two Wells spans the rift (two round holes can still be seen in the floor of the bridge, through which the monks brought up their water). Finally, on the top of the hill stands the Yun yan si Temple Pagoda, usually called the Tiger Hill Pagoda. Its date had always been uncertain until 1956, when the pagoda was restored; a little stone casket was found on the second floor, containing a wooden box, with several things inside it, and an inscription on the bottom indicating that the pagoda was finished in 961. It became unstable and the seventh storey had to be rebuilt in the 17th century. It is clear from this, the top storey (which is not on the same axis as the others), that at that time, the pagoda already leaned towards the south-east. In the 20th century, the centre of gravity moved a yard to the south-east, and the pagoda split from top to bottom. In 1965, the crack was filled in, and the pagoda shored up from the inside.

While this work was going on, the casket which had been put in the pagoda when it was built was found. A workman who was filling a crack in the second storey was astonished at the amount of cement he had put into the crack without filling it; he moved a brick, and found a little passage leading to a cavity 1 yard long, 2 feet 2 ins. wide, and 2 feet high; at the far end were a stone casket and several other things: a pottery incense-burner, pieces of sandalwood, and a series of coins, originally in a fabric bag. In the wooden box inside the casket were eight scrolls of Buddhist texts, wrapped in fabric (one had the donor's name on it).

Another cavity on the third floor, slightly smaller, contained a stone casket (inside was found a metal casket with several ritual objects wrapped in silk) and other things (a bronze mirror, bronze statuettes of the Buddha, prayer beads). On the fourth floor the cavity, shaped like a cross, contained wooden tools, put there haphazardly, used during the building of the pagoda. Lastly, on the fifth floor, three stone statues of the Buddha were found, all headless (some of the objects are on show in the Town Museum).

The pagoda is built on an octagonal base, and is 150 feet high, with seven stories; each facet has an opening. The ground floor consists of an octagonal ambulatory and a square room in the centre (fine workmanship in the ceiling, and in the decoration of the walls). It is no longer possible to climb to the top. To the east of the plateau stands a temple rebuilt under the Qing (several rooms are dedicated to Guan yin).

The **Tombs of the Five** are to the east of the Tiger Hill; after the suppression of the worker's movement in 1626, the people of Su zhou had tombs built here to commemorate the death of the five leaders (Yan Pei wei, Yang Nian ru, Ma jie, Chen Yang and Zhou Wen yuan).

The lands south of the hill belong to a people's commune (the Tiger Hill Commune), which specialises in the cultivation of three kinds of flowers: *mo li hua*, the petals of which are mixed with tea, *bai lan hua*, which has a much sought after perfume, *dai dai hua*, the fruit of which looks like small oranges, and which is used in preparing medecine. All the flowers are grown in pots.

b) The "Liu" Garden and the Western Garden Temple. They are side by side, to the north-west of the town, about half a mile from the walls; the road which leads

JARDIN «LIU» (LIU YUAN)
«LIU» GARDEN (LIU YUAN)

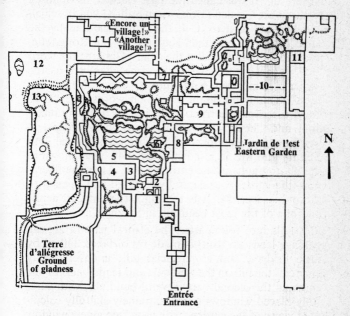

1 Old trees with intertwined trunks
2 «In a green shade»
3 Hall of the *Se* (kind of big lute)
4 Lotus Flower Chamber
5 Cool Terrace
6 Angling Terrace
7 Pavilion of the Blue Distance
8 Western Pavilion
9 Hall of the Immortals of the Five Peaks (Hall of cedarwood)
10 Hall of the Mandarin Ducks
11 Hermitage of the Clouds
12 Vale of the Small Peach-trees
13 Kiosk of Happiness

to them crosses the canal to the west of the town (a section of the Grand Canal); it is interesting to notice the river traffic and the different kinds of boats in use.

The **"Liu" Garden** was laid out under the Ming (Wan li period, 1573–1620) by a civil servant called Xu Shi tai. It was called the East Garden, as opposed to the West Garden (Dong yuan and Xi yuan), which was laid out next to it, at the same time and by the same person. It was then acquired by Liu Rong feng, and people used to call it the "Liu" Garden; the word "liu" is not written with the same character as the owner's name, but with another which means "to keep". This is no doubt a play on words: the "Liu" Garden escaped destruction during the Tai ping rebellion, and "kept" its buildings and rock-gardens. It was however abandoned at the beginning of the 20th century and was in a sad state by 1949, as is shown in the photographs in the entrance hall. After the liberation, the garden was carefully restored and opened to the public in 1954. It is the biggest (nearly 10 acres) and one of the most beautiful in Su zhou.

It falls into four parts. The central part (a zig-zag passage leads up to it) is made up of lakes, linked by little bridges, and an artificial hill; a covered way encircles the hill on the west side and leads back to the east and the second part: several buildings, with carefully-placed windows giving extremely skilfully calculated views of the garden; with each step a new window is discovered, showing a new landscape (the windows are called *huo chuang*, "windows which are alive"); among the buildings is a room which used to be entirely panelled in *nan mu* (a type of cedar found in the southern provinces) and called the *Cedarwood Room* (also called the Hall of the Immortals of the Five Peaks); to the east lies the Hall of the Mandarin Ducks (Yuan yan ting), made up of two large adjacent rooms, separated by a wall (mandarin ducks are the symbol of love and union). The third part of the garden

lies north and north-east of this: several little enclosures are grouped round a lake (fine set of stones from
the lake); then comes a less ornamented stretch, planted with vines, called "Another Village!" *(You yi cun)*
which leads into the fourth and last part, in the western
corner of the park. This consists of a long patch of
ground stretching in a north to south direction, planted
with fruit trees and less artificial than the rest.

The **Western Garden Temple (Xi yuan si)** is also
called Jie chuang lü si; it was built on the site of a
garden laid out at the same time as the Liu yuan by
Xu Shi tai (under the Ming). Xu Shi tai's son gave it
to a Buddhist community; a temple was built straight
away (the present name dates from 1635). It was
destroyed during the Tai ping rebellion, and rebuilt
entirely at the end of the 19th and the beginning of the
20th centuries.

The following parts may be visited: the Hall of
the eighteen *luo han;* to the east, the Hall of the Five
Hundred *luo han* (modelled on the same hall at the
Ling yin si at Hang zhou, now no longer in existence);
the statues of the two monks, Ji gong and Song jiang,
in the middle, are particularly expressive. A large
lake lies next to this, with a central pavilion from
which can be seen giant carp.

c) The Cold Mountain Temple (Han shan si).
This
is to the west of the town; a road starting from Jin
men leads to it, following the course of the old canal.
The temple was founded under the Liang. The name—
the Cold Mountain Temple—came later; it is said
that the two hermits Han shan and Shi de stayed
there under the Tang. Han shan is known to have
been a Buddhist poet, inspired by the Dhyana school;
over three hundred poems attributed to him are

still in existence (they have recently been translated into English: B. Watson, *Cold Mountain*, New York, 1962). The poet's name, Han shan, came from the "Cold Mountain" to which he retired, the Tian tai Mountain (in eastern Zhe jiang). Nothing is known of the true connection between Han shan and the temple. The monastery gained from being near the Grand Canal. A lively trade in grain, fabrics, and wood was carried on in the shadow of its walls and under its protection. Several contemporary poets mention the temple and its bell, which could be heard from far away; Zhang Ji wrote a famous poem: "The moon goes down, the crow cries, cold fills the air; under the Feng bridge, the lantern lights prevent sleep; beyond Su zhou is the Han shan si; through the night, the sound of its bell comes as far as my boat". The buildings were destroyed and rebuilt several times afterwards; the present ones date from the end of the 19th century.

A large screen wall stands in front of the temple; the central hall contains two steles showing Han shan and Shi de. A recent painting hangs in the far hall, with the poem by Zhang Ji already mentioned. The bell pavilion and the steles pavilion are to the east (Zhang Ji's poem is inscribed on one of the steles, and Kang You wei's "reply" on another; he came to Han shan si when the bell had just been taken away by the Japanese: "The sound of the bell has crossed the sea to the east; a cold silence invades the Han shan Temple"). A fine hump-backed bridge spans a little canal in front of the temple; from the top of it, the Grand Canal can be seen.

d) The Ling yan and Shang fang Hills. A road going to the Tai hu, leaving Su zhou to the south-west, leads in their direction; the Shang fang Hill Pagoda can be seen on the left; about 12 miles out of the town, a path leads to the top of Ling yan Hill.

According to various texts, the Wu king Fu Cha had a palace built here for the beautiful lady Xi Shi; stories about her are connected with several spots on the hill. Under the Jin, a Buddhist monk, Zhi ji, retired to the hill. Under the Song, a temple and pagoda were built, later to be destroyed under Wan li, and then rebuilt.

The hill is covered with stones eroded into strange shapes, which have been given names (the Tortoise stone, the Horse stone, the *luo han* stone, etc...). Much of the rock is very fine-grained and was used to make ink-stones (which gave the hill one of its old names: Yan shi shan). In his work on ink stones, the painter and calligrapher Mi Fu (1051–1107) says that the Su zhou stones are like the ones from Gui zhou: "The local people, after they have cut them into the shape of an ink-stone, wrap grass around them, and when this is burned up, roast them slowly in warm ashes, and then the colour changes into purple" (cf. Van Gulik, *Mi Fu on Ink-stones*, Peking, 1938, p. 43).

The little Guan Yin cave is on the left on the way up, with a stone *chuang* near it. The Rock of Spirits Temple (Ling yan si), still in use, stands on the top of the hill. The central part consists of a Hall of the Celestial Guardians, a beautiful courtyard with a bridge, and a large central hall with *luo han*. To the east, beside the refectory, stand the remains of a brick Ming pagoda, in a very sad state; an interesting exhibition on Buddhist art in China has been laid out in the western rooms: large numbers of photographs and reproductions, and a few originals: wooden statues of Bodhisattva, Tang (very fine),

Song and Ming periods; collection of small bronzes, old and Lamaist. The hall housing the exhibition gives on to a terrace, now converted into a garden, where the beautiful Xi Shi is said to have played the lute; the two wells are called after the king of Wu and Zhe ji, the monk. In front of the temple there is an excellent view over the surroundings and Lake Tai hu. The foot of the hill is linked to the lake by a little canal running in a straight line across the plain; it is called the Arrow Canal, because the king of Wu is said to have marked it out by shooting an arrow, or the Canal where Perfumes are gathered, because the king's wives used to pick flowers along its banks.

At the foot of the hill on the western side the tomb of Han Shi zhong, the general who led the Southern Song against the Jin, can still be seen; he was buried here in 1150.

North-east of Ling yan hill is the Tian ping Hill, well-known for its spring, landscape and an excellent view over Lake Tai hu.

e) **The Protection of Sages Temple (Bao sheng si).** The temple is about 25 miles south-east of Su zhou, in the village of Jiao zhi. It was founded under the Liang in 503, and was destroyed and rebuilt several times. The present buildings date from 1860. The only interesting thing left is a set of statues of *luo han* dating from the Song. There were eighteen originally; five still exist today (the Nanking Museum contains two replicas).

Lu zhi

Lu zhi is a little village about 18 miles south-east of Su zhou. The **Protection of the Sages Temple**

(**Bao sheng si**) is in the south of the town. It was founded in the 9th century, under the Tang, and was restored several times in later dynasties. The main gateway, dating from 1761, a *chuang* dating from 1135 and the Hall of the Celestial Guardians, Tian wang dian, are all still standing. In 1930, a hall was built on the site of the original Main Hall to house the statues which were in it, which include an extremely handsome set of *luo han* thought to date from the Song.

THE NORTHERN TOWNS

Nan tong shi

Nan tong shi is on the north bank of the Yang zi, at the centre of a network of canals; it was founded under the Han. It is now an important industrial town (textile mills, flour mills, oil-extracting and food-processing plants).

Tai zhou shi

Tai zhou shi is west of Nan tong shi, at the intersection of two canals, linking the town with the Yang zi to the south, Huai Yin shi to the north and Yang zhou to the west. When Marco Polo saw it, the town was already a lively trading centre (the salt trade was particularly important). It is now well-known for the fishing nets made there.

Yang zhou

Yang zhou is north of the Yang zi, on the left bank of the Grand Canal.

It already existed under the Han. Marco Polo, who visited it in the 13th century, reported that its inhabitants lived by trade and industry, particularly that of equipment for horsemen and men-at-arms. In the 18th century, trade was flourishing and the merchants of Hui zhou (An hui) worked in agreement with the Yang zhou merchants; according to Grosier, "the town is famous for its salt-pans; the salt-farmers have had a pleasure-palace built for the Emperor, all the more astonishing because nothing has yet been seen to equal it. It is a copy of Hai dian, another country house two hours away from Peking." The town was much appreciated by the court (the Qing Emperors visited it on their tours of the south), by painters (a school called the Yang zhou school was formed, Yang zhou hua pai; the eight most famous ones, known as the Yang zhou ba jia, the eight masters of Yang zhou, all came from southern provinces), by scholars, officials and by merchants, who would come to end their lives there. A painter, Shi Tao, is mentioned in contemporary records as being an expert in making artificial rocks, a basic element in all Chinese gardens. Yang zhou had over 24 stone bridges spanning the canals which ran through it. All the travellers of that period (Du Halde, Father Amiot) are generous in their praise of the town. In the 19th century, it suffered during the Tai ping rebellion. It is still much admired as a beautiful town, and it has little industry.

The Yang zhou Story-tellers

From the Ming dynasty onwards, Yang zhou was famous for its story-tellers. In the 18th century, under the Qing, all the streets leading to the gates of the town were lined with platforms *(shu tai)* where the story-tellers would stand to recite episodes from famous novels to an audience grouped round the dais. The Yang zhou Ping hua (Yang zhou story-telling) was incredibly popular, so much so that actors would abandon their stage careers to become story-tellers. Most of the material came from novels such as the *San guo yan yi (Romance of the Three Kingdoms)*, the *Shui hu zhuan (Story of the Water Margin)*, the *Yue zhuan* (the *Story of Yue Fei)*... During the Tai ping rebellion, the town was occupied by the rebels and the story-tellers gave up for a time; many of them moved to other towns in Jiang su, or even to other provinces, to the Huai valley or south An hui. There, they were so successful that their numbers grew considerably; there were soon about a hundred of them. When the Tai ping movement failed, they came back to Yang zhou; the names of the most famous ones still survive: Jin Guo shan (best known for stories from the *Ping yao zhuan* and the *Yue zhuan*), and Gong Wu ting; there is still a saying at Yang zhou which goes: "when you listened to Jin Guo shan, you didn't need to eat, when you listened to Gong Wu ting, you forgot to stop eating!" Whoever went to Yang zhou was inevitably asked afterwards if he had heard Gong Wu ting; if he had to say no, he was the laughing-stock of everyone. Gong Wu ting was considered by his contemporaries to be the story-teller who best conveyed the feelings of the characters in the story. It was an art which was handed down from one generation to the next; each story-teller had one or more novels in which he specialised and he would hand the secrets of his art down to relations or pupils. The repertoire of such story-tellers consisted of 28 novels, 17 of which were historical ones; in 1953, about twenty of them were written down; in 1962, the study group working on the Yang zhou ping hua published a selection of them *(Yang zhou ping hua xuan)*. The two most famous story-tellers now are Wang Shao tang, who specialises in extracts from the *Story of the Water Margin*, and Kang Zhong hua, whose speciality is the *Romance of the Three Kingdoms;* they perform in **Jiao chang Square.**

Several places near the town are worth a visit: 1. The **Lotus Flower Bridge (Lian hua qiao)** north of the town, on Lake Shou xi hu, behind the Lian hua si Temple; its name is supposed to come from its shape, said to be that of a lotus flower; it is also called the Five Kiosk Bridge (Wu ting qiao). It was built under the reign of Qian long in 1755, and has three arches (the central one, topped by a kiosk, is the highest); four blocks of masonry are built up against the central arch, on either side, each of them with four little arches opening in them, and each one surmounted by a kiosk; 2. the **Fa jing si Temple,** near Lake Shou xi hu; it was founded under the Southern Dynasties period and was then called Da ming si (Temple of Bright Light); it was destroyed several times, and the present buildings date from 1934. A *pai lou* stands in front of the temple; left of the main hall is the Ping tang which was built by Ou Yang xiu, when he was prefect of the town (1048); the present building is a modern one; behind the Ping shan tang is the Gu lin tang, and a temple dedicated to Ou Yang xiu (Ou Yang ci) built in 1879; a statue of Ou Yang xiu stands inside. The **Western Garden** (**Xi yuan**) lies to the west of the buildings; it was laid out in 1751, and consists mainly of a lake with trees round it. It is famous for a spring (the fifth spring under heaven). 3. The **Shi gong ci** is a temple dedicated to Shi Ke fa, a national hero who was an official who held a post at Yang zhou at the end of the Ming dynasty; when the Qing seized power, he refused to give in to them, tried to commit suicide and was finally arrested and executed. His body was never recovered, but a temple was built in memory of him, and his clothes were buried in a tomb; several pieces of calligraphy executed by him are kept in the temple. 4. The **Yang zhou Mosque.**

Huai yin shi

It is in the middle of the province, north-west of Lake Hong ze hu, at the intersection of the Grand Canal and the Xin huai he. It acts as a re-distribution centre for the products of the neighbouring areas; it also has some textile factories.

Lian yun gang shi

Lian yun gang shi is the most easterly town of the province, on the railway line from He nan to the sea. It is a busy port; boats sail from there to Shang hai, Qing dao, Tian jin and Lü da. Fishing and the salt industry (south of the town) provide work for most of the inhabitants.

Xu zhou

Xu zhou is in the north-west of the province, at the junction of the railway lines from Tian jin to Pu kou and from Gan su to the sea; traffic between the four provinces of Jiang su, Shan dong, He nan and An hui goes through there. The town is surrounded by hills, in what has always been a strategic position. Iron is mined at Liu guo yi (it was mined there as early as the Han), about 18 miles north of Xu zhou, near the railway line, and coal is to be found even nearer the town; as a result, the town has developed into a flourishing industrial centre (metal industry, and machine industry). The population is 600,000.

The **Xing hua si Temple** on Yun long shan Hill contains a large Buddha carved out of the cliff, about 30 feet high; it dates from the Northern Wei (451).

THE CITY OF SHANG HAI

(Map see p. 1041)

Shang hai is on the left bank of the river Huang pu, a little to the south of the mouth of the Yang zi; it is a flourishing industrial and commercial centre, a great port, and the most densely populated town in China. Today Shang hai and its suburbs form a separate administrative unit, independent of the neighbouring provinces of Zhe jiang and Jiang su; the city covers an area of 3,600 square miles and has 10 million inhabitants (since the extension of its territories in 1958). Its name means "above the sea".

History

The origins of the town date from the Song era, when the lower Yang zi region benefited from the "withdrawal" which followed the invasions from the north. Several organisations responsible for controlling overseas trade had already been based there. Under the Yuan, the settlement was put under the jurisdiction of the administrative centre of Song jiang (south-west of modern Shang hai), and became part of the province of Jiang su. In 1554, ramparts were built round the town to protect it from attacks from Japanese pirates *(wo kou)*. In the 17th and 18th centuries trade flourished and Shang hai cotton was well known; according to Grosier, "In the town of Shang hai alone, which is only a third class town, and in the market towns depending on it, there are over 20,000 calico weavers; large numbers of women are also employed on the weaving".

The real development of the town dates from the 19th century, however. During the Opium War, the English fleet under Vice Admiral Sir William Parker advanced as far as Shang hai, which had to surrender (June 1842). After the signing of the Treaty of Nanking, which opened Shang hai to foreign trade, English, French and American consuls came and settled in the town, and claimed special territories, for their fellow-countrymen to live in; this was the origin of the famous concessions: the British concession, at the meeting point of the rivers Huang pu and Wu song, was created in 1843, and became an international concession in 1863; the French concession, created in 1847, was south of the British one, and stretched round the old Chinese city; and the Japanese concession, to the north, was created when the Treaty of Shimonoseki was signed in 1895.

All was not plain sailing for the Europeans at first; the Tai ping armies reached the outskirts of the town in 1853. At the same time, the Society of Little Swords planned a rising within the town itself (Xiao dao hui, often translated as the "Society of Little Knives"). In April 1854, the foreing residents made a sortie, with the support of their warships' crews; it was known as the Battle of the Muddy Flat, called after the mud flats which then stretched west of the British concession. Finally, the Imperial armies overcame the Tai ping, with the help of the Europeans, and regained control of Shang hai and the surrounding area.

The foreigners became more and more numerous from then on. They controlled the Chinese customs and founded banks, factories and business houses (one of the most famous was Jardine and Matheson). "The Bund" alongside the Huang pu was lined with impressive buildings: the German Club, the Palace Hotel (with its hanging gardens), the Russo-Asian Bank, the Customs Building in Tudor style, complete with a square tower 110 ft. high, with an enormous chiming clock.

At the foot of these magnificent buildings stood several memorial monuments, as though to bear witness to the impact of the Europeans: a monument to Margary (killed in Yun nan in 1873), statues of Sir Harry Parkes (once British Minister in Peking) and Sir Robert Hart (Inspector-General of Customs), a broken, mast in bronze, in memory of the wrecked German gunboat *Iltis*, and finally the pyramid to the "Ever Victorious Army", recording the names of foreigners killed in action against the Tai ping army in 1862. A society of adventurers and a miserable proletariat grew up on the fringe of this conquering soiety.

In the 20th century, the Europeans tightened their hold, and at the same time Chinese national capitalism developed (textiles, shipbuilding). In 1910, the speculation in rubber resulted in a financial crisis which seriously affected the Chinese banks (cf. M.C. Bergère, *Une crise financière à Shang hai, à la fin de l'ancien régime*, Mouton, 1964). Mao Dun gives a good description of the Chinese bourgeoisie of the 1920's in his novel *Midnight*. At the same time, the workers were becoming organised. The Chinese Communist Party was founded in Shang hai on July 1st 1921; its Central Committee sat there for some time. In 1925, the assassination of a Chinese worker by some Japanese caused a protest which resulted in the May 30th Incident. The next year, the Shang hai working class took part in armed risings, in co-ordination with the northern expedition, but in 1927, the movement was savagely put down by Chiang Kai shek, when he broke with the Communists. The town was under enemy occupation during the Sino-Japanese war. Since the liberation, the whole framework of society has changed: the Europeans have gone, business enterprises have been nationalised; the shady elements have been purged; a detachment from the Liberation Army won fame by its supervision of the ex "Nanking Road" (Nan jing lu); it became known as "Hao ba lian".

In an attempt to slow down the growth of the town itself, about ten industrial satellite towns have been founded and enlarged nearby: Min hang, Wu song, Peng pu. At the same time, heavy industry, which was fairly limited before, has expanded. Every branch of industry is now represented in Shang hai: iron and steel, refining of non-ferrous metals, electricity, machine building; textiles (wool, cotton and silk) and foodstuffs are also important.

Shang hai is still one of China's biggest ports; as the products of its industry are intended for the home market first and foremost, the volume of inland traffic handled is growing considerably, and it already exceeds export traffic. At the same time, the proportion of industrial products among the exports is growing.

 Camp des armées Qing
Camp of the Qing armies

 Batterie des Impériaux
Imperial batteries

 Batterie des «Petites épées»
Batterie of the «Little swords»

 Limite des concessions
Limit of concessions

 Routes
Roads

 Remparts de la ville
Town ramparts

1 Consulat britannique
British Consulate

2 Concession britannique
British Concession

3 Manège
Riding-school

4 Hôpital de la mission
Mission Hospital

5 Concession française
French Concession

6 Quai de la famille Wang
Quay of the Wang Family

7 Eglise
Church

8 Bac de la famille Dong (Tonccadu)
Ferry of the Dong Family (Tonccadu

SHANG HAI LORS DU SIÈGE DE 1854
SHANG HAI AT THE TIME OF THE 1854 SIEGE

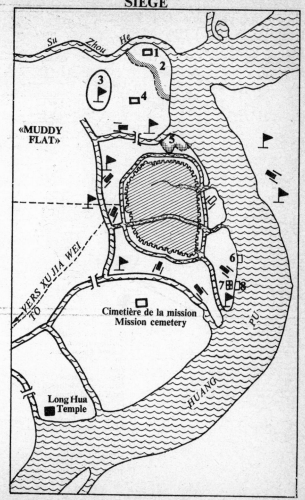

«MUDDY FLAT»

Su Zhou He

VERS XU JIA WEI
TO

Cimetière de la mission
Mission cemetery

Long Hua Temple

HUANG

PU

SHANG HAI VERS 1920
SHANG HAI IN ABOUT 1920

LEGENDE – KEY

Zone construite Built-up area
Jardins publics Public Gardens
Limite des concessions Boundaries Concessions
Limites des murailles de l'ancienne ville Old town Walls
Chemin de fer Railway
Répartition des entrepôts, ateliers et usines
(d'après la carte donnée dans le «Mouvement
ouvrier chinois de 1919 à 1927» de J. Chesneaux)
Warehouses, Workshops and factories (after the
map printed in «The Chinese Workers' Movement
1919 to 1927», by J. Chesneaux)

1 Central police station
2 Customs house
3 Russo-Chinese bank
4 Chartered bank
5 Palace Hotel
6 Sino-Belgianbank
7 Jardine and Matheson Co
8 Bank of Indochina
9 British Consulate
10 Museum
11 Mixed Law Court
12 Public School for Chinese
13 Elgin Market
14 Isolation Hospital
15 General Hospital
16 Astor House Hotel
17 Hong Kong & Shang hai Bank

The rise of Shang hai has led to an impressive development of agriculture in the ten districts which compose the suburbs. Cereals, vegetables, cotton and groundnuts are grown. A few model communes contain well-planned livestock and poultry farms.

Finally, Shang hai is also one of the great intellectual centres. It has twenty-four institutes of higher education (including Fu dan da xue, which has taken over the famous Aurora University); there are also several scientific research centres.

Description

The town lies to the west of a curve in the River Huang pu, about 25 miles upstream of the point where it flows into the Yang zi. The River Wu song (sometimes called Su zhou River: "Soo chow Creek") flows from west to east, and then meets the Huang pu, making a clear dividing line between the northern districts ("northern" and "eastern" districts) and the centre of the town. The Yang king pang Canal used to run parallel to the Wu song, to the south, separating the international concession from the French concession; it was filled in some time ago, and is now Yan an Street. The circular boundaries of the old Chinese town can still be easily traced on the map, south of Yan an Street. The Pu dong district (docks and naval dockyards) is on the right bank of the Wu song; it can be reached by boat only. The town has spread considerably to the north (where the Japanese concession was), to the west and to the south-west. What was once the "Ziccawei suburb" has become part of the town.

The centre (the "Bund" and Nanking Road) will be described first, followed by the old town and its surroundings, then the south-western, western and northern districts.

1. The Centre

This corresponds roughly to the old "central
district"; it runs south of the river Wu song and its
eastern boundary is Zhong shan lu Street, once the
"Bund". The streets are built on a fairly regular plan,
and cross at right angles. The main streets running
from north to south are called after provinces (Yun
nan, Guang xi, Fu jian, Shan xi, He nan, Jiang xi, Si
chuan Streets); the streets running from east to west
are called after towns (Amoy, Peking, Nanking, Jiu
jiang, Han kou, Fu zhou, Canton, Yan an Streets).

The most impressive avenue is still the "Bund",
which begins at the confluence of the rivers Huang pu
and Wu song and runs south (as far as the old town).
On the east side, it is a flowered walk, with a beautiful
view of the Huang pu, its ships and its junks; the Pu
dong docks are in the distance. On the west side, about
fifteen sky-scrapers built in stone and cement recall an
age that has vanished. They were once banks, firms,
clubs, and most are now out of use. Further south, on
the corner of Nanking Road, stands the Peace Hotel
(He ping fan dian, the old Palace Hotel) with its large
tower, surmounted by a pyramid; further south again
are the Central Administrative Offices of the City of
Shang hai, and then the Seamen's Club (Hai yuan
ju le bu), where foreign sailors stay when they put in
at Shang hai. Still further south, the Bund entered
French territory, and changed its name to the "Quai
de France". The tower which used to be the meteorological office is still there; different flags were
hoisted according to the weather, and at midday, a
signal, linked with the Ziccawei Observatory, showed

the exact moment at which the sun passed the meridian, so that all chronometers could be checked by it.

Nanking Road (Nan jing lu), starting at the Bund, south of the Peace Hotel, and running westwards for several miles, is the busiest street. It contains department stores, restaurants, a few cinemas, and two large buildings which are visible for a long way off, because of their high towers: the Radio Building and the Hotel for Overseas Chinese. Further west, south of the Nanking Road, the People's Park and the People's Square occupy what used to be the race course. The Town Library, founded in 1849, is west of the People's Park. Fu zhou Street nearby contains large numbers of secondhand bookshops.

Yan an lu, also nearby, used to mark the boundary between the old French and British concessions; there were once several shops there selling goods from Paris.

At the east end of the street are the **Museum of Natural Sciences** and the **Art and History Museum.** The latter was founded in 1952; the buildings once belonged to a bank. It contains a most valuable collection, arranged in chronological order; it is designed to show the evolution of art, rather than the relationship between art and society.

First Floor. Neolithic Era: a fine set of painted pottery (Yang shao, Ban po, Long shan), several pieces found near Shang hai. *Shang and Zhou civilisations:* very fine collection of bronzes. Unfortunately, most of them were found some time ago, and it is not known where they come from, nor from what strata. Of particular interest: western Zhou bell; *jue* (ritual ewer) with four feet (very rare); a large Shang dynasty axe, inlaid with green stones; a large *ding* (three-legged cauldron), which is the largest after the one in the Peking Historical Museum called "Da ke ding" (circa

850 B.C.); fragments of moulds; bone tools; bone inscription; several pieces of Shang pottery (rare). *The Warring States:* bronze weapons (lances, swords, *ge*); bells; a drum, known as *"chen yu"*, with a handle on the top part; very fine Chu *ding;* articles in gilded bronze; mirrors; fibulae; engraved tiles; jade; *bi* (a sort of flat ring) in a vitrified material *(liu li)*, imitating similar pieces made of jade (rare); beads made of the same material; wine-warmer in the shape of an ox with three openings in the top, found in Shan xi in 1923; lacquer shield found in Hu nan; *mu yong* (wooden tomb figurines), one with jointed arms; seals; iron swords from the state of Yue; bronze objects made by northern minority races.

N.B. A large volume of colour reproductions of the best bronzes in the museum, with an additional volume of rubbings of the inscriptions, and explanations, can be bought in any bookshop.

Second Floor. Qin and Han Periods: Engraved bricks one showing a bridge, found in Si chuan (copy); bas-relief carvings from Shan dong; clay tomb figurines, mainly from Canton, which give a good idea of life under the Han: keep with guards armed with cross-bows, pig-sty, pestle, granary, ovens, well with pulley; very fine animal carvings (ducks, hens, horses, and particularly dogs); clay figures of men, with spades and swords; jade cicadas, found in the mouths of the dead; swords; mirrors and other objects made of bronze; pottery (lamp with a bear); fine painted pottery, with geometric design; large urn found at Luo yang, with a fish motif; examples of art from the steppes; bronzes from Vietnam. *Northern and Southern Dynasties:* Bud-dhist sculpture (some pieces are copies); a large Buddha (Northern Wei); several original pieces of sculpture from Dun huang; a collection of tomb figurines, with a table showing how the shapes developed; "qing" pottery (Southern dynasty). *Sui and Tang Dynasties: large* Bodhisattva (note the *déhanchement*); heads of celestial guardians and of the Buddha; Tang steles, dating from 721; about twenty small Sui and Tang bronzes, most of them gilded; clay tomb figurines (ox-cart, ladies on horseback, polo-players); calligraphy and paintings (replicas) attributed to Wang Xian zhi (c. 400) and to the monk Huai Su (Tang); replicas of Sui wall-paintings, whose originals are at Dun huang; seals and ink-stones; a fine collection of Tang pottery ("three colours"); hairpins; fifteen mirrors, two of them square; small cup with a gilded motive on the bottom; ivory measuring rod.

Third Floor. Song Period: copies of original paintings owned by the museum (paintings by Li Die, Liang Kai, Zhu Ke sou); calligraphy; porcelain (map showing the main centres under the Song); Shan xi celadon ware; Long quan light greenish blue ware. *Yuan Period:* a painting by Wang Meng; porcelain, including one rare grey, pink and white piece from Jing de zhen. *Five Dynasties Period:* head of a *luo han* in wood; bas-relief carvings; mirrors. *Ming Period:* paintings by Lü Ji, Lin Liang and Wen Shu; Jing de Zhen porcelain; Fu jian white porcelain; cloisonné ware; ink-stones; embroidery on silk; illustrated books; lacquer ware; two lutes. *Qing Period:* paintings; calligraphy; porcelain; embroidery. *Present Day:* very interesting exhibition of crafts from different provinces: jade ware (Shang hai, Peking); silver filigree ware (Si chuan); cloisonné ware (Peking); lacquer ware (Fu zhou); ivory ware (Canton, Shang hai, Peking); embroidery (Su zhou); ceramics (Jiang xi); wooden marionnettes (Fu zhou); clay figures (Zhe jiang); paper cut-outs (Tian jin and Zhe jiang); Chinese shadow puppets

(Shân xi); pictures worked in iron (An hui); a few examples of crafts of the minority races: Gao shan figures (Tai wan), Tai fabrics.

The famous **Great World (Da shi jie)** stands at a cross-roads further along Yan an Street, to the west. It was started in the twenties, and housed a number of shows: classical opera, marionnettes, Chinese shadow puppets. Countless Europeans and Chinese would meet there in the evenings in the tea rooms. After the liberation, the establishment was put under supervision and gradually the programmes were changed. It used to occupy buildings on both sides of the street, linked by an underground way. Only one building is left now, consisting of several floors with galleries built round a courtyard in the centre. The visitor takes the lift up to the terrace on the roof, with a good view over the town, then walks down, to look in on various plays etc. going on in different places, all at the same time. The best show is usually given on a large stage in the central courtyard (plays, circus). (It is closed at the moment, 1972.)

The Workers' Cultural Palace is slightly to the north of Yan an lu, near the People's Square.

2. The Old Town and its Surroundings

At the beginning of this century the "Chinese town" was still surrounded by walls, with a circumference of 2 or 3 miles, and it was roughly round. Broad streets have now been laid out to replace the walls (Ren min lu and Zhong Hua lu). The old European guide books strongly advised the tourist not to set foot in the town unless escorted by a Chinese guide, who could be found near the north gate. They were apparently the only ones who could find their way through the labyrinth of streets. The streets may be cleaner than they used to be, but they have not grown any wider, and many are not wide enough to take a car. The visitor on foot will be followed by a crowd of curious children.

An interesting district in the north of the old town is centred round a small lake, in the middle of which stands a tea house, with a zig zag bridge leading to it. The building is an old one, restored in 1965, and used to be well-known under its former name of "Wu xing ting". It was the symbol of Shang hai, and used to be reproduced on plates and curios. A gate near the lake opens into the **Yu yuan (Yu the Mandarin's Garden)**, which closely resembles the garden of Su zhou. It was laid out in 1537 by an official, who later lived there. The Society of Little Swords had its headquarters there during the 1853 rising. The garden was restored in 1956, and is in two parts: an outer garden, fairly big, with pavilions, rockeries, ponds, and an inner garden (nei yuan), laid out on the same pattern, but on a much smaller scale, which is reserved for women. The most striking features are the fine carved bricks (which recall the ones at Su zhou), the small private theatre, the top of the walls separating the two carved in the shape of a dragon, and the large border "with a hundred and eight different kinds of things" (flowers, trees, rocks, etc.). One of the pavilions contains a little museum of the Society of the Little Swords Uprising (swords worn by its members, map of the siege of the town).

The **Temple to the Town Gods (Cheng huang miao)** is nearby. Each town used to possess one, and this is one of the few still surviving. Two statues remain inside: Lao Zi, the patron of the town, and General Huo Guang, a local hero (with a red face and a long beard). The **Garden of the Purple Clouds of Autumn (Qiu xia**

pu), still called the Back Garden (Hou Yuan) lies behind the temple; it was laid out in the Jia jing period (1522–1567) by a high ranking official called Hong Gong. At the end of the Ming dynasty the Hong family were ruined, and the garden (then known as the Hong garden) was sold to a rich salt merchant from An hui. Later on it again belonged to the Hong family, for a short time, and was finally taken over for the Temple to the Town Gods (1726), which occupied some of the buildings in the garden. The park consists of a long ornamental lake, with pavilions and artificial hills round it.

The Temple of Confucius (Wen miao) was in the south-west of the old town; it has been transformed into the Cultural Palace.

Between the eastern boundary of the old town and the river lies the suburb of Dong jia du ("the Dong family ferry"), a busy shopping district. Further south were the French concession's reservoirs and the "Kiang nan" arsenal.

The house in which Sun Yat sen lived while in Shang hai is in the west of the old town, south of Fu xing lu in Zhong qing nan lu; it is now a small museum.

3. The South-western Districts

a) The Ziccawei district (Pekinese: Xu jia hui: "the Xu family village").

At the end of the 16th century, Xu Guang qi (1562-1632), an influential member of the Xu family, held an important post at court; he met Father Ricci, who converted him to Roman Catholicism in 1603; several members of his family followed his example, and a small Christian community was formed here. It was dispersed during the persecutions. The area was ceded to the Jesuits in 1842, and they settled there in 1847. The Vicar apostolic of the Jiang nan mission was based there. The establishment included a library, (over 30,000 books), an orphanage, a printing press (which printed *Variétés Sinologiques*), and above all, the meteorological observatory, founded in 1871, and re-organised in 1900. It was one of the largest in the Far East. All this has vanished now, except for the twin spires of a church. The Communications University (Jiao tong da xue) is to the north.

b) The Long hua Temple District (Long hua si). To the south of the Ziccawei district. The buildings are scattered; the pagoda can be seen from a long way away. It has seven stories with wooden balconies, and since it was the only pagoda in Shang hai, the Europeans who put in here would always come to see it. The temple buildings (Qing dynasty) are large; it consists of four halls, with the future Buddha, the celestial guardians, the hall of the *luo han* and the celestial defenders, with a painted wood ceiling and a cupola, and three Buddhas.

4. The Western District

The **Palace of Sino-Soviet Friendship** is further along Yan an Street to the west; it is built in the same style as the Peking Exhibitions Centre. It houses a permanent exhibition of products manufactured at Shang hai (machines, precision tools, consumer goods, textiles, crafts). To the west again is the **Children's Palace (Shao nian gong),** in a large house which once belonged to a rich businessman. A little to the north, in Nan jing lu, is the **Temple of Serenity (Jing an si),** and opposite it, the Park of Serenity (Jing an gong yuan). A stone column in the middle of the road heralds it; the capital is a copy of the famous Açoka capital. The buildings, which are now reduced in size, date from the 19th century, and although they are not particularly impressive, many people still go on pilgrimage there.

To the north, the Jiang ning lu leads to the **Temple of the Jade Buddha (Yu fo si)**, which has been restored recently (the outside walls are a magnificent yellow). On the first floor of the far pavilion there is a seated statue of the Buddha in white jade, brought from Burma in 1881, by a Chinese monk. The pavilion also contains a recumbent jade statue of the Buddha, with the same history as the first one. Both statues recall the Buddha in the Round Town in Peking, which is also said to come from Burma. The temple still has a very fine collection of Buddhist classics, in Ming editions.

5. The Northern Districts

The Hong kou district is north of the Wu song river; the American concession, which, combined with the British concession, became the International concession in 1863, and the Japanese concession, used to be there. The German, American and Japanese consulates used to be on the bank of the Huang pu, and near the point where the two rivers meet the Astor House Hotel once stood. The long main street, Broadway, ran parallel to the Huang pu and contained shipping company offices and silk factories (its name is now Dong da ming lu). It is still an industrial district today, with shipyards lining the river. Several universities and colleges have been founded there, or moved there, one of which is the former Aurora University, once in the French concession.

Coming from the Bund, one crosses a bridge over the Wu song into the northern district; nearby stands the vast skyscraper of the **Shang hai Hotel (Shang hai da sha)**, with a magnificent view from the top over the town and the Huang pu. The Central Station is to the north-east; to the north is the **Hong kou Park.**

Lu Xun's Tomb and the **Lu Xun Museum (Lu Xun ji nian guan)** are both here. When he died in 1936, Lu Xun was buried in the Wan guo cemetery, in the west of the town. In 1956, his ashes were transferred to the Hong kou Park. There is a seated statue of him in front of the tomb, and the characters on the far wall, which mean "Mr. Lu Xun's Tomb", are in the calligraphy of Chairman Mao.

The Lu Xun museum was opened in 1951, in the house in Shan xian lu where the writer spent the last few years of his life. In 1956, the twentieth anniversary of his death, the museum was transferred to the present building.

It is divided into 24 sections:

1. Childhood and adolescence at Shao xing; 2. education (books, textbooks); 3. stay in Japan; translation of Jules Verne; 4. teaching posts at Shao xing and Hang zhou; Peking, 1912; 5. the May 4th Movement; a copy of the review which Mao Ze dong edited in Hu nan *(Xiang jiang ping lun*, first appeared in 1919); articles published by Lu Xun during the May 4th period; editions of the *True Story of Ah. Q* and various short stories; wood-cuts illustrating them; rubbings which he possessed; a view of the house in Peking in which he wrote *Wanderings* in 1923; 6. his teaching of youth; Peking Teachers' Training College for Girls; his house in Peking; a copy of *Wild Grass;* 7. political activities in Peking; 8. teaching in Amoy and Canton, texts of lectures given in Canton and Hong Kong; 9. Lu Xun "begins to master the Marxist technique"; in 1927 he moves to Shang hai; 10. he becomes a member of the League of the Leftist Writers of China; 11. resistance by left-wing intellectuals; he meets Qu Qiu bai (member of the Communist Party, who works

with Lu Xun); 12. government repression; photographs of intellectuals who were executed; 13. against the Japanese; 14. against fascism; 15. against "the third sort of men"; 16. in favour of mass education and the reform of Chinese characters; copies of works of his published in transcription; article on Chinese characters and latinisation (*Zhong hua ri bao*, August 25th 1934)17. in favour of international culture; contacts with foreign writers (particularly Bernard Shaw); 18. in favour of cultural exchanges with the Russians; his friendship with Gorki; 19. in favour of the development of popular art and wood-cutting; engraving tools; collection of engravings and *nian hua* which belonged to him; 20. his love of children and youth; 21. revolutionary friendship; 22. "entrust China to the Party"; 23. his death; stele from his first tomb and his portrait; articles and reviews which appeared after his death; 24. collection of his works and of works written on him; translations, records, films (adapted from his short stories); an article by Claude Roy entitled *Lu Sin, le Gorki chinois*, which appeared in *Les Lettres Françaises*, December 31st 1953.

6. Song jiang xian

Song jiang xian is about 12½ miles south-west of Shang hai, on the railway line to Hang zhou. The town was founded under the Sui; it was famous, even at this time, for a delicate fish known as "Song perch" (Song lu). At the beginning of the 20th century, Song jiang was also known for its dye works.

West of the Grain Market Bridge (Gu shi qiao), in the south-east of the town, stands the Pagoda belonging to the Xing sheng jiao si Temple; it was built under the Song, in the 11th century, and restored under the

Ming and the Qing. The Pagoda is square, built in brick, and has nine stories, each surmounted by a wooden roof; each facet contains a window, and a staircase goes up to the top.

ZHE JIANG

(Map see Atlas pl. 11)

The province of Zhe jiang is bordered by Shang hai and Jiang su (the southern shores of Lake Tai hu) to the north, An hui and Jiang xi to the west, Fu jian to the south; it faces the sea to the east. It is one of the smallest provinces in China. The River Qian tang jiang (also called the Zhe jiang, hence the name of the province) is its largest waterway; it is 254 miles long, and rises in An hui to run roughly from south-west to north-east, finally forming a huge estuary, the Gulf of Hang zhou, where the famous tidal wave occurs which used to attract crowds of tourists to Hang zhou every year at the autumn equinox. The river Qian tang jiang divides the province into two parts; the north-west consists of some low mountains (the Tian mu shan and the Mo gan shan) and a plain (the plain of Jia xing and Hang zhou, which is the extension of the Jiang su plain from a geographical point of view). The mountains in the south-west are higher (Mount Yan dang shan: 3,672 feet); they are rich in trees and minerals, and famous for their scenery (waterfalls, bamboo forests, seas of clouds). The coastline is long, rocky and fringed by countless islands (the Zhou shan archipelago consists of over 500 altogether). The latitude and the presence of the sea combine to produce a mainly mild and wet climate (sub-tropical plants can be grown).

During the Warring States period, the semi-barbarian kingdoms of Wu and Yue held the north of the province; not until the Han population began to penetrate the south, from the Southern Dynasties onwards, did the area start to develop (see p. 1062, the history of Hang zhou). Under the Five Dynasties, the Song, and most of all the Southern Song, it underwent a period of spectacular economic development, which was accentuated by the Song Dynasty's "retreat" to the south. Agriculture, and particularly sericulture, were stimulated by the presence of the court at Hang zhou. It affected other places as well as Hang zhou, such as Long quan in the south of the province, where the pottery kilns were extremely active from the Five Dynasties up till the end of the Yuan, and Wen zhou, the port which exported the pottery. When the capital was moved to Peking under the Yuan, and later under Yong le of the Ming dynasty, Zhe jiang gradually moved into a period of economic stagnation and difficulty, made worse by the constant attacks of the "Japanese pirates" in the 16th century. In the 19th century, the Tai ping rebellion provoked intense activity in the north of the province; a section of the population joined in, and the areas affected suffered widespread destruction.

From an economic point of view, the Qian tang jiang valley is apart from the rest of the province. The Jia xing and Hang zhou plain is cultivated with the utmost care, forming the most important agricultural area in the province. Like Jiang su, it is covered with a network of canals which facilitate both irrigation and transport; the ponds are used for fish-rearing; the grass at the edge of the fields feeds cattle and sheep (meat and sheepskins); the dead mulberry leaves, the fish, cow-dung and mud from the lakes fertilize the fields; the main crops are rice and mulberry leaves, but flax, cotton, rape, hemp, lotus and water-chestnuts are also grown; the area is densely populated. The railway line from Hang zhou to Jiang xi follows the upper reaches of the river as it cuts a way through the hills; the line also gives access to Shang hai and Canton. The river has been harnessed recently by the great Xin an jiang Dam (upstream from Lan xi, the Qian tang jiang changes its name); the electricity produced is distributed to Hang zhou and even Nanking. The mountains on either side of the Qian tang jiang valley produce wood and bamboo, and tea; as the winters are particularly warm in the south, sugar cane, oranges and mandarin oranges can be grown there (Huang yan is famous for them). There are also mineral resources (sulphur, alum, coal, iron and tin mines). Part of the population of the coastal districts lives off the sea (harbours at Ning bo and Wen zhou); fishing is carried out in the Zhou shan archipelago. A new railway line has recently been opened linking Ning bo and Shao xing with Hang zhou. New branches of light industry have grown up at Ning bo, Hang zhou, Wen zhou; the textile industry is the most widespread. The province has a population of 30 million inhabitants.

Hang zhou, the capital of the province, will be described first, followed by the northern and north-eastern towns; then come the Buddhist centres of Pu tuo and Tian tai, Wan zhou in the south-east, and finally a few places further inland.

HANG ZHOU

(Map see Atlas pl. 12/13)

The town lies to the north-west of the mouth of the river Qian tang jiang (also called Zhe jiang), and to the

east of a famous lake: the Xi hu (Western Lake). When
the Song retreated from the advance of the invaders
from the north, the town became the capital of the
southern empire, and for several centuries it underwent
astonishing development. It is still a large town, famous for its silk, and much appreciated by tourists. It is
the capital of Zhe jiang, and its population is 700,000.

History

1. Its Origins. Unlike Su zhou, Hang zhou is not a town
of ancient foundation. At first, no doubt up to the Han, the
site was a gulf, part of the sea, shut in by the Bao shi shan
Hill to the north and the Wu shan promontory to the south.
Tradition has it that when the emperor Qin shi Huang di was travelling in the south of his empire, he moored his ship to a large
rock on the Bao shi shan. It is a fact that a storm prevented the
emperor from crossing the Qian tang jiang at this point, and
that he had to cross it higher up. The first dyke intended to
protect the countryside from the sea was probably built under
the Han. Little by little, the flow of the Qian tang jiang and the
tide combined to form a coastline which linked the Bao shi shan
and the Wu shan and cut off the Xi hu to the west. A settlement
was formed there, probably on the Wu shan, which the Han
used as a base during their advance towards the south. "The
gradual assimilation of the original inhabitants and the development of agriculture in the region may have contributed to
make this place into a local market" (cf. Maspéro, *Rapport
sommaire sur une mission archéologique au Tcho-Kiang, BEFEO,
1914*).

2. From the Sui to the beginning of the Song. The digging
of the Imperial Canal, and its extension south of the Yang
zi resulted in the enlarging of the city (the last few years of
the 6th century); in 591, Yang Suo, the duke of Yue, had
a wall built round it, whose circumference was 36 *li* (about
11 miles); it cannot now be traced. Well-fortified, the town
grew during the peaceful years at the beginning of the Tang
dynasty. However, its situation, on a sandbank between the
Xin hu and the river, was precarious. The lake flowed into
the river (by way of a tributary, to the north-east) and so threatened the town from the west, in time of flood; to the south-east,
the Qian tang jiang flowed into the sea, and the danger was

FORMATION DU LAC DE L'OUEST
FORMATION OF THE WESTERN LAKE

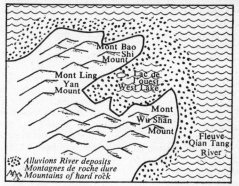

Mont Bao
Shi
Mount

Mont Ling
Yan
Mount

Lac de
l'ouest
West Lake

Mont
Wu Shan
Mount

Fleuve
Qian Tang
River

Alluvions River deposits
Montagnes de roche dure
Mountains of hard rock

*Schéma indiquant la façon dont le Lac de l'Ouest a été séparé
de la mer par les alluvions*
*Diagram showing how the Western Lake has been separated from the
sea by the river deposits*

particularly acute at the equinox, when the high tides produced,
and still do produce, famous tidal waves. Several mentions
of work on dykes under the Tang have been found. Maspéro
will be quoted on this (*Rapport sommaire*, p. 6).

As early as the Tang era, the lake seems to have been divided
into the higher and lower lakes, as it is today, by a sort of
sandbank linking the Gu shan island to the bank; at some
time under the Tang, a dyke was built to support it (Bai sha
ti). It was Li Bi, who was governor of Hang zhou in 799, who
thought of a way to control the flow of the water, and had
two locks with bridges built: one, the Duan Qiao, cut through
the Bai sha ti, and linked or cut off the two parts of the lake as
was needed; the other, the Shi han qiao, controlled the flow
of water at the mouth of the tributary (both still exist today).
Li Bi is also said to be responsible for the digging of six wells
in the town, and for the building of canals to bring in water
from Lake Xi hu.

Soon afterwards, in 824, Bai Ju yi was appointed governor of Hang zhou; he completed Li Bi's work by having the southern bank of the lower lake reinforced by a dyke called after him (the Bai gong ti), of which only traces are left today. This protected the town from dangers from one quarter, but left it still exposed to the terrible tidal waves at the equinox. "Since human strength cannot protect the city adequately", Bai Ju yi tried another way, and addressed prayers to the god of the river. Only a century later, in 910, the governor Qian liu (soon to become king of Wu Yue) began to build the sea wall which still exists today. The waves washing over it night and day prevented the work from going on; so he treated the god as an enemy, and stationed several hundred archers on the bank to shoot at the crests of the waves; at the same time he prayed and composed a propitiatory poem ("To warn the king of the dragons and the government of the waters, that on the river Qian, I have had the Qian wall built"); the waves immediately left the wall and broke against the opposite bank. A bamboo stockade was then put up, with piles of large stones and pieces of timber behind it to reinforce it. The suburbs on this side are built on what was once the river bed.

Work on the dykes continued throughout the centuries which followed; one of the most famous was that which the poet Su Dong po had built when he was governor of Hang zhou (1089-1091); he reinforced the sandbank separating the main lake from its western part by a dyke which still bears his name (Su ti).

In the 10th century (more exactly from 907 to 978 during the so-called "Five Dynasties" period), Hang zhou underwent its first development, under the short dynasty of the kings of Wu Yue. Three large pagodas (one remains: the Pagoda of Six Harmonies) and several big monasteries were built.

3. The Southern Song. After the fall of Bian jing (Kai feng) in 1126, the court wandered for a time in the middle and lower Yang zi region, in search of a new capital. Hang zhou was the final choice, as the surrounding lakes and rice-fields protected it from the advances of the Jin cavalry. The town began to flourish as never before. There are many contemporary sources of information about Hang zhou under the Song, and J. Gernet has used them in a book which has now become a standard work on the period: *Daily Life in China on the Eve of the Mongol Invasion, 1250-1276*, Hachette 1959, trans. H.M. Wright, George Allen and Unwin 1962. Numerous quotations will be made from it here.

We still have a detailed plan of Hang zhou as it was in 1274. "The names of each district, each bridge, of its public buildings, its military camps and its temples, are marked there with the utmost precision... The lay-out was simple: a large thoroughfare (the Imperial Way)... traversed the city from north to south, terminating at the north gate of the Imperial Palace, and then, beyond the Palace, continuing southwards to the altar for the sacrifices to Heaven and Earth. This thoroughfare was crossed at right angles by others running east and west. In addition, several canals ran parallel to the Imperial Way... It is not known how far these suburbs extended to the north and to the south; all that can be said is that it would appear that the whole built-up area must, by 1274, have covered a surface of between seven and eight square miles." (Gernet, op. cit. p. 27).

Hang zhou is therefore one of the most striking examples of the phenomenon of urban development which was happening at that time in the lower Yang zi region. Accurate census figures show how the population increased. "Between 1165 and 1173, 104,669 families were counted, the equivalent, that is, if the current average of four to five individuals per family is accepted, of a population of just below half a million. Between 1241 and 1252, 111,336 families were registered, a figure corresponding to over 500,000 inhabitants. The final figure, about the year 1270, was 186,330 families, that is to say, a total population of around 900 000... 'Still, today,' says an inhabitant of Hangchow in 1275, 'the population of the town continues to increase year by year and month by month'." (op. cit. p. 29–30).

This increase, an astonishing one for that time, brought with it town-planning difficulties. First of all, it became essential to build houses of several stories ("eight or ten", "three to five", depending on the sources). The town was over-populated; fires were frequent (at least four are mentioned for the 12th century); rather than run the constant risk of fire, tradesmen preferred to rent warehouses north-east of the ramparts, where they were surrounded by water and always safe. Transport in town was mainly by canal; hardly any carts were to be seen except on the Imperial Way, where they chiefly carried people.

Supplying a market like this called for strict organisation. A contemporary says: ' "I once had the occasion of hearing the head of the officials employed at the prefecture say, that if one excludes the families who obtain their supplies directly from outside, there are in the city (within the ramparts) 160,000 to

170,000 people who have to buy their rice in the shops. Now, if one reckons an average of 2½ lb. daily consumption per head, it is clear that a supply of at least 210 to 280 tons of rice is required daily. And neither the suburbs to the north and to the south, nor visiting merchants, nor travellers, are included in this calculation."' Apart from rice, pork and salt fish were important forms of food. Marco Polo, who visited the town at the end of the 13th century, says of it: "(there) are ten principal markets, though besides these there are a vast number of others in the different parts of the town... there is always an ample supply of every kind of meat and game,.. and of duck and geese an infinite quantity... From the Ocean sea come daily supplies of fish in great quantity, brought twenty-five miles up the river... All the ten market places are encompassed by lofty houses, and below these are shops where all sorts of crafts are carried on, and all sorts of wares are on sale, including spices and jewels and pearls. Some of these shops are entirely devoted to the sale of wine made from rice and spices, which is constantly made fresh, and is sold very cheap." (*The Book of Ser Marco Polo concerning the Kingdoms and Marvels of the East*, trans. and edited by Sir Henry Yule, 3rd ed. revised by Henri Cordier, 2 vols., London 1926, pp. 201-2 quoted by Gernet, op. cit., p. 47–48).

Since the court, and large numbers of official and people of leisure, had settled in Hang zhou, whole districts were soon turned over entirely to entertainments. '"Quinsai... is the greatest city which may be found in the world,' says Marco Polo, 'where so many pleasures may be found that one fancies himself to be in Paradise."' (*Marco Polo, The Description of the World*, edited by A.C. Moule and Paul Pelliot, London 1938, p. 326, quoted by Gernet, op. cit., p. 48). This was the beginning of a reputation which the town was to keep for a long time. There were countless taverns, large restaurants, theatres, and street entertainers ranging from strolling players and storytellers, operators of marionette and shadow puppet theatres, acrobats, jugglers, tight-rope walkers, to owners of performing animals. One of the most popular places was the Western Lake, where there were fleets of pleasure boats.

The aristocratic districts were to the south. Rich merchants had their houses built on Phoenix Hill (Feng huang shan); the Imperial Palace was north-east of the hill. It had already been destroyed by Marco Polo's time, but he gives a description of it, however, based on information given him by an old merchant: "In the middle part one entered through a very

HANG ZHOU EN 1274
HANG ZHOU IN 1274

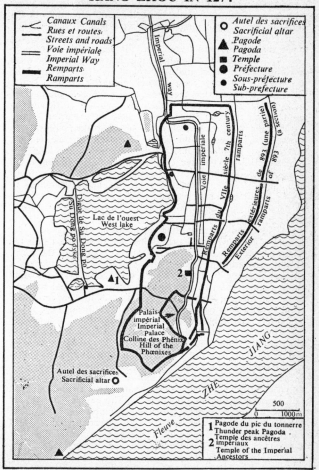

Canaux Canals
Rues et routes
Streets and roads
Voie impériale
Imperial Way
Remparts
Ramparts

○ *Autel des sacrifices*
Sacrificial altar
▲ *Pagode*
Pagoda
● *Temple*
■ *Préfecture*
Sous-préfecture
Sub-prefecture

Imperial way

Voie impériale

remparts du VIIe siècle 7th century ramparts

of 893 (a section) de 893 (une partie)

Digue de Su Dong po Su Tong po Dyke

Lac de l'ouest West lake

Remparts extérieures Exterior ramparts

1 Pagode du pic du tonnerre Thunder peak Pagoda

2 Temple des ancêtres impériaux Temple of the Imperial Ancestors

Palais impérial Imperial Palace
Colline des Phénix Hill of the Phoenixes

Autel des sacrifices Sacrificial altar

ZHE JIANG Fleuve

500
1000 m

1 Pagode du pic du tonnerre
Thunder peak Pagoda
2 Temple des ancêtres impériaux
Temple of the Imperial Ancestors

(d'après le plan reproduit dans J. GERNET, *La vie quotidienne en Chine à la veille de l'invasion mongole 1250-1276*, Hachette, 1959).
(after the plan reproduced in J. GERNET, *Daily life in China on the eve of the Mongol invasion 1250-1276*, Hachette, 1959).

large gate, where were found on one side and on the other very large and broad pavilions on the level ground, with the roof supported by columns which were painted and worked with gold and the finest azures. Then at the head was seen the principal one and larger than all the others, painted in the like way with the pillars gilt, and the ceiling with the most beautiful ornaments of gold; and round about on the walls the stories of past kings were painted with the greatest skill... Beyond... one found another great palace made in the manner of a cloister with its pillars which held up the portico which went round the said cloister, and there were various rooms for the king and queen which were likewise worked with various works, and so were all the walls. Then from this cloister one entered into a walk six paces wide, all covered... so long that it reached down to the lake... The two parts of the said enclosure were laid out with woods, lakes and most beautiful gardens planted with fruit trees, where were enclosed all sorts of animals..."
(A.C. Moule and Paul Pelliot: *Marco Polo, The Description of the World*, London, 1938, vol. I, 338-9, quoted by Gernet, op. cit., p. 119–120).

4. The Yuan and the Ming. Hang zhou was taken by the Mongols in 1276, and South China was assimilated into the Yuan empire, but all this did not immediately ruin the town. It still prospered, in spite of irritating regulations (such as a curfew) imposed by the Mongols. Hang zhou was a trading centre, and stood to profit by the new international network which the Mongol conquest had produced. Numerous foreigners from Central Asia or the South Seas passed through the town; some left invaluable descriptions. Marco Polo has already been quoted; in the 14th century, Odoric de Pordenone and Ibn Battuta visited Hang zhou. De Pordenone says that it is a city "greater than any in the world, and is quite 100 miles round; nor is there any span of ground that is not well inhabited... It has twelve principal gates; and at each of these gates at about eight miles are cities larger than Venice or Padua might be". (quoted by Gernet, op. cit. p. 31, who quotes A.C. Moule: *Quinsai with other notes on Marco Polo*, Cambridge, 1957, p. 25). Ibn Battuta stresses the cosmopolitan aspect of the city, and the different religions to be found side by side there (see H.A.R. Gibb; *Ibn Battuta, Travels in Asia and Africa*, 1325, 1354, London, 1929, p. 293–4).

Under the Ming, the town retained its importance; the silk industry developed there, at the same time as at Su zhou. The walls were rebuilt in 1359.

5. The Qing and the Republic. Although no longer the capital, Hang zhou still had a large population, and its economy flourished. One source of wealth was the endless flow of travellers who came there to rest and enjoy themselves. A proverb claimed that "in heaven there is paradise, on earth, Su zhou and Hang zhou". Several small monographs were published, some of which are true "tourist's guides" (the oldest known one of these is the *Xi hu you lan zhi*, which dates from 1584). Emperors Kang xi and Qian long spent long stays in Hang zhou when travelling in the south, and Qian long had a palace built on the Gu shan hill, cf. below, p. 1072).

Grosier describes the town at the end of the 18th century (*Description*, Vol. I, p. 106): "According to the Chinese, Hang zhou fu, the capital of the province, is an earthly paradise: it can be considered as one of the richest, best situated and largest towns in the empire; it has a circumference of four leagues, without counting the suburbs, and a population of over a million. About sixty thousand silk workers live here... The town's greatest charm, however, is a little lake called Xi hu, which washes the foot of the walls to the west...

"This large city is known above all for the splendour of its triumphal arches, and quaysides, as well as for the network of canals all over it. There are four nine-storey towers... All the streets are paved with large, square stones. The river Qian tang flows near the walls; at this point it is a league wide. The movement of the tide is noticeable throughout the year; a spectacular phenomenon occurs, however, on the 18th day of the eighth lunar month (usually in October), when mountainous waves from the sea travel up the river with such violence and force that it is both wonderful and alarming. At about four o'clock in the afternoon, the magistrates, all the inhabitants of the town, and crowds of strangers gather on the bank to watch the rise of the waters and the prodigious speed of this enormous tide... As it is the provincial capital, the town of Hang zhou fu has a garrison of three thousand men, who are under the viceroy's orders, and seven thousand Tartars, commanded by a Tartar general.

"The inhabitants have chosen the delightful neighbourhood of the Xi hu Lake for their most important cemetery... The tombs are low buildings, only about six or eight feet high, in the shape of little houses. Several will be built together, in line, to form a little street; most of them are painted blue and decorated with white pilasters; some are divided into

into fifteen or twenty cells, alongside each other, each made to take a coffin. The humblest graves are covered only with wood, earth or grass; they belong to the poor... The tombs of the rich are usually half-way up the hill, on semi-circular terraces made to accommodate them. They have walls round them, and the door is a slab of white marble, inscribed with the name, qualities, and a passage in praise of those whose mortal remains are laid there. The terraces are sometimes embellished by obelisks, and nearly always by the dark, melancholy foliage of cyprus trees or weeping evergreens with drooping branches. The tombs and their contents are guarded by priests living in the nearby monasteries; their yearly payment for this represents a large part of their income."

The town suffered heavily during the Tai ping rebellion; most of the temples were burned, which explains why so few are left today. Hang zhou was opened to foreign trade, particularly Japanese, by the treaty of Shimonoseki (1895). The building of the railway, linking the town first with Shang hai, and later with Ning bo, made trade easier; up till then, almost all goods had been carried by the Grand Canal or the river Qian tang jiang.

6. Since the liberation. Light industry has been developed considerably since 1950; machine factories and hemp spinning factories have been built alongside the silk filatures, which still flourish. Satin, brocade, pictures woven in silk, parasols and other products of local crafts (such as sandalwood fans, chopsticks, little knives) are all made there. Thanks to its fertile soil, the region grows rice, hemp, silk worms, and cotton; 'Dragon well' green tea (Long jing cha) enjoys a wide reputation.

Parts of the town have been re-built, especially parts of the centre and to the north of the town (Zhe jiang University, living accommodation for workmen). Old villas round the lake have been converted into convalescent homes, and sanatoria have been built for workers from industrial centres of the lower Yang zi.

Description

The Western Lake will be dealt with first, then the town, and finally the surroundings of the lake (north, west and south).

1. The Western Lake (Xi hu)

History: At the end of the 18th century, Grosier wrote: "The Xi hu Lake, famous throughout the empire for its pleasant situation, its delightful views and its charming walks, washes the western walls of Hang zhou fu. It is about two leagues round... Towards the banks, its surface is covered by the beautiful flowers and floating carpet of leaves of the *lian hua* (lotus)... Long roadways built on piling and paved in the centre with large square stones cross the Lake in several directions. Banana-trees, weeping willows and peach trees are planted on either side of the roadways, along the entire length of them. When the peach trees are in flower, they make the whole lake quite dazzlingly beautiful: all the people from the surrounding coun-tryside and neighbouring towns come in their crowds to see the enchanting sight... An amphitheatre of mountains surrounds the lake to the north, west and south, leaving a circular area of level ground between themselves and the lake. On the moun-tainsides, among the trees and plantations of all kinds, can be seen vast monasteries, pagodas, towers, and tombs, and in the gorges between the hills, bridges of most strange and daring construction span all the streams which run down into the lake."

The countryside had already changed considerably since the Song dynasty, when the surrounding hills were all covered with woods. To the south of the town, the imperial park contained the "Ten thousand pine forest" (Wan song lin), whose name alone survives now, and the Ling yin Hill, to the west, was covered with dense woods, where monkeys lived until the disappearance of the trees drove them elsewhere.

Description. The Xi hu is a small lake, with a surface area of about 1,235 acres; its shape is irregular. It is divided into three by two ancient dykes, built to con-trol the water flowing down from the hills and to pre-vent storms when the wind blew in from the sea. The **Bai Ju yi Dyke (Bai ti)** is to the north; it was in fact built before the famous poet became governor of Hang zhou (8th century) and was called Bai sha ti (the white sand dyke). But as the dyke which Bai Ju yi had built (along the river, south of the town) disappeared very soon, his memory became connected with the northern dyke. This was made easier by the character *bai* which occurred in the original name, and is also the poet's name. The way from the town to the Hang zhou Hotel lies along this dyke. It runs alongside the southern shore of Gu shan Island, and then rejoins the land.

The **Su Dong po dyke (Su ti)** is to the west; it begins to the north, in front of the temple dedicated to Yue Fei, and ends to the south at the foot of the Nan ping shan. Six bridges cut through it, hence its other name: Liu qiao ti ("the six bridge dyke").

There are four islands in the lake, two of which are very small. The largest, to the north-west, is called **Gu shan (The lonely hill),** and is linked to the land by a bridge (to the west) and by the Bai Ju yi dyke (to the east).

History. In the 18th century, Emperor Qian long had a palace built on the southern shore of the island, facing the lake. It included a temple, the Sheng yin si, and a large library, one of six founded by Qian long in 1773 to house a collection of manuscripts of works which made up the Great Encyclopedia of *Si ku quan shu*. To the left of the temple was a stone stupa; on its sixteen facets were reproduced, in outline, a series of sixteen *luo han* (painted by a famous 10th century priest, while he was staying in Hang zhou). The emperor liked contemplating the lake, and he had a little pavilion built in the south-east of the island with a stele bearing the four characters: *Ping hu qiu yue* (Autumn moon on the calm lake). The palace suffered badly during the Tai ping rebellion; the Wen lan ge library was the worst affected (two thirds of the books vanished, either lost, stolen or destroyed, and the massive cupboards which had contained them were destroyed). A local scholar, Ding Bing, restored the library, and tried to replace the missing works by copies. A European house, which was to be the palace of Prince Henry of Prussia, was built on the ruins of the imperial residence. After the 1912 revolution, the gardens were opened to the public, and the Sheng yin Temple was consecrated "to the memory of officers and men of the Zhe jiang revolutionary army who fell at Nanking". The library was once more restored, and a museum was organised in 1929. At the beginning of the 20th century, a small society of scholars who were interested in epigraphs and rubbings settled in the west of the island, and made a collection of ancient inscriptions.

Description. Coming from the Bai Ju yi dyke, there are first of all, on the left, the small pavilion and stele built by Qian long; it is said that autumn is the time to watch the moonlight on the lake from there. The road then passes first the entrance to the old Sheng yin si Temple (with old statues in the gardens), on the right, and then the entrance to the **Zhe jiang Provincial Museum**, which has taken over the old Wen lan ge and its annexes.

The museum consists of a small botanical garden, a section devoted to botany and zoology, a section on physical geography, natural resources and recent changes in the province of Zhe jiang, a section on popular arts and a section on history, which is the largest, and which will be briefly described.

From the origins up to the Han dynasty: prehistoric objects, bronze ploughshares dating from the Warring States period (found near Shao xing in 1959); the seal of an inspector of the waters, Han period; coins; iron tools; eight pieces of pottery found in the tomb of a Han civil servant, at Hang zhou, in 1958. *From the Southern Dynasties up to the Yuan:* irrigation work under the eastern Jin; a fine urn for storing grain and a cage for hens from the Jin period (found at Shao xing); a map of the Sun En rising in 400; a map of the Grand Canal; Tang mirrors, found in Hang zhou; remains of wooden posts from the Tang sea wall, and a model of the work; map of the Qiu Fu rising, in Zhe jiang (859–960); Song iron tools; reproduction of the map of Bian jing (Kai feng); seal belonging to General Yue Fei (whose tomb is at Hang zhou); copy of a picture by Li Song (Song dynasty) showing the Western

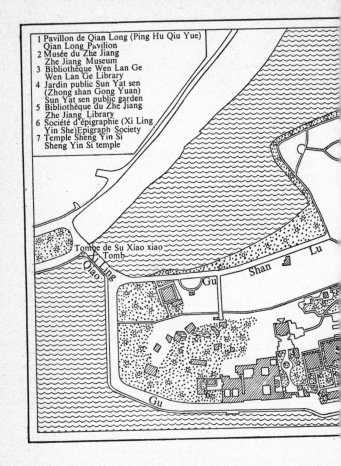

1 Pavillon de Qian Long (Ping Hu Qiu Yue)
  Qian Long Pavilion
2 Musée du Zhe Jiang
  Zhe Jiang Museum
3 Bibliothèque Wen Lan Ge
  Wen Lan Ge Library
4 Jardin public Sun Yat sen
  (Zhong shan Gong Yuan)
  Sun Yat sen public garden
5 Bibliothèque du Zhe Jiang
  Zhe Jiang Library
6 Société d'épigraphie (Xi Ling
  Yin She) Epigraph Society
7 Temple Sheng Yin Si
  Sheng Yin Si temple

Tombe de Su Xiao xiao
Tomb

Li Ling

Qiao

Gu   Shan   Lu

Gu

Lake; rubbing depicting a map of the heavens (the stele is at the Temple of Confucius at Su zhou); model of the Pagoda of Six Harmonies (at Hang zhou);

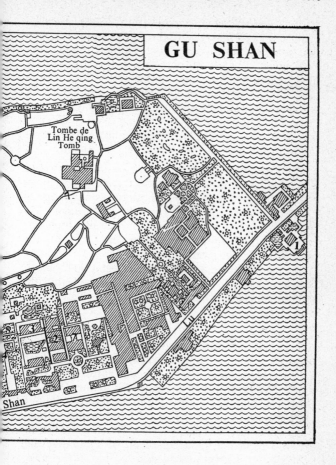

models of Yuan agricultural tools; portraits and works
of the scholar Shen Gua (11th century, a native of
Hang zhou); Yuan bronze cannon, found in the West-

ern Lake. *Ming and Qing:* cadastral registers (so-called "fish-scale", *yu lin ci);* silk (models of looms); model of a boat used for carrying goods on the Grand Canal; very fine collection of porcelain (some from Long quan); documents concerning the resistance to Japanese pirates: portrait of Qi Duan guan (1528–1587), who put up a valiant resistance, painting of a Zhe jiang town attacked by the Japanese; Qing dynasty silk, and paintings. *Present day:* the different phases of the revolution in the province of Zhe jiang.

The skeleton of a whale washed up on the coast of Zhe jiang has a room to itself. At this point it is interesting to turn to a passage in J. Gernet's *Daily Life in China on the Eve of the Mongol Invasion, 1250–1276* (p. 38): "In 1282, a whale over thirty yards long was stranded on the sandbanks of the Che river near the ramparts of Hangchow, and some rascals brought ladders and climbed on to its back to cut it up for meat. Not long after, fire broke out in the town. Notwithstanding the lack of factual evidence, there were people who declared that the fire had been caused by the whale."

The road then passes the entrance to the **Sun Yat sen Gardens (Zhong shan gong yuan),** which have been adapted from what were once the gardens of Qian long's palace, and then the entrance to the **Zhe jiang Provincial Library** (re-arranged in a modern building). On the western tip of the island is the **Xi leng Bridge Epigraph Society (Xi leng yin she).** The slopes of the hill are covered with attractive gardens, with an interesting collection of inscriptions on stone.

The stupa with sixteen facets mentioned on p. 1072 is at the top of the hill. It can be reached by a path perpendicular to Gu Shan lu on the south of the island, or by the path running along the ridge from east to west.

The Gu shan also has several tombs, the most famous of which is that of the Song poet, Lin He qing (967–1028), in the north of the island, near the hermitage to which he retired towards the end of his life. To the west, a bridge links the island with the mainland; the tomb nearby is said to be that of the beautiful Su Xiao xiao, a famous 5th century lady. She is supposed to have seen her lover for the first time here, and a poem tells of the meeting: "She comes in a lacquer chariot,/He arrives on a beautiful black horse,/Where did their hearts meet?/ Under the pines of Xi ling". The tomb of Qiu Jin, a heroine of the revolution, is a little further north (cf. p. 1093).

The little **Xiao ying zhou Island** is in the southern part of the lake. It is said to have been made from earth and rubble during work on the lake undertaken by Su Dong po. A boat goes there from the north shore. The form of the island is unexpected: a surrounding wall of earth encloses four small lakes separated by dykes (which converge in an islet in the middle) and covered with lotus plants, which flower in July and August. A series of small pavilions have been built round the banks. South of the island, about a hundred yards from the shore, three little stupas stick up out of the water; they are shaped "like bottles" (the Chinese say they are shaped "like gourds"); they are known as the *San tan*. The name is an old one, and dates from the Song, but the stupas themselves were built in the early 17th century (Wan li period); even the site is different from the original one (Maspéro). On summer evenings, lamps used to be lit in the upper part of each of the "three tan" and the artificial light mingled with the moonlight.

2. The Town

The ramparts were still standing in 1914, but have now been destroyed entirely. Most of the old temples were burned during the Tai ping rebellion; some were restored at the end of the 19th and the beginning of the 20th centuries, but scarcely any are open to the public now. The centre of the town is completely modern, and even in the oldest districts, archaeological remains are rare.

A possible route for a visit to the town could be as follows: **Lakeside Avenue (Hu bing lu),** where there are several hotels and three memorial monuments, then **Sun Yat sen Avenue (Zhong shan lu),** which follows roughly the same direction as the old Imperial Way, and then some of the canals which have not yet been filled in. In the southern part, the massive base of the old **Drum Tower** can still be seen, and the Mosque can be visited.

The Mosque, known as Feng huang si ("Phoenix Temple"), is number 325, Sun Yat sen Avenue. It still contains four steles, which give some details on its history. They date from 1492, 1648, 1670 and 1743, and indicate that in each year the Mosque was restored. The third one (dated "the ninth year of the Kang xi era") says that "it was founded under the Tang and burned under the Song; that under the Yuan, a man called Aladin from Central Asia gave silk and gold so that it might be rebuilt, but that afterwards it was again destroyed by fire". The Mosque was extensively restored in 1953.

A little corridor leads into the courtyard, which is almost entirely filled by a modern building; going round the right hand side of this, the visitor passes a small collection of steles, and then enters what is left of the old prayer hall. It is the western end of a hall which once extended further east, and was made up of three bays separated by two lines of pillars. The mihrab, which is a fine one, probably dates from the Ming.

South of the town lies the **Wu shan Hill** (so called because it was on the frontier of the State of Wu); the Temple of the Town Gods used to be here. South of the Wu shan is the Phoenix Hill (Feng huang shan); the imperial palace and the rich merchants' villas stood here in the Song dynasty. As far as is known, no diggings have yet been undertaken here.

3. North side of the lake

Just outside the town, and beside the lake, lies the **Zhao qing si Temple,** rebuilt in the 20th century, but now out of use.

A large hill lies north of the lake (it has no name). There is a road, but it is better to climb it by way of the little paths leading to various places of interest. To the south-east, at the foot of the Bao shi shan (Precious Stone Summit), lie the buildings of the **Great Buddha Temple (Da fo si),** called after the large Buddha in the courtyard behind. "A rock about 30 feet high has been carved to represent the head and shoulders of Amitabha emerging from the ground. Tradition has it that Qin shi Huang di moored his boat here in the days when the site of Hang zhou was covered by water, and the Xi hu was a gulf, not a lake. The priest Si jing carved it at the beginning of the 12th century... When the Mongols took Hang zhou in 1276, the temple which housed the statues was burned and the statue fell partly into ruin; a century and a half passed before it was restored, during the Yong le period (1403–1424). The Tai ping destroyed it again in the middle of the last century. Today (1914) the face has entirely disappeared, from the forehead to the chin, revealing marks left by the cramps used in the 15th century restoration... But in spite of its delapidated state, the effect is still striking." (Maspéro, 1914.)

The **Bao shu ta** is on the top of the Bao shi shan, above the Da fo si; it is a tall, slender brick stupa, with no ornaments and no interior staircase. It was founded in the 10th century, by a minister of the king of Wu Yue; since then it has been ruined and restored several times, and it was entirely rebuilt in the 20th century. An esplanade stretches westwards from the tower, with a magnificent view to the south over the lake, and over the modern suburbs of the town to the north.

The **Yellow Dragon Spring (Huang long dong)** rises on the north slope of the hill, near a small Taoist temple, now out of use (in a narrow passage between the rocks east of the spring a large polychrome bas-relief of Manjusri, sitting on a lion, surrounded by clouds, can still be seen).

The next hill top along the ridge from the' Bao shi shan is the **Ge Hong Summit (Ge ling),** where the famous alchemist Ge Hong is supposed to have tried to make an elixir of life from cinnabar in the 4th century; nearby are the remains of a little temple built to his memory. Further west is the **Purple Cloud Cave (Zi yun dong),** a very deep cave, to which people come from Hang zhou in summer, to escape the heat. Next to the cave is the **Tomb of Niu Gao,** a comrade in arms of General Yue Fei, who was executed by treason at the same time (mound and stele).

The **Funerary Temple and Tomb of General Yue Fei** are at the western end of the hill. The road which leads there follows the northern shore of the lake, and passes the Xi leng and Hang zhou hotels. Yue Fei commanded the Southern Song troops, and defeated the

Jin several times; he is said to have been arrested at the height of his career by a jealous general and a treacherous minister, who threw him into prison and put him to death (1141). Popular opinion made him into a national hero; his biography has been written in novel form: the *Yue Fei zhuan*.

The temple was founded in the 12th century. South of the road, beside the lake, in the middle of a little square with shops and restaurants all round it, stands a large stone *pai lou* with three arches, inscribed with the four characters: *Bi xue, dan xin* (Blood of jade, heart of cinnabar); visitors who arrived across the lake would pass under it. The immense door leads on to an enormous courtyard, at the far end of which is the main hall, with a statue of the hero (the ceiling is decorated with cranes, a symbol of immortality). The two pavilions on either side of the courtyard contain statues of Niu Gao and Zhang Xian, comrades in arms of Yue Fei who were executed at the same time as him. West of the courtyard are the tombs of Yue Fei and his son. The way leading up to them is lined with stone statues: lions, rams; horses and civil servants. The tumulus at the end is round, with a stele in front of it; the hero's son has a smaller tomb of the same shape. Facing the tumulus, before the stone statues, stand four cast iron statues of the four traitors responsible for the capture and death of the general; they kneel two by two, their hands tied behind their backs. The present ones date from 1802. The first set, containing only three, was cast in 1513; a fourth was added in about 1600. At the beginning of the 17th century, a governor had two of them thrown into the lake, and the other two moved and placed in front of the funerary temple; these two soon vanished, and a new series was cast in 1731. Three quarters of a century later they were so

badly damaged that the governor Yuan Yuan had to
have them replaced by the present ones. The minister,
Qin Gui, and his wife, who forced him into the act,
stand on one side of the door; Mo qi Xue, the head of
the prison, and Zhang Jun, the jealous general, are on
the other side. Until quite recently, visitors used to
throw stones at them, hit them with their sticks or spit in
their faces. A small notice now asks them not to do so.

The modern buildings of Zhe jiang University lie
north-west of the hill. Just over a mile beyond the Yue
Fei Temple, on the right, a road leads off to the **Qing
lian si Temple,** also called Fang sheng si (the temple
where living beings are given their liberty). The Jade
Spring rises here (Yu quan), and, in a square pond
full of fish stands a little stupa about 18 ins. high,
which "has all the characteristics of similar small monuments in the Song dynasty" (Maspéro). The **Botanical Garden** is to the west of the temple.

4. The Western Side of the Lake

**The Ling Yin si and the "three Indian Temples" (San
tian zhu)** form the largest group of buildings on this
side of the lake; it is one of the most famous spots in
Hang zhou. The Ling yin si, also called Yun lin si
(Temple of the forest of clouds) is certainly the most
interesting of all. It stands to the north of a hill with
many Buddhist bas-reliefs, the **Fei lai feng ("the peak
which flew here").**

The traditional founder of the temple was a certain
Hui Li, who arrived from India at the beginning of the
4th century, and when he saw the hill, claimed to
recognise it as a corner of Mount Grdhrakuta "which
had flown there". The temple is supposed to have been
destroyed and rebuilt in 596, when it was called the
Southern Indian Temple. Some 8th and 9th century

inscriptions (the originals have been lost, but Chinese archaeologists preserved the texts) prove that the Ling yin si existed under this name as far back as the Tang dynasty. It was abandoned when Buddhism was persecuted in 845, but was in use again soon afterwards. The Ling yin si benefited from the development of Hang zhou in the Wu Yue and Song dynasties. (This account comes from Maspéro, *op. cit.*)

The present buildings are all recent. The temple was destroyed during the Tai ping rebellion, and was not rebuilt before the early 20th century. Four *chuang* have survived all the destructions and rebuildings; they almost certainly date from the 10th century, and are the finest things in the temple. Two of them stand, one on each side, at the main door; the king of Wu Yue had them put there in 969; they are inscribed with *dharani* texts; the other two stand to the right and left of the terrace supporting the great hall. They are two octagonal, nine-storey stone stupas, about sixty feet high; they are not dated, and it was thought that they might date from as far back as the Liang era, or from Hui li, but Maspéro claimed that they were 10th century. "The general description is simple. A low infra-structure carries the base, which is an octagonal dado supporting an entablature, also octagonal; the *Fo ding tuo luo ni jing* is inscribed on the facets. Above this is a series of stories decorated with carvings up to the roof. On each storey, the carving on four of the facets imitates the massive doors of real stupas, with the large metal nails used to decorate them; on the first storey, the other panels are exquisitely carved with two bas-reliefs of Guan yin, the second storey is inscribed with the continuation of the *dharani;* above that, still alternating with stupa doors, are panels with Buddhas and Bodhisattvas: the fourth storey is the most striking, with two panels showing Samantabhadra on his elephant and Manjusri on his lion; each one is in a boat with two assistants" (Maspéro).

In the central hall there is a large Buddha built since the liberation, and behind this, a big group showing Guan yin, mistress of the waters. At the west of the temple was a large hall of the five hundred *luo han*, with sculpture dating from the 17th century, which had escaped destruction during the Tai ping period; Maspéro saw them in 1914: the statues, almost life size, were made of gilded clay; among them were the statues of Qian long and Jia qing, put up after their visit to the temple. Although the hall was in the temple enclosure, it did not belong to it, and four monasteries took it in turns to send priests to look after it. It has now disappeared. The **Fei lai feng** rock carvings are the most interesting of all. A stream runs alongside the temple façade, and the other bank is a vertical cliff, with natural caves to the east. The caves were carved in low relief under the Five Dynasties and the Song; the cliff carvings date from the end of the 13th and the beginning of the 14th centuries. They represent one of the rare examples of Yuan rock sculpture which have survived. There are 280 figures altogether.

When approaching the cliff from the east, the visitor first comes upon a little stupa which is supposed to contain the remains of the monk Hui li; the present monument dates from 1590. Behind the stupa are two Vajrapani (defenders of Buddhism), both very expressive, which date from the Yuan. The first cave is a little further on, to the left. There are three of them altogether, and they are called **Long hong dong, Yu ru dong** and **Qing lin dong.**

The statues at the entrance to the **Long hong Cave** represent the people responsible for the main stages in the introduction of Buddhism to China: Matanga and Zhu fa lan (the first to arrive at Luo yang), Boddhidharma (said to have introduced the doctrine of Dhyana under the Liang), and Xuan zang (shown beside the horses which helped him to bring the sutras from India). Inside the cave, there is a 10th century seated statue of Guan yin, and several inscriptions made by Song dynasty tourists (particularly by the poet Su Dong po). The walls of the **Qing lin Cave** are covered with little statues 7 to 15 ins. high representing more or less complete series of the sixteen *luo han*, with a few Buddhas and Bodhisattvas. Short inscriptions show why the pilgrims had them carved: "The disciple Zhu Cheng zan made this *luo han* in order to retain (in future lives) human dignity; June 1001"; "The disciple Huang made this statue of a *luo han* for his dead parents." A large panel carved in 1022, showing Vairocana enthroned between Manjusri, on his lion, and Samantabhadra, on his elephant, decorates the north wall of the east entrance; at the top are two apsaras. On the way out of the cave a genie with bat's wings is depicted.

As has been said, the cliff sculptures all date from the Yuan. The most striking are a large group with a stout Maitreya, surrounded by sixteen *luo han* and two *yaksas* (one at each end); a large panel depicting Guan yin, with two devas standing one on each side, and two other panels, one on either side, with two superposed Vajrapani; a scene showing the Buddha receiving the offering of milk from Sujata and her daughter.

West of the Ling yin si a path with steps in places passes the entrance to the seat of the Zhe jiang Buddhist Society, and leads through a magnificent forest of blue-green bamboos to the **Tao guang**

Hermitage (Tao guang an). Tao guang was a Buddhist priest from Si chuan who settled here in the 8th century; he was a friend of Bai Ju yi, then prefect of Hang zhou, and they used to exchange poems. A small building remains, where tea is served; there is a good view.

East of the Ling yin si a path leads to the first, second and third Indian Temples (Xia, Zhong and Shang tian zhu); the temples are no longer in use, but the walk through the little villages surrounding them is a pleasant one. The path leads past a little stone stupa between the second and third temples; it is about twelve feet high, and dates probably from the 10th or 11th century.

5. Southern Side of the Lake

The **Dragon Well Temple (Long jing si)** and spring are on one of the hills to the south-west. The spring is in fact a double one, and it is pointed out to the visitor that the water from the two does not mix at first. The temple is out of use. Tea has been grown on the surrounding hills for years, and it has a long-standing reputation. It is possible to visit the **Dragon Well People's Commune,** on whose land the plantations are. It is interesting to see how the tea leaves are dried by hand, in metal trays, over a fire of twigs.

A series of three caves, known as the **Yan xia san dong,** lies further to the south. The first contains nothing of interest, but the second, called the "Stone hall" (Shi wu dong) because of its rectangular shape, contains some good sculpture said to date from the 10th century. Little statues of *luo han,* about 8 ins. high, carved out of the rock, cover the walls (518 or so altogether); an altar stands in the centre, opposite the main entrance, with Amitabha surrounded by six other people. The third cave, which dates from the 10th century, is a good fifteen minutes' walk further on. In spite of frequent restoration work, it is one of the finest to be seen at Hang zhou. Two beautiful statues of Guan yin stand on either side of the entrance; a seated statue (added under the Qing) beside the right hand side one probably represents Su Dong po. A seven-storey stupa with people kneeling round it in adoration (some of them—high-ranking officials at the court of Wu Yue—had their names inscribed there) stands beside the other Guan yin. The cave also contains a fine set of seated *luo han*, probably dating from the 10th century.

The **Hu pao si Temple** stands at the foot of the Hu pao shan, a little further on along the road leading to the Pagoda of Six Harmonies. At the beginning of the 9th century, the priest, Xing kong, wanted to build a hermitage here; as there was no water, the mountain god sent two tigers, who scratched at the ground, and revealed a spring. It is still called "the spring dug by tigers" (Hu pao quan). The present buildings are uninteresting; one annex has been converted into a tea room. The spring rises into a rectangular pond beside a pavilion containing statues of the five hundred sages (late 19th century). The spring water has strange properties: numbers of coins can be slid into a bowl already full without making it overflow; the meniscus can reach a height of several millimetres. An esplanade with the ruined base of an old pagoda lies a little further up the hill. A cage in one corner used to house a tiger until very recently.

The **Pagoda of Six Harmonies (Liu he ta)** stands on the banks of the Qian tang jiang, to the south. It was founded in 970, to help protect the town from high tides and to serve as a lighthouse. It was rebuilt under the Song, and considerably modified as time went on. It is nearly 200 ft. high, and consists of seven floors inside and thirteen outside. A broad staircase gives access to the galleries built in wood round the outside of it, which give a good view over the river. A large road and railway bridge spans the Qian tang jiang not far from the pagoda; it was built under the Republic, and before the bridge over the Yang zi was built at Wu han, it was the longest bridge in China.

The Thunder Peak Pagoda (Lei feng ta), an enormous seven-storey brick stupa, similar to the Liu he ta, was still standing at the beginning of the century on the promontory of Xi zhao shan which overlooks the south of the lake. It was founded by Queen Huang, wife of one of the kings of Wu Yue. It fell down in 1924.

The **Jing ci si Temple** lies to the south of Xi zhao shan. It used to be large, but was completely ruined during the Tai ping rebellion. It has been rebuilt recently, but is not open to the public. The monk Ji gong, one of the most highly-coloured figures of the Chinese popular tradition (several "biographies" of him were written, more in the form of novels) is connected by a legend to this temple. Once, when the temple was being restored, the wood proved insufficient. Ji gong drank a large amount of alcohol and slept for three days; when he awoke, the wood which was needed came up out of the temple well. The **Tomb of Zhang Huang yan** lies to the west of Jing ci si; Zhang Huang yan was a national hero who opposed the Manchu in the 17th century, and continued the resistance in east Zhe jiang after the fall of Nanking.

The area south of Xi zhao shan (round the Nan pin, Yu huang and Jian tai Hills) used to be covered with temples which are now either in ruins or closed to the public. Only the Guan yin Caves, containing some Yuan rock sculpture, are worth pointing out. It is possible to climb the Yu huang Hill by a little path which leads past an old Taoist temple (dedicated to the jade emperor) and then through a modern pavilion, near which stand seven large metal jars, with inscriptions in curly script on the outside. They were cast in the reign of Yong zheng of the Qing dynasty, and used to stand on the top of the Yu huang Hill, arranged in the shape of the Great Bear (hence their name: the seven stars). They were always kept full of water, and it was hoped in this way to protect the town from fire (apparently nothing referring to them can be found in the records). From the path on the hillside, the irregular circle of the **Field of the Eight Trigrams (Ba gua tian)** can be seen on the plain below. The Altar of the southern suburbs used to stand here under the Song. The altar of heaven was in the centre; in the 13th century, it was 32 ft. 4 ins high, and the upper terrace was 70 ft. wide. A rounded hillock is all that remains today, with eight rice-fields spreading round it, forming an irregular octagon. The Chinese recognise it as the summit *(tai ji)* surrounded by the traditional eight trigrams, as the name shows. J. Gernet gives a description of the solemn ritual which the Emperor performed there in his book, *Daily Life in China on the Eve of the Mongol Invasion, 1250-1276,* p. 200 onwards. The fields now belong to a people's commune, and are worked by them, but they have still retained their original shape.

NORTH ZHE JIANG

Jia xing

Jia xing is on the Shang hai—Hang zhou railway line; it is an important marketing centre for rice and silk, at the junction of several canals; there are textile and food processing factories in the town. The **Yan yu lou (Pavilion of Mist and Rain)** is to the south-east, on an island in Lake Nan hu; it was built under the Five Dynasties and restored under the Ming and the Qing. In July 1921, it gave shelter to the members of the Communist party, who were being hunted by the Shang hai police after their first meeting. The **Da sheng si Temple Pagoda** is just over half a mile east of the town; it was built in 1887 (brick, with a wooden roof).

Shao xing

Shao xing is on the Hang zhou—Ning bo railway line, about half way between the two.

It is one of the oldest towns in the province; during the Warring States period, the capital of the kingdom of Yue was on this site. Like Hang zhou, Shao xing began to expand under the Tang and developed rapidly under the Song (Southern Song tombs are to be found in the neighbourhood of the town). Its geographical position—inland, without easy access to the sea—meant that it was never on an equal with towns like Hang zhou and Ning bo, however. Grosier visited it at the end of the 18th century, and left this description of it: "It is in the middle of a wide, fertile plain, and the water all round it makes it resemble Venice... Its shores are formed by canals banked with white, with pavements of the same stone on either side" (Grosier, *Description de la Chine*, Vol. II, p. 109). The inhabitants were supposed to have an unusual knowledge of legal matters and the officials used to recruit many of their secretaries there. Part of the population was made up by a class of social outcasts known as "the beggars", supposed to be descendants of prisoners and criminals which had been distributed through the area under the Song; they were barred from all but the most humiliating trades and had to marry among themselves. At the end of the 19th century, Qiu Jin (1875–1907), a heroine of the revolution, was born there, as was the great writer Lu Xun (1881–1936). The network of canals spreading out from the town has made it an important marketing centre for rice and silk; a few branches of industry exist there, the most famous of which is probably the celebrated Shao xing yellow wine, made with the water of a neighbouring lake, which is said to ensure the quality of the wine.

In 1914, Maspéro said that "the most interesting monument in the town from an archaeological point of view (was) the former **Fu xue,** or college, now transformed into a barracks." It contained numerous inscriptions, some of which dated from the Song, and several statues of Confucius and his disciples (its present condition is unknown).

Several places are worth a visit:

1. The **Ying tian si Temple Pagoda** is on the Ta shan ling hill, in the south-west of the town; it was founded under the Song, and restored under the Ming and the Qing, burned during the Tai ping rebellion and restored soon afterwards.

2. The **Da shan si Pagoda** is in the middle of the town; it was founded in 1004 and restored in 1228; it is a hexagonal, seven-storey building, 124 feet high.

3. Two handsome stone bridges, built under the Song, can still be seen: the **Ba zi qiao** (Bridge like the character *ba*, eight) in the south-east of the town, dates from 1256; the **Bao you qiao** in the north of the town was built in 1253 and restored in 1836.

4. Several **murals dating from the Tai ping rebellion** were re-discovered in 1954 in different places in the town. Some of them are in excellent condition and depict interesting mythological and religious scenes. The most well-preserved ones are in the houses

TOMBEAU ET TEMPLE DE YU LE GRAND
TOMB AND TEMPLE OF YU THE GREAT

d'après la Revue «Wen Wu» (1959, No 7)
after the magazine «Wen Wu» (1959, No. 7)

N

Petit temple dédié à Yu le Grand
Small temple dedicated to Yu the Great

Etang
Pool

Pavillon de la stèle devant le tombeau
Pavilion with stele preceding the tomb

Pavillon avec stèles
Pavilion with steles

Pavillon de la source
Spring Pavilion

Source Fei Yin
Fei Yin Spring

Porte d'entrée
Entrance Gateway

Porte d'entrée
Entrance Gateway

Salle Centrale
Central Hall

1 Pavilion with steles from Mount Gou Lou
2 LiangXin Men Gateway
3 Great Gateway
4 Side pavilions
5 Pavilion with steles
6 Central Gateway
7 Side Pavilions
8 Pavilion with Qian Long stele
9 Pavilion with stele
10 Pavilion "Of the Stone Boat"
11 Pavilion with Qing steles
12 Pavilion with Ming steles
13 Gateway leading to the tomb

which used to be called Lai wang fu and Du jia lai
men (Xia da jie street), and Li jia tai men, Tan hua
tai men.

5. The town is full of memories of Lu Xun who
lived there as a child and staged several of his novels
there. The house where he was born is still standing
(and is said to contain some frescoes dating from the
Tai ping); a small museum, the **Lu Xun ji nian guan**
has been opened.

6. A **museum has also been opened in memory of
Qiu Jin,** a heroine of the revolution and a native
of Zhe jiang. She left her husband, an official, and
went to Japan as a student; she joined the Tong
meng hui Society founded by Doctor Sun Yat sen,
edited a newspaper by herself at Shang hai, tried to
organise the taking of Hang zhou, and was captured by
the Emperor's supporters at Hang zhou and shot
in 1907.

7. The **Temple of Yu the Great and his tomb** (Da yu
miao and Da yu ling) are about 3 miles outside the
town, at the foot of Mount Gui ji. According to the
legends, Yu the Great, the founder of the semi-
mythical Xia dynasty, died and was buried there
when on a tour of the south. From the Warring
States period onwards, the kingdom of Yue revered the
memory of the great sovereign; it claimed to have
had the honour of giving him a wife, the mother of
his successor, from whom the kings of Yue claimed
descent. The temple was certainly founded at an
early date, but the present buildings date from the
18th century. The famous tombstone is near the
temple (bian shi); it is a sort of rock about 6 feet
high, with a hole right through the top of it; it is
supposed to have been Emperor Yu's boat; Maspéro

thought that it was "probably a relic of the local religion of the ancient kingdom of Yue".

The **Bao guo si Temple,** founded under the Song (11th century) is near **Yu yao,** on the railway line to Ning bo; the main hall, the Zheng dian, is an excellent example of the architecture of that period.

Ning bo

The town stands at the confluence of the Rivers Yong jiang and Yao jiang; it is an important sea-port and the terminus of the eastern Zhe jiang railway. It is linked to Jin hua and Wen zhou by road.

During the Warring States period, the town was further south, in the mountains; it was then the city of Yin, the western frontier of the little fief of Yue, which the king of Wu granted to the king of Yue when he defeated him in 491. In the 11th century, a town was built on the present site, and was called Ming zhou. Extensive work had to be done to make this possible; like the whole of the alluvial plain south of the Gulf of Hang zhou, the Ning bo area presented most unfavourable natural conditions; the rivers were tidal for a long way inland, as the surroundings are low-lying, so their waters were brackish. The problem seems to have been overcome by digging large lakes at the foot of the hills, with no access to the sea, so that the water from the mountain streams could be collected and distributed through canals which were also closed to the sea (Maspéro). In 832, the local governor began to set up a system of locks and canals. The work was begun under the Tang, at the end of the dynasty, and was continued under the Song; at the end of the 12th century, a breakwater was begun, which when finished protected the whole area. At the same time, the town and its harbour, Zhen hai, became brisk trading centres (most of their exchanges were with Japan). At the beginning of the Ming dynasty (1381), the town was given its present name of Ning bo (calmed waves). The "Japanese pirates" made frequent attacks on it and as early as the 16th century, the Portuguese set up a warehouse depot downstream from the town, at "Liam po". At the end of the 18th century, Grosier reports that: "the silks made at Ning bo are highly valued abroad, particularly in Japan, where the Chinese exchange them for copper, gold and silver." English troops attacked the town in October 1841, during the Opium War; the Treaty of Nanking opened the port to British trade; in December 1843, a British consulate was opened there. The Tai ping armies occupied it in November 1861, but the French and English fleets forced them to retreat in 1862 (in 1916, a pyramid erected "in memory of the officers and men of the French ships 'Etoile' and 'Confucius' killed in action at Ning bo on May 10th 1862" was still standing). Ning bo is now the focal point of land and sea communications in eastern Zhe jiang; a regular service runs between it and Shang hai. It is well known for its textiles, its fishing, its salt pans, and most of all for its food-processing factories (its chief export is tinned bamboo shoots). The population is over 200,000.

In 1914, Maspéro described the Tian hou gong **(Palace of the Celestial Queen),** then used as a club for people from Fu jian (in the eastern suburbs), as the "richest and most beautiful temple in Ning bo"; one of the courts was surrounded by a magnificent stone colonnade, with a dragon carved in high relief twisting round each pillar. Its present condition is not known.

The **Tian feng ta Pagoda** in the south of the town is a large seven storey octagonal brick pagoda, about 90 feet high, founded in the 14th century, and restored under the Ming and the Qing. It is still in good condition; a wooden staircase leads up the inside to the top.

One of the most famous buildings in the town is the **Tian yi ge Library,** south of the Zhong shan lu Avenue, on the western shore of Lake Yue hu. It originally belonged to Fan Qin, a War Ministry official under the reign of the Ming Emperor Jia jing; he settled in Ning bo when he retired, and bought up the Feng family's library, which had been begun in the 11th century. He added to it by having copies made of several manuscripts kept in Xi an, and in twenty years, he amassed a collection of 53,000 volumes. His descendants had to present several rare books to the court when the *Si ku quan shu* was being compiled in 1772. A catalogue dating from 1808 records that it included 1) rare editions of the classics and literary collections; 2) manuscript copies; 3) local histories; 4) differing editions; 5) copies of stone inscriptions. Qian long was so impressed with the design of the library and its buildings that he ordered that the imperial libraries be made on the same principle. The collection has been broken up now, but the buildings are still standing, in an attractive garden surrounded by water.

Mount Yu wang shan, several hours east of Ning bo by boat, was famous for two temples, the Tian tong si and the Yu wang si; the second one was said to contain a relic of the Buddha, which originated near the temple, and an extremely old reliquary.

Pu tuo Island

Pu tuo Island is east of Zhou shan Island. It used to be one of the most widely-known Buddhist sanctuaries, where pilgrims from China, Korea and Japan gathered from the 9th century onwards. Towards 1915, the island belonged to a Buddhist community of about a thousand people, who lived there permanently. Temples and monasteries were scattered over the island, and it was said to be one of the most beautiful spots in south China. Its present condition is not known.

EAST ZHE JIANG

Tian tai

The little town of Tian tai is on the upper reaches
of the River Ling jiang. It used to be the starting
point for the ascent of Mount Tian tai. From the
6th century onwards, the mountain was inhabited
by monks who adapted Buddhism to the Chinese
way of thought; they were in close contact with the
Japanese monasteries of the Tendai sect (an adaptation
of Tian tai). The monasteries flourished under the
Tang, the Song and right up to the Qing, when they
were restored by order of the Emperor. The chief
ones among them were: the **Guo qing si,** founded
in 598 and restored in 1783 (still in good condition);
the **Gao ming si,** which contained the oldest archaeological remains; the **Zhen jue si,** which was rebuilt
at the end of the 19th century; the **Hua ding si** which
was near the top of the highest peak, and the three
Fang guang si Temples.

Xin chang, about 30 miles north-west of Tian tai,
contains two monuments of interest to the tourist:
1) the **Temple to the Town Gods (Cheng huang miao)**
built in 1475, which has a stage, and a beautiful coffered ceiling in the main hall; 2) the **Bao xiang si,** usually
known as the Big Buddha Temple (Da fo si), because
of the stone statue of the Buddha inside: it is about
10 feet high, and is said to date from the end of the
5th century.

Wen zhou

Wen zhou is in the south of the province, 12 miles
upstream of the mouth of the river Ou jiang, on the
south bank; it is a port, with a harbour deep enough

to handle large sea-going boats. It is first mentioned under the Tang; walls were built round the town under the Ming, and the town was opened to European trade in 1877. It used to be famous for its tin vases and lamps. Tea, cotton and oranges are grown in the surrounding area. The town now contains a branch of the food-processing industry (condensed milk), paper mills (stencils), and workshops where trunks, rush matting, umbrellas and oiled paper are made.

INLAND TOWNS

Dong yang

Dong yang is on the road from Ning bo to Jin hua, about 18 miles east of the Hang zhou—Jin hua railway line. It was founded under the Tang; its present name dates from the Song. It is particularly well-known for its large Ming houses, especially the one called Lu zhai, outside the south gate of the town.

Jin hua

Jin hua is in the centre of the province, on the railway line from Hang zhou to Jiang xi. It is a market town, with several branches of industry: machine tool, textile and food-processing industries. Jin hua ham has been famous since the 18th century. It contains two interesting monuments: 1) the former residence of a Tai ping king, with frescoes similar to the ones at Nanking (see p. 981), now converted into a secondary school; 2) the Tian ning si Temple, south of the town, next to the circular road which has replaced the town walls; it was founded under the Song, and rebuilt under the Yuan and the Ming; the Great Hall (Zheng dian), built in 1318, is an excellent example of Yuan architecture (square, with a double roof supported by 16 pillars).

Qu xian

Qu xian is in west Zhe jiang, on the railway line from Hang zhou to Jiang xi. It is a market and mining town; irrigation work has recently been carried out in the neighbourhood.

Long quan

Long quan is in the south-west of the province, on the upper reaches of a tributary of the River Ou jiang. From the Five Dynasties period until the end of the Ming, it was important for its pottery. Remains of several kilns have recently been found nearby, with shards dating mainly from the Song and the Yuan.

AN HUI

(Map see Atlas pl. 4/5)

The province of An hui (created in 1662, when Jiang nan was divided into An hui and Jiang su) is bordered by Jiang su to the north-east, by He nan and Hu nan to the west, Jiang xi to the south and Zhe jiang to the south-east. Two large rivers cross it from west to east: the River Huai to the north and the Yang zi to the south; they break the province up into three parts: north of the Huai (Huai bei), south of the Huai (Huai nan), and the area of Wan nan, south of the Yang zi. The Huai bei area is a low-lying plain, most of which is under 160 feet above sea level, through which flow over ten tributaries of the Huai, all running from north-west to south-east. Before the present canals were dug, and the Huai brought under control, the area was constantly threatened bu floods. Huai nan, lying between the Huai (north) and the Yang zi (south), is a hilly region, with the Da bie shan Mountains in the south-west, partly in Hu bei and partly in An hui, rising to 5,439 feet (their average height is 1,600 feet); their numerous valleys lend themselves well to the building of dams and reservoirs; the eastern hills are lower (630 feet at the most) and cut up by plains and valleys. There are over 15 lakes in Huai nan; the largest is Lake Chao hu, south-east of He fei. The Chao hu plain is criss-crossed by an elaborate network of canals which facilitate irrigation. Wan nan, south of the Yang zi, is also covered with hills, varying between 1,900 and 2,000 feet; the highest of all, the Huang shan (5,433 feet), is a mass of granite, with several sharp peaks. It is a beautiful spot, with mountain tops rising out of the mist, which has often been described by Chinese poets. The Qing yi jiang, a tributary of the Yang zi flows from south to north through the area, forming a wide, fertile valley. The climate of the province is mild and wet, particularly in the south, and is ideal for growing trees and rice.

During the Chun qiu and the Warring States periods, the little principality of Zai held the land north of the Huai; a trade route linking the State of Chu with the northern principalities crossed the province from north to south; the He fei region was famous for its wood, its leather and its fish. From the Qing onwards, and under the Han, agriculture gradually developed. Under the Tang, the south of the province was one of the most important tea-producing areas. Under the

Southern Song, most of the tea and wood was sent to Hang zhou, which was a large consumer town; the area also exported paper, brushes, ink, lacquer ware, oil and bamboo. Under the Ming, trade flourished, especially in the Hui zhou district (now called Wan nan). The She xian merchants were said to be the richest in the province. By the end of the Ming, trade had been enlarged to include products from elsewhere as well; the merchants with some capital traded in salt, fish, coal, metal and soon became rivals of the great Shân xi merchants. Once they had amassed enough money, they went back to their native towns and villages, built magnificent houses with gardens and orchards, and ancestral temples, and spent the end of their lives there, looking after the less fortunate members of their families. The gulf between the great fortunes of the merchants and the poverty of the people in general seems to have grown even wider under the Qing; the population of the region grew and the agricultural land was no longer sufficient to support the increase. The rich merchant class supplied a proportion of the candidates for the imperial examinations; Dai zhen, a famous 18th century scholar, came from the town of Xiu ning, in Hui zhou; his family belonged to the great merchant class, and his father, although not one of the richest, was himself in business. In the 20th century, the west of the province, especially the Da bie shan Mountains, was an important revolutionary stronghold during the second and third civil wars.

An hui is rich in coal (the Huai nan basin) and iron ore (the Ma an shan Mountains and the Wan nan Hills). It had little industry before 1949, but it has developed considerably since the liberation: the Huai nan colliery has been brought up to date and is now one of the largest in China, supplying coal to Shang hai, Jiang su and Zhe jiang; as coal is plentiful, several towns now have iron and steel works and machine tool factories. The Ma an shan iron and steel works on the south bank of the Yang zi on the Jiang su border is one of the biggest in south China. Light industry is based on local products: cigarette making, umbrellas, tea, textiles, the making of a special paper used for traditional Chinese painting (a speciality of Jing xian), bamboo, leather work, ink and ink-stones (She xian district). 90% of the population is still employed in agriculture; there has been an improvement in this domain as well since the liberation, as a wide network of canals has been built to irrigate the province, particularly in the Huai bei region, the Lake Chao hu plain (the chief rice-producing area) and the valley of the Qing yi jiang, in Wan nan. The main crops are rice and wheat

in the north, maize, gao liang, tea on the slopes of the Da bie
shan and the Wan nan hills, and finally oil-bearing plants,
cotton and tobacco. An hui comes second only to Yun nan
as far as tea production is concerned; some of its best known
brands are Meng hong cha and Liu an gu pian, both grown
on the slopes of the Da bie shan Mountains. The hilly regions
are covered with forests (conifers, lac trees and bamboo).
The population numbers 38,000,000.

The towns in Huai bei, Huai nan and Wan nan will be
described in turn.

THE HUAI BEI AREA

Meng cheng

Meng cheng is on the south bank of the Guo
he, 60 miles north-west of Beng bu. The Cha hua
ta Pagoda (also called the Wan fo ta, "Ten Thousand
Buddha Pagoda") stands on a little hillock surrounded
by water in the south-east corner of the town; a
stele set into one wall records that it was founded
under the Song (1102); a temple used to stand there
too, but it has now disappeared. The pagoda is a
thirteen-storey octagonal building in brick, 106 feet
high; four of the eight facets have windows; a staircase,
whose position varies from one floor to the next,
leads up to the top. The base has small square niches,
and the bricks at the back of them still bear traces
of red and green glaze; each brick bears effigies
of the Buddha and his two disciples.

THE HUAI NAN AREA

Beng bu

Beng bu means "Harbour of shells"; it is supposed
to have been a pearl-fishing harbour.

The town is on the south bank of the River Huai, at the junction of the railway lines from Nanking and He fei; as communications (including water traffic communications) are good, it has become a storage and re-distribution centre for the products of the Huai valley; light industry has also developed there. Nan chan Hill, which is now a park, gives an excellent view over the town.

Feng yang

Feng yang is 12 miles south-east of Beng but on the road from Beng bu to He fei, at the foo, of a hill on a plain with a few isolated hills on it. The family of Zhu Yuan zhang, the founder of the Ming dynasty, lived there; in 1372, the new Emperor made it into an "imperial city" enclosed by walls with four gates, and two years later, an earth wall was built outside the enclosure, like the one at Nanking. The Emperor wanted to make it into a subsidiary capital, but money was lacking; in 1755, the earth. wall fell down, and was replaced by a lower wall The "imperial grave" of the Ming Emperors' ancestors is in the western suburbs of the town; it houses the remains of the father and five uncles of Zhu Yuan zhang; the mausoleum was built in 1369.

Huai nan

Huai nan is on the south bank of the River Huai, on the railway line between Beng bu (about 50 miles away) and He fei. The town was founded under the Tang; it is now an industrial centre (coal mining, cigarette making, oil extraction, mirror factories, paper mills). It has a population of 500,000,

He fei

He fei is the provincial capital; it is in the middle of the province, slightly north of Lake Chao hu, and is linked by rail with Peking, to the north, and Shang hai, to the south-east. The town was founded under the Han; the original settlement was north of the present town. It was a small market town until it became the provincial capital in 1949, and could only boast a few handicrafts (oil extracting works, weaving, forges). It has been transformed into a large industrial centre, with iron and steel factories, mines, an electric power station, textile mills and chemicals factories. In 1949, the population was 50,000; it is now 500,000. The old town has been completely changed by new buildings, and several higher educational establishments have been created.

An qing

An qing is in south-west Huai nan, on the north bank of the Yang zi. Roads link it with He fei and Hu bei, and the river links it with Wu hu. Under the Sui, the town was called Tong an; its present name dates from the Song. Under the Qing, it became the provincial capital and walls were built round it; the Tai ping spent six years in the town, and one of their kings had a house there which was still standing at the beginning of the 20th century. The rebels' camps were north of the town; in 1913, the wide, parallel ditches dug for trenches could still be seen. The town as a whole suffered badly from the fighting during the six years of Tai ping rule and most of its old buildings were destroyed. The present town is above all a storage and re-distribution centre for local products. It is built up against the Da long shan Hills, and spreads for several miles along the banks of the Yang zi.

THE WAN NAN AREA

Wu hu

Wu hu is in the east of the province, on the south bank of the Yang zi, on the railway from Nanking to He fei. It was founded under the Han. The harbour was opened to foreign trade in 1877. At the beginning of the 20th century, it was the most flourishing trading centre of the area (rice, tea and wood); its warehouses were owned by rich merchants from Hui zhou. The town still lives by trade and transport of goods; it is one of largest rice-marketing centres in China.

Ma an shan

Ma an shan is 30 miles downstream from Wu hu, on the south bank of the Yang zi, near the Jiang su border; it is linked by water and by rail with Wu hu and Nanking. It is the biggest industrial centre of the province: iron and steel works, iron mines, chemical industries, cement factory.

Tun xi

Tun xi is in the south of Wan nan, on the north bank of the River Xin jiang, south of the Huang shan Hills. The town has been a trading centre since the Song; it is an important marketing centre for tea and wood (which are sent to Zhe jiang); in 1913, the town contained four large banks and about thirty shops where tea was prepared for export. The tea trade is still its main activity; the local brand is known as Tun lü cha. A merchant's house, the Dai song mei zhai, can still be see in the town; it dates from the Ming.

She xian

The town, founded under the Han, is on the north bank of the Xin jiang, 9 miles downstream from Tun xi. From the Song dynasty onwards, and particularly under the Ming, the town and the surrounding area was one of the places in Hui zhou from which the great merchants came. In 1952, research into the question led to the discovery of twenty-three Ming and Qing houses in She xian itself and in neighbouring towns, built by merchants when they retired to their native villages to spend the last years of their lives there. The style and size varies from one to another, but they have a few characteristics in common; they have two stories, and present an austere exterior to the outside world; the ground floor generally has no windows giving on to the outside; wood is the principal material and the interior is luxurious (carved galleries and verandas, painted ceilings and walls). She xian has one house, the Fang jing chu zhai; the villages of Tang mo xiang, Cheng han xiang, Xi ji nan xiang, Zhe lin xiang, Xiong cun xiang each have three; other villages, such as Tan du xiang, Zheng cun xiang, Yan si zhen, Cao shi xiang, Yan cun xiang have one each and Qian kou xiang has two. The report of the archaeological research into the houses was published in 1957, under the title of *Ming Houses in Hui zhou (Hui zhou ming dai zhu zhai)*.

Ji xi

Ji xi is 15 miles north of She xian. It contains a Qing merchant's house, the Zhang she xi zhai. The Zao chi zong ci Temple is 15 miles north-west of Ji xi, south-west of the village of Zhai tan xiang; it contains some Tai ping frescoes (interesting interpretation of Tai ping troops encircling the imperial armies, who are caught in a walled town).

JIANG XI

(Map see Atlas pl. 4/5)

The province of Jiang xi is bordered by Hu bei and An hui to the north, Zhe jiang and Fu jian to the east, Guang dong to the south and Hu nan to the west. Mountains surround it on three sides: to the east, from north to south rise the Fu shan Mountains, the Lu shan Mountains (4,671 feet), the Jiu ling shan Mountains, the Wu gong shan Mountains, the Jing gang shan Mountains; to the south are the Da yu shan Mountains followed by the Jiu lian shan Mountains; the Wu yi shan Mountains stretch to the east. The middle of the province consists of the River Gan jiang basin and the plain surrounding Lake Po yang. The Gan jiang is the biggest river in Jiang xi; it crosses the province from south to north, with tributaries flowing into it from the east, south, and west, before emptying into Lake Po yang, which is also fed by the Xiu shui (west), the Chang jiang and the Xin jiang (east). Lake Po yang is the biggest lake in China; at its fullest, it covers an area of 3,160 square miles. Its warm waters are full of aquatic plants, which makes it particularly suitable for fish-rearing. The plain surrounding it is the largest in the province. Jiang xi is in the middle of the sub-tropical belt, far away from the sea; it is hot in summer, but in winter it is sheltered from the cold by the Da bie shan chain to the north, and the climate is mild. The growing period lasts from 9 to 11 months, so that two crops of rice can be grown each year.

As the Gan jiang is easily navigable, the province became a way through for communications early on in Chinese history. A Shang site has been found at Qing jiang, on the right bank of the Gan jiang. Later on, all the traffic from north China to the province of Guang dong travelled along the river; boats went as far as the frontier between the two provinces, the goods were then carried through the Mei ling guan Pass to Nan xiong (Guang dong) by porters, to be loaded on to boats once more; the postal service used the same route. Even before the Tang, and particularly during the later dynasties, the province played an important part in the economy of the empire because of its porcelain industry; Ji an and Jing de zhen were the main centres. The luxury trade was also an important one: tea and oranges were grown in the province, and wood came from the mountainous regions. In the 20th century Jiang xi was a revolutionary stronghold during the second civil war; most of the mountainous areas, expecially the Jing gang shan Mountains, which are the most suitable, were occupied by the Communist troops and used to establish the first revolutionary bases as early on as 1927. In 1929, the Soviet Central Government was formed at Rui jin, in the south-eastern mountains; when the revolution was at its height, the Soviets occupied over two-thirds of the area of Jiang xi, and included over half the population of the province.

Jiang xi is one of the most important coal-producing provinces in south China. The Ping xiang coal fields have been mined for a long time; since the liberation, the equipment has been brought up to date and new pits have been opened, such as the ones at Feng cheng; as they are near the Zhe jiang—Jiang xi railway line, the coal can be distributed at the least possible expense and supplies Jiang xi, Zhe jiang and other provinces. Branches of the iron and steel, textile and machine building industries have recently been created, mainly at Nan chang and Jiu jiang. The porcelain industry makes goods for the home and foreign markets; the province is also known for handicraft products such as the grass-cloth produced in the districts of Yi chun and Wan zai, and the paper from Shi cheng, Qian shan and Yong feng. Agriculture is highly developed: 30% of the total area of the province is under cultivation, and since the liberation, hundreds of centres have been created where new land is brought under cultivation, especially in the Da mao shan and the Jing gang si areas. Jiang xi is one of the chief rice-producing provinces in China (70% of the farming land is used for rice-growing); the surroundings of Lake Po yang and the Gan jiang valley are the chief areas. Wheat and sweet potatoes are the secondary crops; the main industrial crops are hemp, cotton, oil-bearing plants, tea, sugar-cane, tobacco and oranges (Nan feng oranges are famous throughout China). The forests which cover 10% of the total area of the province are mainly in the hilly districts: pine, cedar and camphor trees are grown. The logs are floated down the Gan jiang; some of the wood is transferred to the Yang zi to be distributed to other provinces. The population is 20,000,000; this figure includes members of the Hui, Miao, She and Yao Minority races, who do not exceed 10,000.

Nan chang, the capital of the province, will be described first, followed by the northern and southern towns, and lastly the south-western towns.

NAN CHANG

Nan chang is north of Lake Po yang, on the left bank of the River Gan jiang; railway lines link it with Jiu jiang to the north, and with Hu nan and Zhe jiang to the south, as the Chang sha—Shang hai line goes through Nan chang. It is the provincial capital, a town with a revolutionary history, and an important industrial centre. It has a population of 500,000.

History

The town was founded under the Han, and was then called Yu zhang. The present name of Nan chang dates from the Five Dynasties period. In the 18th century, Grosier reports that the town produced nothing but porcelain, which was made in the neighbouring areas and brought to the town for storage and distribution. At the beginning of the 20th century the town was a revolutionary centre; in 1927, when Chiang Kai-shek revealed that his position with regard to the left had changed, the Communist Party, determined to carry on the revolution which otherwise was doomed to failure, stirred up an armed rebellion at Nan chang on August 1st. 30,000 men, led by Zhou En lai and Zhu De defeated Chiang Kai-shek's armies, and after four hours' fighting, the town was liberated; a revolutionary committee was founded. The Nan chang rising (known as the Ba yi qi yi, the First of August Rising) was a turning point in the history of the revolution; it marked the birth of a revolutionary army under the direct control of the party, determined to fight against the reactionary element. From 1938 onwards, the town was the headquarters of the new Fourth Army for a time. It is now an industrial centre, producing chemicals, paper, pottery, foodstuffs.

Description

Extensive building has been carried out since the liberation: big modern buildings have grown up (among them 10 hotels), a **Provincial Museum (Jiang xi sheng buo wu guan)** has been created (interesting sections on geography and history, with description of the large-scale work projects) and public gardens have been laid out. A **Museum of the Nan chang Rising** of August 1st 1927 also exists (Nan chang ba yi qi yi ji nian guan), in Zhong shan lu Street, in the buildings which used to be the rebels' headquarters. Near the Temple to the Town Gods is the Yu zhang gong yuan, a little garden with artificial hills and lakes which used to be thought the most beautiful in the town.

The **Ba da shan ren Museum (Ba da shan ren ji nian guan)** is in the suburbs. Ba da Shan ren was a famous 17th century painter, who refused to acknowledge the Qing dynasty and lived most of his life away from the world, in monasteries. Only one of the five or six monasteries where he lived still survives: the **Qing yun pu,** a few miles from Nan chang. He settled there in 1661, when he was 37, and lived there until 1687. After the liberation, the Qing yun pu was converted into a museum. The rooms used by the artist can still be seen; the paintings on show include 20 of his (out of 400 still in existence), works by former painters who influenced him, and paintings by his disciples.

THE NORTHERN AND EASTERN TOWNS

Jiu jiang

Jiu jiang is on the banks of the Yang zi, north of the Lu shan Mountains; it is on the railway line to Nan chang, and is linked by road with Jing de zhen. It was founded under the Han. It has always been an important river port, handling tea and Jing de zhen porcelain. In 1862, the town was opened to foreign

trade and a concession was created on the banks of
the river, west of the town itself. The town still lives
mainly by trade.

Tong yuan zhen is near Jiu jiang; near the Yuan tong
si Temple there is a little Song pagoda, a single
storey octagonal building, 10 feet high, supported
by stone pillars, with one door. The outside walls
are covered with bas-relief carvings. A tiny stone
pagoda stands on a dais just over a foot high inside.

The **Lu shan Mountains,** 6 miles to the south,
are accessible by road from Jiu jiang.

A winding road now leads from Jiu jiang to **Gu ling,**
a summer resort in the mountains about 18 miles
away. The horizon widens with each turn in the
road; Lake Po yang and its junction with the Yang
zi lie spread out on the plain below.

Gu ling, to which tourists used to be carried in
sedan chairs, still shows traces of English influence
in the shape of the roofs and the layout of the villas.
But its gardens, lakes, pavilions, its temples perched
up on the rocks, the memories of scholars, poets
and Emperors—among them Bai Ju yi, Wang Yang
ming and Qian long—who left behind them steles,
poems and inscriptions, all combine to make the
atmosphere entirely Chinese.

The 20th century tourist will still find many things
to see there:

1. The Flowered Walk (hua jing)
2. The Cave of the Immortals (Xian ren dong),
the spring "which flows drop by drop" (I di quan),
the old bell and the statue of the Taoist genie, Lu
Tong ping.
3. The pine tree and the rock (shi song) and the
Dragon's Head Rock (Long shou yan) overlooking
the river.

4. The Black Dragon Pool (Wu long tan).

5. The Five Peaks (Wu lao feng), which have been painted by countless artists.

6. The "Han po kou", where the river drains the lake.

7. The Reed Forest Bridge (Lu lin qiao).

8. The Round Temple (Yuan fo dian).

9. The Dragon's Head Abyss (Long shou ya).

10. The Spring with Three Folds (San die quan).

The alpine botanical garden, begun in 1934, and enlarged later, is well worth a visit; it includes over three thousand different species and the part devoted to medecinal herbs is particularly interesting.

The new regime has kept the former summer residence of its enemy, Chiang Kai-shek, and the buildings used for lectures and interviews attended by high-ranking Guo min dang party cadres from 1928 to 1938, all intact.

Summer is the best time to pay a visit to the Lu shan Mountains, as they rise to nearly 4,917 feet above sea level, and are wonderfully cool after the blistering heat of the Yang zi valley.

Jing de zhen

Jing de zhen is east of Lake Po yang, on the south bank of the River Chang jiang, in the hills. It has been famous for its porcelain for centuries.

Judging by information to be found in old texts, pottery was produced there as early as the Eastern Han dynasty. During the Six Dynasties period, the town (then called Xin ping zhen) received an imperial order for various different pottery objects for use in the building of the palace at Nanking; under the Sui,

statues of animals were made there for the court. Under the
Tang, two factors contributed to the increased demand for
pottery: it was forbidden to use copper for any purpose other
than striking coins (which were already in short supply), and
tea drinking became more widespread. The population of the
town grew and it was promoted to the rank of a district (xian).
Under the Song, still more pottery was required by the court,
and the town was given its present name; a collection of pottery
made for the use of the court during the Jing de period (1004–
1007) was marked as "made during the Jing de period". Fine
pottery became known as pottery from the village of Jing de,
so that gradually the name stuck and the old one disappeared
completely. The kilns were south-east of Jing de zhen, as the
raw materials were to be found there (kaolin, *gao ling tu*, "earth
from Mount Gao ling", was used). More and more pottery
was made over the dynasties which followed, and the quality
improved at the same time; under the Qing, an imperial workshop produced all that was required by the court. European
travellers who visited Jing de zhen in the 18th century were
impressed by the scale on which the work was carried out. Grosier
gives a description of what he saw: "(the town) has a million
inhabitants and over 10,000 loads of rice are consumed each
day; it stretches for a league and a half along the banks of a
beautiful river; instead of consisting of scattered houses and
waste land, the inhabitants complain of the houses being too
close together, and the long streets which they form being
too narrow. Food is expensive as it has to be brought from
some distance away, and even wood comes from almost 100 leagues away. The river forms a sort of harbour about a league
round; rows of boats two or three deep border almost the
whole of the basin. Jing de zhen contains about 500 pottery
kilns, all in use. When night falls, it looks as though the whole
town is on fire; foreigners are not allowed to spend the night
there." Although the raw materials in the area were gradually
exhausted, the kilns did not disappear; kaolin was to be found
further south in the River Xin jiang area, and it was brought
to Jing de zhen by river. The boats came up the lower reaches
of the Chang jiang. Production continued to increase, and the
boats, laden with their precious cargo, went back down the
river, across Lake Po yang, and unloaded at the port of Jing
jiang, where the porcelain was sent all over the empire and
abroad. Improved means of transport in the 20th century have
helped production to continue (motor boats travel up the
Chang jiang and Jing de zhen is linked by road with the places

which now produce the raw materials, and with Hu kou on the south bank of the Yang zi). In 1955, 1,060,000 pieces of porcelain were exported from the kilns.

The town is much the same as it was under the Qing dynasty, though a few streets have been widened to ease traffic and a few modern buildings have appeared. The population is now 200,000. An institute for research into ways of improving production and a training school for workers have been founded since the liberation, as well as a **Jing de zhen Porcelain Museum (Jing de zhen tai qi buo wu guan).** In 1957, the institute of research into Jiang xi porcelain produced a *History of Jing de zhen Porcelain,* written in Chinese: *Jing de zhen tao ci shi gao,* Jiang xi sheng qing gong ye ting tao qi ci yan jiu suo bian.

The **Fu liang cheng Pagoda** is a few miles north of Jing de zhen, on the north bank of the Chang jiang, in the town of Fu liang jiu cheng. It stands on a hillock west of the town, and originally belonged to the Western Pagoda Temple (Xi ta si); it probably dates from the Song. It is a seven-storey brick pagoda, 110 feet high.

THE SOUTH WESTERN TOWNS

Fu zhou

Fu zhou is about 60 miles south-east of Nan chang, on the left bank of the River Xu jiang; it is on the road to Ji an to the south and Jing de Zhen to the north. It is a re-distribution centre. The famous hot springs of the Qing liang shan Mountains are 5 miles west of the town.

Ping xiang shi

Ping xiang shi is on the Hu nan border, on the Shang hai—Chang sha railway lIne. It stands in the hills on the north bank of a tributary of the River Xiang jiang, and is an important industrial centre (coal mines, pottery kilns, paper mills, food-processing factories). The famous miners' strike, involving over 13,000 workers, took place here in 1922.

Ji an

Ji an is 155 miles south-west of Nan chang, on the left bank of the Gan jiang. It was founded under the Han. The town developed from the end of the Tang dynasty onwards, and particularly under the Song, because pottery kilns were built at Ji zhou, 5 miles from the present town; they seem to have fallen into disuse under the Yuan. Excavations carried out in 1957 uncovered the sites of several kilns, and large numbers of shards. The town is now nothing more than a local market town. Near Xi jie Street, in the southern section of Shui xiang Lane, is the **Jiang ren deng ta Pagoda,** which dates from 1082; it is square, with seven stories, each facet of which contains an opening; it is topped by a metal ornament.

Jing gang shan

Jing gang shan is in the mountains 90 miles south-east of Ji an, on the Hu nan border. It is linked by road with Gan zhou and Ji an. It was chosen for the first revolutionary base, because its site made it eminently suitable for this; it is far from other towns, surrounded by hills, and on the borders of two provinces. In December 1927, the revolutionary army of peasants and workers, led by Mao Ze dong, settled there. Once the troops who had taken part in the armed rising at Nan chang and in south Hu nan had reached Jing gang shan, the Fourth Army of the Chinese Workers' and Peasants' Red Army was founded there in 1928 (Gong nong hong jun di si jun). Some of the buildings used by the army have now been converted into a museum.

Gan zhou

Gan zhou is about 15 miles south-east of Ji an, on the left bank of the upper reaches of the River Gan jiang. Roads link it to Guang dong and Fu jian. It is the largest town in the south of the province, with a population of 100,000 inhabitants. East of the Temple of Confucius in the south of the town is the *Ci yun si Temple*, built in the 19th century, under the reign of Guang xu; it has been transformed into a school. A pagoda dated 1024 still stands beside it; it is hexagonal, built in brick, with nine stories and windows in each facet; a staircase used to lead up to the top.

Rui jin

Rui jin is 124 miles east of Gan zhou, on the Fu jian border. Like Chang ding, 30 miles over the border, it was an important revolutionary base during the second civil war. The seat of the Workers' and Peasants' Central Democratic Government (Zhong yang gong nong min zhu zheng fu) was established in the village of Ye ping, a few miles away, in 1931. Some of the buildings used by the revolutionaries were restored to their former state after the liberation, and can be visited today. The hall where the first General Assembly of the Workers' and Peasants' Army was held, which later became the seat of the government, can be seen (before 1931, the building was part of the Xie family temple); the leaders' living-quarters and offices were left of the main hall; three memorials stand nearby: a pagoda erected in memory of the heroes of the revolution; a little kiosk in memory of Huang gong lüe to the right of the pagoda; a fort in memory of Zhao Bao sheng. The village itself still contains the houses (now private houses) where the national bank and finance ministry operated in 1931.

HU BEI

(Map see Atlas pl. 4/5)

The province of Hu bei is bordered by Shân xi and He nan to the north, An hui to the east, Jiang xi and Hu nan to the south, and Si chuan to the west. The name of the province (Hu bei "north of the lake") comes from the fact that it is north of Lake Dong ting. The west of the province is mountainous; the east is fairly low-lying. The average height of the mountains of western Hu bei is under 3,000 feet (Mount Wu dang shan 5,106 feet); the eastern part, bordered to the north-east by the Tong bo shan Mountains and the Da bie shan Mountains (He nan and An hui), mainly consists of a wide alluvial plain, where the Yang zi and the River Han meet. It is a countryside of lakes, rather like the Lake Dong ting basin. The summers are generally hot, except for some places in the western mountains (average for July in Wu han: 85° F). The mountains north of the province form an effective barrier against the cold and the winters are fairly mild (average for January at Wu han: 40° F). The growing period lasts for 300 days each year, the annual rainfall is about 39 inches, so that conditions for agriculture are excellent.

Hu bei is more or less in the centre of China; its capital, Wu han, is roughly equidistant from Peking, Canton, Shang hai and Zhong qing. The Yang zi is a natural channel of communications giving access to towns further downstream and to those in Si chuan. This west-east channel is complemented by waterways, roads and recently the railway line, all leading from north to south. As communications are good, Hu bei has for a long time had an important cultural and urban centre (the capital of the State of Wu was founded there as early as the 3rd century A.D. and it was a revolutionary centre in the 20th century). The province used to be part of that of Hu guang, which was split into two in the first half of the 18th century. Hu guang was famous for its plentiful grain harvests, and was known as the "granary of the empire". East Hu bei has for a long time been one of the richest rice-producing areas.

Since the liberation, an attempt has been made to make the fullest possible use of the waters of the eastern part of the province; the Yang zi embankments have been reinforced and a flood diversion project has been completed on the south bank, and much the same work has been done on the lower reaches of he Han. As well as rice, which has already been mentioned, cotton is also grown (in the River Han basin); wheat and sesame are grown on the non-irrigated land in the north and west; tea and lac trees are grown in the mountains. Pisciculture is carried out in the lakes (fish fry are reared to be sent to other provinces and even abroad). Wu han has always been a centre of communications, and traffic is heavier and easier now that the famous Yang zi bridge has been completed, forming a direct link between north and south China. An iron and steel works has been created north of the Eastern Lake since the liberation. The population is 35,000,000.

Wu han will be described first, followed by other towns in the central Yang zi valley, and a few northern towns.

WU HAN

Wu han consists of three towns arranged round the confluence of the Rivers Han and Yang zi. Han kou is north-west of the confluence, Han yang is south-west and Wu chang is on the right bank of the Yang zi. All three towns are now combined into one city: Wu han, the capital of Hu bei, with a population of over 2,200,000.

WU HAN

1 Concession japonaise
Japonese Concession
2 Concession allemande
German Concession
3 Concession française
French Concession
4 Concession russe
Russian Concession
5 Concession britannique
British Concession
6 Fabrique d'allumettes
Match Factory
7 British-American Tobacco Co.
8 Fabrique de thé en briques
Brick tea Factory
9 Arsenal de Hang Yang
Hang Yang Arsenal

10 Usines métallurgiques
Metallurgical Factories
11 Manufacture de chanvre
Hemp Factory
12 Filature et tissage du coton
Cotton spinning and weaving Mill
13 Filature de coton
Cotton spinning Mill
14 Filature de soie
Silk spinning Factory
15 Verrerie
Glass-works
16 Collège de droit et de sciences politiques
College of Law and Political sciences
17 Ecole des Langues Etrangères
School of Foreign Languages

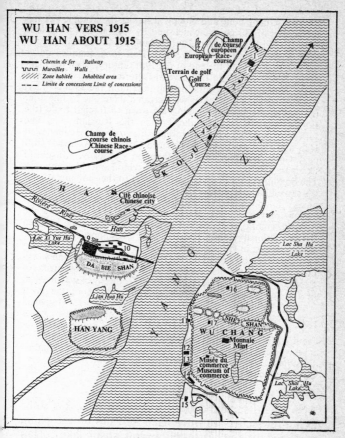

WU HAN VERS 1915
WU HAN ABOUT 1915

―――	*Chemin de fer* Railway
ᴍᴍᴍ	*Murailles* Walls
/////	*Zone habitée* Inhabited area
―――	*Limite de concessions* Limit of concessions

Champ de course européen
European Race-course

Terrain de golf
Golf Course

K O U

Z I

Champ de course chinois
Chinese Race-course

H A N

Cité chinoise
Chinese city

Rivière River

Han

Lac Xi Yue Hu
Lake

DA BIE SHAN

Lian Hua Hu

HAN YANG

Lac Sha Hu
Lake

16

17

SHE SHAN

WU CHANG

Monnaie
Mint

Musée du commerce
Museum of commerce

Lac Shai Hu
Lake

15

History

A settlement existed near the confluence under the Han. In the 3rd century A.D., the Sun family, the founders of the State of Wu, established their capital there for some time. The oldest town is Wu chang. Under the Yuan, it was the capital of Hu guang, which then embraced the present provinces of Hu bei,

Hu nan, Guang dong and Guang xi; under the Ming it was still the capital of Hu guang, which had by then shrunk to include only Hu bei and Hu nan. At the beginning of the century, the town was still surrounded by walls. Han yang, founded under the Sui, expanded at the end of the 19th century, when the mandarin Zhang Zhi dong had several factories and arsenals built there. Han kou was a little fishing port until the 19th century, when European concessions were created there one by one after the agreement of 1861 opening the town to foreign trade (the English arrived in 1861, the French the Russians and the Japanese in 1896). Several foreign firms opened branches at Han kou (British American Tobacco Company, Asiatic Petroleum Company, Jardine and Matheson Company, Mitsubishi Company, Nippon Menkwa Kaisha, Litvinoff and Company...). The building of the railway gave a boost to the economy, but at the same time it resulted in the forming of a proletariat (railwaymen) who were to become more and more sensitive to the revolutionary movement. The revolution which finally overthrew the Manchu empire began at Wu han in 1911. The battle between the revolutionary forces and the imperial supporters lasted for several weeks, in October; most of Han kou was destroyed in a vast fire which broke out during the fighting. The Wu han working class continued to be active after 1911 (the great strike of February 7th, 1923). From 1924 to 1927, the town was the seat of the revolutionary government. The building of the great Yang zi bridge in 1957 (and the bridge over the Han) opened new possibilities for the town. An iron and steel works was built there which in turn resulted in the building of several other factories (machine tools, agricultural machinery, transport material factories); branches of the textile and food-processing industries have also been formed there. The town now has over 20 higher educational establishments.

Description

Wu han, surrounded by water and hills, has some beautiful scenery to offer. Han kou lies on the plain, scattered to the north of several small lakes; Han yang and Wu chang are built round several hills, giving excellent views over the surroundings (the Da bie shan at Han yang, the She shan at Wu chang). Wu chang and the eastern lake will be described first, followed by Han yang and Han kou.

1. Wu chang

Wu chang is no longer isolated as it used to be before the bridge over the Yang zi was built, linking it to Han yang and Han kou; the bridge is nearly a mile long, 260 feet high, and is built on two levels, one for the railways, one for motor traffic.

The town is built round a square plan, and up till the 20th century its walls were still standing; the site of them is still obvious. The She shan Hill divides the town into two parts, north and south; the hill will be described first, then the north and south parts.

a) **The She shan Hill** is the highest in the town. The oldest building in the town stands on the western slope: the **Sheng xiang bao ta Stupa,** which was built under the Yuan in 1343, and originally stood near the walls, west of the Yellow Crane Tower (Huang he lou). (This pavilion was already in existence under the Six Dynasties period; it is said to have

1 Monument to the Strike of 7th February 1923
2 Park of the Liberation and Soviet Aviators' Tomb
3 Children's Library
4 Wu Han Library
5 People's Recreation Centre
6 Handicrafts Pavilion
7 Former Customs house of Wu Han
8 Sailors' Cultural Palace
9 Palace of Sino-Soviet Friendship
10 Hospital No. 2. Annex of the Institute of Medecine
11 Terrace of the Ancient Lute
12 Site of the Peasant Movement Institute directed by Mao Ze dong
13 Site of the headquarters of the 1911 revolution
14 Hu Bei Theatre
15 Terrace where Huang Xing was appointed head of the revolutionary armies in 1911
16 Monument to the memory of the martyrs of the 1911 revolution
17 Remains of the Engineers' garrison which revolted in 1911
18 Hu Bei Provincial Library
19 Taoist Temple of Eternal Spring
20 Wu Chang Railway Station
21 Tomb of the martyr She Yang
22 Institute of Hydraulic Engineering
23 Wu Han Physical Culture Institute
24 Hillock of the Nine Maidens
25 Pavilion of the Shining Lake
26 Pavilion of the Infinite Heavens

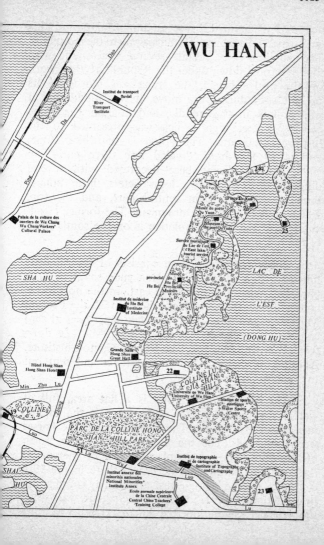

WU HAN

Institut du transport fluvial
River Transport Institute

Palais de la culture des ouvriers de Wu Chang
Wu Chang Workers' Cultural Palace

SHA HU

Institut de médecine du Hu Bei
Institute of Medecine

Place Du Mal
Musée du poète
Qu Yuan
Museum of the poet Qu Yuan

Service touristique du Lac de l'est
East lake tourist service

Musée provincial du Hu Bei
Hu Bei Provincial Museum

LAC DE

L'EST

(DONG HU)

Grande Salle Hong Shan
Hong Shan Great Hall

Hôtel Hong Shan
Hong Shan Hotel

Min   Zhu   Lu

19 COLLINE

COLLINE LU JIA SHAN

Université de Wu Han
University of Wu Han

Station de sports nautiques
Water Sports Centre

SHA HU

PARC DE LA COLLINE HONG SHAN
HILL PARK

Institut de topographie et de cartographie
Institute of Topography and Cartography

Institut annexe des minorités nationales
National Minorities' Institute Annex

École normale supérieure de la Chine Centrale
Central China Teachers' Training College

23

acquired its name because an immortal passed this spot seated on a crane when on his way to the mountain. The pavilion was rebuilt several times, and was finally burned down under the Republic.) When work on the bridge began, the stupa was moved to its present site; during the move, it was found that it was hollow in the middle, and contained a stone *chuang*, 5 feet high, which was presented to the historical museum. The stupa is of white stone, and is 19 feet high, divided into three parts: an eight storey circular base decorated with several different designs (waves, lotus petals, little pillars, birds), a curved, plain central part, and the top, which ends in a bronze ornament. The former **Headquarters of the 1911 Revolution** is on the south slope of the hill.

b) **The north of the town** consists of several little hills (the Yan zhi shan, the Hua yuan shan). A little park has been laid out in the east. In the north-west corner, inside the secondary school no 22, the **Peasant Movement Institute (Nong min yun dong jiang xi suo)** can still be seen; it was directed by Mao Ze dong from 1927 onwards, after he left the Canton institute. About 2,000 cadres were trained there and sent out to organise the peasants.

c) **The South of the Town** is a flat area, full of water; the biggest of the three lakes is the middle one, the Zi yang hu. The **Square where the horses were inspected (Yue ma chang)** used to be north of the lake. The whole place is full of memories: the Tai ping harangued the crowd there in the 19th century; Huang Xing was appointed commander in chief there in 1911; later on, the square was called the Hu bei Revolution Red Square (Hu bei ge ming hong chang). The terrace where Huang Xing was promoted to his post can still be seen. A Monument in Memory of the Martyrs of the 1911 Revolution stands in the street immediately north of Lake Zi yang hu. The former sappers' garrison is north-east of the lake; they were among the first to join in the 1911 rebellion (the buildings were burned down, but have been rebuilt).

2. The Shores of the Eastern Lake (Dong hu).

Wu luo lu Street leads eastwards out of the town into a stretch of hilly countryside. The **Chang chun guan, Taoist Temple of Eternal Spring,** stands at the foot of a hill north of the road. It is an ancient foundation; the legend says that Lao zi used often to come and meditate on a terrace here, and that the temple was built on the same spot. The buildings were destroyed during the Tai ping rebellion, and rebuilt at the end of the 19th century; the temple is still in use, and a community of about 30 monks and nuns lives there. It clings to the slopes of a little hill; the halls contain some interesting statues. The Hong shan Hill with its two pagodas is a little to the east, though still north of the road. The Xing fu si ta, the smaller of the two, now stands on the western slope; it was moved here after the liberation from the courtyard of the Minorities' Institute. It is a stone pagoda 31½ feet high, dating from 1270. The other, more recent, used to belong to the Hong shan si Temple; it is an octagonal pagoda, with seven stories, each one containing windows, and separated from the next by a double roof. The hill has been converted into a park; She yang, the revolutionary hero, lies buried in a tomb at the foot of its southern slope. The lake lies beyond. This is the area chosen for the university; from north to south are: the Physical Training Institute, the Central China Teachers' Training College, the Topography and Cartography Institute, the annex of the Minorities' Institute, the University (it was founded under the Republic; its buildings on the Lu jia shan overlook Wu han and the surrounding area), the Hydraulics Institute, the Medical Institute. The **Provincial Museum** (Hu bei sheng buo wu guan) is here too. It falls into two parts: the first part (ground floor) covers the history of the province from the beginnings up to the Opium War and includes finds from recent excavation work, with an interesting prehistoric section, and a good collection of pottery dating from the Three Kingdoms and the Six Dynasties periods, found in tombs in the Wu han area. The second part (first floor) is devoted to the history of the revolution in the province, from the Opium War to 1949. A small building in memory of the poet Qu yuan (Qu yuan ji nian guan) stands slightly to the north: his works, in several different editions, and studies of them, are on show there. Paths and pavilions have been laid out (the Endless Sky Pavilion, the Sparkling Lake Pavilion...) and boats can be hired on the lake itself.

3. Han yang

Han yang, like Wu chang, has lost the walls that once encircled it. A smaller town, it is divided into four districts by Qin tai lu and He ping lu, two streets which intersect at right angles in the middle. The north-east, north-west, south-west and south-east districts will be described in that order.

a) The north-east district. Most of it is covered by the Da bie shan Hill and Lake Lian hua hu; the Hill is also known as Gui shan, Tortoise Hill, because of its shape. At the beginning of the 20th century, a Temple dedicated to Yu the Great, the mythical founder of the Xia Dynasty, still stood on the eastern slope of the hill. The Jing chuan ge, a two-storey pavilion transformed into a tea house, overlooked the Yang zi from the foot of the hill.

b) The north-west district. Lake Xi yue hu lies in the middle of it, with the Mei zi shan Hill rising to the south-west. The Lute Terrace, Qin tai, also called Bo ya tai, after a famous Qin musician of the Chun qiu period, who is said to have stopped here on his way to Chu to play his lute, is south-east of the lake.

c) The south-west district. The Yuan gui si Temple stands here; it was founded under the Qing, and is famous for its Hall of the Five Hundred *Luo han*.

d) The south-east district. This is the busiest shopping centre in the town; it includes all the big department stores, the Han yang theatre and large public gardens.

4. Han kou

Han kou is the most modern town of the three. It was largely destroyed in 1911, rebuilt afterwards, and has gradually spread west of the railway line; the most recent buildings are interesting from an architectural point of view. Some of the buildings from the old concessions still survive along the riverside. The western suburbs used to be the race course; they have been converted and now include a zoo and stadium to the south, the Liberation Park, and the

Memorial to the 1923 strike to the north. A large
modern bridge spanning the Han shui links Han kou
to Han yang.

OTHER TOWNS IN THE YANG ZI VALLEY

Huang shi

Huang shi is on the south bank of the Yang zi,
about 60 miles downstream from Wu han. It is the
most westerly town on the railway. It is near the
Da ye iron mines and is the biggest industrial centre
in the province after Wu han (iron and steel, building
materials, textiles, foodstuffs). It has a population
of 200,000. Six sites containing Neolithic pottery
were discovered about 18 miles south-west of the
town when work was being done there in 1956.

Sha shi

Sha shi is on the north bank of the Yang zi, 124 miles
upstream of Wu han (by road); canals run between
there and Lake Dong ting. The town was opened
to Japanese trade in the 20th century. It is now a
redistribution centre, handling the products of the
neighbouring areas. Textile factories have been built
there.

Yi chang

Yi chang is about 90 miles upstream of Sha shi,
on the north bank of the Yang zi. It was a town well-
known by the boatmen, as the lower Yang zi steamers
could go no further. The river flows between walls of
rock which are so close together that it is a dangerous
spot. Further upstream the river flows through

gorges, forming rapids, in some of the most beautiful scenery of the whole province. The town was opened to foreign trade in 1877; it was the last town of any size on the river route to Si chuan. A small concession was created there. It is still important as a port, and now contains a little industry as well.

THE NORTHERN TOWNS

Jing shan

Jing shan is 124 miles north-west of Wu han. When the Shi long guo jiang reservoir was being built in 1954, Neolithic remains were discovered (axe heads, black pottery, and red pottery with patterns on it).

Xiang fan shi

Xiang fan shi is in the north of the province, on the Han, near its confluence with the Bai he. It is linked by road with Wu han, Nan yang and He nan, and is the biggest town in the north of the province. Like Guang hua, another town about 50 miles upstream, on the left bank of the Han, it is mainly a redistribution centre.

Jun xian and the Wu dang shan Hills

Jun xian is in the north-west of the province, on the west bank of the Han. The town itself has little to offer, but a road from there leads on to the Wu dang shan Hills, 30 miles to the south. The hills are strictly speaking mountains, for the highest peaks are 5,200 feet above sea level; they are dotted with temples, pavilions, and bridges, most of which date from the Ming (Yong le period, 1403–1425).

1. The **Gu tong dian (Bronze Pavilion)** is dated 1307; it was originally on the Tian zhu feng Peak, but was moved and put up in the Zhuan lan dian Hall on the Xiao lian hua feng Peak. It is made in imitation of wooden architecture, and is 7½ feet high, 8½ feet long and 7¾ feet wide.

2. The **Jin dian (Golden Hall)** is also on the Tian zhu feng Peak (4,800 ft.); it was built in 1416, and is a bronze building which stands on a stone terrace with a parapet round it; twelve pillars carry its double roof; the south-west door has two dragons playing with a ball on it. The inside has a beautiful coffered ceiling and contains several statues: Zhen wu di jun (a Taoist deity) with disciples round him, Zhou gong (to the left) and Tao hua nü (to the right).

3. The **Nan yan gong (Southern Cliff Palace)** is built up against a wall of rock, and dates from 1413; the Stone Hall (Shi dian) is the best preserved part of it, so called because it contains no wood at all.

4. The **Zi xiao gong** is on the slopes of the Zhan qi feng, and also dates from 1413; it stands on a triple stone terrace and has 36 pillars supporting a double roof with slightly upturned eaves corners; it has a fine coffered ceiling inside.

HU NAN

(Map see Atlas pl. 23/24)

The province of Hu nan is bordered by Hu bei to the north, Jiang xi to the east, Guang dong to the south, Gui zhou and Si chuan to the south. Its name (Hu nan, "south of the lake") comes from its position south of Lake Dong ting. Mountains enclose it on the east, the south and the west: the Nan ling Mountains to the south, the Xue feng shan Mountains to the west and the Wu gong shan Mountains to the east; the north of the province is the area round Lake Dong ting. The centre is mountainous, with a few isolated peaks and ridges standing out from the rest, like Mount Heng shan, better known under its other name, Nan yue, a ridge running for about 50 miles, consisting of 72 peaks (it is said); the highest is 4,086 feet. The Xiang jiang, the biggest river in the province, crosses it from south to north to flow into Lake Dong ting, which is fed by the Yuan jiang, the Zi shui and the Li shui to the west; most of the water courses in the province are connected with the lake. It is in fact the second largest lake in China, and as several channels join it and the Yang zi, it regulates the flow of the river to a large extent; the mud and sand brought down by the Yang zi and the other rivers caused it to silt up and consequently floods used to be frequent. This menace has been averted, however, by the Jin jiang flood diversion project in Hu bei, completed after the liberation, which lessens the risk of large volumes of water being emptied by the Yang zi into Lake Dong ting; canalisation work has also been carried out, and embankments have been built to protect the area round the lake. The climate is mild and wet on the whole, though the winters in the north of the province are fairly cold (average for January: 40° F); snow is extremely rare in the south. The growing period lasts for about 330 days of the year; annual rainfall varies between 54 and 78 inches.

The hills and plains of Hu nan have been inhabited for centuries; Shang remains have been found at Heng yang, on the right bank of the Xiang jiang. Under the Warring States period, the province was partly under the control of the Kingdom of Chu; recent excavations have revealed the high level of civilisation attained at this time. The economy of the province gradually developed as the centuries passed. Under the Yuan and the Ming, Hu nan and Hu bei both belonged to the province of Hu guang, which was one of the most important grain-producing areas in the empire; most of the grain was sent to Peking by the Grand Canal. As the saying went, "If the Hu guang harvest is good, no one fears famine". Hu nan, in the centre of the empire, was also a communications centre; as early as the reign of Qin shi Huang di, the Yang zi area was linked to Guang dong and Guang xi by a good system of waterways. The building of the Peking–Canton railway line in the 20th century helped the province to develop further.

Hu nan is still one of the foremost grain producing areas. Rice is the chief crop; every year, a large proportion of the harvest is sent to other provinces. Most of the province, with the exception of the west, is covered with paddy-fields; the richest areas are the Lake Dong ting plain and the Xiang jiang basin. Other crops are maize, wheat, sweet potatoes, soya-beans, hemp, cotton, peanuts, tobacco, sugar-cane, oranges, tea, rape-seed and tea oil, which supplies half of the total amount produced. Forests cover 22% of the total area of the province, growing mainly in the mountainous regions; cedar trees predominate. Those produced by the Yuan jiang basin and the upper Xiang jiang basin are the best known. Strings of logs are floated down the Yuan jiang and the Xiang jiang, across Lake Dong ting and into the Yang zi. Hu nan also has rich mineral resources. It is probably best known for its antimony, lead and zinc. Most of the coalfields are in the south of the province. Both heavy and light industry has been developed since the liberation, particularly the machine-building industry, which specialises in machine tools, electric motors and mining equipment. Handicrafts flourish as well: Li Ling pottery, Liu yang grass cloth, Chang sha embroidery and umbrellas, Liu yang paper, Shao yang bamboo carvings, iron cooking pots, brushes and ink. The population is 40,000,000; the Han population is centred on the plains, while Miao (320,000 of them in the western mountains, forming 10% of the total population of that area), Zhuang, Dong, Yao and Tu jia minority races live in the hills.

The eastern towns will be described first, followed by the western ones.

THE EASTERN TOWNS

Yue yang

Yue yang is in the north of the province, at the Hu bei border, on the Peking—Canton railway line, east of Lake Dong ting, near the channel which leads to the Yang zi jiang. It was founded under the Six Dynasties; the first walls were built in the 5th century, then rebuilt in 750 and enlarged under the Ming in the 14th century. In 1898, the harbour was opened to Europeans. In 1920, the population was 20,000. Yue yang still lives mainly by trade; it is one of the biggest redistribution centres for products from the north of the province.

The site is an attractive one, for the town is opposite Jun shan Hill (on the north shores of the lake). It is chiefly famous for the Yue yang lou, a beautiful tower which stands above the west gate in the old walls. The tower has a long history; during the Three Kingdoms era, Lu Xiao zeng, a Wu general had a tower built here from which to inspect his troops *(yue bing lou);* under the Six Dynasties and the Tang, the tower is mentioned in the poems of Bai Ju yi, Li Bai, Han Yu; poets used to meet there to hold competitions. Under the Song, the gate fell into ruins and in 1045 Teng Zong jing, then governor of the town, had it rebuilt; Fan Zhong yan wrote an essay: *Yue yang lou ji, On the Yue yang Tower,* in memory of the event. At the beginning of the century, the text could still be seen written on one of the walls. The tower was restored several times; the last time was in 1957.

It is a square tower, 45 feet high, with an elegant triple roof of glazed tiles; a balcony runs round the second storey. Two little kiosks, the San cui ting and the Xian wei ting stand in front of it; they were restored in 1867. An iron *ding* over 6 feet high stands in the courtyard in front of the tower, with two round iron receptacles, 4½ feet high, one on each side of it. They bear inscriptions stating that they were cast in

1245; they were originally in the Song sheng si Temple, on Jun shan Hill, and it is not known when they were moved from there. Just outside the west gate (which leads on to the shores of the lake) three iron instruments lie in the sand. Their origin and their use have not yet been determined; they are mentioned in Song texts, which state that there were five of them. The three surviving ones look like a huge X 10 feet long, with a round hole in the middle.

CHANG SHA

Chang sha is on the right bank of the river Xiang jiang, about 45 miles from where it flows into Lake Dong ting. It is the provincial capital and an important regional centre, with a population of over 600,000. The name Chang sha ("long sandbank") no doubt comes from the island in the middle of the river, which makes it easier to cross.

History

The site of Chang sha may have been inhabited even in the Warring States period. Several tombs containing lacquer ware dating probably from the Chu kingdom civilisation have been found in the area, though the name of the town does not appear until the Qin. Little is known of the early history of the town; it became no doubt a centre for the immediate neighbourhood, owing to its position on the banks of the Xiang jiang. The story is told of a certain Jia Yi, a famous scholar, who was sent by the Han emperor Wen to act as counsellor to his son, who had been made king of Chang sha. During the Southern Dynasties and the Five Dynasties, the site was fought over by the various kingdoms, who each wanted to gain control over the area round Lake Dong ting. A famous college was founded on Mount Yue lu (west of the town) under the Song. The well known philosopher Zhu Xi (died 1200) taught there for a time.

At the beginning of the Ming dynasty, under Hong wu, a wall containing nine gates was built round the town. When Hu guang was divided into two provinces in 1664, Chang sha became the capital of Hu nan. In 1747, the wall was enlarged; it can still be

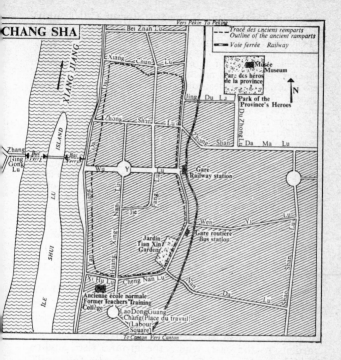

traced on the map. Grosier, writing at the end of the 18th century, stresses its agricultural aspect: "Its territory is a mixture of plain and mountain, it is rich and fertile. The rice harvests never fail, even in the worst droughts, because almost everywhere the farmers can divert water from the lakes and rivers to irrigate their fields. The mountains supply large quantities of soapstone and cinnabar. This city controls ten other third class ones."

When the Tai ping advanced, Chang sha was the only southern town to put up a victorious resistance. A native of the town, the mandarin Zeng Guo fan, played a leading part in the suppression of the rebellion.

The town was opened to foreign trade in 1904; Europeans and Americans were quick to settle there. Business houses, missions

(American Presbyterian, Norwegian, Roman Catholic), and colleges (an off-shoot of Yale) were set up. Towards 1915, the population of the town and its suburbs was reckoned at 280,000 inhabitants. Small industries were set up: powder, paper, jewelry, lacquer ware, porcelain, furniture, and even iron and antimony refineries. The various products of the province were collected here for export: rice, tea, tobacco, cotton, hemp, oil and wood (which was floated here). The building of the Peking-Canton railway line was a great help to the town.

Economic expansion has continued since the liberation. Most agricultural products from the Xiang jiang basin such as rice, tea and "oleaginous tea" *(you cha)* are stored here for redistribution. Heavy industry has been developed, and Chang sha is still the most important town in the province for light industry: tinned meat factories, textile factories, rubber-soled shoe factories, paper mills, porcelain (figurines and little statues of the Buddha as well as everyday products), embroidery workshops, employing men and women (machine and hand embroidery). Buttons, umbrellas, and eiderdowns (filled with duck feathers) are also made. Chang sha is famous for its marionette and shadow puppet theatres.

Description

The old town was enclosed within a rectangular wall which followed the river. A straight paved street divided it into two: the business and shopping district to the west, near the river, and private houses and gardens to the east, where the ground rises slightly. The circumference of the walls was over four miles. They have now almost completely disappeared, and the town has spread considerably eastwards. A large island, Shui lu, splits the river into two channels, and has a few houses scattered over it. A new suburb, centred mainly round the university, has grown up on the left bank of the Xiang jiang and on the slopes of Yue lu Hill (part of the northern foothills of the Heng shan range).

1. The Park of the Province's Heroes is a huge public garden in the north-east of the town, with a large memorial tower, several pavilions and lakes, a small zoo, and the **Hu nan Provincial Museum.**

Finds from recent excavation work in the Chang sha area (particularly the famous lacquer ware) are not yet exhibited (1965). However, the museum has a large collection of documents referring to the history of the revolutionary movement and the part played by the province of Hu nan—Chairman Mao's native province—in the revolution.

Ground floor. First Section: from the Opium War to 1919: documents referring to the Tai ping; good collection of Tai ping coins; map showing the spheres of influence of each European power. *Second Section:* the May 4th Movement and the founding of the Communist Party; map showing towns which brought out new newspapers after the May 4th Movement; copies of the *Xiang jiang ping lun (The Shian kian Weekly Review),* an interesting review edited by Mao Ze dong, which first came out in 1919; copies of the review entitled *Youth;* revolutionary centres in Hu nan; the railwaymen's movement. *Third Section:* the first civil war (1924–1927): picture of a peasant guiding Mao Ze dong (entitled "The People Clear the Chairman's Way"), referring to an incident in 1925: Mao, who had come back to his native village, Shao shan, to preach the revolution, was hunted by the police and would have been caught but for some peasants who helped him to flee; the crossing of Hu nan by soldiers of the northern expedition (a handkerchief in memory) photograph of the house where the first peasant association was formed, in the village of Bai guo, near Heng shan, south-west of Chang sha; development of peasant associations.

First floor. Landing: model of the house in Shao shan where Mao was born. *Fourth Section:* the second civil war (1927–1937): the Nan chang Uprising; revolutionary bases in Jiang xi and Hu nan; model of the Jing gang shan area (Jiang xi) where the first revolutionary base was founded in 1928; map of the Red Army's route from Nan chang to Jing gang shan; the Long March; model of the house where the Zun yi conference was held (1935). *Fifth Section:* the anti-Japanese war (1937–1945): the Lu gou qiao incident (July 7th 1937); Yan an. *Sixth Section:* the third civil war (1945–1959): the liberation of Hu nan.

2. The Former Office of the Hu nan Communist Party Committee (Zhong gong hu nan qu wei yuan hui) is east of the site of the old walls, 500 yards north of the station. At the beginning of this century, there were few houses in the area; a hillock rose beside a pool of clear water, which gave its name to the place: Qing shui tang, Clear Water Pool; the first meeting of the Hu nan Communist Party Committee was held in a house near the pool. The pool has vanished, but the house still stands, and is now a museum **(Qing shui tang ji nian guan).** The rooms used for meetings, and those used as living quarters by Mao and other leaders are visited first of all. A hall beside the house contains a permanent exhibition. *First Section:* creation of the provincial Communist Party committee in 1921, when Mao came back from the first general assembly of the party at Shang hai; founding of the Hu nan University (Hu nan zi xiu da xue); creation of a mill at Chang sha (20 looms), the profits of which were to finance the party; map showing the distribution of basic collective organisations and youth organisations (Qing nian tuan) in the province; *Second Section:* the party's management of workers' movements: founding of evening classes; founding of a workers' club at An yuan; *Third Section:* organisation of the peasants:

training of cadres; the struggle against imperialism. Model of Qing shui tang as it was in 1921.

3. The Tian xian gardens are in the south-eastern corner of the old walls, on the remains of an old fort which the Tai ping attacked, but failed to take, in 1852. It overlooks the town, the river and the southern industrial suburbs (tea shop).

4. The Old Normal School (Hu nan di yi shi fan). It is outside the old south gate. Chairman Mao was here from 1912 to 1918, and held meetings here from 1918 to 1920. The buildings were destroyed during the war, but were carefully rebuilt after the liberation. It contains a small museum: photographs etc. of Mao's teachers; books which he enjoyed; map of the enquiries which he carried out in 1916 and 1917 in Hu nan; *Ti yu yan jiu, Research into sport;* an article written by Mao and published in the review *Xin qing nian, Youth;* model of the normal school before the fire; copy of the review edited by Chinese students abroad *(Hai wai xiang tan)*; the May 4th Movement; new reviews.

In the autobiography which Mao Ze dong dictated to Edgar Snow in 1936, he refers to his time here several times (E. Snow, *Red Star over China*, London, 1937, re-issued 1963, p. 142 sq.): ''Meanwhile, I had been thinking seriously of my 'career' and had about decided that I was best suited for teaching. I had begun reading advertisements again. An attractive announcement of the Hu nan Normal School now came to my attention, and I read with interest of its advantages: no tuition required, and cheap board and cheap lodgings... There were many regulations in the new school and I agreed with very few of them. For one thing, I was opposed to the required courses in natural science. I wanted to specialize in social sciences. ...Most of all I hated a compulsory course in still-life drawing. I thought it extremely stupid... Feeling expansive and the need for a few more intimate companions, I one day inserted an advertisement in a Chang sha paper, inviting young men interested in patriotic work to make a contact with me... gradually I did build up a group of students around myself, and the nucleus was formed of what later was to become a society that was to have a widespread influence on the affairs and destiny of China. It was a serious-minded little group of men and they had no time to discuss trivialities... They had no time for love or 'romance' and considered the times too critical and the need for knowledge too urgent to discuss women or personal matters... We also became ardent physical culturists... At this time my mind was a curious mixture of ideas of liberalism, democratic reformism, and Utopian Socialism. I had somewhat vague passions about 'nineteenth-century democracy', Utopianism and old-fashioned liberalism, and I was definitely anti-militarist and anti-imperialist."

"I had entered the Normal College in 1912. I graduated in 1918."

5. The West Bank Suburbs. Two ferry-boats cross the river (Shui lu island in the middle is crossed on foot), giving a good view of the wide valley of the Xiang jiang and the river traffic (sailing-boats with huge sails, logs). The lower slopes of the Yue lu Hill are covered with higher education and research establishments, recently built: the Normal School, Hu nan University (8,000 students) etc. Paths lead all over the hill (pleasant views of the countryside); there are three memorials to revolutionary heroes, and two old temples.

Visit to Shao shan. Shao shan, where Chairman Mao was born, is near Chang sha. A newly-built hotel provides accommodation for the night it necessary, but it is possible to go there and back in a day, by taxi or by bus (using the local bus service, and leaving from the bus station south of the railway station).

The road leads southwards out of Chang sha and follows the right bank of the Xiang jiang for about 25 miles, before crossing the river by an enormous bridge just before Xiang tan. **Xiang tan** is a large town of nearly 300,000 inhabitants, in an important position on the Xiang jiang, because the river becomes navigable by steamers at this point, as the Lian shui flows into it a little upstream. Its port used to be the final destination for strings of barges coming down from higher up the river, and even from south China (through the canal linking the Xiang jiang with the southern Xi jiang basin). It used to be a storage and redistribution centre for medicinal plants, tea and coal. It is now important for its engineering, textile and food industries, which have been developed in recent years. The town used to be surrounded by walls built in 1754, but these have now disappeared.

Shao shan is 28 miles west of Xiang tan; the road leads through the Hu nan countryside, through paddy-fields, past isolated farms (mostly built recently), with glimpses of what were once landowners' houses. The village of Shao shan is in a low-lying area surrounded by hills. A Taoist hermitage still stands on one of the neighbouring peaks; according to tradition, one of the ministers of a mythical emperor invented the music known as *"shao"* there, and the name of the village, "the *shao* music hill", comes from this legend. The village was chiefly inhabited by the Mao clan, and even now, 60% of them still bear the name. The Chairman's father was a relatively rich peasant, and owned a small farm.

The road ends in a square in front of the hotel; a path leads off to the right, past the vast new village school, the white house where Mao Ze dong first went to school, and the pond where he liked to bathe, to a house on the right: the house where he was born in 1893. It is a typical Hu nan farmhouse, built on the wooded slopes of a little hill, overlooking a pond, which is full of lotus flowers in summer. The rice-fields (where Chairman Mao himself wielded the plough, it is said), and the threshing-floor, are further on, and on the

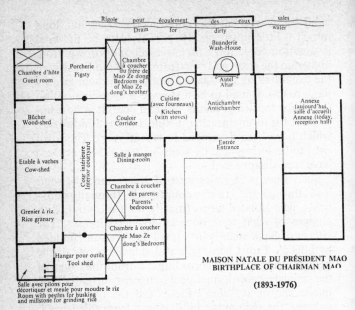

MAISON NATALE DU PRÉSIDENT MAO
BIRTHPLACE OF CHAIRMAN MAO

(1893-1976)

other side of the pond stands the neighbours' house, where a family of peasants still lives.

Before visiting the house where he was born, it is interesting to read a little more of the autobiography from Edgar Snow's book (E. Snow, *Red Star over China*, London, 1937, second edition 1968, p. 130 onwards):

"My father was a poor peasant and while still young was obliged to join the Army because of heavy debts... Later on he returned to the village where I was born, and by saving carefully and gathering together a little money through small trading and other enterprise he managed to buy back his land. As middle peasants then, my family owned 15 *mou* of land (about 2½ acres). At the time my father was a middle peasant he began to deal in

grain transport and selling, by which he made a little money...
I began to work at farming tasks when I was six years old... My
family ate frugally, but had enough always. I began studying in
a local primary school when I was eight and remained there until
I was thirteen years old. In the early morning and at night I
worked on the farm. During the day I read the Confucian
Analects and the *Four Classics*... I knew the classics, but disliked them. What I enjoyed were the romances of old China, and
especially stories of rebellions... I finally left the primary school
when I was thirteen and began long hours on the farm, helping
the hired labourer, doing the full labour of a man during the day
and at night keeping books for my father... At this time an
incident occurred in Hu nan which influenced my whole life...
we students noticed many bean merchants coming back from
Chang sha. We asked them why they were all leaving. They told
us about a big uprising in the city. There had been a severe
famine that year, and in Chang sha thousands were without
food..."

The house is made up of two parts (see plan): to the
right, the house itself, and to the left, the farm buildings. The front door opens on to a courtyard, which
has a wing on either side (the right hand wing has been
emptied of its furniture and converted into a reception
room; on the walls hang photographs of Mao Ze dong
visiting his house, now a museum). The front door
gives on to an antechamber; the altar to the ancestors
is on the far wall. Behind the antechamber is the wash-
house, with an enormous stove and a gutter for the
dirty water. The kitchen is on the left of the ante-
chamber, with a fine, long stove made in masonry.
The kitchen leads on to the dining-room, which gives
on to the parents' bedroom; Mao's bedroom led out
of here. These three rooms constitute the left wing of
the house. A corridor also leads from the kitchen (to
the right is Mao's elder brother's bedroom) to a rectangular courtyard, round which are the outhouses.
The pig-sty is immediately to the right, followed by the
woodshed, which leads to the visitor's room; then

come the cowshed, and the rice storehouse (raised slightly, as a precaution against damp and rats); an outhouse at the far end of the courtyard contains tools: barrow, plough, a small millstone, noria scoops and chain for irrigation; in a small room beyond that are three pestles, operated by the feet, and a small hand threshing-machine.

The old temple of the ancestors of the Mao clan still exists in the village. Mao Ze dong held his first meetings here, when he came back to Hu nan in 1926–27 to organise the peasants' societies and analyse the conditions necessary for a revolutionary movement. In March 1927, after this stay, he published his famous *Investigation of Peasant Movement in Hu nan (Hu nan nong min yun dong kao cha bao gao)*. The temple has now been converted from its original use to an office (there is still a painted wood ceiling). Two other buildings were Mao held meetings are also open to the public.

In 1964, a museum devoted to the Chairman was founded, and housed in a modern building. *First room:* childhood and adolescence; portraits of his parents (who died in 1919), his two brothers, his sister and his wife, all four of whom died during the revolution (either in action or by execution), and his son, who was killed in the Korean war; books which he read as a child (popular novels like *The Romance of the Three Kingdoms*, works of the philosopher Wang Chuan shan). *Second Room:* the founding of the Communist Party. *Third Room:* the founding of the peasants' societies; red flags stamped with white ploughs (their emblems). *Fourth Room:* the founding of the first revolutionary base at Jing gang shan and the extending of the system to other regions.

Xiang xiang

Xiang xiang is about 25 miles east of Xiang tan, on the Chang sha–Xin hua railway line. In Tan shi, near the town, a museum has been created to show a landlord's house beside that of a poor peasant (Di zhu zhuang yuan he ping nong zhu zhai buo wu guan). The former Yang family's house has been used for the museum; it contains 1. a series of rooms with their original furniture, with a few special exhibits (contracts, instruments of torture…) added; 2. next to the house is a workman's cottage with a thatched roof; the man's job was to guard the fish in the landlord's pond, and cultivate a plot of ground, which he leased from the landlord.

Zhu zhou

Zhu zhou is 30 miles south-east of Chang sha, at the junction of the railways between Hu nan and Jiang xi and Peking and Canton; it is now a busy industrial town, with a population of 200,000 (machine building, chemicals, building materials, food processing, paper).

Li ling

Li ling is near the Jiang xi border, on the railway line 30 miles east of Zhu zhou. The town was founded under the Han. The economic growth of the town is more recent however. During the Yong zheng period (1723–1736), Liao Zheng wei, a native of Canton, discovered kaolin near the town; with the help of about twenty workmen he built a kiln and a temple (Fan gong miao) in memory of his former master who taught him the art of pottery-making. For several generations the workmen all had to worship the master,

Fan, and the temple was destroyed only recently. The Li ling workers were famous for white pottery with a blue design. In 1906, an official who was a native of Hu nan obtained the government's permission to set up a porcelain centre at Li ling. The town took part in the Panama exhibition in 1915, and the workers won a prize for their technique; in 1930, production came abruptly to a standstill, as attempts to imitate the European style of the Japanese failed and were followed by bankruptcy. Production began again in 1956, and in 1962, 60 kilns were working, staffed by 7,000 workers. They produce two kinds of pottery: the traditional blue and white for the home market, and porcelain for export. The town is extremely well-placed; the coal used comes from the Ping xiang collieries, on the other side of the border (Jiang xi); raw materials and the finished products are transported by water. In 1962, the production of porcelain, most of which was intended for export, amounted to 7,500,000 pieces. A school has been founded to train the workers; some of them have been sent for training to Shi wan in Guang zhou, and sculptors from Tian jin have been to Li ling to compare experiences.

Heng shan

Heng shan is over 60 miles south of Chang sha, on the west bank of the River Xiang jiang. The road to Heng shan, sometimes called Nan yue, the Southern Mountain, one of the five sacred mountains, begins there (*wu yue*, see Tai shan, p. 715). The mountain is 9 miles west of the town, and a regular bus service runs between Heng shan and the little village at the foot of the mountain; the journey takes half an hour. The Heng shan range consists of 72 peaks; the five highest are the Zhu song feng, the Zi gai feng, the Yun mi feng (still called the Fu rong feng), the Shi lin feng and the Tian zhu feng. Sacrifices were made to the mountain at a very early date; the *Shu jing (Classic of Documents)* reports that Emperor Shun went to Mount Nan yue when he was on a hunting expedition in the south. The tradition was carried on by the Han, but Emperor Wu di decided to offer the sacrifices to the Southern Peak on another mountain, the Huo shan, in the province of An hui; from the Sui onwards, Mount Heng shan was once more regarded as a sacred mountain. As time went on, numerous temples, both Buddhist and Taoist, were built on the mountain. The Qing Emperors constantly sent officials to offer sacrifices for them; many of the temples were restored at the emperor's expense. Under the Republic, people built summer houses on the slopes of Mount Heng shan, as it was known for its pleasant climate during the summer months. Guest houses have been opened there lately, to accommodate visitors; over 10,000 a day arrive there during the pilgrimages which take place every autumn. Taoist and Buddhist communities, consisting of about twenty and over 150 monks respectively, live in over twenty temples which lie scattered over the mountainsides. A few of the temples will be described.

The Zhu sheng si Temple is in the village of Nan yue zhen (at the foot of the mountain), in Dong jie Street. It is one of the biggest temples. It was founded under the Tang, though the present buildings date from the Qing (17th century); their generous scale is explained by the fact that they were built as a palace to accommodate Kang xi on his tours of the south. The Hall of the Classics (Jiang jing tang) contains stone statues of the 500 *luo han.*

The Great Southern Peak Temple (Nan yue da miao)
is also at Nan yue zhen; it was founded in 726, and
was called Zhen jun ci at that stage; it was restored
several times, under the Song (1012), the Yuan (1258),
the Ming (1438) and the Qing (1708), and then was
burned down in 1873. The present buildings date from
1882. The central hall (Zheng dian) stands on a terrace with a beautiful balustrade in Qi yang stone, carved with flowers, birds and beasts; the hall, which is
174 feet long and 114 feet deep, carries a double roof
supported by 72 wooden pillars, each on a stone base.
The 72 pillars and the height of the hall (7 zhang 2 chi)
are said to symbolise the 72 peaks of the Heng shan
range. Statues of the Yue shen (sacred mountain
deities) stand on a carved stone dais inside. The temple
also contains a) a large iron bowl (2¼ feet high and
4¼ feet across) presented to the temple by the Chu
King Ma Yin under the Five Dynasties; it now stands
under the covered way in front of the central hall;
b) an iron bell, dated 1324, hanging in the bell tower;
c) a seated bronze Buddha dating from the end of the
Ming dynasty; d) an incense-burner (iron, 100 feet
high) dated 1633, in the courtyard in front of the central hall; e) several Ming steles.

The Jie long qiao Bridge behind the temple leads
to the road going up to the top of the mountain. It
passes the Luo si tan electric power station, the Nan
yue reservoir, and the Zhong lie ci Temple; after
4 miles, a little kiosk, the Ban shan ting (the kiosk half
way up the mountain) marks the half way mark between the village and the Zhu rong feng Peak. The road
passes several more temples (Shou fu dian, Tie fo si,
Wu yue dian), and then comes to the Shang feng si
Temple, founded under the Sui between 605 and 616,
under the name of Guang tian dian (Fair Sky Temple);

the present buildings were restored under the Qing; the 4 iron statues of the celestial guardians date from the Jia jing period (1522–1567). There are several things to see near the temple: the Shi zi yan (Tiger rock), the Guan yin yan (Guan yin rock), the Luo han Cave (Luo han dong), the Bridge where the Immortals meet (Hui xian qiao) and the **Terrace for looking at the sun (Wang ri tai),** on a peak behind the Shang feng si Temple; built under the Yuan, it was one of the 27 observatories *(ce yan suo)* created by order of the Emperor. The path eventually leads up to the Zhu rong feng Peak (the highest of the Heng shan peaks).

The Fang guang si Temple is at the foot of the Lian hua feng Peak; it was founded in 503 and restored several times in the years which followed. Wang Fu zhi, the great philosopher who refused to acknowledge the new Qing dynasty, retired there in 1643; he had a little house built there, where he lived for several years.

The Fu yan si Temple is at the foot of the Reng bo feng Peak. It was founded in 568, under the Six Dynasties, and was then called Ban ruo si. The present buildings date from the Qing; they contain a bronze statue of the Mountain god (Yue shen) 11 feet high; it is probably earlier than the Song.

Heng yang shi

Heng yang shi is on the east bank of the River Xiang jiang at the point where the railway splits into two; one line goes to Guang xi and the other to Guang dong. As it is at the centre of road, rail and water communications, it is one of the most important towns in the south of the province; it is also an industrial town (chemicals, machine building, textiles, paper and foodstuffs).

THE EASTERN TOWNS

Chang de shi

Chang de shi is on the left bank of the River Yuan shui, about 6 miles from where it flows into Lake Dong ting; mountains encircle it to the north-west, and it opens on to the plain to the south-east. The town was founded under the Han. It used to be an important marketing centre, selling products brought by water, via the Yuan shui, from Gui zhou and Si chuan. In the 19th century, the Europeans asked for the town to be opened to foreign trade. In 1916, it had a population of 180,000. It is now a storage centre for wood-oil, medecines and wood which floated down the River Yuan shui. It also contains a few branches of industry (textiles, food processing, leather).

Yi yang

Yi yang is south-east of Chang de shi, on the north bank of the River Zi shui, 30 miles from the point where it flows into Lake Dong ting. It stretches for over 5 miles along the river bank. The town acts as a storage and redistribution centre for the Zi shui valley products.

Shao yang shi

Shao yang shi is in the middle of the province, on the upper reaches of the River Zi shui; it is linked by road with Heng yang and Xiang tan to the east and with Gui zhou to the west. It is a storage and redistribution centre for the local products.

Hong jiang shi

Hong jiang shi is in the south-west of the province, 30 miles from the Gui zhou border, on the south bank of the River Yuan shui. It is an important marketing centre for wood-oil and wood. Two minority races, the Miao and the Dong live in autonomous districts south of Hong shi: Cheng bu (Miao) and Tong dao (Dong). The Dong have built a beautiful wooden bridge, the Hui long qiao, in the Tong dao xian district; it is in the same style as the bridges in Guang xi.

FU JIAN

(Map see Atlas pl. 4/5)

Fu jian is bordered by Zhe jiang to the north, Jiang xi to the west, Guang dong to the south-west, and to the east and south-east by the Formosa Strait. It is almost entirely mountainous; the plains are limited to the lower reaches of the rivers and a narrow coastal strip. The chief mountain ranges run from north-east to south-west, parallel to the coast; they are formed of hard rock (granite) but long erosion has left few peaks of over 5,000 feet. Most of the rivers in Fu jian are short (the Min jiang is the longest) but as rainfall is abundant, they carry large volumes of water; most of them cut through the mountains at right angles or diagonally, offering excellent conditions for the production of hydro-electric power. The rocky, deeply indented coastline, like the Guang dong coastline, offers some of the best natural harbours in China. Much of the province is still covered with forests, particularly the south.

Until recently, the economy of Fu jian was based entirely on the sea. The mountains made communications with the interior of the country difficult and essential exchanges were carried out by boat. The individuality of the province was striking, both linguistically (see the map of Chinese dialects) and politically (resistance to the Qing Dynasty in the 17th century). Hard natural conditions (mountain soil, rarity of good land) and the severe social system (formation of large estates) turned a large proportion of the population to seek a living from the sea; many of them were fishermen (they salted down the fish and sent it to other parts of the empire) or lived by trade (the forests supplied plentiful wood for boat-building, particularly pine trees for masts). Those who could not scrape a living in the ports or the shipyards left to seek their fortunes abroad, in the Philippines or the south seas (many of the Chinese in Paris, for instance, are from Fu jian). Goods for export were provided by the forests (musk, wood, lacquer ware), the mines (iron, tin, mercury) and handicrafts (steel tools, silk fabrics, pottery); Fu jian tea was extremely sought after until it was rivalled by Indian and Ceylon varieties. Most of the history of the province is to be found in the history of its ports, Fu zhou, Amoy, Quan zhou, never-failing sources of emigrants and busy trading centres, full of foreigners (Moslem, Manichean, Christian colonies in the 12th, 13th and 14th centuries; "Japanese pirates" in the 16th century; Europeans in the open ports in the 19th century).

Now that Chiang-Kai shek has settled in Tai wan, putting an end to all trade across the strait, the whole economy of the province has had to be re-adapted. Trade has fallen off considerably and it is mainly carried out with the interior, by means of the two railway lines, Ying tan–Amoy and Nan ping–Fu zhou, both of which were built after the liberation. They link the main towns in the province and give access to Jiang xi. Agriculture has been developed: rice is grown in the river valleys where there is adequate irrigation (two crops a year), sweet potatoes and maize are grown on drier land, and sugar-cane and tropical fruit are also grown (longans, lichees, oranges, pineapples, bananas and grapefruit). In the mountainous areas, a cereal from South America has been introduced *(ou rou);* tea is still grown, and the forests supply wood to meet the ever-increasing demand (cedar, pine, bamboo, and eucalyptus, which is a recent innovation). Light industry has progressed as well: Zhang zhou now has a sugar refinery, paper mills have been built at Nan ping and Fu zhou. The population was estimated at 13.5 million in about 1930; it has now increased to 17 million (over 100,000 belong to the She minority).

The coastal towns will be described first, followed by the inland towns.

A. THE COAST

San du ao

San du ao is on an island in the middle of San sha wan Bay, which provides an excellent natural harbour It used to be a tea redistribution centre.

Fu zhou shi (Foochow)

Fu zhou is on the north bank of the River Min jiang, about 25 miles upstream from its mouth. It is the provincial capital, with a population of over 500,000 (624,000 in about 1920).

The town was founded by the Chen at the end of the 6th century; the name Fu zhou appears in the 8th century; under the Five Dynasties, the town was the capital of the autonomous state of Min yue. Under the Song and the Yuan, it was a centre of propagation of Manicheism. Marco Polo described the town at the end of the 13th century: "And you may know that great trade is done in this city and there are many merchants and craftsmen. And all of this city, they are idolaters and subject to... the great Kaan. And a great number of armed men stay there, ...because throughout the country many cities and villages very often rebel... And you may know that a great river which is quite a mile wide goes through the middle of this city... They make sugar also in so great abundance that no one could tell it. Great trade in pearls and in other precious stones is done there, and this is because ships from Indie come there in numbers with much merchandise... They have also beautiful gardens and delectable..." (A.C. Moule and Paul Pelliot: *Marco Polo, the Description of the World*, p. 347, 348.) At the beginning of the Ming dynasty, walls were built; the Manchu put a large garrison at Fu zhou (struggle with the loyalist armies of Koxinga). In 1842, the Treaty of Nanking declared Fu zhou am open port and from 1861 onwards, Europeans settled opposite the town, on the south bank of the river. In the 19th century, the town was famous for its tea and lichees, its timber trade (wood was floated down), its handicrafts (silks, lacquer ware, wood engravings, horn combs, umbrellas, matches). Towards 1920, it contained 2 American companies, 15 English companies and 6 Japanese companies. Part of the population were fishermen (oysters were a speciality). The new railway has enabled the town to change from a purely maritime town into one whose economy is based on the rest of the continent. Machine building and chemical industries have been introduced.

The town was laid out on a north-south axis. The suburb where the Europeans settled was to the south, on Nan tai Island. Nan tai was linked to the mainland by two bridges which met on an islet in the middle of the river (Zhong zhou); they measured over half a mile altogether. Sampans could go under the bridge, but junks had to moor downstream of it. The bridge was famous from the end of the 18th century. "Nothing can compare with its magnificent bridge, which has over a hundred arches, and a double parapet running the whole length of it" (Grosier). The district specialising in business and handicrafts lay north of the Min jiang (the Da miao shan hill lay to the west, with a temple dedicated to the founder of the state of Min yue). It had a thoroughfare about 2 miles long running through it as far as the gate of the city, properly speaking. The town walls followed a roughly triangular lay-out, each corner built up against a natural hill, all of which were surmounted by a stupa or a tower (Yue wang shan to the north, the King of Yue's Hill; Wu shi shan to the south-east, the Black Stone Hill; Yu shan or Jiu xian shan to the south-west). The Manchu district used to be in the south-west of the city.

The **Hua lin si** still stands on the southern slope of Bei bing shan, north of Yue wang shan Hill; it is a temple which was founded under the Tang, and later restored several times (under the Song, the Ming and the Qing). The most interesting building is the central hall (Da xiong dian), which is square, with a terrace in front of it, in Song style.

There is a spa nearby, and Mount Gu shan (Drum Hill, c. 3,000 feet) is to the east; it is a famous beauty spot and holiday centre. The hill used to considered as the protector of the town; its name came from a large stone at the top. The Boiling Spring Temple (Yong quan si) stood on the western slope of Gu shan Hill; it was a shrine founded in the 8th century, which used to be famous for the Buddha's tooth which was kept there, which attracted numerous pilgrims, and for animals (pigs, goats, poultry) which were fed by the monks until they died a natural death.

The port of Ma wei (Horse's tail), pronounced Ma moï in the local dialect, is downstream from Fu zhou; it used to contain the famous Fu zhou arsenal (created in 1867 and put in the charge of French officers from 1867 to 1880 and from 1896 to 1908, with foundries, forging presses) and the Temple of the Mother (Ma zu), a Taoist female deity, the patroness of the arsenal.

Quan zhou

Quan zhou lies on a magnificent bay, at the mouth of the River Jin jiang.

The town seems to have been founded at the beginning of the 8th century; under the Tang it was divided into three districts, Ya cheng, Zi cheng and Luo cheng. The walls were in brick, and were replaced by stone walls in the 13th century. The town reached the peak of its activity under the Song and the Yuan, when sea trade developed. In 1086, a special customs office was created to deal with foreign ships, and in the 12th and 13th centuries large numbers of western merchants lived there, all grouped in the same area, on the banks of the Jin jiang, south of the town. Quan zhou was without any doubt Zaytun, the great emporium frequently mentioned in Arabic and Western contemporary documents. People have wondered if the name Zaytun came from Ci tong (a sort of prickly tree which grows near the town) or from Rui tong (the former name of Quan zhou), but the abundant inscriptions in Arabic, Syriac and Latin script are sufficient proof of the existence of a foreign colony. According to Marco Polo: "At this city is the port... to which all the ships from Indie come with many goods and dear, and namely with many precious stones of great value and with many pearls both large and good. And it is this port from which the merchants of Mangi, that is all round this port, come.... Moreover I tell you that for one ship load of pepper which may go to Alexandre or to other place to be carried into Christian lands, there come more than a hundred of them to this port of Caiton... And moreover I tell you that the great Kaan receives in this port and in this town very great duty, because I make you known that all the merchants ships which come from Indie give of all goods, and of all stones and pearls they give, ten per cent, that is the tenth part of everything." (A.C. Moule and Paul Pelliot, p. 351.)

A Christian colony existed there in the 14th century and the names of several of the bishops have been recorded. When the Mongol dynasty fell, the town went into a rapid decline and passed to second place; the harbour became silted up. Local handicrafts still flourish there (lacquer ware, embroidery, basket-making).

The town is rich in archaeological remains, dating mainly from the Song and the Yuan.

a) The town itself

1. The Kai yuan si Temple is in Xi jie; it was founded under the Tang and enlarged under the Song, when it housed over a thousand monks. It was burned down under the Yuan, rebuilt under the Ming Emperor Yong le, and restored under the Qing. The biggest building of all is the Great Hall (Da dian), which dates from the Ming, and has a double roof and a balcony running round it; five statues of the Buddha, statues of Guan yin and the eighteen *luo han* stand on a dais inside. A terrace stretches in front of the Da dian, the Yue tai, 80½ feet long and 27 feet wide; on either side of it, about 200 yards apart, stand the Twin Pagodas (Shuang ta), built in wood under the Tang and rebuilt in brick and stone under the Song. The western one (Ren shou ta) is 144 feet high, and was built in 1228; the eastern one (Zhen guo ta) is 156 feet high and was built in 1237. Both are octagonal, with five stories, and windows in each facet; they are extremely alike (see G. Ecke and P. Demiéville, *The Twin Pagodas of Zayton*, Harvard University Press, 1935).

The **Museum** dealing with the **History of Quan zhou's Foreign Trade (Quan zhou hai wai jiao tong shi buo wu guan)** was opened in the Great Hall in July 1959. It contains 479 exhibits, collected under five headings: 1. the beginnings under the Southern Dynasties, the Tang and the Five Dynasties; 2. trade at its height under the Song and the Yuan; 3. the decline under the Ming and the Qing; 4. the stagnation period from 1850 to 1950; 5. possibilities of future development. Some of the most interesting exhibits are steles inscribed in foreign languages, found during the last

few years (80 or 90 Arabic inscriptions, dating from
between 1009 and 1310; Roman Catholic and Nestorian Christian inscriptions), Manichean steles, bas-
relief of Hindou inspiration (see Wu Wen liang, *Quan
zhou zong jiao shi ke*, Peking 1957).

2. The Mosque is a little to the south-east of the Kai
yuan si. It was built under the Song, restored in the
14th century, and is said to be in poor condition now.

**3. The Museum of Quan zhou's Famous Men (Quan
zhou li shi ren wu ji nian guan)** is in Sun Yat sen Street
(Zhong shan bei lu). It includes sections on Yu Da
xian (1315–1579), who fought the "Japanese pirates";
Li Zhuo wu (1527–1602), the philosopher; Zheng
Cheng gong (1624–1662), known to the Europeans as
Koxinga; Qiu Er liang (1830–1855?), a heroine who
led a peasant revolt.

b) The Surrounding Area

1. Mount Jiu ri shan is in the western suburbs,
3½ miles from Quan zhou, on the north bank of the
Jin jiang. It was famous from the Tang onwards, and
people often used to go into retreat there; temples used
to stand on the two outcrops of the mountain: a large
Buddha, 18 feet high, dating probably from the 10th
century, still stands on the western one. The rocks are
covered with inscriptions, several of which were made
under the Southern Song, engraved by officials sent
to ask for favourable winds before the squadrons set
sail.

2. Mount Hua biao shan is south-west of Quan zhou,
3 miles from the town of Jin jiang. A little temple,
Cao an, stands at the foot of the hill; its iconography
shows Manichean influence.

3. The Three Song Bridges. The Luo yang qiao is north east of Quan zhou, between the districts of Hui an and Jin jiang. It was built under the Song, between 1053 and 1059; it consists of stone slabs resting on 47 pillars, spanning the Luo yang; the Wu li qiao (Five *li* Bridge), which used to be called the Pan guang qiao, built between 1253 and 1258, is nearby; the Fu qiao is west of Quan zhou, spanning the River Xun jiang. It is over 800 feet long and 16 feet wide and was built in 1160. All three are made in the same style: stone slabs lying horizontally on stone pillars.

Amoy

(Peking dialect: Xia men; Amoy is the transcription of the local pronunciation.)

Amoy is on the west coast of an island in the mouth of the River Jiu long jiang. It has a population of about 200,000.

The town was founded at the beginning of the Ming dynasty, at the end of the 14th century. In the 17th century, it was one of the strongholds of Zheng Cheng gong (Koxinga), the Ming general who remained faithful to the fading Ming dynasty, threatened Nanking, drove the Dutch from Tai wan, and held the Formosa Strait for several years against the Manchu. Amoy was declared an open port by the Treaty of Nanking in 1842 and the Europeans soon formed a little colony, living on Gu lang yu Island just off Amoy. The Japanese arrived a little later and were granted a concession on Amoy Island, south-east of the town. At the beginning of the 20th century the town exported tea, sugar, dried fish, salt, tobacco, fruit and manufactured products such as paper umbrellas, paper, bricks, and iron cooking utensils; the value of the imports (cotton fabrics, rice, flour, oil) exceeded the exports and the deficit was made up by money sent home by Chinese working overseas in the Straits Settlements and the Dutch East Indies (from 15 to 18 million taels each year).

Amoy Island has recently been joined to the mainland by a dyke carrying the railway. The fishing industry still employs a large proportion of the inhabitants; chemical industries have now been created in the town as well. Many Overseas Chinese come back to settle in Amoy or nearby, and a special university has been founded for Chinese from the south seas.

The town lies west of some rocky hills famous for their beautiful scenery; some of the best known spots are: Hu tou shan (Tiger Head Mountain), Bai lu dong (White Stag Cave), where the philosopher Zhu Xi is said to have founded a college under the Song. The Nan pu tuo Temple stands about 3 miles east of the town. Gu lang yu island, just off Amoy island, is famous for its scenery and is known as the "Garden on the Sea" (Hai shang hua yuan). The highest point, Ri guang yan, is near the spot where Koxinga camped with his troops.

The **Overseas Chinese Museum (Hua qiao bo wu guan)** was founded in 1959 with financial help from some of them; it has collections of bronzes, pottery, handicrafts dating from the Ming and the Qing, and photographs of the conditions in which the Chinese live overseas.

B. INLAND TOWNS

Zhang zhou

Zhang zhou is in the south-east of the province, on the lower reaches of the River Jiu long jiang, on the railway from Amoy to Jiang xi. The Song philosopher Zhu Xi lived here for a long time; he was prefect of the town, and founded a college for the study of the classics. Zhang zhou is now a re-distribution centre, handling the fruit grown in the area; it has branches of one or two industries.

MAISON COLLECTIVE DE FENG SHENG PRÈS DE YONG DING XIAN
COMMUNAL HOUSE AT FENG SHENG NEAR YONG DING XIAN

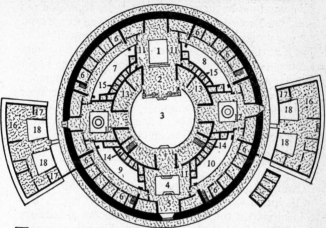

Parties de la maison couvertes par des toitures. Parts of the house which are roofed over.

1 Courtyard	10 Courtyard
2 Great Common hall	11 Balcony
3 Courtyard	12 Courtyard
4 Courtyard	13 Guest room
5 Door	14 Cow-sheds
6 Kitchens	15 Stables
7 Courtyard	16 Mill
8 Courtyard	17 Store-house
9 Courtyard	18 Courtyard

(After Zhong guo jian zhu jian shi: Short History of Chinese Architecture, vol. I, Peking, 1962.)

Yong ding

Yong ding is a small town about 6 miles north of the Guang dong border, on the River Yong ding. The neighbouring village of Feng sheng xiang contains an interesting communal dwelling, of a type which is fairly common in the mountainous areas of the province. It is round, with an outside wall of earth; although it is four stories high, only the top two stories have windows in them, making it easier to defend the building. Three doors lead through the wall to a second circular building with a courtyard in the middle of it. The two lower floors of the outer building contain kitchens, stables and store-rooms for grain; the upper floors and the inner building are living quarters. A large rectangular hall (da ting) in the north of the inner building is used for ceremonial occasions. The largest dwellings of this type have as many as three concentric buildings, and house up to 80 families.

Nan ping

Nan ping is on the upper reaches of the Min jiang, at the point where several tributaries flow into it. It is a local market town; several new branches of industry have been started there since the liberation (wood, chemicals, paper).

Tai ning

Tai ning is in the north-west of the province, on the road to Nan ping. The Gu lu yan Hermitage (Soft Dew Hermitage) is 9 miles south-west of Tai ning, at the foot of an overhanging cliff. It consists of four beautiful buildings which date mainly from the Song (roofs with gracefully upturned eaves corners, remains of frescoes, and large numbers of Song inscriptions).

Chang ting

Chang ting is in the west of the province, on the Jiang xi border. It was a Red Army stronghold during the second civil war. A memorial to Qu Qiu bai has been put there.

TAI WAN (Formosa)

(Map see end of the book)

The island of Tai wan is off the coast of Fu jian, on the other side of the Formosa Strait. The strait is about 186 miles long, 95 miles wide to the north, and 125 miles wide to the south; it is shallow (260 feet deep at the most), and the hot and cold currents which converge there make it an excellent fishing ground. The Peng hu Islands (Pescadores) lie east of the strait, off the coast of Tai wan; there are 64 of them altogether, and the biggest, Peng hu Island, contains an excellent natural harbour: Ma gong. Tai wan is longest from north to south; its area is 22,000 square miles. Two thirds of the island are covered by a chain of mountains with over 60 peaks, running from north to south; the highest of all, Mount Yu shan (Jade Mountain, 12,960 feet) is by far the highest peak in south China. A coastal plain lies along the west of the island. The mountains are rich in mineral resources: coal in the north, oil at the foot of the mountains. The Tropic of Cancer cuts through the middle of the island and its climate is warm and wet. Rainfall is abundant, producing luxuriant vegetation (including dense forests) and swift-flowing rivers which provide hydro-electric power.

It is still not known exactly who the original inhabitants of the island were, nor to which racial group they belonged. As the remains of the early population (about 200,000 people) still live in the mountains in the middle of the island, they have been called Gao shan (mountain dwellers), particularly since 1945. Chinese historians, who are anxious to prove a longstanding connection between the island and the mainland, have been searching for evidence in old documents, which reveal that in 230, the king of Wu sent 10,000 men to the island; in 607 and 610, the Sui sent expeditions there, and the Yuan, followed by the Ming, sent "inspectors" to the Peng hu Islands. The Han population did not start to occupy the island on a large scale until the 17th century; in 1662, the great naval commander Zheng Cheng gong (Koxinga) drove out the Dutch who had built the fort of Zealand there in 1634, and established his leadership over both sides of the strait for several years. When his successor gave in to the Qing in 1684, a government was established on the island (the fu of Tai wan), and placed under the jurisdiction of the Fu jian government. Grosier gives the following information at the end of the 18th century: "Those who want to cross over to the island have to obtain passports from the mandarins in China, which are usually extremely expensive; cautions are required as well... As the Tartars are afraid of a revolt there, the island contains a permanent garrison of 20,000 men who are changed every three years... Nearly all the species of fruit grown in India can be found there, including oranges, bananas, pineapples, gouavas, cocoanuts, and many kinds which are grown in Europe; salt, tobacco, sugar, pepper, camphor, ginger and aloes-wood are all to be found there... The inhabitants of Formosa rear large numbers of oxen, which they ride, as they have no horses or mules... To simplify the collection of taxes and tribute, the government has sent one Chinese to live in each village, to learn the language and act as interpreter for the mandarins." In 1782, Tai wan was devastated by a typhoon which was so violent that in the west it was thought that the island had been swallowed up by the sea. In 1895, after the Sino-Japanese war, the Japanese occupied Tai wan and stayed there for half a century, until the end of the second world war. Finally, as is well known, Chiang Kai-shek's government retreated there in 1949 in the face of the Communist advance.

One quarter of the island consists of cultivable land (the western plain). The main crops are rice and sugar-cane; tea is also grown. The forests on Mounts Tai ping shan, Ba xian shan and A li shan provide wood: Tai wan produces more camphor wood than anywhere else in the world. Several hydro-electric complexes have been built, particularly near Lake Ri yue tan (roughly in the centre of the island). Sugar is the main industry, though metal refineries, machine-building, chemical and food-processing factories are to be found in the main towns: Tai bei (population 2,100,000), Tai zhong (population 560,000), Tai nan (population 550,000). The total population amounts to 16,500,000.

GUANG DONG

(Map at the end of the book)

The province of Guang dong is bordered by Fu jian to the north-east, Jiang xi and Hu nan to the north, the Guang xi Zhuang Autonomous Region to the north-west, and by Vietnam for a short stretch; the sea fringes it to the south. A large island, Hai nan, lies just off the coast (21,000 square miles). The provincial capital, Canton, is about 1,200 miles from Peking as the crow flies. A chain of mountains, the Nan ling, lies in the north of the province, sloping down southwards.

Several passes through the Nan ling give access to the north. The Pearl River (Zhu jiang) basin covers much of the province; it is the biggest watercourse in south China. The river itself is relatively short, but it is fed by three large rivers: the Xi jiang, which rises in Yun nan (1,260 miles long), the Bei jiang and the Dong jiang. As rainfall is abundant, the Pearl River carries a large volume of water; although the area of the river basin is only two thirds that of the Yellow River, it empties eight times as much water into the sea every year. It forms a vast delta; the principal river mouth, Hu men (Tiger gate) was known as "Bocca Tigris" by the first European cartographers. The Tropic of Cancer cuts through the province slightly to the north of Canton, so the climate is hot (average 71° F. over the year) and wet (frequent rain in the summer).

The history of the province is tied up with the trade routes which pass through it:

1. The *northern route* leads through the Nan ling passes to central China; merchandise which came up the Bei jiang to Nan xiong was taken through the Mei guan (Plum-tree Pass) to Jiang xi, where it was sent on northwards. Grosier wrote of it in the 18th century: "The highest point of the gorge was blocked by a wall with a gate in the middle of it, where soldiers were stationed with instructions to keep a check on everything taken through... it was so busy, and the road leading to the pass so full of movement that Father Gaubil said that he had never seen more people in any street in Paris".

2. The *western routes* led from Guang dong to Guang xi, a little further inland (both provinces were often under the same administrative authority in the past) and from there to Yun nan and Tong king.

3. The sea route gave access to the south seas and the West.

At a very early date, Chinese influence from the north began to permeate Guang dong through the northern trade route, whereas the provinces of Yun nan and Guang xi remained virtually untouched by it for some time; Qin shi Huang di sent four armies which met at the sea near Canton in 214 B.C.; the same movement went on under the Han (many Han tombs in the Canton area have yielded tomb furnishings like the ones found in tombs in the middle Yellow River valley).

This situation never changed (even so, the presence of the northern Chinese has not affected the spoken language, which has remained different from that of the north, nor the tendencies to autonomy, which occurred in the 10th century, and again in the 20th century, with Sun Yat sen). The province was sometimes threatened by people from the mountainous regions of Guang xi (Zhuang troops, under Nong Zhi gao, laid siege to Canton in the 11th century), but the reverse was more often true: Cantonese merchants travelled up the Xi jiang and drained off the products of the less-developed areas.

Foreign influence eventually arrived from overseas; a mosque is said to have been built in Canton as early as the 7th century, and a large Moslem colony destroyed Huang chao at the end of the Tang. From then onwards, specialised branches of handicrafts grew up making goods for export (Fo shan pottery and hard-ware). Exchanges with foreign countries were carried out with the help of Overseas Chinese as well as the merchants; the Overseas Chinese (Hua qiao) go abroad for a time, but never forget their own country and constantly send money back home; they like to come back to end their lives in China (in Guang dong alone they number 6,000,000 at the moment). The last (but by no means the least) influence to make itself felt was the Western influence, which dates from the 16th century (the first Portuguese embassy arrived in 1514), and was at its strongest from 1850 onwards. The Europeans were granted land (the Portuguese obtained Macao in about 1553, the British got Hong Kong in 1841–42, and the French received Guang zhou wan in 1898); their impact stimulated Chinese reactions, which started earlier here than elsewhere; Lin Ze xu destroyed the cases of opium imported by the British at Canton, and Sun Yat sen, himself a native of Guang dong, led the Chinese revolution, with the support of the Overseas Chinese.

Twenty per cent of the land in the province is under cultivation; most of it is in the valleys, on the coastal plains, and in the Pearl River delta too, now that recent work has made this possible; in some places, terraced fields have been cut out of the hillsides. The hot, damp climate enable two crops of rice to be grown over most of the province, and sometimes even three, as for instance in east Hai nan Island. Apart from rice, sweet potatoes, sugar-cane (in the delta and the Lei zhou peninsula), fruit (three hundred kinds, the best known of which are oranges, bananas, pineapples, lichees, longans), tobacco, cotton and flax are grown. South Guang dong has a tropical climate, and recently rubber, sisal hemp, coconuts, oil palms, and coffee have been introduced, particularly in Hai nan. Silk worms (7 or 8 harvests a year) and fish are also raised, particularly in the delta. Light industry and the food-processing industry have developed considerably: there are sugar refineries in the delta, food-processing factories (the Canton factories are the biggest in China), flour mills, oil-extracting factories, textile mills (cotton, linen, silk) and paper mills (at Canton and Shan tou).

Coal, iron, and non-ferrous metals are mined in north Guang dong; the metal industry has grown up since 1958. Guang dong has a long tradition of handicrafts: ivory carvings from Canton, Fo shan pottery, Shan tou embroidery. A railway line links Hong Kong and Canton to the north of the country; since the liberation, another has been built from the port of Zhan jiang (Lei zhou peninsula) to Li tang in Guang xi. The population of the province is 37,000,000.

The Chinese consider that the islands in the South China Sea are Chinese territory (Dong sha, Xi sha, Zhong sha and Nan sha); they include over 170 islands or islets (coral reefs).

Canton will be described first, then the inland towns, the coastal towns, and finally Hai nan.

CANTON

(Map, p. 1169)

The Chinese name for the town is **Guang zhou.** It is north of the Pearl River delta, 30 miles north-west of Hu men (Tiger Gate). It is an important industrial centre, a busy port and the provincial capital. The population is 2,000,000.

History

There exists a legend which says that five celestial genies, riding goats, came to bring the first cereals to the inhabitants of the area; the legend has not yet been forgotten at Canton, which is sometimes called Yang cheng (Goat Town), and in the 20th century, a group depicting the five goats was built on the top of a hill north of the town.

The historical origins of the town are not clearly known; the first settlement was probably founded in 214 B.C., when Qin shi Huang di sent his troops down to the sea. The town was then called Pan yu, after two nearby hills. Under the Han, it was for a time the capital of the autonomous state of Nan yue (attached to the empire under the Han Emperor Wu di). During the Three Kingdoms period, the Canton area was under the authority of the state of Wu. The name Guang zhou first appears at this time. Under the Tang, the town was enlarged and several proofs exist of active exchanges with the south seas (a mosque was founded, a large Moslem colony existed). At the end of the dynasty, the town was badly damaged by Huang chao's troops. In the 10th century, it was the capital of an autonomous dynasty, the Southern Han, who called it Xing wang fu; they made several improvements to the town.

The first great period of development occurred during the Song dynasty. Under the Northern Song, the town grew considerably; it was divided into three districts (western, central and eastern towns), walled off from each other. In the *Ling wai dai da* by Zhou Qu fei, information is given on the sea-going boats built in the Canton shipyards. Under the Ming, the town was still flourishing; it spread northwards, as far as Mount Yue xiu shan, and southwards along the Pearl River, whose banks had been altered. Industry (weaving, wrought iron, ship-building, pottery) developed still further. The first European embassy, the Portuguese embassy led by Tome Pires, landed in 1514. Resistance to the Manchu was violent and the Qing had to launch several campaigns before they finally took possession of the town. Canton developed little under the Qing; the arrival of the Europeans gradually created new conditions. The Cantonese were among the first Chinese to come under Western influence, and also among the first to react to the influence.

From the mid-19th century onwards, Canton was a stronghold of democratic and revolutionary ideas. In 1839, the mandarin Lin Ze xu had some of the cases of opium imported by the English destroyed; in 1841, the population of the surroundings

ÉVOLUTION HISTORIQUE DE CANTON
HISTORICAL DEVELOPMENT OF CANTON

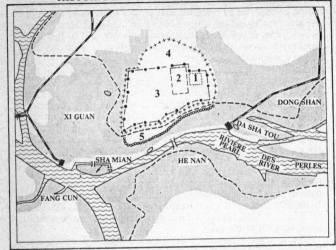

- - - - -	Tracé de l'ancien rivage Former river bank	
O	Anciennes îles Former islands	
-·-·-·1	Ville Qin Qin town	
- - - 2	Ville sous les Sui et les Tang Town under the Sui and the Tang	
-·-·- 3	Ville Song Song town	
4	Première ville Ming First Ming town	+ + + +
5	Deuxième ville Ming Second Ming town	ooooooooooo
	Extensions modernes New Districts	
	Voie ferrée Railway	▬▬▬

of Canton, and particularly of the little town of San yuan li, took arms and opposed a British expeditionary force; in 1854–55, during the Tai ping rebellion, the Li Wan zhong rising took place in the Canton area; in 1911 there was an armed rising against the Manchu (later called the Huang hua gang rising) in which 72 rebels were caught and executed. In 1923, Sun Yat sen came back to Canton and founded the Guo min dang; in 1925 and 1926, Mao Ze dong, with some other Communists, including Zhou En lai and Guo Mo ruo, ran the Peasant Movement Institute in the former Temple of Confucius; in 1925, the Cantonese workers, in agreement with the Hong Kong workers, organised a general strike. In 1927, Chiang Kai-shek suppressed the workers' movements in Shang hai and at the same time crushed the Canton workers' rising (5,000 victims). Canton is now one of the most important industrial centres in south China, and one of China's chief trading ports. It is also a cultural centre; it contains the Sun Yat sen University, several higher education establishments, a museum, libraries; the south China botanical gardens are in the suburbs.

Description

The modernisation of Canton began in the 1920's. A special commission undertook to clean up and organise the vast chaos of tiny streets and shacks which had furnished the 19th century travellers with material for many a horrifying description.

The only sections which had been adapted for traffic were the Franco-British concession on Sha mian Island and the quayside, or Bund, where the foreign trading firms had gathered. The most urgent need was for roads to be cut through the mass of houses, big enough to take lorries and buses. In 18 months, almost 25 miles of wide streets, with pavements and sewers, were laid throughout the town in all directions, most of them crossing at right angles. They are fringed by arcades, which shelter countless tradesmen's and craftsmen's shops from the sun. 3,000 hovels had to be destroyed, a mile and a half of filthy old canals had to be filled in, and part of the old town walls (6 miles) had to be demolished to provide the materials needed. The money was obtained by conceding public transport to a bus and tram company for twenty years, for the price of a million Hong Kong dollars.

The police force was organised at the same time, as well as the prison system, whose tortures had in the past excited the imagination of many writers (see the famous *Jardin des Supplices* by Octave Mirbeau). Energetic measures were taken to improve public hygiene, which put an end to the fearful epidemics, such as the bubonic plague, carried by rats. Large parks were laid out to the north and east of the town. Gambling, which was as flourishing as at Macao, was forbidden, and prostitution, which had developed into a veritable industry in the sampans and flower boats, disappeared almost entirely. Here the authorities were helped by a fire which swept through the boats on the Pearl River. Education was extended and taken in charge by the municipality, who provided schools for 40,000 children out of the total of 100,000; the rest went to the countless private schools, several of which were run by foreigners, Roman Catholics or Protestants.

Modern Canton is mainly the town built by Sun Yat sen, though the regime which emerged victorious after 1949 has put the finishing touches to it. Its most successful contribution is the Pearl River Square, a huge open space by the riverside, bordered by the tall white buildings of the exhibition hall.

The *general lay-out* of the town is fairly simple. It nestles in a bend of the Pearl River, facing south. Its main streets slope gently down towards the river from the rising ground to the north, although they do not always end at the water's edge. The main street is Liberation Avenue (Jie fang lu), the central axis of the town, going from the Yang cheng Hotel to the Exhibitions Centre, and at the same time dividing the town into two parts, east and west. Countless streets of varying sizes cut across it at right angles, from spacious Sun Yat sen Avenue (Zhong shan lu), which is the longest of all, about half-way up, to tiny streets bright with signs, with washing strung across them, teeming with craftsmen and tradesmen of every kind, a permanent market and open air workshop, full of brilliant colours and different smells. When going about the town without a guide, this is the plan to keep in mind.

Sha mian island flanks the town at its south-west tip, like a boat tied up to a large junk. Another island to the south-east, the Er sha tou, is covered with sports grounds. The buildings overflow on to the other bank of the Pearl River, known as He nan.

Canton airport receives planes from Peking, Shang hai and from Phnom Penh, among other places. The traveller who comes from Hong Kong arrives at the station east of the town, almost on the river. Tourists are put up at one of the two hotels open to foreigners: the Ai qun Hotel (Love the Masses Hotel) on the river, a little to the west of Hai zhu qiao Bridge, or the Yang cheng Hotel (Goat Town Hotel) at the north end of Liberation Avenue. The town will be described starting from the north, and from east to west.

The road into town from the airport runs through communes devoted to growing rice and vegetables of various kinds. On the right, in the village of San yuan li, a monument can be seen: a granite stele standing on a mound, in memory of the members of the "Ping ying tuan" movement which was the first to oppose the British armies in 1841. An excellent road, 200 feet wide, leads into the town. A railway bridge carrying the line to Peking spans it just before the Yang cheng Hotel appears on the right.

The **Yang cheng Hotel** consists of five stories of rooms arranged in a horse shoe shape above the hall on the ground floor. The ground and first floors are taken up by services (restaurants, post office, shops, hairdresser, offices, etc...). The eighth floor contains the dining-room and reception rooms. The hotel was built after 1949, in a rather heavy style, clearly influenced by Russian designs, though alleviated by flowers, gardens and a superb view (from the back) of luxurious vegetation and lakes. The new Gymnasium nearby is even more recent; it is built in reinforced concrete, with carvings of tall young athletes.

The west and east of the town will be described first, followed by the south and the surroundings.

1. The West of the Town

Sun Yat sen Street (Zhong shan lu), half-way between the Yang cheng Hotel and the river, leads westwards towards Liu rong jie (Six banyan-trees Street); the **Temple of the Six Banyan-trees (Liu rong si)** opens on to the street. The temple is best known for its pagoda, called the Hua ta, Decorated Pagoda, as opposed to the minaret of the mosque to the south of it which is known as Guang ta (Naked tower). The temple was founded in 479. In 1099, the famous poet Su Dong po visited the temple; he admired the six banyan-trees in the courtyard, and then wrote the two character *liu rong*, six banyan trees. From then on, the temple was known as the Liu rong si, the Temple of the Six Banyan trees. A pagoda was built in 537; it was burned, and restored under the Song in 1098, and under other, later dynasties. The temple is now the head office of the Canton Buddhist Association.

The main hall of the temple contains Qing statues of the Buddha, the god of medecine, eight *luo han* and Guan yin (behind the screen). The pagoda is just behind the hall; it is 180 feet tall, built on an octagonal base, with nine stories separated by little green tiled roofs; each storey has windows in it. A staircase inside leads up to the top, which commands a magnificent view over the town; a niche at the base of the pagoda houses a statue of the Buddha (Ming). A little garden lies east of the pagoda; a stele in the middle is engraved with a portrait of Su dong po.

The **Mosque,** known as **Huai sheng si (Mosque dedicated to the saint)** is south of Zhong shan lu, in Guang ta lu Street. The legend says that is was built in 627 by an uncle of Mohammed; it is said to be the oldest mosque in China. The present buildings are modern and offer little of architectural interest; the minaret (Guang ta), nearly 80 feet high, is a round two-storey tower, faced with grey cement; a staircase leads up to the first storey.

A little to the east, north of Zhong shan lu, is Guang xiao si lu, where the **Guang xiao si Temple** still stands. The Cantonese say that the town of Canton did not exist when the Guang xiao si Temple was founded (Wei you yang cheng, xian you guang xiao); it is in fact one of the oldest temples in the town; it was founded in the 4th century. It used to be a famous temple, which was frequented several times by monks from India. In 1269, part of it was burned; it has been restored many times since; extensive repairs were done in 1832. It is now out of use, and being repaired. The main hall is especially interesting; its style seems to be a happy mixture of several different periods. It is a large rectangular building, 7 bays long and 6 wide, standing on a little terrace with a parapet decorated with stone lions; the double roof is carried by square pillars.

The three statues of the Buddha which used to stand inside were destroyed by mistake several years ago when a school was being moved into the temple; when the statues were broken open, over 70 little

wooden statues were found inside, depicting *luo han*,
donors and the guardians of Buddhism; an enquiry
has brought about twenty of them to light again,
which have been found to date from the Tang; they
are now in the town's history museum. The temple
also contains a little stone pagoda behind the central
hall: the Liu zu fa ta, dating from 676; it is octagonal,
and 21 feet high; each facet contains a niche with
a statue of the Buddha. It also possesses two precious
iron pagodas dating from the Five Dynasties: one,
the Dong ta, to the east, was built in 967; it used
to be in another temple, the Kai yuan si, and was
brought here between 1234 and 1236. A pavilion
was built to house it; it is square, with 7 stories,
and is 13 feet high; each facet contains little niches
with Buddhas which used to be gilded, hence the
name of the pagoda: Tu jin tie ta (Gilded Iron Pagoda).
The base is covered with beautiful dragons and
completed by a lotus design. It is one of the oldest
iron pagodas to survive in such good condition.
The western one (Xi ta), west of the central hall,
dates from 963; a pavilion was built to shelter it
under the Southern Song, but it fell down at the end
of the Qing, damaging four stories of the pagoda;
the first three stories can still be seen; they are in much
the same style as the other one.

Still further west, north of Xia jiu lu Street, is the
Hua lin si Temple, at the end of a narrow little street
giving on to the north side of Xia jiu lu. The temple
was founded in 526; an Indian monk, Da mo, came to
expound the law there in the 6th century. The buildings
which are left are not older than the Qing dynasty:
a huge hall stands at the far end of a rectangular
courtyard on the right, with celestial guardians on
either side of the entrance. It contains statues of the

500 *luo han;* one of them is said to be Marco Polo, recognisable by his large-brimmed hat (at the far end, to the right of the altar). The statues are not as good as the ones in the Temple of the Azure Clouds (Bi yun si) at Peking.

The former **Temple of the Chen Family Ancestors** (Chen jia ci), built between 1840 and 1846, is on the north side of the western section of Zhong shan lu Street; it is outstanding because of its enormous size (it covers an area of 25,000 square feet) and the glazed pottery carvings on its roof; it is now an exhibition centre for the art of Canton and the province (Guang dong min jian gong yi guan).

The **Roman Catholic Cathedral** is between the Love the Masses Hotel (Ai qun da sha) and the Hai zhu guang chang Square; its pointed towers make is conspicuous from a long way off. It was built from 1860 onwards; a French architect, Guillemin, drew up the plans, and it was consecrated in 1863, as two inscriptions on the façade record: Roma-Jerusalem 1863. The grounds, about 1,000 feet long, belonged to the viceroy Ye, whose palace was destroyed during the attack made by the Franco-British troops. The granite was provided by the Chinese government. It is in gothic style, 260 feet long, about 90 feet wide, 80 feet high, with massive towers 160 feet high. It is open at fixed times for services (a notice on the door states the hours) (1965).

The street going down towards the river from the Cathedral ends in the huge Pearl River Square (Hai zhu guang chang); a colossal statue of a revolutionary figure stands in the middle, facing south. The most striking building on the square is the **Exhibitions Centre,** a massive, austere building dating from 1957. It houses an exhibition, spread over a floor space of 98,000 square feet, of the 20,000 or so articles which China makes for export; heavy and light industry, textiles, foodstuffs and handicrafts. Twice a year, in spring and autumn (the autumn session, from 15th October to 30th November, is the most important), buyers from all over the world come to see what New China can produce, and to sign contracts. In this way, Canton, the gate of China, has come into its own again; the authorities stress that unlike the old "unequal treaties", present day exchanges are done on a basis of equality and reciprocity. The tourist will find it interesting as an exhibition of the country's products, particularly of the more artistic ones: silks, embroideries, ivory carvings, porecelain, jewellery, etc.

To the west along the **Quay** (upstream) stand the tall geometric silhouettes of the Post Office building and then the Love the Masses Hotel (Ai qun), 16 stories high, built before the Japanese invasion, in about 1937.

Still further west, the main shopping street, Tai ping lu, turns off to the right, full of trade and administrative buildings, nearly all of which were built by big European or American firms, and which used to attract large amounts of capital to Canton. The **Cultural Park** (Guang zhou wen hua gong yuan) offers a hundred different entertainments, all in an open-air setting. The best time to go there is the evening, when it is crowded with people going to the theatres, cinemas, games rooms and exhibition halls.

Sha mian Island is further west, in the river; it is over half a mile long, about 400 yards wide, and separated from the town by a canal spanned by two bridges, one at the east tip, and one on the north side. One of them has steps up to it and is therefore closed to cars; there are in fact few cars on the island.

The French and British concessions used to be here; when Canton was opened to trade in 1843, at the request of the Europeans, the allies asked to be granted territory, which they obtained in 1859. The island was little more than an uninhabited sand-bank. Stone embankments and other things were built, four fifths of which were paid for by the British, and the other fifth by the French, who had the right to about 44 acres. Magnificent villas grew up rapidly along the water's edge; the French consulate was at the eastern tip, and the British consulate was in the main street. No Chinese were allowed there without permission and the bridges were shut at 10 p.m., by iron gates. It contained administrative buildings, a Protestant Church, a Roman Catholic Church, a masonic lodge, tennis courts, a sailing club, and the offices of several Western banks.

The little island still has a peaceful, residential air about it. The spacious houses are now used by branches of the Chinese administration and schools; they are still well kept up. Handsome trees and lawns line the straight streets. The embankment by the water's edge, overshadowed by enormous banyan-trees, provide a pleasant walk, even in the hottest weather. It commands an excellent view over the river and its traffic.

On the mainland, on the right, on the edge of the quay beside the east bridge, stands a stone stele erected in memory of the demonstrators who were killed on that very spot by bullets from the European soldiers, fired from the concession on June 23rd 1925. It was during one of the episodes in the struggle against the "unequal treaties" which resulted in the general strike which paralysed the harbour of Canton and Hong kong. André Malraux's novel "Les Conquérants" records some of the episodes in the struggle.

2. The East of the Town

The Yue xiu Park is in the east of the town, east of Liberation Street (Jie fang lu); it is the most pleasant of all Canton's parks, and covers an area of over 247 acres. After the revolution, the whole area round Mount Yue xiu shan was turned into a vast public garden with superb views over the surroundings and gardens full of tropical flowers which bloom all the year through; everybody, sportsmen and the casual stroller, can find something to his taste: a **stadium** shaped like the old hippodromes lies up against the south slopes of the hill, two Olympic-size **swimming pools** have been built on the north slope, and an **artificial lake** with islands, bridges and delightful pavilions; a memorial to Sun Yat sen completes the picture.

The most striking building of all is the **Pavilion Overlooking the Sea (Zhen hai lou)**. "The Five-storey Pagoda" as the Europeans called it has never had any religious function. It was built for the first time in 1380, under the Ming, and rebuilt in 1686 as a look-out post, after being burned down; it was at the highest point of the old town walls. It is a dark red, five-storey, rectangular building, with roofs separating the stories, guarded by two monsters in the shape of lions. It has been converted into a **Historical Museum (Guang zhou buo wu guan).**

Ground Floor: miscellaneous exhibits on Canton, maps, models.

First Floor: prehistoric tools found at five sites nearby; the expedition sent by Qin shi Huang di (*ge* found in the town); Han era: extremely handsome tomb figurines found in tombs near Canton (buffalo, sow giving suck to her litter, house built on stilts, mill, dancer with extravagant head-dress); iron implements (spades); a few bronzes; lacquer ware; bronze bells; map of the empire's exchanges with foreign countries; model of a boat; fragment of silk; set of ring-shaped weights; small coins; six drinking goblets with "ears", on a tray; wooden tomb figurines, with a horseman among them; Three kingdoms and Southern Dynasties era: map of the "journey to the south" under the Jin; engraved bricks; remains of an iron sword found east of Canton; mirrors; pottery; the alchemist Ge Hong; the Lu Xun rising (404–411).

Second Floor: Sui and Tang eras: pottery found at Canton; the Guang xiao si Temple (pagoda founded in 676); map of exchanges with the West; tomb figurines depicting Western merchants (large hats, beards and moustaches); Persian gold and silver coins; model of the Canton mosque; the introduction of cotton by the Moslems (?); the rising led by Lin Shi hong, who proclaimed himself king of Nan yue (590–618); the Huang Chao rising; silver ingot sent by the Canton officials as tribute under the Tang; Five Dynasties era: Canton under the Southern Han dynasty; photographs of a pleasure garden in the north of the town (with a metal flower vase), the remains of the Liu hua qiao Bridge, the iron pagodas at the Guang xiao si; lead coins; Song and Yuan

eras: pottery; Su Dong po's stay in Canton (the
calligraphy in the Temple of the Six Banyan-trees;
stele with his portrait); Song Ci (1189–1249), the
author of one of the first treatises on legal medecine,
the *Xi yuan lu;* small scale model (4/10) of a Yuan
clypsedra, formerly kept at Canton and now on
show in the Peking Historical Museum; map of sea
trade under the Song; the compass; rubbing of a
stele found in a Taoist temple in Canton with an
inscription saying that a merchant from San fo qi
(a kingdom in the south seas) had given money for
the temple to be restored; map of the town under
the Song; engraved bricks; model of the Temple
of the Six Banyan-trees Pagoda.

Third Floor: Ming era: development of industry in
Canton;

1. Textiles: photographs of the buildings owned
by the corporation to which textile workers had to
belong in order to get work; model of a loom; fabrics
found in a tomb in 1957;

2. Metal work: main production centres, Fo shan,
Six Banyan-trees Street in Canton; photograph of
a large iron anchor, found in the town in 1958;
Shi wan pottery (west of Canton); enlarging of the
town; building of the Tower which houses the Museum
(1380); photograph of two pagodas (south-east of
the town); Kuang Lu, author of a work on the Guang
xi minority races; two lutes; opposition to the Qing
in the Canton area; Qing era: porcelain; fabrics;
Chinese-English dictionary; clocks; Chinese astronomy and medecine in the 19th century.

Fourth Floor: anti-Manchu and anti-European
movements:

1. the destruction of 20,283 cases of opium imported by English ships in 1839;

2. Canton bombarded by the French and English troops in 1867;

3. Franco-Chinese war after Tong king was annexed in 1881;

4. the 1911 revolution, Sun Yat sen;

Fifth Floor: history of the Communist movement in Canton and the rest of the country.

Several steles found in and near Canton stand in a veranda recently built to house them, in front of the museum. Several late 19th century Krupp guns stand alongside them.

Back in Liberation Avenue (Jie fang lu), one of the next buildings on the right, a new, white one, is the head office of *China Travel Service* (Lü xing she). Beyond the crossroads, a modern street going southwards (left) has an enormous banyan-tree standing in the middle of the roadway. On the right after the gate into the Park (Yue xiu) is the **Guang dong Palace of Science,** a didactic museum for school-children; then comes the **Sun Yat sen Monument,** standing in a large formal garden **(Zhong shan ji nian tang).** It is a compact, elegant building, with a blue glazed tile roof; it now contains an enormous theatre which can seat over 5,000 people. It was built in about 1925, after the death of the great Chinese revolutionary leader; his statue stands in the garden.

South-east of this lies an entirely new district, rebuilt on modern town-planning lines: wide streets, broad pavements, flowers and trees everywhere, buildings which are full of light and not too high (2 or 3 floors). Several temples used to stand here:

the Temple of War, dedicated to Guan Yu, the
god of war; the Temple to the Town Gods (Cheng
huang miao), better known as the temple of horrors.
A long line of cells contained groups of statues
illustrating the different tortures of the Buddhist
hell, in the most realistic way possible: men being
sawn in half, women being devoured by beasts...
and the famous "bell torture", described by Octave
Mirbeau in his book *Le Jardin des Supplices*, which
takes place in Canton. The temples have disappeared.

The former **Temple of Confucius (Kong zi miao)**
is north of Sun Yat sen Street; in July 1924, it was
chosen to house the **Peasant Movement Institute.**
It was in a sense the Communist Party's first school.
It was decided to found it in July 1923, at the third
party congress. As Canton was a suitable place for it,
the temple, already diverted from its original use
by Sun Yat sen, was taken over with the blessing of
the socialist municipality of Canton, and generations
of cadres were trained, drawn mainly from the
peasant classes. The technique upheld by Mao Ze
dong was used, instead of that proposed by the
Soviet delegate, Borodin. Mao himself was in charge
of the Institute from March 1926. 327 students were
trained that year, and emerged at the end of it ready to
spread Communist doctrine and lead the movement
all over China. Most of the theoretical works of the
future statesman grew out of his teaching there,
where he worked alongside Zhou En lai, Qu Qiu bai,
Deng Zhong, Guo Mo ruo and others who were
later to be leaders or heroes of the Chinese revolution.
The school came to a sudden end when the Canton
commune was crushed in 1927.

The building is interesting for two reasons. The
remains of the Temple of Confucius are well worth

a visit; it dates from the Ming (16th century). At the same time, these are the buildings which witnessed the training of the first generation of the present regime. The humble dormitories, the refectory, the white wooden tables which are not very different from the principals' desk, all contributed to mould the craftsmen who built new China as we see it today.

A monument slightly to the east recalls another event in the history of Communism: the **Mausoleum to the Martyrs of the Canton Commune Rising,** put up in 1957. An enormous gate and a stone paved way lead right towards a huge round tumulus encircled by a marble wall, which contains the remains of the 5,000 victims of the crushing of the Canton Commune by the Guo min dang in 1927.

The **Provincial Revolutionary Museum (Guang dong ge ming buo wu guan),** in the east of the park nearby, gives an excellent account of the Guo min dang's role in the revolution from the Opium War up to the liberation; the Sino-Soviet Friendship Pavilion in another part of the park was built in memory of the Russians who shared the fate of the Chinese workers.

The old **Guang dong University,** where Lu Xun taught, is in the south-east of the park, north of Wen ming lu Street; the room where he taught is on the ground floor; the first floor now contains a **museum** devoted to him, the **Lu Xun ji nian guan:** the author's childhood and school-days (1880–1919); Lu Xun in Peking and Amoy (1919–1926); his stay in Canton in 1927, and the political situation in the town at that time; his stay in Shang hai and his activities there between 1927 and 1936; copies of his works and critical studies written on them; his bedroom.

The **former offices of the All-China Federation of Trade Unions (Zhong hua quan guo zong gong hui)** are south of the Lu Xun museum, in the west end of Yue xin nan lu Street. The federation was founded in 1922, during the second All-China Labour Congress; its offices were set up here in 1925. It was here that Liu Shao qi wrote his work on *Trade Union Organisation Methods (Gong hui zu zhi fa)*. The building is now a museum.

A district full of administrative buildings and hospitals is north-east of there, followed by highly industrialised suburbs. The **Tomb of the 72 Martyrs** is about 1½ miles out of town on the road to Huang hua gang Hill. This mausoleum, which covers about 36 acres, is in memory of the 1911 revolution. Before Sun Yat sen finally carried off his victory on October 10th, about ten attempts had failed through lack of arms or efficient methods. The attempt made on March 29th 1911, against the governor's palace, resulted in 88 victims, 72 of whom were buried at Huang hua gang.

In 1918, an appeal was launched to which many Overseas Chinese subscribed as well as those in China, and enough money was collected to build a memorial. The architects had plenty of money, and built an impressive, though rather strange monument, with little about it which is truly Chinese. It includes an Egyptian obelisk, a pavilion rather like the Grand Trianon at Versailles, a smaller copy of Bartholdi's statue of Liberty enlightening the world, and Chinese lions alongside doves of peace. With its mixture of Chinese traditions and Western influences, it is an excellent illustration of the international, progressive revolutionary spirit which existed in the 1920's.

3. The River and the South Bank

The Pearl River (Zhu jiang) is the largest in south China. Its name comes from a rock which breaks its surface as its flows through Canton, which local legends say is a precious stone which the first king of the town dropped into the river. It is 1,200 miles long, and rises in east Yun nan; the Xi jiang, the Bei jiang and the Dong jiang all flow into it. It carries eight times as much water as the Yellow River, because of the abundant rainfall. At Canton, it divides into several different streams, which water the fertile delta stretching from there to the Macao peninsula.

The Hai zhu qiao, was rebuilt in iron in 1952 in strictly utilitarian style to replace the bridge which Chiang Kai-shek's armies destroyed when they left the town in 1949. The bridge upstream of Sha mian Island, built as a railway bridge, has now been adapted to take road traffic as well, acting as the extension of the outer boulevard being built at the same time.

The river no longer offers the strange spectacle described by travellers in the past. At the beginning of the century, the journalist Jean Rodes wrote of it: "Thousands of floating houses tied up to each other along the banks form a colony with a separate existence, with its own trade, rules and habits. It has always been the pleasure district for the Cantonese. After a day shut up in the dark, pestilential entrails of the town, he comes out to enjoy the soft breeze off the delta. Everything is laid out there for the satisfaction of his subtle sensuality. Junks with rooms and furniture encrusted with mother of pearl and marble act as restaurants. Rich Chinese often give dinners there, to the accompaniment of concerts, shrill violins mingling with piercing head voices audible from a long way off, strangely softened by the water. The old three-storey boats inhabited by "flowers" with delicate painted faces were burned two years ago, and have now been replaced, it is true, by enormous "public houses" which a society of rich and honourable Cantonese businessmen has had built on the new quayside. But nearly all the sampans which sail to and fro from one bank to another, from Sha mian to He nan, contain little slave girls, bought from the pirates from the Western River; after rowing stoutly all day, they abandon themselves to more dainty games at nightfall, for the profit of their owners. This piquant mixture of putrefaction and precocity, of austere religion and pagan view of life, is an essential characteristic of the celestial ones and is in complete contradiction with all ideas of a transformed China in the Western sense of the word". Jean Rodes, quoted in *Guide Madrolle, Chine du sud, Java, Japon*, p. 42, 1916.

Not one word of this is true today, even down to the prophecy at the end, for Canton harbour is as clean and well-ordered as many Western ports. Aberdeen, on the east coast of Hong kong island, is the only place to offer similar sights today.

The south bank of the river has little of interest to the tourist from an artistic point of view. It is covered with factories, modern, well-built workers' living-quarters, people's communes; the **Sun Yat sen University (Zhong shan da xue)** is about 2 miles east of the bridge, downstream. It was founded by Sun Yat sen in 1924, and was then called the Guang dong da xue; the name was changed after his death. The university used to be inside the town, in the building now housing the Lu Xun museum; it was moved to its present one in 1931. The university has 9 faculties. The buildings contain an interesting **Sun Yat sen Museum (Sun zhong shan ji nian guan).**

4. The Surroundings of the Town

The Guang dong scenery is held to be among the most beautiful in China. The hills which lie to the south are no higher than 1,500 or 1,600 feet, but they are full of variety, and change as the sky changes. Terraced fields have been made in the hillsides (rice is grown there, although it costs a considerable effort to bring sufficient water); great efforts are being made to re-clothe the bare hills with pines and more exotic trees.

Only one of the many places to visit is accessible by road; a good, tarred road winds up through the woods to the **White Cloud Mountain (Bai yun shan),** about 9 miles north-east of the town. Its peak "which touches the stars" is a little over 1,400 feet, in spite of its resounding title, but it commands a splendid view over the town, the river and its delta.

Its many magnificent temples have made the hill famous: the Temple of Strong Virtue, the White Cloud Temple, helped by beautiful spots such as the cave of luminous vapours, the Tiger's Head Peak, the Nine Dragon Spring, etc,... The temples have been destroyed or abandoned, and the natural beauties of the place have been used methodically to produce the most luxurious mountain resort in China. The former religious centre was already being transformed under the Guo min dang. The new regime has put the finishing touches to their work: large villas, built one above the other, have been changed into hotels, with all the best charac-teristics of both Western and traditional Chinese style houses: large living rooms, bedrooms with big windows, bath rooms with marble baths sunk into the floor. The Chinese come here treading softly as though visiting a museum, dreaming of a China yet to come...

THE INLAND TOWNS

Fo shan

Fo shan is 10 miles south-west of Canton by road and waterway. Its name means "Buddha Hill"; under the Tang, three statues of the Buddha standing on a little hill near the modern Pu jun wei ta jie Street earned it the name of Fo shan. It used to be a well-known religious centre; under the Six Dynasties, Indian pilgrims used to come and preach in the town temples. It was an important economic centre as well; pottery kilns and workshops in Fo shan and the surrounding area produced pottery which was then sold throughout the empire. Recent excavations have uncovered the sites of several kilns; the oldest of them (in the village of Shi wan zhen) appear to have been built under the Song. Metal work grew up under the Ming as well; the cast iron cooking pots used in trade with the south seas were made here. According to Grosier, who visited the place in the 18th century, Fo shan was the biggest and most densely populated village in the world; it was called a village because it had no walls round it, and no governor, although the volume of trade there was considerable, and it contained more people and houses than Canton itself; it was said to have a circumference of three leagues and a population of one million. It is still an important industrial town, with a population of 300,000.

One or two interesting monuments still survive:

1. **The Zu ci miao Taoist Temple.** It was founded under the Ming; the Tai ping took it over in the 19th century, and it has now been converted into a museum. The present buildings, which date from the Qing, are reminiscent of the Temple of the Chen Family Ancestors in Canton; they have the same elaborate glazed pottery ornaments. The temple includes a stage, built in a huge courtyard with verandas and balconies round it; the Tai ping leader had plays put on there while he occupied the temple.

The temple also contains some interesting Qing statues and an exhibition of several things found at Fo shan during excavations there (Han tomb figurines), and from several different places (pottery from Shi wan and Tai ping weapons).

2. The former **Ren shou si Temple** now contains an exhibition of popular art from the town itself (paper cut-outs, lanterns, Shi wan statuettes and new year pictures *(nian hua)* made in Fo shan are all on sale there). The Shi wan potteries can be visited as well; they produce three classes of pottery: building materials, pottery for current use, and more artistic objects. The last of the three is the section usually shown to visitors. The workshops are near the waterway which is used to send away the finished products.

Hua xian

Hua xian is on the Shao guan—Canton railway line, about 25 miles north-west of Canton. Hong Xiu quan, the Tai ping leader, lived in the little village of Guan lu bu nearby; a little museum (Hong xiu quan ji nian guan) has been opened since the liberation

in the temple originally built in memory of the hero
after his death, containing several objects and documents concerning the history of the Tai ping rebellion.

Shao guan

Shao guan is a town in the north of the province,
50 miles from the Hu nan frontier, on the Canton
— Peking railway line, on the left bank of the Bei
jiang. In the 18th century, it was the second most
important town in the province after Canton. It
is now an important centre for trade and industry.
It has a population of 200,000.

THE COASTAL TOWNS AND HAI NAN

Shan tou (Swatow)

Shan tou is on the east coast of the province, 38 miles
from the Fu jian border, on the River Han jiang.
It was opened to Europeans in 1858, after the Treaty
of Tian jin. The first foreigners to settle in the town
were in the opium trade and then dealt in the shipping
abroad of Chinese coolies who left home to seek
their fortune elsewhere. A British consulate was opened
in the town in 1861, and several firms arrived soon
afterwards (Jardine, Matheson and Co., Standard
Oil Co. of New York, the British-American Tobacco
Co., and several import-export firms and transport
companies). Shan tou soon became one of the largest
trading ports in south China.

In the 1920's, the main exports were sugar, tea,
fruit, cotton dyed with indigo (produced in the Shan
tou area), tobacco, bamboo paper (made in south
Fu jian); the imports were mainly coal and matches

from Japan, cotton clothes from England and Italy, paraffin and flour from the United States. New industries have now grown up there alongside the rest: food-processing, pottery. It is the second largest town in the province after Canton, with a population of 300,000.

The town is fan-shaped, spreading over a peninsula and eastwards along the coast. It is surrounded by beautiful hill country: Cong long shan, east of the town, and Jiao shi shan, which overlooks the town, are two of the most famous ones.

Chao an

Chao an is south-east of Shan tou, on the right bank of the River Han; a boat service operates between it and Shan tou. It is a flourishing trading centre. In the 1920's it had a population of 400,000. The Guang ji qiao Bridge near the east gate of the town, or the Xiang zi qiao, as it is sometimes called, was built under the Song. Hu lu shan Hill, north-east of the town, near a little lake, gives a magnificent view over the whole area.

Hong Kong

(Maps see Atlas pl. 14, 15, 16 and city map p. 1201)

Hong Kong, which is Chinese for Incense Port, is the transcription of the local pronunciation, corresponding to the Peking dialect Xiang gang.

The territory now owns an area of about 428 square miles. It is east of the Pearl River estuary, which separates it from the Portuguese colony of Macao, and consists of Hong Kong Island (32 square miles), the Kowloon peninsula (Jiu long, Nine Dragons, 3.8 square miles) on the mainland, and the New Territories (394 square miles) which include about 235 islands and islets; the region as a whole is usually called Hong Kong. The territory is formed of granite hills (lying parallel to the Chinese coast) whose valleys have been flooded by the sea (the To lo strait depression to the north-east, Tu lu in Peking dialect, and countless little islands). The highest peaks are the Tan tau Island mountains (Da yu shan) and the Tai mo shan (Dai mao shan) on the mainland, which reach over 3,200 feet. The low-lying land, along the coastline and north-west of the Dai mao shan Mountains is not very fertile and needs much improvement to be worth cultivating. Apart from the River Shen zhen he, which follows the frontier with the Chinese People's Republic, Hong Kong has practically no streams or rivers (which means that water has to be brought from the Pearl River, and reservoirs have to be made in the hills to catch the rainwater). The climate is ruled by the monsoons: from September to March, the prevailing winds are north or north-east, the weather is dry and sunny, and the temperature rarely exceeds 75° F; this is the most pleasant season; the summer monsoon, however, brings rain from the south, accompanied by constant mist and cloud; in July, the hottest month, the temperature sometimes rises above 86° F.

Hong Kong's territory is full of sheltered bays, and harbours were built there at an early date; the Qing shan wan Bay (which used to be called Tun men wan or Tuan men wan) in the west of the New Territories handled traffic from south-east Asia; under the Southern Dynasties, boats sailed regularly from Tun men to Tong king. Under the Tang, the port grew larger and a garrison was planted at Tun men to guard the harbour. Under the Five Dynasties and the Song, sea trade expanded still further and two more garrisons were built, one on Da yu shan Island, the other at Ru zhou. Under the Yuan and the Ming, a new harbour was opened at Nan tou, on the east bank of the Pearl River estuary, so that Tun men was less active, and from the 16th century onwards, the harbour was constantly attacked by Japanese pirates.

Hong Kong was more than a port, it was an important economic centre; salt pans were created near Nan tou and on the coast of Kowloon Bay under the Han. The salt industry continued under the dynasties which followed, and under the Song, the imperial salt-pans (Guan fu chang) were created on the west coast of Kowloon Bay, and placed under a military guard; at the beginning of the Qing the industry had grown to such proportions that when the census was taken, the salt-pan workers (who inherited their jobs) were counted apart from the ordinary population.

Pearls were to be found off the south coasts of China, and particularly in the Pearl River estuary; a flourishing trade soon grew up. Under the Five Dynasties, the Southern Han princes gained control of the pearl fishing (they were the rulers of Canton at that time) and it was carried out on a large scale, under conditions which were often extremely hard for the fishermen. Several decrees were passed under later dynasties, some of which increased, some of which put a check on the fishing, which was costly; finally it was forbidden altogether. Under the Ming, a plant known as *guan xiang*, used to make incense, was planted for the first time in the north-west of Da yu shan Island. This luxury product was exported from the port of Aberdeen (Xiang gang, Incense

Port, in the south' of Hong Kong Island) and re-distributed in the Yang zi valley; this too stopped under Kang xi. In the 19th century, the whole situation was transformed by the arrival of the Europeans.

The British government had tried several times, in vain, to obtain permission from the Chinese government to establish a permanent base for European merchants who were almost entirely dependent on the local authorities at Canton. In 1841, Hong Kong was ceded to the British after the Opium War. In 1843, when both countries had ratified the treaty, Hong Kong was declared a British colony, and was given the name of Victoria. From 1849 onwards, it became one of the chief ports which sent Chinese coolies to seek their fortunes in south-east Asia and later on in California. The Peking convention of 1860 added the Kowloon Peninsula and the Stonecutters' Islands to the British colony. Finally, when the British had stressed the necessity of a neutral coastal zone for the defense of Hong Kong, the New Territories, stretching for about 18 miles beyond Kowloon, were granted on a 99 years' lease. The population has increased steadily since the 19th century: in 1853, there were 5,000 Chinese (mostly fishermen) and 700 Europeans; in 1865, the Asiatic population amounted to 125,000, with 2,000 Europeans; in 1931, the total population was 849,791; in 1941, it was estimated at 1,600,000, but fell to 600,000 by 1945.

The territory picked up again very quickly after the second World War: in 1961, it had a population of 3,131,131 and in 1978, 4,500,000.

In 1842, the new colony was declared a free port; the beginnings were difficult, however, in spite of excellent geographical surroundings. Once Kowloon was granted, though, business improved and Hong Kong soon became the chief depot in the Far East for goods travelling between China and the rest of the world. Banks, insurance companies, shipping lines, stowage firms, all settled there rapidly and were soon very prosperous (the Hong Kong and Shang hai Banking Corporation, now the biggest bank in the Far East, was founded in 1865). Except for ship-building, industry was negligible until the Korean war. When, in 1950, the U.N.O. put an embargo on everything which could be defined as military equipment destined for the Chinese People's Republic, Hong Kong had to create its own industry and widen its trade outlets. The territory now possesses heavy industry (ship building and repairing, scrap iron industry, machine-building), and extremely varied light industry (building, textiles, plastics, food-processing). In 1964, the chief buyers and suppliers were the United States, some of the capitalist countries, and the Chinese People's Republic.

Agriculture is of only secondary importance in the region's economy; the cultivable land only covers 32,000 acres, that is, 13% of the total area. Fishing is however extremely important: the fishermen amount to 86,000, with 10,000 junks, 4,000 of which are motorised. In 1961, catches amounted to 50,000 tons and the Deep Bay oyster beds, which cover an area of 6,000 acres, yielded 250 tons, most of which were exported. A railway line links Hong Kong to the Chinese People's Republic. The territory includes two towns: Kowloon (on the mainland) and Victoria, also called Hong Kong, on the north shores of the island, which bears the same name. All the hotels sell guides to Hong Kong; the book by Lo Hsiang lin, *Hong Kong and its External Communications before*

1842, Hong Kong 1963, gives an excellent account of the archaeological remains in the country.

Excursions

Hong Kong has few ancient monuments. The tourist will find two different kinds of interests: strolls along the narrow Chinese streets, crowded with people, colourful and full of little shops, and hill walks on the mountainside where it slopes steeply down south-eastwards, and is often quite deserted.

1. The Towns

Victoria is the financial and trading centre of the island, and includes the Governor's Residence, the consulates, the chief banks and two famous hotels, the *Hilton* and the *Mandarin*. Three streets cut through it, parallel to the sea:

Connaught Road along the sea-front, then *Des Vœux Road*, and *Queen's Road* are narrow streets running between tall buildings, full of cars and trams. The little streets perpendicular to them which climb up the hillside are crowded with pedestrians, pedicabs and rickshaws.

Aberdeen, lying on the other side of the island, facing southwards, contains countless sampans moored in its harbour, housing about 150,000 people living in unspeakably poor and dirty conditions. People's China has completed eliminated the famous floating towns which once existed at Canton and Shang hai, and which have inspired countless descriptions given by foreign travellers. Aberdeen is now the only place where one may get an idea of what the floating restaurants, and "flower boats" (often nothing more than plain sampans), the scene of the corruption so dear to writers of exotic literature, were like.

Kowloon which is opposite Hong Kong, on the mainland (the Star Ferry, on the quai opposite the Mandarin Hotel, goes there) has developed enormously during the last few years. A wide street bordered by sky-scrapers, *Nathan Road*, and containing hotels like the *Peninsula*, the *President*, the *Imperial*, etc., cuts through it. Entirely Chinese districts lie behind the high facades of the main street; they are teeming with refugees, and often sordid. Kowloon is more renowned for its night life than is the island.

Kowloon also contains:
1. The airport, which has a magnificent runway along the sea, built by a French company.
2. The station from which the Canton train leaves. The terminus is at the point of the peninsula, near the Star Ferry. Travellers with large amounts of luggage who are bound for People's China will find it easier to take a room in a hotel in Kowloon, to avoid taking it all across by ferry.

Things to see:
The tourist is strongly advised to climb the Victoria Peak, even if he has only a few hours at his disposal. An excellent road winds up to the top (1,674 feet), from which views are to be had over all sides of the island. If a car is unavailable, a funicular railway (Peak tram) which starts just above the Governor's Residence, can be used. The view is one of the most magnificent imaginable. Victoria and its sky-scrapers, the harbour, the bay, the channel and the constant traffic of cargo-boats and junks, followed by Kowloon and its encircling hills and beyond it the province of Guang dong, lie on one side, while on the other, islands of strange shapes and colours lie scattered on a deep blue sea.

A road leads all the way round the island, following the coastline almost all the way, and giving views over the sea. *Cap d'Aguilar* at the south-east tip has wisely been kept free of buildings and in its natural, wild state.

Practical Information

Vaccination certificate. Certificates of vaccination against small-pox and cholera are required (vaccination against small-pox alone is required for entry into China).

Currency. One Hong Kong dollar (H.K.$) is worth 6p; 5.70 H.K.$ are worth 1.00 U.S.$. The dollar is divided into cents.

Time. G.M.T. + 8 hours from November to mid-March
G.M.T. + 9 hours from mid-March to November.

Language: The Hong Kong Chinese speak *Cantonese*. *Mandarin* (Bai hua) is understood by the more educated circles. Hong Kong University gives its classes in Mandarin.

English is widely, though badly, spoken, even among the poorer classes. French is spoken by emigrants from Indo-China or people from the old French concessions in Shang hai or Tian jin.

Most of the large hotels, offices and shops have interpreters speaking other foreign languages.

Transport: It includes trams, buses, taxis, pedicabs and rickshaws (two wheeled vehicles pushed or pulled by a man, which are forbidden in the People's Republic of China).

Chief Hotels:
In Hong Kong itself: the Mandarin, Hong Kong Hilton Hotel.
In Kowloon: the President, the Peninsula, the Ambassador, the Park, the Imperial, the Merlin, the Empress, the Melbourne, the Palace, the Grand Hotel, the Miramar, the Nathan, the Astor, etc...

Travel Agency

For all information, reservations and formalities concerning travel in the People's Republic of China, consult:

China Travel Service, 6 Queen's Road, Hong Kong. Tel. 35841–8.

The Portuguese territory of Macao

Macao is the transcription of the local pronunciation, which corresponds to the Peking dialect Ma jiao; the natives of the island call it O moun (Peking dialect Ao men, meaning "entrance to the creek"). It has a population of 270,000, which includes 8000 Portuguese.

The region of Macao is west of the Pearl River; with the two islands next to it, it covers an area of 5.3 square miles.

The Portuguese first appeared at Canton in 1514, but they settled in Macao a little later on, either in 1553 or in 1557; the exact date is not certain. The colony has gone through serious difficulties, which sometimes hindered the trading activities of its port, but even so, it has managed to survive until now. Industry is growing (textiles) but agriculture non-existent, and food stuffs are imported from the mainland. The town lies at the end of a hilly peninsula, on a magnificent site.

Zhan jiang shi

Zhan jiang shi is on the west coast of the province, on the eastern shore of the Lei zhou peninsula; it used to be called Guang zhou wan (Guang zhou Bay). The Franco-Chinese convention of April 10th 1898 ceded Guang zhou Bay and the surrounding area to France for 99 years; the concession included over 800 villages, with a population, in about 1916, of 200,000 Chinese. The town is now once more part of Chinese territory. Its harbour, sheltered by two little islands, is one of the largest in the province. Zhan jiang shi is on the railway line to Guang xi, making economic exchanges with inland towns easier.

Hai nan Island

It is about 30 miles south of the Lei zhou peninsula.
The Li mu ling Mountains lie in the centre of the
island, running from north-east to south-east; the
highest peak is Wu zhi shan, 6,156 feet; the longest
rivers (Nan du he and Chang he) are in the west
of the island. It contains two roads: one travels
right round the island, and the other cuts through
from north to south, east of the Li mu shan Mountains.

The history of Hai nan is not well known; its
original inhabitants were non-Han. The Chinese
moved in gradually over the years. Officials were
sent into exile there; Su Dong po, one of the great
Song poets, was one of them. The island possessed
valuable natural resources, as Grosier noticed
when he went there in the 18th century: "The surface
of Hai nan Island is cut up into mountains and
plains; most of the mountains are covered with
old, dense forests. The plains and valleys are well
watered and fertile; they usually yield two crops
of rice a year... they also produce sugar, tobacco,
cotton, indigo, betel nuts, coconuts, grapefruit,
and all the kinds of fruit to be found in south China.
Aloes-wood, ebony, rosewood and a sort of wood
said to be incorruptible, are all grown in the mountains;
the last two kinds of wood are considered the best
of all, and are kept for the Emperor's use".

The Island was important during the second
civil war; the Communist troops took refuge in the
mountains, where they were helped by the minority
races who live in the higher regions (Li, Miao).
After the liberation, a Li and Miao Autonomous
Region was created (Hai nan Li zu Miao zu zhi zhou).
Hai nan is one of the main producers of tropical fruit

(sugar-cane, pine apples, grapefruit) and coffee. Rice is also grown there. The biggest town is Hai kou shi, on the north of the island, opposite the Lei zhou peninsula; it is the cultural and economic centre of the island, and the port which handles the traffic with the mainland. Industry has grown up there since the liberation (machine-building, flour mills, sugar refineries, food-processing).

GUANG XI

The Guang xi Zhuang autonomous region is bordered by Yun nan to the west, Gui zhou to the north, Hu nan to the north-east, Guang dong to the south-east and Vietnam to the south-west. Most of it is higher above sea level than Guang dong, but not as high as Yun nan and Gui zhou; roughly speaking, it is highest to the north-west and slopes gently down towards the south-east. The rock is mainly limestone which produces karst formations. The chief rivers (the Xi jiang and its tributaries) rise in the western plateau and flow eastwards towards Guang dong. Although the latitude is much the same as that of northern Guang dong, the climate is slightly less hot and less wet (it is further from the sea, and is affected by waves of cold coming from the north).

Like the other south-western provinces, such as Yun nan and Gui zhou, Guang xi came under Chinese influence fairly late. Most of the population consists of people belonging to the Zhuang minority race. They had developed their own civilisation to a certain extent (oral tradition of literature, theatre, marionettes, handicrafts). In the 11th century, one of their chiefs, Nong Zhi gao, went as far as to lay seige to Canton. Han influence gradually penetrated, both from the north (spread by people such as the poet and official Liu Zong yuan, appointed to Liu zhou under the Tang; he carried out several reforms and finally died there) and from the south (merchants from Canton who sailed up the Xi jiang and its tributaries). The province was a poor one, however, often laid waste by forest fires, and relatively sparsely populated; the inhabitants often emigrated, or took to the bush, and bandits were a constant menace, particularly in the 19th century. The Tai ping movement was born in Guang xi, at Jin tian (the field of gold); it was led by Hong Xiu quan, a Hakka from Guang dong. At the end of the 19th century, the Europeans tried to extend their influence as far as Guang xi. The English sent a steamer every week from the mouth of the Xi jiang up to Nan ning; the French, who were settled in Tong king at that point, and building the railway line in Yun nan, also tried to move into Guang xi, sending merchants and missionaries, one of whom, the famous Father Chapdelaine, was condemned to death by a Chinese mandarin in 1856 at Xi lin. The activities of the banners on the Tong king border worried the mandarins as well as the French, and provided them both with the pretexts they were looking for at the same time.

At the moment, the Zhuang represent only 35 % of the population of Guang xi (22,000,000 inhabitants), but as they occupy 60 % of the area, an autonomous region has been created. Other minority races, the Miao, the Dong, the Yao and the Yi are also represented, but are less numerous. Recently efforts have been made to build reservoirs to hold the water which otherwise often seeps away through cracks in the limestone rocks. Rice is grown in the centre and south of the province (two crops a year), maize and sweet potatoes in the north-west, and sugar-cane and grapefruit in the south. A few forests have survived the frequent fires, mainly containing pine and cedar trees; Liu zhou is the chief forestry area. Star aniseed, cinnamon, and tea-oil are produced. The province also contains mineral deposits (manganese, tin and coal, iron). The machine building, chemical and textile industries are gradually being developed at Liu zhou and Nan ning. The railway line now links the two largest towns, Liu zhou and Nan ning, to Canton and Tong king, and Gui yang and Chang sha. The western towns will be described first, followed by the eastern ones.

THE WESTERN TOWNS

Nan ning

Nan ning is in the south of the province, on the upper reaches of the Yu jiang, near the confluence of the Zuo jiang and the You jiang; it is on the railway to Hu nan and Vietnam. The head office of the people's comittee of the Guang xi Zhuang autonomous region is at Nan ning. The town was founded under the Yuan, and for a long time, it was under the control of Chao ning (15 miles to the south-east), and was no more than a small market town; it began to develop in the 20th century. It is now an industrial centre, with food processing factories, flour mills, sugar refineries, tanneries, printing works, chemical fertilizer factories,

and a cultural centre at the same time; a Minorities'
Institute was created in 1952 (Guang xi min zu xue
yuan). It has a population of 300,000. The town stands
on the north bank of the Yu jiang, and has several
lakes scattered through it; the suburbs stretch out
along the bank of the river. Among the oldest buildings in the town are the Qing feng lou Pavilion, and
the Drum and Bell Towers.

Fu sui

Fu sui is 43 miles south of Nan ning, on the railway
line to Vietnam. Remains found in 1958, in the San
guan yuan Cave (shells, blackened earth) in the Ba gui
shan Hills east of the town suggest that the site may
have been inhabited during the Neolithic era.

The Rock Paintings in the Ming jiang
and Zuo jiang Valley

In 1957, several rock paintings were found 30 miles
east of Ping xiang, north of the railway line to Vietnam,
in the cliffs alongside the Rivers Ming jiang and Zuo
jiang; seven sets have been found so far. The archaeologists and historians who examined them have not yet
made any final statements on the age of the paintings;
it is generally thought that they date from the Tang or
the Song. The subjects treated (ochre paintings of 1.
people, either shown on horseback, with a sword-belt
and sometimes a hat, or dancing; 2. animals; 3. drums
and other objects which have not yet been identified)
suggest that the artists may have belonged to Minority
races. It is thought in some circles that they are Zhuang
paintings, but no documentary evidence exists to sup-

port this view; the only references to them found so far date from the 19th century, and give little information.

The paintings fall into three groups: the *first*, which is the largest, includes four sets of them, all to the north of Ning ming xian. The *first set* is on the right bank of the Ming jiang, 15 miles north of Ning ming xian, on a cliff on Hua shan Hill; most of the paintings are between 15 and 100 feet above the ground. They cover a large expanse of rock; over 1,300 figures have been counted altogether. The tallest of them are 10 feet high, and the smallest 1 foot, but the average size varies between 2 and 5 feet; the paintings include animals and other objects as well. The *second set* is a few miles south of the first, on Gao shan Hill, on either side of the entrance to two caves; it includes about a hundred figures, the tallest of which are 5 feet high and the smallest 1 foot 3 inches, with an average size of between 1½ feet and 3 feet. The *third set* is south of the second, in the Long xia Gorge; the paintings are badly damaged, and include about twenty figures. The *fourth set* is on Zhu shan Hill, on the left bank of the Ming jiang, 5 miles from Ning ming xian; the paintings are mainly near caves hollowed out of the rocks and the cliff face. Several human figures and paintings of animals are scattered over different places. The *second group* of paintings is about 37 miles east of Long zhou, and consists of two sets: the *first* is on the north bank of the Zuo jiang, round the mouths of two caves on Hua shan Hill. The first cave has 180 people round it; the tallest are about 7 feet high, but the average height is between 2 and 5 feet. 230 paintings round the second cave all depict human figures. The *second set* is 15 miles south of the town of Shang jin, north of the Zuo jiang, on a cliff on Hong shan Hill;

EMPLACEMENTS DES PEINTURES
RUPESTRES DANS LES VALLÉES DU MING
JIANG ET DU ZUO JIANG
ROCK PAINTINGS IN THE MING JIANG
AND THE ZUO JIANG VALLEYS.

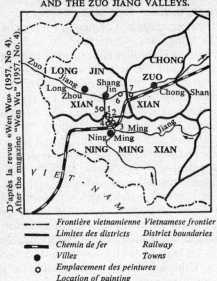

	Frontière vietnamienne	Vietnamese frontier
	Limites des districts	District boundaries
	Chemin de fer	Railway
●	Villes	Towns
○	Emplacement des peintures	
	Location of painting	

Paintings in the Ning Ming Xian	Paintings in the Long Jin Xian
1 Hua Shan	5 Hong Shan
2 Gao Shan	6 Hua Shan
3 Long Xia	Paintings in the Chong Zuo Xian
4 Zhu Shan	7 Hua Shan

four paintings only have been found, all depicting
human figures 2 feet tall. The *third group* is on a cliff
on Hua shan Hill, 15 miles west of Chong shan, and
consists of one set only, which depicts about 10 human
figures of an average height of 2 feet (the paintings are

now very faded). A yard to the left of the paintings is an inscription: it consists of one character, *qiu* (chief), painted in ochre, 7 feet high.

Ping xiang shi

Ping xiang shi is in the south of the province, near the frontier, on the railway line to Vietnam. It is an important centre handling trade between the two countries.

Bai si

Bai si is 125 miles west of Nan ning, on the upper reaches of the River You jiang; it is on the road to Gui zhou, Yun nan, Vietnam and Nan ning. It is an important trading centre; a European traveller who visited the town in 1905 said that the population (estimated at 25,000) lived almost entirely by trade. Local industry was more or less non-existent, and the soil in the surrounding area was so poor that it could not even produce enough to feed the inhabitants of the town, which had to depend entirely on trade. Countless Cantonese merchants kept shops stocked with mainly British and German goods: cotton fabrics, calico of different colours, mirrors, knives, sheets of glass, coloured glass balls to decorate gardens, endoscopes, lamps, oil-cans which came over full from America. These products all arrived at comparatively little expense, and were loaded on to junks on their way to Nan ning, Yu zhou and Canton; Bai si was the storage centre for all goods brought by caravan from Yun nan and Gui zhou. The town now contains some light industry (food-processing factories, sugar refineries, pottery kilns).

THE EASTERN TOWNS

Yu lin

Yu lin is in the south of the province, on the upper reaches of the River Nan liu jiang; the railway, three roads and the river run between there and Guang dong, and it is linked by road and rail to the rest of the province. Under the reign of Qian long, it was a trading centre chiefly frequented by merchants from Canton, who created a guild there. In the 19th century, products from abroad were shipped as far as Yu zhou, and carried the rest of the way by porters; salt, fish and light goods were sent up the River Nan liu jiang by boat. Products for export (medecinal herbs, agricultural produce and wood) were sent to Yu zhou. The town now contains some light industry.

Gui xian

Gui xian is on the Yu jiang, at the point where the railway to Guang dong crosses it. In the 19th century, it was a flourishing trading town; the great merchants who lived there owned 90% of all the surrounding land. It still exports sugar cane, and light industry has also grown up there (sugar refineries and other food processing industries).

Jin tian cun

Jin tian cun is a village 75 miles north-east of Gui xian, south of the River Cheng yang he, a little tributary of the Yu jiang. In 1850, the Tai ping leader Hong Xiu quan proclaimed the beginning of the revolution here. Ten thousand people from surrounding villages and towns came to settle there in response to his appeal;

everyone brought provisions which were pooled together and a community life began. Men and women lived in separate camps; the rebels' military camp was west of the village, in the Xi niu ling Plateau area; it was there that they took the oath to "overcome the waters and the mountains" on January 11th 1851, after beating the imperial troops and electing Hong Xiu quan as their leader. Traces of the camp on the north of the Xi niu ling can still be seen on the hill; it was in fact of an earlier date, as it was built under the Ming, by Yao rebels. It consists of a vast rectangle, 186 feet by 74 feet, with a wall 10 feet high all the way round, and an entrance 22 feet wide to the south, with a gate; the gate has now disappeared, and the walls are falling down. The village still contains the house belonging to Wei Chang hui (one of the Tai ping leaders) and the temple dedicated to him.

San jiang, the Dong Autonomous District

San jiang is 15 miles west of Jin tian cun, on the south bank of the Cheng jiang he; the famous **Feng yu qiao,** or Cheng jiang qiao, a wooden bridge built by the Dong, is near the village of Cheng jiang, not far from San jiang. The bridge rests on stone piers, each one of which carries a little pavilion with a roof built in several layers; a covered way with a tiled roof runs from one pavilion to the next; the bridge is 210 feet long, 11 feet wide and 34 feet high. This type of bridge is often found in areas inhabited by the Dong; seven of them span the Ping tan he, a tributary of the Cheng jiang he, within the space of 6 miles or so.

The village of Ma pang xiang in the San jiang district contains a magnificent tower, built entirely of wood, with a drum and a bell; it is square, with a nine-storey roof. It used to be the cultural and administrative centre of the Dong villages; the people used to meet in the big square nearby, either to settle business together, or for merry-making. The theatre and the kitchens were generally near the tower, as well as the temples and a hall where travellers were welcomed.

Jiang kou

Jiang kou is 9 miles east of Jin tian cun, on the north bank of the Yu jiang. At the beginning of the 18th century, the harbour was on the south bank of the river, and was a market used by the Yao; under the reign of Qian long, the harbour was moved to the opposite bank and the Yao no longer used ti. Trade flourished and merchants came from Guang dong in large numbers; they sold pigs, bamboo and handicrafts there. The development of Wu zhou eclipsed Jiang kou, which is now no more than a small straggling town.

Wu zhou

Wu zhou is on the Yu jiang, at its confluence with the Shui gui jiang a few miles from the Guang dong border. In the 18th century, it was one of the most important towns in the whole province; nearly all the rivers flowed into the Yu jiang upstream of the town, making it easily accessible by watere its position near the border made it an important trading centre. The Cantonese merchants who settled thre ; were considered expert traders; a few of them went in for industry (a match factory). In 1897, the English managed to get the town opened to foreign trade; soon a regular service of English steamers ran between Wu zhou and Canton and Hong Kong. By 1901, an English launch

sailed up to Nan ning once a week from Wu zhou, and
the middle Yu jiang valley was full of English and
American missionary preachers; Wu zhou had a British consulate and an American hospital was built.
After the liberation, industry was introduced alongside the trading activities (factory making chemicals
from resin, wood industry, sugar refineries, and other
food-processing factories).

Liu zhou

Liu zhou is in the centre of the province, at the
junction of the Hu nan—Guang xi and Gui zhou—
Guang xi railway lines, and of roads leading to all four
corners of the province. The town was founded under
the Tang, under the name of Kun zhou; its present
name was given to it soon afterwards. In 815, Liu
Zong yuan, a poet and official who had fallen into disgrace, was sent to Liu zhou, which at that time was a
little town in the midst of a wild countryside where
fierce animals and snakes lived; the city walls were
falling down, and bandits had more or less established
a reign of terror. Within a few years, Liu Zong yuan
improved the town; he had the walls rebuilt, ordered
wells to be dug, and fought against banditry and bond-
age. As time went on, the town gradually developed;
in the 18th century, Grosier describes it as a pleasant
little town, "surrounded by mountains yielding herbs
and rare plants, much frequented by doctors and
botanists". Up till 1949, the town lived mainly by
exporting the products of the surrounding area (wood,
tea-oil, medecinal herbs); it has now been developed
into a large industrial centre (machine-building and
chemical industries, electric power station, metal
refineries, textile mills, food processing factories). It

has a population of 300,000. The temple dedicated to
Liu Zong yuan still stands in the Hou gong yuan Gardens; it was built in 822 under the Tang and restored
several times over the dynasties which followed. The
mountains near by are particularly beautiful; Mount
Li yu feng, south of the town, is one of the most
famous.

Liu jiang

Liu jiang is 9 miles south of Liu zhou. In 1958, a skull
and fragments of human bones dating from the Upper
Paleolithic era (50,000–15,000) were found in a cave
near the town.

Liu cheng

Liu cheng is 30 miles north-west of Liu zhou, on the
lower reaches of the Rong jiang. The town and the
surrounding villages are famous for their ballad-
singers who compose songs in verse for feast days or
to mark any special events in everyday life.

Gui lin

(Map see Atlas pl. 25)

Gui lin is on the upper reaches of the River Li shui,
on the railway line from Nan ning to Hu nan. The
town was founded under Qin shi Huang di (214 B.C.);
it developed as a result of the building of the Ling qu
canal (see p. 1228). Under the Ming, it became the provincial capital, and remained the capital until 1914,
when Nan ning took over; in 1936 it once more became the temporary capital. The town was a revolutionary stronghold during the anti-Japanese war; printing
houses, newspapers, acting companies took refuge

there, and the population grew rapidly. Gui lin is now growing into an industrial town, but it is still famous for its superb landscapes. The underlying rock in this part of Guang xi is limestone; erosion has produced karst scenery full of fantastic shapes. Hundreds of stone hills with strange summits rise out of the plain on either side of the Li jiang, the upper reaches of the Gui jiang, apparently completely unconnected with each other. The curious scenery has attracted many poets and the beauty of Gui lin is praised in countless poems. Han Yu describes the landscape in one of his poems: "The river forms a green gauze belt, the mountains are like blue jade hairpins". The town and its hills will be described first of all, followed by the other hills east and west of it.

1. The Town

The town stretches along the west bank of the Li jiang; the old walls can still be traced in the lay-out of the streets. The River Yang jiang encloses it to the south, and several lakes border it to the west, the largest of which is the Hao tang. Three lakes lie in the south of the town: the Rong hu, the Shan hu and the Yang tang; magnificent rocks are scattered through the north; in the middle is the former palace of the king of Gui lin, known as the Wang cheng.

a) The Former Palace of the King of Jing jiang (Wang cheng)

In 1369, the founder of the Ming Dynasty, Zhu Yuan zhang, made his nephew, Zhu Shou qian, king of Jing jiang. The king had a residence built here *(wang fu)*; in 1393, he had an enclosure built round it *(wang cheng)* with a circumference of three *li* and a door on each side. Under the Qing, the residence was converted into an examination hall *(gong yuan)*; it now houses the Guang xi Province Teachers' Training College *(Guang xi shi fan da xue)*. The site and the gate of the old palace can still be seen.

The Du xiu feng Peak rises in the north of the enclosure; steps lead up the west slope to the top, which overlooks all the surrounding area; a little path on the east slope leads down past a rock shaped like a house, where Yan Yan, a poet who lived during the Six Dynasties period, used to come and work; a little lower down, the cliffs are engraved with characters which date from the Tang and the Ming. The Crescent Moon Pool (Yue ya chi) north of the Du xiu feng was dug under the Ming.

b) The Hills in the North of the Town

Feng bei lu Street (north of the Wang cheng) leads towards the River Li shui and **Fu Bo shan Hill.** It lies in a park, in the north-east corner of which is an enormous cooking pot standing on a terrace; the pot belonged to the Qing ding yue si Temple. A few steps lead on up to the site of the temple dedicated to Ma Yuan, a Han general and a hero of Guang xi, best known under the name of Fu Bo; higher up still is the Da bei gu tong cave, where Guan yin was worshipped from the Ming dynasty onwards; on the east side of the entrance to the cave are engravings of orchids and bamboos, attributed to Li Ping shou, a famous Qing painter. At the foot of the terrace stands an enormous bell weighing over 13 cwt., which also belonged to the Qing ding yue si Temple. The hill gives a superb view over the hills east of the town (Qi xing shan, Xiang bi shan, Chuan shan, Yue ya shan). A legend tells how, when the town

was still surrounded by wild, untamed countryside,
demons, giant snakes and fierce beasts used to come
and seize people's possessions; one day, the sky suddenly grew dark, a violent wind got up and a giant
demon could be seen far off, leaning against the Hill
with a Hole through it (Chuan shan); his hands looked
like a dragon's claws, and in each one he held a boa
spitting poisonous vapours. At that moment, a thun-
derclap was heard on Fu Bo shan Hill and a giant man
appeared amid a blaze of light; he was over 10 feet
high, and carried a huge bow; a great sword hung at
his side; his eyes gave out flashes of lightning and he
spoke in ringing tones. His name was Jie Di; he took
his bow and with one arrow killed the monster and
pierced the mountain through. The other demons and
fierce animals fled, terrified, never to return, and from
that day on, the people of Gui lin lived in peace. On
the way down the south slope is the Returned Pearl
Cave (Huan zhu dong); a legend tells how an old dragon lived in a pool in the cave, and in the evening,
used to play with a pearl of such brilliance that it lit up
the whole cave. An old fisherman, who used often to
stop his boat to watch the mysterious light flickering,
dared one evening to enter the cave. There he found
an old man lying fast asleep, with the pearl which was
the source of the light beside him; he took the pearl
and went back to his boat, but then, overcome by
remorse, he took it back to its owner: hence the name
of the cave. The cave contains a natural pillar of stone
where Jie Di (or according to another legend, Fu Bo)
used to come and try out his swords; the rock is called
Shi jian shi, the Stone where Swords are Tried; one
of the walls has an engraving on it by the Song painter
Mi Wan gong, who was an official at Gui lin. A little
to the left of the cave is the Thousand Buddha Cliff;

there are 300 in fact; some of them date from the Tang.

A little further north, near Die cai lu Street, is **The Hill of Many Colours, Die cai shan Hill,** also called Gui shan or Feng dong shan. It has several peaks: the Si wang shan and the Yu yue shan to the south and the Xian he feng and the Ming yue feng to the north. A path leads up to the Die cai ting Kiosk; east of it is the Yu yue shan, with the Workers' Hospital at the foot of it. The Si wang shan with an annex of the Teachers' Training College at its foot lies to the west; both buildings used to be libraries. At the end of the Qing, Kang You wei, who was studying at Gui lin, used often to come to this hill, so a cave at the foot of the Yu yue shan has been called after him. A little higher up is the Die cai men Gate with a stele near it erected in memory of two late Ming heros, Ju Shi si and Zhang Tong chang, who put up a resistance against the Qing. Further up still is a cliff with statues of the Buddha and a cave called the Wind Cave (Feng tong), because it has an opening at either end, creating a draught, The walls are covered with inscriptions, with a poem by Yuan Mei and engravings by Li Ping shou among them; at the north entrance to the cave are a recumbent statue of the Buddha and an extremely expressive iron statue of a *luo han*. On the Ming yue feng peak is a stone altar, called the Ma wang tai, which was built under the Five Dynasties by Ma yin, King of Chu. Under the Song two more altars were put up here, the Shao shan and the Li shui, where annual sacrifices were made.

The **Treasure Hoard Hill, Bao ji shan,** is east of the Die cai shan, west of Zhong shan bei lu Street. Before the Song, the north gate of the town was between Bao ji shan and Die cai shan, which gave added protection to the town. A famous Taoist master, Jiang, is supposed to have lived in the Hua jing dong

Cave on Bao ji shan; he knew how to hold his breath, and was an experienced doctor. **Yu shan Hill,** also known as Shun shan, is further north, near Yu shan lu Street, east of Bei ji lu Street. At the beginning of the 20th century, two temples still stood at the bottom of the hill, both of which were founded under the Tang; one was dedicated to the mythical Emperor Shun and was called Shun ci, and the other was dedicated to the Emperors of the principality of Yu (Shun's ancestors). Both of them were destroyed during the anti-Japanese war, though the steles belonging to them still survive, one dating from the Tang and the other from the Song. According to the legend, Emperor Shun came for a walk on the hill when on a tour of the south, and died soon afterwards; as he was admired for his just government, it was decided to call the hill after him and build a temple in which to erect his statue. The legend goes on to tell how two wives, who had stayed behind in the north, started out to look for him when he failed to come back; the news of his death reached them when they were on the banks of the Xiang shui, and in their despair, they drowned themselves. The inhabitants of Gui lin had a tomb built for them on Ban yun shan Hill north of the town, and called it the Two Wives' Tomb (Shuang fei zhong).

c) The South of the Town

The **District of the Two Lakes, Rong hu and Shan hu** is one of the most pleasant parts of the town, and has been made into a park. Under the Tang, the lakes were not divided, as they are today, by a bridge in the middle, and they formed a moat which protected the town walls, immediately to the north. The foundations of the South Gate can still be seen in the street to the north of Lake Rong hu. The Green Belt Bridge (Qing dai qiao) was built in the middle of the lake under the Song (its other name is Yang qiao); the names of the lakes, Rong hu (Banyan-tree Lake) and Shan hu (Pine-tree Lake) date from the same time, as banyans and pines were planted round them. The **Kai yuan si Temple** stood on a little island due south of the town, linked to it by a bridge; it was founded under the Sui, and a stupa, once part of it, can still be seen in Wan shou xiang Lane. It was one of the oldest and largest temples in the town, and was destroyed in 1944. The stupa, dated 657, is all that is left of it; it has a square base with an arched doorway on each side, an octagonal first storey and a round second storey topped by a copper ornament. It is the oldest monument in the town.

The **Elephant's Trunk Hill, Xiang bi shan,** lies east of the stupa, near the River Li jiang. The pagoda on its summit is called the Pu xian ta because the statue of the Buddha of Universal Virtue (Pu xian fo) is carved on one side of it. A legend tells how once, when the celestial emperor was on a tour of the south, he crushed the ripe grain in the fields and had the draught animals killed for food. When he arrived at Gui lin, a celestial elephant, which he carried in a precious flask, fell ill; he left it behind beside the road, where upon it was cared for by a human being and decided to work for the service of men. When the celestial emperor heard this, he was furious and sent soldiers to fight the elephant; the elephant was killed by a trick while he was about to drink from the river. He turned into stone immediately, and his trunk can still be seen dipping into the river; the pagoda on his back is the hilt of the sword which killed him, In the 19th century, the hill was used as a camp by the Tai ping.

Shang zhi lu Street leads past the station and on southwards to the **Southern Torrent Hill (Nan xi shan)**, which contains curious rocks and caves.

2. The Hills in the Western Suburbs

After crossing the railway line, Lie jun ji Street leads to **Yin shan Hill** (Hill for going into retreat); its name was given to it in 825 under the Tang, by Li Bo, who had a little pavilion built there, and planted trees and flowers all round it. The hill was completely surrounded by water at that time, but under the Ming, in the 16th century, the water was drained off and disappeared. The **Hua gai an Temple** stands at the foot of the hill; it contains magnificent portraits of the Sixteen Venerable Ones (Shi liu zun), drawn under the Tang by the monk Guan xiu and engraved under the Qing (at the beginning of the dynasty). The hill contains several caves; the Cave which Faces the Sun (Chao yang dong) contains a statue of Lao zi and a recumbent statue of the Buddha.

The **Western Hills (Xi shan)** are on Li shi lu Road, west of Yin shan. The rocks at the Guan yin Peak (guan yin feng) were carved with several hundred Buddhas, dating from the Tang, some of which were 7 feet high. They have unfortunately been destroyed and replaced by a quarry. One has survived, probably because it is in an inaccessible place.

The **Old Man Mountain (Lao ren shan)** is north-east of the Xi shan; it is so called because its outline, when seen from Die cai lu Street or from the Du xiu feng Peak, is not unlike an old man wearing a hood. The legend says that a group of celestial monkeys living on the hill and in the neighbourhood of it used to steal from the inhabitants' fields. The old man who lived on the South Pole Mountain (Nan ji shan) came to

Gui lin, settled on the Lao ren shan Mountain, and made war on the monkeys, who when they saw the mountain, thought it was the old man. Two temples used to stand on the mountain, but they have been destroyed; all that is left is a set of statues of the Buddha carved out of the rocks (dating from the Tang, probably); they are in much the same style as the ones on the Xi shan.

Zhong yin shan Hill is west of the road which goes back towards the Xi shan; it is west of the River Tao hua jiang, and from a distance, it looks like an ox lying down. It contains three curiously shaped caves; the summit overlooks the Peach Flower River (Tao hua jiang). In spring, the river banks are covered with peach blossom, which has given its name to the river.

3. The Hills in the Eastern Suburbs

Liberation Bridge (Jie fang qiao) spans the River Li jiang; Zi jia zhou Island, about half a mile wide and over a mile long, lies south of the bridge, covered with a forest of grapefruit trees. A legend attached to the island tells how a rich landowner had in his employment a girl called Zi Ying, who was an excellent worker, with a beautiful voice, and Gui sheng, a young man who was equally gifted; as they always worked together, they fell in love with each other. When their master heard this, he killed Gui sheng in a fit of rage and threw his body into the river, as for a long time he had intended Zi Ying to be his concubine. A few days later, a patch of ground appeared at the spot where he had thrown the body; it gradually grew larger and became covered with a forest of bamboo. Then one night Zi Ying, standing at the water's edge,

heard Gui sheng's voice, and recognised the song as
the one he always used to sing; she took a boat and
sailed across to the island. At that moment, her master,
who was pursuing her, was swallowed up by the waters;
Zi Ying reached the island, found Gui sheng, and they
lived there happily for the rest of their lives. The
island was called after them: the Zi Family Island.

The Hua qiao Bridge is a little further east; the first
bridge on the site was built of wood in 1456. The present one, a covered bridge built mainly in stone, resting
on twelve arches, was built in 1540. The Crescent
Moon Hill (Yue ya shan) overlooks the bridge, just
south of it. The **Seven Star Hill (Qi xing shan)** rises
north-east of Yue ya shan, so called because its
seven peaks are arranged in almost the same way as
the seven stars of the Great Bear. The four chief stars
of the constellation, which used to have a cult attached
to them, are represented by the four peaks of the Pu
tuo shan, one of the most famous hills at Gui lin;
steles and inscriptions dating from the Tang, the Song
and the Ming, can still be seen there; the hill also contains six large caves, with endless legends attached to
them. Several other smaller hills lie south-east of the
Qi xing shan: Jiu hu shan (Alcohol Flask Hill),
also known as Camel Hill, because it looks like a
camel lying down, has the tomb of Lei Jiu chun at the
foot of it; he was a great lover of beautiful countryside who lived at the end of the Ming, and had a little
house built at the foot of the hill. The Hill where the
Immortals Meet (Hui xian shan) is south of the Jiu hu
shan; it is said to owe its name to four immortals who
used to meet here to drink together.

The road which runs alongside the River Xiao dong
jiang leads southwards to the **Hill with a Hole through**

it (Chuan shan), also called the Cock-fight Hill (Dou ji shan), because it is opposite the Bao ta shan Hill on the other side of the River Xiao dong jiang, and looks like a cock about to a attack. The **Bao ta shan Hill (Pagoda Hill)** has a pagoda on the top of it, as its name suggests. According to an old legend, a cock lived on the Chuan shan a long time ago, and used to sing to greet the morning every day. When people heard it, they quickly got up and set to work; then a demon in the shape of a centipede settled on the opposite hill, and used to rob human beings before they woke up. One day, when the sky was still misted over, the cock chased the centipede and attacked it; it retreated, wounded, to hide in a cave on Bao ta shan Hill, whereupon the people built a pagoda over the entrance to trap the centipede in the cave. The pagoda may still be seen today.

The Ping feng shan Hill lies north of the Hua qiao Bridge (away from the town); the **Chen shan Hill,** also called the Hu shan, or Tiger Hill, is further north again. It has five peaks, sometimes compared to the five fingers of the Buddha's hand; a Taoist called Liu xi lived in retreat on the hill under the Southern Song. The **Celestial Horse Hill (Tian ma shan),** also called Tian sheng shan, full of beautiful natural caves, lies one mile to the north-east; a legend says that horses used to be reared in the meadows near the hills, and it was known that a celestial horse used to mingle with the rest, but no one knew which one it was. One day, however, an old man on his way up the hill to cut wood saw the horse fly past in a blaze of red light; hence the name of the hill.

Yao shan Hill, further along the road to the north-east, is the only hill covered with earth in the neigh-

bourhood of Gui lin. It is said that under the reign of
Qin shi Huang di a temple was built on the hill in
memory of the mythical Emperor Yao; the hill was
called after him. When it is about to rain, the hill is
always encircled with clouds of mist which take on
strange shapes; the farmers used to foretell the weather
by studying the mists. The **Zhu sheng an Temple** is at
the foot of the hill, a little way from the Dragon Pool
(Long chi); a brave monk, Xing yin, lived there at the
end of the Ming dynasty. When he heard that the two
heroes Ju Shi si and Zhang Tong chang had been killed
by the Manchu, he buried them and composed a
ballad in their honour. The path up the hill leads past
the Tian ci tian (field given by the sky), so called because it is the only moist spot on the hill; two temples
stand nearby: the Bai yun guan (White Cloud Temple),
a Taoist temple, and the Shou fo an (Temple of the
Buddha of Longevity), a Buddhist temple. Among the
temple buildings stands one all of stone, built under
Qian long, which overlooks all the surrounding area.
After another mile or so the path reaches the top of the
hill; the White Stag Temple (Bai lu an), also called the
Yu huang ge (Jade Emperor Pavilion) stands on the
summit. According to popular tradition, a Chan sect
monk called the White Stage Master lived there under
the Tang. When he went to the capital to expound the
sutras, a white stag, which had been given as tribute to
Emperor Xuan zong, came to lie at his feet and would
not leave him. The Emperor gave the beast to the
monk, who was known as the White Stage Master,
because he took it back with him to Gui lin. The stag
then became immortal, and it is said still to be living
on the hill. One of the wives of the King of Jing jiang
under the Ming lies buried in a tomb on the east slope
of the hill (some beautiful statues precede the tomb).

Yan shan

Yan shan is 12 miles south-east of Gui lin; a regular
bus service operates between the two towns. In the
19th century, the residence of a great official of the late
Qing dynasty, Tang Zi shi, stood where the Yan shan
gong yuan (Goose Hill Park) now is; the whole place
was sold to the state by Tang Zi shi's descendants,
and an annex of the Teachers' Training College of
Guan xi University and later on the Agricultural
Institute were housed there.

Xing an

Xing an is 45 miles north of Gui lin, on the railway
line.

The Ling qu Canal

The canal forms a link, beginning at Xing an,
between the River Tan shui (south) and the River
Xiang jiang (north), and by extension, links the
Yang zi and the Zhu jiang. It dates from Qin shi
Huang di; the Emperor's campaigns in the south
made it necessary, because the Nan ling Mountains
made communications extremely difficult, and it
was impossible to provide enough grain for the
troops. It was realised that provisions could be
sent by water, and the Ling qu canal was dug so
that they could be sent direct from the Yang zi
to Guang dong. A colossal block of masonry shaped
like a ploughshare, and intented to divide the river
in two, was built in the Xiang jiang at the nearest
point to the Tan shui; part of the water flowed off
through the northern channel to join the lower
reaches of the Xiang jiang, and the rest flowed along
the southern channel, the ling qu, to join the River

Tan shui. The canal was built on a slope and navigation was difficult; in 825, 18 locks were built to regulate the flow. The canal was repaired under the Ming (1368) and 18 new locks were added; further repairs were done under the Qing (1746). The sections of the canal and the remains of the locks can still be seen, as well as the block of masonry in the middle of the Xiang jiang; on the middle of the block stands a pavilion with two steles, one dating from the Ming, the other from the Qing.

Upstream from Xing an, three tombs on the south bank of the canal, just under a mile from the town, are supposed to be the tombs of the three generals sent by Qin shi Huang di to supervise the digging of the canal. A little further on is the Fei lai shi (the Rock which Flew there) and beyond it the Temple of the Four Sages, Si xian ci, built in memory of Shi Lu (who lived under Qin shi huang di), Ma Yuan (the famous Han general), Li Bo and Yu Meng wei (who lived under the Tang).

YUN NAN

(Map, Atlas pl. 23-24

(Map. p. 1233)

The province of Yun nan is bordered by the Tibetan Autonomous Region and Si chuan to the north, Gui zhou and the Guang xi Autonomous Region to the east; Vietnam and Laos lie to the south and Burma to the west. The River Yuan jiang (upper reaches of the Red River) divides it into two different regions. A high plateau lies to the east, which reaches 7,000 feet at its highest points. Mount Wu meng stands on the Gui zhou border. Much of it is karst scenery: "rock forests" (shi lin) interspersed with small fertile low-lying areas, known as ba zi in the local dialect. The plateau has sink-hole lakes scattered over it, and the towns have grown up near them; Lake Er hai with Da li and Xia guan, Lake Dian chi with Kun ming and Jin ning, Lake Fu xian with Jiang chuan. Most of the water-courses on the eastern plateau run northwards, towards the Jin sha jiang (the upper reaches of the Yang zi) or eastwards, towards the Pearl River basin. The area is rich in mineral deposits (tin, iron and coal), which are mined, particularly at Jiu ge. The plateau has a pleasant climate, because the proximity of the Tropic of Cancer is balanced by the altitude. The average for January is 49° F at Kun ming, 48° 5° F at Da li; the average for July is 71.5° F at Kun ming and 69° F at Da li; June is usually the hottest month. The west of the province, on the other side of the Yuan jiang, is completely different; it is a region of valleys and mountain ranges stretching from north to south parallel to the rivers. From east to west lie the Ai lao shan Mountains, the River Ba bian jiang (the upper reaches of the Black River), the Wu liang shan Mountains and the River Lan cang jiang (upper reaches of the Mekong), Mount Nu shan and the River Nu jiang (upper reaches of the Salween), and finally Mount Gao li shan on the Burmese frontier. Differences in climate are determined by differences in altitude; under 5,000 feet, the climate is tropical and very damp; the most pleasant climate is to be found between 5,000 and 10,000 feet; above 10,000 it can be extremely cold. The differences in climate result in great variety in the vegetation; some areas in the province, Xi shuang ban na, for instance, are considered as nature reserves (elephants and parrots).

Yun nan was one of the last provinces to come wholly under Chinese influence. The movement began under the Ming, and in many respects it is still going on now. Today it can be considered as a border province, a Chinese stronghold thrusting into the Vietnam peninsula, but for a long time in the past it was a cross-roads for routes converging there leading from the Yang zi region to Burma, from Tibet to Tong king. This area, considered in the 19th century as a remote, backward region, contains the remains of great civilisations. Among the oldest sites, dating no doubt from the Han, are the Jin ning tumuli, south of Lake Kun ming, where magnificent sets of bronzes have recently been uncovered, including some "drums" which are still puzzling the archaeologists, and the Zhao tong tombs, in the north-east of the province, where Eastern Jin frescoes have been discovered. Under the Han and the Southern Dynasties, the Chinese exercised a vague suzerainty there, from a few outposts. The area developed from the 8th to the 12th centuries, when the state of Nan zhao was formed. It is thought that the leaders came from the Bai ethnic group, a branch of the Yi. Part of the society was converted to Buddhism, and Buddhist caves of high artistic value have been found at Jian chuan, north-west of Da li. In the 13th century, the Mongol dynasty reduced the autonomy of Yun nan (the Bai nobility was wiped out; their tombs can still be seen).

Marco Polo, who visited the area at the same time, refers to the provinces of Karajan (Da li) and Zardandan (Bao shan), both of which were under the control of Mongol princes. He says that the region was famous for its salt and its horses, and that cowries were used for exchange purposes. South of Kun ming, at Tong hai, a little group of Mongols still exists; a Mongol army was kept in the province at this time. From the Ming dynasty onwards, the Han population moved in in larger and larger numbers (voluntary or forced emigration). One of the newcomers, the exiled official Yang Shen, wrote an interesting history of Yun nan (*Nan zhao ye shi*). A Moslem community also developed at this period. Marco Polo mentioned Saracens in his book, and the tomb of a Moslem has recently been found south of Lake Kun ming; he made a pilgrimage to Mecca, and his son, the famous Zheng He, led the south seas maritime expeditions at the beginning of the 15th century. At the end of the Ming dynasty, the province was one of the centres of opposition to the Manchu: the last Ming prince met his end on the Burmese frontier; the uprising led by Li Ding guo took place; the province gained autonomy under Wu San gui. Under the Qing, the Han continued to move into the area, and tried, from the 18th century onwards, to substitute officials appointed by the government for the *ti su*, hereditary chiefs, of the minorities. The resistance of the original races to the Manchu power became more and more pronounced, and resulted in several uprisings; the best known and most violent one was the Moslem revolt which lasted from 1857 till 1872, and was connected with the Tai ping rebellion. It began with quarrels between the Moslems and the Chinese working in the silver mines; the rebels managed to have arms sent to them from Burma. Two of the rebel leaders were the Moslem Ma De jing, who had made the pilgrimage to Mecca, and visited Egypt, Constantinople, Singapore and eastern China, and Du Wen xiu, who took the title of Sultan of Da li. The imperial troops persuaded the Frenchman Jean Dupuis to send them arms from Tong king, and overcame the rebels, who were severely decimated. This explains the composition of the present population of Yun nan. It is now 19,100,000 (it was 10,000,000 in the 1930's). Two thirds are Han, and minority races make up the last third. Half of the fifty or so minority races of China live in this province. The main races are the Yi (in the north and the east), the Bai and the Na xi (north-west of Da li), the Tai (in the south-west), the Ha ni (in the Yuan jiang valley), the Li su, the Jing po and the Wa (in the north-west of the province, near the Burmese frontier).

During the years after the liberation, and as late as 1964, autonomous regions and districts were created in zones where the minorities form large enough communities. The main crops are rice, maize, sweet potato and wheat; for several years, efforts have been made to extend double-crop rice, cotton, rape and sugar-cane to wider areas; in the zones near the Tropic of Cancer, particularly the Tai Autonomous Regions of Xi shuang bananas, cocoanuts and coffee are grown. The mountainous regions produce tea, tobacco and wood (from the Ming dynasty onwards, the wood for the great columns in the Imperial Palace in Peking was sent from Yun nan). Industry, which was virtually non-existent before the liberation, has progressed a little (machine-building and optical instruments at Kun ming), but the whole province is hampered by the poor transport system. The Kun ming — Hanoi railway, built by French engineers in the first ten years of the 20th century, is the only one so far; it is planned to built two more lines, from Kun ming to Si chuan, and to Gui zhou.

List of the autonomous zones (Zi zhi zhou) and autonomous districts (Zi zhi xian) in the province of Yun nan.

Names of autonomous zones and districts	Total population	Non-Han population	Foundation year
Autonomous zones:			
Xi shuang ban na (Tai)	321,000	245,000	1953
De hong (Tai and Jing po)	430,000	220,000	1953
River Hong he (Ha ni and Yi)	1,876,000	929,000	1954
River Nu jiang (Li su)	214,000	192,000	1954
Da li (Bai)	1,621,000	767,000	1956
Di qing (Tibetan)	170,000	138,000	1957
Wen shan (Zhuang and Miao)	1,464,000	812,000	1958
Chu xiong (Yi)	1,592,000	435,000	1958
Autonomous districts:			
E shan (Yi and Bai)	91,000	54,000	1951
Lan cang (La gu)	242,000	177,000	1953
Jiang cheng (Ha ni and Yi)	36,000	28,000	1954
Meng lian (Tai, La gu and Wa)	47,000	45,000	1954
Geng ma (Tai and Wa)	82,000	45,000	1955
Ning lang (Yi)	95,000	79,000	1956
Gong shan (Du long and Nu)	17,000	16,950	1956
Wei shan (Hui and Yi)	148,000	68,000	1956
Lu nan (Yi)	150,000	40,000	(1)
Li jiang (Na xi)	188,000	152,000	1961
He kou (Yao)	33,000	17,000	1963
Bing bian (Miao)	71,000	41,000	1963
Cang yuan (Wa)	71,000	67,000	1964
Xi meng (Wa)	40,000	38,000	(1)
Nan jian (Yi)	11,000	(1)	(1)

Taken from a table in the Cultural Palace of the Minorities. The names of the Minorities are given in brackets. (¹) Figure and date not given.

Kun ming and a few eastern towns will be described first, followed by a few western towns.

KUN MING

Kun ming is in the centre of the east Yun nan tableland, over 6,000 feet above sea level, in a relatively large *ba zi;* Lake Dian chi lies south of the town, which is on the railway line to Vietnam. Other stretches of line, not yet finished, will eventually link Kun ming with Gui zhou and Si chuan. It is the provincial capital, with a population of 900,000.

History

The town was founded under the Han dynasty. Yi zhou jun was founded in 109 B.C., and changed its name several times during the dynasties which followed. Little is known of the early history of Kun ming, though the lake and its surroundings seem to have played an important part in the economy of the region from an early date. According to the *Hou Han shu (History of the Later Han)* the lake was over 200 *li* round; it was wide and deep on the side where the rivers flowed into it, and as it appeared to drain its waters by overflowing, it was called Lake Dian chi, the Lake which Overflows. It was surrounded by a stretch of plain, with fisheries and salt-pans which were a great source of riches to their owners; gold and silver mines made fortunes for those who worked there; the men of Kun ming were considered brave and generous, and the rich governors of the town handed their post down from one generation to the next. Under the Sui and at the beginning of the Tang, it was still under Chinese rule; but in 775 or thereabouts, the Meng family from the kingdom of Nan zhao seized it, fortified it, and called it Tuo dong cheng, Enlarged eastern town. From 809, it was the secondary capital of the kingdom of Da li, known as the Eastern Capital and finally the Main Capital. The town was south-east of the present one and a royal palace was built there in 871.

During the Five Dynasties and under the Song, the town was part of the kingdom of Da li. In 1274, the Mongols took the town by storm; in 1276, it became the headquarters of a department, Zhong qing fu. In 1280, the governor general of Yun nan settled there, and in 1288, the princes of Yun nan chose it as their only capital. Marco Polo visited the town and described it: "At the end of these five days journeys then one finds the capital city and that which is head of the kingdom of Iaci, which is called Iaci, which is very great and noble. There are in it merchants and artisans enough. The people are of several sorts, for there are ... people who worship Mahomet, and idolaters, and few Christians, ... who are Nestorians. There is wheat and rice enough ... they eat no wheat bread because it is unwholesome in that province. But they eat rice, and make a drink of rice with spices which is very good and clear .... They have money in such a way as I shall tell you, for they spend white cowries, those which are found in the sea and which are ... put on the neck of dogs ... They have many salt wells also from which they make much salt ... and all those of this country live by this salt .... They have a lake which is quite a hundred miles round, in which is found a very great quantity of fish of the best in the world. They are very large and of all very fine kinds. And again I tell you that the people of this country, they eat the raw flesh of fowls and of sheep and of oxen and of buffalo ... for the poor men go to the butchers and take and buy the raw liver as soon as it is drawn out of the animal and chops it up small. And then he puts it in ... sauce made with hot water and spices and eats it immediately. And so they do with all the other raw flesh. And in this way all the gentlemen also eat raw flesh, ... they eat it as well as we do the cooked." (*Marco Polo, the Description of the World*, A.C. Moule and Paul Pelliot, p. 277-278).

In 1382, the Ming took Zhong qing fu; a new town was founded north-west of the old one, a wall was built round it, and it was called Yun nan fu. Its site was to remain unchanged until the present day. When the Qing came to power, Yun nan fu was one of the towns which was long in declaring its allegiance to the new dynasty; it supported Wu San gui, who was sent to Yun nan in 1659 to put down the opposition to the Qing, but finally gained the support of all south-west China against the Qing; it did not give in until 1681. The town was badly damaged in the 19th century during the Moslem revolt; it was besieged by the Sultan of Da li several times between 1859 and 1860, and again in 1868; large numbers of old buildings were destroyed. In 1910, the population was so badly decimated by the rebellion that it consisted of only 45,000 inhabitants. It is now an important centre of road, rail and air communications (the China-Burma airline goes through here). Industry is growing up (machine-building, optical instruments).

Description

The town is 3 miles north-west of the lake, and linked to it by a canal. It embraces several hills, the two largest of which are the Wu hua shan (in the middle of the old walled town) and the Yuan tong shan (in the north of the town), and some small lakes.

1. The Town

The two **Pagodas of the East and West Temples** (Dong si ta and Xi si ta) can still be seen in the south of the town. They are traditionally said to have been built at the same time; they were damaged during the Moslem revolt and rebuilt in about 1884. The East Temple Pagoda is in East Temple Street, and is said to have been founded under the Tang; it is built in bricks stamped with pagodas and sanskrit inscriptions. The West Temple Pagoda is in Shu lin jie Street; it is square, with 13 stories and a window in each facet.

The **Wu hua shan (Five Flowers Hill)** is in the centre of the town; it used to be covered with temples and officials' houses. The largest temple was the Wu hua si, on the western slope, supposed to be one of the biggest in the province; it was founded under the Yuan (1277) and restored in 1653 and 1684 (stele dating from 1368). The top of the hill overlooks the town and its surroundings. A park on the banks of Lake Cui hu lies west of the hill.

The **Yuan tong shan Hill,** now a public park, rises in the north of the town; it contains the **Provincial Museum, Yun nan sheng buo wu guan.** The Yuan tong si Temple stands on the southern slope of the hill.

The **Chuan xin ta Pagoda** is beyond the line of the old town walls, in the east of the town; it dates from the Yuan, and is also called the Yan shou ta. It is in the form of a white stupa, rather like the one at the Bai ta si in Peking; all four sides of the base have arched doorways in them. The upper part, which is the stupa, has four little pagodas, one at each corner.

2. The Surroundings of the Town

a) The South

The **Tomb of the Moslem Official, Sai dian chi** (1211–1280), who had a distinguished career as an administrator of the province, is in the suburbs near the town. When he died, he was buried at the north gate of the Yuan town, then called Shan chan; it is said that his court dress was taken to somewhere near Xi an and his turban to Si chuan, once the Vietnamese had come to pay homage to them. Emperor Timur gave him the posthumous title of Prince of Xian yang, and his eldest son succeeded to his post. A stele dating from 1709 stands southwest of the mausoleum, with a text composed by a descendant of Sai dian chi.

Lake Dian chi

The lake is longest from north to south, and bordered by a chain of mountains to the west; the most famous are the **Western Mountains (Xi shan)** which contain the Taoist temple San qing ge (with some beautiful cave temples), and the Guan yin shan (Mount Guan yin), south-west of the lake (18 miles from Kun ming); a temple and a pagoda stand on the top.

Jin ning

Jin ning is south of the lake; it used to be called Kun yang. In 1956, excavations on the Shi zhai shan, near Jin ning, brought to light a graveyard with a large collection of bronzes (drums, weapons, tools, statues...) thought to date from the Han, which provide valuable information on the non-Chinese cultures in the area. The objects are now in the Kun ming Museum. An interesting report on the excavations — a collection of photographs with a text — has been published: *Yun nan Jin ning shi zhai shan gu mu qun fa jue bao gao.*

The tomb of Ma He zhi, father of the famous eunuch Zheng He who made several voyages in the south seas under the Ming, is also at Jin ning; the text of the stele beside the tomb gives interesting information on the life of Ma He zhi.

An ning

An ning is west of Lake Dian chi, 9 miles south west of Kun ming. It was famous under the Ming for its hot springs, and officials used to build houses there; several convalescent homes have been built there recently.

The **Cao xi si Temple** is near the hot springs; it was built under the Tang, by princes from the state of Da li; it was restored under the Yuan and the Qing (handsome wooden architecture).

b) The North

The Golden Temple (Jin dian)

The Golden Temple is about 6 miles north-east of Kun ming, on the Phoenix Song Hill (Ming feng

shan). It was built at the end of the Ming dynasty;
and is supposed to have been embellished by Wu
San gui, for use as a house for the summer (17th century). The temple buildings are in the shape of an
amphitheatre, in tiers; four *pai lou* lead to the gate
of the Hall of Great Peace (Tai he gong men) and
on to the Golden Pavilion (Jin dian), which stands
on a white marble terrace; it used to be gilded, as
its name suggests; the steps and the parapet are of
marble, the pillars are of bronze, the beams are of
gilded wood, and the roof is covered with copper
leaf, like scales.

The Qiong Bamboo Temple (Qiong zhu si)

The temple is about 7 miles west of Kun ming
on Mount Yu feng shan; it is sometimes called Luo
han si (*luo han* temple). It is supposed to have been
founded under the Tang; a Mongol prince used it
for his summer residence in the 14th century. It
was burned down later on, rebuilt in the 17th century,
and restored in the 19th century (1891). The temple
is particularly well situated, hidden in a little wood
to which a path leads from the road, and contains
some magnificent statues, depicting the 500 *luo han*,
supposed to be by Li Guang xiu, a sculptor from
Si chuan.

THE OTHER EASTERN TOWNS

Zhao tong

Zhao tong is in the north-east of the province,
near the Gui zhou border, 155 miles from Kun ming
by road. Excavations carried out since the liberation
have revealed: 1) the site of walls nearly 2 miles

south-west of the present town, apparently dating
from the Yuan or the Ming; no information has
yet been found about it in contemporary texts;
2) several tombs; the most interesting one dates from
the Eastern Jin (4th century A.D.). Frescoes have
been found inside depicting the dead man, his family
and servants, full of valuable details on the material
life of the time. A report of the excavations was
published in the review Wen wu, 1963, No 12.

Lu Nan and the Petrified Forest.

A karst formation known as the Petrified Forest
lies about 60 miles southeast of Kun ming, near Lu
Nan. It covers an area of 27,000 hectares, but only
80 are accessible. A path just over a mile long leads
to the rocks, which have been eroded into extraordinary shapes, some over 100 feet high (the Lotus
Peak, the Pavilion on the rocks, the lake, etc.).

Meng zi

Meng zi is about 120 miles south-east of Kun ming,
on the railway line from there to Vietnam. Its foundation goes back a long way; under the Han, it
came under the authority of Yi zhou jun (present
Kun ming); it was part of the state of Nan zhao,
and was promoted to the rank of district *(xian)*
under the Yuan; in the 19th century it was attacked
by the Moslems in 1858, and then was opened to
Franco-Vietnamese trade in 1890, as a result of the
additional Sino-French convention signed on June
29th 1887. A European district grew up outside the
old town, to the east, and stretched as far as the little
lake which then belonged to the University. At the

beginning of the 20th century, the town was still surrounded by the old walls, built in 1484 and faced with brick in 1615. It was a trading centre above all; the Cantonese and the people from Jiang xi had guilds there. Most of the trade was with Canton and Hong kong; in 1910, it had a population of 12,000.

Ge jiu

Ge jiu is on the railway about 12 miles west of Meng zi. Because of its tin mines, its only source of wealth, it is often known as Xi cheng, Town of Tin. The mines had already been brought up to date at the beginning of the 20th century. In 1905, the 27 furnaces produced 6,000 tons of metal at 95 %. In 1912, production went up to 8,000 tons; the population rose to 10,000, and it is now 100,000.

THE WESTERN TOWNS

Chu xiong

Chu xiong is in the centre of the province, half way along the Kun ming — Xia guan road. It is now the administrative centre of the Yi autonomous zone; a museum is being built there (a prominent figure will be Du Xiu wen, one of the revolutionary heroes who took part in the Moslem revolt in the Chu xiong area between 1855 and 1873).

Xia guan

Xia guan is south of Lake Er hai. It is the seat of the People's Committee of the Da li region. In 1920, the town had a population of 10,000, and was an important trading centre, where products from the west of the province and imports from Burma were collected. It is still mainly a trading town; it lies amidst fertile countryside (rice, wheat, beans, nuts, fish); it is now a centre for the building material industry, with a population of 400,000. The town contains a Cultural Centre (Wen hua guan) with a collection of all the historical finds made in the area. The town library owns some valuable works (old Buddhist manuscripts).

Da li

Da li is on the west bank of Lake Er hai, about 10 miles north of Xia guan. It is at the crossroads of the roads going to Burma and Tibet.

History

Under the Han, the town was under the authority of the Ye yu territory; under the Tang, it was part of the prefecture of Yao zhou, created to rule the non-Chinese *(man)* peoples living in the area. The region was soon taken over by the natives of the area, now thought to have been the ancestors of the Bai people, who set up six principalities, called *zhao* in Chinese. Later on, the southernmost one supplanted the five others and it was known as the Southern Principality (Nan zhao). In 741, Bi luo ge, king of Nan zhao, set up his capital at Tai he cheng, about 5 miles south of present Da li, near a village called Tai he cun. For the whole of the Tang dynasty, bitter struggles took place between the Nan zhao people and the Chinese. In 751, for example, the Chinese troops were beaten off, and in 754 they were completely routed. A famous poem by Bai Ju yi tells of the loss of life suffered by the Chinese and the fear which these wars inspired in them; he describes how a young man broke his arm to avoid having to go and join in the wars in the south, wars from which few returned. (The Tomb of Ten Thousand Men, Wan ren zhong, where the victims of the 754 wars were buried, can still be seen near Xia guan.) In the 10th century, the Kingdom of Nan zhao was replaced by the Kingdom of Da li; under the Song, the Chinese government no longer dared to attack the powerful kingdom of Yun nan. Under the Yuan, however, the state of Da li was annexed to the empire in 1253, and it remained attached to it through the dynasties which followed, though several times under the Ming and the Qing (particularly during the Moslem revolt) the town was in fact entirely independent. The town is said to be one of the most beautiful in west Yun nan; it is now a flourishing economic centre. The working of the famous Da li marble (Da li shi), which is to be found in countless old palaces and temples, has now been brought up to date; over 300 men are employed altogether, about 100 in the quarries, and the rest in the workshops (cutting, polishing, and making various objects).

Description

The present town is just west of Lake Er hai, a vast stretch of water which measures over 25 miles from north to south and 2 or 3 miles across. 18 rivers flow into the lake from the Cang tang Mountains (the highest peak is over 13,000 feet), north-west of Da li.

1. South of the Town. a) **The site of the old capital of the kingdom of Nan zhao,** Tai he cheng; a stele found outside the Tai he men Gate has enabled the site to be identified. b) **The Big Stone Temple (Da shi an),** also called the Guan yin Temple, is about 3 miles south of the town. According to the legend, Chinese troops were on their way to lay seige to Da li, when they met an old woman carrying an enormous stone on her back; the soldiers, surprised at her strength, questioned her; she answered that her strength was nothing in comparison with that of the young men of her country. The soldiers were so alarmed at this that they fled as fast as they could. The old woman was in fact Guan yin; later on, a temple was built on the spot where she laid down her stone, and the statue of Guan yin was worshipped there. The present temple appears to be fairly recent; some nuns still live there. c) **The Serpent's Bones Pagoda (Shi gu ta)** is south of Da li, at the foot of the Ma er feng Peak in the village of Yang pi cun; it was built in 820. A legend attached to it tells that under the Tang, a serpent living in Lake Er hai caused terrible floods, and the king of Meng offered a reward to the man who killed it. A brave stone-cutter called Duan Chi cheng volunteered, waded into the lake armed with his sword and killed the serpent; the remains of the brute were burned and the ashes, mixed with earth, were used to build the pagoda. On the eighth day of the eighth month a meeting is still held on the shores of the lake near the Lin jiang ting Kiosk, when the body of the serpent is supposed to have been recovered from the lake (lao she hui). The pagoda is square, with 13 stories and openings on each facet.

2. West of the Town. The Three San ta si Temple Pagodas are at the foot of the tenth peak of the Cang shan Hills. The Worship the Sages Temple (Chong sheng si), also called the Three Pagoda Temple (San ta si) was founded in 825. The temple was destroyed under the Qing; its three pagodas are among the oldest surviving monuments in the area. The Chinese consider that they date from the Tang; a Ming stele set into the base of one of them records that they were restored after an earthquake. The biggest one (in the middle) is 30 feet high; it is built on a square base, with openings on all four sides of each storey; the other two are much smaller. A temple dedicated to Guan yin, the **Yu zhu Guan yin dian,** stands near them; a legend tells how a monk began work on a bronze statue of Guan yin and had half finished it when he ran out of bronze;

at that moment, little bronze balls fell out of the
sky. The people round about collected them, melted
them down and the monk finished his statue, which
was then called: the Guan yin made of bronze balls
from the sky.

3. North of the Town. The **Sheng yuan si Temple**
is at Xi zhou, a small town 6 miles north of Da li;
the temple was founded under the Tang. The present
buildings were extensively restored under the Qing.
The history of the origins of the Bai state, according
to a text dating from 1706, is carved on the door of
the main hall. The carvings depict religious scenes
and legends, all extremely interesting. A stele known
as the *Shan hua bei*, inscribed with a Ming poem
written in Chinese characters, with transcriptions
of Bai words, is set into the right hand wall of the
hall.

Jian chuan xian

Jian chuan xian is a town over 60 miles north-
west of Da li, on the west bank of the River Yang
bi jiang. The Bai form the majority of the population
of the area. In the Lao jun shan Mountains area,
south-west of the district, some famous cave temples
are to be found, carved by the ancestors of the Bai,
and called the **Stone Rock Hill Caves (Shi zhong shan
shi ku).** The texts which mention the caves are fairly
late (Ming and Qing); several of them state that the
sculpture is the work of craftsmen from Nan zhao
and the state of Da li. Modern archaeologists share
the same opinion. The caves fall into three groups:
the first is near the Stone Bells Temple (Shi zhong
si), the second is near the Lion Pass (Shi zi guan),
and the third is near the village of Sha deng cun.

a) The Shi zhong si Temple Caves

The temple is between the villages of Sha deng cun and Dian tou he, about a mile or so up the hill near Dian tou he. The eight caves are nearby; the biggest is over 36 feet deep and more than 7 feet high, with carvings depicting religious scenes, including effigies of the Buddha, and donors, and scenes from everyday life (statues of kings of Nan zhao with attendants...).

b) The other two groups

are smaller; they are in the same area; the Shi zi guan group is a little lower down than the temple, and includes three caves; the third is west of Sha deng cun, and includes four caves. The iconography of the caves is extremely rich, and provides invaluable material in the study of the history of Nan zhao.

Li jiang

Li jiang is in the north-west of the province, south of the bend formed by the River Jin sha jiang, at the foot of the Yu long xue shan Mountains. The town is now the seat of the Na xi Autonomous District Committee. According to the *Man shu (History of the Man barbarians)*, the Me xie, who were the ancestors of the Na xi, were already living in this area, and on the shores of Lake Er hai, under the Tang; they formed the principality of Me xie (Me xie zhao) which was crushed by Nan zhao. After this interruption, the history of the Na xi continues under the Yuan; the history of a family of *Tu si*, local chiefs, exists; until the end of the Qing, they ruled the Na xi in the Li jiang area. They were known as the Mu shi family; they appear to have been particularly powerful under the Ming and the Qing,

FRESQUES DE LI JIANG ET DE SES ENVIRONS
FRESCOES IN LI JIANG AND THE SURROUNDING AREA

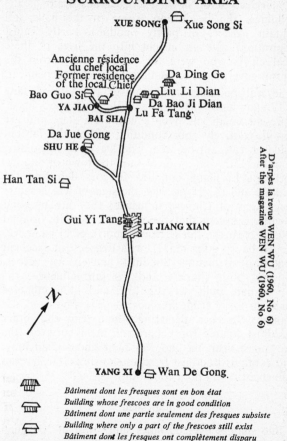

XUE SONG — Xue Song Si

Ancienne résidence du chef local
Former residence of the local Chief

Da Ding Ge

Liu Li Dian

Bao Guo Si
YA JIAO
BAI SHA

Da Bao Ji Dian
Lu Fa Tang

Da Jue Gong
SHU HE

Han Tan Si

Gui Yi Tang — LI JIANG XIAN

N

YANG XI — Wan De Gong

D'après la revue WEN WU (1960, No 6)
After the magazine WEN WU (1960, No 6)

Bâtiment dont les fresques sont en bon état
Building whose frescoes are in good condition
Bâtiment dont une partie seulement des fresques subsiste
Building where only a part of the frescoes still exist
Bâtiment dont les fresques ont complètement disparu
Building where the frescoes have completely disappeared

and left behind them a series of temples and palaces built at this time near Li jiang, which have almost all survived until now. The generous scale of the buildings, the decoration (some of the halls still contain frescoes of partly Buddhist, partly Taoist inspiration) give an insight into the lives of these local chiefs who were far enough away from the central government to be almost entirely independent.

Several buildings still survive: the Gui yi tang in Li jiang itself was built in 1471; the frescoes inside represent Guan yin, Wen shu and Pu xian, and are now in relatively poor conditiin, though the Tibetan influence can still be seen. The Da jue gong, dating from the 15th century, near the little town of Shu he, north of Li jiang, contains frescoes depicting the Buddha and the 18 *luo han*, the style of which shows clear signs of Chinese influence; they are in good condition, except that the paint has lost its original colour. Near the Bai settlement north of Li jiang are: the Ta bao ji gong (1523), with frescoes (in excellent condition) depicting Buddhist and Taoist scenes, showing both Chinese and Tibetan influence; the Liu li dian, built between 1392 and 1406, contains traces of fairly crude frescoes; the Da ding ge (1743) contains frescoes depicting Guan yin and other Buddhist figures (only parts of them survive); the Fu guo si near Ya jiao was built under Qian long, and contains Buddhist frescoes showing clear Tibetan influence (in very poor condition).

Bao shan

Bao shan is over 60 miles south-west of Xia guan by road. It contains an interesting Taoist temple, the **Yu huang ge (Jade Emperor Temple),** which dates from the Ming; the Ming frescoes are still in good condition.

Lu xi

Lu xi is in the Tai De hong Autonomous Region, about 60 miles south-west of Bao shan, near the Burmese frontier; the town contains an interesting temple, the **Da jin si,** also called the Mian si, because it resembles Burmese temples (the Chinese for Burma is Mian dian).

The Buddhist Temples in the Xi shuang ban na Tai Autonomous Zone.

The Xi shuang ban na Tai Autonomous Zone is in the centre of the province, slightly to the south, on either side of the River Lan cang jiang; the centre of the autonomous zone is Jing hong, a town on the west bank of the Lan cang jiang, about 18 miles from the Burmese frontier. The area was a Tai state as early as the 13th century when it was called Meng le guo; its capital, Jing lan, is now the town of Jing hong. Countless Buddhist temples were built during the early years of the state, but they were later abandoned; most of the ones built in the last two or three centuries are on the sites of the old ones. According to an enquiry carried out by Guo Hu sheng in 1959 (see the review Wen wu, 1962, No 2), almost every village has its temple and pagoda, though it sometimes happens that two or three villages share a temple, and they are all one or at the most two centuries old. They have several characteristics in common: 1) they are generally built on rising ground, slightly apart from the village, and surrounded by trees, through which the yellow temple roofs (made of glazed tiles) and the top of the pagoda can be seen; 2) each temple is made up of three parts: the temple

TEMPLE BOUDDHIQUE TAI DE MENG HAI (YUN NAN)

TAI BUDDHIST TEMPLE DE MENG HAI (YUN NAN)

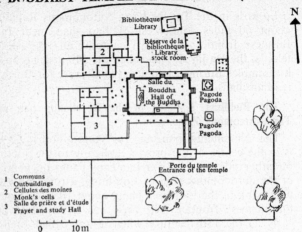

1 Communs
  Outbuildings
2 Cellules des moines
  Monk's cells
3 Salle de prière et d'étude
  Prayer and study Hall

0   10 m

d'après la revue «WEN WU» (1962, No 2).
after the magazine "WEN WU" (1962, No. 2)

itself, rectangular in shape, longest from east to west, with the statue of the Buddha at the east end; the monks' living quarters, to the north and east of the temple; and one or two pagodas, whose position varies; 3) a wall encircling the temple, with a gate in the east or south wall; a covered way (with a roof in tiers) leads from the gate to the temple door.

The Meng hai Temple

Meng hai is 18 miles west of Jing hong by road. Its temple has two walls round it: the first one, with a door to the south-east, encloses a courtyard full of trees; the second, to the north-west, is only partly surrounded by the first, and also has a door to the south-east. A covered way, with roofs overlapping like fish scales, leads to the Great Hall of the Buddha (Fo dian), five bays deep (from west to east) and four bays wide; its double roof has a space between the two parts; a seated, smiling statue of the Buddha is on the dais inside. Three doors lead to the monks' living quarters: cells (varying in size according to the occupant's position in the religious hierarchy), prayer room, common room, kitchen and store-rooms. Two libraries north of the Hall of the Buddha contain the community's collection of sutras; two pagodas stand to the east of the temple. They are square, brick buildings with staircases leading to a little platform with figure of animals at the corners and little pillars all the way round; the central part is octagonal, tapering off towards the top, which is a flattened cone surmounted by a long shaped decoration made of metal.

The Meng zhe Temple

Meng zhe is about 6 miles west of Meng hai by road. The temple is unusual in that its library is built in the shape of a pagoda, a circular wooden building standing on a high stone platform. Its octagonal roof rises in tiers, tapering off to a point.

The Meng han Temple

Meng han is about 6 miles south-east of Jin hong. The temple is unusual for three reasons: 1) the Hall of the Buddha is longest from north to south, the Buddha is in the middle of the building, and the door to the west; 2) it contains no monks' living quarters; 3) the pagoda is much taller than usual (over 60 feet high).

GUI ZHOU

(Map see Atlas pl. 23/24 and p. 1233)

The province of Gui zhou is bordered by Si chuan to the north, Hu nan to the east, Guang xi to the south and Yun nan to the west. It consists of an enormous plateau which is higher than Guang xi, Hu nan and the Si chuan basin, but lower than the Yun nan basin; the average altitude of the mountains is 3,200 feet (Mount Jin ding shan 4,119 feet). The relief is broken up by water-courses, and is so hilly that the province is said to have not a single square mile of level ground. The mountains slope downwards from north-west to south-east, so that the water-courses are scattered; the north-west of Gui zhou, which forms part of the Wu meng shan massif is the highest part of the province. The Wu jiang, the biggest river in the province, rises there and after a few bends in its course, flows north-eastwards into the Si chuan plain; its valley covers most of Gui zhou. The rivers which rise in the east of the province flow into the Yuan jiang in Hu nan (and eventually into Lake Dong ting); all these belong to the Yang zi basin. The Bei pan jiang and the Du jiang are tributaries of the Zhu jiang, flowing south-eastwards into Guang xi; Moung Miao ling divides the two groups. Much of the province is limestone, which produces underground rivers which are sometimes several miles long; in some places, particularly in the south of the province, the underground rivers widen into lakes with no outlet. The Gui zhou plateau is the most cloudy region of China, with the most generous rainfall; showers are frequent in summer, but the sky soon clears after the rain. The growing period lasts for 8 to 10 months and two crops can usually be grown each year.

Gui zhou, a rocky and inaccessible province, came under Chinese influence in the modern era. The population consists above all of Miao, Bu yi, Yi and Dong minority races. The Miao, whose history is little known, lived more or less independently of the Chinese, in fortified towns ruled by hereditary chiefs, who were landlords at the same time; they merely sent tribute to the court. The Chinese did not make themselves felt until the end of the Ming dynasty and under the Qing, when the government decided to replace the local chiefs, who had grown too independent, by officials appointed by the central government. A struggle began from then on between the Miao, who were determined not to submit to the Chinese, and the Chinese who were anxious to move into the area, because they were pushed down there by the pressure of the population in the north, and because they were attracted by the gold, silver, copper and mercury mines. The 18th century was punctuated by bitter fighting, until the Miao finally gave in. Under the Qing the area was raised to the rank of province; it was made up of areas taken from the four neighbouring provinces. The Chinese colonists gradually became more numerous, but they did not venture far from the towns and garrisons, which were kept up by the court at vast expense; they cost more than the tribute brought in. In the 19th century, rebellions broke out again after the Tai ping rebellion, but were once more squashed. Autonomous regions have been created since the liberation in areas where the minority races live in large numbers.

The province is considered to be one of the richest in south China as far as mineral resources are concerned; it has several coalfields, Kai yang is well known for the phosphorous deposits in the area round it, and non-ferrous metals such as copper, silver and manganese are also to be found. Attempts were made before the revolution to use modern methods to mine the coal in the province. In 1887, a commission was sent to England to study the metal industry and buy machinery; coal from the south-east of Gui zhou was analysed, and some was found to be suitable for making coke; all the necessary machinery was bought and shipped up the River Yuan. The factory, when it was built, worked once only, without outstanding results, and they fell back on the old Chinese methods. Since 1949, great stress has been laid on the development of heavy industry (iron and steel, machine-building and chemical industries); its output is now greater than that of light industry (textiles, food-processing, paper-making, distilling — Mao tai, the well-known spirit, comes from Gui zhou). Only 12 % of the land is cultivated, in spite of great efforts to make more terraced fields. Rice is the basic crop, and is grown mainly in the Wu, Qing shui jiang valleys and near Gui yang and Zun yi, all of which are in the east of the province. Maize is grown in the north-west where the land is higher, and the weather colder. Potatoes, rape-seed, tobacco (mainly in the centre of the province; Gui ding tobacco is famous throughout the country) are also grown. The damp climate provides excellent conditions for forestry; cedar and pine trees are grown and floated down the Rivers Qing shui jiang and Du jiang. Other forestry products are wood-oil, unboiled varnish and gallnuts.

The population is relatively small: 16,900,000 inhabitants; the Miao (1,800,000) live in the east and south, in the mountainous areas, and the Bu yi (1,200,000) live in the south. Gui yang, the provincial capital, will be described first, then Zun yi to the north, followed by the small towns in the east and west of the province.

Gui yang

Gui yang is in the centre of the province, on a tributary of the River Wu jiang; it is on the railway line to Guang xi, in the south, and Si chuan, to the north; other stretches are being built, and will eventually link it with Yun nan to the west and Hu nan to the east. It is the centre of a network of roads which covers the whole province. The town was founded under the Han. Under the Ming, walls were built round it, and under the Qing, it became the provincial capital; at the beginning of the century, it was nothing but an administrative centre, with a population of 50,000. The town now has 500,000 inhabitants. Industry — particularly machine-building — is developing rapidly. It is at an altitude of 3,000 feet, and surrounded by beautiful hills; the most famous of them is Qian ling shan, to the north-west. The provincial museum is at Gui yang.

Zun yi

Zun yi is 120 miles north of Gui yang, and the Si chuan-Gui zhou railway line will pass through it once it is completed. Roads link it to the provincial capital and to the northern towns; it is the second biggest town in the province. It became famous as a result of a meeting held there in January 1935, when the members of the Political Bureau of the Party Central Committee brought out a violent criticism of the right-wing policy; its supporters were eliminated, Mao Ze dong became leader of the Party, and his point of view was adopted. It was also decided that the army should be re-organised so that it could keep on the move while fighting, and that the Long March should be continued. The town is now an important economic centre: agricultural products of the area (rice, maize, oil-bearing plants, tobacco, silk) are brought there for re-distribution, and modern industry has been created there (mineral mining, chemical and food-processing industries, silk textiles). The house in which the meeting was held is still standing, and has been converted into a museum.

Zhen yuan

Zhen yuan is on the south bank of the River Wu jiang, on the road from Gui yang to Hu nan. The town was founded under the Yuan; it is now a re-distribution centre for local products (oil-bearing plants), and is sometimes called You xiang: "Oil village".

Tong ren

Tong ren is a town in the north-east of the province, on the south bank of the River Ma yang jiang. It is a re-distribution centre (timber).

Du yun

Du yun is in the south-east, on the Gui yang — Guang xi railway line. It is the seat of the People's Committee of the south Gui zhou Bu yi and Miao Autonomous Department. It possesses iron and steel works, a farm tool factory, linen and paper mills.

Bi jie

Bi jie is in the west of the province, near the Yun nan border; it is on the roads to Si chuan and Gui yang. It is an important marketing centre.

An shun

An shun is in a mountainous area in the south-west of the province, on the roads to Yun nan, Si chuan, Guang xi and Gui yang. It used to be one of the most prosperous towns in the province; a flourishing opium trade existed there, alongside cottons from England, and white wax was sent from there to Hu nan. It then had a population of 50,000. Industry has been created there since the liberation (machine-building, sugar refineries, green tea famous throughout the country). It lies among beautiful scenery; the Yuan tong si is one of the most famous temples in the area.

SI CHUAN

(Map see Atlas, pl. 23/24)

Introduction

West of the great north China plain and the countless hills of south China, Si chuan seems like a third China, somewhat remote from the other two, often clothed in clouds and mist, always green and wet, and astonishingly fertile and densely populated, at least in the central depression.

It is the largest province in China, larger than France or the British Isles (210,000 square miles) and with a larger population (72,160,000 inhabitants); it lies in the bend of the Yang zi, which flows north and then north-east; the river takes on the name of "River of Golden Sand" (Jin sha jiang) from Yi bin onwards.

Broadly speaking, Si chuan falls into two main regions:

a) the Si chuan basin itself, which Richthofen called the "Red Basin",

b) the western stretch of Tibetan plateau which corresponds roughly to the former province of Xi kang, added to Si chuan once more in 1955.

Relief and Rivers

The eastern basin — nearly 70,000 square miles — is framed by chains of mountains varying in altitude from 3,200 feet to 9,800 feet or even more: the Da liang shan to the south-west, the Da ba shan and the Wu shan dividing it from Shân xi and Hu bei to the north and the east, and the limestone plateau of Yun nan to the south. Communications with the outside world are difficult on the whole.

Most of the basin is under 1,600 feet above sea level; it is scattered with red sandstone hills covered with trees (pine) or carefully carved out into terraced fields. The plain of Cheng du is an exception; it is an alluvial plain, generously and regularly watered by the River Min and its canals. It covers 2,000 square miles, and is probably the richest, best cultivated and most densely populated area in China.

Powerful rivers, most of them navigable over almost all their course, flow from north to south across the Red Basin to empty themselves into the Yang zi: the Min jiang, the Tuo jiang, the Jia ling are the largest ones. The only large tributary from the south is the Wu jiang. The Yang zi itself is navigable by steamers as far as Yi bin, 1,800 miles from its mouth.

Most of western Si chuan is over 9,800 feet above sea level, with some high mountains such as the Gong xia in the Da xue shan (Great Snow Mountains) which rises to 24,890 feet above sea level south-west of the town of Kang ding. The plateau slopes gently down from the north-west to the south-east, with deep, narrow valleys cutting into it, such as the upper Yang zi valley, and the valleys of the Ya long and the Da du. The valley formations, the altitude and the situation of the mountain chains all combine to make movement about the province difficult.

Climate

The Si chuan climate naturally reflects the great physical differences between the east and west of the province.

In the eastern basin, the temperature is mild in winter (the average temperature for January varies from 39.5° F to 46° F according to the areas) and hot in summer (75° F). From October to April, the plain is often covered in thick fog, and as the proverb goes, "the dogs bark when they see the sun". The monsoon brings abundant rain and the total for a year sometimes exceeds 40 inches. Two thirds of the total rainfall in Cheng du, for instance, falls in July and August (23.5 inches out of 36.5 inches). This provides excellent conditions for agriculture, and it continues almost all the year round.

The Economy

Si chuan, which is the richest agricultural province in China, saw the beginnings of industrialisation during the Sino-Japanese War; industry has developed still further during the last fifteen years and will certainly go on from strength to strength.

Agriculture, which is rich and continues all the year round, is also varied. Si chuan produces more rice than any other province in China (two crops a year on the whole), and is one of the most important wheat-producing provinces. Barley, maize, sweet potatoes, broad beans, groundnuts and rape-seed are grown more or less everywhere. The Nei jiang area produces large quantities of sugar-cane, the Long chang area produces jute, the Cheng du plain tobacco; cotton is grown in the Fo ling area and tea plantations cover the hills in the Red Basin. Orange trees grow near the Yang zi, and fruit common in temperate climates is also found (apples, grapes). Si chuan is famous for its fine quality silk, made in the Lu shan, San dai and Nan chong areas.

The mountainous western region is less rich: barley, sometimes wheat, are both grown; conifers grow there naturally and stock-breeding (yaks and sheep) is more successful there than in the plains, where pigs, poultry and a few draught animals are found.

Si chuan is also famous for its bamboo, its varnish, its wax trees, and its medecinal herbs which are extremely important in traditional Chinese medecine.

Modern industry first appeared during the Sino-Japanese War (1937-1945) when factories were brought there (arsenals, steelworks, machine tool and textile factories) from the lower and middle Yang zi valley, to be set up once more, sometimes under extremely original managerial systems (Indusco). The present government plans a more systematic development of the area, which will soon be crossed by a railway line from Zhong qing to Cheng du, which was linked to the rest of the network at Bao ji in 1956.

New coal mines have been created or developed in the Zhong qing area (Bei bei, Zhong liang shan), iron works have been built or enlarged to treat ore mined locally (the Ji jiang area south of Zhong qing, and the Wei yuan area).

The province also produces a little copper (near Ya an and Peng xian) and gold (near Sung pan) which have for a long time been treated according to traditional methods.

Oil deposits have been discovered in three or four places (mainly near Zi gong); the quantity is not yet certain. Natural gas is plentiful in the Zi gong area.

For centuries, Si chuan has been famous for the rock salt mines near Zi gong (Zi liu jing and Gong jing), where modern chemical industry is now growing up.

Cheng du and Zhong qing are the two main industrial cities in the province; they will be mentioned again later on.

Transport

The rivers constitute an extremely useful network, particularly as the Yang zi links the province with the rest of the country. Steam and motor boats can sail up as far as Yi bin. Much of the river traffic consists of large junks built in the traditional style. The Jia ling is navigable as far as Nan chong, and the Min as far as Cheng du. Rapids are frequent, however, and the sudden rise in the level of the water at the beginning of the summer changes the currents, so that only the most experienced of boatmen know them. The difference between the lowest and highest levels is sometimes as much as 60 feet, and the river often rises several feet overnight.

The railway lines, all built since 1949 except for a few exceptions in the way of short local lines, consist mainly in the Zhong qing — Cheng du line, opened in 1952, and the extension of the same line towards Bao ji, through the Shân xi mountains. A few branch lines join up with it, particularly the Nei jiang — Zi gong — Yi bin line, which will eventually go as far as Kun ming in Yun nan.

Another line, Zhong qing — Gui yang — Kun ming exists in sections.

It has never been easy to go to Si chuan by road, and all Chinese know the quotation from the poet Du fu which runs:

"How hard the road to Shu is!
It is as hard as the road to heaven."

The Zhong qing — Cheng du road is still the main road through the "red basin". Several other important roads or tracks join it: the road to Tibet from Cheng du to Chang du (Chamdo) and Lhasa, via Ya an, Kang ding, Gan zi, the track from Kang ding to Batang, the track from Ya an to Xi chuan and Hui li.

The Zhong qing — Gui yang road to the south gives easy access to Yun nan. The eastern hills, the high western mountains, the high cost of motor transport and the scarcity of draught animals, all make it difficult to develop an elaborate road network.

The most common forms of transport are still the wheelbarrow, on level ground, and porters who carry goods, using carrying poles, along paths which are often paved. Everywhere, even on the main roads, the traveller comes across interminable processions of peasants carrying or pushing their loads. Si chuan is changing slowly as far as this is concerned.

The internal airlines have planes going to Zhong qing, Cheng du and Xi chang.

Population Distribution

The Chinese population of Si chuan (72 million inhabitants) is mainly Han, as the minority races barely exceed 2 million people (800,000 of whom are Tibetans and 600,000 Yi), scattered over half the area of the province.

The Red Basin is relatively densely populated (over 600 inhabitants to the square kilometre in the Cheng du plain). Village after village lies in the bottom of the valleys, with lightly-built low, white houses with black timbers and wooden shutters, completely different from the yellow or grey houses of north China. The wet climate and the fields spreading over the hillsides enable people to live out of the villages, so that little farms surrounded by bamboos and banana-trees perch on the hillsides right up to the ridges, which are fringed with lines of graceful pine trees or crowned with temples.

The province includes several large, thickly populated cities. Zhong qing and its suburbs contain over 2,400,000 inhabitants, Cheng du has a population of 1,200,000, and Zi gong has 400,000 inhabitants. Nei jiang, Yi bin at the confluence of the Min and the Yang zi, Lu zhou, Wan xian at the entry to the great Yang zi gorges, and Nan chong on the Jia ling are the largest towns in the eastern part of the province.

The Tibetans are the most numerous of the national minorities in the west of Si chuan. They live in the two autonomous *zhou* of A ba, which also contains Jiang and Moslems, and Gan zi (about 500,000 inhabitants in each one).

The *zhou* of Liang shan (800,000 inhabitants) in the southwest contains a majority of Yi, as well as some Tibetans and some Muli. The Yi, who used to be better known under the name of Lolo, are a handsome race of uncertain origin, who still wear their pointed caps and capes; they are a race of mountain farmers more than herdsmen. For a long time they refused to have anything to do with the Han.

Others groups, all less numerous and less well known, such as the Sifan, the Mosso and the Liso live in other areas of the province.

For administrative purposes, Si chuan, with Cheng du as its capital, is divided into 12 special districts containing 181 ordinary sub-prefectures. The three autonomous *zhou* already mentioned (43 sub-prefectures) and three autonomous sub-prefectures exist alongside this organisation.

The Big Towns and places of interest

Cheng du, the provincial capital, which used to be considered one of the most beautiful towns in China, and which is not unlike Peking, has been changing rapidly since 1949.

It is an ancient city, whose history goes back over more than two thousand years. It was already in existence at the time of the "Spring and Autumn Annals" (770–475 B.C.). With Liu Bei it was the capital of the kingdom of Shu during the Three Kingdoms era (221–263) and again during the Five Dynasties period. It was the headquarters of numerous rebellions, and was almost destroyed by the Mongols under the reign of Khubilai Khan. Marco Polo visited the town.

The city was square, and until recently, surrounded by walls and battlements over 12 miles round, with four gates, each facing one of the points of the compass; it was centred round the imperial city, the residence of the viceroy (late 14th century). The tartar city was in the west, the business district in the east. The River Guan xian ran round two sides of it, east and south. Round its walls, villages and gardens mingled with the suburbs. The outward appearance of the city has not changed much; the palace, now used for administrative offices, is still the centre of the town, though it is usually closed to visitors. Wide streets crossing at right angles, with a few large modern shops and the rest smaller ones built in traditional style, with wooden porches, cut through the shopping district. Tea houses open on to the street, full of customers reclining on long bamboo chairs.

The more picturesque elements have not altogether disappeared from the market-places; local handicrafts (bamboo or plaited straw ware, cutlery, pottery,

silks) and sometimes handicrafts from the minority
races (bracelets and necklaces) can still be found.
Cheng du is also a stage on the road to Tibet.

The new industrial districts are spreading outwards
and eastwards, outside the site of the old walls:
they include textile, tool and leather factories.

Cheng du is the chief cultural centre in the south-
west, just as it always has been. Si chuan University
was founded there in 1927, and it now has 5,000 students; about ten more institutes of higher education
including technical institutes, have been created there.

Tourists will find a good modern hotel in the south
of the town; permission can be obtained to visit
the imperial city. The shopping districts, market-
places and public gardens are worth a visit as well.

The **Du Fu Cao tang,** the "cottage" of the great
poet Du Fu (712–770) is outside the town walls.
The modest house in which he lived and worked for
three years after 759 was enlarged and transformed
under the Song, the Ming and the Qing, and restored
in 1955; it is now a delightful group of buildings
between the viceroy's gardens and the former **Cottage
Temple** (Cao tang si), west of the town. A little river,
the "river which bathes the flowers", runs through it.

The paintings inspired by several of Du Fu's
poems on the sufferings of the people have been
collected and are on show; the library contains various
editions of his works and commentaries on them,
and a museum houses a collection of objects of
interest.

The **Wu hou si,** in the south, is the temple dedicated
to the memory of the great scholar and strategist
Zhu Ge liang (181–234), one of the chief heroes
of the **Romance of the Three Kingdoms** and several
plays.

The **tomb of Wang Jian (Wang jian mu)** is also in the southern suburbs; he was an adventurer who became prince of Shu, and was later given the posthumous title of Emperor. The tomb was opened and restored in 1943; its statues and the figurines, representing dancers and musicians, are wonderfully graceful.

A park covering 34 acres lies on the other side of the River Guan xian; over 90 different kinds of bamboo grow there. It also contains the well of Xie Tao, who was a famous Tang singer, and the inventor of a sort of decorated paper.

Near the **Cinnamon Tree Lake (Gui hu),** a little north-east of Cheng du, in the sub-prefecture of Xin du xian, the great Ming sage and scholar Yang Shen (1488–1559) had a country house built. His works and several of his possessions have been collected in a memorial hall to him (Shen en dian).

Zhong qing

Zhong qing, once a stronghold and a trading town, stands on a rocky promontory at the confluence of the Yang zi and the peaceful Jia ling, framed by steep hills, some of them crowned by pine-trees. It is an impressive sight under a louring sky.

Until 1938, before it became the capital from 1939–1945, during the war, the town was still surrounded by its old walls; narrow flights of steps led down towards the ramparts between the huddled houses, and hundreds more led down to the river far below. The only means of transport was by sedan chairs made of light bamboo, or, once outside the walls, on horseback, the mounts were sure-footed ponies who were used to the paved slopes.

Zo hong qing is a martyr town; it suffered savage bombing by the Japanese between 1938 and 1941. Hundreds of shelters were gradually built in the rocks and each time the alarm was raised, the whole population would calmly take to the shelters, line after line of them. From October to April, the heavy fogs protected the city, which took up a more or less normal life once more.

Modern Zhong qing is still striking because of its magnificent site, whether it is seen from the top of the promontory, the middle of the river or from the industrial suburb of Jiang bei, beyond the Jia ling. **Chao tian men (the Gate which looks towards the Sky)** a point overlooking the river, gives a magnificent view over the river; another view can be had by crossing over to the south bank of the Yangzi. The countless stone steps, the picturesque wooden houses built on stilts, clinging to the hillsides or to the remains of the walls, the little steamers and the big junks with their sails and long oars, hauled from the bank as they travel upstream, all present an unforgettable sight.

New modern buildings stand in the central districts or on the point; houses of traditional design, blackened by the weather and the camouflage used during the war, climb up the hillsides towards the slopes of Tian deng po (Celestial Lanterns Hill), and spread alongside the Cheng du road, as far as the suburb of Sha ping pa, where large buildings providing living quarters for the workers, factories or workshops (steel, textiles, farm tools, paper) take over. The technical university is at Sha ping pa.

No ancient monuments or temples are left now (Zhong qing was never a cultural centre); instead a huge many-coloured building dominated by a round edifice with a roof in tiers was built in 1954, and is used for local meetings; one wing is now a hotel. The building as a whole, with the gardens in front of it, is unexpected in a town of dark colours like Zhong qing.

Several easily accessible places round the town show the beauty and richness of the countryside in this part of Si chuan.

After the crossing to the south bank by ferry, a path leads up through cultivated valleys, such as the Huang jue ya, and pine woods, to the **Southern Mountain Gardens (Nan shan gong yuan)**, overlooking a magnificent landscape of terraced fields. The return journey gives a fine view over the town and the river.

The **Southern Hot Springs (Nan wen quan)** are 12 miles away on the right bank; they are sulfurous springs, in a setting of pavilions, lakes and gardens. The Flower Stream (Hua qi), if followed upstream, leads to some caves and beautiful landscapes.

North of Zhong qing, along the banks of the Jia ling, the famous **Bei bei park** (hot springs), spreads out above the river, which flows through deep, narrow gorges at that point; it is possible to have lunch there. Bei bei also has an interesting agricultural school.

The tourist who is interested in modern history can visit the place where the delegation from the 8th Route Army to the Guo min dang government stayed from 1938 to 1946, in the village of **Hong yan cun (Red Cliff),** near Zhong qing. The name of the village sometimes appears in modern novels and plays. Several of the present leaders of China (1966) are natives of Si chuan: Zhu De (former Commander in Chief of the Red Army), Chen Yi (Deputy Prime Minister and Foreign Minister), Deng Xiao ping (Deputy

Prime Minister), Luo Rui qing (Deputy Prime Minister and Chief of the General Staff), Guo Mo ruo (Chairman of the Academy of Science).

The Guan xian Dam

Guan xian, about 30 miles north of Cheng du, is one of the most interesting places in China from the point of view of traditional agricultural waterworks.

In about 250 B.C., the scholar Li Bing had an opening made in a wall of rock at the point where the River Min leaves the mountains, and diverted part of the water towards the plain, using an ingenious system of dams, embankments and bottle-necks. His son carried on the work after him, and it was continued with varying degrees of success over the centuries that followed. The system now irrigates 25 sub-prefectures and 980,000 acres belonging to 351 communes, an area which is the richest agricultural region in China (three crops of rice, rape seed, sugar-cane, tobacco, etc. per year).

Maps, plans and models of the way the system works are on show in a large traditional-style building erected in memory of Li Bing and his son. If possible, it is interesting to go round the offices of the Tuo jiang Project, which is in charge of the supervising and development of the work.

The memorial already mentioned is worth a visit from a touristic point of view, as it contains several inscriptions in memory of Li Bing, recording his saying:

"Dig the canals deep and make embankments low".

A little further north, the **Two Kings Temple** in memory of Li Bing and his son, both of whom received the posthumous title of Wang, overlooks the left bank of the Min; a famous bamboo suspension bridge used to span the river there.

The bridge at Guan xian itself is a covered bridge built of wood, and decorated with painted wooden figures.

E mei shan

The great Buddhist sanctuary of Mount E mei stands on one of the last advance posts of Tibet, 6,500 feet above the Si chuan plain, and 10,143 feet above sea level. It is about 120 miles from Cheng du and 180 miles from Zhong qing, and is still difficult to get at.

It consists of seventy temples spread out near the top of the mountain, which once housed several thousand monks, and was one of the most popular centres of pilgrimages in China. The believers and visitors used to take several days to reach the top, visiting temples and spending the night on the way.

The temples have little real artistic value. They offer much of historic or religious interest, however, and one of the most unusual things quoted is a Buddha riding a life-size bronze elephant in the **Ten Thousand Years Temple (Wan nian si).**

The climb itself, the pleasure of escaping the summer heat, the sight of the great plain, or the sea of clouds, according to the weather, was as important to the lay pilgrims as their devotions once they got to the top, as it was for the pilgrims who climbed Tai shan.

The colossal seated Buddha of Jia ding, cut out of the rock face above the River Min is not far from E mei shan. It is 390 feet high, and is said to be 12 centuries old.

Smaller Towns

Many more towns are interesting for as many different reasons. As it is not easy to visit them at the moment, only their main characteristics will be briefly mentioned.

In the Red Basin: Zi gong, Nei jiang, Nan chong, Lo shan.

Zi gong

Zi gong has a population of 400,000 and is now the third most important town in Si chuan. It has always been famous throughout China for its rock salt (output estimated at 300,000 tons per year), and visitors used to be struck by the ubiquitous bamboo scaffolding, the thousands of water-buffaloes drawing the salt water which came from wells hundreds of feet deep. The extraction of natural gas, and the creation of modern chemical industries, are now changing the countryside considerably.

Nei jiang is a centre of the sugar industry which has become even more important now that sugar from Tai wan no longer helps to supply the mainland.

Nan chong, in the north of the province, is famous for its silks.

On the Yang zi: Yi bin, Lu zhou, Wan xian.

Yi bin is important because it is the terminus for modern river traffic up the Yang zi, and stands at the confluence of the Yang zi and the Min; a road runs from there to Yun nan. Its situation alone will ensure brilliant economic development.

Lu zhou is the port for the rich Tuo jiang valley, famous for its spirits.

Wan xian, the port handling traffic for the east of the province, is at the entrance to the Yang zi

gorges. The town, built on the slopes of the south
bank of the river, probably ranks fourth in importance
in Si chuan.

Finally, the towns marking the stages in the journey
to Tibet and the west: Ya an, Lu ding, Kang ding,
Gan zi, Xi chang.

Ya an probably has a population of about 100,000;
it exports tea and tobacco to Tibet, and imports
skins, musk and medecinal herbs in return.

Lu ding, on the River Da du, is famous for its suspension bridge made of 13 iron chains, which the Red
Army seized during the Long March.

Kang ding (formerly Ta qian lu) is at an altitude
of 8,858 feet, in the midst of majestic mountain
scenery; it used to be a garrison town and a market
centre. Its inhabitants are a mixture of Han and
Tibetan. It used to be famous for its numerous
lamaseries.

Gan zi is the headquarters of a Tibetan *zhou*.

Si chuan was absorbed into the orbit of Chinese
civilisation early on, and possesses countless historical
and archaeological remains of the greatest interest.
A few of them will be touched on here, though they
are scattered and often far away and difficult to get to.

The **Imperial Favour Temple (Huang ze si)** is in
the far north of the province, not far from Guang
yuan, west of the town and the River Jia ling. The
wooden parts of the temple have disappeared, but
6 caves and 28 niches, which have partially fallen
in, can still be seen. The Buddha is generally depicted
surrounded by saints and disciples. The style is that
of the Tang dynasty, although the origins are doubtful
(Later Shu or Five Dynasties).

The **Thousand Buddha Cliff (Qian fo yan)** is also
in the sub-prefecture of Guang yuan. It is considered

to be the richest group of Buddhist sculptures in the province, comparable with Long men and Yun gang. It dates from the beginning of the 8th century, and an inscription records that 17,000 statues of different sizes were carved out of the rock; 400 still exist today.

The carvings and statues on the **Northern Mountain (Bei shan mo ya zao xiang)** are in the sub-prefecture of Da zu, west of Zhong qing. Near them, in the same sub-prefecture, are the carvings and statues on the **Precious Summit Mountain (Bao ding shan mo ya xiang).** This group shows unusual unity of style, although opinions are still divided as to its date of origin (Tang, Song or even Ming).

Some excellent specimens of Tang sculpture (statues, bricks, tiles) have been found since the war in the Qiong lai area; they are now in the historical museum of Cheng du university.

More Buddhist sculpture exists in the east of the province, at **Ba zhong:** 130 niches dating from the Tang.

Remains like these are frequent all over Si chuan; some authors state that they are to be found in 49 sub-prefectures, in 124 different places.

Several *que* dating from the Han still survive in Si chuan. They consist of two large covered pillars, about 60 feet apart as a rule, standing in front of a palace or on either side of the entrance to a tomb, bearing inscriptions and carvings.

One of the best known ones is to be found in the sub-prefecture of Ya an: the *que* belonging to the **tomb of Gao Yi (Gao Yi fen que),** built in 209 A.D.

Another *que* stands in the north of the province, 5 miles north of the sub-prefecture of Mian yang: the **Ping yang fu gan que.**

The sub-prefecture of Qu xian contains two more: the **Fong huan que** and the **Shen fu gun que.** The second one, dating from 121 A.D., is covered with carvings, among them a magnificent "red bird", the emblem of the south.

The tourist should leave Si chuan by river. Steamers cover the distance to Wu han in three days, through the most awe-inspiring and no doubt the most difficult gorges in the world. They stretch over about 120 miles, defying any attempt at detailed description. Every large rock, every rapid, every shoal has a name. Several times the river rushes through narrow passages less than 300 feet wide, between sheer limestone walls several hundred feet high. Not until the beginning of this century did modern boats brave this stretch, although thousands of junks and sampans did so, and still do.

The river flows through three main series of gorges as it leaves Si chuan. The **Qu tang Gorges (Qu tang xia)** cover 5 miles, beginning on a level with Feng jie, about 30 miles from the Hu bei border. The **Wu Gorges (Wu xia)** cut through the Wu Mountains on the border of the two provinces, over about 30 miles.

The last group, the **Xi ling Gorges,** are the most majestic of all; they stretch for 18 miles, ending near Yi chang. Once there, the Yang zi becomes a river of the plain again, and nothing in the countryside recalls the red hills and wooded mountains left behind in Si chuan.

THE AUTONOMOUS
REGION OF TIBET

(Map see Atlas pl. 23/24)

Tibet (Tibetan: Bod, Chinese: Xi zang) is bordered by Xin jiang and Qing hai to the north, Si chuan and Yun nan to the east, Burma, India, Bhutan and Nepal to the south. The present autonomous region covers most of the vast Qing hai — Tibet plateau, which is often over 13,000 feet above sea level ("the roof of the world"). It consists of two completely different regions:

1) to the north, the vast *northern Tibetan tableland*, much of which is over 16,000 feet; to the north, the Kun lun Mountains separate it from the lower lying Tarim (Xin jiang) and Tsai dam (Qing hai basins) ;it has many lakes, and snow-covered mountain peaks; the altitude and the position in the middle of the continent result in an extremely cold and dry climate; "this country makes the Gobi seem fertile in comparison; vast stretches have no vegetation at all; here and there a few small plants grow, leathery and villous, with extraordinarily long, tenacious roots, and a little moss or lichen... "(F. Grenard);

2) the **Zang po valley** to the south (the upper reaches of the Brahmaputra); the river rises to the west, near Mount Kailasa, and runs out of Tibet to the east, to join the Ganges; the valley runs between two chains of mountains, the Gangdis to the north and the Himalaya to the south (several peaks over 25,000 feet); the climate is relatively mild, as damp air from the Indian ocean comes up from the south-east.

Naturally enough, the Tibetan civilisation developed in this valley, and most of the 1,270,000 inhabitants of the autonomous region live there. The wealth of myths and local legends suggests that Tibet has an ancient history; no evidence exists, however, for anything earlier than 600 A.D. At this point the picturesque King Songtsen Gampo (Tibetan spelling: Srongbtsan Sgam-po Chinese: Song zan gan bu), makes his appearance, and his reign begins a period of prosperity for Tibet. His armies pushed as far as the borders of the Tang empire, and reached Yun nan (the state of Nan zhao was for a time the vassal of Tibet, and the north of India. The king married a Chinese princess, the famous **Wen cheng Gong zhu** (a marriage which is often recalled today); he had silk-worms brought from China, and artisans who were specialised in the making of mill-stones, paper and alcohol were sent as well;

he himself sent young Tibetan nobles to Chang an (present day Xi an) to study the Chinese classics. He had also married a Nepalese princess, however, and knew how to make room for Indian influences; the first Tibetan writing, derived from an Indian script, dates from his reign; and little by little Buddhism, also from India, supplanted the primitive religion, Bon. The Tibetan monarchy maintained its power for about a century and then it waned. An obscure period followed, whose chronology is most uncertain. A new upsurge began from the 11th century onwards, but of a different kind; the chief role was taken over by the religious communities, who settled over all the valley and beyond it, as Buddhism became more widespread. Permanent rivalries existed between the communities. At the beginning of the 15th century, a theologian, Tsongkhapa, stressed the need for the discipline imposed by the monastic life, and founded the new order of the Gelugpa ("those who follow virtuous works"), known as the "yellow caps" to distinguish them from their rivals, the "red caps". This order gradually achieved supremacy, thanks to the help of the Mongolian princes, who in 1578 conferred the title of Dalai Lama on one of the successors of Tsongkhapa.

With the beginning of the modern era, the traditional bastion of Tibet began to be the object of envy of its neighbours, who were all jealous of its geographical situation and its strategic position. In the 18th century, the Chinese tried to oust the Mongolian princes from the position of overlord; in 1720, an army was sent by Kang xi, which succeeded in getting as far as Lhasa, and a protectorate was founded which lasted until the end of the Qing dynasty (1911). European missionaries (such as the Jesuit Father Ippolito Desideri, an Italian, who was there from 1716 to 1721) reached Tibet; the Indian empire sent agents to obtain economic advantages; even the Russians dreamed of establishing a protectorate over all the peoples converted to Lamaism (hence the role of the Lama Dorjieff, delegated to Lhasa). In 1904, the English sent a little army towards Lhasa and the Dalai Lama fled to Urga; in 1910, the Chinese advanced in their turn and the Dalai Lama fled to India. When the Manchu dynasty fell in 1912, the Dalai Lama declared himself free of all ties of vassalage. The Chinese Republic had not the means to re-establish their control, but the Tibetans did not try to adapt themselves to their emancipation, and confirm their independence.

Immediately after the liberation, the new regime began to take steps to re-establish Chinese authority over Tibet. It broke first with the Dalai Lama, who fled to India, and then with the Panchen Lama, whose pro-Chinese sympathies had given rise to some hopes of collaboration. Thus the way was cleared for the new order to be established. Three roads were built, linking Tibet with Xin jiang, Qing hai and Si chuan. An airline was opened between Peking and Lhasa. The serfs were emancipated and people's communes gradually began to replace the landlords' estates. Agriculture has been improved in the valley (increase in the frequency of crops, and the introduction of tea growing); livestock is still the main resource on the tableland (yaks, goats, sheep). Hydro-electric stations, assembly works and farming implement factories have been built, but this is only a beginning and the mineral resources are far from being fully exploited.

LHASA AND ITS SURROUNDING AREA

Lhasa is the biggest town in Tibet, and the cultural, religious, economic and political capital. According to traditional sources, it was founded in the 7th century, under the reign of King Song zan gan bu; many of its architectural monuments are supposed to have been built for the Chinese princess whom he married. In any case, a Chinese stele survives at the **Da zhao si** (see below), erected in the 9th century, and known as the **Tang Fan hui meng pai** or the **Chang Qing pai**, inscribed in Tibetan and Chinese, to commemorate the alliance concluded between the two countries.

Next to it stands the **Tang liu**, the "Tang willow tree", said to have been planted by the princess herself, when the **Da zhao si** was built.

Two more steles stand near the tree; one dates from the Qing Emperor Qian long; it has no wall to protect it, and is badly damaged (pieces of the stele, in powder form, were used to make up certain medecines); the other probably dates from Qian long, but it is illegible.

In front of the Potala palace stands a tall memorial stele, put up in the 9th century by King Chi song de

zan. The lower part of the inscription has been
damaged.

The Da zhao Monastery

The oldest architectural monument in Lhasa is the
Da zhao si, the Da zhao monastery. It is built on an
east-west axis; the present main gate, near the street,
is not the original one. The oldest part of all is the
heart of the great hall (dian), and the two first stories.
The main gate used to stand in front of the hall. The
rest of the present monastery consists of buildings or
additions made under the Yuan, the Ming or the Qing.

The architecture of the monastery is remarkable,
because it is a mixture of Tibetan, Chinese, Nepalese
and Indian elements. The carvings and decoration of
the beams, pediments and porches are very fine: the
large gilded bronze statue of the Sakyamuni Buddha
in a niche in the great hall is said to have been brought
from Chang an by the Chinese princess. Four other
statues of Sakya stand grouped two on each side of
the door of the great hall, carved with great vigour.
The Sakya are the ancestors and the descendants of the
kings who reigned at the Potala; their number varies
from 5 to 15,000. Their four sons reigned at Kapilavastu; after the destruction of Kapilavastu, the four
surviving princes founded the kingdoms of Udiana,
Banyan, Himatala, and Sambi. In the side halls stand
statues of King Song zan gan bu, the princess, etc....
In the verandas to the side, the earth and clay which
have accumulated over the centuries have raised the
level of the ground so much that people have to bend
their heads to enter the great gate. The side halls also
contain statues of *Guan yin* (with four arms, or with
eleven faces) dating probably from the 8th century.
There are 12 large gold lamps, and many more

small ones, which have blackened the old frescoes on the walls of the great hall with their smoke. On the first floor is a series of little, low rooms. The treasure chamber contains a collection of old musical instruments (they do not seem to be older than the Ming dynasty, however), table ware, and King Song zan gan bu's helmet.

The Potala

The Potala is known all over the world; it was also built in the 7th century, under the reign of King Song zan gan bu, according to the legends. Judging by the present architecture, however, it was restored in the 17th century, and enlarged. The large buildings date from the fifth and the thirteenth Dalai Lamas; the Red Palace and the White Palace were built by these two. It is said that remains of the original buildings still exist; in the lowest storey of the Potala, at the top of Mount Potala itself, there is an empty room, built in blocks of stone; in the middle of the room is an earthen mound, which is the top of the hill (also called **Mount Pu tuo**); a little pagoda and some ancient banners still exist as well.

Whatever the case may be, the first buildings were certainly begun on this spot on Mount Potala; after going round the "empty" room, a narrow passage leads to the original site of the building. Another narrow path leads to a little room (full of heaps of statues and effigies) built in a very ancient style; it is said to be the "cave" where the marriage between the Chinese princess and King Song zan gan bu took place. Other statues of famous people recall statues in the **Da zhao si.**

Two sets of buildings can be traced in the Potala itself: the first contained the living quarters of the Dalai Lamas (bed-room, living rooms, rooms for

LE POTALA
THE POTALA

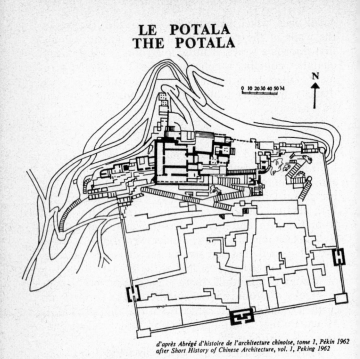

d'après Abrégé d'histoire de l'architecture chinoise, tome 1, Pékin 1962
after Short History of Chinese Architecture, vol. 1, Peking 1962

---

sacred books, little hall of the sutras, big hall of the
sutras, library, treasure-chamber), and the servants'
quarters (rooms of all kinds, bed-rooms, etc.... the
rooms at the back are often very small). The second
consists of **Ling ta dian** (Funerary pagoda halls),
and halls of sutras. The halls of the fifth and the thirteenth Dalai Lamas are the largest and richest of all;
the funerary pagodas are of gilded bronze, and some

are even overlaid with gold leaf. The highest is the one belonging to the thirteenth Dalai Lama, which is over 30 feet high, and in three stories; the body of the pagoda is decorated with carvings of figures, flowers, etc... inlaid with different precious stones. On the altars in front of the Palace are gold lamps, Ming and Qing porcelain, enamels, jade ritual vessels, and banners.

The Hall of the funerary pagoda of the fifth Dalai Lama contains frescoes (one of them depicts his arrival at the Court of Peking, when he was received by the Qing Emperor Shun zi, 1644–1662). The hall of the funerary pagoda of the thirteenth Dalai Lama also contains frescoes describing his visit to the Chinese capital. Although they have been touched up and restored, the frescoes are still invaluable as historical documents.

A helmet is kept in the Potala, supposed to have belonged to King Song zan gan bu; it is made of gold, and seems to be older than the one in the **Da zhao si,** but nothing exists to prove beyond all doubt that it dates from the 7th century.

The **Great Eastern Hall of the Sutras (Dong da jing tang)** was recently sacked by rebels who helped the Dalai Lama to flee; the Buddhas, banners and ritual vessels all have bullet-marks on them, and the hall was abandoned in the most indescribable state of chaos.

Below the Potala Palace stands a large establishment where the sutras were printed. Next to it was the formidable torture chamber of the old regime (the instruments of torture are now exhibited in Lhasa museum)- Nearby was another, known as the "Cave of Scorpions".

Yao wang shan

Opposite the Potala, but some distance away, is the **Yao wang shan,** Mount Yao wang. The little temple on the top of it, the **Yao wang miao,** was built under the Qing, and has been restored several times since then. The monks' cells are built along the mountain ridge. The buildings were badly damaged in the recent disturbances. Books on medecine used to be kept in the temple (hence the name, "Kings of Medecine Temple"), brought to Tibet from China in the 7th century.

Xiao zhao si

The **Xiao zhao si,** which ranked with the **Da zhao si** in importance, is now in ruins; it was sacked in the recent disturbances, but is now being rebuilt and restored. The architecture (particularly the great hall) is completely different from that of the **Da zhao si.**

The Ga dan Monastery

The **Ga dan si,** the **Se la si** and the **Zhe bang si** are the three biggest monasteries in Lhasa, and the most imposing, from an architectural point of view, of all the many monasteries in the town. The three of them, with the **Za shen lun bi si** at Shigatse (Chinese **Ri ga ze**) are the chief religious centres in Tibet; and along with the **Ta er si Monastery** in Qing hai and the **La bu leng si Monastery** in Gan su, they constitute the six most famous Buddhist centres in China, known to believers all over Asia.

The **Ga dan Monastery (Ga dan si)** is about 37 miles east of Lhasa, south of the river, on **Mount Ga dan.** It stands on the peak of the mountain; the buildings huddle together, rising steeply, one on top of each other like a citadel. The monastery was founded by Zong Ka pa (the founder of the yellow sect of Tibetan Buddhism) and built in 1409; it is the oldest of the three big monasteries in Lhasa. The main buildings are the **Great Hall (La ji da dian)** and the **Chi duo kang**; the rest were added later on.

The **La ji da dian** is large and can apparently hold over three thousand lamas. Sutras are recited here, and it also contains some magnificent bronze statues (of Zong Ka pa among others). Behind the great hall, on the left, is a small room with a beautiful carving of Tushita on the door (Tushita is where the Maitreya lives and where the Bodhisattvas are reborn before they appear on earth). The room contains the chair of Zong Ka pa and several relics, as well as numerous things dating from the Ming and the Qing dynasties (ritual vessels, banners); there are some in the great hall too. Diagonally to the left of the great hall, another hall, the **Yang ba jian** ("of the eight gelded calves") contains a large collection of old objects, among them a helmet and suit of armour encrusted with jewels of different kinds which belonged to the Emperor Qian long himself, and which he presented to the Buddha in 1757; they were sent off, addressed to the Buddha, *via* Tibet; the helmet has the explanation inscribed in four languages, Chinese, Manchu, Mongol and Tibetan. It is of the greatest historical interest, and the workmanship is superb. Three verandas run round the **Yang ba jian,** the great hall and the well in front of it; they are decorated with frescoes painted in a fairly rough style, probably very old ones the frescoes in the other rooms, however, have obviously been considerably restored. The **Si dong tuo,** which is the first floor of the **Yang ba jian,** contains a magnificent "funerary pagoda" in memory of Zong

Ka pa. The next floor is the **Tan cheng dian**; above that is the **Chi ba ta dian,** containing six silver "funerary pagodas" and one gold one inset with jewels, which, with the one in memory of Zong Ka pa, is the most beautiful of all.

Zong Ka pa lived in the **Chi duo kang**; a fresco dating from the early Ming dynasty depicts Sakyamuni.

The Ga dan si contains a large collection of works of art, both Tibetan and Chinese. The most famous item of all is the set of 24 rolls of "Tang brocade" (it is said to date from the Tang). A Chinese expert on the subject, Mr. Wang Yi, examined several of them in 1960, and said he thought that it was embroidery from **Jiang su,** dating from the beginning of the Ming dynasty (it is beautiful work; some of the rolls depict Bodhisattvas); he thought it likely that they had been brought back to Tibet by the brother of Zong Ka pa, who visited the court at Nanking.

The Zhe bang Monastery

The **Zhe bang Monastery (Zhe bang si)** is about 6 miles north-west of Lhasa. It is built on a high cliff, up against a high mountain, at whose foot runs the Tibet-Qing hai road. The style is majestic: the buildings join on to each other, and are surmounted by towers, which give them "a very modern air" (so the Chinese say). The style is purely Tibetan. The monastery dates from the Ming (1416) but is slightly more recent than the Ga dan Monastery, and differs from it in style; it is the largest of the three big monasteries at Lhasa.

The main building is the **Great Hall of the Sutras (Da jing tang),** which includes a large hall, four annex halls and most of the monks' cells.

The **Great Hall (Cuo qin dian)** contains some magnificent statues, and some very fine frescoes, which have not been restored, but which have been blackened by smoke from the oil lamps. The **Mi lo dian (Maitreya Hall)** contains a statue of the Maitreya. The main hall and the hall behind it both contain some beautiful statues of Bodhisattvas, influenced by Chinese and Nepalese styles. A pagoda known as the **Yao shi ta** ("of the master of remedies"), covered with copper leaf, and probably earlier than the Ming, judging by the style, is to the left of the great hall. The funerary pagodas of the second, third and fourth Dalai Lamas are there too; the funerary pagodas were not built at the Potala until the death of the fifth Dalai Lama.

The monastery library is on the first floor of the **Da jing tang**; it is an extremely rich one, containing very rare editions of some of the sutras.

The four halls round the Great Hall all contain interesting frescoes and statues. The monastery as a whole possesses a large collection of works of historic and artistic value. The damage resulting from the recent disturbances has been repaired.

The Se la Monastery

The third of the three big monasteries, the **Se la Monastery (Se la si),** was founded in 1419, by the brother of Zong Ka pa, three years later than the **Zhe bang Monastery.** It is about three miles north of Lhasa; it is built up against the mountain nearby, and faces the river; as it stands on the plain, its style is totally different from the two others, but it too is imposing. Like the **Zhe bang Monastery,** it consists mainly of a great hall and annex halls (three), one of them the archives.

The halls used for reciting the sutras all contain old frescoes, probably dating from the Ming; the Buddhist statues are remarkable because they are larger than most, particularly the statue of the Maitreya, in the **Cuo qin da dian.** A hall behind contains some superb statues of the eight Bodhisattvas. The statues, which are large ones, show distinct Indian and Nepalese influence. The monastery owns several objects of value even now, such as scroll paintings *(tankas)* dating from the Ming and the Qing, paintings on silk, etc....

Miscellaneous

These three large monasteries, now all classed as historical monuments, played an extremely important part in the religious and cultural life of ancient Tibet. Several other, smaller monasteries in Lhasa are still worth a visit: the **Cang gu si,** the **Gong de lin miao,** the **Guan di miao.**

The **Luo bu lin ka Palace (Luo bu lin ka gong),** with its ornamental lakes, pavilions, gateways, etc. is also worth a visit.

SHIGATSE (RI GA ZE) AND THE SURROUNDING AREA

The town of Shigatse is about 93 miles south-west of Lhasa, on a small alluvial plain. It always has been, and still is, the next most important town after Lhasa. The Panchen Lamas used to live there. The way from Lhasa to Shigatse passes the mountains of the **Zhe bang Monastery** first of all, then follows the valley, going due north-west, through a landscape of magnificent waterfalls and mountain streams. After **Yang ba jing,** the way goes south-west alongside the **Gang di si** mountains, across a large plain which is blocked all of

a sudden by a mountain lost in the clouds: the famous
Mount Xu ge la (24,600 feet). The way then turns to
twist through rugged mountainous country, sometimes
reaching an altitude of 17,700 feet, before reaching **Ma
jiang,** and after it, the **Shan la Pass** (16,700 feet). The
descent leads through wild, mountainous countryside,
past the village of **Xi ka,** to the banks of the river **Ya
lu zang bu,** which has to be crossed at the ford at
Da zu ka. It sometimes happens that floods make this
impracticable; in this case, as it may mean a delay
of a few days, it is a good opportunity to go and see the
Yong zu ri la lin Temple, further downstream, traditionally meant to have been the high place of the
Tibetan Black Sect. It is on a steep mountainside.

After crossing the river at the ford, the route crosses
the **Ya lu zang bu** a second time, at its confluence with
the river **Nian chu,** in the midst of magnificent countryside. Then it follows the river **Nian chu,** until the citadel
of Shigatse and the great **Za shen lun bu Monastery**
can be seen, encircled by mountains.

The Za shen lun bu Monastery

The **Za shen lun bu Monastery** (**Za shen lun bu si**) is
west of the town; according to the archives there, it was
founded by a brother of **Zong Ka pa, Gen dun zhu ba,**
who was the first Dalai Lama, under the Ming (in
1447). When **Gen dun zhu ba** died, building went on,
and was carried on by the Panchen Lamas (especially
the fourth, fifth and sixth). The result is a mass of
buildings huddled up against the mountainside, like
the three monasteries at Lhasa. The **Za shen lun bu** is
one of the six great centres of Lamaism.

The **Great Hall (Cuo qing da dian)** contains several
funerary pagodas of Panchen Lamas; four halls beside

it contain archives. In the other buildings are 40 *kang cun*, rooms reserved for the Lamas; their number indicates that the monastery is a big one. The Great Hall is built in an old style; it is enormous, and divided into nine halls all extremely simple and pure in structure; frescoes cover all the walls (they depict Zong Ka pa, Sakya Muni, a set of the eighteen *luo han*, etc.). They date from the Ming, and may have been painted as soon as the monastery was built. Four large statues stand among the central pillars, all no doubt later additions. A magnificent statue of the Maitreya stands in the Hall of the Maitreya nearby.

The biggest funerary pagoda in the monastery in the **Jue gan xia dian Hall**. It is in memory of the fourth Panchen Lama, and is overlaid with silver leaf encrusted with jewels.

A large stele exists here in praise of the Emperor of China.

The other halls all contain Buddhist statues, objects dating from the Ming and the Qing, porcelain, bronzes, glass, enamels, seals and rare documents (some date from the Yuan), etc....

The Zong shan

The **Zong shan** in Shigatse is the seat of the government; it is a lofty fortress, visible from far away, forming a complete architectural whole. It was built under the Ming, and enlarged and restored under the Qing. It contains the hall of the sutras, the hall of the Buddha, the archives, the treasure chamber, and a hall with a remarkable set of statues of sitting Lamas, executed with great life and realism.

The La dang Monastery

The **La dang Monastery (La dang si)** is outside the town, about 12 miles beyond the **Za shen lun bi si**, in a little village. It dates from the Song (1235 is the date of foundation). Built by **Dong dun Luo zhu cha**, it was changed considerably as time went on, and is small and at the moment in a bad state of repair. The Hall of the Sutras is still standing, surrounded by verandas resting on pillars cut from single tree-trunks. The ancient statues and frescoes inside are now damaged. The hall where the sutras were printed is also very old; it is the oldest printing works in Tibet (the blocks and the oldest editions are now in the **Za shen lun bi si**). The monastery owns a large collection of magnificent scroll paintings, thought to date from the Yuan, and a collection of ritual vessels (several of them are dated the Yong le period of the Ming dynasty, 1403–1425).

A beautiful pagoda stands near the monastery, known as the **Ji mi luo bu sang cha ta**; it has three stories, and contains statues of the Maitreya, Guan yin, etc... and frescoes, all of them dating from an extremely early period; they recall the style of the **Dun huang caves**. It probably dates from the 12th century.

The Xia lu Monastery

The road going south from **Shigatse** to **Jiang zi** crosses over two wide rivers, goes through **Xi ka**, and the path to the **Xia lu Monastery** leads up through the mountains from there. Unlike the others, it is surrounded by woods and wild vegetation; it is smaller than the great Lhasa monasteries. It used to be a great marketing centre. According to the archives, the monastery was founded in 1087. Under the Yuan, in 1320, it was headed by the Master of the **Bu dun** Law: the sect connected with it is known as the **Bu dun sect,** or the **Xia lu sect**; in 1333, the monastery was repaired, and the powerful wooden structures which can be seen today date from that time.

The main buildings consist of a great hall, called the **Xia lu la kang,** and four annex halls. The style is unusual: a mixture of Chinese and Tibetan traditional architecture. The original tiles have survived throughout: glass tiles, decorated with gilding and old motives (animals, etc....). The lower storey of the great hall contains the Hall of the Sutras; a veranda and annex halls are beside it, all forming a harmonious whole. The frescoes and statues inside are of dazzling beauty and richness (Bodhisattvas, Sakyamuni, Mandjusri, etc....).

The frescoes are among the most beautiful and the most ancient in Tibet, and they are also in a better state than any others; they cover all the verandas and all the walls of the Hall of the Sutras, and all the walls of the two first annex halls. Some show their Chinese influence clearly; others are more influenced by Nepalese art. All are overflowing with life and spontaneity. They are of the greatest possible interest because of the precious details which they give on clothes and architecture as well.

On the wall of the veranda surrounding the courtyard in front of the Great Hall is a magnificent set of frescoes showing "work and days": work in the fields, the harvest, pottery-making, weaving, hunting, etc. The monastery possesses collections of ritual vessels, parts of sutras, rare documents. Remains of an old wall outside are said to date from the Ming.

The Sa jia Monastery

The **Sa jia Monastery (Sa jia si)** is classed as a historical monument, and is about 105 miles south-west of Shigatse; a dangerous road goes through **Xi ka,** and **Zhan zong.** From **Zhan zong,** the last lap of the journey, through marshes, desert-like mountains and valleys, as far as the site of the monastery, about 15 miles from the River **Sa jia,** is done on horseback.

It is a large religious centre, made up of two monasteries, one to the north and the other to the south; to the south, a massive building, surrounded by vertical walls, all based on straight lines, rises out of the plain; the northern part, built up against the mountain in typically Tibetan style, consists of tier upon tier of buildings, with a wide base, narrowing off to the top. The southern part was built in 1268. **Sa jia** was the head of it at the beginning, and **Ben qin** succeeded him when he died; he built the enclosure and the various buildings which still survive today. They have changed little since the Yuan dynasty when they were built, and are in an excellent state of preservation; in spite of a few small additions, they constitute an invaluable source of information on the history of architecture.

The southern monastery consists of a Great Hall of the Sutras surrounded by several other halls full of varied statues. In the back of the great hall, sutras are stored on shelves (some of them extremely rare; there are several thousand of them altogether). In the hall itself are countless statues, some of them magnificent ones, and Chinese porcelain dating from the Qing dynasty mainly, but also from the Ming and the Yuan, precious ritual vessels, brocades etc.... An old flight of stairs leads to the floor above, where the frescoes are. The outer walls are most impressive, with their corner towers, their gates and their battlements,

The northern part dates from the Song (1079); according to some sources, it was built as early as 1034. It is a large, rather haphazard building, which fell on bad days at the beginning of the Ming dynasty. The Great Hall, the **Wu ze la kang,** is the main building; most of the roofs are decorated with gold (dating from the Qing probably) but the main structure of beams and pillars is as it was. It contains some magnificent statues, particularly the statues of Bodhisattvas. It is said that the original wall proved too thin, so that a second one had to be added, hiding the wall paintings on the first one; irregularities in the second wall give glimpses of superb frescoes, which have retained all their former freshness.

The second floor of the great hall consists of three halls, all in perfect state of repair, built in the style of the Yuan dynasty. Frescoes between the beams are also unmistakably Yuan. The double doors are decorated with Yuan carvings, of quite exceptional workmanship.

Two other rooms, the **Xiong ya xiao kang** and the **Gang ka xiao kang** also contain Yuan frescoes, which are unfortunately damaged.

A cave (said to be the original monastery) contains a statue of **Gong ge ning bao** and his wife (**Gong ge ning bao** had the monastery restored 800 years ago).

It is disappointing to find that the monastery has not the usual collection of treasures; it was looted at some time in its history. A few Yuan and Ming objects still remain: the oldest of all are the scroll paintings.

The library, on the other hand, is a particularly rich one, the oldest and richest in Tibet. The library of the southern part of the monastery contains works of various kinds, instead of sutras: chronicles, astronomical treatises, medical treatises, and the chronicles of some famous Lamas, all of which is unusual for a monastery library. Most of the works, and the library contains over 2,500 volumes, date from the Yuan or the Ming. The northern monastery library possesses texts in Sanskrit, Chinese and Mongol, etc.... (about 2,000 volumes), as well as commentaries, glosses on religious subjects, all of which are of the greatest interest. Among them, for examples, is a set of sutras, printed in Peking in 1256 (555 scrolls).

From Shigatse to Ya dong and Jiang zi

The road runs south-east alongside the River **Nian shu** (the way is likely to be impassable from July to September, because of the heavy rain). **Jiang zi** is about 60 miles from Shigatse, at 12,800 feet above sea level. It is worth making a detour to go and see **Ya dong,** near the Himalayas, with magnificent views over the mountains.

The way leads first of all through a precipitous region which is extremely cold, because of the altitude. After the **Sang da Dam,** the country opens out, and when the mists part the third highest peak of the Himalayas, the **Zhe duo la,** and even the second, the **Mu duo la,** can be seen. Then the way runs alongside **Lake Lo mo. Pa li** is 12 miles from there, to the south. Built at an altitude of 14,100 feet, **Pa li** is certainly the highest town in the world. The road leads down from there towards twisting valleys, bare of all vegetation, and then comes out into a stretch of green landscape, before taking an alarmingly steep plunge down through lower mountains amid the din of countless waterfalls and mountain torrents. Finally **Ya dong** is reached, where the traveller is rewarded by a breathtaking view of chains of mountains disappearing into mists tinged with delicate colours.

The **Ya dong** valley has a mild, moist climate; the surrounding mountain-sides are covered with forests of different sorts of trees, and the crops flourish.

Ya dong was a centre of anti-British resistance, like **Kang ma,** about three miles away. The Snow Scrip Monastery, the **Xue nang si,** now in ruins, stands on a cliff at Kang ma.

About 6 miles before reaching **Jiang zi,** the road passes the remains of the **Nai ni Monastery (Nai ni si),** which was converted into a stronghold during the war of resistance.

Jiang zi itself contains several monasteries and monuments of quite exceptional interest: the **Zi jin si,** the **Bai ju si,** the **Da pu ti ta pagoda** and the **Zhuang yuan** or the **Zhuang zi** estate, near **Jiang zi.**

The **Xue nang si** at **Kang ma** will be described first of all.

The Xue nang si at Kang ma

The monastery is a small one, and most of the rooms are now used by the public. The Great Hall contains only five rooms, with 7 statues of the Buddha and one of the Maitreya, of fairly crude workmanship. The lotus flowers which carry them, and the pillars supporting the building, are carved with various designs and animals (lions) executed with great vigour and close attention to detail. The style recalls the pillars in the **Xia lu Monastery** at Shigatse; they were all made under the Yuan or at the beginning of the Ming dynasty.

The walls are covered with paintings which are full of life; they too probably date from the Ming. They have unfortunately suffered badly from the damp.

A brick pagoda stands outside, like the one at the northern monastery at **Sa jia.** It is not tall, but is fairly

big-bellied, unlike most of late Ming or early Qing
pagodas; it may well have been built at an earlier date.
It is open to the public.

The Zhuang zi "Estate"

The village of **Zhuang zi** is about 12 miles from
Jiang zi on the way back to Shigatse, and contains a
remarkable house known as the **Zhuang yuan.** It is
said to be over 600 years old; when Zong Ka pa came
back to Tibet from Qing hai, he is supposed to have
gone to live there two years after his return.

It is five stories high, and its style, structure and even
the materials used, are completely different from those
of similar buildings. It certainly is old; all the wood-
work (staircase, beams, struts) is unchanged. Except
for the fifth storey, which was restored later on, the
style is crude; the inside is in almost complete darkness. It used to be the local landlord's house; the
minute, gloomy rooms housed his relations and other
important people. Each year, the local population was
summoned to pay its respects to the landlord in a
room specially for that purpose, on the fourth floor,
which is still in a good state of repair. The ground floor
was used for storing forage and agricultural tools.
A fixed staircase was built as far as the first floor only:
a ladder was used to reach the floors above.

Zong Ka pa lived for a time in the **Zhuang zi
Monastery (Zhuang zi si)** not far away; it was founded
by one of his brothers. It is later than the **Bai ju si,** but
earlier than the three big monasteries in Lhasa, and
dates from about 1400. It is fairly small; it consists of
a great hall and two rooms of archives. In 1904, it was
looted and partly burned. The frescoes on its walls are
in a rough but lively style, and are probably earlier
than the Qing; there are also some magnificent statues

(among them a bronze statue of Sakyamuni, and two Bodhisattvas). Five pagodas of different sizes stand outside, all probably early Ming.

The Zi jin si

The **Zi jin (Purple gold) Monastery** is several miles away from **Jiang zi**; it is part of the oldest group of monasteries in the region (the others are the **Jiang zi Monastery** and the **Bai ju si**).

It used to have nine annex halls as well as the Great Hall; during the resistance to the British in 1904, it was looted, burned and almost completely destroyed.

The Bai ju si

The **Bai ju si Monastery** (also called the **Ban gen si**) is behind the **Jiang zi Mountain,** west of the town. The central hall contains statues of four terrifying demon kings (Tchaturmaharadjas). The Great Hall is also worth a visit. Documents kept in the monastery give the date of foundation of the main building as 1365. Originally it had 17 rooms of archives as well.

The **Cuo qing da dian,** the Great Hall of the Sutras, has three stories. The ground floor contains paintings of Sakyamuni, statues of the four demon kings, of the masters of the Law, of Bodhisattvas, etc. In the Hall of the Sutras (smaller than the ones in the big monasteries in Lhasa) 48 large pillars support the roof. A side hall contains statues of monsters, suits of armour, weapons and banners. A **Jing tu dian** lies on each side of the Great Hall. The back wall of the Great Hall is covered with a set of very old paintings. Behind them is a statue of the Maitreya whose head reaches to the second floor. The annex halls contain numerous statues and paintings (among them are representations of

Zong Ka pa and his two brothers). A magnificent statue of Guan yin behind the Great Hall has a thousand arms, a thousand eyes and eleven faces. A thousand Buddhas decorate the verandas.

The eastern **Jing tu dian** includes five large halls; the first two are divided into a series of niches with statues (Sakyamuni, Guan yin) and some beautiful carving, including Guan yin, several Tibetan kings, and the masters of the Law. The walls are covered with statues of the Buddha in glory, of simple and vigorous design.

The western **Jing tu dian** is on the same lines; it contains some beautiful caskets, statues, paintings and frescoes.

The second floor of the Great Hall includes the treasure chamber, several halls of the Sutras, frescoes depicting the life of the Buddha, carved doors, etc....

The third floor has a ceiling with a hexagonal design on it, which may be the only one of its kind in Tibet, as well as numerous statues and several sets of wall paintings.

The monastery forms a complete whole, from an architectural point of view and from the point of view of the works of art which it contains; the frescoes and paintings are originals, and have never been touched up or restored.

Da pu ti sa

This magnificent pagoda consists of five stories tapering off towards the top one, surmounted by a three-storey cylindrical tower. It is called the **Ban gen qu de** or **Da pu ti (Great Bodhisattvas) Pagoda. Bu dun** is said to have founded it in 1414, at the beginning of the Ming dynasty; it has altogether 108 doors, 76 niches (20 on the first floor, 16 on the second, 20 on the third, 16 on the fourth, 4 on the fifth; the four remaining floors do not contain separate rooms). All the niches contain different statues (over 1,000 altogether), and paintings (55 of Bodhisattvas, and about 10,000 of the Buddha).

The structure of the building is most unusual: each facet of the base has eight corners, with different designs each time (doors, entrances, etc.); each part has a symbolic function, unfortunately too long to go into here.

The first three stories are decorated with paintings of the Buddha and Bodhisattvas. The fourth has statues of the masters of the Law.

The statues are superb; they show a strong Nepalese influence, whereas the frescoes, painted in an easy, lively style, show Indian or Nepalese influence.

The pagoda contains a large collection of valuable objects: ritual vessels, offerings, carvings, jewels, lamps, gapula (bowls made from crania), rare editions of sutras, etc....

THE ZE DANG REGION

From Lhasa to Ze dang and Nai dong

The Tibet to Qing hai road leaves Lhasa and goes north-west; at **Dong ga zong** it forks, and the southern branch runs along beside the River Lhasa, to cross it at **Qu shui** (The Meanders), near the point where it flows into the **Ya lu tang bu,** about 24 miles from Lhasa. Once over the river, the road divides into two: one leads west (Lhasa to **Jiang zi**); the other goes east, sometimes running alongside the **Ya lu tang bu**; it is rather dangerous (stretches of soft sand, deserted mountain areas). Near this road, a little temple founded 500 years ago by **Tang dong jie bu** stands on a mountain top.

The road finally reaches **Ze dang** (about 142 miles from Lhasa). The area is traditionally thought to be the first one to practise agriculture in Tibet; a cave is pointed out, which was the scene of a goddess' love for a monkey; their child, originally a monkey, gradually turned into a man.

A monastery in Ze dang **(Ga jiu si)** contains a stele dating from the Tang. On the outskirts of the town, to the west, remains of walls dating from the Yuan are still standing in places, with the ruins of several brick pagodas.

Nai dong is a mile and a half south of **Ze dang**; remains of old walls and the **Ze cuo ba Monastery (Se cuo ba si)** lie in a mountainous depression. The annals of the monastery record that it was founded in 1356 by King **Pa mo**; the original building was small, and was west of the present one, which was the archives; the great hall and the side verandas of the old monastery can still be seen. (It contains pillars and frescoes; the side verandas contain statues.) The **Ze cuo ba si** includes five or six stories of buildings spreading down the mountainside; three of them constitute the chief floors, the rest are the monks' cells. The verandas in front of the Great Hall contain frescoes which probably date from the Qing. The Great Hall itself contains a collection of sutras, and some undistinguished statues. Another set of statues behind it show a pronounced Chinese influence; the sutras written in gold on parchment were brought from India by the third Panchen Lama. Among other treasures, the monastery owns a magnificent Buddha embroidered on silk, which even if it is not Tang, as is generally thought, is almost certainly Ming; it is a superb piece of work.

The Zan tang si

The **Zan tang si Monastery** (also called the **Yu yi la kang**) is just under 2 miles south-west of **Nai dong**, near the **Ya long** river. It is supposed to have been founded by one of the wives of King Song zan gan bu. The **Chang zhu Monastery** can be seen opposite it, in the distance.

The **Zan tang si** is relatively small; a gate and a courtyard lead into the main hall and five annex halls: three halls of sutras and two others (constituting the original building). Various frescoes decorate the far wall; the carved colonnade is interesting, as are the beams (they consist of a network of false beams as well as the normal structure). Some fine statues stand in the centre: several Buddhas and eight large Bodhisattvas.

The side verandas contain a set of frescoes and paintings. The floor above has been restored. The architecture as a whole is ancient; the statues are a little rough in style, which is typical of the early Ming carving (they have been changed however by frequent regilding). A pagoda stands about 500 yards behind the monastery; the remains of King **Song zan gan bu** are buried there.

The Yong mu la kang Monastery

The **Yong mu la kang Monastery** stands on the top of a rocky ridge 3 miles or so south-east of **Nai dong**, on the east bank of the River **Ya long**. It is thought to be the oldest monastery in Tibet. A legend tells how when King **Song zan gan bu** went to live at Lhasa, the Tibetan people soon afterwards went to live in the Ya long area, and the king had this monastery built.

It is divided into two parts: first a three storey building, and then another which looks more like a tall fort or tower than a temple. They are built up against each other, and each part is small; they are said to have been built with fragments of stone, rather than blocks (though the fragments are cut, even so). The first set of buildings is square. The main door gives into a large hall with three subdivisions each way, devoid of all ornamentation. The halls which follow contain statues of the Buddha and frescoes depicting the kings Song zan gan bu and Chi song de zan.

There are other statues and frescoes in the side halls (the archives); the most remarkable of them all are the old carvings, one of which is a Sakyamuni in the oldest Tibetan style (short wide face, long slanting eyes, and the ears characteristic of this type of carving), which is unique.

A ladder behind the halls gives access to a wing with some extremely narrow monks' cells; it also leads to the second floor, which is divided into several rooms. It contains a number of bronze statues. The third floor is a flat terrace.

The back of the building is a courtyard surrounded by verandas with frescoes; the verandas are scarcely a yard high.

Beyond this is the tower, which is empty except for a ladder going up to the top.

The monastery as a whole has no traces of old buildings, as might have been expected; all the wooden infrastructure is comparatively recent. The statues, on the other hand, seem to be much earlier than the foundation date of the monastery.

The Chang zhu Monastery

The **Chang zhu Monastery (Chang zhu si)** is on the eastern bank of the Ya long, a mile and a half from **Nai gong,** facing the **Yu yi la kang si** at a distance. It is traditionally supposed to have been founded in the reign of King Song zan gan bu. It is certainly extremely old; the **Nai ding xue** hall bears this out. It is fairly small, and the second floor is called the **Nai ding dang.** Numerous frescoes of the Buddha decorate the far wall of the lower hall. The hall is said to have been built originally of wood and thatch (it is now of wood and brick), and to have been restored by Gong ma (1351) and by the seventh Dalai Lama. The oldest buildings are certainly earlier than King Pa mo. The central part is the **Cuo qing da dian**; behind the great entrance gateway hangs a big bell which is probably Tang or Song, and is a very precious object. A narrow courtyard gives way to the Great Hall, with verandas and statues. The vast hall following it is the hall of the sutras; behind that are halls with very fine intersecting beams and carved pillars. The overall effect of the ground floor of the Great Hall resembles the hall of the **Da zhao si** at Lhasa; but the verandas round it are supported by a system of columns carrying cross beams, some of them extremely old, of a most unusual style (the beams are carved with lotus petals). The walls of the Great Hall are extraordinarily thick; the annex halls are hollowed out of them.

The western hall contains statues of Zong Ka pa and of Dalai Lamas, while the other, to the east, has some arresting statues of **Fa shen:** one, a sitting statue, is black and horrifying; the other is a sort of long-beaked monster, in a vigorous, somewhat rough style. The two statues are unique; they have no equivalent in other Tibetan monasteries. The halls which follow

contain more statues of different kinds, most of them
carved in an ancient, rather crude style, as well as a set
of frescoes. These seven halls contain countless masterpieces which often betray a marked Chinese influence.
In front of the main hall are wooden statues and carved
pillars; in the corners of the verandas preceding it stand
little pagodas.

A beautiful statue of Guan yin with a Thousand
Hands stands in the eighth hall; an annex hall is the
treasure chamber; the ninth hall contains three standing statues of Bodhisattvas; the tenth contains Buddhas, with a superb niche housing a seated Guan yin;
in the eleventh hall are several more niches; the
twelfth hall is the hall of Zong Ka pa. Finally, little
pagodas stand at the ends of the north and south verandas, said to be by **Song zan gan bu.**

The western part of the second floor of the Great
Hall contains rooms for recreation and rest, where
ritual vessels (many of them in bronze) and, for
instance, a bronze cover dating from the Ming (the
Xuan de period), are kept. The halls to the south contain countless statues, a rich library of sutras, frescoes,
a magnificent incense-burner, etc....

This monastery, although a small one, houses an
incredible accumulation of jewels of Buddhist art.

QIONG JIE (TOMBS OF THE TIBETAN KINGS)

The way to the tombs leaves **Ze dang** to the east and
follows the **Ya long** in a south-easterly direction. It
passes the enormous remains of walls and pagodas at
Ma ni, rather like the ones near the **Chang zhu Monastery.** The road from **Ze dang** to **Qiong jie** is extremely
arduous and it takes half a day to cover it, although
the distance is only 30 miles.

A little further along the **Ya long** a group of tombs can be seen south-west of the **Qiong jie Mountains**. They are known as the **Ban shi zhu**. The eight tombs, outlined against the horizon, look exactly like natural hills; one is much larger than the others. They are on three different levels; the top of each one is oval, flat, and 180 paces long from east to west. Earthern ramparts surround them on the side nearest the river, and a sort of bank with sloping sides links them. Hexagonal niches, about 3 feet deep, contain clay figures of Buddhas, pagodas etc... Two magnificent stone lions stand on the second level.

Another tomb rises north of the road, over 38 feet high, with stone steps leading up to the flat top; a little temple in front of it houses statues of Song zan gan bu and his wives, while a wall nearby is engraved with a funerary inscription in Tibetan.

Three tombs rise to the north of the highest one, with a stele near them, surmounted by a square block of stone, its corners upturned towards the sky, and a stone sphere. The stele dates from the Tang; the inscription is still legible, particularly at the top; the calligraphy is simple and powerful in style. It is 7 feet high; it was erected in memory of a victory, by Chi de song zan, and one facet bears an inscription in old Tibetan.

The two tombs near it have enormous hollows in them, caused either by the weather or robbers.

Another Tang stele stands near the road to Qiong jie.

The legends disagree as to the number of tombs in the area, but it is usually thought that there are eight altogether, and eight kings of Tibet: Song zan gan bu, Nang song mang zan, Du song mang bao, Jiang ca la ban, Chi dai zhu dan, Chi song dai zan, Mu nei zan bao, Chi zu dai zan re ba jin, are supposed to be buried there.

The list is taken from old records, and it tallies with the number of tombs visible, but the only way to check it is by systematic archaeological research.

Qiong jie itself is well worth a visit after seeing the tombs; it is a fortress built on a completely inaccessible peak, consisting of five stories with loopholes, battlements and precipitous walls.

Nearby is a little monastery known as **Ri wu de qing,** which was founded 500 years ago by a local figure, Jia er duo qin; it has a small main hall, a minute courtyard with verandas and frescoes, which are uneven in style, although certainly old, a large statue of Mandjusri and statues of the eight Bodhisattvas.

LANG SE LIN

On leaving **Ze dang,** the road follows the **Ya lu tang bu** as far as the Meanders, and then a way leads west to the village of **Za ji,** about 18 miles away, in the **Za cuo** region, which is a fertile alluvial basin. Next comes a stretch of thorny plants and scree, and the best way of reaching the mountain nearby is on foot. A large almond tree can be seen in the distance, and near it, the **Lang se lin,** which is a "country house" not unlike the one already described. It is a seven storey building, 600 years old, and in perfect condition; the inside consists of tiny rooms with narrow ladders leading from one floor to the next, all in almost total darkness. The ground floor is the store-room, the first floor, the treasure chamber; the hall of the sutras is on the third floor; the sixth contains the main living quarters; and the seventh is a terrace with a wide view over the whole of the neighbouring village. The hall of the sutras contains various ritual vessels and offerings, and a statue of **Ga ma ba,** carved in a rather crude, rough style. The house is encircled by two walls, 16½ feet wide at the top, with battlements. A little tower stands south of the house, with a threshing floor of the most astonishing size near it, which gives a good idea of the power of the local landlords (up till recently, none of the villagers dared to enter the house and its surroundings).

MIN ZHU LIN

The **Min zhu lin** is perched high up at the end of a valley, in the o**a cuo** region, under the sub-prefecture of **Za lang,** ab ut 6 miles west of **Lang se lin.**

This large monastery is one of the high places of the Tibetan Red Sect. It was founded in 1671, by Die da lin ba, the first living Buddha to appear in the place. A beautiful white pagoda stands in front of the monastery, made up of five stories built in a strange angular style, with countless niches and statues, topped by a tower.

The monastery has a large group of buildings; the main ones only will be mentioned. Several stone steps lead up to the **Great Hall (Zu la kang),** which is built from east to west; verandas and annex buildings stand in front of it, giving access to the floor above. There are some interesting frescoes and halls of the sutras, statues of saints, monks, the Buddha, the Bodhisattvas.

In the hall behind it are statues of Sakyamuni and the Eight Bodhisattvas, and some frescoes. The **Du kang,** west of the Great Hall (with the largest halls in the monastery) contains a powerful statue of **Die da lin ba.**

Both the **Zu la kang** and the **Du kang** are the original buildings, and have never been restored.

The **Sun qiong,** with the funerary pagoda of Die da lin ba, lies north of the **Du kang.** Another group of buildings, in an unusual style, called the Nan mu jie, are next to it.

All the halls are full of beautiful things, some of them extremely valuable, such as some superb Chinese seals dating from the Ming dynasty.

SANG YUAN SI

The traveller leaves **Za cuo** by car, taking with him a Tibetan leather boat... The road follows the **Ya lu tang bu,** going upstream; then the party takes to the boat, which although made of leather which is so fragile that it has to have a flooring of wooden planks, can still accommodate up to twelve people. After about two hours, a certain spot on the other bank is reached which is only about an hour's ride on horseback from the **Sang yuan Monastery.** The barren stretch in front of the monastery is the site of the former capital of King Chi song de zan (a few remains of it are left).

The **Sang yuan Monastery,** whose old name was **Wu deng bo lai** was founded in the middle of the 8th century; the Great Hall and four pagodas all date from then (the pagodas are red, white, green and black, and with the Great Hall they form a beautiful group).

A magnificent stele stands south of the **Great Hall (Wu ce)** near the main gate, with an inscription in old Tibetan, still intact, which is even older than the steles near the tombs of the kings of Tibet. The top of it is inset with a crescent-shaped jewel; it is altogether an extremely unusual and rare type of stele.

The Chinese inscription over the door of the Great Hall dates from the Qing. The veranda nearby contains a Tang bronze bell, and a superbly powerful stone lion, possibly of a later date.

The Great Hall is on an east-west axis, surrounded by walls and wide verandas supported by pillars. Its three stories are all in different styles: the ground floor is Tibetan, the first floor Chinese, and the third Indian. Although only three stories high, it is a tall building. The verandas contain numerous statues, all different: **Fa shen** riding lions or mules, etc... carved in most forceful style. The Hall of the Sutras contains statues and frescoes. Severals halls lie behind, of unusual style, with walls over 10 feet thick, and magnificent frescoes. A terrace nearby has a niche and a large Sakyamuni, as well as large Bodhisattvas.

The four pagodas of the ministers of King Chi song de zan stand at the corners of the Great Hall, each one different from the rest.

The Green Pagoda: The first and second floors contain statues; the third contains the treasures. The main body of the pagoda is covered in dark green glazed tiles; architecturally speaking, it is a masterpiece.

Tha Black Pagoda: Its shape is strange, rather like three lids one on top of the other; like the green one, it contains treasures. It is made of black bricks.

The Red Pagoda: This is the most unusual shape of all; it is bell-shaped, and made of bricks which look square, but are round. Like the others, it contains treasures. The bricks are red and shiny.

The White Pagoda: It resembles the white pagoda of the Bei hai Lake at Peking, with a square base, tapering off to a dome, all pure white.

This group of pagodas is unique in Tibet. The green one slightly resembles the Shigatse pagoda, but it is a more beautiful version; the red and black ones have no equivalent in Tibet, and the white is of a type which is rare there.

CHAMDO

One place only will be mentioned in eastern Tibet: the great centre where sutras are printed, **Chamdo (Chang du).**

N.B.: Chinese documents have been used here: a table of the kings of Tibet (traditional names, names used in historical documents, Chinese names given in the *Xin Tang Shu*, notes) can be found in *Wen wu* 1961, No 4/5, p. 87.

XIN JIANG

(Map see end of the book)

The Uighur autonomous region of Xin jiang, in the north-west of China, is the largest province in the country. It represents 1/6th of the total Chinese territory. It borders on the People's Republic of Mongolia, the Soviet Union, Afghanistan, Pakistan, India, the Autonomous Region of Tibet, and the provinces of Qing hai and Gan su.

This vast area has 5,640,000 inhabitants, less than 4 inhabitants to the square mile. The population consists of extremely varied ethnic groups. The Uighurs (Chinese *Wei wu er*) alone make up two thirds of the total. The rest is composed of the **Ha long ke** (1/10th of the population), Hui, Mongols, Kazakhs, Tadjiks, Uzbecks, Tatars, Russians, Han, Manchu, Khalkhas, Tahûrs, Olös, Sibos, Tcherkess. Districts and autonomous counties of Khazaks, Mongols, Hui and Khalkhas have been created. The autonomy of the region was officially recognised in 1954.

Xin jiang means the "New Marches". The **Tian shan Mountains** run from east to west, cutting Xin jiang into two natural divisions, the **Nan jiang** (to the south) and the **Bei jiang** (to the north). The average height of the mountains is 10,000 to 13,000 feet, and the highest peak is **Mount Han teng ge li**, 23,165 feet high, near the Soviet frontier. The **Tu lu fan** depression (Turfan) lies between two branches of the chain. It is 500 feet below sea level, and is the lowest point in all China. It is an exceptionally fertile oasis, about 90 miles long. South of the **Tian shan Mountains** lies the Tarim basin, of an average altitude of 3,300 feet, shut in by chains of high mountains, to the north, south and west. The Taklamakan desert occupies most of it.

Oases lie round the edge of the basin: Khotan, at the foot of the **Kun lun Mountains**, Kashgar at the foot of the Pamir Plateau, and Aksu at the foot of the **Tian shan Mountains**. The Tarim river, fed by the mountain snows, is the longest inland watercourse in China. Part of its waters sink into the sand, and part flow into Lake Lob nor. The Dzungarian basin stretches north of the **Tian shan Mountains,** covered mainly by grassland.

The climate in Xin jiang is dry. Agriculture prospers only in the oases or in areas where extensive irrigation work has been undertaken (water is brought by underground canals, *kerese*, in the Turfan and Hami depressions).

Before the invention of the compass in the 12th century enabled the Chinese to travel by sea to Asia and the West, all the communications were based on land routes across Central Asia, and Xin jiang. The road went from one oasis to the next; each one was a little kingdom. The kingdoms totalled 36 under the Western Han (206 B.C. — 25 A.D.), and rose to over 40 under the Eastern Han (25 — 220 A.D.). Han China was threatened by the Huns from the north *(Xiong nu)*, who traded with the oases: they depended on them for their grain supply.

To drive the Huns farther back, the Han Emperor Wu (Han Wu di, 140 — 86 B.C.) launched several large military expeditions to extend the Chinese sphere of influence. China then came into direct contact with Central Asia, India and the Roman Empire (see the expedition of Zhang qian, p. 112) and a strong current of economic and religious exchanges began. Buddhism penetrated from India, moving from oasis to oasis, from the 1st century A.D. (see map, p. 240). China in turn exported silk to the Roman Empire, where it was worth literally its weight in gold. The silk route was divided into two in fact. The northern one started at Lan zhou, and went through **Wu wei, Zhang ye, Jiu quan, An xi, Dun huang,** Turfan, and ran alongside the Tian shan Mountains to the south, through **Wu shi,** Kucha, Aksu, Kashgar, and on to Samarkand. The southern route split off at **Dun huang** and ran alongside the Kun lun Mountains to the north, through **Ruo qiang, Qie mo, Yu tian, He tian** (Khotan) and went on to Afghanistan and India. Under the Northern and Southern Dynasties and the Tang, countless Buddhist pilgrims travelled the two routes to India (Fa Xian, Xuan Zang). Tang China was immensely enriched by its close links with Central Asia (the decorative arts, dancing, music, etc...). When the Chinese empire grew weaker during the second half of the 8th century, the Arab empire grew correspondingly stronger, and extended its influence more and more over Xin jiang.

Since the liberation, the Chinese government has begun to develop the region's natural resources. A railway line has been built to Urumchi (**Wu lu mu qi**). Modern industrial centres have grown up round the numerous deposits of oil, iron, sulphur, phosphorus, salt, etc... The main centres are Urumchi, Yi ning and Kashgar. The most important oil field is at Karamai, near Urumchi. Cotton is grown on a large scale in the Tarim and Turfan depressions, and modern mills now exist at Urumchi,

Kashgar, Khotan, Shihhotse. New land is being brought under
cultivation (Manass is one of the big centres, in the north),
and large mechanised state farms have been created. The People's
Liberation Army has transformed thousands of acres of desert
into fertile fields.

Wheat is grown on half of the total land under cultivation.
Next in order comes rice, then maize, sorgho and millet. Fruit
is grown in large quantities round the oases (grapes, melons,
apricots, apples and other fruit). Owing to its climate, Xin
jiang, if properly irrigated, can eventually be turned into a
fertile and prosperous province. Its mineral resources should
enable it to become one of the most important industrial centres
in China. The government has carried out atomic experiments
in the desert regions.

NORTH XIN JIANG (BEI JIANG)

It has been attached to China since the Yuan dynasty.
Archaeological excavations carried out here have been
scanty so far, and the little work that has been done
had political motives behind it. The British and the
Russians were rivals in Xin jiang as early on as 1900:
as the British had control over India, and the Russians
over Central Asia, the former were anxious to balance
this by extending their influence to Afghanistan and
the neighbouring area; geographical and meteorological expeditions were sent to the **Tian shan Mountains.**
The archaeological finds were disappointing, particularly north of the **Tian shan.** Among them were:

1. Remains of a citadel at **Pu lei** (near a large battlefield, scene of a battle between the Chinese and the
Xiong nu, under the Han), not yet uncovered scientifi-
cally.

2. Tang steles, found near the Tang citadel of **Jin
man** (now **Gu cheng zi**).

3. Remains of the Han citadel of **Shu le**, near modern
Di hua.

4. Various remains near the citadel of **A shan ta,** not far from Siberia.

SOUTH XIN JIANG NAN (JIANG)

From the second century B.C. onwards, several large cultural centres grew up in the south of Xin jiang: Turfan, Kucha, Khotan *(He tian)* on the northern slopes of the **Kun lun Mountains,** and **Yu tian.**

These four centres are all different from each other: Turfan shows marked Indian, Chinese and Iranian influences; Indian sculpture has been found there; the town is the centre of an oasis, and used to be the centre of a powerful empire (music and dancing were particularly popular there, and had a strong influence on Chinese music under the Jin). **Yu tian** was a centre of Indian culture before the Chinese arrived. Generally speaking, they were all flourishing towns towards the second century B.C.; the Indian and Iranian cultures gradually gave way to the growing Chinese influence, until the 7th century. After the victory of the Arabs, Islam became widespread, until the 14th century or thereabouts.

The road from **An xi** to Hami and Turfan goes through the so-called "red" mountains; there, on either side of the **River Tu gu jiang,** monasteries have been hollowed out of the hillside; a temple used to stand here too. Frescoes of different periods still survive: Six Dynasties, Tang, Song, and inscriptions in different languages. 9 miles outside Turfan, the Vine River (the area has always been famous for its vineyards) flows through a narrow gorge, where caves have been hollowed out of the cliffs. The remains of three fortresses can be seen 9 miles from **Sheng jin kou,** dug over in the past by countless

Western archaeologists. The walls and the palace are still standing. It was the area of the **Huo** circuit *(Huo zhou)* under the Yuan.

The town of Turfan itself is divided into two parts, east and west. Outside the west part, 6 miles from the town, lies Lake **Ya er:** under the Han, the citadel of **Jiao he** stood near there, and numerous old tombs dot the area even now.

The **Bo zi ke li ke** caves are about 25 miles southeast of Turfan. A set of caves has been discovered in the mountainside, dating from different periods, from the Six Dynasties to the Tang, the Song, the Ming, with frescoes, documents, etc...

A large well at Turfan itself, called the **Kang er jing,** is said to have been built at the same time as the Great Wall.

To the west, the road goes through **Qian qiang** to **Yan shi,** once the centre of a powerful empire, and one of the Buddhist high places.

A ford below the citadel of **Yan shi** leads across the river to the remains of the **Ming shi** (a Thousand Pieces) about 12 miles away. **Yan shi** contains several temples, caves and monasteries, which have been systematically emptied by English, German and Japanese archaeologists. In the **Tian shan Mountains** north of the **Ming shi** are the remains of an old fortified town. The **Xi ke xin** caves are 24 miles west of **Yan shi.**

The Kucha and **Gui zi** region is west of Turfan. The **Ma za bo he** caves are 18 miles north-east of Kucha, and the **Sen mu sa ma** caves are north-west of them. 3 miles north of Kucha are the **He dun er ga ka** caves; and the **Ku mu tu la** caves are 15 miles southwest of Kucha.

The sub-prefecture of **Sha ya** contains countless remains of caves and monasteries. 18 miles south-west of Kucha, over the **Bridge of the Three Roads (San dao qiao)** spanning the River **Wei gan,** are more caves, on the border of the **Bai cheng** sub-prefecture, which is itself famous for its caves; the latter have been carefully "explored" by Western archaeologists, but many were hidden under the sand and contained beautiful frescoes, and inscriptions in *tu huo luo* (the old language of the country of **Gui zi**). The caves of **Tuo hu la ke dian** are about 2 miles west of **Bai cheng.**

The next town is **Aksu**, followed by a strip of desert, with Kashgar on the other side; Han and Hui minorities live in this area. Near the town of *Shu le* rises the magnificent tomb of Ma za er, who was one of Qian long's concubines. At **Xiao a tu shen,** 9 miles north-west of the town, three caves have been hollowed out of the side of the cliff (they contain the names of a group of archaeologists from several different countries engraved on the rock).

Turfan contains no trace of all the ancient remains which used to exist in the area; the town has no museum. At the same time, no systematic archaeological work has yet been done on the Silk Routes. Many of the tombs at Turfan have not yet been opened. At **Bai cheng** some of the caves have been covered by landslides (a Chinese archaeologist, Mr. Han Le ran, has spent a long time working there).

Historical remains are still standing at the other end of the Silk Route:

1) Remains of the Han Great Wall have survived near the two barriers, **Yu men guan** and **Yang guan ;** at that time, it stretched from **Dun huang** to Ning xia, All the remains have been classed as historical

monuments. In some places, the remains of the wall are over 10 feet high, with a watchtower *(feng dun)* every five or ten *li*.

The Han Great Wall is completely different from the Ming Great Wall; the Ming built theirs as a defensive measure, whereas the Han Wall was built as part of an attack; it encircled all the fertile land in the area, water and grassland, and beyond it was the desert. It had an economic as well as a strategic role, and within it was a military colony in charge of the upkeep. Countless breaches were made in the Ming wall over 300 years, whereas the Han wall is still intact; it was built of a mixture of clay and reeds which can stand up indefinitely to the wind. British archaeologists found documents relevant to the building, and inscriptions on wood dating from about the beginning of the Christian era, with strategical information, armourers' accounts, medical prescriptions, etc... near **Yu men guan.**

2) Going north-eastwards from **Dun huang,** remains of old citadels can still be seen.

3) At **Dun huang** itself are the Thousand Buddha Caves (see Gan su).

4) **Hei cheng,** on the borders of Xin jiang, Gan su and Qing hai, was founded by the *Xi xia* and fell into ruins at the end of the Yuan dynasty. (A Russian archaeological expedition worked there from 1889–1890.)

BAI CHENG (Buddhist Caves)

Under the Han and the Tang, the sub-prefecture of Bai cheng was part of the sub-prefecture of **Ku che** (Kucha), in the country of **Gui zi.** Under the Western Han links were created between China and **Gui zi** which became stronger still under the Tang. In the second century A.D., Indian Buddhism spread to Central Asia; at this time, and during the centuries which followed, the Silk Route, or at least the Northern Silk Route, went through **Gui zi**: the Southern Silk Route (south of the **Tian shan Mountains**) went through **He tian** (Khotan).

Buddhist artistic remains are therefore particularly abundant at **Bai cheng** and at **He tian**.

No documents exist referring to the exact date of the **He se er Caves** (near **Bai cheng**); it is certain, however, that under the Jin and the Northern and Southern Dynasties (3rd to 6th centuries), Buddhism flourished in China, and that there were countless wandering monks. The **Dun huang Caves** date from before the 4th century; the monk **Jiu mo luo shen**, from **Gui zi**, went to China at the beginning of the 5th century; the country of **Gui zi** had reached a high standard of civilisation, and Buddhism was flourishing there; according to contemporary documents, the capital contained "a thousand Buddhist pagodas and temples". The **He se er Caves** are therefore probably earlier than the 4th or 5th century, and they were probably added to under the Tang.

The two sub-prefectures of **Bai cheng** and **Ku che** contain eight groups of "Thousand Buddha Caves" between them. The *He se er Caves* are relatively important because they are numerous and large; they were one of the best known monuments of Buddhist art in Xin jiang. English archaeologists started work there in 1890. They were followed by the Germans, the French and the Japanese (the Berlin museum possessed over twenty frescoes from "eastern Turkestan"). The caves are near a river, in cliffs which have crumbled over the years; 160 out of the total of 235 still have frescoes in them; the paintings have kept their freshness, like the ones at **Dun huang.** The name **He se er** means "red" in Uighur.

The style of the caves is Chinese, but it is nevertheless unusual. Each cave has been hollowed out in such a way that a sort of pagoda has been left standing in the middle, with niches hollowed out of it, or carved with statues of Bodhisattvas; each one is rectangular (not unlike Buddhist remains in Gan su, for example); the far wall is also covered with sculpture. All this is characteristic of the caves in Xin jiang. It may be an example of the direct influence of Indian Buddhist rock carving. Nearly all the caves at **He se er** are made in the same way. Some of them are square, however, and some have carvings on the walls only.

The **He se er** frescoes differ from the **Dun huang** frescoes both in style and in content; symmetrical designs have not been used for the ceilings; the paintings depict religious scenes, sometimes mingling with realistic interpretations of everyday events, or drawings of animals, etc... Other walls are decorated with paintings, as well as the ceilings, with illustrations of scenes from the life of the Buddha, which resemble Sui and Wei frescoes rather than the Tang paintings at Dun huang. The style is composite, and owes much to realistic, popular art.

Nearly all the statues have been mutilated, as has happened everywhere in Xin jiang. The few intact ones are extremely powerful.

GAN SU AND NING XIA

(Atlas, pl. 11)

The province of Gan su is over 880 miles long from north-west to south-east, and forms a natural corridor linking China with Xin jiang and Central Asia. The upper reaches of the Yellow River run perpendicularly through it. The province borders on Inner Mongolia, the Republic of Mongolia, the Xin jiang Autonomous Region, the provinces of Qing hai, Si chuan, Shân xi, and the Autonomous Region of Ning xia. It covers an area of 240,000 square miles and it has a population of about 13 million. Most of the inhabitants are Han. Other ethnic groups represented are the Hui (an autonomous district), the Tibetans (an autonomous district), the Uighurs, the Mongols, the *Dong xiang*, the Khazaks, the *Tu*, the *Sa la*, the *Yu gu* and the *Bao an*. Several of these minority races live in autonomous sub-prefectures.

Gan su falls naturally into three parts. The south-east is a mountainous region, where several rivers rise, to flow down through Shân xi (the Wei, the Han), Hu bei (the Han) and Si chuan (Bao long jiang, Jin ling jian). **Tian shui,** an industrial and commercial town, is the centre of the area. The Yellow River flows through the central area, through three series of gorges east of **Lan zhou:** the Mulberry Tree Garden Gorges *(Sang yuan xia)*, the Red Mountain Gorges *(Hong shan xia)* and the Black Mountain Gorges *(Hei shan xia)*. Lan zhou, the provincial capital, is in the middle of this area. The north-west region stretches from the Yellow River to the edge of the deserts of Xin jiang. It is shaped like a long corridor, with the Mongolian plateau on one side and the **Qi lian shan** mountain range on the other, which is the border of the Qing hai plateau. The climate is cold and dry in the north-west, but becomes milder towards the south-east, where it is mild and wet. Historically speaking, the road from the east to the west has passed through Gan su since the Qin and the Han. For further details on the links between China and Central Asia, see p. 110-2. To protect this route, hundreds of miles of Great Wall were built in Gan su under the Han, parts of which can still be seen today.

The arrival of Buddhism left many traces here, some of which are among the finest monuments of Chinese religious art.

Like Xin jiang, Gan su is an area rich in natural resources: oil, coal, iron, copper, phosphorous and other, non-ferrous,

REGION DE DUN HUANG

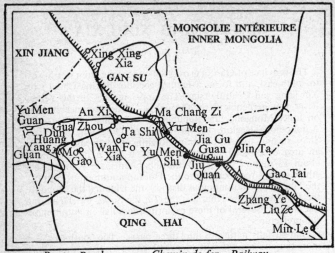

Route Road ┄┄┄┄ Chemin de fer Railway

RÉGION DE DUN HUANG   REGION OF DUN HUANG

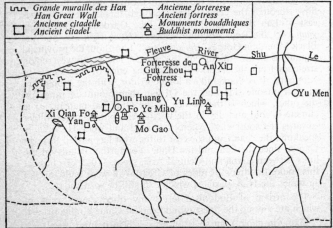

D'après DUN HUANG, par Jiang Liang fu, Shang hai 1956
After DUN HUANG, by Jiang Lianh fu, Shang hai 1956

metals. Several towns are undergoing rapid industrial development: **Tian shui, Lan zhou, Zhang ye, Bai yin, Yu men.** The richest oilfield in China is near **Yu men: Lan zhou,** the provincial capital, is important for its oil-refineries, and chemicals, machine and textile factories. **Gan zhen,** 12 miles south of the town, lies in a coal-bearing area which supplies the energy for the industrial centre. The population of Lan zhou has risen rapidly since the liberation, and as early as 1957, it was 700,000. It is certainly more than that now. Several scientific research institutes and higher educational establishments have been founded in the town: a section of the Chinese Academy of Science, a section of the National Minorities' Institute, Oil Research Institute, etc... Lan zhou is also an important road and railway junction. Since the liberation, railway lines have been built from Shân xi to **Lan zhou,** from **Lan zhou** to Mongolia, Xin jiang and **Xi ning,** the capital of Qing hai, representing a total of over 1,200 miles. **Lan zhou** is linked to Tibet by road, via **Xi ning.**

Agriculture is extremely varied, owing to the differences of climate within the province. Wheat, the main crop, is sown in winter and harvested in May in the south of the province, but sown in spring and harvested in August in the western corridor. Rice and cotton are also grown, using different methods in different parts. Since the liberation, work has been carried out on a large scale to provide protection from the wind by planting screens of trees; the winds from Mongolia used to cover the crops with sand in the corridor region. Tens of thousands of reservoirs and water-tanks have been made to irrigate the desert regions. Stock-breeding is carried out in the Qi lian shan Mountains and in the Tibetan autonomous district (horses, cattle, sheep, camels).

Gan su was one of the provinces picked out for intensive development during the first five-year plan (railways, oil industry, advanced scientific research). As far as communications are concerned, Gan su is now the centre which links all the north-western provinces. It has been made into an industrial centre, as a first step towards the economic conquest of the western territories.

The **Hui Autonomous Region of Ning xia** covers over 40,000 square miles; it is north-east of Lan zhou, between Gan su, Inner Mongolia and Shân xi. The population of 1,800,000 is one third Hui. The capital, Yin chuan, is in the middle of a vast plain, 3,600 or 3,900 feet above sea level, well watered by the Yellow River, which produces large quantities of rice and wheat. This dry plain was reclaimed a long time ago; some of the irrigation canals date from the Qin, the Han and the Tang. It has been further developed since the liberation; in spite of considerable difficulties, a railway line has been laid across shifting sand areas to link Ning xia with **Bao tou** to the north and **Lan zhou** to the south.

THE GAN SU BUDDHIST CAVES

Wu Wei, Zhang ye, Jiu quan and **Dun huang** are in the north-west of the province, west of the Yellow River, in the "corridor west of the River" *(He xi zou lang)*, a zone which used to be under the hegemony of various barbarian minority races *(Xiong nu, Da ya shi,* etc...). From the reign of the Han Emperor Wu onwards, the four settlements of **Wu wei, Zhang ye, Jiu quan** and **Dun huang** were raised to the position of commanderies *(jun)* in strategic control of a region which, economically, was extremely prosperous. The area was also a stronghold of Buddhism: over ten important sites, large and small, still remain. The most well known are the **Mo gao Caves** at **Dun huang**, the **Yu lin Caves** at **An xi**, the **Tian ti shan** at **Wu wei, Chang ma** at **Yu men** (several monasteries), the **Wen shu shan** at **Jiu quan**, the **Ma ti si** at **Zhang ye**, the **Bing ling si** etc. (see map).

THE DUN HUANG CAVES (MO GAO KU)

Dun huang is in the area bordering on Xin jiang and Qing hai, in the most westerly prefecture in Gan su. Two famous mountains rise near Dun huang: **Mount San wei (San wei shan)** and **Mount Ming sha (Ming sha shan)**. A stretch of desert, like a cliff of sand, lies between the two; a tiny oasis is hidden there, invisible until one is on top of it:

Dun huang. It is huddled up against the western side
of a steep river valley. The river still winds past the
caves, which are known as the **Mo gao ku.** The scenery
is striking: desert on the cliff tops, and green valley
below.

The Dun huang caves were discovered at the
beginning of the century. A man called Wang Yuan
lu went to Gan su to take refuge from the famine
which was raging in Hu bei; he settled at Dun huang,
and one day engaged some workmen to clear a cave,
which was sanded up. It was the cave now numbered
as 16. Paintings of Bodhisattvas were revealed (Song),
and then part of the wall fell down. Wang tapped
the rest of the side wall, and thought it sounded
hollow; he broke a way through, found a little door,
opened that, and found himself in a small square
chamber, 5 feet high and 8 feet wide, in total darkness;
there, he found a neat pile of countless documents,
sutras, paintings, ritual vessels, etc... The walls were
covered with Tang frescoes; the objects and documents stored in the chamber were 5th century at
the earliest and 10th at the latest. It might be thought
that this was the treasure belonging to the monks
living at **Mo gao ku:** the door was not sealed, however,
and seemed to have been closed later on (11th century
perhaps). It may be that the monks were intent
on saving as much as possible from the invaders,
the Xi xia, and that they had to flee without being
able to come back, so that the hiding-place remained
a secret.

The world of scholars was extremely excited by
this discovery of inestimably precious documents
900 years old. Wang himself, however, and the Qing
government did not realise their worth; it was suggested
that people should be sent to Gan su to take up the

matter, but the officials reckoned that it would cost at least 5,000 silver taels to bring everything back... the best solution seemed to be to send an official note to Wang asking him to leave the old papers as he had found them, and to shut up the cave!

The fate of the treasures was then in the hands of Wang himself. He took no notice of the orders, naturally enough, and began to sell what he had found, with the result that the documents were scattered far and wide. The Western specialists were quick to recognise them and Sir Aurel Stein appeared at Dun huang for the first time in 1907 (he came five times altogether between 1907 and 1930). He obtained 24 crates of documents and five crates of scrolls and brocades for the ridiculous sum of about 40 *kuai*. In 1914, he paid Wang 500 silver taels for five more crates of miscellaneous scrolls: altogether, he brought back 150 pieces of brocade, over 500 paintings, and over 6,500 scrolls of sutras, as well as documents!

In 1908, the French sinologist, Paul Pelliot, accompanied by C. Nonette, went to Dun huang; he left with 6,000 scrolls, all extremely valuable, and a collection of paintings. Next came some Japanese, then more Englishmen, etc. The Chinese themselves founded a study institute at **Dun huang** in 1943.

The Dun huang Caves

They are in four different groups: **Mo gao ku, Si qian fo ya** (the Four Thousand Buddha Cliff) and **Shui xia kou** (the Entrance to the Gorge). The style is consistent throughout, so that all four sites form a homogeneous artistic whole. Apart from the **Mo gao** caves, they are all small; no documents have been found except in the **Mo gao** caves.

The **Mo gao** group is also called the **Qian fo dong,** the Thousand Buddha Caves; this is in fact a generic name for rock temples, for it recurs at **Yun gang, Long men, Tian shui,** Turfan, etc. The name **Mo gao** comes from the Tang sub-prefecture, **Mo gao xian.**

The position of the caves is as bad as it could be, from a geographical point of view; the south-western caves have already been damaged by wind and sand. When the sand-bearing wind gets up, it blows along the cliff straight into the caves; all the caves and paintings open to the sky, and all the large frontal paintings, have been damaged; water seeping in brings with it risks of the caves falling in, and the River Da chuan erodes them at the base of the cliff.

The whole site has recently been classed as a historical monument.

The **Mo gao** group will be considered first, beginning with the lower part. The caves are of different sizes; some have paintings in them, others are bare and dark. All of them once were lived in by monks. Higher up the cliff, there are others of different shapes again, arranged like cells in a honeycomb; they are on at least five levels, and stretch over above half a mile: over 460 caves have been counted.

Two are different from the rest because they are carved out of the whole height of the cliff, to take two enormous statues of the Buddha, each about 90 feet high.

Most of the caves are rectangular; several of them are extended outwards by a sort of wooden balcony, with an outside system of communication (ladders, etc.). The oldest of them date from the Wei. Of the caves that still survive, 23 date from the Wei, 95 from the Sui, 213 from the Tang, 33 from the Five Dynasties,

DUN HUANG: STRUCTURES COMPARÉES DES GROTTES WEI ET TANG
DIFFERENCES IN STRUCTURE IN WEI AND TANG CAVES

Grottes Wei Wei Caves   **Grottes Tang Tang Caves**

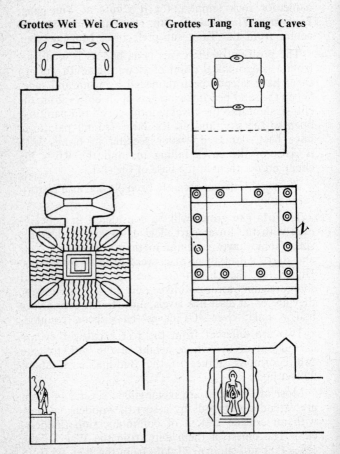

D'après «Dun Huang», par Jiang Liang Fu, Shang Hai 1956
After "Dun Huang", by Jiang Liang Fu, Shang Hai 1956

98 from the Song, 3 from the Xi xia, 9 from the Yuan, and 6 cannot be dated with certainty.

The Wei caves are almost all in the third row; they are the original nucleus. The later caves were cut to the north and below. They included a sort of antechamber, which has often been badly damaged in the case of the Wei caves. The Tang caves are in better condition on the whole; they have been added on to Sui caves in many cases, which suggests that the cliff face was more or less saturated by that time. The outer balconies leading from one to the other were added under the Song. The Song caves were adaptations or restorations of older caves; no new ones were cut. They stand out from the rest as being fairly large. It is thought that the caves must have deteriorated considerably towards the end of the Tang or the Five Dynasties, and that the balconies were built to remedy this; the three-coloured paintings (black, white and green) probably date from the Song as well. Little was added after the Song; from the Xi xia until modern times, only 18 caves have been cut.

The inside of the caves generally follow more or less the same lines: one chamber with right angle corners, either square or rectangular, with a ceiling of an unusual shape (see illustration). The far end of the chamber is usually taken up by a flat dais with paintings or statues. A large statue of the Buddha stands in the middle of the dais, with Bodhisattvas on either side, in varying numbers.

The Wei and Tang caves can be roughly classed as follows: Large caves: 27 feet wide, 30 feet long and 16 feet high; Medium-sized caves: 13 feet wide, 13 ½ feet long, 9 ½ feet high; Small caves: 9 ½ feet wide, 9 ½ feet long, 4 ¼ feet high.

All these are covered with paintings, decorating
the walls and the ceiling, and they are at **Mo gao**.
The caves in the other three sites are much smaller
on the whole, and usually in poor condition.

Countless works of art have been found at the
Mo gao caves, and have inspired many books over
the last thirty years. The aim here is to give the
reader some idea of what can be seen there.

1) Northern and Western Wei Dynasties.

Cave No 290 dates from the Northern Wei, from
520–524; others date from the same period (No 263,
267, 171) but were altered as early as the Sui. Early
alterations are frequent at **Dun huang**. Most of the
Wei caves are about half way up the southern part
of the cliff, scattered over about 200 yards (the later
ones were cut to the right and left of them, and
above them). At that time, the river which runs
close by was larger and swifter; from the Tang
onwards, the current became less violent, and the
lower rows were begun.

The general outline of the largest caves has already
been described. The walls are full of niches holding
Buddhist statues; the central part of the ceiling is a
coffer (caves No 254, 428, etc.), characteristic of
the Wei style. Others are smaller, but similar in
style, such as cave No 249, which is perhaps the
best example. The style originated in India (*zhi ti* or
chatiya caves, which were part of Buddhist monasteries
cut out of the rock, known as *vihara*, like the one
at Ajanta) but was modified by contact with Central
Asian style and Chinese additions.

They contain wall paintings and statues; the statues
have suffered more than the paintings. Many of
the caves are empty, and many of the statues reduced

to mere fragments; it is estimated that 110 caves still contain their original statues, of which 2,415 remain altogether. 318 of these date from the Wei, and are nearly all in perfect condition. The dry climate of Dun huang has preserved them through nearly fifteen centuries.

Judging by the Buddhas and Bodhisattvas at **Dun huang,** the main characteristic of Northern Wei sculpture is the large size of the statues. The faces are unusually wide, the nose high, the eyebrows delicate and long; the thin lips, prominent cheeks, and the curls, are all equally striking. The garments of the Buddhas are light and thin, and look as though they have just emerged from water. A trace of Indian influence can be seen in all these details; Indian influence was widely felt in China during the first phase of Buddhist expansion.

This style continued to satisfy public taste until after the Northern Wei dynasty; then the renewal began south of the river *(Jiang nan)*, particularly with Dai Kui, spread to the north-west and the Marches and reached Dun huang, where traces of the stylistic revolution — in the strictest sense of the word — can be seen in the work of the Sui. Wei sculpture shows relatively few Chinese characteristics, but Chinese sculpture as a whole had already made many essential borrowings from India: the lack of correct proportions in Han work, figures with big heads and little bodies, or with a roughly worked body surmounted by a detailed head, all recall this.

The wall paintings deal with infinitely varied and complicated subjects. A few generalisations should be made however. The **Dun huang paintings** are *tempera* paintings (i.e. water emulsions); this is an important detail, as only one cave with frescoes is known.

and it dates from the Yuan. The technique used was a complex one: a layer of clay and plant fibres was applied first, forming a very strong base when it dried. Next a kind of cement was spread over this, in a layer as thin as an egg-shell; it was evidently intended to countreact the absorbent qualities of the first layer, and was carefully polished; next the background colour was applied, very lightly, either light red or dark grey; then the painting was executed on top of all this. The colours were powder paints, applied in thick layers; the contours were slightly emphasised at the last minute. The materials used to produce the colours were mineral powders, or metal oxides (over ten all together). The type of pigment used has resulted in the paintings lasting for over a thousand years without alteration, and the colours retaining amazing freshness. The colouring matter does not come from Dun huang alone; a certain amount was imported from elsewhere.

Most of the paintings illustrate parables, or Jataka stories. Good examples of these are the caves No 275, 254, 428, 257, etc., all in perfect condition, with frescoes illustrating the stories of **Mo he sa duo, Shi pi, Prince Xu da na.**

Countless little *gong yang ren* are depicted below the paintings; the women wear narrow robes with wide sleeves, and are shown bending forward slightly, the men, all very slender, wear tunics, rather like some of the people in paintings by Gu Kai zhi. The corners and the ceilings are decorated with symmetrical patterns, based on triangles or diamond shapes in different colours, or foliage, with animals playing among it (sparrows, monkeys, etc.). One of the finest of all is the cave No 249, which is decorated with painting inspired entirely by Chinese mythology (dragons, flying horses, winged men, etc., which are referred to in *Tian wen pian* by Qu yuan). The Wei paintings at **Dun huang** show the evolution of Chinese painting after the Han with admirable clarity; outside influences which entered China with Buddhism have already been absorbed, and the amalgamation of the styles has almost been completed. It is interesting to note that great painters of the past like the Han artist Zhang zhi, or Suo jing, Fan zhong, Zhang han, Suo Ji, Suo Yong, who lived under the Jin dynasty, all came from Dun huang. As far as the subject is concerned, all the Wei paintings idealise sacrifice and self-effacement, leaving no room for joy.

2) The Sui Dynasty

This dynasty was a brief one, for it lasted only 38 years; nevertheless, it is still represented by 95 caves at Dun huang. They are mainly north of the Wei caves, and are spread over about 400 yards. Several of them were originally Wei caves, later transformed; a layer of Wei paintings often lies beneath the Sui paintings.

The shape of the caves is fundamentally the same, except that only three of the walls contain niches; the fourth wall is left bare. The niches are fairly deep, almost always containing two floors, and have sloping ceilings; cave No 283 has a ceiling which is different from the rest.

Some of the caves are square; a square dais carrying a statue fills the middle. Others have a niche in the far wall; the ceilings are coffered. Good examples of this can be found in caves No 294, 423, 305. The style anticipates that of the Tang. Like the Wei caves, the Sui caves often had an antechamber attached, but they have fallen in.

Many examples of Sui sculpture still survive, almost all of them in good condition; 140 statues are originals (350 others have been either damaged or restored under later dynasties). They include statues of the Buddha and two Bodhisattvas, as under the Wei, with the addition of statues of Ananda, which appear for the first time under this dynasty. As the niches are deeper, the statues are more stable, and are either sitting or standing; the caves which have a niche in the far wall often have a small chamber joined on to them as well.

The sculpture of this period has a clearly defined style. Under the Wei, the figures were erect, the garnments had sharp folds in them, the emaciated faces suggested majesty, firmness and penetration. Although the faces are smiling, the overall impression is one of reverent fear; this quality of distance disappears under the Sui. An evolution has taken place, sometimes clumsy and not yet fully matured; at the same time, there has been a distinct break with foreign artistic traditions.

The most striking features of the statues are their full faces, the characteristic bridge of the nose, the long ear-lobes, the softly-draped clothes. The most pronounced faults are the over-large head, the long torso, too long for the rest of the body, which is too short, and the lack of proportion in the limbs. This is due at least in part to the rules applied to the carving of the huge statues; the upper part of the body was enormous, to reinforce the impression of majesty. This particular rule was unsuitable when applied to small statues, such as the ones at *Dun huang*. Another fault is the set facial expression in spite of

the power and goodness which the statues radiate.
Yet another step has been made towards the assimilation of the foreign elements to a wholly Chinese
style. Lastly, the clothing under the Sui becomes
much richer.

The subjects of the frescoes of the period are still
Jataka stories; the composition of the pictures,
however, is noticeably richer and the treatment of
the subject more varied, than under the Wei. Cave
295 bears this out. Scenes representing parables or
the expounding of the Law are rarer, but single
Bodhisattvas become more and more frequent.
They are magnificent, and show that the influence
of Central Asian art is much less strongly felt; the
artists reveal rich imagination and daring, but at
the same time, they stay close to reality. The women
portrayed are full of life, and at the same time show
great dignity.

The *gong yang ren* of this period are depicted with
clothes which are no longer Central Asian in style;
nearly all the men wear purely Chinese clothes, and
the women have narrow tunics with long sleeves
(see cave No 64).

The decorative patterns are the most strikingly
successful element in the Sui paintings. They occur
on the richly decorated garments of the Bodhisattvas,
in the halos which surround them, at the back of the
niches, on the ceilings. The ceilings generally have
a large lotus flower in the middle, with symmetrical
patterns at the four corners; the patterns recur again
when the Thousand Buddhas are depicted, adapted to
their role of forming a background to the figures.
The use of patterns contributes much to the dazzling
richness of the Sui paintings.

The themes and compositions of Buddhist art introduced into China are retained, but they are mingled with native elements, from local artistic traditions. From the Wei onwards, the fusion is still more marked; this progress makes the art of the Sui of decisive importance in relation to the art of the Tang.

3) The Tang Dynasty

At the first glimpse of the early Tang caves, the visitor is struck by the force and life of the work of that era, and by the richness of their form and colour. The summit of artistic achievement at **Dun huang** was reached under the Tang.

At the end of the Tang, the great cliff face at **Dun huang** already looked as it does today; many of the caves dating from the end of the dynasty dated in fact from earlier periods, but were transformed or restored at this time. Although the stele of Li Huai rang from **Wu zhou** records that "over a thousand caves" existed, this does not mean that they amounted to one thousand, but simply that they were extremely numerous and that no room was left to cut new ones (unless the caves on the northern face were not included in the count).

213 caves dating from the Tang still exist today; almost half of the total. They show that the Tang dynasty must indeed have been an era of splendour for **Dun huang.**

Most of the Tang caves are square, with an antechamber and another chamber behind (see illustration). Nothing is left of the corner pillars. The statues have been moved to the back chambers; the niches have grown in depth and width until they have become little rooms. In some cases the caves have been made with three levels, communicating with each other, to house the statues which were put there (see cave No 130). Other caves contain a recumbent Buddha, and have been hewn accordingly (see cave No 158). Many others have a sort of side chamber, an annex of the main cave, containing no statues.

Originally, little paths cut out of the rock itself probably ensured communications from one cave to another; by the end of the Tang, the rock face was crumbling, and wooden scaffolding had to be added, a simple structure of ladders and passageways, the upper part of which was soon beautifully decorated, so that it formed little balconies. Only one of these structures is left: cave No 196 still has the framework (the upper part has fallen down), and the paintwork on the beams has retained all its freshness. It now represents a precious relic of the end of the Tang.

As many as 670 pieces of Tang sculpture still survive. Half of them are still intact and are among the most beautiful ever discovered.

Many of the great Tang painters were sculptors as well. Although the two arts had been closely connected before this dynasty, for some reason sculpture was considered a minor art during this period, so that often the artists' names are unknown, and sculptors are rarely mentioned in documents. At **Dun huang,** this injustice is compensated for by the fact that the painters' names are often to be found at the bottom of their works. Some of the most famous are: Yang Hui zhi, Song fa zhi, Wu zhi min, An Sheng, Zhang Jing yan, Han bo tong, Zhang Shou, Song Chao, Zhao yun zhi, Wang Wen, Liu yi er, Li An, Chen yong cheng, Zhang hong du, Wang nai er, Yuan jia er, Yi ming tang, Jin zhong yi, Liu jui lang, Cheng Jin, Li Zheng, Dou hong guo, Mao po luo, Sun ren gui, etc.; countless unknown artists should be added to this list.

Early Tang sculpture was already amazingly accomplished; the faults common in Sui sculpture had been eliminated. The style is more realistic; Buddhas and Bodhisattvas are treated like real people, expressing human sentiments; this profane aspect makes them full of life and easily accessible. Towards the middle of the dynasty, these qualities are still more in evidence, producing unique works of art. The barrier between men and gods disappeared; an artist like Yang Hui zhi created magnificent Buddhas, and at the same time he created superb statues of human beings of astonishing fidelity. Only at the end of the Tang dynasty did this particular art begin to deteriorate and lose its inner force.

Some of the best examples of each period of the Tang can be seen in caves No 57, 77, 332, 444 (early Tang); 194, 320, 322, 458 (middle Tang); 159, 264, 384 (late Tang). The general characteristics can be resumed briefly as follows:

The Buddhas are full of gentleness, goodness, and at the same time, they are majestic and powerful. They are usually portrayed seated, cross-legged, with one hand raised as if beckoning. The folds of their garments seem to move over a perfectly-modelled body; the same is true of the Bodhisattvas, women with bodies and bare arms of faultless beauty. Their faces show perception, clear-sightedness, gentleness, and purity. The mouth is small, the lips smiling, their meek expression seems to show that they are listening to men's prayers; their brocade garments are light and lie close to the body, their folds "float like waves".

The *luo han* are also depicted with astonishing realism, like the heroes *(Vira)*, who are full of strength and firmness of will; they wear helmets and armour, with the upper part of the body left bare, and they are given warlike, determined positions, betraying tense muscles ready for action.

At this time, the Wei and Sui statues were moved from their shallow niches and put up against the side walls: a Buddha in the centre, flanked by his disciples and Bodhisattvas, and by *tian wang* and heroes. The big statues should not go unnoticed: cave No 96 contains a statue over 100 feet high, now housed in a sort of pavilion with nine stories. Cave No 130 has a statue 75 feet high, cut out of three levels of the cliff face. A large statue, damaged, but magnificent nevertheless, stands in cave No 96. Cave No 158 contains another, in perfect condition (like the one in cave 130).

The Tang wall painting are extraordinarily varied. Each cave is full of paintings — *jing bian* — showing various scenes from the Buddhist canon, which are more or less a type of Jataka story. The scenes and paintings are as numerous as the sutras. Caves 152, 320, 171, 172 (Amithaba and Guan yin) have some of the finest of all. This type of painting tends to replace the Jataka story paintings almost entirely, as well as the ones illustrating Buddhist parables, though a few may still be seen.

The fashion for representing one Bodhisattva only appeared at this time; it was generally a large, extremely handsome statue. In some of the caves, it covered almost a whole wall. One of the essential elements in the profane character of Tang sculpture may well be traceable to the importance of the worship of the Bodhisattvas. Their form and their nature brought the Bodhisattvas close to the world of human beings. They were a sort of bridge between the human and the divine. The Buddhist canon says that believers can themselves attain the rank of Bodhisattvas, if their efforts deserve it... Bodhisattvas dressed in profane robes appear in the paintings, wearing ornaments, belts and jewels, clothes which cover their feet; the modelling of the bodies is exquisite; they are in fact statues of handsome Tang nobles. It should be added here that it is recorded in the *Jing huo si ta ji*, dating from the same time, that in the Dao zheng district of Chang an the *tian nü* (female *devas*) in the **Bao ying** monastery were no other than singers from the residence of Wei Yuan zhong, Duke of *Qi*.

At the end of the Tang dynasty, mandalas (Chinese *tan* or *dao chang*), circular shapes intended to help meditation, appeared amongst these varied scenes. Statues of Guan yin with four, six or eight arms, or a thousand hands or eyes, etc..., which recur frequently at Dun huang, appear at the same time.

The *gong yang ren*, who are entirely profane characters, generally appear below the large mural painting. Some of them are sometimes portrayed in the middle of the *jing bian*, however, in an attitude of reverence, beside the Bodhisattvas. An unusual couple can be seen in cave 130 *(Le ting huai fu fu)*; they are nearly 25 feet high. Generally, however, these figures are only slightly bigger than they were under the Wei and the Sui. They are usually portrayed in couples, each with a train of servants engaged in different ceremonial duties, carrying incense-burners, flowers, or with their retinues, groups of singers, etc...

DUN HUANG: COUPE ET PLAN DES GROTTES
CROSS SECTION AND PLAN OF CAVES

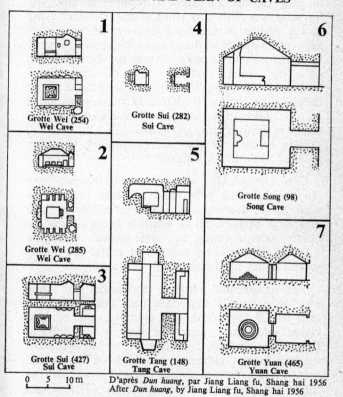

1 Grotte Wei (254)
Wei Cave

2 Grotte Wei (285)
Wei Cave

3 Grotte Sui (427)
Sui Cave

4 Grotte Sui (282)
Sui Cave

5 Grotte Tang (148)
Tang Cave

6 Grotte Song (98)
Song Cave

7 Grotte Yuan (465)
Yuan Cave

0   5   10 m

D'après *Dun huang*, par Jiang Liang fu, Shang hai 1956
After *Dun huang*, by Jiang Liang fu, Shang hai 1956

At the beginning of the Tang dynasty, the *gong yang ren* are shown wearing the same clothes as they wore under the Sui. In the middle of the dynasty,

however, great changes appear. Both men and women
are portrayed as full-figured and thick-set; the couple
in cave 130 are an excellent example of this. The
husband is a faithful portrait of an aristocrat living
in the middle of the Tang dynasty; he wears soft
slippers, an oval head-dress, and a long gown gathered
in to the waist by a belt; his sons are dressed in the
same way, except that they wear different colours
(red and white only). The wife and her retinue are all
dressed alike. Her face is completely round, surmounted
by a head-dress; her silk gown has a many-coloured
design in brilliant reds, greens and white; the graceful,
slender creature of the earlier dynasties has been
replaced by the plump noblewoman.

Generally speaking, the men among the *gong yang
ren* wear flowing robes and turbans; the women
wear loose, floating gowns and their hair is done
in a large chignon, all of which is borne out by the
poetry written during the same period. Cave 156
(Zhang yi chao) also has a vast mural illustrating
several scenes, filled with crowds of people.

The ornamental patterns used under the Tang
play an extremely important part; not an inch of
wall ist lef uncovered, and paintings and patterns
merge into each other. The designs are different
from those used by the Wei and the Sui, and show
marked foreign influence, mainly from Persia and
central India. Various stylised leaf and flower patterns
fill in the gap between the paintings. (The designs
are reproduced in the little book called the *Dun
huang Caves*, published in Chinese at Shang hai
in 1957.) The general effect is one of scrolls and
arabesques of plants and flowers; geometric patterns
have been moved down to second place.

4. The Five Dynasties, the Song dynasty and the Xi xia

The cliff afforded only a limited area, and after the Tang, no new caves could be cut.

Two possibilities were open to those who wanted to add to the caves already there: they could restore or transform existing caves, by changing all the painting and the sculpture; or they could enlarge old caves. Both possibilities needed large teams of workmen, especially the second, and it may be that official help was needed (the government was in favour of Buddhism). The Five Dynasties caves at **Dun huang** were cut by a high-ranking family, the Cao Yi jin. Believers who could not afford as much as that used to have old caves repaired, statues restored, or paintings added below or on top of existing paintings. This situation lasted all through the Five Dynasties and the Song.

Old paintings are often found at Dun huang, hidden underneath Song paintings.

The shape and structure of the caves was the same as it had been earlier on, except that sometimes a new cave was made by digging further into the rock or joining two existing caves from the inside, to make a large square cave. A dais was placed in the middle for the statues, and the back wall was linked to the ceiling by a sort of screen (the same thing is found later in Halls of the Buddha).

33 caves still survive, dating from the Five Dynasties; they are in the lower half of the cliff face, and they are larger than earlier ones. Few pieces of their sculpture remain; out of the 24 in existence at **Dun huang,** only 7 are intact. They resemble Tang sculpture, but they are only outwardly successful, for they lack the life and faith of the Tang work.

The same is true of the paintings; although they are larger than the earlier ones because the caves themselves are larger, when they are studied in detail, it will be seen that they lack the inspiration of the Tang, and that the paintings no longer have any soul to them. As far as the *jing bian* are concerned, no new element can be seen, except for the large painting in cave 146, the composition of which is complex and varied, and which reveals ability to exaggerate and a sense of humour which is unique in this field, as well as great artistic ability on the part of the painter.

The largest painting of *gong yang ren* dates from this period: the painting of the king of **Yü tian,** Li Sheng tian, in cave 98. In general, the clothes and head-dresses are extremely varied, and often people are arranged in line, according to their importance, providing an invaluable document for the history of the Five Dynasties.

18 Song caves have survived. The Xi xia caves are fewer still; there are three. The Xi xia founded their empire in 1038, in the first year of the Bao yuan period of the Song Emperor Ren zong. The empire lasted until 1227, when it fell to the Mongols; it ruled over the western territories for about two hundred years, but as far as **Dun huang** is concerned, the remains left by the Xi xia (documents, miscellaneous works) are meagre, and the few which do exist are indistinguishable from what was produced under the Song; they will therefore be treated together.

Under these dynasties, most of the work done consisted in restoration work on old caves, which had recently been badly damaged by landslides as the result of an earthquake. The Song artists were responsible for large-scale restoration work; large numbers of wooden buildings, roofs and balconies were also put up. They are now in ruins, except for six which are still standing, and which reveal that the work was carried out on a generous scale. The outside of the caves was changed considerably by all this; the inside was left much as it was.

Out of the 74 pieces of Xi xia and Song sculpture still left, only 28 are intact. They show a distinct decline from an artistic point of view for they are stiff and motionless, without a trace of the life which infused the Tang statues; even the ones which are copies of Tang pieces are infinitely inferior to the originals. The realist style which developed under the Song does not seem to have reached a point as far afield as **Dun huang**: it contains nothing comparable to the **Ling yan si** at **Chang Qing,** or the **Mai ji shan** at **Tian shui,** although they are contemporary with it; at the same time, the local economy began to decline, a movement which continued for some time.

The paintings and other decorations in the caves all show the same decline; the general effect is one of confusion. The Bodhisattvas become more and more numerous, but they are always rigid and expressionless; the colours are cold and lack harmony. A few caves dating from the beginning of the Song still retain some of the qualities of the Tang: for example cave 61 contains a magnificent painting dating from the Northern Song, the **Wu tai shan tu.**

This painting belongs to a kind of painting which began to spread in the middle of the 7th century, and which reached places as far away as Turfan and Japan; apart from the two examples at **Dun huang** which date from the Song, but follow the rules of the Tang, no other specimens have survived.

The *gong yang ren* were less frequent by the middle of the period, and by the end they were extremely rare *(Xi xia)*.

In short, the Song and Xi xia period brought nothing new to **Dun huang**: in nearly every case their art consists in a monotonous repetition of identical themes and media. The fact that in the rest of China considerable innovations were introduced makes this all the more striking and disappointing.

5) The Yuan dynasty, etc.

When they had conquered the Xi xia, the Yuan "earned praise for themselves" by restoring a few caves at Dun huang; 9 new ones were cut under the Yuan, mainly in the north face of the cliff, as the south was saturated already.

The caves are small, and contain a circular altar, an idea brought in by the Mongols.

Only 9 statues dating from the Yuan are left (they may have been restored or changed under the Qing) and they are disappointing. The paintings, on the other hand, are interesting; they portray numerous mandalas, Bodhisattvas, etc... The third cave contains a Guan yin with a Thousand Arms and a Thousand Eyes which is a superb work of art.

The paintings of this period were frescoes, a technique which reached **Dun huang** via Nepal, or perhaps directly from Europe.

Apart from an advance in the technique of painting, the dynasty marked the end of a long chapter in the history of art. The Ming added nothing to Dun huang, and the additions made under the Qing are undistinguished. New developments took place in Qing hai and in Tibet after the Yuan; after the centuries of outstanding works in the fields of architecture, sculpture and painting, Dun huang ceased to be an artistic centre.

THE ZHANG YE AREA. MA TI SI

When going from **Dun huang** to **Tian shui**, from west to east, it is worth stopping on the way at the **Qi lian Mountains (Qi lian shan)**, in the sub-prefecture of **Min le**, as there are several things to see: a group of Buddhist caves, the **Ma ti si** monasteries, the Guan yin caves, etc... The groups of caves vary in size, from two to over ten; they were cut over a long period, from the Northern Wei to the Ming; some of them are most unusual. They are hollowed out of a cliff which overhangs a valley, and they are from one to three miles from each other. Some of them are arranged horizontally, others are built up the cliff (at one spot there are many as seven different levels of caves). Monasteries have been built in front of the caves; protective roofs have been built round some of them (particularly the **Ma ti** caves). As the area is inhabited by Tibetans, the monasteries contain Halls of Sutras, Lamas' living quarters, etc...

The **Ma ti Monastery (Ma ti si, Horse's Hoof Monastery)** is about 37 miles south of **Zhang ye**, in the mountain near the boundary of Gan su and Qing hai. It is in a steep mountainous area, with hardly any means of communication; it can be reached on horseback only. A night could be spent at **Hei qiang chuan** to break the journey each way.

1. The Northern Ma ti Monastery Caves

They are on the west bank of the River **Ma ti**, which narrows in July, cut out of the eastern face

of the steep cliff nearby. Several hillocks and hills
in front of the cliff makes it look as though the caves
are on the edge of a sort of basin. Several lamaseries
have been built there (each contains about twenty
to thirty Lamas). They live by raising yaks. Two
Halls of Sutras and a Hall of the Three Buddhas
(**San fo bao dian**) are half way up the foot of the cliff;
the Hall of the Three Buddhas was restored in 1858,
but it is again much in need of repair. The three
large statues of the Buddha inside seem to be older
than the building itself and could date from the
beginning of the Qing dynasty. The **Ma ti Monastery**
is north of the Great Hall; it is an extremely old
foundation; in the Yong le period of the Ming dynasty,
it was called **Pu guan si**: it was restored several times
over the centuries, and became an important religious
centre.

The caves are:

The **Yao wang dong** (Cave 1), also called the
Nan zuo Fo dian, a rectangular cave with a lager
niche in the inside wall housing a statue; on either
side are wall-paintings of the Thousand Buddhas,
in poor condition.

A niche near the entrance to the cave is all that
remains of another cave which was transformed
into a niche after a landslide; it contains a statue
of **Ju lai,** and Bodhisattvas, which are fairly old,
dating probably from the Yuan or the Xi xia.

The **Guan yin ge** (Cave 2), also called the **Nan guan
yin lou,** is above the others; steps lead up to it, and
it has a wooden pavilion at the entrance. A bronze
statue of Guan yin stands inside.

The **San shi san tian** (Cave 3) is really a group of
21 caves, made on seven different levels. The first
level consists of five shallow caves, with niches;

the level immediately above contains five narrow niches; the third level is the same; the fourth contains four niches, and the fifth only one. The sixth level is south of the rest, and the seventh is to the north. The whole group stretches about 200 feet up the cliff; each level is linked to the next by a little path cut out of the rock. From the second level upwards, a wooden door and window have been built on to each entrance. The last three caves have porches as well, restored in 1922.

The first set of five niches contain a set of wall-paintings in poor condition; the colours are cold, and they may date from the Yuan. Many of the statues in the caves higher up, and the red clay figures between the paintings, show a pronounced Tibetan influence. The cave on the sixth level, known as the cave of the "Guan yin dressed in white" was cut in 1632; the seventh level cave dates from the Ming. All the lower ones date from the Yuan, and form a homogeneous whole.

The Bei zuo Fo dong (Cave 4). It contains recent statues.

The Bei yao wang dong (Cave 5), is immediately above the one before. Steps up the cliff give access to it. It contains three niches with a wooden seated statue of the King of Medecine, and Bodhisattvas, all in Ming style, and restored; the wall paintings date from the same period.

The Bei Guan yin dong (Cave 6) is to the right, above Cave 5. The niches, now sealed up, used to contain statues; one statue is left: a Qing Guan yin. On either side of the statue are magnificent Ming wall-paintings, in perfect condition, depicting a Four Armed Guan yin. They are now threatened with damage by water seeping through the wall.

MA TI SI

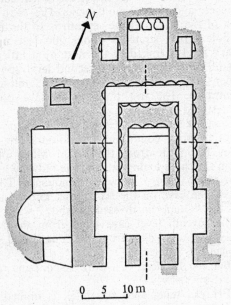

Plan et coupes de la grotte 8 du monastère nord.
Plan and cross sections of cave 8 of the north monastery
D'après la revue «Wen wu» (1965, No 3).
After the magazine «Wen wu» (1965, No.3).

Cave 7 is now in ruins.

The Cang Fo dian (Cave 8) is a huge rectangular cave, made in elaborate style, with niches in all the walls; a second chamber has been built inside the first, opening near the entrance. The style is unusual. It is extremely dark, unfortunately, and in bad condition. As far as it is possible to judge from the remains of the paintings, they were probably painted under the Xi xia, and restored under the Ming and the Qing.

The Ma ti dian is north of Cave 8. It contains a large number of statues, including four celestial kings and sixty *luo han;* it has been restored from top to bottom since the liberation. A pagoda-shaped pillar stands in the centre *(ta zhu);* the three niches on the front of it date from the Northern Dynasties. The horse's hoof carved on the pillar gave its name to the monastery and the mountain.

Three more caves lie next to the Ma ti dian, among them the **Ma wang dian** and the **Gao wang dong** (this one is inaccessible).

2. The Southern Ma ti Monastery Caves

The southern Monastery is over the ridge from the Northern Monastery, and is an extension of it. The Lamas' cells are fewer in numbers. The Great Hall of Sutras dates from the Qing, and it contains some magnificent lacquer statues of the Buddha, about 3 feet high, made using the *tuo tai* technique, in which the core is removed.

Five or six caves still exist nearby, but they are in very poor condition.

3. The Jin ta Monastery Caves

About 30 miles north-east of the Ma ti Monastery, beyond several bare mountains and desert-like valleys, lies a steep mountain with a high cliff on one side of it; a little further on, after crossing stretches of scrub, woods, and climbing a steep wall of rock, the visitor suddenly catches sight of the buttresses of a huge cliff of red earth, about 300 feet high, rising in the middle of a completely wild stretch of countryside. The cliff-face looks as though it has been carved out with one long stroke of the knife. Half way up it are two caves, known by the local shepherds as the **Shi yao dong,** both in the same style, as they were cut at the same time.

The eastern cave is the larger of the two; it is rectangular. The front wall has disappeared, leaving a hollow about 18 feet deep, and exposing the outer part to the weather, which has eroded most of it. The central pillar, or *ta zhu*, is in the shape of a pagoda rising up to the ceiling, like the one in the **Ma ti** caves. "Pearl-shaped" niches in all four sides contain statues of Ju lai and Bodhisattvas in excellent condition; sets of "Thousand Buddhas" are carved above the niches (about ten to each facet); Bodhisattvas fill the space from them to the ceiling. The sculpture bears a striking resemblance to the work at **Dun huang,** in the Northern Wei caves; the difference lies in the fact that here, the statues are much larger, and even more lifelike and powerful than the sculpture at the **Mo gao** caves at **Dun huang,** which dates from the same time. Unfortunately many of the **Jin ta si (Golden Pagoda Monastery)** statues have been restored, and some have been changed slightly; others were damaged, particularly under the Ming. No trace remains of the wall paintings; they have been destroyed by water seeping through the porous red rock.

The southern cave is smaller, but no smaller than the Dun huang caves, which date from the same period. Like the other, it has a central pillar shaped like a pagoda, but the style is cruder. It is made up of three stories, each covered with a great variety

of carvings; the middle section is the most handsome
of the three. Later restoration work can be seen here
too, and the facet of the pillar facing the entrance
to the cave has been transformed into a statue of
Guan yin, which probably dates from the Ming.
As the cave is a small one, the pillar has been eroded
by the weather; pilgrims have written poems in ink
on some of the statues.

Judging by all these details, it seems reasonable
to assume that this valley was much frequented by
Buddhists under the Northern Wei dynasty. Later
on, Lamaists settled there too. Buildings probably
existed there too, along with the caves; nothing
is left of them now but the name, **Jin ta si.**

4. The Upper Guan yin Caves (Shang Guan yin dong).

Another name for the site is the **Guan yin Caves
Upper Monastery (Guan yin dong shang si).** It is about
2 miles north of the **Jin ta si,** on a steep, lonely outcrop
of particularly hard rock, forming a wall on one side,
with the caves scattered over it, wherever a suitable
place for them can be found. This too is the site of
an ancient Buddhist settlement; the caves are now
deserted, except for a group of six near the top,
three of which contain statues, which are watched
over by a Lama.

The far wall of the central cave contains a niche
with a statue of Guan yin. Another cave above it
contains a statue of Ju lai, and other niches and
paintings, on all the other walls. The cave to the right
contains a statue of Guan yin with a Thousand
Arms and a Thousand Eyes, and some excellent
frescoes depicting Guan yin as well, which are touched
up with gold. The statues and paintings of these three

caves show a marked Tibetan influence; most of them are recent (late Qing), and further additions have changed the original work considerably.

5. The Middle Guan yin Caves (Zhong Guan yin dong)

They are about 1 ½ miles north of the Upper Caves, on the highest peak of this group of mountains. The pavilions, built in a daring style, which is most impressive, can be seen from a long way off; the inside of them is unfortunately in ruins. All the buildings were restored under the Qing, but most of them are now on the verge of falling down. The seven caves beside them are either empty, or contain very mediocre Qing statues.

6. The Lower Guan yin Caves (Xia Guan yin dong)

The Lower Caves are about a mile north of the Middle Caves; they are cut out of an enormous wall of rock. One of the four is in excellent condition, and dates from the Northern Wei; it contains a pagoda shaped central pillar *(ta zhu)*. The paintings were restored in 1883.

7. The Thousand Buddha Caves

The **Qi lian shan** begin about 2 miles north-east of **Ma ti**. The way from **Zhang ye** via **Min le** leads past the caves just before it reaches **Ma ti**. They are on the west bank of the River **Ma ti**, separated from the river by a narrow strip of plain, where several buildings stands, housing a colony of Lamas. The ten caves have magnificent wooden buildings in front of them. Both buildings and caves have been damaged by weather and age, but some are in relatively good condition.

The first cave, starting from the southern end, is in the style of the Northern Dynasty; the front of it has fallen in, as far as the central pagoda-shaped pillar, which is bare of carving except for one facet, which contains a niche reaching up to the ceiling, with a statue which is now no more than a mixture of styles, owing to numerous restorations. As the cave is cut out of friable red rock, the paintings are badly damaged. Remains of Ming paintings, although partly obliterated, are touched up with gold and were obviously beautiful in their time.

The second cave is the most handsome of all. It dates from the Northern Dynasty, and contains a central pagoda-shaped pillar covered with superb carvings, arranged in four stories, depicting Buddhist figures (even at Dun huang there is nothing to compare with it); the statues of Ju lai are particularly fine. Although it has been frequently touched up and restored, the overall style closely resembles the style of the Northern Wei. Paintings cover most of the side walls; in some places, there are as many as four different layers of them. The upper layer is very fine.

The third cave has partly collapsed, and the statues have been removed, but remains of Ming paintings still survive. The cave dates from the Northern Dynasty.

The fourth cave dates from the same period; the central pagoda-shaped pillar has one niche only, which suggests that it might possibly have been made at the same time as the first one (?). The statues, which are old, have been slightly re-touched. The paintings are recent.

The central cave is called **Zhan Fo dian, Hall of the Standing Buddha,** by the Lamas; it is large

and square. The statues are also generously proportio-
ned; several details (full faces, nose and eyes fairly
close together, round cheeks, domed heads, tightly-
fitting clothing, rich ornaments, etc.) suggest that
they may date from the Sui dynasty. Four of the
side walls are covered with paintings, which until
recently were under a thin layer of mud. The Lamas
had carefully washed the walls, and the archaeologists
had the greatest difficulty to persuade them not to
go on doing so!

Another cave to the north also dates from the
Northern Dynasty, and is an excellent example of
the style of the caves of that period; the central
pagoda-shaped pillar is carved on all four sides,
and the side walls contain niches. The whole cave
was restored in 1934, and great care was taken to
keep the cave as it was originally.

The other caves have all suffered badly, either
from the inclemencies of the weather or man's efforts;
the restoration work carried out by Lamaists has
transformed the original work entirely. In some cases,
the contents have simply been removed, and the
caves left empty.

The Qi lian shan area contains several groups of
caves. Seven groups survive near the **Ma ti si,** five
of which are still in fairly good condition; when
the caves near the Northern Monastery **(San shi
san tian)** are added to these, the total number is
as large as the **He se er** group, at **Bai cheng** (Xin
jiang). When these are added to the large group
formed by the **Mo gao** caves **(Dun huang),** and the
Mai ji shan and the **Bing ling** groups, it gives a good
idea of the importance of the **Zhang ye** region in
the history of Buddhism. (See the general map.)

As far as the dating of the caves is concerned, a few can be dated with certainty: there are 9 caves dating from the Northern Dynasty, one dating from the Sui, 3 dating from the Xi xia, 1 from the Yuan and 2 from the Ming. It is impossible to say when the first ones were cut. It is certain, however, that new ones were cut from the Sui dynasty onwards, in spite of the dynastic changes and reversals which were going on (the Tibetans took **Zhang ye** in 766, then the Xi xia took it from them in 1038, the Mongols took over in 1225, and the Ming in 1372). All these secular disturbances seem to have affected the work very little, for it went on without a break from the Northern Wei until quite recently. The development of these caves is linked with the fact that Buddhism prospered in this area, and it is even more closely linked with the development of the nearby groups at **Mo gao, Yu lin** and **Tian ti shan,** etc... Although no documentary evidence, such as steles or documents, exists to prove the date of the first ones, the style and general structure suggest that they were begun under the last period of the Northern Wei.

The caves enable the history of Buddhism to be followed in fairly close detail, with the Xi xia period forming the turning-point for a time; the Yuan remains show the development of Lamaism, which was to continue without interruption.

As far as the history of religious art in China is concerned, the caves are important there too. Although systematic research work was only begun in 1956, two facts have already come to light: the **Dun huang** and the **Mai ji shan** caves contain the richest and most interesting collection of sculpture; on the other hand, the carving in the Thousand Buddha Cave at the **Jin ta si** is unique. The architecture of the

San shi san tian cave, with its balconies both inside and outside, is also unlike that of any of the caves at **Mo gao** or **Yu lin,** etc...

THE BING LING SI CAVES

The **Bing ling si** caves at **Yong jing** were discovered recently; a group of archaeologists began on a study of them in 1952. The name, **Bing ling si,** is comparatively modern; under the Tang, the monastery was known as **Ling yan si** (Supernatural Cliff Monastery). **Bing ling si** is a transcription of the Tibetan for "a hundred thousand Buddhas", a name often given to Buddhist cave temples. The caves are mentioned in documents from the 5th century onwards.

The way to the caves leads out of the north gate of **Yong jing,** across the Yellow River, over the "Camel's Hump" and through **Yan dun:** it then takes a southerly direction, through an area of steep, almost unsurmountable cliffs, with a view of the pointed peaks of the **Xiao ji shi,** about 3 miles away, into a fantastic world of mountain peaks, sheer cliffs and deep ravines. The "Upper Monastery" of the **Bing ling si,** which contains one cave with a Tang niche, is here. The way goes on along the bottom of a valley, past a ridge of hills; the chief monastery, with the caves and the Big Buddha alongside it, come into sight, visible from a long way off. The "Lower Monastery" is a little further on, at the end of the valley near the north bank of the Yellow River. A complete description of the site can be found in old texts, for instance in the *Fa yuan zhu lin* (chap. 53) which dates from 668.

The "discovery" of the **Bing ling si** caves is only a partial discovery; the caves were in fact forgotten for about a century, after being one of the high places of Buddhism for many hundreds of years. The town of **Yong jing** was an important centre of communications; the sub-prefecture of **Yong jing** is part of the **Lin xia** district, formerly **He zhou**. A legend says that Yu the Great re-shaped the course of the Yellow River from **Ji shi** as far as **Long men: Ji shi,** which is a group of strangely shaped mountain peaks, is near the site of the caves.

The date at which the caves were cut is known with comparative certainty, as an inscription dated 513 (Northern Wei) has been found. A magnificent set of Northern Wei statues has also been found, spreading round three walls of one of the caves.

New caves were added under each succeeding dynasty; under the Wei, 10 caves and 2 niches were cut; 21 caves and 85 niches date from the Tang; 5 caves and 1 niche date from the Ming. On the whole, the style is much the same as that of the **Yun gang, Long men** and **Dun huang** caves. The cliff face is pitted with niches, however, which are of a most unusual type, made in the shape of an Indian pagoda; very few examples of this have been found elsewhere.

The **Bing ling si** was particularly flourishing under the Song and the Ming, as the numerous wall-paintings dating from these two dynasties show. (**He zhou** was also a stronghold of considerable strategic importance under the Song.)

Pilgrimages used to be made to the **Bing ling si** and it was constantly restored and renewed, which resulted in many old works of art being spoiled; what is more, the red rock of which the cliff is made

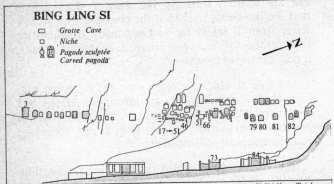

D'après Bing Ling Si Shi Ku, rapport officiel, Pékin 1953   After Bing Ling Si Shi Ku, official repor

is particularly vulnerable, and easily eroded by the
wind, so that many of the statues exposed to the
outside air deteriorated rapidly. The head of one
Buddha was found to have been worn away so that
only a ball of rock was left. The caves were often
damaged by fire, or sacked by soldiers through the
many wars which have followed their creation,
although on the whole they are in fairly good condition.
The site has been classed as a historical monument.

The most interesting pieces of sculpture and painting
are as follows:

Cave 84: Song paintings.

Cave 73: Ming paintings.

Caves 17 to 51: a set of pagoda-shaped niches of all
sizes.

Caves 79, 80, 81: Wei statues (a Thousand Buddhas,
lions, Guan yin...).

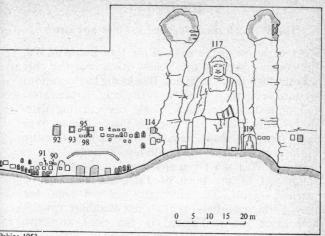

Peking 1953

Cave 82: Recumbent Buddha. Statues, wall-paintings.
Cave 90: Head of the Buddha (Wei).
Cave 3: stone pagodas (Tang). Tang statues of various subjects. Wall-paintings.
Cave 46: Tang Buddha; Guan yin; Bodhisattvas.
Cave 51: Guan yin (Tang), Standing Buddha, Bodhisattvas.
Cave 56: Tang Guan yin.
Cave 95: stone pagodas carved out of the cliff face (Tang).
Cave 91: Tang Guan yin.
Caves 92 and 93: "Celestial Kings" *(tian wang)*, Tang.
Cave 98: bust of Guan yin (Tang).
Cave 114: Tang paintings.
Cave 117: Big Tang Buddha.
Cave 1: Big Ming Buddha.
Cave 73: Ming paintings.

JIU QUAN

The Wen wu shan Buddhist temples and caves

As early on as the reign of the Han Emperor Wu, the corridor west of the Yellow River was the only way through from **An xi** and **Dun huang** to the various western empires. It is an extremely fertile area, full of historical remains. Some caves dating from the Northern Wei still survive there; **Mount Wen shu (Wen shu shan)** was the chief religious centre in the area from the Wei up till modern times.

Mount Wen shu (Wen shu shan) is about 9 miles south-west of the town of **Jiu quan**, and can be reached by car. The mountains are not high, but they form countless peaks; the Buddhist temples and caves are well-placed in the most attractive sites in the area. Unlike most other places, the caves here are not cut out of cliffs; instead they are cut out of gaps in the hillsides, prepared for them beforehand. The soil is mixed with gravel, and fairly loose, so the caves are relatively small, and of only medium height. They fall into two main groups, one on each side of a large river bed. The first group is in the "front mountain" and the second in the "back mountain"; when approached from **Jiu quan,** the "front mountain", which lies to the north, has to be climbed to reach the "back mountain" to the south. The view opens out over a vast plain with snow-covered mountains beyond: the **Qi lian shan.** Tibetan herdsmen form the population of the plain.

Large numbers of caves still exist, particularly in the "back mountain". Big buildings have been put up at the entrance to the caves; instead of porches, there are buildings more like little temple halls, with gateways, halls of the Buddha, reception halls,

offices, annex buildings, etc. The architecture is of
an elaborate style; they contain paintings and carved
beams inside. Most of the pavilions are built on a
somewhat massive base, topped by roofs with sharply
upturned eaves corners; the heights vary according
to the mountains around them. The general effect is
one of great variety of buildings. A local chronicle
dating from the beginning of the Qian long period,
the *Chong xiu Su zhou xin zhi*, refers to the monastery
here as the "three hundred Buddhist cells" or *xiao
xi tian*, and affirms that it is one of the most famous
places in the area. From 1865 onwards, however,
the three hundred cells were demolished by Hui
minority peoples who rebelled against the Qing
government. The present buildings were restored
later on. Many of the little temples still survive,
particularly in the hills behind, for example: the
Dou mu gong, the **Sun huang gong**, the **Wu liang dian**,
the **Yan guang niang niang dian**, the **Ling guan dong**,
the **Long wang gong**, the **Ri yue gong**, the **Dong yue
miao** to name only a few; these are all Taoist temples.
The Buddhist temples are fewer in number, though
Qian Fo lou, the **Guan yin dong**, the **Wen shu si**,
the **Shan Fo dong**, the **Shou yuan si**, the **Shui Fo si**,
the **Qian Fo dong** are all still standing. They are all
recent buildings; nothing earlier than the Qian long
period has been found. The remains in the front mountain show that from the beginning of the Qing dynasty
onwards, many temples must have existed; they were
built by the rich families in the neighbourhood.
They were owned in common by groups of believers
or by several villages; no monks, either Buddhist
or Taoist, lived there for a long period at a time. On
the eighth day of the fourth lunar month, and on
other feast days, people would gather there for

several days' merry-making. For the rest of the year, the place was deserted.

Remains of some interesting old buildings stand on the little cliff near the river, in front of the mountain: the **Tai zi si** and the **Yu huang ge,** built between 627 and 649, and the **Sheng shou si,** which dates from the Liang (502–556), restored in 1326. On the front mountain are several Lamaist Halls of the Sutras. Most of the Buddhist temples are on the front mountain, and the temples on the back mountain are mainly Taoist.

Buddhism flourished in this area until quite recently. Under the Northern Wei, the Sui and the Tang, the **Wen shu shan** caves constituted an important Buddhist centre. As early on as the end of the 5th century, Buddhism was already widespread in the area; caves had already been cut near there, in the **San wei shan** and in the southern **Liang zhou** mountains (they resembled the ones at **Yu lin, An xi,** and the **Tian ti shan** caves at **Wu hei).** The first caves in the **Wen shu shan** were no doubt cut at the same time. A brief description will be given of the most interesting ones.

The **Qian Fo dong (Thousand Buddha Cave)** is in the front mountain, half-way up the cliff at the entrance to the valley, which stretches south-west. A building with three openings stands at the entrance to the cave, which is typical of the Northern Wei: it is 11 ½ feet deep, 12 feet wide, 11 feet high, like a large cube, and the entrance is 2 1/5 feet wide and 5 feet high. A pagoda-shaped pillar *(ta zhu)* stands in the centre, with two rows of carvings in "pearl-shaped" niches, which are also typical of the period. The pillar is still intact; the statues are original ones, restored later on. The wall-paintings are in poor condition, but parts of them are still recognisable as Ming. The ceiling is covered with Buddhist paintings as well (scenes of the Law, Bodhisattvas, *gong yang ren*). As a whole, it is exactly like the caves at Dun huang which date from the end of the Northern Wei dynasty. This cave is the oldest in the **Wen shu shan.** To the left is another, probably also dating from the same period; the front of it has fallen in.

The **Wan Fo dong (Ten Thousand Buddha Cave)** is also in the front mountain, near the first one, in a sort of steep hill. Three lovely pavilions with curved roofs conceal the entrance; their interiors were restored under the Ming. The inside of the cave is late Wei. It is the same size as the Thousand Buddha Cave, with a central pagoda-shaped pillar, again with two rows of statues; the statues and the wall-paintings have been changed during restoration. The present paintings date from the Yuan and the Ming; some of them show a Tibetan influence. The inscriptions in the cave are in Chinese, Mongolian and Tibetan.

The **Tai zi si** stands on a little hillock at the foot of the front mountain; its handsome buildings are on a sort of earth terrace on several levels, which raises them considerably above ground level. They consist of two pavilions with triple curved roofs, their corners turning gracefully upwards towards the sky, and other, smaller annex buildings; the overall impression is one of life and vigour, to which the different levels lend a pleasant note of variety. The large cave behind dates from the Tang, but it is in poor condition; the surviving statues are nearly all in Tibetan style. The remains of a Wei statue were found there.

Six or seven **small caves** are to be found in the front mountain, opening towards the river. They are in Tibetan style, and may be Lamaist cave temples cut under the Yuan dynasty.

The **Gu Fo dong (Old Buddha Cave)** is in a deep valley in the back mountain. A porch built in 1889 shelters the entrance. The cave was first cut under the Northern Wei; it is 17 feet deep, 16 feet wide and 11 feet high, extremely dark and blackened by soot. The front and back of the central pagoda-shaped pillar are 7 ¼ feet across, and the other two sides are 7 feet across. It is divided into three parts: a base, a row of niches, and a row of paintings. The niches are "pearl-shaped"; they are an excellent example of Northern Wei architecture. The statues are in Tibetan style and are later additions. The paintings are blackened, but otherwise in fairly good condition. A set of Sui or Tang Buddhas can be seen, and several Ming additions.

The **Qian Fo dong (Thousand Buddha Cave)** is in the back mountain. The porch dates from 1909. The inside of the cave is in the same style as the Old Buddha Cave, with a central pillar; it dates from the Northern Wei as well. The statues in the niches are ugly late Qing additions. The paintings are in poor condition, though they are recognisable as Ming.

The **Guan yin dong (Guan yin Cave)** is a square cave in the back mountain. The paintings are in excellent condition and appear to be Tang works, restored under the Ming.

YU MEN. THE CHANG MA CAVES

The **Chang ma Caves** are about 38 miles southeast of the sub-prefecture of Yu men; they consist of several groups: **Xia jiao, Da ba, Hong shan si.** The area is surrounded by mountains, and forms a sort of basin; the only way in winds through the **Da ban shan Mountains.** The river which flows through it splits into two as it leaves; one branch goes eastwards towards **Yu men** and the other goes westwards towards **An xi.** The surrounding area is a prosperous one.

Xia jiao is on the west bank of the river; it is a cliff in which caves have been hollowed out of clay which is not very durable. They are about 50 yards from each other, and there are eleven altogether, divided into three groups: four caves to the south, four in the centre, and three to the north. The northern and southern groups are in very poor condition and no longer contain anything of interest. The only ones which have survived are the second and fourth caves in the centre; they contain some old statues and others dating from the Five Dynasties and the beginning of the Song dynasty.

The Second Central Cave

It is square; but a pillar in the middle divided the cave into two chambers. The first one is rectangular, with two doors and a two-storey carved colonnade between them; the upper storey has shallow niches cut out of it, and the lower storey has one large empty niche.

The wall-paintings are the most interesting feature of the cave. The four walls of the ante-chamber have some particularly fine designs (peonies) among the paintings; a magnificent Bodhisattva stands above the doors, carrying a fan in one hand and a jewel in the other. The other paintings on either side of the doors depict processions of *gong yang ren*, a lion, an elephant and two Bodhisattvas. On the northern and southern walls are a set of terraces, pavilions and

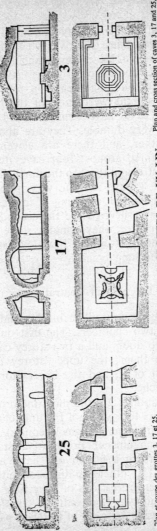

PLAN ET COUPE DES GROTTES DE YU LIN
PLAN AND CROSS SECTION OF THE YU LIN CAVES

Plan et coupe des grottes 3, 17 et 25.
D'après la revue «Wen Wu» (1956, No 10)

Plan and cross section of caves 3, 17 and 25.
After the magazine "Wen Wu" (1956, No.10)

summer-houses. The ceiling opposite the entrance
is decorated with seven Buddhas, with lotus designs
between them.

The central pillar in the back chamber has niches
on each facet, each one containing a seated Buddha
flanked by two Bodhisattvas. It also contains a set
of 20 Bodhisattvas, and a decorated ceiling which
is exactly the same as the ceiling in Cave 327 at
Dun huang, which dates from the beginning of the
Song dynasty.

The Fourth Central Cave

This cave is rectangular, with a central pillar
reaching up to the ceiling; the base of the pillar
forms a terrace or altar, with two rows of niches
and statues above it (each niche contains a Buddha
and two Bodhisattvas). The statues are in a crude,
antiquated style, with clumsy features, strongly
reminiscent of the statues in Cave 259 at Dun huang.
The top row of paintings depicts banners; the bottom
row portrays some very handsome Bodhisattvas
nearly 6 feet tall, surrounded by a lotus flower design.

The shape and the surviving statues suggest that
these two caves were made at a very early date.
The style of the frescoes and the folds of the Bodhisattvas' garments closely resembles the same things in
Caves 328 and 327 at Dun huang and Cave 17 at
Yu lin. Bright reds and greens predominate; the
style has not the ease of Tang work. The ornamentation is profuse and intricate; the Bodhisattvas
have a slightly set air about them, unlike the Tang
figures, which are full of life. The Chang ma work
as a whole is clearly influenced by the Mo gao and
Yu lin caves; the caves may possibly have been cut

by order of members of the rich families in the area,
such as Zhang Yi chao and Cao Yi jin, who had
caves cut at **Mo gao** and **Yu lin** to "win merit for
themselves", and thus became the patrons of numerous
painters and other artists.

YU LIN SI (WAN FO XIA)

The **Yu lin** (Elm Forest) Buddhist caves, also
called **Wan Fo xia** (the Ten Thousand Buddha Gorges)
are some of the most famous in China, and form
part of the large group of caves at Dun huang. They
are about 43 miles south of the town of **An xi** (Gan
su), in the mountains. The road to them leaves **An
xi** by the gate, and goes through **Shi gong**, about
9 miles away, and then through **Wen jia zhuang**.
Han and Tang remains are scattered throughout
the area. The way enters the mountains (**San wei
shan**) and goes on to **Mo gu tai zi,** near the caves.

The mountains form gorges, and the caves are
hollowed out of lofty cliffs like the one at **Dun huang,**
which form the sides of the gorge, about a hundred
yards away from each other. The whole landscape
is breathtakingly beautiful.

41 caves exist at the moment (30 to the east and
11 to the west): 3 date from the Tang, 8 date from
the Five Dynasties, 13 from the Song, one from the
Xi xia, 7 from the Yuan and 9 from the Qing.

No remains of steles giving the exact date at which
work began on the caves have been found; but the
central pillars in caves 17 and 28 are exactly like
the ones in the Wei and Sui caves at **Dun huang
(Mo gao).** Several layers of wall-paintings cover
the walls of some of the caves, and the bottom layer
is in the style of the Tang (the beginning of the dynasty).

Caves 17 and 28 also contain Tang frescoes in niches in the walls which have survived intact. The **Yu lin** caves were hollowed out probably before the Tang, under the Wei or the Sui, at much the same time as the **Dun huang** caves. From the Five Dynasties onwards, the work went steadily on, in spite of the troubled times; existing caves were decorated, and new ones cut, for example caves 33 and 35. Under the Yuan, the work was continued; several of the Xi xia caves were restored and transformed (for example Caves 2, 29). Much less interest was shown under the Ming and the caves were gradually abandoned; under the Qing, however, particularly between 1796 and 1851, interest was revived.

The caves fall into three groups, according to their structure: some are made with a central pillar, some have coffered ceilings, and some have ceilings in the shape of a flattened cone.

1. Three caves only have central pillars (and they may be old ones which were transformed later on). The most striking of these is Cave 17, in the east cliff.

2. Most of the caves at **Yu lin** have coffered ceilings; examples of this style date from the Tang, the Five Dynasties, the Song and the Yuan. They contain an altar rising towards the coffered ceiling, which may be double; in the Yuan caves, the altar is round, while in the Tang and Song caves it is square.

3. The third type is extremely rare, and at **Yu lin** only one example exists (Cave 6, **Da Fo dong**): the ceiling is in the shape of a flattened cone, low and wide. The cave closely resembles Cave 5 at **Yun gang**, but no proof exists to show that is was cut at the same early date.

GROTTES DE YU LIN
YU LIN CAVES

Grottes de la face est.
Caves on the east face.

D'après la revue «Wen Wu» (1956, No 10). Les numéros se réfèrent à la description donnée dans le texte.
After the magazine "Wen Wu" (1956, No. 10). The numbers refer to the description given in the text.

The wall-paintings are in poor condition on the whole, though a few large ones have survived, such as the paintings in Caves 25 and 26. The oldest ones date from the Tang; Cave 15 contains celestial kings, and Cave 20 Bodhisattvas, all of them superb works of art. The most interesting of all are in Cave 25; they are also Tang paintings, and are some of the most beautiful in existence.

The five Dynasties and the Song paintings are equally rich and varied in content; Caves 16, 17, 19 and 35 are good examples of this.

The Yuan caves also contain wall-paintings; they are unusual in that each one shows a different style, as Caves 6 and 3 show. Cave 39 contains paintings dating from the Xi xia.

Yu lin and its caves have been classed as a historical monument.

TIAN SHUI — THE MAI JI SHAN CAVES

The **Mai ji shan** is an odd-shaped hill about 15 miles south of **Tian shui** station, in a stretch of beautiful countryside. The caves which are cut into the sides of it are in fairly loose soil, easily eroded by wind and water, in a cliff which itself is friable. Because of these geographical and geological features, the sculpture inside the caves is generally of clay, or clay with a stone core; it has survived for a thousand years and is now as hard as terra cotta.

The hill contains over 190 caves. The sculpture dates from the Northern Wei at the earliest, and was restored and added to under the Sui, the Tang, etc., and even under the Qing. Some of the caves contain paintings on the side walls or the ceilings, as well as sculpture; some magnificent ones still survive dating from the Western Wei and the Northern Zhou.

The Mount **Mai ji** caves contain about a thousand pieces of sculpture altogether; a few of the most interesting ones will be briefly described.

The western side of the hill contains caves which have been left untouched for years; although they contain statues which were touched up or restored under the Tang and the Song, many of them have been left as they were, and date from the Northern Wei, the Western Wei or the Northern Zhou. Cave 100, for instance, contains a statue dating from the beginning of the Northern Wei, which shows a definite Alexandrian influence in the features, shoulders and bearing (the Hellenic influence reached as far as Central Asia, through India and Afghanistan). The slight body and floating garments prove, however, that two different styles were mingled in the statue, and the traditional Chinese style of the Han and the Jin is equally clear.

Cave 133 is the richest of all the **Mai ji shan** caves. It contains engraved stones as well as sculpture, and the stone is of a fine, hard kind which does not come from the surrounding area. Out of the 18 engraved stones, some date from the Western Wei and the Northern Zhou; one of them depicts a Buddha flanked by two other Buddhas, with hands raised, and sleeves and robes falling about them in graceful folds. Two Tang standing Buddhas fill the centre of the cave; the larger of the two, bowing slightly and full of goodwill, is most impressive. The smaller one also shows great strength and grace.

The two clay Bodhisattvas in Cave 121 appear to date roughly from the Western Wei.

The most outstanding Song work at **Mai ji shan** is in Cave 165. A large roofless niche (perhaps unfinished) contains a set of Buddhas portrayed with astonishing realism; they probably date from the beginning of the Song.

The eastern side of the mountain is more easily accessible, and the caves are in poorer condition. Many of the statues have been restored, often without great success. Cave 4 is worth a visit to see its paintings, which have escaped restoration (the cave is so small that it is impossible to get far enough away from the paintings to have a good overall view of them, and at the same time, the details need close examination). Seven pavilions and 41 magnificent Bodhisattvas stand out against an ornamental background, dating probably from the beginning of the Song, if not the Tang; they are full of life and extremely varied.

Cave 43 contains the bowed figure of a hero (Vira), of great power.

Cave 7, known as the **Niu er tang,** is west of the caves already mentioned; it is so called because it contains a statue of a calf, which shows remarkably close observation in the large, round, obstinate eyes, the folds of skin on the neck, the position, and the brute strength.

As a whole, the sculpture at the **Mai ji shan** contains some of the most interesting examples of China's artistic heritage.

THE QING YANG AND
THE ZHEN YUAN CAVES

They were discovered in about 1960. The group at **Qing yang** consists of 224 caves, containing 948 statues, near the confluence of the Rivers **Pu** and **Ru:** the style of both caves and statues suggests that most of them are extremely old. A stele near the entrance bears an inscription which tallies with an account given in the local records, which say that the caves were cut under the Northern Wei and restored under the Tang and the Song; only four large caves are in good condition now, and the rest are almost entirely in ruins. A magnificent statue of the Buddha Devaradja has survived in perfect condition. Numerous statues have been dug up and are now being restored.

A few more places in Gan su are also worth a visit:

The **Han xing lou** is in the Southern Pass Monastery **(Nan guan da si)** at **Lin xia**: it is a little pavilion with three roofs, each one smaller than the last, with upturned eaves corners; the floors between them consist of a plain framework of balustrades, open at the sides.

The Mosque **(Da he jia qing zhen si)** at Lin xia is also called the **Hai yi si**. The gateway is decorated with carvings and paintings, and the main building has an unusually large, sharply sloping roof, built all of one piece.

Lin xia also contains a beautiful carved gateway.

THE YUAN GUANG MONASTERY AND THE XU MI SHAN CAVES (NING XIA)

The **Xu mi shan Mountains** are 28 miles north-west of **Gu yuan**: they are part of the **He lan shan** chain which separates Ning xia from Inner Mongolia. The **Yuan guang Monastery (Yuan guang si)** is at the foot of the mountains, to the east, on a promontory of rock which gives a view over the Big Buddha and the **Xu mi shan Caves,** which face westwards, stretching over about half a mile.

The monastery was built comparatively late; the caves probably date from about the 5th century

A.D. (some of the sculpture has all the characteristics of Wei carving), with numerous additions dating from the Tang, the Song, and even the Ming (paintings). There have been frequent landslides, particularly in the central part. Many of the statues have been damaged or have disappeared over the last hundred years.

About 60 caves have survived; 17 of these contain statues. Two date from the Wei, two from the Sui, two from the beginning of the Tang, and 13 from the Tang; several niches date from the Song and the Jin.

Cave 1 is at the southern end; it contains a standing statue of the Buddha which probably dates from the Tang.

Cave 2 is north of the first one, and is the largest of all (over 65 feet high); as a result of landslides, the huge Buddha inside it is now in the open. It is a Maitreya, 65 feet high, portrayed sitting, with its hands on its knees; the ears reach down to the shoulders; the whole statue stands out against an ornamental background. A Tang pilgrim's inscription can be seen behind it. The eastern part contains several niches with little figures.

Cave 3 is one of the oldest; it is further along the valley from the second one. It is over 13 feet wide, and 4 feet deep. It contains three tiers of carvings: a prince travelling, a Buddha and two Bodhisattvas. It may well date from the Northern Dynasty.

The remains of the Song monastery, **Jin yun**, and the Ming monastery **Yuan guang** are near the third cave; the caves nearby all date from the Sui or the beginning of the Tang dynasty.

Cave 4 is north of the last one; it contains badly damaged statues.

Cave 5 is north again; it is 19 ½ feet square, and contains niches and several statues of the Buddha and Bodhisattvas, dating from the beginning of the Tang at the latest. Next to it is:

Cave 6, which contains a large niche with a Buddha (a Song copy).

Cave 7 contains a Song copy of a Buddha.

Cave 8 contains damaged statues, but the Bodhisattvas in the niches are full of life and recall the ones at **Long men,** in the **Fang xian si:** the paintings probably date from the Ming.

The other caves which are north of these contain paintings and niches of particular interest (Cave 12 contains some Tang statues; Cave 13 some Song statues, and Caves 14 and 15 contain Tang sculpture).

Only two Wei caves are left, built like the inside of a pagoda, with pillars and vaulted ceilings; the sculpture is typical of the Northern Dynasty.

Most of the Sui and Tang caves have been restored; they contain central pillars *(ta zhu)* and vaulted ceilings. The sculpture resembles the statues at the **Yun men shan** in Shan dong.

The late Tang caves are more numerous than the rest; the sculpture resembles statues of the same period in Gan su.

THE GAN SU — QING HAI REGION: THE GREAT BUDDHIST MONASTERIES

Introduction

A Tibetan Autonomous District **(Gan nan Cang zu zi zhi zhou)** in the south of Gan su borders on Si chuan and Qing hai.

Almost half of the inhabitants are Tibetans; the rest are Chinese, Hui, Manchu, and Mongol. The region is particularly rich in temples and monasteries, lamaseries and mosques. There are relatively few Chinese Buddhist monasteries.

Over a hundred monasteries contain more than ten Lamas each, and there are several hundred smaller religious centres (usually a little Hall of Sutras).

One of the six Great Monasteries of China, the **La bu leng si,** is in this area; 47 other monasteries come under it, and there are several dozen others which are independent of it. The **La bu leng si** is one of the most important centres of the Yellow Sect.

Originally several large sects existed side by side: the Red sect *(Ning ma pai)*, the White Sect *(Jia ju pai)*, the "Many-coloured" Sect *(Pu jia pai)*, and the Yellow Sect *(Ge lu pai)*. The Yellow Sect gradually predominated towards the middle of the Ming dynasty, and rapidly gained control over Lamaism. Under the Qing, the regime gave it considerable support; during the Kang xi period, both temples and monasteries developed as never before. Most of the religious centre in southern Gan su belong to the Yellow Sect. The other sects are poorly represented, and the introduction will be devoted entirely to the Yellow Sect.

All the monasteries have grown up near towns or villages, and are often very large. The largest stand out from the rest: the **La bu leng si** at **Xia he,** the **Za mu ka er si** at **Hei cuo,** the **Chan ding si** at **Zhuo ni.**

The buildings often back on to the hillside; they are impressively tall, and rest on solid foundations; the outside is often brightly coloured. Lamaseries only use black and white for decoration, but red, gold and yellow are frequent elsewhere.

Most of the monasteries are built following a strict rule. The structure on the whole is more or less the same, and the style varies little from one monastery to another; they are generally extremely satisfying buildings, both from an artistic and a technical point of view.

Lamaist establishments fall into several clearly defined categories.

1. The rank of the monastery depends on whether one or several living Buddhas are in residence there, or whether the monastery is an offering made by an individual (feudal landlord). A further distinction is made between principal monasteries, monasteries under the jurisdiction of a principal monastery, and small monasteries.

2. The principal monasteries are independent and their authority may extend over numerous other religious establishments falling into the other two categories, which need not necessarily be in the same neighbourhood. The **La bu leng si,** a principal monastery, has control over 47 others in the **Xia he** area; its authority extends to eleven others, at **Lin tan, Lin xia,** in Qing hai, in Tibet, Si chuan, Inner Mongolia, Shan xi and in Peking! The Lamas in the principal monasteries are well-educated; the monasteries spread over a large area, and house over a thousand monks. The same is true of all principal monasteries. There are over three thousand monks at the **La bu leng si.**

3. The secondary monasteries are directly dependent on the principal ones. Some of them receive administrative, religious or financial help; others are simply offshoots of the main one, under its control. They do not necessarily depend on the nearest principal monastery. The **Za nu ka er si,** a large and important

monastery, comes under the authority of a principal monastery in Qing hai. The secondary monasteries are run by monks of a lower level of education; the buildings are smaller, and house about a hundred monks.

4. The small monasteries come under the control of the secondary or the principal monasteries. They are generally small; one or two Living Buddhas with a relatively low standard of education live there, and the monks do not number more than a hundred.

As distances are so great, some towns or villages have a small religious centre *(ma ni fang)* run by one or two Lamas. The buildings are fairly rough in style.

5. The Yellow Sect monasteries often run temples belonging to the other sects.

6. Each monastery is run according to an established pattern: the Lamas pursue a strict study cycle, with examinations and a system of promotion. They live in different parts of the monastery, according to their rank.

A Lamaist monastery consists of several different pats:

A *Za Cang* is a type of institute. The **La bu leng si** has six of them, for the study of doctrine, astronomy, medecine, etc... Each *za cang* includes a hall of the Sutras *(jing tang)*, and a hall of the Buddha *(Fo dian)*, which always has verandas, statues, annex halls, and sometimes two stories. The hall of the Sutras is used for the reading of the canon; it is often on a large scale, and has a *tian jing* in front of it, with statues and frescoes. General meetings of all the Lamas are held in this hall several times a year (known as *du kang*). The hall at the **La bu leng si** is a huge one;

it contains 15 rooms across the width of it and 11 from back to front. High-ranking Living Buddhas administer the *za cang*. In the secondary monasteries, the *za cang* are often smaller; the small monasteries have one only. There is always another building to one side containing several large copper vats in which tea is made for the Lamas.

Near the *za cang* is the *xia jing yuan*, where the sutras are read in summer; it is a courtyard surrounded by low walls, full of trees.

The *la kang* (which means "monastery of the Buddha") are also important. Some monasteries have several Living Buddhas; others may have as few as one. The *la kang* is devoted entirely to the worship of the Buddha, and consists of one hall with verandas round it, with no hall of the Sutras. The halls are usually square and can be tall buildings (examples of these halls are the **Lu wa si** and the **Shou xi si** in the **La bu leng Monastery:** the nine-storey pagoda called the **ge da he** at the **Za mu ka er Monastery**). The Lamas' living quarters and the outbuildings and offices are attached to these halls.

The *nang qian* are administrative centres; the rooms where the Living Buddhas sleep or give audience are here too. A hall of the Sutras is reserved for the use of the Living Buddhas alone; the higher their rank, the bigger the hall. (The **Da nang** at the **La bu leng si** is one of these.) They are painted yellow on the outside, with a roof of green glazed tiles, and magnificent ornamentation.

The *ma ni ka la* verandas *(ma ni ka la lang)* are places where series of Sutras are read (they are printed on large vertical scrolls which are inserted into the wall and turned gradually). Every monastery has a veranda for this purpose. The one in the **La bu leng si** runs all the way round all the buildings.

Qiao deng (pagodas) are also numerous. Two kinds exist: pagodas with Sutras or statues of the Buddha, usually at the entrance to the monastery courtyard, and funerary pagodas, containing the remains of Living Buddhas, kept inside the Halls of the Buddha, and often overlaid with gold leaf (they are sometimes outside). They all have the same, characteristic shape: white Lamaist pagodas, but some are particularly fine specimens, such as the **Gong tang pagoda** at the **La bu leng si.**

The *bian jing tan* is a sort of altar where discussions between the highest-ranking Living Buddhas take place. It is a small raised platform.

The *yin jing yuan* is the workshop where the Sutras are printed; the printing blocks are kept there.

The *cang jing lou* is a hall for reading or reciting the Sutras, attached to large monasteries; it is also a library of sorts.

The Lamas' living quarters occupy many of the monastery buildings. The Living Buddhas have a special residence, as mentioned above. Rich Lamas also have special living quarters, and can take in poor Lamas. The other, ordinary, Lamas each have a cell to themselves; the cells are in groups of two or three, and several groups fill a building. The outside of these buildings is painted white, as laid down by the rules, and the doors are black, so that they stand out among the rest. The style is generally fairly rough. Inside, they look like typical Tibetan houses; the wooden walls are full of niches. The ordinary Lamas live in the plainest buildings of the monastery; those of higher rank live in the *za cang*, the *la kang* and the *nang qian*. The living quarters are built as they are needed, when the numbers increase; the buildings themselves and the narrow dark lanes alongside them follow no specified pattern.

The most interesting monasteries in the Gan su — Qing hai area will be briefly described.

The La bu leng si

The monasteries in southern Gan su contain several elements of traditional Tibetan architecture. The buildings are arranged in accordance with a general plan, and it is interesting to note how they are placed in relation to the central elements, and how they are decorated.

They are arranged in two ways: some consist of elements of different styles which combine to form a homogeneous whole (in this case the contrast between the unity of the whole and the incoherence of the details needs to be analysed); others are made up of elements of identical style, in which case the relation of each element to the whole should be determined.

Most of the monasteries are built up against the mountainside, facing the river; when they lie along a flat cliff, each building is encircled by an enclosure, and no particular order is imposed on the buildings. The **Chan ding si** at **Zhuo ni** is an example of this.

When the style is the same throughout all the buildings, it produces a most striking architectural whole; this is true of the **La bu leng si**. Building went on almost without a break from 1710 to 1949; it has nevertheless resulted in a coherent whole. One reason for this is the strict observance of the rule of this monastery that the monks' living quarters should all form the lowest tier of the monastery, and that they should be painted white. They therefore form the base for the rest. The halls of the Buddha, the *za cang*, *nang qian*, and the other buildings back on to the mountainside and often rise high above the lowest tier; their bright colours (red or yellow walls, golden or glazed roofs, and so on) enhance this effect. The verandas or walls round the building, all following the same design, also provide an element of unity. Skilful use of ornaments on the Guan Yin Hall roof, for instance, makes this comparatively low building stand out among the rest of the lowest tier. The *ma ni ka la* verandas, which contain over five hundred big vertical scrolls (each as high as a man, giving the impression that the rows of tall cylinders go on as far as the eye can see), surround all the buildings and bind them together as a whole. The interior style of the buildings is ancient in most cases, and fairly homogeneous.

The Za nu ka er si

The **Za nu ka er si** is on a large cliff at the foot of the mountain; the buildings follow a strict plan. It spreads down from the mountain towards the valley and the plain. The chief buildings are on the mountainside; the Lamas' living quarters begin up against the rest and fall away towards the plain. This natural development has produced an ordered, coherent group of buildings, with the main buildings standing out clearly above the rest; they are more than simply higher buildings among the one-storey monks' quarters. The effect is unfortunately partly spoiled by the fact that they are up against the mountainside, for only the highest, nine-storey buildings (the **Ge da he**) can be seen to full advantage. The latter also gains from being in front of a depression in the hillside. The Lamas' quarters are built in tiers, and the lowest tier is an enormous *ma ki na la* veranda. Here again, the verandas produce a most striking effect: they hold together all the different elements of the monastery, and create a sharply defined architectural border with long straight sections, like a regular polygon standing out against the emptiness around it.

The Lin tan

This monastery, unlike the last one, is built on a narrow cliff; some of its buildings are consequently very tall, and built on neighbouring peaks. It is a remarkable group of buildings, spreading over a large area, with many-coloured buildings shooting high up towards the sky. The upper line of buildings follows the mountainside like a succession of spirals, linked by clearly-marked paths; this again gives the impression of a well-planned whole. At the same time, the paths reveal new views and angles at every turn.

To sum up, it is obvious that the three monasteries mentioned are in fact collections of buildings which have grown up without any formal plan, though they are held together by a few accepted practices, so that the final effect is both coherent and varied. Although the exteriors are more or less unified in style, the interiors are all different. Details may vary, but the overall effect is homogeneous (for instance, the colour combinations, the doors, the surrounding halls), for the basic style is identical, but carried out in slightly different ways. The *ma ni ka la* verandas should be mentioned here: they are level, fairly low, and travel round all the buildings of each group;

a pointed pagoda often stands near the entrance,
by way of contrast with the low arcades.

The Structure of the Main Buildings

Their chief characteristic is their large size, calculated to give them dignity and majesty; added to this
is the elaborate use of ornamentation, which is
intended to give the onlooker an impression of utmost
grandeur.

The size is due to one of the most effective aspects
of Tibetan architecture, for the secret lies in the
creation of a tall, imposing pile out of buildings
which individually are relatively small. It is achieved
through skilful arrangement. The **La bu leng si,**
for instance, includes a hall called the **Shou xi si**
which is not a large building; but the façade consists
of four stories, each one of them different, and five
more stretch downwards. The visitor is deceived
by the different levels into thinking that he is looking
at an enormous building. The Hall of Guan yin
with a Thousand Arms consists of one modest single
storey building; the top of the hall ends in a little
two-storey pavilion, however, so that when it is
seen from the little courtyard next to it, it seems
very tall... Again, the Hall of the Sutras in the same
monastery is only three stories high, but the tangle
of roofs is executed in such an ingenious way that
they seem to disappear into the clouds.

Another way of suggesting several stories is to
use repeated horizontal lines. The Halls of the Sutras
and the Monasteries of the Buddha often have only
two or three stories, unlikely though this may seem.
Tiers of buildings spreading downwards over a slope
at the foot of a mountain contribute to the general
impression of height.

Yet another artifice used is that by which a whole
collection of buildings is made to look larger by simply
magnifying an insignificant detail in one part of it.
When the windows are outlined in black paint, not
only they, but the whole building is made to appear
larger. High verandas and tall pillars are other devices
used.

The use of false doors and windows is a good
example of the devices employed. The **Shou xi si**
for instance has only four stories, but they are made
to look like six from the outside. The nine-storey
pagoda, the **Ge da he**, at the **Za nu ka er Monastery** is a
skilfully devised six-storey pagoda.

A device often used in the *za cang* is the addition
of a new element reflecting the base of the building
at the top of it.

The skilful use of contrasts has an important role
to play as well. The main buildings present elaborately
decorated pointed shapes, alongside the long lines
of the stone walls and wooden verandas, or the
juxtaposition of different colours: red, yellow, white,
brown, green tiles, golden roofs, standing out against
stone walls; all these join with the vision of the whole
to produce an impression of majesty and power.

Ornaments and decoration

Countless different forms of decoration are to be
found. Some of them seem to be aimed at producing
an effect of magnificence and nothing more (carpets,
frescoes, screens, façades, statues, etc...); in many
cases the ornaments are survivals of earlier styles
which have not changed with the times. The Chinese
government has organised groups to study some
features in detail, so that this artistic tradition,

which is still full of life, may be continued; one of the fields which has excited interest is that of interior decoration.

The monks' living quarters are lined with richly panelled walls and niches. The colour combinations in the halls like the *nang qian* are particularly interesting, especially in the context of the surrounding wood carvings and carved bricks. It is unfortunately impossible to go into further detail in the space available here.

The Lamas' Living Quarters

The Lamas' living quarters fill a large area in the monasteries. They are built to meet certain practical needs, and may have several floors, cellars or basements; they are extremely varied. In order to save space and materials, they often have to serve several purposes; this is true of most of the buildings, except for the Halls of the Buddha and the Halls where the Sutras are recited. The basic structure is usually made of wood; the buildings may contain two, three, four or five rooms, and they are surrounded by verandas built in a characteristic style, between 6 and 8 feet high, with a little hearth, and stools round it. The shape and decoration of the windows are interesting.

The Tibetan traditions of architecture have been mingled with many Chinese elements, brought in by the local workmen, in the building of these monasteries. The roof ridges, the sculpture, the style of the doors and windows, all show this. Even the design itself of some of the *nang qian* halls shows clear Chinese influence.

The monastery walls are often works of art in themselves, with their elaborate ornaments.

Annex: The La bu leng si

This monastery is the most interesting of all those in the area. It was originally called the **Za xi qi si.** It has played such an important part in the religious life of western China that its name, **La bu leng,** is sometimes used to indicate all the regions round it: Gan su, Qing hai, Si chuan and Tibet.

The site on which it stands was originally the property of a Mongol prince who settled in Qing hai, and who founded the monastery under the Kang xi period of the Qing dynasty, in 1708, after making a pilgrimage to Lhasa. Building continued throughout the next two centuries, until the buildings now cover an area of 1,234 *mu.* The monastery includes six institutes *(za cang)*, 18 monasteries of the Buddha of different sizes, 18 large *nang qian* and over twenty normal sized nang *qian*, over a thousand rooms containing Lamas' living quarters, over a mile of *ma ni ka la* verandas, a printing-shop for printing Sutras, a library of Sutras, a gilded bronze pagoda, and three ordinary Lamaist pagodas. At first there were several dozen Lamas, then a few hundred. Before 1949 they numbered over 3,000. 108 other religious establishments come under the authority of the monastery, scattered over Gan su, Si chuan, Tibet, Inner Mongolia, Shan xi and Peking; the annex monasteries contain more than 20,000 Lamas. Six neighbouring towns and villages come under the control of the **La bu leng si,** which is, as has been said before, one of the six Great Monasteries of the Yellow Sect. The other five are: the **Zhe bang si,** the **Se la si,** the **Ga deng si,** the **Za shen lun bu si** (all in Tibet) and the **Ta er si** (in the sub-prefecture of **Huang zhong** in **Qing hai**). The sixth

Living Buddha *Jia mu yang (Jia mu yang huo Fo)* lives there; the first *Jia mu yang huo Fo* settled there in 1648.

The chief *nang qian* have housed 18 Living Buddhas, and have been embellished over the years.

THE GREAT WALL

Some of the finest remaining sections of the Great Wall are to be seen in Gan su and Mongolia. A few brief remarks will be made about the western and eastern parts.

The parts of the Wall near **Jiu quan,** at **Jia yu guan,** date from the Ming; all the remains are classed as a historical monument. It was originally the westernmost stretch of the Great Wall, on the edge of the Gobi desert. The gateway through it (with a tower and walls) standing today has been restored since the liberation: the original buildings date from 1372.

The overall length of the Wall is about 10,000 *li*, as its Chinese name suggests (Wan li chang cheng). Most of it follows the ridges and mountain tops. The Qin Emperor Shi huang is the figure always associated with the Wall; from the Tang dynasty onwards, it was a common mistake to think that he had it built. In fact, stretches of the Wall existed long before that; under the Warring States, six kingdoms joined in an effort to build them, and when the Qin empire had defeated them (220 B.C.) General Meng Tian was ordered to assemble a force of 300,000 men to extend the Wall. At that time it stretched from **Lin tao** (Gan su) as far as **Jie shen** at Liao ning, over a total of more than 10,000 *li*. The Wall now ends at **Jia yu guan** (Gan su) and **Shan hai guan**

(Liao ning), two points very near the two given by
the old texts. The two Walls which ran parallel
in east China were built to ward off the barbarians;
many stretches of the Qin wall merely linked up
existing stretches of Wall. The eastern part of the Wall
built by Meng Tian joined on to the old wall of the
Kingdom of Yan, which ran from **Zao yang** (now
Zhang jia kou) to **Xiang ping**. The western section
of the Wall (Shân xi and Gan su) was built by Emperor
Zhao of the kingdom of Qin. The Wall as a whole
was far from being the work of **Qin shi Huang di**
alone.

Only a few traces of the Qin Wall are left today
(the kingdom of Qin stretched well to the north of
the present Wall); parts of it can be seen near Tsihar
(it is purple).

Even so, the existing Wall is over 1,400 years old;
the eastern section is largely made up of stretches
built by the kingdom of Qi. The kingdom of Qi
used to include He bei, Shan dong, part of He nan
and part of Shan xi. In the middle of the 6th century,
it was extended as far as the sea, which made it over
3,000 *li* long. In 557, a second Wall was built inside
it; it ran from modern **Pian guan**, in Shan xi, to
modern **Ping xing guan** in the North-East. In 565, it
was extended again, as far as **Ju yong guan.** This stretch
of Wall, going from **Yan men guan** (reached in 579)
eastwards to **Ping zhou** (in the present **Chang li xian**
district in He bei), built by the Qi and the Later
Zhou, formed the foundation for the inner Ming
Wall. Finally, a stretch of Wall was built under the
Ming which stretched from **Dao ma, Long quan,**
as far as **Niang zi guan** and **Gu guan** (along the borders
of He bei and Shan xi), and linked various old remains
dating from the Warring States period.

The old texts say that the Great Wall stretched eastwards as far as the sea, but the exact point at which it met the sea is never stated. In 598 it reached **Lin yu guan,** about 60 miles east of **Ping zhou:** and **Lin yu guan** is not far from modern **Shan hai guan.**

The western section of the Wall probably dates from the 7th century (Sui dynasty). The main structure dates from 585; at that date it stretched as far as **Shuo fang** (west of the present sub-prefecture of **Heng shan,** Shân xi) and **Ling wu** (on the east bank of the Yellow River, in the present sub-prefecture of **Ling wu,** Gan su). When the Ming Wall was built, it was based on this wall in Shân xi and Gan su. The Sui Wall began either at **Wu wei,** or **Yu zhong xian,** south-east of **Lan zhou,** or at **Xi ning xian,** west of **Lan zhou.** It is thought that a section of Wall must also have been built in the corridor west of the Yellow River. Under the Han, walls existed near **Yu men guan** and **Yang guan:** remains of the Han wall have been found west of **Dun huang.** From the Ming onwards, the western stretch of the Wall reached no further than **Jia yu guan.**

It is hard to calculate the exact length of the Wall; as the crow flies, it measures 5,000 *li* from east to west, but it is made up of endless windings. The stretch in He bei, from **Shan hai guan** to **Ju yong guan,** known as the *jiu zhen,* which was constantly repaired under the Ming, measures 1,200 *li*. 1,023 *li* can be added for the stretch going westwards as far as the frontier of He bei and Shan xi **(Da tong):** 647 *li* on as far as **Ya gu shan:** 254 *li* from **Tai yuan zhen** to the bank of the Yellow River **(Bao de xian):** 1,770 *li* from **Yan sui** to **Hua ma chi:** 1,800 *li* from north-east Gan su to Ning xia **(Gu yuan zhen):** a stretch measuring 200 *li* north of **Gu yuan zhen:** 1,600 *li* from **Jin**

cheng xian (Gan su; the north bank of the Yellow
River, north-west of modern **Lan zhou**) to **Jia gu guan.**
This makes a total of 8,494 *li*, much less than the
real figures (other smaller stretches should be added).
When the double walls, built inside the other, are
added, the total easily exceeds 10,000 *li*. Over 10 walls
were built at some spots of special strategic importance.
Near **Yan men guan** there are three large walls and
more than twenty smaller ones, all parallel. Other
stretches of double walls can be seen at **Mi yun
xian** (He bei) and at **Ju yong guan,** north of Peking.
This point can be reached by train from Peking; the
train goes north westwards, through **Sha he** and **Nan
kou.** The Wall lies in the **Ba da ling Mountains** north of
Ju yong, stretching eastwards and westwards as
far as the eye can see. Beyond **Qing long qiao,** the
train passes another Wall; the wall at **Ba da ling**
is the inner Wall, and the outer Wall is crossed at
Feng zhen. The stretches at **Nan kou** and **Ba da ling**
are in fact remains of a third series of walls; nothing
is left of the point at which the Walls joined up;
originally, they were completely hermetic.

The gates in the Wall at **Ju yong guan** are extremely
fine; the outer gates lie outside the town of **Ju yong guan
(Ju yong wai zhen),** and the north gate, the **Guo
jie ta,** contains Buddhist sculpture dating from
1439 (Ming).

QING HAI

(Map see Atlas pl. 23/24)

Qing hai is a plateau of an average altitude of 9,800 feet, bordering on the Autonomous Regions of Tibet and Xin jiang and the provinces of Gan su and Si chuan. Its total area is 270,000 square miles, and it has a population of over two million. Half of these are Han; the rest are mainly Tibetan, though Mongols, *Ha long ke*, Hui, *Tu* and *Sa la* also live there.

Qing hai means "blue sea". It was originally the name of the huge lake in the east of the province, which is better known under its Mongol name of Kuku-nor; it later became the name of the province itself. The area round the lake and the basin round **Xi ning**, the capital, form one of the natural divisions of the province. The closed-in Tsaidam basin (area 84,000 square miles, the same as the Si chuan basin) stretches away to the north-west. The south of the province consists of a huge mountainous plateau crossed by the extension of the Kun lun Mountains, which are of an average height of 16,400 to 19,600 feet above sea level, with one peak reaching 23,497 feet. The Yellow River rises in the north of the mountains, and the Yang zi River in the south.

A railway line has been built between **Xi ning** and **Lan zhou** since the liberation, and several industries have been created there (dairy products, wool). The River Huang basin, where **Xi ning** stands, is the main agricultural area in the province. It was considered as the only cultivable land in Qing hai; in fact, most of the province has fertile soil, an abundant water supply and a suitable climate. It is now being systematically developed in several zones, and the traditional pastoral emphasis of the economy is changing, though stock-breeding is still the most important activity. The **Kun lun Mountains** and the **Qi lian shan Mountains** are covered with rich natural forests, which are now being worked properly (the timber is sent away down the rivers). The steppe country and the forests are full of bears, wolves, foxes, deer and other wild animals.

Until recently, the Tsaidam basin was inhabited by a scattered population of Khazak, Mongol and Tibetan herdsmen. No towns or roads existed. After the liberation, the area was prospected and found to contain large deposits of oil, coal, nonferrous metals, some of them rare ones, non-metallic minerals and vast salt reserves. In some places the salt is so abundant that

it is used for everything: roads are paved with it, bridges are
built with it, blocks of it are even used to build houses. It comes
in the form of red, blue or white transparent crystals, or "pearl
salt", and is extracted either from salt lakes, which replenish
themselves automatically, or mines, in which case it is as hard
as stone.

The Tsaidam basin is rich from all points of view: its sub-soil
contains large mineral deposits, which in time will result in
the creation of large industrial centres, and it is potentially
excellent agricultural land. Water flowing down from the
melting snows of the **Kun lun Mountains** can be used for irrigation.
All the conditions for future economic development are therefore fulfilled.

One large project has already been carried out since the
liberation: thousands of miles of roads have been built. They
now run from **Xi ning** to **Da chai dan,** in the north of the basin,
and on to Gan su; from **Xi ning** to **Golmo** (Go er mu), in the
south of the basin, and from there to Xin jiang in one direction
and Tibet (via the **Tang gu la Pass**) in the other; from **Xi ning**
to the mountains in the south of the province, where the road
forks, and one stretch leads to **Cheng du,** Si chuan, while the
other goes through west Si chuan to **Jiang da** and **Chang du**
(Chamdo), and on towards Lhasa.

The Qu tan Monastery

The **Qu tan Monastery** (Qu tan si) is near **Le du,**
east of **Xi ning,** in Qing hai. The River Huang flows
nearby and ever since the Han, the area has been
called **Huang zhong.** Routes from China to the
western regions run through it and it has always
been a prosperous area. Remains dating from the
Ming dynasty are particularly abundant. The two
chief monuments to see are the **Jin ta si** (one of the
six great monasteries of China) and the **Qu tan
Monastery.**

The **Qu tan si** lies amidst magnificent scenery 12
miles south of the town of **Le du,** surrounded by two
yellow earth walls.

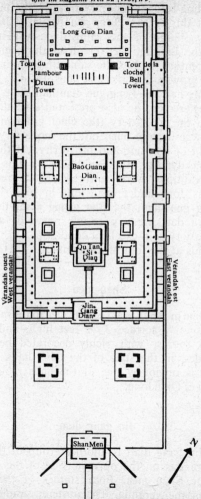

QU TAN SI

d'après la revue Wen wu (1964, nº 5)
after the magazine Wen wu (1964, nº 5)

Long Guo Dian

Tour du tambour
Drum Tower

Tour de la cloche
Bell Tower

Bao Guang Dian

Qu Tan Si Dian

Vérandah ouest
West verandah

Vérandah est
East verandah

Jin Gang Dian

Shan Men

N

According to contemporary records, the monastery was built during the Hong wu period (1368–1399), at the beginning of the Ming dynasty. The Great Hall of the Buddha was rebuilt at the beginning of the 15th century, and at the same time the monastery began to grow both in size and fame. In 1427, Emperor Xuan zong had the **Long guo dian** hall built, and had two steles erected; he also presented several valuable things to the monastery (the chief gift consisted of several large incense burners); the monastery reached the height of its fame and prosperity. At the end of the Ming dynasty, the buildings, by this time in poor condition, were restored. More restoration work was done under Qian long in 1644. Later on, the **Long guo dian,** the **Bao guang dian,** the northwest verandas, etc... were all repaired, and now the monastery is in excellent condition.

It stands at the foot of a mountain.

Shan men

The **Shan men** hall is at the entrance to the monastery; it stands on a terrace 3 ½ feet high, and consists of three rooms, with richly decorated beams and colonnades, in the style of the Qing halls near **Lan zhou.** It is obviously one of the halls rebuilt under the reign of Qian long.

Jin gang dian

The Jin gang dian is another group of three halls with verandas on the opposite side of the courtyard from the **Shan men.** Four statues of the Buddha stand on the veranda. The austere, simple style of the beam structure suggests that the building dates from before the Qing dynasty.

Qu tan si dian

Some sections of the beam structure on the outside of the hall recall the style of the Song and the Yuan in their build and decoration; the brick facing inside recalls the style of the **Dong pei dian** at the **Da zhong si** at **Jiu quan** (Gan su), which is also a feature of many of the Lamaist monasteries of Inner Mongolia. The inside walls are entirely covered with frescoes; a large sign written in golden characters on a red background outside the door gives the name of the monastery, and is dated the 26th year of the Hong wu period (1394) of the Ming dynasty; it is the oldest building in the monastery. The verandas round it contain some very fine mural paintings.

Bao guang dian

The Bao guang dian is a series of halls with magnificent beam structures, all very intricate and richly decorated.

Long guo dian

This is the largest hall in the monastery. The Great Hall, a masterpiece which dates from the Ming dynasty, is as brilliant a success as the **Ju lai dian si** at Peking. The pillars and roofs are in the same style as those at the **Shi san long ming lou,** also at Peking; it contains a mirror-column.

Hou zhong gu lou

The Bell and Drum Towers, east and west of the
Long guo dian show a masterly use of the elements
of beams, roofs and balustrades.

INNER MONGOLIA

The Autonomous Region of Inner Mongolia is the northern-most part of China. It is the largest province after Xin jiang and Tibet. It borders on the Mongolian People's Republic and the provinces of Gan su, Ning xia, Shân xi, Shan xi, He bei, Liao ning, Ji lin and Hei long jiang, stretching like an immense bow over 1,800 miles long. It has a population of 1,100,000 inhabitants. Mongols are the most numerous, but the Han, the Manchu, the Hui and the Dawor are also represented. Inner Mongolia was the first autonomous region to be created by the Party, in 1947. As far as the administration is concerned, districts and municipalities exist in the industrial and agricultural regions, peopled mainly by Han Chinese; confederations *(meng)* and banners *(qi)* exist in the regions where stock-breeding is the main activity, and where the population is chiefly Mongol.

Inner Mongolia is a plateau of an average altitude of 3,200 feet, slightly lower to the north-east, where the Xing an Mountains (Xing an shan) separate it from the plateau of Manchuria. East of the mountains, another stretch of steppe country links Mongolia to the north-eastern provinces. In the west, the Yellow River flows through the province, cutting off the Yin shan Mountains in the north from the Ordos plateau to the south. The province has a continental climate, generally cold and dry, with hot summers (maximum and minimum temperatures: — 30° F in winter and 97° F in Summer) on the higher plateaux; the eastern part has a damper climate, which produces good grazing grounds.

The economy of Mongolia is centred round stock-breeding (sheep, cattle, horses, camels). The introduction of communes is gradually extinguishing the nomadic methods of stock-breeding. The pasture lands, which used to be under constant threat of being sanded up (dunes of moving sands pushed by the wind) are now better protected; trees are being planted to keep the sand from blowing away, and to provide shelter from the wind. Factories are being built to deal with the animal products (tanneries, sheep and camel wool factories, dairy produce factories). Other branches of the economy are developing too: agriculture (wheat and potatoes) regularly produces more than expected; the eastern forests (12% of the province's total area) represent 17 % of the forest land in China. Mongolia also possesses rich mineral reserves: coal, iron, salt and soda.

The **Bao tou** area boasts large coal and iron mines. **Bao tou,** which is on the railway to **Peking** and **Lan zhou,** and which is in a position to take advantage of the hydraulic energy produced by the Yellow River, is well on the way to becoming a large industrial centre. Large rolling-mills have been built there since the liberation. Other branches of industry (machine-building, electrical, food-processing, textiles and transformers) also exist in the towns of **Bao tou, Huhehot** and **Hailar.**

Huhehot (Chinese: **Hu he hao te**) is the capital of Inner Mongolia. As far as industrial production goes, it comes second only to **Bao tou.** It now possesses a university, a Teachers' Training College and an Animal Husbandry and Veterinary Institute.

The Mongolian language spoken in Inner Mongolia differs considerably from that spoken in the Mongolian People's Republic; in Chinese territory the classical Mongolian alphabet, written vertically, is still in use, whereas in Outer Mongolia it has been replaced by the Cyrillic alphabet.

History and historical monuments

It has been established that west Mongolia was inhabited by the Huns (*Xiong nu*), a pastoral and hunting people, a thousand years before the birth of Christ. During the Spring and Autumn period, several clans settled in the south-east (*Dong hu*): they formed a confederation during the Warring States period, and the Chnese kingdom of **Yan** began work on the Great Wall to defend themselves against them. Other Chinese continued the building later on (Yan, Zhao, Qin) and completed the "Great Ten Thousand *li* Wall" (*Wan li chang cheng*). Under the Han, the **Xiong nu** became gradually more and more of a menace; their khan (*chan yu*) established his court in the area of modern **Yi ke zhao.** He constantly made war on the Chinese. Under the Han Emperor Wu, the Chinese themselves went to war against the Xiong nu, and occupied the land south and west of the Yellow River, in what is now Gan su, and the Yellow River area in the present province of Inner Mongolia, as they were anxious to keep clear the trade route to the West. The tomb figurines (*ming qi*) and other things uncovered during recent excavations show that the Mongols of this period had attained a high level of civilisation as far as art, architecture etc. are concerned (rich collections in the **Bao tou** Museum).

Later on, several clans: the *He lian*, the *Xian bei*, the *Tuo ba*, to name a few, settled in Inner Mongolia and in the north of the Chinese territories under the Jin and the Wei dynasties, and even established a dynasty of their own, the Xia dynasty (407) with He lian bo bo, and an imposing capital, **Tong wan cheng** (413); the remains of it are in the modern Banner of Wu chen.

In 630, the Tang Emperor Tai zong (Li Shi min) founded **Jiu zhou** in Mongolia, not a trace of which is left today.

In 916, the powerful Kitan *(Ji dan)* founded the Liao dynasty and established their capital at **Shang jing** (in the present Banner of **Ba lin, Ba lin zuo qi**), and occupied almost all of what is now Inner Mongolia. Numerous remains dating from this period still survive, particularly octagonal pagodas, 7 to 13 stories high which taper off to the top, and are characteristic of the architecture of the time. One of the most handsome of them is at **Shang jing**: the **Nan ta**, in the Banner of **Ba lin**. (The North Pagoda, four stories of which still stand, with their roofs, is not in such good condition, but it is just as fine.)

The magnificent White Pagoda **(Bai ta)** at **Qing zhou**, near the tombs of three Liao Emperors, with its walls covered with carvings of *luo han*, is still intact, and is one of the masterpieces of this type of architecture.

Other relics of the same period are:

1) the big pagoda at **Zhong jing** (the present sub-prefecture of **Ning cheng**), which has 13 stories following close on one another, built on a large base covered with carvings;

2) the little **Zhong jing** pagoda, near the first one; it consists of 13 stories resting on a slender base;

3) the broken pagoda at **Zhong jing** (in ruins); only the sturdy base is left;

4) the **Wan bu hua yan jing** pagoda, in the present **Tu mo te Banner,** which was built under the Liao, and restored under the Jin; it has 7 stories with elaborately carved roofs.

The Liao left other remains which have survived until now, such as the amazing stone lion at **Zhong jing**, which is as powerful as the lions of Delos; a huge stone torso at **Shang jing (Ba lin Banner)** and a column *(chuang)* at **Lin dong**.

In 1115, the Jin dynasty was founded, and it controlled about half of present Inner Mongolia. It was short-lived, and the only artistic relic which has survived is a beautiful stone lion which was dug up in the sub-prefecture of **Qing shui he.**

In the 12th century, Genghis Khan subdued all the other clans and in 1206, the Mongol Dynasty (the Yuan), set its first Emperor *(Tai zu)* to rule over China after the fall of the Southern Song dynasty. Mongolia still contains remains of the artistic splendour of the Yuan:

1) the walls of the citadel of **Shang du** (near modern **Duo lun nuo er**):

2) the remains of **Zhong du** (modern sub-prefecture of **Xing he**):

3) the white pagoda in the present sub-prefecture of **Kai lu** (built in the characteristic shape: a base surmounted by a dome, in turn carrying a sort of slender pagoda);

4) capitals and various steles (for instance the **Ji ning** stele).

Once the Mongol empire fell, feudal wars followed in close succession, leaving no artistic monuments. The Chinese dynasty of the Ming, however, still threatened by invasions from the north, built a new section of the Great Wall in the south of Inner Mongolia; the watch towers still stand in the sub-prefecture of **Qing he shui**, for instance.

Next the Manchu invaded and reduced Inner Mongolia; then they spread southwards to subdue the entire empire. In the Kang xi and Qian long periods (end of the 18th century) large lamaseries were built on the steppes of Mongolia, for instance at **Duo lun nuo er**, at **Cheng de** and in the Huhehot area. By the end of the Qing dynasty, over 1,000 of them had been built, scattered throughout Mongolia, about 20 to each Banner.

The monasteries were built in one of three styles:

1) **Tibetan style.** The **Ge gen** (in the *meng* of **Hu lun bei er**), the **Wu dang Monastery** (at **Bao tou**) are examples of this style: no real structural connection exists between the buildings; the wings are arranged haphazardly round the Great Hall, which is generally square, with a large, empty ground floor used for reciting the sutras. The Hall of the Buddha, like the Great Hall, is a tall building, usually with two to four floors; the windows are usually rectangular, and outlined in black (a wide band at the bottom and a narrow one at the top, giving an impression of heaviness and stability). The roof ridges are decorated with various kinds of gilded ornaments. The verandas contain numerous murals, executed with thick layers of paint.

2) **The Sino-Tibetan Style.** This is the most usual style in Inner Mongolia. The **Da zhao**, the Five Pagoda Monastery at Huhehot, the **Fu en Monastery** in the **A la shan Banner**, the **Yan fu si** at **Ba yin hot**, and many others, are examples of this. The Great Hall and the Hall of the Buddha are often joined together, with a double or even triple ridged roof, of enormous size; the Great Hall often has covered ways with pillars linking it with the buildings alongside; the decoration of the ceilings is another characteristic feature. Apart from these details, the rest is more like the Tibetan style buildings. The ornamentation is often extremely elaborate, and the carvings very rich. The monasteries often contain countless Lamas' pagodas (sometimes over a hundred) which are very fine.

3) **The Chinese Style.** The **Bei zi miao** (at **Xi lin hao te**) and the **Xi da miao** (in the **Ba lin Banner**) are good examples of this. The style is the same as that in similar monuments in China; everything is built as a coherent whole round a given focal point. In most cases the Great Hall is square. Verandas with pillars run round the buildings, the roofs have the characteristic Chinese shape; the details are nearer the Tibetan style (gilded points to the pagodas). The halls round the Great Hall are often smaller; the Hall of the Sutras may be built in one of several styles, but it is always a building of great magnificence.

Before moving on to consider several of the monuments in more detail, it should be added that Moslem monuments are fairly frequent in Inner Mongolia. Nearly all the large towns possess something: Huhehot has a mosque and a minaret, both dating from the Qing, **Duo lun nuo er** has a mosque as well, etc...

The steppes themselves abound in different kinds of tents and huts.

HUHEHOT

The Wan bu hua yan jing Pagoda

The pagoda is in the eastern suburbs of Huhehot, south-west of the village of **Bai ta cun**, near a disused monastery. It is an octagonal brick pagoda, about 20 feet long on each side. Each storey is divided off from the next by a fringe of roof. In its general outlines, the pagoda is like the one at the **Zhe du Monastery** in the sub-prefecture of **Zhou,** in He bei. The top is missing.

The first story, or base, ends in three rows of lotus petals; the second, fourth, sixth and eighth ones have arched doorways through the north and south facades, with statues of heroes *(Vira)* on the second and third. All the other façades have false windows and statues of different people (Bodhisattvas etc.) scattered over them, all masterpieces of the Liao dynasty art of sculpture. Each façade has slightly oval colonnades surmounted by dragons. A balcony runs round each floor inside, with false doors, and a staircase leads up to the top; round the walls are seven lintels with inscriptions on them *(pai)*. The pagoda was built between 983 and 1031, under the reign of the Liao Emperor Sheng zong. Several inscriptions dating from the Yuan can be seen inside. The pagoda has been restored several times.

The Wu ta zhao Pagoda

The pagoda is in the **Ping kang** district of the old town in Huhehot, and is also called the **Ga deng si** or the **Jin gang bao zuo ta.** It is all that is left of the monastery of the same name. It is a splendid building, standing on a large terrace surrounded by sturdy ramparts; its seven stories with green glazed tile roofs and white stone parapets stand on a white brick base. The tops of the little pagodas on the terrace are of yellow and white glass which can be seen shimmering from far away. The terrace at the base is 25 feet high, 36 ½ feet from west to east and 31 feet from north to south. It is covered with carvings (lions, *luo han*, etc.). The narrow strips of roofing jutting out from the seven stories shelter niches, also with carvings. Handsome Qing statues flank the door; inside is an altar to the Buddha. Five pagodas stand on the terrace; the middle one is over 20 feet high. The little pagodas are covered with beautiful carvings, all extremely varied. According to local records, the building dates from 1740. The most interesting parts of the neighbouring monastery, the **Jin gan bao,** are the halls of the sutras and the library.

Huhehot also contains a mosque, which has already been mentioned, and which is worth a visit, and various other monuments.

The Drum Tower (Gu lou)

The tower is part of the Great Wall built by the Qing, and has survived in perfect condition; it consists of a massive, plain base, supporting a huge two-story pavilion, with two sets of wide balconies and roofs parallel with each other, decorated with little bronze statues. The lines of the building are simple and austere; the impression of symmetry is sustained by the pillars (one at each corner, and four along each side, dividing the building into three).

Xi li tu zhao

This Sino-Tibetan style monastery is also called **Yan shou si.** The Great Hall of the Sutras dates from the Ming, and has a wide veranda supported by pillars, characteristic of this style. The roof is covered with elaborate ornaments, little bells, bronze animals, and magnificent dragons and clouds at the corners.

The monastery also contains a large wooden Ming gate *(ma pai fang)* with inscriptions in Mongolian; the beams and the roofs are extremely complex, and yet light at the same time. The shafts are decorated with symmetrical geometric patterns.

The famous Two Ears Pagoda **(Shuang er ta)** stands nearby; it is a magnificent white pagoda of classic lines, which compares favourably with the **Miao ying Pagoda** at Peking. Two graceful carved lobes curve outwards and downwards from the thirteenth ridge of the pointed section at the top. The base is unusual; four graded tiers engraved with inscriptions rest on a stone plinth with columns, its walls decorated with a pattern of clouds and mushrooms, representing longevity.

The various buildings forming the monastery are grouped round the central hall.

The Da zhao

The **Da zhao** is another Sino-Tibetan style monastery, dating from the Ming, which differs, however, from the **Xi li tu zhao.** The Great Hall of the Sutras stands at the end of a huge courtyard containing several stone plinths carrying bronze lions and large bronze vases. The Great Hall is a massive two-storey building with slightly oblique walls, which stress the overall impression of power and stability which it conveys. The roofs, built in Chinese style, slope gently down to the corners, which are sharply up-turned, with the customary sets of little statues decorating the ridge. The first floor, with lattice windows opening on to a balcony with a balustrade, is divided off from the floor below by a strip of straight roofing. Here again, the buildings are centred round the main hall, on roughly the same plan as the last one. The different

vases, animals etc. in the courtyard in front of the
Great Hall are known as the *tiao gui*, Devils' Leap.

Wu su tu zhao

The **Wu su tu zhao** is also a Sino-Tibetan monastery,
and dates from the Ming; it stands in the middle of a
stretch of semi-desert, and looks like a confused
jumble of roofs when seen from a distance. Oddly
enough, the roofs are unmistakably Chinese in
style; they belong to the annex buildings. The Great
Hall itself is completely different; all its lines are
vertical or horizontal, and the general effect is heavy
and graceless. A flight of steps leads up to the door,
which is flanked by two small wall-paintings standing
out against the wall, which is painted white. The
building is three stories high; balconies with balustrades divide each floor from the one above. The
one colourful element which relieves the rest is provided by the carvings and paintings on the four
pillars supporting the first floor balcony, and the
round ends to the tiles, all painted in different colours.
A large wooden panel bearing the name of the monastery in Chinese characters hangs from the upper
balcony.

Xiao zhao

This monastery is the Qing counterpart of the
Da zhao already mentioned. It is also known as the
Chong fu si. It is now in poor condition, but it is
none the less beautiful for that. The eastern courtyard
contains a very fine pavilion with a glazed tile roof,
built on austere, vertical lines which are broken
by two roofs: the first is fairly severe, a long, wide
strip with only a hint of a curve; the other crowns

the whole building, sloping steeply down from a
narrow ridge to sharply up-turned corners. The
general effect is at once powerful and graceful. A
slender openwork column stands in front of the
pavilion.

A massive column stands on a plinth in the eastern
courtyard; the base consists of rows of petals, surmounted by tortuous carvings ending in dragons'
heads; it is executed in glazed tiles.

The courtyard in front of the Great Hall is decorated
with various objects, as is the **Da zhao** courtyard;
this is another characteristic of Sino-Tibetan architecture.

The Wu ta si

This monastery is famous for its pagoda, a masterpiece whose only rival is the **Jin gang bao zuo** pagoda
of the **Zheng jue Monastery** in Peking.

It is an impressive building: the seven-storey base
has narrow strips of tile roofing separating the rows
of statues of the Buddha. The base is entirely symmetrical; the middle section of the main façade containing
the door juts out slightly from the rest, but the rows
of Buddhas and the roofing continue uninterrupted.

Five pagodas built in the same style stand on the
flat roof formed by this block of masonry: one at
each corner and one in the middle. The whole building
dates from the Qing.

E mu qi zhao

The E mu qi zhao monastery dates from the Qing,
and is built in massive style, particularly the Hall
of the Sutras and the Hall of the Buddha. It bears
a strong resemblance to many purely Chinese Qing

buildings, though it contains one or two Sino-Tibetan elements, such as the **Devils' Leap (Tiao gui)** in front of the Great Hall: an enormous incense-burner with a base shaped like a tripod *(ding)*, ending in a two-storey pagoda-shaped building, with roofs, open at the sides. Bronze lions flank the entrance to the hall.

The Lamaist pagoda is entirely classic in style: the base is shaped like a pyramid, with indented corners, surmounted by a slightly egg-shaped dome ending in a roof and a point with thirteen stories. The ornament at the top is round.

BAO TOU

The Kun du lun zhao White Pagoda

The White Pagoda is striking mainly because the material used is unusual. It is small, and is the same shape as most Lamaist pagodas, except that the base is different: it consists of two plinths, one on top of the other, the second one smaller and lower than the first. Out of the second one grows yet another base, taller than the others, square like them. though each corner has seven indentations in it; finally the dome above it has four openings alternating with delicate carvings and ends in a point whose base echoes the base of the dome, with its indented corners; the top of the point has thirteen tiny stories.

Bao tou also contains a handsome doorway, the **A wang fu** door, which dates from the Qing.

The Wu dang zhao

The Wu dang zhao, also known as the **Guang jue si,** is a large group of light-coloured buildings, dating from the Qing, in a valley framed by hills. The architecture is Tibetan throughout. Most of the buildings, (the Lamas' living-quarters), have two stories, and are scattered over the valley instead of being grouped round the Great Hall, which is on the hillside. The buildings are isolated, with paths running from one to another, instead of covered ways. All of them are well kept up, painted white, with bands of black, wider at the bottom than at the top, on the window recesses. The flat roofs are characteristic of Tibetan architecture. An interesting comparison can be made between this group and the **La bu leng si:** a temple of the same name exists here too. It is relatively small, but built so that it appears to have more floors than it has in reality; a large veranda in front of the main door has some handsome paintings on the walls.

As a group, the building may at first sight appear to lack cohesion; the individual buildings, however, are built in a powerful and entirely homogeneous style.

BAYINHOT (Ba yin hao te)

The Ding Yuan Wall

The **Ding yuan ying** was built under the Qing; a short section of the wall, a colossal gate and a tower are still standing.

The surviving gate is the north gate of the wall; a colossal tower shaped like a flattened cone stands beside it, with battlements at the top. A graceful two-story pavilion stands on top of the tower; built in wood, it has two parallel roofs, the lower one larger than the other, both with strikingly up-turned corners; the bottom floor is plain, with columns;

the second floor, above the lower roof, is a bare wooden cube, surmounted by an elegant roof.

The Mu pai fang

The **Mu pai fang** is a graceful wooden arch spanning the street. It consists of a wooden panel placed vertically, with a plaque engraved with characters supported by slender columns, on either side; the roof looks as though it has alighted there, with its elegant upturned corners, resting on a complicated system of beams and tracery, like Chinese roofs. Little bronze bells hang one at each corner of the roof; bronze statuettes stand on the ridges. This masterpiece dates from the Qing.

The Da wang fu

The Da wang fu is a large group of buildings of purely Chinese style, enclosed by a wall, all dating from the Qing; it is well worth a visit. The buildings include:

a) the **Fang ting zi,** a square pavilion, built entirely of straight lines, with a flat roof;

b) a tall kiosk, the **Gao ting zi,** which is square, built on a high base and surrounded by a little parapet of open brickwork; the style is light and plain; the curve of the eaves corners is so pronounced that the ridge is crescent-shaped. The beam structure supporting the roof is unusual.

c) the park is also walled, with glimpses of Chinese style pavilions among the trees.

The Yan fu si

This Sino-Tibetan style monastery again dates from the Qing. It is on a vast scale, with the Great

Hall in the middle; its roofs are extravagantly decorated, and built in several horizontal layers. A veranda running along the main facade of the building is supported by painted and carved pillars; murals decorate the walls. The pillars and beams inside are in the traditional Tibetan style: they are covered from top to bottom in paintings, like the walls themselves, depicting dragons twisting round the columns; vast Buddhist scenes cover the walls, geometric patterns the top and bottom of the pillars, and scroll-like patterns of clouds the angles formed by the beams, and the ceiling. The monastery is built on a ridge; the upper stories of the Hall of the Buddha commands a magnificent view over the varied scenery which unfolds below.

Private houses

Several houses at Bayinhot reflect the style of houses in Ning xia: a symmetrical combination of pillars, lattice windows and doors, carved beams at the corners and below the roofs.

ULANHOT (Wu lan hao te)

The Mo li miao

The **Mo li miao** is a little Buddhist temple which is interesting above all because of one or two details: the ceiling in the Great Hall of the Sutras is divided up by the beams into a sort of chequerboard shape, and each section is decorated with highly stylised symmetrical paintings: cloud patterns in the corner angles, and a circle with inscriptions in the middle.

A stele with a statue of the Buddha stands in the courtyard, with a little Chinese style roof sheltering it.

The **Mo li si,** which is another example of Sino-Tibetan style, dates from the Qing. The stele, like the one at the **Guang zong si** in the **A la shan Banner,** is of Lamaist inspiration, and relatively rare.

The A la shan Banner (A la shan qi)

The **Jia lan shan Monastery (Jia lan shan bei si)** is in the A la shan Banner. It consists of a large group of Sino-Tibetan style buildings dating from the Qing. The chief buildings are on the hillside, and the annex buildings spread out below, forming two smaller groups, apparently un-connected except for the walls and covered ways running from one to another. The monastery is also known as the **Fu yin si.**

The scale of the buildings is impressive: the Great Hall of the Sutras stands at the far end of a vast courtyard completely enclosed by covered ways several rows of pillars deep, with all the pillars carved and painted in Tibetan style. The Hall itself is a colossal, heavy building, where the dominant feature is furnished by horizontal lines. It too is preceded by a veranda carried by thick pillars.

The **Qie lin zhao Hall** next to it is a curious edifice; a tall, elegant incense-burner stands on a plinth in front of it. The roof shows distinct Chinese influence, as it slopes steeply down from a narrow ridge, then becomes almost flat as it reaches the edge; the rest of the building combines traditional Tibetan style with the earth-bound, solid aspect of some Chinese buildings. When seen from the front, the hall, which is raised above ground level, seems to consist of one storey only; pillars on either side of the door support a deep veranda; then right and left of the veranda are two stretches of wall, covered with elaborate decoration executed in glazed tiles. A balcony with an open work balustrade and several bronze ornaments runs the length of the façade between the two side walls. The building is massive when considered as a whole, but it is lightened by the profusion of detail. The courtyard round it has covered ways running along the walls, in Chinese style.

The **Hutuketu Family Temple** in the monastery is a handsome Tibetan style building, painted white, with the windows outlined in black like the windows in the Lamas' living quarters. It is built on a large raised base, with a flight of steps leading up to the door; the style is plain and symmetrical; a veranda with two slender pillars in front of the door runs along the front of the building. It has no mural paintings.

The **Temple of the Maitreya Buddha (Mai de er miao)** is not far away; it stands on a massive stone base overlooking a valley; the gate and the roof are Chinese in style, but the rest is Tibetan: white walls, black outlines to the windows, verandas, and a hall which recalls the **Qie lin zhao**.

The monastery is north of the Jia lan Hills (hence its full name, **Jia lan shan bei si**).

Its counterpart, on the south side of the mountains, is the **Jia lan shan nan si**, also called the **Guang zong si**. From a distance, it gives the impression of a coherent, well-planned whole; the little white Lamas' dwellings are linked by walls or covered ways. Unlike the northern monastery, the buildings are not scattered; though they have clearly been added gradually as needed, a certain order has been maintained, and they follow the line of the valley. All the houses are more or less alike; they are small, and the main façade has a door with a lattice window on each side, giving on to a veranda supported by plain wooden pillars; the flat roofs are made of puddled clay. The houses are built in groups, or added on to each other cornerwise.

The main buildings are the most interesting from an architectural point of view, and are excellent examples of "pure" Sino-Tibetan style, where the different elements (Chinese roofs, and the Tibetan ideas of proportion) are successfully combined to make a harmonious whole. The roofs are steeper than Chinese roofs (a slope of about 45°); then main halls form a block which gathers the surrounding buildings towards it, using walls and covered ways.

The Great Hall is an extremely handsome building, with an interesting feature in the gables, which are covered with series of different little scenes disguising the struts and beams.

The monastery also contains a carved rock.

The A sa ke Banner (A sa ke qi)

The **A sa ke zhao Monastery,** a Qing Sino-Tibetan style monastery, is in this banner. The Great Hall of the Sutras is the most impressive building in it. It is square: the bottom story has one main door and two side doors on the front façade, opening on to a veranda with four slim carved pillars; slender beams and tracery join the pillars to the first roof. The other sides are plain white walls, with two pointed arched windows. A gently sloping roof covers the lower story. The second story is narrow, with a balcony which is almost hidden under a second roof in classic Chinese style. The hall is unusual because the first roof is much longer and wider than is generally the case in this type of building.

The Wu shen Banner (Wu shen qi)

The Wu shan Banner contains a magnificent Qing monastery, the **Wu shen zhao,** built in Sino-Tibetan style.

The Great Hall is striking above all for the balance in its lines between symmetry and power. The façade, which is raised above ground level, has a large main door (covered with paintings and carvings) flanked by lattice windows, covered by a sort of porch running almost the whole length of the façade, whose roof, sloping gently down to the up-turned corners, juts out beyond the rest of the ground floor. Another roof of the same height covers the rest of the building; the two of them give the impression that the whole building is dominated by horizontal lines. A second, smaller story grows out of this, lower than the first and with four blind walls; its roof follows the same lines up-turned at the corners, as the other two. The whole effect is most striking and is rendered even more so by a single white Lamaist pagoda on the right, emerging from the roofs, accentuating the symmetry of the rest by breaking into it; no other example of this exists in Mongolia.

The monastery is also famous for its countless pagodas. The Great Hall of the Sutras is enclosed in an empty courtyard; beyond the wall is a veritable forest of pagodas. They are of all sizes; most of them are traditional Lamaist pagodas; some of the walls are bordered by a line of fairly small ones, which form a screen of white domes and points hiding the bases of the bigger ones. The variations of style are usually to be found in the base, which is made up of tiers of stone. One pagoda is worth describing in detail: the "octagonal" pagoda *(ba jiao la ma ta)*, which dates from the Qing, though its style is far more ancient. It stands on a massive base with battered walls tapering slightly towards the top; the steps or tiers are decorated, and on a generous scale. The dome grows out of an octagonal base, and is spherical, with a row of little dormer windows; an elongated pyramid-shaped point ends in an open work cylindrical iron ornament, with a fringe of little tassel-shaped ornaments round the bottom of it. The whole pagoda is white, and apart from the windows, has no opening except for a door at the bottom. A graceful little wooden porch precedes the door, in Chinese style, with its eaves corners turning skywards, supported by four slim pillars. The beams are beautifully worked.

By way of contrast, another pagoda, equally beautiful in a different way, is entirely round and plain, resting on a cubic plinth covered with interesting carvings.

SILINHOT (Xi lin hao te)

The **Bei zi miao** is the chief temple of interest at Silinhot. The Great Hall of the Sutras and the other main halls are purely Chinese in style, but they have verandas in front of them. The complicated roof structure is characteristic of Qing architecture. The Great Hall is curious, as its entrance is approached first of all through a little wooden hut, and then through a white Mongolian tent, which gives on to the door of the hall. The hall itself contains an excellent statue of the Maitreya.

The same monastery contains the strange **ao bao**: first a row of cylindrical tumuli, made of earth and stone, with tufts of vegetation growing out of them, and then a kind of white terrace, on the top of which Mongolian staves and banners have been fixed.

The Da er han and the Mao ming an Banners

The huge Sino-Tibetan monastery here forms a
completely homogeneous whole. The majority of the
buildings are Tibetan, and the Tibetan influence
is noticeable in many different aspects: the arrangement of the annex buildings round the main halls,
the monolithic effect of the great halls on their
raised platforms, their white walls and flat roofs.
The general overall impression is of horizontal
lines emphasised by black painted outlines broken
only by the slanting lines of the walls, wider at the
bottom than at the top. The monastery is known
as **Guang fu si**, or **Bei le si**.

The Great Hall and the main halls are austere in
their outline, but the decoration used is chosen with
the utmost care: inscriptions, geometric patterns,
stylised cloud designs, etc.. The roofs sweep down
from the intricately carved ridges decorated with
bronze animals, resting on magnificent carved beams.

The monastery also contains several handsome
Lamaist pagodas, in classic, plain style.

A ba ga Banner (A ba ga qi)

The **Han bai Temple (Han bai miao)**, dating from
the Qing, is in this banner. It is built in Chinese
style; the most striking element in it is the magnificent
stone Lamaist pagoda. It consists of a carved stone
base, followed by plain stone tiers, out of which rises
the dome; it is almost spherical, and carved with
lotus petals at the base and in the middle. Above it
several thick, tall stone rectangles give way to the
point, ringed with horizontal ridges and ending
in a round base supporting an ornament.

The paintings in the Great Hall of the Sutras of the same temple are some of the most beautiful in the whole of Mongolia. They are highly stylised, so much so that their technique is almost too perfect.

Yue wu zhu mu qin Banner

This banner contains a very fine temple in Chinese style, the **La ma ku lun miao.** The Great Hall is entirely Chinese in its general lines, though a few additions, such as the decoration of the top of the pillars supporting the veranda, show slight Tibetan influence. An annex hall, behind the Great Hall, is square, and consists of a tall base supporting a wooden pavilion. The first story has a flat roof with a low parapet round it, in Tibetan style, and the pavilion stands in the middle; its most striking feature is the roof, with very pronounced ridges, and ornaments at the corners.

The same temple includes another hall, with three stories, of curious construction: the outer walls are of pure Tibetan style (the massive walls slant slightly inwards towards the top, the windows are deep-set and narrow, the roof is flat), while the frontal veranda, set back between two massive walls, is Chinese, with pillars supporting strips of roofing and balconies (the reverse phenomenon is more usual). Another unusual feature is that the two stories of the façade resemble each other closely, whereas the third is set very much further back.

The whole effect is one of great strength. The wall paintings inside are executed in a simple, almost sophisticated style.

Zhun ge er Banner

The western monastery (**Zhun ge er xi zhao**) is a mixture of strange buildings of confused styles, probably dating from the end of the Qing.

This list of monuments is far from exhaustive, though it helps to show something of Mongolian Lamaist art. Other monasteries are well worth a visit:

The **San de miao** at **Wu la de** (Tibetan).

· The **Hui zong si** and the **Shan yin si** at **Duo lun nuo er**.

The **Xi da miao** in the **Ba lin Banner**.

On the whole, the monuments and buildings in Sino-Tibetan style are the most frequent of all, and at the same time, they are the most interesting from an artistic point of view, as they show how the two different styles may be combined with more or less success.

A group of caves and several recent archaeological discoveries should be visited if possible.

The Ba lin Banner (Ba lin zuo qi)

An ancient Liao citadel stands in the **Zhao wu da** confederation, south of the town of **Lin dong**. Four groups of cave monasteries are to be found in the **Ba lin zuo qi** area as well. The largest monastery is about 18 miles from the old citadel (at **Dong shan**); natural caves are used as well as caves hollowed out artifically: over 100 of them have been counted altogether.

Ten more caves lie 45 miles away, near **San shan dun.** Finally, two large temples stand south of the citadel: the **Qian zhao miao** and the **Hou zhao miao.** Between them they constitute the most complete group of buildings from an artistic and archaeological point of view still to be seen in Inner Mongolia.

To reach them, the best way is to start from **Lin dong,** crossing the River **Bai yin ge lou** (or **Sha li**), and follow the river southwards until after about 6 miles, the river enters a mountainous area, with some of the most exciting scenery in north China. A narrow path leads through this for about 12 miles, and ends in a thickly wooded valley full of monasteries. The **Hou zhao miao** is on a steep rock about 160 feet high in the middle of the valley.

The three caves are now sheltered by a lamasery built in front of them under the Qing, the **Shan fu si,** usually called the **Hou zhao miao.** It consists of a Great Hall and verandas; the caves are behind the Great Hall. A statue of the Buddha stands at the entrance; then come two groups of Bodhisattvas, the fifteen disciples of the Buddha, all weeping, and wall paintings of the Thousand Buddhas. At the far end are three sets of 18 statues and to the south, three sets of 10 statues, all about 18 inches high. The north cave, slightly above the other, also contains some magnificent statues, including the Buddha and his disciples, Bodhisattvas, and stone lions, all dating from the Liao. East of the valley are more statues in excellent condition.

The **Qian zhao miao** is about 2 miles from there, on a cliff south of the ridge. A Lamasery was founded there under the Qing, in front of caves dating from the Liao. It includes ten halls, and countless stone niches imitating the style of wooden niches, which is useful from a documentary point of view. The numerous statues are on the whole less lovely than the ones at the **Hou zhao miao,** both in the material used and in the style. A circular stele made of several blocks may have been restored.

Ning cheng

The old citadel of **Zhong jing,** dating from the Liao, is in the sub-prefecture of **Ning cheng** (in the **Zhao wu da** confederation); remains of strongholds of the Peking circuit (under the Jin) and the **Da ning** circuit (under the Yuan and the Ming) are also to be found there. Excavations have yielded a rich collection of remains which are extremely important for the study of the history of the Ji dan as well as that of Mongolia. Excavation work began in 1959, and the site has been classed as a historical monument.

Buildings on several different levels have been uncovered, as in the case of the **di tan** (altar of the earth) and of the citadel itself (an account was published in *Wen wu,* 1961, 9, p. 34); remains of the **Ou fo** monastery have also been uncovered, with coins, fragments of statues, etc.; among them is a remarkable mask of a "hero" *(Vira).*

Tombs have been found outside the walls of the citadel itself, and large quantities of Liao porcelain, pottery, statuettes, bronzes and jade ware (see *Wen wu,* 1961, 9).

Ku lun qi

In 1953, a royal tomb yielding an extremely rich collection of objects was found about 12 miles from **Ku lun qi,** near the village of **Wu li bu ge:** pottery and porcelain were found near it, as well as other tombs. They all appear to be Liao tombs.

Ling dong

In 1953, remains of an old citadel, dating probably from the Liao, were found there, along with a large group of tombs. Large quantities of stone tools were uncovered west of the town.

Another group of tombs were found at **Feng huang shan.** Work is still going on in the **Shi jia zi** area on remains of the site of **Qing zhou.**

THE NORTH-EAST

The three north-eastern provinces: Liao ning, Hei long jiang and Ji lin, usually referred to as Manchuria by Western geographers, are interesting for two reasons. The Manchu dynasty, the Qing (Ch'ing), who ruled China from 1644 to 1911, came from there, and it is now the most important industrial area in the country.

For centuries the north-eastern steppe country was virtually empty of inhabitants, until it was opened to Chinese emigrants at the beginning of this century. As it was rich in natural resources, potentially good agricultural land, and gave easy access to Peking, the neighbouring foreign powers each tried to gain control over it, until the Japanese finally occupied it, and founded the state of Manchukuo in 1933; they then began to industrialise the whole area. Its economy has developed considerably since 1949, with the help of the Soviet Union, who at first took it over as part of their share at the end of the war in 1945.

The North-East, whose natural resources make it one of the richest areas in the whole country, differs from the rest in that it is fairly thinly populated: its 60 million inhabitants live in an area covering 380,000 square miles, as compared, for instance with Shan dong, where the same number of inhabitants live in an area of 68,000 square miles. Most of the emigrants to the North-East are in fact natives of Shan dong. Liao ning, the most densely populated of the three provinces, has only 80 inhabitants to the square kilometre. Roughly a third of China's industry is concentrated in the North-East; heavy industry and the machine-building industry form the backbone of this. When seen from the train, the plain covering the centre of the region, now carefully cultivated and yielding good harvests, immediately brings to mind the great monotonous stretches of recently re-claimed agricultural land in the Soviet Union or the United States.

The mountains which fringe the plain to the east and the north are covered with forests; several rivers rise there, carrying heavy traffic in summer. Facilities exist for ski-ing and skating; in the winter of 1964–65, the Chinese ski championships were held at Tong hua.

The towns are modern; the streets and squares in the town centres are flanked by Western style buildings, a legacy from the Japanese, or buildings dating from after the liberation.

Shen yang, better known in the West under its Manchu name of Mukden, is the only town which has any ancient monuments.

A regular train service exists between Peking and the North-East; the trains are frequent and fairly fast. The expresses cover the 719 miles from Peking to Chang chun in 16 hours 35 minutes, at an average speed of 45 m.p.h., and the 193 miles from Chang chun to Shen yang take 4 hours, at an average speed of 50 m.p.h. Several planes a week fly from Peking to Shen yang, and there is a weekly service from Peking to Chang chun and Ha er bin. Planes from Peking to Pyong yang make a stop at Shen yang.

Shen yang

The former city of Mukden now has a population of 2,800,000 as compared with 100,000 in 1910 and 581,000 in 1937. Its wide streets, tall buildings and spacious squares give a modern look to the town; its plan and buildings recall Western cities. This, combined with a noticeably better and more carefully dressed population than is usual in Chinese towns, give it an air of prosperity.

As it was the capital of the Manchu dynasty from 1625, it is the only town in the North-East which can boast any historical monuments.

It is now an important and flourishing industrial town, and the capital of the rich province of Liao ning, near the An shan iron works and mines; it possesses a large arsenal and numerous factories.

The Exhibition of Industrial Products of Shen yang and the province of Liao ning gives an idea of the town's capacities in this field. It is a permanent exhibition, like the one at Shang hai covering the Shang hai area, housed in a vast building with a floor space of 50,000 square yards, built in 1959 in a style which clearly shows its Russian influence. The exhibits include the most modern industrial products made in the province.

Diagrams and hotels illustrate the main industries in Liao ning. The following factories are the ones most often shown to visitors to Shen yang:

a) The Sino-Czechoslovak Friendship machine tools factory,

b) The transformer factory,

c) The machine-building factory,

d) The metal-works.

Each factory employs several thousand workmen and is well equiped with good-quality tools and machines. The products themselves reveal fairly advanced techniques.

Tourists who are interested may ask to be shown several teaching establishments, such as the Medical Faculty and the three hospitals attached to it, or the Conservatoire of music, founded at Yan an about 20 years ago and moved here.

The Imperial Palace

The Qing sovereigns lived there from 1625 to 1643; once the dynasty made Peking its capital, in 1644, the palace became merely an object of pilgrimage for the Manchu rulers when they came to pay homage to their ancestors. The buildings as a whole recall the style and lay-out of the Imperial Palace at Peking.

The little pavilions on either side of the way leading from the main gate to the great halls contain collections of porcelain, furniture, etc.

The Northern Imperial Tomb (Bei ling)

This tomb contains the remains of Qing tai zong, the founder of the Qing dynasty, who died in 1643, and of his wife. Once the dynasty had settled in

Peking, the Emperors used to come from time to time to visit the tomb and offer sacrifices to their ancestors.

The whole place was neglected under the Republic, when it began to fall into ruins, but it has been carefully restored since the liberation. It has now been transformed into a magnificent park, full of beautiful trees and scattered with lakes and pavilions. The tomb itself is at the end of a way starting at an archway, and lined with twelve statue of animals, at the end of which is a little temple with the Emperor's stele, inscribed in Chinese and Manchu. The Dragon Gate leads from there into a square enclosure surrounded by battlemented walls, containing a round tumulus covered with trees. It has not yet been opened.

Useful Information

The Liao ning Hotel, the chief hotel at Shen yang, is in Sun Yat sen Square, in the middle of the town. There is an antique shop in Tai yuan street. The Roman Catholic church is still open, and Mass is said every Sunday morning (1966).

Chang chun

Chang chun has a population of 1,400,000, and is the capital of Ji lin, on the same latitude as Vladivostok; its name means "Eternal Spring". It is an industrial and a university town, with no historical monument, and chiefly known for its car factory.

From 1933 to 1945, it was promoted by the Japanese to the rank of capital of Manchukuo, under the name of Xin jing; an ambitious plan was drawn up for the town, and it still possesses some imposing administrative buildings and several parks, roundabouts, and wide tree-lined avenues.

An atmosphere of provincial calm now reigns in the district which was once the centre of the Manchukuo government, still full of huge, cold buildings built in different styles and surrounded by trees.

The buildings dating from the Japanese period — the Government building, the Department of Justice, the Foreign Office, the Communications Department, the Treasury and Trade Department, the Ministry of the Interior, the Supreme Court and the Bank — are nearly all used for sections of the university now.

The biggest factory, in the south-west suburbs, west of the railway line, is the car factory. It was built between 1953 and 1956, and was the first factory of its kind in China; it is still by far the most important. It employs 23,000 people altogether, and produces 32,000 lorries each year, known as "Liberation", 2.5 tons to 4 tons, with 2 or 3 axles. It is about to be brought up to date, and will then produce new models.

It also produces "Red Flag" cars, in small numbers.

Tourists are taken to see other things at Chang chun as well:

a) the Ji lin University, which has been in the capital since 1958. It includes 10 faculties, 7 of which are arts and the other 4 science faculties. It contains 4,377 students, 60 % of whom are reading scientific subjects.

b) the Drama school,

c) the Film Studios, which are among the most famous in China.

Useful Information

There are two large hotels in Chang chun. There is also an antique shop.

An shan

An shan holds pride of place in China's heavy industry, and is willingly shown off to foreigners. It includes the biggest iron and steel works in the country, and since it began to be developed in 1949, the population has risen from 120,000 to 900,000. The town is entirely centred round the factories and has grown up near them; it is well laid out, with wide avenues lined with trees and flowers, a rare sight in an iron town.

The complex also includes the iron mines close by the town, one of which produces 8 million metric tons of iron ore per year; the ten blast-furnaces, with a capacity of over 4 million tons, the steelworks, the rolling-mills and the seamless steel tubing mill form an impressive industrial landscape.

Tang gang zi is easily accessible from An shan; it is a convalescent home about 6 miles south-east of the town. The hot spring, which rises at a temperature of 161.5° F, is particularly beneficial in the case of rheumatism.

Several houses are scattered through the park; two are pointed out to the visitor: one is the unattractive house which the warlord Zhang Zuo lin had built here, and the other is the one which Pu Yi, the Emperor of Manchukuo, lived in; he later became a member of the National Assembly (Pu Yi died in 1967.)

Visitors to Tang Gang zi can take baths in private rooms; there is no swimming pool.

Practical
Information

CHINA

This chapter has been brought up to date as far as possible, but readers may still find some changes. It should be noted that the Chinese spelling of Peking is now BEIJING, in accordance with the official transcription of Chinese characters, known as pinyin. *The old western spelling of the name has been left unchanged in most places in this guide, however.*

INDEX

A FEW TOWNS

Peking

PRACTICAL INFORMATION

As soon as they set foot on Chinese territory, most tourists are taken in hand by the one state-run tourist agency in existence in China, Lü xing she, the China International Travel Service, or by the commercial, political or social organisations whose guests they are. The difficulty of both the written and spoken language in a country where foreign languages are not widely known as yet, and are certainly more widely read than spoken, cuts the foreigner off more effectively than any other kind of barrier, and makes it essential for him to have a guide-interpreter with him constantly from morning till night, except at meal times, for interpreters never eat meals with him, and once the day's programme is over. Great efforts are being made to train interpreters speaking Western European languages, but they are relatively few and often lack practice. The personality of the guide-interpreter and his capabilities can to some extent make or mar one's trip to China.

The tours organized by Lü xing she are limited to the towns and regions which are open to foreigners, which are (1979): Peking, with a trip to the Great Wall and the Ming Tombs; Tientsin (Tian jin); Shanghai; Ha er bin (Harbin) (Hei long jiang province); Chang chun, Ji lin (Ji lin province); Shen yang, An shan, Fu shun, Da lian (Liao ning province); Shi jia zhuang, Tang shan (He bei province); Tai yuan, Da tong, Da zhai (Shan xi); Ji nan, Qing dao (Shan dong province); Xi an, Yan an (Shânxi province); Zheng zhou, An yang, Lin xian, Xin xiang, Hui xian, Yu xian, Gong xian, Luo yang, Kai feng (He nan province); Nanking, Su zhou, Wu xi, Yang zhou (Jiang su province); Hang zhou (Zhe jiang province); Wu han (Hu bei province); Chang sha (Hu nan province); Nan chang, Jing gang shan, Jiu jiang, Lu shan (Jiang xi province); Canton, Chao jing (Guang dong province); Nan ning, Gui lin, (Guang xi province); Cheng du, Zhong jing (Si chuan province), with a trip down the River Yang zi to Wu han; Kun ming (Yun nan province).

The sight-seeing programmes in the open towns combine ancient monuments and creations of the new regime, which is justly proud to show off its economic and social achievements. Visits to people's communes, factories, technical institutes, schools of all kinds, workers' living quarters, hospitals, kindergartens can be included in the programme to suit the taste or special field of each visitor. Foreigners are welcomed by a director who gives a brief outline of the history and characteristics of the establishment, accompanied by cups of tea. Questions can be asked, and answers are given as far as possible.

Receptionists and telephone operators in the hotels have the greatest difficulty in understanding foreign names. You are advised to give your room number to anyone in town who may want to get in touch with you to make sure that messages and telephone communications reach you.

During their stay in People's China, visitors will notice numerous differences between the present regime and the preceding ones which may seem startling to those who have not seen China again since 1949: honesty, cleanliness and punctuality, among other things. Wherever they go, tourists are certain to stay and take their meals in places which are constantly kept clean, and this applies to most of what they see around them. Flies are extremely rare, in spite of fly swats-which are to be seen in public places and trains.

The tourist will find that the strict honesty which is now the rule throughout China generates a peace of mind which is rare in other countries. Money, cameras or jewellery present no worries at all. If anything is left behind in a car or a hotel room, it will be brought back as soon as it is found. Everybody knows the story of the tourist who left an old pair of shoes behind in the waste paper basket in his hotel room, only to be confronted with them as he was getting into the aeroplane.

When shopping, anyone unsure of the value of the notes he is handling can be certain that his change will be given him with scrupulous care; should a mistake occur, it will be corrected immediately and the difference will be sent to him, even if he has already left the town.

Tipping is strictly forbidden and foreigners risk offending anyone to whom they offer a tip.

Begging does not exist in China.

Strict punctuality is observed on all occasions, in theatres or cinemas, in the case of arrival or departure times of trains or aeroplanes, or at official receptions. It should be noted that Chinese guests often arrive several minutes earlier than the time indicated on the invitation.

Visas and Vaccination Certificates

Entrance and exit visas are compulsory for all foreigners. They are delivered for a particular frontier post ([1]). Should anyone want to enter the country at a post other than the one specified on the visa, he should apply for the change to be made at the Chinese Embassy in the country where the original request for a visa was made.

Foreigners should report to the police within three days after their arrival in China through the Public Security Office in Dong jiao min xiang Street, in the old Legation Quarter in Peking, not far from the Peking and Xin qiao hotels. It is as well to ascertain at the same time, through an interpreter, if the exit visa is the correct one..

Should they want to leave China by a different post from the one marked on the visa, they may apply to have this changed at the Public Security Office; it takes several days, at times even a week. As no-one in the office speaks anything but Chinese, it is as well to go there with an interpreter.

When leaving China for the Soviet Union, a Soviet visa is needed, as well as a Mongolian visa, in the case of the trans-Mongolian railway line.

The international certificate of vaccination against small-pox, less than three years old, is the only one needed for entry into China. People leaving China via Hong Kong need a certificate of vaccination against cholera less than six months old. Foreigners can be vaccinated against cholera at Peking, at the Shou du yi yuan Hospital, Shuai fu yuan Street.

Customs and Exchange Regulations

Everybody entering China has to fill in a form for the customs authorities stating how much foreign currency and how many objects of value he has in his possession: jewellery, watches, alarm clocks, fountain pens, cameras and cine cameras, type-writers, all come under this. In theory, only one of each of these things may be brought into the country.

---

[1] The chief frontier posts are: Peking, Shang hai, Canton, Kun ming, Shun chun (the land frontier with Hong Kong), Man zhou li, on the frontier of Hei long jiang and Siberia, and Er lian, on the frontier between China and the People's Republic of Mongolia. As the visas are in Chinese, it is difficult for a foreigner who cannot read the language to check the entrance and exit points on his visa.

The customs authorities allow a limited quantity — corresponding to "what may reasonably be consumed by one person" — of cigarettes, tobacco and alcohol to be brought in, though no paper exists confirming this. About 200 cigarettes and 2 or 3 three bottles of spirits seems to be the allowance for each person.

All foreign exchange operations carried out in China must be mentioned on the form which must be handed over to the authorities on leaving the country. Any *yuan* which are left are then repaid in foreign currency. The exporting of Chinese money is forbidden.

Chinese Currency — Exchange Rates — Banks

The money in use in China is the YUAN or J.M.P. (Ren min piao, or People's Currency), which is divided into 10 *mao* and 100 *fen*. The *yuan* is known as the *kuai* in everyday speech. It is worth approximately U.S. $ 0.50.

No foreign banks exist in China, and the Bank of China alone is qualified to change money. The head office of its foreign department is in an old building in the former Legation Quarter, Xi jiao min xiang Street. Exchange offices have now been opened in the hotels (hours: 8.30 to 12.00, 2.00 to 5.00).

10 *yuan* notes are the highest ones issued, so that large sums are awkward to carry about.

	10 *yuan*, black
Large size notes	5 *yuan*, reddish brown
	2 *yuan:* blue
	1 *yuan*, red or black
	5 *mao*, purple, with a picture of a dam
	2 *mao*, green, with a picture of a dam, and
Small size notes	green, with a picture of an engine
	1 *mao*, red, with a picture of peasants, and brown, with a picture of a tractor
	1 *mao:* brown and green, with a picture of peasants going off to work.

5, 2 and 1 *fen* aluminium coins.

It is advisable to obtain travellers' cheques in currency which is negotiable in every country in the world, making sure that the bank which issues them does not omit to mention this.

Seasons for Visiting China

Differences in climate are so enormous in China that the tourist must expect to experience considerable changes in temperature, whatever the season, especially if travelling from north to south or vice versa.

The summer is hot throughout the country, though it is wettest in the south. The hotels have no air-conditioning and rooms facing south and west should be avoided. The winter is hard in the north, and in Peking the temperature may fall as low as − 4° F (− 20 °C); fine weather and blue skies last for six months and the air becomes very dry; from time to time bitter winds blow down from Mongolia, bringing with them clouds of dust: the "Yellow Wind". The recent planting of trees in the town itself and round the outskirts has, according to old inhabitants of Peking, lessened the winds somewhat and changed the climate slightly, for the winters have been less severe for several years now. In the south it never freezes in winter, but the temperature at Shang hai may go down to about 32° F. (0 °C.). The most pleasant seasons for tourism are spring, which unfortunately lasts a very short time, and autumn. May Day and October 1st, the National Day, also give the tourist the chance of seeing large gatherings and impressive parades throughout the country, and especially in Peking.

Foreign Languages

The Chinese with whom the tourist is most likely to speak are interpreters supplied by agencies or by the organisations who are their hosts. The Chinese are rarely able to speak to foreigners without the help of an interpreter.

A limited number of people have some knowledge of foreign languages, and they generally read more easily than they speak. From 1950 to 1960, Russian was the chief foreign language taught in schools. English has replaced it, and an effort is now being made to teach French. The Chinese recruit French teachers and send students to France to study the language.

The import and export corporations with whom foreign business men and industrial representatives do business have their own interpreters, most of whom speak English.

Suggested Trips

Tai yuan, Da tong, Xi an, Zheng zhou, An yang, Luo yang, Gong xian, Kai feng, Su zhou, Nanking, Hang zhou and Cheng du are the most attractive towns for tourists interested in art and history. Hang zhou, the seaside town of Qing dao, the boat trip down the River Yang zi from Zhong jing to Wu han, the Jing gang shan Mountains, and the towns of Gui lin and Kun ming offer landscapes of great natural beauty. Shanghai, which is the second largest town in the world, the biggest in China and essentially a modern town, gives an impressive picture of the power of Chinese industry and its capacity. This aspect of China is also illustrated by the towns of the North-eastern provinces: Ha er bin (Hei long jiang province), Chang chun, Ji lin (Ji lin province), and Shen yang, An shan, Fu shun, Da lian (Liao ning province), and the town of Wu han (Hu bei). Other towns, such as Xin xiang in He nan province (Red Flag Canal) and Da zhai in Shan xi province (model commune) show recent achievements in other fields, or are landmarks in the history of the revolution (Yan an, Jing gang shan, etc.) Canton is a tropical town with a personality of its own, but few ancient monuments. Whatever itinerary the visitor chooses, a third of his time should be devoted to Peking and its neighbourhood.

No passenger lines exist enabling passengers to come to a Chinese port but those who enjoy sea journeys may travel as far as Hong Kong by sea and take the train there for Canton.

Tourists may come to China by air or train. Passengers taking the Trans-Siberian railway or coming into China via Hong Kong enter by train. Passengers travelling by air have a choice between the northern route via Moscow and Siberia or one of the southern routes to Kun ming, Canton or Shang hai.

Once in China it is a good idea to travel part of the way by train, preferably when south of the Yang zi, from Wu han to Canton or from Shang hai to Canton, for instance. The countryside is more picturesque than that of the northern plains. Anyone travelling via Hong Kong has to travel a little way by train, as 90 miles separate Canton and Hong Kong; the line goes through Shun chun, the frontier post between China and the British colony. N° regular airline exists between Canton and though in 1978 a service using jumbo jets was introduced between Hong Kong and Canton during the Canton Fair.

Clothes

Winter: in the north, woollen clothes, fur coats and hats, fur-lined boots. In the south, between-season clothes.

Summer: very light tropical clothes; something woollen for evenings in the north, where it can get chilly once the sun has set; sun glasses; light raincoats.

Short-sleeved, open-necked shirts are widely worn and tourists should take advantage of this. Chinese officials are instructed to wear them, as in summer they are allowed to leave off the dark jackets with high necks which they wear for the rest of the year.

Spring and Autumn: Between-season clothes, and light coats for northern evenings. Light clothes in the south.

Cars

The number of cars in Peking has never been published. They consist of taxis, cars used by government officials, and those belonging to members of the diplomatic corps. In other towns there are fewer.

Cars used for tourists are sometimes from Chinese factories — the "Red Flag", made to order by the factory at Chang chun, or the "Phoenix", made in Shang hai; most of them are either of Soviet, Czech or Polish make; there are Japanese, French and British cars as well, and Japanese minibuses.

The number of lorries in use is not high yet either, even in industrial cities. Many of them are of foreign make, Soviet, French or Czech, and they are estimated at a total of 650,000 units.

Motor Travel

Foreigners have few opportunities to travel by car in China. No foreigners' cars are allowed into the country, except in the case of residents. Even then, they are not allowed outside limits corresponding roughly to the outskirts of the town, which are clearly marked by notices in Chinese, Russian and English indicating that special permission is needed to travel beyond that point. In Peking, foreigners are allowed within a radius of about 15 miles from the centre of the town, though three points outside that — the airport, the Ming Tombs and the Great Wall — can be visited freely. Permission is needed to go to Tian jin (Tientsin) and the port of Xin gang (Hsin kang), but it is almost always granted.

Railway Travel

Every tourist is advised to travel part of the way in China by train, especially in south China, between Shang hai and

Canton, for instance. It provides an excellent opportunity to admire the beautifully tended countryside, and the peasants' work.

Chinese trains travel at an average of 35 to 50 m.p.h., depending on the lines, and are always on time. Most of them are hauled by steam engines, but the Ministry of Railways has drawn up an ambitious plan to introduce diesel engines; electrified lines as rare as yet.

The total mileage is now 23,000 miles. All the rolling stock is made in China, and large numbers of engines are now being made too.

The sleeping cars are comfortable, with four bunks to a compartment; the restaurant cars serve Western and Chinese food.

Each compartment contains a loudspeaker which broadcasts military music, news and physical training exercises from dawn onwards.

Daily services exist between Peking and all large towns; it should be remembered that distances are often considerable. The journey from Peking to Canton takes 43 hours via Wuhan, and over 48 hours via Shanghai; it takes 25 hours to get from Peking to Shanghai, and 36 hours from Shanghai to Canton. The journey from Peking to Shen yang takes over 10 hours, and it takes 15 and a half hours to go from Peking to Chang chun, and 19 hours to get from Peking to Ha er bin. Two trains a week leave Peking for Moscow: the Trans-Mongolian crosses the frontier at Er lian, and goes through Ulan Bator; the journey takes 6 days. The Trans-Siberian goes through Man zhou li on the Siberian frontier, and gets to Moscow in 7 days. Twice-weekly services exist between Peking and Ulan Bator (the journey takes 36 hours 30 minutes), Pyongyang (the journey takes 23 hours) and Hanoi (the journey takes 49 hours). There are several trains a day between Canton and Shun chun, the Hong Kong land frontier post, and one through train daily between Canton and Kowloon. A hovercraft service was introduced between Hong Kong and Canton in 1978.

Civil Air Lines

The lines run by the C.A.A.C. are extending constantly and now connect all the main towns in the country. The pilots are Chinese, but the aeroplanes are foreign.

Security rules are rigorous and strictly observed. Aircraft will often delay departure if atmospheric conditions are not considered good enough. The services between Peking and Shanghai and Canton use both big and small aircraft; the latter stop several times on the way. Those who dislike low flying and frequent stops are advised to state their preference for big aircraft, and to arrange their travelling dates accordingly.

Several international airlines now operate flights to China, and CAAC in turn operates flights abroad. In 1979, the following towns were connected with Peking:

— Hanoi (CAAC)

— Phnom-Penh (CAAC)

— Pyongyang (CAAC, Civil Aviation Administration of the Democratic People's Republic of Korea)

— (Kun ming) Rangoon (CAAC)

— Moscow (CAAC, Aeroflot)

— Teheran, Bucharest (CAAC)

— (Shanghai), Osaka, Tokyo (CAAC, JAL)

— Tokyo (Peking), Athens, Karachi, Paris (CAAC, Air France)

— Karachi, Bombay, Aden, Addis Ababa (CAAC, Ethiopian Airlines)

— Urumchi, Bombay, Athens, Belgrade, Geneva, Zurich (CAAC, Swissair)

— Karachi, Bucharest (CAAC, Tarom)

— Tokyo (Peking), Rawalpindi, Karachi (CAAC, PIA)

— Tokyo (Peking), Teheran (CAAC, Iran Air)

— Teheran, Bucharest, Francfurt (CAAC, Lufthansa)

Time

Peking time applies to the whole country. No summer-time.

It is 7 hours ahead of G.M.T. in summer, and 8 in winter. When it is 12 o'clock midday in London, it is 7 or 8 o'clock in Peking, depending on the season.

To find out the time in Peking, dial 117.

Timetables

The Chinese get up early and go to bed early.

The Imperial Palace in Peking closes its gates to visitors at 3 p.m. in winter and 4.30 p.m. in summer; visitors have to leave at 4 p.m. in winter and at 5.30 in summer. The museums close at 4 p.m. (they close for a whole day once a week, on Mondays), the antique shops close at 6.30 and the department stores at 8.30 p.m.

Chinese official dinners begin at about 7 o'clock and end between 9.30 and 10 o'clock p.m. All Peking is asleep by that time. The last buses leave at 10.30 p.m. or 11 p.m. in some cases. Night life is absolutely non-existent.

Weights and Measures

The Chinese system of weights and measures is relatively coherent. In the past, the value attributed to the units of the system varied considerably, according to the period in question, the province, professions and the thing measured. This often produces hideous difficulties for anyone studying Chinese history, and even modern history (see *Zhong guo du liang heng shi, A History of Chinese Weights and Measures* by Wu Cheng luo, Shang hai 1937, re-printed Peking 1957, 257 p.; *Introduction aux études d'histoire contemporaine de Chine* by J. Chesneaux and J. Lust, Mouton, Paris 1964, 148 p.).

To put an end to the confusion, the Chinese governement has drawn up a a conversion table showing equivalent metric weights and measures alongside the traditional system. Both systems are in use at the moment. In the case of distances, kilometres and metres are gaining ground over the *zhang* and the *li*, but fabrics are still measured in the traditional inches *(cun)* and feet *(chi)*. Areas of provinces or countries are given in square kilometres *(ping fang gong li)*, but agricultural land is still measured in *mu*. Everything bought in the shops is measured in *liang* (a tenth of a pound) and *jin* (a pound). In restaurants, the Chinese order their rice, noodles and steamed rolls by the *liang* or the *jin*. In practice, the two systems do not double up on each other, and are used more or less frequently, depending on the field in question.

A conversion table follows:

Chinese unit	Contains	Metric equivalent	English equivalent	Chinese name for metric unit
Length				
1 li (league)	180 zhang	0.576 km	1/3 mile	km *gong li*
1 zhang	10 chi	3.3 m	10 ft 8 ins	m *mi*, *gong chi*
1 chi (cubit, foot)	10 cun	33 cm	1 ft 1 in	cm *gong fen*
1 cun (inch)	10 fen	33 mm	1 1/10 in	mm *gong li*
1 fen				
Weight				
1 dan	100 jin	50 kg	133 lbs	kg *gong jin*
1 jin (catty, pound)	10 liang	0.5 kg	1 1/3 lb	
1 liang (tael)		50 gr	2 ½ ozs	gr. *gong fen*, *ke*
Volume				
1 dan (picul)	10 dou	100 lb	133 lb	
1 dou (bushel)	10 sheng	10 lb	13 1/3 lb	
1 sheng		1 lb	1 1/3 lb	lb *gong sheng*

AREA is measured in square kilometres, square metres, etc. (square is translated into Chinese by the prefix *ping fang*, hence *ping fang gong li*, *ping fang mi*, etc.). The old system is still used for measuring agricultural land:

1 qing = 100 mu = 6.6 hectares = 16.5 acres

1 mu = 0.66 hectares = 0.165 acres

For further details and conversion tables, see the tables in most pocket dictionaries and almanacs, especially the *Xin hua zi dian*, the *Xin hua Dictionary*.

The Postal and Telephone Systems

Post offices exist in all hotels. They are open from 8 to 1 in the morning and from 4 to 7 in the afternoon; on Sundays they are open from 8 to 12.

Surface mail from China to Europe and Asia costs 25 *fen* a letter.

Air mail to Europe costs 70 *fen* for up to 10 gms., and 1 *yuan* for 20 gms.

The air mail rate for Asia is 60 *fen* for 10 gms., and 90 *fen* for 20 gms.

Postcards abroad cost 60 *fen*.

Letters to other parts of China and Hong Kong cost 8 *fen* by surface mail and 10 *fen* by air mail.

Letters usually take about 6 days to reach Europe from China.

Parcels can be sent by rail (Trans-Siberian). They take about a month to reach Europe. The cost from Peking is 8.70 *yuan* for 1 kg., 13.70 *yuan* for 2 to 3 kgs., 17.20 *yuan* for 3 to 5 kgs., and 29 *yuan* for 5 to 10 kgs. The air mail rate for parcels starts at 19.80 *yuan* for 1 kg.

If trunks or suitcases are sent, keys should be sent with them so that they can be opened by the customs officials.

Telegrams: They may be sent in foreign languages, but may be distorted if they are not written in capital letters.

Telephones: They work well, and extensions are to be found in all hotel rooms. Calls to numbers within the Peking area are free from the hotel, and they can be dialled directly, after dialling a single number, usually O, to get an outside line. Other rooms in the hotel can be called by dialling their room numbers only.

Public telephones exist in houses or shops in Peking; they are indicated by a yellow sign, with the characters *gong yong dian hua* written in red. The cost is 5 *fen*.

Calls can be made abroad. Some European countries have direct, lines: Great Britain, France, Denmark, Norway, Holland, Sweden and Switzerland. For long distance international calls, dial 33.74.31

OFFICIAL FEAST DAYS

National Day: October 1st. It commemorates the proclamation of the People's Republic by Chairman Mao Ze dong at Tian an men Square in Peking in 1949.

The capital is decorated and lit up for three days. A banquet for 5,000 guests is held at the National People's Congress Building, attended by the Chinese leaders and officials, the Diplomatic Corps, the foreign experts, teachers, guests and tourists.

On the lst October, a huge parade takes place, in which several hundred thousand people take part, representing different aspects of national life: agriculture, industry, culture, religion and sport, with floats, banners, flights of pigeons and many-coloured balloons. A sumptuous firework display is given in the evening on Tian an men Square. Similar merry-making takes place throughout the country.

The Spring Festival. Although this falls in January or February, it is called the Spring Festival because it marks the end of winter according to the lunar calendar. The Chinese who work away from their families are allowed a few days' holiday, so that they can go home. Businessmen may find that things slow down as people are absent.

In the old days, a fair used to be held over the festival (it was held at Liu li chang in Peking; children's toys, mainly wind-mills, kites and diabolos, used to be sold in countless little shops of boards and matting, alongside stalls selling cakes, fabrics, china ware, and books. The shops were moved to other parts of the town in 1965, because the crowds were too dense).

May Day is celebrated either by a parade like the one on October lst or by popular entertainments (singing, dancing, miming) given in the largest parks in the town (in Peking, these are the Summer Palace, the Sun yat sen Park, the Bei hai and the Workers' Cultural Palace Park) by students from the universities, institutes and colleges. Admission to the parks is by invitation only. A firework display is given in the evening at Tian an men, beginning at 7.30 p.m.

For other feast days, see p. 336.

Cigarettes and Tobacco

The Chinese make about twenty different kinds of cigarettes, mostly using tobacco of the type used for English or American cigarettes. The best Chinese cigars come from Si chuan. Foreigners are allowed to bring a reasonable amount of cigarettes with them (see Customs etc.).

Drinking Water and Non-Alcoholic Drinks

It is advisable to drink boiled water only, as the Chinese town-dwellers themselves do. The water served in carafes in hotels has been boiled. There is an excellent Chinese mineral water, not unlike the French Vichy, from a spring near Qing dao (Shan dong), called *Lao shan*. Fizzy drinks are available *(Qi shui)*: orangeade, lemonade, etc., and also soda water *(su da shui)*.

The drink most suited to the climate is China tea or green tea, as it is also called. It is drunk at all hours of the day, without sugar, and is refreshing and thirst-quenching. It comes in jasmine, red rose and magnolia-scented varieties. Another type of tea also exists, known as red tea, which is cheaper than green tea and resembles Indian tea.

Those who prefer coffee are advised to bring their own instant coffee with them; thermos flasks of boiling water are available at all hours.

Alcoholic Drinks

The Chinese are reluctant to spend foreign currency on consumer goods, and they import Russian vodka and Georgian champagne only. Tourists will find that other drinks are not available in their hotels. Chinese spirits and wines exist, however, some of them imitations of foreign drinks: *fu de jia* (vodka), *wei shi ji* (whisky), brandy, gin, wines and champagnes; others, the traditional Chinese drinks, are only drunk on special occasions, such as banquets to which foreigners are invited, by the Chinese, who are frugal and abstemious on the whole. They raise their glasses proposing the traditional *gan bei* ("cheers") to the health of their guests, who may drink either *mao tai*, a grape wine, or rice spirits in response; all three drinks are often drunk at the same meal. *Mao tai* is a spirit made from sorghum and left to age for several years in stone jars. Its name comes from a place in the southern province of Gui zhou, where it is made.

Rice spirit, known as yellow wine, is drunk warm, from little china bowls. The most famous variety comes from Shao xing, in the province of Zhe jiang, a town which is well-known for its opera as well, and its Tang mirrors.

Grape wines, both red and white, are made in the Peking area and in the North-East; they are reminiscent of French dessert wines, as they are sweet.

Beer is brewed in most large towns, particularly Peking and Qing dao (Shan dong) and is of good quality.

Eating Out in Chinese Restaurants

Chinese gastronomy still lives up to its reputation and visitors to China will find that meals in Chinese restaurants in China are incomparably better than in Chinese restaurants abroad. Restaurants abound, especially at Peking, and the dishes range from the most simple to the most elaborate. In large restaurants, some of which are proud of their age, it is advisable to order dinner in the morning of the same day, or on the day before, in the case of lunch, as the more elaborate dishes cannot be prepared at short notice.

Each one has its specialities, and some have a hundred or more different dishes on the menu. They cannot all be described here; authors such as the Frenchman Nachbaur do so with all the authority which long experience gives. Suffice it to say that among other things, sharks' fins and bird's nest soup are served; the latter is the most expensive dish of all, as the best quality costs 248 *yuan* a pound in the shops. Europeans usually enjoy dishes containing chicken or duck which are cooked in different ways in different provinces, and especially the Peking roast duck, mandarin fish, lamb cooked on the spit as served in Moslem restaurants, and the grilled lamb and sauce to be found in Mongolian restaurants.

Round tables are traditionally used, except in some restaurants which have been recently done up, and which have adopted the European habit of using rectangular tables. The tables take twelve people easily, and are perfectly suited to the Chinese habit of placing the dish in the middle of the table, instead of offering it to each guest in turn. Meals which are ordered in advance are served in small private rooms which also have armchairs and sofas to enable the guests to drink their tea in comfort before and after the meal. A towel, either hot or cold, depending on the season, is handed to each person at that point, a custom which is both pleasant and hygienic.

As each dish is the same size, however many people are there to eat it, the number of dishes varies with the number of guests; it used to be the custom to serve as many dishes, and one more, as there were guests. Soup is served in the middle and at the end of the meal, instead of at the beginning.

The host helps his guests, using either chopsticks or a china spoon, depending on whether the dish is solid or liquid; the waiter generally takes no part in this, but merely brings the dishes to the table. In Hong Kong a revolving tray is often used so that guests may help themselves to the hors d'œuvres, but this is rare in Shanghai and unknown in Peking.

It is considered incorrect to drink one's wine or spirits before the host has proposed the health of his guests, which he does by saying *gan bei* and emptying his glass at one draught. It is polite to reply to the first toast by emptying one's own glass and turning it upside down to show that not a drop remains; for the rest of the toasts, it is then sufficient to drink a sip or two if preferred, or as the Chinese say, to drink *sui bian*, as one likes. It is also polite for the chief guest and others to propose one or several toasts to their host's health.

As foreigners may have some difficulty in using chopsticks, all the restaurants frequented by them will provide knives and forks if needed.

Chinese dinners begin at 6.30 p.m. or even earlier, and end two or three hours later. Foreigners tend to sit over their meal occasionally or linger over their tea afterwards. The restaurant staff wait until they are ready to go, but it is more polite to leave a Chinese restaurant at about 10 o'clock at the latest.

Foreigners must not be surprised if the head-waiter insists on their taking away with them various things left over from the meal, such as fruit, cakes and cigarettes, as this is the custom among the Chinese.

Prices in the bigger restaurants vary between about 12 and 15 *yuan* per head, when the menu includes particular delicacies (sharks' fins, bird's nest soup, sea-slugs); drinks are included in this. In more modest restaurants, an excellent meal costs only one or two *yuan*.

The Press

All the daily papers printed in China are in Chinese. The only source of local news for foreigners who do not read Chinese is the daily news bulletin published in English, French and Russian by the New China News Agency (Xin Hua). A daily news bulletin in English—a summary of news published by the Agence France Presse and Reuter—is now available to foreigners, and is on sale in hotels.

Hotels put reviews printed in Peking in foreign languages at their clients' disposal — Peking Information, China Reconstructs, etc. and large amounts of political publications.

Photographs

Black and white films made in China can be bought and developed on the spot. Peking has several shops dealing in this, two or three of which are in Wang fu jing, for instance no. 182. They also take passport photographs and develop them in 24 hours.

Photographs should be taken tactfully, taking care not to offend people. It is as well to ask people's permission before taking photographs of them. It is not advisable to take photographs of soldiers. It is forbidden to take photographs from aircraft flying over Chinese territory.

Films taken in China can usually be taken out to be developed abroad without difficulty.

A FEW TOWNS

I. PEKING

The Airport

It is about 18 miles north-east of the town, at the end of a cement surfaced road lined with young trees, several rows deep. No coaches, buses, taxi-ranks or pedicabs are to be found there; visitors and travellers are met by representatives from Lü xing she or by their hosts, who take them back to town. If necessary, a taxi can be called from town (tel. 557461).

The airport buildings are recent and include a restaurant, a children's waiting-room, shops and V.I.P. lounges, among other things.

It is possible to go right down on to the tarmac when meeting people or seeing them off. Enquiries, particularly about arrival and departure times, can be made by telephone: no. 55 32 45; they may be made in Chinese or English.

Restrictions

No foreigners, whether they are resident in Peking or visitors spending a short time there only, are allowed to go beyond certain limits which are clearly marked by notices in Chinese, Russian and English, unless they have special permission from the authorities. The boundaries to this area lie about 15 miles from the centre of the town; the line goes past the Bridge of Ba li qiao to the east and the Bridge of Lu gou qiao (Marco Polo Bridge) to the south-west. The two exceptions to this rule are the roads to the airport, which is 18 miles north-east of Peking, and to the Ming Tombs and the Great Wall, which are 28 and 43 miles away respectively.

This ruling is strictly observed and special permission is almost invariably refused, except to those wanting to drive to Tian jin and Xin gang, the sea port nearest to Peking.

Traffic and Public Transport

The traffic moves easily along the main streets through the town, supervised by countless policemen from raised shelters or platforms in the middle of the road, all armed with megaphones to enable them to call pedestrians and cyclists to order if they neglect their highway code. The traffic lights, though always respected by the few motor vehicles to be seen in Peking, are much less carefully obeyed by pedestrians, cyclists and the endless streams of pedicabs, who frequently find themselves stopped by the police. As the Chinese police do not have the right to impose fines, they can do no more than deliver a series of warnings.

The maximum speed by day for motor vehicles is fixed at 30 miles per hour, as long as the road is a wide one, traffic light and visibility excellent. Their speed must not exceed 10 miles per hour at road junctions or in places where pedestrians are particularly numerous. Drivers are allowed to use their horns, and it is compulsory to sound one's horn when overtaking; Peking drivers use them constantly, and considering the enormous numbers of pedestrians, cyclists, pedicabs and other vehicles drawn both by men and animals, they are justified in doing so.

The *Hu tong*, narrow little streets running between the main thoroughfares, are not closed to cars, but the crowds of children and bicycles make driving dangerous and slow.

Few cyclists use lights at night.

As third party insurance does not exist, drivers are usually careful.

Taxis

The chief taxi rank is at 54 Dong an men nan jie (tel. 55 74 61). This the number to use when in need of a taxi anywhere in town.

Peking has several other taxi ranks, at the following places:

Wan ming lu	Xin jie kou
Wang fu da jie	Wang fu jing
Dong si	Yong ding men
Xi an men	Xi si
He ping li	Xi dan
Nan he yan	Dong wu yuan
Xuan nei da jie	Qian men

Tourists are advised to keep their taxis when going round different places in town, as if they do not, they will have to telephone in Chinese for another to take them back to their hotel, which may involve a long wait if they are far from the centre; taxis never cruise on the look-out for fares as they do in the West.

The drivers, many of whom are women, are careful and drive very slowly. At the end, they hand over slips of paper with the fare printed on them.

The unit price is 50 *fen* a kilometre for a Shanghai sedan and a Crown sedan, and 45 *fen* a kilometre for a Toyota sedan. The initial charge for a journey of 4 kilometres or less is 2.00 *yuan* for the Shanghai and Crown sedan classes, and 1.80 *yuan* for the Toyota sedan class; every additional kilometre exceeding 4 kilometres is charged for at the unit price. The charge for waiting is 1 *yuan* for half and hour or less, and 1 *yuan* for every additional half hour, with reduced charges on journeys of 40 kilometres or more. Hiring a taxi for a trip to the Ming Tombs or the Great Wall costs 80 to 100 *yuan*. A return journey to the taxi rank without passengers is charged up at half the original fare, and cancellations are also charged for.

Buses and Trolleybuses

Town and suburban buses are numerous (see maps of bus and trolleybus lines, p. 529-561). Peking has about 25 bus lines and 10 trolleybus lines. Only one tram line is still in use (1966).

Fares depend on the distance covered, except in the case of the No 1 bus: 4 *fen* for 3 stops, then 7, 9, 11, 13 and 17 *fen* for the longest distance, such as, for instance, the No 103 trolleybus from Hatamen Gate to the Zoo. It is advisable to avoid travelling during the rush hours, i.e. from 6-8 a.m. and round about 6 in the evening. Passengers often give up their seats to foreigners.

Free travel for children depends not on age but on size (under 3ft 7in, or a metre 20). This height is marked up on the wall to avoid argument.

ADDRESSES

Foreign Legations

They are centred in two districts: San li tun, the more recent
of the two, is in the modern industrial suburbs north-east of
the old walled city, on the way to the airport. Countries who
have opened diplomatic relations with China recently have
embassies in this area, and blocks of flats have been built there
to lodge diplomats and their families.

Most of the Socialist countries, and a few others, among
them Great Britain, Cambodia and Finland, have their embassies in a district about a mile east of the old walls; near them
is a large compound full of blocks of flats reserved for diplomats, known as *Wai jiao da lou.*

The Soviet Embassy occupies a vast territory inside the town
walls, in the north-east corner of the town, covering an area
of nearly 100 acres, on the site of the old Orthodox mission.
The site was ceded by Emperor Kang xi in 1685 to some Cossacks
who had been taken prisoner on the banks of the River Amur.
The Orthodox mission was transferred here in 1958.

Embassy Addresses

Afghanistan (A Fu Han): Tong Zhi Men Wai Da Jie 8, tel.
52 15 82.

Albania (A Er Ba Ni Ya): Guang Hua Lu 28, tel. 52 11 20.

Algeria (A Er Ji Li Ya): San Li Tun Lu 7, tel. 52 12 31, 52 12 32.

Argentina (A Gen Ting): San Li Tun Tong Wu Jie 11, tel.
52 22 81 and 52 20 90.

Australia (Ao Da Li Ya): Tong Zhi Men Wai Da Jie 15, tel.
52 23 31 and 52 23 32.

Austria (Ao Di Li): Jie Guo Men Wai Xiu Shui Nan Jie 5,
tel. 52 20 62 and 52 20 63.

Bangladesh (Men Jia La): Guang Hua Lu 42, tel. 52 25 21
and 52 37 06.

Belgium (Bi Li Shi): San Li Tun Lu 6, tel. 52 17 36 and 52 17 37.

Benin (Bei Ning): Guang Hua Lu 38, tel. 52 27 41.

Brazil (Ba Xi): Guang Hua Lu 27, tel. 52 27 40 and 52 28 04.

Bulgaria (Bao Jia Li Ya): Jie Guo Men Wai Xiu Shui Bei Jie 4,
tel. 52 22 32 and 52 22 33.

Burma (Mian Dian): Tong Zhi Men Wai Da Jie 6, tel. 52 14 25
and 52 14 88.

Burundi (Bu Long Di): Guang Hua Lu 25, tel. 52 23 28.

Cambodia (Jie Pu Zhai): Guang Hua Lu 34, tel. 52 18 89 and 52 18 18.

Cameroun (Ka Mai Long): San Li Tun Tong Wu Jie 7, tel. 52 17 67 and 52 18 28.

Canada (Jia Na Da): San Li Tun Lu 10, tel. 52 14 75 and 52 15 71.

Chad (Zha De): Guang Hua Lu 21, tel. 52 12 96 and 52 20 68.

Central African Empire (Zhong Fei Di Guo): San Li Tun Wai Jiao Ren Yuan Ban Gong Lou 1-61, tel. 52 17 89 and 52 38 03.

Chile (Zhi Li): San Li Tun Tong Si Jie 1, tel. 52 15 22 and 52 15 91.

Congo (Gang Guo): San Li Tun Tong Si Jie 7, tel. 52 22 57 and 52 16 58.

Cuba (Gu Ba): Jie Guo Men Wai Xiu Shui Nan Jie 1, tel. 52 28 22 and 52 17 14.

Czechoslovakia (Jie Ke Si Luo Fa Ke), Jie Guo Men Wai Ri Tan Lu, tel. 52 15 30 and 52 15 31.

Denmark (Dan Mai): San Li Tun Tong Wu Jie 1, tel. 52 24 31 and 52 24 32.

Egypt (Ai Ji): Ri Tan Tong Lu 2, tel. 52 18 25 and 52 18 80.

Equatorial Guinea (Chi Dao Ji Nei Ya): San Li Tun Wai Jiao Ren Yuan Ban Gong Lou 2-41, tel. 52 36 79.

Ethiopia (Ai Sai E Bi Ya): Jie Guo Men Wai Shui Nan Jie 3, tel. 52 17 82 and 52 17 21.

Federal Republic of Germany (De Yi Zhi Lian Bang): Tong Zhi Men Wai Da Jie 5, tel. 52 21 61 and 52 21 62.

Finland (Fen Lan): Guang Hua Lu 30, tel. 52 17 53 and 52 19 96.

France (Fa Guo): San Li Tun Tong San Jie 3, tel. 52 13 31 and 52 13 32.

Gabon (Jia Pong): Guang Hua Lu 36, tel. 52 28 10 and 52 38 24.

German Democratic Republic (Min Zhu De Guo): San Li Tun Tong Si Jie 3, tel. 52 16 31 and 52 16 32.

Ghana (Jia Na): San Li Tun Lu 8, tel. 52 13 19 and 52 36 17.

Greece (Xi La): Guang Hua Lu 19, tel. 52 13 91,

Guinea (Ji Nei Ya): San Li Tun Tong San Jie 7, tel. 52 36 49 and 52 16 97.

Guyana (Guei Ya Na): Jie Guo Men Wai Xiu Shui Tong Jie 1, tel. 52 13 37.

Hungary (Xiong Ya Li): Tong Zhi Men Wai Da Jie 10, tel. 52 12 73 and 52 14 31.

India (Yin Du): Ri Tan Tong Lu 1, tel. 52 18 56 and 52 19 08.

Iran (Yi Land): Tong Zhi Men Wai Da Jie 9, tel. 52 13 85 and 52 20 40.

Iraq (Yi La Ke): Ri Tan Tong Lu 3, tel. 52 18 53 and 52 18 73.

Italy (Yi Da Li): San Li Tun Tong Er Jie 2, tel. 52 21 31 and 52 21 32.

Japan (Ri Ben): Ri Tan Lu 7, tel. 52 23 61 and 52 13 01.

Korea (Chao Xian): Jian Guo Men Wai Ri Tan Bei Lu, tel. 52 11 86 and 52 11 54.

Kuwait (Ke Wei Te): Guang Hua Lu 3, tel. 52 22 16 and 52 21 82.

Laos (Lao Wo): San Li Tun Tong Si Jie 11, tel. 52 12 24.

Lebanon (Li Ba Nen): San Li Tun Tong Liu Jie 51, tel. 52 27 70 and 52 21 97.

Liberia (Li Bi Li Ya): San Li Tun Wai Jiao Ren Yuan Ban Gong Lu 2-62, tel. 52 35 49 and 52 35 23.

Madagascar (Ma Da Jia Si Jia): San Li Tun Tong Jie 3, tel. 52 13 53 and 52 16 43.

Malaysia (Ma Lai Yi Ya): Tong Zhi Men Wai Da Jie 13, tel. 52 25 31 and 52 25 32.

Mali (Ma Li): San Li Tun Tong Si Jie 8, tel. 52 17 04 and 52 13 89.

Mauritania (Mo Li Ta Ni Ya): San Li Tun Tong San Jie 9, tel. 52 13 96 and 52 13 46.

Mexico (Muo Xi Ge): San Li Tun Tong Wu Jie 5, tel. 52 20 70 and 52 25 74.

Mongolia (Mong Gu): Jie Guo Men Wai Xiu Shui Bei Jie 2, tel. 52 12 03 and 52 18 10.

Morocco (Mo Luo Ge): San Li Tun Lu 16, tel. 52 17 96 and 52 14 89.

Nepal (Ni Po Er): San Li Tun Lu 12, tel. 52 17 95.

Netherlands (He Lan): San Li Tun Tong Si Jie 10, tel. 52 17 31 and 52 17 32.

New Zealand (Xin Xi Lan): Ri Tan Lu Tong Er Jie 1, tel. 52 27 31 and 52 27 32.

Niger (Ni Ri Er): San Li Tun Tong Liu Jie 50, tel. 52 22 14 and 52 27 68.

Nigeria (Ni Ri Li Ya): San Li Tun Tong Wu Jie 2, tel. 52 16 50 and 52 36 31.

Norway (Nuo Wei): San Li Tun Tong Yi Jie 1, tel. 52 22 61 and 52 22 62.

Pakistan (Pa Ji Si Tan): Jie Guo Men Wai Xiu Shui Bei Jie 3, tel. 52 25 04 and 52 26 95.

Peru (Mi Lu): San Li Tun Wai Jiao Ren Yuan Ban Gong Lou 2-82, tel. 52 21 78 and 52 29 13.

Philippines (Fei Li Bin): Jie Guo Men Wai Xiu Shui Bei Jie 23, tel. 52 27 94.

Poland (Po Lan): Jie Guo Men Wai Ri Tan Lu, tel. 52 12 35 and 52 19 04.

Romania (Luo Ma Ni Ya): Ri Tan Lu Tong Er Jie 2, tel. 52 33 15 and 52 32 55.

Rwanda (Lu Wang Da): Xiu Shi Bei Jie 307, tel. 52 21 93 and 52 17 62.

Senegal (Sai Nei Jia Er): Jie Guo Men Wai Ri Tan Tong Yi Jie 1, tel. 52 26 46 and 52 25 93.

Sierra Leone (Sai La Li Ang): Tong Zhi Men Wai Da Jie 7, tel. 52 14 46 and 52 12 22.

Somalia (So Ma Li): San Li Tun Lu 2, tel. 52 23 12 and 52 17 52.

Spain (Xi Ban Ya): San Li Tun Lu 9, tel. 52 19 67.

Sri Lanka (Si Li Lan Ka): Jie Guo Men Wai Jie Hua Lu 3, tel. 52 18 61 and 52 18 62.

Sudan (Su Dan): San Li Tun Tong Er Jie 1, tel. 52 37 15.

Sweden (Rui Dian): Tong Zhi Men Wai Da Jie 3, tel. 52 17 70 and 52 12 52.

Switzerland (Rui Shi): San Li Tun Tong Wu Jie 3, tel. 52 28 31 and 52 28 32.

Syria (A La Bo Xu Li Ya): San Li Tun Tong Si Jie 6, tel. 52 13 72 and 52 13 47.

Thailand (Tai Guo): Guang Hua Lu 40, tel. 52 19 03 and 52 22 82.

Tanzania (Tan Sang Ni Ya): San Li Tun Lu 14, tel. 52 14 91 and 52 17 19.

Togo (Duo Ge): Tong Zhi Men Wai Da Jie 11, tel. 52 22 02.

Tunisia (Tu Ni Si): San Li Tun Tong Jie 1, tel. 52 24 35 and 52 24 36.

Turkey (Tu Er Qi): San Li Tun Tong Wu Jie 9, tel. 52 26 50 and 52 21 84.

Uganda (Wu Gan Da): San Li Tun Tong Jie 5, tel. 52 17 08.

United Kingdom (Yin Guo): Guang Hua Lu 11, tel. 52 19 61 and 52 19 62.

United States of America: (see below).

Upper Volta (Shang Fu Er Te): San Li Tun Tong Liu Jie 52, tel. 52 25 50.

USSR (Su Lian): Fan Di Lu 1, tel. 52 20 51 and 52 13 81.

Venezuela (Wei Nei Rui La): San Li Tun Wai Jiao Ren Yuan Ban Gong Lou 2-72, tel. 52 12 95 and 52 38 41.

Vietnam (Yue Nan): Guang Hua Lu 32, tel. 52 11 31 and 52 11 55.

Yemen Arab Republic (A La Po Yie Men): Tong Zhi Men Wai Ta Jie 4, tel. 52 13 62 and 52 33 46.

Yemen, Democratic Republic (Min Zhu Ye Men): San Li Tun Tong San Jie 5, tel. 52 15 58.

Yugoslavia (Nan Si La Fu): San Li Tun Tong Si Jie 2, tel. 52 15 62.

Zaïre (Zai Yi Er): San Li Tun Tong Wu Jie 6, tel. 52 19 95.

Zambia (Zan Bi Ya): San Li Tun Tong Si Jie 5, tel. 52 15 54 and 52 17 78.

***

United States Liaison Office (Mei Lien Chu): Guang Hua Lu 17, tel. 52 20 33.

Office of Palestine Liberation Organisation (Ba Le Si Tan Zhu Jin Ban Shi Chu): San Li Tun Tong San Jie 2, tel. 52 13 61.

Press Agencies

Albania, *Zeri i Popullit*, 10-1-33 Jian guo men wai, tel. 52-2915

Australia, *Australian Broadcasting Commission*, 8-122 Qi jia yuan, tel. 52-2410

    The Sydney Morning Herald, 10-72 Qi jia yuan, tel. 52-2778

Britain, *British Broadcasting Corporation*, Ban gong lou 2-31 San li tun, tel. 52-3777

    Daily Telegraph, 1-3-71 Jian guo men wai, tel. 52-2877

    Reuter, Ban gong lou 2-21 San li tun, tel. 52-1921

Bulgaria, *BTA*, 1-4-13 Jian guo men wai, tel. 52-1226

Canada, *The Globe and Mail (Toronto)*, 2-2-31 San li tun (north), tel. 52-1661.

Cuba, *Prensa Latina*, 6-2-12 Qi jia yuan, tel. 52-1914

Czechoslovakia, *CTK*, 10-43 Qi jia yuan, tel. 52-2704

France, *Agence France Presse*, 10-83 Qi jia yuan, tel. 52-1992

    Le Monde, 7-2-34 Qi jia yuan, tel. 52-1467

German Federal Republic, *ARD*, Ban gong lou 2-32, San li tun, tel. 52-3696

Die Welt, 2-2-52 Jian guo men wai, tel. 52-3215

DPA, Ban gong lou 1-31, San li tun, tel. 52-1473

German Democratic Republic, *ADN*, 7-3-62 Qi jia yuan, tel. 52-1805

Hungary, *MTI*, Ban gong lou 1-42, San li tun, tel. 52-1755

Italy, *ANSA*, Ban gong lou 2-81, San li tun, tel. 52-1954

Japan, *Asahi Shimbun*, 8-62 Qi jia yuan, tel. 52-1998

Chunichi Shimbun, Nishinihon Shimbun, Hokkaido Shimbun, 8-22 San li tun, tel. 52-1674

Jiji Press, 9-1-13 Jian guo men wai, tel. 52-2924

Kyodo News Service, 8-41 Qi jia yuan, tel. 52-2680

Mainichi Shimbun, 10-1-13 Jian guo men wai, tel. 52-2856

NHK, 2-3-33 San li tun (north), tel. 52-1251

Nihon Keizai Shimbun, 2-3-21 San li tun (north), tel. 52-1664

TBS, NTV, ANB, 5-1-32 San li tun, tel. 52-2720

Yomiuri Shimbun, 10-2-72 San li tun (north), tel. 52-2053

North Korea, *Korean Central News Agency*, Embassy of North Korea, tel. 52-1186

Rodong Sinmun, Embassy of North Korea, 52-1186

Outer Mongolia, *Montsame*, Embassy of Outer Mongolia, tel. 52-1810

Poland, *PAP*, Central Residential Building, 32, tel. 52-1918

Trybuna Ludu, Central Residential Building, 23, tel. 52-1750

Scandinavia, *The Nordic News Agencies: NTB, RB, STT, TT*, 2-2-41 Jian guo men wai, tel. 52-1622

Dagens Nyheter, Politiken, Helsingin Sanomat, Dagbladet, 10-32 Qi jia yuan, tel. 52-2747

USSR, *Tass*, 1-9 Qi jia yuan, tel. 52-1895

Vietnam, *Nhan Dan*, Vietnam Embassy Compound, tel. 52-1131

VNTTX, Vietnam Embassy Compound, tel. 52-1131

Yugoslavia, *Politika*, Ban gong lou 1-11, San li tun, tel. 52-2887

Tanjug, 9-25 Qi jia yuan, tel. 52-2406

MUSEUMS AND EXHIBITIONS

As all the written information is in Chinese only, and apart from the dates of the dynasties, those who cannot read Chinese will find nothing to help them to understand what they see, it is advisable to ask for a guide.

Most museums and public parks charge an entrance fee, but it is negligible. The museums close at 5 p.m.

The Museum of the Revolution is to the left, and the *Museum of Chinese History* is to the right in the imposing building put up in 1959, forming the east side of Tian an men Square (see p. 426-462).

The Museum of the Army is outside the town, to the west, in Fu xing men wai da jie (see p. 642).

The Cultural Palace of the Minorities is in Fu xing men nei da jie (the extension of Chang an jie Avenue) (see p. 523).

The Planetarium is opposite the zoo (see p. 564).

The Sun Yat sen Museum: see the Temple of the Azure Clouds, p. 602.

The Agriculture Exhibition Centre is in the eastern suburbs at San li tun, near the new Embassy quarter.

The Old Observatory is in Jian guo men nei da jie (see p. 521).

The Exhibition Centre is west of Xi zhi men Gate, next to the zoo (see p. 566).

The Imperial Palace Museum is in the Imperial Palace. Entrance tickets are sold from 8.30 a.m. to 3 p.m. in the winter, and from 8.30 a.m. to 4.30 p.m. in summer. Visitors must leave at 4 p.m. in winter and 5.30 p.m. in summer (see p. 464).

The Natural History Museum is near the Bridge of Heaven (see p. 539).

The Institute of Musicology Museum is north-west of the town, in Xue yuan lu Street (see p. 572).

The Lu Xun Museum is next to the house in which the writer lived, which is also open to visitors, in Xi san tiao Street, near Fu cheng Gate (see p. 507).

Exhibitions of paintings

Exhibitions of paintings, sculpture, and handicrafts, both Chinese and foreign, are usually held in a modern building in semi-traditional style at the junction of Wang fu jing and Han hua yuan da jie Streets. (See Exhibition Centre of the Chinese Artists' Association, p. 515).

Flower exhibitions are held in the Bei hai gardens and the Summer Palace, among other places.

The Foreign Trade Corporations

The Import and Export Corporations are buying and selling centres with a complete monopoly of foreign trade in their own field. Foreign business men deal with these organisations and never with those who actually use imported products and materials or those who make products for export.

There are sixteen corporations altogether, some at Er li gou, north-west of the town, about 6 miles from the Xin qiao hotel, and the others in the centre, not far from the Peking hotel, to the north. They have branches in the largest provincial towns. Their addresses in Peking are as follows:

— *China National Cereals, Oils and Foodstuffs Import and Export Corporation,*

  82 Dong an men Street, Beijing.
  Telegrams: CEROILFOOD BEIJING
  Telex: 22281 CEROF CN, 22111 CEROF CN
  Tel: 55-8831, 55-5180

— *China National Native Produce and Animal By-Products Import and Export Corporation,*

  82 Dong an men Street, Beijing.
  Telegrams: CHINATUHSU BEIJING
  Telex: 22283 TUHSU CN
  Tel: 55-8831, 55-4124

— *China National Textiles Import and Export Corporation,*

  82 Dong an men Street, Beijing.
  Telegrams: CHINATEX BEIJING
  Telex: 22280 CNTEX CN
  Tel: 55-3793, 55-8831

— *China National Light Industrial Products Import and Export Corporation,*

  82 Dong an men Street, Beijing.

Telegrams: INDUSTRY BEIJING
Telex: 22282 LIGHT CN
Tel: 55-8831, 55-6749

— *China National Arts and Crafts Import and Export Corporation,*

82 Dong an men Street, Beijing.
Telegrams: ARTCHINA BEIJING
Telex: 22155 CNART CN
Tel: 55-8831, 55-2187

— *China National Chemicals Import and Export Corporation,*

Er li gou, Xi jiao, Beijing.
Telegrams: SINOCHEM BEIJING
Telex: 22243 CHEMI CN
Tel: 89-0931, 89-1289

— *China National Machinery Import and Export Corporation,*

Er li gou, Xi jiao, Beijing.
Telegrams: MACHIMPEX BEIJING
Telex: 22242 CMIEC CN
Tel: 89-0931, 89-1974

— *China National Metals and Minerals Import and Export Corporation,*

Er li gou, Xi jiao, Beijing.
Telegrams: MINNERAIS BEIJING
Telex: 22241 MINET CN
Tel: 89-0931, 89-2376

— *China National Technical Import Corporation,*

Er li gou, Xi jiao, Beijing.
Telegrams: TECHIMPORT BEIJING
Telex: 22244 CNTIC CN
Tel: 890931, 892116

— *China National Foreign Trade Transportation Corporation,*

Er li gou, Xi jiao, Beijing.
Telegrams: ZHONGWQIYUN BEIJING
Telex: 22153 TRANS CN, 22154 TRANS CN, 22265 TRANS CN

— *China National Complete Plant Export Corporation,*

An ding men wai, Beijing.
Telegrams: COMPLANT BEIJING

— *China National Export Commodities Packaging Corporation*,
2 Dong Chang an jie, Beijing. Telegrams: CHINAPACK
BEIJING
Telegrams: CHINAPACK BEIJING

— *China National Chartering Corporation*,
Er li gou, Xi jiao, Beijing.
Telegrams: ZHONGZU BEIJING
Telex: 22153 TRANS CN, 22154 TRANS CN, 22265
TRANS CN

— *China Ocean Shipping Company*,
6 Dong Chang an jie Street, Beijing.
Telegrams: COSCO BEIJING
Telex: 22264 CPC PK CN

— *China National Publications Import Corporations*,
P.O. Box 88, Beijing.
Telegrams: PUBLIM BEIJING

— *China National Machinery and Equipment Export Corporation*,
12 Fu xing men wai Street, Beijing.
Telegrams: EQUIPEX BEIJING

Medical Treatment

Medical treatment is excellent in China; both doctors and
surgeons are first class.

Doctors from the hospital will visit patients who are seriously
ill only, and rarely at that. In almost all cases, foreigners who
fall ill have to go to the Shou du yi yuan Hospital in Shuai fu
yuan Street, a little street perpendicular to Wang fu jing, not
far from the Peking Hotel (Tel.: 55 37 31 and 55 65 93).

The chemists stock a large variety of medecine, from aspirin
to antibiotics, all made in China and of excellent quality. They
are all cheap, but their plain wrappings give instructions for
use in Chinese only, so that those who do not understand the
language may find some difficulty here. Tourists are advised
to bring any medecine which they may need with them, and
to lay in a small stock to ward off 'flu, coughs, stomach and
liver upsets. In winter, it is as well to bring some sort of hand
and face cream because of the cold and the dryness.

Those who belong to the rhesus negative blood group should
note that it does not exist among the Chinese.

Public bath houses exist, where massage treatments are given at the same time, such as the one as 241 Dong dan bei da jie.

Shopping

Peking has something to offer everyone in this field; the shops, ranging from very small ones to large department stores like Western shops have countless, varied articles to offer.

The range of goods is astonishingly large for a country where the purchasing power is still low, and austerity still the rule. The shops are full of products of every kind and crowded with idlers and serious customers, particularly on Sundays. The numbers of shops give liveliness to the streets, and this is one of the greatest charms of the capital. The present regime has managed to retain them although the economic structure of the country has been transformed and private ownership almost entirely abolished. A stroll through the busy shopping districts is a source of endless amusement, even when one has no intention of buying anything. It gives an idea of the immensely varied products of China's industry and handicrafts; except for a few rare examples, such as Swiss watches and Albanian cigarettes, no foreign consumer goods are imported, as the country saves its foreign currency to buy raw materials and equipment.

Business hours are extremely convenient for the customer, and China is an exception to the rule in this respect. The shops are open all day, from early morning until 6.30 p.m. or even 8.30 p.m. in some cases, every day, including Sunday. Most of them are closed on public holidays, however (May Day, October 1st, Spring Festival).

The friendly shop assistants, and their anxiety to give priority to foreigners, in spite of language difficulties, also makes China different from many other countries, especially countries with a state economy. The fact that employees have no material interest in business turnover makes them all the more praiseworthy. The only reward which they can hope for in return for their enthusiasm and success is promotion in their work. They are all scrupulously honest, too, a quality which is especially valuable in the case of antique dealers and jewellers.

Bargaining is out of the question. Prices are marked in Arabic numerals and can never be argued over. They are fixed by specialised organisations and the shop assistants have not the power to change them.

The busiest shopping streets are: 1) south of Chang an jie Avenue: the main street running southwards from Qian men Gate, known as Qian men da jie, and all the smaller streets perpendicular to it; 2) north of Chang an jie: Wang fu jing Street, which is to the east of the Imperial Palace, and another, symmetrical street west of the Palace, called Xi dan da jie, and its extension, Xi si da jie; Dong dan da jie and Dong si da jie, east of Wang fu jing, and Di an men wai da jie Street which runs northwards from Coal Hill towards the Drum Tower.

Shops for Tourists

The tourist who has neither the time nor the inclination to stroll about the shopping streets will find an interesting selection of goods at several shops reserved for foreign visitors.

No. 64 Dong hua men da jie is in a street perpendicular to Wang fu jing, running westwards. It sells curios, pieces of old embroidery and brocade, and traditional Chinese, Mongolian and Manchu costumes.

No. 16 Dong hua men da jie sells records.

The Friendship Store (You yi shang dian), Jian guo men wai da jie, is a department store and food market. It also includes a bank, a dry cleaner's, a flower shop and a packing, moving and shipping department.

The Friendship Furniture Store, 16 Dong da qiao lu, sells *modern* furniture.

Antique Shops Peking still has a few antique shops, most of which are in Liu li chang Street, the traditional centre of the antique-dealing trade, south-west of Qian men Gate. It is a most attractive street, with little low houses and old-fashioned shops behind wooden-framed windows, their cupboards and shelves crowded with a most varied collection of objects. Porcelain and pottery ware is more common than anything else, and varies enormously in quality: vases, bowls, plates, brush-pots, hat-stands, statues of deities and animals. The curios include countless snuff-bottles made of porcelain, glass, agate or jade, peach and other fruit-stones covered with minute carving, ornaments recalling customs and ways of life under the empire which have been abolished or abandoned: buttons for mandarins' hats, whose different colours denoted different ranks, beads, plaques, pendants, beard-combs; remains of fashions and pastimes of days gone by: pipes, cages for singing crickets with finely-worked ivory and tortoise-shell lids, boxes for fighting crickets, pigeon-whistles, which used to be fixed to the birds' tails... and paintings on glass, or rather pictures painted on the back of glass plaques, which are much sought after in Europe.

The shops in Liu li chang (which has an east and a west portion) are part of the *Peking Antique Store* and handle various specialities. To the east, no. 80 specializes in china and earthenware, no. 70 in bronzes, wood carvings and cloisonné ware, no. 108 in jade and soapstone, nos. 86, 63 (the oldest shop of all), 60 and 58 sell paintings and calligraphy, no. 91 sells artists' materials (brushes and paper), no. 92 sells lampshades and Chinese lanterns, and no. 115 is a bookshop. To the west, no. 17 sells chinaware, and no. 19, Rong bao zhai, artists' materials, and original modern paintings; it also specializes in the art of reproduction and restoration of paintings. You can also get paintings mounted on scrolls here, and at no. 31, another shop which specializes in restoration. No. 34 sells seals, paintings and ink sticks and stones, while no. 20 has old stone rubbings, books of calligraphy, and paintings.

With the exception of the professional buyers who deal directly with the Art and Crafts Corporation, no foreigner can hope to buy anything earlier than the reign of Jia Qing (1796–1820), the son of Qian Long. However, in spite of what some manuals and art books have to say on the subject, articles of high quality are still to be found in Peking: the 19th century craftsmen had taste and skill, and many things dating from the reigns of Dao Guang (1821-1850), or Xian feng (1851-1862), Tong zhi (1862-1875) and Guang xu (1875-1908) are of interest to art-lovers, and even collectors. Restrictions on the export of works of art are not always based on age alone. Some things made in the 19th century are not allowed out of the country because they are of exceptional artistic quality, or in the case of furniture, because they are made of precious woods such as rosewood or sandal-wood.

Bills, which have to be signed when the purchase is made, and the red sealing-wax seal attached to all old things by the service in control of the exporting of antiques, must be kept carefully, as the seal denotes permission to export the article, and both this and the bill have to be shown to the customs authorities when you leave China.

Useful Addresses

Bookshops are to be seen everywhere. The largest of all, selling Chinese books only, are in Wang fu jing. Publications and translations in foreign languages are sold at the Wai wen shu dian, no. 235 Wang fu jing, and at no. 16 Dong hua men da jie Street; reviews in foreign languages are for sale at no. 219 Wang fu jing.

The Furriers' selections of sable, ermine and mink are not of first class quality, but the prices are far lower than in Europe. Mongolia and the North-Eastern provinces are close to Peking, and the severe cold in winter makes it necessary to wear furs, all of which explains the abundance of different kinds on sale: wild cat, lynx, marten, otter, marmot, rabbit, as well as sheep and goatskins, tiger and leopard skins. Fur coats and hats can be found, as well as fur-lined gloves, jackets and raincoats. No. 192 Wang fu jing, shops in the Western Covered Market and a department of the Bai huo da lou, all sell furs.

Theatrical costumes and Properties: Turn east along Zhu shi kou out of Qian men wai, then take the first *hutong, Xi cao shi jie*, on the right. The shop is in the first modern building on the left, but has no number or sign.

Carpets: Apart from carpets made in Peking, the most highly prized carpets come from Bao tou, Ning xia and the province of Xin jiang, all of which are Persian in inspiration. Modern copies can be bought at no 208 Qian men da jie, near the Bridge of Heaven.

Modern China: 149 Qian men da jie (Jing de zhen ware).

Tea Shops: Countless varieties of tea exist: green tea is the most expensive, and may have jasmine, magnolia or red roses added to it; fermented black tea, packed sometimes in round bricks (Yun nan) or square ones (Si chuan); white tea from Fu jian. One of the most famous shops is the one at no. 142, Wang fu jing. The tea sold in the shops in the hotels can be bought without rationing cards.

Chemists' Shops: Some of them sell European style medicine only, such as no. 139 Wang fu jing, which sells ordinary medicine, and no. 267 Wang fu jing da jie which sells more specialised kinds; others specialise in traditional Chinese medicines, which use fresh or dried medicinal herbs, fruit stones, seaweed, fish-skins, tiger bones, deer and rhinoceros horns, snakes, sea-horses, centipedes, scorpions, toads, dried grasshoppers and silk-worms, oyster-shell powder, tortoise-shell powder, cinnabar, amber and orpiment powder, etc... The most famous of these is Tong ren tang, in Da zha lan Street.

Shops selling food of various kinds: Peking contains countless grocer's and other food shops, but some are older and more famous than the rest:

Xin yuan zhai, in Liu li chang street, which is over 100 years old and famous for its plum syrup;

Liu bi ju, no. 2 Liang shi dian jie, near Qian men Gate, is over 400 years old, as its old sign bears out; it specialises in sauces and condiments.

Xiang ju gong, no. 176 Qian men da jie specialises in Moslem food: sesame seed cakes.

Tong san yi, no. 19 Qian men, specialises in Chinese cakes dried and preserved fruits, and pear syrup for coughs.

Fruit and Vegetables: Most of Peking's fruit and vegetables come from people's communes in the neighbourhood; market gardening has developed enormously over recent years, and many of the vegetables are grown under glass. Both fruit and vegetables are in plentiful supply in shops all over the town, and prices are low, especially for vegetables. The apples, peaches, grapes and persimmons are all delicious. Citrus fruits and bananas from the southern provinces are on sale in Peking almost all the year round. Medlars threaded on sticks and dipped in caramel are a great winter delicacy *(Tang hu lu).*

Department Stores and Bazaars: The *Bai huo da lou* is similar to Western department stores; it is a large three-story building, no. 99 Wang fu jing. All consumer goods which are obtainable can be found there (it is open from 9 a.m. to 8.30 p.m.).

The *Dong feng shi chang,* opposite the *Bai huo da lou,* is a large, modern department store, all on ground level, with entrances in Wang fu jing and Jin yu hu tong. It is one of the most interesting shopping centres in Peking.

The *Western Covered Market (Xi dan shang chang),* in Xi dan bei da jie, was built in 1932, west of the Forbidden City, and is the counter-part of the old *Dong an shi chang* (now the *Dong feng shi chang),* though not so large or so picturesque.

The *Children's Shop* is at no. 172 Wang fu jing.

Commission shops (Xin tuo shang dian) deal in secondhand clothes, watches, spectacles, crockery, cameras, wireless sets, etc., and furniture. Some of the largest are at these addresses: 113 Dong dan da jie, 67 Wang fu jing, 119 Qian men wai, 32 Chong wen men da jie, and 137 Xin jie kou da jie.

A few sell furniture only: 18 Luo ma shi da jie, near Liu li chang Street, 35 Dong hua men da jie, 200 Dong si bei da jie; old furniture which has been restored can be found at no. 26 Wang fu jing.

Stamps. Stamp-collectors will find a large choice of Chinese stamps at the post offices on the ground floor of the hotels; a shop at 26 Dong hua men da jie, specialises in Chinese and foreign stamps.

Handicrafts from all over China can be found at the Arts and Crafts Store, 200 Wang fu jing, and at the Artcompany Store, 289 Wang fu jing.

T-shirt stencilling is done at 155 Xi dan north.

Flowers and Florists. Horticulture has been an art for a long time in China, and much appreciated at that. Exhibitions are held all the year round, particularly in Bei hai Park and at the Summer Palace. The public gardens are famous for their peonies in spring and chrysanthemums in autumn.

The flower shops are well stocked with gladioli, roses, chrysanthemums, pinks, marguerites, sweet peas, plants in pots, shrubs and cacti. Baskets of flowers are delivered to order.

The best known florists are near the Xin qiao Hotel, no. 68. Chong wen men da jie. They sell Christmas trees at Christmas time.

Massage Treatments: At the hairdresser's shops at the International Club, Jian guo men wai, and the Xin Qiao Hotel, 2 Dong jiao min xiang.

Musical Instruments, both Chinese and Western, are to be found at 231 Wang fu jing, which is a branch of the Bai huo da lou.

Chinese records and musical scores: 42 Wang fu jing da jie.

Clocks and Watches: No. 170 and 174 Wang fu jing are both clockmakers' shops which sell and repair clocks and watches.

Transport of Goods: A national company, the Peking Friendship Company (Transport Department) takes charge of the packing, customs clearance and sending off of all parcels to Europe (Frienship Store, Jian Guo Men Wai).

Hotels

Peking contains about 300 hotels and boarding houses, but very few of them take in foreigners. The main ones which cater for them are:

The Peking Hotel (Bei jing fan dian). Tel. 55 22 31. It stands on the wide east-west avenue, Chang an jie, near Tian an men and Wang fu jing. Its main clientele consists of foreign delegations and missions invited by the Chinese government; tourists rarely stay there.

The Xin qiao Hotel (Xin qiao fan dian) Tel. 55 77 31, is in the south-east corner of the old Legation Quarter, and is reserved for foreign businessmen and tourists. The bar is open until late in the evening.

The Nationalities' Hotel (Min zu fan dian). Tel. 66 85 41, is next to the Minorities' Cultural Palace, on the wide east-west avenue, Chang an jie, west of the Imperial Palace.

The Qian men Hotel (Qian men fan dian) Tel. 33 87 31, is a new building, south of Liu li chang.

Guests of the Chinese government sometimes stay at the *Peace Hotel* (He ping bin guan — tel. 55 51 31) Mi shi da jie, Jin yu hu tong no 3.

The rooms are comfortable, and usually have a bathroom attached. They are not air-conditioned. Heating is turned on on about October 15th and is counted as an extra, over and above the price of the room. Soap, a comb, clothes brush and slippers are provided in each room as a rule. The telephone, which has extensions in every room, has direct lines communicating with outside numbers. Few of the staff in the big hotels understand foreign languages, though the switchboard operators understand room numbers in English.

Laundering, pressing and dry-cleaning are done on the premises, quickly and well.

As well as the post office and foreign exchange office, hotels usually have a ladies' and gentlemen's hairdresser on the ground floor (in the case of special treatment, such as dyeing or tinting, it is advisable to supply one's own products). A hair-cut costs about 2 *yuan*, and a shampoo and set 4 *yuan* 80 *fen*. The International Club also has a hairdressing salon, and another exists at San li tun.

Shops on the ground floor of most hotels also sell toilet articles, stationery, fruit, sweets, drinks, cigarettes and souvenirs.

A simple meal can be ordered and sent up to your room in most hotels.

Electric current

230 volts, 50 c/s, A.C.

The wall sockets are slightly different from the international type; adapters with extensions can be borrowed from the hotels.

Restaurants

The Peking Duck (Quan ju de, "Meeting of all the virtues") has two branches: one, a few hundred yards south of Qian men Gate (tel. 75 13 79) was done up and enlarged in 1964; the other (tel. 55 33 10) which has been left unchanged as yet is in Shuai fu yuan, a little street perpendicular to Wang fu jing.

The Quan ju de, which is 130 years old, is one of the oldest restaurants in Peking. A whole meal consisting of nothing but duck can be ordered; the main dish is roast duck. The ducks come from people's communes in the Peking area; they are crammed so that when they are 60 days old their average weight is 5 to 6 lbs. It is possible to visit the kitchens, to see how they are cooked: the birds are filled with water, painted with sugar, and cooked for 40 minutes over a fire of jujube or pear wood, in huge ovens.

The Garden of the Horn of Plenty (Feng ze yuan, tel. 33 28 28) is in Qian men wai, mei shi jie; it is about a hundred years old. The cooking is excellent. Two of its specialities are a soup of cuttle-fish eggs, which are cut into thin strips (Wu yu dan tang) and duck marrow soup.

The Pei hai Lake Restaurant (Fang shan, tel. 44 25 73) is relatively cool in summer, as it is at the water's edge. Its name means that it imitates the cooking in the old imperial kitchens, and one of the specialities on the menu consists of a selection of the sweetmeats of which Empress Ci xi was particularly fond.

The Shou Du *Kao Rou* ("the Grill", tel. 44 59 21) was done up in the winter of 1964–65; it is in a most attractive spot, on a lake near the Drum Tower, no. 36 Yi liu hu tong, and is approached through a network of little winding lanes. Its speciality is lamb grilled in Mongolian style.

The *Hong bin lou fan zhuang* ("Distinguished Guests Restaurant", tel. 33 09 67) is a Moslem restaurant, no. 80 Xi chang an jie, opposite the Central Post Office Building. It specialises in meat cooked on the spit and sweet cakes.

The *E mei* (called after a famous mountain in Si chuan, one of the five sacred mountains in ancient China, tel. 86 30 68-69) is in Xi dan market and specialises in Si chuan dishes.

The *Jin yang fan zhuang*, 241 Hu fang qiao lu (tel. 33 16 60), specialises in Shan xi dishes.

The *Sha guo ju* ("the Clay Saucepan", tel. 66 11 26), no. 60 Gang wa shi Street, Xi si wang nan, specialises in pork dishes only.

The *Qing hai can ting* (tel. 44 28 46) is called after the province next to Tibet, and is at Dong si pai lou; its speciality is meat cooked on the spit.

The *Bei jing su cai* Restaurant, 74 Xuan wu men nei, tel. 33-4296, is a vegetarian restaurant.

The *Huai yang* Restaurant, 217 Xi dan north, tel. 66-4018, 66-0521, is a Jiangsu restaurant—braised crabs, eels, prawns.

The *Hui min kao rou wan*, 102 Xuan wu men (south Xi dan), tel. 33-0700, is a Moslem restaurant.

The restaurant at the *International Club*, Jian guo men wai, tel. 55-2144, serves Chinese and Western food.   Closed on Mondays.

The *Kang le* Restaurant, 259 An ding men nei da jie, tel. 44-3884, specializes in dishes from Fu jian and Yun nan.

Min zu fan zhuang, 16 Dong hua men, tel. 55-0069, 55-1098, is a Moslem restaurant famous for its Peking hot pot and shashlik.   Book in advance.

Nationalities Hotel, 51 Fu xing men nei da jie, tel. 66-8551, Chinese and Western food.

The *Peace Café*, Dong feng Market, tel. 55-4552, serves Western food.

The *San li tun* Restaurant in the foreigners' residential compound serves Chinese and western food, and is open in the afternoon for drinks.   Tel. 52-1084.

The *Shou du fan zhuang*, 60 Ren min lu, tel. 55-4581, specializes in Shantung dishes.

The *Si chuan* Restaurant, 51 Rong xian hutong, tel. 33-6356, serves Si chuan dishes, in an old house with several inner courtyards.

The *Tong he ju*, 3 Xi si south, tel. 66-0925, serves Shan dong dishes.

The *Xiang jiang* Restaurant, 133 Xi dan north, tel. 66-1414, specializes in Hu nan dishes.

The *Xin Qiao* Hotel, 2 Dong jiao min xiang, tel. 55-7731, has separate Chinese and western restaurants (Pakistani curries in western one).

The *Zhen jiang* Restaurant, Xi dan crossroads, tel. 66-1289, specializes in dishes from Jiangsu.

Suburban Restaurants and others in the Neighbourhood.

The *Xin jiang* restaurant, Er li gou Street, is near the Exhibitions Centre and the chief Foreign Trade Corporations.

The *Ting li guan* ("The Orioles' Rendez-vous") is in a temple in the Summer Palace, about ten minutes' walk from the entrance.

The *Xiang shan fan dian* ("The Fragrant Hills Restaurant") is in the former Hunting Park, 18 miles west of the town. It is extremely popular in summer, so it is advisable to book a table by telephone (tel. 81 92 44).

Foreign Style Cooking

The big hotels in Peking serve western dishes cooked by Chinese chefs. The menus are written out in Chinese and English. They have a good choice, including fish, hors d'œuvres, chicken, mixed grill, Mongolian cheese, yoghourt, fruit, tart, pancakes, and one can have a good meal there.

A few restaurants specialise in foreign cooking:

Russian cooking: Mo si ke can ting (Moscow Restaurant), at the exhibition Centre.

A western-style restaurant now exists in the San li tun district.

Churches, Mosques and Temples

Roman Catholic services are held at the Nan tang, 79 Sheng cheng jie Street (tel. 33 27 07) at 9.30 a.m. on Sundays.

Mosques. The largest mosque is in Niu jie Street (Ox Street). Others are to be found in Dong si da jie, Jin shi fang jie Street and Hua shi Street.

Buddhist Temple. The Guang ji si Temple, in the north west of the town.

Entertainments

No specialised publication exists, and programmes are to be found in the daily papers.

Classical Opera: (*Jing ju* or Peking Opera, when accompanied by string instruments, *Kun ju* when accompanied by wind instruments). Some famous classical operas—the *White Snake*, the *Good Judge*, the *Mandarin with Three Daughters*, the *Monkey King*, the *Boars' Forest*, *Driven to Revolt* and the *Innkeeper*—are performed now (1979).

Modern Peking Opera—such as *The Red Lantern*, *Taking the Bandits' Stronghold*—has retained the classical instruments and style of singing, but the subjects are taken from the present day or recent history.

Modern operas from Shao xing, Canton, Wu han and other Chinese towns are occasionally performed by troupes from the provinces who come to Peking. *Western style opera* including singing *(Ge ju)* or singing and dancing *(Ge wu ju)* has been introduced recently, and also 'modern revolutionary' ballet *(wu ju)*, two of which are: *The White-haired Girl* and *The Red Detachment of Women*.

Foreign companies, mainly folk-dance companies, come to China nearly every year. The famous Chinese acrobat companies are nearly always either abroad or touring the provinces, and can rarely be seen in Peking.

Although Western music is taught in the conservatoires with growing success, concerts are rare occurrences. They are usually held in the Bridge of Heaven Theatre or at the Minorities' Cultural Palace. Foreign artists sometimes come to give recitals.

Plays etc. begin between 7 and 7.30 p.m.; they begin punctually and last about two and a half hours, with a ten-minute interval. Seats are extremely cheap; they cost from 50 *fen* to 1 *yuan* 20. Some theatres act as cinemas in the afternoon and theatres in the evening.

Tourists wishing to go to the cinema or the theatre should apply to Lü xing she, as tickets are extremely hard to get.

Peking contains about 15 large and medium-sized theatres. The four largest are recent buildings:

- the Capital Theatre (Shou dou ju chang) in the extension of Wang fu jing, which seats 1,120;
  the Bridge of Heaven Theatre (Tian qiao ju chang), in the Bridge of Heaven district;

- the People's Theatre (Ren min ju chang) in Hu guo si da jie;

- the Exhibition Centre Theatre (Bei jing zhan lan guan ju chang), which is the largest in Peking, and which lies away from the centre, outside the walls, next to the Zoo;
- the Peking Workers' Club Theatre (Bei jing gong ren ju le bu), Hu fang qiao;
- the Minorities' Cultural Palace Theatre (Min zu wen hua gong li tang), Xi chang an da jie;
- the February 7th Theatre (Er qi ju chang), Fu xing men wai;
- the Great Harmony Theatre (Guang he ju chang), which is very old, in Qian men wai;
- the Masses' Theatre (Qun zhong ju chang), Chao wai da jie;
- the Chinese Youth Art Theatre (Zhong guo qing nian yi shu ju chang), Dong chang an jie;
- the Chang an Theatre, Xi chang an jie, near Xi dan;
- the Theatre of Democracy (Min zu ju chang), Zhu shi kóu, outside Qian men;
- the Yin yue tang theatre, in the Sun Yat sen Park, open in the summer only.

The Peking cinemas show foreign films. Several theatres show films during the day, such as the Guang he (Qian men). The first showing begins between 8 and 9 a.m., and the least between 8 and 9 p.m.

Seats cost between 30 and 40 *fen*.

The main cinemas which show new films are:

- the Capital (Shou dou dian ying yuan), Xi chang an jie, near Xi dan; not to be confused with the Capital Theatre (Shou dou ju chang), in the extension of Wang fu jing;
- the Great China (Da hua), in Dong dan;
- the Er tong dian ying yuan, Dong chang an jie;
- the Red Star (Hong xing), Dong dan, which specialises in newsreels;

Sports and Games

Tourists may play tennis, ping pong and bathe in the swimming-pool at the *International Club* (Jian Guo Men Wai tel. 52 21 44), once they have paid a subscription covering the length of their stay. Foreigners are also able to use the swimming-pool at the Workers' Stadium. Admission to both pools is only granted to holders of a medical certificate, delivered by the Shou du Hospital, Shuai fu yuan Street, after an examiination. In summer, bathing is allowed in the Summer Palace Lake.

The beach at Bei dai he (Pei tai ho), on the Gulf of Bei zhi li (Chihli) is open to foreigners from June 15th to August 31st; it is 6 hours from Peking by train.

Skating takes place in several places in winter: the International Club, the moat round the Imperial City, and the Bei hai Lake. Rinks are made there, which are well-lit, and where skating goes on from 4 or 5 p.m. onwards.

Horse and dog-racing, betting and gambling are all forbidden in China.

SHANG HAI

Airports

The *Hong qiao* airport (Rainbow Bridge Airport), south-west of the city, next to the zoo, has been modernised.

Japan Air Lines runs four flights a week between Tokyo and Peking (1979), via Shanghai; it is the only international company to use Shanghai airport. The agency is at 1202 Huai hai zhong lu, tel. 37-8467. Airport office tel. 53-6530, ext. 368.

Hotels

— Peace Hotel (He ping fan dian), 20 Nanking Road east, tel. 21-1244, at the corner of Zhong shan dong yi (Sun Yat sen) which runs alongside the river, and Nanking Road; an annex has been opened on the other side of Nanking road.

— International Hotel (Guo ji fan dian), 170 Nanking Road west, tel. 56-3040.

— Jing jiang Hotel, 59 Mao ming nan Street, tel. 53-4242.

Restaurants

— Hong fang zi (The Red House), 37 Shân xi Road south, tel. 56-5748, 56-5220 (Western food; Grand Marnier soufflé, but bring your own Grand Marnier; baked Alaska; order these in advance).

— De da Restaurant, 805 Nanking Road west, tel. 53-5202 (ground floor: coffee, Shanghai cakes and pastries, first floor: western food).

- International Hotel Restaurant, 170 Nanking Road west, tel. 56-3040 (Peking dishes).

- Si chuan fan dian (Si chuan Restaurant), 457 Nanking Road east, tel. 22-1965.

- Guangzhou Restaurant, Nanking Road east, tel. 28-1393.

- Lu yang cun Restaurant, 763 Nanking Road east, tel. 53-7221, 53-8427.

- Peking Restaurant, Nanking Road east, tel. 28-1298 (northern style food).

- Yang zhou Restaurant, Nanking Road east, tel. 22-2779.

The following Restaurants existed in 1966, and most of them are still open, but the visitor would be well advised to check before going there (1979):

- Xing hua lou (Cantonese) 343 Fu zhou Street, tel. 29 35 55.

- Xin ya (Cantonese), 719 Nanking Road, tel. 29 00 80, on the corner of Nanking Road and Guang xi Street;

- Hua qiao fan dian (Overseas Chinese Restaurant, serving Chinese and European dishes), 104 Nanking Road (West), tel. 29 41 86.

- Heng shan fan dian (formerly the Picardie, Si chuan and Cantonese dishes) 534 Heng shan lu, tel. 37 70 50;

- Shang hai da sha (Chinese and European dishes), tel. 24 62 60;

- Hong chang xing yang rou guan (Moslem restaurant, Mongolian stew), 6 Lian yun lu, tel. 53 60 66;

- Gong de lin shu shi chu (vegetarian restaurant), 4, 41st Lane, Huang he lu, tel. 55 1313;

- Zhi wei guan hang cai jiu jia (Hang zhou dishes), 345 Fu jian lu, tel. 29 02 40;

- Jie er jing chuan cai cha shi (Clean and Delicate Restaurant, Si chuan dishes), near the Fu xing Park, 82 Yan tang lu, tel. 28 28 14;

- Lao zheng xing (Ancient Prosperity, Shang hai dishes), 566 Jiu jiang lu, tel. 29 31 53.

- Mei long zhen jiu jia (Yang zhou dishes) 22, Lane 1081, Nanking Road (West), tel. 53 53 53.

Shops

Friendship Store, 33 Zhongs han dong lu. It includes antiques and modern handicraft products.

Antique Shop: 218 Canton Road. Closing time: 6 p.m. The china is arranged in different sections, one for each dynasty. It also contains jewellery, soapstone and jade carvings, lacquer ware, boxes and bronzes.

Arts and Crafts Store (Gong yi mei shu), Nanking Road east.

Calligraphy and Paper Arts Company, Nanking Road east.

Foreign Languages Book Store (Wai wen shu dian), Fu zhou Road.

Commission Shops (secondhand clocks, watches, spectacles, glass, crockery, etc.; furniture) 1297 Huai hai Road central, 557 Yan an Road central.

Old Books Store, Fu zhou Road.

The *Old Town shopping district* starts at the main entrance to Yu Gardens (Yu Yuan).

Shang hai Museum

Is at 16 He nan Road; it is open every day except Monday, from 9-11 a.m. and from 1.30-4.0 p.m. It has an excellent collection of bronzes.

The Handicraft Research Institute

Master-craftsmen teach about a dozen crafts: stone, bamboo, ivory, box-wood carving, artificial flower making, paper cut-outs, tapestry work, embroidery, knitting, coloured lantern making.

Theatres: the largest theatre is the Da wu tai, Han kou Road.

Shang hai theatres give performances of Shang hai Opera *(Hu ju)*, Shao xing Opera and Peking Opera mainly.

Circus: a new circular building in Nanking Road houses a circus.

The Great World (Da shi jie): it contains all kinds of entertainments, including theatres, cinemas and a circus, among others.

The Roman Catholic Church, Xu jia hui, is on the road to the Long hua Airport.

The Mosque is in Canton Road.

Factories

Foreigners are usually taken to see the following:

— the Wu song oil refinery;

— the Wu jing ammonia fertilizer and urea factory;

— the Min hang heavy machinery factory, and its model workers' city, which was built in the space of a few months, about 12 miles south-west of Shang hai.

One of these factories has built a 12,000 metric ton hydraulic press.

Electric current

220 volts in the city centre, and in the chief hotels; 110 volts in some districts.

Trips to nearby Towns

Hang zhou, Su zhou and Wu xi are all easily accessible by train from Shang hai. It takes 2 hours 47 minutes to cover the 117 miles from Shang hai to Hang zhou.

Shang hai is 53 miles (1 hour 4 minutes) by train from Su zhou; it is possible to make a day trip there.

The train covers the 78 miles from Shang hai to Wu xi in 1 hour 41 minutes.

CANTON

Airport

The Bai yun (White Clouds) Airport is a few miles north of the town, in a valley bordered by the White Cloud Hills to the east.

Station

The station for the Canton — Shen zheng (Shun chun) — Kowloon (Hong kong) line is in the south-east of the town, near the Pearl River.

Hotels

— Bai Yun Guest House, Huan shi Road, east, tel. 67-700.

— Bei jing fan dian (Peking Hotel), Chang ti, 21-799.

— Dong fang Guest House (Dong fang bing guan), Ren min Road north, tel. 69-900, 32-644, 30-690, 32-227.

— Hua qiao da sha (Overseas Chinese Hotel), Hai zhu Square, tel. 61-112.

— People's Mansion (Ren min da sha), Yuan jiang Road I, tel. 61-445, 23-518.

Restaurants

— Ban xi Restaurant, Xiang yang Road I, tel. 85-655 (Cantonese food).

— Nam yuen Restaurant (Nan yuan jiu jia), Qian jin Road, tel. 50-542, 50-532.

— Bei Xiu Restaurant, Da bei Street, tel. 31-154 (Cantonese).

— Dong fang Guest House, Ren min Road north, tel. 69-900 (Cantonese, northern and western food).

— Guang chuan Villa, San yuan li, tel. 32-540 (Cantonese and western food).

— Guang Hui Restaurant, Chang ti Road, tel. 23-054 (Cantonese and western food).

— Guangzhou Restaurant, Wen chang Road south, tel. 87-136, 87-840. (Cantonese).

— Liu hua Guest House, Ren min Road north, tel. 68-800 (Cantonese and western food).

— Moslem Restaurant, Zhong shan Road VI, tel. 88-414 (mutton, no pork).

— North China Restaurant, Zhong shan Road V, tel. 33-837 (northern dishes).

— Overseas Chinese Hotel, Hai zhu Square, tel. 61-112 (Cantonese).

— Sheng li Guest House, Sha mian, tel. 61-223 (Cantonese and western food).

— Tai ping House, Peking Road north (35-529 (Cantonese and western food).

The following restaurants existed in 1966 and may still be open, but the visitor would be well advised to check before going there (1979):

- the "Listen to the rain falling" restaurant on the shores of the lake in the Yuet sau (Yue xiu) Park, Tai pak (Da bei) Street, tel. 33387; 30876.

- the So hung (Shu hong) Restaurant, in Liu fa (Liu hua hu) Park, west of the Yang cheng Hotel, tel. 31770 and 31914.

- the Au tam (E tam) floating restaurant, on Shameen Island (Sha mian), tel. 75996.
- the Zoo Restaurant (tel. 70101), Martyrs' Street; it specialises in game.
- the "Birds, Flowers and Music" Tea House, 54 Liberation Street north (tel. 30919).

The Exhibition Centre

It stands on the Ai qun Square, at the end of the new bridge spanning the Pearl River. The "Canton Fair" is held there twice a year, for a month at a time, beginning on the 15th May and the 15th October (see Chinese Economy, p. 263).

In the same square, near the bridge, stands a second building which houses the arts and crafts section of the exhibition.

Shops

— Canton Antique shop, 146 Wen de north Street.
— Canton Sporting Goods Store, 333-339 Peking Road.
— Department Store for Women and Children, Xiu li Road II.
— Friendship Store (You yi shang dian), Yuan jiang Road I.
— Jiang nan Native Produce Store, 399 Zhong shan Road IV.
— Nan fang Department Store, Yuan jiang Road I.
— Zhong shan Road V Department Store, Shong shan Road V.

Trips to Places of Interest

The Cong hua Hot Springs are 50 miles north of Canton. The waters rise at a temperature of 112° F., and are used for treating rheumatism, hypertension, and neurasthenia. Tourists can bathe in the swimming-pools.

The Seven Star Cliffs are 69 miles north of Canton. They contain caves, the Temple of Great Illumination, the Tower of the Celestial Pillar; boats are for hire on the Star Lake.

INDEX

This index should provide the reader with a quicker means of finding the provinces, towns and other important places described, than the Table of Contents (p. 5) at the beginning of the book. Names which are frequently quoted are entered under their Anglo-Saxon or French transcriptions, with the official *pinyin* transcription, as used in the guide, alongside them. A few poets, writers, historical (hist.) or political (polit.) figures, and the most important Chinese dynasties (dyn.), are included as well.

For information on the different transcriptions and pronunciation tables, see p. 91. The names given in *pinyin* in the index are recognisable because no hyphens are used.

Other glossaries, word lists, etc., are also available for the reader: (drawn up in *pinyin*):

Chronological list of Ming and Qing Emperors, p. 130

Practical vocabulary, p. 101

Glossary of Chinese deities and religious terms, p. 160

Glossary of Chinese historical, architectural and archaeological terms, p. 256

Chinese names are explained on p. 326

A rich vocabulary on cooking is to be found in the chapter on Chinese cooking, p. 370

Printed in Switzerland

This Encyclopedia-Guide has been set, printed and bound by
Nagel Publishers in Geneva (Switzerland)

Legal Deposit No. 731

Printed in Switzerland

CHINE

Cartes et plans

CHINA

Maps and plans

CARTOGRAPHIE NAGEL

SOMMAIRE / CONTENTS

Pl. 1

PROVINCE DU HE BEI
PROVINCE OF HE BEI

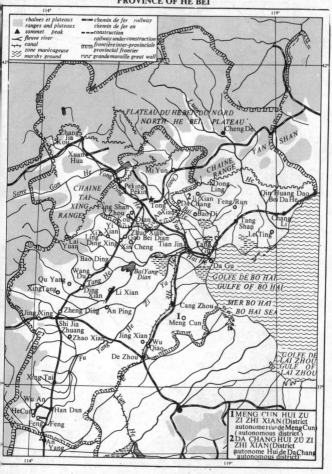

chaînes et plateaux
ranges and plateaus
▲ sommet peak
fleuve river
canal
zone marécageuse
marshy ground
━━ chemin de fer railway
chemin de fer en
construction
╌╌ railway under construction
frontière inter-provinciale
provincial frontier
grande muraille great wall

PLATEAU DU HEBEI DU NORD
NORTH HE BEI PLATEAU

Cheng De

YAN SHAN

Zhang Jia Kou

Xuan Hua

CHAINE RANGE

He Yong

Mi Yun

Dong Ling

Qin Huang Dao
Bei Da He

Sang Gan

CHAINE TAI XING RANGE

Peking Pékin

Li Xian

Feng Run

Tong Xian

Da Chang

Bao Di

Fang Shan

Zhou Kou Dian

Yi Xian

Zhuo Xian

Gao Bei Dian

Xin Cheng

Tang Shan

Chang Li

Le Ting

Lai Yuan

Lin Ji

Ding Xing

Tian Jin

Bao Ding

Tang Gu

Wang Du

Tang He

BaiYang Dian

Hai He

Da Gu

GOLFE DE BO HAI
GULFE OF BO HAI

Qu Yang

Ding Xian

Li Xian

Ya Zi

MER BO HAI
BO HAI SEA

XingTang

Zheng Ding

An Ping

Cang Zhou

Jing Xing

Shi Jia Zhuang

Zhao Xian

Jing Xian

Meng Cun

Wu Qiao

Fu

De Zhou

Yang

GOLFE DE LAI ZHOU
GULF OF LAI ZHOU

Xing Tai

Wu An

HeCun

Han Dan

Feng Feng

An Yang

He

1 MENG CUN HUI ZU
ZI ZHI XIAN (District
autonome Hui de Meng Cun
(autonomous
district)

2 DA CHANG HUI ZŪ ZI
ZHI XIAN (District
(autonome Hui de Da Chang
autonomous district)

Pl. 2

ENVIRONS DE PÉKIN - AREA SURROUNDING PEKING

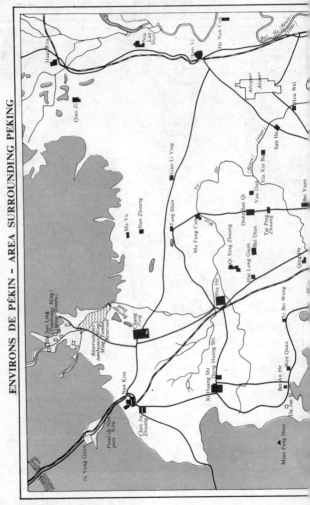

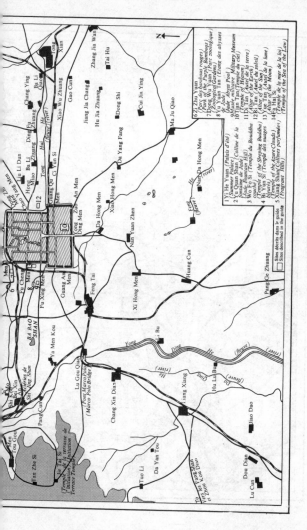

Pl. 3

Pl. 4

PROVINCE DU JIANG SU, AN HUI, ZHE JIANG
PROVINCE OF JIANG SU, AN HUI, ZHE JIANG

1 MONT HUO SHAN (1751 m)
  MOUNT
2 MONTAGNE JIU HUA SHAN
3 MONT HUANG SHAN
4 COLLINE HUI SHAN HILL
5 MONT MO GAN SHAN
6 MONT BEI YAN DANG
  SHAN (1001 m)
7 MONT NAN YAN DANG
  SHAN (1121 m)
8 MONT XIAN XIA LING
  (1423 m)
9 MONT WU YI SHAN
  (2120 m)

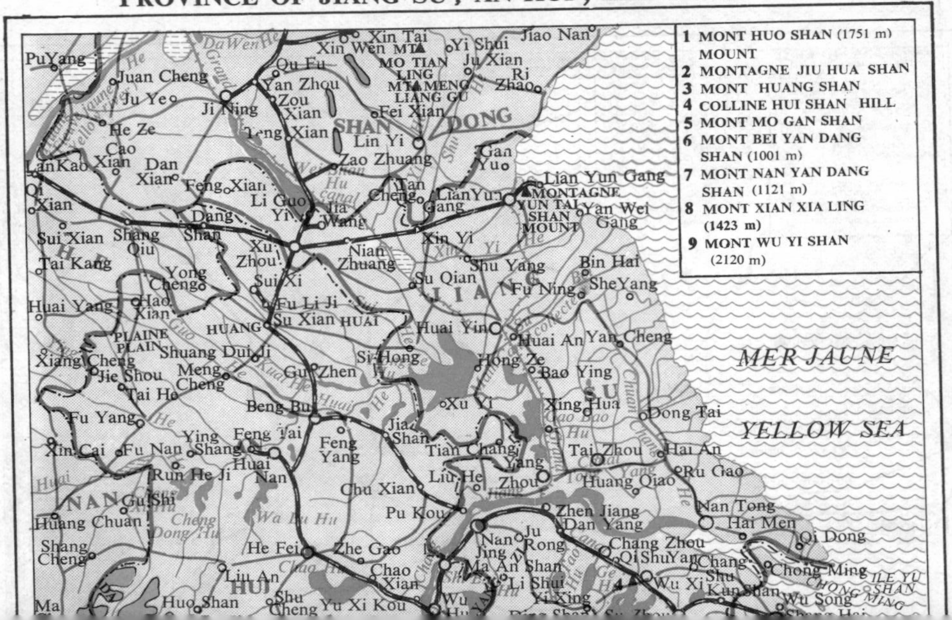

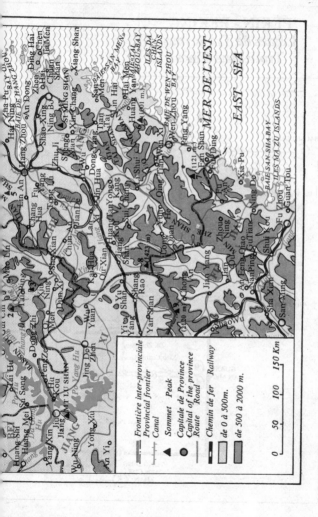

Pl. 5

MER DE L'EST

EAST SEA

BAIE DE HANG-ZHOU

BAIE DE WEN-ZHOU

ÎLES DA CHEN ISLANDS

ÎLES MA ZU ISLANDS

Frontière inter-provinciale
Provincial frontier

Canal

▲ Sommet   Peak

● Capitale de Province
Capital of the province

Route   Road

Chemin de fer   Railway

de 0 à 500m.

de 500 à 2000 m.

0   50   100   150 Km

Pl. 6

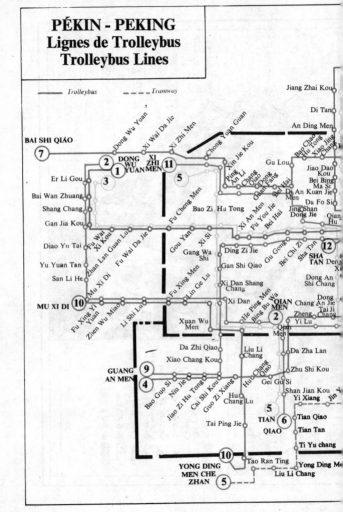

PÉKIN - PEKING
Lignes de Trolleybus
Trolleybus Lines

— Trolleybus   - - - Tramway

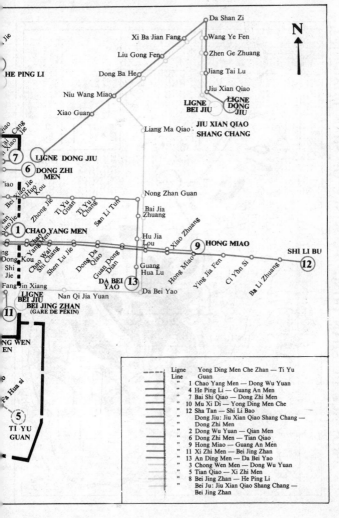

Pl. 7

N

Da Shan Zi

Xi Ba Jian Fang ○ ○ Wang Ye Fen

Liu Gong Fen ○ ○ Zhen Ge Zhuang

HE PING LI

Dong Ba He ○ ○ Jiang Tai Lu

Niu Wang Miao ○ ○ Jiu Xian Qiao

Xiao Guan ○ **LIGNE BEI JIU** **LIGNE DONG JIU**

JIU XIAN QIAO SHANG CHANG

Liang Ma Qiao

⑦ **LIGNE DONG JIU**

⑥ **DONG ZHI MEN**

Nong Zhan Guan

Zhong Jie ○ Ti Yu Guan ○ Ti Yu Chang ○ San Li Tun

Bai Jia Zhuang

① **CHAO YANG MEN**

Chao Yang Men ○ Chao Wai Shi Chang ○ Shen Lu Jie ○ Dong Da Qiao ○ Guan Dong Dian

Hu Jia Lou

Xiao Zhuang ⑨ **HONG MIAO** **SHI LI BU** ⑫

DA BEI YAO ⑬

Guang Hua Lu

Hong Miao ○ Ying Jia Fen ○ Ci Yun Si ○ Ba Li Zhuang

Nan Qi Jia Yuan

Da Bei Yao

LIGNE BEI JIU **BEI JING ZHAN (GARE DE PÉKIN)**

⑪

NG WEN EN

Fa Hua si

⑤ **TI YU GUAN**

Ligne Line	Yong Ding Men Che Zhan — Ti Yu Guan
" 1	Chao Yang Men — Dong Wu Yuan
" 4	He Ping Li — Guang An Men
" 7	Bai Shi Qiao — Dong Zhi Men
" 10	Mu Xi Di — Yong Ding Men Che
" 12	Sha Tan — Shi Li Bao
"	Dong Jiu: Jiu Xian Qiao Shang Chang — Dong Zhi Men
" 2	Dong Wu Yuan — Qian Men
" 6	Dong Zhi Men — Tian Qiao
" 9	Hong Miao — Guang An Men
" 11	Xi Zhi Men — Bei Jing Zhan
" 13	An Ding Men — Da Bei Yao
" 3	Chong Wen Men — Dong Wu Yuan
" 5	Tian Qiao — Xi Zhi Men
" 8	Bei Jing Zhan — He Ping Li
"	Bei Ju: Jiu Xian Qiao Shang Chang — Bei Jing Zhan

Pl. 8

PROVINCE DU SHAN DONG PROVINCE OF SHAN DONG

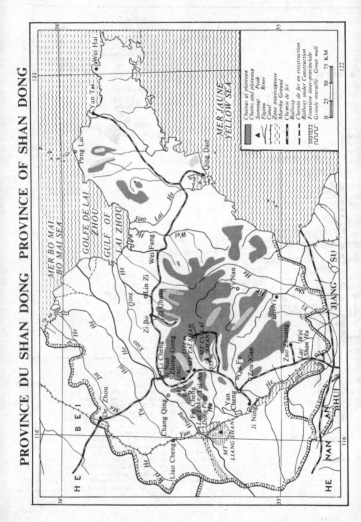

MER BO MAI
BO MAI SEA

MER JAUNE
YELLOW SEA

GOLFE DE LAI
ZHOU
GULF OF
LAI ZHOU

Wei Hai
Yan Tai
Peng Lai
Qing Dao
Wei Fang
Wei He
Jiao Lai He
Lai He
Zi Bo
Qing He
Xiao Qing He
Jiao He
Zi He
Zi Chuan
Ji Nan
Yi Nan
Lin Zi
Lin Yi
Yi He
Shu He
Le Cheng
Nan Zhong Gong
MT TAI SHAN
1524 m
955 m
MT CUI SHAN
Qu Fu
Zao Zhuang
Lac Wei Shan Hu
Lake Wei Shan Hu
Chang Qing
Ma He
Tu He
Zhou
Yun He
Liao Cheng
MT LIANG SHAN
Fei Cheng
Tai An
Lac Loke
Dong Ping Hu
Yan
Cheng
Ji Ning

HE BEI

HE NAN

AN HUI

JIANG SU

Légende

	Chaînes et plateaux	Chains and plateaux
▲	Sommet	Peak
	Fleuve	River
	Canal	Canal
	Zone marécageuse	Marshy Ground
	Chemin de fer	Railway
	Chemin de fer en construction	Railway under Construction
	Frontière inter-provinciale	
	Grande muraille	Great Wall

0 25 50 75 KM

116 122
35 38

Pl. 9

PROVINCE DU SHAN XI
PROVINCE OF SHAN XI

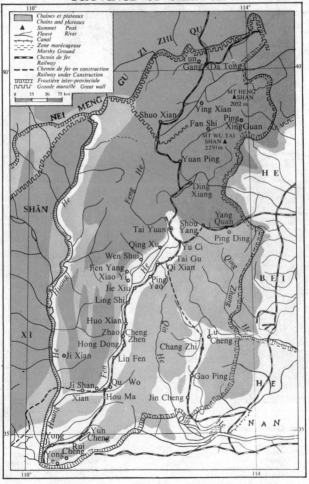

Chaînes et plateaux
Chains and plateaux
Sommet   Peak
Fleuve   River
Canal
Zone marécageuse
Marshy Ground
Chemin de fer
Railway
Chemin de fer en construction
Railway under Construction
Frontière inter-provinciale
Great wall
Grande muraille

0 25 50 75 km

Pl. 10

PROVINCE DU HE NAN   PROVINCE OF HE NAN

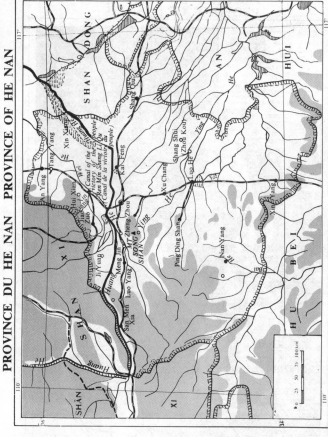

Chaînes et plateaux
Chains and plateaux

▲ Sommet   Peak

Fleuve   River
Canal

Zone marécageuse
Marshy Ground

Chemin de fer
Railway

Chemin de fer en construction
Railway under Construction

Frontière inter-provinciale
Grande muraille   Great wall

Pl. 11

PROVINCE DU SHÂN XI
PROVINCE OF SHÂN XI

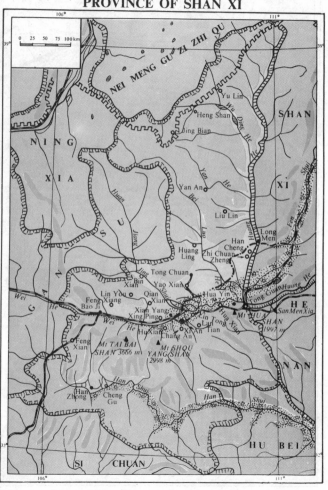

NEI MENG GU ZI ZHI QU

SHAN

Yu Lin

Heng Shan

Ding Bian

Wu Ding He

NING

Yan Bei

Yan An

XI

Huan Jiang

XIA

Liu Lin

Fen Shui

GAN

Long Men

Luo

Huang Ling

Han Cheng

Zhi Chuan

Zheng

SU

Jing

Tong Chuan

Yao Xian

Bin Xian

Lin You

Qian Xian

Feng Xiang

Xian Yang

Hua Yin

Tong Guan

Huang He

Bao Ji

Xing Ping

HE

Wei He

Lan

San Men Xia

Wei He

Hu Xian

Chang An

Lin Tong

Xi An

Tian

Feng Xian

Mt TAI BAI SHAN 3666 m

Mt SHOU YANG SHAN 2998 m

Mt HUA SHAN 1997 m

NAN

Han Zhong

Han Shui

Cheng Gu

Han Shui

SI CHUAN

HU BEI

0   25 50 75 100 km

Pl. 12

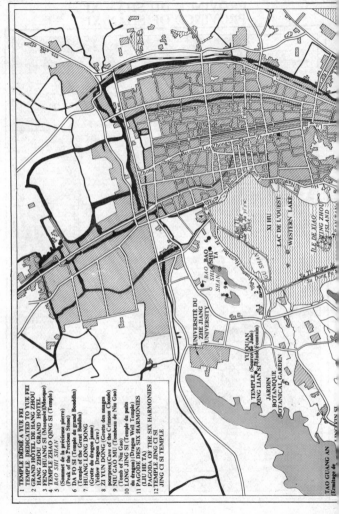

1 TEMPLE DÉDIÉ À YUE FEI
  (Temple dedicated to Yue Fei)
2 GRAND HÔTEL DE HANG ZHOU
  HANG ZHOU GRAND HOTEL
3 FENG HUANG SI (Mosquée/Mosque)
4 TEMPLE ZHAO QING SI (Temple)
5 *BAO SHI SHAN*
  (Sommet de la précieuse pierre)
  (Peak of the Precious Stone)
6 DA FO SI (Temple du grand Bouddha)
  (Temple of the Great Buddha)
7 HUANG LONG DONG
  (Grotte du dragon jaune)
  (Yellow Dragon's Cave)
8 ZI YUN DONG (Grotte des nuages
  pourpres/Cave of the Crimson Clouds)
9 NIU GAO MU (Tombeau de Niu Gao)
  (Tomb of Niu Gao)
10 LONG JING SI (Temple du puits
   du dragon/Dragon's Well Temple)
11 PAGODE DES SIX HARMONIES
   (LIU HE TA)
   PAGODA OF THE SIX HARMONIES
12 TEMPLE JING CI SI
   JING CI SI TEMPLE

UNIVERSITÉ DU ZHE JIANG
ZHE JIANG UNIVERSITY

YU QUAN
TEMPLE (Source/Fountain)
QING LIAN SI

JARDIN
BOTANIQUE
BOTANICAL GARDEN

TAO GUANG AN
(Ermitage de

BAO SHI SHAN
BAO SHI TA

SHAN

XI HU
LAC DE L'OUEST
WESTERN LAKE

ÎLE DE XIAO
YING ZHOU
ISLAND

Pl. 13

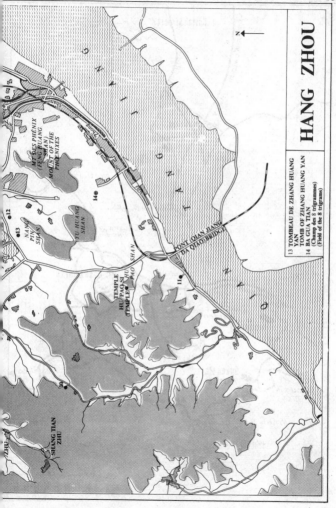

HANG ZHOU

13 TOMBEAU DE ZHANG HUANG YAN
TOMB OF ZHANG HUANG YAN
14 BA GUA TIAN
(Champ des 8 trigrammes)
(Field of the 8 trigrams)

MT. DES PHÉNIX
(FENG HUANG SHAN)
MOUNT OF THE PHOENIXES

NAN PIN SHAN

FU HUANG SHAN

TEMPLE HU PAO SHAN
TEMPLE HU PAO SI

SHANG TIAN ZHU

DA QIAO BRIDGE
PONT QIAO JIANG

QIAN TANG JIANG

Pl. 14

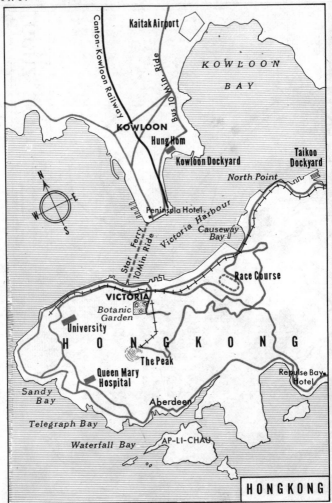

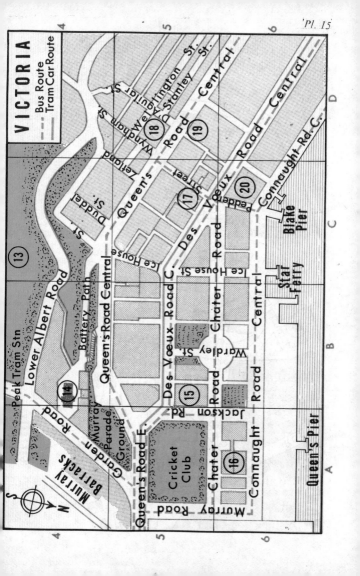

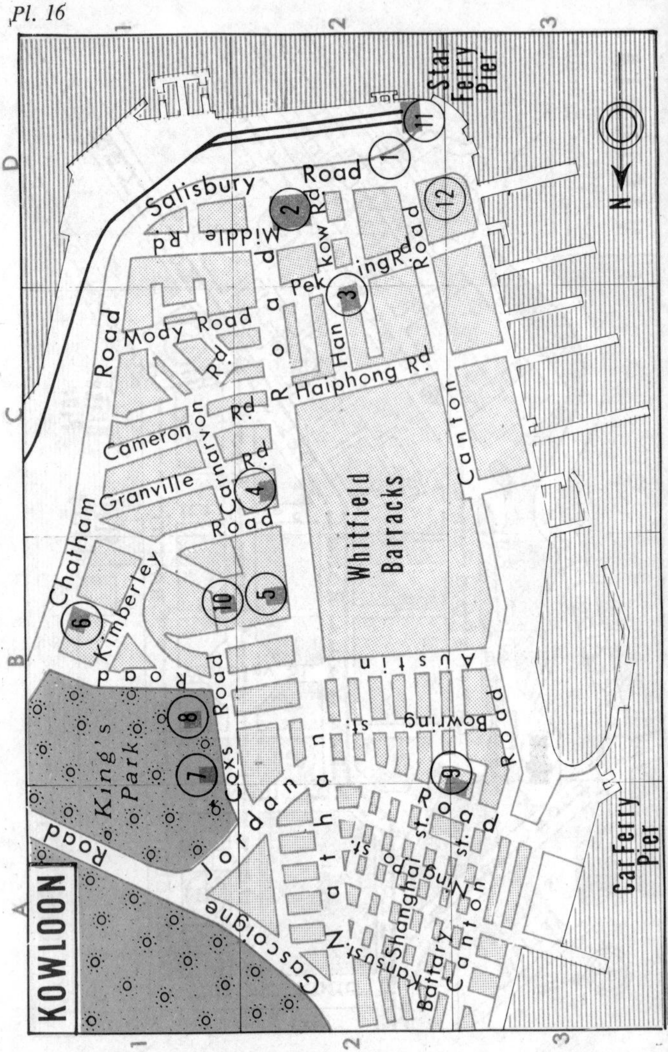
KOWLOON
Star Ferry Pier
Car Ferry Pier
Whitfield Barracks
King's Park
Salisbury Road
Middle Rd
Peking Rd
Hankow Rd
Mody Road
Chatham Road
Cameron Rd
Granville Rd
Carnarvon Road
Kimberley Road
Haiphong Rd
Canton Road
Austin Road
Bowring st.
Nathan Road
Jordan Road
Coxs Road
Gascoigne Road
Kansu st.
Shanghai st.
Ningpo st.
Battary st.
Canton Road
N
1
2
3
4
5
6
7
8
9
10
11
12
A
B
C
D
1
2
3

Pl 17

TIAO QI

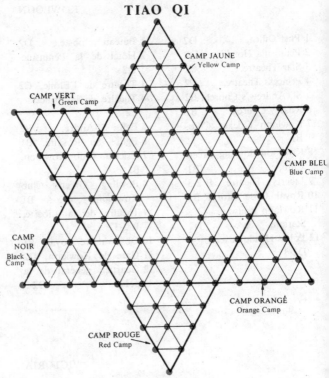

CAMP JAUNE
Yellow Camp

CAMP VERT
Green Camp

CAMP BLEU
Blue Camp

CAMP NOIR
Black Camp

CAMP ORANGÉ
Orange Camp

CAMP ROUGE
Red Camp

fig. 1

Pl. 18

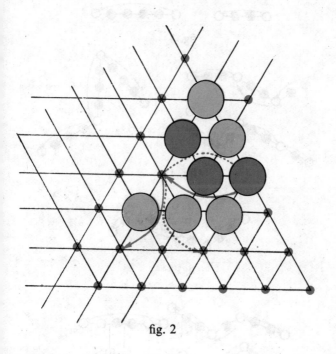

fig. 2

Pl. 19

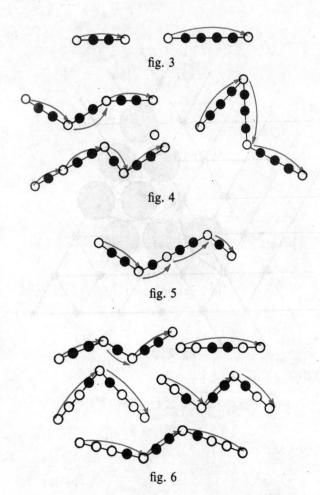

fig. 3

fig. 4

fig. 5

fig. 6

Pl. 20

ÉCHECS CHINOIS (XIANG QI)
CHINESE CHESS (XIANG QI)

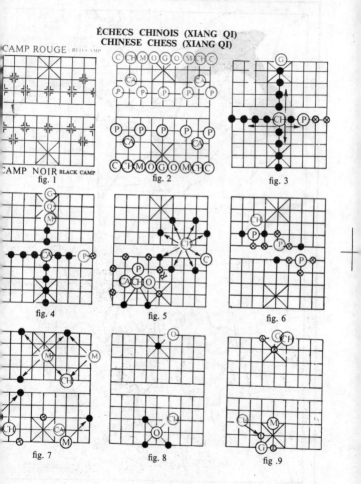

CAMP ROUGE RED CAMP

CAMP NOIR BLACK CAMP

fig. 1

fig. 2

fig. 3

fig. 4

fig. 5

fig. 6

fig. 7

fig. 8

fig. 9

Pl. 21.

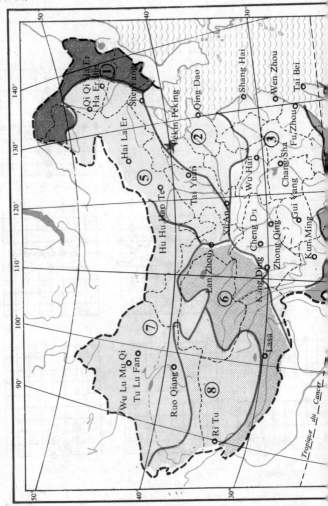

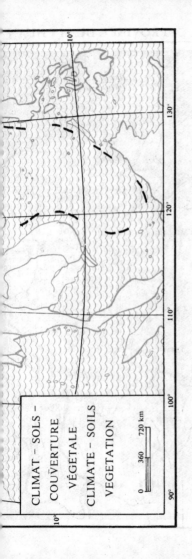

Pl. 22

CLIMAT – SOLS –
COUVERTURE
VÉGÉTALE

CLIMATE – SOILS –
VEGETATION

0   360   720 km

① Zone tempérée froide — Sols podzoliques — Forêts de conifères
et d'arbres à feuilles caduques.
Cold temperate zone — Podzolic soils — Forests of conifers
and deciduous trees.

② Zone tempérée chaude — Sols bruns et beiges — Arbres à
feuilles caduques.
Warm temperate zone — Brown and beige soils —
Deciduous trees.

③ Zone subtropicale — Sols rouges et jaunes, terres à riz —
Végétation subtropicale.
Sub-tropical zone — Red and yellow soils, ricelands —
Sub-tropical vegetation

④ Zone tropicale (Moussons) — Sols latéritiques, terres à riz —
Végétation tropicale (forêts).
Tropical zone (Monsoons) — Lateritic soils, ricelands —
Tropical vegetation (forests).

⑤ Zone tempérée — Sols lœssiques — Steppe.
Temperate zone — Loess soils — Steppe.

⑥ Zone froide d'altitude — Sols steppiques.
Elevated cold zone — Steppe soils.

⑦ Zone tempérée continentale — Sols désertiques (avec oasis).
Continental temperate zone — Desert soils (with oases).

⑧ Zone froide d'altitude — Sols désertiques.
Elevated cold zone — Desert soils.

Pl. 23

PROVINCE DU SI CHUAN

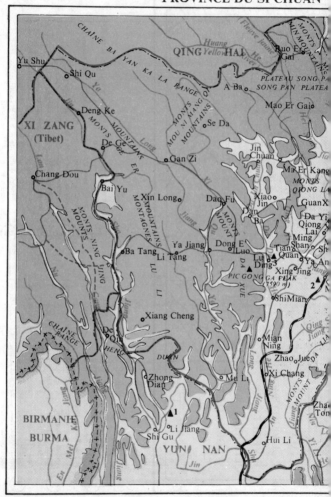